WILEY

Practitioner's Guide to

GAAS 2017

Covering All SASs, SSAEs, SSARSs, and Interpretations

Subscriber Update Service

BECOME A SUBSCRIBER!

Did you purchase this product from a bookstore?

If you did, it's important for you to become a subscriber. John Wiley & Sons, Inc. may publish, on a periodic basis, supplements and new editions to reflect the latest changes in the subject matter that you *need to know* in order stay competitive in this ever-changing industry. By contacting the Wiley office nearest you, you'll receive any current update at no additional charge. In addition, you'll receive future updates and revised or related volumes on a thirty-day examination review.

If you purchased this product directly from John Wiley & Sons, Inc., we have already recorded your subscription for this update service.

To become a subscriber, please call 1-877-762-2974 or send your name, company name (if applicable), address, and the title of the product to

mailing address: **Supplement Department**
John Wiley & Sons, Inc.
One Wiley Drive
Somerset, NJ 08875

e-mail: subscriber@wiley.com
fax: 1-732-302-2300
online: www.wiley.com

For customers outside the United States, please contact the Wiley office nearest you:

Professional & Reference Division
John Wiley & Sons Canada, Ltd.
22 Worcester Road
CANADA
416-236-4433
Phone: 1-800-567-4797
Fax: 416-236-4447
Email: canada@jwiley.com

John Wiley & Sons, Ltd.
The Atrium
Southern Gate, Chichester
West Sussex, PO 198SQ
ENGLAND
Phone: 44-1243-779777
Fax: 44-1243-775878
Email: customer@wiley.co.uk

John Wiley & Sons Australia, Ltd.
33 Park Road
P.O. Box 1226
Milton, Queensland 4064
AUSTRALIA
Phone: 61-7-3859-9755
Fax: 61-7-3859-9715
Email: brisbane@johnwiley.com.au

John Wiley & Sons (Asia) Pte. Ltd.
2 Clementi Loop # 02-01
SINGAPORE 129809
Phone: 65-64632400
Fax: 65-64634604/5/6
Customer Service: 65-64604280
Email: enquiry@wiley.com.sg

WILEY

Practitioner's Guide to GAAS 2017

Covering All SASs, SSAEs, SSARSs, and Interpretations

Joanne M. Flood

WILEY

This book is printed on acid-free paper. ♾

Published by John Wiley & Sons, Ltd, Chichester

Published simultaneously in Canada.

For general information on our other products and services please contact our Customer Care

Department within the US at 800-762-2974, outside the US at 317-572-3993, or fax 317-572-4002.

Wiley also publishes its books in a variety of electronic formats. Some content that appears in print may not be available in electronic books. For more information about Wiley products, visit our website at www.wiley.com.

ISBN 978-1-119-37377-3 (paperback)
ISBN 978-1-119-37375-9 (ebk)
ISBN 978-1-119-37369-8 (ebk)
ISBN 978-1-119-37380-3 (ebk)

Printed in the United States of America

10 9 8 7 6 5 4 3 2 1

CONTENTS

PREFACE

THE AICPA's CLARITY PROJECTS

AUDITING STANDARDS

Following the creation of the Public Company Accounting Oversight Board (PCAOB), the AICPA's Auditing Standards Board (ASB) reassessed its mission. The ASB developed a plan to converge US generally accepted auditing standards (GAAS) with the International Standards on Auditing (ISAs) issued by the International Auditing and Assurance Standards Board (IAASB). Thus, the ASB's clarity project began work to:

- Redraft the auditing standards for clarity—to make the standards easier to read, understand, and apply
- Converge US standards with the ISAs

The ASB has completed its project. While clarity and convergence, not change, were the goals of the clarity project, the project did create some changes that require auditors to make changes in practice. For ease of use, this book arranges information according to the sections of the AICPA's auditing standards codification.

PREPARATION, COMPILATION, AND REVIEW STANDARDS

In May 2010, the AICPA's Accounting and Review Services Committee (ARSC) approved a clarity project with the purpose of aligning the conventions of its standards with the ASB standards and making the compilation and review standards easier to read, understand, and apply. One divergence from the ASB approach is that the ARSC decided not to include application guidance for governmental and smaller, less complex entities. Otherwise, the formats are similar and include:

- *Objectives*—define the context in which the requirements are set
- *Definitions*—explain, where relevant, specific terms
- *Requirements*—what the practitioners must do to meet the objectives of the standard
- *Application and other explanatory matters*—provide further guidance for carrying out the requirements of the standard. These paragraphs use an "A" prefix and are in a separate section that follows the requirements section.

As a result of the ARSC clarity project, a new section identifier, "AR-C," was established for the clarified standards in order to avoid confusion with references to the extant "AR" sections.

SSARS No. 21

Statement on Standards for Accounting and Review Services (SSARS) No. 21, *Clarification and Recodification*, is a product of the SSARS clarity project. There have long been practice problems around when an accountant is associated with or involved in the preparation of financial statements. Questions circled around the accountant's responsibilities and the users' perceptions of the meaning of the accountant's involvement. With the advent first of computers and then the cloud, these issues became even more complex.

In an effort to clarify the accountant's role under various scenarios, in October 2014 the AICPA released SSARS No. 21. This standard significantly affects public practitioners who prepare financial statements and is effective for reviews, compilations, and presentations of financial statements for periods ending on or after December 15, 2015.

SSARS No. 21 supersedes all extant AR sections, except for AR Section 120, which will be the subject of a future clarified standard. SSARS No. 21 eliminates all existing SSARS interpretations and incorporates them into the clarified guidance. SSARS No. 21 contains substantive changes to standards for compilations and engagements to prepare financial statements. Those changes are highlighted in the Technical Alert sections and incorporated into the relevant chapters of this book.

SSARS No. 21 results in the following structure:

- Section 60, *General Principles for Engagements Performed in Accordance with Statements on Standards for Accounting and Review Services*
- Section 70, *Preparation of Financial Statements*
- Section 80, *Compilation Engagements*
- Section 90, *Review of Financial Statements*

In September 2016, the AICPA completed the clarity project with the issuance of SSARS no. 22, *Compilation of Pro Forma Financial Information.* The guidance is included in the chapter on AR-C 120.

Attestation Standards

In April 2016, the ASB issued SSAE 18, *Attestation Standards: Clarification and Recodification.* The standards are effective in May 2017 and are included in this publication.

Resources

Wiley Practitioner's Guide to GAAS 2017 contains robust tools to help practitioners implement the clarified standards. Each chapter begins with the source of the code section, the clarified objectives, and definitions, followed by practice guidance. Exhibits and illustrations are integrated into the chapter and clearly identified. Clarified standard references are preceded by "AR-C."

The AICPA has dedicated a page on its site to the SSARS clarity project, with links to additional resources that may be helpful in implementing the changes: http://www.aicpa.org/SSARSClarity.

Other New Projects

To clarify jurisdictional issues, in January 2016, the ASB issued SAS No. 131, *Amendment to Auditing Standards No. 122 Section 700, Forming an Opinion and Reporting on Financial Statements*. The amendment clarifies the format of the auditor's report when conducting an audit in accordance with PCAOB standards and in accordance with GAAS. SAS No. 131 is effective for audits of financial statements for periods ending on or after June 15, 2016.

In October 2015, the ASB issued SAS No. 130, *An Audit of Internal Control over Financial Reporting That Is Integrated with an Audit of Financial Statements.* SAS No. 130 moves the guidance in AT 501 and related Interpretation No. 1, *Reporting under Section 112 of the Federal Deposit Insurance Corporation Improvement Act (AT 9501)* to the guidance for generally accepted auditing standards. SAS No. 130 creates a new AU-C section—940.

Guidance from both of these documents is incorporated into this volume.

ABOUT THE AUTHOR

Joanne M. Flood, CPA, is an author and independent consultant on accounting and auditing technical topics and e-learning. She has experience as an auditor in both an international firm and a local firm and worked as a senior manager in the AICPA's Professional Development group. She received her MBA summa cum laude in accounting from Adelphi University and her bachelor's degree in English from Molloy College.

While in public accounting, Joanne worked on major clients in retail, manufacturing, and finance and on small business clients in construction, manufacturing, and professional services. At the AICPA, Joanne developed and wrote e-learning, text, and instructor-led training courses on US and international standards. She also produced training materials in a wide variety of media, including print, video, and audio, and pioneered the AICPA's e-learning product line. Joanne resides on Long Island, New York, with her daughter, Elizabeth. Joanne is the author of several articles for and a contributor to Wiley Insight IFRS and the following Wiley publications:

Financial Disclosure Checklist
Wiley GAAP 2017: Interpretation and Application of Generally Accepted Accounting Principles
Wiley Practitioner's Guide to GAAS 2017: Covering All SASs, SSAEs, SSARSs, and Interpretations
Wiley GAAP: Financial Statement Disclosures Manual (Wiley Regulatory Reporting), coming soon
Wiley Revenue Recognition

And the following AICPA online and live CPE programs:

Audit Staff Essentials, Level 1—New Hire
Audit Staff Essentials, Level 2—Experienced Staff
Audit Staff Essentials, Level 3—Audit Senior/In-Charge

ORGANIZATION AND KEY CHANGES

This book reduces the official language of Statements on Auditing Standards (SASs), Statements on Standards for Attestation Engagements (SSAEs), Statements on Standards for Accounting and Review Services (SSARSs), and the interpretations of those standards into easy-to-read and understandable advice. It is designed to help CPAs in the application of, and compliance with, authoritative standards.

Clarified Auditing Standards

The AICPA's clarified auditing standards are now fully implemented. The Preface contains additional information on the clarity project.

This book follows the sequence of sections of the AICPA *Codification of Statements on Auditing Standards*, the *Codification of Statements on Standards for Attestation Engagements*, and the *Codification of Statements on Standards for Accounting and Review Services*. Sections are divided into the following easy-to-understand parts:

Original Pronouncement. A handy, brief identification of the original standard for the Section.

Definitions of Terms. A glossary of official definitions that gathers in one place explanations of terms that are ordinarily scattered throughout a standard.

Objectives of Section. A behind-the-scenes explanation of the reasons for the pronouncement and a capsule explanation of the most basic ideas of the section.

Requirements. Concise listing and descriptions of those things specifically mandated by the section, and helpful techniques for complying with the fundamental requirements of the section.

Interpretations. A brief summary of each Interpretation.

On the Horizon

Clarified Attestation Standards

SSAE 18 supersedes all existing AT sections and is effective for reports dated after April 30, 2017. The guidance from SSAE is codified in the AT-C sections of AICPA professional standards and appears in the AT-C chapters of this book.

Accounting and Review Standards

The AICPA has issued an exposure draft to amend AR-C 90 on review engagements. The exposure draft includes a technical correction for supplementary information that accompanies reviewed financial statements and the accountant's review report thereon. The proposed SSARS is expected to be effective upon issuance.

Auditing Standards

The Auditing Standards Board (ASB) has two exposure drafts. The first is on auditor involvement with exempt offering documents. If adopted and issued as a final standard, the proposed SAS will be codified in AU-C sec. 945 and will be effective for exempt offering documents with which the auditor is involved that are initially distributed, circulated, or submitted on or after June 15, 2018. Early application of the SAS will be permitted. The second exposure draft is on an auditor's consideration of an entity's ability to continue as a going concern. At the time the current auditing guidance on going concern was issued, the Financial Accounting Standards Board (FASB) had not issued its guidance on management's consideration of going concern. This proposed guidance would better align the AICPA with the FASB, the Governmental Accounting Standards Board (GASB), and International guidance. If adopted, the guidance will be effective for audits of financial statements for periods ending on or after December 15, 2017, and for interim periods beginning thereafter.

This publication is current through SAS No. 131, SSARS 22, and SSAE 18.

Joanne M. Flood
September 2017

AU-C 200 Overall Objectives of the Independent Auditor and the Conduct of an Audit in Accordance with Generally Accepted Auditing Standards

AU-C ORIGINAL PRONOUNCEMENTS

Sources Statements on Auditing Standards (SASs) 122, 123, 128, and 130.

TECHNICAL ALERT

In October 2015, the Auditing Standards Board (ASB) issued Statement on Auditing Standards (SAS) No. 130. SAS No. 130 contains amendments to this section. Any relevant changes are incorporated into the information that follows.

AU-C 200 DEFINITIONS OF TERMS

Source: AU-C 200.14

Applicable financial reporting framework. The financial reporting framework adopted by management and, when appropriate, those charged with governance in the preparation and fair presentation of the financial statements that is acceptable in view of the nature of the entity and the objective of the financial statements, or that is required by law or regulation.

Audit evidence. Information used by the auditor in arriving at the conclusions on which the auditor's opinion is based. Audit evidence includes both information contained in the accounting records underlying the financial statements and other information. *Sufficiency of audit evidence* is the measure of the quantity of audit evidence. The quantity of the audit evidence needed is affected by the auditor's assessment of the risks of material misstatement and also by the quality of such audit evidence. *Appropriateness of audit evidence* is the measure of the quality of audit evidence; that is, its relevance and its reliability in providing support for the conclusions on which the auditor's opinion is based.

Audit risk. The risk that the auditor expresses an inappropriate audit opinion when the financial statements are materially misstated. Audit risk is a function of the risk of material misstatement and detection risk.

Auditor. The term used to refer to the person or persons conducting the audit, usually the engagement partner or other members of the engagement team or, as applicable, the firm. When an AU-C section expressly intends that a requirement or responsibility be fulfilled by the engagement partner, the term *engagement partner* rather than *auditor* is used. *Engagement partner* and *firm* are to be read as referring to their governmental equivalents when relevant.

Detection risk. The risk that the procedures performed by the auditor to reduce audit risk to an acceptably low level will not detect a misstatement that exists and that could be material, either individually or when aggregated with other misstatements.

Financial reporting framework. A set of criteria used to determine measurement, recognition, presentation, and disclosure of all material items appearing in the financial statements; for example, US generally accepted accounting principles, International Financial Reporting Standards (IFRSs) promulgated by the International Accounting Standards Board (IASB), or a special purpose framework.

The term *fair presentation framework* is used to refer to a financial reporting framework that requires compliance with the requirements of the framework and:

1. Acknowledges explicitly or implicitly that, to achieve fair presentation of the financial statements, it may be necessary for management to provide disclosures beyond those specifically required by the framework; or
2. Acknowledges explicitly that it may be necessary for management to depart from a requirement of the framework to achieve fair presentation of the financial statements. Such departures are expected to be necessary only in extremely rare circumstances.

A financial reporting framework that requires compliance with the requirements of the framework but does not contain the acknowledgments in 1 or 2 is not a fair presentation framework.

Financial statements. A structured representation of historical financial information, including related notes, intended to communicate an entity's economic resources and obligations at a point in time or the changes therein for a period of time in accordance with a financial reporting framework. The related notes ordinarily comprise a summary of significant accounting policies and other explanatory information. The term *financial statements* ordinarily refers to a complete set of financial statements as determined by the requirements of the applicable financial reporting framework, but can also refer to a single financial statement.

Historical financial information. Information expressed in financial terms regarding a particular entity, derived primarily from that entity's accounting system, about economic events occurring in past time periods or about economic conditions or circumstances at points in time in the past.

Interpretive publications. Auditing interpretations of generally accepted accounting standards (GAAS), exhibits to GAAS, auditing guidance included in the American Institute of Certified Public Accountants (AICPA) Audit and Accounting Guides, and the AICPA Auditing Statements of Position (SOPs).

Management. The person(s) with executive responsibility for the conduct of the entity's operations. For some entities, management includes some or all of those charged with governance; for example, executive members of a governance board or an owner-manager.

Misstatement. A difference between the amount, classification, presentation, or disclosure of a reported financial statement item and the amount, classification, presentation, or disclosure that is required for the item to be presented fairly in accordance with the applicable financial reporting framework. Misstatements can arise from fraud or error.

Other auditing publications. Publications other than interpretive publications; these include AICPA auditing publications not defined as interpretive publications; auditing articles in the *Journal of Accountancy* and other professional journals; continuing professional education programs and other instruction materials, textbooks, guidebooks, audit programs, and checklists; and other auditing publications from state certified public accountant (CPA) societies, other organizations, and individuals.

Premise, relating to the responsibilities of management and, when appropriate, those charged with governance, on which an audit is conducted (the premise). Management and, when appropriate, those charged with governance have acknowledged and understand that they have the following responsibilities that are fundamental to the conduct of an audit in accordance with GAAS; that is, responsibility:

1. For the preparation and fair presentation of the financial statements in accordance with the applicable financial reporting framework;
2. For the design, implementation, and maintenance of internal control relevant to the preparation and fair presentation of financial statements that are free from material misstatement, whether due to fraud or error; and
3. To provide the auditor with:
    a. Access to all information of which management and, when appropriate, those charged with governance are aware that is relevant to the preparation and fair presentation of the financial statements, such as records, documentation, and other matters;
    b. Additional information that the auditor may request from management and, when appropriate, those charged with governance for the purpose of the audit; and
    c. Unrestricted access to persons within the entity from whom the auditor determines it necessary to obtain audit evidence.

The premise, relating to the responsibilities of management and, when appropriate, those charged with governance, on which an audit is conducted may also be referred to as the premise.

Professional judgment. The application of relevant training, knowledge, and experience within the context provided by auditing, accounting, and ethical standards in making informed decisions about the courses of action that are appropriate in the circumstances of the audit engagement.

Professional skepticism. An attitude that includes a questioning mind, being alert to conditions that may indicate possible misstatement due to fraud or error, and a critical assessment of audit evidence.

Reasonable assurance. In the context of an audit of financial statements, a high, but not absolute, level of assurance.

Risk of material misstatement. The risk that the financial statements are materially misstated prior to the audit. This consists of two components, described as follows at the assertion level:

- **Inherent risk.** The susceptibility of an assertion about a class of transaction, account balance, or disclosure to a misstatement that could be material, either individually or when aggregated with other misstatements, before consideration of any related controls.
- **Control risk.** The risk that a misstatement that could occur in an assertion about a class of transaction, account balance, or disclosure and that could be material, either individually or when aggregated with other misstatements, will not be prevented, or detected and corrected, on a timely basis by the entity's internal control.

Those charged with governance. The person(s) or organization(s) (for example, a corporate trustee) with responsibility for overseeing the strategic direction of the entity and the obligations related to the accountability of the entity. This includes overseeing the financial reporting process. Those charged with governance may include management personnel; for example, executive members of a governance board or an owner-manager.

OBJECTIVES OF AU-C SECTION 200

AU-C Section 200.12 states that:

. . . *The overall objectives of the auditor, in conducting an audit of financial statements, are to*

a. *obtain reasonable assurance about whether the financial statements as a whole are free from material misstatement, whether due to fraud or error, thereby enabling the auditor to express an opinion on whether the financial statements are presented fairly, in all material respects, in accordance with an applicable financial reporting framework; and*
b. *report on the financial statements, and communicate as required by GAAS, in accordance with the auditor's findings.*

If reasonable assurance cannot be obtained and a qualified opinion is insufficient, the auditor must either disclaim an opinion or withdraw from the engagement, when possible under applicable law or regulation. (AU-C 200.13)

REQUIREMENTS

MANAGEMENT'S RESPONSIBILITIES

Financial statements are prepared by management with oversight from those charged with governance. GAAS do not *impose* requirements on management or those charged with governance, but rather an audit is conducted on the premise that management and those charged with governance *understand* their responsibilities. (AU-C 200.05)

Many times clients do not understand their responsibilities for audited financial statements. The financial statements are *management's*. They contain management's representations. The form and content of the financial statements are management's responsibility, even if the auditor prepared them or participated in their preparation.

Management also is responsible for implementing and maintaining an effective system of internal control.

AUDITOR'S RESPONSIBILITIES

The auditor's responsibilities for the financial statements are confined to the expression of an opinion on the financial statements being audited. In performing the audit, the auditor is responsible for compliance with GAAS. Under GAAS, the auditor has a responsibility to consider AU-C sections and interpretive publications in all audits. If such guidance is not followed, an auditor must be prepared:

- For AU-C sections, to justify a departure from GAAS
- For interpretive publications, to explain that an alternative approach achieved the objectives of GAAS

To provide reasonable assurance that it is conforming with generally accepted auditing standards in its audit engagements, an accounting firm should establish quality control policies and procedures. These policies and procedures should apply not only to audit engagements but also to attest and accounting and review services for which professional standards have been established. (AU-C 200.A20) The AICPA's Quality Control Standards detail the firm's responsibility for establishing and maintaining a system of quality control for auditors. See QC Section 10, *A Firm's System of Quality Control*, for more information.

In every audit, the auditor has to obtain reasonable assurance[1] about whether the financial statements are free of material misstatement, whether due to errors or to fraud. (AU-C 200.06) Materiality is taken into account when planning and performing the audit. Misstatements are considered material, individually or in the aggregate, when they influence economic decisions made by financial statement users. Materiality considers qualitative and quantitative elements and should be viewed in context. (AU-C 200.07)

Ethical Requirements

The auditor must be independent. If not independent, the auditor cannot issue a report under GAAS. The only exception is if GAAS provides otherwise or law or regulation requires the auditor to accept the engagement and report on the financial statements. (AU-C 200.15)

To *be* independent, the auditor must be intellectually honest; to be *recognized* as independent, he or she must be free from any obligation to or interest in the client, its management, or its owners. For specific guidance, the auditor should look to the AICPA and the state society codes of conduct and, if relevant, the requirements of the Securities and Exchange Commission (SEC).[2]

Policies and procedures should provide reasonable assurance that personnel maintain independence when required and perform all responsibilities with integrity, objectivity, and due care.

1. Independence is an impartiality that recognizes an obligation for fairness.
2. Integrity pertains to being honest and candid, and requires that service and public trust not be subordinated to personal gain.
3. Objectivity is a state of mind that imposes an obligation to be impartial, intellectually honest, and free of conflicts of interest.
4. Due care requires the auditor to discharge professional responsibilities with the competence and diligence necessary to perform the audit and issue an appropriate report and to render services promptly, thoroughly, and carefully, while observing applicable standards.

(See the AICPA's Code of Professional Conduct, Section 300.)

---

1 *See Definitions of Terms.*

2 *Section 201 of the Sarbanes-Oxley Act of 2002 and the related SEC implementing rules created significant new independence requirements for auditors of public companies. For example, the SEC prohibits certain nonaudit services such as bookkeeping, internal audit outsourcing, and valuation services. All audit and nonaudit services performed by the auditor, including tax services, must be preapproved by the company's audit committee. In March 2003, the SEC issued final rules implementing Section 201 of the Act. The rules,* Strengthening the Commission's Requirements Regarding Auditor Independence, *can be found at www.sec.gov/rules/final/33-8183.htm.*

Professional Skepticism and Judgment

The auditor must perform the audit with professional skepticism and exercise professional judgment in planning and performing an audit of financial statements. (AU-C 200.17-18) The auditor should:

- Observe GAAS,
- Possess the degree of skill commonly possessed by other auditors, and
- Exercise that skill with reasonable care and diligence.

The auditor should also exercise *professional skepticism*, that is, *an attitude that includes a questioning mind and a critical assessment of audit evidence.*

In practice, this means that auditors should be alert for:

- Contradictory evidence,
- Indications of fraud,
- Unusual circumstances,
- Evidence that calls into question the reliability of documents and responses to inquiries,
- The possibility of collusion when performing the audit, and
- How management may override controls in a way that would make the fraud particularly difficult to detect.

(AU-C 200.A22-A23)

However, the auditor is not an insurer, and the audit report does not constitute a guarantee. It is based on *reasonable assurance*. Thus, it is possible that an audit conducted in accordance with GAAS may not detect a material misstatement.

COMPLYING WITH GAAS

Auditors must comply with and understand AU-C sections. (AU-C 200.20 and .21) AU-C Section 200.25-26 clarifies that the SASs use two categories of professional requirements to describe the degree of responsibility the standards impose on auditors.

1. *Unconditional requirements.* The auditor is required to comply with an unconditional requirement in all cases in which the circumstances exist to which the unconditional requirement applies. SASs use the word *must* to indicate an unconditional requirement.
2. *Presumptively mandatory requirements.* The auditor is also required to comply with a presumptively mandatory requirement in all circumstances where the presumptively mandatory requirement exists and applies. However, in rare circumstances, the auditor may depart from a presumptively mandatory requirement. The departure should only relate to a specific procedure when the auditors determine that the procedure would be ineffective in the specific circumstances. The auditors must document their justification for the departure and how the alternative procedures performed in the circumstances were sufficient to achieve the objectives of the presumptively mandatory requirement. GAAS use the word *should* to indicate a presumptively mandatory requirement.

(AU-C 200.25-.26)

The term *should consider* means that the consideration of the procedure or action is presumptively required, whereas carrying out the procedure or action is not.

AU-C Section 200 also clarifies that explanatory material is intended to explain the objective of the professional requirements, rather than imposing a professional requirement for the auditor to perform.

GAAS AND THE GAAS HIERARCHY

The auditor is responsible for planning, conducting, and reporting the results of an audit according to GAAS.[3] GAAS provide the standards for the auditors' work in fulfilling their objectives. Each AU-C section contains objectives that provide a link between the requirements and the overall objectives of the auditors. Auditors should have sufficient knowledge of the AU-C sections to determine when they apply and should be prepared to justify departures from them.

Interpretive Publications

Interpretive publications are not auditing standards, but are recommendations, issued under the authority of the ASB, on how to apply the SASs in specific circumstances, including engagements for entities in specialized industries. Interpretive publications are not auditing standards. They consist of the following:

- Auditing Interpretations of SASs, listed in each chapter of this book that has a related Interpretation.
- AICPA Audit and Accounting Guides and Statements of Position, listed in Appendix B of this book.

(AU-C 200.A81)

Auditors should consider interpretive publications that apply to their audits.

Other Auditing Publications

Other auditing publications, listed in Appendix C of this book, are not authoritative but may help auditors to understand and apply SASs. An auditor should evaluate such guidance to determine whether it is both (1) *relevant* for a particular engagement and (2) *appropriate* for the particular situation. When evaluating whether the guidance is appropriate, the auditor should consider whether the publication is recognized as helpful in understanding and applying SASs, and whether the author is recognized as an auditing authority. AICPA auditing publications that have been reviewed by the AICPA Audit and Attest Standards staff are presumed to be appropriate. (AU-C 200.A84)

---

[3] *Generally accepted auditing standards are issued in the form of Statements on Auditing Standards and codified into AU-C sections in the AICPA's Professional Standards.*

AU-C 210 Terms of Engagement

AU-C ORIGINAL PRONOUNCEMENT

Source Statement on Auditing Standards (SAS) 122.

APPLICABILITY

This section states the requirements and provides application guidance on the auditor's responsibilities in agreeing upon terms of engagement with management and those charged with governance. It establishes preconditions for an audit, for which management is responsible. AU-C 220, *Quality Control for an Engagement Conducted in Accordance with Generally Accepted Auditing Standards*, addresses those aspects of engagement acceptance that the auditor can control. AU-C 580, *Written Representations*, discusses management's responsibilities. (AU-C 210.01)

AU-C 210 DEFINITIONS OF TERMS

Source: AU-C 210.04

Preconditions for an audit. The use by management of an acceptable financial reporting framework in the preparation and fair presentation of the financial statements and the agreement of management and, when appropriate, those charged with governance, to the premise on which an audit is conducted.

Recurring audit. An audit engagement for an existing audit client for whom the auditor performed the preceding audit.

OBJECTIVES

AU-C Section 210.03 states that:

. . . the objective of the auditor is to accept an audit engagement for a new or existing audit client only when the basis upon which it is to be performed has been agreed upon through

a. establishing whether the preconditions for an audit are present and
b. confirming that a common understanding of the terms of the audit engagement exists between the auditor and management and, when appropriate, those charged with governance.

FUNDAMENTAL REQUIREMENTS

ENGAGEMENT ACCEPTANCE

Preconditions

Unless required to do so by law or regulation, an auditor should not accept an engagement when the preconditions (see "Definitions of Terms" section above) are not met. (AU-C 210.08) To assess whether those preconditions are met, the auditor should:

a. *determine whether the financial reporting framework*[1] *to be applied in the preparation of the financial statements is acceptable and*

b. *obtain the agreement of management that it acknowledges and understands its responsibility*

   i. *for the preparation and fair presentation of the financial statements in accordance with the applicable financial reporting framework;*

   ii. *for the design, implementation, and maintenance of internal control relevant to the preparation and fair presentation of financial statements that are free from material misstatement, whether due to fraud or error; and*

   iii. *to provide the auditor with*

      1. *access to all information of which management is aware that is relevant to the preparation and fair presentation of the financial statements, such as records, documentation, and other matters;*
      2. *additional information that the auditor may request from management for the purpose of the audit; and*
      3. *unrestricted access to persons within the entity from whom the auditor determines it necessary to obtain audit evidence.*

(AU-C 210.06)

Limitation of Scope

If management limits the scope of the auditor's work so that the auditor will have to disclaim an opinion, the auditor should not accept the engagement. The exception to this is when management is required by law or regulation to have an audit and the disclaimer of opinion is acceptable under law or regulation, for example with audits of employee benefit plans. Then the auditor can accept the engagement, but is not required to do so. (AU-C 210.07)

Agreement on Terms

The auditor should establish an understanding with management or those charged with governance[2] about the services to be performed for each audit, review of a public company's

---

1 *Acceptable reporting frameworks contain established accounting principles promulgated by a body designated by the Council of the AICPA under Rule 203 in the AICPA Code of Professional Conduct. These bodies include FASB, FASAB, IFRS, GASB, AICPA, and PCAOB.*

2 *In this chapter, references to management should be read as "management and, when appropriate, those charged with governance," unless the context suggests otherwise. Those charged with governance are those "with responsibility for overseeing the strategic direction of the entity and obligations related to the accountability of the entity," including the financial reporting process. (AU-C Glossary of Terms)*

financial statements, or agreed-upon procedures engagement. The understanding should include:

1. The engagement's objectives and scope
2. Management's responsibilities
3. Auditor's responsibilities
4. The audit's limitations, the inherent limitations of internal control, and the risk that some misstatements may not be detected
5. Financial reporting framework
6. Expected form and content of the report

In addition, the auditor may want to:

- Elaborate on the scope of the audit by referencing regulations, laws, GAAS, ethical codes, and pronouncements of professional bodies, as applicable.
- Identify any communications in addition to the auditor's report.
- Discuss audit planning and performance, including composition of the audit team.
- Remind management about the expectation of written representation, the agreement to make available draft financial statements on a timely basis, and the agreement for management to inform the auditor of subsequent events or facts discovered after the date of the financial statements that may affect the financial statements.
- Detail fees and billing arrangements.
- Request management to acknowledge receipt of the engagement letter and to agree to the terms by signing the letter.

The auditor may also choose to address arrangements concerning the involvement of other auditors, specialists, internal auditors and other entity staff, and predecessor auditors. Restrictions on auditor's liability, when not prohibited, audit documentation to be provided to other parties, additional services, arrangements with component auditors, and any other agreements with the entity may be included in the engagement letter. (AU-C 210.A23-.A26)

The auditor should document the understanding in writing. If the auditor fails to establish an understanding, the auditor should decline the engagement. (AU-C 210.09-.10) A sample engagement letter is included at the end of this chapter.

Initial Audits, Including Reaudits

Inquiry of the predecessor auditor is required because the predecessor may provide information that will assist the successor auditor in deciding whether to accept the engagement. The communication may be either written or oral. Both the predecessor and successor auditors should treat any information obtained from each other as confidential information. The successor auditor should request permission from the prospective client to make an inquiry of the predecessor *prior to final acceptance of the engagement.* However, the successor auditor may make a proposal for an audit engagement before having permission to inquire of the predecessor auditor.

The successor auditor should ask the prospective client to authorize the predecessor to respond fully to the successor auditor's inquiries. If a prospective client refuses to permit the predecessor auditor to respond or limits the response, the successor auditor should inquire as to the reasons and consider the implications of that refusal in deciding whether to accept the engagement. (AU-C 210.11) The successor auditor should make specific and reasonable inquiries of the predecessor about the following four matters:

1. Information about management's integrity
2. Disagreements with management about accounting principles, auditing procedures, or other significant matters
3. Communications to those charged with governance and responsibility regarding fraud, noncompliance with laws or regulations, and matters related to internal control
4. The predecessor auditor's understanding of the reasons for the change of auditors

(AU-C 210.A31)

The predecessor auditor should respond promptly, fully, and factually. However, if the predecessor decides, due to unusual circumstances such as impending, threatened, or potential litigation; disciplinary proceedings; or other unusual circumstances, not to respond fully, he or she should indicate that the response is limited. Also, if more than one auditor is considering accepting the audit, the predecessor auditor does not have to respond to inquiries until an auditor has been selected by the entity and has accepted the engagement. Any information exchanged between the predecessor and successor auditors should be considered confidential. (AU-C 210.A28-A30)

If the successor auditor receives a limited response, that auditor should consider the implications of the limited response in deciding whether to accept the engagement.

Recurring Audits

For a recurring audit, the auditor should evaluate whether the terms of the engagement need to be changed. The auditor should also remind the client about the existing terms of engagement.

Change in Terms

If the client requests a change in the terms, the auditor must ensure that there is a reasonable justification for the change. So, too, if prior to completion of an audit, the client requests a change to an engagement with a lower level of assurance, the auditor must be satisfied that a reasonable justification for doing so exists.

Certain factors may warrant a change in the terms of engagement for a recurring engagement. These might include, for example, changes in management or ownership, in legal or regulatory requirements, in the size of the entity, or in the financial reporting framework. (AU-C 210.A33) If the terms are changed, the auditor and management should document in writing the mutually agreed-upon change. (AU-C 210.13-16) If, however, the auditor concludes there is no reasonable justification for a change in terms and management does not allow the auditor to continue the original audit, the auditor must take these three steps:

1. Withdraw from the engagement.
2. Communicate the situation to those charged with governance.
3. Determine whether the auditor has any legal, contractual, or other obligation to report the circumstances to owners, regulators, or other parties.

(AU-C 210.17)

ILLUSTRATION

ILLUSTRATION 1. EXAMPLE OF AN AUDIT ENGAGEMENT LETTER (FROM AU-C 210.A42)

The following is an example of an audit engagement letter for an audit of general purpose financial statements prepared in accordance with US GAAP. This letter is intended only to be a guide that may be used in conjunction with the considerations outlined in AU-C Section 210. The letter will vary according to individual requirements and circumstances and is drafted to refer to the audit of financial statements for a single reporting period. The auditor may seek legal advice about whether a proposed letter is suitable.

Auditor's letterhead	Smith and Jones Certified Public Accountants October 7, 20XX
Addressed to the appropriate representative of those charged with governance	Brock Warner Plainsmen, Inc. 2320 Tiger Blvd. Lancaster, PA 19701
The objective and scope of the audit	You have requested that we audit the financial statements of Plainsmen, Inc., which comprise the balance sheet as of December 31, 20XX, and the related statements of income, changes in stockholders' equity, and cash flows for the year then ended, and the related notes to the financial statements. We are pleased to confirm our acceptance and our understanding of this audit engagement by means of this letter. Our audit will be conducted with the objective of our expressing an opinion on the financial statements.
The responsibilities of the auditor	We will conduct our audit in accordance with auditing standards generally accepted in the United States of America (GAAS). Those standards require that we plan and perform the audit to obtain reasonable assurance about whether the financial statements are free from material misstatement. An audit involves performing procedures to obtain audit evidence about the amounts and disclosures in the financial statements. The procedures selected depend on the auditor's judgment, including the assessment of the risks of material misstatement of the financial statements, whether due to fraud or to error. An audit also includes evaluating the appropriateness of accounting policies used and the reasonableness of significant accounting estimates made by management, as well as evaluating the overall presentation of the financial statements. Because of the inherent limitations of an audit, together with the inherent limitations of internal control, an unavoidable risk exists that some material misstatements may not be detected, even though the audit is properly planned and performed in accordance with GAAS. In making our risk assessments, we consider internal control relevant to the entity's preparation and fair presentation of the financial statements in order to design audit procedures that are appropriate in the circumstances but not for the purpose of expressing an opinion on the effectiveness of the entity's internal control. However, we will communicate to you in writing concerning any significant deficiencies or material weaknesses in internal control relevant to the audit of the financial statements that we have identified during the audit.

The responsibilities of management and identification of the applicable financial reporting framework	Our audit will be conducted on the basis that [*management and, when appropriate, those charged with governance*] acknowledge and understand that they have responsibility: 1. For the preparation and fair presentation of the financial statements in accordance with accounting principles generally accepted in the United States of America; 2. For the design, implementation, and maintenance of internal control relevant to the preparation and fair presentation of financial statements that are free from material misstatement, whether due to fraud or to error; and 3. To provide us with: a. Access to all information of which [*management*] is aware that is relevant to the preparation and fair presentation of the financial statements such as records, documentation, and other matters; b. Additional information that we may request from [*management*] for the purpose of the audit; and c. Unrestricted access to persons within the entity from whom we determine it necessary to obtain audit evidence. As part of our audit process, we will request from [*management and, when appropriate, those charged with governance*] written confirmation concerning representations made to us in connection with the audit.
Other relevant information:	
Insert other information, such as fee arrangements, billings, and other specific terms, as appropriate.	
Reporting	[*Insert appropriate reference to the expected form and content of the auditor's report. Example follows:*] We will issue a written report upon completion of our audit of Plainsmen, Inc.'s financial statements. Our report will be addressed to the board of directors of Plainsmen, Inc. We cannot provide assurance that an unmodified opinion will be expressed. Circumstances may arise in which it is necessary for us to modify our opinion, add an emphasis-of-matter or other-matter paragraph(s), or withdraw from the engagement. We also will issue a written report on [*insert appropriate reference to other auditors' reports expected to be issued*] upon completion of our audit.
Signed *Name and Title* *Date*	Please sign and return the attached copy of this letter to indicate your acknowledgment of, and agreement with, the arrangements for our audit of the financial statements including our respective responsibilities. Smith and Jones. Acknowledged and agreed on behalf of Plainsmen, Inc. by __________

AU-C 220 Quality Control for an Engagement Conducted in Accordance with Generally Accepted Auditing Standards

AU-C ORIGINAL PRONOUNCEMENTS

Sources Statements on Auditing Standards (SASs) 122 and 128.

APPLICABILITY

AU-C 220 addresses specific responsibilities of the auditor regarding quality control standards for an audit of financial statements. Quality control is the responsibility of the audit firm. AU-C 220 also addresses supervision of an audit.

AU-C 220 DEFINITIONS OF TERMS

Source: AU-C 220.09

Engagement partner. The partner or other person in the firm who is responsible for the audit engagement and its performance and for the auditor's report issued on behalf of the firm and who, when required, has the appropriate authority from a professional, legal, or regulatory body.

Engagement quality control review. A process designed to provide an objective evaluation, before the report is released, of the significant judgments the engagement team made and the conclusions it reached in formulating the auditor's report. The engagement quality control review process is only for those audit engagements, if any, for which the firm has determined that an engagement quality control review is required, in accordance with its policies and procedures.

Engagement quality control reviewer. A partner, other person in the firm, suitably qualified external person, or team made up of such individuals, none of whom is part of the engagement team, with sufficient and appropriate experience and authority to objectively evaluate the significant judgments that the engagement team made and the conclusions it reached in formulating the auditor's report.

Engagement team. All partners and staff performing the engagement and any individuals engaged by the firm or a network firm who perform audit procedures on the engagement. This excludes an auditor's external specialist engaged by the firm or a network firm.

The term *engagement team* also excludes individuals within the client's internal audit function who provide direct assistance on an audit engagement when the external auditor complies with the requirements of Section 610, *Using the Work of Internal Auditors*.[1]

Firm. A form of organization permitted by law or regulation whose characteristics conform to resolutions of the Council of the AICPA and which is engaged in the practice of public accounting.

Monitoring. A process comprising an ongoing consideration and evaluation of the firm's system of quality control, including inspection or a periodic review of engagement documentation, reports, and clients' financial statements for a selection of completed engagements, designed to provide the firm with reasonable assurance that its system of quality control is designed appropriately and operating effectively.

Network. An association of entities, as defined in ET Section 92, *Definitions*.

Network firm. A firm or other entity that belongs to a network, as defined in ET Section 92.

Partner. Any individual with authority to bind the firm with respect to the performance of a professional services engagement. For purposes of this definition, *partner* may include an employee with this authority who has not assumed the risks and benefits of ownership. Firms may use different titles to refer to individuals with this authority.

Personnel. Partners and staff.

Professional standards. Standards promulgated by the AICPA Auditing Standards Board or the AICPA Accounting and Review Services Committee under Rule 201, *General Standards* (ET sec. 201 par. .01), or Rule 202, *Compliance with Standards* (ET sec. 202 par. .01), of the AICPA Code of Professional Conduct, or other standards-setting bodies that set auditing and attest standards applicable to the engagement being performed and relevant ethical requirements.

Relevant ethical requirements. Ethical requirements to which the engagement team and engagement quality control reviewer are subject, which consist of the AICPA Code of Professional Conduct together with rules of applicable state boards of accountancy and applicable regulatory agencies that are more restrictive.

Staff. Professionals, other than partners, including any specialists that the firm employs.

Suitably qualified external person. An individual outside the firm with the competence and capabilities to act as an engagement partner (for example, a partner of another firm).

OBJECTIVES OF AU-C SECTION 220

AU-C Section 220.08 states that:

. . . the objective of the auditor is to implement quality control procedures at the engagement level that provide the auditor with reasonable assurance that

a. *the audit complies with professional standards and applicable legal and regulatory requirements and*
b. *the auditor's report issued is appropriate in the circumstances.*

---

1 *This paragraph was added by SAS No. 128.*

REQUIREMENTS

QUALITY CONTROL STANDARDS

The engagement partner is responsible for the overall quality of the engagements to which the partner is assigned. An audit firm should establish a quality control system to provide it with reasonable assurance that its staff meets the requirements of professional standards and applicable legal and regulatory requirements and that reports are appropriate. (AC 220.03)

SYSTEM OF QUALITY CONTROL

The nature and extent of a firm's quality control policies and procedures depend on the following five factors:

1. Firm size and the number of its offices
2. The degree of autonomy of personnel and practice offices
3. The knowledge and experience of its personnel
4. The nature and complexity of the firm's practice
5. The cost of developing and implementing quality control policies and procedures in relation to the benefits provided

When a firm establishes quality control policies and procedures, it should do the following:

1. Assign responsibilities to qualified personnel to implement quality control policies and procedures.
2. Communicate quality control policies and procedures to personnel (see below).
3. Monitor the effectiveness of the quality control system. The purpose is to determine that policies and procedures and the methods of implementing and communicating them are still appropriate.

NOTE: Flaws in, or a violation of, a firm's quality control do not necessarily indicate that an audit was not performed in accordance with GAAS.

ELEMENTS OF QUALITY CONTROL

When establishing its quality control policies and procedures, a firm should consider the elements of quality control:

- Leadership responsibilities for quality
- Ethical requirements
- Acceptance and continuance of clients
- Assignment of engagement terms
- Engagement performance
- Monitoring

NOTE: CPA firms or individuals that are enrolled in an AICPA-approved practice-monitoring program are obligated to adhere to quality control standards. In addition, the Principles of Professional Conduct indicate that members should practice in firms that have in place quality control procedures to provide reasonable assurance that services are competently delivered and adequately supervised. The Statements on Quality Control apply to a CPA firm's accounting, auditing, and attest practices.

Independence[2]

The engagement partner is responsible for the independence requirements for each audit and ensuring that these requirements are met. The engagement partner should:

- Evaluate the threats to independence,
- Evaluate any breaches, and
- Take appropriate action to eliminate or reduce threats to an appropriate level. If that cannot be done, the firm may have to withdraw from the engagement. (AU-C 220.13)

To *be* independent, auditors must be intellectually honest; to be *recognized* as independent, they must be free from any obligation to or interest in the client, its management, or its owners. For specific guidance, the auditor should look to AICPA and the state society codes of conduct and, if relevant, the requirements of the Securities and Exchange Commission (SEC).

Acceptance and Continuance of Client Relationships

The engagement partner must be satisfied that appropriate procedures regarding acceptance and continuance of clients have been performed and that appropriate conclusions were reached. (AU-C 220.14)

Policies and procedures should provide reasonable assurance that the firm will not be associated with clients whose management lacks integrity. A firm should:

- Undertake only engagements that can be completed with professional competence,
- Consider the client's integrity,
- Ensure that ethical requirements can be met, and
- Evaluate significant issues during current or previous audits and their implications for continuance.

(AU-C 220.A7)

Assignment of Engagement Teams

The engagement partner must be comfortable that the engagement team and external specialists are capable and have the appropriate competencies. (AU-C 220.16)

Direction, Supervision, and Performance

The engagement partner is responsible for the direction, supervision, and performance of the engagement with compliance with GAAS and the appropriateness of the report, performance of reviews, and that sufficient appropriate evidence has been obtained. (AU-C220.17)

---

2 *Section 201 of the Sarbanes-Oxley Act of 2002 and the related SEC implementing rules contain significant independence requirements for auditors of public companies. For example, the SEC prohibits certain nonaudit services such as bookkeeping, internal audit outsourcing, and valuation services. All audit and nonaudit services performed by the auditor, including tax services, must be preapproved by the company's audit committee. In March 2003, the SEC issued final rules implementing Section 201 of the Act. The rules,* Strengthening the Commission's Requirements Regarding Auditor Independence, *can be found at www .sec.gov/rules/final/33-8183.htm.*

The auditor with final responsibility for the audit should inform members of the engagement team about:

- Their responsibilities
- The responsibilities of the partners
- The objectives of the procedures they are to perform
- Aspects of the entity's business relevant to their assignment
- Risk-related issues
- Problems that may arise
- Details of the approach to the engagement

(AU-C 220.A12)

Supervision includes:

- Tracking the engagement progress
- Considering the competence of engagement team members
- Addressing significant findings or issues
- Identifying matters for consultation or referral to other team members

(AU-C 220.A13)

Engagement Performance

Reviewing Work

The engagement partners are responsible for the reviews following the firm's policies and procedures. In order to be sure that they are satisfied that the audit audience is sufficient and appropriate to support the conclusion, the engagement partners should review the audit documentation and discuss the engagement with the auditor. Then, this should be done on or before the date of the auditor's report. (AU-C 220.18-19)

The suitably experienced auditors should review the work of each team member and consider if:

1. The work was performed in accordance with professional standards and legal and regulatory requirements.
2. Significant issues were raised and considered.
3. Consultations, if necessary, took place and were documented.
4. The nature, timing, and extent of the work were appropriate.
5. Work performed supports the conclusion and is documented, and the evidence supports the auditor's report.
6. Objectives were achieved.

(AU-C 220.A16)

The engagement partner's review should allow time to resolve issues. (AU-C 220.A17)

Difference of Opinion

If differences of opinion arise among firm personnel about accounting or auditing issues in an audit, there should be:

1. Consultation to attempt resolution
2. Documentation of an assistant's disagreement, if he or she wants to be disassociated from the final resolution

3. Documentation of the basis for the final resolution

(AU-C 220.A23)

Assignment of Engagement Teams

When evaluating the competence of the engagement team, the engagement partner may consider:

1. Professional standards
2. Regulatory requirements
3. Relevant IT and specialized areas of accounting and auditing
4. The firm's quality control policies and procedures
5. The industry environment

Personnel should have experience in similar engagements through training and participation. Policies and procedures should also provide reasonable assurance that personnel refer to authoritative literature and consult, on a timely basis, with appropriate individuals when dealing with complex, unusual, or unfamiliar issues. (AU-C 220.A10)

Monitoring

The audit firm must establish a monitoring process. Policies and procedures should provide reasonable assurance that the above elements of quality control are suitably designed and effectively applied. (AU-C 220.A32) Monitoring involves:

1. Relevant and adequate policies and procedures that are complied with by members of the firm
2. Appropriate guidance and practice aids
3. Effective professional development activities

AU-C 230 Audit Documentation

AU-C ORIGINAL PRONOUNCEMENTS

Sources Statements on Auditing Standards (SASs) 122, 123, and 128.

AU-C 230 DEFINITIONS OF TERMS

Source: AU-C 230.06

Audit documentation. The record of audit procedures performed, relevant audit evidence obtained, and conclusions the auditor reached (terms such as *working papers* or *workpapers* are also sometimes used).

Audit file. One or more folders or other storage media, in physical or electronic form, containing the records that constitute the audit documentation for a specific engagement.

Documentation completion date. The date, no later than 60 days following the report release date, on which the auditor has assembled for retention a complete and final set of documentation in an audit file.

Experienced auditor. An individual (whether internal or external to the firm) who has practical audit experience and a reasonable understanding of:

1. Audit processes;
2. GAAS and applicable legal and regulatory requirements;
3. The business environment in which the entity operates; and
4. Auditing and financial reporting issues relevant to the entity's industry.

Report release date. The date the auditor grants the entity permission to use the auditor's report in connection with the financial statements.

OBJECTIVES OF AU-C SECTION 230

AU-C Section 230.05 states that:

. . . the objective of the auditor is to prepare documentation that provides

a. a sufficient and appropriate record of the basis for the auditor's report; and
b. evidence that the audit was planned and performed in accordance with GAAS and applicable legal and regulatory requirements.

REQUIREMENTS

Requirement for Audit Documentation

The auditor must prepare audit documentation, on a timely basis, in sufficient detail to provide a clear understanding of:

- The work performed, including the nature, timing, extent, and results of audit procedures performed;
- The evidence obtained and its source, and the conclusions reached; and
- The fact that the audit was planned and performed in accordance with GAAS and relevant legal and regulatory requirements.

(AU-C 230.02)

The form and content of the audit documentation should be designed for the specific engagement.

Form, Content, and Extent of Audit Documentation

The quantity, type, and content of the audit documentation are based on the auditor's professional judgment and vary with the engagement. Factors to consider in determining the content of audit documentation are discussed in the following paragraphs.

The Audience

The auditor should prepare audit documentation that would allow an experienced auditor[1] having no previous connection with the audit to understand:

- The nature, timing, and extent of auditing procedures performed to comply with GAAS and applicable legal and regulatory requirements;
- The results of the audit procedures performed and the audit evidence obtained; and
- The significant findings for issues that arose during the audit, the conclusions reached on those significant matters, and professional judgments made in reaching those conclusions.

(AU-C 230.08)

Sufficiency of Audit Documentation

Audit documentation should include:

- Who reviewed specific audit work and the date the work was completed
- Who performed the audit documentation and the date of such review
- Identifying characteristics of specific items tested

(AU-C 230.09)

Audit documentation should also include abstracts or copies of significant contracts or agreements that involved audit procedure. (AU-C 230.10)

Documentation of Significant Findings

The auditor should document *significant* audit findings or issues, actions taken to address them (including additional evidence obtained), and the basis of the conclusions reached. Significant audit findings or issues include:

---

1 *See "Definitions of Terms" section.*

- Matters that are both significant and involve the appropriate selection, application, and consistency of accounting principles with regard to the financial statements, including related disclosures. Such matters often relate to (1) accounting for complex or unusual transactions or (2) estimates and uncertainties, and the related management assumptions, if applicable.
  - Results of auditing procedures that indicate that the financial statements or disclosures could be materially misstated or that the auditing procedures need to be significantly modified.
  - Circumstances that cause significant difficulty in applying necessary auditing procedures.
  - Other findings that could result in a modified auditor's report.

The auditor should document discussions with management and those charged with governance, including when and with whom, about significant findings. (AU-C 230.11)

Departures from a Relevant Requirement

The auditor may find it necessary to not perform a required procedure. If so, the auditor should document the reason for the departure and how alternative procedures enabled the auditor to fulfill the objectives of the audit. (AU-C 230.13)

This documentation is required only if the required procedure is relevant to the audit. For example, if the entity does not have an internal audit function, procedures in AU-C 610 would not be relevant.

Factors to Consider in Determining the Nature and Extent of Audit Documentation

The auditor should consider the following factors in determining the nature and extent of the documentation for an audit area or auditing procedure:

- What is the risk of material misstatement associated with the assertion, or account or class of transactions?
- What is the extent of judgment involved in performing the work and evaluating results?
- What is the nature of the auditing procedure?
- What is the significance of evidence obtained to the tested assertion?
- What is the nature and extent of identified exceptions?
- Is there a need to document a conclusion or basis for a conclusion not readily determinable from the documentation of the work performed?
- What are the methodologies or tools used?

(AU-C 230.A4)

Documentation of Report Release Date and Revisions

The auditor should document the report release date and complete the assembly of the final audit file on a timely basis, but no later than 60 days following the report release date. (AU-C 230.15-.16) After this date, the auditor must not delete or discard existing audit documentation before the end of the specified retention period, not less than five years. If changes are made to the audit documentation after this date, the auditor should document the change, when and by whom the changes were made, the specific reasons for the change, and the effect of the changes, if any, on the auditor's previous conclusions. (AU-C 230.14 and .18)

Ownership and Confidentiality

The auditor owns the audit documentation, but his or her ownership rights are limited by ethical and legal rules on confidential relationships with clients. The auditor should adopt reasonable procedures to protect the confidentiality of client information. (AU-C 230.15-19) The auditor should also adopt reasonable procedures to prevent unauthorized access to the audit documentation. Sometimes audit documentation may serve as a source of reference for the client, but it should not be considered as a part of, or a substitute for, the client's accounting records.

Standardization of Audit Documentation

Audit documentation should be designed for the specific engagement; however, audit documentation supporting certain accounting records may be standardized.

The auditor should analyze the nature of his or her clients and the complexity of their accounting systems. This analysis will indicate accounts for which audit documentation may be standardized. An auditor ordinarily may be able to standardize audit documentation for a small-business client as follows:

1. Cash, including cash on hand
2. Short-term investments
3. Trade accounts receivable
4. Notes receivable
5. Other receivables
6. Prepaid expenses
7. Property, plant, and equipment
8. Long-term investments
9. Intangible assets
10. Deposits
11. Accrued expenses
12. Taxes payable
13. Long-term debt
14. Stockholders' equity accounts

Preparation of Audit Documentation

All audit documentation should have certain basic information, such as the following:

1. Heading
    a. Name of client
    b. Description of audit documentation, such as:
        i. Proof of cash—Fishkill Bank & Trust Company
        ii. Accounts receivable—confirmation statistics
    c. Period covered by engagement
        i. For the year ended . . .
2. An index number
    a. All audit documentation should be numbered for easy reference. Audit documentation is identified using various systems, such as the following:

i. Alphabetical
ii. Numbers
iii. Roman numerals
iv. General ledger account numbers
v. A combination of the preceding

3. Preparer and reviewer identification

   a. Identification of person who prepared audit documentation and date of preparation:

      i. If client prepared the audit documentation, this should be noted. Person who checked papers also should be identified.

   b. Identification of person who reviewed the audit documentation and date of review

4. Explanation of symbols

   a. Symbols used in the audit documentation should be explained. Symbols indicate matters such as the following:

      i. Columns were footed.
      ii. Columns were cross-footed.
      iii. Data were traced to original sources.

5. Source of information

   a. The audit documentation should indicate source of information:

      i. Client records
      ii. Client personnel

Related Accounts

One page of audit documentation may provide documentation for more than one account. Many balance sheet accounts are related to income statement accounts. In these circumstances, the audit work on the accounts should be documented in one page of audit documentation. Examples of related accounts are the following:

1. Notes receivable and interest income
2. Depreciable assets, depreciation expense, and accumulated depreciation
3. Prepaid expenses and the related income statement expenses, such as insurance, interest, and supplies
4. Long-term debt and interest expense
5. Deferred income taxes and income tax expense

Client Preparation of Audit Documentation

It is advisable to have the client's employees prepare as much as possible of the auditor's audit documentation. This increases the efficiency of the audit. The auditor should identify the audit documentation as "Prepared by the Client" (PBC) and note the auditor who reviewed the client-prepared audit documentation. The preparation of audit documentation by the client does not impair the auditor's independence. However, the auditor should test the information in client-prepared audit documentation.

Quality of Audit Documentation

Audit documentation aids the execution and supervision of the current year's engagement. Also, such documentation helps the auditor in planning and executing the following year's audit. Audit documentation also serves as the auditor's reference for answering questions from the client. For example, a bank or a credit agency may want information that the auditor can provide to the client for submission to the third party from the audit documentation.

In case of litigation against the client, the auditor's audit documentation may be subpoenaed. In litigation against the auditor, the audit documentation will be used as evidence. Therefore audit documentation should be accurate, complete, and understandable. After audit documentation is reviewed, additional work, if any, is done, and modifications are made to the audit documentation, superseded drafts, corrected documents, duplicate documents, and review notes, and all to-do points should be discarded because the issues they addressed have been appropriately responded to in the audit documentation. (AU-C 230.A6)

Likewise, miscellaneous notes, memoranda, e-mails, and other communications among members of the audit engagement team created during the audit should be included or summarized in the audit documentation when needed to identify issues or support audit conclusions; otherwise, they should be discarded. Any information added after completion of fieldwork should be dated at the date added.

Oral Explanations

Oral explanations on their own do not represent sufficient support for the work the auditor performed or conclusions the auditor reached but may be used by the auditor to clarify or explain information contained in the audit documentation. (AU-C 230.A7)

NOTE: For example, if the auditing standards state that the auditor should obtain an understanding of the entity's control environment, but there is no evidence that he or she obtained such an understanding, then the auditor cannot make a plausible claim that the understanding was obtained but just not documented.

Audit Documentation Deficiencies

Some of the more common audit documentation deficiencies are failure to:

1. Express a conclusion on the account being analyzed.
2. Explain exceptions noted.
3. Obtain sufficient information for note disclosure.
4. Reference information.
5. Update and revise permanent file.
6. Post adjusting and reclassification journal entries to appropriate audit documentation.
7. Indicate source of information.
8. Promptly review audit documentation prepared by assistants.
9. Sign or date audit documentation.
10. Foot client-prepared schedules.
11. Explain tick marks.

Documentation Requirements in Other Sections

Certain other sections require documentation of specific matters. These requirements are presented in Illustration 4 at the end of this chapter. In addition, other standards, such as government auditing standards, laws, or regulations, may also contain specific documentation requirements.

INTERPRETATIONS

PROVIDING ACCESS TO OR COPIES OF AUDIT DOCUMENTATION TO A REGULATOR (ISSUED JULY 1994; REVISED JUNE 1996; REVISED OCTOBER 2000; REVISED JANUARY 2002; REVISED DECEMBER 2005; REVISED DECEMBER 15, 2012)

A regulator may request access to an auditor's audit documentation to fulfill a quality review requirement or to assist in establishing the scope of a regulatory examination. In making the request, the regulator may ask to make photocopies and may also make such copies available to others. When regulators make a request for access, the auditor should:

1. Consider advising the client about the request and indicating that he or she intends to comply. In some cases the auditor may wish or be required to confirm in writing the requirements to provide access (see Illustration 1).
2. Make arrangements with the regulator for the review.
3. Maintain control over the original audit documentation.
4. Consider submitting a letter to the regulator (see Illustration 2).
5. Obtain the client's consent, preferably in writing, to provide access when not required to provide access (see Illustration 3).

AU-C ILLUSTRATIONS

Illustrations 1, 2, and 3 are adapted from AICPA Interpretations of AU-230 (AU-C 9230).

1. An auditor's written communication to client when wishing to or required to provide access
2. An auditor's letter to a regulator
3. A written communication to the client when regulator may request access to audit documentation when not required by law or regulation

Illustration 4, which lists audit documentation requirements in other sections, is adapted from the application guidance in AU-C 230.

ILLUSTRATION 1. AUDITOR'S WRITTEN COMMUNICATION TO CLIENT WHEN THE AUDITOR MAY WISH AND IN SOME CASES MAY BE REQUIRED TO PROVIDE ACCESS (ADAPTED FROM AU-C INTERPRETATION AU-C 9230.1 AND FOOTNOTE 4)

The audit documentation for this engagement is the property of Guy & Co. and constitutes confidential information. However, we may be requested to make certain audit documentation available to [*name of regulator*] pursuant to authority given to it by law or regulation. If requested, access to such audit documentation will be provided under the supervision of [*name of auditor*]. Furthermore, upon request, we may provide copies of selected audit documentation to [*name of regulator*]. The [*name of regulator*] may intend or may decide to distribute the copies of information contained therein to others, including other governmental agencies.

You have authorized Guy & Co. to allow [*name of regulator*] access to the audit documentation in the manner discussed above. Please confirm your agreement to the above by signing below and returning it [*name of auditor, address*].

Firm signature

____

Agreed and acknowledged:

____

[Name and title]

____

[Date]

ILLUSTRATION 2. AUDITOR'S LETTER TO REGULATOR (FROM AU-C INTERPRETATION OF AU-C 230.06)

[Date]

[Name and address of regulatory agency]

Your representatives have requested access to our audit documentation in connection with our audit of December 31, 20X1 financial statements of Widget Company. It is our understanding that the purpose of your request is [*state purpose: for example, "to facilitate your regulatory examination"*].

Our audit of Widget Company December 31, 20X1 financial statements was conducted in accordance with auditing standards generally accepted in the United States of America, the objective of which is to form an opinion as to whether the financial statements, which are the responsibility and representations of management, present fairly, in all material respects, the financial position, results of operations, and cash flows in conformity with generally accepted accounting principles. Under generally accepted auditing standards, we have the responsibility, within the inherent limitations of the auditing process, to design our audit to provide reasonable assurance that errors and fraud that have a material effect on the financial statements will be detected, and to exercise due care in the conduct of our audit. The concept of selective testing of the data being audited, which involves judgment both as to the number of transactions to be audited and as to the areas to be tested, has been generally accepted as a valid and sufficient basis for any auditor to express an opinion on financial statements. Thus, our audit, based on the concept of selective testing, is subject to the inherent risk that material errors or fraud, if they exist, would not be detected. In addition, an audit does not address the possibility that material errors or fraud may occur in the future. Also, our use of professional judgment and the assessment of materiality for the purpose of our audit means that matters may have existed that would have been assessed differently by you.

The audit documentation was prepared for the purpose of providing principal support for our report on Widget Company December 31, 20X1 financial statements and to aid in the conduct and supervision of our audit. The audit documentation is the principal record of the auditing procedures performed, the evidence obtained, and the conclusions reached in the engagement. The auditing procedures that we performed were limited to those we considered necessary under generally accepted auditing standards to enable us to formulate and express an opinion on the financial statements taken as a whole. Accordingly, we make no representation as to the sufficiency or appropriateness, for your purposes, of either the information contained in our audit documentation or our audit procedures. In addition, any notations, comments, and individual conclusions appearing on any of the audit documentation do not stand alone, and should not be read as an opinion on any individual amounts, accounts, balances, or transactions.

Our audit of Widget Company December 31, 20X1 financial statements was performed for the purpose stated above and has not been planned or conducted in contemplation of your [*state purpose: for example, "regulatory examination"*] or for the purpose of assessing Widget Company compliance with laws and regulations. Therefore, items of possible interest to you may not have been specifically addressed. Accordingly, our audit and the audit documentation prepared in connection therewith should not supplant other inquiries and procedures that should be undertaken by the [*name of regulatory agency*] for the purpose of monitoring and regulating statements of Widget Company. In addition, we have not audited any financial statements of Widget Company since [*date of audited balance sheet referred to in the first paragraph above*], nor have we performed any audit procedures since [*date*], the date of our auditor's report, and significant events or circumstances may have occurred since that date.

The audit documentation constitutes and reflects work performed or evidence obtained by [*name of auditor*] in its capacity as independent auditor for Widget Company. The documents contain trade secrets and confidential commercial and financial information of our firms and Widget Company that are privileged and confidential, and we expressly reserve all rights with respect to disclosures to third parties. Accordingly, we request confidential treatment under the Freedom of Information Act or similar laws and regulations when requests are made for the audit documentation or information contained therein or any documents created by the [*name of regulatory agency*] containing information derived therefrom. We further request that written notice be given to our firm before distribution of the information in the audit documentation (or photocopies thereof) to others, including other governmental agencies, except when such distribution is required by law or regulation.

[*If it is expected that photocopies will be requested, add:*]

Any photocopies of our audit documentation we agree to provide you will be identified as "Confidential Treatment Requested by [*name of auditor, address, telephone number*]."

Firm signature

____

Illustration 3. Written Communication to the Client When Regulator May Request Access to Audit Documentation When Not Required by Law or Regulation (from AU-C Interpretation 9230.13)

The audit documentation for this engagement is the property of [*name of auditor*] and constitutes confidential information. However, we may be requested to make certain audit documentation available to [*name of regulator*] for [*describe the regulator's basis for its request*]. If requested, access to such audit documentation will be provided under the supervision of [*name of auditor*] personnel. Furthermore, upon request, we may provide photocopies of selected audit documentation to [*name of regulator*]. The [*name of regulator*] may intend or decide to distribute the copies of information contained therein to others, including other government agencies.

You have authorized [*name of auditor*] to allow [*name of regulator*] access to the audit documentation in the manner discussed above. Please confirm your agreement to the above by signing below and returning to [*name of auditor, address*].

Firm signature

____

Agreed and acknowledged:

____

[Name and title]

____

[Date]

ILLUSTRATION 4. AUDIT DOCUMENTATION REQUIREMENTS IN OTHER AU-C SECTIONS (FROM AU-C 230.A30)

The following lists the main paragraphs in other AU-C sections that contain specific documentation requirements. See the related chapters in this book for additional information.

a.	Paragraphs .10, .13, and .16 of Section 210, *Terms of Engagement*
b.	Paragraphs .25–.26 of Section 220, *Quality Control for an Engagement Conducted in Accordance with Generally Accepted Auditing Standards*
c.	Paragraphs .43–.46 of Section 240, *Consideration of Fraud in a Financial Statement Audit*
d.	Paragraph .28 of Section 250, *Consideration of Laws and Regulations in an Audit of Financial Statements*
e.	Paragraph .20 of Section 260, *The Auditor's Communication with Those Charged with Governance*
f.	Paragraph .12 of Section 265, *Communicating Internal Control Related Matters Identified in an Audit*
g.	Paragraph .14 of Section 300, *Planning an Audit*
h.	Paragraph .33 of Section 315, *Understanding the Entity and Its Environment and Assessing the Risks of Material Misstatement*
i.	Paragraph .14 of Section 320, *Materiality in Planning and Performing an Audit*
j.	Paragraphs .30–.33 of Section 330, *Performing Audit Procedures in Response to Assessed Risks and Evaluating the Audit Evidence Obtained*
k.	Paragraph .12 of Section 450, *Evaluation of Misstatements Identified during the Audit*
l.	Paragraph .20 of Section 501, *Audit Evidence—Specific Considerations for Selected Items*
m.	Paragraph .08 of Section 520, *Analytical Procedures*
n.	Paragraph .22 of Section 540, *Auditing Accounting Estimates, Including Fair Value Accounting Estimates, and Related Disclosures*
o.	Paragraph .28 of Section 550, *Related Parties*
p.	Paragraph .22 of Section 570, *The Auditor's Consideration of an Entity's Ability to Continue as a Going Concern*
q.	Paragraphs .49 and .64 of Section 600, *Special Considerations—Audits of Group Financial Statements (Including the Work of Component Auditors)*
r.	Paragraph .13 of Section 915, *Reports on Application of Requirements of an Applicable Financial Reporting Framework*
s.	Paragraphs .42–.43 of Section 930, *Interim Financial Information*
t.	Paragraphs .39–.42 of Section 935, *Compliance Audits*

AU-C 240 Consideration of Fraud in a Financial Statement Audit

AU-C ORIGINAL PRONOUNCEMENTS

Sources Statements on Auditing Standards (SASs) 122 and 128.

AU-C 240 DEFINITIONS OF TERMS

Source: AU-C 240.11

Fraud. An intentional act by one or more individuals among management, those charged with governance, employees, or third parties, involving the use of deception that results in a misstatement in financial statements that are the subject of an audit.

Fraud risk factors. Events or conditions that indicate an incentive or pressure to perpetrate fraud, provide an opportunity to commit fraud, or indicate attitudes or rationalizations to justify a fraudulent action.

OBJECTIVES OF AU-C SECTION 240

AU-C Section 240.10 states that the objectives of the auditor are to:

1. *Identify and assess the risks of material misstatement of the financial statements due to fraud;*
2. *Obtain sufficient appropriate audit evidence regarding the assessed risks of material misstatement due to fraud, through designing and implementing appropriate responses; and*
3. *Respond appropriately to fraud or suspected fraud identified during the audit.*

REQUIREMENTS

DESCRIPTION AND CHARACTERISTICS OF FRAUD

Although fraud is a broad legal concept, the auditor's interest specifically relates to fraudulent acts that cause a material misstatement of financial statements. Two types of misstatements are relevant to the auditor's consideration in a financial statement audit.

1. Misstatements arising from fraudulent financial reporting

NOTE: Fraudulent financial reporting does not need to involve a grand plan or conspiracy. Management may rationalize that a misstatement is appropriate because it is an aggressive interpretation of accounting rules, or that it is a temporary misstatement that will be corrected later.

2. Misstatements arising from misappropriation of assets
(AU-C 240.02-.03)

Fraudulent financial reporting and misappropriation of assets differ in that fraudulent financial reporting is committed, usually by management, to deceive financial statement users, whereas misappropriation of assets is committed against an entity, most often by employees.

Fraud generally involves the following three conditions:

1. A pressure or an incentive to commit fraud
2. A perceived opportunity to do so
3. Rationalization of the fraud by the individual(s) committing it
(AU-C 240.A1)

However, not all three conditions must be observed to conclude that there is an identified risk. It is particularly difficult to observe that the correct environment for rationalizing fraud is present.

The auditor should be aware that the presence of each of the three conditions may vary, and is influenced by factors such as the size, complexity, and ownership of the entity. These three conditions usually are present for both types of fraud.

The auditor should also be alert to the fact that fraudulent financial reporting often involves the override of controls, and that management's override of controls can occur in unpredictable ways. Also, fraud may be concealed through collusion, making it particularly difficult to detect.

Although fraud usually is concealed, the presence of risk factors or other conditions may alert the auditor to its possible existence.

Basic Requirement

In every audit, the auditor is obligated to plan and perform the audit to obtain reasonable assurance about whether the financial statements are free of material misstatement, whether caused by error or by fraud. (AU-C 240.05)

Professional Skepticism

As defined in AU-C Section 200, professional skepticism is an attitude that includes a questioning mind and critical assessment of audit evidence. The auditor should conduct the entire engagement with an attitude of professional skepticism, recognizing that fraud could be present, regardless of past experience with the entity or beliefs about management's integrity. (AU-C 240.12) The auditor should not let his or her beliefs about management's integrity allow the auditor to be satisfied with any audit evidence that is less than persuasive. Finally, the auditor should continuously question whether information and evidence obtained suggest that material misstatement caused by fraud has occurred.

Engagement Team Discussion about Fraud (Brainstorming)

When planning the audit, members of the audit team should discuss where and how the financial statements may be susceptible to material misstatement caused by fraud. This discussion should include the following:

- Exchange ideas and brainstorm about where the financial statements are susceptible to fraud, how assets could be stolen, and how management might engage in fraudulent financial reporting.

- Emphasize the need to maintain the proper mindset throughout the audit regarding the potential for fraud. As previously discussed, the auditor should continually exercise professional skepticism and have a questioning mind when performing the audit and evaluating audit evidence. Engagement team members should thoroughly probe issues, acquire additional evidence when necessary, and consult with other team members and firm experts as needed.
- Consider known external and internal factors affecting the entity that might create incentives and opportunities to commit fraud, and indicate an environment that enables rationalizations for committing fraud.
- Consider indications of earnings management.
- Consider the risk that management might override controls.
- Consider how to respond to the susceptibility of the financial statements to material misstatement caused by fraud.
- For the purposes of this discussion, set aside any of the audit team's prior beliefs about management's honesty and integrity.

The discussion would normally include key audit team members. Other factors that should be considered when planning the discussion include:

- Whether to have multiple discussions if the audit involves more than one location
- Whether to include specialists assigned to the audit

Audit team members should continue to communicate throughout the audit about the risks of material misstatement due to fraud. (AU-C 240.15)

Obtaining Information Needed to Identify Fraud Risks

In addition to performing procedures required under Section 315, *Understanding the Entity and Its Environment and Assessing the Risks of Material Misstatements*, the auditor should obtain information needed to identify the risks of material misstatement due to fraud by:

- Asking management and others within the entity about their views on the risk of fraud and how such risks are addressed.
- Considering unusual or unexpected relationships identified by analytical procedures performed while planning the audit.
- Considering whether any fraud risk factors exist.
- Considering other information that may be helpful in identifying fraud risk.

Inquiries of Management

Management is responsible for designing and implementing programs to prevent, deter, and detect fraud. When management and others, such as the audit committee and board of directors, set the proper tone of ethical conduct, the opportunities for fraud are significantly reduced.

The auditor should make the following inquiries of management:

- Does management or others within the entity know about actual or suspected fraud?
- Have there been any allegations of actual or suspected fraud from employees, former employees, analysts, regulators, short sellers, and others?
- Does management understand the entity's fraud risk, including any identified risk factors or account balances or classes of transactions for which a fraud risk is likely to exist?

- What programs and controls does the entity have to help prevent, deter, and detect fraud? How does management monitor such programs?
- When there are multiple locations, how are operating locations or business segments monitored? Is fraud more likely to exist at any one of the locations or business segments?
- Does management communicate its views on business practices and ethical behavior to employees, and, if so, how?
- Has management communicated to those charged with governance how the entity's internal control prevents, deters, and detects fraud?

(AU-C 240.17-.18)

When evaluating management's responses to these inquiries, auditors should remember that management is often in the best position to commit fraud. Therefore, the auditor should determine when it is necessary to corroborate those responses with other information. When responses are inconsistent, the auditor should obtain additional audit evidence.

Inquiries of Those Charged with Governance

The auditor should understand how those charged with governance oversee the entity's assessment of fraud risks and the mitigating programs and controls. (AU-C 240.20) The auditor should make the following inquiries of those charged with governance:

- What are those charged with governance's (or the audit committee's or at least the chair's) views of the risk of fraud?
- Do they know about actual, alleged, or suspected fraud in the entity?

(AU-C 240.21)

Inquiries of Internal Auditors

The auditor should make the following inquiries of appropriate individuals within the internal audit function:

- What are their views on the risk of fraud?
- Have they performed procedures to identify or detect fraud during the year?
- Has management satisfactorily responded to any finding from procedures performed to identify or detect fraud?
- Are they aware of any actual, suspected, or alleged fraud?

(AU-C 240.19)

Inquiries of Others within the Organization

The auditor should also ask others within the entity whether they are aware of actual or suspected fraud, using professional judgment to determine to whom these inquiries are made and how extensive the inquiries should be. The following are examples of people who may provide helpful information and, therefore, to whom the auditor may wish to consider directing inquiries:

1. Anyone at varying levels of authority whom the auditor deals with during the audit, such as when the auditor is obtaining an understanding of the entity's internal controls, observing inventory, performing cutoff procedures, or getting explanations for fluctuations noted during analytical procedures
2. Operating staff not directly involved in financial reporting

3. Employees involved in initiating, recording, or processing complex or unusual transactions
4. In-house legal counsel

(AU-C 240.A19)

Considering the Results of Analytical Procedures

When performing the required analytical procedures in planning the audit as discussed in Section 520, *Analytical Procedures*, the auditor may find unusual or unexpected relationships as a result of comparing the auditor's expectations with recorded amounts or ratios developed from such amounts. The auditor should consider those results in identifying the risk of material misstatement due to fraud. (AU-C 240.23)

The auditor should also perform analytical procedures relating to revenue with the objective of identifying unusual or unexpected relationships involving revenue accounts that may indicate a material misstatement due to fraudulent financial reporting. Examples of such procedures include:

- Comparing sales volume with production capacity (sales volume greater than production capacity might indicate fraudulent sales).
- Trend analysis of revenues by month and sales return by month shortly before and after the reporting period (the analysis may point to undisclosed side agreements with customers to return goods).

(AU-C 240.25)

Although analytical procedures performed during audit planning may be helpful in identifying the risk of material misstatement due to fraud, they may only provide a broad indication, since such procedures use data aggregated at a high level. Therefore, the results of such procedures should be considered along with other information obtained by the auditor in identifying fraud risk. (AU-C 240.26)

Considering Fraud Risk Factors

Using professional judgment, the auditor should consider whether information obtained about the entity and its environment indicates that fraud risk factors are present, and, if so, whether it should be considered when identifying and assessing the risk of material misstatement due to fraud. (AU-C 240.24)

Examples of fraud risk factors are presented in Illustrations 1 and 2 at the end of this chapter. These risk factors are classified based on the three conditions usually present when fraud exists:

1. Incentive/pressure
2. Opportunity
3. Attitude/rationalization

(AU-C 240.A30)

The auditor should not assume that all three conditions must be present or observed. In addition, the extent to which any condition is present may vary.

The size, complexity, and ownership of the entity may also affect the identification of fraud risks. (AU-C 240.A31)

In planning the audit, the auditor will most likely use a list of fraud risk factors to serve as a memory jogger. This list may be taken from the examples listed in the AU-C Illustrations at the end of this chapter, or the examples provided may be tailored to the client. The documentation of this list of fraud risk factors to be considered is *not* required, but represents good practice.

During the planning and performance of the audit, the auditor may identify some of the fraud risk factors from the list as being present at the client. Of those risk factors present, some will be addressed sufficiently by the planned audit procedures; others may require the auditor to extend audit procedures.

Considering Other Information

The auditor should evaluate other information that may be helpful in identifying fraud risk. The auditor should consider:

- Any information from procedures performed when deciding to accept or continue with a client
- Results of review of interim financial statements
- Identified inherent risks
- Information from the discussion among engagement team members

IDENTIFYING FRAUD RISKS

Fraud risk factors may come to the auditor's attention while performing procedures relating to acceptance or continuance of clients, during engagement planning or obtaining an understanding of an entity's internal control, or while conducting fieldwork. Accordingly, the assessment of the risk of material misstatement due to fraud is a cumulative process that includes a consideration of risk factors individually and in combination. As noted earlier, assessment of fraud risk factors is not a simple matter of counting the factors present and converting the result to a level of fraud risk. A few risk factors or even a single risk factor may heighten the risk of fraud significantly.

Attributes

The auditor should use professional judgment and information obtained when identifying the risks of material misstatement due to fraud. The auditor should consider the following attributes of the risk when identifying risks:

- *Type* (Does the risk involve fraudulent financial reporting or misappropriation of assets?)
- *Significance* (Could the risk lead to a material misstatement of the financial statements?)
- *Likelihood* (How likely is it that the risk would lead to a material misstatement of the financial statements?)
- *Pervasiveness* (Does the risk impact the financial statements as a whole, or does it relate to an assertion, account, or class of transactions?)

Throughout the audit, the auditor should evaluate whether identified fraud risks can be related to certain account balances or classes of transactions and related assertions, or whether they relate to the financial statements as a whole. (AU-C 240.25) Examples of accounts or classes of transactions that might be more susceptible to fraud risk include:

- Liabilities from a restructuring because of the subjectivity in estimating them
- Revenues for a software developer, because of their complexity

---

NOTE: The auditor should document the identified fraud risks.

Presumption about Improper Revenue Recognition as a Fraud Risk

Since fraudulent financial reporting often involves improper revenue recognition, the auditor should ordinarily presume that there is a risk of material misstatement due to fraudulent revenue recognition. (AU-C 240.26)

NOTE: The auditor should document the reasons supporting his or her conclusion when improper revenue recognition is not identified as a fraud risk. (AU-C 240.46)

Consideration of the Risk of Management Override of Controls

The auditor should also recognize that, even when other specific risks of material misstatement are not identified, there is a risk that management can override controls. (AU-C 240.31) The auditor should address this risk as discussed in the later section on "Addressing the Risk of Management Override."

Assessing Identified Risks

As part of the understanding of internal control required by Section 319, the auditor should:

1. Evaluate whether the entity's programs and controls that address identified risks have been appropriately designed and placed in operation. Programs and controls may involve specific controls, such as those designed to prevent theft, or broad programs, such as one that promotes ethical behavior.
2. Consider whether programs and controls mitigate identified risks of material misstatement due to fraud or whether control deficiencies exacerbate risks.
3. Assess identified risks, taking into account the evaluation of programs and controls.
4. Consider this assessment when responding to the identified risks of material misstatement due to fraud.

Responding to the Results of the Assessment

The auditor responds to assessment of risk of material misstatement due to fraud by:

- Exercising professional skepticism
- Evaluating audit evidence
- Considering programs and controls to address those risks

Examples of the use of professional skepticism would include:

- Designing additional or different audit procedures to obtain more reliable evidence
- Obtaining additional corroboration of management's responses or representations

The auditor should respond to the risk of material misstatement in the following ways:

1. Evaluate the overall conduct of the audit.
2. Adjust the nature, timing, and extent of audit procedures performed in response to identified risks.
3. Perform certain procedures to address the risk that management will override controls.

NOTE: The auditor should document a description of the auditor's response to identified fraud risks.

If the auditor concludes that it is not practical to design audit procedures to sufficiently address the risks of material misstatement due to fraud, the auditor should consider withdrawing from the engagement and communicating the reason to the audit committee.

Overall Response to Risk

Judgments about the risk of material misstatements due to fraud may affect the audit in the following ways:

1. **Assignment of personnel and supervision.** The personnel assigned to the engagement should have the knowledge, skill, and experience necessary to address the auditor's assessment of the level of risk of the engagement. The extent of supervision should also reflect the level of risk.
2. **Accounting principles.** The auditor should evaluate management's selection and application of significant accounting principles, particularly those relating to subjective measurements and complex transactions. The auditor should also consider whether the collective application of the principles indicates a bias that may create a material misstatement.
3. **Predictability of audit procedures.** The auditor should vary procedures from year to year to create an element of unpredictability. For example, the auditor may perform unannounced procedures or use a different sampling method.

(AU-C 240.29)

Adjusting the Nature, Timing, and Extent of Audit Procedures to Address Risk

The auditor may respond to identified risks by adjusting the nature, timing, and extent of audit procedures performed. Specifically:

- The *nature* of procedures may need to be modified to provide more reliable and persuasive evidence, or to corroborate management's representations. For example, the auditor may need to rely more on independent sources, physical observation of assets, or computer-assisted audit techniques (CAATs).
- The *timing* of procedures may need to be changed. For example, the auditor may decide to perform more procedures at year-end, rather than relying on tests from an interim date.
- The *extent* of procedures applied should reflect the assessment of fraud risk and may need to be adjusted. For example, the auditor may increase sample sizes, perform more detailed analytical procedures, or perform more computer-assisted audit techniques.

Appendix B of AU-C 240 contains the following examples of ways to modify the nature, timing, and extent of tests in response to identified risks of material misstatement due to fraud:

- Perform unannounced or surprise procedures at locations.
- Ask that inventories be counted as closely as possible to the end of the reporting period.
- Orally confirm with major customers and suppliers in addition to sending written confirmations.
- Send confirm requests to a specific party in an organization.
- Perform substantive analytical procedures using disaggregated data, such as comparing gross profit or operating margins by location, line of business, or month to auditor-developed expectations.

- Interview personnel involved in areas where a fraud risk has been identified to get their views about the risk and how controls address the risk.
- Discuss with other independent auditors auditing other subsidiaries, divisions, or branches the extent of work that should be performed to address the risk of fraud resulting from transactions and activities among those components.
- If the work of an expert becomes particularly significant with respect to a financial statement item for which the assessed risk of misstatement due to fraud is high, perform additional procedures relating to some or all of the expert's assumptions, methods, or findings to determine that the findings are not unreasonable, or engage another expert for that purpose.
- Perform audit procedures to analyze selected opening balance sheet accounts of previously audited financial statements to assess how certain issues involving accounting estimates and judgments (for example, an allowance for sales returns) were resolved with the benefit of hindsight.

Examples of Responses to Identified Risks of Misstatements from Fraudulent Financial Reporting

The following examples are from AU-C 240 Appendix B:
Revenue recognition. The auditor may consider:

- Performing substantive analytical procedures relating to revenue using disaggregated data, such as comparing revenue reported by month or by product line or business segment during the current reporting period with comparable prior periods.
- Confirming with customers certain relevant contract terms and the absence of side agreements, because the appropriate accounting often is influenced by such terms or agreements (for example, acceptance criteria, delivery and payment terms, the absence of future or continuing vendor obligations, the right to return the product, guaranteed resale amounts, and cancellation or refund provisions often are relevant in such circumstances).
- Inquiring of the entity's sales and marketing personnel or in-house legal counsel regarding sales or shipments near the end of the period and their knowledge of any unusual terms or conditions associated with these transactions.
- Being physically present at one or more locations at period-end to observe goods being shipped or being readied for shipment (or returns processing) and performing other appropriate cutoff procedures.
- For those situations for which revenue transactions are electronically initiated, processed, and recorded, testing controls to determine whether they provide assurance that recorded revenue transactions occurred and are properly recorded.

Inventory quantities. The auditor may consider:

- Examining the entity's inventory records to identify locations or items that require specific attention during or after the physical inventory count.
- Performing additional procedures during the count, such as rigorously examining the contents of boxes, checking for hollow squares in the manner in which goods are stacked, or examining the quality of liquid substances for purity, grade, or concentration.
- Performing additional testing of count sheets, tags, or other records to reduce the possibility of subsequent alteration or inappropriate compilation.

- Performing additional procedures to test the reasonableness of quantities counted, such as comparing quantities for the current period with prior periods by class or category of inventory or location.
- Using CAATs.

Management estimates. The auditor may want to supplement the audit evidence obtained. The auditor may:

- Engage a specialist to develop an independent estimate for comparison.
- Extend inquiries to individuals outside of management and the accounting department to corroborate management's ability and intent to carry out plans that are relevant to developing the estimate.

Examples of Responses to Identified Risks of Misstatements Arising from Misappropriation of Assets

The auditor will usually direct a response to identified risks of misstatements arising from misappropriation of assets to certain account balances. The scope of the work should be linked to the specific information about the identified misappropriation risk. (AU-C 240 Appendix B) The auditor may consider some of the procedures listed in the preceding section, "Examples of Responses to Identified Risks of Misstatements Arising from Fraudulent Financial Reporting." However, in some cases, the auditor may:

- Obtain an understanding of the controls related to preventing or detecting the misappropriation and testing of such controls.
- Physically inspect assets near the end of the period.
- Apply substantive analytical procedures, such as the development by the auditor of an expected dollar amount at a high level of precision to be compared with a recorded amount.

NOTE: Audit procedures may involve both substantive tests and tests of controls. However, since management may be able to override controls, it is unlikely that audit risk can be reduced to an appropriate level by performing only tests of controls.

Addressing the Risk of Management Override

The auditor should perform the following procedures to specifically address the risk for management's override of controls.

Examining journal entries and other adjustments for evidence of possible material misstatement due to fraud, and testing the appropriateness and authorization of such entries. (AU-C 240.A49-.A50) The following procedures should help the auditor in addressing possible recording of inappropriate or unauthorized journal entries or making financial statement adjustments, such as consolidating adjustments, report combinations, or reclassifications not reflected in formal journal entries. The auditor should specifically:

1. Understand the financial reporting process, understand the design of controls over journal entries and other adjustments, and determine that such controls are suitably designed and placed in operation.

2. Identify and select journal entries and other adjustments for testing, while considering the following:
   - What is our assessment of the risk of material misstatement due to fraud? (The auditor may identify a specific class of journal entries to examine after considering a specific fraud risk factor.)
   - How effective are controls over journal entries and other adjustments? (Even if controls are implemented and operating effectively, the auditor should identify and test specific items.)
   - Based on our understanding of the entity's financial reporting process, what is the nature of evidence that can be examined? (Regardless of whether journal entries are automated or processed manually, the auditor should select journal entries to be tested from the general ledger, and examine support for those items. In addition, if journal entries and adjustments are in electronic form only, the auditor may require that an information technology [IT] specialist extract the data.)

   NOTE: Computer-assisted audit techniques (CAATs) such as data extraction applications frequently are the most effective and efficient means for identifying and selecting journal entries and adjustments for testing.

   - What are the characteristics of fraudulent entries or adjustments, or the nature and complexity of accounts? Illustration 3 at the end of this chapter provides a worksheet to use in identifying characteristics of fraudulent journal entries or adjustments, or accounts that may be more likely to contain inappropriate journal entries or adjustments. (When audits involve multiple locations, the auditor should consider whether to select journal entries from various locations.)
   - Are there any journal entries or other adjustments processed outside the normal course of business (i.e., nonstandard or nonrecurring entries)? The auditor should consider placing additional emphasis on identifying and testing items processed outside the normal course of business, because such items may not be subject to the same level of internal control as other entries.
3. Determine the timing of testing. Fraud may occur throughout a period, so the auditor should consider the need to test journal entries throughout the period under audit. However, the auditor should also consider that fraudulent journal entries are often made at the end of the reporting period and should focus on entries made during that time.
4. Ask individuals in the financial reporting process about inappropriate or unusual activity relating to journal entries and adjustments.

NOTE: The auditor should document the results of procedures performed to address the possibility that management might override controls.

Reviewing accounting estimates for biases that could result in fraud. (AU-C 240.A52-.A53) The auditor should consider whether differences between amounts supported by audit evidence and the estimates included in the financial statements, even if individually reasonable, indicate a possible bias on the part of entity's management. If so, the auditor should reconsider the estimates taken as a whole.

The auditor should retrospectively review significant accounting estimates in prior years' financial statements to determine whether there is a possible bias on the part of management. (Significant accounting estimates are those based on highly sensitive assumptions or significantly affected by management's judgment.) The review should provide information to the auditor about a possible management bias that can be helpful in evaluating the current year's estimates. If a management bias is identified, the auditor should evaluate whether the bias represents a risk for material misstatement due to fraud.

Evaluating whether the rationale for significant unusual transactions is appropriate. (AU-C 240.A54) Personnel at the entity engaged in trying to hide a theft or commit fraudulent financial reporting might use unusual or nonstandard transactions to conceal the fraud. The auditor should understand the business rationale for such transactions and whether the rationale suggests that the transactions are fraudulent. When evaluating the transactions, the auditor should consider:

- Is the transaction overly complex?
- Has management discussed the nature and accounting for the transaction with the audit committee or board of directors?
- Is management focusing more on achieving a particular accounting treatment than the underlying economics?
- Have any transactions involving special purpose entities or other unconsolidated related parties been approved by the audit committee or board of directors?
- Do transactions involve previously unidentified related parties?
- Do transactions involve parties that cannot support the transaction without the help of the audited entity?

Evaluating Audit Evidence

The auditor should:

1. Assess the risk of material misstatement due to fraud throughout the audit.
2. Evaluate whether analytical procedures performed as substantive tests or in the overall review indicate a previously unidentified fraud risk.
3. Evaluate the risk of material misstatement due to fraud at or near the completion of fieldwork.
4. Respond to misstatements that may result from fraud.
5. Consider whether identified misstatements may be indicative of fraud, and, if so, evaluate their implications.

(AU-C 240.34-.37)

Evaluating Analytical Procedures

The auditor should consider whether analytical procedures performed as substantive tests or in the overall review stage of the audit indicate a risk of material misstatement due to fraud. The auditor should perform analytical procedures relating to revenue through the end of the reporting period, either as part of the overall review of the audit or separately. If such procedures are not included during the overall review stage of the audit, the auditor should perform analytical procedures specifically related to potentially fraudulent revenue recognition.

The auditor should be alert to responses to inquiries about analytical relationships that are:

- Vague or implausible
- Inconsistent with other audit evidence

NOTE: The auditor should document other conditions or analytical relationships that result in additional procedures, and any other responses the auditor feels are necessary.

As part of the auditor's evaluation of analytical procedures performed as substantive tests or in the overall review stage of the audit, and those analytical procedures that relate to revenue through the end of the reporting period, the auditor may find it helpful to consider the following issues:

1. Are there any unusual relationships involving revenues and income at year-end, such as an unexpectedly large amount of revenue reported at the very end of the reporting period from nonstandard transactions, or income that is not consistent with cash flow trends from operations?
2. Are there other unusual or unexpected analytical relationships that should be evaluated? The guidance provides the following examples:
   - An unusual relationship between net income and cash flows from operations may occur if management recorded fictitious revenues and receivables but was unable to manipulate cash.
   - Inconsistent changes in inventory, accounts payable, sales, or cost of sales between the prior period and the current period may indicate a possible employee theft of inventory, because the employee was unable to manipulate all of the related accounts.
   - Comparing the entity's profitability to industry trends, which management cannot manipulate, may indicate trends or differences for further consideration.
   - Unexplained relationships between bad debt write-offs and comparable industry data, which employees cannot manipulate, may indicate a possible theft of cash receipts.
   - Unusual relationships between sales volume taken from the accounting records and production statistics maintained by operating personnel—which may be more difficult for management to manipulate—may indicate a possible misstatement of sales.

(AU-C 240.A58)

Evaluating Fraud Risk at or Near the Completion of Fieldwork

The auditor should, at or near the end of fieldwork, evaluate whether the results of auditing procedures and observations affect the earlier assessment of the risk of material misstatement due to fraud. When making this evaluation, the auditor with final responsibility for the audit should confirm that all audit team members have been communicating information about fraud risks to each other throughout the audit.

Responding to misstatements that may result from fraud. When misstatements are identified, the auditor should consider whether they are indicative of fraud. The auditor may need to consider the impact on materiality and other related responses.

If the auditor believes that the misstatements are fraudulent or may result from fraud, but the effect is not material to the financial statements, the auditor should evaluate the implications for the rest of the audit. If the auditor determines that there are implications, such as implications about management's integrity, the auditor would reevaluate the assessment of the risk of material misstatement due to fraud and its impact on the nature, timing, and extent of substantive tests and the assessment of control risk if control risk were assessed below the maximum.

If the auditor believes that the misstatements are fraudulent or may result from fraud, and the effect is material (or if the auditor cannot evaluate the materiality of the effect), the auditor should:

1. Try to obtain additional evidence to determine whether fraud occurred and what its effect would be.
2. Consider how it affects the rest of the audit.
3. Discuss the matter and a plan for further investigation with a level of management at least one level above those involved, as well as senior management and those charged with governance (if senior management is involved, it may be appropriate for the auditor to hold the discussion with those charged with governance).
4. Consider suggesting that the client consult legal counsel.

After evaluating the risk of material misstatement, the auditor may determine that he or she should withdraw from the engagement and communicate the reason to those charged with governance. The auditor may wish to consult legal counsel when considering withdrawing from the engagement.

NOTE: Because of the wide variety of circumstances involved, it is not possible to definitively point out when the auditor should withdraw. However, the auditor may want to consider the implications of the fraud for management's integrity and the cooperation and effectiveness of management and/or the board of directors when considering whether to withdraw.

Communication about Possible Fraud to Management and Those Charged with Governance

When the auditor discovers or suspects fraud, the actions and communications required are somewhat complex, especially when an SEC client is involved. The actions/communications required by Title III of the Private Securities Litigation Reform Act of 1995, by the SEC Practice Section (SECPS) for its members, and by the SEC in Form 8-K add to the complexity.

The auditor should communicate on a timely basis any evidence that fraud may exist, even if such fraud is inconsequential, to the appropriate level of management. (AU-C 240.39)

The auditor should directly inform those charged with governance about:

- Fraud involving management
- Fraud involving employees who have significant roles in internal control
- Fraud that causes a material misstatement of the financial statements

(AU-C 240.40)

The auditor should reach an understanding with those charged with governance about the nature and extent of communications that need to be made to them about misappropriations committed by lower-level employees.

The auditor should consider whether the following are reportable conditions that should be communicated to senior management and those charged with governance:

- Identified risks of material misstatement due to fraud that have continuing control implications (whether or not transactions or adjustments that could result from fraud have been detected)
- A lack of, or deficiencies in, programs and controls to mitigate the risk of fraud

The auditor may also want to communicate other identified risks of fraud to those charged with governance, either in the overall communication of business and financial statement risks affecting the entity or in the communication about the quality of the entity's accounting principles (see Section 260).

Ordinarily, the auditor is not required to disclose possible fraud to anyone other than the client's senior management and those charged with governance, and in fact would be prevented by the duty of confidentiality from doing so. However, a duty to disclose to others outside the entity may exist when:

1. Complying with certain legal and regulatory requirements
2. Responding to a successor auditor's inquiries
3. Responding to a subpoena
4. Complying with requirements of a funding agency or other specified agency for audits that receive governmental financial assistance

(AU-C 240.A72)

The auditor may wish to consult legal counsel before discussing these matters outside the client to evaluate the auditor's ethical and legal obligations for client confidentiality. (AU-C 240.A73)

NOTE: The auditor should document these communications to management, the audit committee, and others.

When deciding on how to communicate, the best approach is to decide which of the following three situations governs, and to follow the guidance presented for the applicable situation.

Situation 1

Any Fraud Involving Senior Management for Non-SEC Clients
Auditor should:

1. Consider the implications for other aspects of the audit.
2. Reevaluate the assessment of the risk of fraud.
3. Discuss the matter and the approach to further investigation with the appropriate level of management.[1]
4. Obtain additional evidentiary matter, including suggesting that the client consult with legal counsel.
5. Consider whether any risk factors identified represent reportable conditions (Section 325).
6. Consider withdrawing from the engagement and communicating the reasons to those charged with governance.
7. Report the fraud to the audit committee or, in a small business, to the owner-manager.

NOTE: If the perpetrator controls the audit committee or board of directors, go directly to client's legal counsel. If the perpetrator is a general partner acting against the interests of the limited partners, obtain legal advice and consider communicating to the limited partners. If the perpetrator is the owner-manager of a small business, the auditor has little choice but to communicate with the perpetrator and has no obvious course of action but to withdraw. However, first the auditor should consult with his or her legal counsel.

---

[1] *Fraud that involves senior management or fraud that causes a material misstatement of the financial statements should be reported directly to those charged with governance.*

8. Insist that the financial statements be revised and, if they are not, express a qualified or adverse opinion (if precluded from obtaining needed evidence, disclaim an opinion or withdraw).

Situation 2

Any Fraud Involving Senior Management for SEC Clients
Auditor should:

1. Follow the steps in the Situation 1 checklist plus additional items 2–4 below.
2. Consider Section 10A(b) of the Securities Exchange Act of 1934 (Title III, Private Securities Litigation Reform Act of 1995):

   a. Matter is reported to board of directors and it does not take appropriate action.
   b. Auditor concludes that failure to take remedial action is expected to cause departure from standard audit report or cause withdrawal.
   c. Auditor should report conclusion in item b of this list to board of directors as soon as practicable (e.g., on Monday).
   d. Client is required to notify SEC (within one business day) of auditor's conclusion described in item b (e.g., by Tuesday).
   e. Client is required to furnish report to SEC in item d to auditor within one business day (e.g., by Tuesday).
   f. If auditor doesn't receive report in item e, auditor notifies SEC within one business day following failure to receive (e.g., on Wednesday).

3. If the auditor withdraws or resigns from the engagement, the auditor must send a copy of resignation to the SEC within five business days.
4. Follow SEC requirements for reporting on Form 8-K:

   a. Upon auditor's withdrawal, client must disclose within four business days the following information on a Form 8-K, filed with the SEC, with a copy to the auditor on the same day:

      - Auditor's resignation
      - Auditor's conclusion that the information coming to his or her attention *has a material impact* on the fairness or reliability of the client's financial statements or audit report and that this matter was not resolved to the auditor's satisfaction before resignation

   b. Auditor must prepare a letter stating agreement or disagreement with client's statements after reading Form 8-K. If auditor disagrees, he or she must disclose differences of opinion in a letter to client as promptly as possible. Client must then file the letter with the SEC within ten business days after filing the Form 8-K. Notwithstanding the ten-business-day requirement, client has two business days from the date of receipt to file the letter with the SEC.

Situation 3

Any Fraud Not Involving Senior Management for All Clients (Public and Nonpublic)
Auditor should:

1. Evaluate the implications for other aspects of the audit, especially organizational positions of persons involved.

2. Bring to the attention of, and discuss with, the appropriate level of management (even if inconsequential).
3. Communicate the matter to those charged with governance unless the matter is clearly below the communication threshold previously agreed to by the auditor and those charged with governance.
4. Consider whether any risk factors identified represent reportable conditions (Section 265).

Documentation

The auditor should document:

- The engagement team's discussion, when planning the audit, about the entity's susceptibility to fraud; the documentation should include how and when the discussion occurred, audit team members participating, and the subject matter covered.
- Procedures performed to obtain the information for identifying and assessing the risks of material misstatements due to fraud.
- Specific risks of material misstatement due to fraud identified by the auditor, and a description of the auditor's response to those risks.
- If improper revenue recognition has not been identified as a risk factor, the reasons supporting such conclusion.
- The results of procedures performed that addressed the risk that management would override controls.
- Other conditions and analytical relationships that caused the auditor to believe that additional procedures or responses were required, and any other further responses to address risks or other conditions.
- The nature of communications about fraud to management, those charged with governance, and others.

(AU-C 240.43-.46)

Antifraud Programs and Controls

The Committee of Sponsoring Organizations of the Treadway Commission (COSO) Internal Control—Integrated Framework (2013) includes a discussion of expectations related to preventing and detecting fraud. The guidance in AU-C 240 is based on the presumption that entity management has both the responsibility and the means to take action to reduce the occurrence of fraud at the entity. To fulfill this responsibility, management should:

- Create and maintain a culture of honesty and high ethics.
- Evaluate the risks of fraud and implement the processes, procedures, and controls needed to mitigate the risks and reduce the opportunities for fraud.
- Develop an appropriate oversight process.

Culture of Honesty and Ethics

A culture of honesty and ethics includes these elements:

- A value system founded on integrity
- A positive workplace environment where employees have positive feelings about the entity
- Human resource policies that minimize the chance of hiring or promoting individuals with low levels of honesty, especially for positions of trust

- Training—both at the time of hire and on an ongoing basis—about the entity's values and its code of conduct
- Confirmation from employees that they understand and have complied with the entity's code of conduct and that they are not aware of any violations of the code
- Appropriate investigation and response to incidents of alleged or suspected fraud

Evaluating Antifraud Programs and Controls

The entity's risk assessment process (as described in the separate chapter on AU-C 315) should include the consideration of fraud risk. With an aim toward reducing fraud opportunities, the entity should take steps to:

- Identify and measure fraud risk.
- Mitigate fraud risk by making changes to the entity's activities and procedures.
- Implement and monitor an appropriate system of internal control.

Develop an Appropriate Oversight Process

The entity's audit committee or board of directors should take an active role in evaluating management's:

- Creation of an appropriate culture
- Identification of fraud risks
- Implementation of antifraud measures

To fulfill its oversight responsibilities, audit committee members should be financially literate, and each committee should have at least one financial expert. Additionally, the committee should consider establishing an open line of communication with members of management one or two levels below senior management to assist in identifying fraud at the highest levels of the organization or investigating any fraudulent activity that might occur.

AU-C ILLUSTRATIONS

ILLUSTRATION 1. RISK FACTORS—FRAUDULENT FINANCIAL REPORTING

The following are examples of risk factors, reproduced with permission from AU-C Section 240 Appendix A, relating to misstatements arising from fraudulent financial reporting:

Incentives/Pressures

a. Financial stability or profitability is threatened by economic, industry, or entity operating conditions, such as (or indicated by):

   - High degree of competition or market saturation, accompanied by declining margins.
   - High vulnerability to rapid changes, such as changes in technology, product obsolescence, or interest rates.
   - Significant declines in customer demand and increasing business failures in either the industry or overall economy.
   - Operating losses making the threat of bankruptcy, foreclosure, or hostile takeover imminent.
   - Recurring negative cash flows from operations or an inability to generate cash flows from operations while reporting earnings and earnings growth.

- Rapid growth or unusual profitability, especially compared to that of other companies in the same industry.
- New accounting, statutory, or regulatory requirements.

b. Excessive pressure exists for management to meet the requirements or expectations of third parties due to the following:

- Profitability or trend level expectations of investment analysts, institutional investors, significant creditors, or other external parties (particularly expectations that are unduly aggressive or unrealistic), including expectations created by management in, for example, overly optimistic press releases or annual report messages.
- Need to obtain additional debt or equity financing to stay competitive—including financing of major research and development or capital expenditures.
- Marginal ability to meet exchange listing requirements or debt repayment or other debt covenant requirements.
- Perceived or real adverse effects of reporting poor financial results on significant pending transactions, such as business combinations or contract awards.
- A need to achieve financial targets required in bond covenants.
- Pressure for management to meet the expectations of legislative or oversight bodies or to achieve political outcomes, or both.

c. Information available indicates that management's or the board of directors' personal financial situation is threatened by the entity's financial performance arising from the following:

- Significant financial interests in the entity.
- Significant portions of their compensation (for example, bonuses, stock options, and earn-out arrangements) being contingent upon achieving aggressive targets for stock price, operating results, financial position, or cash flow.[2]
- Personal guarantees of debts of the entity.

d. There is excessive pressure on management or operating personnel to meet financial targets set up by the board of directors or management, including sales or profitability incentive goals.

Opportunities

a. The nature of the industry or the entity's operations provide opportunities to engage in fraudulent financial reporting that can arise from the following:

- Significant related-party transactions not in the ordinary course of business or with related entities not audited or audited by another firm.
- A strong financial presence or ability to dominate a certain industry sector that allows the entity to dictate terms or conditions to suppliers or customers that may result in inappropriate or non-arm's-length transactions.
- Assets, liabilities, revenues, or expenses based on significant estimates that involve subjective judgments or uncertainties that are difficult to corroborate.
- Significant, unusual, or highly complex transactions, especially those close to period end that pose difficult "substance over form" questions.
- Significant operations located or conducted across international borders in jurisdictions where differing business environments and cultures exist.
- Significant bank accounts or subsidiary or branch operations in tax-haven jurisdictions for which there appears to be no clear business justification.

---

2 *Management incentive plans may be contingent upon achieving targets relating only to certain accounts or selected activities of the entity, even though the related accounts or activities may not be material to the entity as a whole.*

b. There is ineffective monitoring of management as a result of the following:
   - Domination of management by a single person or small group (in a nonowner-managed business) without compensating controls.
   - Ineffective board of directors or audit committee oversight over the financial reporting process and internal control.

c. There is a complex or unstable organizational structure, as evidenced by the following:
   - Difficulty in determining the organization or individuals that have controlling interest in the entity.
   - Overly complex organizational structure involving unusual legal entities or managerial lines of authority.
   - High turnover of senior management, counsel, or board members.

d. Internal control components are deficient as a result of the following:
   - Inadequate monitoring of controls, including automated controls and controls over interim financial reporting (where external reporting is required).
   - High turnover rates or employment of ineffective accounting, internal audit, or information technology staff.
   - Ineffective accounting and information systems, including situations involving reportable conditions.
   - Weak controls over budget preparation and development and compliance with law or regulation.

Attitudes/Rationalizations

Risk factors reflective of attitudes/rationalizations by board members, management, or employees that allow them to engage in and/or justify fraudulent financial reporting may not be susceptible to observation by the auditor. Nevertheless, the auditor who becomes aware of the existence of such information should consider it in identifying the risks of material misstatement arising from fraudulent financial reporting. For example, auditors may become aware of the following information that may indicate a risk factor:

- Ineffective communication, implementation, support, or enforcement of the entity's values or ethical standards by management or the communication of inappropriate values or ethical standards.
- Nonfinancial management's excessive participation in or preoccupation with the selection of accounting principles or the determination of significant estimates.
- Known history of violations of securities laws or other laws and regulations, or claims against the entity, its senior management, or board members alleging fraud or violations of laws and regulations.
- Excessive interest by management in maintaining or increasing the entity's stock price or earnings trend.
- A practice by management of committing analysts, creditors, and other third parties to achieve aggressive or unrealistic forecasts.
- Management failing to correct known reportable conditions on a timely basis.
- An interest by management in employing inappropriate means to minimize reported earnings for tax-motivated reasons.
- Low morale among senior management.
- The owner-manager making no distinction between personal and business transactions.
- Dispute between shareholders in a closely held entity.
- Recurring attempts by management to justify marginal or inappropriate accounting on the basis of materiality.

- Strained relationship between management and the current or predecessor auditor, as exhibited by the following:
  - Frequent disputes with the current or predecessor auditor on accounting, auditing, or reporting matters.
  - Unreasonable demands on the auditor, such as unreasonable time constraints regarding the completion of the audit or the issuance of the auditor's report.
  - Restrictions on the auditor that inappropriately limit access to people or information or the ability to communicate effectively with the board of directors or audit committee.
  - Domineering management behavior in dealing with the auditor involving attempts to influence the scope of the auditor's work or the selection or continuance of personnel assigned to or consulted on the audit engagement.

ILLUSTRATION 2. RISK FACTORS—MISAPPROPRIATION OF ASSETS

The following are examples of risk factors, reproduced with permission from AU-C Section 240, Appendix A, relating to misstatements arising from misappropriation of assets:

Incentives/Pressures

a. Personal financial obligations may create pressure on management or employees with access to cash or other assets susceptible to theft to misappropriate those assets.
b. Adverse relationships between the entity and employees with access to cash or other assets susceptible to theft may motivate those employees to misappropriate those assets. For example, adverse relationships may be created by the following:
   - Known or anticipated future employee layoffs.
   - Recent or anticipated changes to employee compensation or benefit plans.
   - Promotions, compensation, or other rewards inconsistent with expectations.

Opportunities

a. Certain characteristics or circumstances may increase the susceptibility of assets to misappropriation. For example, opportunities to misappropriate assets increase when there are the following:
   - Large amounts of cash on hand or processed.
   - Inventory items that are small in size, of high value, or in high demand.
   - Easily convertible assets, such as bearer bonds, diamonds, or computer chips.
   - Fixed assets that are small in size, marketable, or lacking observable identification of ownership.
b. Inadequate internal control over assets may increase the susceptibility of misappropriation of those assets. For example, the misappropriation of assets may occur because there is the following:
   - Inadequate segregation of duties or independent checks.
   - Inadequate oversight of senior management expenditures, such as travel and other disbursements.
   - Inadequate management oversight of employees responsible for assets; for example, inadequate supervision or monitoring of remote locations.
   - Inadequate job applicant screening of employees with access to assets.
   - Inadequate record keeping with respect to assets.
   - Inadequate system of authorization and approval of transactions (for example, in purchasing).
   - Inadequate physical safeguards over cash, investments, inventory, or fixed assets.
   - Lack of complete and timely reconciliations of assets.
   - Lack of timely and appropriate documentation of transactions, for example, credits for merchandise returns.

- Lack of mandatory vacations for employees performing key control functions.
- Inadequate management understanding of information technology, which enables information technology employees to perpetrate a misappropriation.
- Inadequate access controls over automated records, including controls over and review of computer systems events logs.

Attitudes/Rationalizations

Risk factors reflective of employee attitudes/rationalizations that allow them to justify misappropriation of assets are generally not susceptible to observation by the auditor. Nevertheless, the auditor who becomes aware of the existence of such information should consider it in identifying the risks of material misstatement arising from misappropriation of assets. For example, auditors may become aware of the following attitudes or behavior of employees who have access to assets susceptible to misappropriation:

- Disregard for the need for monitoring or reducing risks related to misappropriation of assets.
- Disregard for internal control over misappropriation of assets by overriding existing controls or by failing to correct known internal control deficiencies.
- Behavior indicating displeasure or dissatisfaction with the company or its treatment of the employee.
- Changes in behavior or lifestyle that may indicate assets have been misappropriated.
- The belief by some government or other officials that their level of authority justifies a certain level of compensation and personal privileges.
- Tolerance of petty theft.

Illustration 3. Worksheet to Identify Fraudulent Entries or Adjustments (Adapted from AU-C 240.49)

Inappropriate journal entries and other adjustments often have certain unique characteristics. The auditor should use the following questions to help identify characteristics of inappropriate journal entries and other adjustments:

- Is the entry made to an unrelated, unusual, or seldom-used account?
- Is the entry made by an individual who typically does not make journal entries?
- Is the entry made at closing of the period or postclosing with little or no explanation or description?
- Do entries made during the preparation of financial statements lack account numbers?
- Does the entry contain round numbers or a consistent ending number?

The auditor should use the following questions to identify journal entries and adjustments made to accounts that have the following characteristics:

- Does the account consist of transactions that are complex or unusual in nature?
- Does the account contain significant estimates and period-end adjustments?
- Has the account been prone to errors in the past?
- Has the account not been regularly reconciled on a timely basis?
- Does the account contain unreconciled differences?
- Does the account contain intercompany transactions?
- Is the account otherwise associated with an identified risk of material misstatement due to fraud?

Illustration 4. List of Circumstances That May Indicate the Possibility of Fraud (from AU-C 240 Appendix C)

Conditions may be identified during fieldwork that change or support a judgment regarding the assessment of the risks, such as the following:

- Discrepancies in the accounting records, including:
  - Transactions that are not recorded in a complete or timely manner or are improperly recorded as to amount, accounting period, classification, or entity policy.
  - Unsupported or unauthorized balances or transactions.
  - Last-minute adjustments that significantly affect financial results.
  - Evidence of employees' access to systems and records inconsistent with that necessary to perform their authorized duties.
  - Tips or complaints to the auditor about alleged fraud.
- Conflicting or missing evidential matter, including:
  - Missing documents.
  - Documents that appear to have been altered.
  - Unavailability of other than photocopies or electronically transmitted documents when documents in original form are expected to exist.
  - Significant unexplained items on reconciliations.
  - Unusual balance sheet changes, or changes in trends or important financial statement ratios or relationships; for example, receivables growing faster than revenues.
  - Inconsistent, vague, or implausible responses from management or employees arising from inquiries procedures.
  - Unusual discrepancies between the entity's records and confirmation replies.
  - Large numbers of credit entries and other adjustments made to accounts receivable records.
  - Unexplained or inadequately explained differences between the accounts receivable subledger and the control account, or between the customer statements and the accounts receivable subledger.
  - Missing inventory or physical assets of significant magnitude.
  - Unavailable or missing electronic evidence, inconsistent with the entity's record retention practices or policies.
  - Fewer responses to confirmations than anticipated or a greater number of responses than anticipated.
  - Inability to produce evidence of key systems development and program change testing and implementation activities for current-year system changes and deployments.
- Problematic or unusual relationships between the auditor and management, including:
  - Denial of access to records, facilities, certain employees, customers, vendors, or others from whom audit evidence might be sought.
  - Undue time pressures imposed by management to resolve complex or contentious issues.
  - Complaints by management about the conduct of the audit or management intimidation of audit team members, particularly in connection with the auditor's critical assessment of audit evidence or in the resolution of potential disagreements with management.
  - Unusual delays by the entity in providing requested information.
  - Unwillingness to facilitate auditor access to key electronic files for testing through the use of computer-assisted audit techniques.
  - Denial of access to key IT operations staff and facilities, including security, operations, and systems development personnel.
  - An unwillingness to add or revise disclosures in the financial statements to make them more complete and transparent.
  - An unwillingness to address identified deficiencies in internal control on a timely basis.

ILLUSTRATION 5. EXAMPLE PROGRAM FOR MANAGEMENT OVERRIDE OF INTERNAL CONTROL

Audit Program for Management Override of Internal Control	Page ________ of ________
Company:	Balance Sheet Date:

Audit Objective	Audit Procedure for Consideration	N/A Performed By	Workpaper Index
	AUDIT OBJECTIVES A. To identify risk of material misstatement due to fraud caused by inappropriate or unauthorized journal entries B. To determine whether management is not unduly biased in the preparation of significant accounting estimates C. To determine whether significant unusual transactions have not been entered into to engage in fraudulent financial reporting or to conceal a misappropriation of assets		
	Review of Journal Entries		
A.	1. Obtain an understanding of the company's financial reporting process and the controls over nonstandard journal entries. Document the following: a. The sources of entries posted to the general ledger (for example, subledgers, cash receipts journal, etc.) b. How the journal entries are recorded and whether physical documentation exists c. The individuals responsible for: (a) initiating, (b) reviewing, and (c) approving the journal entries d. The controls in place to prevent and detect unauthorized entries		
A.	2. Obtain an understanding of the adjustments posted by the entity to prepare its financial statements (for example, reclassification or consolidating entries). Document the following: a. The nature of the adjustments posted to the financial statements that are not posted to the general ledger b. How the adjustments are posted to the financial statements c. The individuals responsible for: (a) initiating, (b) reviewing, and (c) approving the adjustments d. The controls in place to prevent and detect unauthorized adjustments		

Audit Objective	Audit Procedure for Consideration	N/A Performed By	Workpaper Index
A.	3. Identify and select significant nonstandard journal entries and other significant adjustments for testing. In making this selection, consider the following: a. The effectiveness of the company's controls over journal entries and adjustments b. The characteristics of fraudulent entries or adjustments, such as: • Made to unrelated, unusual, or seldom-used accounts • Made by individuals who typically do not make journal entries • Recorded at the end of the reporting period or as postclosing entries • Having few or no explanations or account numbers • Containing round numbers or a consistent ending number c. The nature and complexity of the accounts. Examples include accounts that: • Contain transactions that are complex or unusual in nature • Contain significant estimates or period-end adjustments • Have been prone to errors in the past • Cannot be reconciled on a timely basis or that contain significant unreconciled differences • Contain intercompany transactions • Are otherwise associated with an identified risk of material misstatement due to fraud d. Contain journal entries or other adjustments processed outside the normal course of business		
A.	4. Ask individuals involved in the financial reporting process, including IT personnel (if appropriate), about the presence or observations of inappropriate or unusual activity relating to the processing of journal entries or other adjustments.		
A.	5. Document the following: a. The journal entries and adjustments selected for testing b. The nature and purpose of the journal entry or adjustment c. Whether the journal entries and adjustments were properly approved d. A conclusion regarding the propriety of the journal entries and adjustments tested		

Audit Objective	Audit Procedure for Consideration	N/A Performed By	Workpaper Index
	Retrospective Review of Estimates		
B.	6. Identify and document: a. Accounting estimates that are significant to the financial statements b. For each significant estimate, the key underlying assumptions made by management		
B.	7. For the prior reporting period, compare the key assumptions made by management at the time the financial statements were prepared to actual events, management actions, or results obtained subsequent to that time.		
B.	8. Determine whether the results of your procedures indicate a bias on the part of management that may affect the financial statements. If no bias is detected, document this conclusion.		
	Significant Unusual Transactions		
C.	9. Identify and document significant unusual transactions entered into during the reporting period. Consider documenting: • The counterparty(ies) to the transaction • How the transaction was accounted, presented, and disclosed in the financial statements • The process followed by the entity to approve the transaction and its accounting treatment • Management's stated business rationale for the transaction		
C.	10. Determine and document whether the management's rationale for the transaction (or lack thereof) suggests that the transaction may have been entered into to engage in fraudulent financial reporting or conceal a misappropriation of assets. In making your determination, consider whether: • The form of such transactions is overly complex. • Management has discussed the nature of an accounting for such transactions with ABC Co., the audit committee, or board of directors. • Management is placing more emphasis on the need for a particular accounting treatment than on the underlying economics of the transaction. • Transactions that involve unconsolidated related parties have been properly reviewed and approved by the audit committee or board of directors. • The transactions involve previously unidentifiable related parties or parties that do not have the substance or the financial strength to support the transaction without assistance from the entity under the audit.		

Audit Objective	Audit Procedure for Consideration	N/A Performed By	Workpaper Index
	CONCLUSION We have performed procedures sufficient to achieve the stated audit objective, and the results of these procedures are adequately presented in the accompanying workpapers. (If you are unable to conclude on the objective, prepare a memo documenting your reason.) ____ ____ ____		

AU-C 250 Consideration of Laws and Regulations in an Audit of Financial Statements

AU-C ORIGINAL PRONOUNCEMENT

Source Statement on Auditing Standards (SAS) 122.

AU-C 250 DEFINITION OF TERM

Source: AU-C 250.11

Noncompliance. Acts of omission or commission by the entity, either intentional or unintentional, which are contrary to the prevailing laws or regulations. Such acts include transactions entered into by, or in the name of, the entity or on its behalf by those charged with governance, management, or employees. Noncompliance does not include personal misconduct (unrelated to the business activities of the entity) by those charged with governance, management, or employees of the entity.

OBJECTIVES OF AU SECTION 250

AU-C Section 250.10 states that:

. . . *the objectives of the auditor are to*

a. *obtain sufficient appropriate audit evidence regarding material amounts and disclosures in the financial statements that are determined by the provisions of those laws and regulations generally recognized to have a direct effect on their determination (see paragraph .06a),*
b. *perform specified audit procedures that may identify instances of noncompliance with other laws and regulations that may have a material effect on the financial statements (see paragraph .06b), and*
c. *respond appropriately to noncompliance or suspected noncompliance with laws and regulations identified during the audit.*

REQUIREMENTS

Auditor's Responsibilities

Noncompliance with laws and regulations is so diverse that articulating the auditor's responsibility for their detection and reporting has proven to be very complex. Some laws and regulations, such as the Internal Revenue Code regulations concerning income tax expense, clearly fall within the auditor's expertise, and the audit of financial statements normally includes testing compliance with such laws and regulations. Other laws and regulations, such as those on occupational safety and health or food and drug administration, are clearly outside the auditor's expertise and are not susceptible to testing by customary auditing procedures.

Categories of Laws and Regulations

AU-C 250 makes a distinction in the auditor's responsibility between two categories of laws and regulations:

1. Those that have a direct effect on the determination of financial statement amounts—for example, pension and tax laws and regulations. (AU-C 250.6a)
2. Those that do not have a direct effect but compliance may be fundamental to operating and continuing the business, and which may carry material penalties for noncompliance—for example, operating licenses and environmental regulation. (AU-C 250.06b)

AU-C Section 250 requires the performance of procedures to identify *material* misstatements resulting from noncompliance with laws and regulations. The auditor is not expected to detect noncompliance with all laws and regulations. (AU-C 250.04) Because of the inherent limitations of an audit, some material misstatements in the financial statements may not be detected even when the audit is properly planned and performed in accordance with GAAS. (AU-C 250.05)

Audit Procedures

The auditor is explicitly required to:

- Obtain an understanding of the legal and regulatory framework.
- Obtain an understanding of how the entity is complying with that framework.

(AU-C 250.12)

To obtain an understanding of the entity's legal and regulatory framework, the auditor may, among other procedures,

- Use the auditor's existing understanding of the entity's industry and regulatory and other external factors and update the understanding of those regulations that directly determine the reported amounts and disclosures in the financial statements.
- Inquire of management concerning the client's compliance with laws and regulations, policies on prevention of noncompliance, and the use of directives and periodic representations obtained from management at appropriate levels of authority concerning compliance with laws and regulations.
- Consider the entity's history of noncompliance.

(AU-C 250.A8)

For laws and regulations category 1 above, the auditor must obtain sufficient evidence regarding material amounts in the financial statements that are determined by those laws and regulations. (AU-C 250.13)

For category 2, the auditor's responsibility is to perform specified audit procedures that may identify noncompliance having a material effect on the financial statements. (AU-C 250.07) These are:

- Inquire of management and, if appropriate, those charged with governance about whether the entity is complying with laws and regulations.
- Inspect correspondence with the relevant licensing or regulatory authorities.

(AU-C 250.14)

During the audit, the auditor should remain alert to instances of noncompliance that may be revealed by other audit procedures. (AU-C 250.15) Examples of customary audit procedures that might bring possible noncompliance to the auditor's attention include:

1. Reading minutes
2. Making inquiries of management and legal counsel concerning litigation, claims, and assessments
3. Performing substantive tests of sensitive transactions

(AU-C 250.A17)

However, aside from the requirements above and absent specific information concerning possible noncompliance, the auditor does not need to perform any further procedures in this area. AU-C 580, *Written Representations*, requires the auditor to obtain a written representation from management concerning the absence of noncompliance with laws or regulations. (AU-C 250.16)

Response to Identified or Suspected Noncompliance with Laws and Regulations

When the auditor becomes aware of information about a possible noncompliance, the auditor should obtain an understanding of:

1. The nature of the possible noncompliance,
2. The circumstances in which the act occurred, and
3. Sufficient other information to allow the auditor to consider the effect on the financial statements.

(AU-C 250.17)

According to AU-C 250.A19, the auditor should be aware that specific information such as the following may raise a question concerning possible noncompliance:

1. Noncompliance with laws or regulations cited in reports of examinations by regulatory agencies that have been made available to the auditor
2. Unusual payments in cash
3. Large payments for unspecified services to consultants, affiliates, or employees
4. Failure to file tax returns or pay government duties or similar fees that are common to the entity's industry or the nature of its business

In addition to procedures previously mentioned, the auditor may apply other procedures, if necessary, to further understand the nature of noncompliance that has come to the auditor's attention. The additional procedures might include:

a. Examining supporting documents, such as invoices
b. Confirming significant information with other parties to the transaction
c. Determining if the transaction was properly authorized
d. Considering whether other similar transactions may have occurred
e. Applying procedures to identify other similar transactions

(AU-C 250.A20)

The auditor should inquire of management at a level above those involved, if possible. If the effect may be material and management or those charged with management do not provide satisfactory information that there has been no noncompliance, the auditor should:

- Consider the need to seek legal advice (AU-C 250.18)
- Evaluate the effect on the opinion (AU-C 250.19)
- Evaluate the implication on other area of the audit—for example, the assessment of audit risk (AU-C 250.20)

If management or those charged with governance do not provide sufficient evidence to support the entity's compliance, the auditor may consider consulting with the client's legal counsel (with the client's permission) or other specialists about applying relevant laws and regulations to the circumstances and the possible effects on the financial statements. (AU-C 250.A23)

Evaluation of Detected or Suspected Noncompliance with Laws and Regulations

The auditor should consider the quantitative and qualitative aspects of the noncompliance. Loss contingencies resulting from noncompliance that may be required to be disclosed should be evaluated similar to other loss contingencies. (AU-C 250.A21)

The auditor should consider the implications of noncompliance for the rest of the audit, particularly whether the auditor can rely on client representations. (AU-C 250.A24) Factors to consider include the relationship of the perpetration and concealment, if any, of the noncompliance to specific control procedures and the level of management or employees involved.

Even when the noncompliance is not material to the financial statements, the auditor may decide to withdraw from the engagement when the client does not take the remedial action the auditor considers necessary in the circumstances. (AU-C 250.A25)

Reporting Identified or Suspected Noncompliance

Internal Communications

The auditor should communicate with those charged with governance to make sure they are adequately informed about noncompliance that came to the auditor's attention. (AU-C 250.21) (If senior management is involved in the noncompliance, the auditor should communicate directly with those charged with governance.) If the noncompliance is believed to be intentional and material, the auditor should communicate with those charged with governance as soon as practicable.

Since clearly inconsequential matters need not be communicated to those charged with governance, the auditor may agree in advance with the audit committee on the nature of matters to be communicated.

Any communication regarding noncompliance or suspected noncompliance should describe:

1. The noncompliance
2. The circumstances of its occurrence
3. The financial statement effect

(AU-C 250.A26)

Effect on the Audit Report

If the auditor concludes that the noncompliance that has a material effect on the financial statements has not been properly accounted for or disclosed, the auditor should issue a qualified or an adverse opinion in accordance with AU-C 705, *Modifications to the Opinion in the Independent Auditor's Report.* (AU-C 250.24)

If the client prevents the auditor from obtaining sufficient competent evidential matter to evaluate whether noncompliance that could be material to the financial statements has occurred or is likely to have occurred, the auditor should express a qualified opinion or disclaim an opinion in accordance with AU-C 705. (AU-C 250.25)

If the client refuses to accept the auditor's report as modified because of noncompliance, the auditor should withdraw from the engagement and communicate, in writing, the reasons for withdrawal to the audit committee or to those charged with governance. (AU-C 250.A27)

External Communications

Normally, disclosing noncompliance with laws or regulations outside the client's organization would be precluded by the auditor's ethical or legal obligation of confidentiality. However, the auditor should determine whether there is a responsibility to report the matter to outside parties. (AU-C 250.27) The auditor should recognize that in the following circumstances, a duty to notify parties outside the client may exist:

1. To the SEC when the client reports an auditor change on Form 8-K (or to comply with other legal and regulatory requirements, such as Section 10A of the Securities Exchange Act of 1934)
2. To a successor auditor under Section 210
3. To a court order
4. To a funding agency or other specified agency in audits of entities that receive financial assistance from a government agency

(AU-C 250.A28)

Documentation

The auditor should document identified or suspected noncompliance and the related discussions with management, those charged with governance, and other internal or external parties. (AU-C 250.28)

AU-C 260 The Auditor's Communication with Those Charged with Governance

AU-C ORIGINAL PRONOUNCEMENTS

Sources Statements on Auditing Standards (SASs) 122, 123, 125, and 128.

AU-C DEFINITIONS OF TERMS

Source: AU-C 260.06

Management. The person(s) with executive responsibility for the conduct of the entity's operations. For some entities, management includes some or all of those charged with governance; for example, executive members of a governance board or an owner-manager.

Those charged with governance. The person(s) or organization(s) (for example, a corporate trustee) with responsibility for overseeing the strategic direction of the entity and the obligations related to the accountability of the entity. This includes overseeing the financial reporting process. Those charged with governance may include management personnel; for example, executive members of a governance board or an owner-manager.

OBJECTIVES OF AU-C SECTION 260

AU-C Section 260.05 states that the objectives of the auditor are to:

a. *communicate clearly with those charged with governance the responsibilities of the auditor regarding the financial statement audit and an overview of the planned scope and timing of the audit.*
b. *obtain from those charged with governance information relevant to the audit.*
c. *provide those charged with governance with timely observations arising from the audit that are significant and relevant to their responsibility to oversee the financial reporting process.*
d. *promote effective two-way communication between the auditor and those charged with governance.*

REQUIREMENTS

AUDITOR'S GENERAL RESPONSIBILITY

The auditor *must* communicate with those charged with governance matters related to the financial statement audit that are, in the auditor's professional judgment, significant and relevant to the responsibilities of those charged with governance in overseeing the financial reporting process. Certain matters *should* be communicated in each audit (as described below); however, the auditor is not required to perform procedures specifically to identify these matters.

THOSE CHARGED WITH GOVERNANCE

AU-C 260.09 and AU-C 206.A6-.A9 provide some guidance on how the auditor should determine which persons or bodies are "those charged with governance" (see "Definitions of Terms"). Governance structures vary by entity; however, in most entities, governance is the collective responsibility of a governing body, such as a board of directors, a supervisory board, partners, proprietors, a committee of management, trustees, or equivalent. In some entities, one person, such as the owner-manager, may be the sole person charged with governance of the entity.

When "those charged with governance" are not clearly identifiable, the auditor and the engaging party should agree on the person(s) with whom the auditor will communicate. In those situations where the entity's governance structure includes subgroups (e.g., an audit committee), the auditor also should evaluate whether communication with a subgroup is sufficient.

MATTERS TO BE COMMUNICATED

The auditor should communicate with those charged with governance:

1. The auditor's responsibility under generally accepted auditing standards, that is, forming and expressing an opinion on statements prepared by management with oversight by those charged with governance in accordance with the applicable financial reporting framework.
2. The fact that the audit of the financial statements does not relieve management or those charged with governance of their responsibilities.
3. An overview of the planned scope and timing of the audit.
4. Significant findings from the audit.

(AU-C 260.10-11)

The auditor may communicate matters such as:

- The auditor is responsible for performing the audit in accordance with GAAS.
- An audit is designed to obtain reasonable, not absolute, assurance.
- An audit includes consideration of internal control as a basis for designing audit procedures, but not for expressing an opinion on the effectiveness of internal control over financial reporting.
- The auditor is responsible for communicating significant matters related to the audit that are relevant to the responsibilities of those charged with governance.
- The auditor is responsible for communicating particular matters required by laws or regulations, agreement with the entity, or additional requirements applicable to the engagement.

(AU-C 260.A13)

Overview of the Planned Scope and Timing of the Audit

The auditor should communicate an overview of the planned scope and timing of the audit. To meet that general requirement, the auditor *may* communicate matters such as the following:

- How the auditor proposes to address the significant risks of material misstatement.
- The auditor's approach to internal control.
- The concept of materiality in planning and executing the audit.
- Where the entity has an internal audit function and the internal auditors can work together in a constructive manner, the extent to which the auditor will use internal auditors.
- The views of those charged with governance about:
  - The appropriate person(s) in the entity's governance structure with whom to communicate
  - The allocation of responsibilities between those charged with governance and management
  - The entity's objectives and strategies, and the related business risks that may result in material misstatements
  - Matters those charged with governance consider warrant particular attention during the audit, and any areas where they request additional procedures to be undertaken
  - Significant communications with regulators
  - Other matters those charged with governance believe are relevant to the audit of the financial statements
- The attitudes, awareness, and actions of those charged with governance concerning (1) the entity's internal control and its importance in the entity and (2) the detection or the possibility of fraud.
- The actions of those charged with governance in response to developments in financial reporting, laws, accounting standards, corporate governance practices, and other related matters.
- The actions of those charged with governance in response to previous communications with the auditor.

(AU-C 260.A20-A21)

Significant Findings

The auditor should communicate the following matters:

- The auditor's views about qualitative aspects of the entity's significant accounting practices, including accounting policies, accounting estimates, and financial statement disclosures.
- Significant difficulties, if any, encountered during the audit.
- Disagreements with management, if any.
- Other findings or issues, if any, arising from the audit that are significant and relevant to those charged with governance.

(AU-C 260.12)

The auditor *should* communicate significant difficulties, if any, encountered during the audit; these may include:

- Significant delays in management providing required information.
- An unnecessarily brief time within which to complete the audit.

- Extensive unexpected effort required to obtain sufficient appropriate audit evidence.
- The unavailability of expected information.
- Restrictions imposed on the auditors by management.
- Management's unwillingness to provide information about management's plans for dealing with the adverse effects of the conditions or events that lead the auditor to believe there is substantial doubt about the entity's ability to continue as a going concern.

(AU-C 260.A26)

The auditor should also communicate uncorrected misstatements, other than those the auditor believes are trivial. This information should include the effect they may have, individually or in the aggregate, on the auditor's opinion. Material uncorrected misstatements should be identified individually, and the auditor should request that they be corrected. So, too, the auditor should communicate the effect of uncorrected misstatements related to prior periods. (AU-C 260.13)

Unless all of those charged with governance are involved in managing the entity, the auditor also should communicate:

- Material corrected misstatements that were brought to the attention of management as a result of audit procedures.
- Written representations the auditor is requesting from management.
- The auditor's view of management's consultations with other accountants.
- Significant issues, if any, that were discussed, or the subject of correspondence, with management.

(AU-C 260.14)

Communication Process

The auditor should communicate, on a timely basis, with those charged with governance regarding the timing and expected general content of communications. (AU-C 260.15) The auditor may also communicate matters such as:

- The purpose of communications. When the purpose is clear, the auditor and those charged with governance are in a better position to have a mutual understanding of relevant issues and the expected actions arising from the communication process.
- The person(s) on the audit team and among those charged with governance who will communicate regarding particular matters.
- The form of communication.
- The auditor's expectation that communication will be two-way, and that those charged with governance will communicate with the auditor matters they consider relevant to the audit. Such matters might include strategic decisions that may significantly affect the nature, timing, and the extent of audit procedures; the suspicion or the detection of fraud; or concerns about the integrity or competence of senior management.
- The process for taking action and reporting back on matters communicated by the auditor.
- The process for taking action and reporting back on matters communicated by those charged with governance.

(AU-C 260.A35)

The auditor may discuss matters with management before approaching those charged with governance. In some circumstances, for instance where management's competence or integrity are involved, it would be appropriate to go directly to those charged with governance. In other circumstances, it might be helpful to go to management or to those in the internal audit function to clarify facts. (AU-C 260.A38)

Form of Communication

If it is the auditor's judgment that communication is not adequate, the auditor should communicate in writing significant findings from the audit (see "Matters to be Communicated"). If matters are communicated during the audit and satisfactorily resolved, those matters do not have to be documented. (AU-C 260.16) All other communications may be oral or in writing. When matters are communicated orally, the auditor should document them.

Timing of Communication

The auditor should communicate with those charged with governance on a sufficiently timely basis to enable those charged with governance to take appropriate action. (AU-C 260.18)

Evaluating the Communication Process

The auditor should evaluate whether the two-way communication between the auditor and those charged with governance has been adequate for the purpose of the audit. If the communication between the auditor and those charged with governance has not been adequate, the auditor should assess the effect on risk and the ability to obtain sufficient audit evidence, and should take appropriate action. (AU-C 216.19)

Qualitative Aspects of Accounting Practices

Auditors should seek to have an open and constructive communication with those charged with governance about the qualitative aspects of the entity's significant accounting practices. This communication may include comment on the acceptability of significant accounting practices.

When making this communication, the auditor should explain why he or she considers the practice not to be appropriate. When necessary, the auditor should request changes. If requested changes are not made, the auditor should inform those charged with governance that the auditor will consider the effect of this on the financial statements of the current and future years, and on the auditor's report.

The AU-C 260.A48 Appendix includes matters that may be communicated, such as the following:

Accounting Policies

- The appropriateness of the accounting policies to the particular circumstances of the entity, considering the need to balance the cost of providing information with the likely benefit to users of the entity's financial statements. Where acceptable alternative accounting policies exist, the communication may include identification of the financial statement items that are affected by the choice of significant policies as well as information on accounting policies used by similar entities.
- The initial selection of, and changes in, significant accounting policies, including the application of new accounting pronouncements. The communication may include the effect of the timing and method of adoption of a change in accounting policy on the current and future earnings of the entity, and the timing of a change in accounting policies in relation to expected new accounting pronouncements.

- The effect of significant accounting policies in controversial or emerging areas (or those unique to an industry, particularly when there is a lack of authoritative guidance or consensus).
- The effect of the timing of transactions in relation to the period in which they are recorded.

Accounting Estimates

For items for which estimates are significant, issues discussed in AU-C 540, *Auditing Accounting Estimates, Including Fair Value Accounting Estimates and Related Disclosures*, include, for example:

- Management's identification of accounting estimates
- Management's process for making accounting estimates
- Risks of material misstatement
- Indicators of possible management bias

Financial Statement Disclosures

- The issues involved, and related judgments made, in formulating particularly sensitive financial statement disclosures (for example, disclosures related to revenue recognition, going concern, subsequent events, and contingency issues)
- The overall neutrality, consistency, and clarity of the disclosures in the financial statements

Related Matters

- The potential effect on the financial statements of significant risks and exposures, and uncertainties, such as pending litigation, that are disclosed in the financial statements.
- The extent to which the financial statements are affected by unusual transactions, including nonrecurring amounts recognized during the period, and the extent to which such transactions are separately disclosed in the financial statements.
- The factors affecting asset and liability carrying values, including the entity's bases for determining useful lives assigned to tangible and intangible assets. The communication may explain how factors affecting carrying values were selected and how alternative selections would have affected the financial statements.
- The selective correction of misstatements—for example, correcting misstatements with the effect of increasing reported earnings, but not those that have the effect of decreasing reported earnings.

OTHER AU-C SECTIONS

Requirements to communicate with those charged with governance are included in other AU-C sections, and readers should refer to those sections in this book: AU-C Sections 210, 240, 250, 265, 550, 560, 570, 600, 705, 706, 720, 730, 930, and 935.

AU-C 265 Communicating Internal Control Related Matters Identified in an Audit

AU-C ORIGINAL PRONOUNCEMENTS

Sources Statements on Auditing Standards (SASs) 122, 125, and 128.

TECHNICAL ALERT

In October 2015, the Auditing Standards Board (ASB) issued Statement on Auditing Standards (SAS) No. 130. SAS No. 130 contains amendments to this section. Any relevant changes are incorporated into the information that follows.

AU-C DEFINITIONS OF TERMS

Source: AU-C Section 265.07

Deficiency in internal control. A deficiency in internal control over financial reporting exists when the design or operation of a control does not allow management or employees, in the normal course of performing their assigned functions, to prevent, or detect and correct, misstatements on a timely basis. A deficiency in *design* exists when (1) a control necessary to meet the control objective is missing, or (2) an existing control is not properly designed so that, even if the control operates as designed, the control objective would not be met. A deficiency in *operation* exists when a properly designed control does not operate as designed or when the person performing the control does not possess the necessary authority or competence to perform the control effectively.

Material weakness. A deficiency or a combination of deficiencies in internal control over financial reporting, such that there is a reasonable possibility that a material misstatement of the entity's financial statements will not be prevented, or detected and corrected, on a timely basis. A reasonable possibility exists when the likelihood of an event occurring is either reasonably possible or probable as defined as follows:

a. Reasonably possible. The chance of the future event or events occurring is more than remote, but less than likely.
b. Probable. The future event or events are likely to occur.

Significant deficiency. A deficiency, or a combination of deficiencies, in internal control over financial reporting that is less severe than a material weakness yet important enough to merit attention by those charged with governance.

OBJECTIVES

AU-C Section 265.06 states that:

> *. . . the objective of the auditor is to appropriately communicate to those charged with governance and management deficiencies in internal control that the auditor has identified during the audit and that, in the auditor's professional judgment, are of sufficient importance to merit their respective attentions.*

REQUIREMENTS

Determining Whether Deficiencies in Internal Control Have Been Identified

The auditors must determine whether, on the basis of the audit work performed, they have identified one or more deficiencies in internal control. (AU-C 265.08) The auditor must evaluate the severity of the control deficiencies identified during the audit to determine whether those deficiencies, individually or in combination, are significant deficiencies or material weaknesses. See "Definitions of Terms" for definitions of these terms. (AU-C 265.09)

NOTE: The auditor is not required to search out or have procedures in place to identify control deficiencies. In other words, when an auditor "trips across" an internal control deficiency in the course of an audit, the auditor must then evaluate the deficiency.

Determination of Deficiency Severity

The auditor must evaluate identified control deficiencies to determine whether they are—individually or in the aggregate—significant deficiencies or material weaknesses. (AU-C 265.09) When evaluating control deficiencies, the auditor should consider both the possibility and the magnitude of the misstatement that could result from the deficiency. Determining the severity of a deficiency depends on:

1. The magnitude of a misstatement resulting from the deficiency, and
2. Whether there is a reasonable possibility that the entity's controls will fail to prevent, or detect and correct, a misstatement. Notice that the determination of severity of a deficiency *does not* depend on whether the misstatement actually occurred.

(AU-C 265.A5)

The magnitude of a misstatement can be impacted by such factors as the amounts or transaction volume that is exposed to the deficiency. When evaluating the magnitude of a potential misstatement, the recorded amount is considered the maximum amount by which an account balance can be overstated. (AU-C 265.A6-.A7)

Risk Factors

The reasonable possibility that one or more deficiencies will result in a financial statement misstatement is affected by risk factors. Risk factors include the following:

- The nature of the financial statement, transaction types, account balances, disclosures, and assertions
- The susceptibility of assets or liabilities to loss or fraud

- The extent of judgment required to determine amounts, as well as the level of subjectivity and complexity in these decisions
- The interaction of controls with each other
- The interaction of deficiencies with each other
- The future consequences of the deficiency
- The importance of the controls to the financial reporting process

(AU-C 265.A8)

One can evaluate whether a deficiency presents a reasonable possibility of misstatement without quantifying a specific range for the probability of occurrence. It is quite possible that the probability of a small misstatement will exceed the probability of a large misstatement. (AU-C 265.A9)

Possibility of the misstatement. The possibility of a misstatement is a continuous spectrum that ranges from "remote" to "reasonably possible" to "probable." The following diagram illustrates this range, with "probable" as somewhat less than 100% certainty and "remote" as greater than a 0% chance, while "reasonably possible" is when the chance is more than remote.

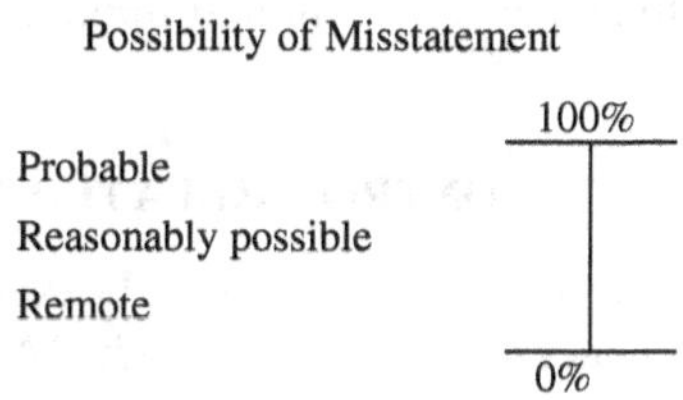

The evaluation may be made without quantifying an amount. Factors that may increase the possibility of misstatement include the nature of the item involved, the cause and frequency of noted exceptions, the susceptibility of the related item to loss or fraud, the extent of judgment required to determine the amount involved, the interaction with other deficiencies, possible future consequences, and the importance of the control to the financial reporting process. (AU-C 265.A8)

Magnitude of the misstatement. The magnitude of a misstatement also is a continuous spectrum with two key thresholds, "inconsequential" to "material," as illustrated in the following diagram.

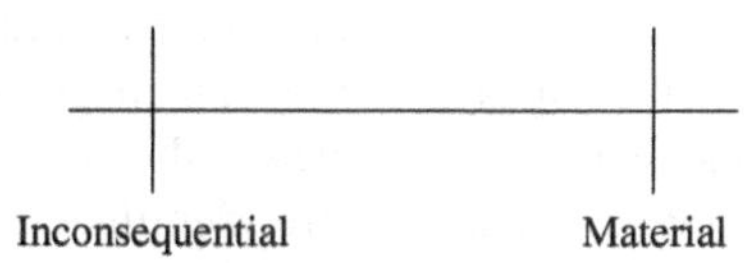

The combination of possibility and magnitude. The evaluation of control deficiencies requires the auditor to consider both the possibility and the magnitude of the misstatement. Combining the previous two diagrams illustrates this concept.

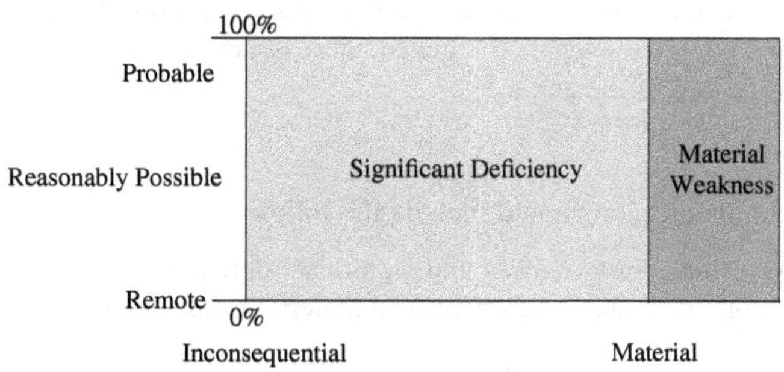

When a control deficiency exists, there is a chance that the internal control system will fail to either prevent or detect a misstatement. This diagram illustrates that if the possibility of the misstatement being included in the financial statements is greater than remote and the magnitude of the misstatement is greater than inconsequential, then the deficiency is at least a significant deficiency. If the magnitude of the potential misstatement is greater than material, then a material weakness exists.

Indicators of Material Weakness

The following are indicators of material weaknesses in internal controls:

- Fraud by senior management, even if immaterial
- Restatement of previously issued financial statements
- Correction of a material misstatement due to error or fraud
- Identification of a material misstatement that would not have been detected by the entity's internal controls
- Ineffective oversight of financial reporting and internal controls

(AU-C 265.A11)

Communication of Internal Control Related Matters

Significant deficiencies and material weaknesses must be communicated in writing to management and those charged with governance as a part of each audit. [AU-C 265.11-12(a)] In this context, senior management includes the principal extent and financial access and any other members of senior management who play a significant role on the entity's financial reporting process.

The auditor may communicate matters in writing or orally that he or she does not consider to be reportable conditions but which nonetheless may be of benefit to the entity. If the communication is oral, it should be documented. [AU-C 265.12(b)] The auditor is not required to communicate such matters if they have been communicated by the auditor in a prior period or by others, such as internal auditors. (AU-C 265.A26)

If significant deficiencies and material weaknesses were not remediated following previous audits, this communication should repeat the description or reference the prior communications. While management may have made a conscious decision to accept the risk of a control deficiency, the auditor must still communicate the issue regardless of management's decision. (AU-C 265.A20)

To avoid potential misunderstanding or misuse, the auditor should not issue a written communication that no significant deficiencies were identified during the audit. (AU-C 265.16)

Timing

Communication of internal control related matters should be made no later than 60 days following the report release date. (AU-C 265.13) For significant issues in need of immediate correction, the auditor may choose to communicate those issues during the audit and can do so other than in writing; however, even if remediated, these issues should still be included in a written communication at the end of the audit.

Content

The written communication should include the following items:

- Definitions of material weakness and significant deficiency
- Description of significant deficiencies and material weaknesses and their potential effects

- Information that enables those charged with governance and management to understand the context of the communications, particularly statements that:
  - The auditor is expressing an opinion on the financial statements.
  - The audit included consideration of internal control to design audit procedures, not for the purpose of expressing an opinion on internal control.
  - The auditor is not expressing an opinion on the effectiveness of internal control.
  - The auditor's consideration of internal control may not identify all significant deficiencies or material control weaknesses.
- An appropriate alert in accordance with AU-C 905, *Alert That Restricts the Use of the Auditor's Written Communication*

(AU-C 265.14)

The content of the communication can contain additional topics, such as recommendations for improvement in such areas as administrative or operational efficiency, as well as less than significant deficiencies or immaterial weaknesses. Any verbal communications should be documented. The auditor may also note the general inherent limitations of internal control, including the possibility of management override of those controls. It may also be acceptable to specifically describe the extent of the auditor's consideration of internal control.

The auditor may be asked to issue a communication indicating that no material weaknesses were identified, which then would be submitted to governmental authorities. The "AU-C 265 Illustrations" section contains a sample communication that may be used.

Management Response

Management may prepare a written response to the auditor's communication. Such responses typically describe corrective actions taken, plans to issue new controls, or management's belief that the cost of new controls exceeds their benefit. If this response is included in a document that also contains the auditor's controls communication, the auditor may include a disclaimer paragraph, such as:

> ABC Company's written response to the significant deficiencies [and material weaknesses] identified in our audit was not subjected to the auditing procedures applied in the audit of the financial statements and, accordingly, we express no opinion on it.
> (AU-C 265.A33)

INTERPRETATIONS

Communication of Significant Deficiencies and Material Weaknesses Prior to the Completion of the Compliance Audit for Participants in Office of Management and Budget Single-Audit Pilot Project (Issued November 1994; Revised March 2010; January 2012, Effective for Audits of Financial Statements for Periods Ending on or after December 15, 2012)

Section 265 permits an auditor to communicate deficiencies and material weaknesses in writing to management before completing a financial statement audit, and this also applies to a compliance audit.

Communication of Significant Deficiencies and Material Weaknesses Prior to the Completion of the Compliance Audit for Auditors That Are Not Participants in Office of Management and Budget Pilot Project (Issued November 2009; Revised March 2010; January 2012, Effective for Audits of Financial Statements on or after December 15, 2012)

If the auditor decides to communicate with management regarding any significant deficiencies or material weaknesses in internal control, he or she may do so using the guidelines in Section 265, *Communicating Internal Control Related Matters Identified in an Audit.*

Appropriateness of Identifying No Significant Deficiencies or No Material Weaknesses in an Interim Communication (Issued November 2009; Revised March 2010; January 2012, Effective for Audits of Financial Statements for Periods Ending on or after December 15, 2012)

In the scenarios in these interpretations, the auditor should not issue a written communication stating that no significant deficiencies were identified during an audit as of an interim date, only at the end of an audit.

AU-C 265 ILLUSTRATIONS

Illustration 1. Examples of Circumstances That May Be Control Deficiencies, Significant Deficiencies, or Material Weaknesses

The appendix to Section 265.A37 lists the following as examples of circumstances that may be control deficiencies in the design of controls, or failures in the operation of internal control. As such, auditors should consider these matters when designing and performing risk assessment procedures to gain an understanding of the design and implementation of internal control and when performing and evaluating the results of further audit procedures.

Deficiencies in Internal Control Design

- Inadequate design of internal control over the preparation of the financial statements being audited.
- Inadequate design of internal control over a significant account or process.
- Inadequate documentation of the components of internal control.
- Insufficient control consciousness within the organization—for example, the tone at the top and the control environment.
- Absent or inadequate segregation of duties within a significant account or process.
- Absent or inadequate controls over the safeguarding of assets (this applies to controls that the auditor determines would be necessary for effective internal control over financial reporting).
- Inadequate design of information technology (IT) general and application controls that prevents the information system from providing complete and accurate information consistent with financial reporting objectives and current needs.
- Employees or management who lack the qualifications and training to fulfill their assigned functions (for example, in an entity that prepares financial statements in accordance with generally accepted accounting principles (GAAP), the person responsible for the accounting and reporting function lacks the skills and knowledge to apply GAAP in recording the entity's financial transactions or preparing its financial statements).

- Inadequate design of monitoring controls used to assess the design and operating effectiveness of the entity's internal control over time.
- The absence of any internal process to report deficiencies in internal control to management on a timely basis.
- Evidence of ineffective aspects of the control environment, such as indications that significant transactions in which management is financially interested are not being appropriately scrutinized by those charged with governance.
- Evidence of an ineffective entity risk assessment process, such as management's failure to identify a risk of material misstatement that the auditor would expect the entity's risk assessment process to have identified.
- Evidence of an ineffective response to identified significant risks (for example, absence of controls over such a risk).
- Absence of a risk assessment process within the entity when such a process would ordinarily be expected to have been established.

Failures in the Operation of Internal Control

- Failure in the operation of effectively designed controls over a significant account or process; for example, the failure of a control such as dual authorization for significant disbursements within the purchasing process.
- Failure of the information and communication component of internal control to provide complete and accurate output because of deficiencies in timeliness, completeness, or accuracy; for example, the failure to obtain timely and accurate consolidating information from remote locations that is needed to prepare the financial statements.
- Failure of controls designed to safeguard assets from loss, damage, or misappropriation. This circumstance may need careful consideration before it is evaluated as a significant deficiency or material weakness. For example, assume that a company uses security devices to safeguard inventory (preventive controls) and also performs periodic physical inventory counts (detective control) timely in relation to its financial reporting. Although the physical inventory count does not safeguard the inventory from theft or loss, it prevents a material misstatement of the financial statements if performed effectively and timely. Therefore, given that the definitions of material weakness and significant deficiency relate to likelihood of misstatement of financial statements, the failure of a preventive control such as inventory tags will not result in a significant deficiency or material weakness if the detective control (physical inventory) prevents a misstatement of the financial statements. Material weaknesses relating to controls over the safeguarding of assets would exist only if the company does not have effective controls (considering both safeguarding and other controls) to prevent or detect and correct a material misstatement of the financial statements.
- Failure to perform reconciliations of significant accounts. For example, accounts receivable subsidiary ledgers are not reconciled to the general ledger account in a timely or accurate manner.
- Undue bias or lack of objectivity by those responsible for accounting decisions; for example, consistent understatement of expenses or overstatement of allowances at the direction of management.
- Misrepresentation by client personnel to the auditor (an indicator of fraud).
- Management override of controls.
- Failure of an application control caused by a deficiency in the design or operation of an IT general control.
- An observed deviation rate that exceeds the number of deviations expected by the auditor in a test of the operating effectiveness of a control. For example, if the auditor designs a test in which he or she selects a sample and expects no deviations, the finding of one deviation is a nonnegligible deviation rate because, based on the results of the auditor's test of the sample, the desired level of confidence was not obtained.

ILLUSTRATION 2. AUDITOR'S COMMUNICATION REGARDING SIGNIFICANT DEFICIENCES AND MATERIAL WEAKNESSES (AU-C 265.A38)

To Management and [*identify the body or individuals charged with governance, such as the entity's board of directors*] of ABC Company

In planning and performing our audit of the financial statements of ABC Company (the "Company") as of and for the year ended December 31, 20XX, in accordance with auditing standards generally accepted in the United States of America, we considered the Company's internal control over financial reporting (internal control) as a basis for designing audit procedures that are appropriate in the circumstances for the purpose of expressing our opinion on the financial statements, but not for the purpose of expressing an opinion on the effectiveness of the Company's internal control. Accordingly, we do not express an opinion on the effectiveness of the Company's internal control.

Our consideration of internal control was for the limited purpose described in the preceding paragraph and was not designed to identify all deficiencies in internal control that might be [*material weaknesses or significant deficiencies*] and therefore [*material weaknesses or significant deficiencies*] may exist that were not identified. However, as discussed below, we identified certain deficiencies in internal control that we consider to be [*material weaknesses or significant deficiencies or material weaknesses and significant deficiencies*].

A deficiency in internal control exists when the design or operation of a control does not allow management or employees, in the normal course of performing their assigned functions, to prevent, or detect and correct, misstatements on a timely basis. A material weakness is a deficiency, or a combination of deficiencies, in internal control, such that there is a reasonable possibility that a material misstatement of the entity's financial statements will not be prevented, or detected and corrected, on a timely basis. [*We consider the following deficiencies in the Company's internal control to be material weaknesses:*]
[*Describe the material weaknesses that were identified and explain their potential effects.*]

[*A significant deficiency is a deficiency, or a combination of deficiencies, in internal control that is less severe than a material weakness, yet important enough to merit attention by those charged with governance. We consider the following deficiencies in the Company's internal control to be significant deficiencies:*]

[*Describe the significant deficiencies that were identified and explain their potential effects.*]

[*If the auditor is communicating significant deficiencies and did not identify any material weaknesses, the auditor may state that none of the identified significant deficiencies are considered to be material weaknesses.*]

This communication is intended solely for the information and use of management, [*identify the body or individuals charged with governance*], others within the organization, and [*identify any governmental authorities to which the auditor is required to report*] and is not intended to be, and should not be, used by anyone other than these specified parties.
[*Auditor's signature*]

[*Auditor's city and state*]

[*Date*]

ILLUSTRATION 3. AUDITOR'S COMMUNICATION INDICATING THAT NO MATERIAL WEAKNESSES WERE IDENTIFIED (AU-C 265.A39)

To Management and [*identify the body or individuals charged with governance, such as the entity's board of directors*] of NPO Organization:

In planning and performing our audit of the financial statements of NPO Organization (the "Organization") as of and for the year ended December 31, 20XX, in accordance with auditing standards generally accepted in the United States of America, we considered the Organization's internal control over financial reporting (internal control) as a basis for designing audit procedures that are appropriate in the circumstances for the purpose of expressing our opinion on the financial statements, but not for the purpose of expressing an opinion on the effectiveness of the Organization's internal control. Accordingly, we do not express an opinion on the effectiveness of the Organization's internal control.

A deficiency in internal control exists when the design or operation of a control does not allow management or employees, in the normal course of performing their assigned functions, to prevent, or detect and correct, misstatements on a timely basis. A material weakness is a deficiency, or a combination of deficiencies, in internal control, such that there is a reasonable possibility that a material misstatement of the entity's financial statements will not be prevented, or detected and corrected, on a timely basis.

Our consideration of internal control was for the limited purpose described in the first paragraph and was not designed to identify all deficiencies in internal control that might be material weaknesses. Given these limitations, during our audit we did not identify any deficiencies in internal control that we consider to be material weaknesses. However, material weaknesses may exist that have not been identified.

[*If one or more significant deficiencies have been identified, the auditor may add the following:*]

Our audit was also not designed to identify deficiencies in internal control that might be significant deficiencies. A significant deficiency is a deficiency, or a combination of deficiencies, in internal control that is less severe than a material weakness, yet important enough to merit attention by those charged with governance. We communicated the significant deficiencies identified during our audit in a separate communication dated [*date*].

This communication is intended solely for the information and use of management, [*identify the body or individuals charged with governance*], others within the organization, and [*identify any governmental authorities to which the auditor is required to report*], and is not intended to be, and should not be, used by anyone other than these specified parties.

[*Auditor's signature*]

[*Auditor's city and state*]

[*Date*]

AU-C 300 Planning an Audit

AU-C ORIGINAL PRONOUNCEMENTS

Sources Statements on Accounting Standards (SASs) 122 and 128.

OBJECTIVE OF AU-C SECTION 300

AU-C Section 300.04 states that:

. . . *the objective of the auditor is to plan the audit so that it will be performed in an effective manner.*

REQUIREMENTS

Preliminary Engagement Activities

It's important for the engagement partner and other key members of the engagement team to be involved in planning the audit. (AU-C 300.05) The auditor should perform the following activities at the beginning of the current audit engagement:

- Perform procedures regarding the continuance of the client relationship and the specific audit engagement. (AU-C 220)
- Evaluate the auditor's compliance with ethical requirements, including independence. (AU-C 220)
- Establish the terms of the engagement. (AU-C 210)

(AU-C 300.06)

The purpose of performing these preliminary engagement activities is to consider any events or circumstances that either may adversely affect the auditor's ability to plan and perform the audit or may pose an unacceptable level of risk to the auditor.

The Overall Audit Strategy

The auditor should establish and document the overall audit strategy for the audit. (AU-C 300.07)

The overall audit strategy involves the determination of:

- The characteristics of the audit that define its scope
- The reporting objectives of the engagement related to the timing of the audit and the required communications
- Important factors that determine the focus of the audit team's efforts
- Factors to be considered from preliminary work or previous engagements
- Nature, timing, and resources needed

(AU-C 300.08)

The audit strategy helps the auditor determine the resources necessary to perform the engagement.

Communications with Those Charged with Governance and Management

As required by AU-C 260, the auditor must discuss elements of planning and the scope with those charged with governance and the entity's management. (AU-C 300.A13)

The Audit Plan

The audit plan is a more detailed, tactical plan that addresses the various audit matters identified in the audit strategy. The auditor must develop and document an audit plan for every audit.

The audit plan should include a description of:

- The nature, timing, and extent of planned risk assessment procedures (AU-C 315)
- The nature, timing, and extent of planned further audit procedures at the relevant assertion level for each material class of transactions, account balance, and disclosure (AU-C 330)
- Other audit procedures to be carried out to comply with GAAS

(AU-C 300.09)

Developing an audit strategy and an audit plan is intended to be an iterative process. As information becomes available over the course of the audit, the auditor should reconsider the audit strategy and audit plan to determine whether they remain relevant. (AU-C 300.10) All changes to audit strategy and plan should be documented.

Establishing an audit strategy varies according to the size of the entity and the complexity of the audit. In audits of small entities, a very small audit team may conduct the entire audit. With a smaller team, coordination and communication between team members are easier. Consequently, establishing the overall audit strategy need not be a complex or time-consuming exercise.

As part of audit planning, the auditor plans the direction and supervision of engagement team members and plans for the review of their work. (AU-C 300.11)

Determining the Extent of Involvement of Professionals Possessing Specialized Skills

The auditor should consider whether specialized skills are needed in performing the audit. (AU-C 300.12) For example, the auditor may need to involve the use of an information technology (IT) specialist to:

- Determine the effect of IT on the audit
- Understand the IT controls
- Design and perform tests of IT controls or substantive procedures

In determining whether an IT professional is needed, the auditor should consider factors such as the following:

- The complexity of the entity's systems and IT controls and the manner in which they are used in conducting the entity's business
- The significance of changes made to existing systems, or the implementation of new systems
- The extent to which data is shared among systems
- The extent of the entity's participation in electronic commerce
- The entity's use of emerging technologies
- The significance of audit evidence that is available only in electronic form

(AU-C 300.A18)

Additional Considerations in Initial Audit Engagements

Before starting an initial audit, the auditor should:

- Perform procedures regarding the acceptance of the client relationship and the specific audit engagement (see AU-C 220).
- Communicate with the previous auditor, where there has been a change of auditors (see Section 210).

(AU-C 300.13)

When developing the overall audit strategy and audit plan, the auditor should consider:

- Arrangements to be made with the previous auditor—for example, to review the previous auditor's audit documentation.
- Any major issues (including the application of accounting principles or of auditing and reporting standards) discussed with management in connection with the initial selection as auditors, the communication of these matters to those charged with governance, and how these matters affect the overall audit strategy and audit plan.
- The planned audit procedures to obtain sufficient appropriate audit evidence regarding opening balances.
- Other procedures required by the firm's system of quality control for initial audit engagements (for example, the firm's system of quality control may require the involvement of another partner or senior individual to review the overall audit strategy prior to commencing significant audit procedures or to review reports prior to their issuance).

(AU-C 300.A20)

Matters to Consider in Developing an Audit Strategy

AU-C 300.A25 *Appendix—Considerations in Establishing the Overall Audit*

The appendix to AU-C 300 provides examples of matters the auditor may consider in establishing the overall audit strategy, and many of these matters also will influence the detailed audit plan. The examples provided cover a broad range of matters applicable to many engagements. Although some of the following matters may be required by other AU-C sections, not all matters are relevant to every audit engagement, and the list is not necessarily complete.

Characteristics of the Engagement

The following are some examples of characteristics of the engagement:

- The financial reporting framework on which the financial information to be audited has been prepared, including any need for reconciliations to another financial reporting framework
- Industry-specific reporting requirements, such as reports mandated by industry regulators
- The expected audit coverage, including the number and locations of components to be included
- The nature of the control relationships between a parent and its components that determine how the group is to be consolidated
- The extent to which components are audited by other auditors
- The nature of the business divisions to be audited, including the need for specialized knowledge

- The reporting currency to be used, including any need for currency translation for the audited financial information
- The need for statutory or regulatory audit requirements (for example, OMB Circular A-133, *Audits of States, Local Governments, and Nonprofit Organizations*)
- The availability of the work of the internal auditor function and the extent of the auditor's potential direct use of such work
- The entity's use of service organizations and how the auditor may obtain evidence concerning the design or operation of controls performed by them
- The expected use of audit evidence obtained in previous audits (for example, audit evidence related to risk assessment procedures and tests of controls)
- The effect of IT on the audit procedures, including the availability of data and the expected use of computer-assisted audit techniques
- The coordination of the expected coverage and timing of the audit work with any reviews of interim financial information, and the effect on the audit of the information obtained during such reviews
- The availability of client personnel and data

Reporting Objectives, Timing of the Audit, and Nature of Communications

The following examples illustrate reporting objectives, timing of the audit, and nature of communications:

- The entity's timetable for reporting, including interim periods
- The organization of meetings with management and those charged with governance to discuss the nature, timing, and extent of the audit work
- The discussion with management and those charged with governance regarding the expected type and timing of reports to be issued and other communications, both written and oral, including the auditor's report, management letters, and communications to those charged with governance
- The discussion with management regarding the expected communications on the status of audit work throughout the engagement
- Communication with auditors of components regarding the expected types and timing of reports to be issued and other communications in connection with the audit of components
- The expected nature and timing of communications among engagement team members, including the nature and timing of team meetings and timing of the review of work performed
- Whether there are any other expected communications with third parties, including any statutory or contractual reporting responsibilities arising from the audit

Significant Factors, Preliminary Engagement Activities, and Knowledge Gained on Other Engagements

The following examples illustrate significant factors, preliminary engagement activities, and knowledge gained on other engagements:

- The determination of materiality, in accordance with AU-C Section 320, *Materiality in Planning and Performing an Audit*, and, when applicable, the following:
  - The determination of materiality for components and communication thereof to component auditors in accordance with AU-C Section 600, *Special Considerations—Audits of Group Financial Statements (Including the Work of Component Auditors)*

- The preliminary identification of significant components and material classes of transactions, account balances, and disclosures

- Preliminary identification of areas in which there may be a higher risk of material misstatement
- The effect of the assessed risk of material misstatement at the overall financial statement level on direction, supervision, and review
- The manner in which the auditor emphasizes to engagement team members the need to maintain a questioning mind and exercise professional skepticism in gathering and evaluating audit evidence
- Results of previous audits that involved evaluating the operating effectiveness of internal control, including the nature of identified deficiencies and action taken to address them
- The discussion of matters that may affect the audit with firm personnel responsible for performing other services to the entity
- Evidence of management's commitment to the design, implementation, and maintenance of sound internal control, including evidence of appropriate documentation of such internal control
- Volume of transactions, which may determine whether it is more efficient for the auditor to rely on internal control
- Importance attached to internal control throughout the entity to the successful operation of the business
- Significant business developments affecting the entity, including changes in IT and business processes; changes in key management; and acquisitions, mergers, and divestments
- Significant industry developments, such as changes in industry regulations and new reporting requirements
- Significant changes in the financial reporting framework, such as changes in accounting standards
- Other significant relevant developments, such as changes in the legal environment affecting the entity

Nature, Timing, and Extent of Resources

The following examples illustrate the nature, timing, and extent of resources:

- The selection of the engagement team (including, when necessary, the engagement quality control reviewer; see AU-C Section 220, *Quality Control for an Engagement Conducted in Accordance with Generally Accepted Auditing Standards*) and the assignment of audit work to the team members, including the assignment of appropriately experienced team members to areas in which there may be higher risks of material misstatement.
- Engagement budgeting, including considering the appropriate amount of time to set aside for areas in which there may be higher risks of material misstatement.

AU-C 315 Understanding the Entity and Its Environment and Assessing the Risks of Material Misstatement

AU-C ORIGINAL PRONOUNCEMENTS

Sources Statements on Auditing Standards (SASs) 122 and 128.

TECHNICAL ALERT

In October 2015, the Auditing Standards Board (ASB) issued Statement on Auditing Standards (SAS) No. 130. SAS No. 130 contains amendments to this section. Any relevant changes are incorporated into the information that follows.

DEFINITIONS OF TERMS

Source: AU-C 315.04

Assertions. Representations by management, explicit or otherwise, that are embodied in the financial statements as used by the auditor to consider the different types of potential misstatements that may occur.

Business risk. A risk resulting from significant conditions, events, circumstances, actions, or inactions that could adversely affect an entity's ability to achieve its objectives and execute its strategies, or resulting from the setting of inappropriate objectives and strategies.

Internal control. A process effected by those charged with governance, management, and other personnel that is designed to provide reasonable assurance about the achievement of the entity's objectives with regard to the reliability of financial reporting, effectiveness and efficiency of operations, and compliance with applicable laws and regulations. Internal control over safeguarding of assets against unauthorized acquisition, use, or disposition may include controls relating to financial reporting and operations objectives.

Relevant assertion. A financial statement assertion that has a reasonable possibility of containing a misstatement or misstatements that would cause the financial statements to be materially misstated. The determination of whether an assertion is a relevant assertion is made without regard to the effect of internal controls.

Risk assessment procedures. The audit procedures performed to obtain an understanding of the entity and its environment (including the entity's internal control) to identify and assess the risks of material misstatement, whether due to fraud or to error, at the financial statement and relevant assertion levels.

Significant risk. An identified and assessed risk of material misstatement that, in the auditor's professional judgment, requires special audit consideration.

OBJECTIVES OF AU-C SECTION 315

AU-C Section 315.03 states that:

. . . the objective of the auditor is to identify and assess the risks of material misstatement, whether due to fraud or error, at the financial statement and relevant assertion levels through understanding the entity and its environment, including the entity's internal control, thereby providing a basis for designing and implementing responses to the assessed risks of material misstatement.

OVERVIEW

The audit risk model describes audit risk as:

$$AR = RMM \times DR$$

where AR is audit risk, RMM is the risk of material misstatement, and DR is detection risk. The risk of material misstatement is a combination of inherent and control risk. Although the standard describes a combined risk assessment, the auditor may perform separate assessments of inherent and control risks.

Section 315 describes how the auditor should identify and assess the risk of material misstatement, which provides a basis for designing further audit procedures. These further audit procedures (which consist of tests of controls and substantive tests) must be clearly linked and responsive to assessed risks.

Section 315 also includes the concept of *significant risks*, which are risks that require special audit consideration. (See "Definitions of Terms.") One or more significant risks arise on all audits.

The following is an overview of how the process is described in Section 315:

1. Perform risk assessment procedures to gather information and gain an understanding of the entity and its environment, including internal control.
2. Based on this understanding, identify risks of material misstatement, which may exist at either the financial statement or the relevant assertion level.
3. Assess the risk of material misstatement, which requires the auditor to:
   - Identify the risk of material misstatement.
   - Describe the identified risks in terms of what can go wrong in specific assertions.
   - Consider the significance and likelihood of material misstatement for each identified risk.

NOTE: This process for assessing risk is consistent with the process for assessing the risk of material misstatement due to fraud. Essentially it is an information gathering, assessment, and response process, in which the auditor gathers information about the entity, assimilates and synthesizes that information to make an assessment of risk, and then designs audit procedures that are responsive to those risks.

The assessment of the risk of material misstatement enables the auditor to design appropriate further audit procedures, which are clearly linked and responsive to the assessed risks.

NOTE: Section 315 describes risks as existing at one of two levels: the financial statement level or the relevant assertion level. This distinction is important because the nature of the auditor's response differs depending on whether the risk is at the financial statement level or the assertion level.

- *The risk of material misstatement at the financial statement level has a pervasive effect on the financial statements and affects many assertions. The control environment is an example of a financial-statement-level risk. In addition to developing assertion-specific responses, financial-statement-level risks may require the auditor to develop an overall response, such as assigning more experienced team members.*
- *Assertion-level risks pertain to a single assertion or related group of assertions. Assertion-level risks will require the auditor to design and perform specific further audit procedures such as tests of controls and/or substantive procedures that are directly responsive to the assessed risk.*

Section 330 provides guidance on the design and performance of further audit procedures.

In all audits, the auditor must obtain a sufficient understanding of the entity and its environment, including its internal control, to assess the risk of material misstatement of the financial statements whether due to error or to fraud, and to design the nature, timing, and extent of further audit procedures.

This assessment of the risk of material misstatement becomes the basis for the proper design of further audit procedures.

NOTE: Obtaining an understanding of the entity and its environment also allows the auditor to make judgments about other audit matters, such as:

- *Materiality*
- *Whether the entity's selection and application of accounting policies are appropriate and financial statement disclosures are adequate*
- *Areas where special audit consideration may be necessary—for example, related-party transactions*
- *The expectation of recorded amounts used for performing analytical procedures*
- *The evaluation of audit evidence*

Even if the auditor plans a purely substantive audit, he or she still is required to obtain an understanding of internal control. Such an understanding is necessary to:

- Identify missing or ineffective controls.
- Evaluate identified control deficiencies.
- Confirm that substantive procedures alone are sufficient to design and perform an appropriate audit strategy and provide sufficient appropriate audit evidence to support the audit opinion.

REQUIREMENTS

Risk Assessment Procedures

The auditor should perform risk assessment procedures to provide a basis for the assessment of material misstatement. (AU-C 315.05) Risk assessment procedures include:

1. Inquiries of management, individuals in the internal audit function, and others at the client
2. Analytical procedures
3. Observation and inspection

(AU-C 315.06)

The auditor's risk assessment procedures provide the audit evidence necessary to support the auditor's risk assessments, which in turn support the determination of the nature, timing, and extent of further audit procedures. Thus, the results of the auditor's risk assessment procedures are an integral part of the audit evidence obtained to support the opinion on the financial statements.

NOTE: Under the previous auditing standards, it was common for auditors to declare control risk to be maximum simply for audit efficiency, without any basis for making that assessment. Section 315 eliminates that practice by requiring auditors to document their rationale for assessing control risk. This rationale should be based on the information gathered from the performance of risk assessment procedures. The elimination of the auditor's ability to default to maximum control risk without justification is a significant change from previous practice.

A Mix of Procedures

Except for the five components of internal control, the auditor is not required to perform all the procedures for each of the five aspects of the client and its environment listed in the upcoming subsection, "The Entity and Its Environment." However, in the course of gathering information about the client, the auditor should perform all the risk assessment procedures.

Other procedures may provide relevant information about the entity. For example:

- When relevant to the audit, the auditor should consider other information, which may include:
  - Information obtained from the client acceptance or continuance process (AU-C 315.07)
  - Experience gained on other engagements performed for the entity (AU-C 315.08)
- Some of the procedures the auditor performs to assess the risks of material misstatement due to fraud also may help gather information about the entity and its environment, particularly its internal control. (AU-C 315.09)

NOTE: Because of the close connection between the assessment of the risk of material misstatement and the procedures performed to assess fraud risk, the auditor will want to:

- *Coordinate the procedures he or she performs to assess the risk of material misstatement due to fraud with the other risk assessment procedures.*
- *Consider the results of his or her assessment of fraud risk when identifying the risk of material misstatement.*

Updating Information from Prior Periods

If certain conditions are met, the auditor may use information obtained in prior periods as audit evidence in the current period audit. However, when the auditor intends to use information from prior periods in the current period audit, the auditor should determine whether changes have occurred that may affect the relevance of the information for the current audit. (AU-C 315.10) To make this determination, the auditor should make inquiries and perform other appropriate audit procedures, such as walk-throughs of systems. (AU-C 315.A20)

Discussion by the Audit Team

The members of the audit team should discuss the susceptibility of the client's financial statements to material misstatement. (AU-C 315.11) This discussion will allow team members to exchange information and create a shared understanding of the client and its environment, which in turn will enable each team member to:

- Share his or her knowledge.
- Gain a better understanding of the potential for material misstatement resulting from fraud or error in the assertions that are relevant to the areas assigned to them.
- Exchange information about business risks.
- Understand how the results of the audit procedures that they perform may affect other aspects of the audit.

This "brainstorming session" of the audit team could be held at the same time as the team's discussion related to fraud, which is required by Section 240. (AU-C 315.A21)

Understanding the Entity and Its Environment, Including Internal Control

The Entity and Its Environment

The auditor should obtain an understanding of the following five elements of the entity and its environment:

1. *External factors*, including:
   - Industry factors, such as the competitive environment, supplier and customer relationships, and technological developments.
   - The regulatory environment, which includes the applicable financial reporting framework, the legal and political environment, and environmental requirements that affect the industry.
   - Other matters, such as general economic conditions
2. *Nature of the client*, which includes its operations, its ownership, governance, the types of investments it makes and plans to make, how it is financed, and how it is structured.
3. *Accounting policies*, including the entity's selection and application of accounting policies, the reasons for any changes, and whether the entity's accounting policies are appropriate for its business and consistent with the applicable financial reporting framework and accounting policies used in the relevant industry.
4. *Objectives and strategies and related business risks*, which may result in material misstatement of the financial statements taken as a whole or as individual assertions.
5. *Measurement and review of the client's financial performance*, which tell the auditor which aspects of the client's performance management considers important.

(AU-C 315.12)

NOTE: The purpose of understanding the entity and its environment is to help identify and assess risk. For example:

- *Information about the client's industry may allow the auditor to identify characteristics of the industry that could give rise to specific misstatements.*
- *Information about the ownership of the client, how it is structured, and other elements of its nature will help identify related-party transactions that, if not properly accounted for and adequately disclosed, could lead to a material misstatement.*
- *The auditor's identification and understanding of the business risks facing the entity increase the chance of identifying financial reporting risks.*
- *Information about the performance measures used by the entity may lead the auditor to identify pressures or incentives that could motivate entity personnel to misstate the financial statements.*
- *Information about the design and implementation of internal control may identify deficiencies in control design, which increase the risk of material misstatement.*

Evaluating the Design of Internal Control

On every audit, the auditor should obtain an understanding of internal control that is of sufficient depth to enable the auditor to:

1. Assess the risks of material misstatement of the financial statements, whether due to error or to fraud.
2. Design the nature, timing, and extent of further audit procedures.

To meet these requirements, the auditor should:

1. Evaluate the design of controls that are relevant to the audit and determine whether the control—either individually or in combination—is capable of effectively preventing or detecting and correcting material misstatements.
2. Determine that the control has been implemented—that is, that the control exists and that the entity is using it.

(AU-C 315.13-14)

The auditor's evaluation of internal control design and the determination of whether controls have been implemented are critical to the assessment of the risks of material misstatement. Remember that even if the auditor's overall audit strategy contemplates performing only substantive procedures for all relevant assertions related to material transactions, account balances, and disclosures, the auditor still needs to evaluate the design of the client's internal control.

NOTE: In evaluating control design, it is helpful to consider:

- *Whether control objectives that are specific to the unique circumstances of the client have been considered for all relevant assertions for all significant accounts and disclosures*
- *Whether the control or combination of controls would—if operated as designed—meet the control objective*
- *Whether all controls necessary to meet the control objective are in place*

When obtaining an understanding about the design of internal controls and determining whether those controls have been implemented, inquiry alone is not sufficient. Thus, for these purposes, the auditor should supplement inquiries with other risk assessment procedures. (AU-C 315.14)

NOTE: To evaluate the design and implementation of internal controls relevant to the audit, the auditor should perform procedures such as:

- *Inquiry*
- *Observation*
- *Inspection of documentation*
- *Walk-throughs—tracing transactions through the information systems*

(AU-C 315.A76)

Distinguishing between Evaluation of Design and Tests of Controls

Obtaining an understanding of the design and implementation of internal controls is different from testing their operating effectiveness.

- *Understanding the design and implementation* is required on every audit as part of the process of assessing the risks of material misstatement.
- *Testing the operating effectiveness* is necessary only when the auditor will rely on the operating effectiveness of controls to modify the nature, timing, and extent of substantive procedures or when substantive procedures alone do not provide the auditor with sufficient audit evidence at the assertion level.

The procedures necessary to understand the design and implementation of controls do provide some limited evidence regarding the operation of the controls. However, the procedures necessary to understand the design and implementation of controls generally are not sufficient to serve as a test of their operating effectiveness for the purpose of placing significant reliance on their operation.

Examples of situations where the procedures the auditor performs to understand the design and implementation of controls may provide sufficient audit evidence about their operating effectiveness include:

- Controls that are automated to the degree that they can be performed consistently provided that general information technology (IT) controls over those automated controls operate effectively during the period.
- Controls that operate only at a point in time rather than continuously throughout the period. For example, if the client performs an annual physical inventory count, the auditor's observation of that count and other procedures to evaluate its design and implementation provide audit evidence that may affect the design of the auditor's substantive procedures.

The required understanding of internal control must include all five components of internal control:

1. The control environment,
2. Risk assessment,
3. Information and communication,
4. Control activities, and
5. Monitoring.

(AU-C 315.A57)

These components may operate at the entity level or the individual transaction level. Obtaining an appropriate understanding of internal control requires the auditor to understand and evaluate the design of all five components of internal control and to determine whether the controls are in use by the client.

Control Environment

The auditor should obtain a sufficient knowledge of the control environment to understand management's and the board of directors' attitudes, awareness, and actions concerning the environment. (AU-C 315.15) Control environment factors include:

1. Communication and enforcement of integrity and ethical values
2. Commitment to competence
3. Participation by those charged with governance
4. Management's philosophy and operating style
5. Organizational structure
6. Assignment of authority and responsibility
7. Human resource policies and practices

(AU-C 315.A79)

NOTE: The auditor should concentrate on the substance of controls (established and acted upon), not their form.

Risk Assessment

The auditor should obtain an understanding of the entity's procedures for business risk, specifically:

- Identifying the risks
- Estimating significance
- Assessing the likelihood of occurrence
- Deciding on an action plan to address the risk

(AU-C 315.16)

Risks can occur because of the following:

1. Changes in operating environment
2. New personnel
3. New or revamped information systems
4. Rapid growth
5. New technology
6. New business models, products, or activities
7. Corporate restructurings
8. Expanded foreign operations
9. New accounting pronouncements
10. Changes in economic conditions

(AU-C 315.A90)

NOTE: The auditor's assessment of inherent and control risks is a separate consideration and not part of the entity's risk assessment.

Information and Communication

The auditor should obtain sufficient knowledge of the accounting information system to understand:

1. The classes of transactions that are significant to the financial statements
2. The procedures, both automated and manual, by which those transactions are initiated, recorded, processed, and reported from their occurrence to inclusion in the financial statements
3. The related accounting records, whether electronic or manual, supporting information, and specific accounts involved in initiating, recording, processing, and reporting transactions
4. How the information system captures other events and conditions that are significant to the financial statements
5. The financial reporting process
6. Controls surrounding journal entries, including nonstandard journal entries used to record nonrecurring, unusual transactions, or adjustments

(AU-C 315.19)

The auditor should understand the automated and manual procedures used to prepare financial statements and related disclosures, and how misstatements may occur. Such procedures include:

1. The procedures used to enter transaction totals into the general ledger

---

NOTE: The auditor should be aware that when information technology (IT) is used to automatically transfer information from transaction processing systems to general ledger or financial reporting systems, there may be little or no visible evidence of intervention in the information systems (e.g., an individual may inappropriately override automated processes by changing the amounts being automatically passed to the general ledger or financial reporting system).

---

2. The procedures used to initiate, record, and process standard (e.g., monthly sales and purchase transactions) and nonstandard (e.g., business combinations or disposals, or a nonrecurring accounting estimate) journal entries in the general ledger

---

NOTE: Auditors should be aware that:

- *When IT is used to maintain the general ledger and prepare financial statements, such nonstandard entries may exist only in electronic form and may be more difficult to identify through physical inspection of printed documents.*
- *Financial statement misstatements are often perpetrated by using nonstandard entries to record fictitious transactions or other events and circumstances, particularly near the end of the reporting period.*

---

3. Other procedures used to record recurring and nonrecurring adjustments (e.g., consolidating adjustments and reclassifications that are not made by formal journal entries)

The auditor should also obtain sufficient knowledge of the means the entity uses to communicate financial reporting roles and responsibilities and significant matters about financial reporting. (AU-C 315.20)

Control Activities

The auditor should obtain an understanding of those control activities that are relevant to the audit. (AU-C 315.21) Control activities are relevant to the audit if they are related to *significant risks*, as discussed later in this section. Examples of specific control activities include:

1. Authorization
2. Performance reviews
3. Information processing
4. Physical controls
5. Segregation of duties (e.g., assigning different people the responsibility for authorizing transactions, recording transactions, and maintaining custody of assets)

(AU-C 315.A99)

The auditor should also obtain an understanding of the process of reconciling detail to the general ledger for significant accounts. (AU-C 315.21)

Monitoring

The auditor should obtain sufficient knowledge of the major types of activities that the entity uses to monitor internal control over financial reporting, including the internal audit function—how it works, its responsibilities, and how it fits into the organization. (Section 610)

NOTE: Section 315 requires the auditor to gain an understanding of some controls that previously did not have to be addressed, including the following:

- *How the incorrect processing of significant transactions is resolved*
- *The process of reconciling detail to the general ledger for significant accounts*
- *Control activities related to "significant risks," as defined in the standard*

Assessing the Risk of Material Misstatement

The auditor's understanding of the entity and its environment—which includes an evaluation of the design and implementation of internal control—is used to assess the risk of material misstatement. To assess the risk of material misstatement, the auditor should:

1. Identify risks throughout the process of obtaining an understanding of the entity, its internal control, and its environment.
2. Relate the identified risks to what can go wrong at the relevant assertion level.
3. Consider whether the risks could result in a material misstatement to the financial statements.
4. Consider the likelihood that the risks could result in a material misstatement of the financial statements.

(AU-C 315.27)

Financial-statement-level and assertion-level risks. The auditor should identify and assess the risks of material misstatement at both the financial statement level and the relevant assertion level. (AU-C 315.26)

1. **Financial-statement-level risks.** Some risks of material misstatement relate pervasively to the financial statements taken as a whole and potentially affect many relevant assertions.

These risks at the financial statement level may be identifiable with specific assertions at the class of transaction, account balance, or disclosure level. (AU-C 315.122)

2. **Assertion-level risks.** Other risks of material misstatement relate to specific classes of transactions, account balances, and disclosures at the assertion level. The auditor's assessment of risks at the assertion level provides a basis for considering the appropriate audit approach for designing and performing further audit procedures. (AU-C 315.A126)

Risks that exist at the financial statement level—for example, those that pertain to a weak control environment or to management's process for making significant accounting estimates—should be related to specific assertions. In other instances, it may not be possible to relate financial-statement-level risks to a particular assertion or group of assertions. (AU-C 315.A123-.A124) Financial-statement-level assertions that cannot be related to specific assertions will require an overall response, such as the way in which the audit is staffed or supervised. Section 330 provides additional guidance on the auditor's overall responses to financial-statement-level risks.

How to consider internal control when assessing risks. When making risk assessments, the auditor should identify the controls that are likely to either prevent or detect and correct material misstatements in specific assertions.

Individual controls often do not address a risk completely in themselves. Often, only multiple control activities, together with other components of internal control (for example, the control environment, risk assessment, information and communication, or monitoring), will be sufficient to address a risk. For this reason, when determining whether identified controls are likely to prevent or detect and correct material misstatements, the auditor generally considers controls in relation to significant transactions and accounting processes (for example, sales, cash receipts, or payroll), rather than ledger accounts.

Identification of Significant Risks

As part of assessing the risks of material misstatement, the auditor should identify significant risks, which are defined as those risks that require special audit consideration. Significant risks should be determined without regard to internal controls—that is, by considering inherent risk only. (AU-C 315.28) For example, if the entity is named as a defendant in a patent infringement lawsuit that may threaten the viability of its principal product, the auditor could consider significant the risks that the lawsuit (1) would not be appropriately recorded or disclosed in accordance with GAAP or (2) may affect the entity's ability to continue as a going concern.

Significant risks arise on most audits. When the auditor determines that a risk is a significant risk, the audit procedures should include (but not be limited to):

- Obtaining an understanding of internal control, including relevant control activities, related specifically to those significant risks
- Evaluating whether the controls have been designed and implemented to mitigate the risks
- Substantive procedures specifically designed to address the significant risk

(AU-C 315.30)

Significant risks frequently arise from unusual, nonroutine transactions and from judgmental matters such as estimates. In addition, significant risks may relate to matters such as the following:

- **External circumstances.** External circumstances giving rise to business risks influence the determination of whether the risk requires special audit attention. For example, technological developments might make a particular product obsolete, thereby causing inventory to be more susceptible to overstatement. Recent significant economic, accounting, or other developments also may require special attention.

- **Factors in the client and its environment.** Factors in the client and its environment that relate to several or all of the classes of transactions, account balances, or disclosures may influence the relative significance of the risk. For example, a lack of sufficient working capital to continue operations or a declining industry characterized by a large number of business failures may have a pervasive effect on risk for several account balances, classes of transactions, or disclosures.
- **Recent developments.** Recent significant economic, accounting, or other developments can affect the relative significance of a risk.
- **Complex calculations.** Complex calculations are more likely to be misstated than are simple calculations.
- **Risk of fraud or theft.** Revenue recognition is presumed to be a financial reporting fraud risk; cash is more susceptible to misappropriation than an inventory of coal.
- **Estimates.** Accounts consisting of amounts derived from accounting estimates that are subject to significant measurement uncertainty pose greater risks than do accounts consisting of relatively routine, factual data.
- **Related-party transactions.** Related-party transactions may create business risks that can result in a material misstatement of the financial statements.

Risks for Which Substantive Procedures Alone Do Not Provide Sufficient Appropriate Audit Evidence

For some risks it is not possible or practicable to reduce detection risk to an acceptably low level with audit evidence obtained only from substantive procedures. (AU-C 315.31) Examples of such situations include:

- An entity that conducts its business using IT to initiate orders for the purchase and delivery of goods based on predetermined rules of what to order and in what quantities, and to pay the related accounts payable based on system-generated decisions initiated upon the confirmed receipt of goods and terms of payment.
- An entity that provides services to customers via electronic media and uses IT to create a log of the services provided to its customers, to initiate and process its billings for the services, and to automatically record such amounts in the accounting records.

Revision of Risk Assessment

During the course of the audit, new information may surface that causes the auditor to change his or her assessment of the risk of material misstatements. If so, the auditor should revise the assessment and the planned audit procedures. (AU-C 315.32)

Documentation

The auditor should document the following:

1. The discussion among members of the audit team regarding the susceptibility of the entity's financial statements to material misstatement due to error or fraud, including how and when the discussion occurred, the subject matter discussed, the audit team members who participated, and significant decisions reached concerning planned responses at the financial statement and relevant assertion levels.

2. Key elements of the understanding obtained regarding each of the aspects of the entity and its environment, including each of the five components of internal control, to assess the risks of material misstatement of the financial statements, the sources of information from which the understanding was obtained, and the risk assessment procedures.
3. The assessment of the risks of material misstatement both at the financial statement level and at the relevant assertion level and the basis for the assessment.
4. The risks identified as significant risks.

(AU-C 315.33)

Examples of Matters to Consider When Obtaining an Understanding of the Entity and Its Environment

The extent of the auditor's planning depends on the nature of the client and the experience of the auditor with that client. For example, planning for the audit of a new client is more extensive than planning for the audit of an existing client. When planning an audit, the auditor should consider the following:

1. The economy
2. The client's industry
3. The client's business
4. Firm requirements

These factors are in Appendix A of AU-C 315.A156 and are discussed next. All factors are not appropriate for every audit. The size and complexity of the client determine which factors are relevant.

The Economy

There are certain economic conditions that significantly influence the industry and the business of the client. The auditor should be aware of these conditions and should consider them when planning the audit. Some economic factors that might affect client operations and, therefore, should be considered in planning an audit include:

1. Interest rates and availability of financing
2. Unemployment rates
3. Money supply
4. Foreign currency exchange rates and contracts
5. Tariff trade restrictions
6. Government regulations and legislation
7. Overall business conditions—depression, recession, inflation

The Client's Industry

When planning the audit, the auditor should be aware of conditions in the client's industry. Factors to consider include the following:

1. Growth and financial results of the industry; possible sources of this information are:
   a. Industry trade association literature
   b. Publications issued by agencies such as Moody's, Standard & Poor's, and Robert Morris Associates
   c. Government publications issued by the Government Printing Office, Washington, D.C.

2. Cyclical and seasonal nature of the industry
3. Product technology
4. Supply availability and cost
5. Is the industry labor intensive or capital intensive?
6. Industry labor conditions:
   a. Is the industry unionized?
   b. Has the industry recently experienced a strike?
7. Accounting principles and industry accounting practices; this information may be obtained from firm members with clients in the same industry and the American Institute of Certified Public Accountants (AICPA) Industry Audit and Accounting Guides.
8. Industry price patterns and consumer reactions to price changes
9. Regulatory environment
10. Taxation:
    a. Number of bankruptcies during the past year
    b. Number of new companies organized during the current year

In addition to the information the auditor obtains about the client's industry from industry-related publications, he or she may obtain industry information from bankers, client management, auditors with clients in the same industry, and general business publications, such as the *Wall Street Journal*, *Bloomberg Businessweek*, *Forbes*, and *Fortune*.

The Client's Business: New Client

When planning the audit, the auditor should have a knowledge of the client's operations. For a new client, the primary sources of information are discussions with the predecessor auditor and inquiries of client management.

For a new client, the auditor should learn about the client and plan the audit by doing the following:

1. Communicate with predecessor auditor.
2. Visit client's administrative office and major facilities.
3. Review year-end financial statements of prior year and interim financial statements of current and prior year.
4. Review auditor's report on prior year's financial statements:
   a. Was there a scope limitation?
   b. Were certain matters emphasized?
   c. Did the auditor disclaim an opinion or issue an adverse opinion?
   d. Were there other modifications of the auditor's standard report?
5. Review prior year's income tax returns.
6. Obtain the results of the most recent income tax examination.
7. Review reports issued to agencies, such as the following:
   a. Securities and Exchange Commission (SEC)
   b. Federal Housing Administration, Small Business Administration, and Department of Labor
   c. Credit agencies and banks

Visit to Administrative Office

During a visit to the client's administrative office, the auditor should do the following:

1. Meet with in-house legal counsel and inquire about:
   a. Litigation
   b. Compliance with laws and regulations
   c. Knowledge of fraud or suspected fraud
   d. Warranties
   e. Postsales obligations
   f. Arrangements, such as joint ventures, with business partners
   g. The meaning of contract terms
2. Meet with financial and administrative officers and obtain or determine the following:
   a. The functions of each executive
   b. The executive responsible for the audit
   c. The existence of an internal audit function
   d. Organization charts
   e. Locations and relative importance of all offices, showrooms, warehouses, and factories
   f. Corporate manuals or memoranda that provide information about the following:
      1. Nature and description of the entity's products
      2. Production and distribution methods
      3. Internal control
      4. General ledger chart of accounts
   g. Methods of financing the entity's operations
   h. Schedule of long-term debt
   i. Names of banks and account executive at each bank; for each bank, determine the following:
      1. Outstanding indebtedness and terms of payment
      2. Lines of credit
      3. Other banking services
   j. For nonpublic companies, a schedule of stockholders with the following information:
      1. Names
      2. Addresses
      3. Certificate numbers
      4. Number of shares held
      5. Shareholder function in the business
   k. Purchase terms:
      1. Terms of payment
      2. Are letters of credit used for foreign purchases?
   l. Sales terms:
      1. Terms of payment
      2. Are letters of credit used for foreign sales?

m. Changes in the entity's marketing strategies, sales trends, or contractual arrangements with its customers
n. The existence of related-party transactions such as the following:
    1. Purchases and sales
    2. Loans
    3. Receiving or providing services, such as management, legal, and administrative
o. Information systems:
    1. System changes
    2. Systemic control failures
    3. Other information systems-related risks
p. Schedule of all affiliates and nonconsolidated subsidiaries
q. Customers and suppliers on whom the entity is economically dependent
r. Most recent trial balance
s. General ledger and books of original entry:
    1. Are accounting records up to date?
    2. What is the quality of accounting records?
t. Extent of client responsibility, including the involvement of the internal audit function, for preparation of the following:
    1. Trial balance
    2. Schedules
    3. Adjustments and accruals
    4. Confirmations
    5. Inventory instructions
    6. Financial statements
    7. Income tax returns
u. Tentative audit schedule; agree to dates for the following:
    1. Physical inventory
    2. Cash and securities count
    3. Mailing and confirmations
    4. Start of fieldwork

3. Obtain the entity's forms and documents, such as the following:
    a. Purchase requisitions
    b. Purchase orders
    c. Sales authorizations
    d. Sales orders
    e. Sales invoices
    f. Production orders
    g. Production requisitions
    h. Receipts
    i. Checks
    j. Payroll cards
    k. Sales returns and credits
    l. Purchase returns and credits

4. Examine work area that will be allocated to the auditor.
5. Walk through the accounting area:
   a. Observe work conditions.
   b. Meet employees.
   c. Determine employee functions.

Visit to Facility

During the visit to the client's facility, the auditor should do the following:

1. Meet with management.
2. Walk through a production cycle and note the following:
   a. Initiation of order
   b. Requisition of materials
   c. Movement of production
   d. Completion of production
   e. Storage of completed product
   f. Shipment to customer
3. Document flow of production.
4. Note conditions of facility and equipment.
5. Visit materials stockroom, observe condition of the inventory, and review the following:
   a. Inventory records
   b. Receiving reports
   c. Inventory reports

THE CLIENT'S BUSINESS: CONTINUING CLIENT

For a continuing client, information about the business is obtained from the following:

1. Client's permanent file
2. Prior year's audit documentation
3. Prior year's audit team
4. Client's current year budgets
5. Client's current year interim financial statements
6. Members who had professional assignments with the client during the year; these assignments include the following:
   a. Review of interim financial statements
   b. Income tax planning
   c. Systems and other consulting services
7. Discussions with client management

Discussions with Client Management

The in-charge auditor and the staff member who will supervise the audit should visit the client before beginning the audit to determine the following:

1. Change in product line
2. Addition or deletion of factories, offices, warehouses, or showrooms

3. Addition of new administrative departments
4. Acquisition of subsidiaries
5. Existence of new or continuing related parties
6. Changes in production or distribution methods
7. Changes in sources of financing
8. Changes in internal control
9. Acquisition of new office equipment, such as computers
10. Changes in key personnel
11. New long-term commitments, such as:
    a. Leases
    b. Employment contracts
12. Adoption of employee compensation and benefit plans

Using a Risk-Based, Top-Down Approach to Evaluate Internal Control

Section 315 does not provide any definitive guidance on how auditors can most effectively and efficiently comply with the requirement to evaluate control design on every engagement. However, auditors of nonpublic companies would be well served to apply the lessons learned by auditors of public companies who have been required to audit their clients' internal controls ever since the Sarbanes-Oxley Act became effective.

Lessons from SOX 404

In the years immediately following the effective dates of Section 404 of the Sarbanes-Oxley Act (SOX 404), many auditors adopted an evaluation approach that started by identifying all (or nearly all) of the company's controls and then documenting and testing each of these to determine whether internal control as a whole was effective. As can be imagined, this approach was extremely time-consuming and costly. Moreover, this "bottom-up" approach was unnecessary to achieve the overall objective of management's evaluation.

In 2007, the SEC revised its rules and described a "risk-based, top-down" approach to understanding internal control. Auditors of nonpublic companies are not required to use this approach. However, applying its basic principles will provide an effective and efficient approach to meeting the requirements of Section 315.

In general, the key steps in this approach include the following:

1. Ask "what can go wrong?" in the preparation of the financial statements. The auditor should use knowledge of the client, external events and circumstances, and the application of GAAP to identify risks that the entity's financial statements could be misstated. Once they are identified, the auditor should assess the relative magnitude of these risks.
2. Identify controls that address the "what can go wrongs." The entity should have controls in place to mitigate those misstatement risks that are of some significance. The auditor will focus attention on those controls whose failure is most likely to result in a material misstatement. To make this determination, the auditor will consider both:
    a. The likelihood that the control will fail, and
    b. If it did fail, the significance of the misstatement that would result.

For example, an entity may have controls over its bank balances (e.g., month-end bank reconciliations) and its petty cash on hand. Auditors will focus on the controls over the company's bank balances, because the risks related to the control failure of the reconciliation are greater than the risks related to the petty cash. That is, if the bank reconciliations fail, the misstatement of the financial statements could be material; if petty cash was misstated, the misstatement would not be material.

3. Obtain an understanding of relevant controls from the "top" down. This process of identifying controls should begin at the "top," with the broadest, most pervasive controls, and then proceed "downward" to more direct, specific controls.

A Top-Down Approach to Evaluating Controls

The consideration of the risk of material misstatement is crucial when planning and performing an evaluation of internal control. It is this consideration that helps direct the auditor's focus to the most critical areas of the company's internal control system. In a similar fashion, beginning at the "top" of the system and working "down" will help drive efficiency and direct the focus of the evaluation of internal control design.

But where is the "top" of an internal control system? And once the auditor is there, what direction is "down"? To answer these questions requires an understanding of three key principles of internal control design:

1. Within any organization, controls operate at two distinct levels: the broad, general *entity level* and the more focused and specific *activity level*.
2. Controls are designed to mitigate risks. Some controls address risks *directly*, whereas other controls address the same risks *indirectly*.
3. At the activity level, controls can be designed to either:
   a. Prevent errors from entering the financial information system, or
   b. Detect and correct errors that have already entered the system.

Entity-level controls sit at the "top" of the internal control structure. For example, these controls might include the company's hiring and training policies and the firewall protecting its network. There are relatively few entity-level controls. This is because, by their nature, entity-level controls have a broad (though indirect) effect on the company's financial reporting risks (as indicated by the relative size of the sphere). For example, a firewall might cover the company's inventory system, billing and receivables, and general ledger system all at once.

Entity-level controls have a very indirect effect on the financial statements. For example, the quality of the company's training can improve job performance and reduce the risk of misstatement, but training alone is not sufficient to prevent or detect an error.

At the lowest level of the pyramid are the company's most specific, narrowly focused activity-level controls. For example, an edit check to ensure that a date is formatted mm/dd/yyyy is an activity-level control. This control is specifically directed to one field on a single data entry form. The control is designed to *prevent* an error from entering the information, and it is typical for controls at this level of the pyramid to be preventive controls, designed to be performed on every transaction.

In a typical control system there are many, many activity-level controls. There are two reasons for this relative abundance of preventive activity-level controls:

1. Activity-level controls address very specific risks and have a very narrow (but direct) effect on financial reporting risks. Entities enter into many different types of transactions. In our

example, paying suppliers is just one of dozens of different types of financial activities, and an organization will have activity-level controls for each of these activities. Additionally, for each transaction type, the company may face many different kinds of risk, each requiring a different kind of activity-level control. For example, not only will companies want to make sure that they pay only approved suppliers, but they also will want to make sure they pay the correct amount.

2. Many internal control systems include redundant controls—multiple controls that achieve the same objective. For example, the company may use a purchase order system to make sure that its buyers are approved to enter into transactions. In addition, a manager may periodically compare actual purchases to the budget to make sure that company buyers are staying within their approved limits.

Between the entity-level controls and preventive activity-level controls are the broad-based activity-level controls. A bank reconciliation is a good example of such a control. A bank reconciliation does not prevent the bookkeeper from entering an incorrect amount as a cash disbursement, but if such an error were made, a properly performed bank reconciliation should detect and correct it. Many broad-based activity-level controls are detective in nature and usually performed periodically, rather than on every transaction.

A top-down approach to internal control evaluation means that the auditor starts with entity-level controls, which have the broadest span but the most *indirect* effect on reducing financial statement misstatements. Once the auditor has evaluated entity-level controls, he or she then proceeds "down" to the more specific activity-level controls. At the activity level, the auditor again begins at the "top," with those controls that are furthest along in the information processing stream. Usually, these are *detective* controls.

After evaluating detective controls, the auditor may then proceed back down the information processing stream, back to the inception of the transaction, evaluating controls along the way.

The key to applying the top-down approach is to ask—at each step of the evaluation—"Are the controls I have evaluated so far capable of appropriately addressing the related risk of material misstatement?" If the answer is "yes," then there is no need to evaluate more controls. If the answer is "no," then the auditor should continue to evaluate more controls further down in the structure until reaching a point where he or she has evaluated enough controls to evaluate the risk.

Effect of IT on Internal Control

Information technology (IT) affects the way in which transactions are initiated, recorded, processed, and reported. IT controls consist of automated controls (e.g., controls embedded in computer programs) and manual controls. Manual controls may be independent of IT, may use information produced by IT, or may be limited to (1) monitoring the effective function of IT and of automated controls and (2) handling exceptions. An entity's mix of controls varies with the nature and complexity of its use of IT. IT enables an entity to:

1. Consistently apply predefined business rules and perform complex calculations in processing large volumes of transactions or data.
2. Enhance the timeliness, availability, and accuracy of information.
3. Facilitate the additional analysis of information.
4. Enhance the ability to monitor the performance of activities and the policies and procedures.

5. Reduce the risk that controls will be circumvented.
6. Enhance the ability to achieve effective segregation of duties by implementing security controls.

IT also poses specific risks to an entity's internal control, including:

1. Reliance on systems or programs that are inaccurately processing data, processing inaccurate data, or both
2. Unauthorized access to data that may result in destruction of data or improper changes to data, including the recording of unauthorized or nonexistent transactions or inaccurate recording of transactions
3. Unauthorized changes to data in master files
4. Unauthorized changes to systems or programs
5. Failure to make necessary changes to systems or programs
6. Inappropriate manual intervention
7. Potential loss of data

IT General Controls

IT general controls are entity-wide controls that apply to many if not all application systems and help ensure their continued proper operation. For example, the effectiveness of an entity's controls relating to the access of its database will determine whether it will be successful in maintaining the integrity of that data, which may be used in a number of different applications.

If there are inadequate general controls, controls at the application level may not function properly, and the information produced by the system may be largely unreliable. For that reason, IT general controls are typically included within the evaluation of internal control effectiveness.

But which IT general controls are used?

To answer this question, it is helpful to think of IT general controls as operating within three different domains, or stacks:

1. Database
2. Operating system
3. Network

There are three control objectives within each of these domains:

1. Systems are appropriately tested and validated prior to being placed into production.
2. Data are protected from unauthorized change.
3. Any problems or incidents in operations are properly responded to, recorded, investigated, and resolved.

To determine which IT general controls should be used for the evaluation, apply the risk-based, top-down approach. IT general controls will vary in how directly they affect the financial reporting process and therefore in the risk that their failure could result in a material misstatement of the financial statements.

IT General Controls That Are Unlikely to Affect the Financial Statements

Some IT control frameworks include controls that have only an indirect effect on IT systems. For example, the IT strategic plan and the overall IT organization and infrastructure may contribute indirectly to the effective functioning of IT systems and could be an area of interest for an IT auditor. However, these controls are so far removed from the financial reporting process that, in most situations, they will have only a negligible effect on the financial statements. The risk that a failure in one of these controls could result in a financial statement misstatement likewise is negligible. Thus, typically, these controls would not be included in an evaluation of controls over financial reporting.

IT General Controls That May Affect the Financial Reporting Process

Some IT systems process information that is not reflected in the financial statements. For example, an organization may have a sales and marketing system that tracks lead generation, customer contact information, and purchase history. IT general controls that affect the functioning of this system may or may not be included within the scope of an evaluation of financial reporting controls, depending on how management uses the information generated by the system.

For example, management and the sales team may use the information only to manage the sales process, in which case the sales system is not important to the financial reporting process. Or management may use the information generated from the sales system to monitor financial results, generate financial information, or perform some other control procedure.

For example, information in the sales system could be used to:

- Calculate bonuses to salespeople, an amount that is reported in the financial statements.
- Generate a key performance indicator, which management uses to identify anomalies in the accounting records or financial statements.
- Generate nonfinancial information, which management uses in its monitoring process.

General controls related to nonfinancial systems may be included in management's evaluation if the risk of failure of the control is significant. If the risk is small, then the system can be excluded from the scope of the evaluation.

General Controls Directly Related to Financial Information

Other IT systems at an organization are directly related to the processing of financial information; these systems include the accounting system, the sales system, or the inventory management system. To the extent that these systems process significant financial information where a material misstatement could occur, they will be included within the scope of the auditor's evaluation.

IT systems that have a more direct effect on the financial reporting process typically are included within the scope of management's evaluation. Relevant IT general control objectives usually relate to:

- Logical access to programs and data
- Physical access to computer hardware and the physical environment within which the hardware operates
- System development and change
- Effect on the internal audit function

ILLUSTRATIONS

The following questionnaire will help the auditor assess risk. The existence of a condition covered by the questionnaire does not mean errors or fraud have occurred; it is a warning sign indicating increased risk in the audit areas affected. The questionnaire should be modified in accordance with the size and complexity of the entity.

ILLUSTRATION 1. RISK ASSESSMENT QUESTIONNAIRE

____

[*Client*]

____

[*Audit date*]

___________ ___________

[*Prepared by/Date*] [*Reviewed by/Date*]

Instructions

The purpose of this questionnaire is to document and assess audit risk. It should be part of audit planning and updated during the audit. (AU-C 260.15)

The information required to complete this questionnaire comes from the following sources:

1. Client responses to our inquiries
2. Our knowledge of general and industry economic conditions
3. Our knowledge of the client

This questionnaire is divided into two major sections: external and internal factors. It is designed so that every "Yes" answer adversely affects risk exposure.

For every "Yes" answer, the item should be referenced to the appropriate audit documentation. The audit documentation should state our assessment of the effect of the condition on the risk of material errors or fraud.

External Factors

	Yes	No	Working paper reference
General Economic and Financial Conditions			
1. Are there trade or other barriers to the client's international business?			
2. Have the client's domestic markets suffered from high unemployment?			
3. Have the client's domestic markets suffered from high inflation?			
4. Has legislation passed that adversely affects the client?			
5. Are interest rates high in relation to the client's capital needs?			
6. Has the client's business been adversely affected by changes in the following:			
a. Interest rates?			
b. Unemployment rates?			
c. Money supply?			
d. Foreign currency exchange rates?			
e. Overall business conditions (depression, recession, inflation)?			
Industry Economic and Financial Conditions			
1. Are the products of this industry subject to rapid obsolescence?			
2. Is the industry highly competitive?			
3. Have there been an unusual number of bankruptcies in this industry?			
4. Does the estimated income for the year deviate significantly from the industry average?			
5. Did the industry experience a strike or other labor unrest?			
Uses and Users of Financial Statements			
1. Will the financial statements be filed with the SEC?			
2. Will the financial statements be submitted to the client's bank?			
3. Will the financial statements be submitted to credit agencies?			
4. Will the financial statements be submitted to stockholders?			
5. Will the financial statements be submitted to employees with reference to:			
a. Profit-sharing plans?			
b. Pension plans?			
c. Bonus arrangements?			
d. Other compensation arrangements?			
6. Will the financial statements be used in connection with negotiations relating to an acquisition or a disposal of a business or a segment of a business?			
7. Will the financial statements be used in connection with negotiations for:			
a. A loan?			
b. A performance bond?			
c. Private sale of stock?			
8. Are there other uses or users of these financial statements that may affect our risk? If so, list.			

INTERNAL FACTORS

	Yes	*No*	*Working paper reference*
Management's Integrity			
1. Are there any indications that management may lack integrity?			
2. Does management desire favorable company earnings because of the following:			
a. Need to meet forecasts?			
b. Need to support the price of the entity's stock?			
c. Existence of management profit-sharing agreements?			
3. Does management desire low company earnings to reduce income taxes?			
4. Is management dominated by one or a few individuals?			
5. Does management have a poor reputation in the industry?			
6. Does management have a reputation for taking unusual or unnecessary risks?			
7. Has there been considerable turnover in senior management positions?			
8. Are there other characteristics of management personnel that may affect our risk? If so, list.			
Entity Organization			
1. Does the entity lack an audit committee?			
2. Does the entity fail to document its accounting system?			
3. Does the entity fail to use the internal audit function?			
4. Does the internal audit function, if any, not report to the audit committee or some other high organizational level of the entity?			
5. Is the organization owner- or manager-dominated?			
6. Does the entity fail to document job requirements?			
7. Does management lack an understanding of accounting and administrative controls?			
8. Does management fail to implement accounting and administrative controls?			
9. Has management failed to correct material weaknesses in internal accounting control that can be corrected?			
10. Are the entity's records generated to a significant degree by an electronic data processing (EDP) system?			
11. Does the entity fail to maintain perpetual records of:			
a. Inventories?			
b. Long-lived assets?			
c. Investments?			
12. If the entity maintains perpetual records, does it fail to periodically compare them with physical counts?			
13. Does management fail to communicate to other personnel a commitment to control?			
14. Does the entity fail to maintain policy and procedures manuals?			
15. Is there a high turnover of accounting and finance personnel?			
16. Has the client recently changed auditors or attorneys?			
17. Does a hostile relationship exist between our staff and management?			
18. Has the client recently organized or acquired a subsidiary?			

	Yes	*No*	*Working paper reference*
Financial Condition of Entity			
1. Does the entity have insufficient working capital?			
2. Does the entity have insufficient lines of credit?			
3. Does the entity depend on relatively few customers?			
4. Does the entity depend on relatively few suppliers?			
5. Are there violations of debt covenants?			
6. Has the entity recently experienced a significant period of losses?			
7. Is the entity using short-term obligations to finance long-term projects?			
8. Does the entity have excess productive capacity?			
9. Does the entity have high fixed costs?			
10. Has the entity experienced rapid expansion?			
11. Does the entity have a significantly long operating cycle?			
12. Does the entity have significant contingent liabilities?			
13. Is the entity the defendant in any significant litigation?			
14. Do major valuation problems exist, such as:			
a. Allowance for doubtful accounts?			
b. Inventories?			
c. Investment?			
d. Long-term construction contracts?			
15. Has the client experienced severe losses from investments or joint ventures?			
Nature of Transactions			
1. Does the entity engage in a significant number of consignment purchases or sales?			
2. Does the entity engage in significant cash transactions?			
3. Does the entity engage in significant related-party transactions?			
4. Has the entity engaged in significant unusual transactions during the year or near the end of the year?			
5. Are there any questions on the timing of revenue recognition?			

Illustration 2. Example Control Objectives

Business Objective	*Example Control Objectives*
Corporate Culture Establish a culture and a tone at the top that fosters integrity, shared values, and teamwork in pursuit of the entity's objectives.	• Articulate and communicate codes of conduct and other policies regarding acceptable business practice, conflicts of interest, and expected standards of ethical and moral behavior. • Reduce incentives and temptations that can motivate employees to act in a manner that is unethical, opposed to the entity's objectives, or both. • Reinforce written policies about ethical behavior through action and leadership by example.

Business Objective	*Example Control Objectives*
Personnel Policies The entity's personnel have been provided with the information, resources, and support necessary to effectively carry out their responsibilities.	• Identify, articulate, and communicate to entity personnel the information and skills needed to perform their jobs effectively. • Provide entity personnel with the resources needed to perform their jobs effectively. • Supervise and monitor individuals with internal control responsibilities. • Delegate authority and responsibility to appropriate individuals within the organization.

IT General Controls
The entity's general IT policies enable the effective functioning of computer applications related to the financial reporting process.
	• Logical access control protects the following, which are used in the financial reporting process:
	  ◦ Systems
	  ◦ Data
	  ◦ Application, utility, and other programs
	  ◦ Spreadsheets
	• Installation of suitable computer operating environment and controls over the physical access to hardware.
	• Proper functioning of new, upgraded, and modified systems and applications, including plans for migration, conversion, testing, and acceptance.

Risk Identification Implement a process that effectively identifies and responds to conditions that can significantly affect the entity's ability to achieve its financial reporting objectives.	• Identify what can go wrong in the preparation of the financial statements at a sufficient level of detail that allows management to design and implement controls to mitigate risk effectively. • Continuously identify and assess risk to account for changes in external and internal conditions.
Antifraud Programs and Controls Reduce the incidence of fraud.	• Create a culture of honesty and high ethics. • Evaluate antifraud processes and controls. • Develop an effective antifraud oversight process.

Period-End Financial Reporting Processes
Nonroutine, nonsystematic financial reporting adjustments are appropriately identified and approved.
	• Management is aware of and understands the need for certain financial reporting adjustments.
	• Information required for decision-making purposes is:
	  ◦ Identified, gathered, and communicated
	  ◦ Relevant and reliable
	• Management analyzes the information and responds appropriately.
	• Management's response is reviewed and approved.

Business Objective	*Example Control Objectives*
Selection and application of accounting principles result in financial statements that are "fairly presented."	• Management identifies events and transactions for which accounting policy choices should be made or existing policies reconsidered. • The accounting policies chosen by management have general acceptance and result in a fair presentation of financial statement information. • Information processing and internal control policies and procedures are designed to apply the accounting principles selected appropriately.

Monitoring
Identify material weaknesses and changes in internal control that require disclosure.
	• Monitoring controls operate at a level of precision that would allow management to identify a material misstatement of the financial statements. This objective applies both to:
	  • Controls that monitor other controls
	  • Controls that monitor financial information

Activity-Level Control Objectives Adequately control the initiation, processing, and disclosure of transactions.	• Identify, analyze, and manage risks that may cause material misstatements of the financial statements. • Design and implement an information system to record, process, summarize, and report transactions accurately. • Design and implement control activities, including policies and procedures applied in the processing of transactions that flow through the accounting system, in order to prevent or promptly detect material misstatements. • Monitor the design and operating effectiveness of activity-level internal controls to determine if they are operating as intended and, if not, to take corrective action.

AU-C 320 Materiality in Planning and Performing an Audit

AU-C PRONOUNCEMENT

Source Statement on Accounting Standards (SAS) 122.

NOTE: The auditor may want to consider the guidance provided in the SEC's Staff Accounting Bulletin (SAB) 99, Materiality. *This SAB addresses the application of materiality thresholds to the preparation and audit of financial statements filed with the SEC and provides guidance on qualitative factors to consider when evaluating materiality.*

DEFINITION OF TERM

Source: AU-C Section 320.09

Performance materiality. The amount or amounts set by the auditor at less than materiality for the financial statements as a whole to reduce to an appropriately low level the probability that the aggregate of uncorrected and undetected misstatements exceeds materiality for the financial statements as a whole. If applicable, *performance materiality* also refers to the amount or amounts set by the auditor at less than the materiality level or levels for particular classes of transactions, account balances, or disclosures. Performance materiality is to be distinguished from tolerable misstatement.

OBJECTIVE OF AU-C SECTION 320

AU-C Section 320.08 states:

. . . *that the objective of the auditor is to apply the concept of materiality appropriately in planning and performing the audit.*

OVERVIEW

The concept of materiality recognizes that some matters are more important for the fair presentation of the financial statements than others. In performing the audit, the auditor is concerned with matters that, individually or in the aggregate, could be material to the financial statements. The auditor's responsibility is to plan and perform the audit to obtain reasonable assurance that the auditor detects all material misstatements, whether caused by error or by fraud.

The accounting standards define materiality as "the magnitude of an omission or misstatement of accounting information that, in light of surrounding circumstances, makes it probable that the judgment of a reasonable person relying on the information would have been changed by the omission or misstatement." Thus, materiality is influenced by the auditor's perception of the needs of financial statement users who will rely on the financial statements to make economic decisions. (AU-C 320.104) Specific needs of users may vary widely, and those are not considered.

Materiality and Audit Risk

Audit risk is the risk that the financial statements are materially misstated and the auditor expresses an inappropriate audit opinion. The auditor must perform the audit to reduce audit risk to a low level. Audit risk is a function of two components:

1. *Risk of material misstatement*, which is the risk that the financial statements are materially misstated prior to the audit, and
2. *Detection risk*, which is the risk that the auditor will not detect such misstatements.

The model AR = Risk of material misstatement (RMM) × Detection risk (DR) expresses the general relationship of audit risk and the risks associated with the auditor's assessment risk of material misstatement (inherent and control risks) and detection risk. (AU-C 320.A1)

Reducing audit risk to a low level requires the auditor to:

1. Assess the risk of material misstatement and, based on that assessment,
2. Design and perform further audit procedures to reduce overall audit risk to an appropriately low level.

The auditor must consider materiality and audit risk during the audit, especially when:

- Determining the nature and extent of risk assessment procedures
- Identifying and assessing the risks of material misstatements
- Determining the nature, timing, and extent of further audit procedures
- Assessing the effect of uncorrected misstatements on the financial statements and auditor's opinion

(AU-C 320.A1)

REQUIREMENTS

Determining Materiality and Performance Materiality

In considering audit risk at the overall financial statement level, the auditor should consider risks of material misstatement that relate pervasively to the financial statements taken as a whole and often potentially relate to many assertions. It is also possible that specific classes of transactions, account balances, or disclosures may exist for which misstatements at a lower amount than the materiality of the financial statements taken as a whole may influence the decisions of users, so the auditor must determine the materiality level for those items. (AU-C 320.10)

Making a Judgment about Materiality when Planning the Audit

When making a judgment during the planning phase about the amount to be considered material to the financial statements, the auditor should first recognize the nature of this amount. It is an allowance or "cushion" for undetected or uncorrected misstatements remaining in the financial statements after all audit procedures have been applied. The auditor's goal is to plan audit procedures so that if misstatements exceed this amount, there is a relatively low risk of failing to detect them.

It is usually efficient and effective to estimate a single dollar amount to be used in planning the audit. Since the amount is to be used as an aid in planning the scope of auditing procedures, use of a general benchmark is both practical and acceptable. (AU-C 320.A5) For example, many auditors use 5% to 10% of before-tax income or 0.5% to 1% of the larger of total assets or total revenues. Adoption of a benchmark requires consideration of the appropriate base and the percentage of that base to be used to make the calculation.

Determining materiality in the planning phase is a matter of professional judgment. Typically, auditors apply a percentage to an appropriate basis (e.g., total revenues, total assets, etc.) as a starting point for determining materiality. When identifying an appropriate benchmark, the auditor may consider:

- How the users use the entity's financial statements to make decisions
- The nature of the entity and the industry in which it operates
- The size of the entity, the nature of its ownership, and the way it is financed
- The elements of the financial statements
- The entity's ownership and financing structures
- The reliability of the benchmark

(AU-C 320.A5)

Determining the Base

If the current financial statements are available, amounts from these statements may be used, or interim financial statements may be annualized. However, if significant audit adjustments are expected, an average from prior financial statements may be used. When historical data are used, the auditor should adjust the data for unusual items that affected prior years and for any known changes that can be expected to affect the current period. (AU-C 320.A7)

Usually a single base is necessary because the auditor expresses an opinion on the financial statements taken as a whole rather than on individual financial statements. The most common bases for materiality judgments are:

1. Profit before tax
2. Total revenues
3. Net asset value

Other benchmarks the auditor may use include gross profit and total expenses, total equity, and profit before tax from continuing operations. (AU-C 320.A6)

Some common approaches to using these bases include, but are not limited to, the following:

1. Select from among the bases recognizing differences in client and industry circumstances. For example:

    a. If income fluctuates significantly or approaches breakeven, use total revenues.
    b. If the entity is in an industry that is asset intensive, such as a financial institution, use total assets; if the entity is a nonprofit organization, use total revenues.
    c. Otherwise, use income before taxes.

2. Use a single base that is likely to be valid across most client circumstances or industries. For example, always use the larger of total assets or total revenues.
3. Consider using appropriate percentages applied to different bases as the outside limits on a range, and select an amount within the range based on judgment. For example, select an amount between X% of income before taxes and Y% of total revenues.

The choice of approach is influenced by judgments about the importance of stability of the base versus flexibility in using judgment in the circumstances.

Nature of a Materiality Benchmark

Several matters should be recognized in using a benchmark to estimate an amount to be used for planning materiality. First, the amount expresses the auditor's judgment about the total acceptable amount of undetected misstatement and detected but uncorrected misstatement. Thus, this amount in some circumstances may be larger than some auditors have considered to be material.

Second, because the amount includes an allowance for *undetected* misstatements and includes the *combined* effect of misstatements, it is not suitable as a threshold for evaluating the materiality of individual misstatements. Also, when evaluating, the auditor should consider qualitative matters and additional information obtained during the audit.

Finally, a benchmark is in no sense a rule. It is simply a guide to making a planning decision. If the benchmark produces an amount that an auditor believes is unreasonable, the auditor's considered judgment should prevail over arbitrary adherence to the benchmark.

For smaller entities, where the owner takes a significant amount of before-tax profit, it might be prudent to use another benchmark, such as profit before distribution and tax. (AU-C 320.A10)

The auditor should determine a materiality level for the financial statements taken as a whole when establishing the overall audit strategy. This materiality, developed during the planning stage, helps guide the auditor's judgments in:

- Assessing the risks of material misstatement, and
- Planning the nature, timing, and extent of further audit procedures.

(AU-C 320.11)

Revision of Materiality

During the audit, the auditor may become aware of information that indicates that a lower level of materiality is more appropriate. In that case, the auditor should consider the necessity of revising performance materiality and whether further audit procedures need to be considered. (AU-C 320.12-.13)

Documentation Requirements

The auditor should document the following:

- The level of materiality for the financial statements as a whole
- Materiality levels for particular classes of transactions, account balances, and disclosures
- Performance materiality
- Any revisions to the above during the audit

(AU-C 320.14)

AU-C 330 Performing Audit Procedures in Response to Assessed Risks and Evaluating the Audit Evidence Obtained

AU-C ORIGINAL PRONOUNCEMENT

Source Statement on Auditing Standards (SAS) 122.

DEFINITIONS OF TERMS

Substantive procedure. An audit procedure designed to detect material misstatements at the assertion level. Substantive procedures comprise:

1. Tests of details (classes of transactions, account balances, and disclosures), and
2. Substantive analytical procedures

Test of controls. An audit procedure designed to evaluate the operating effectiveness of controls in preventing, or detecting and correcting, material misstatements at the assertion level.

OBJECTIVE OF AU-C SECTION 330

AU-C Section 330.03 states that:

> *. . . the objective of the auditor is to obtain sufficient appropriate audit evidence regarding the assessed risks of material misstatement through designing and implementing appropriate responses to those risks.*

OVERVIEW

Sections 330 and 315 are the centerpiece of the risk assessment standards. Together, these two sections provide detailed guidance on how to apply the audit risk model described in Section 320. That model describes audit risk as:

$$AR = RMM \times DR$$

where AR is audit risk, RMM is the risk of material misstatement, and DR is detection risk. The RMM is a combination of inherent and control risk. Although the standard describes a combined risk assessment, the auditor may perform separate assessments of inherent and control risks.

Section 330 provides guidance on the design, performance, and evaluation of further audit procedures, which consist of tests of controls (an element of RMM), and substantive procedures, which are related to detection risk.

The assessment of the risk of material misstatement serves as the basis for the design of further audit procedures. Further audit procedures should be clearly linked and responsive to the assessed risks.

NOTE: Risk exists at one of two levels: the financial statement level or the relevant assertion level. This distinction is important because the nature of the auditor's response differs depending on whether the risk is at the financial statement level or the assertion level.

- *The risk of material misstatement at the financial statement level has a pervasive effect on the financial statements and affects many assertions. The control environment is an example of a financial-statement-level risk. In addition to developing assertion-specific responses, financial-statement-level risks may require the auditor to develop an overall response, such as assigning more experienced audit team members.*
- *Assertion-level risks pertain to a single assertion or related group of assertions. Assertion-level risks require the auditor to design and perform specific further audit procedures, such as tests of controls and/or substantive procedures that are directly responsive to the assessed risk.*

To reduce audit risk to an acceptably low level, the auditor should:

- Determine overall responses to address the assessed risks of material misstatement at the *financial statement* level, and
- Design and perform further audit procedures responsive to the assessed risks of material misstatement at the relevant *assertion* level.

(AU-C 330.05-06)

NOTE: Further audit procedures consist of either tests of controls or substantive tests. Often, a combined approach using both tests of controls and substantive procedures is an effective approach.

Audit procedures performed in previous audits and example procedures provided by illustrative audit programs may help the auditor understand the types of further audit procedures that are possible to perform. However, prior-year procedures and example audit programs do not provide a sufficient basis for determining the nature, timing, and extent of audit procedures to perform in the current audit. The assessment of the risk of material misstatement in the current period is the primary basis for designing further audit procedures in the current period.

REQUIREMENTS

OVERALL RESPONSES

The overall responses to financial-statement-level risks of material misstatement may include:

- Emphasizing to the audit team the need to maintain professional skepticism in gathering and evaluating audit evidence.
- Assigning more experienced staff or those with specialized skills.
- Using specialists.

- Providing more supervision.
- Incorporating additional elements of unpredictability in the selection of further audit procedures.
- Making general changes to the nature, timing, or extent of further audit procedures, such as performing substantive procedures at period end instead of at an interim date.

(AU-C 330.A1)

Designing the Nature, Timing, and Extent of Further Audit Procedures

The auditor should design and perform further audit procedures whose nature, timing, and extent are responsive to and clearly linked with the assessment of the risk of material misstatement. (AU-C 330.06) In designing further audit procedures, the auditor should consider matters such as:

- The significance of the risk.
- The likelihood that a material misstatement will occur.
- The characteristics of the class of transactions, account balance, or disclosure involved.
- The nature of the specific controls used by the entity, in particular whether they are manual or automated.
- Whether the auditor expects to obtain audit evidence to determine if the entity's controls are effective in preventing or detecting material misstatements.

(AU-C 330.07)

Regardless of the audit approach selected, the auditor should design and perform substantive procedures for all relevant assertions related to each material class of transactions, account balance, and disclosure.

Nature

The nature of an audit procedure refers to its type (inspection, reperformance, etc.) and its purpose (tests of controls and substantive procedures). Selecting the type of audit procedure to perform is critical to designing tests that are an effective response to assessed risks.

The higher the auditor's assessment of risk, the more reliable and relevant is the audit evidence sought by the auditor from substantive procedures. Section 500 provides guidance on the relative reliability of various types of audit evidence.

In some instances, the auditor may use information produced by the entity's information system in performing audit procedures. For example, the auditor may use the entity's aging of accounts receivable to test the adequacy of their allowance for doubtful accounts. When the auditor uses information from the entity's system in this manner, the auditor should obtain audit evidence about the accuracy and completeness of the information. This audit evidence may come from tests of controls, substantive procedures, or both.

Timing

Timing refers to:

- When audit procedures are performed,
- The period for which the auditor intends to rely on those controls, or
- The period or date to which the audit evidence applies.

Tests of controls may be performed either at an interim date or throughout the period for which the auditor intends to rely on those controls. (AU-C 330.11) In considering when to perform audit procedures, the auditor should consider matters such as:

- The control environment.
- When relevant information is available (for example, electronic files may subsequently be overwritten, or procedures to be observed may occur only at certain times).
- The nature of the risk (for example, if there is a risk of inflated revenues to meet earnings expectations by subsequent creation of false sales agreements, the auditor may examine contracts available on the date of the period end).
- The period or date to which the audit evidence relates.

Extent

Extent refers to the quantity of a specific audit procedure to be performed—for example, a sample size. The auditor determines the extent of an audit procedure after considering:

- Materiality
- The assessed risk of material misstatement
- The degree of assurance the auditor plans to obtain

As the risk of material misstatement increases, the extent of audit procedures also should increase. (AU-C 330.A16)

NOTE: Increasing the extent of audit procedures is effective only if the nature of the procedures is responsive to the risk of material misstatement. For example, the confirmation of accounts receivable is a test primarily directed to the existence assertion. If the auditor is concerned about the completeness assertion, increasing the number of confirmations sent to customers will not be effective.

TESTS OF CONTROLS

The auditor should test controls when:

- The auditor will rely on the operating effectiveness of controls to modify the nature, timing, and extent of substantive procedures, or
- Substantive procedures alone will not be sufficient. Section 330 provides guidance on determining when substantive procedures alone will not be sufficient.

(AU-C 330.08)

NOTE: When determining whether to rely on the operating effectiveness of controls to modify the nature, timing, and extent of substantive procedures, the auditor may consider matters such as the following:

- *The incremental cost of testing controls, which includes the cost of testing not just the controls that have a direct effect on the assertion, but also those controls upon which the direct controls depend. When considering incremental testing costs, consider that the costs of evaluating control design already have been incurred (because the auditor must evaluate control design on every audit) and that the incremental cost of obtaining audit evidence about the effective operation of controls may not be substantial.*
- *In many circumstances, audit evidence obtained from tests of controls may be relevant for a three-year period. That is, the costs of testing controls may provide benefit for three audit periods.*

- *The benefits to be derived from testing controls. In many cases, testing controls may have benefits that extend beyond the relevant assertion to be addressed by the substantive procedures. For example, testing controls may provide audit evidence about the reliability of the entity's IT system, which can allow the auditor to rely on other information produced by the system to perform substantive tests. For example, information obtained from a reliable IT system can contribute to more reliable analytical procedures.*

The auditor will perform risk assessment procedures to evaluate the design of the entity's internal control, and these procedures may provide some limited audit evidence about the operating effectiveness of internal control. But risk assessment procedures by themselves generally will not provide sufficient appropriate audit evidence to support relying on controls to modify the nature, timing, and extent of substantive procedures.

Nature

As the planned level of assurance increases, the auditor should seek more reliable or more extensive audit evidence about the operating effectiveness of controls. For example, if the auditor has determined that, for a particular assertion, substantive procedures alone will not be sufficient, then the auditor would want to select tests of controls that will provide more reliable audit evidence.

When designing tests of controls, the auditor should consider the need to obtain audit evidence supporting the effective operation of controls directly related to the relevant assertion, as well as other indirect controls on which those controls depend. For example, if the auditor tests an IT application control, he or she should consider the need to test the IT general controls upon which the effective operation of the application control depends.

Timing

When determining the timing of tests of controls, the auditor should consider whether audit evidence is needed about how the control operated as of a point in time or how it operated throughout the audit period. This determination will depend on the auditor's overall objective. For example, to test the controls over the entity's physical inventory count, the auditor's objective would be related to how the control operated at the point in time the physical inventory count was taken. However, to modify the nature, timing, and extent of, say, revenue transactions or accounts payable, the auditor would want to test the operation of controls throughout the audit period.

When further audit procedures are performed at an interim date, the auditor should consider obtaining information about significant changes to controls tested and the additional evidence that is necessary for the remaining period. (AU-C 330.12)

If certain conditions are met, the auditor may use audit evidence about the operating effectiveness of controls obtained in prior audits. These conditions include the following:

- The auditor should obtain audit evidence about whether changes to the controls have occurred since the prior audit. If the controls have changed since they were last tested, the auditor should test the controls in the current period to the extent they affect the relevance of the audit evidence from the prior period.
- The auditor should test the operating effectiveness of controls at least once every third year in an annual audit. When there are a number of controls for which the auditor determines that it is appropriate to use audit evidence in prior audits, the auditor should test the operating effectiveness of some controls each year.

(AU-C 330.14)

NOTE: When considering whether it is appropriate to use audit evidence about the operating effectiveness of controls obtained in prior audits, the auditor should consider matters such as:

- *The effectiveness of other elements of internal control, including the control environment, the entity's monitoring of controls, and the entity's risk assessment process*
- *The risks arising from the characteristics of the control, including whether controls are manual or automated*
- *The effectiveness of IT general controls*
- *The effectiveness of the control and its application by the entity, including the nature and extent of deviations in the application of the control from tests of operating effectiveness in prior audits*
- *Whether the lack of a change in a particular control poses a risk due to changing circumstances*
- *The risk of material misstatement and the extent of reliance on the control*

(AU-C 330.13)

In general, the higher the risk of material misstatement, or the greater the auditor's reliance on controls, the shorter the time period that should elapse between tests of the controls.

Extent

In general, the greater the auditor's planned reliance on the operating effectiveness of controls, the greater the extent of testing. (AU-C 330.A16) Other factors that the auditor should consider when determining the extent of tests of controls include the following:

- The frequency of the performance of the control by the entity during the period
- The length of time during the audit period that the auditor is relying on the operating effectiveness of the control
- The relevance and reliability of the audit evidence to be obtained in supporting that the control prevents, or detects and corrects, material misstatements at the relevant assertion level
- The extent to which audit evidence is obtained from tests of other controls related to the relevant assertion
- The expected deviation from the control

Generally, IT processing is inherently consistent. Therefore, the auditor may be able to limit the testing to one or a few instances of the control operations, providing that IT general controls operate effectively.

Substantive Procedures

The auditor's substantive procedures should include:

- Performing tests directed to the relevant assertions related to each material class of transactions, account balance, and disclosures (AU-C 330.18),
- Agreeing the financial statements, including their accompanying notes to the underlying accounting records, and
- Examining material journal entries and other adjustments made during the course of preparing the financial statements.

(AU-C 330.21)

The auditor is required to use external confirmation procedures for accounts receivable, except when the account balance is immaterial, external confirmations would be ineffective, or the assessed level of risk at the relevant assertion level is low and other procedures address the risk. (AU-C 330.20)

Section 315 describes *significant risks* and how the auditor identifies significant risks. With regard to performing procedures related to significant risks, the auditor should perform tests of details or a combination of tests of details and substantive analytical procedures. That is, the auditor is precluded from performing only substantive analytical procedures in response to significant risks. (AU-C 330.22)

Timing

In some circumstances, the auditor may perform substantive procedures as of an interim date, which increases the risk that misstatements that exist at the period end will not be detected by the auditor. Therefore, when substantive tests are performed at an interim date, the auditor should perform further substantive procedures or substantive procedures combined with tests of controls to cover the period between the interim tests and period end. (AU-C 330.23)

When considering whether to perform substantive procedures at an interim date, the auditor should consider factors such as:

- The control environment and other relevant controls
- The availability of information at a later date that is necessary for the auditor's procedures
- The objective of the substantive procedure
- The assessed risk of material misstatement
- The nature of the class of transactions or account balance and relevant assertions
- The auditor's ability to reduce detection risk for misstatements that exist at the period end by performing substantive procedures or substantive procedures combined with tests of controls to cover the remaining period

(AU-C 330.A61)

If the auditor detects misstatements at an interim date, the auditor should consider modifying the planned nature, timing, or extent of the substantive procedures covering the remaining period. (AU-C 330.24)

Extent

The greater the risk of material misstatement, the greater the extent of substantive procedures. In designing tests of details, the auditor normally thinks of the extent of testing in terms of the sample size, which is affected by the planned level of detection risk, tolerable misstatement, expected misstatement, and the nature of the population. However, the auditor also should consider other matters, such as selecting large or unusual items from a population rather than sampling items from the population. (AU-C 330.A68)

Evaluating the Sufficiency and Appropriateness of the Audit Evidence Obtained

The auditor must form a conclusion as to whether sufficient appropriate audit evidence has been obtained to reduce to an appropriately low level the risk of material misstatements in the financial statements. (AU-C 330.27 and .28) The auditor's judgment as to what constitutes sufficient appropriate audit evidence is influenced by factors such as the following:

- Significance of the potential misstatement in the relevant assertion and the likelihood of its having a material effect, individually or aggregated with other potential misstatements, on the financial statements

- Effectiveness of management's responses and controls to address the risks
- Experience gained during previous audits with respect to similar potential misstatements
- Results of audit procedures performed, including whether such audit procedures identified specific instances of fraud or error
- Source and reliability of available information
- Persuasiveness of the audit evidence
- Understanding of the entity and its environment, including its internal control

If the auditor concludes that he or she has not obtained sufficient evidence, the auditor:

- Attempts to obtain such evidence.
- Expresses a qualified opinion or disclaims an opinion if unable to obtain that evidence.

(AU-C 330.29)

DOCUMENTATION

The auditor should document the following:

1. The overall responses to address the assessed risks of misstatement at the financial statement level
2. The nature, timing, and extent of the further audit procedures
3. The linkage of those procedures with the assessed risks at the relevant assertion level
4. The results of the audit procedures
5. The conclusions reached with regard to the use in the current audit of audit evidence about the operating effectiveness of controls that was obtained in a prior audit
6. Basis for not using external confirmations
7. Agreement of financial statements with underlying accounting records

(AU-C 330.30-.33)

TESTING AT INTERIM DATES

Convenience-Timed Tests

Some audit tests can be applied at any convenient selected date before the balance sheet date and completed as part of year-end procedures. Examples are:

1. Tests of details of the additions to, and reduction of, accounts such as property, investments, debt, and equity
2. Tests of details of transactions affecting income and expense accounts
3. Tests of accounts that are not generally audited by testing the details of items composing the balance sheet, such as warranty reserves and certain deferred charges
4. Analytical procedures applied to income or expense accounts

The common denominator in these tests is that the nature and extent of procedures applied are not necessarily influenced by doing a portion of the testing before the balance sheet date. For example, the auditor may decide to vouch all property additions and retirements over a specified dollar amount. The nature and extent of the test are not influenced by whether the testing is done all at year-end or one portion is done at an interim date and the remainder at year-end.

Misstatements Detected at Interim Dates

If the auditor confirms accounts receivable as of October 31 and discovers an error in the receivables balance, how should that misstatement be handled, given that the opinion is on the balance sheet as of December 31, not October 31?

As a practical matter, the auditor should evaluate the results of interim testing to assess the possibility of misstatement at the balance sheet date. This evaluation is influenced by:

1. The potential implications of the nature and cause of the misstatements detected at the interim date
2. The possible relationship to other phases of the audit; for example, do the misstatements detected indicate a need to reconsider the assessment of control risk?
3. Corrections that the entity subsequently records
4. The results of auditing procedures that cover the remaining period

This assessment may cause the auditor to reperform principal substantive tests at year-end or to otherwise expand the scope of substantive tests at year-end. (AU-C 330.A64)

NOTE: Even if the misstatement detected at an interim date is corrected prior to year-end, there may be implications for evaluation of misstatements at year-end. Unless the auditor has applied procedures sufficient to provide reasonable assurance that similar misstatements have not occurred, the auditor may need to project a misstatement from interim to year-end.

Considering Control Risk When Testing at an Interim Date

When performing principal substantive tests at an interim date, the primary control focus is on asset safeguarding and controls that address the completeness assertion. If the design of these controls is not effective, then the substantive tests related to existence and completeness assertions should be applied at year-end.

Keep in mind that this consideration is tied to specific assertions, not to the overall account. For example, confirmation of receivables does not address the completeness assertion, which means that receivables could be confirmed at an interim date even if controls to address completeness were not effectively designed. However, the auditor would still need to consider the nature, timing, and extent of further audit procedures related to the completeness assertion.

Length of Remaining Period

How long can the remaining period be? Section 330 offers only the general observation that the potential for increased audit risk tends to become greater as the remaining period becomes longer.

In practice, many auditors believe the remaining period should not exceed three months (i.e., for a December 31 audit, testing certain balances as of September 30). Another rule of thumb is to consider a remaining period of one month as creating a relatively low increase in audit risk. Ordinarily, if the remaining period is one month, substantive tests to cover the remaining period can be restricted to tests such as:

- Comparison of the account balance at year-end with the balance at the interim date to identify unusual amounts or relationships.
- Investigation of unusual amounts or relationships.
- Application of other analytical procedures to the year-end balance.

Naturally, as with any rule of thumb, the auditor should be aware that in specific circumstances, factors may increase audit risk, and the principal substantive tests will have to be applied at year-end.

Designing Audit Procedures

There is an almost infinite variety of approaches that an auditor can use in practice to achieve the objectives of Section 330. The following chart shows some examples of further audit procedures that may be performed to meet certain audit objectives.

Illustrative assertions about account balances	*Examples of substantive procedures*
	Existence or Occurrence
Inventories included in the balance sheet physically exist.	Observing physical inventory counts. Obtaining confirmation of inventories at locations outside the entity. Testing of inventory transactions between a preliminary physical inventory date and the balance sheet date.
Inventories represent items held for sale or use in the normal course of business.	Reviewing perpetual inventory records, production records, and purchasing records for indication of current activity. Comparing inventories with a current sales catalog and subsequent sales and delivery reports. Using the work of specialists to corroborate the nature of specialized products.
	Completeness
Inventory quantities include all products, materials, and supplies on hand.	Observing physical inventory counts. Analytically comparing the relationship of inventory balances to recent purchasing, production, and sales activities. Testing shipping and receiving cutoff procedures.
Inventory quantities include all products, materials, and supplies owned by the entity that are in transit or stored at outside locations.	Obtaining confirmation of inventories at locations outside the entity. Analytically comparing the relationship of inventory balances to recent purchasing, production, and sales activities. Testing shipping and receiving cutoff procedures.
Inventory listings are accurately compiled and the totals are properly included in the inventory accounts.	Tracing test counts recorded during the physical inventory observation to the inventory listing. Accounting for all inventory tags and count sheets used in recording the physical inventory counts. Testing the clerical accuracy of inventory listing. Reconciling physical counts with perpetual records and general ledger balances and investigating significant fluctuations.
	Rights and Obligations
The entity has legal title or similar rights of ownership to the inventories.	Observing physical inventory counts. Obtaining confirmation of inventories at locations outside the entity. Examining paid vendors' invoices, consignment agreements, and contracts.
Inventories exclude items billed to customers or owned by others.	Examining paid vendors' invoices, consignment agreements, and contracts. Testing shipping and receiving cutoff procedures.

Valuation or Allocation	
Inventories are properly stated at cost (except when market value is lower).	Examining paid vendors' invoices. Reviewing direct labor rates. Testing the computation of standard overhead rates. Examining analyses of purchasing and manufacturing standard cost variances.
Existence or Occurrence	
Slow-moving, excess, defective, and obsolete items included in inventories are properly identified.	Examining an analysis of inventory turnover. Reviewing industry experience and trends. Analytically comparing the relationship of inventory balances to anticipated sales volume. Touring the plant. Inquiring of production and sales personnel concerning possible excess of obsolete inventory items.
Inventories are reduced, when appropriate, to replacement cost or net realizable value.	Obtaining current market value quotations. Reviewing current production costs. Examining sales after year-end and open purchase order commitments.
Presentation and Disclosure	
Inventories are properly classified in the balance sheet as current assets.	Reviewing drafts of the financial statements.
The major categories of inventories and their bases of valuation are adequately disclosed in the financial statements.	Reviewing drafts of the financial statements. Comparing the disclosures made in the financial statements to the requirements of generally accepted accounting principles.
The pledge or assignment of any inventories is appropriately disclosed.	Obtaining confirmation of inventories pledged under loan agreements.

This approach can be time-consuming and result in a substantial amount of repetition. For example, developing specific audit objectives for the existence of each asset normally results in the repetitive statement that the particular asset does, in fact, exist and is available for its intended use. There is more variation for specific audit objectives related to presentation and disclosure, but disclosure checklists are available for that assertion and related specific objectives.

TESTS OF INTERNAL CONTROL OPERATING EFFECTIVENESS

Test Design Considerations

Your tests of operating effectiveness should be designed to determine:

- How the control procedure was performed
- The consistency with which it was applied
- By whom it was applied

Risk-Based Approach to Designing Tests

The reliability of a test is influenced by three factors:

1. *Nature.* The type of the test you perform is referred to as its "nature."

There are four types of tests:

- **Inquiry.** Think of inquiry as providing circumstantial evidence about the performance of a control. For example, if you ask the accounting clerk "Did you perform the month-end reconciliation?" the reply "Yes" does not provide you with as much evidence as you would get from reviewing the actual reconciliation. For controls related to higher risks of misstatement, you will want to supplement your inquiries with other tests.
- **Observation.** You may observe the performance of a control procedure. For example, the annual count of inventory and an edit check built into a computer application are controls whose performance you might observe. The observation of a control is a reliable test, but it applies only to the point in time when you observed the control. If the control is performed only once during the period (e.g., the inventory count), that one observation may be sufficient. But if the control is performed throughout a period (e.g., the edit check), you will need to perform other tests if you want evidence that the control was performed consistently.
- **Documentation.** You may inspect the documentation of the performance of the control. For example, if cash disbursements over a certain dollar amount require dual signatures, then you could inspect a number of checks over that amount to determine that they contain two signatures.
- **Combination.** In many instances, particularly for controls associated with higher risks, you will perform a combination of procedures. A walk-through is an example of a combination of inquiry, observation, and inspection of documentation.

2. *Timing.* You are required to determine whether controls are operating effectively as of the company's fiscal year-end. The closer your tests are to year-end, the more reliable; the further away from year-end, the less reliable. Ideally, you would perform all your tests as of the balance sheet date, but as a practical matter this is not possible. Some tests will be performed in advance of year-end. For example, you may decide to test the controls relating to payroll as of October 31.

   The bigger the difference between the "as of" date of the tests and year-end, the less reliable the tests. In our example, if payroll controls are tested as of October 31, there is a chance that the operating effectiveness of those controls changed during the two months from October 31 to December 31.

   Plan on testing controls related to low risks of material misstatement in advance of year-end. Controls related to higher risks should be performed as closely to year-end as possible.
3. *Extent.* The extent of your procedures refers to the number of tests you perform. In the previous example of certain cash disbursements requiring dual signatures, the question is "How many checks should I examine?" The greater the extent of your tests—in this case, the more checks you examine—the more reliable your conclusion. Controls related to higher risk of misstatement will require more extensive testing than those related to lower risk.

When you do test controls in advance of year-end, you will want to consider the need to perform additional tests to establish the effectiveness of the control procedure from the time the tests were performed until year-end.

For example, if you tested the effectiveness of bank reconciliations as of June 30 and the reporting date was December 31, you should consider performing tests to cover the period from

July 1 through December 31. These tests may *not* require you to repeat the detailed tests performed at June 30 for the subsequent six-month period. If you establish the effectiveness of the control procedure at June 30, you may be able to support a conclusion about the effectiveness of the control at the reporting date indirectly through the consideration of entity-level controls and other procedures, such as:

- *The effectiveness of personnel-related controls, such as the training and supervision of personnel who perform control procedures.* For example, are the people performing the bank reconciliations adequately supervised, and was their work reviewed during the second half of the year?
- *The effectiveness of risk identification and management controls, including change management.* For example, would management be able to identify changes in the entity's business or its circumstances that would affect the continued effectiveness of bank reconciliations as a control procedure?
- *The effectiveness of the monitoring component of the entity's internal control.*
- *Inquiries of personnel to determine what changes, if any, occurred during the period that would affect the performance of controls.*
- *Repeating the procedures performed earlier in the year, focusing primarily on elements of the control procedure that have changed during the period.* For example, if the entity added new bank accounts or new personnel performing certain bank reconciliations, you would focus your tests on those accounts and individuals.

Information Technology Application Controls

Again, the types of procedures you perform for the period between June 30 and December 31 will depend on the risk related to the control. Application controls are the structure, policies, and procedures that apply to separate, individual business process application systems. They include both the automated control procedures (i.e., those routines contained within the computer program) and the policies and procedures associated with user activities, such as the manual follow-up required to investigate potential errors identified during processing.

As with all other control procedures, information technology (IT) application controls should be designed to achieve specified control objectives, which in turn are driven by the risks to achieving certain business objectives. In general, the objectives of a computer application are to ensure that:

- Data remain complete, accurate, and valid during their input, update, and storage.
- Output files and reports are distributed and made available only to authorized users.

Specific application-level controls should address the risks to achieving these objectives.

The way in which IT control objectives are met will depend on the types of technologies used by the entity. For example, the specific control procedures used to control access to an online, real-time database will be different from those procedures related to access of a "flat file" stored on a disk.

An IT controls specialist most likely will be needed to understand the risks involved in various technologies and the related activity-level controls.

Shared Activities

Some activities in a company are performed centrally and affect several different financial account balances. For example, cash disbursements affect not only cash balances but also accounts payable and payroll. The most common types of shared activities include:

- Cash receipts
- Cash disbursements
- Payroll
- Data processing

When designing your activity-level tests, you should be sure to coordinate your tests of shared activities with your tests of individual processing streams. For example, you should plan on testing cash disbursements only once, not several times for each different processing stream that includes cash disbursements.

Sample Sizes and Extent of Tests

Whenever you test activity-level controls, you will have to determine the extent of your tests. If you are testing the reconciliation of significant general ledger accounts to the underlying detailed trial balance, how many reconciliations should you look at? If the control is something that is performed on every transaction—for example, the authorization of payments to vendors—how many should you test?

The extent of your tests should be sufficient to support your conclusion on whether the control is operating effectively at a given point in time. Determining the sufficiency of the extent of your tests is a matter of judgment that is affected by a number of factors. Exhibit 1 lists these factors and indicates how they will affect the extent of your tests.

Exhibit 1 Determining the Extent of Tests

	Effect on the Extent of Tests	
Factor to consider	***Increase number of tests***	***Decrease number of tests***
How frequently the control procedure is performed	Procedure performed often (e.g., daily)	Procedure performed occasionally (e.g., once a month)
Importance of control	Important control (e.g., control addresses multiple assertions or is a period-end detective control)	Less important control
Degree of judgment required to perform the control	High degree of judgment	Low degree of judgment
Complexity of control procedure	Relatively complex control procedure	Relatively simple control procedure
Level of competence of the person performing the control procedure	Highly competent	Less competent

When determining the extent of tests, you also should consider whether the control is manual or automated. When a control is performed manually, the consistency with which that control is performed can vary greatly. In contrast, once a control becomes automated, it is performed the same way each and every time. For that reason, you should plan on performing more extensive tests of manual controls than you will for automated controls.

In some circumstances, testing a single operation of an automated control may be sufficient to obtain a high level of assurance that the control operated effectively, *provided that* IT general controls operated effectively throughout the period.

Sample Sizes for Tests of Transactions

You do not have to test every performance of a control to draw a valid conclusion about the operating effectiveness of the control. For example, suppose that one of the controls a manufacturing company performs in its revenue cycle is to match the shipping report to the customer's invoice to make sure that the customer was billed for the right number of items and the revenue was recorded in the proper period. Over the course of a year, the company has thousands of shipments. How many of those should be tested to draw a conclusion?

Statistical Sampling Principles

You do not have to perform a statistical sample to determine your sample size, but it does help to apply the basic principles of statistical sampling theory. In a nutshell, the size of your sample is driven by three variables:

1. *Confidence level.* This variable has to do with how confident you are in your conclusion. If you want to be very confident that you reached the correct conclusion (say, 95% confident), then your sample size will be larger than if you want a lower confidence level (say, 60%).
2. *Tolerable rate of error.* This variable addresses the issue of how many deviations in the performance of the control would be acceptable for you still to conclude that the control is operating effectively. If you can accept a high rate of error (the procedure is performed incorrectly 20% of the time), then your sample size can be smaller than if you can accept only a slight rate of error (the procedure is performed incorrectly only 2% of the time).
3. *Expected error rate of the population.* This variable has to do with your expectation of the true error rate in the population. Do you think that the control procedure was performed correctly every single time it was performed (0% deviation rate), or do you think that a few errors might have been made? The lower the expected error rate, the lower the sample size.

Note that the size of the population does not affect the sample size unless it is very small (e.g., when a control procedure is performed only once a month, in which case the population consists of only 12 items).

In practice, most companies have chosen sample sizes for tests of transactions that range from 20 items to 60 items. It is common for independent auditors to offer some guidance on sample sizes.

Be careful about simply accepting sample sizes without questioning the underlying assumptions for the three variables just listed. In reviewing these assumptions, you should ask:

- Am I comfortable with the assumed confidence level? Given the importance of the control and other considerations, do I need a higher level of confidence (which would result in testing more items), or is the assumed level sufficient?
- Is the tolerable rate of error acceptable? Can I accept that percentage of errors in the application of the control procedure and still conclude that the control is operating effectively?

- Is the expected population deviation rate greater than 0%? Some sample sizes are determined using the assumption that the expected population deviation rate is 0%. Although this assumption reduces the initial sample size, if a deviation is discovered, the sample size must be increased to reach the same conclusion about control effectiveness. Unless you have a strong basis for assuming a population deviation rate of 0%, you should assume that the population contains some errors. That assumption will increase your initial sample size, but it usually is more efficient to start with a slightly higher sample size rather than increasing sample sizes subsequently as deviations are discovered.

Sample Sizes for Tests of Other Controls

You also will need to determine sample sizes for controls that are performed less frequently than every transaction or every day. Because the population sizes for these types of controls are so small, traditional sampling methodologies need to be adjusted. Exhibit 2 lists the sample sizes that have evolved in practice for tests of smaller populations.

Exhibit 2 Sample Sizes for Small Populations

Frequency of control performance	*Typical sample sizes*
Annually	1
Quarterly	2 or 3
Monthly	2 to 6
Weekly	5 to 15

Types of Tests

Inquiry and Focus Groups

Formal inquiries of entity personnel—either individually or as part of a focus group—can be a reliable source of evidence about the operating effectiveness of application-level controls. Inquiries can serve two main purposes:

1. To confirm your understanding of the design of the control (what should happen).
2. To identify exceptions to the entity's stated control procedures (what *really* happens).

Confirming control design. Typically, this process consists primarily of a review of documentation (such as policies and procedures manuals) and limited inquiries of high-level individuals or those in the accounting department. To confirm this understanding of the processing stream and control procedures, you should expand your inquiries to include operating personnel and those responsible for performing the control.

When conducting your inquiries, consider the following:

Focus first on what should happen and whether the employees' understanding of the control procedure is consistent with your understanding. This strategy accomplishes two important objectives:

1. It provides you with a baseline understanding of the procedure that everyone can agree on. It helps to start with everyone on the same page. You can then discuss exceptions to the norm later.

2. If the employees' understanding of what should happen varies significantly from what is documented, that may indicate a weakness in entity-level controls. For example, you may determine that a weakness in the entity's hiring or training policies is the cause of the lack of understanding of what should happen. This weakness may have implications for the operating effectiveness of other application-level controls.

Differences between the documentation and the employees' understanding of the procedures also may indicate that the implementation or use of the entity's automated documentation tool was poorly planned or executed. For example, documentation of a new control may have been created without informing operating personnel of the change.

- *Ask open-ended questions.* Open-ended questions get people talking and allow them to *volunteer information*. The results of your inquiries are more reliable when individuals volunteer information that is consistent with your own understanding rather than simply confirming that understanding with a direct statement.
- *Focus on how the procedure is applied and documented.* As described earlier, operating effectiveness is determined by how the procedure was applied, the consistency with which it was applied, and by whom (e.g., whether the person performing the control has other, conflicting duties). The last two elements will be the subject of your inquiries to identify exceptions to the stated policy. Questions about what somebody does or how he or she documents control performance (e.g., by initialing a source document) typically are less threatening than questions related to consistency ("Under what circumstances do you *not* follow the required procedure?") or possible incompatible functions.
- *Interviewers should share their findings and observations with each other.* Research indicates that the effectiveness of inquiries as an evidence-gathering technique improves when engagement team members debrief the results.
- *Ask "What could go wrong?"* Interviewees will easily understand a line of questioning that starts with: "Tell me what could go wrong in processing this information," followed by: "What do you do to make sure those errors don't occur?"

  Toward that end, consider using the financial statement assertions model to frame your questions. As described previously, one way to organize your understanding of activity-level controls is to link them to financial statement assertions. You can use these assertions to formulate questions. For example, the question "What procedures do you perform to make sure that you capture all the transactions?" is related to the completeness assertion.
- *Consider the difference between processes and controls.* A process changes or manipulates the information in the stream. Processes introduce the possibility of error. Controls detect errors or prevent them from occurring during the processing of information. Your inquiries should confirm your understanding of *both* the steps involved in processing the information *and* the related controls.

The duties of an individual employee may include the processing of information (e.g., the manual input of data into the computer system or the preparation of source documents), control procedures (e.g., the performance of a reconciliation or the follow-up on items identified in an exception report), or both. In making your inquiries, you should remain cognizant of the distinction between processes and controls and the responsibilities of the individual being interviewed.

Identify exceptions. In every entity, there will be differences between the company's stated procedures and what individuals actually do in the course of everyday work. The existence of differences is normal. In testing the effectiveness of application-level controls, you should anticipate that these differences will exist, and you should plan your procedures to identify them and assess how they affect the effectiveness of activity-level controls. Differences between what *should* happen and what *really* happens can arise from:

- The existence of transactions that were not contemplated in the design of the system.
- Different application of the procedure according to division, location, or differences between people.
- Changes in personnel or in their assigned responsibilities during the period under review.
- Practical, field-level work-arounds, a way to satisfy other objectives, such as bypassing a control to better respond to customer needs.

Once you and the interviewee reach a common understanding of the company's stated procedures, you should be prepared to discuss the circumstances that result in a variation from these procedures. When making these inquiries:

- *Don't make value judgments.* In any organization, the information that flows through a processing stream will follow the path of least resistance. Controls that are seen as barriers to the processing of legitimate transactions that meet the company's overall objectives may be bypassed. The employee may not be at fault. More important, if you adopt a judgmental attitude toward the interviewee, he or she will be less inclined to participate productively in the information-gathering process, and your interview will lose effectiveness.
- *Separate information gathering from evaluation.* Remember that this phase of your inquiries is a two-step process: (1) identify the exceptions to the stated policy, and (2) assess the effect that these have on operating effectiveness. Keep these two objectives separate. Be careful that you don't perform your evaluation prematurely, before you gather all the necessary information. When performing your inquiries, remember that your only objective is to gather information; you will perform your evaluation once you have completed your inquiries.
- *Use hypothetical or indirect questions to probe sensitive areas.* Many interviewees will feel uncomfortable describing to you how they circumvent company policies or how they have incompatible duties that could leave the company vulnerable to fraud. To gather this type of information, use indirect questioning techniques that do not confront employees directly or otherwise put them on the defensive. For example, you might preface your questions with qualifying statements, such as:
  - "If a situation arose in which . . ."
  - "Suppose that . . ."
  - "If someone wanted to . . ."
- Ask interviewees directly about their opinions of control effectiveness. The overall objective of your inquiry is to gather information to assess the effectiveness of controls. The opinions of those who perform the control procedures on a daily basis are important. Ask them to share those opinions. Do they think the controls are effective? Why or why not?

Qualifications of employees. Assessing the operating effectiveness of control activities requires you to consider who performs such activities. Your inquiries should determine whether the interviewee is qualified to perform the required procedures. To be qualified, the individual should have the necessary skills, training, and experience and should have no incompatible functions.

Focus groups. As a supplement to, or perhaps instead of, interviewing people individually, you may wish to facilitate a group discussion about the entity's activity-level control activities and their effectiveness. The purpose of the group discussion would be the same as a discussion with individuals: to confirm your understanding of control design and to gather information about operating effectiveness. However, group discussions are advantageous in that they:

- *Enable you to see the whole process.* You may be able to convene a group of individuals who represent every step in the processing stream, from the initiation of the transaction through to its posting in the general ledger. A group discussion that includes these members will help you to understand more quickly how the entire process fits together.
- *Foster communication and understanding.* In conducting your group discussion, you will bring together people in the company who may not interact on a regular basis, and you will engage them in a discussion about operating procedures and controls. By participating in this process, employees will gain a greater understanding of their responsibilities and how these fit into the larger picture. This improved understanding among employees will allow your project to provide value to the company that goes beyond mere compliance.

To conduct a group discussion, follow these five steps:

1. *Review the documentation of the processing stream and determine who should be invited to participate.* Groups of five to ten people usually work best—everyone can make a meaningful contribution to the conversation without things getting out of hand. Try to make sure that someone is present who has experience with every process, control, document, or electronic file described in your documentation of the processing stream.
2. *Prepare a flowchart of the process on a large sheet of paper.* Use sticky notes to document processes and control points. Your group discussion will be highly interactive, and the participants will have the opportunity to change your original flowchart to provide a more accurate description of what really happens in the process. Therefore, you should prepare your flowchart in a way that allows the group to work with it easily. Low-tech, high-touch works best.
3. *Assemble the group and explain:*
    - The *purpose of the discussion*, as described previously.
    - The *process*, in which you will facilitate a discussion of how the process really works and the participants will be free to describe what happens by modifying the flowchart.
    - *How long the discussion will take.* Usually, one to two hours is the longest that group discussion of this nature can remain productive. If you need more time, it is better to have more sessions rather than have longer sessions.
4. *Post the flowchart on the wall, and walk the participants through your understanding of the process.*

5. *Facilitate a discussion among the participants.* Be sure to:
   a. Reach an understanding about what should happen.
   b. Identify those instances in which exceptions exist (what really happens).

Throughout the discussion, encourage the participants to change the flowchart as necessary so that it reflects what they have said.

Tests of Transactions

Some control procedures allow you to select a sample of transactions that were recorded during the period and:

- Examine the documentation indicating that the control procedure was performed.
- Reperform the procedure to determine that the control was performed properly. For example, the process for recording inventory purchases may require physically matching a paper-based warehouse receiving report with an approved purchase order.
- Determine that the purchase order was properly approved, as indicated by a signature.
- Determine that the vendor is an approved vendor.
- Observe evidence (e.g., checkmarks, initials) that warehouse personnel counted the goods received.

To test the effectiveness of this control procedure, you could:

- Examine documentation that the control was performed, including:
  - Documents were matched.
  - Purchase order was signed.
  - Receiving report was marked.
- Determine that the control was performed properly, including:
  - Purchase order and receiving report are for the same transaction.
  - Vendor is an approved vendor.
  - Signer of the purchase order has the authority to approve the transaction.

Computer application controls also may lend themselves to similar testing techniques. For example, suppose that purchased goods are accompanied by a bar code that identifies the goods received and their quantities. The bar code is scanned, and the information is matched electronically to purchase order files and approved vendor master files. Unmatched transactions are placed in a suspense file for subsequent follow-up. (As indicated previously, the computer application control consists of both the programmed elements of the control and the manual follow-up of identified errors.) To test the effectiveness of this control, you could:

- Prepare a file of test transactions and run through the system to determine that all errors are identified.
- Review the resolution of the suspense account items performed throughout the period to determine that they were resolved properly.

When performing tests of transactions, you will have to address issues related to the extent of testing: how many items to test. Suggestions for considering the extent of tests were provided earlier in this chapter.

Before performing your tests of transactions, you also should define what you will consider a control procedure error. In instances in which the evidence of performing the procedure is documented (e.g., an initial or a signature), the lack of documentation (a missing signature) should be considered an error in the operation of the control. That is, in order for a documented control to be considered properly performed, *both* of these points must be true:

- The documentation indicates that the control procedure was performed.
- Your reperformance of the procedure indicates it was performed properly.

Reconciliations

Reconciliations are a common control procedure; examples are bank reconciliations or the reconciliation of the general ledger account total to a subsidiary ledger. In some instances, a well-designed reconciliation can provide an effective control over most of a processing stream. Testing the effectiveness of a reconciliation is similar to tests of transactions.

- Review documentation that the test was performed on a timely basis throughout the period.
- Reperform the test to determine that all reconciling items were identified properly.
- Investigate the resolution of significant reconciling items.

Observation

You may be able to observe the application of some control procedures, such as computer input controls like edit checks. A physical inventory count also lends itself to observation as a means of assessing effectiveness. For a control performed only occasionally, such as a physical count, it may be possible to observe the control each time it is performed. For controls that are performed continuously for large volumes of transactions, you will need to supplement your observations with other tests, such as:

- Inquiry
- Test of entity-level controls

Evaluating Test Results

The results of your tests of activity-level controls should support your conclusion about their operating effectiveness. If your tests revealed no deviations or exceptions in the performance of control procedures, then you should be able to conclude that the control is operating effectively (assuming that the scope of your test work, as discussed earlier in this chapter, was sufficient).

When your tests of operating effectiveness uncover exceptions to the company's prescribed control procedures, you should determine whether additional tests are required to assess operating effectiveness. A control testing exception is not necessarily a control deficiency. You may determine that the exception was an isolated instance of noncompliance with the established control procedure. However, if you do conclude that a testing exception is not a control deficiency, then you should perform and document additional test work to support your conclusion. In most instances, control testing exceptions usually are not considered to be isolated instances of noncompliance.

For example, when your test work reveals deficiencies in either the design or the operating effectiveness of a control procedure, you will need to exercise your judgment in order to reach a conclusion about control effectiveness.

Ultimately, you should consider that you are making a conclusion about the effectiveness of internal control *as a whole*. When you evaluate activity-level controls, you should consider the effectiveness of the entire information-processing stream, not individual control procedures in isolation.

EXAMPLES OF EVIDENTIAL MATTER THAT MAY SUPPORT THE SPECIFIC ASSERTIONS EMBODIED IN FINANCIAL STATEMENTS

Another approach is a source list of procedures or evidential matter to be used as a resource in developing audit programs. Exhibit 3 indicates what this approach might look like for some common financial statement components. Usually such source lists present either evidential matter or procedures but, to avoid repetition, not both. For example, if the evidential matter is minutes of board meetings, the procedure is to read the minutes. Or if the procedure is to inspect a broker's advice, the evidential matter is the broker's advice.

Another approach is to use standardized audit programs developed for common components of financial statements. This approach is not illustrated here. Many auditors prefer source lists to packaged programs because of a concern that standardized programs promote routine application and do not encourage exercise of judgment.

Exhibit 3 Source List of Procedures or Evidential Matter

Elements of financial statements	*Existence or occurrence*	*Completeness*	*Rights and obligations*	*Valuation or allocation*	*Presentation and disclosure*
Cash	Bank confirmations	Bank reconciliations	Bank confirmations	Foreign currency exchange rates from newspapers, and so on	Confirmation of restrictions on bank balances
	Cash counts	Interbank transfer schedules			Contractual agreements relating to escrow funds, compensating balances, sinking funds, and so on
	Certificates of deposit and savings account books	Subsequent cutoff bank statements			
		Review of controls over cash receipts and disbursements			
Marketable securities	Security counts	Analyses of general ledger account activity	Certificate of ownership	Broker's advices and documents supporting purchases of securities	Representation and other information regarding management's intention to retain securities
	Security confirmations	Confirmations of security positions with brokers and dealers	Security confirmations	Market value quotations	Minutes of board or committee meetings
	Custodian's reports	Custodian's reports		Appraised values of infrequently traded securities	Contractual terms of debt securities and preferred stocks
		Review of subsequent transactions		Foreign currency exchange rates from newspapers, and so on	Confirmation of securities pledged under loan agreements, and so on
		Review of controls over security of investments and transactions			
Receivables	Confirmation of account balances	Tests of year-end sales and shipping cutoff procedures	Confirmation of account balances	Aging of open balances	Confirmation of terms with debtors
	Underlying customer orders and agreements, invoices, and shipping documents	Reconciliation of trial balances and general control accounts	Subsequent collections	Credit experience and terms	Sales agreement and contract terms

Elements of financial statements	*Existence or occurrence*	*Completeness*	*Rights and obligations*	*Valuation or allocation*	*Presentation and disclosure*
Receivables (continued)	Subsequent collections	Analytical relationship of balances to recent sales volume	Sales records	Credit reports on customers	Terms of notes receivable and collateral held
	Customer correspondence	Analyses of general ledger account activity	Customer correspondence	Correspondence on collection follow-up	Confirmation of receivables sold with recourse, discounted, pledged, and so on
	Sales records	Review of controls over billings and cash receipts	Promissory notes	History of sales returns and allowances Industry experience and trends Subsequent collections, credits, and write-offs Discussion with credit and collection personnel Review of controls over credit extension and collection Foreign currency exchange rates from newspapers, and so on	
Inventory	Physical counts	Tests of year-end shipping and receiving cutoff procedures	Physical counts and confirmations	Purchasing and manufacturing cost records	Confirmation of inventories pledged under loan agreements, and so on
	Confirmation of inventories not on hand	Reconciliations of physical counts with perpetual records and general ledger balances	Paid vendors' invoices	Vendors' invoices	
	Perpetual inventory records	Analytical relationship of balances to recent purchasing, production, and sales activity	Consignment agreements	Review of labor rates	
	Underlying purchasing records, including purchase orders, vendors' invoices, and receiving reports	Analyses of general ledger account activity	Purchase agreements and contracts	Analyses of purchasing and manufacturing standard cost variances	

Elements of financial statements	*Existence or occurrence*	*Completeness*	*Rights and obligations*	*Valuation or allocation*	*Presentation and disclosure*
Inventory (continued)	Underlying production records	Review of controls over accounting for receiving, production, and shipping activities	Physical observations and confirmations	Open purchase commitments	
	Subsequent sales and delivery reports	Review of controls over inventory records		Current market value quotations and replacement cost information Plant tour for possible excess and obsolescence Discussion with production and sales personnel Inventory turnover schedules Industry experience and trends Analytical relationship of balances to anticipated sales volume	
Prepaid assets and deferred charges	Invoices, contracts, agreements, and other documents supporting additions to balances	Analyses of general ledger account activity	Documents supporting additions to balances	Documents supporting additions to balances	Terms of insurance policies, tax bills, and so on (current vs. noncurrent)
		Review of controls over accounts payable and cash disbursements Review of subsequent transactions		Recalculation of amortization Recomputation of ending account balances Analytical relationship of balances to estimated future utilization of assets Discussion of realizability of deferred charges with appropriate personnel Industry experience and trends	

Elements of financial statements	*Existence or occurrence*	*Completeness*	*Rights and obligations*	*Valuation or allocation*	*Presentation and disclosure*
Fixed assets	Physical observations	Plant tour	Documents supporting confirmations	Documents supporting acquisitions	Minutes, representations, and other information regarding management's intention to abandon or dispose of fixed assets
	Documents supporting acquisitions, including authorizations in minutes, construction contracts, purchase orders, invoices, work orders, and so on	Analyses of general ledger activity	Lease agreements	Lease agreement terms	Confirmation of fixed assets pledged under loan agreements, and so on
	Confirmation of equipment maintained at outside locations	Reconciliation of account activity to subsidiary property records		Appraisal reports, replacement cost quotations, and so on	Terms of lease agreements
		Analytical relationship of fixed asset dispositions to replacements		Recalculation of depreciation and amortization	
		Confirmation of construction contracts payable		Analytical relationship of current year's depreciation and amortization to fixed asset costs	
		Vouching of repair and maintenance expense accounts		Industry experience and trends	
		Review of controls over accounts payable and cash disbursements			
		Review of controls over construction work in progress			

Elements of financial statements	*Existence or occurrence*	*Completeness*	*Rights and obligations*	*Valuation or allocation*	*Presentation and disclosure*
Intangible assets	Documents supporting acquisitions, including authorizations in minutes, purchase agreements, contracts, and so on	Review of controls over accounts payable and cash disbursements	Documents supporting acquisitions	Documents supporting acquisitions	Terms of contracts and purchase agreement
				Appraisal reports	Minutes of board or committee meetings
				Recalculation of amortization	
				Representations and other information regarding use and realizability of assets	
				Industry experience and trends	
				Verification of foreign currency exchange rates	
Accounts payable	Confirmation of selected accounts	Circularization of vendors	Confirmation of selected balances	Foreign currency exchange rates from newspapers, and so on	Confirmation of terms with creditors
	Supporting documents, including purchase orders, invoices, receiving reports, check requests, and so on	Tests of year-end purchasing and receiving cutoff procedures	Purchase contracts and vendor statements		Purchase agreement and contract terms
	Vendor statements	Reconciliation of trial balances and general ledger control accounts			
		Review of subsequent payments			
		Review of unmatched vendor invoices and receiving reports			
		Review of controls over purchasing, receiving, and cash disbursements			

Elements of financial statements	*Existence or occurrence*	*Completeness*	*Rights and obligations*	*Valuation or allocation*	*Presentation and disclosure*
Accrued taxes and other expenses	Tax bills, invoices, and other documents supporting charges for services	Analysis of general ledger account activity	Tax bills, invoices, and other documents supporting charges for services	Documents relating to items accrued	Terms of tax bills, and so on
	Subsequent payments	Comparison of account balances between years	Subsequent payments	Recalculation of amortization	Internal Revenue Service agents' reports
	Industry experience	Review of controls over recording of cash disbursements		Recomputation of ending account balance	
				Discussion of estimated future costs with entity personnel	
Debt	Confirmation with lenders	Bank confirmations	Notes and loan agreements	Current interest rate quotations	Confirmation of terms with lenders
	Note and loan agreements	Representations from management	Lease agreements	Foreign currency exchange rates from newspapers, and so on	Terms of note and loan agreements
	Lease agreements	Reference in minutes to commitments, obligations, acquisitions, and so on			Terms of lease
	Authorization in minutes of board meetings	Correspondence from legal counsel			Current bank prime rate schedules
Revenue	Documents in support of selected revenue transactions, including customer orders, contracts, shipping documents, and sales invoices	Tests of year-end sales and shipping cutoff procedures	Not applicable	Discussions with engineers regarding percentage of completion of long-term projects	Terms of documents supporting revenue transactions, including long-term contracts
	Review of controls over shipping and billing activities	Review of subsequent transactions		Recalculations of percentage of completion computations	
	Documents in support of selected expense transactions, including	Review of controls over shipping and billing activities		History of sales returns and allowances	

Elements of financial statements	*Existence or occurrence*	*Completeness*	*Rights and obligations*	*Valuation or allocation*	*Presentation and disclosure*
	purchase orders, contracts, check requests, and so on				
	Review of controls over recording long-term contract activity		Industry experience and trends	Subsequent credit memos	

NOTE: Revenue recognition continues to pose significant audit risk to auditors. Therefore, auditors should be aware that the AICPA's Audit and Accounting Guide, Auditing Revenue in Certain Industries, summarizes key accounting guidance regarding whether and when revenue should be recognized in accordance with GAAP, identifies circumstances and transactions that may signal improper revenue recognition, and provides guidance on auditing revenue transactions in selected industries not covered by existing AICPA Audit and Accounting Guides. In addition, the SEC has issued Staff Accounting Bulletin 104, Revenue Recognition, which summarized certain of the SEC staff's views in applying GAAP to revenue recognition in financial statements. These two publications may be useful to auditors in evaluating revenue recognition issues.

Elements of financial statements	*Existence or occurrence*	*Completeness*	*Rights and obligations*	*Valuation or allocation*	*Presentation and disclosure*
Expense	Documents in support of selected expense transactions, including purchase orders, contracts, check requests, and so on	Test of year-end purchasing cutoff procedures	Not applicable	Recomputation of depreciation and amortization	Terms of documents supporting selected expense transactions, including large and unusual purchases
	Confirmation of large and unusual purchases with suppliers	Review of subsequent transactions		Recomputation of amortization of prepaid and accrued expense and deferred charges	
	Review of controls over accounts payable and cash disbursements	Comparison of account balances between years		Analytical relationship of balances to total revenue	
		Review of controls over accounts payable and cash disbursements			

AU: Shouldn't above "NOTE" be treated like other NOTEs rather than part of table?--CE

AU-C 402 Audit Considerations Relating to an Entity Using a Service Organization

AU-C ORIGINAL PRONOUNCEMENTS

Sources Statements on Auditing Standards (SASs) 122 and 128.

AU-C 402 contains guidance only for *user* auditors. Guidance for *service* auditors is contained in SSAE No. 16 (AT Section 901).

TECHNICAL ALERT

In October 2015, the Auditing Standards Board (ASB) issued Statement on Auditing Standards (SAS) No. 130. SAS No. 130 contains amendments to this section. Any relevant changes are incorporated into the information that follows.

DEFINITIONS OF TERMS

Source: AU-C 402.08

Complementary user entity controls. Controls that management of the service organization, in the design of its service, assumes will be implemented by user entities and which, if necessary to achieve the control objectives stated in management's description of the service organization's system, are identified as such in that description.

Report on management's description of a service organization's system and the suitability of the design of controls (referred to in this section as a *type 1 report*). A report that comprises the following:

1. Management's description of the service organization's system
2. A written assertion by management of the service organization about whether, in all material respects and based on suitable criteria:
    a. Management's description of the service organization's system fairly presents the service organization's system that was designed and implemented as of a specified date.
    b. The controls related to the control objectives stated in management's description of the service organization's system were suitably designed to achieve those control objectives as of the specified date.
3. A service auditor's report that expresses an opinion on the matters in 2(a–b)

Report on management's description of a service organization's system and the suitability of the design and operating effectiveness of controls (referred to in this section as a *type 2 report*). A report that comprises the following:

1. Management's description of the service organization's system
2. A written assertion by management of the service organization about whether, in all material respects and based on suitable criteria:
    a. Management's description of the service organization's system fairly presents the service organization's system that was designed and implemented throughout the specified period.
    b. The controls related to the control objectives stated in management's description of the service organization's system were suitably designed throughout the specified period to achieve those control objectives.
    c. The controls related to the control objectives stated in management's description of the service organization's system operated effectively throughout the specified period to achieve those control objectives.
3. A service auditor's report that:
    a. Expresses an opinion on the matters in 2(a–c)
    b. Includes a description of the service auditor's tests of controls and the results thereof

Service auditor. A practitioner who reports on controls at a service organization.

Service organization. An organization or segment of an organization that provides user entities with services that are relevant to those user entities' internal control over financial reporting.

Service organization's system. The policies and procedures designed, implemented, and documented by management of the service organization to provide user entities with the services covered by the service auditor's report. Management's description of the service organization's system identifies the services covered, the period to which the description relates (or in the case of a type 1 report, the date to which the description relates), the control objectives specified by management or an outside party, the party specifying the control objectives (if not specified by management), and the related controls.

Subservice organization. A service organization used by another service organization to perform some of the services provided to user entities that are relevant to those user entities' internal control over financial reporting.

User auditor. An auditor who audits and reports on the financial statements of a user entity.

User entity. An entity that uses a service organization and whose financial statements are being audited.

OBJECTIVES OF AU-C SECTION 402

AU-C Section 402.07 states that:

. . . the objectives of the user auditor, when the user entity uses the services of a service organization, are to

a. *obtain an understanding of the nature and significance of the services provided by the service organization and their effect on the user entity's internal control relevant to the audit, sufficient to identify and assess the risks of material misstatement.*
b. *design and perform audit procedures responsive to those risks.*

OVERVIEW

More and more entities are outsourcing activities to service organizations. There is often a belief by the user organization that the service organization can be totally relied upon and that the user organization needs only to have limited, if any, controls. Section 402 is intended to help auditors determine what additional information they might need when auditing an entity that uses a service organization. It also makes it clear that the guidance applies if an entity obtains services from another organization that is part of the entity's information system. Also, it clarifies the factors that an auditor should use in determining the significance of a service organization's controls to the user organization's controls. In other words, the audit procedures that are appropriate when a service organization's procedures are significant to the audited entity are not optional. The auditor has to evaluate the interaction between the audited entity and all service organizations used by that entity.

SCOPE

This Section provides guidance to auditors of financial statements of an entity that uses a service organization to process transactions that are part of its information system. A service organization's services are part of an entity's information system if they affect any of the following:

1. Significant classes of transactions
2. Transaction initiation, authorization, recording, processing, correction, and reporting
3. Accounting records, supplemental detail, and specific accounts used to initiate, authorize, record, process, correct, transfer to the general ledger, and report
4. Processing of significant accounting information other than transactions
5. Financial reporting and journal entry processes
6. Journal entry controls.

(AU-C 402.03)

For example, bank trust departments are service organizations because they invest and service assets for others. An example of a user organization for a bank trust department is an employee benefit plan. Data processing service centers are service organizations because they process transactions and related data for others. Similarly, mortgage bankers that service mortgages for other entities are service organizations.

A bank that processes checking account transactions or a broker who executes securities transactions is not included under the Section's definition of *service organizations*. That is because when services are limited to executing transactions specifically authorized by the client, Section 402 is not applicable. The Section also is not applicable to the audit of transactions arising from financial interest in partnerships, corporations, and joint ventures. (AU-C 402.05)

REQUIREMENTS

When an entity uses a service organization, part of the processing that the auditor usually finds in the client's internal control is physically and operationally separate from that entity (the user entity). In some circumstances, the user entity may be able to implement effective internal controls. This occurs when the user entity authorizes all transactions and maintains accountability that would detect unauthorized transactions or activity.

In other circumstances, the service organization's procedures relevant to the user entity need to be included when the user auditor is obtaining an understanding of internal control in accordance with Section 315. One source of additional information to obtain this understanding is a service auditor's report. (AU-C 330.12)

The key factors for a user auditor to consider in deciding whether additional information, such as a service auditor's report, is needed are:

1. The nature and significance of the sources provided by the service organization
2. The nature of the relationship between the user entity and the service organization, including contractual terms
3. The degree of interaction between the activity at the service organization and that of the user organization
4. The nature of the transactions processed
5. The materiality of the transactions processed

(AU-C 330.09)

Information about a service organization's controls may be obtained from various sources, including:

- User and technical manuals
- System overviews
- The contract between the user organization and the service organization
- Reports by service auditors, internal auditors, or regulatory authorities on the service organization's controls
- The user auditor's prior experience with the service organization (if the services and the service organization's controls are highly standardized)

The auditor's understanding of internal control should be sufficient to "plan the audit." Additional information from the service center or a service auditor's report may not be needed if the auditor obtains at the user entity a sufficient understanding of the controls placed in operation by the service organizations to:

- Identify types of potential misstatements,
- Consider factors that affect the risk of material misstatement, and
- Design substantive tests.

If the user auditor cannot obtain a sufficient inventory from the user entity, the auditor should consider the following procedures:

- Request specific information from the service organization.
- Visit the service organization and perform procedures to obtain the necessary information.
- Use another auditor to perform the necessary procedures.
- Obtain and read a type 1 or type 2 service organization report.

(AU-C 402.12)

Before deciding to use a type 1 or type 2 report, the user auditor should be satisfied about:

- The service auditor's professional competence and independence
- The adequacy of the standards used to issue the report

(AU-C 402.13)

When using a Type 1 or 2 report as audit evidence, the auditor should:

- Determine whether the report is as of a date (type 1) or is for a period (type 2) that is appropriate for the audit's progress,
- Assess the efficiency and appropriateness of the report,
- Evaluate whether complementary user entity controls identified by the service organization are relevant to addressing the user of national misstatements, and
- If those controls are relevant, obtain an understanding of whether the user entity has designed and implemented those controls.

(AU-C 402.14)

If the user auditor cannot obtain sufficient evidence to achieve the audit objectives, the user auditor should issue a qualified opinion or disclaim an opinion because of a scope limitation.

Types of Service Auditor's Reports

AU-C 402.08 defines two types of service auditor's reports:

1. Report on controls placed in operation

NOTE: This type of report can help in obtaining an understanding of internal control to plan the audit, but it is not usually in and of itself an adequate basis for reducing the assessed level of control risk below the maximum.

---

2. Report on controls placed in operation and tests of operating effectiveness

Both types of service auditor's reports provide an opinion on whether:

1. The accompanying description presents fairly, in all material respects, the aspects of the service organization's controls that may be relevant to a user organization's internal control;
2. The controls have been placed in operation as of a date; and
3. The controls are suitably designed to provide reasonable assurance that the specified control objectives would be achieved.

The second type of service auditor's report adds a list of tests of controls performed by the service auditor and an opinion on whether the controls tested were operating with sufficient effectiveness to provide reasonable, but not absolute, assurance that the related control objectives were achieved during the period specified.

Before using a service auditor's report, the user auditor should make inquiries about the service auditor's professional reputation. Also, the user auditor should consider:

1. Discussing the audit procedures and their results with the service auditor
2. Reviewing the service auditor's audit program
3. Reviewing the service auditor's audit documentation

Reports on Controls Placed in Operation (Type 1)

This report has two elements:

1. The service auditor's report on whether the service organization's description of its controls presents fairly the controls placed in operation as of a specific date, and
2. The service auditor's opinion that the controls have been suitably designed to provide reasonable assurance that the stated control objectives would be achieved if the controls were complied with satisfactorily.

This type of report generally helps in obtaining an understanding of the entity's internal control sufficient to plan the audit. It does not allow the user auditor to reduce the assessed level of control risk below the maximum.

Report on Controls Placed in Operation and Tests of Operating Effectiveness (Type 2)

This report includes both elements of a type 1 report and adds a third; it refers to a list of tests performed by the service auditor of specific controls. The test period covered is described and is a minimum of six months. The user auditor is responsible for deciding what evidential matter is needed to reduce the assessed level of control risk. In some cases, the tests of operating effectiveness performed by the service auditor may provide such evidence. (Other potential sources of this evidence are tests of the user entity's controls over the activities of the service organization, or tests of controls performed by the user auditor at the service organization.)

The user auditor selects the audit approach:

1. Is it more efficient to obtain evidential matter about the operating effectiveness to permit assessing control risk below the maximum, or
2. Is the more efficient approach to assess control risk at the maximum and plan other audit procedures suitable for that level of risk of material misstatement?

Considerations in Using a Service Auditor's Report

A service auditor's report with a "clean opinion" does not mean the service organization controls are effective for the user organization. It means that the control objectives listed and their related controls are described accurately. For example:

1. The report may not address all of the control objectives that the user auditor would find helpful. Key control objectives relating to transactions processed by service organizations are often defined in the description as responsibilities of the user organization, not of the service organization.
2. The description may state that the system was designed with the assumption that certain internal controls would be implemented by the user organization. In this case, the service auditor's report includes "and user organizations applied the internal controls contemplated in the design of the service organization's controls" in the scope and opinion paragraphs.
3. One criterion used by service auditors to determine whether a *significant deficiency* exists is whether user organizations would "generally be expected to have controls in place to mitigate such design deficiencies." The user auditor needs to consider whether his or her client has these expected controls in place.

Obtaining a service auditor's report and carefully reading the description are the starting point for obtaining an understanding of internal control and how it is integrated between the service organization and the user entity.

The user auditor should make inquiries concerning the service auditor's professional reputation. The user auditor should consider the scope and results of the service auditor's work to decide whether the report provides the needed information and evidential matter that the user auditor needs to achieve the audit objectives. In some cases, the user auditor may clarify his or her understanding of the service auditor's procedures and conclusions by discussing the scope and results of the work with the service auditor and reviewing the service auditor's audit program and workpapers.

To explain a modification of the user auditor's opinion, a user auditor may make reference to the work of a service auditor. In that case, the user auditor's report must indicate that such reference does not diminish the user auditor's responsibility for that opinion. (AU-C 330.22) However, if the report is not modified, the user auditor's audit report on the financial statements should *not* refer to the report of the service auditor. (AU-C 330.21) The service auditor is not responsible for examining any portion of the financial statements.

When the user auditor wishes to reduce the assessed level of control risk and is using a service auditor's report that reports the results of tests of controls over a specified time period, the user auditor should consider the appropriateness of the time period covered in evaluating the tests performed and results to assess the level of control risk for the user entity.

ILLUSTRATION 1. AUDIT PROGRAM FOR AN AUDITOR'S REVIEW OF A SERVICE AUDITOR'S REPORT

	Page__________ of __________		
	Audit Program for Consideration of Type 1 and Type 2 Reports		
Company:		Balance Sheet Date:	
Audit Objective	**Audit Procedure for Consideration**	**N/A Performed By**	**Workpaper Index**
	Audit Objectives A. Determine whether a **type 1 or type 2** report is required to: • Obtain an understanding of the design of internal controls and whether they have been placed in operation (all audits) • Assess control risk below the maximum for certain financial statement assertions (if applicable) B. Read and understand the **type 1 or type 2** report to determine how service organization's controls affect the: • Types of potential misstatements to the entity's financial statements		

	• Factors that affect the risk of material misstatement • Design of substantive audit tests • Assessment of control risk for individual assertions		
	Planning		
A.	1. Identify transactions that are processed by a service organization.		
A.	2. Link the transactions identified in step 1 to the entity's financial statements and relevant assertions.		
A.	3. Determine whether a **type 1 or type 2** report is needed for each of the transactions identified in step 1. a. If a **type 1 or type 2** report is not needed or is unavailable, then either: i. Perform alternative procedures to obtain the information necessary to plan the audit, or ii. Modify the auditor's report for a scope limitation.		
A.	4. Obtain the necessary Section 324 report(s), either from the client or directly from the service organization.		
	Read and Assess the Implication of the Type 1 or Type 2 Report		
B.	5. Read the service auditor's report and assess its implications for the audit of the entity's financial statements, including: a. Whether the service auditor prepares a type I or type II report b. The nature of the opinions rendered and whether these included any modifications to the standard reporting language c. The timing of the engagement, that is, i. The date "as of" which the description of controls applies ii. The period of time covered by the tests of operating effectiveness of controls, if control risk is to be assessed below the maximum		
B.	6. Read the description of the service organization's controls and evaluate the effect of the following on the audit of the entity's financial statements: a. Whether the description includes all significant transactions, processes, computer applications,		

	or business units that affect the audit of the entity's financial statements b. Whether the description includes all five components of internal control c. Whether the description is sufficiently detailed to understand how the service organization's processing affects the entity's financial statements, including estimates and disclosures d. Changes to service organization controls e. Instances of noncompliance with service organization controls f. Whether the description of controls is adequate to provide an understanding of those elements of the entity's accounting information system maintained by the service organization		
B.	7. List all complementary user organization controls identified in the **type 1 or type 2** report that the service auditor assumed were maintained by the entity. Cross-reference this list to the audit work performed to: a. Understand the design of these complementary user controls and whether they have been placed in operation, and b. If applicable, tests of operating effectiveness of these controls.		
	Tests of Operating Effectiveness (if applicable)		
B.	8. Review the service auditor's description of the tests of controls and assess their adequacy for your purposes. Consider: a. The link between the financial statement assertion and the control objective b. The link between the control objective and the controls tested c. The nature, timing, and extent of the tests performed		
B.	9. Evaluate the results of the tests of controls and determine whether they support assessing control risk below the maximum.		

AU-C 450 Evaluation of Misstatements Identified during the Audit

AU-C ORIGINAL PRONOUNCEMENT

Source Statement on Accounting Standards (SAS) 122.

DEFINITIONS OF TERMS

Source: AU-C Section 450.04

Misstatement. A difference between the amount, classification, presentation, or disclosure of a reported financial statement item and the amount, classification, presentation, or disclosure required for the item to be presented fairly in accordance with the applicable financial reporting framework. Misstatements can arise from fraud or error.

Misstatements also include those adjustments of amounts, classifications, presentations, or disclosures that, in the auditor's professional judgment, are necessary for the financial statements to be presented fairly, in all material respects.

Uncorrected misstatements. Misstatements that the auditor has accumulated during the audit and that have not been corrected.

OBJECTIVES OF AU-C SECTION 450

AU-C Section 450.03 states that the objective of the auditor is to evaluate the effect of:

a. *Identified misstatements on the audit and*
b. *Uncorrected misstatements, if any, on the financial statements*

THE NATURE AND CAUSES OF MISSTATEMENTS

A misstatement may consist of:

- An inaccuracy in gathering or processing data from which financial statements are prepared
- An omission of a financial statement element, account, or item, or information required to be disclosed under the applicable financial reporting framework
- Financial statement disclosures that are not in accordance with the applicable financial reporting framework
- An incorrect accounting estimate arising, for example, from an oversight or misinterpretation of facts

- Differences between management's and the auditor's judgments concerning accounting estimates, or the selection and application of accounting policies that the auditor considers inappropriate (for example, a departure from GAAP).

(AU-C 450.A1)

REQUIREMENTS

Accumulation of Misstatements

The auditor must accumulate misstatements identified during the audit, other than those that the auditor believes are clearly trivial, and communicate them on a timely basis to the appropriate level of management. (AU-C 450.05) *Clearly trivial* is not the same as immaterial. Clearly trivial matters are quantitatively and qualitatively inconsequential, individually or in the aggregate.

Considerations as the Audit Progresses

The auditor should not assume that a misstatement is an isolated occurrence. If the nature of the identified misstatements and the circumstances of their occurrence indicate that other misstatements may exist that could be material, or if the aggregate of misstatements approaches materiality, the auditor should consider whether the overall audit strategy and audit plan need to be revised. (AU-C 450.06)

Communication and Correction of Misstatements to Management

The auditor must accumulate all misstatements and communicate them to the appropriate level of management on a timely basis. The auditor should ask management to record the adjustments needed to correct all misstatements identified during the audit. (AU-C 450.07) If the entity makes the corrections, the auditor should confirm that through additional procedures. (AU-C 450.08)

The auditor may request that management examine a class of transactions, account balance, or disclosure in order to correct misstatements therein. If the misstatement involves a difference in an estimate, the auditor should ask management to review the assumptions and methods used in developing the estimate. After management has responded to the auditor's request, the auditor should reevaluate the amount of likely misstatement and, if necessary, perform further audit procedures. (AU-C 450.A9-.A11)

Evaluating the Effect of Uncorrected Misstatements

It is ordinarily not feasible when planning an audit to anticipate all of the circumstances that may ultimately influence judgment about materiality levels in evaluating audit findings at the completion of the audit. Thus, materiality levels at the planning and performing phases will ordinarily differ from the judgment about materiality levels used in evaluating audit findings. (AU-C 450.A16) Therefore, before evaluating the effect of uncorrected misstatements, the auditor should reconsider materiality. (AU-C 450.10)

The auditor should consider the effects, both individually and in the aggregate, of uncorrected misstatements.

The aggregation should consist of:

a. Factual misstatements
b. Projected misstatements from substantive audit samples

c. Differences between any estimated amounts in the financial statements that the auditor considers unreasonable and the *closest reasonable* estimates

(AU-C 450.A3)

Misstatements should be aggregated in a way that enables the auditor to consider whether, in relation to individual amounts, subtotals, or totals in the financial statements, they materially misstate the financial statements.

Qualitative as well as quantitative considerations should be included in evaluating materiality. (AU-C 450.A22)

The Qualitative Characteristics of Misstatements

The auditor should also consider qualitative factors when evaluating misstatements, since misstatements of relatively small amounts may have a material effect on the financial statement. This interpretation lists a number of qualitative factors that the auditor may want to consider, including:

- What are the possible effects of the misstatement on profitability or other trends, or compliance with loan covenants, other contractual agreements, and regulatory provisions?
- Does the misstatement change a loss into income (or vice versa) or increase management's compensation?
- What is the effect of the misstatement on segment information or the effect of a misclassification (e.g., a misclassification between operating and nonoperating income)?
- Are there statutory or regulatory requirements that affect materiality thresholds?
- How sensitive are the circumstances of the misstatements (e.g., a misstatement that involves a fraud or illegal act)?
- How significant is the financial statement element impacted by the misstatement (e.g., a misstatement that affects recurring earnings versus a nonrecurring charge or credit), or what is the significance of the misstatement or disclosures as they relate to the needs of users (e.g., the effect of misstatements on earnings contrasted with expectations)?
- What is the character of the misstatement (e.g., an error in an objectively determinable amount versus an error in an estimate, which by its nature involves a degree of subjectivity)?
- What is management's motivation?
- Do individually significant but different misstatements have offsetting effects?
- What is the likelihood that a currently immaterial misstatement may become material?
- What is the cost of correcting the misstatement?
- How great is the risk that there are possible additional undetected misstatements that might impact the auditor's evaluation?

(AU-C 450.A23)

Prior Period Misstatements

Section 450.A25 requires that prior period misstatements be considered. Two common approaches are the *rollover* and the *iron curtain* approaches. Under the iron curtain approach, the effects of all cumulative uncorrected misstatements are deemed to affect the current period's income statement as well as the balance sheet. Under the rollover approach, the cumulative uncorrected misstatements, net of the uncorrected misstatements carried over from the prior year, are deemed to affect the current period's income statement. If, for example, warranties payable were understated by $150 in the prior period and $200 in the current period, the rollover approach would compare only $50 to the current income to evaluate quantitative materiality, whereas the iron curtain approach would compare the full $200. The auditor should be alert to the fact that neither the iron curtain approach nor the rollover approach can be applied mechanically.

The two approaches are clear alternatives only in complex situations in which a misstatement accumulates in the balance sheet. In fact, the mechanical application of the iron curtain approach in a more complex situation may have the opposite effect from what is intended. For example, if warranties payable were *overstated* in the prior period by $300 and *understated* in the current period by $200, the aggregate effect on the current period income statement would be a $500 overstatement of income before tax. The uncorrected prior period misstatement would have a $300 carryover effect in the current period income statement. Therefore, careful consideration of the impact of prior period adjustments is needed, and individual facts and circumstances must be considered.

Misstatement Worksheet

Usually the only practical way to consider whether financial statements are materially misstated at the conclusion of the audit is to use a worksheet that determines the combined effect of uncorrected misstatements on important totals or subtotals in the financial statements (e.g., current assets, current liabilities, income before taxes, income taxes, net income, total assets, total liabilities, and stockholders' equity). It may be helpful to categorize the misstatements by their nature: factual, judgmental, or projected from a sample. Use of such worksheets is fairly common in auditing practice. However, it is important to recognize that the auditor may use a different amount in evaluating whether the financial statements are materially misstated than was used in planning the audit. Qualitative considerations may cause the auditor to consider smaller detected misstatements to be material. Also, for misstatements that have an effect only on the balance sheet or that affect only classification within a financial statement, an amount may have to be larger to be considered material.

Documentation Requirements

The auditor should document the following:

- The benchmark below which misstatements are considered clearly trivial
- All misstatements, indicating corrected or uncorrected, accumulated during the audit
- The auditor's conclusion as to whether uncorrected misstatements, individually or in the aggregate, do or do not cause the financial statements to be materially misstated and the basis of that conclusion

(AU-C 450.12)

The auditor should create a summary of uncorrected misstatements, other than those that are trivial, related to misstatements; this summary should be documented in a way that allows the auditor to consider:

- The aggregate effect of uncorrected misstatements on the financial statements,
- The evaluation of whether materiality levels have been exceeded, and
- The effect of uncorrected misstatements on ratios, trends, and legal, regulatory, and contractual segments.

(AU-C 450.28)

AU-C 500 Audit Evidence

AU-C ORIGINAL PRONOUNCEMENTS

Sources Statements on Accounting Standards (SASs) 122 and 128.

DEFINITIONS OF TERMS

Source: AU-C 500.05

Accounting records. The records of initial accounting entries and supporting records, such as checks and records of electronic fund transfers; invoices; contracts; the general and subsidiary ledgers; journal entries and other adjustments to the financial statements that are not reflected in journal entries; and records, such as worksheets and spreadsheets, supporting cost allocations, computations, reconciliations, and disclosures.

Appropriateness (of audit evidence). The measure of the quality of audit evidence (that is, its relevance and reliability in providing support for the conclusions on which the auditor's opinion is based).

Audit evidence. Information used by the auditor in arriving at the conclusions on which the auditor's opinion is based. Audit evidence includes both information contained in the accounting records underlying the financial statements and other information.

Management's specialist. An individual or organization possessing expertise in a field other than accounting or auditing, whose work in that field is used by the entity to assist the entity in preparing the financial statements.

Sufficiency (of audit evidence). The measure of the quantity of audit evidence. The quantity of the audit evidence needed is affected by the auditor's assessment of the risks of material misstatement and also by the quality of such audit evidence.

OBJECTIVE

AU-C Section 500.04 states that:

> *. . . the objective of the auditor is to design and perform audit procedures that enable the auditor to obtain sufficient appropriate audit evidence to be able to draw reasonable conclusions on which to base the auditor's opinion.*

SCOPE

AU-C-500 is applicable to all audit evidence. Other sections address specific aspects of an audit, audit evidence to be obtained related to a particular topic, specific audit procedures, and the evaluation of whether sufficient evidence has been obtained. (AU-C 500.02)

REQUIREMENTS

General Guides to Appropriateness of Evidence

The auditor should consider the relevance and reliability of the audit evidence. (AU-C 500.07) Appropriateness of evidence depends on the circumstances, so there are important exceptions to the following presumptions. They are, however, useful general guides.

1. Evidential matter from independent sources outside an entity is more reliable than that secured solely within the entity.
2. Accounting data are more reliable when developed under effective internal control.
3. Direct personal knowledge obtained from the auditor's own physical examination, inspection, observation, or computation is more reliable than information obtained indirectly.
4. Audit evidence is more reliable when it exists in documentary form.
5. Audit evidence provided by original documents is more reliable than audit evidence provided by photocopies or facsimiles.

(AU-C 500.A32)

When information produced by the entity is used by the auditor to perform further audit procedures (for example, analytical procedures), the auditor should obtain audit evidence about the accuracy and completeness of the information.

Using a Management's Specialist

If audit evidence is created using the work of a management's specialist, the auditor should be careful to evaluate the competence and objectivity of the specialist, get an understanding of the work, and evaluate the appropriateness of the work relevant to the related assertion. (AU-C 500.08)

The auditor should ensure the information produced by the entity is accurate, complete, sufficiently precise, and detailed. (AU-C 500.09)

General Guides to Sufficiency of Evidence

The amount of competent evidential matter necessary to provide a reasonable basis for an opinion depends largely on the exercise of professional judgment. Usually the auditor must rely on evidence that is persuasive rather than convincing; an auditor is seldom convinced beyond all doubt about all aspects of the statements being audited. There should be a rational relationship between the cost and the usefulness of evidence, but the difficulty and expense of a test are not valid reasons for omitting it.

Audit Procedures for Obtaining Audit Evidence

The auditor should obtain audit evidence to draw reasonable conclusions on which to base the audit opinion by performing audit procedures to:

1. Obtain an understanding of the entity and its environment, including its internal control, to assess the risks of material misstatement. These procedures are referred to as *risk assessment procedures*.
2. When necessary, or when the auditor has determined to do so, test the operating effectiveness of controls.

3. Detect material misstatements by performing substantive procedures, which are substantive analytical procedures, tests of details, or a combination of both.

Risk assessment procedures must be performed in order to provide a basis for the assessment of risk. (AU-C 500.A10)

The auditor should use one or more types of the following audit procedures:

- Inspection of records or documents such as checks, invoices, contracts, and minutes of meetings.
- Inspection of tangible assets, such as inventory.
- Observation of a process or procedure being performed by entity personnel.
- Inquiry of knowledgeable persons inside or outside the entity.
- Obtaining confirmation and other written representation from knowledgeable people within and outside the entity.
- Recalculation by checking the mathematical accuracy of documents or records.
- Reperformance of the entity's procedures or controls.
- Analytical procedures, as described in Section 520.

(AU-C 500.A14-.A21)

INTERPRETATIONS

The Effect of an Inability to Obtain Evidential Matter Relating to Income Tax Accruals (Issued March 1981; Revised April 2003; Revised December 2005; Revised March 2006; Revised March 2008; Revised June 2009; Revised October 2011)

1. Occasionally, the client may not (a) prepare or maintain appropriate documentation of the calculation or contents of the income tax accrual, or (b) permit the auditor access to the documentation or necessary information, or to entity personnel with information about the income tax accrual.
2. In these circumstances, the client has imposed a scope limitation on the audit, and the auditor should determine the effect of the limitation on his or her ability to express an opinion on the financial statements. The auditor may express an unqualified opinion or a qualified opinion, or may disclaim an opinion.
3. The auditor should document all relevant information that he or she obtains about the income tax accrual. The documentation should include results of auditing procedures and should include significant elements of the client's analysis of the tax contingencies or reserves. The documentation should be sufficient for an experienced auditor to understand the extent and results of auditing procedures performed. It should include the client's analysis of tax contingencies and reserves, support for related disclosures, and support for assessing deferred tax assets.
4. The opinion of the client's legal counsel about the appropriateness of the income tax accrual is **not** sufficient competent evidential matter for the accrual.
5. If a client is basing its position on a material tax accrual on an outside advisor's opinion, the auditor should obtain the opinion, or the client's summarization of that opinion.
6. Similarly, an auditor cannot rely solely on the conclusions of a third-party tax advisor without careful consideration by the auditor. The auditor should have access to the tax

advisor's opinions and supporting evidence. If the auditor cannot obtain sufficient competent evidence, the auditor has a scope limitation.

Auditor of Participating Employer in a Governmental Cost-Sharing Multiple-Employer Pension Plan (Issued April 2014)

Auditor of Participating Employer in a Governmental Agent Multiple-Employer Pension Plan (Issued June 2014)

In June 2012, the Governmental Accounting Standards Board (GASB) issued statements No. 67 and No. 68 that change the reporting of public employee pension plans and the state and local governments that participate in those plans. In response, the Auditing Standards Board (ASB) issued three interpretations to assist plan and employer auditors in implementing those standards. Auditors of entities that have implemented the standards should reference AU-C Sections 9500, 9600, and 9805 for more information.

AU-C 501 Audit Evidence—Specific Considerations for Selected Items

AU-C ORIGINAL PRONOUNCEMENT

Source Statement on Auditing Standards (SAS) 122.

DEFINITIONS OF TERMS

AU-C 501 contains no definitions.

OBJECTIVES OF AU SECTION 501

AU-C Section 501.03 states that the objective of the auditor is to obtain sufficient appropriate audit evidence regarding the:

a. *Valuation of investments in securities and derivative instruments;*
b. *Existence and condition of inventory;*
c. *Completeness of litigation, claims, and assessments involving the entity; and*
d. *Presentation and disclosure of segment information, in accordance with the applicable financial reporting framework.*

REQUIREMENTS—INVESTMENTS IN SECURITIES AND DERIVATIVE INSTRUMENTS

As the accounting standards for investing and related activities have become more complex and detailed, the related auditing guidance has followed suit. Section 501 applies to investments in all securities as well as to derivative instruments and hedging activities.

There are two types of securities—debt securities and equity securities. This section uses the definitions of debt security and equity security that are in the FASB Master Glossary.

Section 501 contains the basic notion that an investee's unaudited financial statements generally do not provide sufficient evidential matter. However, it adds a cautionary note that even audited financial statements might not be sufficient because of factors such as significant differences in fiscal year-ends or accounting principles between the investor and investee, or changes in ownership or conditions.

Section 501 includes substantial guidance on the effect on audit approach and procedures of complexities and risks related to derivatives, involvement of service organizations, and accounting requirements applicable to hedging activities.

The AICPA publishes *Special Considerations in Auditing Financial Instruments—AICPA Audit Guide*. The guide contains many illustrative examples of both the accounting for and the auditing of the most common types of derivatives, particularly those that are prevalent at small business entities. The Committee of Sponsoring Organizations of the Treadway Commission (COSO) issued *Internal Control Issues in Derivatives Usage: An Information Tool for Considering the COSO "Internal Control—Integrated Framework" in Derivatives Applications* in 1996. Although the COSO document precedes FASB ASC 815, its guidance may be useful to entities in developing controls over derivatives transactions and to auditors in assessing control risk for assertions about those transactions.

Required Risk Assessment in Planning

The auditor should consider inherent risk and control risk for assertions about derivative instruments and securities when designing audit procedures.

Assessing Inherent Risk for an Assertion about a Derivative Instrument or a Security

The primary inherent risk is the susceptibility of an assertion about a security or derivative instrument to a material misstatement, assuming there are no related controls. Examples of considerations that might affect the auditor's assessment of inherent risk are as follows:

- *Management's objectives.* The complexity of accounting requirements based on management's objectives may increase the inherent risk for certain assertions.
- *The complexity of the features of the security or derivative instrument.* The complexity of the features of the security or derivative instrument may increase the complexity of measurement and disclosure considerations required by the applicable financial reporting framework.
- *Whether the transaction that gave rise to the security or derivative instrument involved the exchange of cash.* Derivatives that do not involve an initial exchange of cash are subject to an increased risk that they will not be identified for valuation and disclosure considerations.
- *The entity's experience with the security or derivative instrument.* An entity's inexperience with a security or derivative instrument increases the inherent risk for assertions about it.
- *Whether a derivative is freestanding or an embedded feature of an agreement.* Embedded derivatives are less likely to be identified by management, which increases the inherent risk for certain assertions.
- *Whether external factors affect the assertion.* Assertions about securities or derivative instruments may be affected by a variety of risks related to external factors, such as:
    - *Credit risk,* which exposes the entity to the risk of loss as a result of the issuer of a debt security or the counterparty to a derivative failing to meet its obligation.
    - *Market risk,* which exposes the entity to the risk of loss from adverse changes in market factors that affect the fair value of a security or derivative instrument, such as interest rates, foreign exchange rates, and market indexes for equity securities.
    - *Basis risk,* which exposes the entity to the risk of loss from ineffective hedging activities. Basis risk is the difference between the fair value (or cash flows) of the hedged item and the fair value (or cash flows) of the hedging derivative. The entity is

subject to the risk that fair values (or cash flows) will change so that the hedge will no longer be effective.
- *Legal risk*, which exposes the entity to the risk of loss from a legal or regulatory action that invalidates or otherwise precludes performance by one or both parties to the derivative or security.

Changes in external factors can also affect assertions about derivatives and securities. The following are examples:

- The increase in credit risk associated with amounts due under debt securities issued by entities that operate in declining industries increases the inherent risk for valuation assertions about those securities.
- Significant changes in, and the volatility of, general interest rates increase the inherent risk for the valuation of derivatives whose value is significantly affected by interest rates.
- Significant changes in default rates and prepayments increase the inherent risk for the valuation of retained interests in a securitization.
- The fair value of a foreign currency forward contract will be affected by changes in the exchange rate, and the fair value of a put option for an available-for-sale security will be affected by changes in the fair value of the underlying security.

- *The evolving nature of derivatives and the applicable financial reporting framework.* As new forms of derivatives are developed, interpretive accounting guidance for them may not be issued until after the derivatives are broadly used in the marketplace. In addition, the applicable financial reporting framework for derivatives may be subject to frequent interpretation by various standard-setting bodies. Evolving interpretative guidance and its applicability increase the inherent risk for valuation and other assertions about existing forms of derivatives.
- *Significant reliance on outside parties.* An entity that relies on external expertise may be unable to appropriately challenge the specialist's methodology or assumptions. This may occur, for example, when a valuation specialist values a derivative.
- *Assumptions about future conditions.* The applicable financial reporting framework may require developing assumptions about future conditions. As the number and subjectivity of those assumptions increase, the inherent risk of material misstatement increases for certain assertions. For example, inherent risk for valuation assertions based on assumptions about debt securities whose value fluctuates with changes in prepayments (for example, interest-only strips) increases as the expected holding period lengthens. Similarly, the inherent risk for assertions about cash flow hedges fluctuates with the subjectivity of the assumptions and the probability, timing, and amounts of future cash flows.

Control Risk Assessment

The auditor should assess control risk for the related assertions after obtaining an understanding of internal control over derivatives and securities transactions. For assertions for which the auditor plans to assess control risk below the maximum, the auditor should:

- Identify specific controls relevant to the assertions that are likely to prevent or detect material misstatements that have been placed in operation by either the entity or a service organization.
- Gather evidential matter about whether controls are operating effectively.

NOTE: Gathering evidential matter about the operating effectiveness of controls is often referred to simply as testing controls.

To achieve its objectives, management of an entity with extensive derivatives transactions should consider the following:

- Are derivatives transactions monitored by a control staff that is fully independent of derivatives activities?
- Do derivatives personnel obtain at least oral approval from senior management independent of derivatives activities prior to exceeding limits?
- Does senior management properly address limit excesses and divergences from approved derivatives strategies?
- Are derivatives positions accurately transmitted to the risk measurement systems?
- Are appropriate reconciliations performed to ensure data integrity across the full range of derivatives, including any new or existing derivatives that may be monitored apart from the main processing networks?
- Do derivatives traders, risk managers, and senior management define constraints on derivatives activities and justify identified excesses?
- Does senior management, an independent group, or an individual whom management designates perform a regular review of the identified controls and financial results of the derivatives activities to determine whether controls are being effectively implemented and the entity's business objectives and strategies are being achieved?
- Are limits reviewed in the context of changes in strategy, risk tolerance of the entity, and market conditions?

The required extent of the auditor's understanding of internal control over derivatives and securities depends on how much information the auditor needs to identify the types of potential misstatements, consider factors that affect the risk of material misstatement, design tests of controls where appropriate, and design substantive tests. The understanding could include controls over derivatives and securities transactions from initiation to inclusion in the financial statements, and might encompass controls placed in operation by the entity and by service organizations whose services are part of the entity's information system.

THE EFFECT OF A SERVICE ORGANIZATION ON AUDIT APPROACHES AND PROCEDURES FOR SECURITIES AND DERIVATIVE INSTRUMENTS

Confirmations of balances or transactions from a service organization do not provide evidence about its controls.

AU-C 402 provides guidance on how service organizations apply to audits.

1. *Determining applicability of Section 402*, Audit Considerations Relating to an Entity Using a Service Organization. A service organization's services are part of an entity's information system for securities and derivative instruments if they affect any of the following:

   - The initiation of the entity's derivatives and securities transactions
   - The accounting records, supporting information, and specific accounts involved in processing and reporting derivatives and securities transactions

- The processing of accounting transactions from their initiation to their inclusion in the financial statements, including electronic means (such as computers and electronic data interchange) used to transmit, process, maintain, and access information
- The entity's process for reporting information about derivatives and securities transactions in its financial statements, including significant accounting estimates and disclosures

2. *Examples where Section 402 applies*. A service organization's services that would be part of an entity's information system include, for example:

- Initiating the purchase or sale of equity securities by a service organization acting as investment advisor or manager.
- Services that are ancillary to holding an entity's securities, such as:
  - The collection of dividend and interest income and the distribution of that income to the entity
  - Receipt of notice of corporate actions
  - Receipt of security purchase and sale transactions
  - Receipt of payments from purchasers and disbursing proceeds to sellers for security purchase and sale transactions
  - Recording securities transactions for the entity
- Maintaining custody of securities, either in physical or electronic form, is referred to as *holding* securities; performing ancillary services is referred to as *servicing* securities.
- A pricing service providing fair values of derivatives and securities through paper documents or electronic downloads that the entity uses to value its derivatives and securities for financial statement reporting.

A service organization's services that would not be part of an entity's information system include, for example:

- Executing trades by a securities broker that are initiated by either the entity or its investment advisor
- Holding an entity's securities

3. *Obtaining information*. Information about the nature of a service organization's services that are part of an entity's information system for derivatives and securities transactions, or its controls over those services, may be gathered from various sources, such as:

- User manuals
- System overviews
- Technical manuals
- The contract between the entity and the service organization
- Reports by auditors, internal auditors, or regulatory authorities on the information system and other controls placed in operation by a service organization
- Asking or observing personnel at the entity or at the service organization
- Prior experience with the service organization if the services and the service organization's controls over those services are highly standardized

4. *Effect on audit procedures*. Providing services that are part of an entity's information system may affect the nature, timing, and extent of the auditor's substantive procedures for

assertions about derivatives and securities in a variety of ways. The following are examples:

- Supporting documentation, such as derivatives contracts and securities purchases and sales advices, may need to be inspected at the service organization's facilities.
- Service organizations may electronically transmit, process, maintain, or access significant information about an entity's securities. To reduce audit risk to an acceptable level, the auditor may be required to identify controls placed in operation by the service organization or the entity and gather evidential matter about the operating effectiveness of those controls.
- Service organizations may initiate securities transactions, and hold and service securities for an entity. In determining the level of detection risk for substantive tests, the auditor should consider whether duties are segregated and other controls for the services are provided. For example:
  - One service organization initiates transactions as an investment advisor and another service organization holds and services those securities. In this case, the auditor may corroborate the information provided by the two organizations by confirming holdings with the holder of the securities and applying other substantive tests to transactions reported by the entity based on information provided by the investment advisor. In certain situations, the auditor also may confirm transactions or holdings with the investment advisor and review the reconciliation of differences.
  - If one service organization both initiates transactions as an investment advisor and holds and services the securities, the auditor may be unable to sufficiently limit audit risk without obtaining evidential matter about the operating effectiveness of one or more of the service organization's controls, since all of the information that the auditor has is based on the service organization's information. An example of such controls is when independent departments are established that provide the investment advisory services and the holding and servicing of securities, and then reconcile the information about the securities that is provided by each department.

Designing Auditing Procedures

In designing auditing procedures for assertions about derivatives and securities, the auditor should consider the following about the entity:

- Its size
- Its organizational structure
- The nature of the entity's operations
- The types, frequency, and complexity of its derivatives and securities transactions
- Its controls over those transactions

Importance of Identifying and Testing Controls

In some circumstances, the auditor will need to identify controls placed in operation by the entity or service organization and gather evidence about the operating effectiveness of the controls to reduce audit risk to an acceptable level.

For example, the auditor likely would be unable to reduce audit risk to an acceptable level without identifying and testing controls for assertions about the occurrence of earnings if the entity has a large number of derivatives or securities transactions. Relevant controls include those over the authorization, recording, custody, and segregation of duties.

Designing Substantive Procedures Based on Risk Assessment

When determining the nature, timing, and extent of substantive procedures to be performed to detect material misstatements of the financial statement assertions, the auditor should use the assessed levels of inherent risk and control risk for assertions about derivatives and securities.

The auditor should consider whether the results of other audit procedures conflict with management's assertions about derivatives and securities, and, if so, consider the impact on the sufficiency of evidential matter.

Completeness Assertion for Derivatives

In designing tests of the completeness assertion for derivatives, the auditor should not focus exclusively on evidence relating to cash receipts and disbursements. Derivatives may involve only a commitment to perform under a contract and not an initial exchange of tangible considerations.

The auditor should consider the following procedures:

1. Make inquiries, including inquiries about operating activities that might present risks hedged by derivatives.
2. Inspect agreements.
3. Read minutes of meetings of the board of directors or the finance, investment, or other committees.
4. Read any other relevant information.

Valuation

Valuation Based on an Investee's Financial Results

If the applicable financial reporting framework requires that the derivative or security be valued based on the investee's financial results, the auditor should obtain sufficient evidence to support those financial results. The investor's auditor should:

- Read financial statements and the audited report of the investee, if available. Audited financial statements of the investee and an audit report satisfactory for the investor auditor's purpose may constitute sufficient evidential matter.
- Ask that the investor arrange with the investee to have another auditor apply appropriate auditing procedures if the investee's financial statements are not audited or the investee's audit report is not satisfactory, taking into account the materiality of the investment.
- Obtain sufficient evidence to support the carrying amount of the security if this amount reflects factors not recognized in the investee's financial statements or if the asset's fair values are materially different from the carrying amounts.
- If the difference between financial statement period of the entity and the investee could have a material effect,
  - Determine whether management has considered the lack of comparability, and
  - Determine the effect on the auditor's report.
- If the auditor is not able to get sufficient audit evidence because one or more of these procedures could not be performed, consider the effect on the auditor's report.

(AU-C 501.04)

NOTE: A time lag in reporting between the date of the financial statements of the investor and the investee should be consistent from period to period. The effect may be material when, for example, the time lag is not consistent with the prior period in comparative statements or if a significant transaction occurred during the time lag. In this case, the auditor should determine if management has properly considered the lack of comparability. (AU-C 501.A9)

The audior should also read the investee's interim financial statements and make inquiries of the investor to identify subsequent events (those occurring after the date of the investee's financial statements but before the date of the investor auditor's report) that are material to the investor's financial statements. Subsequent events discussed in Section 560, *Subsequent Events and Subsequently Disclosed Facts*, should be disclosed in the notes to the investor's financial statements and labeled "unaudited." (AU-C 501.05)

NOTE: The events or transactions discussed in Section 560 should be recognized when recording the investor's share of the investee's results of operations.

Valuation Based on Fair Value

If the applicable financial reporting framework requires that the derivative or security be valued based on fair value, the auditor should obtain evidence supporting management's assertions about the fair value of derivatives and securities measured or disclosed at fair value. The auditor should:

- Determine whether the applicable financial reporting framework specifies the method to be used for calculating the fair value of the derivatives and securities, and evaluate whether the fair value calculations are consistent with that valuation method. (AU-C 501.06)
- If management or a third party uses a valuation model to determine fair value, the auditor should understand the method used and obtain evidence supporting the fair value determined. (AU-C 501.07-.08)
- Consider the guidance in Section 540, *Auditing Accounting Estimates, Including Fair Value Accounting Estimates, and Related Disclosures*, if appropriate. (AU-C 501.A12)

Sources of Fair Value Information

If derivatives or securities are listed on national exchanges or over-the-counter markets, quoted market prices are available in financial publications, the exchange, NASDAQ (originally the National Association of Securities Dealers Automated Quotations System), pricing services, and other sources. (AU-C 501.A13)

Quoted market prices for other derivatives and securities can be obtained from broker-dealers who are market makers or through the National Quotation Bureau. However, special knowledge may be necessary for understanding the way in which the quote was developed. For example, National Quotation Bureau quotes may not be based on recent trades and may only indicate interest and not an actual price for the underlying derivative or security. (AU-C 501.A14)

If quoted market prices are not available, broker-dealers or other third-party sources can often develop fair value estimates using internally or externally developed valuation models. The auditor should understand the method used in developing the estimate. The auditor may also decide to obtain estimates from more than one pricing source. This may be appropriate if either:

- There is a relationship between the pricing source and the entity that might impair objectivity, or
- The valuation is based on highly subjective or particularly sensitive assumptions.

(AU-C 501.A15)

NOTE: When fair value estimates are obtained from broker-dealers and other third-party sources, the auditor should consider whether guidance in Section 620, Using the Work of an Auditor's Specialist, *applies. The guidance in Section 530,* Audit Sampling, *may be applicable if the third-party source derives the fair value of the derivative or security by using modeling or similar techniques. If the entity uses a pricing service to obtain prices of securities and derivatives, the guidance in Section 402,* Audit Considerations Relating to an Entity Using a Service Organization, *may be appropriate.*

Fair Value Determined Using a Model

The entity may use a valuation model, such as the present value of expected future cash flows, option-pricing models, matrix pricing, or option-adjusted spread models, as well as fundamental analysis, to value a derivative or security. (AU-C 501.A16)

NOTE: When the entity uses a valuation model, the auditor should not assume the role of an appraiser and is not expected to substitute his or her judgment for that of management. When the applicable financial reporting framework requires that quoted market prices be used to determine fair value, a valuation model should not *be used.*

The auditor should perform procedures such as the following to obtain evidence about management's assertions about fair value as determined by the model: (AU-C 540.A75-.A77)

- Assess whether the model is reasonable and appropriate. (For example, estimates of future cash flows should be based on reasonable and supportable assumptions.) Since evaluating appropriateness may require knowledge of valuation techniques and other factors, the auditor may need to involve a specialist to assess the model.
- Calculate the value using the auditor's model or a model developed by the auditor's specialist to corroborate the reasonableness of the entity's value.
- Compare the fair value with subsequent or recent transactions.

Impairment Losses

If the applicable financial reporting framework requires that the derivative or security be valued based on cost, the auditor should evaluate management's conclusion about recognizing an impairment loss for an other-than-temporary decline in a security's fair value below its cost and obtain audit evidence supporting the amount of impairment and whether it complies with the applicable financial reporting framework. (AU-C 501.09)

In evaluating management's conclusion, the auditor should evaluate (1) whether management has considered relevant information about whether a decline is other than temporary and (2) management's conclusions about recognizing an impairment loss. (AU-C 501.A18) The auditor is required to obtain evidence about such factors that tend to corroborate or conflict with management's conclusions. Factors include:

- Fair value is below cost or carrying value, and
    - The decline has continued for an extended period of time and is attributable to adverse conditions related to the specific security, and
    - The entity intends to sell or will likely be forced to sell the security.
- A rating agency has downgraded the security.
- The issuer's financial condition has deteriorated.
- After the end of the reporting period, the entity recorded losses.
- Dividend or interest payments have been reduced or eliminated.

(AU-C 501.A17)

Unrealized Appreciation or Depreciation in Fair Value of a Derivative

The auditor should obtain evidence to support the amount of unrealized appreciation or depreciation in the fair value of a derivative that is recognized in earnings or other comprehensive income or that is disclosed because of the ineffectiveness of a hedge. (AU-C 501.10)

NOTE: The applicable financial reporting framework may specify how to account for unrealized appreciation and depreciation of the fair value of the entity's derivatives and securities. For example, GAAP requires the entity to report a change in the unrealized appreciation or depreciation in the fair value of a derivative designated as:

- *A fair value hedge in earnings, with the ineffective portion of the hedge disclosed*
- *A cash flow hedge in two components, with the ineffective portion reported in earnings and the effective portion reported in other comprehensive income*

GAAP also requires reporting of a change in the unrealized appreciation or depreciation in fair value of:

- *A derivative that was previously designated as a hedge but is no longer highly effective, or a derivative that is not designated as a hedge, reported in earnings*
- *An available-for-sale security, reported in other comprehensive income*

The applicable financial reporting framework may also require reclassification of amounts from accumulated other comprehensive income to earnings. For example, such reclassifications may be required because a hedged transaction is determined to be no longer probable of occurring.

Additional Considerations Related to Gathering Evidential Matter about Hedging Activities

The auditor should gather evidential matter to:

- Determine whether management complied with hedge accounting requirements, including designation and documentation requirements.
- Support management's expectation at the inception of the hedge that the relationship will be highly effective, and periodically assess ongoing effectiveness.
- Support the recorded change in the hedged item's fair value attributable to the hedged risk.

- Determine whether management has properly applied the applicable financial reporting framework to the hedged item.
- Evaluate whether a forecasted transaction that is hedged is probable of occurring.

NOTE: The likelihood that a forecasted transaction will take place cannot be based solely on management intent.

Special Skill or Knowledge Might Be Needed to Plan or Perform Auditing Procedures Related to Derivatives or Securities[1]

Examples of situations that might require special skill or knowledge to plan or perform auditing procedures related to derivatives or securities are when the auditor:

- Obtains an understanding of an entity's information system for derivatives and securities, including services provided by a service organization. The auditor may need to have special skills or knowledge about computer applications when significant information about derivatives and securities is transmitted, processed, maintained, or accessed electronically.
- Identifies controls placed in operation by a service organization that provides services to an entity that are part of the entity's information system for derivatives and securities. The auditor may need to have an understanding of the operating characteristics of entities in a certain industry.
- Gains an understanding of the applicable financial reporting framework for assertions about derivatives. The auditor may need special knowledge because of the complexity of those principles. In addition, a complex derivative may require the auditor to have special knowledge to evaluate the measurement and disclosure of the derivative in conformity with the applicable financial reporting framework.
- Gains an understanding of how fair values of derivatives and securities are determined, including the appropriateness of various types of valuation models and the reasonableness of key factors and assumptions. The auditor may need to know about valuation concepts.
- Assesses inherent risk and control risk for assertions about derivatives used in hedging activities. The auditor may need an understanding of general risk management concepts and typical asset/liability management strategies.

If the auditor seeks assistance from employees of the auditor's firm, or others outside the firm, with the necessary skill or knowledge, the auditor should consider the guidance in Section 500, *Audit Evidence*. If the auditor plans to use the work of a specialist, the auditor should consider the guidance in Section 620, *Using the Work of an Auditor's Specialist*.

---

1 AICPA Guide, Special Considerations in Auditing Financial Instruments, para 2.10, Copyright AICPA, New York.

ILLUSTRATIONS—INVESTMENTS IN SECURITIES AND DERIVATIVE INSTRUMENTS

ILLUSTRATION 1. EXAMPLES OF SUBSTANTIVE PROCEDURES FOR EXISTENCE OR OCCURRENCE ASSERTIONS[2]

Examples of substantive procedures for existence or occurrence assertions about derivatives and securities are:

- Confirmation with the issuer of the security.
- Confirmation with the holder of the security, including securities in electronic form, or with the counterparty to the derivative.
- Confirmation of settled transactions with the broker-dealer or counterparty.
- Confirmation of unsettled transactions with the broker-dealer or counterparty.
- Physical inspection of the security or derivative contract.
- Reading executed partnership or similar agreements.
- Inspecting underlying agreements and other forms of supporting documentation, in paper or electronic form, for:
  - Amounts reported
  - Evidence that would preclude the sales treatment of a transfer
  - Unrecorded repurchase agreements
- Inspecting supporting documentation for subsequent realization or settlement after the end of the reporting period.
- Performing analytical procedures. For example, the absence of a material difference from an expectation that interest income will be a fixed percentage of a debt security based on the effective interest rate determined when the entity purchased the security provides evidence about existence of the security.

2 *Existence assertions relate to whether the derivatives and securities reported in the financial statements through recognition or disclosure exist at the date of the statement of financial position. Occurrence assertions relate to whether derivatives and securities transactions reported in the financial statements, as a part of earnings, other comprehensive income, or cash flows, or through disclosure, occurred.*

ILLUSTRATION 2. EXAMPLES OF SUBSTANTIVE PROCEDURES FOR COMPLETENESS ASSERTIONS[3]

Examples of substantive procedures for completeness assertions about derivatives and securities are:

- Requesting the counterparty to a derivative or the holder of a security to provide information about it, such as whether there are any side agreements or agreements to repurchase securities sold.
- Requesting counterparties or holders who are frequently used, but with whom the accounting records indicate there are no derivatives or securities at present, to state whether they are counterparties to derivatives with the entity or holders of its securities.
- Inspecting financial instruments and other agreements to identify embedded derivatives.
- Inspecting documentation in paper or electronic form for activity subsequent to the end of the reporting period.
- Performing analytical procedures. For example, a difference from an expectation that interest expense is a fixed percentage of a note based on the interest provisions of the underlying agreement may indicate the existence of an interest rate swap agreement.
- Comparing previous and current account detail to identify assets that have been removed from the accounts, and testing those items further to determine that the criteria for sales treatment have been met.
- Reading other information, such as minutes of meetings of the board of directors or finance, asset/ liability, investment, or other committees.

Derivatives may involve only a commitment to perform under a contract and not an initial exchange of tangible consideration. Thus, auditors designing tests related to the completeness assertion should not focus exclusively on evidence relating to cash receipts and disbursements. When testing for completeness, auditors should consider making inquiries, inspecting agreements, and reading other information, such as minutes of meetings of the board of directors or finance, asset/liability, investment, or other committees. Auditors should also consider making inquiries about aspects of operating activities that might present risks hedged using derivatives. For example, if the entity conducts business with foreign entities, the auditor should inquire about any arrangements the entity has made for purchasing foreign currency. Or, if an entity is in an industry in which commodity contracts are common, the auditor should inquire about any commodity contracts with fixed prices that run for unusual durations or involve unusually large quantities. The auditor also should consider inquiring as to whether the entity has converted interest-bearing debt from fixed to variable, or vice versa, using derivatives.

If one or more service organizations provide services that are part of the entity's information system for derivatives, the auditor may be unable to sufficiently limit audit risk for assertions about the completeness of derivatives without obtaining evidential matter about the operating effectiveness of controls at one or more of the service organizations. Testing reconciliations of information provided by two or more of the service organizations may not sufficiently limit audit risk for assertions about the completeness of derivatives.

---

3 *Completeness assertions relate to whether all the entity's derivatives and securities are reported in the financial statements through recognition or disclosure. They also relate to whether all derivatives and securities transactions are reported in the financial statements as a part of earnings, other comprehensive income, or cash flows, or through disclosure. The extent of substantive procedures for completeness may vary in relation to the assessed level of control risk. The auditor should consider that derivatives may not involve an initial exchange of tangible consideration, and thus it may be difficult to limit audit risk for assertions about the completeness of derivatives to an acceptable level with an assessed level of control risk at the maximum.*

Illustration 3. Examples of Substantive Procedures for Rights and Obligations Assertions[4]

Examples of substantive procedures for assertions about rights and obligations associated with derivatives and securities are:

- Confirming significant terms with the counterparty to a derivative or the holder of a security, including the absence of any side agreements.
- Inspecting underlying agreements and other forms of supporting documentation, in paper or electronic form.
- Considering whether the findings or other auditing procedures, such as reviewing minutes of meetings of the board of directors and reading contracts and other agreements, provide evidence about rights and obligations, such as pledging of securities as collateral or selling securities with a commitment to repurchase them.

REQUIREMENTS—INVENTORY EXISTENCE AND CONDITION

When inventory is material to the financial statements, the auditor needs to get sufficient evidence regarding the existence and condition of inventory. This can be done through being present at a physical inventory count. Observation of inventories has been a "generally accepted auditing procedure" (GAAP) since 1939. The first auditing statement, SAP 1, was issued as a result of a study of the McKesson & Robbins fraud.

The auditor should also:

- Evaluate management's instructions and procedures for the count,
- Inspect the inventory,
- Perform test counts, and
- Perform procedures on the final inventory records to assess whether the records reflect the count results.

(AU-C 501.11)

Depending on the date of the count, it may be necessary for the auditor to obtain evidence that changes in inventory between the count date and the report date are reflected properly. (AU-C 501.12)

If the auditor cannot attend the count because of unforeseen circumstances, the auditor should make or observe counts on another date and audit the intervening transactions. (AU-C 501.13)

If it is impractical to attend the count, the auditor must perform procedures that produce sufficient evidence about the existence and condition of inventory. If the alternative is not possible, the auditor must modify the opinion, per Section 705. (AU-C 501.14)

If the inventory is under the physical control of a third party, the auditor must request a confirmation and/or perform inspection or other appropriate audit procedures. (AU-C 501.15)

Timing and Extent of Inventory Observation

The timing and extent of inventory observation are determined by the client's inventory system and the effectiveness of its inventory controls. If the client maintains perpetual inventory

---

4 *Assertions about rights and obligations relate to whether the entity has the rights and obligations associated with derivatives and securities, including pledging arrangements, reported in the financial statements.*

records and the inventory controls are effective, the auditor may limit the extent of his or her observation and may observe the physical count at various times during the year.

Periodic Inventory System

If the client has a periodic inventory system, a physical inventory should be taken at least once during the year. No matter how many times during the year the client takes a physical inventory, the auditor should observe the count that occurs at or near year-end.

For purposes of this section, it is assumed that the client has a periodic inventory system. However, the same procedures, with minor modifications, may be used when observing inventory accounted for under a perpetual system.

Inventory Held by a Third Party

Occasionally, the client's inventory is held by a consignee or a subcontractor.

Procedures

When the amount held by the third party is significant and depending on the circumstances, the auditor should perform other audit procedures. The auditor may observe or arrange for another auditor to observe the count of the inventory, if it is practicable. If observation is not practicable, the auditor should do the following:

1. Inspect documents regarding the inventory.
2. Determine the reliability of the third party by obtaining another auditor's report on the adequacy of the third party's internal control.
3. Confirm with the third party as to quantities and condition of inventory held.

(AU-C 501.15 and AU-C 501.A38)

Steps in the Observation of Inventory

Preplanning for Inventory Observation

Before the client counts the inventory, the auditor should prepare his or her program for the observation. Before preparing this program, the auditor should do the following:

1. Review last year's inventory observation audit documentation to ascertain the:
    a. Nature of inventory
    b. Materiality of specific items
    c. Components of inventory
    d. Nature of any problems
2. Review and discuss with client its physical inventory plan.
3. Visit all locations where significant amounts of inventory are held. Determine if the location is conducive to the physical count.
4. Consider the need for using the services of an outside specialist to assist in identification and valuation problems of certain inventory items.
5. Prepare personnel assignments for inventory observation.

The two major steps in the observation of a physical inventory are:

1. Planning the physical inventory
2. Taking the physical inventory

Planning the Physical Inventory

Planning the physical inventory is essential. The auditor should review or prepare the client instructions and should work closely with the client in the planning stage. The inventory should be taken at a time when operations are suspended or minimal.

The client has primary responsibility for planning and conducting the physical inventory. Because of the auditor's important role in the taking of the inventory, however, he or she should participate in the planning stage.

Before taking the inventory, the client should submit a plan containing the following:

1. Date and time inventory is to be taken
2. Locations of inventory
3. Method of counting and recording
4. Instructions to employees
5. Provisions for the following:
   a. Receipts and shipments of inventory during the counts
   b. Segregation of inventory not owned by client
   c. Physical arrangement of inventory

Date and time of inventory. If the client has a periodic inventory system, the physical inventory should be taken at or near year-end. The inventory should be taken at a time when operations have ceased or are at a reduced level. Ideally, the physical inventory should be taken when the client is not operating, such as weekends or after hours.

Locations of inventory. The client's plan should indicate the location of all inventory. Inventory usually is located at the following:

1. Client's premises; client should indicate where on its premises inventory is located.
2. Plants at locations other than the client's major premises.
3. In transit.
4. On consignment.
5. In a public warehouse.
6. At nonrelated factories for processing.

The client's plan should indicate how inventory will be taken at the various locations.

Method of counting and recording. When a physical inventory is taken, it ordinarily requires two people: one to call the count and the other to record it, or one to count the inventory and the other to check the count. Ordinarily, it is recorded in duplicate on one of the following:

1. Prenumbered inventory sheets
2. Prenumbered inventory tags

When the count is completed, the auditor keeps one copy of the sheets or tags.

Instructions to employees. Before the client counts the inventory, the auditor should review the instructions to the employees. Instructions should include the following:

1. Method of counting and recording:
   a. Will one person count and record and then have another check?
   b. Will one person call the count to a second person, who will record it?

2. Method of arranging inventory before physical count:
   a. Will inventory be segregated by style number, serial number, or in some other way?
   b. Will inventory be moved to a specific area?
3. Method of description (how inventory will be described when recorded):
   a. Style number
   b. Serial number
   c. Part number
   d. Other
4. Method of controlling inventory tags or inventory sheets:
   a. Who will have custody?
   b. How will they be distributed to employees taking the physical inventory?
5. How and when inventory tags or sheets should be gathered
6. Custody of inventory tags or sheets when the count is completed

If the client is a manufacturer, the instructions to the employees also should indicate how the stage of completion is determined for work in process.

Other considerations. The plan for the physical inventory also should provide for the following:

1. Receipts and shipments of inventory during the count:
   a. Whenever possible, no merchandise should be shipped until after the physical count. If this is not feasible, merchandise that will be shipped should be segregated.
   b. A designated area on the client's premises should be used for merchandise received during the count.
2. Segregation of inventory not owned by the client, such as the following:
   a. Inventory on consignment
   b. Bill-and-hold merchandise (merchandise invoiced to a customer but not yet shipped)
   c. Customer merchandise being repaired by the client
3. The physical arrangement of the inventory

TAKING THE PHYSICAL INVENTORY

Audit Program for Inventory Observation

After preliminary reviews, the auditor should prepare his or her observation program (see the "AU-C Illustrations—Inventory Observation" section later in this chapter). The program should include the following:

1. Obtain cutoff numbers (i.e., last receiving number and last shipping number prior to physical count).
2. Inform staff of client inventory procedures.
3. Assign sufficient staff to observe that client procedures are properly executed.
4. Determine the extent to which client counts will be test counted.

5. Randomly select cartons of inventory and have them opened to ascertain that inventory does, in fact, exist.
6. Randomly select inventory items and, as appropriate, do the following:

    a. Have client measure them.
    b. Have client weigh them.

7. When client counts are test counted, compare count with what appears on inventory tag, sheet, or card. Also, compare inventory serial number, style number, and description with what appears on the inventory tag, sheet, or card. List numbers where these procedures were applied.
8. Obtain the range of numbers for the inventory tags, sheets, or cards used to record the inventory:

    a. At conclusion of count, ascertain that all numbers distributed for the count are accounted for.
    b. Be sure to specifically identify for later reference the numbers of all unused inventory tags, sheets, or cards.

9. Make a note of all tags, sheets, or cards that represent obsolete, defective, excess, or slow-moving inventory.
10. For work in process, review with knowledgeable employees the following:

    a. Estimated cost to complete per production records.
    b. Estimated costs to date; review, on a test basis, documentation such as:

        1. Material invoices
        2. Labor costs

11. After the inventory has been completed, tour area with supervisor and ascertain that all items have been tagged.
12. Account for all numbers distributed.
13. Supervise the collection of all tags, sheets, or cards, being careful to note that none of the inventory is moved.
14. Make certain that inventory not owned by the client is not included in the count.
15. If specialists are used, observe their procedures.
16. For finished goods inventory, do the following on a test basis:

    a. Inspect the goods to ascertain that they are complete.
    b. If feasible, have some units disassembled to ascertain that all components have been included.

17. After all tags, sheets, or cards have been collected, review numbers to ascertain that all numbers are accounted for (see 8a and b).
18. Separate the original and the copy of the tags, sheets, or cards, leaving the original with the client and taking the copy for audit files.

At completion of the physical inventory, the auditor should prepare an inventory observation memorandum that includes the following:

1. Receiving and shipping cutoff numbers
2. Entity personnel who supervised the count
3. Number range for inventory tags, sheets, or cards

OUTSIDE INVENTORY-TAKING FIRM

Clients may retain outside firms of nonaccountants to take their physical inventories. This does not relieve the auditor, however, of the responsibility to observe physical inventories.

Auditor's Procedures

If a client retains an outside inventory firm to count its inventories, the auditor's primary concern is the effectiveness of the outside firm's procedures. To evaluate the procedures of the outside firm, the auditor should do the following:

1. Examine the firm's inventory observation program.
2. Observe the firm's procedures and controls.
3. Observe some physical counts of inventory.
4. Recompute calculations of the submitted inventory on a test basis.

If the auditor is satisfied with the procedures of the outside firm, he or she may reduce, *not eliminate*, his or her work on the physical count of the inventory.

Restrictions on Auditor

Any restrictions on the auditor's judgment concerning the extent of his or her contact with the inventory counted by an outside firm is a scope limitation.

INVENTORY OBSERVATION CHECKLIST

To make certain all procedures have been applied in the observation of inventories, the auditor should design an inventory observation checklist. One is presented next in "AU-C Illustrations—Inventory Observation," along with examples of confirmations.

AU-C ILLUSTRATIONS—INVENTORY OBSERVATION

This section contains illustrations of the following:

1. Inventory observation checklist
2. Confirmation of inventories on consignment
3. Confirmation of inventories in public warehouses

ILLUSTRATION 1. INVENTORY OBSERVATION CHECKLIST

____
[*Client*]
____
[*Audit date*]
____
[*Date of physical inventory*]

Instructions

This checklist is divided into four sections.

1. General information
2. Procedures performed prior to date of physical inventory
3. Procedures performed at date of physical inventory
4. Procedures performed after date of physical inventory

If a procedure is not applicable, insert N/A in the column "Performed by" and explain why in the "Explanation" column.

General

1. List inventory locations.
   a. _______________
   b. _______________
   c. _______________
   d. _______________
2. List staff members assigned to observe the inventory count.
   a. _______________
   b. _______________
   c. _______________
   d. _______________
   e. _______________
   f. _______________
3. List client personnel supervising the inventory count.
   a. _______________
   b. _______________
   c. _______________
   d. _______________
4. If inventory was ticketed (inventory tags, etc.), indicate range of ticket numbers.
   a. From _______________
   b. To _______________
5. If inventory was not ticketed, explain briefly how inventory was counted. _________________
6. Nature of inventory.
   a. Finished goods _____
   b. Work in process _____
   c. Raw materials _____
7. Describe client's physical inventory procedures. ________________ Instead of this description, attach copy of client's instructions.
8. Indicate the following:
   a. Last receiving number prior to physical count _____
   b. Last sales number prior to physical count.
      1. Bill of lading number _____
      2. Sales invoice number _____
9. Indicate the following:
   a. Inventory tickets.
      1. Number used _____
      2. Number checked _____
   b. Inventory value.
      1. Total $_____
      2. Amount checked $_____

Procedure	*Performed by*	*Date*	*Explanation*
Prior to Date of Physical Inventory			
1. Visit inventory locations. Note critical areas.			
a. Receiving			
b. Shipping			
c. Production			
d. Stock			
e. ____			
2. Review inventory instructions.			
a. Date and time			
b. Locations			
c. Method of counting and recording			
d. Segregation of inventory			
(1) By style number			
(2) By serial number			
(3) By part number			
(4) ____			
3. Discuss with client the following:			
a. Physical arrangement of inventory			
b. Segregation of inventory not owned			
c. Receipts and shipments of inventory during count			
d. Production during count			
4. Ascertain other locations of inventory.			
a. In transit			
b. On consignment			
c. In public warehouse			
d. At contractor			
e. Bill and hold			
f. Merchandise for repair			
5. Review prior year's observation audit documentation for:			
a. Nature of inventory			
b. Materiality of specific items			
c. Components of inventory			
d. Nature of any problems			
6. Consider need for using services of outside specialist.			
7. Discuss inventory observation with staff.			
At Date of Physical Inventory			
1. Obtain cutoff numbers for shipments and receipts.			
2. Obtain first and last inventory ticket numbers.			
3. Ascertain that inventory was arranged and segregated as required by inventory instructions.			
4. Ascertain that operations were halted during the count.			
a. Receiving			
b. Shipping			
c. Production			

Procedure	*Performed by*	*Date*	*Explanation*
5. If operations were not halted during the count, prepare memo indicating how control was maintained.			
6. Ascertain when counting and tagging was completed.			
a. Before your arrival			
b. After your arrival			
7. If inventory is counted and tagged after your arrival, observe if method of counting and tagging conforms with instructions.			
8. Determine that all inventory was tagged.			
9. Count the inventory on a test basis and compare with quantity entered on inventory tag.			
10. Prepare schedule indicating your count and client's count for tags checked.			
11. If test count indicates significant difference, increase number of tags tested.			
12. Have client correct tags with errors.			
13. Where inventory is in sealed containers:			
a. Have client open them on a test basis and count inventory.			
b. Compare count with that indicated on tag.			
14. For finished goods, ascertain on a test basis that they are in fact completed.			
a. Lift some of them.			
b. Have some of them disassembled, if feasible.			
15. For work in process, note on a test basis the following:			
a. Amount of material			
b. Amount of labor			
16. Review inventory for old and obsolete items.			
a. Discussion with client			
b. Amount of labor			
17. Tour inventory area and ascertain that all inventory has been tagged or otherwise counted.			
18. Observe the pulling of the inventory tickets, and obtain your copies immediately. Make certain that none of the tickets are altered.			
19. Account for all inventory ticket numbers.			
After Date of Physical Inventory			
1. Compare client's inventory sheets with your copies of inventory tickets for the following:			
a. All ticket numbers have been accounted for.			
b. Description and quantity on tickets agree with inventory sheets.			
2. If client maintains perpetual inventory records, test check inventory tickets against those records.			

ILLUSTRATION 2. CONFIRMATION OF INVENTORIES ON CONSIGNMENT

[*Control number*]

[*Client letterhead*]

[*Date*]

[*Name and address of consignee*]

Gentlemen:

Our auditors, [*name and address*], are conducting an audit of our financial statements. Please confirm to them our merchandise consigned to you as of [*date*], as described below:

Description	Quantity

Your prompt attention to this request will be appreciated. An envelope is enclosed for your reply.

Very truly yours,

____

[*Client signature and title*]

Confirmation:

The consigned merchandise listed above is all that is held by us as of [*date*] except as noted below:

____

[*Consignee name*]

Date ______ By ________________

ILLUSTRATION 3. CONFIRMATION OF INVENTORIES IN PUBLIC WAREHOUSES

[*Control number*]

[*Client letterhead*]

[*Date*]

[*Name and address of warehouse*]

Gentlemen:

Our auditors, [*name and address*], are conducting an audit of our financial statements. Please furnish them with a list of our inventory at your warehouse as of [*date*] and a statement that this merchandise was stored on your premises for our account at that date.

Your prompt attention to this request will be appreciated. An envelope is enclosed for your reply.

Very truly yours,

____

[*Client signature and title*]

Confirmation:

The attached list, prepared by us, represents all merchandise stored on our premises as of [*date*] for the account of [*client name*].

____

[*Warehouse name*]

Date ______ By ________________

REQUIREMENTS—LITIGATION, CLAIMS, AND ASSESSMENTS INVOLVING THE ENTITY

AU-C 501 takes a principle-based approach. It requires the auditor to seek direct communication with the entity's external legal counsel (through a letter of inquiry) if the auditor assesses a risk of material misstatement regarding litigation or claims, or when audit procedures performed indicate that material litigation or claims may exist.

This section establishes requirements in four areas:

1. Accounting considerations
2. Audit procedures other than inquiry of lawyers
3. Inquiry of the client's lawyer and related considerations
4. Evaluation of the lawyer's response

ACCOUNTING CONSIDERATIONS

The relevant accounting standards are found in FASB Accounting Standards Codification (ASC) 450, *Contingencies*.

1. Accrual of a loss is required if:

   a. The amount can be reasonably estimated, and
   b. At the date of the financial statements, it is *probable* that an asset has been impaired or a liability incurred. (That is, it is probable that a future event will occur confirming the loss.)

2. Disclosure of a loss contingency is required if:

   a. No accrual is made because either the amount cannot be estimated or it was not probable that an asset was impaired or a liability incurred at the financial statement date, or there is exposure to loss in excess of an accrual.
   b. There is at least a reasonable possibility that a loss or an additional loss may have been incurred.

3. Disclosure should be made of:

   a. The nature of the contingency.
   b. The possible loss or range of loss, or a statement should be given that an estimate cannot be made.

4. Disclosure of the nature of an accrual, and sometimes the amount accrued, should be made if it is necessary for the financial statements not to be misleading.
5. Disclosure of an unasserted claim or assessment is required if:

   a. It is probable that a claim will be asserted.
   b. There is at least a reasonable possibility that the outcome will be unfavorable.

6. In evaluating whether accrual or disclosure is required of pending or threatened litigation or possible claims or assessments, the following factors must be considered:

   a. The period in which the cause for legal action occurred (the date of the underlying cause of action rather than the date of a lawsuit or claim affects whether accrual is appropriate)
   b. The likelihood of an unfavorable outcome
   c. The ability to estimate the loss

NOTE: These same factors are the focus of the auditor's procedures. (AU-C 501.17)

7. In evaluating the likelihood of an unfavorable outcome, the following factors must be considered:
   a. The nature of the litigation, claim, or assessment
   b. The progress of the case up to the date the financial statements are issued
   c. The opinions of legal counsel and other advisors
   d. The experience of the entity or other entities in similar cases
   e. Any decision of management on how the entity intends to respond

NOTE: The same factors are the focus of the auditor's inquiry of the client's lawyer.

AUDIT PROCEDURES OTHER THAN INQUIRY OF LAWYERS

Several customary audit procedures other than inquiry of the client's lawyer are required:

1. Inquire of, and discuss with, the client's management and others within the entity, including in-house legal counsel, its procedures for identifying, evaluating, and accounting for litigation, claims, and assessments.
2. Get from management a description and evaluation of litigation, claims, and assessments that existed at the date of the financial statements being reported on and the period from the date of the financial statements to the date the information is furnished, including matters referred to legal counsel.
3. Examine documents held by the client, such as correspondence and invoices from lawyers, and review legal expense accounts.

NOTE: This does not include documents subject to the lawyer-client privilege.

4. Review minutes of meetings of those charged with governance.

(AU-C 501.16)

Client without a Lawyer

A client not having a lawyer should not present unusual audit problems. Inquiry of a client's lawyer is a procedure applied by the auditor to identify pending or threatened litigation. The auditor may perform the procedure described previously.

Client Assertions

When the client does not retain an attorney, it ordinarily will state that there are no asserted or unasserted litigation, claims, and assessments. In these circumstances, the client should include these assertions on absence of litigation and lack of an attorney in the client representation letter (see "AU-C Illustration—Litigation, Claims, and Assessments").

Auditor Discovery of Claims

In the application of other procedures, the auditor may discover the following:

1. A material asserted claim
2. A situation in which a material unasserted claim exists

In these circumstances, the auditor should recommend that the client seek legal advice. If the client does not accept this recommendation, the auditor should consider it a scope limitation and may need to modify his or her report.

Inquiry of Client's Lawyer

The primary audit procedures for litigation, claims, and assessments are a combination of inquiries of the client's management and lawyers. Unless the audit procedures indicate no actual or potential litigation claims, or assessments that may give rise to a risk of material misstatement, the auditor should:

1. Ask the client's management to prepare letters of inquiry to those lawyers consulted on litigation, claims, and assessments. The letter should be sent by the auditor and request that the attorney communicate directly with the auditor. (AU-C 501.18)
2. Obtain written assurances from management that:
   a. It has disclosed all matters required to be disclosed by FASB ASC 450.
   b. It has disclosed all unasserted claims that the lawyer has advised are probable of assertion and must be disclosed under ASC 450.

   NOTE: These two assurances obviously overlap, but the separate assurance is required for unasserted claims because of the different treatment accorded them to preserve the lawyer-client privilege. These assurances may be included in the management representation letter (see Section 580, Written Representations*).*

3. Inform the lawyer, with the client's permission, that the client has given the assurance concerning unasserted claims.

   NOTE: This is usually covered in the inquiry letter.

(AU-C 501.18)

Content of Inquiry to Lawyer

According to AU-C 501.22, the inquiry letter to the lawyer should cover the following matters:

1. Identification of the entity, the financial statements under audit, and the date of the audit.
2. A list, prepared by management, that describes and evaluates pending or threatened litigation, claims, and assessments for which legal counsel has been engaged and on which legal counsel has spent substantive time. For each matter on the list, the lawyer should be asked to furnish:
   a. A description of the nature of the matter
   b. The progress of the case to date
   c. The action the entity intends to take
   d. An evaluation of the likelihood of an unfavorable outcome and an estimate, if possible, of the amount or range of possible loss
   e. An identification of any omissions or a statement that the list of matters is complete

NOTE: The list may be prepared by management or by the lawyer. Under either approach, management normally consults with the lawyer on the response to the auditor.

3. A list, prepared by management, that describes and evaluates unasserted claims or assertions that:
   a. Management considers probability of assertion
   b. There is a reasonable possibility of unfavorable outcome
   c. The legal counsel has been engaged, and
   d. The legal counsel has devoted substantive attention
4. The lawyer should be asked to comment on each of these items where its view differs from management's view as to the description or evaluation.
5. A statement on the management's understanding of the lawyer's professional responsibility concerning unasserted claims.
6. A request that the lawyer confirm the understanding stated in item 4.
7. A request that the lawyer specifically identify the nature of and reasons for any limitation on his or her response.
8. The date by which the lawyer's response should be sent to the auditor.
9. A request that the lawyer specify the latest date covered by his or her review (the effective date).

(AU-C 501.22)

Client Changes Lawyer or Lawyer Resigns

Because the special treatment accorded unasserted claims rests on the lawyer's professional responsibility, the auditor should consider the need to make inquiries concerning why the lawyer is no longer associated with the client. (AU-C 501.23)

The auditor always should be concerned when a client's attorney is replaced or has resigned. If the auditor has reason to believe an attorney has been replaced or has resigned, he or she should ask management about the reasons for the resignation or replacement. If an attorney has resigned, the auditor, with the client's consent, should discuss the matter with the attorney.

Evaluation of Lawyer's Response

The auditor does not have the expertise of a lawyer. Therefore, he or she requires the opinion of a lawyer on legal matters relating to the client. It is the lawyer's opinion on litigation, claims, and assessments that helps the auditor reach a conclusion on the appropriateness of accounting for, and disclosure of, litigation and other contingent liabilities. However, the lawyer's opinion on a legal matter might not be clear and, thus, might not be acceptable for the auditor's purposes. Examples of such responses are presented in "Interpretations."

In evaluating the lawyer's response, the auditor needs to be aware that some limitations on responses may affect his or her opinion. Others have no effect.

Limitations with No Effect

A lawyer may appropriately limit his or her response in the following ways:

1. To matters to which the lawyer has given substantive attention in the form of legal consultation or representation

NOTE: This means essentially that the lawyer does not do a legal audit. He or she does not undertake to evaluate all legal exposures or reconsider earlier conclusions.

2. To matters that are considered individually or collectively material, provided the lawyer and auditor have agreed on the amounts to be used

(AU-C 501.A56)

Limitations with Effect

A limitation such as either of the following may preclude an unmodified opinion:

1. *Scope.* If a lawyer refuses to furnish information requested in the ordinary inquiry letter, it is a limitation on the scope of the audit that results in a qualified or disclaimed opinion. (AU501.24A)
2. *Uncertainty.* If a lawyer is unable to evaluate the likelihood of an unfavorable outcome or estimate the amount or range of potential loss, it is an uncertainty. The guidance in Section 705, *Modifications to the Opinion in the Independent Auditor's Report*, should be followed, which may result in the auditor modifying the opinion because of the scope limitation. (AU-C 501.A57)

If management refuses to allow the auditor to contact the attorney, the auditor should modify the auditor's report, per Section 705. (AU501.24B)

Refusal of Attorney to Respond

An auditor may encounter a situation in which the attorney refuses to respond to the client's letter of inquiry. In these situations, the auditor is faced with a scope limitation sufficient to preclude an unqualified opinion.

If the attorney refuses to respond, the auditor should attempt to have a meeting with the attorney and the client to resolve the problem. If the attorney continues to refuse to respond to the letter of inquiry, the auditor should decide whether to issue an "except for" opinion or to disclaim an opinion (see Section 705, *Modification to the Opinion in the Independent Auditor's Report*).

Effective Date of Lawyer's Response

If the effective date of the lawyer's response is the balance sheet date or a date not close enough to the date the fieldwork is completed, the auditor will have to initiate a second inquiry to the lawyer. This second inquiry may be either another letter to the lawyer or a telephone call from the auditor to the lawyer. Responses to a telephone call should be documented.

Unacceptable Attorney Response

If the auditor receives a response from a client attorney that is not helpful in evaluating the litigation for accounting purposes, he or she should review the matter with the attorney and the client. The purpose of this review is to obtain a more complete and acceptable response from the attorney.

The auditor may not be able to obtain a satisfactory response from the client's attorney and may not be able to obtain sufficient other corroborating evidence to support management's evaluation of the litigation. In these circumstances, the auditor has a scope limitation that may require a qualified or disclaimed opinion.

Avoidance of Unacceptable Attorney Response

To avoid unacceptable attorney responses, the letter of inquiry should specifically request that the evaluation of the litigation reflect the attorney's opinion. Also, the attorney should be requested to specify litigation for which he or she can express no opinion on a probable outcome or a range of potential loss. The attorney should be requested to state reasons for this type of response.

Lawyer on Board of Directors

In response to the client's letter of inquiry, the lawyer is not required to include information he or she received as a director or an officer of the client unless he or she also received the information in the capacity of attorney for the client.

A reply that excludes information the attorney obtained solely as a member of the board of directors or as an officer of the client is acceptable. The letter of inquiry should request that the attorney indicate if he or she is excluding such information. If the attorney indicates that he or she is excluding this information, the auditor may wish to obtain specific written representations from the attorney concerning the information.

Litigation Not Investigated by Lawyer

A lawyer's response is limited to those matters to which he or she has given substantive attention. If a lawyer is not able to investigate a matter adequately and render a satisfactory opinion regarding material litigation, the auditor generally should attempt to arrange a meeting with the client's management and the lawyer. The purpose of this meeting is to determine what can be done to enable the lawyer to respond satisfactorily.

Delay Issuance of Financial Statements

If a lawyer cannot render a satisfactory opinion concerning material litigation because he or she has not given the matter substantive attention, the problem may be resolved if the client is able to and agrees to delay the issuance of its financial statements. The delay will give the lawyer time to study the matter and formulate a satisfactory opinion.

Audit Scope Limitation

A lawyer's *inability* to evaluate material litigation is not a limitation on the scope of an audit. If the lawyer cannot evaluate the litigation, and if the auditor cannot obtain sufficient other evidence to corroborate the information about the matter, however, the matter is a limitation on the scope of the audit.

Litigation with Insurance Company

In some cases, litigation, claims, and assessments are defended by the client's insurance company. In these circumstances, the client's attorney may decline to provide an opinion. The attorney may be knowledgeable, however, about the litigation and its probable outcome, especially those matters in which there is a reasonable prospect that the liability will exceed the insurance coverage. In these circumstances, the client should request that the lawyer provide the auditor with an opinion on the probable outcome of the litigation.

If the client's lawyer cannot render an opinion on litigation handled by the client's insurance company, the auditor should ask the client to send a letter of inquiry to the insurance company or the insurance company's counsel.

Reliance on House or Inside Counsel

The letter to the client's lawyer is the auditor's primary means of obtaining corroboration of the information furnished by management concerning litigation, claims, and assessments. In certain circumstances the corroboration may come from evidential matter provided by the client's legal department or inside general counsel.

Many entities employ inside counsel or house counsel. Some entities maintain legal departments. Attorneys employed by the client are bound by the American Bar Association's Code of Professional Ethics. Therefore, the auditor may accept as corroborative evidence responses from house counsel. In these circumstances, the usual distinction between internal evidence and external independent evidence does not apply.

A response from house counsel is generally acceptable; however, it cannot be substituted for a response from outside counsel when outside counsel refuses to respond to a valid inquiry or when outside counsel is clearly more knowledgeable about litigation.

House counsel and outside counsel may have devoted substantive attention to a matter, and their opinions may differ on the possible outcome. In this situation, the auditor should attempt to resolve the difference by discussion with the parties involved.

Although inside counsel and outside counsel are both subject to the same ethical responsibilities, the auditor has to be aware that house counsel is a member of management and operates within the client's control environment. Thus, the auditor has to consider the presence of fraud risk indicators and the nature of the representations in evaluating a response from house counsel.

Review of Interim Financial Information

When an accountant reviews interim financial information under Section 930, *Interim Financial Information*, it is not necessary to send an inquiry letter to the client's lawyer concerning litigation, claims, and assessments. The accountant would be prudent, however, to communicate, at least orally, with the attorney regarding updated information on the previous audit inquiry responses concerning litigation, claims, and assessments.

Securities Act of 1933

When an accountant's report on audited financial statements is included in a filing under the Securities Act of 1933, regardless of whether unaudited interim information is included, he or she should inquire of the client's legal counsel concerning litigation, claims, and assessments. In this situation, the lawyer should be requested to update his or her previous audit inquiry response to the estimated effective date of the registration statement.

Ordinarily, a request to the lawyer to update a previous audit inquiry response is limited to the following:

1. Changes from the lawyer's previous evaluation of litigation, claims, and assessments
2. Any new matters arising since the previous response

AU-C ILLUSTRATION—Litigation, Claims, and Assessments

ILLUSTRATION 1. INQUIRY OF A CLIENT'S LAWYER CONCERNING LITIGATION, CLAIMS, AND ASSESSMENTS: STANDARD FORM LETTER OF INQUIRY (FROM AU-C 501.A69)

[*Client letterhead*]

[*Date*]

[*Name and address*
of lawyer and salutation]

In connection with an audit of our financial statements at [*balance sheet date*] and for the [*period*] then ended, management of the Company has prepared, and furnished to our auditors [*name and address of auditors*], a description and evaluation of certain contingencies, including those set forth below involving matters with respect to which you have been engaged and to which you have devoted substantive attention on behalf of the Company in the form of legal consultation or representation. These contingencies are regarded by management of the Company as material for this purpose [*management may indicate a materiality limit if an understanding has been reached with the auditor*]. Your response should include matters that existed at [*balance sheet date*] and during the period from that date to the date of your response.

[*Alternative wording when management requests the lawyer to prepare the list that describes and evaluates pending or threatened litigation, claims, and assessments is as follows:*]

In connection with an audit of our financial statements as of [*balance sheet date*] and for the [*period*] then ended, please furnish our auditors, [*name and address of auditors*], with the information requested below concerning certain contingencies involving matters with respect to which you have devoted substantive attention on behalf of the Company in the form of legal consultation or representation. [*When a materiality limit has been established based on an understanding between management and the auditor, the following sentence should be added:*] This request is limited to contingencies amounting to [*amount*] individually or items involving lesser amounts that exceed [*amount*] in the aggregate.

Pending or Threatened Litigation (Excluding Unasserted Claims)

[Ordinarily the information would include the following: (1) the nature of the litigation, (2) the progress of the case to date, (3) how management is responding or intends to respond to the litigation (for example, to contest the case vigorously or to seek an out-of-court settlement), and (4) an evaluation of the likelihood of an unfavorable outcome and an estimate, if one can be made, of the amount or range of potential loss.]

This letter will serve as our consent for you to furnish to our auditor all the information requested herein. Accordingly, please furnish to our auditors such explanation, if any, that you consider necessary to supplement the foregoing information, including an explanation of those matters for which your views may differ from those stated and an identification of the omission of any pending or threatened litigation, claims, and assessments or a statement that the list of such matters is complete.

[*Alternative wording when management requests the lawyer to prepare the list that describes and evaluates pending or threatened litigation, claims, and assessments is as follows:*]

Regarding pending or threatened litigation, claims, and assessments, please include in your response: (1) the nature of each matter, (2) the progress of each matter to date, (3) how the Company is responding or intends to respond (for example, to contest the case vigorously or seek an out-of-court settlement), and (4) an evaluation of the likelihood of an unfavorable outcome and an estimate, if one can be made, of the amount or range of potential loss.

Unasserted Claims and Assessments (Considered by Management to be Probable of Assertion and That, If Asserted, Would Have at Least a Reasonable Possibility of an Unfavorable Outcome)

[*Ordinarily management's information would include the following: (1) the nature of the matter, (2) how management intends to respond if the claim is asserted, and (3) an evaluation of the likelihood of an unfavorable outcome and an estimate, if one can be made, of the amount or range of potential loss.*] Please furnish to our auditors such explanation, if any, that you consider necessary to supplement the foregoing information, including an explanation of those matters for which your views may differ from those stated.

We understand that whenever, in the course of performing legal services for us with respect to a matter recognized to involve an unasserted possible claim or assessment that may call for financial statement disclosure, if you have formed a professional conclusion that we should disclose or consider disclosure concerning such possible claim or assessment, as a matter of professional responsibility to us, you will so advise us and will consult with us concerning the question of such disclosure and the applicable requirements of Financial Accounting Standards Board (FASB) Accounting Standards Codification (ASC) 450, *Contingencies*. Please specifically confirm to our auditors that our understanding is correct.

[*Alternative wording when management requests the lawyer to prepare the list that describes and evaluates pending or threatened litigation, claims, and assessments is as follows:*]

We have represented to our auditors that there are no unasserted possible claims or assessments that you have advised us are probable of assertion and must be disclosed in accordance with FASB ASC 450. We understand that whenever, in the course of performing legal services for us with respect to a matter recognized to involve an unasserted possible claim or assessment that may call for financial statement disclosure, you have formed a professional conclusion that we should disclose or consider disclosure concerning such possible claim or assessment, as a matter of professional responsibility to us, you will so advise us and will consult with us concerning the question of such disclosure and the applicable requirements of FASB ASC 450. Please specifically confirm to our auditors that our understanding is correct.

Please specifically identify the nature of and reasons for any limitation on your response.

[*The auditor may request the client to inquire about additional matters—for example, unpaid or unbilled charges or specified information on certain contractually assumed obligations of the Company, such as guarantees of indebtedness of others.*]

[*Alternative wording when management requests the lawyer to prepare the list that describes and evaluates pending or threatened litigation, claims, and assessments is as follows:*]

Your response should include matters that existed as of [*balance sheet date*] and during the period from that date to the effective date of your response. Please specifically identify the nature of and reasons for any limitations on your response. Our auditors expect to have the audit completed about [*expected completion date*]. They would appreciate receiving your reply by that date with a specified effective date no earlier than [*ordinarily two weeks before expected completion date*].

[*Wording that could be used in an audit inquiry letter, instead of the heading and first paragraph, when the client believes that there are no unasserted claims or assessments (to be specified to the lawyer for comment) that are probable of assertion and that, if asserted, would have a reasonable possibility of an unfavorable outcome as specified by Financial Accounting Standards Board Accounting Standards Codification 450, Contingencies, is as follows:*]

Unasserted claims and assessments—We have represented to our auditors that there are no unasserted possible claims that you have advised us are probable of assertion and must be disclosed, in accordance with Financial Accounting Standards Board Accounting Standards Codification 450, *Contingencies*. [*The second paragraph in the section relating to unasserted claims and assessments would not be altered.*]

Very truly yours,

____

[Client signature and title]

REQUIREMENTS—SEGMENT REPORTING

AU-C 501 requires the auditor to obtain sufficient evidence regarding the presentation disclosure of segment information. The auditor must understand the methods management used to determine segment information, evaluate whether those methods will result in the required disclosures, test the application of those methods (if appropriate), and perform analytical procedures or other appropriate procedures. (AU-C 501.25)

AU-C 505 External Confirmations

AU-C ORIGINAL PRONOUNCEMENT

Source Statement on Auditing Standards (SAS) 122.

DEFINITIONS OF TERMS

Source: AU-C 505.06

Exception. A response that indicates a difference between information requested to be confirmed or contained in the entity's records, and information provided by the confirming party.

External confirmation. Audit evidence obtained as a direct written response to the auditor from a third party (the confirming party), either in paper form or by electronic or other medium (for example, through the auditor's direct access to information held by a third party).

Negative confirmation request. A request that the confirming party respond directly to the auditor only if the confirming party disagrees with the information provided in the request.

Nonresponse. A failure of the confirming party to respond, or fully respond, to a positive confirmation request or a confirmation request returned undelivered.

Positive confirmation request. A request that the confirming party respond directly to the auditor by providing the requested information or indicating whether the confirming party agrees or disagrees with the information in the request.

OBJECTIVE OF AU-C SECTION 505

AU-C Section 505.05 states:

The objective of the auditor, when using external confirmation procedures, is to design and perform such procedures to obtain relevant and reliable audit evidence.

REQUIREMENTS

RELATED AU-C 330 REQUIREMENTS

AU-C 330.20 requires the auditor to consider whether external confirmations are to be performed, and requires the use of confirmations for accounts receivable unless to do so would be ineffective, the balance is immaterial, or the assessed level of risk of material misstatement is low and other procedures address the assessed risk. If the auditor does not confirm accounts receivable, he or she should document the reasons for not doing so.

An auditor may use confirmations to reduce the risk of material misstatement due to fraud at the assertion level. (AU-C 505.03)

The auditor should consider the materiality of an account balance and his or her assessment of inherent risk and control risk when deciding whether the evidence provided by confirmations reduces audit risk for the related assertions to an acceptably low level.

RESULTS OF CONFIRMATION PROCEDURES

The auditor should maintain control over the external confirmations by determining the information to be requested and from whom, and designing and sending the requests, including the follow-up requests. (AU-C 505.07)

The auditor should perform additional procedures when he or she concludes that evidence provided by confirmations alone is not reliable. (AU-C 505.10) For example, the auditor may perform sales cutoff tests in addition to confirming accounts receivable to obtain sufficient evidence concerning the completeness and existence assertions for accounts receivable.

Oral Responses

AU-C 505.A27 clarifies that the receipt of an oral response to a confirmation request does not meet the definition of an external confirmation. When the auditor concludes that an oral or other confirmation response is unreliable, the auditor may need to revise the assessment of the risks of material misstatement at the assertion level and modify planned audit procedures.

AU-C 505.A24 offers examples of alternative procedures:

- For accounts receivable balances, examining specific subsequent cash receipts (including matching such receipts with the actual items being paid), shipping documentation, or other client documentation providing evidence for the existence assertion
- For accounts payable balances, examining subsequent cash disbursements or correspondence from third parties and other records, such as receiving reports and statements that the client receives from vendors providing evidence for the completeness assertion

Electronic Confirmations

The term *external confirmation* includes audit evidence obtained by electronic or other medium. For electronic confirmations to be reliable:

- Access to the information must come from the third party.
- Access provided by management to the auditor does not meet the definition of an external confirmation.

Even when audit evidence is received from external sources, the auditor must consider the risk that the electronic confirmation process is not secure or is improperly controlled.

MANAGEMENT'S REFUSAL TO ALLOW CONFIRMATIONS

AU-C 505.08 addresses the responsibilities of the auditor when management refuses to allow the auditor to send a confirmation request. If management refuses to allow the auditor to perform external confirmation procedures, the auditor should:

1. Inquire about management's reasons for the refusal and get audit evidence to assess the validity and reasonableness of the refusal;

2. Evaluate the implications of management's refusal on the auditor's assessment of the relevant risks of material misstatement and on the nature, timing, and extent of other audit procedures; and
3. Perform alternative audit procedures.

If the auditor considers management's refusal unreasonable or cannot get alternative audit evidence, the auditor should inform those charged with governance and consider the implications for the auditor's opinion. (AU-C 505.09)

DESIGNING THE CONFIRMATION REQUEST

The auditor should design the confirmation request to satisfy the specific audit objective. Factors the auditor should consider include the following:

1. Assertions addressed
2. Specific identified risks, including fraud risks
3. Conditions likely to affect the reliability of the confirmations
4. Form of the confirmation request
5. Method of communication (paper, online, or other)
6. Prior experience on the audit or similar engagements
7. Nature of information being confirmed
8. Intended respondent's ability to confirm or provide requested information
9. Management's authorization or discouragement to the confirming party to respond to the auditor

(AU-C 505.A5)

When using negative confirmations, the auditor should:

1. Perform other substantive procedures to supplement the use of the negative confirmations.
2. Investigate relevant information provided on returned negative confirmations.
3. Reconsider the combined assessed level of inherent and control risk and consider the effect on planned audit procedures when investigation of responses indicates a pattern of misstatements.
4. Be aware that unreturned negative confirmation requests rarely provide significant evidence concerning financial statement assertions.
5. Be aware that negative confirmation requests are more likely to generate responses indicating misstatements if a larger number of requests are sent.

The auditor should consider the type of information respondents will be readily able to confirm when designing confirmation requests. For example, respondents, because of the nature of their accounting system, may not be able to confirm account balances but may be able to confirm transactions, terms of loans, and other information.

The auditor should obtain an understanding of the substance of the client's arrangements and transactions with third parties to determine the appropriate information to include on the confirmation request. For example:

1. The auditor should consider confirming the *terms* of unusual transactions or sales, such as bill-and-hold sales, in addition to amounts.
2. If the auditor believes there is at least a moderate degree of risk that there may be significant oral modifications to agreements (for example, unusual payment terms or liberal rights of

return), he or she should inquire about those modifications. A method of doing this is to confirm both the terms of the agreement and whether oral modifications exist.

The Respondent

The confirmation request should be addressed to a person who the auditor believes is knowledgeable about the information to be confirmed.

If a question arises about the respondent's competence, knowledge, motivation, ability, objectivity, or willingness to respond, the auditor should consider the effect in designing the confirmation request and evaluating the response. In those circumstances, the auditor should also determine whether other procedures are necessary.

If there are unusual circumstances where the auditor should exercise a heightened degree of professional skepticism concerning the respondent's competence, knowledge, motivation, ability, objectivity, or willingness to respond, the auditor should consider whether there is sufficient basis for concluding that the confirmation request is being sent to a respondent who the auditor believes will provide meaningful and competent evidence. Examples of such circumstances are significant unusual year-end transactions that have a material effect on the financial statements and when the respondent is the custodian of a material amount of the audited entity's assets.

Timing of Confirmation Request

For both positive and negative confirmation requests, the debtor is provided with the balance as of a specified date. The date may be:

1. Year-end date
2. Date prior to year-end (generally one or two months prior to year-end)

It is recommended that confirmation requests be sent to debtors approximately a week before the date specified in the request. If the debtor is in a foreign country, the request should be mailed earlier.

Confirming Prior to Year-End

The auditor may decide to request that the debtor confirm the balance as of a date before year-end. If the auditor follows this procedure, however, he or she should perform the following procedures during the year-end procedures:

1. Perform selective other substantive tests of transactions from the confirmation date to the balance sheet date. These tests would include the following:
   a. Review subsequent sales invoices and related bills of lading.
   b. Review subsequent customer cash receipts and related remittance advices.
2. If balances change significantly from confirmation date to year-end, it is recommended that the auditor reconfirm.

Use of Negative Form of Confirmation Request

Negative confirmations provide less persuasive evidence than positive confirmations. Therefore, the auditor should not use negative confirmations as the sole evidence unless the assessed risk of material misstatement is low and the auditor has obtained sufficient audit evidence regarding the effectiveness of controls; the population for negative confirmations consists of a large number of small, homogeneous balances; the auditor expects a low exception rate; and the auditor does not expect the recipients not to disregard the requests. (AU-C 505.15)

If the negative form of confirmation request is used, the auditor should normally do one of the following:

1. Send out more requests than if the positive form is used.
2. Apply other auditing procedures to a greater extent than if the positive form is used. Other auditing procedures include examination of the following:
   a. Subsequent cash receipts
   b. Subsequent cash remittance advices
   c. Sales and shipping documents

Steps in Confirmation of Accounts Receivable

The steps in the process of confirming receivables follow:

1. Obtain aged schedule of accounts receivable.
2. Select accounts for confirmation.
3. Prepare and mail confirmation requests.
4. Process responses to confirmation requests.
5. Summarize confirmation results.

Obtain Aged Schedule of Accounts Receivable

The auditor should obtain an aged schedule of accounts receivable as of the confirmation date. He or she should apply the following procedures to this schedule:

1. Determine that totals are correct.
2. Compare all or a selected sample of account balances with the account balances in the accounts receivable subsidiary ledger.
3. Investigate credit balances.

Select Accounts for Confirmation

Auditors have used, and some continue to use, judgment in selecting accounts for confirmation. Statistical sampling methods, however, are ideal for the selection process. Whatever method of selection is used, the auditor generally considers the following accounts:

1. All accounts with a balance over a predetermined amount; the predetermined amount is based on the auditor's assessment of materiality.
2. Some or all accounts with zero balances.
3. Accounts with old unpaid items, especially when subsequent sales have been paid.
4. Accounts written off during the year under review.
5. Accounts with entities related to the client but not audited by the auditor.
6. Certain accounts that appeared on the prior year's accounts receivable schedule but not on the current year's.
7. Accounts with credit balances:
   a. Occasionally, the client will not want confirmation requests sent to these accounts. If the amounts are material, this might result in a scope limitation; however, this is generally not the case.

b. If accounts with credit balances are not confirmed, alternative auditing procedures should be applied.

8. Of the remaining accounts, a representative portion both in dollar amount and number of accounts should be selected.

Prepare and Send Confirmation Requests

The auditor should observe the following procedures in preparing and sending confirmation requests:

1. Prepare schedule of accounts to be confirmed (see the section "AU-C Illustrations" later in the chapter):
   a. Organize the accounts alphabetically.
   b. Include the address.
   c. Include the amount.
   d. Assign each account a number. This number also should be placed on the confirmation request.
   e. Total the dollar amount of receivables selected for confirmation, and compute it as a percentage of the total dollar amount of the receivables.
   f. Determine the number of confirmation requests, and compute it as a percentage of the total number of accounts.
   g. Leave sufficient blank columns after the customer's name to insert the following information when the confirmation reply is received:
      1. Date reply received
      2. Amount confirmed
      3. Explanation of difference between amount customer confirmed and client amount
   h. Leave a blank column for insertion of the date the second request is mailed.
   i. Indicate at bottom the date the first requests were mailed.
2. Request that client address confirmation forms and prepare customer statements:
   a. If auditor desires that client not know which accounts are to be confirmed, he or she should have his or her staff address confirmations.
   b. If auditor desires that client not know which accounts are to be confirmed but wants client to address confirmations, he or she should request client to address confirmation to all accounts and then eliminate the accounts not selected for confirmation.
3. When the auditor receives the addressed confirmation with the account balance and the customer statement, he or she should compare that balance with the balance on the schedule.
4. Independently, some customer addresses should be checked. These tests can be made by comparing the address on the confirmation with the address in the telephone book or a reliable online source.
5. After confirmations have been reviewed and numbered, the auditor should insert them and the customer statement in his or her firm's envelopes—that is, envelopes with the firm's return address.

6. In addition to inserting the confirmation request in the envelope, insert a postage-paid return envelope bearing the auditor's address.
7. When the requests have been stamped, the auditor should mail them.

From the time the auditor receives the addressed confirmation requests containing the account balances, he or she should never lose control. The confirmation requests should always remain in the auditor's custody or under his or her supervision until mailed.

CONTROL OF CONFIRMATIONS

The auditor should maintain control of the confirmation requests and responses. There should be no client intervention from the mailing of the requests to the receipt of the responses.

Because of the risks associated with facsimile responses (difficulty of ascertaining the sources of the responses), the auditor should consider performing the following in order to treat the confirmation as valid audit evidence:

1. Verifying the source and contents of the response through a telephone call to the purported sender
2. Asking the purported sender to mail the original confirmation directly to the auditor

Oral confirmations should be documented in the workpapers. If the information is significant, the auditor should ask the parties involved to submit written confirmation of that information directly to the auditor.

Process Responses to Confirmation Requests

When confirmation replies are received, the auditor should do the following:

1. Enter for each account the following:
   a. Date received
   b. Amount confirmed
2. If the amount confirmed differs from the account balance, the following should be done:
   a. Copy confirmation reply.
   b. Give copy to client and request that the difference be reconciled and provide documentation for reconciling items.
   c. Review documentation for reconciling items.
   d. If documentation is satisfactory, enter reasons for difference in receivable confirmation schedule.
3. If the amount confirmed differs from the account balance and the client cannot satisfactorily reconcile the difference, the auditor should do the following:
   a. If the difference is small, the auditor may ignore it. If there are a significant number of small differences, however, the auditor should analyze them. If the analysis of the significant number of small differences indicates a deficiency in the receivable controls, the auditor may have to apply additional auditing procedures to satisfy himself or herself of the accounts receivable balance.
   b. If the difference is significant, request the client to correspond with the debtor. Make certain the correspondence states that the debtor response should be sent directly to the auditor.

A CPA firm needs to establish a mechanism for ensuring that responses mailed to the CPA firm are obtained and considered by the audit team in the field on a timely basis. Also, a firm needs to ensure that responses that relate to transaction terms and other complex matters (such as compliance with laws and regulations for a governmental entity) are considered by appropriately experienced audit team members.

NONRESPONSE TO CONFIRMATION REQUESTS

If the recipients do not respond to the confirmation requests, other than negative confirmation requests, the auditor should generally follow up with a second and sometimes a third request to those who did not respond.

If the auditor does not receive replies to positive confirmation requests, he or she should apply alternative procedures to the nonresponse to obtain the necessary evidence (see below). (AU-C 550.12)

The auditor does not have to apply alternative procedures if:

1. He or she has not identified unusual qualitative factors or systematic characteristics related to the nonresponses (for example, all nonresponses pertain to year-end transactions).
2. He or she is testing for overstatement, and the nonresponses in the aggregate, when projected as 100% misstatements to the population and added to the total of all other unadjusted differences, would not affect the auditor's decision about whether the financial statements are materially misstated.

(AU-C 505.A26)

If a second request is sent, the auditor should note in the accounts receivable confirmation worksheet the date the second request was mailed.

Telephone Call to Debtor

If the nonresponse pertains to an account with a significant balance, the auditor should consider making a telephone call to the customer. If the auditor confirms by telephone, he or she should do the following:

1. Obtain the name and title of the person providing the information.
2. Request that the information provided be confirmed in writing.

Other Auditing Procedures

If the nonresponse pertains to an account with a significant balance, the auditor should consider reviewing the customer file to determine the following:

1. Cash receipts subsequent to year-end.
2. Items paid for subsequent to year-end; this is done by reviewing customer remittance advices.

NONDELIVERY OF CONFIRMATION REQUEST

If a confirmation request is returned to the auditor because it was not delivered, the auditor should do the following:

1. Determine customer's new address and remail confirmation request.
2. If customer went out of business, ascertain that client has established appropriate allowance.

CONFIRMATION RESPONSES NOT EXPECTED

Sometimes the auditor does not expect a response to a confirmation request based on past experience with the entity or with customers similar to those of the entity.

When the auditor does not expect a response to a traditional confirmation request, he or she should do the following:

1. Request confirmation of specific items included in the account balance.
2. Review subsequent customer remittances. Where these amounts are significant, it is recommended that for a period of time subsequent to the balance sheet date the auditor be present whenever the client receives mail. The auditor should open all mail from customers unable to confirm balances, and should compare remittance advices to ledger balances.
3. Undertake other procedures to validate the existence of the customer and sales to the customer. (For example, the customer could be looked up in a phone directory and called.)

When fraud risk factors are present and confirmation of receivables is not possible, the auditor should employ unusual procedures if necessary to validate the existence of the customer and the sales to that customer.

Summarize Confirmation Results

Near the conclusion of the engagement, the auditor should prepare a worksheet summarizing confirmation results. The worksheet should contain the following:

1. Number and dollar amount of confirmations sent and the percentage of these to the total receivables
2. Number and dollar amount of confirmations received with no exceptions indicated and the percentage of these to the total confirmations requests
3. Number and dollar amount of confirmations received with exceptions that were satisfactorily reconciled by the client; compute the percentage of these to the total confirmations requested
4. Number and dollar amount of confirmations received with exceptions that were not satisfactorily reconciled by the client:

   a. Determine total dollar amount of differences between client records and confirmation responses.
   b. Determine reasons for differences and materiality of differences.
   c. Compute the percentage of these to the total confirmations requested.

5. Review of statistics with a determination of whether the results of the confirmation procedures provided sufficient competent evidential matter as to the existence of the receivables; if the auditor is not satisfied with the results of the confirmation procedures, he or she should perform other procedures such as the following:

   a. Review subsequent cash receipts and accompanying remittance advices.
   b. Review individual sales invoices and related shipping documents.

A confirmation worksheet is presented in "AU-C Illustrations."

EVALUATING THE RESULTS

If the auditor has determined that an external confirmation is needed and does not receive a response, the auditor should consider the implications for the audit and the audit opinion. (AU-C 505.13)

The auditor should evaluate the combined evidence provided by the confirmations and the alternative procedures to determine whether sufficient evidence has been obtained. In performing the evaluation, the auditor should consider the following:

1. The reliability of the evidence
2. The nature of any exceptions, including quantitative and qualitative implications of those exceptions
3. The evidence provided by other procedures
4. Whether additional evidence is necessary

(AU-C 505.14 and 505.A16)

If additional evidence is needed, the auditor should request additional confirmations or extend other tests, such as tests of details or analytical procedures.

The auditor should also evaluate the risks associated with electronic requests and consider whether the information may not be from an authentic source or the integrity of the information may have been compromised. The auditor may decide to mitigate risk by using an electronic confirmation system. (AU-C 505.A14)

CONFIRMATION CHECKLIST

To make certain all procedures have been applied in the confirmation of receivables, the auditor should design a confirmation checklist. One is presented next in "AU-C Illustrations," along with examples of confirmations.

AU-C ILLUSTRATIONS

This section contains illustrations of the following for accounts receivable:

1. Confirmation checklist
2. Positive confirmation with statement
3. Positive confirmation without statement
4. Negative confirmation
5. Subsequent payments confirmation
6. Confirmation of selected transactions
7. Description of confirmation worksheet

ILLUSTRATION 1. ACCOUNTS RECEIVABLE CONFIRMATION CHECKLIST

____

[*Client*]

____

[*Audit date*]

Instructions. This checklist is divided into two sections:

1. General information
2. Procedures

If a procedure listed is not applicable, insert "N/A" in the column "Performed by" and explain why in the "Explanation" column.

General Information

1. Date confirmation sent.

	Positive confirmation	*Negative confirmation*
First request		
Second request		N/A
Third request		N/A

2. For positive confirmation, list the following:

	Number of receivables	*Amount of receivables*
a. Accounts receivable		
b. Confirmations sent		
c. Percentage		
d. Responses		
e. Percentage of confirmations sent		
f. Percentage of total receivables		

3. For negative confirmation, list the following:

	Number of receivables	*Amount of receivables*
a. Accounts receivable		
b. Confirmations sent		
c. Percentage		
d. Responses		
e. Percentage of confirmations sent		
f. Percentage of total receivables		

Procedure	Performed by	Date	Explanation
1. Obtain from client aged schedule of accounts receivable.			
2. Determine that all accounts listed in the accounts receivable schedule are customer accounts.			
3. Check that total in accounts receivable is correct, and compare total with balance for accounts receivable in general ledger.			
4. Compare all or a selected sample of account balances in the schedule with account balances in the accounts receivable subsidiary ledger.			
5. Select accounts for positive confirmations.			
6. Select accounts for negative confirmations.			
7. Prepare schedule of accounts to be confirmed, listing the following:			
a. Confirmation number			
b. Name of account			
c. Address of account			
d. Receivables balance			
e. Balance confirmed			
f. Difference			
g. Explanation of difference			
8. On a test basis, check account addresses to source independent of accounts receivable department, such as:			
a. Customer file			
b. Telephone book			
9. Mail confirmation requests in envelope with firm return address. Include the following:			
a. Customer statement			
b. Letter requesting confirmation			
c. Firm postage-paid envelope			
10. For confirmation responses, do the following:			
a. Enter balance confirmed.			
b. Require client to reconcile any differences.			
c. Review documentation for reconciling items.			
11. Send second requests.			
12. Send third requests.			
13. For nonresponses of significant balances, do the following:			
a. Review subsequent cash receipts.			
b. Review customer remittance advices.			
14. If customer indicates it cannot confirm balance owed, request confirmation of:			
a. Specified invoices			
b. Specified cash receipts			
15. If nondelivery of request, remail to new address.			

Procedure	*Performed by*	*Date*	*Explanation*
16. Facsimile response: a. Photocopy response. b. Verify source and contents of response by telephone call to sender. c. Request sender to mail original confirmation request.			

ILLUSTRATION 2. ACCOUNTS RECEIVABLE: POSITIVE CONFIRMATION WITH STATEMENT

[*Control number*]

[*Client letterhead*]

[*Date*]

[*Name and address of customer*]

Gentlemen:

Our auditors, [*name and address*], are conducting an audit of our financial statements. Please examine the accompanying statement and either confirm its correctness or report any differences to our auditors.

Your prompt attention to this request will be appreciated. An envelope is enclosed for your reply.

Very truly yours,

____

[*Client signature and title*]

Confirmation

The balance receivable from us of [*amount*] as of [*date*] is correct except as noted below:

____

[*Debtor name*]

Date ____________________________ By ____________________________

NOTE: This confirmation also may be used as a second request by stamping or printing in a prominent location "SECOND REQUEST" and mailing with a copy of the statement.

ILLUSTRATION 3. ACCOUNTS RECEIVABLE: POSITIVE CONFIRMATION WITHOUT STATEMENT

[*Control number*]

[*Client letterhead*]

[*Date*]

[*Name and address of customer*]

Gentlemen:

Our auditors, [*name and address*], are conducting an audit of our financial statements. Please confirm to them our receivable from you of [*amount*] as of [*date*].

Your prompt attention to this request will be appreciated. An envelope is enclosed for your reply.

Very truly yours,

____

[*Client signature and title*]

Confirmation

The balance receivable from us of [*amount*] as of [*date*] is correct except as noted below:

____

[*Debtor name*]

Date _______________________ By_______________________

NOTE: This confirmation also may be used as a second request by stamping or printing in a prominent location "SECOND REQUEST."

ILLUSTRATION 4. ACCOUNTS RECEIVABLE: NEGATIVE CONFIRMATION WITH STATEMENT, GUMMED STICKER, OR RUBBER STAMP

Auditor's Confirmation Request

Please examine this statement. If it does not agree with your records, please report any exceptions directly to our auditors,

[*Auditor's name*]
[*Auditor's address*]

who are conducting an audit of our financial statements. An envelope is enclosed for your reply.

NOTE: This format may be used as a gummed sticker attached to a statement or as a rubber stamp imprinted on a statement.

ILLUSTRATION 5. ACCOUNTS RECEIVABLE: SUBSEQUENT PAYMENTS CONFIRMATION

[*Control number*]

[*Client letterhead*]

[*Date*]

[*Name and address of customer*]

Gentlemen:

Our records indicate that between [*date*] and [*date*], you made payments to us of [*amount*].

In connection with an audit of our financial statements, please confirm the payments and their allocation listed below or report any differences to our auditors, [*name and address*].

Check or voucher				*Applicable to invoices dated*	
Date	Number	Amount	Deductions	Before	After

Your prompt attention to this request will be appreciated. An envelope is enclosed for your reply.

Very truly yours,

____

[*Client signature and title*]

Confirmation

The payments and their allocation listed above agree with our records except as noted below:

____

[*Debtor name*]

Date _______________________________ By _______________________________

ILLUSTRATION 6. ACCOUNTS RECEIVABLE: CONFIRMATION OF SELECTED TRANSACTIONS, OPEN INVOICE SYSTEM

[*Control number*]

[*Client letterhead*]

[*Date*]

[*Name and address of customer*]

Gentlemen:

We understand that you do not maintain an accounts payable ledger showing balances due each vendor. However, we would appreciate your assistance in providing limited confirmation of specific transactions to permit the completion of our annual audit.

Please confirm to our auditors, [*name and address*], that the invoices listed below were proper and were unpaid as of [*date*].

Invoice		*Customer*		
No.	Date	P.O. No.	Location	Amount

Your prompt response will be appreciated. An envelope is enclosed for your reply.

Very truly yours,

____

[*Client signature and title*]

Confirmation

The invoices listed above were properly charged to our account and were unpaid as of [*date*] except as noted below.

____

[*Debtor name*]

Date _______________________________ By _______________________________

Illustration 7. Accounts Receivable: Description of Confirmation Worksheet

Description. An accounts receivable confirmation worksheet ordinarily should include the following columns:

1. Customer name
2. Control number
3. Indication of second request
4. Balance per client
5. Amount confirmed
6. Differences
7. Explanation of differences:
    a. Receipts in transit:
        1. Date deposited
        2. Amount
    b. Credits issued:
        1. Date issued
        2. Amount
    c. Shipments in transit:
        1. Date shipped
        2. Amount
    d. Other

AU-C 510 Opening Balances—Initial Audit Engagements, Including Reaudit Engagements

AU-C ORIGINAL PRONOUNCEMENT

Source Statement on Auditing Standards (SAS) 122.

APPLICABILITY

This section relates to the auditor's responsibilities for the opening balance in an initial audit engagement, including a reaudit. The section does not apply to the predecessor auditor if the most recent audited financial statements are more than one year prior to the beginning of the earliest period to be audited by the successor auditor. (AU-C 510.01-.02)

DEFINITIONS OF TERMS

Source: AU-C Section 510.05

Initial audit engagement. An engagement in which either (1) the financial statements for the prior period were not audited, or (2) the financial statements for the prior period were audited by a predecessor auditor.

Opening balances. Those account balances that exist at the beginning of the period. Opening balances are based upon the closing balances of the prior period and reflect the effects of transactions and events of prior periods and accounting policies applied in the prior period. Opening balances also include matters requiring disclosure that existed at the beginning of the period, such as contingencies and commitments.

Predecessor auditor. The auditor from a different audit firm who has reported on the most recent audited financial statements or was engaged to perform but did not complete an audit of the financial statements.

Reaudit. An initial audit engagement to audit financial statements that have been previously audited by a predecessor auditor.

OBJECTIVES OF AU-C SECTION 510

AU-C Section 510.04 states that:

. . . the objective of the auditor, in conducting an initial audit engagement, including a reaudit engagement, is to obtain sufficient appropriate audit evidence regarding opening balances about whether

a. opening balances contain misstatements that materially affect the current period's financial statements and
b. appropriate accounting policies reflected in the opening balances have been consistently applied in the current period's financial statements or changes thereto are appropriately accounted for and adequately presented and disclosed in accordance with the applicable financial reporting framework.

REQUIREMENTS

For an initial audit or reaudit, the auditor must read the most recent financial statements and auditor's opinion for information on opening balances and consistency of disclosures. (AU-C 510.06) In order to have the information necessary to plan and perform the engagement, the auditor should request that management authorize the predecessor auditor to respond fully to inquiries from the auditor, and allow a review of the prior year's documentation. (AU-C 510.07) The auditor may make this request before or after accepting the engagement. (AU-C 510.A3) The predecessor auditor may request a consent and acknowledgment letter from the entity to document this authorization. (AU-C 510.A4) The predecessor auditor may also request written confirmation of the auditor's agreement regarding the use of the audit documentation. (AU-C 510.A6) Also, see the illustrations later in this chapter.

As the auditor reviews the opening balances, the auditor should:

- Determine whether the closing balances from the prior period were brought forward correctly and reflect the application of appropriate accounting policies.
- Evaluate whether audit procedures in the current period provide evidence relevant to the opening balances by reviewing the predecessor's audit documentation and/or performing specific procedures to obtain evidence regarding the opening balances. (AU-C 510.08)

The evidence gathered should also address whether the accounting policies reflected in the opening balances have been consistently applied. The auditor must also evaluate whether changes in accounting policies have been properly presented and disclosed. (AU-C 510.10)

Material Misstatement in Prior Year Financial Statements

During the review of the opening balances, the auditor may gather evidence that suggests that the prior period statements may contain a material misstatement. In that case, the auditor must perform additional procedures to determine the effect on the current period statements. If the auditor concludes that the material misstatements exist in the current statements, the auditor must communicate the misstatements to management and those charged with governance. (AU-C 510.09)

If the prior period financial statements were audited and may need revision, the auditor should ask management to inform the predecessor auditor and arrange for a meeting of the three parties to try to resolve the matter. (AU-C 510.12)

Management may refuse to inform the processor auditor that the financial statements may need revision, or the auditor may not be satisfied with the resolution. In such cases, the auditor should consider withdrawal. If withdrawal is not possible under applicable law or regulation, the auditor should disclaim an opinion. (AU-C 510.13)

Audit Conclusions and Reporting

The auditor should not reference the predecessor's report as the basis, in part, for the auditor's opinion. (AU-C 510.14)

If the auditor has not been able to obtain sufficient evidence regarding opening balances, the auditor should disclaim an opinion or express a qualified opinion, in accordance with Section 705. (AU-C 510.15)

The auditor should express a qualified or adverse opinion if the auditor concludes that:

- The opening balances contain a material misstatement that affects the current statements, and the effect is not appropriately accounted for or adequately disclosed.
- A change in accounting policies is not consistently applied or accounted for, or adequately presented or disclosed as to opening balances.

(AU-C 510.16-.17)

If the prior period opinion included a modification relevant and material to the current financial statements, the auditor should modify the current opinion in accordance with Section 705. (AU-C 510.18)

ILLUSTRATIONS

ILLUSTRATION 1. REPORT WITH DISCLAIMER OF OPINION ON RESULTS OF OPERATIONS AND CASH FLOWS AND UNMODIFIED OPINION ON FINANCIAL POSITION (FROM AU-C 510.A19)

Circumstances include the following:

- The auditor did not observe the counting of the physical inventory at the beginning of the current period and was unable to obtain sufficient appropriate audit evidence regarding the opening balances of inventory.
- The possible effects of the inability to obtain sufficient appropriate audit evidence regarding opening balances of inventory are deemed to be material and pervasive to the entity's results of operations and cash flows.
- The financial position at year-end is fairly presented.
- A disclaimer of opinion regarding the results of operations and cash flows and an unmodified opinion regarding financial position are considered appropriate in the circumstances.

Independent Auditor's Report

[*Appropriate addressee*]

Report on the Financial Statements

We have audited the accompanying balance sheet of ABC Company as of December 31, 20X1, and were engaged to audit the related statements of income, changes in stockholders' equity, and cash flows for the year then ended, and the related notes to the financial statements.

Management's Responsibility for the Financial Statements

Management is responsible for the preparation and fair presentation of these financial statements in accordance with accounting principles generally accepted in the United States of America; this includes the design, implementation, and maintenance of internal control relevant to the preparation and fair presentation of financial statements that are free from material misstatement, whether due to fraud or to error.

Auditor's Responsibility

Our responsibility is to express an opinion on these financial statements based on conducting the audit in accordance with auditing standards generally accepted in the United States of America. Because of the matters described in the Basis for Disclaimer of Opinion paragraph, however, we were not able to obtain sufficient appropriate audit evidence to provide a basis for an audit opinion on the income statement and the cash flow statement.

We conducted our audit of the balance sheet in accordance with auditing standards generally accepted in the United States of America. Those standards require that we plan and perform the audit to obtain reasonable assurance about whether the balance sheet is free from material misstatement.

An audit involves performing procedures to obtain audit evidence about the amounts and disclosures in the financial statements. The procedures selected depend on the auditor's judgment, including the assessment of the risks of material misstatement of the financial statements, whether due to fraud or to error. In making those risk assessments, the auditor considers internal control relevant to the entity's preparation and fair presentation of the financial statements in order to design audit procedures that are appropriate in the circumstances, but not for the purpose of expressing an opinion on the effectiveness of the entity's internal control. Accordingly, we express no such opinion. An audit also includes evaluating the appropriateness of accounting policies used and the reasonableness of significant accounting estimates made by management, as well as evaluating the overall presentation of the financial statements.

We believe that the audit evidence we have obtained is sufficient and appropriate to provide a basis for our unmodified opinion on the financial position.

Basis for Disclaimer of Opinion on the Results of Operations and Cash Flows

We were not engaged as auditors of the Company until after December 31, 20X0, and, therefore, did not observe the counting of physical inventories at the beginning of the year. We were unable to satisfy ourselves by performing other auditing procedures concerning the inventory held at December 31, 20X0. Since opening inventories enter into the determination of net income and cash flows, we were unable to determine whether any adjustments might have been necessary in respect of the profit for the year reported in the income statement and the net cash flows from operating activities reported in the cash flow statement.

Disclaimer of Opinion on the Results of Operations and Cash Flows

Because of the significance of the matter described in the Basis for Disclaimer of Opinion paragraph, we have not been able to obtain sufficient appropriate audit evidence to provide a basis for an audit opinion on the results of operations and cash flows for the year ended December 31, 20X1.

Accordingly, we do not express an opinion on the results of operations and cash flows for the year ended December 31, 20X1.

Opinion on the Financial Position

In our opinion, the balance sheet presents fairly, in all material respects, the financial position of ABC Company as of December 31, 20X1, in accordance with accounting principles generally accepted in the United States of America.

Report on Other Legal and Regulatory Requirements

[*Form and content of this section of the auditor's report will vary depending on the nature of the auditor's other reporting responsibilities.*]

[*Auditor's signature*]

[*Auditor's city and state*]

[*Date of the auditor's report*]

ILLUSTRATION 2. ENTITY CONSENT AND ACKNOWLEDGMENT LETTER (FROM AU-C 510.A20)

The following letter is presented for illustrative purposes only and is not required by professional standards.

[*Date*]

ABC Enterprises

[*Address*]

You have given your consent to allow [*name of successor CPA firm*], as independent auditors for ABC Enterprises (ABC), access to our audit documentation for our audit of the December 31, 20X1 financial statements of ABC. You also have given your consent to us to respond fully to [*name of successor CPA firm*] inquiries. You understand and agree that the review of our audit documentation is undertaken solely for the purpose of obtaining an understanding about ABC and certain information about our audit to assist [*name of successor CPA firm*] in planning and performing the audit of the December 31, 20X2 financial statements of ABC.

Please confirm your agreement with the foregoing by signing and dating a copy of this letter and returning it to us.

Attached is the form of the letter we will furnish [*name of successor CPA firm*] regarding the use of the audit documentation.

Very truly yours,

[*Predecessor auditor*]

By: ______________________

Accepted:

ABC Enterprises

By: ______________________

Date: ____________

ILLUSTRATION 3. ILLUSTRATIVE SUCCESSOR AUDITOR ACKNOWLEDGMENT LETTER (FROM AU-C 510.A21)

The following letter is presented for illustrative purposes only and is not required by professional standards.

[*Date*]

[*Successor auditor*]

[*Address*]

We have previously audited, in accordance with auditing standards generally accepted in the United States of America, the December 31, 20X1 financial statements of ABC Enterprises (ABC). We rendered a report on those financial statements and have not performed any audit procedures subsequent to the audit report date. In connection with your audit of ABC's 20X2 financial statements, you have requested access to our audit documentation prepared in connection with that audit. ABC has authorized our firm to allow you to review that audit documentation.

Our audit, and the audit documentation prepared in connection therewith, of ABC's financial statements were not planned or conducted in contemplation of your review. Therefore, items of possible interest to you may not have been specifically addressed. Our use of professional judgment and the assessment of audit risk and materiality for the purpose of our audit mean that matters may have existed that would have been assessed differently by you. We make no representation about the sufficiency or appropriateness of the information in our audit documentation for your purposes.

We understand that the purpose of your review is to obtain information about ABC and our 20X1 audit results to assist you in planning and performing your 20X2 audit of ABC. For that purpose only, we will provide you access to our audit documentation that relates to that objective.

Upon request, we will provide copies of audit documentation that provides factual information about ABC. You agree to subject any such copies or information otherwise derived from our audit documentation to your normal policy for retention of audit documentation and protection of confidential entity information. Furthermore, in the event of a third-party request for access to your audit documentation prepared in connection with your audits of ABC, you agree to obtain our permission before voluntarily allowing any such access to our audit documentation or information otherwise derived from our audit documentation, and to obtain on our behalf any releases that you obtain from such third party. You agree to advise us promptly and provide us a copy of any subpoena, summons, or other court order for access to your audit documentation that includes copies of our audit documentation or information otherwise derived therefrom.

Please confirm your agreement with the foregoing by signing and dating a copy of this letter and returning it to us.

Very truly yours,

[*Predecessor auditor*]

By: ___________________

Accepted:

[*Successor auditor*]

By: ___________________

Date: _____________

Even with management's consent, access to the predecessor auditor's audit documentation may still be limited. Experience has shown that the predecessor auditor may be willing to grant broader access if given additional assurance concerning the use of the audit documentation. Accordingly, the auditor might consider agreeing to the following additional limitations on the review of the predecessor auditor's audit documentation in order to obtain broader access:

- The auditor will not comment, orally or in writing, to anyone as a result of the review about whether the predecessor auditor's engagement was performed in accordance with generally accepted auditing standards.
- The auditor will not provide expert testimony or litigation support services or otherwise accept an engagement to comment on issues relating to the quality of the predecessor auditor's audit.
- The auditor accepts sole responsibility for the nature, timing, and extent of audit work performed and the conclusions reached in expressing an opinion on the 20X2 financial statements of ABC.

The following paragraph illustrates the previous text:

Because your review of our audit documentation is undertaken solely for the purpose described previously and may not entail a review of all our audit documentation, you agree that (1) the information obtained from the review will not be used by you for any other purpose; (2) you will not comment, orally or in writing, to anyone as a result of that review about whether our audit was performed in accordance with generally accepted auditing standards; (3) you will not provide expert testimony or litigation support services or otherwise accept an engagement to comment on issues relating to the quality of our audit; and (4) you accept sole responsibility for the nature, timing, and extent of audit work performed and the conclusions reached in expressing your opinion on the 20X2 financial statements of ABC.

AU-C 520 Analytical Procedures

AU-C ORIGINAL PRONOUNCEMENT

Source Statement on Auditing Standards (SAS) No. 122.

AU-C DEFINITION OF TERM

Source: AU-C 520.04

Analytical procedures. Evaluations of financial information through analysis of plausible relationships among both financial and nonfinancial data. Analytical procedures also encompass such investigation as is necessary of identified fluctuations or relationships that are inconsistent with other relevant information or that differ from expected values by a significant amount.

OBJECTIVES OF AU-C SECTION 520

AU-C Section 520.03 states that:

. . . the objectives of the auditor are to

a. obtain relevant and reliable audit evidence when using substantive analytical procedures and

b. design and perform analytical procedures near the end of the audit that assist the auditor when forming an overall conclusion about whether the financial statements are consistent with the auditor's understanding of the entity.

OVERVIEW

How to Use Analytical Procedures

AU-C 315 addresses the use of analytical procedures in risk assessment when planning the audit, and AU-C330 addresses the nature, timing, and extent of procedures in response to assessed risk. Those procedures may include substantive analytical procedures.

As Substantive Procedures

The auditor may, but is not required to, use analytical procedures as a substantive test. When used as a substantive test, the objective of analytical procedures is to accumulate evidence supporting the validity of a specific account balance assertion. For example, the results of applying an average interest rate to average debt outstanding would provide evidence supporting the amount of interest expense.

During the Overall Review

The objective of using analytical procedures in the overall review of the audited financial statements near the end of the audit is to help the auditor in forming a conclusion about whether the financial statements are consistent with the auditor's understanding of the entity and to help form a conclusion. (AU-C 520.06)

This chapter begins with a discussion of analytical procedures.

REQUIREMENTS

ANALYTICAL PROCEDURES

Introduction

Analytical procedures include:

1. Comparisons,
2. Ratio analysis,
3. Trend analysis,
4. Variance analysis,
5. Preparation of common-size financial statements, and
6. Regression analysis.

The specific procedures used are determined by the nature of the client's business and its industry, availability of data, degree of precision required, and auditor judgment.

When applying analytical procedures, the auditor may use data from outside the accounting system or financial statements, such as:

1. Units produced or sold
2. Number of employees
3. Hours worked by nonsalaried employees
4. Square feet of selling space
5. Budget information; if, however, the budget is primarily a motivational tool (goals instead of expectations) its usefulness for analytical procedures is limited.

The remainder of this section contains a general discussion of various techniques for the application of analytical procedures, followed by an explanation of how these procedures could be applied to the specific phases of the audit—planning, accumulation of audit evidence (substantive tests), and overall review.

Analytical Procedures: General

When the auditor applies analytical procedures, he or she usually *computes*, *compares*, and *analyzes ratios*, *trends*, and *variances*. Generally, ratio analysis, trend analysis, and variance analysis are used together. In addition to these analyses, some auditors use regression analysis in applying analytical procedures.

Ratio analysis involves the following:

1. The computation of significant financial relationships, such as current assets to current liabilities

2. The comparison of current period ratios with one or more of the following:
   a. Similar ratios of a prior period or periods
   b. Similar ratios of the industry
   c. Similar ratios generally viewed as acceptable by bankers or other credit grantors
3. The analysis of unexpected deviations between current period ratios and those with which they are compared

Trend analysis involves the following:

1. The selection of a base period
2. The computation of subsequent periods' financial data, such as sales as a percentage of base period data
3. The comparison of current period's percentages with those of prior periods
4. The analysis of unexpected changes in percentages between the current period and prior periods

Variance analysis involves the following:

1. The determination of acceptable levels for the financial data being analyzed
2. The comparison of current period financial data with the acceptable levels
3. The analysis of unexpected deviations between current period financial data and the acceptable level for such data

Comparisons with Industry

In applying analytical procedures, the auditor may wish to compare the financial data of the client with those of the client's industry. For a diversified entity, however, comparisons may not be effective unless the auditor compares client segment data with appropriate industry data.

Comparisons with National Economic Data

The auditor may wish to compare the client's financial data with national economic data such as the following:

1. Economic indicators—leading, lagging, coincident
2. Gross domestic product
3. Disposable income
4. Consumer price index
5. Wholesale price index
6. Unemployment rate

The data are issued monthly, the first five by the US Department of Commerce and the sixth by the US Department of Labor. All of the data and other national economic data are reported in the *Wall Street Journal.*

Ratio Analysis

The most common analytical procedure is ratio analysis. Ratios may be classified based on their sources as follows:

1. Balance sheet ratios
2. Income statement ratios
3. Mixed ratios (these ratios contain numbers from more than one financial statement)

Some of the more common ratios, their classification, method of computation, and the attribute measured are shown in the following list:

Ratio	*Formula*	*Purpose*
Liquidity ratios—Measure the entity's ability to meet its short-term obligations, and provide an indication of the entity's solvency.		
Current ratio	$=\frac{\text{Current assets}}{\text{Current liabilities}}$	Indicates whether claims of short-term creditors can be met with current assets.
Quick ratio or acid test	$=\frac{\text{Current assets} - \text{Inventory}}{\text{Current liabilities}}$	Measures the entity's ability to pay off short-term creditors without relying on the sale of inventories.
Leverage ratios—Measure the extent to which the entity is financed by debt and provide a measure of the risk of the entity borne by the creditors.		
Debt ratio	$=\frac{\text{Total debt}}{\text{Total assets}}$	Indicates percentage of total funds provided by creditors; high ratios when economy is in downturn indicate more risk for creditors.
Times interest earned	$=\frac{\text{Earnings before interest and taxes}}{\text{Interest charges}}$	Measures extent to which earnings can decline and still provide entity with ability to meet annual interest costs; failure to meet this obligation may result in legal action by creditors, possibly resulting in bankruptcy.
Long-term debt to equity	$=\frac{\text{Long-term debt}}{\text{Stockholders' equity}}$	Indicates the proportion of the entity financed through long-term debt vs. owners' equity.
Activity ratios—Measure how effectively an entity employs its resources.		
Inventory turnover	$=\frac{\text{Cost of goods sold}}{\text{Average inventory}}$	Estimates how many times a year inventory is sold.
Age of inventory	$=\frac{\text{360 days}}{\text{Inventory turnover}}$	Indicates number of days of inventory on hand at year-end.
Accounts receivable turnover	$=\frac{\text{Net credit sales}}{\text{Average accounts receivable}}$	Estimates how many times a year accounts receivable are collected.
Age of accounts receivable	$=\frac{\text{360 days}}{\text{Accounts receivable turnover}}$	Indicates the age of accounts receivable or number of days sales not collected.
Total asset turnover	$=\frac{\text{Net sales}}{\text{Total assets}}$	Estimates volume of sales based on total assets.
Profitability ratios—Measure how effectively the entity is being managed.		
Sales to total assets	$=\frac{\text{Net sales}}{\text{Total assets}}$	Indicates the ability of an entity to use its assets to generate sales.
Gross margin	$=\frac{\text{Gross margin}}{\text{Net sales}}$	Provides a percentage relationship based on sales.
Profit margin on sales	$=\frac{\text{Net income}}{\text{Net sales}}$	Indicates the return an entity receives on sales.

Net operating margin	$= \frac{\text{Operating income}}{\text{Net sales}}$	Indicates management's effectiveness at using entity's assets to generate operating income.
Return on total assets	$= \frac{\text{Net income + Interest expense}}{\text{Total assets}}$	Indicates the return an entity receives for its assets.
Return on common stockholders' equity	$= \frac{\text{Net income} - \text{Preferred dividends}}{\text{Average stockholders'equity}}$	Indicates return on investment to common stockholders.

These ratios are some, but not all, of the ratios that may be used in applying analytical procedures. The auditor should use his or her knowledge of the client and its industry to develop relevant and meaningful ratios.

Ratio analysis has limitations in that it concentrates on the past and deals in aggregates. However, ratios serve as warning signs and indicators that are helpful in discovering existing or potential trouble spots when applied in trend analysis and variance analysis.

Trend Analysis

Trend analysis indicates the relevant changes in data from period to period. For example, assume the following sales in successive income statements:

Year	20X1	20X2	20X3	20X4	20X5
Sales	$200	$300	$350	$450	$500

If 20X1 is selected as the base year, sales for that year are 100% and sales for 20X2 are 150% (300 ÷ 200). Sales in a trend statement are as follows:

Year	20X1	20X2	20X3	20X4	20X5
Sales	100%	150%	175%	225%	250%

Any year may be the base year, and the auditor may select a moving base year. At the end of 20X6, he or she may decide to develop a new five-year trend statement by eliminating 20X1 and making 20X2 the base year or 100%.

Trend statements may be developed from any data. For example, assume the following gross profit percentages:

Year	20X1	20X2	20X3	20X4	20X5
Profit	42%	43%	45%	45%	40%

If 20X1 is selected as the base year, its gross profit percentage would be 100.0%, and 20X2 would be 102.4% (43% ÷ 42%). Gross profit percentages in a trend statement are as follows:

Year	20X1	20X2	20X3	20X4	20X5
Profit	100.0%	102.4%	107.1%	107.1%	95.2%

The unusual decline in the trend from 20X4 to 20X5 alerts the auditor to an area (sales and cost of goods sold) requiring special attention and, perhaps, additional audit procedures.

Maintaining trend statements for significant numbers, sales, cost of goods sold, repairs and maintenance, selling expenses, and so on, and for significant ratios aids the auditor in detecting unusual deviations from prior periods.

Variance Analysis

An auditor may wish to compare current data with predetermined acceptable levels (the norms). Deviations from these levels require investigation. This process is known as variance analysis.

When applying variance analysis, the auditor may use data for his or her norms from the following sources:

1. Entity budgets
2. Entity forecasts
3. Industry data
4. Prior period data

When using industry data in analytical procedures, the auditor may convert the client's financial statements to common-size financial statements.

Common-Size Financial Statements

A common-size financial statement is one in which the numbers are converted to percentages. The dollars of cash, receivables, inventory, and other assets in the balance sheet are converted to percentages based on the relationship of each asset to total assets.

Common-size financial statements aid the auditor in comparing financial data of businesses of different sizes because not numbers but proportions are being compared. Further, most industry data such as those issued by Dun & Bradstreet are common size.

The following balance sheet is presented in amounts and in common size:

	Amount	*Common size*
Cash	$ 200	6.7%
Accounts receivable	500	16.7
Inventories	700	23.3
Property, plant, and equipment, net	1,500	50.0
Other assets	100	3.3
Total	$3,000	100.0%
Accounts payable	$ 300	10.0%
Other current liabilities	100	3.3
Long-term debt	900	30.0
Stockholders' equity	1,700	56.7
Total	$ 3,000	100.0%

Common-size income statements also may be prepared based on sales as the 100% figure.

Regression Analysis

Regression analysis is the means by which a relation between variables is used to make inferences about such variables. The relationships are expressed in terms of a dependent variable and one or more independent variables.

Regression is used in auditing to make inferences as to what account balances *should be* for comparison with what account balances *are*. Ordinarily, a linear regression model is used when the auditor applies regression analysis.

Linear Regression.

The linear regression model defines the relationship between the dependent variable and the independent variable or variables in terms of a straight line. To determine meaningful relationships, the auditor should identify those independent variables that affect the dependent variable. Although these relationships will never be exact and will differ at various times, useful inferences are possible as long as the relationships indicate that a relatively stable pattern exists between the dependent variable and the independent variable or variables.

Defining the Variables.

To develop the regression model, the auditor should define the variables. In defining the variables, the auditor will use his or her knowledge of the client and previously audited historical data. In developing regression models, the auditor also may use external independent variables, such as gross national product, disposable net income, unemployment rate, and so on.

The Linear Regression Formula.

The linear regression formula is as follows:

$$Y = a + bX$$

In this formula, a is the value of Y when X is equal to 0. The slope of the regression line is b, which indicates the change in Y for each unit of change in X. For example, assume the auditor wishes to make inferences about the amount of recorded selling expenses. Based on his or her knowledge of the client, the auditor determines the following:

1. Fixed selling expenses amount to $10,000. In the regression formula, this amount is a.
2. Selling expenses (Y) increase as sales (X) increase.
3. From prior data, the auditor determines that for each dollar of sales, selling expenses increase by $.05. In the regression formula, this amount is b.

In the regression formula, the preceding information is expressed as follows:

$$\text{Selling expense }(Y) = \$10,000(a) + [.50(b) \times \text{Sales}(X)]$$

Therefore, if sales were $10 million, the auditor would expect selling expenses to be $510,000, determined as follows:

$$Y = \$10,000 + .50 \times \$10,000,000$$
$$Y = \$510,000$$

Applying Regression Analysis.

After defining the variables and determining the values for a and b, the auditor should perform other steps before making inferences. These steps are as follows:

1. Calculate the correlation coefficient.
2. Calculate point estimates.
3. Determine the standard deviation.
4. Determine the standard error.
5. Calculate the precision interval.
6. Calculate the confidence interval.

SUBSTANTIVE TESTS

The auditor may determine that the use of analytical procedures to obtain evidential matter about particular assertions related to account balances or classes of transactions is appropriate. When used for this purpose, analytical procedures are substantive tests.

1. When using analytical procedures for substantive testing, the auditor should assess the reliability of the data by considering:
   - Was the data obtained from independent sources outside the entity?
   - Are the data sources in the entity independent of those who are responsible for the data being audited?
   - Was the data developed under a reliable system with adequate controls?
   - Was the data subject to audit testing in the current or prior year?
   - Were the expectations developed from data using various sources?
2. The auditor should consider the amount of difference from his or her expectation that can be accepted without additional investigation.
3. The auditor should evaluate significant unexpected differences.
4. Management explanations should ordinarily be corroborated with other evidence.
5. If an explanation for a difference cannot be obtained, the auditor should perform other audit procedures if a likely misstatement has occurred.
6. The auditor should consider that an unexplained difference might increase the risk of material misstatement.

(AU-C 520.05)

NOTE: To be used as a substantive test, an analytical procedure has to provide persuasive evidence. Audit objectives cannot be achieved by the application of analytical procedures that only provide overall comfort—the evidence has to be persuasive.

The extent to which the auditor uses analytical procedures as a substantive test depends on the level of assurance he or she wants in achieving a particular audit objective. The higher the level of assurance desired, the more predictable the relationship should be. As a general rule, relationships involving income statement accounts are more predictable than relationships involving only balance sheet accounts.

It may be difficult or impossible to achieve certain substantive audit objectives without relying to some extent on analytical procedures (e.g., this is often the case in testing for unrecorded transactions).

Some audit objectives may be difficult or impossible to achieve by relying solely on analytical procedures (e.g., testing an account balance that is not expected to show a predictable relationship with other operating or financial data).

Analytical procedures may be more effective and efficient than tests of details for assertions in which potential misstatements would not be apparent from an examination of the detailed evidence or in which detailed evidence is not readily available (e.g., comparison of aggregate purchases with quantities received may indicate duplication payments that may not be apparent from testing individual transactions).

Differences from expected relationships would often be good indicators of potential omissions, whereas evidence that an individual transaction should have been recorded may not be readily available.

The expected effectiveness and efficiency of an analytical procedure in addressing risk of material misstatement depends on, among other things:

- The nature of the assertion
- The plausibility and practibility of the relationship
- The reliability and availability of the data used to develop the expectation
- The precision of the expectation

(AU-C 520.A8)

Availability and Reliability of Data

The auditor obtains assurance from analytical procedures based upon the consistency of the recorded amounts with the expectations developed from data derived from other sources. Other sources for data include industry trade associations; data service organizations, such as Dun & Bradstreet and Standard & Poor's Corp. industry trade journals; and the client's prior year's audited financial statements. In circumstances where the auditor specializes in a specific industry, the auditor may use clients' data to develop plausible expectations (for example, gross margin percentage, other income statement ratios, and accounts receivable and inventory turnover ratios).

The reliability of the data used to develop the expectations should be appropriate for the desired level of assurance from the analytical procedures.

In general, the following factors influence the reliability of data used for analytical procedures:

- Whether the data was obtained from independent sources outside the entity or from sources within the entity.
- Whether sources within the entity were independent of those who are responsible for the amount being audited.
- Whether the data was developed under a reliable system with effectively designed controls.
- Whether the data was subjected to audit testing in the current or prior year.
- Whether the expectations were developed using data from a variety of sources.

Precision of the Expectation

The expectation of the relationship that exists should be precise enough to provide the desired level of assurance that differences that may be potential material misstatements would be identified for the auditor to investigate. Expectations developed at a detailed level ordinarily have a greater chance of detecting misstatements of a given amount than do broad comparisons. (AU-C 520.A23) For example, expectations developed at a division level will have a greater chance of detecting misstatement than expectations developed at an entity level.

Overall Review

The auditor should use analytical procedures in the overall review near the end of the audit. The results of this review may indicate that additional audit evidence may be needed. (AU-C 520.06)

The application of analytical procedures in the overall conclusion phase near the end of the audit is one of the last tests of the audit. Analytical procedures at this stage of the audit assist the auditor in assessing the conclusions reached concerning certain account balances and in evaluating the overall financial statement presentation.

Recommended Procedures

The overall conclusion stage generally includes reading the financial statements and accompanying notes for reasonableness and adequacy of notes and considering the following:

1. The adequacy of evidence accumulated for account balances considered unusual or unexpected in the planning stage or during the audit
2. Unusual or unexpected balances or relationships that were not previously identified

(AU-C 520.A25)

In addition to reading the financial statements and accompanying notes, the auditor may consider using other analytical procedures, such as the following:

1. Comparison to similar financial data for the prior year or the client's industry
2. Ratio analysis
3. Trend analysis
4. Development of common-size financial statements

Results of Overall Conclusion Procedures

The results of the overall conclusion phase may indicate that additional audit evidence is needed. Because of this possibility, the auditor should try to complete this phase before the end of fieldwork. (AU-C 520.A26)

Documentation

As with any other auditing procedure, the auditor should document the application of analytical procedures. AU-C 230, *Audit Documentation*, applies to substantive analytical procedures and analytical procedures performed near the end of the audit. The auditor should comply with that guidance in addition to the documentation guidance in AU-C 520. The auditor should document all of the following when an analytical procedure is used as the principal substantive test for an assertion:

- The expectation and factors considered in its development, when the expectation is not readily determinable from the existing documentation.
- Results of comparing the expectation to the recorded amounts or ratios developed from the recorded amounts.
- If analytical procedures indicated unexpected fluctuations or inconsistent relationships, an explanation of these anomalies and the results of additional procedures should appear in the audit documentation. The results of the auditor's investigation of those fluctuations should include audit evidence supporting that explanation and the results of additional procedures.

(AU-C 520.08)

In addition, the following are recommended:

1. Procedures to be applied should be listed in the audit program.
2. Auditor conclusions should appear in the audit documentation.
3. If procedures applied in the overall review indicated that additional procedures were required, reference should be made in the audit documentation to those sections that document the additional procedures.

PERMANENT FILE FOR ANALYTICAL PROCEDURES

Because analytical procedures are based in part on industry data and client prior period data, these data may be maintained in the client permanent file for subsequent use. The data to be maintained depend on the nature of the analytical procedures.

When the auditor compares current period results with prior periods, the comparisons may include the following:

1. Quarter to quarter during the current year
2. Month to month during the current year
3. Season to season during the current year
4. Current year's quarter, month, or season with the similar periods of prior years

The auditor may maintain in the client permanent file all periodic data used in the analysis. The auditor also may include in the permanent file, when applicable, the following:

1. The percentages used in trend analysis
2. The percentages used in common-size financial statements
3. The ratios used in ratio analysis
4. The industry data used and the source of the data

There is no specified period of time for which permanent file data should be retained; however, it is advisable to retain these data for at least five years.

AU-C ILLUSTRATIONS

The following illustrations give examples of the application of analytical procedures and suggested follow-up audit procedures.

ILLUSTRATION 1

Facts

A company had sales (all credit) for the year of $120,000. Its accounts receivable at year-end amounted to $20,000. Its day's sales in accounts receivable is computed as follows:

1. Sales	$120,000
2. Accounts receivable	20,000
3. Average daily sales (Sales $120,000 ÷ 360 days)	333
4. Day's sales in accounts receivable [Accounts receivable ÷ Average daily sales ($20,000 ÷ $333)]	60

In the previous year, the day's sales in accounts receivable was 45.

Analysis

The company is not collecting its receivables as rapidly as it did in the previous year. This increase in the day's sales in accounts receivable indicates a possible problem in the collectibility of the receivables.

Auditing Procedures

The auditor may consider doing some or all of the following:

1. Review cash receipts and remittance advices for the subsequent period.
2. Obtain credit reports on significant past due accounts.

3. Analyze year-end sales to determine any unusually large sales. Determine the nature of these sales and ascertain that they were recorded in the proper accounting period.

ILLUSTRATION 2

Facts

A company has cost of sales for the year of $108,000. Its inventory amounted to $20,000 at the beginning of the year and $16,000 at the end of the year. Its inventory turnover is determined as follows:

1. Average inventory		
Beginning balance	$20,000	
Ending balance	16,000	
Total	$36,000	
Total divided by 2		$18,000

NOTE: A better indication of the average inventory may be obtained by using month-end inventories, if available.

2. Cost of goods sold	$108,000
3. Cost of goods sold ÷ Average inventory = Inventory turnover	6

In the previous year, the inventory turnover was four times.

Analysis

An increase in the inventory turnover ratio may occur because of improved purchasing, production, and pricing policies. It may also be caused by one of the following:

1. Poor credit rating of client. If the client has a poor credit rating, it may not be getting all of the inventory it requires. This will cause inventory levels to decline, and if sales do not decline as rapidly, the inventory turnover ratio will increase.
2. Unrecorded purchases.
3. Unusual inventory shrinkage.
4. Overly conservative inventory valuation.
5. Error in computing the inventory.

Auditing Procedures

There are no specific auditing procedures when the high turnover is caused by insufficient inventory because of a poor credit rating. In that situation, however, the auditor might want to obtain a credit report on the client and should approach the audit with more skepticism than usual.

If the auditor believes the high turnover is caused by other than a poor credit rating, he or she may do the following:

1. Review debit balances in the accounts payable schedule. A debit balance might indicate a payment without the accompanying entry for a purchase.
2. Review inventory controls to determine the possibility of theft. Also, if the company is a manufacturer, review production records to determine spoilage and waste.
3. Compare inventory costs with inventory values.
4. Review inventory computations.

ILLUSTRATION 3

Facts

Following is a trend statement of selected income and expense items:

Year	20X1	20X2	20X3	20X4	20X5
Sales	100	116	133	151	168
Selling expenses	100	115	132	150	175

Analysis

Sales have increased at a steady rate over the five-year period, and selling expenses matched this increase for the first four years. In the fifth year, however, the increase in selling expenses was disproportionate to previous years' increases and to the current year's increase in sales. The increase may have been caused by one of the following:

1. Misclassification of expenses
2. Classification of prepayments as expenses
3. Recording of nonbusiness expenses

Auditing Procedures

If a trend statement indicates a disproportionate increase in an expense, the auditor should apply additional substantive tests to this expense. To determine the reason for the disproportionate increase in selling expenses in the preceding example, the auditor may review invoices for major expense items in order to answer the following:

1. Were administrative or nonselling expenses classified as selling expenses?
2. At year-end, did the entity make advance payments for the subsequent year's selling program and classify these payments as an expense rather than as a prepayment?
3. Are expenses of executives that are personal in nature being charged to the entity?

AU-C 530 Audit Sampling

AU-C ORIGINAL PRONOUNCEMENT

Source Statement on Auditing Standards (SAS) 122.

AU-C DEFINITIONS OF TERMS

Source: AU-C 530.04

Audit sampling (sampling). The selection and evaluation of less than 100% of the population of audit relevance such that the auditor expects the items selected (the sample) to be representative of the population and, thus, likely to provide a reasonable basis for conclusions about the population. In this context, *representative* means that evaluation of the sample will result in conclusions that, subject to the limitations of sampling risk, are similar to those that would be drawn if the same procedures were applied to the entire population.

Nonsampling risk. The risk that the auditor reaches an erroneous conclusion for any reason not related to sampling risk.

Population. The entire set of data from which a sample is selected and about which the auditor wishes to draw conclusions.

Sampling risk. The risk that the auditor's conclusion based on a sample may be different from the conclusion if the entire population were subjected to the same audit procedure. Sampling risk can lead to two types of erroneous conclusions:

1. In the case of a test of controls, that controls are more effective than they actually are, or in the case of a test of details, that a material misstatement does not exist when, in fact, it does. The auditor is primarily concerned with this type of erroneous conclusion because it affects audit effectiveness and is more likely to lead to an inappropriate audit opinion.
2. In the case of a test of controls, that controls are less effective than they actually are, or in the case of a test of details, that a material misstatement exists when, in fact, it does not. This type of erroneous conclusion affects audit efficiency because it would usually lead to additional work to establish that initial conclusions were incorrect.

Sampling unit. The individual items constituting a population.

Statistical sampling. An approach to sampling that has the following characteristics:

1. Random selection of the sample items
2. The use of an appropriate statistical technique to evaluate sample results, including measurement of sampling risk

A sampling approach that does not have these two characteristics is considered nonstatistical sampling.

Stratification. The process of dividing a population into subpopulations, each of which is a group of sampling units that have similar characteristics.

Tolerable misstatement. A monetary amount set by the auditor, in respect of which the auditor seeks to obtain an appropriate level of assurance that the monetary amount set by the auditor is not exceeded by the actual misstatement in the population.

Tolerable rate of deviation. A rate of deviation set by the auditor, in respect of which the auditor seeks to obtain an appropriate level of assurance that the rate of deviation set by the auditor is not exceeded by the actual rate of deviation in the population.

OBJECTIVES OF AU-C SECTION 530

AU-C Section 530.04 states that:

the objective of the auditor, when using audit sampling, is to provide a reasonable basis for the auditor to draw conclusions about the population from which the sample is selected.

OVERVIEW

The Section is not just for statistical samplers. It applies equally to nonstatistical and statistical sampling. (AU-C 530.01) Either approach to audit sampling, *when properly applied*, can provide sufficient evidential matter. And, the Section establishes specific requirements essential for proper application.

Because the Section establishes requirements that apply whenever audit sampling is used, the definition of audit sampling becomes very important. Audit sampling is the application of an audit procedure to less than 100% of the items within an account balance or class of transactions for the purpose of evaluating some characteristic of the balance or class. Thus, whenever the auditor intends to reach a conclusion about whether an account balance or class of transactions is misstated based on an examination of less than all the items in the balance or class, he or she should adhere to the requirements. (AU-C 530)

One effect of the Section on practice should be to place a premium on the auditor's decision to sample. If the auditor is sampling, he or she should adhere to the Section. If the auditor has some other audit objective, the Section does not apply. Thus, the auditor cannot simply decide that a procedure will be applied on a test basis. Careful consideration should go into a decision that the best approach to an audit test involves use of audit sampling.

If the auditor is sampling, the selection of sample items should not be judgmental. It must be expected to be representative. All audit sampling has to be either statistical or nonstatistical.

REQUIREMENTS

In planning a particular sample, the auditor should:

1. Determine the specific audit objective to be achieved.
2. Determine that the audit procedure, or combination of procedures, to be applied will achieve that objective.
3. Determine that the population from which the auditor draws the sample is appropriate for the specific audit objective.

(AU-C 530.06)

NOTE: The following requirements apply equally to nonstatistical and statistical audit samples.

EXAMINED 100%

Some items exist for which, in the auditor's judgment, acceptance of some sampling risk is not justified. All of these items should be examined. (Items examined 100% are not part of the items subject to sampling.)

NOTE: Some items may individually be so significant or may have such a high likelihood of being misstated that they should not be sampled.

SAMPLE SELECTION

Sample items should be selected in such a way that the sample can be expected to be representative of the population and likely to provide the auditor with a basis for conclusion about the population. (AU-C 530.08) That is, the auditor should select a sample he or she believes is representative of the items composing the pertinent account balance or class of transactions. The sample size depends on the level of risk the auditor is willing to accept. (AU-C 530.A12)

STRATIFICATION

The auditor may be able to decrease required sample size by separating items subject to sampling into relatively homogeneous groups on the basis of some characteristic related to the specific audit objective. (AU-C 530.A11)

UNEXAMINED SAMPLE ITEMS

The treatment of unexamined selected sample items depends on their effect on the auditor's evaluation of the sample. In a substantive test, if considering the unexamined items to be misstated would not alter the auditor's evaluation of sample results, the items may be ignored. If the evaluation would be changed, the auditor should apply alternative procedures for those items and consider the implications of the reasons for the inability to examine the items. In a test of controls, selected items that cannot be examined should be treated as deviations.

NOTE: Before ignoring or simply considering unexamined or missing items as misstated or deviations, the auditor should consider whether the unexamined items might be indicative of fraud.

SAMPLE SIZE: SUBSTANTIVE TEST

To determine the number of items to be selected in a sample for a particular substantive test of details, the auditor should consider:

1. Tolerable misstatement
2. Risk of material misstatement
3. Characteristics of the population
4. Assurance obtained from other procedures
5. Expected misstatement
6. Stratification

(AU-C 530.A13)

NOTE: For a statistical audit sample, these factors should be reduced to specific amounts for use in a formula or table to calculate sample size. For a nonstatistical sample, specific amounts are often neither required nor possible, and the auditor considers qualitative relationships. For example, as tolerable misstatement increases, sample size decreases.

Sample Size: Test of Controls

To determine the number of items to be selected for a particular sample for a test of controls, the auditor should consider:

1. Tolerable rate of deviation from controls being tested, based on the planned assessed level of control risk
2. Expected or likely rate of deviation
3. Allowable risk of assessing control risk too low

(AU-C 530.A13)

Projection of Misstatements

The auditor should project the misstatement results of the sample to the account balance or class of transactions from which the sample was selected.

Aggregation of Misstatements

The auditor should aggregate projected misstatements for all audit sampling applications and all known misstatements from nonsampling applications when he or she evaluates whether the financial statements taken as a whole may be materially misstated.

Qualitative Aspects

In addition to evaluating quantitative sample results (frequency of deviations or frequency and amount of monetary misstatements), the auditor should consider the qualitative aspects of sample results, such as the nature and cause of deviations or monetary misstatements.

NOTE: The qualitative evaluation includes consideration of whether sample results might be indicative of fraud.

Relating Balance Sheet and Income Statement Sampling

Accounts in the balance sheet and income statement are often related. In obtaining assurance from balance sheet accounts, an auditor can frequently also obtain some assurance regarding related income statement accounts and vice versa. Thus, the extent of tests performed on balance sheet accounts may be considered when determining whether additional audit evidence regarding one or more assertions needs to be obtained from direct tests of income statement accounts.

NONSAMPLING TECHNIQUES

Distinguishing Sampling from Other Audit Tests

Because Section 530 applies equally to nonstatistical sampling and statistical sampling, whether a procedure involves audit sampling becomes a critical decision. Some audit procedures obviously do not involve sampling, such as:

- Analytical procedures
- Inquiries and observation used in tests of controls that do not result in documentary evidence of performance and in audit planning
- Examination of 100% of the items in an account balance or class of transactions

In general, an audit procedure involves sampling whenever evidence relating to individual items is used as a basis for a conclusion about the population from which the items were selected. However, there are two types of audit tests that do not involve audit sampling that should be carefully distinguished because they are commonly thought of as being done on a test basis:

1. Key-item tests
2. Flow-of-transactions tests (walk-throughs)

Key-Item Tests

Key-item tests are substantive tests of details of all the items in a population that individually or in total could contain monetary misstatements that approximate tolerable misstatement. This approach does not test those items that in total are not material. The results of this kind of test cannot be projected to the balance or class as a whole. The evidence obtained only supports evaluation of the items tested.

This kind of test can be used primarily when most of the dollar amount of an account balance is concentrated in a comparatively few key items such that the remainder of the items in the account balance could be entirely misstated without having a material effect on the financial statements.

Flow-of-Transactions Tests

If the auditor's objective is to obtain a better understanding of the flow of a particular class of transactions through the accounting system, sampling is not involved. In a flow-of-transactions test, the auditor traces one or a few of the different types of transactions through the related documents and records. It is often called a walk-through. This test does not involve sampling if the auditor is trying to confirm his or her understanding of how the accounting system works.

NONSTATISTICAL AUDIT SAMPLING TECHNIQUES[1]

INTRODUCTION

The auditor performs two separate groups of procedures in audit sampling:

1. Sample selection and evaluation of the sample results
2. Audit procedures in examining the sample items

The audit procedures performed on the sample items do not depend on the method of sample selection. Items selected by either nonstatistical or statistical sampling methods are subject to the same audit procedures.

A properly designed nonstatistical sampling plan can provide results that are as effective as results from a properly designed statistical sampling plan. The significant difference between nonstatistical and statistical sampling is that statistical sampling measures the sampling risk associated with sampling procedures. Sampling risk arises from the possibility that when a test of

[1] *The American Institute of Certified Public Accountants' (AICPA) Audit Sampling Guide includes case studies and an in-depth look at nonstatistical audit sampling. The appendices include sampling tables, testing considerations, and a comparison of the key provisions of the risk assessment standards.*

controls or substantive test is applied to a sample, the auditor's conclusions might be different from those that would have been made if the tests were applied in the same way to all items in the population. That is, the sample selected from the population might not be representative of that population. For tests of controls, sampling risk is the risk of assessing control risk too low or too high. For substantive testing, sampling risk is the risk of incorrect acceptance or incorrect rejection of the amount tested.

METHODS OF SAMPLE SELECTION

Sample items should be selected in a way so that the sample can be expected to be representative of the population; therefore, all items in the population should have a chance of being selected. Common methods of selecting samples are:

- Block sampling
- Haphazard sampling
- Random number sampling
- Systematic random sampling

Block sampling does not meet the requirements for a representative sample. The other three do. Ordinarily, only the last two methods are used in statistical sampling. In addition to the detailed discussion in this chapter, the AICPA Audit Guide *Audit Sampling* contains detailed discussion of selected techniques.

Block Sampling

A block sample is obtained by selecting several items in sequence. Once the first item in the block is selected, the remainder of the block is chosen automatically. For example, the sample may consist of all vouchers processed during a two-week period or all vouchers processed on specific days. Block samples could theoretically be representative samples but are rarely used because they are inefficient. The time and expense to select sufficient blocks so that the sample could be considered representative of the total population is prohibitive.

Haphazard Sampling

A haphazard sample is obtained by selecting, without any conscious bias, items regardless of their size, source, or other distinguishing characteristics. This does not mean it is the selection of sampling units in a careless manner; the units are selected in a manner so that the sample can be expected to be representative of the population. For example, the sample may consist of vouchers pulled from all vouchers processed for the year. Excluding items from the sample on the basis of judgment invalidates the requirement for a representative sample.

Random Number Sampling

A random number sample is obtained by selecting numbers from a random number table or by generating numbers randomly by computer and matching them with document numbers, such as check numbers and invoice numbers.

Systematic Random Sampling

A systematic random sample is obtained by selecting items at uniform intervals. The interval is determined by dividing the number of physical units in the population by the sample size. A starting point is selected at random in the first interval, and one item is selected from the population at each of the uniform intervals from the random starting point. For example, in a population of 20,000 units and a desired sample of 100 units, every 200th item will be selected from the starting point. Neither the size nor the unusualness of an item should be allowed to influence selection. The auditor can select large and unusual items in addition to items sampled, however.

TESTS OF CONTROLS

After the auditor obtains and documents an understanding of internal control, he or she may wish to assess control risk at below the maximum for certain assertions. For these assertions, the auditor should perform tests of controls (see Section 319). When testing controls, the auditor may use attribute sampling.

Attribute Sampling

An attribute is a characteristic of interest. For example, some attributes of a sale that are of interest to the auditor may be the following:

1. Authorization by the sales order department
2. Approval by the credit department
3. Comparison of merchandise shipped and merchandise listed on the sales invoice for agreement

In testing for attributes, the auditor is concerned with how many times a prescribed internal control failed to operate; every deviation from a prescribed control is given equal weight in the sample evaluation, regardless of the dollar amount of the transaction. Based on the occurrence rate in the sample, the auditor decides if he or she can assess control risk at below the maximum.

For nonstatistical attribute sampling, the auditor does the following:

1. Judgmentally determines sample size.
2. Selects the sample.
3. Applies audit procedures to the sampling units.
4. Evaluates the results of the application of audit procedures to the sample.

Determination of sample size. The auditor determines sample size and evaluates sample results using subjective judgment to apply the criteria specified in Section 530 and his or her own experience with the client. The auditor may, but is not required to, use statistical tables to determine sample size for nonstatistical compliance tests. (See Tables 1 and 2.) Sample sizes should be based on the tolerable rate of deviation from the control procedures being tested, the expected rate of deviations, and the allowable risk of assessing control risk too low.

The auditor is not required to select a number of items comparable to a statistical sample size. If past experience with a continuing client has been good, the auditor might continue to use sample sizes that have proven effective.

Selection of sampling units. The auditor may use one of the methods described earlier for selecting the sample. In selecting the sample, the auditor may encounter the following:

1. Voided documents
2. Unused or inapplicable documents
3. Inability to examine selected items

Voided documents. If the auditor selects a voided document—for example, a voided sales invoice—it should be replaced with another. The auditor should obtain reasonable assurance, however, that the document was properly voided and was not a deviation from prescribed internal control.

Unused or inapplicable documents. If the auditor selects an unused or inapplicable document, it should be treated the same as a voided document.

Inability to examine selected items. If for any reason a selected item cannot be examined—for example, the document cannot be located—the auditor should consider this a deviation from prescribed policies or procedures. Also, the auditor should consider reasons for this deviation and the effect it has on his or her understanding and assessed level of control risk of particular control procedures.

Evaluating sample results. After completing the examination of the sampling units and having noted the deviation from prescribed policies or procedures, the auditor:

1. Calculates the deviation rate.
2. Considers sampling risk.
3. Considers qualitative aspects of deviations.
4. Extends the sample when control deviations are found.
5. Assesses the potential magnitude of a control deficiency.
6. Reaches a conclusion.

Calculation of deviation rate. The deviation rate is the number of observed deviations divided by the sample size. This is the auditor's best estimate of the deviation rate for the population from which the sample was selected. In statistics, it is called a point estimate.

Consideration of sampling risk. When evaluating a sample for a test of controls, the auditor should consider sampling risk (see "AU-C Definitions of Terms"). For a nonstatistical sample, sampling risk cannot be quantified. Generally, however, sample results do not support assessed risk below the maximum if the actual deviation rate is close to or exceeds the expected population deviation rate used in designing the sample.

Qualitative aspects of deviations. The qualitative aspects of the observed deviations should be considered by the auditor. Each deviation from a prescribed policy procedure should be analyzed to determine its nature and cause. Deviations that occurred when the person responsible for performing the task was on vacation are not as serious as intentional failure to perform prescribed policies or procedures or misunderstood instructions of prescribed policies or procedures. The nature and cause of deviations may influence the auditor's decision to assess control risk below the maximum or perform additional audit procedures.

Reaching a conclusion. Based on the sample results and on experience and judgment, the auditor reaches a conclusion about the level of control risk. If the auditor concludes that he or she cannot assess control risk below the maximum, the auditor may:

- Test additional items with the hope of reducing sampling risk
- Modify planned substantive tests

Documentation of Sampling Procedures

AU-C 530 does not require specific documentation of audit sampling applications; however, the auditor might consider including the following in the audit documentation:

1. A description of the control tested
2. Objectives of the sampling application, including its relationship to planned substantive testing
3. Definitions of the population and the sampling unit
4. Definition of a deviation

5. Assessments of:
   a. Risk of assessing control risk too low
   b. Tolerable deviation rate
   c. Expected population deviation rate
6. Method of determining sample size
7. Method of selecting sample
8. Description of how sampling procedure was performed and a list of sample deviations
9. Evaluation of sample and summary of conclusions, including:
   a. Number of sample deviations
   b. Explanation of how sampling risk was considered
   c. Determination of whether sample results supported planned assessed level of control risk
   d. Qualitative aspects of deviations
   e. Effects of evaluation of results on planned substantive tests

SUBSTANTIVE TESTS

In using nonstatistical sampling for substantive tests, the auditor should do the following:

1. Identify individually significant items.
2. Define the population.
3. Define the sampling unit.
4. Determine the sample size.
5. Select the sample.
6. Evaluate the sample results (quantitatively and qualitatively).
7. Consider sampling risk.
8. Document the sampling procedures.

Identify Individually Significant Items

In using sampling for substantive tests, the auditor may decide that for certain items accepting some sampling risk is not justified. For example, the auditor may decide to examine *all* items over a specified dollar amount. Items tested 100% are not part of the sample. Dividing a population into relatively homogeneous units is known as stratification. Excluding individually significant items provides an initial stratification. The auditor may further subdivide the remaining population, however, into subgroups of items with similar values.

Define the Population

The population consists of the class of transactions or the account balance to be tested. Because the auditor will project the results of the sample to the population, he or she must specify the population so that the sampling units come from that population. For example, accounts receivable has four different populations:

1. All accounts
2. Accounts with zero balances
3. Accounts with debit balances
4. Accounts with credit balances

The audit objective determines which population is appropriate.

Define the Period Covered by the Test

When testing during interim work, the auditor should consider what additional evidence needs to be obtained for the remaining period. If the testing is not extended to all transactions occurring in the remaining period, the population consists only of transactions for the interim period and the results of the test can only be projected to that period. In this case, the auditor obtains other evidence to conclude on the operating effectiveness of those controls during the period not covered by the tests.

When the auditor requires assurance regarding the effectiveness of controls as of a specific date, the transactions on or close to that date constitute the population from which a sample is selected. If it is impractical to perform these tests in that period, it may be appropriate to conduct tests for an earlier period instead.

Define the Sampling Unit

A sampling unit is any item in the population. For example, a sampling unit may be a customer account or an individual transaction.

Determine Sample Size

For nonstatistical sampling, sample size can be subjectively determined. Factors 1 to 4 should be considered and 5 might be considered:

1. Amounts of the individual items in the population
2. Variability and size of the population
3. Risk of incorrect acceptance or rejection
4. Tolerable misstatement and expected misstatement
5. Statistical table or formula

Amounts of individual items. Accounting populations usually include a few very large amounts, a number of moderately large amounts, and a large number of small amounts. In these circumstances, if the population is not stratified, much larger sample sizes are necessary.

Variability and size of the population. Populations are characterized by some variability; that is, not every item in the population is the same amount. Statistically, this variation is measured by the standard deviation. The larger the variability of the population, the larger the standard deviation. For nonstatistical sampling, the standard deviation is not quantified; it is estimated in qualitative terms, such as small variability or large variability. *The larger the estimated variability of the population, the larger the sample size required.* To estimate variability, the auditor may use:

- His or her judgment
- Prior year results
- A pilot sample

The number of items in the population generally has little effect on the sample size for substantive tests; therefore, it is generally not efficient to determine sample size as a fixed percentage of the population.

Risk of incorrect acceptance. In determining sample size, the auditor should consider the risk of incorrect acceptance (an aspect of sampling risk). As the level of risk of incorrect acceptance increases, the sample size for the substantive test decreases. For example, a 10% level of risk of incorrect acceptance requires a smaller sample to achieve the same results than does a 5% level of risk. If he or she assessed control risk at lower than the maximum for a given assertion, the auditor can accept a larger risk of incorrect acceptance for the substantive test related to the assertion.

Risk of incorrect rejection. The auditor should also consider the risk of incorrect rejection when determining the sample size. To limit the risk of incorrect rejection, one can increase the sample size. An alternative solution is to perform additional procedures when testing finds a higher amount of misstatement than expected.

Tolerable misstatement and expected misstatement. For an account balance or a class of transactions, the sample size, given the risk of incorrect acceptance, increases as the tolerable misstatement for that balance or class of transactions decreases. As the size or frequency of expected misstatements decreases, the sample size also decreases.

Statistical table or formula. After determining sample size for nonstatistical sampling, the auditor may wish to, but is not required to, compare it with the sample size from a statistical table or formula. The auditor may also use a statistical table or formula to determine sample size for a nonstatistical sample. The distinguishing feature of statistical sampling is mathematical evaluation of sample results using the laws of probability. Use of statistical methods for sample size determination and selection of sample items do not by themselves make the audit sample a statistical sample.

Select the Sample

The auditor should select the sampling units by using any method that can be expected to result in a representative sample. For substantive tests of account balances, the auditor ordinarily stratifies the population before selecting the sample.

Evaluate Sample Results

The Section requires the auditor to project the misstatement results of the sample to the population from which the sample was selected.

One method of projecting the misstatement is to divide the dollar amount of the misstatement in the sample by the percentage of the sample dollars out of the total dollars in the population. For example, if the sample amounted to 5% of the population (in dollars), and if $1,000 of misstatement was observed in the sample, the misstatement projected to the population is $20,000 ($1,000 ÷ 5%). This is the best estimate of the misstatement in the population.

Another method of projecting the misstatement is to multiply the average unit misstatement in the sample by the number of units in the population. For example, if there were 200 units in the sample and $600 in misstatements was observed, the average misstatement in the sample is $3 ($600 ÷ 200). If there are 30,000 units in the population, the misstatement projected to the population is $90,000 (30,000 × $3).

Projected misstatement is the best estimate of the misstatement in the population. In statistics, it is called the point estimate.

Consider Sampling Risk

For nonstatistical sampling, the auditor uses his or her experience with the client and professional judgment when considering sampling risk. If the projected misstatement does not exceed the expected misstatement, the auditor may reasonably conclude that there is an acceptably low risk that the true misstatement exceeds the tolerable misstatement. However, if the projected misstatement exceeds or approximates the expected misstatement, the auditor may reasonably conclude that there is an unacceptably high risk that the true misstatement exceeds the tolerable misstatement.

If he or she believes the recorded amount may be misstated, the auditor ordinarily suggests that the entity investigate the misstatements and, if appropriate, adjust the recorded amount.

Document Sampling Procedures

This section does not require specific documentation of audit sampling applications; however, the auditor might consider including the following in the audit documentation:

1. Objectives of the test and a description of other procedures, if any, directed to these same objectives
2. Definitions of the population and the sampling unit
3. Definition of a misstatement
4. Assessment of:
   a. Risk of incorrect acceptance
   b. Risk of incorrect rejection (solely a matter of efficiency)
   c. Tolerable misstatement
   d. Expected population misstatement
5. Sampling technique used
6. Method of selecting sample
7. Description of how sampling procedure was performed and a list of sample errors
8. Evaluation of sample and summary of conclusions, including:
   a. Projection of misstatements
   b. Consideration of sampling risk
   c. Qualitative aspects of the misstatements

STATISTICAL AUDIT SAMPLING TECHNIQUES

INTRODUCTION

There are many valid ways of applying statistical sampling. The method described in this section is a highly efficient application.

Statistical samples can be designed to satisfy either or both of the following objectives:

1. *The detection objective.* The detection of a misstatement or deviation if it exists in the population at a specified rate or amount.
2. *The estimation objective.* The estimation of the extent of detected misstatements or deviations.

Random sampling enables the auditor to project sample results mathematically and to state, with measurable precision and confidence, the estimated rate of deviation in the population under audit (attribute sampling), or the estimated dollar amount of misstatement in the population (dollar value,[2] or variables, sampling).

CALCULATING SAMPLE SIZE

Given that the auditor is willing to accept some sampling risk, the most important risk to consider in the planning of a test procedure is the risk of incorrect acceptance (or risk of assessing control risk too low). In the simplified approach to be presented below, this risk, whether for substantive tests or tests of control, will be referred to as the detection risk. Detection risk is the

---

[2] *Dollar value sampling is also referred to as probability proportional to size sampling.*

chance that an audit sample will fail to disclose misstatement if the misstatement in the population exceeds the tolerable misstatement (or tolerable rate of deviation). The complement of the detection risk is the detection confidence. The sample size approach that controls the detection risk is known as a discovery sample size.

Discovery Sampling

A discovery sample is the smallest sample size capable of providing a specified chance (confidence) of detecting misstatement when the misstatement in the population exceeds tolerable misstatement. If a discovery sample is selected and discloses no misstatement, then the auditor can assert, with specified confidence, that the population misstatement does not exceed tolerable misstatement.

Discovery sampling is an efficient, yet powerful, approach in determining the extent of testing required to satisfy an audit test objective and is especially useful for testing populations that are nearly free of misstatement. If misstatements exist, they are likely to be detected. If misstatements are detected, the sample results can then be used to project the detected misstatements to the population from which the sample was selected.

Discovery sample sizes are easily calculated. For tests of controls, the sample size (n) is obtained by dividing the confidence factors (CF) by the tolerable deviation rate (TDR), or:

$$n = \mathrm{CF}/\mathrm{TDR}$$

Confidence factors for discovery sample size are:

Confidence level (%)	80.0	90.0	95.0	97.5	99.0	99.5
Risk (%) (1 – Confidence level)	20.0	10.0	5.0	2.5	1.0	0.5
Confidence factor (CF)	1.61	2.31	3.00	3.69	4.61	5.30

For substantive tests, the confidence factor is multiplied by the population book value (B) and divided by the tolerable misstatement amount (TMA), or:

$$n = (\mathrm{B} \times \mathrm{CF})/\mathrm{TMA}$$

For example, assume that a population has a book value of $3,530,000. The auditor wishes to have an 80% chance of detecting misstatement in the sample if the amount of misstatement in the population exceeds $70,000. The discovery sample size is:

$$\begin{aligned} n &= (3{,}530{,}000 \times 1.61)/70{,}000 \\ &= 82 \text{ items (rounded up)} \end{aligned}$$

Note that when the foregoing method is applied to samples selected with equal chance, it is assumed that misstatements tend to be randomly distributed throughout the population. If this is not likely to be the case, the auditor should consider stratifying the population so as to segregate those portions of the population that, in the auditor's judgment, are more likely to be prone to misstatement.

Sample Sizes When Deviations or Misstatements Are Expected

If a population is not expected to be nearly free of deviation or misstatement, a discovery sample size will often be too small to enable the auditor to conclude that the population deviation or misstatement is less than tolerable deviation or misstatement. In addition to the aforementioned factors, the auditor considers the expected deviation rate (EDR) when planning a test of controls or the expected misstatement amount (EMA) when planning a substantive test. For a test of controls, the sample size formula is:

$$n = \left(\frac{\text{CF}}{\text{TDR} - \text{EDR}}\right)\left[1 + \left(\frac{\text{EDR}}{\text{TDR} - \text{EDR}}\right)\right]$$

For a substantive test using dollar unit sampling, or when sampling with equal chance for randomly distributed errors or overstatement:

$$n = \left[\frac{(\text{B})(\text{CF})}{\text{TMA} - \text{EMA}}\right]\left[1 + \left(\frac{\text{EMA}}{\text{TMA} - \text{EMA}}\right)\right]$$

The confidence factor is determined from the table of confidence factors given earlier. There is a tendency to understate somewhat the sample size for confidence levels of 97.5% or higher. This can be corrected by using the following factors:

Confidence level	*Confidence factor*
97.5	3.84
99.0	5.43
99.5	6.63

Suppose, in the previous example, the auditor expects as much as $20,000 of misstatement in the population, based on previous experience. The sample size is:

$$n = \left[\frac{(5{,}530{,}000)(1.61)}{70{,}000 - 20{,}000}\right]\left[1 + \left(\frac{20{,}000}{70{,}000 - 20{,}000}\right)\right]$$
$$= 160 \text{ items (rounded up)}$$

Note that the foregoing formula applies only when EDR is less than TDR (or EMA is less than TMA). As a practical matter, the auditor should consider applying this formula only if EDR or EMA is no more than TDR/2 or TMA/2, respectively.

As the expected deviation or misstatement approaches or exceeds one-half the tolerable deviation or misstatement, it becomes increasingly difficult to establish, with a reasonable sample size, that the population deviation or misstatement does not exceed the specified tolerable level. Tests of controls may not be appropriate when numerous deviations are expected—the auditor may choose not to assess control risk lower than the maximum. Accordingly, the auditor may modify the substantive testing objective to obtaining an estimate of the dollar amount of misstatement in the population.

In this case, the auditor specifies the desired precision (P) for the estimate to be obtained. This is usually an amount between TMA/2 and TMA. The sample size formula is:

$$n = \left(\frac{(\text{B})(\text{CF})}{\text{P}}\right)\left(1 + \frac{\text{EMA}}{\text{P}}\right)$$

For example, the expected misstatement in a $9,450,000 population may be as high as $600,000. The auditor wishes to obtain an estimate of the maximum amount of overstatement that could exist. The auditor's desired precision is $400,000. The confidence level is 97.5%. The sample size is:

$$n = \left[\frac{(9{,}450{,}000)(3.84)}{400{,}000}\right]\left[1 + \left(\frac{600{,}000}{400{,}000}\right)\right]$$
$$= 227 \text{ items (rounded up)}$$

Small Populations

Some important controls do not operate frequently, but still require testing. For example, controls over the year-end close occur only once a year, whereas controls over a semimonthly payroll occur 24 times per year. The following table provides a sample size guidance for these smaller populations:

Control frequency and population size	*Sample size*
Quarterly (4)	2
Monthly (12)	2–4
Semimonthly (24)	3–8
Weekly (52)	5–9

Other Methods for Calculating Sample Size

The preceding parts of this section describe the simplest methods for calculating sample sizes. The methods are well suited to testing controls and substantive tests for overstatement (such as tests of existence, collectibility, or lower of cost or market). Numerous other methods exist, particularly for substantive tests.

Risk and Confidence in Substantive Tests of Details

The *detection risk* is the chance that the statistical sampling results will lead the auditor to conclude incorrectly that the misstatement in the population does not exceed the tolerable misstatement.

The complement of the detection risk is a one-sided confidence level that may be expressed in either of two ways: (1) the confidence that the magnitude of misstatement in the population is greater than zero, or (2) the confidence that the magnitude of misstatement in the population is less than the tolerable misstatement.

The audit test risk is associated with the detection objective. When planning a test, it is specified by the auditor.

The *estimation risk* or the risk of incorrect rejection is the chance that the calculated confidence interval does not include the true value of the population. This confidence interval is two-sided because it makes simultaneous use of two confidence limits, an upper misstatement limit and a lower misstatement limit.

The simultaneous use of two confidence limits is associated with the estimation objective. When planning to achieve the estimation objective, the auditor specifies a two-sided confidence level that will achieve the auditor-specified precision. When evaluating the results of a sample, the auditor calculates the precision (and confidence limits) associated with the specified confidence level.

The following table gives the relationship between a one-sided confidence level and a two-sided confidence level:

One-sided confidence level (%)	*Two-sided confidence level (%)*
99.5	99.0
99.0	98.0
97.5	95.0
95.0	90.0
90.0	80.0
80.0	60.0
75.0	50.0

Statistical Evaluation of a Sample in Substantive Tests of Details

The auditor can evaluate a statistical sample by calculating a *point estimate* and a *confidence interval* around the point estimate at the specified *confidence level*. The point estimate is the projection of the detected misstatements to the population from which the sample was selected. The confidence interval and the confidence level are related measurements. The confidence level is the chance that a confidence interval that is calculated as a result of a random sample will include the actual misstatement within its limits. The width of this interval indicates the amount of precision that the auditor has achieved with the estimate. The two end points of the confidence interval are called the upper and lower confidence limits (UCL and LCL, respectively).

The confidence interval for a specified confidence level can be expressed in three ways:

1. The population misstatement is not more than the UCL (a one-sided confidence limit).
2. The population misstatement is not less than the LCL (a one-sided confidence limit).
3. The population misstatement is included between the LCL and the UCL (two-sided confidence limits).

For example, suppose the evaluation is as follows:
Two-sided confidence: 90%

$LCL	=	$5,000 of overstatement error
$UCL	=	$15,000 of overstatement error

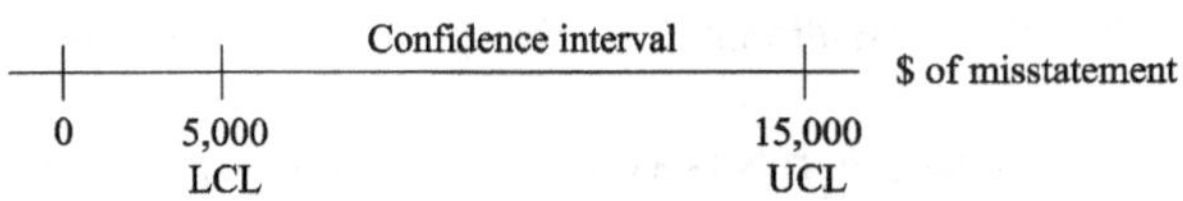

The auditor could conclude, with 90% confidence (two-sided), that the misstatement in the population is $5,000 – $15,000 of overstatement. The auditor could, alternatively, conclude, with 95% confidence, that the misstatement was no less than $5,000 of overstatement, or that the misstatement was no more than $15,000 of overstatement. If the tolerable misstatement is $10,000, the auditor concludes that the population is overstated (because the lower confidence limit is greater than $0) and that the misstatement may exceed the tolerable misstatement (because the upper confidence limit is greater than the tolerable misstatement). Only if the upper confidence limit were less than $10,000 would the auditor be able to conclude that any existing misstatement was not likely to exceed the tolerable misstatement.

The complement of confidence is risk. In statistical sampling there are two aspects of risk: detection risk, which is associated with the detection objective, and estimation risk, which is associated with the estimation objective. Both aspects and their related confidence levels are discussed in the following sections.

Calculating Confidence Limits

The calculations for a point estimate and confidence limits depend on the method by which the sample was selected and on certain data assumptions—for example, the assumption that an item cannot be overstated by more than its recorded value. A variety of evaluation methods are given in Arkin's *Handbook of Sampling for Auditing and Accounting*.

Three basic methods for evaluating statistical samples are presented next. The methods presented do not cover all situations, but they provide the auditor with the means to evaluate samples on an attributes basis for tests of controls and on a dollar value basis for substantive tests for overstatement.

Equal-Probability Sampling: Attributes Evaluation

Point Estimate

The point estimate of the rate of deviation in the population (D) is obtained by dividing the number of deviations (m) that occurred in the sample by the sample size (n). The formula is:

$$D\% = (100)(m/n)$$

For example, if three deviations are disclosed in a sample of 150 items, the point estimate is:

$$\begin{aligned} D\% &= (100)(3/150) \\ &= 2.0\% \end{aligned}$$

Confidence Limits

The upper confidence limit (UCL%) of the rate of deviation in the population is obtained by dividing the upper confidence limit factor (ULF) in Table 1 by the sample size (n). The formula is:

$$\text{UCL\%} = (100)(\text{ULF}/n)$$

The appropriate row in Table 1 is determined by the number of deviations in the sample. The appropriate column is determined by the auditor's specified confidence level, which, in Table 1, is given as a one-sided confidence level.

A lower confidence limit is obtained in the same manner, except that Table 2 is used to obtain the lower limit factor (LLF). The formula is:

$$\text{LCL\%} = (100)(\text{LLF}/n)$$

For example, to obtain an upper 95% confidence limit for a sample of 150 that disclosed three deviations, first obtain the upper limit factor from Table 1 (ULF = 7.76). The upper limit is:

$$\begin{aligned} \text{UCL\%} &= (100)(7.76/150) \\ &= 5.17\% \end{aligned}$$

Thus, the auditor can be 95% confident that the population deviation rate does not exceed 5.17%.

To obtain a lower 95% confidence limit for the same sample outcome, obtain the lower limit factor from Table 2 (LLF = 0.81). The lower limit is:

$$\begin{aligned} \text{LCL\%} &= (100)(.81/150) \\ &= .54\% \end{aligned}$$

Thus, the auditor can also be 95% confident that the population deviation rate is at least 0.54%.

If the auditor wishes to express the sample results on a two-sided basis, he or she would be 90% confident that the population deviation rate is between 0.54% and 5.17%. (See the list given earlier for the relationship between one-sided and two-sided confidence levels.)

Dollar Value Evaluation

The following procedures are applicable to the most common type of substantive tests of details—the test for overstatement in an account balance or class of transactions. They may be used (1) for tests of the existence assertion, such as in the confirmation of receivables; (2) for tests of the valuation assertion, such as collectibility, lower of cost or market, or obsolescence;

or (3) for tests of the classification assertion. The following conditions should apply to the population:

1. The population does not consist of commingled debit-balance, or credit-balance, and zero-balance items. For example, if the auditor is testing an asset account, the population should consist only of debit-balance items.
2. The maximum amount by which an item may be overstated is its recorded value.

It should be noted that these data conditions are not unduly restrictive and are appropriate for testing the aforementioned financial statement assertions.

EQUAL-PROBABILITY SAMPLING: VARIABLES EVALUATION

Point Estimate

The point estimate of the amount of misstatement in the population ($M_\$$) is determined by (1) calculating the ratio (R) of the total overstatement misstatement in the sample (Σm) to the total book value of the sample (Σb), and (2) multiplying the ratio by the total book value (B) of the population from which the sample was selected. The formula is:

$$\begin{aligned} M_\$ &= (B)(R) \\ &= (B)(\Sigma m/\Sigma b) \end{aligned}$$

For example, three misstatements are disclosed in a sample of 150 items. The total misstatement in the three items is \$225. The total book value of the 150 items is \$15,300. The total book value of the population is \$1,492,000. The misstatement ratio R is:

$$\begin{aligned} R &= 225/15{,}300 \\ &= .0147 \end{aligned}$$

The point estimate of the total misstatement in the population is:

$$\begin{aligned} M_\$ &= 1{,}492{,}000 \times 0.147 \\ &= \$21{,}932 \end{aligned}$$

Confidence Limits

The upper confidence limit ($UCL_\$$) of the amount of overstatement misstatement in the population is obtained by dividing the upper confidence limit factor (ULF) in Table 1 by the sample size (n) and multiplying the result by the population book value (B). The formula is:

$$UCL_\$ = (B)(ULF/n)$$

The appropriate row in Table 1 depends on the sample total equivalent misstatement (TEM) (m'), which is obtained by multiplying the misstatement ratio (R) by the sample size (n). The formula is:

$$m' = (n)(R)$$

In the example the total equivalent misstatement is:

$$\begin{aligned} m' &= (150)(.0147) \\ &= 2.21 \end{aligned}$$

Locate the upper limit factor in the column of Table 1 that is headed by the desired one-sided confidence level. Note that it may be necessary to interpolate between two successive values of TEM. In the example, the 95% confidence ULF is 6.30 for m equal to 2. The ULF is 7.76 for m equal to 3. Thus, the appropriate ULF, obtained by linear interpolation, is 6.61. The calculation is:

$$ULF = 6.30 + (.21)(7.76 - 6.30)$$
$$6.61 \text{ (rounded off)}$$

The upper 95% confidence limit of the amount of misstatement in the population is:

$$UCL_{\$} = (1{,}492{,}000)(6.61/150)$$
$$= \$65{,}700 \text{ (rounded off)}$$

The lower confidence limit is calculated using the sample procedure, except that the lower confidence limit factor is obtained from Table 2. The formula is:

$$LCL_{\$} = (B)(LLF/n)$$

In the example, the 95% confidence LLF, obtained by interpolation, is 0.45. Thus, the lower confidence limit is:

$$LCL_{\$} = (1{,}492{,}000)(.45/150)$$
$$= \$4{,}500 \text{ (rounded off)}$$

Thus, the auditor can be 95% confident that the total misstatement in the population is no more than $65,700. The auditor can also be 95% confident that the total misstatement is at least $4,500. Furthermore, the auditor can be 90% confident that the total misstatement is between $4,500 and $65,700. (See the earlier list for the relationship between one-sided and two-sided confidence levels.)

It should be noted that to apply the foregoing procedure, the total book value of the population (B) must be known to be accurately footed, because both the estimate and the confidence limits are obtained directly from this number.

Table 1 Upper Limit Factors, *m* Deviations or Misstatements in Sample (*m′* Equivalent Deviations of Misstatements)

Deviations or Misstatements in Sample (m)	Confidence (One-sided)						
	99.5	99.0	97.5	95.0	90.0	80.0	75.0
0	5.30	4.61	3.69	3.00	2.31	1.61	1.39
1	7.43	6.64	5.58	4.75	3.89	3.00	2.70
2	9.28	8.41	7.23	6.30	5.33	4.28	3.93
3	10.98	10.05	8.77	7.76	6.69	5.52	5.11
4	12.60	11.61	10.25	9.16	8.00	6.73	6.28
5	14.15	13.11	11.67	10.52	9.28	7.91	7.43
6	15.66	14.58	13.06	11.85	10.54	9.08	8.56
7	17.14	16.00	14.43	13.15	11.78	10.24	9.69

Table 1 (*Continued*)

Deviations or Misstatements in Sample (*m*)	Confidence (One-sided)						
	99.5	99.0	97.5	95.0	90.0	80.0	75.0
8	18.58	17.41	15.77	14.44	13.00	11.38	10.81
9	20.00	18.79	17.09	15.71	14.21	12.52	11.92
10	21.40	20.15	18.40	16.97	15.41	13.66	13.02
11	22.78	21.50	19.69	18.21	16.60	14.78	14.13
12	24.15	22.83	20.97	19.45	17.79	15.90	15.22
13	25.50	24.14	22.24	20.67	18.96	17.02	16.32
14	26.84	25.45	23.49	21.89	20.13	18.13	17.40
15	28.17	26.75	24.75	23.10	21.30	19.24	18.49
16	29.49	28.04	25.99	24.31	22.46	20.34	19.58
17	30.80	29.31	27.22	25.50	23.61	21.44	20.66
18	32.10	30.59	28.45	26.70	24.76	22.54	21.74
19	33.39	31.85	29.68	27.88	25.91	23.64	22.81
20	34.67	33.11	30.89	29.07	27.05	24.73	23.89
21	35.95	34.36	32.11	30.25	28.19	25.82	24.96
22	37.22	35.61	33.31	31.42	29.33	26.91	26.03
23	38.49	36.85	34.52	32.59	30.46	28.00	27.10
24	39.75	38.08	35.72	33.76	31.59	29.09	28.17
25	41.01	39.31	36.91	34.92	32.72	30.17	29.24
26	42.26	40.54	38.10	36.08	33.84	31.25	30.31
27	43.50	41.76	39.29	37.24	34.96	32.33	31.37
28	44.74	42.98	40.47	38.39	36.08	33.41	32.43
29	45.98	44.19	41.65	39.55	37.20	34.49	33.50
30	47.21	45.41	42.83	40.70	38.32	35.57	34.56
31	48.44	46.61	44.01	41.84	39.43	36.64	35.62
32	49.67	47.82	45.18	42.99	40.55	37.72	36.68
33	50.89	49.02	46.35	44.13	41.66	38.79	37.74
34	52.11	50.22	47.52	45.27	42.77	39.86	38.79
35	53.33	51.41	48.68	46.41	43.88	40.93	39.85
36	54.54	52.61	49.84	47.55	44.98	42.00	40.91
37	55.75	53.80	51.00	48.68	46.09	43.07	41.96
38	56.96	54.98	52.16	49.81	47.19	44.14	43.02
39	58.17	56.17	53.32	50.94	48.29	45.21	44.07
40	59.37	57.35	54.47	52.07	49.39	46.27	45.12
41	60.57	58.53	55.63	53.20	50.49	47.34	46.18
42	61.77	59.71	56.78	54.33	51.59	48.40	47.23
43	62.96	60.89	57.93	55.45	52.69	49.47	48.28
44	64.15	62.06	59.07	56.58	53.79	50.53	49.33
45	65.35	63.24	60.22	57.70	54.88	51.59	50.38
46	66.53	64.41	61.36	58.82	55.98	52.66	51.43
47	67.72	65.58	62.51	59.94	57.07	53.72	52.48
48	68.91	66.74	63.65	61.08	58.16	54.78	53.53
49	70.09	67.91	64.79	62.18	59.25	55.84	54.58
50	71.27	69.07	65.92	63.29	60.34	56.90	55.62

Table 2 Lower Limit Factors, *m* Deviations or Misstatements in Sample (*m′* Equivalent Deviations of Misstatements)

Deviations or Misstatements in Sample (*m*)	Confidence (One-sided)						
	99.5	99.0	97.5	95.0	90.0	80.0	75.0
0	0.0	0.0	0.0	0.0	0.0	0.0	0.0
1	0.01	0.01	0.03	0.05	0.11	0.22	0.29
2	0.10	0.14	0.24	0.35	0.53	0.82	0.96
3	0.33	0.43	0.61	0.81	1.10	1.53	1.72
4	0.67	0.82	1.08	1.36	1.74	2.29	2.53
5	1.07	1.27	1.62	1.97	2.43	3.08	3.36
6	1.53	1.78	2.20	2.61	3.15	3.90	4.21
7	2.03	2.33	2.81	3.28	3.89	4.73	5.08
8	2.57	2.90	3.45	3.98	4.65	5.57	5.95
9	3.13	3.50	4.11	4.69	5.43	6.42	6.83
10	3.71	4.13	4.79	5.42	6.22	7.28	7.72
11	4.32	4.77	5.49	6.16	7.02	8.15	8.61
12	4.94	5.42	6.20	6.92	7.82	9.03	9.51
13	5.58	6.09	6.92	7.68	8.64	9.91	10.42
14	6.23	6.78	7.65	8.46	9.46	10.79	11.32
15	6.89	7.47	8.39	9.24	10.29	11.68	12.23
16	7.56	8.18	9.14	10.03	11.13	12.57	13.15
17	8.25	8.89	9.90	10.83	11.97	13.46	14.06
18	8.94	9.61	10.66	11.63	12.82	14.36	14.98
19	9.64	10.34	11.43	12.44	13.67	15.26	15.90
20	10.35	11.08	12.21	13.25	14.52	16.17	16.83
21	11.06	11.82	12.99	14.07	15.38	17.07	17.75
22	11.79	12.57	13.78	14.89	16.24	17.98	18.68
23	12.52	13.32	14.58	15.71	17.10	18.89	19.60
24	13.25	14.08	15.37	16.54	17.97	19.81	20.53
25	13.99	14.85	16.17	17.38	18.84	20.72	21.47
26	14.74	15.62	16.98	18.21	19.71	21.64	22.40
27	15.49	16.39	17.79	19.05	20.59	22.55	23.33
28	16.24	17.17	18.60	19.90	21.46	23.47	24.27
29	17.00	17.95	19.42	20.74	22.34	24.39	25.20
30	17.76	18.74	20.24	21.59	23.22	25.32	26.14
31	18.53	19.53	21.06	22.44	24.11	26.24	27.08
32	19.30	20.32	21.88	23.29	24.99	27.16	28.02
33	20.07	21.12	22.71	24.15	25.88	28.09	28.96
34	20.85	21.91	23.54	25.01	26.77	29.02	29.90
35	21.63	22.72	24.37	25.86	27.66	29.94	30.84
36	22.42	23.52	25.21	26.73	28.55	30.87	31.79
37	23.20	24.33	26.05	27.59	29.44	31.80	32.73
38	23.99	25.14	26.89	28.45	30.34	32.73	33.68
39	24.79	25.95	27.73	29.32	31.24	33.67	34.62
40	25.58	26.77	28.57	30.19	32.13	34.60	35.57
41	26.38	27.58	29.42	31.06	33.03	35.53	36.51
42	27.18	28.40	30.26	31.93	33.93	36.47	37.46
43	27.98	29.22	31.11	32.81	34.83	37.40	38.41

Table 2 *(Continued)*

Deviations or Misstatements in Sample (m)	Confidence (One-sided) 99.5	99.0	97.5	95.0	90.0	80.0	75.0
44	28.79	30.05	31.97	33.68	35.74	38.34	39.36
45	29.59	30.87	32.82	34.56	36.64	39.27	40.31
46	30.40	31.70	33.87	35.44	37.55	40.21	41.28
47	31.21	32.53	34.53	36.31	38.45	41.15	42.21
48	32.03	33.38	35.39	37.20	39.36	42.09	43.16
49	32.84	34.19	36.25	38.08	40.27	43.03	44.11
50	33.86	35.03	37.11	38.96	41.17	43.97	45.06

Point Estimate

The point estimate of the amount ($M_\$$) of overstatement misstatement in the population is obtained by multiplying the population book value (B) by the average item misstatement ratio (r). The misstatement ratio (r) for a sample item is obtained by dividing the amount of misstatement (m) in the item by the item's book value (b). Thus:

$$r_i = m/b$$

for each item in the sample. Note that r will be zero for most of the sample items in a typical audit application. This greatly simplifies the calculation of the average ratio r. The formula for the average misstatement ratio is:

$$r = (\Sigma r)/n$$

or the total equivalent misstatement (m), which is the sum of the item ratios divided by the sample size. The formula for the point estimate of the population misstatement amount is:

$$M_\$ = (B)(r)$$

Suppose the data of the previous example were obtained for a sample that was selected with probability proportional to size (that is, dollar unit sampling), instead of equal-probability sampling. The sample data follow:

Population book value (B): $1,492,000

Sample size: 150 items

	Item	Book value (b)	Misstatement amount (m)	Misstatement ratio (r)	
	1	183	37	0.20	
	2	452	185	0.41	
	3	3	3	1.00	
	4	95	0	0.00	
	–	–	–	–	
	–	–	–	–	
	–	–	–	–	
$n =$	150	214	0	0.00	
		$15,300	$225	1.61	$= m'$

The average misstatement ratio is:

$$\begin{aligned} r &= 1.61/150 \\ &= .011 \end{aligned}$$

The point estimate of population misstatement is:

$$\begin{aligned} M_\$ &= 1{,}492{,}000 \times .011 \\ &= \$16{,}412 \end{aligned}$$

Confidence Limits

The upper confidence limit ($UCL_\$$) of the amount of overstatement misstatement in the population is obtained by dividing the upper confidence limit factor (ULF) in Table 1 by the sample size (n), and multiplying the result by the population book value (B). The formula is:

$$UCL_\$ = (B)(ULF/n)$$

For any specified confidence level the ULF is determined by the total equivalent misstatement (m'), which, in dollar unit sampling, is the sum of the sample item misstatement ratios (Σr). The formula is:

$$m' = \Sigma r$$

If the calculated m' is between two successive values of m in Table 1, the auditor can determine the ULF by interpolation. In the example, m' is calculated to be 1.61 equivalent misstatements. The 95% confidence factors for one and two misstatements are 4.75 and 6.30, respectively. Thus, the interpolated confidence factor for $m' = 1.61$ is:

$$\begin{aligned} \text{ULF} &= 4.75 + (.61)(6.30-4.75) \\ &= 5.70 \text{ (rounded off)} \end{aligned}$$

Thus, the upper 95% confidence limit is:

$$\begin{aligned} UCL_\$ &= (1{,}492{,}000)(5.70/150) \\ &= \$56{,}700 \text{ (rounded off)} \end{aligned}$$

The lower confidence limit is calculated in the same manner, except that the lower limit factor is obtained by interpolating between successive values of LLF in Table 2. Thus:

$$LCL_\$ = (B)(LLF/n)$$

In the example, the lower 95% confidence factor is:

$$\begin{aligned} \text{LLF} &= .05 + (.61)(.35 - .05) \\ &= .23 \text{ (rounded off)} \end{aligned}$$

The lower confidence limit is:

$$\begin{aligned} LCL_\$ &= (1{,}492{,}000)(.23/150) \\ &= \$2{,}300 \text{ (rounded off)} \end{aligned}$$

The auditor can state, with 95% confidence, that the population overstatement does not exceed \$56,700. The auditor can also state, with 95% confidence, that the misstatement is at least \$2,300. Moreover, the auditor can be 90% confident that the actual population overstatement misstatement is between \$2,300 and \$56,700. (See the earlier list for the relationship between one-sided and two-sided confidence levels.)

AU-C 540 Auditing Accounting Estimates, Including Fair Value Accounting Estimates and Related Disclosures

AU-C ORIGINAL PRONOUNCEMENT

Source Statement on Auditing Standards (SAS) 122.

DEFINITIONS OF TERMS

Source: AU-C 540.07

Accounting estimate. An approximation of a monetary amount in the absence of a precise means of measurement. This term is used for an amount measured at fair value when there is estimation uncertainty, as well as for other amounts that require estimation. When this section addresses only accounting estimates involving measurement at fair value, the term *fair value accounting estimates* is used.

Auditor's point estimate or auditor's range. The amount or range of amounts, respectively, derived from audit evidence for use in evaluating the recorded or disclosed amount(s).

Estimation uncertainty. The susceptibility of an accounting estimate and related disclosures to an inherent lack of precision in its measurement.

Management bias. A lack of neutrality by management in the preparation and fair presentation of information.

Management's point estimate. The amount selected by management for recognition or disclosure in the financial statements as an accounting estimate.

Outcome of an accounting estimate. The actual monetary amount that results from the resolution of the underlying transaction(s), event(s), or condition(s) addressed by the accounting estimate.

OBJECTIVE OF AU-C SECTION 540

AU-C Section 540.06 states that:

. . . the objective of the auditor is to obtain sufficient appropriate audit evidence about whether, in the context of the applicable financial reporting framework

a. *accounting estimates, including fair value accounting estimates, in the financial statements, whether recognized or disclosed, are reasonable and*
b. *related disclosures in the financial statements are adequate.*

OVERVIEW

Estimation is essential in the preparation of financial statements. Exact measurement of some amounts or the valuation of some accounts is uncertain until (1) the outcome of future events is known, or (2) all relevant data concerning events that have already occurred are accumulated.

More and more accounting pronouncements require the use of estimates and fair value measurements when presenting and disclosing certain elements in the financial statements. Such measurements have become both increasingly complex and yet important for financial statement users. Because they involve uncertainty and subjectivity and because controls over them are more difficult to establish than controls over factual information, accounting estimates ordinarily are more susceptible to material misstatements. It is, therefore, necessary for the auditor to devote adequate audit resources to accounting estimates considering the degree of uncertainty and subjectivity, quality of controls, and other relevant circumstances.

REQUIREMENTS

RISK ASSESSMENT PROCEDURES

The auditor is required to evaluate whether the accounting estimates and disclosures in the financial statements conform with the applicable financial reporting framework. The auditor must also understand how management identifies items that need estimation and how management makes those estimates, and the data on which the estimates are based. (AU-C 540.08) The auditor uses the understanding of the applicable financial reporting framework requirements, knowledge of the entity's business and industry, and the results of audit procedures to evaluate the accounting for and disclosure of estimates. The auditor's understanding of the business is particularly important in certain cases, such as the following:

- When the asset or liability or the valuation method is highly complex, such as when valuing complex derivatives.
- When valuing items that may be affected by the entity's circumstances and operations, such as the valuation of intangible assets acquired in a business combination.
- When assessing the need to recognize an impairment loss under the applicable financial reporting framework. The results of audit procedures should also be considered when making this assessment.

An entity's internal control may reduce the likelihood that accounting estimates may be materially misstated. Aspects of control related to accounting estimates include the following:

1. Does management communicate the need for proper accounting estimates?
2. Are appropriate data on which to base the estimate accumulated?
3. Are estimates prepared by qualified personnel?
4. Are accounting estimates and supporting data adequately reviewed and approved?
5. Are past accounting estimates compared with actual results?
6. Has management considered whether the accounting estimate is consistent with its plans?

When the auditor documents his or her understanding of the entity's internal controls, he or she should document those aspects that are related to accounting estimates.

ENGAGING A SPECIALIST

The auditor should consider whether to engage and use the work of a specialist as evidential matter in performing substantive tests of material financial statement assertions. (AU-C 540.14) This consideration usually is part of forming an overall audit strategy. If the auditor decides to use a specialist, he or she considers whether the specialist's understanding of estimates and the method to be used by the specialist are consistent with those of management and with the applicable financial reporting framework. The auditor may discuss such matters with the specialist or read the specialist's report. The auditor should also apply the guidance in Section 620, *Using the Work of an Auditor's Specialist.*

MANAGEMENT'S INTENT AND ABILITY

The auditor should also evaluate the intent and ability of management to carry out specific courses of action where intent is relevant to the use of estimates, the related presentation and disclosure requirements, and how changes in estimates are reported in the financial statements. (AU-C 540.15) The auditor's procedures ordinarily include reviewing budgets, minutes, written plans, and other documentation, and making inquiries of management, corroborating management's responses as necessary, to evaluate:

1. Management's history of carrying out its stated intentions regarding assets or liabilities
2. Management's reasons for choosing a particular course of action and its ability to carry out the action in light of economic circumstances and contractual commitments

Valuation Methods

When the entity uses a valuation method, the auditor should evaluate whether the entity's measurement method is appropriate in the circumstances. The evaluation requires the use of professional judgment along with an understanding of management's rationale for selecting a particular method, obtained by discussing the reasons for selecting the valuation method with management. The auditor also considers the following:

1. Has management sufficiently evaluated and applied the required applicable financial reporting framework criteria, if any, to support the selected method?
2. Is the valuation method appropriate in light of the nature of the item valued and the entity's business, industry, and operating environment?
3. If different valuation methods result in significantly different estimates, how has the entity investigated the reasons for these differences in establishing its fair value measurements?

Consistency of Methodology

The auditor should evaluate whether the entity's method for determining estimates is applied consistently, and, if so, whether such consistency is appropriate in light of any changes in the entity's circumstances or environment, or changes in accounting principles.

If management changes the method for determining estimates, the auditor considers whether management can adequately demonstrate that the new method is more appropriate.

NOTE: An example of an appropriate change might be discontinuing an old valuation method when an active market for an equity security is created.

Use of Collateral in Evaluating Fair Value

If collateral is important in evaluating an investment, the auditor should obtain evidence regarding:

- The collateral's existence
- Its fair value
- Its transferability
- Investor's rights to the collateral

(AU-C 540.A56)

NOTE: Negotiable securities, real estate, chattels, or other property is often assigned as collateral for debt securities.

Auditor's Responsibility

The auditor is responsible for evaluating the reasonableness of accounting estimates made by management. (AU-C 540.18) The auditor should consider, with an attitude of professional skepticism, both the subjective and objective factors on which accounting estimates are based in planning and performing procedures to evaluate those estimates.

Identifying Circumstances That Require Material Accounting Estimates

When evaluating whether management has identified all material accounting estimates, the auditor should consider performing the following procedures:

1. Consider assertions embodied in the financial statements to determine what accounting estimates are needed.
2. Consider information obtained when performing other auditing procedures.
3. Ask management about whether circumstances exist that may indicate the need to make an accounting estimate.

The following are more detailed procedures:

1. *Read the financial statements.* The auditor should read the financial statements, including the notes, to determine if any elements, accounts, or items require an accounting estimate. The auditor's knowledge of the client's operations and industry help the auditor determine those components of the financial statements that require accounting estimates.
2. *Obtain information by performing other procedures.* By performing customary auditing procedures—reading minutes, inquiries, and substantive tests of account balances—the auditor may obtain information that might indicate the need for an accounting estimate. The auditor should evaluate this information, which includes the following:

    a. Information about changes made or to be made in the entity's business that may indicate that an account estimate is needed. For example, estimates must be made if the entity has disposed of, or plans to dispose of, a segment of the business.
    b. Changes in the process for accumulating financial information. Documenting the auditor's understanding of the entity's internal control would provide this information.

c. Information about identified litigation, claims, and assessments, as well as other contingencies. Inquiring of the client's lawyer and analysis of the client's legal expenses would provide this information (see Section 337, *Inquiry of a Client's Lawyer Concerning Litigation, Claims and Assessments*).
d. Information from reading available minutes of meetings of stockholders, directors, and appropriate committees.
e. Information included in regulatory or examination reports, supervisory correspondence, and similar materials from regulatory agencies.

In addition, other auditing procedures, such as confirmation of receivables and observation of inventories, might provide information about the need to reconsider the estimate for allowance for doubtful accounts or provide an estimate for inventory obsolescence.

3. *Make inquiries of management.* Throughout the audit the auditor makes inquiries of management. An inquiry should be made concerning the need for an accounting estimate.

In addition to the guidance provided by Section 540:

- Section 240, *Consideration of Fraud in a Financial Statement Audit*, states that the auditor should perform a retrospective review of estimates to respond to the risk of management override.
- Section 330, *Performing Audit Procedures in Response to Assessed Risks and Evaluating the Audit Evidence Obtained*, alerts the auditor that accounting estimates often are the source of significant risks.

NOTE: In evaluating whether all material estimates have been identified, the auditor considers the circumstances of the industry, the entity's method of conducting business, new accounting pronouncements, and other relevant internal or external factors.

EVALUATING REASONABLENESS

In evaluating reasonableness of accounting estimates, the auditor should do the following:

1. As a general rule, consider the historical experience of the entity in making past estimates and the auditor's experience in the industry.
2. Understand how management developed the estimate and whether there are any indications of management bias.
3. Based on the understanding obtained in item 2, the auditor should do one or a combination of the following:

   a. Review and test management's process for developing the estimate.
   b. Develop an independent expectation of the estimate to corroborate whether management's estimate is reasonable.
   c. Review subsequent events or transactions occurring before the completion of fieldwork.

NOTE: In evaluating reasonableness, the auditor should concentrate on key factors and assumptions that are:

1. *Significant*
2. *Sensitive to variations*
3. *Deviations from historical patterns*
4. *Subjective and susceptible to misstatement and bias*

Review and Test Management's Process

In evaluating the reasonableness of accounting estimates, the auditor may consider performing the following procedures:

1. Identify the sources of information that management used in forming the assumptions, and consider whether the information is reliable and sufficient for the purpose based on information gathered in other audit tests.
2. Evaluate whether the assumptions are consistent with one another, the supporting data, and relevant historical data.

NOTE: The auditor should consider whether management used available market information in developing assumptions.

---

3. Analyze historical data used in developing the assumptions to assess its comparability and consistency with data of the period under audit, and determine whether it is sufficiently reliable for the purpose.
4. Consider whether changes in the business or industry may cause other factors to significantly affect the assumptions.
5. Review available documentation of the assumptions used to develop the accounting estimates, and inquire about any of the entity's other plans, goals, and objectives, as well as considering their relationship to the assumptions.
6. Test the calculations used to translate the assumptions and key factors into the accounting estimate.
7. Consider whether there are more appropriate ways to translate assumptions into estimates.
8. Consider obtaining the opinion of a specialist regarding certain assumptions (see Section 620, *Using the Work of an Auditor's Specialist*).

The auditor should also consider the following when obtaining an understanding of the entity's process for determining estimates and disclosures:

1. General considerations, including:
   a. The role of information technology in the process
   b. The types of accounts or transactions requiring estimates (e.g., do the accounts consist of routine recurring transactions or unusual transactions?)
   c. Whether the entity uses a service organization
2. Information about controls over:
   a. The process for determining estimates, including data controls and whether duties are segregated between personnel responsible for committing the entity to the underlying transactions and those responsible for making the estimates
   b. The ability to change controls and security procedures for valuation models and the associated information systems
   c. Consistency, timeliness, and reliability of the data for valuation models
3. Information about the personnel involved, including:
   a. The expertise and experience of the personnel making the estimates
   b. Whether a specialist is used

Fair Value Considerations

Fair value of an asset, liability, or component of equity may be measured when the item is initially recorded or at a later date when the value of the item changes. The applicable financial reporting framework requires that certain items be recorded at fair value, but may provide for different treatments of changes in fair value that occur over time. For example, certain changes in fair value are reflected in net income, whereas others may be shown as an element of other comprehensive income.

The Nature of Fair Value Measurements

Fair value measurements, other than those with observable market prices, are inherently imprecise because such measurements involve uncertainty and are based on assumptions that may change over time. The auditor is responsible for considering information available to him or her at the time of the audit and is not responsible for predicting future conditions, transactions, or events that, had they been known at the time of the audit, might affect actions and assumptions underlying fair value measurements and disclosures.

Measuring fair value may be relatively simple for certain assets or liabilities, such as actively traded securities. For other items, fair value measurement may be much more complex and require the use of a valuation method.

Develop an Expectation

Based on his or her understanding of the facts and circumstances and knowledge of the client and its industry, the auditor may develop an independent expectation of the estimate by using factors and assumptions not used by the entity, and compare that to the client's estimate. Analytical procedures are a common method used in this approach (see Section 520, *Analytical Procedures*).

Review Subsequent Events

In evaluating the reasonableness of an accounting estimate, the auditor may review subsequent events to confirm the estimate or the appropriateness of the factors and assumptions used to develop the estimate or to obtain additional relevant information. For example, a loan that was 60 days past due at year-end might be 180 days past due near the completion of the audit.

Relation to Other Audit Procedures

Other audit procedures may also provide evidence about estimates and disclosures. For example, examining an asset to verify its existence may also provide evidence about the physical condition that would affect its valuation.

TESTING THE ENTITY'S ESTIMATES AND DISCLOSURES

Complex fair value measurements normally tend to be more uncertain, resulting from:

- A longer forecast period
- More significant and complex assumptions
- Greater subjectivity in the assumptions and factors used in the process
- Greater uncertainty as to future events underlying the assumptions used
- Less or no objective data when highly subjective factors are used

Examples of considerations when developing auditing procedures include:

- Estimates may be made at a date other than the required financial statement reporting date. When this happens, the auditor obtains evidence that management has accounted for any changes affecting the measurements that occur between the measurement and reporting dates.
- If collateral is a factor when measuring fair value, the auditor obtains sufficient competent audit evidence regarding the existence, value, rights, and access to or transferability of the collateral. The auditor should consider whether all appropriate liens have been filed and whether the collateral has been appropriately disclosed.
- The auditor considers whether additional procedures are needed to obtain sufficient competent audit evidence about the appropriateness of an estimate, such as physically inspecting an asset to verify the current physical condition and the effect on fair value.

Tests of Significant Assumptions

When evaluating significant assumptions used by management, the auditor considers the following:

- Assumptions will vary depending upon the characteristics of the item valued and the valuation method used.
- Assumptions will be supported by different types of internal and external evidence, and the auditor evaluates the source and reliability of such evidence.
- Because assumptions are often interdependent, assumptions should be evaluated individually and as a whole. Auditors should be alert to the fact that an assumption can appear reasonable when considered individually but not when considered along with other assumptions.
- The valuation may be sensitive to changes in significant assumptions, such as market conditions. If necessary, the auditor encourages management to use sensitivity analysis or other techniques to identify sensitive assumptions. If management does not do so, the auditor should consider whether to employ such techniques.
- If assumptions are based on historical information, the auditor should consider whether that basis is justified.

Assumptions should be realistic and consistent with:

- The overall economic climate, the economic climate of the industry, the entity's own economic circumstances, and market information
- The entity's plans
- Prior period assumptions, if still appropriate, and any applicable past experience
- Risk related to cash flows, including possible variations in the amount and timing of cash flows and the effect on the discount rate, if applicable
- The extent to which management relies on historical financial information and whether such reliance is appropriate
- Any other financial statement matters, such as assumptions used for other types of accounting estimates

The auditor may also compare estimates from prior periods to help evaluate the reliability of the entity's process for making such measurements. If variances from prior period measurements exist, the auditor considers whether they result from changes in market or economic circumstances.

Testing the Valuation Model

The auditor does not function as an appraiser and does not substitute his or her judgment for management's when evaluating valuation models. Instead, the auditor should review the model and determine whether:

- The assumptions are reasonable.
- The model is appropriate for that entity.

NOTE: Section 540 notes that an example of where a method might not be appropriate is the use of discounted cash flows by a start-up entity for valuing an equity investment if there is no current revenue stream on which to base future forecasts of earnings or cash flows.

ILLUSTRATION

The following list is taken from the Section 540 Appendix. It is not all-inclusive.

ILLUSTRATION 1. EXAMPLES OF ACCOUNTING ESTIMATES (FROM AU-C 540.A136)

Receivables:

Uncollectible receivables
Allowance for loan losses
Uncollectible pledges

Inventories:

Obsolete inventory
Net realizable value of inventories where future selling prices and future costs are involved
Losses on purchase commitments

Financial instruments:

Valuation of securities
Trading vs. investment security classification
Probability of high correlation of a hedge
Sales of securities with puts and calls

Productive facilities, natural resources, and intangibles:

Useful lives and residual values
Depreciation and amortization methods
Recoverability of costs
Recoverable reserves

Accruals:

Property and casualty insurance company loss reserves
Compensation in stock option plans and deferred plans
Warranty claims
Taxes on real and personal property
Renegotiation refunds
Actuarial assumptions in pension costs

Revenues:

Airline passenger revenue
Subscription income
Freight and cargo revenue
Dues income
Losses on sales contracts

Contracts:

Revenue to be earned
Costs to be incurred
Percent of completion

Leases:

Initial direct costs
Executory costs

Litigation:

Probability of loss
Amount of loss

Rates:

Annual effective tax rate in interim reporting
Imputed interest rates on receivables and payables
Gross profit rates under program method of accounting

Other:

Losses and net realizable value on disposal of segment or restructuring of a business
Fair values in nonmonetary exchanges
Interim period costs in interim reporting
Current values in personal financial statements

RESPONDING TO THE ASSESSED RISKS OF MATERIAL MISSTATEMENT

Based on the auditor's assessment of the risk of material misstatement, the auditor should test the entity's accounting estimates and disclosures. The nature, timing, and extent of audit procedures may vary widely because of differences in the complexity of estimates and levels of the risk of material misstatement. Such substantive tests may involve:

1. Testing management's significant assumptions, the valuation model, and the underlying data;
2. Developing corroborating independent estimates; or
3. Reviewing subsequent events and transactions.

The auditor evaluates the following when testing the entity's estimates and disclosures:

1. Are management's assumptions reasonable and consistent with market information?
2. Was the value determined using an appropriate model?
3. Did management use relevant and reasonably available information?

The auditor should evaluate whether management's significant assumptions, taken individually and as a whole, provide a reasonable basis for the entity's estimates and disclosures. The auditor pays particular attention to significant assumptions that support complex valuation methods and considers whether they are reasonable and consistent with market information. The auditor should keep in mind, however, that he or she is not required to obtain evidence to provide an opinion on the assumptions, but rather to evaluate whether such assumptions provide a reasonable basis for the estimates in the context of the audit.

The auditor should test the data used in preparing the estimates and disclosures and evaluate whether the estimates have been properly determined from the data and assumptions. The auditor evaluates whether the data are accurate, complete, and relevant. The auditor also evaluates whether the data and management's assumptions support the measurements. Such tests of data may include:

- Verification of the data's source
- Mathematical recomputation of inputs
- Review of the consistency of information, including consistency with management's intent and ability to carry out planned actions

Developing Corroborating Independent Estimates

If the auditor decides to develop an independent estimate to corroborate management's estimate, the auditor evaluates management's assumptions. The auditor may decide to develop his or her own assumptions to make a comparison with management's estimates. However, the auditor should still understand and evaluate management's assumptions. This understanding will help to ensure that the auditor's independent estimate considers all significant variables, and will help in evaluating significant differences in the auditor's estimate and management's estimate. The auditor should also test the data that management uses to develop the estimates, as discussed previously.

Reviewing Subsequent Events and Transactions

Subsequent events and transactions that reflect circumstances existing at the balance sheet date may substantiate estimates and reduce the need to apply other audit procedures to substantiate the measurements. However, if subsequent events or transactions reflect changes in circumstances occurring after the balance sheet date, then such events are not competent evidence of the estimates at the balance sheet date.

NOTE: For example, a change in the price of an equity security with an active market change reflects a change in circumstances and would not provide competent evidence of the fair value measurement of the security at the balance sheet date. The section notes that this consideration of subsequent events is a substantive test and differs from the review of subsequent events in Section 560, Subsequent Events.

Disclosures

The auditor should evaluate whether the entity's disclosures related to estimates are adequate and are in conformity with the applicable financial reporting framework. (AU-C 540.19) The auditor would use essentially the same procedures to audit the estimate disclosures as are used in auditing estimates in the financial statements. The auditor obtains sufficient competent audit evidence that the valuation principles are appropriate and consistently applied, and that the valuation method and significant assumptions used are properly disclosed as required by the applicable financial reporting framework.

When evaluating the adequacy of disclosure, the auditor considers whether disclosures of items with a high degree of measurement uncertainty sufficiently inform users of this uncertainty.

When estimates required under the applicable financial reporting framework are not included because it is not practicable to reliably determine the amount, the auditor evaluates whether the disclosures in these circumstances are adequate or the lack of disclosure causes the financial statements to be materially misstated.

Voluntary Information Presented

The entity may include information not required by the applicable financial reporting framework but that provides useful information to the stakeholders. In that case, the auditor should obtain sufficient audit evidence about whether the disclosures are in accordance with the requirements of the applicable financial reporting framework. (AU-C 540.A128)

Written Representations

In accordance with Section 580, the auditor should obtain written representations from management about whether significant assumptions are reasonable and whether they appropriately reflect management's intent and ability to carry out specific courses of action relevant to the use of estimates and disclosures. (AU-C 540.A126)

Communication with Audit Committees

Section 260, *The Auditor's Communication with Those Charged with Governance*, requires that certain significant accounting estimates be communicated to those charged with governance. The auditor should determine that those charged with governance are informed about management's process for formulating sensitive accounting estimates, including fair value estimates, and the basis for the auditor's conclusions about those estimates. (AU 540.A127)

The auditor may consider communicating:

- The nature of significant assumptions underlying fair value measurements
- The subjectivity of the assumptions
- The materiality of the measurements to the financial statements as a whole

Only Required Information Presented

Assuming no audit report modifications are needed, the auditor may issue a standard audit report. The auditor may elect to add an emphasis-of-matter paragraph calling attention to the nature and possible range of fair values. (AU-C 540.A120) If required information is not presented, the auditor should look to the guidance in AU-C 700.A33.

DOCUMENTATION

The auditor should document any indicators of bias on the part of management. For those estimates giving rise to significant risks, the auditor should document the basis for his or her conclusions about the reasonableness of those estimates and their disclosures in the financial statements. (AU-C 540.22)

MANAGEMENT'S RESPONSIBILITIES

In applying procedures to identify circumstances that require accounting estimates and to evaluate the reasonableness of the estimates, the auditor should be aware of the entity's responsibilities in the development of accounting estimates.

Management is responsible for determining the estimates and disclosures in the financial statements, including:

1. Establishing the process for determining estimates
2. Selecting appropriate valuation methods
3. Identifying and supporting significant assumptions
4. Performing the valuation
5. Determining that the presentation and disclosure of the estimates are in conformity with the applicable financial reporting framework

Developing Accounting Estimates

Management should establish the process for preparing accounting estimates. The process may not be documented or formally applied; however, it usually consists of:

1. Determining when accounting estimates are required
2. Determining the factors that influence the accounting estimate
3. Assembling data on which to base the estimate
4. Developing appropriate assumptions
5. Estimating the amount
6. Determining that the estimate is presented in the financial statements in conformity with appropriate accounting principles and that disclosure is adequate

If management's process for developing accounting estimates is documented, generally the auditor should review the documentation. If the process is not documented, the auditor should make inquiries of management to determine how management developed its accounting estimates.

AU-C 550 Related Parties

AU-C ORIGINAL PRONOUNCEMENTS

Sources Statements on Accounting Standards (SASs) 122 and 128.

DEFINITIONS OF TERMS

Arm's-length transaction. A transaction conducted on such terms and conditions between a willing buyer and a willing seller who are unrelated and are acting independently of each other and pursuing their own best interests.

Related party. A party defined as a related party in GAAP.

OBJECTIVES OF AU SECTION 550

AU-C Section 550.09 states that:

. . . the objectives of the auditor are to

a. obtain an understanding of related-party relationships and transactions sufficient to be able to

i. recognize fraud risk factors, if any, arising from related-party relationships and transactions that are relevant to the identification and assessment of the risks of material misstatement due to fraud.

ii. conclude, based on the audit evidence obtained, whether the financial statements, insofar as they are affected by those relationships and transactions, achieve fair presentation.

b. obtain sufficient appropriate audit evidence about whether related-party relationships and transactions have been appropriately identified, accounted for, and disclosed in the financial statements.

AU-C 550 is framework-neutral. It encompasses financial reporting frameworks in addition to US GAAP promulgated by the bodies designated by the Council of the AICPA, such as International Financial Reporting Standards, as well as special-purpose frameworks described in AU-C Section 800, *Special Considerations—Audits of Financial Statements Prepared in Accordance with Special Purpose Frameworks*. (AU-C 550.11)

Special attention to related parties has a long history in auditing. From the auditor's perspective, related-party transactions have two distinct, but not mutually exclusive, aspects: adequate disclosure and fraud detection.

The disclosure aspect is emphasized in FASB ASC 850. Some related-party transactions may be the direct result of the relationship. Without that relationship, the transaction might not have occurred at all or might have had substantially different terms. Thus, disclosure of the nature and amount of transactions with related parties is necessary for a proper understanding of the financial statements.

Inadequate disclosure of related-party transactions may result in misleading financial statements, so the auditor should be concerned with identifying such transactions in the audit and evaluating the adequacy of their disclosure. The auditor should also be concerned, however, with the possibility that an undisclosed relationship with a party to a material transaction has been used to fabricate transactions. That is, the transactions may be fraudulent or without substance. Section 550 clearly acknowledges the possibility that a related-party relationship may be a tool for fraud by management.

SAS 6 was issued in 1975 primarily in response to some spectacular fraud cases in which management's involvement in material transactions was obscured by either inadequate disclosure or outright concealment. The SAS was more disclosure-oriented than fraud-oriented, however, because fraud is the exception rather than the norm. Nevertheless, the auditor should be aware of the possibility of fraud. The SAS observed:

> *In the absence of evidence to the contrary, transactions with related parties should not be assumed to be outside the ordinary course of business.*
>
> *The auditor should view related-party transactions within the framework of existing pronouncements, placing primary emphasis on the adequacy of disclosure. In addition, the auditor should be aware that the substance of a particular transaction could be significantly different from its form.*

REQUIREMENTS

The auditor must perform audit procedures to identify, assess, and respond to the risk of material misstatement from failure to properly account for or disclose related-party items. (AU-C 550.04) Professional skepticism is especially important when auditing for related-party items. (AU-C 550.07)

ACCOUNTING CONSIDERATIONS

FASB ASC 850, *Related-Party Disclosures*, provides that:

1. Material related-party transactions other than compensation arrangements, expense allowances, and other similar items in the ordinary course of business should be disclosed. (Disclosure of transactions eliminated in consolidated or combined statements is not required in those statements.)
2. The disclosures must include:

    a. The nature of the relationship(s).
    b. A description of the transactions for each of the periods for which income statements are presented and such other information necessary to understand the effects of the transactions on the financial statements (including transactions to which no amounts or nominal amounts were ascribed).
    c. The dollar amounts of transactions for each period for which an income statement is presented. (The effects of any change in the method of establishing the terms from the prior period should also be disclosed.)
    d. Amounts due from or to related parties as of each balance sheet date presented and the terms and manner of settlement.

AUDIT PROCEDURES

An audit cannot be expected to provide assurance that all related-party transactions will be discovered. (AU-C 550.06) Nevertheless, the auditor should be aware of:

1. The possibility that material related-party transactions exist that could affect the financial statements
2. Common ownership or management control relationships that are required by FASB ASC 850 to be disclosed even though there are no transactions

A preliminary evaluation concerning the likelihood of related-party transactions is usually made during the planning of the audit when the risk assessment questionnaire is completed. This evaluation includes:

1. Obtaining an understanding of the structure of the entity and management responsibilities.
2. Considering the business purpose of the various components of the entity.
3. Considering the control consciousness within the entity and controls over management activities.

In determining the scope of work to be performed, the auditor should obtain an understanding of management responsibilities and the relationship of each of the entity's components to the total entity. The work performed should be sufficient to meet the objectives articulated earlier in this chapter.

The auditor should consider controls over management activities and the business purpose served by the various components. The auditors should specifically consider the susceptibility to fraud or error due to an entity's related-party relationships and transactions. (AU-C 550.13)

NOTE: Business structure and operating style are occasionally deliberately designed to obscure related-party transactions.

The auditor should recognize that the following transactions may indicate related parties:

1. Transactions to borrow or lend at no interest or at rates significantly different from market rates
2. The sale of real estate at a price significantly different from its appraised value
3. A nonmonetary exchange of property for similar property
4. Loans made with no scheduled terms for the time or method of repayment

(AU-C 550.A4)

The following are factors that the auditor should be aware of that may motivate transactions with related parties:

1. Is there a lack of sufficient working capital or credit to continue the business?
2. Does management have an urgent desire for a continued favorable earnings record to support the price of the entity's stock?
3. Is the earnings forecast overly optimistic?
4. Does the entity depend on one or a few products, customers, or transactions for continued success?
5. Is the entity in a declining industry with many business failures?
6. Does the entity have excess capacity?

7. Is the entity involved in significant litigation, especially between stockholders and management?
8. Are there significant dangers of obsolescence because the entity is in a high-technology industry?

(AU-C 550.A5)

NOTE: These are fraud warning signs or risk factors. The presence of one or more factors is not proof of fraud, but the auditor should increase his or her awareness of the possibility of fraud. If the risk is high, the auditor might increase the scope of substantive tests designed to identify undisclosed relationships or use some of the expanded procedures enumerated in Section 550. (See also Section 240, Consideration of Fraud in a Financial Statement Audit.*)*

Basic Approach

To identify material related-party transactions, the auditor should:

1. Identify related parties (through inquiry and review of relevant information to determine the identity of related parties so that material transactions with these parties known to be related can be examined).

NOTE: According to Section 550, the auditor should place emphasis on testing identified material related-party transactions.

---

2. Identify material transactions (consider whether there are indications of previously undisclosed relationships for material transactions).
3. Examine identified material related-party transactions.

(AU-C 550.14)

NOTE: In Section 550 the procedures are grouped essentially in the preceding categories. In the following discussion, a different grouping is used to emphasize distinctions between specific procedures for related parties and general procedures.

Specific Procedures for Identifying Related Parties

Related-party transactions and similar transactions that require disclosure may be classified as follows:

1. Those recognized in the accounting records
2. No-charge transactions
3. Those that create economic dependence

Related-Party Transactions Recognized in the Accounting Records

To identify these transactions, specific audit procedures are necessary. These procedures were described in "Requirements" and are listed in the related-party checklist in the "Illustration" section later in this chapter.

No-Charge Transactions

Sometimes a related party provides services that are not given accounting recognition. Examples of these services are the following:

1. Accounting and managerial
2. Credit and collection
3. Professional

To identify no-charge transactions, the auditor should compare expenses with sales and investigate deviations from:

1. Industry standards
2. Prior year

These are essentially analytical procedures (see Section 520, *Analytical Procedures*).

Transactions That Create Economic Dependence

FAS ASC 850 does not address the issue of economic dependence. Related parties do not exist solely because one party is economically dependent on another. If one party exercises significant influence over the other, however, a related-party situation does exist and should be disclosed. In situations where economic dependence does not create related parties, disclosure may still be necessary to keep the financial statements from being misleading.

Section 550 includes some procedures performed solely for the purpose of identifying related parties or related-party transactions, including items that should be addressed in discussions with the audit team.

1. Inquire of management:
   a. Names of all related parties and the nature of the relationships between the entity and those related parties,
   b. Whether there were any transactions with these parties during the period, and
   c. Whether the entity has procedures for identifying and properly accounting for related-party transactions, authorizing and approving significant transactions with related parties and those outside the normal course of business; if so, evaluate these procedures. (AU-C 550.15)

NOTE: This is covered in the written representations. It is helpful to give management the technical definition of related parties at the time of initial inquiry and in the letter.

---

2. Obtain the names of all pension and other trusts established for the benefit of employees and the names of officers and trustees of the trusts.
3. Review stockholder listings of closely held entities and identify principal stockholders.
4. Provide audit staff with the names of known related parties so that they can identify transactions with such parties. (AU-C 550.18)
5. For indications of undisclosed relationships, review the nature and extent of business transacted with major:
   a. Customers
   b. Suppliers

c. Borrowers
d. Lenders

6. Consider whether transactions are occurring but not being given accounting recognition, such as the client receiving or providing accounting, management, or other services at no charge, or a major stockholder absorbing corporate expenses.

General Procedures

The procedures in Section 550 for identifying related parties and for identifying transactions with related parties include several procedures that are usually performed in an audit. These are normal procedures performed for several purposes that may also identify related parties.

General procedure	*Relevance to related parties*
Review prior years' audit documentation.	Identify names of known related parties.
Review minutes of meetings of board of directors and executive or operating committees.	Obtain information on material transactions authorized or discussed.
Review confirmations of compensating balance arrangements.	Identify whether balances are or were maintained for or by related parties.
Review invoices from law firms for regular or special services.	Identify indications of related parties or related-party transactions.
Review confirmations of loans receivable and payable.	Identify whether there are guarantees and the nature of relationship to guarantor.
Review material investment transactions.	Determine whether investment created related party.
Review accounting records for large, unusual, or nonrecurring transactions or balances, particularly at or near end of reporting period.	Consider whether transactions are with related parties.
Inquire of predecessor, principal, or other auditors of related entities (this inquiry should be made at an early stage of the audit).	Obtain their knowledge of related parties or related-party transactions.

Procedures: Public Companies

Some procedures in Section 550 are relevant only for public companies:

1. Review filings with the SEC and other regulatory agencies for the names of related parties and for other businesses in which officers and directors occupy directorships or other management positions.
2. Review proxy and other material filed with the SEC and comparable data filed with other regulatory agencies for information on material transactions with related parties.
3. Review conflict-of-interest statements obtained by the entity from its management.

Procedures for Identified Related Parties or Related-Party Transactions

The auditor may identify related parties or significant related-party transactions that the entity had not previously disclosed to the auditor. In that case, the auditor should:

- Communicate the information to the members of the audit team,
- Request that management identify all transactions with those related parties,
- Ask why the entity's controls did not identify the parties or transactions,
- Perform substantive procedures,

- Reconsider the risk that other related parties or items have not been identified and perform appropriate procedures, and
- Evaluate the implications for the audit if the nondisclosure appears intentional. (AU-C 550.23)

When the auditor identifies a related-party transaction, he or she should analyze it to determine the following:

1. The purpose of the transaction
2. The nature of the transaction
3. The extent of the transaction
4. The effect of the transaction on the financial statements

To determine the preceding, the auditor applies normal auditing procedures and also may have to apply extended auditing procedures.

After a related-party transaction is identified, the auditor should apply substantive tests to that transaction. Inquiry of management is not sufficient. Procedures that should be considered are:

1. Obtaining an understanding of the transaction's business purpose.

NOTE: Until the auditor understands the business sense of the transaction, the audit cannot be completed.

---

2. Examining invoices, executed copies of agreements, contracts, and other pertinent documents, such as receiving reports and shipping documents.
3. Determining whether the transaction has been approved by the board of directors or other appropriate officials.
4. Testing for reasonableness the compilation of amounts to be disclosed or considered for disclosure.
5. Inspecting or confirming and obtaining satisfaction that collateral is transferable and appropriately valued.
6. For intercompany account balances:
   a. Arranging for examination at concurrent dates, even if fiscal years differ.
   b. Arranging for examination of specified, important, and representative related-party transactions by auditors for each of the parties with an exchange of relevant information.

NOTE: In the case of a group engagement, the component not audited by the group engagement team may have related-party transactions that are complex or unusual. In such a case, the group engagement team should request access to the component auditor's audit documentation concerning this matter.

Expanded Procedures

If the auditor concludes that it is necessary to fully understand a related-party transaction, he or she should consider the following procedures that might otherwise be unnecessary:

1. Confirm the amount and terms of the transaction, including guarantees and other significant data, with the other party.

2. Inspect evidence in the other party's possession.
3. Confirm or discuss significant information with intermediaries (banks, guarantors, agents, or attorneys).
4. If there is reason to believe that material transactions with unfamiliar customers, suppliers, or others may lack substance, refer to financial publications, trade journals, credit agencies, and other information sources.
5. Obtain information on the financial capability of the other party for material uncollected balances, guarantees, or other obligations.

Equivalence Representations

No representations need be made in the financial statements that related-party transactions were consummated on terms equivalent to those that prevail in arm's-length transactions. If representations are made that state or imply that, AU-C 550.25 requires that the entity be able to substantiate them. Thus, the auditor should consider whether there is sufficient support for such a representation, if made, and consider, per Section 705, the implications for the audit and on the audit opinion. (AU-C 550.A49)

NOTE: Lack of substantiation of representations made on equivalence of material related-party transactions should result in a qualified or adverse opinion because of a departure from GAAP.

Written Representations

Much of the information about related parties is obtained through inquiry of management. The responses to these inquiries should be formalized in the written representations from management (see Section 580, *Written Representations*).

If no related-party transactions occurred, a statement to that effect should appear in the written representations. If related-party transactions occurred, management should verify in writing that:

- It has disclosed to the auditor the related parties and all related-party transactions of which it is aware.
- It has accounted for and disclosed the related-party relationships and transactions.

(AU-C 550.A13)

The auditor should also consider obtaining written representations from the client's senior management and those charged with governance about whether they or other related parties engaged in any transactions with the entity.

ILLUSTRATION

ILLUSTRATION 1. RELATED-PARTY CHECKLIST

Checklist

Related Parties

[*Client*]

[*Audit date*]	[*Date completed*]	[*Reviewed by*]	[*Date*]

Instructions. This checklist is designed to assist the auditor in complying with the requirement that material related-party transactions be identified and evaluated for disclosure. This checklist is not meant to be comprehensive, and the auditor should tailor it for each engagement. If this checklist is not used, the audit program should include appropriate procedures for related-party transactions. This checklist does not apply to transactions that are eliminated in consolidation.

Many procedures performed for related-party transactions are normal auditing procedures executed during other phases of the audit. These procedures are indicated in this checklist by an asterisk (*).

Procedures for auditing related-party transactions involve the following:

1. Gaining an understanding of management's responsibilities, internal accounting controls related to management's activities, and the relationship of each component of the entity to the total business.
2. Obtaining knowledge of related parties and planning and executing the audit so that material transactions—individually or in the aggregate—with related parties are identified and evaluated for disclosure.

Part 1 of this checklist is concerned with the existence and identification of related parties and related-party transactions. Part 2 is concerned with the examination and evaluation of identified related-party transactions and the adequacy of disclosure of these transactions in the client's financial statements. Part 2 should *not* be done if Part 1 has been completed and it is concluded that no related-party transactions exist.

The "Inquiry of, W/P reference" column should provide the name and position of the client personnel queried and, where applicable, reference to the supporting audit documentation (working papers or workpapers), including client permanent files. If a procedure is not applicable, "N/A" should be placed in the "Inquiry of, W/P reference" column.

PART 1: EXISTENCE AND IDENTIFICATION

Procedure	*Performed by*	*Inquiry of, W/P reference*
*1. Review prior year's audit documentation for names of known related parties and related-party transactions.		
2. Evaluate client procedures for identifying, accounting for, and disclosing related-party transactions, including procedures established to monitor or avoid conflicts of interest in purchasing, contracting, or similar business activities.		
3. Review conflict-of-interest statements obtained by the entity from its management.		
4. For nonpublic entities, review stock certificate book or schedule of stockholders to identify principal stockholders.		
*5. Review material filed with the SEC, taxing authorities, and other regulatory bodies.		
6. Inquire about the names of related parties and whether there were transactions with them.		
7. Inquire about whether the client is under common ownership or management control with another entity.		
8. Obtain the names of all pension and profit-sharing trusts established for the benefit of employees, and the names of the officers and trustees and their trusts. (If the trusts are managed by or under the trusteeship of management, they are related parties.)		
*9. Inquire of predecessor auditor and principal auditor or other auditors of related entities about their knowledge of existing related parties and the extent of management involvement in material transactions.		
*10. Review the extent and nature of business transacted with major customers, suppliers, borrowers, and lenders for indications of previously undisclosed relationships.		
11. Inquire about transactions occurring but not being given accounting recognition, such as receiving or providing accounting, management, or other services at no charge, or a major stockholder absorbing corporate expenses.		
*12. Review confirmations or compensating balance arrangements for indications that balances are maintained for or by related parties.		
*13. Review confirmations of loans receivable and payable for indications of guarantees. If guarantees are indicated, determine their nature and the relationship of the guarantors to the client.		
*14. Review material investment transactions to determine if the nature and extent of the investments created related parties.		
*15. Review minutes of meetings of shareholders and those charged with governance for discussions or authorization of material or unusual transactions. (AU-C 550.16B)		
*16. Review large, unusual, or nonrecurring transactions, especially those recognized at or near the end of the period under audit and transactions outside the normal course of business. (AU-C 550.17) If appropriate, inquire about the nature of the		

Procedure	*Performed by*	*Inquiry of, W/P reference*
transactions and whether the transactions involved a related party.		
*17. Review invoices from law firms and other specialists for indications of related parties or related-party transactions.		
*18. Review life insurance policies acquired by the entity.		
19. In the audit team discussion, explore the nature and extent of the entity's related parties and related-party transactions, including how related parties may be involved in fraud.		
20. Prepare or update a carryforward schedule of related parties and information on known continuing related-party transactions. Provide copy of schedule to audit personnel and other auditors of related entities.		

PART 2: EXAMINATION AND EVALUATION

(To be filled out only if Part 1 indicates the existence of related-party transactions.)

Procedure	*Performed by*	*Inquiry of, W/P reference*
1. Obtain an understanding of the business purpose of the transactions. If necessary, consult with attorney or other specialist.		
2. Examine invoices, agreements, contracts (especially significant contracts renegotiated during the period), and other relevant documents, such as receiving reports and shipping documents.		
3. Determine that the transactions have been authorized by the appropriate party.		
4. Arrange for audits of intercompany account balances at the same date.		
5. Arrange for the examination of specific related-party transactions by auditors for each of the parties and for the exchange of relevant information.		
6. Inspect or confirm collateral received in connection with related-party transactions, and obtain satisfaction regarding the value and transferability of the collateral.		
7. To understand fully a specific related-party transaction, consider doing the following:		
a. Confirm transaction amounts and terms, including guarantees and other significant data, with other parties to the transaction.		
b. Inspect evidence in the possession of other parties to the transaction.		
c. Confirm or discuss significant information with intermediaries, such as banks, guarantors, agents, or lawyers.		
d. Refer to financial publications, trade journals, credit agencies, and other sources if there is reason to believe that unfamiliar customers, suppliers, or other business enterprises with which material amounts of business have been transacted may lack substance.		

Procedure	*Performed by*	*Inquiry of, W/P reference*
e. For material uncollected balances, guarantees, and other obligations, obtain information about the financial capability of other parties to the transaction.		
8. Review reports of the internal audit function.		
9. Recompute the compilation of amounts to be disclosed.		
10. Determine that the financial statements adequately disclose related-party transactions.		

AU-C 560 Subsequent Events and Subsequently Discovered Facts

AU-C ORIGINAL PRONOUNCEMENT

Source Statement on Auditing Standards (SAS) 122.

DEFINITIONS OF TERMS

Source: AU-C 560.07

Date of the auditor's report. The date that the auditor dates the report on the financial statements, in accordance with Section 700 (Ref: par. .A14).

Date of the financial statements. The date of the end of the latest period covered by the financial statements.

Subsequent events. Events occurring between the date of the financial statements and the date of the auditor's report.

Subsequently discovered facts. Facts that become known to the auditor after the date of the auditor's report that, had they been known to the auditor at that date, may have caused the auditor to revise the auditor's report.

OBJECTIVES OF AU-C SECTION 560

AU-C Section 560.05 states that:

. . . the objectives of the auditor are to

a. *obtain sufficient appropriate audit evidence about whether events occurring between the date of the financial statements and the date of the auditor's report that require adjustment of, or disclosure in, the financial statements are appropriately reflected in those financial statements in accordance with the applicable financial reporting framework and*
b. *respond appropriately to facts that become known to the auditor after the date of the auditor's report that, had they been known to the auditor at that date, may have caused the auditor to revise the auditor's report.*

Predecessor auditor. AU-C 560 also addresses situations where a predecessor auditor is asked to reissue a previously issued auditor's report on financial statements that are to be presented on a comparative basis. The predecessor auditor should perform specific procedures to determine whether the auditor's report is still appropriate. (AU-C 560.06)

OVERVIEW

Subsequently discovered facts. Before the issuance of SAP 41 in 1982, there was no authoritative guidance for auditors if, after issuing a report on the financial statements, they became aware of facts that existed at the date of the report that would have required them to change their report had they been aware of those facts. SAP 41 was a direct result of *Fischer v. Kletz*, commonly known as the *Yale Express* case.

In the *Yale Express* case, a large CPA firm did not promptly disclose material errors in financial statements covered by its issued report that were subsequently discovered during a consulting services engagement. The court rejected the contention in the defendant's motion to dismiss the case that an auditor has no duty to those still relying on the report to disclose subsequently discovered errors in that report. The case was settled out of court, however, and the precise nature and extent of an auditor's duty to those relying on a previous report were unclear. SAP 41 was issued to delineate the nature and extent of the auditor's responsibility.

AU-C 560 confirms the auditor's *continuing responsibility* for the validity of the report. It provides guidance on procedures the auditor should follow after the date of the report if he or she becomes aware of certain facts that may have existed when the report was issued.

Subsequent events. The date of the auditor's report is generally the cutoff point for important facts that arise after the date of the financial statements. Up through that date, auditors should apply procedures specifically directed to keeping informed about events that have a material effect on the financial statements. After that date, they cannot be expected to know of such events unless the information is brought to their attention. (AU-C 560.03)

Many financial reporting frameworks provide guidance on subsequent events. Those frameworks usually identify two categories of events:

1. Those that provide evidence of conditions that existed at the date of the financial statements, and
2. Those that provide evidence of conditions that arose after the date of the financial statements.

(AU-C 560.02)

REQUIREMENTS

SUBSEQUENT EVENTS

Auditing Procedures

The auditor's procedures should cover the period from the date of the financial statements to the date of the auditor's report or as near as practical to that date. For this subsequent period, the auditor should apply the following procedures to determine if all subsequent events that require adjustment or disclosure have been identified: (AU-C 560.09)

1. Understand management's procedures to ensure that subsequent events are identified.
2. Read minutes of meetings, held after the date of the financial statements, of management, owners, and those charged with governance. Ask about matters dealt with at meetings for which minutes are not available.
3. Compare latest interim financial statements with the financial statements being audited.
4. Ask management and, when appropriate, those charged with governance whether any subsequent event occurred that might affect the financial statements. For example, ask if:

a. Interim financial statements are prepared on the same basis as annual financial statements
b. During the subsequent period there were:
   1. Unusual adjustments
   2. Significant changes in:
      a. Capital stock
      b. Long-term debt
      c. Working capital
      d. Status of items accounted for on the basis of tentative or inconclusive data
      e. Existence of substantial contingent liabilities or commitments

(AU-C 560.10)

Accounting Considerations

If the auditor identifies subsequent events that require adjustment of or disclosure in the financial statements, the auditor must determine whether those events are reflected properly in the financial statements. (AU-C 560.11) The auditor should evaluate whether management has:

1. Adjusted the financial statements for any changes in estimates resulting from relevant events after the date of the statements but before issuance—*adjustment events.*

   NOTE: This is a nudge toward adjustment. That is, there is encouragement to adjust for events that affect asset realization or settlement of estimated liabilities. The only exception is changes in quoted market prices of securities, because the changes represent concurrent evaluation of new conditions rather than the culmination of existing conditions.

2. Disclosed events that occurred in the subsequent period that do not require adjustment but that require disclosure to keep the financial statements from being misleading.

   NOTE: A substantial amount of judgment is required in evaluating these events, but they usually involve significant changes in the composition or valuation of assets or liabilities presented in the financial statements being reported on, such as the issuance of bonds or stock, purchase of a business, or loss of plant or inventories from catastrophes.

Application Techniques

General

For subsequent events, the auditor is concerned about the following:

1. Types of events
2. Procedures for becoming aware of them
3. Their effect on the audit report

Types of Subsequent Events

Subsequent events may be classified as follows:

1. Require adjustment
2. Require disclosure

Require adjustment. Ordinarily, the following subsequent events require adjustment of the current financial statements:

1. Customer bankruptcy arising from other than the customer's major casualty subsequent to the balance sheet date
2. Investee bankruptcy arising from other than the investee's major casualty subsequent to the balance sheet date
3. Resolution of an uncertainty concerning loss contingencies or asset realization

Require disclosure. Ordinarily, the following subsequent events require disclosure in the current financial statements:

1. Issuing bonds or capital stock
2. Business combination
3. Loss of assets or decline in value of assets because of the following events occurring in the subsequent period:
   a. Expropriation
   b. Earthquake or similar event
   c. Major casualty such as fire experienced by customer or investee

Events that require disclosure may be presented as follows:

1. Explanatory information in the notes to financial statements
2. Pro forma (as if) financial information in the notes to financial statements
3. Pro forma (as if) financial statements on the face of the historical statements

Ordinarily, subsequent events that require disclosure are explained in the notes to financial statements. Sometimes the effect of this type of event is so significant, however, that disclosure should be made by using pro forma financial information or by presenting pro forma financial statements. In those circumstances, the pro forma presentation may be marked "unaudited."

Procedures

Specific procedures for becoming aware of subsequent events are in the checklist in the "Illustration" section later in this chapter. These procedures may be classified as inquiring, reviewing, and reading.

Inquiry. Get written representations from management and where appropriate those charged with governance (see Section 580, *Written Representations*) that includes information concerning subsequent events. (AU-C 560.A8)

In the letter to the client's lawyer (see Section 501), the auditor should make certain that he or she inquires about events that occurred up to the approximate date of the conclusion of the audit. When the inquiry is sent, the auditor will estimate the date the audit will end. If the response is received significantly before the audit report date, an updated response should be obtained.

Review. The auditor should review the accounting records for unusual material transactions from the date of the balance sheet to the date of the auditor's report. Records to be reviewed include the general ledger, the general journal, and other books of original entry.

The auditor should inquire about any subsequent unusual material transactions that come to his or her attention and determine their effect on the audited financial statements.

Reading. The auditor should read subsequent client minutes and financial statements.

Minutes. The auditor should read minutes of meetings of those charged with governance that occurred between the balance sheet date and the date of the auditor's report. Items of concern include the following:

1. Issuance of debt or equity securities
2. Declaration of stock dividends, stock splits, and reverse stock splits
3. Debt modification
4. Refinancing of short-term debt with long-term debt
5. Business combinations
6. Disposal or discontinuance of a segment
7. Reduction in carrying value of assets
8. Adoption of pension or profit-sharing plan
9. Approval of long-term commitments

Unavailability of minutes. Minutes for all meetings may not have been prepared by the completion of the audit. In these circumstances, the auditor should do the following:

1. Meet with the secretary of the entity or whoever is responsible for preparing the minutes.
2. Review notes of the person who will prepare the minutes.
3. Obtain a letter from the person responsible for preparing the minutes, confirming matters discussed and decisions made.

Financial statements. The auditor should read the most recent interim financial statements of the entity. He or she should compare these statements with those of the corresponding prior period and the current audited statements. Explanations should be obtained for material fluctuations.

Subsequently Discovered Facts Known to the Auditor before the Report Release Date

Auditor Action

After the date of the auditor's report, the auditor is not required to perform any procedures. However, the auditor may become aware, before the release of the report, of a subsequently discovered fact. If so, the auditor should determine its reliability, whether it existed at the date of the report, and whether the financial statements need revision. The auditor should discuss the matter with whatever level of management is appropriate, including those charged with governance, and ask how management intends to handle the matter in the financial statements. (AU-C 560.12) If management revises the financial statements, the auditor should perform whatever procedures are necessary. (AU-C 560.13)

If management has revised the financial statements, the auditor should decide whether to update or to dual date the report. If the auditor changes the date of the report to a later date, the auditor must extend the audit procedures discussed in the Auditing Procedures paragraphs in the "Subsequent Events" section earlier in this chapter and request from management written representations as of the new date. (AU-C 560.13a)

Dating the auditor's report. The report date signals the end of the auditor's responsibility for applying procedures specifically directed to obtaining knowledge of subsequent events. AU-C 700.41, *Forming an Opinion and Reporting on Financial Statements*, states:

The auditor's report should be dated no earlier than the date on which the auditor has obtained sufficient appropriate audit evidence on which to base the auditor's opinion on the financial statements, including evidence that:

a. The audit documentation has been reviewed;
b. All the statements that the financial statements comprise, including the related notes, have been prepared; and
c. Management has asserted that they have taken responsibility for those financial statements.

(AU-C 560.A10)

Dual dating the auditor's report. Because updating the report makes the auditor liable for reviewing for events occurring up to the new date, he or she ordinarily will dual date the report. (AU-C 560.A11) To limit liability and avoid extending his or her procedures, the auditor dual dates the report for the revision. Ordinarily, the revision is described in a separate note to the financial statements. The auditor should apply appropriate auditing procedures asking management if any other matters have come to its attention that would require adjustment or disclosure or if management believes any of the previous representations should be modified. (AU-C 560.13b) For example, if the subsequent event was the issuance of debt or stock, the auditor would examine documents pertaining to the issuance and accounting records recording the event. The auditor also would consider confirming the event directly with the other party to the transaction.

When the auditor's report is dual dated, the date of the report is presented in a manner such as the following:

> February 10, 20X1, except as to Note Y, which is as of March 31, 20X1.
>
> Where February 10, 20X1 is the date of the auditor's report and March 31, 20X1 is the date of completion of audit procedures limited to revision disclosed in Note Y. (AU-C 560.A13)

Management Does Not Revise Financial Statements

If the facts are discovered before the issuance of the report and management does not revise the financial statements, the auditor should modify the opinion. The auditor should express a qualified or adverse opinion in accordance with AU-C 705, *Modifications to the Opinion in the Independent Auditor's Report*. (AU-C 560.14)

NOTE: In this situation, if the auditor has not already done so, it is prudent to consult his or her attorney.

Subsequently Discovered Facts Known to the Auditor after the Report Release Date

Reissuing auditor's report. Sometimes, financial statements are reissued. The auditor generally has no responsibility to apply procedures to search for events that occur after issuance of the financial statements. However, sometimes events that are significant to the financial statements, but that occurred after the financial statements and audit report were originally issued, come to the auditor's attention. Events that occurred between the issuance date and the reissuance date do not require adjustment of the financial statements, unless the adjustment meets the criteria for the correction of an error or the subsequent discovery of facts existing at the date of the auditor's report. The auditor should discuss the subsequently discovered fact with management and those charged with governance, to determine whether the financial statements need revision. If the financial statements need to be revised, the auditor should ask how management intends to handle the matter. (AU-C 560.15)

To prevent financial statements from being misleading, subsequent events between issuance date and reissuance date might have to be disclosed. This disclosure may be labeled "unaudited" and does not require a change of date or a dual dating of the auditor's report. (AU-C 560.A16)

Management Revises Financial Statements

In the case of a subsequently discovered fact that causes management to revise the financial statements, the auditor should apply the procedures in AU-C 560.13 discussed previously. (AU-C 560.16a)

The auditor should advise the client to disclose the newly discovered facts and their effect on the financial statements to anyone known to be currently relying, or who is likely to rely, on the previously issued financial statements and the related auditor's report if the auditor believes there is anyone who would attach importance to the information. (AU-C 560.16b)

If the auditor's opinion on the revised financial statements differs from that which the auditor previously expressed, the following matters should be disclosed in an emphasis-of-matter or other-matter paragraph (see AU-C 708):

a. The date of the previous report
b. The type of opinion previously expressed
c. The substantive reasons for the different opinion
d. That the auditor's opinion on the revised financial statements is different from the auditor's previous opinion

(AU-C 560.16c)

The auditor should take whatever steps he or she believes necessary to satisfy himself or herself that the client has made the requested disclosures (see the section "Application Techniques" for methods of disclosure).

NOTE: Information about facts existing at the date of the auditor's report may come from many sources, such as:

1. *Tax engagements*
2. *Consulting engagements*
3. *Client executive or any other current or former employee of the client*
4. *Audit staff performing interim work*
5. *Unattributable rumors or an anonymous informant*

Management Does Not Revise Financial Statements

If management refuses to make the revisions requested, the auditor should notify management and those charged with governance not to make the financial statements available to third parties before the revisions are made and a new auditor's report has been provided. If the audited financial statements have been made available to third parties, the auditor should assess whether management has taken steps to inform anyone in receipt of the financial statements that they are not to be relied on. (AU-C 560.17)

If management does not take those steps, the auditor should notify management and those charged with governance that the auditor will try to prevent further reliance on the auditor's report. If management still does not respond appropriately, the auditor should take action to prevent reliance on the auditor's report. (AU-C 560.18)

Auditor Action

Parties to Be Notified

When the auditor has concluded that subsequently discovered information should be disclosed, some or all of the following might be notified:

1. Stockholders
2. Banks
3. Bond trustees
4. Major note holders, such as insurance companies
5. Major suppliers
6. Credit agencies
7. Securities and Exchange Commission (SEC)
8. Stock exchanges
9. Regulatory agencies
10. Other persons known to be currently relying or likely to rely on the financial statements and related auditor's report

Notification of parties other than the client is a serious step and should be undertaken only under the guidance of legal counsel. The requirement to notify applies only for persons actually known by the auditor to be relying on the financial statements and related auditor's report and not to persons that the auditor might infer could be relying on them. However, whether to notify and whom to notify should be considered with the advice of legal counsel. (AU-C 560.A23)

If the report has been released, unless his or her attorney recommends otherwise, the auditor should take the following steps when the client fails to make the requested disclosures:

1. Notify management and those charged with governance that the auditor's report is not to be relied on.
2. Notify regulatory agencies with jurisdiction over the client that the report should no longer be relied on.
3. Notify each person known specifically by the auditor to be relying on the financial statements that the report should no longer be relied on (see section on "Application Techniques").

(AU-C 560.A24)

Content of auditor disclosure to those in receipt of the financial statements. If the auditor determines that the information is unreliable and the client refuses to make appropriate disclosures, the auditor should disclose:

1. The nature of the subsequently acquired information and its effect on the financial statements
2. What effect the subsequently acquired information would have had on the auditor's report had it been known at the date of the report and not reflected in the financial statements

(AU-C 560.A25)

NOTE: The disclosure should be precise and factual and should avoid comments concerning the conduct or motives of any person.

If the auditor takes the steps described previously when the client refuses to make disclosures, and has not been able to determine the reliability of the information, the auditor should disclose that, if the information is true, the auditor believes the report must no longer be relied on or associated with the client's financial statements. (AU-C 560.A26)

NOTE: These disclosures should be made only if the auditor believes that the financial statements may be misleading and that the report should not be relied on.

REISSUANCE OF PREDECESSOR AUDITOR'S REPORT

Predecessor's Procedures

Before reissuing or consenting to the reuse of a report previously issued on financial statements of a prior period, when those financial statements are to be presented on a comparative basis with audited financial statements of a subsequent period, a predecessor auditor should consider whether the previous report on those statements is still appropriate. The predecessor should do the following:

1. Read the current period financial statements.
2. Compare the prior period financial statements that the predecessor reported on with the financial statements to be presented on a comparative basis.
3. Inquire of and obtain written representation from management about whether:
    a. Any information has come to management's attention that would cause it to believe that any previous representations should be modified.
    b. Any events have occurred subsequent to the date of the latest prior period financial statements reported on by the predecessor auditor that would require adjustment to, or disclosure in, those financial statements.
4. Obtain a representation letter from the successor auditor stating whether the successor auditor's audit revealed any matters that might have a material effect on, or require disclosure in, the financial statements reported on by the predecessor auditor.

(AU-C 560.19)

Based on these procedures, if the auditor becomes aware of a subsequently discovered fact, the auditor should discuss the matter with management and those charged with governance and determine whether the financial statements need revision and how management intends to handle the matter. (AU-C 560.20a)

Management may not revise the financial statements, or the predecessor auditor may not plan to issue a new auditor's report. In those cases, the predecessor auditor should determine if the audited financial statements have been made available to third parties and, if so, whether management is informing those third parties not to rely on the financial statements. (AU-C 560.20c)

Revision of Previously Issued Report

If the predecessor auditor concludes that the previously issued report should be revised, the updated report should disclose all substantive reasons for the different opinion in an emphasis-of-matter or other-matter paragraph in accordance with AU-C 706 requirements. The explanatory paragraph should disclose the following:

1. The auditor's previous report date.
2. The type of opinion previously issued.
3. The circumstances or events that have caused the auditor to express a different opinion.
4. That the updated opinion on the prior period financial statements is different from the opinion previously expressed on those financial statements.

(AU-C 560.20b)

Dating of Reissued Report

When reissuing the auditor's report on prior period financial statements, the predecessor auditor should use the date of the previous report.

If the predecessor revises the report or the previously reported-on financial statements are restated, the predecessor auditor should dual date the report.

ILLUSTRATION

The following pages illustrate a subsequent events checklist.

ILLUSTRATION 1. SUBSEQUENT EVENTS CHECKLIST

________	________	________
[Client]	*[Prepared by]*	*[Date]*
________	________	________
[Period ended]	*[Reviewed by]*	*[Date]*

Instructions

This checklist is designed to assist in complying with the requirement that a review be made of transactions and events occurring between the date of financial statements being audited and the date of the auditor's report. The purpose of the review is to determine whether transactions or events occurred that require adjustment of the financial statements or disclosure in the notes to the financial statements. If this checklist is not used, the audit program should include appropriate procedures concerning subsequent events. This checklist may be modified to fit the needs of a specific audit.

Subsequent events are classified as follows:

1. Events that provide additional evidence about conditions that existed at the balance sheet date and affect estimates in the financial statements. The financial statements should be adjusted for changes in estimates resulting from the use of this evidence.

NOTE: Events affecting the realization of assets, such as receivables and inventories, or the settlement of estimated liabilities, ordinarily result in adjustment.

2. Events that provide evidence about conditions that did not exist at the balance sheet date but arose subsequent to that date. These events, except for stock dividends, stock splits, or reverse stock splits, do not result in adjustment of the financial statements. Some, however, may require disclosure to keep the financial statements from being misleading.

Ordinarily, the review of subsequent events is limited to transactions and events occurring between the date of the audited financial statements and the auditor's report date. If there are circumstances in which significant time lags exist between those dates, however, the subsequent events review may have to be extended.

This checklist includes procedures to be performed before the release of the financial statements. These procedures should be coordinated with other auditing procedures, such as cutoff tests, confirmation follow-up, review of subsequent cash collections, and so on. In some circumstances, this checklist might be supplemented by supporting audit documentation.

For all procedures listed below, the "Completed by" and "Date" columns should be completed. The "Inquiry of" and "W/P reference" columns should include the name of the client personnel queried or a reference to supporting audit documentation. If a procedure is not applicable, "N/A" should be entered in the "Inquiry of" and "W/P reference" columns.

Procedure	*Completed by*	*Date*	*Inquiry of*	*W/P reference*
1. Read minutes of meetings of those charged with governance up to the date of the auditor's report.				
2. Read the most recent interim financial statements prepared after the balance sheet date and compare them with the financial statements being reported on, budgets and forecasts if available, and interim financial statements for the same period of the prior year.				
3. Review accounting records—general ledger, general journal, and other books of original entry—for unusual material transactions from the balance sheet date to the date of the auditor's report.				
4. Review reports of internal auditors prepared after the balance sheet date. If reports have not been prepared, inquire about the findings of the internal auditors.				
5. Inquire of appropriate executives about matters and events such as the following:				
a. The most recent interim financial statements				
(1) Accounting practices that differ from those in the financial statements being reported on				
(2) Components of operating results				
(3) Significant changes in working capital				
b. Property, plant, and equipment				
(1) Commitments for major additions or dispositions				
(2) New or modified leases				
(3) New or modified mortgages or other liens				
(4) Fire or other casualty losses				

Procedure	*Completed by*	*Date*	*Inquiry of*	*W/P reference*
c. Long-term debt and capital stock				
(1) New borrowings or modifications of existing debt				
(2) Early extinguishment of debt				
(3) Compliance with debt covenants				
(4) Stock conversions or conversions of debt to stock				
(5) Transactions involving equity securities, such as stock splits, stock options, and warrants				
(6) Declaration of dividends				
d. Personnel				
(1) Labor disputes				
(2) Adoption of new or amended employee benefit plans				
e. Contingencies				
(1) Status of contingencies existing at the balance sheet date				
(2) New contingencies				
(3) Notice of deficiencies from regulatory agencies				
f. Other				
(1) Significant sales, purchases, or other commitments				
(2) Unusual adjustments made subsequent to the balance sheet date				
(3) Negotiations or agreements involving business combinations or dispositions of corporate assets				
(4) Status of transactions with related parties entered into before or after the balance sheet date				
(5) New information about items in the financial statements being reported on that were accounted for on the basis of tentative or inconclusive data				
(6) Decisions that may affect carrying value or classification of assets or liabilities				
(7) Changes in lines of credit or compensating balances				
(8) Changes in financial policies				
6. Review letters received from entity lawyers in response to inquiries on litigation, claims, and assessments. If these letters are not dated close to the report date, consider whether it is necessary to obtain an updated letter.				

Procedure	*Completed by*	*Date*	*Inquiry of*	*W/P reference*
7. Review documents and financial statements provided to regulatory agencies, credit agencies, financial institutions, potential investors, and others subsequent to the balance sheet date.				
8. For documents prepared by the client that include audited financial statements and other information, read the other information.				
9. Review the written representations to determine that they include matters pertaining to subsequent events.				

AU-C 570 The Auditor's Consideration of an Entity's Ability to Continue as a Going Concern

AU-C ORIGINAL PRONOUNCEMENT

Source Statement on Auditing Standards (SAS) 126.

AU-C DEFINITION OF TERM

Source: AU-C 570.07

Reasonable period of time. A period of time not to exceed one year beyond the date of the financial statements being audited.

OBJECTIVES OF AU-C SECTION 570

AU-C Section 570.06 states that:

. . . *the objectives of the auditor are to*

a. *evaluate and conclude, based on the audit evidence obtained, whether there is substantial doubt about the entity's ability to continue as a going concern for a reasonable period of time;*
b. *assess the possible financial statement effects, including the adequacy of disclosure regarding uncertainties about the entity's ability to continue as a going concern for a reasonable period of time; and*
c. *determine the implications for the auditor's report.*

NOTE: The Statement applies in the audit of any type of entity. It is applicable to both profit-making and not-for-profit organizations. Thus, it would apply, for example, in the audit of a municipality. Also, the Statement applies to financial statements prepared using a general-purpose or special-purpose framework. However, it does not apply to liquidation-basis financial statements. (AU-C 570.01)

REQUIREMENTS

AUDITOR'S RESPONSIBILITY

The auditor's responsibility is to evaluate whether there is substantial doubt about the entity's ability to continue as a going concern for a reasonable period of time, not to exceed one year beyond the date of the financial statements being audited (i.e., the balance sheet date). (AU-C 570.08)

However, the auditor is *not* required to design audit procedures specifically to identify conditions and events that indicate a "going concern" problem.

Procedures Required

The auditor should consider whether the results of the usual audit procedures indicate that there could be substantial doubt. (AU-C 570.09)

Specific Procedures

The auditor's evaluation of whether there is a substantial doubt about the entity's ability to continue as a going concern for a reasonable period of time (not to exceed one year beyond the balance sheet date) is based on his or her knowledge of relevant *conditions* and *events* that exist at, or occurred before, the date of the auditor's report. It is not necessary for the auditor to design audit procedures specifically to identify conditions and events that indicate a going concern problem. *Regular auditing procedures are sufficient.* (AU-C 570.A1)

Regular auditing procedures that may identify conditions and events that indicate a going concern problem include the following:

1. **Analytical procedures.** Analytical procedures used as a substantive test or used in the planning and overall review stages of the audit may indicate:

   a. Negative trends
   b. Slow-moving inventory
   c. Receivable collectibility problems
   d. Liquidity and solvency problems

2. **Review of subsequent events.** Subsequent events, such as the bankruptcy of a major customer, confirm adverse conditions that existed at the balance sheet date. Other subsequent events that indicate a possible going concern problem include:

   a. Collapse of the market price of the entity's inventory
   b. Withdrawal of a line of credit by a bank
   c. Expropriation of the entity's assets

3. **Review of compliance with the terms of debt and loan agreements.** Violation of debt covenants results in debt default.
4. **Reading of minutes.** Minutes of meetings of stockholders, board of directors, and board committees may indicate:

   a. Potentially expensive litigation
   b. Loss of lines of credit
   c. Loss of a major supplier
   d. Changes in the operation of the business that could result in significant losses

5. **Inquiry of legal counsel.** Responses to inquiries of the entity's legal counsel about litigation, claims, and assessments could indicate possible significant losses because of product liability claims, copyright or patent infringement, contract violations, or illegal acts.
6. **Confirmations concerning financial support.** Confirmation with related parties and third parties of the details of arrangements to provide or maintain financial support may indicate loss of bank lines of credit or loss of third-party guarantees of entity indebtedness.

Indications of Going Concern Problems

Regular audit procedures such as those described above may reveal conditions and events that indicate there could be substantial doubt about the entity's ability to continue as a going concern for a reasonable period of time. Examples of these conditions and events (going concern warning signs or red flags) are:

1. Negative trends:
   a. Declining sales
   b. Increasing costs
   c. Recurring operating losses
   d. Working capital deficiencies
   e. Negative cash flows from operations
   f. Adverse key financial ratios
2. Internal matters:
   a. Chaotic and inefficient accounting system
   b. Loss of key management or operations personnel
   c. Work stoppages or other labor difficulties
   d. Substantial dependence on the success of a particular project
   e. Uneconomic long-term commitments
   f. Need to significantly revise operations
3. External events that have occurred:
   a. Legal proceedings
   b. Legislation or similar matters that might jeopardize operating ability
   c. Loss of a key franchise, license, or patent
   d. Loss of a principal customer or supplier
   e. Uninsured catastrophes such as drought, earthquake, or flood
4. Other indications of possible financial difficulties:
   a. Default on loan or similar agreements
   b. Arrearages in dividends
   c. Denial of usual trade credit from suppliers
   d. Noncompliance with statutory capital requirements
   e. Seeking new sources or methods of financing

Consideration of Management's Plans

If, after considering the conditions and events described above, the auditor believes there is substantial doubt about the entity's ability to continue as a going concern for a reasonable period of time, he or she should consider management's plans for addressing these conditions and events.

Management's plans may be classified as follows:

1. Plans to dispose of assets
2. Plans to borrow money or restructure debt
3. Plans to reduce or delay expenditures
4. Plans to increase ownership equity

Plans to Dispose of Assets

If management plans to dispose of assets, the auditor should consider the following:

1. How marketable are the assets that management plans to sell?
2. Are there any restrictions on the disposal of assets?
3. What are the possible effects of disposal?

Marketability of Assets

The auditor should do the following:

1. If the assets are securities, review market quotations to determine price and volume.
   a. If the securities are unlisted, review management documentation and correspondence with prospective buyer.
2. If the assets are intangible assets—patents, franchises, copyrights—review the following:
   a. Cash generated by the asset over the previous years
   b. Management's documentation of estimated sales price
   c. Correspondence with prospective buyer
3. If the assets are long-lived assets—property, plant, and equipment—review the following:
   a. Current market for the assets and current market value
   b. Management's documentation of estimated sales prices
   c. Correspondence with prospective buyers
4. If management contemplates sales of receivables to a financial institution, review the following:
   a. Allowances for doubtful accounts, and sales returns and allowances
   b. Management's documentation of estimated sales price
   c. Correspondence with financial institution
5. If the assets are a complete segment of the entity, review the following:
   a. Segment operations over previous years
   b. Management's documentation of estimated sales price
   c. Correspondence with prospective buyer

Restrictions on Disposal of Assets

Under certain circumstances, the entity may be prohibited from disposing of assets. If management contemplates disposal, the auditor should do the following:

1. Review all loan agreements.
2. Review mortgages, financing arrangements, and other asset encumbrances.

Effects of Disposal

The auditor should consider possible adverse effects of the proposed disposal of assets. He or she should:

1. Discuss with management the estimated effect of the disposal on the continuing operations of the entity.

2. Prepare pro forma financial statements of the entity, after excluding the assets that will be disposed of.
3. Analyze the pro forma financial statements to determine the effect of the disposal on operations and cash flows.

Plans to Borrow Money or Restructure Debt

If management plans to borrow money or restructure debt, the auditor should consider the following:

1. How available is debt financing?
2. Is collateral available and sufficient?
3. Are there restrictions on additional borrowing?
4. Are there existing or committed arrangements to restructure or subordinate debt or to obtain guarantees of loans to the entity?

Availability of Debt Financing

The auditor should do the following:

1. Review management's plan.
2. Determine if there are existing or committed arrangements, such as lines of credit.
3. Determine feasibility of factoring receivables. Consider the impact on operations of factor's fees and interest charges.
4. Ascertain the availability of assets for sale-leaseback arrangements.

Availability and Sufficiency of Collateral

If there is a question about an entity's continued existence, it is probable that it will not be able to borrow funds without collateral. The auditor should consider the availability and sufficiency of assets as collateral. Assets to be considered are the following:

1. Marketable securities
2. Receivables
3. Inventories
4. Property, plant, and equipment

Restrictions on Additional Borrowing

Existing loan agreements may prohibit the entity from borrowing additional funds. To determine this, the auditor should review:

1. Mortgage agreements
2. Bond indentures
3. Bank loan agreements

Existing or Committed Arrangements

If there are existing plans or commitments to modify existing loans or to guarantee existing or new loans, the auditor should:

1. Review management's plans for:

    a. Debt restructuring
    b. Subordination of existing debt
    c. Obtaining loan guarantees

2. Review correspondence and documents pertaining to the arrangements.
3. Confirm the arrangement with the other party—for example, the bank.

Plans to Reduce or Delay Expenditures

When a question arises about the continued existence of an entity, it is not uncommon for the entity to reduce or delay expenditures, such as the following:

1. Repairs and maintenance
2. Advertising
3. Research and development
4. Additions to property, plant, and equipment

If management plans to reduce or delay these expenditures, the auditor should:

1. Review management's plans.
2. Discuss with management the plan's effects on operations.

Plans to Increase Ownership Equity

When a question arises about the continued existence, it is not uncommon for the entity to offer equity capital to an investor. Also, it is not uncommon for investors to search for entities in need of additional capital.

Ordinarily, in these circumstances, the entity will sell its stock to the investor at a discount from market value. In certain circumstances, the investor may have plans to bring profitable businesses into the troubled entity to use the troubled entity's net operating loss carryforward. In these situations, the auditor should:

1. Review the plan.
2. Determine the tax consequences of the plan.
3. Determine the plan's impact on existing shareholders.
4. Discuss with management the adequacy of the investment.

The auditor's concern is that the funds will be sufficient to ease the liquidity problem and to provide sufficient working capital.

Consideration of Management Forecasts

The auditor is not required to examine management forecasts; however, he or she should read these forecasts and apply his or her knowledge of the client. The auditor should pay special attention to cash flows and the implementation of management plans. The auditor is interested in whether the forecasts provide a reasonable basis for the belief that the entity will still be in business a year from the current balance sheet date.

Obtain Management Assumptions

The auditor should ask management for its assumptions, especially assumptions about the following:

1. General economic conditions
2. Industry economic conditions
3. Sales
4. Cost of sales
5. Cost of labor
6. Expenditures for plant and equipment

7. Selling, general, and administrative expenses
8. Borrowings, interest expense, and extension of lines of credit
9. Income taxes, if any

Sources of Management Assumptions

The auditor should ask management for sources for its assumptions in developing the prospective data, especially assumptions that:

1. Are material to the forecasts or projections.
2. Are unusually uncertain or sensitive to variation.
3. Deviate from historical trends.

Possible sources for assumptions are the following:

1. Government publications
2. Industry publications
3. Economic forecasts
4. Entity budgets
5. Labor agreements
6. Sales backlog
7. Debt agreements

When the auditor reads management's assumptions, he or she may want to consider the following:

1. Historical trends of the entity
2. Historical trends of the industry
3. Comparison of prior year's forecasts with actual results

Internal Consistency of Assumptions

Management assumptions should be internally consistent. Examples of this internal consistency are the following:

1. There should be a logical relationship between net cash flow and the following:
   a. Sales
   b. Expenses
   c. Expenditures
   d. Receivables
   e. Payables
2. There should be a logical relationship between sales and the following:
   a. Cost of sales
   b. Labor
   c. Rent
   d. Advertising
3. There should be a logical relationship between income statement items and balance sheet items such as the following:
   a. Sales to receivables
   b. Cost of sales to inventories
   c. Sales to working capital

If the auditor has substantial doubt about the entity's ability to continue as a going concern for a reasonable period of time, he or she should:

1. Obtain information about management's plans to mitigate the problem.
2. Assess the likelihood of effective implementation of the plans.
3. Identify those elements that are especially significant to mitigating the going concern problem and plan, and perform auditing procedures to obtain evidential matter about those elements.

(AU-C 570.10)

The auditors should also obtain written representations from management about its plans to mitigate the problem causing the doubt and that the financial statements disclose all the matters that management is aware of relevant to the entity's ability to continue as a going concern. (AU-C 570.14)

Prospective Financial Information

If prospective financial information is significant to management's plans, the auditor should obtain that information and should consider the adequacy of support for the significant assumptions. The auditor should pay special attention to those assumptions that are:

1. Material to the prospective financial information
2. Particularly sensitive or susceptible to change
3. Not consistent with historical trends

The auditors should base their assessment on knowledge of the business, read prospective financial information and underlying assumptions, and compare that information to actual results from prior periods and results year to date. (AU-C 570.11)

Auditor Conclusions—Substantial Doubt Exists

If the auditor concludes that there is substantial doubt about the entity's ability to continue as a going concern for a reasonable period of time, he or she should (1) consider whether the condition is adequately disclosed (AU-C 570.12) and (2) modify the auditor's standard report by including an emphasis-of-matter paragraph. (AU-C 570.15) The auditor's conclusion should be expressed in the report using the terms "substantial doubt" and "going concern." (AU-C 570.16)

The auditor may also disclaim an opinion. If so, the emphasis-of-matter paragraph should not be used. Rather, the auditors should describe the reasons for the disclaimer as required by AU-C 705.18.

Disclosure might include the following:

1. Conditions and events creating the doubt, such as recurring operating losses, negative cash flows, working capital deficiency, and violation of debt covenants
2. Possible effect of conditions and events, such as a cutback in operations, a layoff of employees, or a bankruptcy filing
3. Management's evaluation of the significance of the conditions and events and any mitigating factors
4. Whether operations may need to be discontinued
5. Management's plans, including relevant prospective financial information
6. Information about recoverability or classification of recorded asset amounts or the amounts or classification of liabilities

The auditor should communicate to those charged with governance the nature of the condition or events identified, their possible effects on the financial statements, the adequacy of related disclosures, and the effects on the auditor's report. (AU-C 570.19)

EFFECTS ON THE AUDITOR'S REPORT

If the auditor concludes that substantial doubt exists about the entity's ability to continue as a going concern for a reasonable period of time, the auditor's standard report should include an emphasis-of-matter paragraph to reflect that conclusion. In these circumstances, the auditor ordinarily expresses an unqualified opinion (see the next section, "Disclaimer of Opinion"). The auditor's conclusion should be expressed using a phrase such as "substantial doubt about its (the entity's) ability to continue as a going concern." The report wording must include the terms "substantial doubt" and "going concern" and should be stated unconditionally.

The following (from AU-C 570.A6) is an example of an explanatory paragraph:

> The accompanying financial statements have been prepared assuming that the Company will continue as a going concern. As discussed in Note X to the financial statements, the Company has suffered recurring losses from operations and has a net capital deficiency that raises substantial doubt about its ability to continue as a going concern. Management's plans in regard to these matters are also described in Note X. The financial statements do not include any adjustments that might result from the outcome of this uncertainty. Our opinion is not modified with respect to the matter.

Disclaimer of Opinion

Instead of issuing an unqualified opinion with an emphasis-of-matter paragraph, the auditor may disclaim an opinion. The auditor should include an emphasis-of-matter paragraph articulating the reasons for the disclaimer. (AU-C 570.A8)

Inadequate Disclosure

If the auditor concludes that the entity's disclosures about its ability to continue as a going concern for a reasonable period of time are not adequate, the auditor's report should be modified for a departure from generally accepted accounting principles (GAAP). This may result in either a qualified or an adverse opinion. (AU-C 705.A1)

Prior Period Audit Report

The fact that the auditor is issuing a "going concern" report on the current period financial statements does not imply that a going concern problem existed in the prior period. Therefore, the auditor's report on prior period financial statements presented for comparative purposes with the current period financial statements need not be changed. (AU-C 570.A9)

AUDITOR CONCLUSIONS—SUBSTANTIAL DOUBT HAS BEEN ALLEVIATED

After considering management's plans, the auditor may conclude that substantial doubt about the entity's ability to continue as a going concern for a reasonable period of time does not exist. In these circumstances, the auditor should nonetheless consider the need to disclose the conditions and events responsible for the initial doubt and any mitigating factors, including management's plans. (AU-C 570.13)

NOTE: The absence of reference to substantial doubt in the auditor's report does not mean that the auditor is providing assurance about an entity's ability to continue as a going concern.

Subsequent Period Audit Report

The auditor may have issued a "going concern" report on the prior period financial statements that are presented for comparative purposes with the current period financial statements. If the going concern problem has been resolved during the current period, the explanatory paragraph included in the auditor's report on those prior period financial statements should *not* be repeated. (AU-C 570.20)

INADEQUATE DISCLOSURE

If the auditor concludes that the entity's disclosures about its ability to continue as a going concern for a reasonable period of time are inadequate, the auditor's report should be qualified or adverse because of a departure from GAAP, according to AU-C 705. (AU-C 570.17)

NOTE: The need to consider the adequacy of disclosure of going concern problems is independent of the auditor's decision to modify the audit report; that is, disclosure may be necessary even when the report is not modified.

ELIMINATING A GOING CONCERN EXPLANATORY PARAGRAPH FROM A REISSUED REPORT

An auditor may be asked by the client to reissue the audit report and eliminate the going concern paragraph. Such requests usually occur after the going concern matter has been resolved. The auditor has no obligation to reissue the audit report. However, if the auditor decides to reissue the report, he or she should:

1. Audit the event or transaction that prompted the request to reissue.
2. Perform the procedures in Section 560.
3. Consider at the date of reissue the conditions and events that related to negative trends, internal matters, external matters, and other indications of financial difficulty. Also consider at the date of reissue management plans, including prospective financial information, the financial statement effects, and the effects on the audit report.
4. Consider the implications for the auditor's report per AU-C 560.

DOCUMENTATION REQUIREMENTS

If, after considering the aggregate of events and conditions identified during the audit, the auditor believes that there is substantial doubt about the ability of the entity to continue as a going concern for a reasonable period of time, the auditor should document all of the following:

1. The conditions or events that led to the auditor's belief that there is substantial doubt about the entity's ability to continue as a going concern.
2. Those parts of management's plans that are particularly significant to overcoming the adverse effects of conditions or events.
3. The auditing procedures performed and evidence obtained to evaluate management's plans.
4. The auditor's conclusions about whether substantial doubt about the going concern issue remains.
   - If substantial doubt remains, document the possible effects of the conditions or events on the financial statements and the adequacy of the related disclosures.

- If substantial doubt is alleviated, document the conclusion about whether disclosure of the principal conditions and events that led the auditor to believe there was substantial doubt is needed.

5. The auditor's conclusion with respect to the auditor's report emphasis-of-matter paragraph. (AU-C 570.22)

ILLUSTRATION

The following checklist may be used by the auditor to assess his or her doubt about a client's ability to continue as a going concern and to evaluate management's plans for addressing the issue.

ILLUSTRATION 1. GOING CONCERN CHECKLIST

____
[*Client*]

____
[*Audit Date*]

Instructions

This checklist should be used in every audit of financial statements to assess whether there is significant doubt about the "going concern" assumption. It is divided into two parts. Part I should always be completed. Part II should be completed only when, as a result of completing Part I, the auditor concludes that significant doubt may exist.

If an item is not applicable, insert "N/A" in the Yes/No column.

Part I

	Yes/No	*Date*	*Comment*
1. Have audit procedures identified any of the following conditions or events that may raise a question about the client's continued existence?			
a. Recurring operating losses			
b. Working capital deficiencies			
c. Negative cash flows from operations			
d. Adverse key financial ratios, such as the current ratio and the quick asset ratio			
e. Default on loan or similar agreements			
f. Dividend arrearages			
g. Denial of usual trade credit from suppliers			
h. Noncompliance with statutory capital requirements			
i. Necessity of seeking new sources or methods of financing			
j. Loss of key management or operations personnel			
k. Work stoppages or other labor difficulties			

	Yes/No	*Date*	*Comment*
l. Substantial dependence on the success of a particular project			
m. Uneconomic long-term commitments			
n. Legal proceedings, legislation, or similar matters that might jeopardize entity's ability to operate			
o. Loss of key franchise, license, or patent			
p. Loss of a principal customer or supplier			
q. Uninsured catastrophe			
r. Other factors that create an uncertainty about going concern status			
2. Analyze the conditions or events identified in question 1 and conclude whether they raise a question about ability to continue as a going concern. (If the conclusion is "Yes," complete the procedures described in Part II.)			

Part II

	Performed by	*Date*	*Explanation or conclusion*
Consideration of Management Plans			
1. Discuss situation with management and determine plans for correcting conditions. Is management planning to:			
a. Dispose of assets?			
b. Borrow money or restructure debt?			
c. Reduce or delay expenditures?			
d. Increase ownership equity?			
2. Fill out appropriate section or sections below:			
Liquidate assets			
3. Inquire about marketability of assets.			
4. Inquire about restrictions on the disposal of assets.			
5. Inquire about effects on operations of disposal.			
Borrow money or restructure debt			
6. Inquire about the availability of new debt.			
7. Inquire about the availability of collateral to support new debt.			

	Performed by	*Date*	*Explanation or conclusion*
8. Inquire about restrictions on additional debt.			
9. Read management's plans for:			
a. Debt restructuring			
b. Subordination of existing debt			
c. Obtaining loan guarantees			
Reduce or delay expenditures			
10. Read management's plans for reducing or delaying expenditures for the following:			
a. Repairs and maintenance			
b. Advertising			
c. Research and development			
d. Property, plant, and equipment			
e. Other			
11. Discuss with management the effect on operations of the reduction or delay.			
12. Read management's plan to sell equity securities.			
13. Discuss tax consequences of plan with auditor's tax department.			
14. Inquire about plan's impact on existing shareholders.			
15. Discuss with management the adequacy of the investment.			
Management Forecasts			
1. Read management's assumptions about the following:			
a. General economic conditions			
b. Industry economic conditions			
c. Sales			
d. Cost of sales			
e. Cost of labor			
f. Capital expenditures			
g. Selling, general, and administrative expenses			
h. Interest expenses			
i. New borrowings			

	Performed by	Date	Explanation or conclusion
j. Income taxes			
2. Recompute mathematical calculations.			
3. Consider the internal consistency of the forecasts.			
Adequacy of Disclosure and Auditor's Report			
1. Consider the need to disclose the following:			
a. Conditions and events that created the doubt about continued existence			
b. Possible effects of significant conditions and events			
c. Management's evaluation of conditions and events			
d. Possible disposal of a component of an entity			
e. Management's plans, including relevant prospective financial information			
f. Information about recoverability or classification of recorded asset amounts or the amounts or classification of liabilities			
2. Consider the need to modify report.			
a. Add emphasis-of-matter paragraph.			
b. Disclaim an opinion (discretionary).			

INTERPRETATIONS

In August 2014, the Financial Accounting Standards Board (FASB) issued ASU 2014-15, *Presentation of Financial Statements—Going Concern (Subtopic 205-40): Disclosure of Uncertainties about an Entity's Ability to Continue as a Going Concern*. This ASU essentially, with some changes, mirrors going concern requirements for auditors currently found in Public Company Accounting Oversight Board (PCAOB) and American Institute of Certified Public Accountants (AICPA) standards. Now, management must perform at least annually an evaluation of the entity's ability to continue as a going concern.

Guidance. Management must evaluate, in the aggregate, conditions and events that are known or reasonably knowable at the evaluation date. Management must assess whether it is probable that the entity will be able to meet its obligations that are due within one year after the date that the financial statements are issued or available to be issued. The probability threshold is the same as that used for accounting for contingencies—more likely than not. When making the assessment, management may consider mitigating plans to determine whether substantial doubt is alleviated. These plans can be considered only if both of the following conditions are met:

- It is probable that the plan will be effectively implemented within the year.
- It is probable that the plan when implemented will mitigate the conditions or events that raise substantial doubt about going concern.

In order for these plans to be considered, generally management or those with authority must approve the plans before the issuance date of the financial statements.

Disclosure requirements. If, after considering all the facts and management's plans, management concludes that substantial doubt remains, the financial statements must include a statement that there is substantial doubt about the entity's ability to continue as a going concern within one year after the date that the financial statements are issued or available to be issued. The financial statements must also include disclosures that allow users to understand:

- Principal conditions or events that raised substantial doubt,
- Management's evaluation of the significance of those conditions or events in relation to the entity's ability to meet its obligations, and
- Management's plans to mitigate the conditions or events.

These disclosures must be made even if management concludes that the substantial doubt has been alleviated.

Implementation information. ASU 2014-14 is effective for annual periods ending after December 15, 2016 and for annual periods and interim periods thereafter. Early adoption is permitted.

In response, the Auditing Standards Board (ASB) issued three interpretations to AU-C Section 570 and found in Section 9570.

Interpretation No. 1, "Definition of Substantial Doubt about an Entity's Ability to Continue as a Going Concern" (Issued January 2015)

Entities should apply the definition of going concern in the applicable financial reporting framework.

Interpretation No. 2, "Definition of Reasonable Period of Time" (Issued January 2014; Issued January 2015)

Section 570 required the auditor to assess going concern based on a reasonable period of time, further defined as not to exceed one year from the date of the financial statements. However, Interpretation No. 1 above guides auditors to use the time period dictated by the guidance in the applicable financial reporting framework. Therefore, those auditing US GAAP financial statements should apply the guidance in ASU 205-40. That time period is one year from the date the financial statements are issued or available to be issued.

Interpretation No. 3, "Interim Financial Information" (Issued January 2015)

Section 930 contains guidance on an auditor's review of interim financial information. The interpretation clarifies that when performing those reviews the auditors should use the guidelines in the applicable financial reporting framework to evaluate management's evaluations and disclosures.

Interpretation No. 4, "Consideration of Financial Statements Effects" (Issued January 2015)

If the applicable financial reporting framework required disclosures not detailed in Section 570, such as in ASC 205-40, which requires management's going concern evaluation.

AU-C 580 Written Representations

AU-C ORIGINAL PRONOUNCEMENT

Source Statement on Auditing Standards (SAS) 122.

AU-C DEFINITION OF TERM

Source: AU-C 580.07

Written representation. A written statement by management[1] provided to the auditor to confirm certain matters or to support other audit evidence. Written representations in this context do not include financial statements, the assertions therein, or supporting books and records.

OBJECTIVES OF AU-C SECTION 580

AU-C Section 580.06 states that:

> *. . . the objectives of the auditor are to*
>
> a. *obtain written representations from management and, when appropriate, those charged with governance that they believe that they have fulfilled their responsibility for the preparation and fair presentation of the financial statements and for the completeness of the information provided to the auditor;*
>
> b. *support other audit evidence relevant to the financial statements or specific assertions in the financial statements by means of written representations if determined necessary by the auditor or required by other AU-C sections; and*
>
> c. *respond appropriately to written representations provided by management and, when appropriate, those charged with governance or if management or, when appropriate, those charged with governance do not provide the written representations requested by the auditor.*

REQUIREMENTS

RELIANCE ON MANAGEMENT REPRESENTATIONS

Management representation letters are audit evidence, and they serve to:

1. Establish and remind management that they are primarily responsible for the financial statements.

[1] *References to management in this section should be read as "management and, when appropriate, those charged with governance."*

2. Document representations explicitly or implicitly given to the auditor.
3. Reduce the possibility of misunderstanding.

Representation letters complement other auditing procedures and are not a substitute for those auditing procedures needed to support an opinion on the financial statements.

The representation letter should be obtained from those with appropriate knowledge and responsibility for the financial statements. (AU-C 580.09)

According to AU-C 580.23, if a representation made by management is contradicted by other audit evidence, the auditor should investigate the circumstances and consider the reliability of the other representations made. In this situation, the auditor should consider whether reliance on other representations made by management is appropriate and justified, and consider the effect on the opinion. (AU-C 580.24)

Obtaining Written Representations

The written representations should cover all financial statements and periods covered by the auditor's report. (AU-C 580.20)

NOTE: If the auditor is reporting on consolidated financial statements, the representation letter should relate to those statements. If the auditor is reporting on the separate financial statements of a component of a consolidated group, including the parent company, the representation letter should also relate to the separate statements.

According to AU-C 580.10-.18, specific representations in a representation letter for financial statements presented in accordance with the applicable financial reporting framework should cover the following (see "Illustrations" for an illustrative management representation letter):

Financial Statements

1. Management's acknowledgment that it has fulfilled its responsibility as detailed in the engagement letter
2. That management has fulfilled its responsibilities for the design, implementation, and maintenance of internal controls related to the financial statements that are free from material misstatements whether due to fraud or to error.
3. Management's acknowledgment of its responsibility for the fair presentation in the financial statements of financial position, results of operations, and cash flows in conformity with the applicable financial reporting framework
4. Management's belief that the financial statements are fairly presented in conformity with the applicable financial reporting framework

Completeness of Information

5. Availability of all financial records and related data
6. Completeness and availability of all minutes of meetings of stockholders, directors, and committees of directors
7. Communications from regulatory agencies concerning noncompliance with, or deficiencies in, financial reporting practices
8. Absence of unrecorded transactions
9. Management's belief that all transactions have been recorded and are reflected in the financial statements

Fraud

10. Management's acknowledgment of its responsibility for designing and implementing programs and controls to prevent and detect fraud
11. Knowledge of actual or suspected fraud involving (1) management, (2) employees who have significant roles in internal control, or (3) others where the fraud could have a material effect on the financial statements
12. Knowledge of any allegations of actual or suspected fraud made by current or former employees, analysts, regulators, short sellers, or others

Recognition, Measurement, and Disclosure

13. Management's belief that any uncorrected misstatements (a summary of which is included in or attached to the letter) are immaterial, both individually and in the aggregate
14. Plans or intentions that may affect the carrying value or classification of assets or liabilities
15. Information concerning related-party transactions and amounts receivable from, or payable to, related parties
16. Guarantees, whether written or oral, under which the entity is contingently liable
17. Management's belief that significant estimates are reasonable
18. Noncompliances or possible noncompliance with laws and regulations whose effects should be considered for disclosure in the financial statements or as a basis for recording a loss contingency
19. Uncorrected misstatements are immaterial
20. Other liabilities or loss contingencies that are required to be accrued or disclosed by the applicable reporting framework
21. Management's belief that all known or possible litigation has been disclosed and accounted for
22. Satisfactory title to assets, liens or encumbrances on assets, and assets pledged as collateral
23. Compliance with aspects of contractual agreements that may affect the financial statements

Subsequent Events

24. Information concerning subsequent events

Tailoring the Representation Letter

Ordinarily, the representation letter should also be modified to include additional representations from management covering matters specific to the entity's business or industry.

NOTE: Consult relevant AICPA industry audit and accounting guides for additional representations that are unique to a particular industry.

Materiality Considerations

Management's representations may be limited to material matters, provided management and the auditor have reached an understanding on materiality. Materiality may be different for different representations. Materiality may be addressed explicitly in the representation letter, in either qualitative or quantitative terms. Materiality considerations do not apply to items that are not directly related to amounts included in the financial statements—for example, items 1, 3, 4, and 5 under "Obtaining Written Representations." Likewise, materiality does not apply to item 9 for management and employees who have significant roles in internal control.

Addressing and Dating the Letter

The representation letter should be addressed to the auditor and should be dated as of the date of the auditor's report. (AU-C 580.20-.21) If the report is dual dated, the auditor should consider whether to obtain additional representations for subsequent events. (AU-C 580.A17)

Signing the Letter

The management representation letter should be signed by those in management with overall financial and operating responsibility who the auditor believes are responsible for, and knowledgeable about, directly or through others in the organization, the matters covered by the representations. Normally this includes the chief executive officer and chief financial officer or others with equivalent positions in the entity.

The auditor should obtain a representation letter from current management for all periods covered by the auditor's report, even if current management was not present during all such periods.

The auditor may also want to have other individuals provide written representations. For example, the auditor could obtain from the person responsible for keeping minutes of stockholders, directors, and committees of directors a written representation stating that such minutes are complete.

Doubt about Reliability of Written Representation

The auditor may have reason to doubt management's competence, integrity, or diligence in preparation of the written representations. If so, the auditor should determine the effect on the audit. The auditor may choose to perform additional audit procedures. If the concerns are not alleviated, the auditor should consider the effect on the opinion in the auditor's report. (AU-C 550.22-24)

Requested Representation Letter Not Provided

If management refuses to furnish a representation letter, the auditor should ordinarily issue a disclaimer of opinion in accordance with Section 705 because of the limitation on audit scope or withdraw from the engagement. (AU-C 580.26) If the auditor concludes that a qualified opinion is appropriate, he or she should consider the effects of the refusal in relying on other management representations. (AU-C 580.25)

If the auditor is precluded from performing necessary procedures on a matter that is material to the financial statements, even though management has given representations on the matter, the auditor should qualify the opinion or disclaim an opinion because of the limitation.

Representations Required by Other AU-C Sections

Other AU-C sections contain requirements for specific written representations that may not be required for every audit:

- AU-C 260, *The Auditor's Communication with Those Charged with Governance*
- AU-C 560.19, *Subsequent Events and Subsequently Discovered Facts*
- AU-C 700.52, *Forming an Opinion and Reporting on Financial Statements*

- AU-C 725.07g, *Supplementary Information in Relation to the Financial Statements as a Whole*
- AU-C 935.23, *Compliance Audits*

Certain AICPA Audit and Accounting Guides suggest written representations concerning matters that are unique to a particular industry.

AUDITOR'S RELATIONSHIP WITH A SMALL OR NONPUBLIC CLIENT

The *independent* auditor's relationship with a small or nonpublic client usually is closer than the relationship with a large or publicly held client. In these circumstances, the independent auditor may significantly influence *client* decisions, such as the following:

1. Depreciation methods
2. Accounting for start-up and similar costs
3. Accounting for revenues
4. Accounting for leases
5. Inventory valuation methods

Even though the auditor's influence may be significant, it is management's responsibility to decide whether to accept the auditor's recommendations. The representation letter is management's acknowledgment of this responsibility.

To avoid problems when the auditor asks management to sign the representation letter, he or she should consider some or all of the following approaches:

1. Describe management's responsibilities in the engagement letter.
2. Discuss accounting policies and choices with management during the year and at the end of the year.
3. Define technical terms that appear in the representation letter.

When the engagement letter is signed, it is advisable to tell the client that at the end of the audit management must sign a representation letter in which it acknowledges its responsibility.

Although it is important to agree about management responsibility at the beginning of the engagement, it is equally important to remind management of its responsibility during the year. (AU-C 580.A8)

Procedures during the Year

For the audit of a nonpublic client, the auditor usually is involved throughout the year. Decisions about accounting principles and methods are made during the year. For example, depreciation methods are determined, decisions are made to capitalize start-up costs and similar expenditures, and the method of accounting for various revenue streams may be established. In these circumstances, it is recommended that the auditor do the following:

1. Review the decision with management.
2. Explain to management the decision's effect on financial statements.
3. Document the decision.

NOTE: Include name of person who made the decision.

Procedures at End of Year

At the end of the year, the auditor should review with management the accounting principles applied during the year. The auditor should prepare a list of the accounting principles and explain their financial statement effect.

Before asking management to sign the representation letter, the auditor should review with it the draft of the financial statements, including the notes and the auditor's report. If the auditor has not prepared the notes and the report, he or she should tell management about their content.

Explicitly Addressing Materiality in the Written Representations

The auditor is permitted to reach an understanding with management on materiality, and then management representations may be limited to material matters, except for certain items. Materiality may be addressed in quantitative or qualitative terms. An example of a quantitative expression would be 3% of before-tax income. A qualitative expression would be, for example, a significant change in the trend of earnings or revenue. The Financial Accounting Standards Board's (FASB) definition of materiality from Concepts Statement 2 is applicable to both quantitative and qualitative aspects of materiality. The conceptual description used alone, if read literally, would permit management to omit items larger than would be quantitatively material based on qualitative considerations. The author does not recommend using it for that reason. The author recommends that a quantitative expression of materiality well below the planning materiality amount be used, in conjunction with the FASB's conceptual definition. A common rule of thumb is one-sixth of planning materiality for the quantitative expression.

AU-C 580 ILLUSTRATIONS[2]

The following items presented in this section are from Section 580, *Written Representations*:

1. Illustrative management representation letter for GAAP financial statements
2. Additional illustrative representations
3. Illustrative updating management representation letter

Illustration 1. Illustrative Representation Letter (from AU-C 580.A35)

The following illustrative letter includes written representations that are required by this and other AU-C sections in effect for audits of financial statements for periods ending on or after December 15, 2012. It is assumed in this illustration that the applicable financial reporting framework is accounting principles generally accepted in the United States, that the requirement in Section 570, *The Auditor's Consideration of an Entity's Ability to Continue as a Going Concern*, to obtain a written representation is not relevant, and that no exceptions exist to the requested written representations. If there were exceptions, the representations would need to be modified to reflect the exceptions.

[Entity letterhead]

[To auditor]

[Date]

---

2 *Illustrations 1, 2, and 3 are designed for nonissuers. Auditors of issuers should consider the standards of the PCAOB and other SEC requirements for public companies.*

This representation letter is provided in connection with your audit of the financial statements of ABC Company, which comprise the balance sheet as of December 31, 20XX, and the related statements of income, changes in stockholders' equity, and cash flows for the year then ended, and the related notes to the financial statements, for the purpose of expressing an opinion on whether the financial statements are presented fairly, in all material respects, in accordance with accounting principles generally accepted in the United States (US GAAP).

Certain representations in this letter are described as being limited to matters that are material. Items are considered material, regardless of size, if they involve an omission or misstatement of accounting information that, in the light of surrounding circumstances, makes it probable that the judgment of a reasonable person relying on the information would be changed or influenced by the omission or misstatement.

Except where otherwise stated below, immaterial matters less than $[*insert amount*] collectively are not considered to be exceptions that require disclosure for the purpose of the following representations. This amount is not necessarily indicative of amounts that would require adjustment to or disclosure in the financial statements.

We confirm that, to the best of our knowledge and belief, having made such inquiries as we considered necessary for the purpose of appropriately informing ourselves, as of [*date of auditor's report*]:

Financial Statements

- We have fulfilled our responsibilities, as set out in the terms of the audit engagement dated [*insert date*], for the preparation and fair presentation of the financial statements in accordance with US GAAP.
- We acknowledge our responsibility for the design, implementation, and maintenance of internal control relevant to the preparation and fair presentation of financial statements that are free from material misstatement, whether due to fraud or error.
- We acknowledge our responsibility for the design, implementation, and maintenance of internal control to prevent and detect fraud.
- Significant assumptions used by us in making accounting estimates, including those measured at fair value, are reasonable.
- Related-party relationships and transactions have been appropriately accounted for and disclosed in accordance with the requirements of US GAAP.
- All events subsequent to the date of the financial statements and for which US GAAP requires adjustment or disclosure have been adjusted or disclosed.
- The effects of uncorrected misstatements are immaterial, both individually and in the aggregate, to the financial statements as a whole. A list of the uncorrected misstatements is attached to the representation letter.
- The effects of all known actual or possible litigation and claims have been accounted for and disclosed in accordance with US GAAP.

[*Any other matters that the auditor may consider appropriate.*]

Information Provided

- We have provided you with:
  - Access to all information of which we are aware that is relevant to the preparation and fair presentation of the financial statements such as records, documentation, and other matters;
  - Additional information that you have requested from us for the purpose of the audit; and
  - Unrestricted access to persons within the entity from whom you determined it necessary to obtain audit evidence.

- All transactions have been recorded in the accounting records and are reflected in the financial statements.
- We have disclosed to you the results of our assessment of the risk that the financial statements may be materially misstated as a result of fraud.
- We have [*no knowledge of any*] [*disclosed to you all information that we are aware of regarding*] fraud or suspected fraud that affects the entity and involves:
  - Management;
  - Employees who have significant roles in internal control; or
  - Others when the fraud could have a material effect on the financial statements.
- We have [*no knowledge of any*] [*disclosed to you all information that we are aware of regarding*] allegations of fraud, or suspected fraud, affecting the entity's financial statements communicated by employees, former employees, analysts, regulators, or others.
- We have disclosed to you all known instances of noncompliance or suspected noncompliance with laws and regulations whose effects should be considered when preparing financial statements.
- We [*have disclosed to you all known actual or possible*] [*are not aware of any pending or threatened*] litigation, claims, and assessments whose effects should be considered when preparing the financial statements [*and we have not consulted legal counsel concerning litigation, claims, or assessments*].
- We have disclosed to you the identity of the entity's related parties and all the related-party relationships and transactions of which we are aware.

[*Any other matters that the auditor may consider necessary.*]

____

[*Name of Chief Executive Officer and Title*]

____

[*Name of Chief Financial Officer and Title*]

ILLUSTRATION 2. ILLUSTRATIVE SPECIFIC WRITTEN REPRESENTATIONS (FROM AU-C 580.A36)

Condition	*Illustrative specific written representation*
General	
Unaudited interim information accompanies the financial statements.	The unaudited interim financial information accompanying [*presented in Note X to*] the financial statements for the [*identify all related periods*] has been prepared and fairly presented in conformity with generally accepted accounting principles (GAAP) applicable to interim financial information. The accounting principles used to prepare the unaudited interim financial information are consistent with those used to prepare the audited financial statements.
The effect of a new accounting principle is not known.	We have not completed the process of evaluating the effect that will result from adopting the guidance in Financial Accounting Standards Board (FASB) Accounting Standards Update 20YY-XX, as discussed in Note [X]. The company is therefore unable to disclose the effect

Condition	*Illustrative Specific Written Representation*
	that adopting the guidance in FASB Accounting Standards Update 20YY-XX will have on its financial position and the results of operations when such guidance is adopted.
Financial circumstances are strained, with disclosure of management's intentions and the entity's ability to continue as a going concern.	Note [X] to the financial statements discloses all of the matters of which we are aware that are relevant to the company's ability to continue as a going concern, including significant conditions and events and management's plans.
The possibility exists that the value of specific significant long-lived assets or certain identifiable intangibles may be impaired.	We have reviewed long-lived assets and certain identifiable intangibles to be held and used for impairment whenever events or changes in circumstances have indicated that the carrying amount of the assets might not be recoverable, and have appropriately recorded the adjustment.
The entity has a variable interest in another entity.	Variable interest entities (VIEs) and potential VIEs and transactions with VIEs and potential VIEs have been properly recorded and disclosed in the financial statements in accordance with GAAP. We have considered both implicit and explicit variable interests in (1) determining whether potential VIEs should be considered VIEs; (2) calculating expected losses and residual returns; and (3) determining which party, if any, is the primary beneficiary. We have provided you with lists of all identified variable interests in (1) VIEs, (2) potential VIEs that we considered but judged not to be VIEs, and (3) entities that were afforded the scope exceptions of Financial Accounting Standards Board (FASB) *Accounting Standards Codification* (ASC) 810, *Consolidation.* We have advised you of all transactions with identified VIEs, potential VIEs, or entities afforded the scope exceptions of FASB ASC 810. We have made available all relevant information about financial interests and contractual arrangements with related parties, de facto agents, and other entities, including but not limited to their governing documents, equity and debt instruments, contracts, leases, guarantee arrangements, and other financial contracts and arrangements. The information we provided about financial interests and contractual arrangements with related parties, de facto agents, and other entities includes information about all transactions, unwritten understandings, agreement modifications, and written and oral side agreements.

Condition	*Illustrative Specific Written Representation*
	Our computations of expected losses and expected residual returns of entities that are VIEs and potential VIEs are based on the best information available and include all reasonably possible outcomes.
	Regarding entities in which the company has variable interests (implicit and explicit), we have provided all information about events and changes in circumstances that could potentially cause reconsideration about whether the entities are VIEs or whether the company is the primary beneficiary or has a significant variable interest in the entity.
	We have made and continue to make exhaustive efforts to obtain information about entities in which the company has an implicit or explicit interest but that were excluded from complete analysis under FASB ASC 810 due to lack of essential information to determine one or more of the following: whether the entity is a VIE, whether the company is the primary beneficiary, or the accounting required to consolidate the entity.
The work of a specialist has been used by the entity.	We agree with the findings of specialists in evaluating the [*describe assertion*] and have adequately considered the qualifications of the specialist in determining the amounts and disclosures used in the financial statements and underlying accounting records. We did not give or cause any instructions to be given to specialists with respect to the values or amounts derived in an attempt to bias their work, and we are not otherwise aware of any matters that have had an effect on the independence or objectivity of the specialists.
Assets	
Cash	
Disclosure is required of compensating balances or other arrangements involving restrictions on cash balances, lines of credit, or similar arrangements.	Arrangements with financial institutions involving compensating balances or other arrangements involving restrictions on cash balances, line of credit, or similar arrangements have been properly disclosed.
Financial Instruments	
Management intends to and has the ability to hold to maturity debt securities classified as held to maturity.	Debt securities that have been classified as held to maturity have been so classified due to the company's intent to hold such securities to maturity and the company's ability to do so. All other debt securities have been classified as available for sale or trading.
Management considers the decline in value of debt or equity securities to be temporary.	We consider the decline in value of debt or equity securities classified as either available for sale or held to maturity to be temporary.

Condition	*Illustrative Specific Written Representation*
Management has determined the fair value of significant financial instruments that do not have readily determinable market values.	The methods and significant assumptions used to determine fair values of financial instruments are as follows: [*describe methods and significant assumptions used to determine fair values of financial instruments*]. The methods and significant assumptions used result in a measure of fair value appropriate for financial statement measurement and disclosure purposes.
Financial instruments with off-balance-sheet risk and financial instruments with concentrations of credit risk exist.	The following information about financial instruments with off-balance-sheet risk and financial instruments with concentrations of credit risk has been properly disclosed in the financial statements: 1. The extent, nature, and terms of financial instruments with off-balance-sheet risk 2. The amount of credit risk of financial instruments with off-balance-sheet risk and information about the collateral supporting such financial instruments 3. Significant concentrations of credit risk arising from all financial instruments and information about the collateral supporting such financial instruments
Investments Unusual considerations are involved in determining the application of equity accounting.	[*For investments in common stock that are either nonmarketable or of which the entity has a 20% or greater ownership interest, select the appropriate representation from the following*:] The equity method is used to account for the company's investment in the common stock of [*investee*] because the company has the ability to exercise significant influence over the investee's operating and financial policies. The cost method is used to account for the company's investment in the common stock of [*investee*] because the company does not have the ability to exercise significant influence over the investee's operating and financial policies.
The entity had loans to executive officers, nonaccrued loans, or zero interest rate loans.	Loans to executive officers have been properly accounted for and disclosed.
Liabilities	
Debt Short-term debt could be refinanced on a long-term basis, and management intends to do so.	The company has excluded short-term obligations totaling $[*amount*] from current liabilities because it intends to refinance the obligations on a long-term basis. [*Complete with appropriate wording detailing how amounts will be refinanced as follows*:] The company has issued a long-term obligation [*debt security*] after the

Condition	*Illustrative Specific Written Representation*
	date of the balance sheet but prior to the issuance of the financial statements for the purpose of refinancing the short-term obligations on a long-term basis.
	The company has the ability to consummate the refinancing by using the financing agreement referred to in Note [X] to the financial statements.
Tax-exempt bonds have been issued.	Tax-exempt bonds issued have retained their tax-exempt status.
Taxes Management intends to reinvest undistributed earnings of a foreign subsidiary.	We intend to reinvest the undistributed earnings of [*name of foreign subsidiary*].
Pension and Postretirement Benefits An actuary has been used to measure pension liabilities and costs.	We believe that the actuarial assumptions and methods used to measure pension liabilities and costs for financial accounting purposes are appropriate in the circumstances.
Involvement with a multiemployer plan exists.	We are unable to determine the possibility of a withdrawal liability in a multiemployer benefit plan. *or* We have determined that there is the possibility of a withdrawal liability in a multiemployer plan in the amount of $[XX].
Postretirement benefits have been eliminated.	We do not intend to compensate for the elimination of postretirement benefits by granting an increase in pension benefits. *or* We plan to compensate for the elimination of postretirement benefits by granting an increase in pension benefits in the amount of $[XX].
Employee layoffs that would otherwise lead to a curtailment of a benefit plan are intended to be temporary.	Current employee layoffs are intended to be temporary.
Management intends to either continue to make or not make frequent amendments to its pension or other postretirement benefit plans, which may affect the amortization period of prior service cost, or has expressed a substantive commitment to increase benefit obligations.	We plan to continue to make frequent amendments to the pension or other postretirement benefit plans, which may affect the amortization period of prior service cost. *or* We do not plan to make frequent amendments to the pension or other postretirement benefit plans.
Equity Capital stock repurchase options or agreements or capital stock reserved for options, warrants, conversions, or other requirements exist.	Capital stock repurchase options or agreements or capital stock reserved for options, warrants, conversions, or other requirements have been properly disclosed.

ILLUSTRATION 3. ILLUSTRATIVE UPDATING MANAGEMENT REPRESENTATION LETTER (FROM AU-C 580.A37)

The following letter is presented for illustrative purposes only. It may be used in the circumstances described in AU-C 580.A17. Management need not repeat all of the representations made in the previous representation letter.

If matters to be disclosed to the auditor exist, they may be listed following the representation. For example, if an event subsequent to the date of the balance sheet has been disclosed in the financial statements, the final paragraph could be modified as follows: "To the best of our knowledge and belief, except as discussed in Note X to the financial statements, no events have occurred . . . ."

[*Date*]

To [*Auditor*]

In connection with your audit(s) of the [*identification of financial statements*] of [*name of entity*] as of [*dates*] and for the [*periods*] for the purpose of expressing an opinion as to whether the [*consolidated*] financial statements present fairly, in all material respects, the financial position, results of operations, and cash flows of [*name of entity*] in accordance with accounting principles generally accepted in the United States of America, you were previously provided with a representation letter under date of [*date of previous representation letter*]. No information has come to our attention that would cause us to believe that any of those previous representations should be modified.

To the best of our knowledge and belief, no events have occurred subsequent to [*date of latest balance sheet reported on by the auditor*] and through the date of this letter that would require adjustment to or disclosure in the aforementioned financial statements.

____

[*Name of Chief Executive Officer and Title*]

____

[*Name of Chief Financial Officer and Title*]

AU-C 585 Consideration of Omitted Procedures after the Report Release Date

AU-C ORIGINAL PRONOUNCEMENT

Source Statement on Auditing Standards (SAS) 122.

DEFINITION OF TERM

Source: AU 585.05

Omitted procedure. An auditing procedure that the auditor considered necessary in the circumstances existing at the time of the audit of the financial statements but which was not performed.

OVERVIEW

PROFESSIONAL DISAGREEMENTS

This section does not apply to professional disagreements about whether an auditing procedure is necessary in a specific engagement under circumstances existing at the time of the audit. For example, a peer reviewer may suggest that an auditing procedure was necessary (e.g., confirming additional receivables), and the auditor may disagree.

The alleged omitted auditing procedure might be one that professionals could reasonably disagree about (e.g., judgments about materiality). In these circumstances, every effort should be made to convince the reviewer that the auditor's judgment was appropriate.

NO SUBSTITUTE FOR OMITTED PROCEDURES

The omitted procedure may be one for which there is no alternative (e.g., making or observing some inventory counts), or the omission may be the failure to apply any auditing procedures to obtain evidential matter for a significant audit objective (e.g., accepting management representations and not testing percentage of completion on a material construction contract). In these circumstances, the auditor cannot maintain that these are matters about which reasonable professionals might disagree.

DISTINCTION FROM SECTION 560

Section 560, *Subsequent Events and Subsequently Discovered Facts*, provides guidance when the auditor becomes aware, subsequent to the date of the report on the audited financial statements, that facts may have existed at that date that might have affected the financial statements or the audit report had the auditor been aware of those facts. These facts usually relate to the financial statements and whether those financial statements are presented fairly in all material respects in conformity with generally accepted accounting principles (GAAP).

Section 560 applies to facts that indicate possible misstatement of financial statements, whereas Section 585 applies to the possible omission of auditing procedures. The application of Section 560 is initiated by a possible GAAP failure; the application of Section 585 is initiated by a possible GAAS failure. However, when omitted auditing procedures are applied, the auditor may become aware that facts may have existed at the date of the auditor's report and might have affected the report had the auditor been aware of those facts (see "Requirements"). In that situation, Section 560 is applicable.

OBJECTIVES OF AU SECTION 585

AU Section 585.04 states that:

. . . the objectives of the auditor are to

a. *assess the effect of omitted procedures of which the auditor becomes aware on the auditor's present ability to support the previously expressed opinion on the financial statements, and*
b. *respond appropriately.*

SCOPE

This section applies when subsequent to the date of the auditor's report on audited financial statements, the auditor concludes that one or more auditing procedures considered necessary at the time of the audit in the circumstances then existing were omitted from the audit. (AU 585.01)

This section does not apply in an engagement in which an auditor's work is at issue in a threatened or pending legal proceeding (see "Definition of Term" section) or regulatory investigation. (AU 585.02)

REQUIREMENTS

IMPORTANCE OF OMITTED PROCEDURES

If the auditor decides that a situation involving an omitted procedure exists, he or she should determine if the omitted procedure currently affects the ability to support the previously expressed opinion. (AU 585.06)

NOTE: In these circumstances, the auditor would be well advised to consult with his or her attorney.

The objective of the auditor's assessment of the importance of the omitted procedure is to determine if it is:

1. Necessary to apply the omitted procedure
2. Necessary to apply alternative procedures
3. Appropriate not to apply either the omitted procedure or alternative procedures

APPLYING OMITTED PROCEDURES

The client may be able to wait a short period of time (to be determined by the client, the auditor, and their lawyers) for the matter to be resolved; however, it cannot wait too long before notifying interested parties. The urgency of resolution may differ for public versus nonpublic companies. (AU 585.A4)

Public Companies

Public companies file audited financial statements with the Securities and Exchange Commission (SEC). If the auditor becomes aware of an omitted procedure concerning these financial statements, he or she should consider the client's possible obligation for timely disclosure of significant events. Form 8-K must be filed within four business days after occurrence of most significant events.

Nonpublic Companies

Nonpublic companies may submit audited financial statements to banks, bonding companies, credit agencies, and others. If these financial statements were not audited properly *and* are misleading, the client should notify immediately anyone relying on them. Although there is no specified time period within which to notify interested parties, the client probably will consider its reputation and its exposure to lawsuits in determining when to notify them. It would therefore be prudent for the auditor to complete all procedures before a significant period of time has elapsed.

The auditor should promptly attempt to apply the omitted procedure or alternative procedures that would provide a satisfactory basis for the original opinion on the financial statements if he or she:

1. Decides that the omitted procedure impairs his or her present ability to support the previously expressed opinion, and
2. Believes that there are persons relying currently, or likely to rely, on the financial statements and the related auditor's report.

(AU-C 585.07)

When the auditor subsequently applies the omitted procedure or alternative procedures, he or she may become aware of facts regarding the financial statements that existed at the date of the auditor's report and would have affected the report had the auditor been aware of them. In these circumstances, the auditor should apply the provisions of Section 560. (AU 585.08)

The auditor also would be well advised to consult with his or her attorney.

If the client refuses to make the disclosures requested, the auditor should follow the guidance in Section 560 under "Requirements."

INABILITY TO APPLY OMITTED PROCEDURES

If the auditor is not able to apply the omitted procedure or appropriate alternative procedures, the auditor should consult his or her attorney to determine the proper action concerning the auditor's responsibilities to:

1. The client
2. Regulatory authorities having jurisdiction over the client
3. Persons relying, or likely to rely, on the auditor's report

(AU-C 585.A5)

NOTE: This section does not require the auditor to notify the client of the omitted auditing procedures.

DETERMINING IMPORTANCE OF OMITTED PROCEDURES

To determine the importance of the omitted procedure to the auditor's present ability to support the previously expressed opinion, the auditor should:

1. Review documentation of the audit.
2. Discuss circumstances with audit personnel and others.
3. Review documentation of the subsequent audit.
4. Reevaluate the overall scope of the audit.

(AU 585.A3)

Review of Audit Documentation

The auditor should review relevant audit documentation to determine if:

1. Other procedures were applied that compensated for the one omitted or made the one omitted less important. For example, the review of subsequent cash collected and the related customer remittance advices might compensate for inadequate confirmation of receivables or make the failure to obtain enough receivable confirmations less important than usual.
2. A lower level of control risk was justified so that the omitted procedure was not necessary. The auditor should review audit documentations on:
   a. The documentation of the understanding of internal control
   b. Tests of controls

Discussions with Audit Personnel

The auditor should discuss the audit with audit personnel to determine if:

1. The omitted procedure or a related procedure was discussed.
2. The omitted procedure was performed but not documented.
3. The omitted procedure affected an item considered not material.

The auditor should determine if the alleged omitted procedure was performed, and if not, why not.

Review of Subsequent Period Audit Documentation

The auditor should review audit documentation for the subsequent period to determine if procedures applied provide audit evidence to support the previously expressed opinion. For example:

1. Costing of subsequent period sales may provide audit evidence about existence of prior period inventory.
2. A review of subsequent period changes in receivables may provide audit evidence about existence of prior period receivables.
3. A review of subsequent period liabilities may provide evidence that a contingency did not exist at the end of the prior period.

ILLUSTRATION

ILLUSTRATION 1. APPLYING THE OMITTED PROCEDURE

If the auditor concludes that the omitted procedure should be performed, he or she should apply it promptly. In these circumstances, the auditor would have to discuss the matter with the client. Following are possible omitted procedures and suggested methods of correcting the omission.

Possible Omitted Procedure	*Remedy*
1. Failure to obtain written representations.	Obtain letter retroactive to date of auditor's report.
2. Failure to obtain a sufficient number of confirmations of receivables.	Confirm retroactive to balance sheet date.
	If control risk is assessed at less than the maximum, confirm currently, and work back to balance sheet date.
3. Failure to observe a sufficient quantity of inventory.	If control risk is assessed at less than the maximum, observe count of specific styles or components, and work back to year-end.
	If control risk is assessed at the maximum, the entire inventory may have to be taken currently before the auditor can work back to year-end.
4. Failure to make inquiry of client's lawyer.	Make inquiry retroactive to date of auditor's report.
5. Failure to obtain sufficient evidence about the value of investments in nonpublic investees.	Review recent audited financial statements, if available.
	If recent audited financial statements are not available, review recent unaudited financial statements, and apply selected audit procedures.
	Consult with investee's accountant.
6. Failure to apply procedures for identifying related-party transactions.	Apply procedures for current and prior period (see Section 550, *Related Parties*).

AU-C 600 Special Considerations—Audits of Group Financial Statements (Including the Work of Component Auditors)

AU-C ORIGINAL PRONOUNCEMENTS

Sources Statements on Auditing Standards (SASs) 122, 127, and 128.

TECHNICAL ALERT

In October 2015, the Auditing Standards Board (ASB) issued SAS No. 130. SAS No. 130 contains amendments to this section. Any relevant changes are incorporated into the information that follows.

INTRODUCTION

SAS No. 127 clarifies that the group engagement team is required to determine component materiality for those components on which the group engagement team will assume responsibility for the work of a component auditor who performs an audit or a review.

The AICPA has issued Technical Questions and Answers on Audits of Group Financial Statements and Work of Others. The Q and As address these areas of practice issues:

- Applicability of AU-C 600
- Making reference to any or all component auditors
- Deciding to act as auditor of group financial statements
- Factors to consider regarding component auditors
- Governmental financial statements that include a GAAP-basis component
- Component audit performed in accordance with Government Auditing Standards
- Component audit performed by other engagement teams of the same firm
- Terms of the group audit engagement
- Criteria for identifying components
- Criteria for identifying significant components
- No significant components are identified
- Restricted access to component auditor documentation
- Responsibilities with respect to fraud in a group audit
- Inclusion of component auditor in engagement team discussions
- Determining component materiality

- Understanding of component auditor whose work will not be used
- Involvement in the work of a component auditor
- Factors affecting involvement in the work of a component auditor
- Form of communication with component auditors
- Use of component materiality when the component is not reported on separately
- Applicability of AU-C Section 600 when only one engagement team is involved
- Applicability of AU-C Section 600 when making reference to the audit of an equity method investee
- Procedures required when making reference to the audit of an equity method investee
- Circumstances in which making reference is inappropriate
- Determining if the audit of the component was performed in accordance with the relevant requirements of GAAS
- Making reference when different financial reporting frameworks have been used
- Lack of response from a component auditor
- Equity investee's financial statements reviewed, and investment is a significant component
- Making reference to a review report
- Review of a component that is not significant performed by another practitioner
- Issuance of component auditor's report
- Structure of component auditor engagement
- Subsequent events procedures relating to a component
- Component and group having different year-ends
- Investments held in a financial institution presented at cost or fair value
- Employee benefit plan using investee results to calculate fair value
- Using net asset value to calculate fair value
- Disaggregation of account balances or classes of transactions
- Variable interest entities (VIEs) as a component
- Component using a different basis of accounting than the group
- Component audit report of balance sheet only
- Using another accounting firm to perform inventory observation

AU-C 600 DEFINITIONS OF TERMS

Source: AU-C 600.11

Component. An entity or business activity for which group or component management prepares financial information that is required by the applicable financial reporting framework to be included in the group financial statements.

Component auditor. An auditor who performs work on the financial information of a component that will be used as audit evidence for the group audit. A component auditor may be part of the group engagement partner's firm, a network firm of the group engagement partner's firm, or another firm.

Component management. Management responsible for preparing the financial information of a component.

Component materiality. The materiality for a component determined by the group engagement team for the purposes of the group audit.

Group. All the components whose financial information is included in the group financial statements. A group always has more than one component.

Group audit. The audit of group financial statements.

Group audit opinion. The audit opinion on the group financial statements.

Group engagement partner. The partner or other person in the firm who is responsible for the group audit engagement and its performance and for the auditor's report on the group financial statements that is issued on behalf of the firm. When joint auditors conduct the group audit, the joint engagement partners and their engagement teams collectively constitute the group engagement partner and the group engagement team. This section does not, however, address the relationship between joint auditors or the work that one joint auditor performs in relation to the work of the other joint auditor.

Group engagement team. Partners, including the group engagement partner, and staff who establish the overall group audit strategy, communicate with component auditors, perform work on the consolidation process, and evaluate the conclusions drawn from the audit evidence as the basis for forming an opinion on the group financial statements.

Group financial statements. Financial statements that include the financial information of more than one component. The term *group financial statements* also refers to combined financial statements aggregating the financial information prepared by components that are under common control.

Group management. Management responsible for the preparation and fair presentation of the group financial statements.

Group-wide controls. Controls designed, implemented, and maintained by group management over group financial reporting.

Significant component. A component identified by the group engagement team (a) that is of individual financial significance to the group, or (b) that, due to its specific nature or circumstances, is likely to include significant risks of material misstatement of the group financial statements.

NOTE: Auditors who do not meet the definition of a member of the group engagement team are considered component auditors.

OBJECTIVES OF AU-C SECTION 600

AU-C Section 600.10 states that:

. . . the objectives of the auditor are to determine whether to act as the auditor of the group financial statements and, if so, to

- *a. determine whether to make reference to the audit of a component auditor in the auditor's report on the group financial statements;*
- *b. communicate clearly with component auditors; and*
- *c. obtain sufficient appropriate audit evidence regarding the financial information of the components and the consolidation process to express an opinion about whether the group financial statements are prepared, in all material respects, in accordance with the applicable financial reporting framework.*

OVERVIEW

The following is an overview of major decisions and performance requirements under AU-C 600.

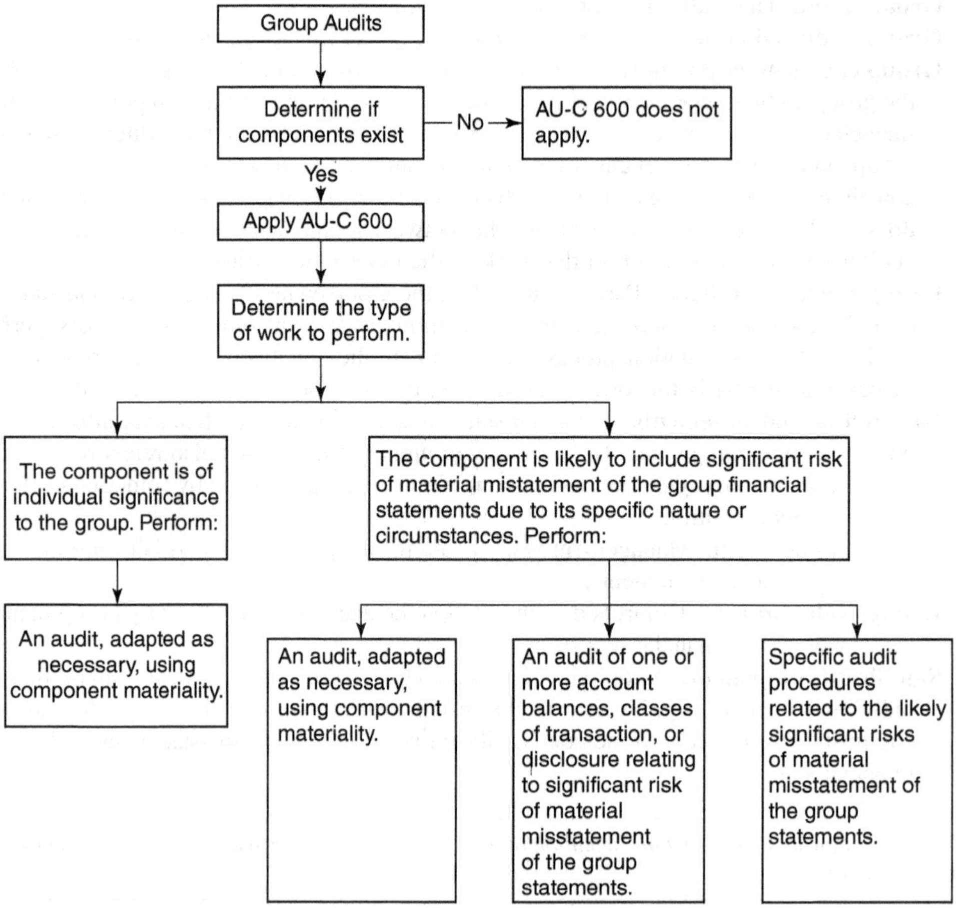

REQUIREMENTS

AU-C 600 applies whenever the audited financial statements include more than one component, including:

- Combined financial statement of components under common control, or
- Group financial statements

Practice pointer: AU-C 600 applies to all audits of group financial statements, even if the same engagement team is auditing all the components of the financial statements. The AU-C 600 guidelines related to component auditors are not relevant in those circumstances, but other AU-C 600 requirements are. Group financial statements are statements that contain more than one component.

AU-C 600 articulates the degree of involvement required when reference is made to component auditors in the auditor's report. If the group engagement partner does not make reference to a component auditor in the auditor's report, all of the requirements of AU-C 600 apply. If the group engagement partner does make reference to the component auditor in the auditor's report, some of the requirements do not apply.

Identifying Components

The auditor must exercise professional judgement to determine if an activity represents an AU-C 600 component. Auditors should look closely at the following to determine if they have a group start that falls under the requirements of AU-C 600:

- Entity under common control is centered.
- It is a consolidated affiliate.
- It is an equity method investment.
- It is a joint venture investment.
- Entity is a head office and branches that are separately managed and have separate financial statements.
- It is a cost method investment where reports of other auditors are a major element of evidence of the investment.
- A separate function, process, product, service, or location is separately managed and provides separate financial reporting to the head office.

Responsibilities

AU-C 600 includes requirements and guidance relating to work to be performed on all components for which the group engagement partner is assuming responsibility for the work of the component auditor, whether that work is performed by the group engagement team or by component auditors. AU-C 600 includes requirements and guidance specifying the nature, timing, and extent of the group engagement team's involvement in the work of the component auditors.

The auditor must audit components that are financially significant. For components considered significant due to their likelihood of including significant risks of material misstatements, an audit or other audit procedures are performed. For components that are not significant, the group engagement team performs analytical procedures at the group level.

AU-C 600 also includes requirements and guidance related to:

- Internal controls,
- The consolidation process, and
- Subsequent events.

According to AU-C 600.13, the group engagement partner is responsible for:

- Direction, supervision, and performance of the group audit engagement in compliance with professional standards and regulatory and legal requirements, and
- Determining whether the auditor's report is appropriate.

The group engagement team or the firm may assist the group engagement partner in fulfilling the group audit responsibilities. AU-C 600 provides guidance on when such assistance is permitted. Reference the definitions section of this chapter for more on roles and responsibilities.

Engagement Acceptance and Continuance

Auditors must base their determination on whether or not to accept an engagement or continue with a client on whether the auditor believes they will be able to obtain sufficient appropriate audit evidence over the group financial statements, including whether the group engagement team will have appropriate access to information. (AU-C 600.15)

Risk Assessment Standards

AU-C 600 incorporates application of the risk assessment standards into the performance of group audits and discusses specific applications. For example, detection risk includes the risk that a component auditor may not detect a material misstatement. (AU-C 600.07)

Involvement with Component Auditors

AU-C 600.22 requires the group engagement team to gain an understanding of the component auditor, including:

- Professional competence,
- Ethical requirements, particularly independence,
- Whether a component auditor operates in a regulatory environment that oversees auditors,
- Whether the team will be able to get consolidation process information from a component auditor, and
- The extent to which the group engagement team will be able to be involved in the work of the component auditor.

After gaining an understanding of the component auditor, the group engagement partner may choose to either:

- Assume responsibility for, and thus be required to be involved in, the work of component auditors, insofar as that work relates to the expression of an opinion on the group financial statements, or
- Not assume responsibility for, and accordingly not make reference to, the audit of a component auditor in the auditor's report on the group financial statements.
(AU-C 600.08)

Involvement in the work performed by a component auditor involves the group engagement team:

- Establishing component materiality to be used by the component auditor,
- Performing risk assessment procedures, and
- Participating in the assessment of risks of material misstatement and the planned audit response.

These may be performed together with the component auditor or by the group engagement team.

Materiality

AU-C 600.32 requires the group engagement team to determine:

- Materiality, including performance materiality for the group as a whole,
- Whether certain transactions, account balances, or disclosures pose more risk and, therefore, should have a lower materiality level,
- Component materiality for those components in which the group engagement team will assume responsibility for the work of a component auditor who performs an audit or review—determined by the group engagement team, whether or not the group engagement partner is making reference to the audit of a component auditor—and
- Thresholds for recording passed adjustments.

Component materiality, including performance materiality, must be lower than group materiality.

The group engagement team does not have to determine materiality for:

- Components where the group auditor refers to the work of a component auditor, or
- Those components where analytical procedures only will be performed.

Communication with Others

The group engagement team is required to:

- Communicate specific items to the component auditor:
  - A request that the component auditor confirm that he or she will cooperate with the group engagement team
  - Relevant ethical requirements
  - A list of related parties
  - Significant risks of material misstatements

  (AU-C 600.41)
- Request that the component auditor communicate with the group engagement team about certain matters, such as compliance with ethical requirements; identification of the financial information on which the component auditor is reporting; and the overall findings, conclusions, or opinions. (AU-C 600.42)
- Communicate specific items to group management and those charged with governance of the group, including material weaknesses and significant deficiencies in internal control, fraud, and significant matters. (AU-C 600.46-.48)
- Communicate with those charged with governance, including an overview of the group engagement's planned involvement in the work to be performed, concerns about the quantity of a component auditor's work, limitations on the group audit, and any fraud or suspected fraud involving a material misstatement. (AU-C 600.49)

Documentation

AU-C 600.50 requires specific documentation, including:

- An analysis of the components indicating the significant components and the type of work performed on the components
- Nature, timing, and extent of involvement of group team with component auditors
- Written communications between the group team and component auditors
- The financial statements and audit reports of those components to which the group auditor is making reference

INTERPRETATIONS

In June 2012, the Governmental Accounting Standards Board (GASB) issued statements No. 67 and No. 68 that change the reporting of public employee pension plans and the state and local governments that participate in those plans. In response, the ASB issued three interpretations to assist plan and employer auditors in implementing those standards. Auditors of entities that have implemented the standards should reference the interpretation below and AU-C Sections 9805 and 9500 for more information.

INTERPRETATION NO. 1, "AUDITOR OF PARTICIPATING EMPLOYER IN A GOVERNMENTAL PENSION PLAN," OF AU-C SECTION 600, *SPECIAL CONSIDERATIONS—AUDITS OF GROUP FINANCIAL STATEMENTS (INCLUDING THE WORK OF COMPONENT AUDITORS)* (ISSUED APRIL 2014)

If a governmental entity provides pension benefits through governmental pension plans, in order to report pension amounts in accordance with GASB Statement No. 68, the entity may obtain information from the governmental pension plan. In that case, a governmental pension plan is not considered a component of the employer for purposes of AU-C Section 600. Therefore, it would not be appropriate for the entity's auditor to make reference to the audit report of the governmental pension plan auditor.

ILLUSTRATIONS

The following appendices and exhibits are from AU-C 600:

- Appendix A. Understanding the Group, Its Components, and Their Environments—Examples of Matters about Which the Group Engagement Team Obtains an Understanding
- Appendix B. Examples of Conditions or Events That May Indicate Risks of Material Misstatement of the Group Financial Statements
- Appendix C. Required and Additional Matters Included in the Group Engagement Team's Letter of Instruction
- Exhibit A. Illustrations of Auditor's Reports on Group Financial Statements
- Illustration 1—A Report with a Qualified Opinion When the Group Engagement Team Is Not Able to Obtain Sufficient Appropriate Audit Evidence on Which to Base the Group Audit Opinion
- Illustration 2—A Report in Which the Auditor of the Group Financial Statements Is Making Reference to the Audit of Financial Statements of a Component Auditor Prepared Using the Same Financial Reporting Framework as That Used for the Group Financial Statements and Performed by a Component Auditor in Accordance with Generally Accepted Auditing Standards
- Illustration 3—A Report in Which the Auditor of the Group Financial Statements Is Making Reference to the Audit of Financial Statements of a Component Auditor Prepared Using a Different Financial Reporting Framework from That Used for the Group Financial Statements and Performed by a Component Auditor in Accordance with Generally Accepted Auditing Standards
- Illustration 4—A Report in Which the Auditor of the Group Financial Statements Is Making Reference to the Audit of the Financial Statements of a Component Prepared Using the Same Financial Reporting Framework as That Used for the Group Financial Statements and Performed by a Component Auditor in Accordance with Auditing Standards Other Than GAAS
- Exhibit B. Illustrative Component Auditor's Confirmation Letter
- Exhibit C. Sources of Information

APPENDIX A. UNDERSTANDING THE GROUP, ITS COMPONENTS, AND THEIR ENVIRONMENTS—EXAMPLES OF MATTERS ABOUT WHICH THE GROUP ENGAGEMENT TEAM OBTAINS AN UNDERSTANDING

The examples provided cover a broad range of matters; however, not all matters are relevant to every group audit engagement, and the list of examples is not necessarily complete.

Group-Wide Controls

Group-wide controls may include a combination of the following:

- Regular meetings between group and component management to discuss business developments and review performance
- Monitoring of components' operations and their financial results, including regular reporting routines, which enables group management to monitor components' performance against budgets and take appropriate action
- Group management's risk assessment process (that is, the process for identifying, analyzing, and managing business risks, including the risk of fraud, that may result in material misstatement of the group financial statements)
- Monitoring, controlling, reconciling, and eliminating intragroup account balances, transactions, and unrealized profits or losses at group level
- A process for monitoring the timeliness and assessing the accuracy and completeness of financial information received from components
- A central IT system controlled by the same general IT controls for all or part of the group
- Control activities within an IT system that are common for all or some components
- Monitoring of controls, including activities of the internal audit function and self-assessment programs
- Consistent policies and procedures, including a group financial reporting procedures manual
- Group-wide programs, such as codes of conduct and fraud prevention programs
- Arrangements for assigning authority and responsibility to component management

The internal audit function may be regarded as part of group-wide controls, for example, when the internal audit function is centralized. Section 610, *Using the Work of Internal Auditors*, addresses:

- The group engagement team's evaluation of whether the internal audit function's organizational status and relevant policies and procedures adequately support the objectivity of external auditors,
- The level of competence of the internal audit function, and
- Whether the function applies a systematic and disciplined approach when the group engagement team expects to use the function's work.

Consolidation Process

The group engagement team's understanding of the consolidation process may include matters such as the following:

- Matters relating to the applicable financial reporting framework, such as:
    - The extent to which component management has an understanding of the applicable financial reporting framework

- The process for identifying and accounting for components, in accordance with the applicable financial reporting framework
- The process for identifying reportable segments for segment reporting, in accordance with the applicable financial reporting framework
- The process for identifying related-party relationships and related-party transactions for reporting, in accordance with the applicable financial reporting framework
- The accounting policies applied to the group financial statements, changes from those of the previous financial year, and changes resulting from new or revised standards under the applicable financial reporting framework
- The procedures for dealing with components with financial year-ends different from the group's year-end

- Matters relating to the consolidation process, such as:
  - Group management's process for obtaining an understanding of the accounting policies used by components and, when applicable, ensuring that uniform accounting policies are used to prepare the financial information of the components for the group financial statements and that differences in accounting policies are identified and adjusted, when required, in terms of the applicable financial reporting framework. Uniform accounting policies are the specific principles, bases, conventions, rules, and practices adopted by the group, based on the applicable financial reporting framework, that the components use to report similar transactions consistently. These policies are ordinarily described in the financial reporting procedures manual and reporting package issued by group management.
  - Group management's process for ensuring complete, accurate, and timely financial reporting by the components for the consolidation
  - The process for translating the financial information of foreign components into the currency of the group financial statements
  - How IT is organized for the consolidation, including the manual and automated stages of the process and the manual and programmed controls in place at various stages of the consolidation process
  - Group management's process for obtaining information on subsequent events

- Matters relating to consolidation adjustments, such as:
  - The process for recording consolidation adjustments, including the preparation, authorization, and processing of related journal entries and the experience of personnel responsible for the consolidation
  - The consolidation adjustments required by the applicable financial reporting framework
  - Business rationale for the events and transactions that gave rise to the consolidation adjustments
  - Frequency, nature, and size of transactions between components
  - Procedures for monitoring, controlling, reconciling, and eliminating intragroup account balances, transactions, and unrealized profits or losses
  - Steps taken to arrive at the fair value of acquired assets and liabilities, procedures for amortizing goodwill (when applicable), and impairment testing of goodwill, in accordance with the applicable financial reporting framework
  - Arrangements with a controlling interest or noncontrolling interest regarding losses incurred by a component (for example, an obligation of the noncontrolling interest to compensate such losses)

Appendix B. Examples of Conditions or Events That May Indicate Risks of Material Misstatement of the Group Financial Statements

The examples provided cover a broad range of conditions or events; however, not all conditions or events are relevant to every group audit engagement, and the following list of examples is not necessarily complete:

- A complex group structure, especially when there are frequent acquisitions, disposals, or reorganizations
- Poor corporate governance structures, including decision-making processes, that are not transparent
- Nonexistent or ineffective group-wide controls, including inadequate group management information on monitoring of components' operations and their results
- Components operating in foreign jurisdictions that may be exposed to factors such as unusual government intervention in areas such as trade and fiscal policy, restrictions on currency and dividend movements, and fluctuations in exchange rates
- Business activities of components that involve high risk, such as long-term contracts or trading in innovative or complex financial instruments
- Uncertainties regarding which components' financial information requires incorporation in the group financial statements, in accordance with the applicable financial reporting framework (for example, whether any special purpose entities or nontrading entities exist and require incorporation)
- Unusual related-party relationships and transactions
- Prior occurrences of intragroup account balances that did not balance or reconcile on consolidation
- The existence of complex transactions that are accounted for in more than one component
- Components' application of accounting policies that differ from those applied to the group financial statements
- Components with different financial year-ends, which may be utilized to manipulate the timing of transactions
- Prior occurrences of unauthorized or incomplete consolidation adjustments
- Aggressive tax planning within the group or large cash transactions with entities in tax havens
- Frequent changes of auditors engaged to audit the financial statements of components

Appendix C. Required and Additional Matters Included in the Group Engagement Team's Letter of Instruction

The following matters are relevant to the planning of the work of a component auditor. *Required matters are italicized.*

- *A request for the component auditor, knowing the context in which the group engagement team will use the work of the component auditor, to confirm that the component auditor will cooperate with the group engagement team*
- The timetable for completing the audit
- Dates of planned visits by group management and the group engagement team and dates of planned meetings with component management and the component auditor
- A list of key contacts
- *The work to be performed by the component auditor, the use to be made of that work,* and arrangements for coordinating efforts at the initial stage of and during the audit,

including the group engagement team's planned involvement in the work of the component auditor
- *The ethical requirements that are relevant to the group audit and, in particular, the independence requirements*
- In the case of an audit or review of the financial information of the component, component materiality
- *In the case of an audit or review of, or specified audit procedures performed on, the financial information of the component, the threshold above which misstatements cannot be regarded as clearly trivial to the group financial statements*
- *A list of related parties prepared by group management and any other related parties of which the group engagement team is aware, and a request that the component auditor communicates on a timely basis to the group engagement team related parties not previously identified by group management or the group engagement team*
- Work to be performed on intragroup account balances, transactions, and unrealized profits or losses
- Guidance on other statutory reporting responsibilities (for example, reporting on group management's assertion on the effectiveness of internal control)
- When a time lag between completion of the work on the financial information of the components and the group engagement team's conclusion on the group financial statements is likely, specific instructions for a subsequent events review

The following matters are relevant to the conduct of the work of the component auditor:

- The findings of the group engagement team's tests of control activities of a processing system that is common for all or some components and tests of controls to be performed by the component auditor
- *Identified significant risks of material misstatement of the group financial statements, due to fraud or error, that are relevant to the work of the component auditor, and a request that the component auditor communicate on a timely basis any other significant risks of material misstatement of the group financial statements, due to fraud or error, identified in the component and the component auditor's response to such risks*
- The findings of the internal audit function, based on work performed on controls at or relevant to components
- A request for timely communication of audit evidence obtained from performing work on the financial information of the components that contradicts the audit evidence on which the group engagement team originally based the risk assessment performed at group level
- A request for a written representation on component management's compliance with the applicable financial reporting framework or a statement that differences between the accounting policies applied to the financial information of the component and those applied to the group financial statements have been disclosed
- Matters to be documented by the component auditor

Other information, such as the following:

- A request that the following be reported to the group engagement team on a timely basis:
  - Significant accounting, financial reporting, and auditing matters, including accounting estimates and related judgments
  - Matters relating to the going concern status of the component
  - Matters relating to litigation and claims

- Material weaknesses in controls that have come to the attention of the component auditor during the performance of the work on the financial information of the component and information that indicates the existence of fraud

- A request that the group engagement team be notified of any significant or unusual events as early as possible
- A request that the matters listed be communicated to the group engagement team when the work on the financial information of the component is completed

EXHIBIT A. ILLUSTRATIONS OF AUDITOR'S REPORTS ON GROUP FINANCIAL STATEMENTS

ILLUSTRATION 1. A REPORT WITH A QUALIFIED OPINION WHEN THE GROUP ENGAGEMENT TEAM IS NOT ABLE TO OBTAIN SUFFICIENT APPROPRIATE AUDIT EVIDENCE ON WHICH TO BASE THE GROUP AUDIT OPINION

In this example, the group engagement team is unable to obtain sufficient appropriate audit evidence relating to a significant component accounted for by the equity method because the group engagement team was unable to obtain the audited financial statements of the component as of December 31, 20X1 and 20X0, including the auditor's report thereon. In this example, the auditor of the group financial statements is not making reference to the report of a component auditor.

In the auditor's professional judgment, the effect on the group financial statements of this inability to obtain sufficient appropriate audit evidence is material but not pervasive.

If, in the auditor's professional judgment, the effect on the group financial statements of the inability to obtain sufficient appropriate audit evidence is material and pervasive, the auditor would disclaim an opinion, in accordance with Section 705, *Modifications to the Opinion in the Independent Auditor's Report*.

Independent Auditor's Report

[*Appropriate addressee*]

Report on the Consolidated Financial Statements

We have audited the accompanying consolidated financial statements of ABC Company and its subsidiaries, which comprise the consolidated balance sheets as of December 31, 20X1 and 20X0, and the related consolidated statements of income, changes in stockholders' equity, and cash flows for the years then ended, and the related notes to the financial statements.

Management's Responsibility for the Financial Statements

Management is responsible for the preparation and fair presentation of these consolidated financial statements in accordance with accounting principles generally accepted in the United States of America; this includes the design, implementation, and maintenance of internal control relevant to the preparation and fair presentation of consolidated financial statements that are free from material misstatement, whether due to fraud or to error.

Auditor's Responsibility

Our responsibility is to express an opinion on these consolidated financial statements based on our audits. We conducted our audits in accordance with auditing standards generally accepted in the United States of America. Those standards require that we plan and perform the audit to obtain reasonable assurance whether the consolidated financial statements are free from material misstatement.

The audit involves performing procedures to obtain audit evidence about the amounts and disclosures in the consolidated financial statements. The procedures selected depend on the auditor's judgment, including the assessment of the risks of material misstatement of the consolidated financial statements, whether due to fraud or to error. In making those risk assessments, the auditor considers internal control relevant to the entity's preparation and fair presentation of the consolidated financial statements in order to design audit procedures that are appropriate in the circumstances, but not for the purpose of expressing an opinion on the effectiveness of the entity's internal control. Accordingly, we express no such opinion.

An audit also includes evaluating the appropriateness of accounting policies used and the reasonableness of significant accounting estimates made by management, as well as evaluating the overall presentation of the consolidated financial statements.

We believe that the audit evidence we have obtained is sufficient and appropriate to provide a basis for our qualified audit opinion.

Basis for Qualified Opinion

We were unable to obtain audited financial statements supporting the Company's investment in a foreign affiliate stated at $_ and $_ at December 31, 20X1 and 20X0, respectively, or its equity in earnings of that affiliate of $_ and $___, which is included in net income for the years then ended as described in Note X to the consolidated financial statements; nor were we able to satisfy ourselves as to the carrying value of the investment in the foreign affiliate or the equity in its earnings by other auditing procedures.

Qualified Opinion

In our opinion, except for the possible effects of the matter described in the Basis for Qualified Opinion paragraph, the consolidated financial statements referred to above present fairly, in all material respects, the financial position of ABC Company and its subsidiaries as of December 31, 20X1 and 20X0, and the results of their operations and their cash flows for the years then ended in accordance with accounting principles generally accepted in the United States of America.

Report on Other Legal and Regulatory Requirements

[*Form and content of this section of the auditor's report will vary depending on the nature of the auditor's other reporting responsibilities.*]

[*Auditor's signature*]

[*Auditor's city and state*]

[*Date of the auditor's report*]

ILLUSTRATION 2. A REPORT IN WHICH THE AUDITOR OF THE GROUP FINANCIAL STATEMENTS IS MAKING REFERENCE TO THE AUDIT OF THE FINANCIAL STATEMENTS OF A COMPONENT PREPARED USING THE SAME FINANCIAL REPORTING FRAMEWORK AS THAT USED FOR THE GROUP FINANCIAL STATEMENTS AND PERFORMED BY A COMPONENT AUDITOR IN ACCORDANCE WITH GENERALLY ACCEPTED AUDITING STANDARDS

In this example, the auditor of the group financial statements is making reference to the audit of the financial statements of a component prepared using the same financial reporting framework as that used for the group financial statements and performed by a component auditor in accordance with generally accepted auditing standards (GAAS).

Independent Auditor's Report

[Appropriate addressee]

Report on the Consolidated Financial Statements

We have audited the accompanying consolidated financial statements of ABC Company and its subsidiaries, which comprise the consolidated balance sheets as of December 31, 20X1 and 20X0, and the related consolidated statements of income, changes in stockholders' equity, and cash flows for the years then ended, and the related notes to the financial statements.

Management's Responsibility for the Financial Statements

Management is responsible for the preparation and fair presentation of these consolidated financial statements in accordance with accounting principles generally accepted in the United States of America; this includes the design, implementation, and maintenance of internal control relevant to the preparation and fair presentation of consolidated financial statements that are free from material misstatement, whether due to fraud or to error.

Auditor's Responsibility

Our responsibility is to express an opinion on these consolidated financial statements based on our audits. We did not audit the financial statements of B Company, a wholly owned subsidiary, which statements reflect total assets constituting 20% and 22%, respectively, of consolidated total assets at December 31, 20X1 and 20X0, and total revenues constituting 18% and 20%, respectively, of consolidated total revenues for the years then ended. Those statements were audited by other auditors, whose report has been furnished to us, and our opinion, insofar as it relates to the amounts included for B Company, is based solely on the report of the other auditors. We conducted our audits in accordance with auditing standards generally accepted in the United States of America. Those standards require that we plan and perform the audit to obtain reasonable assurance about whether the consolidated financial statements are free from material misstatement.

An audit involves performing procedures to obtain audit evidence about the amounts and disclosures in the consolidated financial statements. The procedures selected depend on the auditor's judgment, including the assessment of the risks of material misstatement of the consolidated financial statements, whether due to fraud or to error. In making those risk assessments, the auditor considers internal control relevant to the entity's preparation and fair presentation of the consolidated financial statements in order to design audit procedures that are appropriate in the circumstances, but not for the purpose of expressing an opinion on the effectiveness of the entity's internal control. Accordingly, we express no such opinion. An audit also includes evaluating the appropriateness of accounting policies used and the reasonableness of significant accounting estimates made by management, as well as evaluating the overall presentation of the consolidated financial statements.

We believe that the audit evidence we have obtained is sufficient and appropriate to provide a basis for our audit opinion.

Opinion

In our opinion, based on our audit and the report of the other auditors, the consolidated financial statements referred to above present fairly, in all material respects, the financial position of ABC Company and its subsidiaries as of December 31, 20X1 and 20X0, and the results of their operations and their cash flows for the years then ended in accordance with accounting principles generally accepted in the United States of America.

Report on Other Legal and Regulatory Requirements

[*Form and content of this section of the auditor's report will vary depending on the nature of the auditor's other reporting responsibilities.*]

[*Auditor's signature*]

[*Auditor's city and state*]

[*Date of the auditor's report*]

ILLUSTRATION 3. A REPORT IN WHICH THE AUDITOR OF THE GROUP FINANCIAL STATEMENTS IS MAKING REFERENCE TO THE AUDIT OF THE FINANCIAL STATEMENTS OF A COMPONENT PREPARED USING A DIFFERENT FINANCIAL REPORTING FRAMEWORK FROM THAT USED FOR THE GROUP FINANCIAL STATEMENTS AND PERFORMED BY A COMPONENT AUDITOR IN ACCORDANCE WITH GENERALLY ACCEPTED AUDITING STANDARDS

In this example, the auditor of the group financial statements is making reference to the audit of the financial statements of a component prepared using a different financial reporting framework than that used for the group financial statements and performed by a component auditor in accordance with GAAS.

Independent Auditor's Report

[*Appropriate addressee*]

Report on the Consolidated Financial Statements

We have audited the accompanying consolidated financial statements of ABC Company and its subsidiaries, which comprise the consolidated balance sheets as of December 31, 20X1 and 20X0, and the related consolidated statements of income, changes in stockholders' equity, and cash flows for the years then ended, and the related notes to the financial statements.

Management's Responsibility for the Financial Statements

Management is responsible for the preparation and fair presentation of these consolidated financial statements in accordance with accounting principles generally accepted in the United States of America; this includes the design, implementation, and maintenance of internal control relevant to the preparation and fair presentation of consolidated financial statements that are free from material misstatement, whether due to fraud or to error.

Auditor's Responsibility

Our responsibility is to express an opinion on these consolidated financial statements based on our audits. We did not audit the financial statements of B Company, a wholly owned subsidiary, which statements reflect total assets constituting 20% and 22%, respectively, of consolidated total assets at December 31, 20X1 and 20X0, and total revenues constituting 18% and 20%, respectively, of consolidated total revenues for the years then ended. Those statements, which were prepared in accordance with International Financial Reporting Standards as issued by the International Accounting Standards Board, were audited by other auditors, whose report has been furnished to us. We have applied audit procedures on the conversion adjustments to the financial statements of B Company, which conform those financial statements to accounting principles generally accepted in the United States of America. Our opinion, insofar as it relates to the amounts included for B Company, prior to these conversion adjustments, is based solely on the report of the other auditors. We conducted our audits in accordance with auditing standards generally accepted in the United States of America. Those standards require that we plan and perform the audit to obtain reasonable assurance about whether the consolidated financial statements are free from material misstatement.

An audit involves performing procedures to obtain audit evidence about the amounts and disclosures in the consolidated financial statements. The procedures selected depend on the auditor's judgment, including the assessment of the risks of material misstatement of the consolidated financial statements, whether due to fraud or to error. In making those risk assessments, the auditor considers internal control relevant to the entity's preparation and fair presentation of the consolidated financial statements in order to design audit procedures that are appropriate in the circumstances, but not for the purpose of expressing an opinion on the effectiveness of the entity's internal control. Accordingly, we express no such opinion. An audit also includes evaluating the appropriateness of accounting policies used and the reasonableness of significant accounting estimates made by management, as well as evaluating the overall presentation of the consolidated financial statements.

We believe that the audit evidence we have obtained is sufficient and appropriate to provide a basis for our audit opinion.

Opinion

In our opinion, based on our audits and the report of the other auditors, the consolidated financial statements referred to above present fairly, in all material respects, the financial position of ABC Company and its subsidiaries as of December 31, 20X1 and 20X0, and the results of their operations and their cash flows for the years then ended in accordance with accounting principles generally accepted in the United States of America.

Report on Other Legal and Regulatory Requirements

[*Form and content of this section of the auditor's report will vary depending on the nature of the auditor's other reporting responsibilities.*]

[*Auditor's signature*]

[*Auditor's city and state*]

[*Date of the auditor's report*]

ILLUSTRATION 4. A REPORT IN WHICH THE AUDITOR OF THE GROUP FINANCIAL STATEMENTS IS MAKING REFERENCE TO THE AUDIT OF THE FINANCIAL STATEMENTS OF A COMPONENT PREPARED USING THE SAME FINANCIAL REPORTING FRAMEWORK AS THAT USED FOR THE GROUP FINANCIAL STATEMENTS AND PERFORMED BY A COMPONENT AUDITOR IN ACCORDANCE WITH AUDITING STANDARDS OTHER THAN GAAS

In this example, the auditor of the group financial statements is making reference to the audit of the financial statements of a component prepared using the same financial reporting framework as that used for the group financial statements and performed by a component auditor in accordance with auditing standards other than GAAS or standards promulgated by the Public Company Accounting Oversight Board. The group engagement partner has determined that the component auditor performed additional audit procedures to meet the relevant requirements of GAAS. If additional procedures were not necessary for the audit of the component auditor to meet the relevant requirements of GAAS, Illustration 2 is applicable.

Independent Auditor's Report

[*Appropriate addressee*]

Report on the Consolidated Financial Statements

We have audited the accompanying consolidated financial statements of ABC Company and its subsidiaries, which comprise the consolidated balance sheets as of December 31, 20X1 and 20X0, and the related consolidated statements of income, changes in stockholders' equity, and cash flows for the years then ended, and the related notes to the financial statements.

Management's Responsibility for the Financial Statements

Management is responsible for the preparation and fair presentation of these consolidated financial statements in accordance with accounting principles generally accepted in the United States of America; this includes the design, implementation, and maintenance of internal control relevant to the preparation and fair presentation of consolidated financial statements that are free from material misstatement, whether due to fraud or to error.

Auditor's Responsibility

Our responsibility is to express an opinion on these consolidated financial statements based on our audits. We did not audit the financial statements of B Company, a wholly owned subsidiary, which statements reflect total assets constituting 20% and 22%, respectively, of consolidated total assets at December 31, 20X1 and 20X0, and total revenues constituting 18% and 20%, respectively, of consolidated total revenues for the years then ended. Those statements were audited by other auditors in accordance with [*describe the set of auditing standards*], whose report has been furnished to us, and our opinion, insofar as it relates to the amounts included for B Company, is based solely on the report of, and additional audit procedures to meet the relevant requirements of auditing standards generally accepted in the United States of America performed by, the other auditors. We conducted our audits in accordance with auditing standards generally accepted in the United States of America. Those standards require that we plan and perform the audit to obtain reasonable assurance about whether the consolidated financial statements are free of material misstatement.

An audit involves performing procedures to obtain audit evidence about the amounts and disclosures in the consolidated financial statements. The procedures selected depend on the auditor's judgment, including the assessment of the risks of material misstatement of the consolidated financial statements, whether due to fraud or to error. In making those risk assessments, the auditor considers internal control relevant to the entity's preparation and fair presentation of the consolidated financial statements in order to design audit procedures that are appropriate in the circumstances, but not for the purpose of expressing an opinion on the effectiveness of the entity's internal control. Accordingly, we express no such opinion. An audit also includes evaluating the appropriateness of accounting policies used and the reasonableness of significant accounting estimates made by management, as well as evaluating the overall presentation of the consolidated financial statements.

We believe that the audit evidence we have obtained is sufficient and appropriate to provide a basis for our audit opinion.

Opinion

In our opinion, based on our audits and the report of, and additional audit procedures performed by, the other auditors, the consolidated financial statements referred to above present fairly, in all material respects, the financial position of ABC Company and its subsidiaries as of December 31, 20X1 and 20X0, and the results of their operations and their cash flows for the years then ended in accordance with accounting principles generally accepted in the United States of America.

Report on Other Legal and Regulatory Requirements

[*Form and content of this section of the auditor's report will vary depending on the nature of the auditor's other reporting responsibilities.*]

[*Auditor's signature*]

[*Auditor's city and state*]

[*Date of the auditor's report*]

EXHIBIT B. ILLUSTRATIVE COMPONENT AUDITOR'S CONFIRMATION LETTER

The following is not intended to be a standard letter. Confirmations may vary from one component auditor to another and from one period to the next. In this example, confirmations expected only when the auditor of the group financial statements is assuming responsibility have been italicized.

Confirmations often are obtained before work on the financial information of the component commences.

[*Component auditor letterhead*]

[*Date*]

To [*audit firm*]

This letter is provided in connection with your audit of the group financial statements of [*name of parent*] as of and for the year ended [*date*] for the purpose of expressing an opinion on whether the group financial statements present fairly, in all material respects, the financial position of the group as of [*date*] and of the results of its operations and its cash flows for the year then ended in accordance with [*indicate applicable financial reporting framework*].

We acknowledge receipt of your instructions dated [*date*], requesting us to perform the specified work on the financial information of [*name of component*] as of and for the year ended [*date*].

We confirm that:

1. *We will be able to comply with the instructions./We advise you that we will not be able to comply with the following instructions* [specify instructions] *for the following reasons* [specify reasons].
2. *The instructions are clear, and we understand them./We would appreciate it if you could clarify the following instructions* [specify instructions].
3. *We will cooperate with you and provide you with access to relevant audit documentation.*

We acknowledge that:

1. *The financial information of* [name of component] *will be included in the group financial statements of* [name of parent].
2. *You may consider it necessary to be further involved in the work you have requested us to perform on the financial information of* [name of component] *as of and for the year ended* [date].
3. *You intend to evaluate and, if considered appropriate, use our work for the audit of the group financial statements of* [name of parent].

In connection with the work that we will perform on the financial information of [*name of component*], a [*describe component, e.g., wholly owned subsidiary, subsidiary, joint venture, investee accounted for by the equity or cost methods of accounting*] of [*name of parent*], we confirm the following:

1. We have an understanding of [*indicate relevant ethical requirements*] that is sufficient to fulfill our responsibilities in the audit of the group financial statements and will comply therewith. In particular, and with respect to [*name of parent*] and the other components in the group, we are independent

within the meaning of [*indicate relevant ethical requirements*] and comply with the applicable requirements of [*refer to rules*] promulgated by [*name of regulatory agency*].

2. We have an understanding of auditing standards generally accepted in the United States of America and [*indicate other auditing standards applicable to the audit of the group financial statements, such as Government Auditing Standards*] that is sufficient to fulfill our responsibilities in the audit of the group financial statements and will conduct our work on the financial information of [*name of component*] as of and for the year ended [*date*] in accordance with those standards.
3. We possess the special skills (e.g., industry-specific knowledge) necessary to perform the work on the financial information of the particular component.
4. We have an understanding of [*indicate applicable financial reporting framework or group financial reporting procedures manual*] that is sufficient to fulfill our responsibilities in the audit of the group financial statements.

We will inform you of any changes in the above representations during the course of our work on the financial information of [*name of component*].

[*Auditor's signature*]

Illustration of Potential Component Auditor Representations in Governmental Entities and Not-for-Profit Organizations

5. We have an understanding of relevant laws and regulations that may have a direct and material effect on the financial statements of [*name of component*]. In particular, we have an understanding of [*indicate relevant laws and regulations*].

EXHIBIT C. SOURCES OF INFORMATION

The American Institute of Certified Public Accountants (AICPA) Professional Ethics Team can respond to inquiries about whether individuals are members of the AICPA and whether complaints against members have been adjudicated by the Joint Trial Board. The team cannot respond to inquiries about public accounting firms or provide information about letters of required corrective action issued by the team or pending disciplinary proceedings or investigations. The AICPA Peer Review Program staff or the applicable state CPA society administering entity can respond to inquiries about whether specific public accounting firms are enrolled in the AICPA Peer Review Program, the date of acceptance, and the period covered by the firm's most recently accepted peer review.

AU-C 610 Using the Work of Internal Auditors

AU-C ORIGINAL PRONOUNCEMENT

Source Statement on Auditing Standards (SAS) 128.

OBJECTIVES OF AU-C SECTION 610

AU-C Section 610.11 states:

The objectives of the external auditor, when the entity has an internal audit function and the external auditor expects to use the work of internal auditors to modify the nature or timing, or reduce the extent, of audit procedures to be performed directly by the external auditor, are as follows:

a. *To determine whether to use the work of the internal audit function in obtaining audit evidence or to use internal auditors to provide direct assistance, and if so, in which areas and to what extent*
b. *If using the work of the internal audit function in obtaining audit evidence, to determine whether that work is adequate for purposes of the audit*
c. *If using internal auditors to provide direct assistance, to appropriately direct, supervise, and review their work*

APPLICABILITY OF AU-C SECTION 610

AU-C 610 addresses the external auditor's responsibilities if using the work of internal auditors. The external auditor may use internal audit to:

1. *Obtain* audit evidence.
2. *Provide direct assistance* under the direction, supervision, and review of the external auditor.

AU-C 610's requirements are, for the most part, organized around those two uses.

AU-C 610 does *not* apply if:

- The entity does not have an internal audit function,
- The internal audit function is not relevant to the audit, or
- The external auditor does not intend to use the work of the internal audit function.

(AU-C 610.03)

It's worth noting that the external auditor is not required to use internal audit. However, using the internal audit function can result in cost savings and a more effective audit.

DEFINITIONS OF TERMS

Source: AU-C 610.12

Direct assistance. The use of internal auditors to perform audit procedures under the direction, supervision, and review of the external auditor.

Internal audit function. A function of an entity that performs assurance and consulting activities designed to evaluate and improve the effectiveness of the entity's governance, risk management, and internal control processes.

OVERVIEW

SECTION 315 AND UNDERSTANDING INTERNAL CONTROL

According to Section 315, the external auditor's understanding of the entity's internal control should include knowledge about the design of relevant policies, procedures, and records and whether they have been placed in operation. The external auditor may review entity documentation, such as flowcharts prepared by the internal auditors, to obtain information about the design of policies and procedures. To obtain information about whether the controls have been placed in operation, the external auditor may consider the results of procedures performed by the internal auditors on the controls.

In addition to a role in the design and implementation of internal control, the company's internal audit function also plays a role in the monitoring component of internal control. The auditor's understanding of internal audit will therefore provide evidence about the design and possibly operating effectiveness of management's monitoring of internal control. (AU-C 610.A112)

The knowledge gained about the internal audit function while complying with Section 315 is useful when applying Section 610. The external auditor's understanding of the entity's internal control should include knowledge about the design of relevant policies, procedures, and records and whether they have been placed in operation (see Section 315). The external auditor, when obtaining an understanding of the internal audit function (see below), may review flowcharts prepared by the internal auditors to obtain information about the design of policies and procedures.

To obtain information about whether the controls have been placed in operation, the external auditor may consider the results of procedures performed by the internal auditors on the controls.

The company's internal audit function also plays a role in the monitoring component of internal control. The auditor's understanding of internal audit will therefore provide evidence about the design and possibly operating effectiveness of management's monitoring of internal control. (AU-C 315.A112)

Illustrations 1 and 2 at the end of this chapter contain detailed steps for obtaining an understanding of the internal audit function and its role in assisting the external auditor.

RESPONSIBILITY OF THE EXTERNAL AUDITOR

Assuming that the external auditor is satisfied with the competence, objectivity, and work performance, the only limitation on the use of the internal audit function for any purpose is that significant audit judgments should be made by the external auditor.

The work of internal auditors may affect the external auditor's procedures; however, the external auditor should perform enough of his or her own procedures to obtain sufficient, competent evidential matter to support the auditor's report. In making judgments about the extent of the effect of the internal audit functions' work on the external auditor's procedures, the external auditor considers the following about the financial statement amounts worked on by internal auditors:

- The materiality of financial statement amounts; that is, account balances or classes of transactions.
- The risk, inherent risk and control risk, of material misstatement of the assertions related to these financial statement amounts.
- The degree of subjectivity involved in the evaluation of the audit evidence gathered in support of the assertions.

As the materiality of the financial statement amounts increases and either the risk of material misstatement or the degree of subjectivity increases, the need for the auditor to perform his or her own tests of the assertions increases. As these factors decrease, the need for the external auditor to perform his or her own tests of the assertions decreases.

Practice pointer. PCAOB inspection reports have remarked on instances where the external auditors did not have a basis for relying on internal auditors. Based on those experiences, some auditors may have shied away from using external auditors. A recent joint report by the Center for Audit Quality (CAQ) and the Institute of Internal Auditors (IIA), *Intersecting Roles: Fostering Effective Working Relationships among External Audit, Internal Audit, and the Audit Committee,* suggests tactics for effective use of the internal audit function:

- Early frequent communication
- Training internal auditors on evidence needed by external auditors
- Engaging audit committees in the communication process

The report may be useful for audits of nonpublic companies and is available online on the CAQ website at thecaq.org.

Although Section 610 does not require the external auditor to use the work of internal auditors, AU-C 300, *Planning an Audit*, requires the external auditor to obtain a sufficient understanding of internal control to plan the audit. The internal audit function is part of internal control and of the control environment. If the entity has an internal audit function that acts as a higher level of control over the operation of control procedures, it will usually influence the external auditor's assessment of control risk and, as a result, may influence the audit plan and procedures. Section 610 provides sources of information and appropriate inquiries for the external auditor to make to obtain the required understanding.

As a practical matter, the section permits the external auditor to use the work of the internal function to reduce audit costs. In effect, the section officially sanctions the use of internal auditors, but the section does not provide a mandate on minimum use.

Another important point to recognize is that the section is concerned with the internal audit *function* and not client personnel who simply have the title of internal auditor. For example, personnel who reconcile bank accounts or recompute the amount of invoices might be called auditors, but the external auditor would not view their work any differently from that of other personnel who perform those specific procedures. The section is concerned with internal auditors who act as a higher level of control—an additional layer of control to ensure that routine control procedures are operating.

Uses of the Internal Audit Function

The external auditor should determine what work of the internal audit function is relevant to a financial statement audit and whether:

1. It is efficient to use the internal audit function in *obtaining evidence*, and/or
2. Internal auditors may be used to *provide direct assistance* to the external auditor by performing substantive tests or tests of controls.

For either use (item 1 or 2), the external auditor should review the competence and objectivity of the internal audit function and evaluate its work.

REQUIREMENTS

Effect of Use of Internal Auditors' Work on the Audit

The use of the internal auditors' work affects the scope of the audit, especially when the external auditor performs:

1. Procedures to obtain an understanding of the entity's internal control
2. Procedures to assess risk
3. Substantive procedures

Risk Assessment

The results of the internal auditors' tests of controls may provide information about the effectiveness of the entity's internal control and change the nature, timing, and extent of testing the auditor would otherwise need to perform. (AU-C 610.20)

Substantive Procedures

Internal auditors may perform substantive tests, such as the confirmation of receivables and the observation of inventories. The external auditor, therefore, may be able to change the timing of the confirmation procedures, the number of receivables to be confirmed, or the number of locations of inventories to be observed. (AU-C 610.A20)

When the external auditor obtains an understanding of internal control, he or she should obtain an understanding of the internal audit function that is sufficient to identify internal audit activities that are relevant to planning the audit.

Determining Whether Internal Audit Can Be Used to Obtain Evidence

To determine whether the work of the internal audit function can be used in *obtaining* audit evidence, the external auditor ordinarily should make inquiries, listed in AU-C 610.13, of appropriate management and internal audit personnel about the internal auditors':

- Organizational status within the entity and whether the status and policies and procedures allow the internal audit function to be objective
- Level of competence
- Application of a systematic and disciplined approach, including quality control

If the external auditor decides to consider how the internal auditors' work might affect the audit plan and procedures, he or she should assess the competence and objectivity of the internal auditors and the approach to the internal auditors to their work.

Assessing Competence

According to AU-C 610.A8, when the external auditor assesses the internal audit function's competence, he or she should obtain or update information from prior years about whether the internal audit function has:

- Adequate appropriate resources,
- Policies for hiring, training, and assigning internal auditors,
- Internal auditors who have adequate training and proficiency,
- Internal auditors who are knowledgeable about the entity's financial reporting system and the applicable financial reporting framework and have the skills needed to assist the external auditors, and
- Internal auditors who have current certification from professional bodies.

Assessing Objectivity

When the external auditor assesses the internal auditors' objectivity, he or she should obtain or update information from prior years about factors such as:

- The organizational status of the person responsible for the internal audit function, and
- Policies to maintain the internal auditors' objectivity about the areas audited.

(AU-C 610.A7)

Systematic and Disciplined Approach

AU-C 610 contains the concept of a "systematic and disciplined approach." (AU-C 610.13) The section requires that the internal audit function apply a systematic and disciplined approach, including quality control, to its work, and the external auditor must evaluate the application of that approach. Indicators of such an approach may be the existence of documented procedures and quality control procedures. (AU-C 610.A13) This evaluation is in addition to the assessment required by Section 315.

NOTE: Standards for the professional practice of internal auditing have been developed by the Institute of Internal Auditors and the General Accountability Office.

Deciding to Use the Internal Audit Function

After obtaining the required understanding of the internal audit function, the auditor may decide that the internal auditors' work is not relevant to the audit or that it is not efficient to use their work.

If the external auditor decides to use the internal audit function's work to obtain audit evidence, the auditor must then review the nature, timing, and extent of the internal audit work and how it is relevant for the audit plan. (AU-C 610.15) Generally, the external auditor will perform more of the work and rely less on the internal audit function where:

- More judgment is involved,
- The assessed risk is higher at the assertion level, especially for areas of significant risk,
- The organization has a lower level of support for the objectivity of the internal function, and
- The level of competence of the internal audit function is lower.

(AU-C 610.17)

Communicating with Those Charged with Governance

Once the external auditor has planned how to use the work of the internal audit function, that plan should be communicated to those charged with governance. (AU-C 610.19)

PROCEDURES WHEN USING THE INTERNAL AUDIT FUNCTION

The external auditor should also discuss the plan with the internal audit function so that efforts can be coordinated efficiently and effectively. (AU-C 610.20)

Coordination of Work

If the internal auditors' work will have an effect on the external auditor's procedures, it would be efficient for them to coordinate their work by doing the following:

1. Holding periodic meetings
2. Scheduling audit work
3. Providing access to internal auditors' audit documentation
4. Reviewing audit reports
5. Discussing possible accounting and auditing issues

(AU-C 610.A29-.A30)

In addition, the external auditor should:

- Review internal audit reports relevant to the work the internal auditors will perform.
- Perform tests on the internal audit work as a whole to determine its adequacy for the audit, making sure that:
  - It was adequately planned, performed, supervised, reviewed, and documented.
  - Adequate evidence was obtained.
  - Conclusions reached are appropriate, and reports are consistent.
- Re-perform some of the internal audit function's work that the auditor intends to use in obtaining audit evidence.

(AU-C 610.22-.23)

Before the conclusion of the audit, the external auditor should perform another evaluation to ensure that the nature and extent of the work of the internal audit function remains appropriate. (AU-C 610.24)

DETERMINING WHETHER INTERNAL AUDIT CAN BE USED TO PROVIDE DIRECT ASSISTANCE

To use the internal audit function to provide direct assistance with the audit, the external auditor must evaluate:

- Any threats to the internal auditors' objectivity,
- Safeguards to reduce or eliminate those threats,
- The competence of the internal auditors, and
- Judgment needed in planning and performing the procedures and evaluating the evidence obtained.

(AU-C 610.25)

Factors affecting the extent of the effect of the internal auditors' work on the audit plan and procedures are (1) objectivity, (2) risk, and (3) judgment. (AU-C 610.27)

The external auditor may decide to use the internal auditors' work for assertions related to material financial statement amounts where the risk of material misstatement or the degree of subjectivity involved is high. In these circumstances, the internal auditors' work cannot alone reduce audit risk to a level that would eliminate the need for the external auditor to apply any procedures to those assertions. Examples of those assertions are: (1) valuation of assets and liabilities involving significant accounting estimates (for example, accounts receivable; property, plant, and equipment; product warranties), (2) existence and disclosure of related-party transactions, (3) contingencies, (4) uncertainties, and (5) subsequent events. The external auditor should apply some audit procedures to these assertions, in addition to considering the internal auditors' work.

The external auditor may decide to use the internal auditors' work for assertions related to less material financial statement amounts where the risk of material misstatement or the degree of subjectivity involved is low. In these circumstances, the internal auditors' work may reduce audit risk to an acceptable level so that the external auditor does not have to apply any further procedures to those assertions. Examples of those assertions are the existence of cash, prepaid assets, and fixed-asset additions.

Communicating with Those Charged with Governance Regarding Internal Auditors Providing Direct Assistance

Before using internal auditors to provide direct assistance, the external auditor should get acknowledgment, in writing, from management or those charged with governance that those providing assistance will be allowed to follow the external auditor's direction and will not be interfered with by the entity. (AU-C 610.30) This acknowledgement may be included in the engagement letter or other written document. (AU-C 610.A45)

Managing the Internal Audit Function When It Is Providing Direct Assistance

Following the guidance in AU-C 220, the external auditor should direct, supervise, and review the work performed. In particular, the work should be responsive to the outcome of the evaluation factors in AU-C 610.27 mentioned above. Internal auditors should be instructed to bring issues to the external auditor. The external auditor should test some of the work performed by the internal auditors. (AU-C 610.31)

Evaluating and Testing Effectiveness of Internal Auditors' Work

The external auditor must test the work of internal audit to ensure that:

- It was adequately planned, performed, and documented, and
- Sufficient appropriate audit evidence was gathered.

Part of this testing must include the external auditor re-performing a portion of the internal auditor's work.

Procedures for Evaluating the Work Performed by Internal Audit

Procedures to evaluate the work of internal auditors include a review of the following:

1. Scope of work
2. Instructions to internal audit staff
3. Audit documentation

Scope of work. The external auditor should review the scope of the internal auditors' work to determine that it was established by them and was in no way restricted.

Instructions to staff. To determine that the internal auditors were properly instructed, the external auditor should read all written instructions. The external auditor also should review audit programs to determine that they were adequate.

Review of audit documentation. To determine the quality of internal auditors' work, the external auditor should review their audit documentation to determine that:

1. Audit documentation adequately records work performed, including evidence of supervision and review.
2. There is evidence of follow-up and disposition of questions and errors.
3. Conclusions are appropriate in the circumstances.
4. Reports are consistent with the results of work performed.

Testing

To determine the effectiveness of the internal auditors' work, the external auditor should test their work by examining documentary evidence of work performed. The external auditor should either (1) examine some of the controls, transactions, or balances examined by the internal auditors or (2) examine similar controls, transactions, or balances not actually examined by the internal auditors. In either case, the external auditor should compare the results of his or her tests with the results of the internal auditors' work.

DOCUMENTATION

If the external auditor uses the internal audit to obtain audit evidence, the external auditor should document:

- The results of the evaluation of internal audit's function status and relevant policies and procedures,
- The internal audit's level of competence,
- The audit procedures performed to evaluate the adequacy of the work used, and
- The work re-performed by the external auditor.

(AU-C 610.33)

If internal auditors provide direct assistance, the external auditor should document:

- The evaluation of threats and safeguards related to the internal auditors' objectivity,
- The internal auditors' level of competence,
- How the nature and extent of the work performed by internal auditors was decided,
- The nature and extent of the review by the external auditor of the internal auditors' work, and
- The workpapers prepared by the internal auditors.

(AU-C 610.34)

ILLUSTRATIONS

ILLUSTRATION 1. OBTAINING AN UNDERSTANDING OF THE INTERNAL AUDIT FUNCTION

As part of the external auditor's obtaining an understanding of internal control, he or she should obtain an understanding of the internal audit function.

To obtain an understanding of the internal audit function, the external auditor might do the following:

1. Read the entity's manuals.
2. Review the entity's policies and management directives concerning the internal audit function.
3. Make inquiries of management and internal audit personnel about the internal audit function, as described in "Requirements."
4. Review internal auditors' audit documentation.
5. Consider the entity's organization chart and organization chart of the internal audit department.

Inquiries

The external auditor should make inquiries of appropriate management and internal audit personnel about the internal auditors' work. The inquiries should answer the following questions:

1. What are the primary responsibilities of internal auditors?
2. What do internal auditors do when:
   a. They believe misstatements have occurred?
   b. They believe the entity's policies are not being properly executed?
   c. They believe weaknesses exist in internal control?
3. What importance does management attach to the internal audit function?
4. What does management do with recommendations and reports of internal auditors?

To determine how the internal audit department functions, the external auditor should seek answers to the following questions:

1. How are scopes of examinations determined?
2. How are audit procedures determined?
3. How are reports prepared?
4. Who receives the reports?
5. What are the follow-up procedures?

Review of Audit Documentation

Section 315 requires the external auditor to obtain an understanding of internal control and to determine whether relevant policies, procedures, and records have been placed in operation. A review of the internal auditors' audit documentation, schedules, flowcharts, questionnaires, checklists, and so on will help the external auditor determine whether the relevant policies, procedures, and records have been placed in operation. It also will help the external auditor obtain an understanding of the internal audit function.

Organization Charts

To determine the position of the internal audit department in the organization, the external auditor might obtain an organization chart of the entity. The external auditor would then determine the following:

1. To whom do internal auditors report?
2. To what extent do internal auditors have access to top management and to the audit committee or the full board of directors?

Ready access to top management and to the audit committee indicates that the internal audit department could act independently.

To determine the size of the internal audit department and the responsibilities of each member, the external auditor might obtain an organization chart of the department. The responsibilities of the members indicate whether the department performs an internal audit function or an accounting control function.

Assessing Relevance and Efficiency

Relevance

When the external auditor reviews the internal auditors' audit documentation (see above, "Obtaining an Understanding of the Internal Audit Function"), he or she can determine which of the internal auditors' work is relevant to a financial statement audit. Other procedures that may be used by the external auditor to determine the relevancy of the internal auditors' work include the following:

1. Consider knowledge from prior audits.
2. Review how the internal auditors allocate their resources to financial or operating areas of the entity.
3. Read internal audit reports to obtain a detailed understanding about the scope of internal audit activities.

Efficiency

Determining whether it is efficient to use the internal auditors' work requires the professional judgment of the external auditor. The external auditor should answer the question: Is it less time-consuming and cheaper, and as effective, to use the internal auditors' work than to do original work himself or herself?

This section contains a checklist that may be used by the external auditor when he or she uses the work of internal auditors.

ILLUSTRATION 2. CHECKLIST FOR USING WORK OF INTERNAL AUDITORS

____
[*Client*]

____
[*Audit date*]

This checklist should be used on all engagements where the firm intends to use the work of internal auditors.

The work of internal auditors should be evaluated in two situations, as follows:

1. When obtaining audit evidence
2. When providing direct assistance

	Performed by	*Date*
Acquire an Understanding of Internal Audit Function		
1. Review internal audit department and note the following:		
a. Hiring policies		
b. Total number of employees		
c. Number of employees by title; for example, supervisor, senior, and so on		
d. Department's place in organization structure		
e. To whom department reports		
2. Review current year's reports and note the following:		
a. Number and nature of audits		
b. Scope of audits		
c. Recommendations		
d. To whom issued		
e. Action on recommendations		
Relevancy and Efficiency		
1. Determine what work of the internal auditors is relevant to a financial statement audit.		
2. Determine whether it is efficient to use the internal auditors' work as part of the audit.		
Competence of Internal Auditors		
1. Determine if entity conducts training programs for internal auditors.		
2. If entity does not conduct training programs, determine if internal auditors attend outside seminars.		
3. Review personnel files and compare with hiring policies.		
4. Review department library.		
5. Review, on a test basis, current year's audit documentation and note the following:		
a. Quality of work		
b. Adequacy of documentation		
c. Adequacy of supervision		
Objectivity of the Internal Audit Function		
1. Review, on a test basis, scope of audits.		
2. Determine how scope was established.		
3. Determine work performed by internal auditors and ascertain that work was independent of accounting functions.		
4. Review, on a test basis, reports of internal audit department:		
a. Recommendations		
b. To whom issued		
c. Action on recommendations		
Evaluating Work of the Internal Audit Function		
1. Select, on a test basis, audits performed by the department during the year and do the following:		
a. Determine if scope is appropriate for job.		
b. Review audit programs.		

	Performed by	*Date*

c. Review preaudit instructions.
d. Review audit documentation for:

(1) Completeness of documentation
(2) Follow-up and disposition of questions and errors

2. Determine if audit reports and conclusions are consistent with findings noted in audit documentation.
3. Test work of internal auditors:

a. Examine the same transactions and account balances.
b. Examine similar transactions and account balances.
c. Compare results to findings of internal auditors.

Direct Assistance of Internal Auditors

1. Meet with internal auditors:

a. Discuss areas of work.
b. Review program.
c. Review procedures.

2. Review completed audit documentation of internal auditors.
3. Consider the need to test the work performed by internal auditors.

Documentation

1. If the external auditor uses internal audit to obtain audit evidence, the external auditor should document:

- The results of the evaluation of internal audit's function status and relevant policies and procedures,
- The internal audit's level of competence,
- The audit procedures performed to evaluate the adequacy of the work used, and
- The work re-performed by the external auditor.

(AU-C 610.33)

2. If internal auditors provide direct assistance, the external auditor should document:

- The evaluation of threats and safeguards related to the internal auditors' objectivity,
- The internal auditors' level of competence,
- How the nature and extent of the work performed by internal auditors was decided,
- The nature and extent of the review by the external auditor of the internal auditors' work, and
- The workpapers prepared by the internal auditors.

(AU-C 610.34)

	Performed by	*Date*
Communication		
1. Engagement letter: External auditors who intend to use the direct assistance of internal audit must make specific mention of that in the engagement letter.		
2. Once the external auditor has planned how to use the work of the internal audit function, that plan should be communicated to those charged with governance.		
3. If planning to use the internal audit function to provide direct assistance, the external auditor obtains management's written acknowledgment that internal auditors will be taking direction from external auditors.		

AU-C 620 Using the Work of an Auditor's Specialist

AU-C ORIGINAL PRONOUNCEMENT

Source Statement on Auditing Standards (SAS) 122.

AU-C DEFINITIONS OF TERMS

Source: AU-C 620.06

Auditor's specialist. An individual or organization possessing expertise in a field other than accounting or auditing, whose work in that field is used by the auditor to assist the auditor in obtaining sufficient appropriate audit evidence. An auditor's specialist may be either an auditor's internal specialist (who is a partner or staff, including temporary staff, of the auditor's firm or a network firm) or an auditor's external specialist.

Expertise. Skills, knowledge, and experience in a particular field.

Management's specialist. An individual or organization possessing expertise in a field other than accounting or auditing, whose work in that field is used by the entity to assist the entity in preparing the financial statements.

OBJECTIVES OF AU-C SECTION 620

AU-C Section 620.04 states that:

. . . the objectives of the auditor are

a. to determine whether to use the work of an auditor's specialist and

b. if using the work of an auditor's specialist, to determine whether that work is adequate for the auditor's purposes.

REQUIREMENTS

NOTE: Typically, the auditor will consider the need to use a specialist as part of forming an overall audit strategy.

QUALIFICATIONS OF A SPECIALIST

The auditor should consider the following to evaluate whether the specialist has the necessary qualifications:

1. Competence, capabilities, and objectivity
2. Professional certification, license, or other recognition of competence

3. Reputation and standing in the view of peers and other knowledgeable parties
4. Experience in the kind of work under consideration

(AU-C 620.09)

NOTE: For example, an actuary determining property and casualty loss reserves should have experience in the property and casualty insurance field.

Agreement with the Specialist

The auditor should agree in writing with the specialist regarding:

- Nature, scope, and objectives of the assignment
- Roles and responsibilities
- Communication, including form of the report by the specialist
- Confidentiality

(AU-C 620.11)

Work of a Specialist

The auditor should obtain an understanding of the specialist's work that covers the following:

1. Nature
2. Objectives and scope
3. Evaluation of the adequacy of the specialist's work relative to the auditor's purpose

(AU-C 620.10)

NOTE: Sometimes it may be necessary to contact the specialist to ensure the specialist is aware of the auditor's intended use of the work.

Relationship to Client

The auditor should evaluate whether the specialist's relationship to the client, if any, might impair the specialist's objectivity; if so, the auditor should perform additional procedures to determine whether the specialist's assumptions, methods, or findings are not unreasonable, or engage another specialist for that purpose.

Evaluating Findings

The auditor should perform procedures to:

1. Obtain an understanding of the methods and assumptions used
2. Test data (accounting and other data) provided to the specialist and, in considering the extent of testing, assess the control risk relevant to the data
3. Evaluate whether the findings are relevant, reasonable, and consistent with other audit evidence
4. In the circumstance in which the auditor believes the findings are unreasonable, apply additional procedures

(AU-C 620.12-.13)

NOTE: Additional procedures might include obtaining the opinion of another specialist.

Effect on Audit Report

If there is a material difference between the specialist's findings and the assertions in the financial statements, the auditor should do the following:

1. If the matter cannot be resolved by applying additional audit procedures, obtain the opinion of another specialist, unless it appears that the matter cannot be resolved.
2. If the matter has not been resolved, qualify the opinion or disclaim an opinion because of the inability to obtain sufficient competent evidence.
3. If the auditor concludes that the difference indicates the assertions are not in conformity with generally accepted accounting principles (GAAP), qualify the opinion or express an adverse opinion.

Report Reference to Specialist

The auditor should not refer to the work or findings of or identify the specialist in the audit report containing an unmodified opinion. (AU-C 620.14) However, if an auditor makes reference to the specialist's work because he or she believes the reference is relevant to understanding a modification, the auditor should state that such reference does not lessen the auditor's responsibility of the opinion. (AU-C 620.15)

Examples of Use of a Specialist

The following are examples of common uses of specialists:

1. Determination of postemployment and postretirement benefit-related amounts by an actuary
2. Determination of environmental cleanup obligations by an environmental consultant
3. Determination of oil and gas reserves by a petroleum engineer
4. Valuation of a financial institution's real estate investments or real estate collateral by an appraiser
5. Determination of loss reserves of an insurance company by an actuary

The auditor is not required to use a specialist automatically whenever the client has engaged a specialist. The distinction between the circumstances that require use and other circumstances involving use of real estate appraisers discussed by the Auditing Standards Board provides an instructive example. The key is the relation of the specialist's work to the financial statement assertions. A financial institution normally obtains a real estate appraisal for loans collateralized by real estate as part of the loan origination process. In testing controls over the loan origination process, the auditor normally would inspect the appraisal to see that it conformed with the institution's policies and procedures. This is not use of a specialist's work that requires application of the guidance in Section 620. This is a test of controls, not a substantive test, and the specialist's work is not being used to evaluate a material financial statement assertion.

In contrast, in the evaluation of the need for a reserve on a problem loan, the auditor might inspect an appraisal to consider whether the collateral value is below the loan amount. This is a substantive test involving the valuation assertion, and loss reserves are usually material to a financial institution's financial statements. Application of the guidance in Section 620 is required.

Specialist Related to Client

Section 620 clearly indicates that the purpose of considering the specialist's relationship is to evaluate whether there are circumstances that might impair the specialist's objectivity. If the client has the ability to directly or indirectly control or significantly influence the specialist, objectivity might be impaired. The influence might arise from employment, ownership, contractual right, family relationship, or otherwise.

A specialist without a relationship to the client is more likely to be objective, and that specialist's work will provide the auditor with greater assurance of reliability.

If the specialist has a relationship with the client, the auditor should assess the risk that the specialist's objectivity might be impaired. If the auditor believes the relationship might impair the specialist's objectivity, the auditor should perform additional procedures.

The additional procedures involve heightened scrutiny of the specialist's assumptions, methods, or findings to determine that the findings are not unreasonable. The auditor might decide that another specialist should be engaged for this purpose.

The "Illustrations" section contains an engagement letter and a statement of the specialist's independence that can be used to document information concerning the relationship of the specialist to the client.

SPECIALIST EMPLOYED BY CPA FIRM

Some CPA firms have employed specialists to provide consulting services to clients. For example, some CPA firms employ actuaries, real estate appraisers, or environmental specialists.

If the client has engaged a specialist employed by the CPA firm to determine an amount or disclosure that is material to the financial statements, the guidance in Section 620 applies to the auditor's use of that specialist's work. This means the auditor has to apply the same procedures that Section 620 would require to be applied to the work of a specialist unrelated to the CPA firm. For example, the auditor would have to obtain an understanding of the methods and assumptions used by the specialist and evaluate whether the specialist's findings support the related assertions in the financial statements.

In some cases, the auditor might decide to engage a specialist. For example, a specialist might be engaged by the auditor to apply additional procedures when the client uses a related specialist. In these circumstances, a specialist employed by the CPA firm might be used. In this case, the specialist is functioning as a member of the audit team. The auditor would need to provide proper supervision of that specialist in the same manner as any other member of the audit team. However, if the auditor engages a specialist not employed by the CPA firm, then the guidance in Section 620 applies. When the CPA firm uses a firm specialist as a member of the audit team, the specialist is an assistant on the audit with all that such status implies. The specialist has to adhere to GAAS and be properly supervised. Extra supervision is required when the specialist is not knowledgeable about GAAP, GAAS, and the Code of Professional Conduct.

TESTS OF DATA USED BY THE SPECIALIST

In many cases, the client has to provide data to the specialist. For example, the management of an insurance company would provide data on insurance in force to an actuary engaged to determine loss reserves, and a financial institution might provide a real estate appraiser with income statements of a project that collateralizes a loan.

Section 620 indicates that the auditor should make appropriate tests of data provided to the specialist. In other words, the data to be tested is not limited to accounting data.

In deciding the extent of testing of data that is necessary, the auditor should consider the control risk associated with production of the data. Section 620 does not mention inherent risk. Thus, the implication is that the auditor would need to substantiate data provided to the specialist unless the data are produced by a system with a relatively low control risk. Also, the extent of testing considered necessary would depend on the nature and materiality of the related financial statement assertion.

Need to Refer to Audit Guides

If there is more specific guidance on the use of a specialist in an audit guide, the auditor should refer to the more detailed guidance. An audit guide cannot reduce the procedures needed when a specialist's work is used. However, the guidance might specify additional procedures or limit the auditor's discretion in determining the scope of procedures.

An AICPA audit guide might also provide informative guidance on the methods and assumptions of a specialist that is useful in evaluating whether a specialist's findings support financial statement assertions. For example, there is an AICPA guide on real estate appraisals that describes the various methods used by an appraiser. Some methods might produce a value that is not suitable for supporting financial statement assertions in certain circumstances. For example, the market value determined by an appraiser based on stabilized net operating income might not be appropriate when the real estate's fair value is the appropriate measure.

AU-C INTERPRETATIONS

The Use of Legal Interpretations as Audit Evidence to Support Management's Assertion That a Transfer of Financial Assets Has Met the Isolation Criterion in Paragraphs 7-14 of Financial Accounting Standards Board Codification 860-10-40 (December 2001); Revised March 2006, June 2009, October 2011; Effective for Audits of Financial Statements for Periods Ending on or after December 15, 2012[1]

Financial Accounting Standards Board (FASB) Accounting Standards Codification (ASC) 860, *Transfers and Servicing*, requires that a transferor of financial assets must surrender control over the financial assets to account for the transfer as a sale. Paragraph 9(a) states several conditions that must be met to provide evidence of surrender of control. One of these conditions is that the transferred assets must have been isolated from the transferor and its creditors. The determination of whether this isolation criterion has been met depends on facts and circumstances and should be assessed primarily from a legal perspective. The interpretation has not been updated to reflect the issuance of SFAS No. 166, now incorporated in FASB ASC 860. Likewise, the interpretation has not been updated for the September 2010 changes to the Federal Deposit Insurance Corporation's (FDIC) safe harbor for financial assets transferred in connection with securitizations and participations. The AICPA's Auditing Standards Board is currently in the process of revising the interpretation. However, the guidance continues to be relevant.

Decision to Use a Specialist

The auditor should first consider whether to use the work of a legal specialist to support management's assertion that the isolation criterion has been met. The specialist can be the client's internal or external attorney who is knowledgeable about applicable law. While the use of a legal

---

1 While this interpretation guidance continues to be relevant, readers should be aware that it has not yet been updated for FASB Statement No. 166 and the FDIC's September 2010 changes to safe harbor rules. An update is planned, and readers should keep an eye out for changes.

specialist will not be necessary for routine transfers of assets, a legal specialist is necessary for transfers involving complex legal structures, continuing involvement by the transferor, or other legal issues.

If the auditor uses a legal opinion to support the accounting conclusion, the auditor may need, in certain circumstances, to obtain updates of the opinion to confirm that there have been no subsequent changes in relevant law or applicable regulations or in the pertinent facts of the transaction that would change the previous opinion. Updates may be necessary when:

- The legal opinion relates to multiple transfers under a single structure, and such transfers occur over an extended period of time under that structure.
- Management asserts that a new transaction has a structure that is the same as a prior structure for which a legal opinion that complies with this interpretation was used as evidence to support an assertion that the transfer of assets met the isolation criterion.

The auditor should also consider whether management needs to obtain periodic updates to confirm that there have been no subsequent changes in relevant law or applicable regulations that may affect the conclusions in the previous opinion in the case of other transfers.

Assessing the Adequacy of the Legal Opinion

In assessing the adequacy of the legal opinion, the auditor should:

- Consider whether the legal specialist has experience with relevant matters, including knowledge of the US Bankruptcy Code and other federal, state, and foreign law.
- Consider whether the legal specialist has knowledge of the transaction on which management's assertion is based.
- For transactions that may be affected by provisions of the Federal Deposit Insurance Act, consider whether the legal specialist has experience with the rights and powers of receivers, conservators, and liquidating agents under that Act.
- Obtain an understanding of the assumptions used by the legal specialist and make appropriate tests of information.
- Consider the form and content of the document provided by the legal specialist.
- Evaluate whether the legal specialist's findings support management's assertions about the isolation criterion.

A legal opinion that includes any of the following would not be persuasive evidence that a transfer of assets has met the isolation criterion:

- An inadequate opinion, an inappropriate opinion, or a disclaimer of opinion
- A limit on the scope of the opinion to facts and circumstances that are not applicable to the transaction
- Language that does not provide persuasive evidence, such as the following examples provided in the interpretation:
  - "We are unable to express an opinion . . ."
  - "It is our opinion, based upon limited facts . . ."
  - "We are of the view . . ." or "it appears . . ."
  - "There is a reasonable basis to conclude that . . ."
  - "In our opinion, the transfer would be *either* a sale *or* a grant of a perfected security interest . . ."
  - "In our opinion, there is a reasonable possibility . . ."

- "In our opinion, the transfer *should* be considered a sale . . ."
- "It is our opinion that the entity will be able to assert meritorious arguments . . ."
- "In our opinion, it is more likely than not . . ."
- "In our opinion, the transfer would *presumptively* be . . ."
- "In our opinion, it is probable that . . ."

- Conclusions about hypothetical transactions if they are not relevant to management's assertions or do not contemplate all the facts and circumstances of the transaction

If a legal specialist's response does not provide persuasive evidence that a transfer of assets has met the isolation criterion, and no other relevant evidential matter exists, derecognition of the transferred assets is not in conformity with GAAP, and the auditor should consider expressing a qualified or adverse opinion (see Section 508, *Reports on Audited Financial Statements*).

Restricted-Use Legal Opinions

Legal opinions that restrict the use of the opinion to the client or to third parties other than the auditor would *not* be acceptable audit evidence. In this case, the auditor should ask the client to obtain the legal specialist's written permission for the auditor to use the opinion for the purpose of evaluating management's assertion that the isolation criterion has been met.

If the legal specialist does not grant permission for the auditor to use a legal opinion that is restricted to the client or to third parties other than the auditor, a scope limitation exists, and the auditor should consider qualifying or disclaiming an opinion (see Section 508).

The following example from the interpretation illustrates a letter from a legal specialist to a client that adequately communicates permission for the auditor to use the legal specialist's opinion for the purpose of evaluating management's assertion that a transfer of financial assets meets the isolation criterion of FAS ASC 860:

> Notwithstanding any language to the contrary in our opinions of even date with respect to certain bankruptcy issues relating to the above-referenced transaction, you are authorized to make available to your auditors such opinions solely as evidential matter in support of their evaluation of management's assertion that the transfer of the receivables meets the isolation criterion of ASC 860, provided a copy of this letter is furnished to them in connection therewith. In authorizing you to make copies of such opinions available to your auditors for such purpose, we are not undertaking or assuming any duty or obligation to your auditors or establishing any lawyer–client relationship with them. Further, we do not undertake or assume any responsibility with respect to financial statements of you or your affiliates.

The following would *not* adequately communicate permission for the auditor to use:

- "Use but not rely on" language in which a letter from a legal specialist authorizes the client to make copies available to the auditor but states that the auditor is not authorized to rely thereon
- Other language that similarly restricts the auditor's use of the legal specialist's opinion

The auditor may wish to consult with legal counsel in circumstances where it is not clear that the auditor may use the legal specialist's opinion.

Finally, the interpretation provides:

- Two examples of the conclusions in a legal opinion for an entity that is subject to receivership or conservatorship under provisions of the Federal Deposit Insurance Act. The conclusions in the examples provide persuasive evidence, in the absence of contradictory evidence, to support management's assertion that the transferred financial assets have been put presumptively beyond the reach of the entity and its creditors, even in conservatorship or receivership.

- Examples of additional paragraphs addressing substantive consolidation that applies when the entity to which the assets are sold or transferred is an affiliate of the selling entity. These paragraphs may also apply in other situations as noted by the legal specialist.

ILLUSTRATIONS

The following are illustrations of:

1. An engagement letter from a client to a specialist
2. An independence letter for a specialist

ILLUSTRATION 1. ENGAGEMENT LETTER FROM CLIENT TO SPECIALIST

[*Client's letterhead*]

[*Addressed to specialist's firm*]

This letter confirms our understanding for the services you provide as an independent specialist in connection with the audit of the financial statements of [*name of client*] for the year ended [*date*]. If you agree to this understanding, please sign one copy of this letter and return it to us.

Our understanding is as follows:

1. You understand that the results of your work will be used by our auditors, [*name of auditors*], as corroborating evidence in connection with their audit of the aforementioned financial statements for the purpose of expressing an opinion on whether the statements are presented fairly in all material respects in conformity with accounting principles generally accepted in the United States of America.
2. The objectives of your work are as follows:

   [*List objectives, such as determining fair market value of inventory, fair value of stock in a closely held corporation, pension expense, pension liability, etc.*]
3. The scope of your work is as follows:

   [*List procedures that it is anticipated the specialist will apply. In this list, indicate that scope is in no way restricted.*]
4. The methods and assumptions you will use will cover the following areas:

   [*List methods and assumptions such as the following: estimated rate of return and estimated life expectancy of employees for pension expense and pension liability, estimated rate of return and estimated cash flows for valuation of stock in a closely held corporation, etc.*]
5. Your report will be submitted directly to us with a copy to our auditors no later than [*date*]. Your report will include the following:

   a. Scope of work
   b. Methods used and statement of consistency of the methods used with those used in the prior year
   c. Assumptions used
   d. Results, in detail, of your work

e. Your opinion on the information that will appear in our financial statements and accompanying notes

6. You are independent with respect to us and our management. Principals, officers, owners of your firm and members of their immediate families, and members of your staff in the office working on this engagement are not in any way—nor have you been in any way—associated with us and our management except in your capacity as an outside specialist.
[*This paragraph would be modified if there is a relationship between the specialist and the client.*]
7. Fees for your services will be at your usual per diem rate of [*amount*].

Very truly yours,

____

[*Client's name*]

____

[*Signature and title*]

Agreed to:

____

[*Name and title of specialist*] [*Date*]

ILLUSTRATION 2. STATEMENT OF SPECIALIST'S INDEPENDENCE

[*Client's letterhead*]

[*Addressed to specialist's firm*]

In connection with their audit of our financial statements for the year ended [*date*], please describe directly to our auditors, [*name of firm*], the nature and extent of any relationship noted below that you have with the entity, exclusive of your engagement as [*type of work, i.e., actuary, appraiser, etc.*]. A stamped, self-addressed envelope is enclosed for your convenience.

Very truly yours,

____

[*Client's name*]

By ______________

____

[*Title*]

Specialist Representation

Except as noted below, the principals, officers, owners of our firm and members of their immediate families, and members of our staff in the office doing the work described above are not associated with [*name of client*], as follows:

1. By direct or indirect financial interest
2. As an officer, employee, or member of the board of directors

3. In any capacity, other than our normal business relationship, where we have a vested interest in the success of the entity

   Exceptions: ____
   ____
   ____
   ____
   ____

________	____________	____________	________
[*Date*]	[*Firm*]	[*Signature*]	[*Title*]

AU-C 700 Forming an Opinion and Reporting on Financial Statements

AU-C ORIGINAL PRONOUNCEMENT

Sources Statements on Auditing Standards (SASs) 122 and 130.

TECHNICAL ALERT

In January 2016, the Auditing Standards Board (ASB) issued SAS No. 131, *Amendment to Auditing Standards No. 122 Section 700, Forming an Opinion and Reporting on Financial Statements*. The SAS clarifies the format's auditor's report that should be used when the auditor conducts an audit in accordance with the status of Public Company Accounting Oversight Board (PCAOB) standards when the audit is not under the jurisdiction of the PCAOB. Amendments are effective for audits of financial statements for periods ending on or after June 15, 2016. Earlier application is permitted. The amendments are incorporated into this chapter.

AU-C DEFINITIONS OF TERMS

Source: AU-C 700.11

Comparative financial statements. A complete set of financial statements for one or more prior periods included for comparison with the financial statements of the current period.

Comparative information. Prior period information presented for purposes of comparison with current period amounts or disclosures that is not in the form of a complete set of financial statements. Comparative information includes prior period information presented as condensed financial statements or summarized financial information.

Condensed financial statements. Historical financial information that is presented in less detail than a complete set of financial statements, in accordance with an appropriate financial reporting framework. Condensed financial statements may be separately presented as unaudited financial information or may be presented as comparative information.

General purpose financial statements. Financial statements prepared in accordance with a general purpose framework.

General purpose framework. A financial reporting framework designed to meet the common financial information needs of a wide range of users.

Unmodified opinion. The opinion expressed by the auditor when the auditor concludes that the financial statements are presented fairly, in all material respects, in accordance with the applicable financial reporting framework.

OBJECTIVES OF AU-C SECTION 700

AU-C 700.10 states that:

. . . *the objectives of the auditor are to*

a. form an opinion on the financial statements based on an evaluation of the audit evidence obtained, including evidence obtained about comparative financial statements or comparative financial information, and
b. express clearly that opinion on the financial statements through a written report that also describes the basis for that opinion.

REQUIREMENTS: FORMING AN OPINION

In order to form an opinion, the auditor must make a conclusion as to whether she or he has obtained reasonable assurance about whether the financial statements in accordance with the applicable financial reporting framework are presented fairly in all material aspects. (AU-C 700.13) In order to make that conclusion, the auditor must evaluate whether:

1. Sufficient, appropriate evidence has been obtained (see AU-C 330).
2. Uncorrected misstatements are material, individually or in the aggregate (see AU-C 450).
3. There are any indications of management bias.
4. The financial statements are prepared in accordance with requirements of the applicable financial reporting framework (AU-C 700.15), particularly in respect to:

   a. Adequate disclosure of the significant accounting policies selected and applied
   b. Consistency of those accounting policies with the applicable financial reporting framework and their appropriateness
   c. The reasonableness of accounting estimates
   d. The relevance, reliability, comparability, and understandability of information
   e. Adequacy of disclosures to enable the intended users to understand the effect of material transactions and events on the information conveyed in the financial statements
   f. The appropriateness of the terminology used in the financial statements, including the title of each financial statement
   g. The overall presentation, structure, and content of the financial statements
   h. Whether the presentation represents fairly the underlying transactions and events
   i. Whether the financial statements adequately refer to or describe the applicable financial reporting framework

   (AU-C 700.14-.18)

If the auditor concludes that the financial statements are presented fairly, in all material respects, in accordance with the appropriate financial reporting framework, the auditor should express an unmodified opinion. (AU-C 700.19)

However, if the auditor concludes that the financial statements are materially misstated or the auditor is unable to obtain the evidence needed to make a conclusion, the auditor should modify the opinion in accordance with AU-C 705. (AU-C 700.20)

REQUIREMENTS: AUDITOR'S STANDARD REPORT

COMPONENTS OF AUDITOR'S STANDARD REPORT

The auditor's standard report must be in writing (AU-C 700.22) and should include the following:

1. A title that includes the word *independent* (for example, Independent Auditor's Report). (AU-C 700.23) AU-C 200 provides guidance when the auditor is not independent. (AU-C 700.A18)
2. An introductory paragraph with statements that:
   a. Identify the entity audited.
   b. The financial statements explicitly identified in the report as to title and date were audited.

   (AU-C 700.25)
3. A section titled "Management's Responsibility for the Financial Statements" (AU-C 700.26) that:
   a. Describes management's responsibility for the preparation and fair presentation of the financial statements, including:
      1. An explanation that management is responsible for the preparation and fair presentation of the financial statements in accordance with the applicable financial reporting framework, and that
      2. This responsibility includes the design, implementation, and maintenance of internal control relevant to the preparation and fair presentation of financial statements that are free from material misstatement, whether due to fraud or to error.

      (AU-C 700.27)
4. A section headed "Auditor's Responsibility" (AU-C 700.29) that includes:
   a. A statement related to the auditor's responsibility to express an opinion on the financial statements based on an audit (AU-C 700.30), and
   b. Another statement that the audit was conducted in accordance with GAAS and an identification of the United States of America as the country of origin of those standards (e.g., auditing standards generally accepted in the United States of America, or US GAAS). The report should go on to explain that GAAS requires that the auditor plan and perform the audit to obtain reasonable assurance about whether the financial statements are free from material misstatement. (AU-C 700.31)
   c. A description of an audit that states an audit includes:
      1. Performing procedures to obtain audit evidence about the amounts and disclosures in the financial statements. (AU-C 700.32a)
      2. Selecting procedures based on the auditor's judgment, including the assessment of the risks of material misstatement of the financial statements, whether due to fraud or to error. In making those risk assessments, the auditor considers internal control relevant to the entity's preparation and fair presentation of the financial statements in order to design audit procedures that are appropriate in the circumstances but not

for the purpose of expressing an opinion on the effectiveness of the entity's internal control, and accordingly, no such opinion is expressed. (AU-C 700.32b)

3. Evaluating the accounting principles used and significant estimates made by management. (AU-C 700.32c)
4. Evaluating the overall financial statement presentation.

d. A statement that the auditor believes that the audit evidence is sufficient and appropriate to provide a reasonable basis for the opinion. (AU-C 700.33)

5. A section with the heading "Opinion." (AU-C 700.34) An opinion paragraph presents the auditor's opinion as to whether the financial statements present fairly, in all material respects, the financial position of the entity as of the balance sheet date and the result of its operations and its cash flows for the period then ended in conformity with the applicable financial reporting framework. (AU-C 700.35) The opinion should identify the applicable financial reporting framework. (AU-C 700.36)
6. The manual or printed signature of the auditing firm (AU-C 700.39), the city and state where the auditor practices (AU-C 700.40), and the date of the audit report, which should be no earlier than the date on which the auditor has obtained sufficient appropriate audit evidence on which to base the opinion. (AU-C 700.41)

Addressee

The auditor's report may be addressed to the entity whose financial statements are being audited or those charged with governance. For an unincorporated entity, the report should be addressed as circumstances dictate. For example:

- **Unincorporated entity.** The report should be addressed to the partners, or to the general partner of a limited partnership, to joint venturers, or to the proprietor of a sole proprietorship.
- **Audit of entity not the client of the auditor.** When an auditor is retained to audit the financial statements of an entity that is not the auditor's client, the report should be addressed to the one who retained the auditor and not to those charged with governance whose financial statements were audited.

(AU-C 700.A19-23)

NOTE: Under Section 301, Public Company Audit Committees, and the SEC's related implementing Rule No. 33-8138, "Strengthening the Commission's Requirements Regarding Auditor Independence," the audit committee is "directly responsible for the appointment, compensation, and oversight of the work of any registered public accounting firm employed by that issuer . . . for the purpose of preparing or issuing an audit report or related work, and each such registered public accounting firm shall report directly to the audit committee." Therefore, audit reports of listed companies should be addressed to the audit committee. It is acceptable to also address the report to the stockholders and boards of directors.

The "AU-C 700 Illustrations" section at the end of this chapter contains examples of the auditor's standard report on financial statements covering a single year and on comparative financial statements.

At times an auditor may conduct an audit that is not under the jurisdiction of the PCAOB, but the entity under audit wants to have such an audit or the audit may be required to be conducted in accordance with the standards of the PCAOB by:

- Requirements of an urgency or a regulator
- Contractual agreement

Certain SEC filings require audits to be performed in accordance with PCAOB standards even though the entity is not within the jurisdiction of the PCAOB.

Some agencies that may want PCAOB audits are:

- Clearing agencies
- Future commission merchants registered with the Commodity Futures Trading Commission (CFTC)
- Often agencies registered with the CFTC

Auditors performing such audits must also comply with GAAS. If the report refers to the PCAOB standards in addition to GAAS, the audits should use the form of report required by the PCAOB standards. (AU-C 700.44) The "AU-C 700 Illustrations" section shows examples of reporting on those circumstances.

REQUIREMENTS: REPORTS ON COMPARATIVE FINANCIAL STATEMENTS

General

A continuing auditor should update his or her report on the prior period financial statements presented on a comparative basis with the current period financial statements. When updating his or her report, the auditor should consider the effects of circumstances or events coming to his or her attention during the audit of the current period financial statements that may affect the prior period financial statements. (AU-C 700.45)

Change of Opinion

In an updated report, if the auditor expresses an opinion different from the one previously expressed on prior period financial statements, he or she should do the following:

1. Disclose all substantive reasons for the different opinion in an emphasis-of-matter paragraph
2. The emphasis-of-matter paragraph should disclose the following:
    a. The date of the auditor's previous report
    b. The kind of opinion previously expressed
    c. The circumstances or events that caused the auditor to express a different opinion
    d. That the auditor's opinion on the amended, prior period financial statements is different from the opinion previously expressed on those financial statements

    (AU-C 700.53)

Reissuance of Predecessor Auditor's Report

Predecessor's Procedures

Before reissuing or consenting to the reuse of a report previously issued on financial statements of a prior period, when those financial statements are to be presented on a comparative basis with audited financial statements of a subsequent period, a predecessor auditor should consider whether the previous report on those statements is still appropriate. The predecessor should do the following:

1. Read the current period financial statements.
2. Compare the prior period financial statements that the predecessor reported on with the financial statements to be presented on a comparative basis.
3. Obtain letters of representation from:
    a. The successor auditor, stating whether the successor's audit revealed matters that might have a material effect on, or require disclosure in, the financial statements reported on by the predecessor auditor, and
    b. Management of the former client, stating:
        1. Whether any information has come to management's attention that would cause it to believe that any previous representations should be modified, and
        2. Whether any events have occurred subsequent to the balance sheet date of the latest prior period financial statements reported on by the predecessor auditor that would require adjustment to, or disclosure in, those financial statements.

Based on these procedures, if the predecessor auditor believes the previously issued report must be revised, he or she should make inquiries about the matter and perform other procedures considered necessary.

Revision of Previously Issued Report

If the predecessor auditor concludes that the previously issued report should be revised, the updated report should disclose all substantive reasons for the different opinion in a separate explanatory paragraph *preceding* the opinion paragraph of the report. The explanatory paragraph should disclose the following:

1. The auditor's previous report date
2. The kind of opinion previously expressed
3. The circumstances or events that caused the auditor to express a different opinion
4. The updated opinion on the prior period financial statements is different from the opinion previously expressed on those financial statements

Dating of Reissued Report

When reissuing the auditor's report on prior period financial statements, the predecessor auditor should use the date of the previous report.

If the predecessor revises the report or the previously reported-on financial statements are restated, the predecessor auditor should dual date the report.

PREDECESSOR AUDITOR'S REPORT NOT PRESENTED

General

When the predecessor auditor's report on prior period financial statements is not reissued, the successor auditor should disclose in an other-matter paragraph of his or her report the following:

1. That the prior period financial statements were audited by another auditor
2. The predecessor auditor's report date

3. The type of opinion expressed by the predecessor auditor and, if the opinion was modified, the reasons why
4. The nature of an emphasis-of-matter or other-matter paragraph included in the predecessor's report, if any

(AU-C 700.54)

Prior Period Financial Statements Restated

When the prior period financial statements have been restated and the predecessor auditor agrees to issue a new auditor's report on the restated financial statements, the auditor should express an opinion on only the current period. (AU-C 700.55)

INTERPRETATIONS

INTERPRETATION NO. 1, "REPORTING ON FINANCIAL STATEMENTS PREPARED ON A LIQUIDATION BASIS OF ACCOUNTING" (ISSUED DECEMBER 1984; REVISED JUNE 1993 AND FEBRUARY 1997; REVISED OCTOBER 2000; REVISED JUNE 2009; REVISED OCTOBER 2011, EFFECTIVE FOR AUDITS OF FINANCIAL STATEMENTS FOR PERIODS ENDING ON OR AFTER DECEMBER 15, 2012; REVISED MAY 2014; REVISED SEPTEMBER 2014)

INTERPRETATION NO. 2, "SUSTAINABILITY FINANCIAL STATEMENTS UNDER FEDERAL FINANCIAL ACCOUNTING STANDARDS—AUDITOR REPORTING" (ISSUED OCTOBER 2015)

This interpretation applies to financial statements of the U.S. government. Auditors involved in such a report should refer to the AICPA's text in AU-C 9700.06-.07.

An entity is not viewed as a going concern if liquidation is imminent. In these circumstances, the liquidation basis of accounting is GAAP. If the liquidation basis has been properly applied and adequate disclosures are made, the auditor may issue an unqualified opinion.

If financial statements on the liquidation basis are presented in comparative form with a prior period's going-concern-basis financial statements and a matter presented in the financial statements is of such importance that it is fundamental to the user's understanding of the financial statements, the auditor's report must include an emphasis-of-matter paragraph that describes the change in basis of accounting.

AU-C 700 ILLUSTRATIONS (SOURCE: AU-C 700.58)

1. An Auditor's Report on Consolidated Comparative Financial Statements Prepared in Accordance with Accounting Principles Generally Accepted in the United States of America
2. An Auditor's Report on a Single Year Prepared in Accordance with Accounting Principles Generally Accepted in the United States of America
3. An Auditor's Report on Consolidated Comparative Financial Statements Prepared in Accordance with Accounting Principles Generally Accepted in the United States of America When the Audit Has Been Conducted in Accordance with Both Auditing Standards Generally Accepted in the United States of America and International Standards on Auditing

4. An Auditor's Report on a Single Year Prepared in Accordance with Accounting Principles Generally Accepted in the United States of America When Comparative Summarized Financial Information Derived from Audited Financial Statements for the Prior Year Is Presented
5. An Auditor's Report on a Single Year Prepared in Accordance with Accounting Principles Generally Accepted in the United States of America When Comparative Summarized Financial Information Derived from Unaudited Financial Statements for the Prior Year Is Presented

ILLUSTRATION 1. AN AUDITOR'S REPORT ON CONSOLIDATED COMPARATIVE FINANCIAL STATEMENTS PREPARED IN ACCORDANCE WITH ACCOUNTING PRINCIPLES GENERALLY ACCEPTED IN THE UNITED STATES OF AMERICA

Circumstances include the following:

- Audit of a complete set of general purpose consolidated financial statements (comparative).
- The financial statements are prepared in accordance with accounting principles generally accepted in the United States of America.

Independent Auditor's Report

[*Appropriate addressee*]

Report on the Financial Statements

We have audited the accompanying consolidated financial statements of ABC Company and its subsidiaries, which comprise the consolidated balance sheets as of December 31, 20X1 and 20X0; the related consolidated statements of income, changes in stockholders' equity, and cash flows for the years then ended; and the related notes to the financial statements.

Management's Responsibility for the Financial Statements

Management is responsible for the preparation and fair presentation of these consolidated financial statements in accordance with accounting principles generally accepted in the United States of America; this includes the design, implementation, and maintenance of internal control relevant to the preparation and fair presentation of consolidated financial statements that are free from material misstatement, whether due to fraud or to error.

Auditor's Responsibility

Our responsibility is to express an opinion on these consolidated financial statements based on our audits. We conducted our audits in accordance with auditing standards generally accepted in the United States of America. Those standards require that we plan and perform the audit to obtain reasonable assurance about whether the consolidated financial statements are free from material misstatement.

An audit involves performing procedures to obtain audit evidence about the amounts and disclosures in the consolidated financial statements. The procedures selected depend on the auditor's judgment, including the assessment of the risks of material misstatement of the consolidated financial statements, whether due to fraud or to error. In making those risk assessments, the auditor considers internal control relevant to the entity's preparation and fair presentation of the consolidated financial statements in order to design audit procedures that are appropriate in the circumstances, but not for the purpose of expressing an opinion on the effectiveness of the entity's internal control. Accordingly, we express no such opinion.

An audit also includes evaluating the appropriateness of accounting policies used and the reasonableness of significant accounting estimates made by management, as well as evaluating the overall presentation of the consolidated financial statements.

We believe that the audit evidence we have obtained is sufficient and appropriate to provide a basis for our audit opinion.

Opinion

In our opinion, the consolidated financial statements referred to above present fairly, in all material respects, the financial position of ABC Company and its subsidiaries as of December 31, 20X1 and 20X0, and the results of their operations and their cash flows for the years then ended in accordance with accounting principles generally accepted in the United States of America.

Report on Other Legal and Regulatory Requirements

[*Form and content of this section of the auditor's report will vary depending on the nature of the auditor's other reporting responsibilities.*]

[*Auditor's signature*]

[*Auditor's city and state*]

[*Date of the auditor's report*]

Illustration 2. An Auditor's Report on a Single Year Prepared in Accordance with Accounting Principles Generally Accepted in the United States of America

Circumstances include the following:

- Audit of a complete set of general purpose financial statements (single year).
- The financial statements are prepared in accordance with accounting principles generally accepted in the United States of America.

Independent Auditor's Report

[*Appropriate addressee*]

Report on the Financial Statements

We have audited the accompanying financial statements of ABC Company, which comprise the balance sheet as of December 31, 20X1, and the related statements of income, changes in stockholders' equity, and cash flows for the year then ended, and the related notes to the financial statements.

Management's Responsibility for the Financial Statements

Management is responsible for the preparation and fair presentation of these financial statements in accordance with accounting principles generally accepted in the United States of America; this includes the design, implementation, and maintenance of internal control relevant to the preparation and fair presentation of financial statements that are free from material misstatement, whether due to fraud or to error.

Auditor's Responsibility

Our responsibility is to express an opinion on these financial statements based on our audit. We conducted our audit in accordance with auditing standards generally accepted in the United States of America. Those standards require that we plan and perform the audit to obtain reasonable assurance about whether the financial statements are free from material misstatement.

An audit involves performing procedures to obtain audit evidence about the amounts and disclosures in the financial statements. The procedures selected depend on the auditor's judgment, including the assessment of the risks of material misstatement of the financial statements, whether due to fraud or to error. In making those risk assessments, the auditor considers internal control relevant to the entity's preparation and fair presentation of the financial statements in order to design audit procedures that are appropriate in the circumstances, but not for the purpose of expressing an opinion on the effectiveness of the entity's internal control. Accordingly, we express no such opinion. An audit also includes evaluating the appropriateness of accounting policies used and the reasonableness of significant accounting estimates made by management, as well as evaluating the overall presentation of the financial statements.

We believe that the audit evidence we have obtained is sufficient and appropriate to provide a basis for our audit opinion.

Opinion

In our opinion, the financial statements referred to above present fairly, in all material respects, the financial position of ABC Company as of December 31, 20X1, and the results of its operations and its cash flows for the year then ended in accordance with accounting principles generally accepted in the United States of America.

Report on Other Legal and Regulatory Requirements

[*Form and content of this section of the auditor's report will vary depending on the nature of the auditor's other reporting responsibilities.*]

[*Auditor's signature*]

[*Auditor's city and state*]

[*Date of the auditor's report*]

ILLUSTRATION 3. AN AUDITOR'S REPORT ON CONSOLIDATED COMPARATIVE FINANCIAL STATEMENTS PREPARED IN ACCORDANCE WITH ACCOUNTING PRINCIPLES GENERALLY ACCEPTED IN THE UNITED STATES OF AMERICA WHEN THE AUDIT HAS BEEN CONDUCTED IN ACCORDANCE WITH BOTH AUDITING STANDARDS GENERALLY ACCEPTED IN THE UNITED STATES OF AMERICA AND INTERNATIONAL STANDARDS ON AUDITING

Circumstances include the following:

- Audit of a complete set of general purpose financial statements (comparative).
- The financial statements are prepared in accordance with accounting principles generally accepted in the United States of America.
- The financial statements are audited in accordance with auditing standards generally accepted in the United States of America and International Standards on Auditing.

Independent Auditor's Report

[*Appropriate addressee*]

Report on the Financial Statements

We have audited the accompanying financial statements of ABC Company, which comprise the balance sheets as of December 31, 20X1 and 20X0, and the related statements of income, changes in stockholders' equity, and cash flows for the years then ended, and the related notes to the financial statements.

Management's Responsibility for the Financial Statements

Management is responsible for the preparation and fair presentation of these financial statements in accordance with accounting principles generally accepted in the United States of America; this includes the design, implementation, and maintenance of internal control relevant to the preparation and fair presentation of financial statements that are free from material misstatement, whether due to fraud or to error.

Auditor's Responsibility

Our responsibility is to express an opinion on these financial statements based on our audits. We conducted our audits in accordance with auditing standards generally accepted in the United States of America and in accordance with International Standards on Auditing. Those standards require that we plan and perform the audit to obtain reasonable assurance about whether the financial statements are free from material misstatement.

An audit involves performing procedures to obtain audit evidence about the amounts and disclosures in the financial statements. The procedures selected depend on the auditor's judgment, including the assessment of the risks of material misstatement of the financial statements, whether due to fraud or to error. In making those risk assessments, the auditor considers internal control relevant to the entity's preparation and fair presentation of the financial statements in order to design audit procedures that are appropriate in the circumstances, but not for the purpose of expressing an opinion on the effectiveness of the entity's internal control. Accordingly, we express no such opinion. An audit also includes evaluating the appropriateness of accounting policies used and the reasonableness of significant accounting estimates made by management, as well as evaluating the overall presentation of the financial statements.

We believe that the audit evidence we have obtained is sufficient and appropriate to provide a basis for our audit opinion.

Opinion

In our opinion, the financial statements referred to above present fairly, in all material respects, the financial position of ABC Company as of December 31, 20X1 and 20X0, and the results of its operations and its cash flows for the years then ended in accordance with accounting principles generally accepted in the United States of America.

Report on Other Legal and Regulatory Requirements

[*Form and content of this section of the auditor's report will vary depending on the nature of the auditor's other reporting responsibilities.*]

[*Auditor's signature*]

[*Auditor's city and state*]

[*Date of the auditor's report*]

ILLUSTRATION 4. AN AUDITOR'S REPORT ON A SINGLE YEAR PREPARED IN ACCORDANCE WITH ACCOUNTING PRINCIPLES GENERALLY ACCEPTED IN THE UNITED STATES OF AMERICA WHEN COMPARATIVE SUMMARIZED FINANCIAL INFORMATION DERIVED FROM AUDITED FINANCIAL STATEMENTS FOR THE PRIOR YEAR IS PRESENTED

Circumstances include the following:

- Audit of a complete set of general purpose financial statements (single year).
- Prior year summarized comparative financial information derived from audited financial statements is presented.

- The financial statements are prepared in accordance with accounting principles generally accepted in the United States of America.

Independent Auditor's Report

[Appropriate addressee]

Report on the Financial Statements

We have audited the accompanying financial statements of XYZ Not-for-Profit Organization, which comprise the statement of financial position as of September 30, 20X1, and the related statements of activities and cash flows for the year then ended, and the related notes to the financial statements.

Management's Responsibility for the Financial Statements

Management is responsible for the preparation and fair presentation of these financial statements in accordance with accounting principles generally accepted in the United States of America; this includes the design, implementation, and maintenance of internal control relevant to the preparation and fair presentation of financial statements that are free from material misstatement, whether due to fraud or to error.

Auditor's Responsibility

Our responsibility is to express an opinion on these financial statements based on our audit. We conducted our audit in accordance with auditing standards generally accepted in the United States of America. Those standards require that we plan and perform the audit to obtain reasonable assurance about whether the financial statements are free from material misstatement.

An audit involves performing procedures to obtain audit evidence about the amounts and disclosures in the financial statements. The procedures selected depend on the auditor's judgment, including the assessment of the risks of material misstatement of the financial statements, whether due to fraud or to error. In making those risk assessments, the auditor considers internal control relevant to the organization's preparation and fair presentation of the financial statements in order to design audit procedures that are appropriate in the circumstances, but not for the purpose of expressing an opinion on the effectiveness of the organization's internal control. Accordingly, we express no such opinion. An audit also includes evaluating the appropriateness of accounting policies used and the reasonableness of significant accounting estimates made by management, as well as evaluating the overall presentation of the financial statements.

We believe that the audit evidence we have obtained is sufficient and appropriate to provide a basis for our audit opinion.

Opinion

In our opinion, the financial statements referred to above present fairly, in all material respects, the financial position of XYZ Not-for-Profit Organization as of September 30, 20X1, and the changes in its net assets and its cash flows for the year then ended in accordance with accounting principles generally accepted in the United States of America.

Report on Summarized Comparative Information

We have previously audited the XYZ Not-for-Profit Organization's 20X0 financial statements, and we expressed an unmodified audit opinion on those audited financial statements in our report dated December 15, 20X0. In our opinion, the summarized comparative information presented herein as of and for the year ended September 30, 20X0 is consistent, in all material respects, with the audited financial statements from which it has been derived.

Report on Other Legal and Regulatory Requirements

[*Form and content of this section of the auditor's report will vary depending on the nature of the auditor's other reporting responsibilities.*]

[*Auditor's signature*]

[*Auditor's city and state*]

[*Date of the auditor's report*]

ILLUSTRATION 5. AN AUDITOR'S REPORT ON A SINGLE YEAR PREPARED IN ACCORDANCE WITH ACCOUNTING PRINCIPLES GENERALLY ACCEPTED IN THE UNITED STATES OF AMERICA WHEN COMPARATIVE SUMMARIZED FINANCIAL INFORMATION DERIVED FROM UNAUDITED FINANCIAL STATEMENTS FOR THE PRIOR YEAR IS PRESENTED

Circumstances include the following:

- Audit of a complete set of general purpose financial statements (single year).
- Prior year summarized comparative financial information derived from unaudited financial statements is presented.
- The financial statements are prepared in accordance with accounting principles generally accepted in the United States of America.

Independent Auditor's Report

[*Appropriate addressee*]

Report on the Financial Statements

We have audited the accompanying financial statements of XYZ Not-for-Profit Organization, which comprise the statement of financial position as of September 30, 20X1, and the related statements of activities and cash flows for the year then ended, and the related notes to the financial statements.

Management's Responsibility for the Financial Statements

Management is responsible for the preparation and fair presentation of these financial statements in accordance with accounting principles generally accepted in the United States of America; this includes the design, implementation, and maintenance of internal control relevant to the preparation and fair presentation of financial statements that are free from material misstatement, whether due to fraud or to error.

Auditor's Responsibility

Our responsibility is to express an opinion on these financial statements based on our audit. We conducted our audit in accordance with auditing standards generally accepted in the United States of America. Those standards require that we plan and perform the audit to obtain reasonable assurance about whether the financial statements are free from material misstatement.

An audit involves performing procedures to obtain audit evidence about the amounts and disclosures in the financial statements. The procedures selected depend on the auditor's judgment, including the assessment of the risks of material misstatement of the financial statements, whether due to fraud or to error. In making those risk assessments, the auditor considers internal control relevant to the organization's preparation and fair presentation of the financial statements in order to design audit procedures that are appropriate in the circumstances, but not for the purpose of expressing an opinion on the effectiveness of the organization's internal control. Accordingly, we express no such opinion. An audit also includes evaluating the appropriateness of accounting policies used and the reasonableness of significant accounting estimates made by management, as well as evaluating the overall presentation of the financial statements.

We believe that the audit evidence we have obtained is sufficient and appropriate to provide a basis for our audit opinion.

Opinion

In our opinion, the financial statements referred to above present fairly, in all material respects, the financial position of XYZ Not-for-Profit Organization as of September 30, 20X1, and the changes in its net assets and its cash flows for the year then ended in accordance with accounting principles generally accepted in the United States of America.

Report on Summarized Comparative Information

The summarized comparative information presented herein as of and for the year ended September 30, 20X0, derived from those unaudited financial statements, has not been audited, reviewed, or compiled and, accordingly, we express no opinion on it.

Report on Other Legal and Regulatory Requirements

[*Form and content of this section of the auditor's report will vary depending on the nature of the auditor's other reporting responsibilities.*]

[*Auditor's signature*]

[*Auditor's city and state*]

[*Date of the auditor's report*]

AU-C 705 Modifications to the Opinion in the Independent Auditor's Report

AU-C ORIGINAL PRONOUNCEMENTS

Sources Statements on Accounting Standards (SASs) 122 and 123.

AU-C DEFINITIONS OF TERMS

Source: AU-C 705.06

Modified opinion. A qualified opinion, an adverse opinion, or a disclaimer of opinion.

Pervasive. A term used in the context of misstatements to describe the effects or possible effects on the financial statements of misstatements, if any, that are undetected due to an inability to obtain sufficient appropriate audit evidence. Pervasive effects on the financial statements are those that, in the auditor's professional judgment:

- Are not confined to specific elements, accounts, or items of the financial statements;
- If so confined, represent or could represent a substantial proportion of the financial statements; or
- With regard to disclosures, are fundamental to users' understanding of the financial statements.

OBJECTIVE OF AU-C SECTION 705

AU-C Section 705.05 states that:

. . . the objective of the auditor is to express clearly an appropriately modified opinion on the financial statements that is necessary when

a. the auditor concludes, based on the audit evidence obtained, that the financial statements as a whole are materially misstated or

b. the auditor is unable to obtain sufficient appropriate audit evidence to conclude that the financial statements as a whole are free from material misstatement.

REQUIREMENTS

TYPES OF MODIFIED OPINIONS

Circumstances may require that the auditor not express an unqualified opinion on the financial statements. This section establishes three types of modified opinions: (AU-C 705.01)

1. Qualified opinions, expressed when the auditor:
   a. Has sufficient evidence and concludes that misstatements are material, but not pervasive to the financial statements, or
   b. Does not have the evidence on which to base an opinion, but concludes that the effects of undetected misstatements, although possibly material, are not pervasive.

   (AU-C 705.08)
2. Adverse opinions, expressed when the auditor concludes that misstatements are both material and pervasive. (AU-C 705.09)
3. A disclaimer of opinion, used when the auditor is unable to obtain sufficient audit evidence and concludes that the possible effects of undetected misstatements could be both material and pervasive. (AU-C 705.10)

Types of Modified Opinions

Reason for Modification	Effect on Financial Statements	
	Material, not pervasive	Material and pervasive
Financial statements are materially misstated.	Qualified opinion	Adverse opinion
Auditor is unable to obtain sufficient appropriate audit evidence.	Qualified opinion	Disclaimer of opinion

MODIFIED OPINION FORMAT

When the auditor modifies the opinion, he or she should:

1. Use a heading that describes the opinion, such as "Qualified Opinion." (AU-C 705.23)
2. Add a separate basis for modification paragraph(s) immediately *preceding* the opinion paragraph of the report that disclose(s) all of the substantive reasons for the qualified opinion. The paragraph should be headed "Basis for Qualified Opinion."

(AU-C 705.17)

3. Add appropriate qualifying language to the opinion paragraph, including the word *except* or *exception* in a phrase such as *except for* or *with the exception of.*
4. Add a reference in the opinion paragraph to the basis of qualified opinion paragraph(s).

(AU-C 705.24)

NOTE: Disclosing all the substantive reasons for an opinion means that all GAAP departures and scope limitations that are material and known to the auditor should be disclosed. For example, the auditor should disclose a known misapplication of the lower of cost or market method in inventory evaluation, even though the opinion has been qualified for a scope limitation related to inventory.

DISCLAIMER OF OPINION

The auditor disclaims an opinion when he or she has not performed an audit sufficient in scope to enable him or her to form an opinion on the financial statements. Ordinarily, the auditor should disclaim an opinion on the financial statements when significant scope restrictions are imposed by the client. The rationale for a disclaimer in these circumstances is that the client is in a position to avoid the limitation and the auditor cannot know what would be found by release of the restriction.

The auditor should *not* disclaim an opinion because he or she believes there are material departures from the applicable financial reporting framework.

When disclaiming an opinion because of a scope limitation, the auditor should state in the opinion paragraph that:

a. Because of the significance of the matter described in the basis for disclaimer of opinion paragraph, the auditor has not been able to obtain sufficient appropriate audit evidence to provide a basis for an audit opinion, and
b. Accordingly, the auditor does not express an opinion on the financial statements.

(AU-C 705.26)

NOTE: Even though the auditor disclaims an opinion, the auditor should disclose any known departures from the applicable financial reporting framework.

INABILITY TO OBTAIN SUFFICIENT APPROPRIATE AUDIT EVIDENCE

General

The decision to qualify the opinion or to disclaim an opinion because of a limitation on scope depends on the auditor's assessment of the importance of the omitted procedure to his or her ability to form an opinion on the financial statements being audited. The auditor's assessment is affected by the following:

1. Nature and magnitude of the potential effects
2. Significance to financial statements of the item to scope limitation
3. Pervasiveness of the item

Pervasiveness generally relates to the number of items in the financial statement or a substantial portion of the financial statements; that is, is the matter isolated to a few items or does it affect many? For example, ending inventory affects many items—current assets, current ratio, gross profit, income taxes, and net income—whereas an investment accounted for by the equity method affects few line items in the financial statements.

Common Restrictions on Scope

Common restrictions on the scope of the audit involve (1) observation of physical inventories, (2) confirmation of accounts receivable, and (3) long-term investments accounted for by the equity method when the auditor is unable to obtain audited financial statements of the investee.

If the auditor did not observe the ending inventory because of circumstances such as appointment after year-end, he or she should apply alternative procedures. Alternative procedures may include observing all or part of the physical inventory after year-end and rolling it back to year-end by adjusting for additions and sales between year-end and the date the physical inventory was observed. Whatever alternative procedures are used, the auditor should always make, or observe, some physical counts of the inventory and apply appropriate tests to the transactions between year-end and the date of the observation.

If the auditor did not confirm accounts receivable at year-end because of circumstances such as appointment after year-end, he or she might do either of the following at the time of appointment:

1. Try to confirm year-end balances or individual sales and cash receipts.
2. Confirm balances at a date subsequent to year-end and apply appropriate tests to transactions between year-end and the confirmation date.

Some debtors are unable to confirm balances at any time. In these circumstances, the auditor should consider examining subsequent cash receipts or specific sales invoices. In all instances in which accounts receivable are not substantiated by confirmation, the auditor has to document how the presumption that receivables will be confirmed was overcome.

If the auditor is unable to obtain audited financial statements of the investee for investments accounted for by the equity method, he or she should examine other types of financial statements (compiled, reviewed, internal) and, depending on the materiality of the investment, apply appropriate auditing procedures to these statements. If there is a scope limitation and the auditor satisfies himself or herself as to the account balance by applying alternate procedures, the auditor's report should not make reference to these circumstances.

Management-Imposed Limitation

When management imposes limitations on the audit's scope, the auditor should:

- Request that management remove the limitation
- Communicate the matter to those charged with governance, if management refuses to remove the limitation, and
- Determine if it is possible to obtain sufficient evidence by using alternative procedures

(AU-C 705.11-12)

The auditor should disclaim an opinion on the financial statement or, when practicable, withdraw from the engagement, when the auditor is unable to obtain sufficient evidence because of a management-imposed scope limitation and the possible effects of undetected misstatements could be material and pervasive. (AU-C 705.13)

Lack of Independence

If the auditor is not independent but law or regulation requires her or him to report on the financial statements, the auditor should:

- Disclaim an opinion.
- Specifically state that the auditor is not independent.

The auditor is not required to explain the reasons for the lack of independence. However, if the auditor explains the lack of independence, the auditor must include *all* the reasons for the lack of independence. (AU-C 705.16)

Material Misstatement in the Financial Statements

When financial statements are materially affected by a material misstatement in the financial statements, the auditor should issue a qualified opinion or an adverse opinion, depending on whether misstatements are pervasive.

When the auditor expresses a qualified opinion, he or she should include a separate basis for qualified opinion paragraph or paragraphs disclosing:

1. All substantive reasons that led to the conclusion that there was a material misstatement of the financial statements related to specific amounts, and
2. The principal effects of the departure on the financial statements, if practicable.

(AU-C 705.18)

The opinion paragraph of a report qualified because of a departure from GAAP should include appropriate qualifying language and refer to the basis for qualified opinion paragraph(s). (AU-C 705.24)

Inadequate disclosure. If the financial statements, including the notes, do not disclose information required by the applicable financial reporting framework, the auditor should:

- Discuss the omission with those charged with governance describing the omitted information,
- Issue a qualified or adverse opinion describing the omitted information, and
- Provide the omitted information in the auditor's report, if practical.

(AU-C 705.19 and .20)

Adverse Opinions

When the auditor expresses an adverse opinion, the auditor should state in the opinion paragraph that the financial statements taken as a whole are not presented fairly in conformity with the applicable financial reporting framework. (AU-C 705.25)

When the auditor expresses an adverse opinion, he or she should do the following:

1. Disclose in a separate paragraph immediately *before* the opinion paragraph of the report all substantive reasons for the opinion.
2. State the principal effects of the subject matter that caused the adverse opinion on financial position, results of operations, and cash flows, if practicable. If the effects are not reasonably determinable, the auditor's report should state this fact.
3. Include in the opinion paragraph a direct reference to the separate basis for an adverse opinion paragraph.

(See Illustration 3 later in this chapter.)

Departure from the Applicable Financial Reporting Framework

The decision to express a qualified or an adverse opinion because of a departure from GAAP depends on the degree of materiality of the departure. Criteria for determining the degree of materiality of a departure from the applicable financial reporting framework are:

1. Dollar magnitude of the effects
2. Significance of the item to the entity (for example, inventories to a manufacturing company)
3. Pervasiveness of the misstatements
4. Impact of the misstatement on the financial statements taken as a whole

In practice, auditors also consider the likely purpose of management in departing from the applicable financial reporting framework. A judgment that management intended to mislead users would ordinarily cause the auditor to express an adverse opinion.

AU-C 705 ILLUSTRATIONS (SOURCE: AU-C 705.A32)

The following auditor's reports with modifications to the opinion are illustrated:

1. An Auditor's Report Containing a Qualified Opinion Due to a Material Misstatement of the Financial Statements
2. An Auditor's Report Containing a Qualified Opinion for Inadequate Disclosure
3. An Auditor's Report Containing an Adverse Opinion Due to a Material Misstatement of the Financial Statements
4. An Auditor's Report Containing a Qualified Opinion Due to the Auditor's Inability to Obtain Sufficient Appropriate Audit Evidence
5. An Auditor's Report Containing a Disclaimer of Opinion Due to the Auditor's Inability to Obtain Sufficient Appropriate Audit Evidence about a Single Element of the Financial Statements
6. An Auditor's Report Containing a Disclaimer of Opinion Due to the Auditor's Inability to Obtain Sufficient Appropriate Audit Evidence about Multiple Elements of the Financial Statements
7. An Auditor's Report in Which the Auditor Is Expressing an Unmodified Opinion in the Prior Year and a Modified Opinion (Qualified Opinion) in the Current Year
8. An Auditor's Report in Which the Auditor Is Expressing an Unmodified Opinion in the Current Year and a Disclaimer of Opinion on the Prior-Year Statements of Income, Changes in Stockholders' Equity, and Cash Flows

ILLUSTRATION 1. AN AUDITOR'S REPORT CONTAINING A QUALIFIED OPINION DUE TO A MATERIAL MISSTATEMENT OF THE FINANCIAL STATEMENTS

Circumstances include the following:

- Audit of a complete set of general purpose financial statements (comparative) prepared in accordance with accounting principles generally accepted in the United States of America.
- Inventories are misstated. The misstatement is deemed to be material but not pervasive to the financial statements. Accordingly, the auditor's report contains a qualified opinion.

Independent Auditor's Report

[*Appropriate addressee*]

Report on the Financial Statements

We have audited the accompanying financial statements of ABC Company, which comprise the balance sheets as of December 31, 20X1 and 20X0, and the related statements of income, changes in stockholders' equity, and cash flows for the years then ended, and the related notes to the financial statements.

Management's Responsibility for the Financial Statements

Management is responsible for the preparation and fair presentation of these financial statements in accordance with accounting principles generally accepted in the United States of America; this includes the design, implementation, and maintenance of internal control relevant to the preparation and fair presentation of financial statements that are free from material misstatement, whether due to fraud or to error.

Auditor's Responsibility

Our responsibility is to express an opinion on these financial statements based on our audits. We conducted our audits in accordance with auditing standards generally accepted in the United States of America. Those standards require that we plan and perform the audit to obtain reasonable assurance about whether the financial statements are free from material misstatement.

An audit involves performing procedures to obtain audit evidence about the amounts and disclosures in the financial statements. The procedures selected depend on the auditor's judgment, including the assessment of the risks of material misstatement of the financial statements, whether due to fraud or to error. In making those risk assessments, the auditor considers internal control relevant to the entity's preparation and fair presentation of the financial statements in order to design audit procedures that are appropriate in the circumstances, but not for the purpose of expressing an opinion on the effectiveness of the entity's internal control. Accordingly, we express no such opinion. An audit also includes evaluating the appropriateness of accounting policies used and the reasonableness of significant accounting estimates made by management, as well as evaluating the overall presentation of the financial statements.

We believe that the audit evidence we have obtained is sufficient and appropriate to provide a basis for our qualified audit opinion.

Basis for Qualified Opinion

The Company has stated inventories at cost in the accompanying balance sheets. Accounting principles generally accepted in the United States of America require inventories to be stated at the lower of cost or market. If the Company stated inventories at the lower of cost or market, a write-down of $XXX and $XXX would have been required as of December 31, 20X1 and 20X0, respectively. Accordingly, cost of sales would have been increased by $XXX and $XXX, and net income, income taxes, and stockholders' equity would have been reduced by $XXX, $XXX, and $XXX, and $XXX, $XXX, and $XXX, as of and for the years ended December 31, 20X1 and 20X0, respectively.

Qualified Opinion

In our opinion, except for the effects of the matter described in the Basis for Qualified Opinion paragraph, the financial statements referred to above present fairly, in all material respects, the financial position of ABC Company as of December 31, 20X1 and 20X0, and the results of its operations and its cash flows for the years then ended in accordance with accounting principles generally accepted in the United States of America.

Report on Other Legal and Regulatory Requirements

[*Form and content of this section of the auditor's report will vary depending on the nature of the auditor's other reporting responsibilities.*]

[*Auditor's signature*]

[*Auditor's city and state*]

[*Date of the auditor's report*]

ILLUSTRATION 2. AN AUDITOR'S REPORT CONTAINING A QUALIFIED OPINION FOR INADEQUATE DISCLOSURE

Circumstances include the following:

- Audit of a complete set of general purpose financial statements (comparative) prepared in accordance with accounting principles generally accepted in the United States of America.

- The financial statements have inadequate disclosures. The auditor has concluded that (1) it is not practicable to present the required information and (2) the effects are such that an adverse opinion is not appropriate. Accordingly, the auditor's report contains a qualified opinion.

Independent Auditor's Report

[*Appropriate addressee*]

Report on the Financial Statements

We have audited the accompanying financial statements of ABC Company, which comprise the balance sheets as of December 31, 20X1 and 20X0, and the related statements of income, changes in stockholders' equity, and cash flows for the years then ended, and the related notes to the financial statements.

Management's Responsibility for the Financial Statements

Management is responsible for the preparation and fair presentation of these financial statements in accordance with accounting principles generally accepted in the United States of America; this includes the design, implementation, and maintenance of internal control relevant to the preparation and fair presentation of financial statements that are free from material misstatement, whether due to fraud or to error.

Auditor's Responsibility

Our responsibility is to express an opinion on these financial statements based on our audits. We conducted our audits in accordance with auditing standards generally accepted in the United States of America. Those standards require that we plan and perform the audit to obtain reasonable assurance about whether the financial statements are free from material misstatement.

An audit involves performing procedures to obtain audit evidence about the amounts and disclosures in the financial statements. The procedures selected depend on the auditor's judgment, including the assessment of the risks of material misstatement of the financial statements, whether due to fraud or to error. In making those risk assessments, the auditor considers internal control relevant to the entity's preparation and fair presentation of the financial statements in order to design audit procedures that are appropriate in the circumstances, but not for the purpose of expressing an opinion on the effectiveness of the entity's internal control. Accordingly, we express no such opinion. An audit also includes evaluating the appropriateness of accounting policies used and the reasonableness of significant accounting estimates made by management, as well as evaluating the overall presentation of the financial statements.

We believe that the audit evidence we have obtained is sufficient and appropriate to provide a basis for our qualified audit opinion.

Basis for Qualified Opinion

The Company's financial statements do not disclose [*describe the nature of the omitted information that is not practicable to present in the auditor's report*]. In our opinion, disclosure of this information is required by accounting principles generally accepted in the United States of America.

Qualified Opinion

In our opinion, except for the omission of the information described in the Basis for Qualified Opinion paragraph, the financial statements referred to above present fairly, in all material respects, the financial position of ABC Company as of December 31, 20X1 and 20X0, and the results of its operations and its cash flows for the years then ended in accordance with accounting principles generally accepted in the United States of America.

Report on Other Legal and Regulatory Requirements

[*Form and content of this section of the auditor's report will vary depending on the nature of the auditor's other reporting responsibilities.*]

[*Auditor's signature*]

[*Auditor's city and state*]

[*Date of the auditor's report*]

ILLUSTRATION 3. AN AUDITOR'S REPORT CONTAINING AN ADVERSE OPINION DUE TO A MATERIAL MISSTATEMENT OF THE FINANCIAL STATEMENTS

Circumstances include the following:

- Audit of a complete set of consolidated general purpose financial statements (single year) prepared in accordance with accounting principles generally accepted in the United States of America.
- The financial statements are materially misstated due to the nonconsolidation of a subsidiary. The material misstatement is deemed to be pervasive to the financial statements. Accordingly, the auditor's report contains an adverse opinion. The effects of the misstatement on the financial statements have not been determined because it was not practicable to do so.

Independent Auditor's Report

[*Appropriate addressee*]

Report on the Consolidated Financial Statements

We have audited the accompanying consolidated financial statements of ABC Company and its subsidiaries, which comprise the consolidated balance sheet as of December 31, 20X1, and the related consolidated statements of income, changes in stockholders' equity, and cash flows for the year then ended, and the related notes to the financial statements.

Management's Responsibility for the Financial Statements

Management is responsible for the preparation and fair presentation of these consolidated financial statements in accordance with accounting principles generally accepted in the United States of America; this includes the design, implementation, and maintenance of internal control relevant to the preparation and fair presentation of consolidated financial statements that are free from material misstatement, whether due to fraud or to error.

Auditor's Responsibility

Our responsibility is to express an opinion on these consolidated financial statements based on our audit. We conducted our audit in accordance with auditing standards generally accepted in the United States of America. Those standards require that we plan and perform the audit to obtain reasonable assurance about whether the consolidated financial statements are free from material misstatement.

An audit involves performing procedures to obtain audit evidence about the amounts and disclosures in the consolidated financial statements. The procedures selected depend on the auditor's judgment, including the assessment of the risks of material misstatement of the consolidated financial statements, whether due to fraud or to error. In making those risk assessments, the auditor considers internal control relevant to the entity's preparation and fair presentation of the consolidated financial statements in order to design audit procedures that are appropriate in the circumstances, but not for the purpose of expressing an opinion on the effectiveness of the entity's internal control. Accordingly, we express no such opinion. An audit also includes evaluating the appropriateness of accounting policies used and the reasonableness of significant accounting estimates made by management, as well as evaluating the overall presentation of the consolidated financial statements.

We believe that the audit evidence we have obtained is sufficient and appropriate to provide a basis for our adverse audit opinion.

Basis for Adverse Opinion

As described in Note X, the Company has not consolidated the financial statements of subsidiary XYZ Company that it acquired during 20X1 because it has not yet been able to ascertain the fair values of certain of the subsidiary's material assets and liabilities at the acquisition date. This investment is therefore accounted for on a cost basis by the Company. Under accounting principles generally accepted in the United States of America, the subsidiary should have been consolidated because it is controlled by the Company. Had XYZ Company been consolidated, many elements in the accompanying consolidated financial statements would have been materially affected. The effects on the consolidated financial statements of the failure to consolidate have not been determined.

Adverse Opinion

In our opinion, because of the significance of the matter discussed in the Basis for Adverse Opinion paragraph, the consolidated financial statements referred to above do not present fairly the financial position of ABC Company and its subsidiaries as of December 31, 20X1, or the results of its operations or its cash flows for the year then ended.

Report on Other Legal and Regulatory Requirements

[*Form and content of this section of the auditor's report will vary depending on the nature of the auditor's other reporting responsibilities.*]

[*Auditor's signature*]

[*Auditor's city and state*]

[*Date of the auditor's report*]

ILLUSTRATION 4. AN AUDITOR'S REPORT CONTAINING A QUALIFIED OPINION DUE TO THE AUDITOR'S INABILITY TO OBTAIN SUFFICIENT APPROPRIATE AUDIT EVIDENCE

Circumstances include the following:

- Audit of a complete set of general purpose financial statements (single year) prepared in accordance with accounting principles generally accepted in the United States of America.
- The auditor was unable to obtain sufficient appropriate audit evidence regarding an investment in a foreign affiliate. The possible effects of the inability to obtain sufficient appropriate audit evidence are deemed to be material but not pervasive to the financial statements. Accordingly, the auditor's report contains a qualified opinion.

Independent Auditor's Report

[*Appropriate addressee*]

Report on the Financial Statements

We have audited the accompanying financial statements of ABC Company, which comprise the balance sheet as of December 31, 20X1, and the related statements of income, changes in stockholders' equity, and cash flows for the year then ended, and the related notes to the financial statements.

Management's Responsibility for the Financial Statements

Management is responsible for the preparation and fair presentation of these financial statements in accordance with accounting principles generally accepted in the United States of America; this includes the design, implementation, and maintenance of internal control relevant to the preparation and fair presentation of financial statements that are free from material misstatement, whether due to fraud or to error.

Auditor's Responsibility

Our responsibility is to express an opinion on these financial statements based on our audit. We conducted our audit in accordance with auditing standards generally accepted in the United States of America. Those standards require that we plan and perform the audit to obtain reasonable assurance about whether the financial statements are free from material misstatement.

An audit involves performing procedures to obtain audit evidence about the amounts and disclosures in the financial statements. The procedures selected depend on the auditor's judgment, including the assessment of the risks of material misstatement of the financial statements, whether due to fraud or to error. In making those risk assessments, the auditor considers internal control relevant to the entity's preparation and fair presentation of the financial statements in order to design audit procedures that are appropriate in the circumstances, but not for the purpose of expressing an opinion on the effectiveness of the entity's internal control. Accordingly, we express no such opinion. An audit also includes evaluating the appropriateness of accounting policies used and the reasonableness of significant accounting estimates made by management, as well as evaluating the overall presentation of the financial statements.

We believe that the audit evidence we have obtained is sufficient and appropriate to provide a basis for our qualified audit opinion.

Basis for Qualified Opinion

ABC Company's investment in XYZ Company, a foreign affiliate acquired during the year and accounted for under the equity method, is carried at $XXX on the balance sheet at December 31, 20X1, and ABC Company's share of XYZ Company's net income of $XXX is included in ABC Company's net income for the year then ended. We were unable to obtain sufficient appropriate audit evidence about the carrying amount of ABC Company's investment in XYZ Company as of December 31, 20X1 and ABC Company's share of XYZ Company's net income for the year then ended because we were denied access to the financial information, management, and auditors of XYZ Company. Consequently, we were unable to determine whether any adjustments to these amounts were necessary.

Qualified Opinion

In our opinion, except for the possible effects of the matter described in the Basis for Qualified Opinion paragraph, the financial statements referred to above present fairly, in all material respects, the financial position of ABC Company as of December 31, 20X1, and the results of its operations and its cash flows for the year then ended in accordance with accounting principles generally accepted in the United States of America.

Report on Other Legal and Regulatory Requirements

[*Form and content of this section of the auditor's report will vary depending on the nature of the auditor's other reporting responsibilities.*]

[*Auditor's signature*]

[*Auditor's city and state*]

[*Date of the auditor's report*]

ILLUSTRATION 5. AN AUDITOR'S REPORT CONTAINING A DISCLAIMER OF OPINION DUE TO THE AUDITOR'S INABILITY TO OBTAIN SUFFICIENT APPROPRIATE AUDIT EVIDENCE ABOUT A SINGLE ELEMENT OF THE FINANCIAL STATEMENTS

Circumstances include the following:

- Audit of a complete set of general purpose financial statements (single year) prepared in accordance with accounting principles generally accepted in the United States of America.
- The auditor was unable to obtain sufficient appropriate audit evidence about a single element of the financial statements. That is, the auditor was unable to obtain audit evidence about the financial information of a joint venture investment accounted for under the proportionate consolidation approach. The investment represents more than 90% of the Company's net assets. The possible effects of this inability to obtain sufficient appropriate audit evidence are deemed to be both material and pervasive to the financial statements. Accordingly, the auditor's report contains a disclaimer of opinion.
- The auditor concluded that it was unnecessary to include in the auditor's report specific amounts for the Company's proportional share of the assets, liabilities, income, and expenses of the joint venture investment because the investment represents more than 90% of the Company's net assets, and that fact is disclosed in the auditor's report.

Independent Auditor's Report

[*Appropriate addressee*]

Report on the Financial Statements

We were engaged to audit the accompanying financial statements of ABC Company, which comprise the balance sheet as of December 31, 20X1, and the related statements of income, changes in stockholders' equity, and cash flows for the year then ended, and the related notes to the financial statements.

Management's Responsibility for the Financial Statements

Management is responsible for the preparation and fair presentation of these financial statements in accordance with accounting principles generally accepted in the United States of America; this includes the design, implementation, and maintenance of internal control relevant to the preparation and fair presentation of financial statements that are free from material misstatement, whether due to fraud or to error.

Auditor's Responsibility

Our responsibility is to express an opinion on these financial statements based on conducting the audit in accordance with auditing standards generally accepted in the United States of America. Because of the matter described in the Basis for Disclaimer of Opinion paragraph, however, we were not able to obtain sufficient appropriate audit evidence to provide a basis for an audit opinion.

Basis for Disclaimer of Opinion

The Company's investment in XYZ Company, a joint venture, is carried at $XXX on the Company's balance sheet, which represents more than 90% of the Company's net assets as of December 31, 20X1. We were not allowed access to the management and the auditors of XYZ Company. As a result, we were unable to determine whether any adjustments were necessary relating to the Company's proportional share of XYZ Company's assets that it controls jointly, its proportional share of XYZ Company's liabilities for which it is jointly responsible, its proportional share of XYZ Company's income and expenses for the year, and the elements making up the statements of changes in stockholders' equity and cash flows.

Disclaimer of Opinion

Because of the significance of the matter described in the Basis for Disclaimer of Opinion paragraph, we have not been able to obtain sufficient appropriate audit evidence to provide a basis for an audit opinion. Accordingly, we do not express an opinion on these financial statements.

Report on Other Legal and Regulatory Requirements

[*Form and content of this section of the auditor's report will vary depending on the nature of the auditor's other reporting responsibilities.*]

[*Auditor's signature*]

[*Auditor's city and state*]

[*Date of the auditor's report*]

Illustration 6. An Auditor's Report Containing a Disclaimer of Opinion Due to the Auditor's Inability to Obtain Sufficient Appropriate Audit Evidence about Multiple Elements of the Financial Statements

Circumstances include the following:

- Audit of a complete set of general purpose financial statements (single year) prepared in accordance with accounting principles generally accepted in the United States of America.
- The auditor was unable to obtain sufficient appropriate audit evidence about multiple elements of the financial statements, that is, the entity's inventories and accounts receivable. The possible effects of this inability to obtain sufficient appropriate audit evidence are deemed to be both material and pervasive to the financial statements. Accordingly, the auditor's opinion contains a disclaimer of opinion.

Independent Auditor's Report

[*Appropriate addressee*]

Report on the Financial Statements

We were engaged to audit the accompanying financial statements of ABC Company, which comprise the balance sheet as of December 31, 20X1, and the related statements of income, changes in stockholders' equity, and cash flows for the year then ended, and the related notes to the financial statements.

Management's Responsibility for the Financial Statements

Management is responsible for the preparation and fair presentation of these financial statements in accordance with accounting principles generally accepted in the United States of America; this includes the design, implementation, and maintenance of internal control relevant to the preparation and fair presentation of financial statements that are free from material misstatement, whether due to fraud or to error.

Auditor's Responsibility

Our responsibility is to express an opinion on these financial statements based on conducting the audit in accordance with auditing standards generally accepted in the United States of America. Because of the matters described in the Basis for Disclaimer of Opinion paragraph, however, we were not able to obtain sufficient appropriate audit evidence to provide a basis for an audit opinion.

Basis for Disclaimer of Opinion

We were not engaged as auditors of the Company until after December 31, 20X1, and, therefore, did not observe the counting of physical inventories at the beginning or end of the year. We were unable to satisfy ourselves by other auditing procedures concerning the inventory held at December 31, 20X1, which is stated in the balance sheet at $XXX. In addition, the introduction of a new computerized accounts receivable system in September 20X1 resulted in numerous misstatements in accounts receivable. As of the date of our audit report, management was still in the process of rectifying the system deficiencies and correcting the misstatements. We were unable to confirm or verify by alternative means accounts receivable included in the balance sheet at a total amount of $XXX at December 31, 20X1. As a result of these matters, we were unable to determine whether any adjustments might have been found necessary in respect of recorded or unrecorded inventories and accounts receivable, and the elements making up the statements of income, changes in stockholders' equity, and cash flows.

Disclaimer of Opinion

Because of the significance of the matters described in the Basis for Disclaimer of Opinion paragraph, we have not been able to obtain sufficient appropriate audit evidence to provide a basis for an audit opinion. Accordingly, we do not express an opinion on these financial statements.

Report on Other Legal and Regulatory Requirements

[*Form and content of this section of the auditor's report will vary depending on the nature of the auditor's other reporting responsibilities.*]

[*Auditor's signature*]

[*Auditor's city and state*]

[*Date of the auditor's report*]

ILLUSTRATION 7. AN AUDITOR'S REPORT IN WHICH THE AUDITOR IS EXPRESSING AN UNMODIFIED OPINION IN THE PRIOR YEAR AND A MODIFIED OPINION (QUALIFIED OPINION) IN THE CURRENT YEAR

Circumstances include the following:

- Audit of a complete set of general purpose financial statements (comparative) prepared in accordance with accounting principles generally accepted in the United States of America.
- Certain lease obligations have been excluded from the financial statements in the current year. The effect of the exclusion is material but not pervasive. The auditor expressed an unmodified opinion in the prior year and is expressing a modified opinion (qualified opinion) in the current year.

Independent Auditor's Report

[*Appropriate addressee*]

Report on the Financial Statements

We have audited the accompanying financial statements of ABC Company, which comprise the balance sheets as of December 31, 20X1 and 20X0, and the related statements of income, changes in stockholders' equity, and cash flows for the years then ended, and the related notes to the financial statements.

Management's Responsibility for the Financial Statements

Management is responsible for the preparation and fair presentation of these financial statements in accordance with accounting principles generally accepted in the United States of America; this includes the design, implementation, and maintenance of internal control relevant to the preparation and fair presentation of financial statements that are free from material misstatement, whether due to fraud or to error.

Auditor's Responsibility

Our responsibility is to express an opinion on these financial statements based on our audits. We conducted our audits in accordance with auditing standards generally accepted in the United States of America. Those standards require that we plan and perform the audit to obtain reasonable assurance about whether the financial statements are free from material misstatement.

An audit involves performing procedures to obtain audit evidence about the amounts and disclosures in the financial statements. The procedures selected depend on the auditor's judgment, including the assessment of the risks of material misstatement of the financial statements, whether due to fraud or to error. In making those risk assessments, the auditor considers internal control relevant to the entity's preparation and fair presentation of the financial statements in order to design audit procedures that are appropriate in the circumstances, but not for the purpose of expressing an opinion on the effectiveness of the entity's internal control. Accordingly, we express no such opinion. An audit also includes evaluating the appropriateness of accounting policies used and the reasonableness of significant accounting estimates made by management, as well as evaluating the overall presentation of the financial statements.

We believe that the audit evidence we have obtained is sufficient and appropriate to provide a basis for our qualified audit opinion.

Basis for Qualified Opinion

The Company has excluded from property and debt in the accompanying 20X1 balance sheet certain lease obligations that were entered into in 20X1 that, in our opinion, should be capitalized in accordance with accounting principles generally accepted in the United States of America. If these lease obligations were capitalized, property would be increased by $XXX, long-term debt by $XXX, and retained earnings by $XXX as of December 31, 20X1, and net income and earnings per share would be increased (decreased) by $XXX and $XXX, respectively, for the year then ended.

Qualified Opinion

In our opinion, except for the effects on the 20X1 financial statements of not capitalizing certain lease obligations as described in the Basis for Qualified Opinion paragraph, the financial statements referred to above present fairly, in all material respects, the financial position of ABC Company as of December 31, 20X1 and 20X0, and the results of its operations and its cash flows for the years then ended in accordance with accounting principles generally accepted in the United States of America.

Report on Other Legal and Regulatory Requirements

[*Form and content of this section of the auditor's report will vary depending on the nature of the auditor's other reporting responsibilities.*]

[*Auditor's signature*]

[*Auditor's city and state*]

[*Date of the auditor's report*]

Illustration 8. An Auditor's Report in Which the Auditor Is Expressing an Unmodified Opinion in the Current Year and a Disclaimer of Opinion on the Prior-Year Statements of Income, Changes in Stockholders' Equity, and Cash Flows

Circumstances include the following:

- Audit of a complete set of general purpose financial statements (comparative) prepared in accordance with accounting principles generally accepted in the United States of America.
- The auditor was unable to observe the physical inventory as of December 31, 20X0, as at that time the auditor had not been engaged. Accordingly, the auditor was unable to obtain sufficient appropriate audit evidence regarding the net income and cash flows for the year ended December 31, 20X1. The effects of the inability to obtain sufficient appropriate audit evidence are deemed material and pervasive.
- The auditor expressed an unmodified opinion on the December 31, 20X2 and 20X1 balance sheets and a disclaimer of opinion on the 20X1 statements of income, changes in stockholders' equity, and cash flows.

Independent Auditor's Report

[*Appropriate addressee*]

Report on the Financial Statements

We have audited the accompanying financial statements of ABC Company, which comprise the balance sheets as of December 31, 20X2 and 20X1, and the related statements of income, changes in stockholders' equity, and cash flows for the years then ended, and the related notes to the financial statements.

Management's Responsibility for the Financial Statements

Management is responsible for the preparation and fair presentation of these financial statements in accordance with accounting principles generally accepted in the United States of America; this includes the design, implementation, and maintenance of internal control relevant to the preparation and fair presentation of financial statements that are free from material misstatement, whether due to fraud or to error.

Auditor's Responsibility

Our responsibility is to express an opinion on these financial statements based on our audits. Except as explained in the Basis for Disclaimer of Opinion paragraph, we conducted our audits in accordance with auditing standards generally accepted in the United States of America. Those standards require that we plan and perform the audit to obtain reasonable assurance about whether the financial statements are free from material misstatement.

An audit involves performing procedures to obtain audit evidence about the amounts and disclosures in the financial statements. The procedures selected depend on the auditor's judgment, including the assessment of the risks of material misstatement of the financial statements, whether due to fraud or to error. In making those risk assessments, the auditor considers internal control relevant to the entity's preparation and fair presentation of the financial statements in order to design audit procedures that are appropriate in the circumstances, but not for the purpose of expressing an opinion on the effectiveness of the entity's internal control. Accordingly, we express no such opinion. An audit also includes evaluating the appropriateness of accounting policies used and the reasonableness of significant accounting estimates made by management, as well as evaluating the overall presentation of the financial statements.

We believe that the audit evidence we have obtained is sufficient and appropriate to provide a basis for our audit opinions on the balance sheets as of December 31, 20X2 and 20X1, and the statements of income, changes in stockholders' equity, and cash flows for the year ended December 31, 20X2.

Basis for Disclaimer of Opinion on 20X1 Operations and Cash Flows

We did not observe the taking of the physical inventory as of December 31, 20X0, since that date was prior to our engagement as auditors for the Company, and we were unable to satisfy ourselves regarding inventory quantities by means of other auditing procedures. Inventory amounts as of December 31, 20X0 enter into the determination of net income and cash flows for the year ended December 31, 20X1.

Disclaimer of Opinion on 20X1 Operations and Cash Flows

Because of the significance of the matter described in the Basis for Disclaimer of Opinion paragraph, we have not been able to obtain sufficient appropriate audit evidence to provide a basis for an audit opinion on the results of operations and cash flows for the year ended December 31, 20X1. Accordingly, we do not express an opinion on the results of operations and cash flows for the year ended December 31, 20X1.

Opinion

In our opinion, the balance sheets of ABC Company as of December 31, 20X2 and 20X1, and the statements of income, changes in stockholders' equity, and cash flows for the year ended December 31, 20X2, present fairly, in all material respects, the financial position of ABC Company as of December 31, 20X2 and 20X1, and the results of its operations and its cash flows for the year ended December 31, 20X2 in accordance with accounting principles generally accepted in the United States of America.

Report on Other Legal and Regulatory Requirements

[*Form and content of this section of the auditor's report will vary depending on the nature of the auditor's other reporting responsibilities.*]

[*Auditor's signature*]

[*Auditor's city and state*]

[*Date of the auditor's report*]

AU-C 706 Emphasis-of-Matter Paragraphs and Other-Matter Paragraphs in the Independent Auditor's Report

AU-C ORIGINAL PRONOUNCEMENT

Source Statement on Auditing Standards (SAS) 122.

AU-C DEFINITIONS OF TERMS

Source: 706.05

Emphasis-of-matter paragraph. A paragraph included in the auditor's report that is required by GAAS, or is included at the auditor's discretion, and that refers to a matter appropriately presented or disclosed in the financial statements that, in the auditor's professional judgment, is of such importance that it is fundamental to users' understanding of the financial statements.

Other-matter paragraph. A paragraph included in the auditor's report that is required by GAAS, or is included at the auditor's discretion, and that refers to a matter other than those presented or disclosed in the financial statements that, in the auditor's professional judgment, is relevant to users' understanding of the audit, the auditor's responsibilities, or the auditor's report.

OBJECTIVES OF AU-C SECTION 706.04

AU-C Section 706.04 states that:

. . . the objective of the auditor, having formed an opinion on the financial statements, is to draw users' attention, when in the auditor's judgment it is necessary to do so, by way of clear additional communication in the auditor's report, to

a. a matter, although appropriately presented or disclosed in the financial statements, that is of such importance that it is fundamental to users' understanding of the financial statements or
b. as appropriate, any other matter that is relevant to users' understanding of the audit, the auditor's responsibilities, or the auditor's report.

REQUIREMENTS

Emphasis-of-Matter and Other-Matter Paragraphs

AU-C Section 706 describes two paragraphs in the auditor's report:

1. An *emphasis-of-matter* paragraph refers to a matter appropriately presented or disclosed in the financial statements. It is any paragraph added to the auditor's report that relates to a matter that is fundamental to users' understanding of the financial statements.

   Certain standards require an emphasis-of-matter paragraph, whereas other emphasis-of-matter paragraphs are added at the discretion of the auditor, consistent with current practice. However, all such paragraphs are to be considered emphasis-of-matter paragraphs, because they are intended to draw the users' attention to a particular matter.
2. An *other-matter* as a paragraph included in the auditor's report refers to a matter other than those presented or disclosed in the financial statements that, in the auditor's judgment, is relevant to the users' understanding of the audit, the auditor's responsibilities, or the auditor's report.

(AU-C 706.01)

Circumstances may require the auditor to add an emphasis-of-matter paragraph or other-matter paragraph to the standard report, even though the circumstances do not affect the auditor's opinion. If the auditor expects to add such a paragraph, he or she should communicate that and the expected wording to those charged with governance.

Emphasis-of-Matter Paragraph

The auditor may decide that it is fundamental to the users' understanding of the financial statements to draw their attention to a matter that is disclosed or presented in the financial statements. In such a case, the auditor adds an emphasis-of-matter paragraph that only refers to information in the financial statements. (AU-C 706.06)

An emphasis-of-matter paragraph should:

- Immediately follow the opinion paragraph.
- Use a heading, such as "Emphasis of Matter" or other appropriate heading.
- Include a clear reference to the matter emphasized and where relevant disclosures can be found in the financial statements.
- Indicate that the auditor's opinion is not modified with respect to the matter emphasized.

(AU-C 706.07)

AU-C 706.14 identifies paragraphs in other AU-C sections that require the auditor to include an emphasis-of-matter paragraph in the auditor's report in certain circumstances.

- Paragraph .16c of Section 560, *Subsequent Events and Subsequently Discovered Facts*
- Paragraphs .15–.16 of Section 570, *The Auditor's Consideration of an Entity's Ability to Continue as a Going Concern*
- Paragraphs .08–.09 and .11–.13 of Section 708, *Consistency of Financial Statements*
- Paragraphs .19 and .21 of Section 800, *Special Considerations—Audits of Financial Statements Prepared in Accordance with Special Purpose Frameworks*

Other Matters in the Auditor's Report

The auditor may find it necessary to communicate a matter that is *not* disclosed or presented in the financial statements, but is relevant to the:

- Understanding of the audit,
- Auditor's responsibilities, or
- Auditor's report.

In that case, the auditor should include the information in a paragraph headed "Other Matter" or other appropriate heading. The paragraph should appear immediately after the opinion paragraph or any emphasis-of-matter paragraph. However, the paragraph may appear elsewhere if it is relevant to the "Other Reporting Responsibilities" section.

AU-C 706.A15 lists the following circumstances that necessitate paragraphs in other AU-C sections that require the auditor to include an other-matter paragraph in the auditor's report in certain circumstances. The list is not a substitute for considering the requirements and related application and other explanatory material in AU-C sections.

- Paragraph .16c of Section 560, *Subsequent Events and Subsequently Discovered Facts*
- Paragraphs .53–.54 and .56–.57 of Section 700, *Forming an Opinion and Reporting on Financial Statements*
- Paragraph .12 of Section 720, *Other Information in Documents Containing Audited Financial Statements*
- Paragraph .09 of Section 725, *Supplementary Information in Relation to the Financial Statements as a Whole*
- Paragraph .07 of Section 730, *Required Supplementary Information*
- Paragraph .20 of Section 800, *Special Considerations—Audits of Financial Statements Prepared in Accordance with Special Purpose Frameworks*
- Paragraph .13 of Section 806, *Reporting on Compliance with Aspects of Contractual Agreements or Regulatory Requirements in Connection with Audited Financial Statements*
- Paragraph .07 of Section 905, *Alert That Restricts the Use of the Auditor's Written Communication*

Communication

If the auditor intends to include an emphasis-of-matter or other-matter paragraph, the auditor should communicate that to those charged with governance and discuss the content of the paragraph. (AU-C 706.09)

AU-C 706 ILLUSTRATIONS

The following auditor's reports with emphasis-of-matter or other-matter paragraphs are illustrated:

1. An Auditor's Report with an Emphasis-of-Matter Paragraph Because There Is Uncertainty Relating to a Pending Unusually Important Litigation Matter
2. An Auditor's Report with an Other-Matter Paragraph That May Be Appropriate When an Auditor Issues an Updated Report on the Financial Statements of a Prior Period That Contains an Opinion Different from the Opinion Previously Expressed

3. An Auditor's Report with a Qualified Opinion Due to a Material Misstatement of the Financial Statements and an Emphasis-of-Matter Paragraph Because There Is Uncertainty Relating to a Pending Unusually Important Litigation Matter

ILLUSTRATION 1. AN AUDITOR'S REPORT WITH AN EMPHASIS-OF-MATTER PARAGRAPH BECAUSE THERE IS UNCERTAINTY RELATING TO A PENDING UNUSUALLY IMPORTANT LITIGATION MATTER

Circumstances include the following:

- Audit of a complete set of general purpose financial statements (single year) prepared in accordance with accounting principles generally accepted in the United States of America.
- There is uncertainty relating to a pending unusually important litigation matter.
- The auditor's report includes an emphasis-of-matter paragraph.

Independent Auditor's Report

[*Appropriate addressee*]

Report on the Financial Statements

We have audited the accompanying financial statements of ABC Company, which comprise the balance sheet as of December 31, 20X1 and the related statements of income, changes in stockholders' equity, and cash flows for the year then ended, and the related notes to the financial statements.

Management's Responsibility for the Financial Statements

Management is responsible for the preparation and fair presentation of these financial statements in accordance with accounting principles generally accepted in the United States of America; this includes the design, implementation, and maintenance of internal control relevant to the preparation and fair presentation of financial statements that are free from material misstatement, whether due to fraud or to error.

Auditor's Responsibility

Our responsibility is to express an opinion on these financial statements based on our audit. We conducted our audit in accordance with auditing standards generally accepted in the United States of America. Those standards require that we plan and perform the audit to obtain reasonable assurance about whether the financial statements are free from material misstatement.

An audit involves performing procedures to obtain audit evidence about the amounts and disclosures in the financial statements. The procedures selected depend on the auditor's judgment, including the assessment of the risks of material misstatement of the financial statements, whether due to fraud or to error. In making those risk assessments, the auditor considers internal control relevant to the entity's preparation and fair presentation of the financial statements in order to design audit procedures that are appropriate in the circumstances, but not for the purpose of expressing an opinion on the effectiveness of the entity's internal control. Accordingly, we express no such opinion. An audit also includes evaluating the appropriateness of accounting policies used and the reasonableness of significant accounting estimates made by management, as well as evaluating the overall presentation of the financial statements.

We believe that the audit evidence that we have obtained is sufficient and appropriate to provide a basis for our audit opinion.

Opinion

In our opinion, the financial statements referred to above present fairly, in all material respects, the financial position of ABC Company as of December 31, 20X1, and the results of its operations and its cash flows for the year then ended in accordance with accounting principles generally accepted in the United States of America.

Emphasis of Matter

As discussed in Note X to the financial statements, the Company is a defendant in a lawsuit [briefly describe the nature of the litigation consistent with the Company's description in the note to the financial statements]. Our opinion is not modified with respect to this matter.

Report on Other Legal and Regulatory Requirements

[Form and content of this section of the auditor's report will vary depending on the nature of the auditor's other reporting responsibilities.]

[*Auditor's signature*]

[*Auditor's city and state*]

[*Date of the auditor's report*]

ILLUSTRATION 2. AN AUDITOR'S REPORT WITH AN OTHER-MATTER PARAGRAPH THAT MAY BE APPROPRIATE WHEN AN AUDITOR ISSUES AN UPDATED REPORT ON THE FINANCIAL STATEMENTS OF A PRIOR PERIOD THAT CONTAINS AN OPINION DIFFERENT FROM THE OPINION PREVIOUSLY EXPRESSED

Circumstances include the following:

- Audit of a complete set of general purpose financial statements (comparative) prepared in accordance with accounting principles generally accepted in the United States of America.
- The auditor's report on the prior period financial statements expressed an adverse opinion due to identified departures from accounting principles generally accepted in the United States of America that resulted in the financial statements being materially misstated. The entity has elected to change its method of accounting for the matters that gave rise to the adverse opinion in the prior period, and has restated the prior period financial statements. Therefore, the auditor has expressed an unmodified opinion on the comparative financial statements.
- The auditor's report includes an other-matter paragraph indicating that the updated report on the financial statements of the prior period contains an opinion different from the opinion previously expressed, as required by Section 700, *Forming an Opinion and Reporting on Financial Statements*.
- Although the entity changed its method of accounting for the matters that gave rise to the adverse opinion in the prior period, the principal objective of the communication in the other-matter paragraph is to draw users' attention to the change in the auditor's opinion on the prior period financial statements. The other-matter paragraph also refers to the change in accounting principle and the related disclosure in the financial statements. Therefore, the other-matter paragraph also meets the objective of communicating the change in accounting principle as required by Section 708, *Consistency of Financial Statements*, and a separate emphasis-of-matter paragraph is not considered necessary.

Independent Auditor's Report

[*Appropriate addressee*]

Report on the Financial Statements

We have audited the accompanying financial statements of ABC Company, which comprise the balance sheets as of December 31, 20X1 and 20X0, and the related statements of income, changes in stockholders' equity, and cash flows for the years then ended, and the related notes to the financial statements.

Management's Responsibility for the Financial Statements

Management is responsible for the preparation and fair presentation of these financial statements in accordance with accounting principles generally accepted in the United States of America; this includes the design, implementation, and maintenance of internal control relevant to the preparation and fair presentation of financial statements that are free from material misstatement, whether due to fraud or to error.

Auditor's Responsibility

Our responsibility is to express an opinion on these financial statements based on our audits. We conducted our audits in accordance with auditing standards generally accepted in the United States of America. Those standards require that we plan and perform the audit to obtain reasonable assurance about whether the financial statements are free from material misstatement.

An audit involves performing procedures to obtain audit evidence about the amounts and disclosures in the financial statements. The procedures selected depend on the auditor's judgment, including the assessment of the risks of material misstatement of the financial statements, whether due to fraud or to error. In making those risk assessments, the auditor considers internal control relevant to the entity's preparation and fair presentation of the financial statements in order to design audit procedures that are appropriate in the circumstances, but not for the purpose of expressing an opinion on the effectiveness of the entity's internal control. Accordingly, we express no such opinion. An audit also includes evaluating the appropriateness of accounting policies used and the reasonableness of significant accounting estimates made by management, as well as evaluating the overall presentation of the financial statements.

We believe that the audit evidence that we have obtained is sufficient and appropriate to provide a basis for our audit opinion.

Opinion

In our opinion, the financial statements referred to above present fairly, in all material respects, the financial position of ABC Company as of December 31, 20X1 and 20X0, and the results of its operations and its cash flows for the years then ended in accordance with accounting principles generally accepted in the United States of America.

Other Matter

In our report dated March 1, 20X1, we expressed an opinion that the 20X0 financial statements did not fairly present the financial position, results of operations, and cash flows of ABC Company in accordance with accounting principles generally accepted in the United States of America because of two departures from such principles: (1) ABC Company carried its property, plant, and equipment at appraisal values and provided for depreciation on the basis of such values, and (2) ABC Company did not provide for deferred income taxes with respect to differences between income for financial reporting purposes and taxable income. As described in Note X, the Company has changed its method of accounting for these items and restated its 20X0 financial statements to conform with accounting principles generally accepted in the United States of America. Accordingly, our present opinion on the restated 20X0 financial statements, as presented herein, is different from that expressed in our previous report.

Report on Other Legal and Regulatory Requirements

[*Form and content of this section of the auditor's report will vary depending on the nature of the auditor's other reporting responsibilities.*]

[*Auditor's signature*]

[*Auditor's city and state*]

[*Date of the auditor's report*]

ILLUSTRATION 3. AN AUDITOR'S REPORT WITH A QUALIFIED OPINION DUE TO A MATERIAL MISSTATEMENT OF THE FINANCIAL STATEMENTS AND AN EMPHASIS-OF-MATTER PARAGRAPH BECAUSE THERE IS UNCERTAINTY RELATING TO A PENDING UNUSUALLY IMPORTANT LITIGATION MATTER

Circumstances include the following:

- Audit of a complete set of general purpose financial statements (single year) prepared in accordance with accounting principles generally accepted in the United States of America.
- Inventories are misstated. The misstatement is deemed to be material but not pervasive to the financial statements.
- There is uncertainty relating to a pending unusually important litigation matter.
- The auditor's report includes a qualified opinion and also includes an emphasis-of-matter paragraph.

Independent Auditor's Report

[*Appropriate addressee*]

Report on the Financial Statements

We have audited the accompanying financial statements of ABC Company, which comprise the balance sheet as of December 31, 20X1, and related statements of income, changes in stockholders' equity, and cash flows for the year then ended, and the related notes to the financial statements.

Management's Responsibility for the Financial Statements

Management is responsible for the preparation and fair presentation of these financial statements in accordance with accounting principles generally accepted in the United States of America; this includes the design, implementation, and maintenance of internal control relevant to the preparation and fair presentation of financial statements that are free from material misstatement, whether due to fraud or to error.

Auditor's Responsibility

Our responsibility is to express an opinion on these financial statements based on our audit. We conducted our audit in accordance with auditing standards generally accepted in the United States of America. Those standards require that we plan and perform the audit to obtain reasonable assurance about whether the financial statements are free from material misstatement.

An audit involves performing procedures to obtain audit evidence about the amounts and disclosures in the financial statements. The procedures selected depend on the auditor's judgment, including the assessment of the risks of material misstatement of the financial statements, whether due to fraud or to error. In making those risk assessments, the auditor considers internal control relevant to the entity's preparation and fair presentation of the financial statements in order to design audit procedures that are appropriate in the circumstances, but not for the purpose of expressing an opinion on the effectiveness of the entity's internal control. Accordingly, we express no such opinion. An audit also includes evaluating the appropriateness of accounting policies used and the reasonableness of significant accounting estimates made by management, as well as evaluating the overall presentation of the financial statements.

We believe that the audit evidence we have obtained is sufficient and appropriate to provide a basis for our qualified audit opinion.

Basis for Qualified Opinion

The Company has stated inventories at cost in the accompanying balance sheet. Accounting principles generally accepted in the United States of America require inventories to be stated at the lower of cost or market. If the Company stated inventories at the lower of cost or market, a write-down of $XXX would have been required as of December 31, 20X1. Accordingly, cost of sales would have been increased by $XXX, and net income, income taxes, and stockholders' equity would have been reduced by $XXX, $XXX, and $XXX, respectively, as of and for the year ended December 31, 20X1.

Qualified Opinion

In our opinion, except for the effects of the matter described in the Basis for Qualified Opinion paragraph, the financial statements referred to above present fairly, in all material respects, the financial position of ABC Company as of December 31, 20X1, and the results of its operations and its cash flows for the year then ended in accordance with accounting principles generally accepted in the United States of America.

Emphasis of Matter

As discussed in Note X to the financial statements, the Company is a defendant in a lawsuit [briefly describe the nature of the litigation consistent with the Company's description in the note to the financial statements]. Our opinion is not modified with respect to this matter.

Report on Other Legal and Regulatory Requirements

[*Form and content of this section of the auditor's report will vary depending on the nature of the auditor's other reporting responsibilities.*]

[*Auditor's signature*]

[*Auditor's city and state*]

[*Date of the auditor's report*]

AU-C 708 Consistency of Financial Statements

AU-C ORIGINAL PRONOUNCEMENT

Source Statement on Auditing Standards (SAS) 122.

AU-C DEFINITION OF TERM

Source: AU-C 708.04

Current period. The most recent period upon which the auditor is reporting.

OBJECTIVES OF AU-C SECTION 708

AU-C Section 708.03 states that:

. . . *the objectives of the auditor are to*

a. evaluate the consistency of the financial statements for the periods presented and
b. communicate appropriately in the auditor's report when the comparability of financial statements between periods has been materially affected by a change in accounting principle or by adjustments to correct a material misstatement in previously issued financial statements.

REQUIREMENTS

CONSISTENCY IMPLICATION OF AUDITOR'S STANDARD REPORT

According to AU-C 708.05, the auditor must be satisfied that the comparability of financial statements between periods has not been materially affected by adjustments to correct a material misstatement in previously issued financial statements or by changes in accounting principles and that such principles have been consistently applied between or among periods because either (1) no change in accounting principles has occurred, or (2) there has been a change in accounting principles or in the method of their application, but the effect of the change on the comparability of the financial statements is not material. In these cases, the auditor would not refer to consistency in his or her report.

Periods to Which Consistency Standard Relates

The financial statements included in the consistency implication depend on what financial statements are covered by the auditor's report:

1. *Current period only*—the consistency of application of accounting principles in relation to the preceding period only (even if financial statements for one or more preceding periods are presented)
2. *Two or more years (no other statements presented)*—the consistency of application of accounting principles between such years
3. *Two or more years (prior year presented but not included in auditor's report)*—consistency between years included in report and also the consistency of such years with the prior year

(AU-C 708.06)

Changes Affecting Consistency

The following changes, if they have a material effect, require the addition of an emphasis-of-matter paragraph after the opinion paragraph that describes the inconsistency.

1. Change in Accounting Principle

Adoption of an accounting principle from the applicable financial reporting framework that is different from the one used in the prior period. An example is a change from the straight-line method to the declining balance method of depreciation for all newly acquired assets in a class. An investee accounted for by the equity method may change an accounting principle. (AU-C 708.12) If this change causes a material lack of comparability in the financial statements of the investor, the auditor should add an emphasis-of-matter paragraph to the auditor's report. (AU-C 708.07-.08)

2. Change in Reporting Entity

A special type of change in accounting principle that is limited mainly to:

a. A presentation of consolidated or combined statements instead of statements of individual entities
b. A change in specific subsidiaries included in the group of entities in the consolidation

(AU-C 708.A11)

NOTE: This means a change in consolidation policy and not the creation, cessation, purchase, or disposition of a subsidiary.

---

c. A change in entities included in combined financial statements

3. Change in Principle Inseparable from Change in Estimate

A change in estimate that is achieved by changing an accounting principle. An example is changing from deferring and amortizing a cost to expensing it when incurred because future benefits of the cost have become doubtful. (AU-C 708.10)

NOTE: Although the accounting treatment is that for a change in estimate, the change in principle affects audit reporting.

---

4. Changes in Presentation of Cash Flows

A change in an entity's policy for determining which items are treated as cash equivalents. This type of change, if material, should be effected by restating financial statements for earlier years presented for comparative purposes. This change in the presentation of cash flows requires the addition of an emphasis-of-matter paragraph. (AU-C 708.A15)

5. Correction of a Material Misstatement in Previously Issued Financial Statements

Correction of an error not involving an accounting principle, such as mathematical mistakes, oversights, or misuse of facts that existed when the financial statements were originally prepared. An emphasis-of-matter paragraph is required when the corrections are material. (AU-C 708.13)

The emphasis-of-matter paragraph should reference the entity's related disclosure and include a statement that the previously issued financial statements have been restated for the correction of a material misstatement. (AU-C 708.14)

CHANGES NOT AFFECTING CONSISTENCY

The following changes, if they have a material effect on comparability, require disclosure in the financial statements but have no effect on the auditor's report and its implications for consistency. If the disclosure is not adequate, the auditor should look to AU-C 705, *Modification to the Opinion in the Independent Auditor's Report.*

1. Change in Accounting Estimate

Examples of items for which estimates are made include uncollectible receivables, inventory obsolescence, warranty costs, and service lives and salvage values of depreciable assets. As new events occur or additional information is obtained, a change in such accounting estimates may be necessary.

2. Changes in Classification or Reclassification

Use of classifications within the financial statements different from classifications in prior years may be made. For example, "cash on hand" might be combined with "cash in bank" in a new classification, "cash."

NOTE: The auditor should evaluate whether the change is also a change in accounting principle or an adjustment to correct a material misstatement in previously issued financial statements and may require a consistency modification. (AU-C 708.16)

FIRST-YEAR AUDITS

If the independent auditor has not audited an entity's financial statements for the preceding year, he or she should apply reasonable and practicable procedures, such as reviewing underlying financial records and the predecessor auditor's audit documentation, to obtain assurance as to the consistency of accounting principles employed in the current year and the preceding year. (AU-C 708.A2)

AU-C 720 Other Information in Documents Containing Audited Financial Statements

AU-C ORIGINAL PRONOUNCEMENTS

Sources Statements on Auditing Standards (SASs) 118, 122, and 123.

AU-C EFFECTIVE DATE AND SUMMARY OF CHANGES

SAS No. 118 was codified in AU 550 when issued, but was moved to AU-C 720 with the issuance of SAS No. 122. Some conforming changes were made in specific paragraphs and footnotes due to the issuance of SAS No. 122, but no substantive changes were made.

AU-C DEFINITIONS OF TERMS

Source: AU-C 720.05

Inconsistency. Other information that conflicts with information contained in the audited financial statements. A material inconsistency may raise doubt about the audit conclusions drawn from audit evidence previously obtained and possibly about the basis for the auditor's opinion on the financial statements.

Misstatement of fact. Other information that is unrelated to matters appearing in the audited financial statements that is incorrectly stated or presented. A material misstatement of fact may undermine the credibility of the document containing audited financial statements.

Other information. Financial and nonfinancial information (other than the financial statements and the auditor's report thereon) that is included in a document containing audited financial statements and the auditor's report thereon, excluding required supplementary information.

OBJECTIVE OF AU-C SECTION 720

AU-C Section 720.04 states that:

> *. . . the objective of the auditor is to respond appropriately when the auditor becomes aware that documents containing audited financial statements and the auditor's report thereon include other information that could undermine the credibility of those financial statements and the auditor's report.*

Other information may include a report by management or those charged with governance on operations, financial summaries or highlights, employment data, planned capital expenditures, financial ratios, names of officers and directors, and selected quarterly data. Other information does not include a press release or similar memorandum or cover letter accompanying the document containing audited financial statements and the auditor's report thereon, information contained in analyst briefings, or information contained on the entity's website. (AU-C 720.A3-.A4)

REQUIREMENTS

The auditor should take the following steps:

1. **Read other information.** Read the other information in the document, looking for any inconsistencies with the audited financial statements. (AU-C 720.06) The auditor should obtain this information from management or those charged with governance prior to the report release date; if the information is not available prior to the report release date, then read the information as soon as practicable thereafter. (AU-C 720.07)

   NOTE: The auditor may delay the release of the auditor's report until management provides the other information to the auditor.

2. **Procedures.** Inform those charged with governance of the auditor's responsibility regarding the other information, as well as any procedures performed on it and the results. (AU-C 720.08)
3. **Treatment of material inconsistencies.** If there is a material inconsistency in the other information, determine whether the audited financial statements or the other information should be revised. (AU-C 720.09)

   Use the following table to select the correct treatment, which assumes that the report has not yet been released:

Identified before Report Release Date

Situation	*Auditor action*
There is a material inconsistency identified before the date of the auditor's report that requires revision of the financial statements, and management refuses to make the revision.	Modify the auditor's opinion in accordance with Section 705, *Modifications to the Opinion in Independent Auditor's Report.* (AU-C 720.10)
There is a material inconsistency identified after the date of the auditor's report that requires revision of the audited financial statements.	Apply the relevant requirements in AU-C 560.11, *Subsequent Events and Subsequently Discovered Facts.* (AU-C 720.11)
There is a material inconsistency identified prior to the report release date that requires revision of the other information, and management refuses to make the revision.	Communicate the issue to those charged with governance. Also, include in the auditor's report an other-matter paragraph, withhold the auditor's report, or withdraw from the engagement. (AU-C 720.12)

If the report has already been released, then instead use the following table to select the correct treatment:

Identified before Report Release Date	
Situation	*Auditor action*
There is a material inconsistency that requires revision of the financial statements.	Apply AU-C 560. (AU-C 720.13)
There is a material inconsistency that requires revision of the other information, and management agrees to make the revision.	Complete those procedures necessary under the circumstances. (AU-C 720.14)
There is a material inconsistency that requires revision of the other information, but management refuses to make the revision.	Notify those charged with governance, and take further actions as appropriate. (AU-C 720.15)

NOTE: When management agrees to make a revision to a document that has already been issued, the auditor may review the steps taken by management to ensure that those in receipt of the previous document version are informed of the need for a revised document.

4. *Treatment of material misstatements.* If there is a material misstatement of fact, discuss the situation with management. (AU-C 720.16) Then, if there is still an apparent material misstatement of fact, ask management to consult with a qualified third party; the auditor should consider any advice received from this third party. (AU-C 720.17) If there is still a material misstatement of fact and management refuses to correct it, then notify those charged with governance of the situation, and take further actions as appropriate. (AU-C 720.18)

NOTE: Following discussion of an apparent material misstatement of fact with management, the auditor may conclude that there are valid differences of judgment or opinion.

ILLUSTRATION

It is not necessary to reference the other information in the auditor's report on the financial statements. However, if the auditor believes that he or she could be associated with the information, this may imply a level of assurance that the auditor did not intend. Accordingly, consider using the disclaimer in Illustration 1 to disclaim an opinion on the other information. (AU-C 720.A2)

ILLUSTRATION 1. OTHER-MATTER PARAGRAPH TO DISCLAIM AN OPINION ON OTHER INFORMATION (FROM AU-C 720.A13)

Our audit was conducted for the purpose of forming an opinion on the basic financial statements as a whole. The [*identify the other information*] is presented for purposes of additional analysis and is not a required part of the basic financial statements. Such information has not been subjected to the auditing procedures applied in the audit of the basic financial statements, and accordingly we do not express an opinion or provide any assurance on it.

AU-C 725 Supplementary Information in Relation to Financial Statements as a Whole

AU-C ORIGINAL PRONOUNCEMENTS

Sources Statements on Auditing Standards (SASs) 119, 122, and 125.

AU-C DEFINITION OF TERM

Source: AU-C 725.04

Supplementary information. Information presented outside the basic financial statements, excluding required supplementary information that is not considered necessary for the financial statements to be fairly presented in accordance with the applicable financial reporting framework. Such information may be presented in a document containing the audited financial statements or separate from the financial statements.

OBJECTIVE OF AU-C SECTION 725

AU-C Section 725.03 states:

The objective of the auditor, when engaged to report on supplementary information in relation to the financial statements as a whole, is to

a. evaluate the presentation of the supplementary information in relation to the financial statements as a whole and

b. report on whether the supplementary information is fairly stated, in all material respects, in relation to the financial statements as a whole.

REQUIREMENTS

An auditor should determine that all of the following conditions are met in order to determine whether supplementary information is fairly stated, in all material respects, in relation to the financial statements as a whole:

- *Source of material.* The supplementary information was derived from the accounting records used to prepare the financial statements.
- *Period.* The supplementary information encompasses the same period as the financial statements.

- *Opinion type.* Neither an adverse opinion nor a disclaimer of opinion was issued on the financial statements.
- *Accompaniment.* The supplementary information will accompany the audited financial statements, or the entity will make the audited financial statements available.

(AU-C 725.05)

Further, management must acknowledge that it is responsible for the following:

- *Supplementary information.* The preparation of supplementary information.
- *Representations.* The following written representations:
    - It acknowledges responsibility for presentation of the supplementary information.
    - It believes the supplementary information is fairly presented.
    - The measurement and presentation methods have not changed from those used in the prior period, or the reasons for such changes are given.
    - Any significant assumptions or interpretations underlying the supplementary information are given.
    - It will make the audited financial statements available whenever the supplementary information is not presented with those statements.
- *Audit report inclusion.* The inclusion of the auditor's report on the supplementary information in any documents containing such information.
- *Inclusion with financials.* The inclusion of the supplementary information with the audited financial statements, or to make the financial statements available.

(AU-C 725.06 and .07)

Finally, the auditor should perform the following procedures, using the same materiality level used in the audit of the financial statements:

1. *Inquiries.* Inquire about the purpose of the supplementary information and the criteria used to prepare it.
2. *Form and content.* Determine whether the form and content of the supplementary information comply with any applicable criteria.
3. *Preparation methods.* Gain an understanding of the methods used to prepare the supplementary information, whether these methods have changed from those used in previous periods, and, if so, why the changes were made.
4. *Reconciliation.* Reconcile the supplementary information to the accounting records used to prepare the financial statements.
5. *Assumptions.* Make inquiries about significant assumptions used in the preparation of the supplementary information.
6. *Appropriateness and completeness.* Evaluate the appropriateness and completeness of the supplementary information.

(AU-C 725.07)

When the entity includes the supplementary information with its financial statements, the auditor reports on this additional information either in an other-matter paragraph or in a separate report. The other-matter paragraph or separate report should include the following items:

1. The audit was conducted to form an opinion on the financial statements as a whole.
2. The supplementary information provides additional analysis and is not a required part of the financial statements.

3. Management is responsible for the supplementary information, and this information was derived from the accounting records used to prepare the financial statements.
4. The supplementary information has been subjected to the auditing procedures used in the financial statements audit, along with additional procedures such as reconciling the information to the records used to prepare the financial statements, in accordance with GAAS.
5. If the opinion is unmodified and the supplementary information is fairly stated, then the supplementary information is fairly stated, in all material respects, in relation to the financial statements as a whole.
6. If the opinion is qualified and that qualification affects the supplementary information, in the auditor's opinion, such information is fairly stated, in all material respects, in relation to the financial statements as a whole.

(AU-C 725.09)

NOTE: If the financial statements are presented without the supplementary information, the auditor should report on the supplementary information in a separate report. When preparing this separate report, the report should include a reference to the report on the financial statements, the report's date, and report modifications, as well as the nature of the opinion expressed therein.

Opinion on Supplementary Information

If the auditor issues an adverse opinion or a disclaimer of opinion on an entity's financial statements and has also been engaged to deliver an opinion on the supplementary information, he or she cannot express a separate opinion on the supplementary information. When permitted by law, the auditor can withdraw from the engagement to report on the supplementary information. If the auditor cannot withdraw, then the report on the supplementary information should state that, due to the significance of the matter disclosed in the auditor's report, it is inappropriate to express an opinion on the supplementary information. (AU-C 725.11)

If the auditor concludes that the supplementary information is misstated, then he or she should discuss the matter with management and propose appropriate revisions. If management does not revise the supplementary material accordingly, then the auditor should either modify the auditor's opinion on the supplementary information and describe the misstatements, or withhold the report. (AU-C 725.13)

INTERPRETATION

Supplementary Information in Relation to the Financial Statements as a Whole: Auditing Interpretations of Section 725 (Issued July 2011; Revised October 2011)

The auditor's report on supplementary information should not be dated earlier than the date on which the auditor completed the procedures required listed previously. When the auditor completes those procedures subsequent to the date of the auditor's report on the audited financial statements, the auditor is not required to obtain additional evidence with respect to the audited financial statements. (AU-C 725.08)

AU-C 725 ILLUSTRATIONS

The following are illustrations from AU-C 725.17:

1. An Other-Matter Paragraph When the Auditor Is Issuing an Unmodified Opinion on the Financial Statements and an Unmodified Opinion on the Supplementary Information
2. An Other-Matter Paragraph When the Auditor Is Issuing a Qualified Opinion on the Financial Statements and a Qualified Opinion on the Supplementary Information
3. An Other-Matter Paragraph When the Auditor Is Disclaiming an Opinion on the Financial Statements
4. An Other-Matter Paragraph When the Auditor Is Issuing an Adverse Opinion on the Financial Statements
5. A Separate Report When the Auditor Is Issuing an Unmodified Opinion on the Financial Statements and an Unmodified Opinion on the Supplementary Information
6. A Separate Report When the Auditor Is Issuing a Qualified Opinion on the Financial Statements and a Qualified Opinion on the Supplementary Information
7. A Separate Report When the Auditor Is Disclaiming an Opinion on the Financial Statements
8. A Separate Report When the Auditor Is Issuing an Adverse Opinion on the Financial Statements

ILLUSTRATION 1. AN OTHER-MATTER PARAGRAPH WHEN THE AUDITOR IS ISSUING AN UNMODIFIED OPINION ON THE FINANCIAL STATEMENTS AND AN UNMODIFIED OPINION ON THE SUPPLEMENTARY INFORMATION

Our audit was conducted for the purpose of forming an opinion on the financial statements as a whole. The [*identify accompanying supplementary information*] is presented for purposes of additional analysis and is not a required part of the financial statements. Such information is the responsibility of management and was derived from and relates directly to the underlying accounting and other records used to prepare the financial statements. The information has been subjected to the auditing procedures applied in the audit of the financial statements and certain additional procedures, including comparing and reconciling such information directly to the underlying accounting and other records used to prepare the financial statements or to the financial statements themselves, and other additional procedures in accordance with auditing standards generally accepted in the United States of America. In our opinion, the information is fairly stated in all material respects in relation to the financial statements as a whole.

ILLUSTRATION 2. AN OTHER-MATTER PARAGRAPH WHEN THE AUDITOR IS ISSUING A QUALIFIED OPINION ON THE FINANCIAL STATEMENTS AND A QUALIFIED OPINION ON THE SUPPLEMENTARY INFORMATION

Our audit was conducted for the purpose of forming an opinion on the financial statements as a whole. The [*identify accompanying supplementary information*] is presented for purposes of additional analysis and is not a required part of the financial statements. Such information is the responsibility of management and was derived from and relates directly to the underlying accounting and other records used to prepare the financial statements. The information has been subjected to the auditing procedures applied in the audit of the financial statements and certain additional procedures, including comparing and reconciling such information directly to the underlying accounting and other records used to prepare the financial statements or to the financial statements themselves, and other additional procedures in accordance with auditing standards generally accepted in the United States of America. In our opinion, except for the effect on the supplementary information of [*describe reason for qualification of the auditor's opinion on the financial statements, and reference the other-matter paragraph*], the information is fairly stated in all material respects in relation to the financial statements as a whole.

Illustration 3. An Other-Matter Paragraph When the Auditor Is Disclaiming an Opinion on the Financial Statements

We were engaged for the purpose of forming an opinion on the basic financial statements as a whole. The [*identify accompanying supplementary information*] is presented for the purposes of additional analysis and is not a required part of the financial statements. Because of the significance of the matter described above [*the auditor may describe the basis for the disclaimer of opinion*], it is inappropriate to express an opinion on the supplementary information referred to above, and we express no such opinion.

Illustration 4. An Other-Matter Paragraph When the Auditor Is Issuing an Adverse Opinion on the Financial Statements

Our audit was conducted for the purpose of forming an opinion on the financial statements as a whole. The [*identify accompanying supplementary information*] is presented for the purposes of additional analysis and is not a required part of the financial statements. Because of the significance of the matter described above [*the auditor may describe the basis for the adverse opinion*], it is inappropriate to express an opinion on the supplementary information referred to above, and we express no such opinion.

Illustration 5. A Separate Report When the Auditor Is Issuing an Unmodified Opinion on the Financial Statements and an Unmodified Opinion on the Supplementary Information

We have audited the financial statements of XYZ Entity as of and for the year ended June 30, 20X1, and have issued our report thereon dated [*date of the auditor's report on the financial statements*] which contained an unmodified opinion on those financial statements. Our audit was performed for the purpose of forming an opinion on the financial statements as a whole. The [*identify supplementary information*] is presented for the purpose of additional analysis and is not a required part of the financial statements. Such information is the responsibility of management and was derived from and relates directly to the underlying accounting and other records used to prepare the financial statements. The information has been subjected to the auditing procedures applied in the audit of the financial statements and certain additional procedures, including comparing and reconciling such information directly to the underlying accounting and other records used to prepare the financial statements or to the financial statements themselves, and other additional procedures in accordance with auditing standards generally accepted in the United States of America. In our opinion, the information is fairly stated in all material respects in relation to the financial statements as a whole.

Illustration 6. A Separate Report When the Auditor Is Issuing a Qualified Opinion on the Financial Statements and a Qualified Opinion on the Supplementary Information

We have audited the financial statements of XYZ Entity as of and for the year ended June 30, 20X1, and have issued our report thereon dated [*date of the auditor's report on the financial statements, the nature of the opinion expressed on the financial statements, and a description of the report modifications*]. Our audit was performed for the purpose of forming an opinion on the financial statements as a whole. The [*identify supplementary information*] is presented for the purpose of additional analysis and is not a required part of the financial statements. Such information is the responsibility of management and was derived from and relates directly to the underlying accounting and other records used to prepare the financial statements. The information has been subjected to the auditing procedures applied in the audit of the financial statements and certain additional procedures, including comparing and reconciling such information directly to the underlying accounting and other records used to prepare the financial statements or to the financial statements themselves, and other additional procedures in accordance with auditing standards generally accepted in the United States of America. In our opinion, except for the effect on the accompanying information of the qualified opinion on the financial statements as described above, the information is fairly stated in all material respects in relation to the financial statements as a whole.

ILLUSTRATION 7. A SEPARATE REPORT WHEN THE AUDITOR IS DISCLAIMING AN OPINION ON THE FINANCIAL STATEMENTS

We were engaged to audit the financial statements of XYZ Entity as of and for the year ended June 30, 20X1, and have issued our report thereon dated [*date of the auditor's report on the financial statements*]. However, the scope of our audit of the financial statements was not sufficient to enable us to express an opinion because [*describe reasons*], and accordingly we did not express an opinion on such financial statements. The [*identify the supplementary information*] is presented for purposes of additional analysis and is not a required part of the basic financial statements. Because of the significance of the matter discussed above, it is inappropriate to express an opinion on the supplementary information referred to above, and we express no such opinion.

ILLUSTRATION 8. A SEPARATE REPORT WHEN THE AUDITOR IS ISSUING AN ADVERSE OPINION ON THE FINANCIAL STATEMENTS

We have audited the financial statements of XYZ Entity as of and for the year ended June 30, 20X1, and have issued our report thereon dated [*date of the auditor's report on the financial statements*] which stated that the financial statements are not presented fairly in accordance with [*identify the applicable financial reporting framework, such as accounting principles generally accepted in the United States of America (GAAP)*] because [*describe reasons*]. The [*identify the supplementary information*] is presented for purposes of additional analysis and is not a required part of the basic financial statements. Because of the significance of the matter discussed above, it is inappropriate to express an opinion on the supplementary information referred to above, and we express no such opinion.

AU-C 730 Required Supplementary Information

AU-C ORIGINAL PRONOUNCEMENTS

Sources Statements on Auditing Standards (SASs) 120 and 122.

AU-C DEFINITIONS OF TERMS

Source: AU-C 730.04

Applicable financial reporting framework. The financial reporting framework adopted by management and, when appropriate, those charged with governance in the preparation and fair presentation of the financial statements that is acceptable in view of the nature of the entity and the objective of the financial statements, or that is required by law or regulation.

Basic financial statements. Financial statements presented in accordance with an applicable financial reporting framework as established by a designated accounting standards setter, excluding required supplementary information.

Designated accounting standards setter. A body designated by the Council of the AICPA to promulgate GAAP pursuant to the "Compliance with Standards Rule" (ET sec. 1.310.001) and the "Accounting Principles Rule" (ET sec. 1.320.001) of the AICPA Code of Professional Conduct.

Prescribed guidelines. The authoritative guidelines established by the designated accounting standards setter for the methods of measurement and presentation of the required supplementary information.

Required supplementary information. Information that a designated accounting standards setter requires to accompany an entity's basic financial statements. Required supplementary information is not part of the basic financial statements; however, a designated accounting standards setter considers the information to be an essential part of financial reporting for placing the basic financial statements in an appropriate operational, economic, or historical context. In addition, authoritative guidelines for the methods of measurement and presentation of the information have been established.

OBJECTIVES OF AU-C SECTION 730

AU-C Section 730.03 states that:

. . . the objectives of the auditor when a designated accounting standards setter requires information to accompany an entity's basic financial statements are to perform specified procedures in order to

a. describe, in the auditor's report, whether required supplementary information is presented and

b. communicate therein when some or all of the required supplementary information has not been presented in accordance with guidelines established by a designated accounting standards setter or when the auditor has identified material modifications that should be made to the required supplementary information for it to be in accordance with guidelines established by the designated accounting standards setter.

REQUIREMENTS

PROCEDURES

The auditor should apply these procedures to required supplementary information (see "AU-C Definitions of Terms"):

1. *Preparation methods.* Make inquiries regarding the preparation of supplementary information. This should include whether the information is being measured and presented in accordance with specific guidelines, whether these methods have changed and the reasons for doing so, and whether there were any significant assumptions underlying these methods.
2. *Consistency review.* Compare the information for consistency with the responses to the inquiries in step 1, as well as to the basic financial statements and other knowledge obtained during the basic financial statements audit.
3. *Written representations.* Obtain written representations from management that it acknowledges its responsibility for the required supplementary information, that the information is measured and presented in accordance with specific guidelines, whether these methods have changed and the reasons for doing so, and regarding any significant assumptions underlying these methods.

(AU-C 730.05)

NOTE: If the auditor cannot complete these procedures due to significant difficulties in dealing with management, then inform those charged with governance. (AU-C 730.06)

COORDINATION WITH OTHER AUDIT AREAS

The auditor should coordinate the application of procedures to supplementary information with procedures applied in other areas. For example, for an entity engaged in oil- and gas-producing activities, the entity might be required to pay state or federal taxes on oil and gas produced in particular geographical areas. In this circumstance, the auditor would want to coordinate work on tax expense and payables and segment disclosures with work on the required supplementary oil and gas information.

Reporting on Supplementary Information

Include an other-matter paragraph in the auditor's report after the opinion paragraph that refers to the supplementary information. This paragraph should explain the following items, as applicable:

1. *The required supplementary information is included, and the auditor has applied the procedures noted above.* If so, state that the applicable financial reporting framework requires that the supplementary information be presented to supplement the basic financial statements. Also, state that such information, although not a part of the basic financial statements, is required by the designated accounting standards setter, which considers it to be an essential part of financial reporting for placing the context. Further, state that the auditor has applied certain limited procedures to the required supplementary information in accordance with auditing standards generally accepted in the United States of America, which consisted of inquiries of management about the methods of preparing the information and comparing the information for consistency with management's responses to the auditor's inquiries, the basic financial statements, and other knowledge the auditor obtained during the audit of the basic financial statements. Finally, state that the auditor does not express an opinion or provide any assurance on the information, because the limited procedures do not provide the auditor with sufficient evidence to express an opinion or provide any assurance.
2. *The required supplementary information is omitted.* If so, state that management has omitted the information that is required to be presented by the designated accounting standards setter. Also, state that such missing information, although not a part of the basic financial statements, is required by the designated accounting standards setter, which considers it to be an essential part of financial reporting for placing the basic financial statements in an appropriate operational, economic, or historical context. Finally, state that the auditor's opinion on the basic financial statements is not affected by the missing information.
3. *Some required supplementary information is missing, and some is presented in accordance with the guidelines.* If so, state that management has omitted some information that the designated accounting standards setter requires be presented to supplement the basic financial statements. Also state that such missing information, although not a part of the basic financial statements, is required by the designated accounting standards setter, which considers it to be an essential part of financial reporting for placing the basic financial statements in an appropriate operational, economic, or historical context. Finally, state that the auditor's opinion on the basic financial statements is not affected by the missing information.
4. *There are material departures from the guidelines.* If so, state that although the auditor's opinion on the basic financial statements is not affected, there are material departures from the guidelines (and describe the material departures).
5. *The auditor was unable to complete the procedures noted above.* If so, state that the auditor was unable to apply certain limited procedures to the required supplementary information in accordance with auditing standards generally accepted in the United States, and state the reasons. Also state that the auditor does not express an opinion or provide any assurance on the information.
6. *The auditor has unresolved doubts about whether the supplementary information is presented in accordance with the guidelines.* If so, state that although the auditor's opinion

on the basic financial statements is not affected, the results of the limited procedures have raised doubts about whether material modifications should be made to the required supplementary information for it to be presented in accordance with the guidelines established by the designated accounting standards setter.

NOTE: Required supplementary information is not part of the basic financial statements, so the auditor's opinion on the fairness of presentation of financial statements is not affected by the presentation of the supplementary information or the failure to present some or all of it.

(AU-C 730.07-.09)

Examples of the above variations on the auditor's report regarding required supplementary information are noted next under "AU-C 730 Illustrations."

AU-C 730 ILLUSTRATIONS

The following examples from AU-C 730.A3 illustrate the separate other-matter paragraphs that might be added to the standard report in the indicated circumstances.

ILLUSTRATION 1. THE REQUIRED SUPPLEMENTARY INFORMATION IS INCLUDED, THE AUDITOR HAS APPLIED THE SPECIFIED PROCEDURES, AND NO MATERIAL DEPARTURES FROM PRESCRIBED GUIDELINES HAVE BEEN IDENTIFIED

[*Identify the applicable financial reporting framework (for example, accounting principles generally accepted in the United States of America)*] require that the [*identify the required supplementary information*] on page XX be presented to supplement the basic financial statements. Such information, although not a part of the basic financial statements, is required by [*identify designated accounting standards setter*], which considers it to be an essential part of financial reporting for placing the basic financial statements in an appropriate operational, economic, or historical context. We have applied certain limited procedures to the required supplementary information in accordance with auditing standards generally accepted in the United States of America, which consisted of inquiries of management about the methods of preparing the information and comparing the information for consistency with management's responses to our inquiries, the basic financial statements, and other knowledge we obtained during our audit of the basic financial statements. We do not express an opinion or provide any assurance on the information, because the limited procedures do not provide us with sufficient evidence to express an opinion or provide any assurance.

ILLUSTRATION 2. ALL REQUIRED SUPPLEMENTARY INFORMATION IS OMITTED

Management has omitted [*describe the missing required supplementary information*] that [*identify the applicable financial reporting framework (for example, accounting principles generally accepted in the United States of America)*] require to be presented to supplement the basic financial statements. Such missing information, although not a part of the basic financial statements, is required by [*identify designated accounting standards setter*], which considers it to be an essential part of financial reporting for placing the basic financial statements in an appropriate operational, economic, or historical context. Our opinion on the basic financial statements is not affected by this missing information.

ILLUSTRATION 3. SOME REQUIRED SUPPLEMENTARY INFORMATION IS OMITTED, AND SOME IS PRESENTED IN ACCORDANCE WITH THE PRESCRIBED GUIDELINES

[*Identify the applicable financial reporting framework (for example, accounting principles generally accepted in the United States of America)*] require that [*identify the included supplementary information*] be presented to supplement the basic financial statements. Such information, although not a part of the basic financial statements, is required by [*identify designated accounting standards setter*], which considers it to be an essential part of financial reporting for placing the basic financial statements in an appropriate operational, economic, or historical context. We have applied certain limited procedures to the required supplementary information in accordance with auditing standards generally accepted in the United States of America, which consisted of inquiries of management about the methods of preparing the information and comparing the information for consistency with management's responses to our inquiries, the basic financial statements, and other knowledge we obtained during our audit of the basic financial statements. We do not express an opinion or provide any assurance on the information because the limited procedures do not provide us with evidence sufficient to express an opinion or provide any assurance.

Management has omitted [*describe the missing required supplementary information*] that [*identify the applicable financial reporting framework*] require to be presented to supplement the basic financial statements. Such missing information, although not a part of the basic financial statements, is required by [*identify designated accounting standards setter*], which considers it to be an essential part of financial reporting for placing the basic financial statements in an appropriate operational, economic, or historical context. Our opinion on the basic financial statements is not affected by this missing information.

ILLUSTRATION 4. MATERIAL DEPARTURES FROM PRESCRIBED GUIDELINES ARE IDENTIFIED

[*Identify the applicable financial reporting framework (for example, accounting principles generally accepted in the United States of America)*] require that the [*identify the supplementary information*] on page XX be presented to supplement the basic financial statements. Such information, although not a part of the basic financial statements, is required by [*identify designated accounting standards setter*], which considers it to be an essential part of financial reporting for placing the basic financial statements in an appropriate operational, economic, or historical context. We have applied certain limited procedures to the required supplementary information in accordance with auditing standards generally accepted in the United States of America, which consisted of inquiries of management about the methods of preparing the information and comparing the information for consistency with management's responses to our inquiries, the basic financial statements, and other knowledge we obtained during our audit of the basic financial statements.

Although our opinion on the basic financial statements is not affected, the following material departures from the prescribed guidelines exist [*identify the required supplementary information, and describe the material departures from the prescribed guidelines*]. We do not express an opinion or provide any assurance on the information.

ILLUSTRATION 5. SPECIFIED PROCEDURES ARE NOT COMPLETED

[*Identify the applicable financial reporting framework (for example, accounting principles generally accepted in the United States of America)*] require that the [*identify the supplementary information*] *on page XX be presented to supplement the basic financial statements. Such information, although not a part of the basic financial statements, is required by [identify designated accounting standards setter*], which considers it to be an essential part of financial reporting for placing the basic financial statements in an appropriate operational, economic, or historical context. We were unable to apply certain limited procedures to the required supplementary information in accordance with auditing standards generally accepted in the United States of America because [*state the reasons*]. We do not express an opinion or provide any assurance on the information.

Illustration 6. Unresolved Doubts about Whether the Required Supplementary Information Is in Accordance with Prescribed Guidelines

[*Identify the applicable financial reporting framework (for example, accounting principles generally accepted in the United States of America)*] require that the [*identify the supplementary information] on page XX be presented to supplement the basic financial statements. Such information, although not a part of the basic financial statements, is required by [identify designated accounting standards setter*], which considers it to be an essential part of financial reporting for placing the basic financial statements in an appropriate operational, economic, or historical context. We have applied certain limited procedures to the required supplementary information in accordance with auditing standards generally accepted in the United States of America, which consisted of inquiries of management about the methods of preparing the information and comparing the information for consistency with management's responses to our inquiries, the basic financial statements, and other knowledge we obtained during our audit of the basic financial statements. We do not express an opinion or provide any assurance on the information because the limited procedures do not provide us with sufficient evidence to express an opinion or provide any assurance. Although our opinion on the basic financial statements is not affected, the results of the limited procedures have raised doubts about whether material modifications should be made to the required supplementary information for it to be presented in accordance with guidelines established by [*identify designated accounting standards setter*]. [*The auditor may consider including in the report the reason(s) for being unable to resolve these doubts.*]

AU-C 800 Special Considerations—Audits of Financial Statements Prepared in Accordance with Special Purpose Frameworks

AU-C ORIGINAL PRONOUNCEMENTS

Sources Statements on Auditing Standards (SASs) 122, 125, and 127.

AU-C DEFINITIONS OF TERMS

Source: AU-C 800.07

Special purpose financial statements. Financial statements prepared in accordance with a special purpose framework.

Special purpose framework. A financial reporting framework other than GAAP that is one of the following bases of accounting:

1. **Cash basis.** A basis of accounting that the entity uses to record cash receipts and disbursements and modifications of the cash basis having substantial support (for example, recording depreciation on fixed assets).
2. **Tax basis.** A basis of accounting that the entity uses to file its income tax return for the period covered by the financial statements.
3. **Regulatory basis.** A basis of accounting that the entity uses to comply with the requirements or financial reporting provisions of a regulatory agency to whose jurisdiction the entity is subject (for example, a basis of accounting that insurance companies use pursuant to the accounting practices prescribed or permitted by a state insurance commission).
4. **Contractual basis.** A basis of accounting that the entity uses to comply with an agreement between the entity and one or more third parties other than the auditor.
5. **Other basis.** A basis of accounting that uses a definite set of logical, reasonable criteria that is applied to all material items appearing in financial statements.

The cash, tax, and regulatory bases of accounting are commonly referred to as *other comprehensive bases of accounting* (*OCBOA*).

OBJECTIVES OF AU-C SECTION 800

AU-C Section 800 states that:

. . . the objective of the auditor, when applying generally accepted auditing standards (GAAS) in an audit of financial statements prepared in accordance with a special-purpose framework, is to address appropriately the special considerations that are relevant to

a. the acceptance of the engagement,
b. the planning and performance of that engagement, and
c. forming an opinion and reporting on the financial statements.

SCOPE

This section applies to auditor's reports issued in connection with a complete set of financial statements prepared in accordance with a special purpose framework—cash, tax, regulatory, contractual, or another basis of accounting. (AU-C 800.01)

REQUIREMENTS

PRECONDITION FOR AN AUDIT

The auditor must determine the acceptability of the financial reporting framework and obtain an understanding of the purpose for which the financial statements are prepared, the intended users, and the steps taken by management to determine the acceptability of the financial reporting framework. (AU-C 800.10)

In compliance with AU-C 210, the auditor must determine whether the preconditions for an audit are present. Those preconditions include determining that the financial statement's financial reporting framework is acceptable. If an audit involves special purpose frameworks, the auditor must also obtain management's acknowledgment of its responsibility to include all informative disclosures. (AU-C 800.11)

The auditor of special purpose financial statements should adopt and apply all relevant AU-C sections. (AU-C 800.12) So, too, the auditor should apply AU-C 315 and understand the entity's selection and application of accounting policies. In particular, an auditor working with financial statements prepared using a contractual basis of accounting should understand any significant interpretations of the contract that management made when preparing the financial statements. (AU-C 800.13)

COMPONENTS OF AUDITOR'S STANDARD REPORT

When reporting on special purpose financial statements, the auditor should evaluate whether the financial statements

- Are suitably titled,
- Include a summary of significant accounting policies, and
- Describe adequately how the special purpose framework differs from GAAP.

(AU-C 800.15)

If the financial statements are prepared in accordance with a contractual basis of accounting, the auditor must assess whether the financial statements adequately describe any significant interpretations of the contract. (AU-C 800.16) The auditor's report, in the explanation of management's responsibility, should make reference to its responsibility for determining that the framework is acceptable. It should also describe the purpose for which the financial statements are prepared or refer to a note in the financial statements when the financial statements are prepared in accordance with:

a. A regulatory or contractual basis of accounting or
b. Another basis of accounting, and the auditor is required to restrict use of the report per AU-C 905.06a-b.

(AU-C 905.18)

With an exception described below, the auditor's report should include an emphasis-of-matter paragraph that indicates that the financial statements are prepared in accordance with the applicable special purpose framework, refers to the note that describes that framework, and states that the basis is other than GAAP. (AU-C 800.19) The report should also include an other-matter paragraph restricting the use of the report when the special purpose financial statements are prepared in accordance with contractual, regulatory, or other basis of accounting when required by AU-C 905.06a-b. (AU-C 800.20)

However, if the special purpose financial statements are prepared in accordance with a regulatory basis of accounting and the statements together with the auditor's report are intended for general use, the auditor should not include the emphasis-of-matter or other-matter paragraphs described above. Rather, the auditor should express an opinion about whether the financial statements are presented fairly in accordance with GAAP. In a separate paragraph, the auditor should express an opinion about whether the financial statements are prepared in accordance with the special purpose framework. (AU-C 800.21)

AU-C 800 ILLUSTRATIONS (SOURCE: AU-C 800.A36)

1. An Auditor's Report on a Complete Set of Financial Statements Prepared in Accordance with the Cash Basis of Accounting

2. An Auditor's Report on a Complete Set of Financial Statements Prepared in Accordance with the Tax Basis of Accounting

3. An Auditor's Report on a Complete Set of Financial Statements Prepared in Accordance with a Regulatory Basis of Accounting (the Financial Statements Together with the Auditor's Report Are Not Intended for General Use)

4. An Auditor's Report on a Complete Set of Financial Statements Prepared in Accordance with a Regulatory Basis of Accounting (the Financial Statements Together with the Auditor's Report Are Intended for General Use)

5. An Auditor's Report on a Complete Set of Financial Statements Prepared in Accordance with a Contractual Basis of Accounting

ILLUSTRATION 1. AN AUDITOR'S REPORT ON A COMPLETE SET OF FINANCIAL STATEMENTS PREPARED IN ACCORDANCE WITH THE CASH BASIS OF ACCOUNTING

Circumstances include the following:

- The financial statements have been prepared by management of the entity in accordance with the cash basis of accounting (that is, a special purpose framework).
- Management has a choice of financial reporting frameworks.

Independent Auditor's Report

[*Appropriate addressee*]

Report on the Financial Statements

We have audited the accompanying financial statements of ABC Partnership, which comprise the statement of assets and liabilities arising from cash transactions as of December 31, 20X1, and the related statement of revenue collected and expenses paid for the year then ended, and the related notes to the financial statements.

Management's Responsibility for the Financial Statements

Management is responsible for the preparation and fair presentation of these financial statements in accordance with the cash basis of accounting described in Note X; this includes determining that the cash basis of accounting is an acceptable basis for the preparation of the financial statements in the circumstances. Management is also responsible for the design, implementation, and maintenance of internal control relevant to the preparation and fair presentation of financial statements that are free from material misstatement, whether due to fraud or to error.

Auditor's Responsibility

Our responsibility is to express an opinion on these financial statements based on our audit. We conducted our audit in accordance with auditing standards generally accepted in the United States of America. Those standards require that we plan and perform the audit to obtain reasonable assurance about whether the financial statements are free from material misstatement.

An audit involves performing procedures to obtain audit evidence about the amounts and disclosures in the financial statements. The procedures selected depend on the auditor's judgment, including the assessment of the risks of material misstatement of the financial statements, whether due to fraud or to error. In making those risk assessments, the auditor considers internal control relevant to the partnership's preparation and fair presentation of the financial statements in order to design audit procedures that are appropriate in the circumstances, but not for the purpose of expressing an opinion on the effectiveness of the partnership's internal control. Accordingly, we express no such opinion. An audit also includes evaluating the appropriateness of accounting policies used and the reasonableness of significant accounting estimates made by management, as well as evaluating the overall presentation of the financial statements.

We believe that the audit evidence we have obtained is sufficient and appropriate to provide a basis for our audit opinion.

Opinion

In our opinion, the financial statements referred to above present fairly, in all material respects, the assets and liabilities arising from cash transactions of ABC Partnership as of December 31, 20X1, and its revenue collected and expenses paid during the year then ended in accordance with the cash basis of accounting described in Note X.

Basis of Accounting

We draw attention to Note X of the financial statements, which describes the basis of accounting. The financial statements are prepared on the cash basis of accounting, which is a basis of accounting other than accounting principles generally accepted in the United States of America. Our opinion is not modified with respect to this matter.

Report on Other Legal and Regulatory Requirements

[*Form and content of this section of the auditor's report will vary depending on the nature of the auditor's other reporting responsibilities.*]

[*Auditor's signature*]

[*Auditor's city and state*]

[*Date of the auditor's report*]

ILLUSTRATION 2. AN AUDITOR'S REPORT ON A COMPLETE SET OF FINANCIAL STATEMENTS PREPARED IN ACCORDANCE WITH THE TAX BASIS OF ACCOUNTING

Circumstances include the following:

- The financial statements have been prepared by management of a partnership in accordance with the basis of accounting the partnership uses for income tax purposes (that is, a special purpose framework).
- Based on the partnership agreement, management does not have a choice of financial reporting frameworks.

Independent Auditor's Report

[*Appropriate addressee*]

Report on the Financial Statements

We have audited the accompanying financial statements of ABC Partnership, which comprise the statements of assets, liabilities, and capital-income tax basis as of December 31, 20X1, and the related statements of revenue and expenses—income tax basis and of changes in partners' capital accounts—income tax basis for the year then ended, and the related notes to the financial statements.

Management's Responsibility for the Financial Statements

Management is responsible for the preparation and fair presentation of these financial statements in accordance with the basis of accounting the Partnership uses for income tax purposes; this includes the design, implementation, and maintenance of internal control relevant to the preparation and fair presentation of financial statements that are free from material misstatement, whether due to fraud or to error.

Auditor's Responsibility

Our responsibility is to express an opinion on these financial statements based on our audit. We conducted our audit in accordance with auditing standards generally accepted in the United States of America. Those standards require that we plan and perform the audit to obtain reasonable assurance about whether the financial statements are free from material misstatement.

An audit involves performing procedures to obtain audit evidence about the amounts and disclosures in the financial statements. The procedures selected depend on the auditor's judgment, including the assessment of the risks of material misstatement of the financial statements, whether due to fraud or to error. In making those risk assessments, the auditor considers internal control relevant to the partnership's preparation and fair presentation of the financial statements in order to design audit procedures that are appropriate in the circumstances, but not for the purpose of expressing an opinion on the effectiveness of the partnership's internal control. Accordingly, we express no such opinion. An audit also includes evaluating the appropriateness of accounting policies used and the reasonableness of significant accounting estimates made by management, as well as evaluating the overall presentation of the financial statements.

We believe that the audit evidence we have obtained is sufficient and appropriate to provide a basis for our audit opinion.

Opinion

In our opinion, the financial statements referred to above present fairly, in all material respects, the assets, liabilities, and capital of ABC Partnership as of December 31, 20X1, and its revenue and expenses and changes in partners' capital accounts for the year then ended in accordance with the basis of accounting the Partnership uses for income tax purposes described in Note X.

Basis of Accounting

We draw attention to Note X of the financial statements, which describes the basis of accounting. The financial statements are prepared on the basis of accounting the Partnership uses for income tax purposes, which is a basis of accounting other than accounting principles generally accepted in the United States of America. Our opinion is not modified with respect to this matter.

Report on Other Legal and Regulatory Requirements

[Form and content of this section of the auditor's report will vary depending on the nature of the auditor's other reporting responsibilities.]

[Auditor's signature]

[Auditor's city and state]

[Date of the auditor's report]

ILLUSTRATION 3. AN AUDITOR'S REPORT ON A COMPLETE SET OF FINANCIAL STATEMENTS PREPARED IN ACCORDANCE WITH A REGULATORY BASIS OF ACCOUNTING (THE FINANCIAL STATEMENTS TOGETHER WITH THE AUDITOR'S REPORT ARE NOT INTENDED FOR GENERAL USE)

Circumstances include the following:

- The financial statements have been prepared by management of the entity in accordance with the financial reporting provisions established by a regulatory agency (that is, a special purpose framework).
- The financial statements together with the auditor's report are not intended for general use.
- Based on the regulatory requirements, management does not have a choice of financial reporting frameworks.

Independent Auditor's Report

[Appropriate addressee]

Report on the Financial Statements

We have audited the accompanying financial statements of ABC City, Any State, which comprise cash and unencumbered cash for each fund as of December 31, 20X1, and the related statements of cash receipts and disbursements and disbursements—budget and actual for the year then ended, and the related notes to the financial statements.

Management's Responsibility for the Financial Statements

Management is responsible for the preparation and fair presentation of these financial statements in accordance with the financial reporting provisions of Section Y of Regulation Z of Any State. Management is also responsible for the design, implementation, and maintenance of internal control relevant to the preparation and fair presentation of financial statements that are free from material misstatement, whether due to fraud or to error.

Auditor's Responsibility

Our responsibility is to express an opinion on these financial statements based on our audit. We conducted our audit in accordance with auditing standards generally accepted in the United States of America. Those standards require that we plan and perform the audit to obtain reasonable assurance about whether the financial statements are free from material misstatement.

An audit involves performing procedures to obtain audit evidence about the amounts and disclosures in the financial statements. The procedures selected depend on the auditor's judgment, including the assessment of the risks of material misstatement of the financial statements, whether due to fraud or to error. In making those risk assessments, the auditor considers internal control relevant to the entity's preparation and fair presentation of the financial statements in order to design audit procedures that are appropriate in the circumstances, but not for the purpose of expressing an opinion on the effectiveness of the entity's internal control. Accordingly, we express no such opinion. An audit also includes evaluating the appropriateness of accounting policies used and the reasonableness of significant accounting estimates made by management, as well as evaluating the overall presentation of the financial statements.

We believe that the audit evidence we have obtained is sufficient and appropriate to provide a basis for our audit opinion.

Opinion

In our opinion, the financial statements referred to above present fairly, in all material respects, the cash and unencumbered cash of each fund of ABC City as of December 31, 20X1, and their respective cash receipts and disbursements, and budgetary results for the year then ended in accordance with the financial reporting provisions of Section Y of Regulation Z of Any State described in Note X.

Basis of Accounting

We draw attention to Note X of the financial statements, which describes the basis of accounting. As described in Note X to the financial statements, the financial statements are prepared by ABC City on the basis of the financial reporting provisions of Section Y of Regulation Z of Any State, which is a basis of accounting other than accounting principles generally accepted in the United States of America, to meet the requirements of Any State. Our opinion is not modified with respect to this matter.

Restriction on Use

Our report is intended solely for the information and use of ABC City and Any State and is not intended to be and should not be used by anyone other than these specified parties.

Report on Other Legal and Regulatory Requirements

[*Form and content of this section of the auditor's report will vary depending on the nature of the auditor's other reporting responsibilities.*]

[*Auditor's signature*]

[*Auditor's city and state*]

[*Date of the auditor's report*]

ILLUSTRATION 4. AN AUDITOR'S REPORT ON A COMPLETE SET OF FINANCIAL STATEMENTS PREPARED IN ACCORDANCE WITH A REGULATORY BASIS OF ACCOUNTING (THE FINANCIAL STATEMENTS TOGETHER WITH THE AUDITOR'S REPORT ARE INTENDED FOR GENERAL USE)

Circumstances include the following:

- The financial statements have been prepared by management of the entity in accordance with the financial reporting provisions established by a regulatory agency (that is, a special purpose framework).
- The financial statements together with the auditor's report are intended for general use.
- Based on the regulatory requirements, management does not have a choice of financial reporting frameworks.
- The variances between the regulatory basis of accounting and accounting principles generally accepted in the United States of America (US GAAP) are not reasonably determinable and are presumed to be material.

Independent Auditor's Report

[*Appropriate addressee*]

Report on the Financial Statements

We have audited the accompanying financial statements of XYZ City, Any State, which comprise cash and unencumbered cash for each fund as of December 31, 20X1, and the related statements of cash receipts and disbursements and disbursements—budget and actual for the year then ended, and the related notes to the financial statements.

Management's Responsibility for the Financial Statements

Management is responsible for the preparation and fair presentation of these financial statements in accordance with the financial reporting provisions of Section Y of Regulation Z of Any State. Management is also responsible for the design, implementation, and maintenance of internal control relevant to the preparation and fair presentation of financial statements that are free from material misstatement, whether due to fraud or to error.

Auditor's Responsibility

Our responsibility is to express an opinion on these financial statements based on our audit. We conducted our audit in accordance with auditing standards generally accepted in the United States of America. Those standards require that we plan and perform the audit to obtain reasonable assurance about whether the financial statements are free from material misstatement.

An audit involves performing procedures to obtain audit evidence about the amounts and disclosures in the financial statements. The procedures selected depend on the auditor's judgment, including the assessment of the risks of material misstatement of the financial statements, whether due to fraud or to error. In making those risk assessments, the auditor considers internal control relevant to the entity's preparation and fair presentation of the financial statements in order to design audit procedures that are appropriate in the circumstances, but not for the purpose of expressing an opinion on the effectiveness of the entity's internal control. Accordingly, we express no such opinion. An audit also includes evaluating the appropriateness of accounting policies used and the reasonableness of significant accounting estimates made by management, as well as evaluating the overall presentation of the financial statements.

We believe that the audit evidence we have obtained is sufficient and appropriate to provide a basis for our audit opinions.

Basis for Adverse Opinion on US Generally Accepted Accounting Principles

As described in Note X of the financial statements, the financial statements are prepared by XYZ City on the basis of the financial reporting provisions of Section Y of Regulation Z of Any State, which is a basis of accounting other than accounting principles generally accepted in the United States of America, to meet the requirements of Any State.

The effects on the financial statements of the variances between the regulatory basis of accounting described in Note X and accounting principles generally accepted in the United States of America, although not reasonably determinable, are presumed to be material.

Adverse Opinion on US Generally Accepted Accounting Principles

In our opinion, because of the significance of the matter discussed in the "Basis for Adverse Opinion on US Generally Accepted Accounting Principles" paragraph, the financial statements referred to above do not present fairly, in accordance with accounting principles generally accepted in the United States of America, the financial position of each fund of XYZ City as of December 31, 20X1, or changes in financial position or cash flows thereof for the year then ended.

Opinion on Regulatory Basis of Accounting

In our opinion, the financial statements referred to above present fairly, in all material respects, the cash and unencumbered cash of each fund of XYZ City as of December 31, 20X1, and their respective cash receipts and disbursements, and budgetary results for the year then ended in accordance with the financial reporting provisions of Section Y of Regulation Z of Any State described in Note X.

Report on Other Legal and Regulatory Requirements

[*Form and content of this section of the auditor's report will vary depending on the nature of the auditor's other reporting responsibilities.*]

[*Auditor's signature*]

[*Auditor's city and state*]

[*Date of the auditor's report*]

ILLUSTRATION 5. AN AUDITOR'S REPORT ON A COMPLETE SET OF FINANCIAL STATEMENTS PREPARED IN ACCORDANCE WITH A CONTRACTUAL BASIS OF ACCOUNTING

Circumstances include the following:

- The financial statements have been prepared by management of the entity in accordance with a contractual basis of accounting (that is, a special purpose framework) to comply with the provisions of that contract.
- Based on the provisions of the contract, management does not have a choice of financial reporting frameworks.

Independent Auditor's Report

[*Appropriate addressee*]

Report on the Financial Statements

We have audited the accompanying financial statements of ABC Company, which comprise the assets and liabilities—contractual basis as of December 31, 20X1, and the revenues and expenses—

contractual basis, changes in equity—contractual basis, and cash flows—contractual basis for the year then ended, and the related notes to the financial statements.

Management's Responsibility for the Financial Statements

Management is responsible for the preparation and fair presentation of these financial statements in accordance with the financial reporting provisions of Section Z of the contract between ABC Company and DEF Company dated January 1, 20X1 (the contract). Management is also responsible for the design, implementation, and maintenance of internal control relevant to the preparation and fair presentation of financial statements that are free from material misstatement, whether due to fraud or to error.

Auditor's Responsibility

Our responsibility is to express an opinion on these financial statements based on our audit. We conducted our audit in accordance with auditing standards generally accepted in the United States of America. Those standards require that we plan and perform the audit to obtain reasonable assurance about whether the financial statements are free from material misstatement.

An audit involves performing procedures to obtain audit evidence about the amounts and disclosures in the financial statements. The procedures selected depend on the auditor's judgment, including the assessment of the risks of material misstatement of the financial statements, whether due to fraud or to error. In making those risk assessments, the auditor considers internal control relevant to the entity's preparation and fair presentation of the financial statements in order to design audit procedures that are appropriate in the circumstances, but not for the purpose of expressing an opinion on the effectiveness of the entity's internal control. Accordingly, we express no such opinion. An audit also includes evaluating the appropriateness of accounting policies used and the reasonableness of significant accounting estimates made by management, as well as evaluating the overall presentation of the financial statements.

We believe that the audit evidence we have obtained is sufficient and appropriate to provide a basis for our audit opinion.

Opinion

In our opinion, the financial statements referred to above present fairly, in all material respects, the assets and liabilities of ABC Company as of December 31, 20X1, and revenues, expenses, changes in equity, and cash flows for the year then ended in accordance with the financial reporting provisions of Section Z of the contract.

Basis of Accounting

We draw attention to Note X of the financial statements, which describes the basis of accounting. The financial statements are prepared by ABC Company on the basis of the financial reporting provisions of Section Z of the contract, which is a basis of accounting other than accounting principles generally accepted in the United States of America, to comply with the financial reporting provisions of the contract referred to above. Our opinion is not modified with respect to this matter.

Restriction on Use

Our report is intended solely for the information and use of ABC Company and DEF Company and is not intended to be and should not be used by anyone other than these specified parties.

Report on Other Legal and Regulatory Requirements

[*Form and content of this section of the auditor's report will vary depending on the nature of the auditor's other reporting responsibilities.*]

[*Auditor's signature*]

[*Auditor's city and state*]

[*Date of the auditor's report*]

AU-C 805 Special Considerations—Audits of Single Financial Statements and Specific Elements, Accounts, or Items of a Financial Statement

AU-C ORIGINAL PRONOUNCEMENT

Source Statement on Auditing Standards (SAS) 122.

AU-C DEFINITIONS OF TERMS

AU-C 805 does not contain any definitions, but does provide the following guidance in AU-C 805.06.

For purposes of this section, reference to

a. an element of a financial statement or an element means an element, account, or item of a financial statement.
b. a single financial statement or a specific element of a financial statement includes the related notes. The related notes ordinarily comprise a summary of significant accounting policies and other explanatory information relevant to the financial statement or the specific element.

OBJECTIVES OF AU-C SECTION 805

AU-C Section 805.05 states that:

> . . . the objective of the auditor, when applying generally accepted auditing standards (GAAS) in an audit of a single financial statement or of a specific element, account, or item of a financial statement, is to address appropriately the special considerations that are relevant to
>
> *a. the acceptance of the engagement;*
> *b. the planning and performance of that engagement; and*
> *c. forming an opinion and reporting on the single financial statement or the specific element, account, or item of a financial statement.*

SCOPE

This section applies to auditor's reports issued in connection with audit of a single financial statement or of a specific element, account, or item of a financial statement. This section does not apply to the report of a component auditor issued as a result of work performed on a component as part of a group audit under AU-C 600. (AU-C 805.01-.02)

REQUIREMENTS

Examples and Other Services

An auditor may accept an engagement to express an opinion on one or more specified elements, accounts, or items of a financial statement, either as a separate engagement or in conjunction with the audit of the financial statements. The specified elements, accounts, or items may be presented in the auditor's report or in a document accompanying the report.

Examples of specified elements, accounts, or items of a financial statement on which an auditor may report include accounts receivable, investments, rentals, royalties, provision for income taxes, and total expenses. For specified elements, accounts, or items, the accountant may review the specified elements, accounts, or items in accordance with attestation standards (see Section AT 201).

Application of GAAS

The AU-C 200 requirement for the auditor to comply with all AU-C sections relevant to the audit applies to an audit of a single financial statement or a specific element of a financial statement whether or not the auditor is engaged to audit the full set of financial statements. (AU-C 805.08) When not engaged to audit the complete financial statements, the auditor must consider carefully whether he or she will be able to perform procedures on interrelated items. (AU-C 805.09)

Financial Reporting Framework

As required by AU-C 210, the auditor should consider the acceptability of the financial reporting framework applied to the single statement or specific element. The auditor should also understand:

- The intended user
- The purpose
- How management has determined that the framework is acceptable in the circumstances
- Whether the framework will provide adequate disclosure

(AU-C 805.10-11)

Scope of Audit and Level of Materiality

Many financial statement elements, such as sales and receivables, inventory and payables, long-lived assets and depreciation, are interrelated. The auditor may therefore also apply audit procedures to elements, accounts, or items that are interrelated with those on which he or she has been engaged to express an opinion. The auditor should have performed procedures necessary to obtain sufficient evidence to express an opinion about financial position and results of operations, excluding classification or disclosure matters, when expressing an opinion on a specified element, account, or item when that specified element, account, or item is, or is based upon, an entity's stockholders' equity or equivalent. (AU-C 805.13)

In these types of engagements, the auditor expresses an opinion on *each* of the specified elements, accounts, or items encompassed by the auditor's report. The measurement of materiality, therefore, should be related to each individual element, account, or item reported on, and not to the aggregate of them or to the financial statements taken as a whole. (AU-C 805.14)

Because the amount considered material is usually smaller in an audit of this nature, the audit of the specified element, account, or item usually is more extensive than it is when the same information is being considered in conjunction with an audit of the financial statements taken as a whole. (AU-C 805.A16)

The Auditor's Report

The auditor's report on one or more specified elements, accounts, or items of a financial statement should reflect the requirements in AU-C 700. (AU-C 805.15) The report should be separate from the report on the full set of financial statements but indicate the date and nature of the opinion in the report on the full set of financial statements. (AU-C 805.16)

The individual statement or specific elements can be published together with the completed, audited financial statements but should be differentiated. (AU-C 805.17) If not properly differentiated the auditor should ask management to do so and, if this is not done, the auditor should not release the report on the single financial statement or element. (AU-C 805.18)

If the auditor's opinion on the complete set of financial statements is modified, the auditor should consider the effect on the opinion on the single financial statement or specific element. (AU-C 805.19)

When reporting on the audit of a specific element of a financial statement if the modified opinion on the complete set of statements is considered relevant to the audit of that element, the auditor should form an opinion based on the reason for the modified opinion. If the opinion on the full set is a result of a material misstatement, the auditor should express an adverse opinion on the element. If the modification on the full set is a result of an inability to obtain sufficient appropriate evidence, the auditor should disclaim an opinion on the specific element. (AU-C 805.20)

An auditor may have expressed an adverse opinion or disclaimed an opinion on the basic financial statements. In these circumstances, the auditor still may report on one or more specified elements, accounts, or items of the basic financial statements only if the following conditions exist:

1. The matters to be reported on and the scope of the audit were not intended to and did not include so many elements, accounts, or items that they compose a major portion of the basic financial statements.
2. The report on the elements, accounts, or items should be presented separately from the report on the financial statements of the entity.

(AU-C 805.21)

Likewise, a single financial statement is considered a major portion of a complete set of financial statements, and, therefore, the auditor cannot express an unmodified opinion on a single statement if the auditor has expressed an adverse opinion or disclaimed an opinion on the complete set. (AU-C 805.22)

If the complete set includes an emphasis-of-matter or an other-matter paragraph that is relevant to the audit of the single financial statement or specific element, the auditor must include a similar paragraph in the auditor's report on the single financial statement or specific element. (AU-C 805.23)

INTERPRETATION

SPECIAL CONSIDERATIONS—AUDITS OF SINGLE FINANCIAL STATEMENTS AND SPECIFIC ELEMENTS, ACCOUNTS, OR ITEMS OF A FINANCIAL STATEMENT: AUDITING INTERPRETATIONS OF SECTION 805

In June 2012, the Governmental Accounting Standards Board (GASB) issued statements No. 67 and No. 68 that change the reporting of public employee pension plans and the state and local governments that participate in those plans. In response, the Auditing Standards Board (ASB) issued three interpretations to assist plan and employer auditors in implementing those standards. Auditors of entities that have implemented the standards should reference AU-C Sections 9805, 9600, and 9500 for more information.

ILLUSTRATIONS OF AUDITOR'S REPORTS ON A SINGLE FINANCIAL STATEMENT AND A SPECIFIC ELEMENT OF A FINANCIAL STATEMENT (SOURCE: AU-C 805.25)

1. An Auditor's Report on a Single Financial Statement Prepared in Accordance with a General Purpose Framework

2. An Auditor's Report on a Single Financial Statement Prepared in Accordance with a Special Purpose Framework

3. An Auditor's Report on a Specific Element, Account, or Item of a Financial Statement Prepared in Accordance with a General Purpose Framework

4. An Auditor's Report on a Specific Element, Account, or Item of a Financial Statement Prepared in Accordance with a Special Purpose Framework

5. An Auditor's Report on an Incomplete Presentation but One That Is Otherwise in Accordance with Generally Accepted Accounting Principles

ILLUSTRATION 1. AN AUDITOR'S REPORT ON A SINGLE FINANCIAL STATEMENT PREPARED IN ACCORDANCE WITH A GENERAL PURPOSE FRAMEWORK

Circumstances include the following:

- Audit of a balance sheet (that is, a single financial statement).
- The balance sheet has been prepared by management of the entity in accordance with accounting principles generally accepted in the United States of America.

Independent Auditor's Report

[*Appropriate addressee*]

Report on the Financial Statement

We have audited the accompanying balance sheet of ABC Company as of December 31, 20X1, and the related notes (the financial statement).

Management's Responsibility for the Financial Statement

Management is responsible for the preparation and fair presentation of this financial statement in accordance with accounting principles generally accepted in the United States of America; this includes the design, implementation, and maintenance of internal control relevant to the preparation and fair presentation of the financial statement that is free from material misstatement, whether due to fraud or to error.

Auditor's Responsibility

Our responsibility is to express an opinion on the financial statement based on our audit. We conducted our audit in accordance with auditing standards generally accepted in the United States of America. Those standards require that we plan and perform the audit to obtain reasonable assurance about whether the financial statement is free from material misstatement.

An audit involves performing procedures to obtain audit evidence about the amounts and disclosures in the financial statement. The procedures selected depend on the auditor's judgment, including the assessment of the risks of material misstatement of the financial statement, whether due to fraud or to error. In making those risk assessments, the auditor considers internal control relevant to the entity's preparation and fair presentation of the financial statement in order to design audit procedures that are appropriate in the circumstances, but not for the purpose of expressing an opinion on the effectiveness of the entity's internal control. Accordingly, we express no such opinion. An audit also includes evaluating the appropriateness of accounting policies used and the reasonableness of significant accounting estimates made by management, as well as evaluating the overall presentation of the financial statement.

We believe that the audit evidence we have obtained is sufficient and appropriate to provide a basis for our audit opinion.

Opinion

In our opinion, the financial statement referred to above presents fairly, in all material respects, the financial position of ABC Company as of December 31, 20X1, in accordance with accounting principles generally accepted in the United States of America.

Report on Other Legal and Regulatory Requirements

[*Form and content of this section of the auditor's report will vary depending on the nature of the auditor's other reporting responsibilities.*]

[*Auditor's signature*]

[*Auditor's city and state*]

[*Date of the auditor's report*]

ILLUSTRATION 2. AN AUDITOR'S REPORT ON A SINGLE FINANCIAL STATEMENT PREPARED IN ACCORDANCE WITH A SPECIAL PURPOSE FRAMEWORK

Circumstances include the following:

- Audit of a statement of cash receipts and disbursements (that is, a single financial statement).
- The financial statement has been prepared by management of the entity in accordance with the cash basis of accounting (a special purpose framework) to respond to a request for cash flow information received from a creditor.
- Management has a choice of financial reporting frameworks.

Independent Auditor's Report

[Appropriate addressee]

Report on the Financial Statement

We have audited the accompanying statement of cash receipts and disbursements of ABC Company for the year ended December 31, 20X1, and the related notes (the financial statement).

Management's Responsibility for the Financial Statement

Management is responsible for the preparation and fair presentation of this financial statement in accordance with the cash basis of accounting described in Note X; this includes determining that the cash basis of accounting is an acceptable basis for the preparation of the financial statement in the circumstances. Management is also responsible for the design, implementation, and maintenance of internal control relevant to the preparation and fair presentation of the financial statement that is free from material misstatement, whether due to fraud or to error.

Auditor's Responsibility

Our responsibility is to express an opinion on the financial statement based on our audit. We conducted our audit in accordance with auditing standards generally accepted in the United States of America. Those standards require that we plan and perform the audit to obtain reasonable assurance about whether the financial statement is free from material misstatement.

An audit involves performing procedures to obtain audit evidence about the amounts and disclosures in the financial statement. The procedures selected depend on the auditor's judgment, including the assessment of the risks of material misstatement of the financial statement, whether due to fraud or to error. In making those risk assessments, the auditor considers internal control relevant to the entity's preparation and fair presentation of the financial statement in order to design audit procedures that are appropriate in the circumstances, but not for the purpose of expressing an opinion on the effectiveness of the entity's internal control. Accordingly, we express no such opinion. An audit also includes evaluating the appropriateness of accounting policies used and the reasonableness of significant accounting estimates made by management, as well as evaluating the overall presentation of the financial statement.

We believe that the audit evidence we have obtained is sufficient and appropriate to provide a basis for our audit opinion.

Opinion

In our opinion, the financial statement referred to above presents fairly, in all material respects, the cash receipts and disbursements of ABC Company for the year ended December 31, 20X1, in accordance with the cash basis of accounting described in Note X.

Basis of Accounting

We draw attention to Note X to the financial statement, which describes the basis of accounting. The financial statement is prepared on the cash basis of accounting, which is a basis of accounting other than accounting principles generally accepted in the United States of America. Our opinion is not modified with respect to this matter.

Report on Other Legal and Regulatory Requirements

[Form and content of this section of the auditor's report will vary depending on the nature of the auditor's other reporting responsibilities.]

[Auditor's signature]

[Auditor's city and state]

[Date of the auditor's report]

ILLUSTRATION 3. AN AUDITOR'S REPORT ON A SPECIFIC ELEMENT, ACCOUNT, OR ITEM OF A FINANCIAL STATEMENT PREPARED IN ACCORDANCE WITH A GENERAL PURPOSE FRAMEWORK

Circumstances include the following:

- Audit of a schedule of accounts receivable (that is, a specific element, account, or item of a financial statement).
- The schedule of accounts receivable has been prepared by management of the entity in accordance with accounting principles generally accepted in the United States of America.
- The audit of the schedule of accounts receivable was performed in conjunction with an engagement to audit the entity's complete set of financial statements. The opinion on those financial statements was not modified, and the report did not include an emphasis-of-matter paragraph or other-matter paragraph.

Independent Auditor's Report

[*Appropriate addressee*]

Report on the Schedule

We have audited the accompanying schedule of accounts receivable of ABC Company as of December 31, 20X1, and the related notes (the schedule).

Management's Responsibility for the Schedule

Management is responsible for the preparation and fair presentation of this schedule in accordance with accounting principles generally accepted in the United States of America; this includes the design, implementation, and maintenance of internal control relevant to the preparation and fair presentation of the schedule that is free from material misstatement, whether due to fraud or to error.

Auditor's Responsibility

Our responsibility is to express an opinion on the schedule based on our audit. We conducted our audit in accordance with auditing standards generally accepted in the United States of America. Those standards require that we plan and perform the audit to obtain reasonable assurance about whether the schedule is free from material misstatement.

An audit involves performing procedures to obtain audit evidence about the amounts and disclosures in the schedule. The procedures selected depend on the auditor's judgment, including the assessment of the risks of material misstatement of the schedule, whether due to fraud or to error. In making those risk assessments, the auditor considers internal control relevant to the entity's preparation and fair presentation of the schedule in order to design audit procedures that are appropriate in the circumstances, but not for the purpose of expressing an opinion on the effectiveness of the entity's internal control. Accordingly, we express no such opinion. An audit also includes evaluating the appropriateness of accounting policies used and the reasonableness of significant accounting estimates made by management, as well as evaluating the overall presentation of the schedule.

We believe that the audit evidence we have obtained is sufficient and appropriate to provide a basis for our audit opinion.

Opinion

In our opinion, the schedule referred to above presents fairly, in all material respects, the accounts receivable of ABC Company as of December 31, 20X1, in accordance with accounting principles generally accepted in the United States of America.

Other Matter

We have audited, in accordance with auditing standards generally accepted in the United States of America, the financial statements of ABC Company as of and for the year ended December 31, 20X1, and our report thereon, dated March 15, 20X2, expressed an unmodified opinion on those financial statements.

Report on Other Legal and Regulatory Requirements

[*Form and content of this section of the auditor's report will vary depending on the nature of the auditor's other reporting responsibilities.*]

[*Auditor's signature*]

[*Auditor's city and state*]

[*Date of the auditor's report*]

ILLUSTRATION 4. AN AUDITOR'S REPORT ON A SPECIFIC ELEMENT, ACCOUNT, OR ITEM OF A FINANCIAL STATEMENT PREPARED IN ACCORDANCE WITH A SPECIAL PURPOSE FRAMEWORK

Circumstances include the following:

- Audit of a schedule of royalties applicable to engine production (that is, a specific element, account, or item of a financial statement).
- The financial information has been prepared by management of the entity in accordance with a contractual basis of accounting (that is, a special purpose framework) to comply with the provisions of that contract.
- Based on the provisions of the contract, management does not have a choice of financial reporting frameworks.
- The audit of the schedule was not performed in conjunction with an engagement to audit the entity's complete set of financial statements.

Independent Auditor's Report

[*Appropriate addressee*]

Report on the Schedule

We have audited the accompanying schedule of royalties applicable to engine production of the Q Division of ABC Company for the year ended December 31, 20X1, and the related notes (the schedule).

Management's Responsibility for the Schedule

Management is responsible for the preparation and fair presentation of the schedule in accordance with the financial reporting provisions of Section Z of the license agreement between ABC Company and XYZ Corporation dated January 1, 20X1 (the contract). Management is also responsible for the design, implementation, and maintenance of internal control relevant to the preparation and fair presentation of the schedule that is free from material misstatement, whether due to fraud or to error.

Auditor's Responsibility

Our responsibility is to express an opinion on the schedule based on our audit. We conducted our audit in accordance with auditing standards generally accepted in the United States of America. Those standards require that we plan and perform the audit to obtain reasonable assurance about whether the schedule is free from material misstatement.

An audit involves performing procedures to obtain audit evidence about the amounts and disclosures in the schedule. The procedures selected depend on the auditor's judgment, including the assessment of the risks of material misstatement of the schedule, whether due to fraud or to error. In making those risk assessments, the auditor considers internal control relevant to the entity's preparation and fair presentation of the schedule in order to design audit procedures that are appropriate in the circumstances, but not for the purpose of expressing an opinion on the effectiveness of the entity's internal control. Accordingly, we express no such opinion. An audit also includes evaluating the appropriateness of accounting policies used and the reasonableness of significant accounting estimates made by management, as well as evaluating the overall presentation of the schedule.

We believe that the audit evidence we have obtained is sufficient and appropriate to provide a basis for our audit opinion.

Opinion

In our opinion, the schedule referred to above presents fairly, in all material respects, the royalties applicable to engine production of the Q Division of ABC Company for the year ended December 31, 20X1, in accordance with the financial reporting provisions of Section Z of the contract.

Basis of Accounting

We draw attention to Note X to the schedule, which describes the basis of accounting. The schedule was prepared by ABC Company on the basis of the financial reporting provisions of Section Z of the contract, which is a basis of accounting other than accounting principles generally accepted in the United States of America, to comply with the financial reporting provisions of the contract referred to above. Our opinion is not modified with respect to this matter.

Restriction on Use

Our report is intended solely for the information and use of ABC Company and XYZ Corporation and is not intended to be and should not be used by anyone other than these specified parties.

Report on Other Legal and Regulatory Requirements

[*Form and content of this section of the auditor's report will vary depending on the nature of the auditor's other reporting responsibilities.*]

[*Auditor's signature*]

[*Auditor's city and state*]

[*Date of the auditor's report*]

Illustration 5. An Auditor's Report on an Incomplete Presentation but One That Is Otherwise in Accordance with Generally Accepted Accounting Principles

Circumstances include the following:

- Audit of the historical summaries of gross income and direct operating expenses (that is, a single financial statement).
- The historical summaries have been prepared by management of the entity in accordance with accounting principles generally accepted in the United States of America but are an incomplete presentation of revenues and expenses.

Independent Auditor's Report

[*Appropriate addressee*]

Report on the Historical Summaries

We have audited the accompanying Historical Summaries of Gross Income and Direct Operating Expenses of ABC Apartments for each of the three years in the period ended December 31, 20X1, and the related notes (the historical summaries).

Management's Responsibility for the Historical Summaries

Management is responsible for the preparation and fair presentation of these historical summaries in accordance with accounting principles generally accepted in the United States of America; this includes the design, implementation, and maintenance of internal control relevant to the preparation and fair presentation of the historical summaries that are free from material misstatement, whether due to fraud or to error.

Auditor's Responsibility

Our responsibility is to express an opinion on the historical summaries based on our audit. We conducted our audit in accordance with auditing standards generally accepted in the United States of America. Those standards require that we plan and perform the audit to obtain reasonable assurance about whether the historical summaries are free from material misstatement.

An audit involves performing procedures to obtain audit evidence about the amounts and disclosures in the historical summaries. The procedures selected depend on the auditor's judgment, including the assessment of the risks of material misstatement of the historical summaries, whether due to fraud or to error. In making those risk assessments, the auditor considers internal control relevant to the entity's preparation and fair presentation of the historical summaries in order to design audit procedures that are appropriate in the circumstances, but not for the purpose of expressing an opinion on the effectiveness of the entity's internal control. Accordingly, we express no such opinion. An audit also includes evaluating the appropriateness of accounting policies used and the reasonableness of significant accounting estimates made by management, as well as evaluating the overall presentation of the historical summaries.

We believe that the audit evidence we have obtained is sufficient and appropriate to provide a basis for our audit opinion.

Opinion

In our opinion, the historical summaries referred to above present fairly, in all material respects, the gross income and direct operating expenses described in Note X of ABC Apartments for each of the three years in the period ended December 31, 20X1, in accordance with accounting principles generally accepted in the United States of America.

Emphasis of Matter

We draw attention to Note X to the historical summaries, which describes that the accompanying historical summaries were prepared for the purpose of complying with the rules and regulations of Regulator DEF (for inclusion in the filing of Form Z of ABC Company) and are not intended to be a complete presentation of the Company's revenues and expenses. Our opinion is not modified with respect to this matter.

Report on Other Legal and Regulatory Requirements

[*Form and content of this section of the auditor's report will vary depending on the nature of the auditor's other reporting responsibilities.*]

[*Auditor's signature*]

[*Auditor's city and state*]

[*Date of the auditor's report*]

AU-C 806 Reporting on Compliance with Aspects of Contractual Agreements or Regulatory Requirements in Connection with Audited Financial Statements

AU-C ORIGINAL PRONOUNCEMENTS

Sources Statements on Auditing Standards (SASs) 122 and 125.

AU-C DEFINITIONS OF TERMS

AU-C 806 does not contain any definitions.

OBJECTIVE OF AU-C SECTION 806

AU-C Section 806.06 states that:

the objective of the auditor is to report appropriately on an entity's compliance with aspects of contractual agreements or regulatory requirements, in connection with the audit of financial statements, when the auditor is requested to report on such matters.

SCOPE

Auditor's reports issued in connection with compliance with aspects of contractual agreements or regulatory requirements related to accounting matters connected with audited financial statements. (AU-C 806.01)

If the auditor is testing compliance with laws and regulations in an audit in accordance with the *Government Auditing Standards* (the "Yellow Book") issued by the Comptroller General of the United States or a single audit act in accordance with an Office of Management and Budget circular, he or she should follow the guidance in Section 935, *Compliance Audits.* (AU-C 806.03)

REQUIREMENTS

AGREEMENTS REQUIRING COMPLIANCE REPORTS

Bond indentures, loan and other agreements, or regulatory agencies may require compliance reports by independent auditors. For example, loan agreements may contain covenants for borrowers, such as payments into sinking funds, payments of interest, maintenance of current ratios, restriction of dividend payments, and use of proceeds of sales of property. Also, these agreements may require that the borrower provide annual financial statements that have been audited by an independent auditor. (AU-C 806.02)

REQUEST FOR ASSURANCE

In certain circumstances, lenders request from the independent auditor assurance that the borrower has complied with the covenants of the agreements relating to accounting or auditing matters. (The lender's request is made to the client, not the auditor.) The independent auditor usually satisfies this request by giving negative assurance concerning the applicable covenants. Such assurance may *not* be given if the auditor has not audited the financial statements related to the contractual agreements or regulatory requirements, if the auditor has issued an adverse opinion or disclaimer of opinion on those statements, or if the assurance extends to covenants addressing matters not subjected to auditing procedures. (AU-C 806.07)

The negative assurance given by the auditor may be provided in a separate report or in one or more paragraphs of the auditor's report accompanying the financial statements.

SEPARATE AUDITOR'S REPORT

If an auditor's report on compliance with contractual agreements or regulatory provisions is a separate report, it should include the following:

1. A title that includes the word *independent* and an appropriate addressee.
2. A paragraph stating that the financial statements were audited in accordance with auditing standards generally accepted in the United States of America and the date of the auditor's report on the financial statements. Any departure from the auditor's standard report on the financial statements should be disclosed.
3. If no instances of noncompliance are identified:
    a. Reference to the specific covenants or paragraphs of the agreement
    b. Provides negative assurance relative to compliance with the applicable covenants
4. If instances of noncompliance are identified:
    a. Reference to the specific covenants or paragraphs
    b. Description of the identified instances or noncompliance
5. Specification that the report is being given in connection with the audit of the financial statements.
6. A statement that the audit was not directed primarily toward obtaining knowledge regarding compliance.

7. A paragraph that describes and states the source of any significant interpretations made by the entity's management relating to provisions of the agreement.
8. A paragraph, in accordance with AU-C 905, that restricts the use of the report to those within the entity and the parties to the contract or agreement or for filing with the regulatory agency, if appropriate.
9. The manual or printed signature of the auditing firm and the city and state where the auditor practices.
10. The date of the report, which should be the same date as the auditor's report on the financial statements.

(AU-C 806.12)

Assurance Given in Auditor's Report on the Financial Statements

The auditor may include his or her report on compliance with contractual agreements or regulatory provisions in the auditor's report on the financial statements. In this case, the auditor should include an other-matter paragraph, after the opinion paragraph, that provides the negative assurance relative to compliance with the applicable covenants of the agreement, insofar as they relate to accounting matters. If instances of noncompliance are found, the paragraph should describe the identified instances of noncompliance. The paragraph also should state that (1) the negative assurance is being given in connection with the audit of the financial statements and (2) the audit was not directed primarily toward obtaining knowledge regarding compliance.

The auditor's report should also include a paragraph that describes and states the source of any significant interpretations made by the entity's management and a paragraph that, in accordance with AU-C 905, restricts its use to those within the entity and the parties to the contract or agreement or for filing with the regulatory agency, if appropriate. (AU-C 806.13)

AU-C 806 ILLUSTRATIONS (SOURCE: AU-C 806.A8)

The following reports on compliance with aspects of contractual agreements or regulatory requirements in connection with audited financial statements are illustrated:

1. A Report on Compliance with Aspects of Contractual Agreements Provided in a Separate Report When No Instances of Noncompliance Are Identified
2. A Report on Compliance with Aspects of Contractual Agreements Provided in a Separate Report When Instances of Noncompliance Are Identified
3. A Report on Compliance with Aspects of Contractual Agreements Provided in a Separate Report When Instances of Noncompliance Are Identified and a Waiver Has Been Obtained
4. A Report on Compliance with Aspects of Contractual Agreements Provided in a Separate Report When Instances of Noncompliance Are Identified, and the Auditor Has Disclaimed an Opinion on the Financial Statements
5. A Report on Compliance with Aspects of Contractual Agreements Provided in a Separate Report When No Instances of Noncompliance Are Identified

ILLUSTRATION 1. A REPORT ON COMPLIANCE WITH ASPECTS OF CONTRACTUAL AGREEMENTS PROVIDED IN A SEPARATE REPORT WHEN NO INSTANCES OF NONCOMPLIANCE ARE IDENTIFIED

Independent Auditor's Report

[*Appropriate addressee*]

We have audited, in accordance with auditing standards generally accepted in the United States of America, the financial statements of XYZ Company, which comprise the balance sheet as of December 31, 20X2, and the related statements of income, changes in stockholders' equity, and cash flows for the year then ended, and the related notes to the financial statements, and have issued our report thereon dated February 16, 20X3.

In connection with our audit, nothing came to our attention that caused us to believe that XYZ Company failed to comply with the terms, covenants, provisions, or conditions of sections XX to YY, inclusive, of the Indenture dated July 21, 20X0, with ABC Bank, insofar as they relate to accounting matters. However, our audit was not directed primarily toward obtaining knowledge of such noncompliance. Accordingly, had we performed additional procedures, other matters may have come to our attention regarding the Company's noncompliance with the above-referenced terms, covenants, provisions, or conditions of the Indenture, insofar as they relate to accounting matters.

This report is intended solely for the information and use of the board of directors and management of XYZ Company and ABC Bank and is not intended to be and should not be used by anyone other than these specified parties.

[*Auditor's signature*]

[*Auditor's city and state*]

[*Date of the auditor's report*]

ILLUSTRATION 2. A REPORT ON COMPLIANCE WITH ASPECTS OF CONTRACTUAL AGREEMENTS PROVIDED IN A SEPARATE REPORT WHEN INSTANCES OF NONCOMPLIANCE ARE IDENTIFIED

Independent Auditor's Report

[*Appropriate addressee*]

We have audited, in accordance with auditing standards generally accepted in the United States of America, the financial statements of XYZ Company, which comprise the balance sheet as of December 31, 20X2, and the related statements of income, changes in stockholders' equity, and cash flows for the year then ended, and the related notes to the financial statements, and have issued our report thereon dated March 5, 20X3.

In connection with our audit, we noted that XYZ Company failed to comply with the "Working Capital" provision of section XX of the Loan Agreement dated March 1, 20X2, with ABC Bank. Our audit was not directed primarily toward obtaining knowledge as to whether XYZ Company failed to comply with the terms, covenants, provisions, or conditions of sections XX to YY, inclusive, of the Loan Agreement, insofar as they relate to accounting matters. Accordingly, had we performed additional procedures, other matters may have come to our attention regarding noncompliance with the above-referenced terms, covenants, provisions, or conditions of the Loan Agreement, insofar as they relate to accounting matters.

This report is intended solely for the information and use of the board of directors and management of XYZ Company and ABC Bank and is not intended to be and should not be used by anyone other than these specified parties.

[*Auditor's signature*]

[*Auditor's city and state*]

[*Date of the auditor's report*]

ILLUSTRATION 3. A REPORT ON COMPLIANCE WITH ASPECTS OF CONTRACTUAL AGREEMENTS PROVIDED IN A SEPARATE REPORT WHEN INSTANCES OF NONCOMPLIANCE ARE IDENTIFIED AND A WAIVER HAS BEEN OBTAINED

Independent Auditor's Report

[*Appropriate addressee*]

We have audited, in accordance with auditing standards generally accepted in the United States of America, the financial statements of XYZ Company, which comprise the balance sheet as of December 31, 20X2, and the related statements of income, changes in stockholders' equity, and cash flows for the year then ended, and the related notes to the financial statements, and have issued our report thereon dated March 5, 20X3.

In connection with our audit, we noted that XYZ Company failed to comply with the "Working Capital" provision of section XX of the Loan Agreement dated March 1, 20X2, with ABC Bank. The Company has received a waiver dated February 5, 20X3, from ABC Bank. Our audit was not directed primarily toward obtaining knowledge as to whether XYZ Company failed to comply with the terms, covenants, provisions, or conditions of sections XX to YY, inclusive, of the Loan Agreement, insofar as they relate to accounting matters. Accordingly, had we performed additional procedures, other matters may have come to our attention regarding noncompliance with the above-referenced terms, covenants, provisions, or conditions of the Loan Agreement, insofar as they relate to accounting matters.

This report is intended solely for the information and use of the board of directors and management of XYZ Company and ABC Bank and is not intended to be and should not be used by anyone other than these specified parties.

[*Auditor's signature*]

[*Auditor's city and state*]

[*Date of the auditor's report*]

ILLUSTRATION 4. REPORT ON COMPLIANCE WITH ASPECTS OF CONTRACTUAL AGREEMENTS PROVIDED IN A SEPARATE REPORT WHEN INSTANCES OF NONCOMPLIANCE ARE IDENTIFIED, AND THE AUDITOR HAS DISCLAIMED AN OPINION ON THE FINANCIAL STATEMENTS

Independent Auditor's Report

[*Appropriate addressee*]

We were engaged to audit, in accordance with auditing standards generally accepted in the United States of America, the financial statements of XYZ Company, which comprise the balance sheet as of

December 31, 20X2, and the related statements of income, changes in stockholders' equity, and cash flows for the year then ended, and the related notes to the financial statements, and have issued our report thereon dated March 5, 20X3. Our report disclaims an opinion on such financial statements because of [*describe the scope limitation or matter causing the disclaimer*].

In connection with our engagement, we noted that XYZ Company failed to comply with the "Working Capital" provision of section XX of the Loan Agreement dated March 1, 20X2, with ABC Bank. Our engagement was not directed primarily toward obtaining knowledge as to whether XYZ Company failed to comply with the terms, covenants, provisions, or conditions of sections XX to YY, inclusive, of the Loan Agreement, insofar as they relate to accounting matters. Accordingly, had we been able to complete the audit, other matters may have come to our attention regarding noncompliance with the above-referenced terms, covenants, provisions, or conditions of the Loan Agreement, insofar as they relate to accounting matters.

This report is intended solely for the information and use of the board of directors and management of XYZ Company and ABC Bank and is not intended to be and should not be used by anyone other than these specified parties.

[*Auditor's signature*]

[*Auditor's city and state*]

[*Date of the auditor's report*]

Illustration 5. A Report on Compliance with Aspects of Contractual Agreements Provided in a Separate Report When No Instances of Noncompliance Are Identified

Independent Auditor's Report

[*Appropriate addressee*]

Report on the Financial Statements

We have audited the accompanying financial statements of ABC Company, which comprise the balance sheet as of December 31, 20X1, and the related statements of income, changes in stockholders' equity, and cash flows for the year then ended, and the related notes to the financial statements.

Management's Responsibility for the Financial Statements

Management is responsible for the preparation and fair presentation of these financial statements in accordance with accounting principles generally accepted in the United States of America; this includes the design, implementation, and maintenance of internal control relevant to the preparation and fair presentation of financial statements that are free from material misstatement, whether due to fraud or to error.

Auditor's Responsibility

Our responsibility is to express an opinion on these financial statements based on our audit. We conducted our audit in accordance with auditing standards generally accepted in the United States of America. Those standards require that we plan and perform the audit to obtain reasonable assurance about whether the financial statements are free from material misstatement.

An audit involves performing procedures to obtain audit evidence about the amounts and disclosures in the financial statements. The procedures selected depend on the auditor's judgment, including the assessment of the risks of material misstatement of the financial statements, whether due to fraud or to error. In making those risk assessments, the auditor considers internal control relevant to the entity's preparation and fair presentation of the financial statements in order to design audit procedures that are appropriate in the circumstances, but not for the purpose of expressing an opinion on the effectiveness of the entity's internal control. Accordingly, we express no such opinion. An audit also includes evaluating the appropriateness of accounting policies used and the reasonableness of significant accounting estimates made by management, as well as evaluating the overall presentation of the financial statements.

We believe that the audit evidence we have obtained is sufficient and appropriate to provide a basis for our audit option.

Opinion

In our opinion, the financial statements referred to above present fairly, in all material respects, the financial position of ABC Company as of December 31, 20X1, and the results of its operations and its cash flows for the year then ended in accordance with accounting principles generally accepted in the United States of America.

Other Matter

In connection with our audit, nothing came to our attention that caused us to believe that ABC Company failed to comply with the terms, covenants, provisions, or conditions of sections XX to YY, inclusive, of the Indenture dated July 21, 20X0 with XYZ Bank, insofar as they relate to accounting matters. However, our audit was not directed primarily toward obtaining knowledge of such non-compliance. Accordingly, had we performed additional procedures, other matters may have come to our attention regarding the Company's noncompliance with the above-referenced terms, covenants, provisions, or conditions of the Indenture, insofar as they relate to accounting matters.

Restricted Use Relating to the Other Matter

The communication related to compliance with the aforementioned Indenture described in the Other Matter paragraph is intended solely for the information and use of the boards of directors and management of ABC Company and XYZ Bank and is not intended to be and should not be used by anyone other than these specified parties.

Report on Other Legal and Regulatory Requirements

[*Form and content of this section of the auditor's report will vary depending on the nature of the auditor's other reporting responsibilities.*]

[*Auditor's signature*]

[*Auditor's city and state*]

[*Date of the auditor's report*]

[*Illustration added, December 2011, to reflect conforming changes necessary due to the issuance of SAS No. 125.*]

AU-C 810 Engagements to Report on Summary Financial Statements

AU-C ORIGINAL PRONOUNCEMENT

Source Statement on Auditing Standards (SAS) 122.

DEFINITIONS OF TERMS

Source: AU-C 810.06

Applied criteria. The criteria applied by management in the preparation of the summary financial statements.

Summary financial statements. Historical financial information that is derived from financial statements but that contains less detail than the financial statements, while still providing a structured representation consistent with that provided by the financial statements of the entity's economic resources or obligations at a point in time or the changes therein for a period of time. Summary financial statements are separately presented and are not presented as comparative information.

OBJECTIVES OF AU-C SECTION 810

AU-C Section 810.05 states that:

. . . *the objectives of the auditor are*

a. to determine whether it is appropriate to accept the engagement to report on summary financial statements and,

b. if engaged to report on summary financial statements, to

i. perform the procedures necessary as the basis for the auditor's opinion on the summary financial statements;

ii. form an opinion on whether the summary financial statements are consistent, in all material respects, with the audited financial statements from which they have been derived, in accordance with the applied criteria, based on an evaluation of the conclusions drawn from the evidence obtained; and

iii. express clearly that opinion through a written report that also describes the basis for that opinion.

SCOPE

AU-C 810 addresses the auditor's responsibilities when reporting on summary financial statements derived from financial statements audited by that same auditor. Accordingly, an auditor cannot report on summary financial statements unless the auditor has audited the financial statements from which the summary financial statements are derived.

REQUIREMENTS

ENGAGEMENT ACCEPTANCE

In order to accept an engagement to report on summary financial statements, the auditor must be engaged to conduct a GAAS audit of the financial statements from which the summary financial statements are derived. The auditor should determine whether the applied criteria are free from bias, obtain written acknowledgment from management of its responsibility, and get the written agreement of management about the expected form and content of the report. (AU-C 810.08-.09)

PROCEDURES

AU-C 810 contains the notion of criteria for preparing summary financial statements and requires the auditor to determine whether the criteria applied by management in the preparation of the summary financial statements are acceptable.

AU-C 810.11 stipulates specific procedures to be performed as the basis for the auditor's opinion in the summary financial statements.

The auditor should determine whether the summary financial statements adequately disclose that the financial statements are summarized and the financial statements are identified.

If the summary financial statements are not accompanied by the audited financial statements, the auditor should determine whether the summary financial statements clearly describe where the audited financial statements are available and if those statements are readily available to the intended users of summary statements.

The auditor must determine whether the applied criteria are adequately disclosed. The auditor must also agree the summary financial information to that in the audited financial statements, make sure that the summary financial information is prepared in accordance with the applied criteria, and determine whether the summary financial statements contain the information necessary to fulfill their purpose and at an appropriate level of aggregation.

Written Representations

Management must provide a written representation letter to the auditor affirming that it has:

- Fulfilled its responsibility for the preparation of the summary financial statements in accordance with acceptable, applied criteria, and
- Made the audited financial statements readily available to the intended users of the summary information.

If the date of the auditor's report on the summary financial statements is later than the date of the report on the audited financial statements, management must indicate whether information has come to light that would lead management to modify any previous representation, or any subsequent events have occurred that require adjustment to or disclosure of the audited financial statements. (AU-C 810.12)

Form of Opinion

When the auditor has concluded that an unmodified opinion on the summary financial statements is appropriate, the auditor's opinion must state that the summary financial statements are consistent, in all material respects, with the audited financial statements from which they have been derived, in accordance with the applied criteria. (AU-C 810.14)

The auditor may find that the summary financial statements are not consistent with the audited financial statements and management does not agree to make the changes. In that case, the auditor should express an adverse opinion on the summary statements. (AU-C 810.15)

When the auditor's report on the audited financial statements contains an adverse opinion or a disclaimer of opinion, the auditor must withdraw from the engagement when withdrawal is possible under applicable law or regulation. Otherwise, the auditor is required to state in the report that it is inappropriate to express, and the auditor does not express, an opinion on the summary financial statements. (AU-C 810.16)

Form of Report

The auditor's report on summary financial statements should include:

1. Title that includes the word *independent*
2. Addressee
3. Identification of the summary financial statements on which the auditor is reporting and the audited financial statements from which that summary information is derived
4. A statement that the auditor has audited and expressed an opinion on the complete financial statements, that refers to the date of that report, and, if appropriate, that an unmodified opinion is expressed on the audited financial statements
5. If the date of the report on the summary statements is later than the date of the report on the audited statements, a statement that the summary statements and the audited financial statements do not reflect the effects of events that occurred subsequent to the date of the auditor's report on the audited financial statements
6. An indication that the summary information does not include all the disclosure information required by the applicable financial reporting framework, and that reading the summary information is not a substitute for reading the audited financial statements
7. A description of management's responsibility
8. A statement that the auditor is responsible for expressing an opinion about whether the summary financial statements are consistent, in all material respects, with the audited financial statements based on the procedures required by GAAS, including explaining that the procedures consisted principally of comparing the summary statements with the related information in the audited financial statements from which the summary statements were prepared in accordance with the applicable criteria, and, if the date of the report on the summary statements is later than the date on audited statements, that the auditor did not perform any audit procedures regarding the audited financial statements after the date of the report on those financial statements
9. The type of opinion issued
10. Auditor's signature, auditor's city and state, and date of the report
    (AU-C 810.17)

An example of this form of report is given in "AU-C 810 Illustrations."

Dating Report

Similar to the requirement for dating a report on audited financial statements, the auditor should date the auditor's report on the summary financial statements no earlier than the date on which the auditor has obtained sufficient appropriate evidence on which to base an opinion. And, of course, the date cannot be earlier than the date of the auditor's report on the audited financial statements. (AU-C 810.18)

When the date on the summary financial statements is later than the date of the auditor's report on the audited financial statements and the auditor becomes aware of subsequently discovered facts, the auditor should not release the auditor's report on the summary statements until the auditor's consideration of subsequently discovered facts in accordance with AU 560 has been completed. (AU-C 810.19)

Restriction on Use or Alerting Readers to the Basis of Accounting

If the auditor's report on the audited financial statements is restricted or alerts users that the audited financial statements are prepared in accordance with a special purpose framework, the auditor should include a similar restriction and/or alert in the report on the summary financial statements. (AU-C 810.20)

Unaudited Information Presented with Summary Financial Statements

The auditor must make sure that any unaudited financial information is clearly differentiated from the summary financial information. If it is not clearly differentiated, the auditor must ask management to change presentation of the unaudited information. If management does not do so, the auditor should explain in his or her report that such information is not covered by the report and no opinion is expressed on it. (AU-C 810.25)

Auditor Association

If the entity plans to state that the auditor has reported on summary financial statements in a document containing the summary statements and the auditor becomes aware of this, the auditor must request that management includes the auditor's report. If management still does not include the report, the auditor should decide on and carry out appropriate actions to prevent management from inappropriately associating the auditor with the summary statement in that document. (AU-C 810.28)

AU-C 810 ILLUSTRATIONS (SOURCE: AU-C 810.a22)

The following reports on summary financial statements are illustrated:

1. An Unmodified Opinion Is Expressed on the Summary Financial Statements (the Auditor's Report on the Summary Financial Statements Is Dated Later Than the Date of the Auditor's Report on the Financial Statements from Which the Summary Financial Statements Are Derived)
2. An Unmodified Opinion Is Expressed on the Summary Financial Statements and a Qualified Opinion Is Expressed on the Audited Financial Statements
3. An Adverse Opinion Is Expressed on the Audited Financial Statements (as a Result of the Adverse Opinion on the Audited Financial Statements, It Is Inappropriate to Express, and the Auditor Does Not Express, an Opinion on the Summary Financial Statements)
4. An Adverse Opinion Is Expressed on the Summary Financial Statements Because They Are Not Consistent, in All Material Respects, with the Audited Financial Statements, in Accordance with the Applied Criteria

ILLUSTRATION 1. AN UNMODIFIED OPINION IS EXPRESSED ON THE SUMMARY FINANCIAL STATEMENTS (THE AUDITOR'S REPORT ON THE SUMMARY FINANCIAL STATEMENTS IS DATED LATER THAN THE DATE OF THE AUDITOR'S REPORT ON THE FINANCIAL STATEMENTS FROM WHICH THE SUMMARY FINANCIAL STATEMENTS ARE DERIVED)

Circumstances include all of the following:

- An unmodified opinion is expressed on the audited financial statements.
- Criteria are developed by management for the preparation of the summary financial statements and are adequately disclosed in Note X. The auditor has determined that the criteria are acceptable in the circumstances.
- An unmodified opinion is expressed on the summary financial statements.
- The auditor's report on the summary financial statements is dated later than the date of the auditor's report on the financial statements from which the summary financial statements are derived.

Independent Auditor's Report on Summary Financial Statements

[*Appropriate addressee*]

The accompanying summary financial statements, which comprise the summary balance sheet as of December 31, 20X1, the summary income statement, summary statement of changes in stockholders' equity, and summary cash flow statement for the year then ended, and the related notes, are derived from the audited financial statements of ABC Company as of and for the year ended December 31, 20X1. We expressed an unmodified audit opinion on those audited financial statements in our report dated February 15, 20X2. The audited financial statements, and the summary financial statements derived therefrom, do not reflect the effects of events, if any, that occurred subsequent to the date of our report on the audited financial statements.

The summary financial statements do not contain all the disclosures required by [*describe financial reporting framework applied in the preparation of the financial statements of ABC Company*]. Reading the summary financial statements, therefore, is not a substitute for reading the audited financial statements of ABC Company.

Management's Responsibility for the Summary Financial Statements

Management is responsible for the preparation of the summary financial statements on the basis described in Note X.

Auditor's Responsibility

Our responsibility is to express an opinion about whether the summary financial statements are consistent, in all material respects, with the audited financial statements based on our procedures, which were conducted in accordance with auditing standards generally accepted in the United States of America. The procedures consisted principally of comparing the summary financial statements with the related information in the audited financial statements from which the summary financial statements have been derived, and evaluating whether the summary financial statements are prepared in accordance with the basis described in Note X. We did not perform any audit procedures regarding the audited financial statements after the date of our report on those financial statements.

Opinion

In our opinion, the summary financial statements of ABC Company as of and for the year ended December 31, 20X1 referred to above are consistent, in all material respects, with the audited financial statements from which they have been derived, on the basis described in Note X.

[*Auditor's signature*]

[*Auditor's city and state*]

[*Date of the auditor's report*]

ILLUSTRATION 2. AN UNMODIFIED OPINION IS EXPRESSED ON THE SUMMARY FINANCIAL STATEMENTS AND A QUALIFIED OPINION IS EXPRESSED ON THE AUDITED FINANCIAL STATEMENTS

Circumstances include all of the following:

- A qualified opinion is expressed on the audited financial statements.
- Criteria are developed by management for the preparation of the summary financial statements and are adequately disclosed in Note X. The auditor has determined that the criteria are acceptable in the circumstances.
- An unmodified opinion is expressed on the summary financial statements.

Independent Auditor's Report on Summary Financial Statements

[*Appropriate addressee*]

The accompanying summary financial statements, which comprise the summary balance sheet as of December 31, 20X1, the summary income statement, summary statement of changes in stockholders' equity, and summary cash flow statement for the year then ended, and the related notes, are derived from the audited financial statements of ABC Company as of and for the year ended December 31, 20X1. We expressed a qualified audit opinion on those audited financial statements in our report dated February 15, 20X2 (see below).

The summary financial statements do not contain all the disclosures required by [*describe financial reporting framework applied in the preparation of the financial statements of ABC Company*]. Reading the summary financial statements, therefore, is not a substitute for reading the audited financial statements of ABC Company.

Management's Responsibility for the Summary Financial Statements

Management is responsible for the preparation of the summary financial statements on the basis described in Note X.

Auditor's Responsibility

Our responsibility is to express an opinion about whether the summary financial statements are consistent, in all material respects, with the audited financial statements based on our procedures, which were conducted in accordance with auditing standards generally accepted in the United States of America. The procedures consisted principally of comparing the summary financial statements with the related information in the audited financial statements from which the summary financial statements have been derived, and evaluating whether the summary financial statements are prepared in accordance with the basis described in Note X.

Opinion

In our opinion, the summary financial statements of ABC Company as of and for the year ended December 31, 20X1 referred to above are consistent, in all material respects, with the audited financial statements from which they have been derived, on the basis described in Note X.

The summary financial statements are misstated to the equivalent extent as the audited financial statements of ABC Company as of and for the year ended December 31, 20X1. The misstatement of the audited financial statements is described in our qualified audit opinion in our report dated February 15, 20X2. Our qualified audit opinion is based on the fact that the Company's inventories are carried in the balance sheet in those audited financial statements at $XXX. Management has not stated the inventories at the lower of cost or net realizable value but has stated them solely at cost, which constitutes a departure from [*describe financial reporting framework applied in the preparation of the financial statements of ABC Company*]. The Company's records indicate that, had management stated the inventories at the lower of cost or net realizable value, an amount of $XXX would have been required to write the inventories down to their net realizable value. Accordingly, cost of sales would have been increased by $XXX, and income tax, net income, and stockholders' equity would have been reduced by $XXX, $XXX, and $XXX, respectively. Our qualified audit opinion states that, except for the effects of the described matter, those financial statements present fairly, in all material respects, the financial position of ABC Company as of December 31, 20X1, and the results of its operations and its cash flows for the year then ended in accordance with [*describe financial reporting framework applied in the preparation of the financial statements of ABC Company*].

[*Auditor's signature*]

[*Auditor's city and state*]

[*Date of the auditor's report*]

ILLUSTRATION 3. AN ADVERSE OPINION IS EXPRESSED ON THE AUDITED FINANCIAL STATEMENTS (AS A RESULT OF THE ADVERSE OPINION ON THE AUDITED FINANCIAL STATEMENTS, IT IS INAPPROPRIATE TO EXPRESS, AND THE AUDITOR DOES NOT EXPRESS, AN OPINION ON THE SUMMARY FINANCIAL STATEMENTS)

Circumstances include both of the following:

- An adverse opinion is expressed on the audited financial statements. As a result of the adverse opinion on the audited financial statements, it is inappropriate to express, and the auditor does not express, an opinion on the summary financial statements, as described in paragraph .16.
- Criteria are developed by management for the preparation of the summary financial statements and are adequately disclosed in Note X. The auditor has determined that the criteria are acceptable in the circumstances.

Independent Auditor's Report on Summary Financial Statements

[*Appropriate addressee*]

Management derived the accompanying summary financial statements, which comprise the summary balance sheet as of December 31, 20X1, the summary income statement, summary statement of changes in stockholders' equity, and summary cash flow statement for the year then ended, and the related notes, from the audited financial statements of ABC Company as of and for the year ended December 31, 20X1. Management is responsible for the preparation of these summary financial statements on the basis described in Note X.

In our report dated February 15, 20X2, we expressed an adverse audit opinion on the financial statements of ABC Company as of and for the year ended December 31, 20X1. The basis for our adverse audit opinion was [*describe basis for adverse audit opinion*]. Our adverse audit opinion stated that [*describe adverse audit opinion*].

Because of the significance of the matter discussed above, it is inappropriate to express, and we do not express, an opinion on the summary financial statements of ABC Company as of and for the year ended December 31, 20X1.

[*Auditor's signature*]

[*Auditor's city and state*]

[*Date of the auditor's report*]

ILLUSTRATION 4. AN ADVERSE OPINION IS EXPRESSED ON THE SUMMARY FINANCIAL STATEMENTS BECAUSE THEY ARE NOT CONSISTENT, IN ALL MATERIAL RESPECTS, WITH THE AUDITED FINANCIAL STATEMENTS, IN ACCORDANCE WITH THE APPLIED CRITERIA

Circumstances include all of the following:

- An unmodified opinion is expressed on the audited financial statements.
- Established criteria for the preparation of summary financial statements exist.
- The auditor expresses an adverse opinion on the summary financial statements because they are not consistent, in all material respects, with the audited financial statements, in accordance with the applied criteria.

Independent Auditor's Report on Summary Financial Statements

[*Appropriate addressee*]

The accompanying summary financial statements, which comprise the summary balance sheet as of December 31, 20X1, the summary income statement, summary statement of changes in stockholders' equity, and summary cash flow statement for the year then ended, and the related notes, are derived from the audited financial statements of ABC Company as of and for the year ended December 31, 20X1. We expressed an unmodified audit opinion on those audited financial statements in our report dated February 15, 20X2.

The summary financial statements do not contain all the disclosures required by [*describe financial reporting framework applied in the preparation of the financial statements of ABC Company*]. Reading the summary financial statements, therefore, is not a substitute for reading the audited financial statements of ABC Company.

Management's Responsibility for the Summary Financial Statements

Management is responsible for the preparation of the summary financial statements on the basis described in Note X.

Auditor's Responsibility

Our responsibility is to express an opinion about whether the summary financial statements are consistent, in all material respects, with the audited financial statements based on our procedures, which were conducted in accordance with auditing standards generally accepted in the United States of America. The procedures consisted principally of comparing the summary financial statements with the related information in the audited financial statements from which the summary financial statements have been derived, and evaluating whether the summary financial statements are prepared in accordance with the basis described in Note X.

Basis for Adverse Opinion

[*Describe matter that caused the summary financial statements not to be consistent, in all material respects, with the audited financial statements, in accordance with the applied criteria.*]

Adverse Opinion

In our opinion, because of the significance of the matter discussed in the Basis for Adverse Opinion paragraph, the summary financial statements of ABC Company as of and for the year ended December 31, 20X1 referred to above are not consistent with the audited financial statements from which they have been derived, on the basis described in Note X.

[*Auditor's signature*]

[*Auditor's city and state*]

[*Date of the auditor's report*]

AU-C 905 Alert That Restricts the Use of the Auditor's Written Communication

AU-C ORIGINAL PRONOUNCEMENT

Source Statement on Auditing Standards (SAS) 125.

AU-C DEFINITION OF TERM

Source: AU-C 905

Specified parties. The intended users of the auditor's written communication.[1]

OBJECTIVES OF AU-C SECTION 905

AU-C Section 905.04 states that:

> *. . . the objective of the auditor is to restrict the use of the auditor's written communication by including an alert when the potential exists for the auditor's written communication to be misunderstood if taken out of the context in which the auditor's written communication is intended to be used.*

REQUIREMENTS

REPORTS REQUIRED TO BE RESTRICTED

AU-C 905 applies to auditor's reports and other written communications issued in connection with a GAAS engagement and requires an alert that restricts the use of the auditor's written communication, in a separate paragraph, when the subject matter of that communication is based on:

1. Measurement or disclosure criteria that are determined by the auditor to be suitable only for a limited number of users who can be presumed to have an adequate understanding of the criteria,
2. Measurement or disclosure criteria that are available only to the specified parties, or

---

[1] *In addition to auditor's reports, auditor's written communications may include letters or presentation materials (for example, letters communicating internal control related matters or presentations addressing communications with those charged with governance). (AU-C 905.A1)*

3. Matters identified by the auditor during the course of the audit engagement when the identification of such matters is not the primary objective of the audit engagement (commonly referred to as a by-product report).

(AU-C 905.06)

Required Restricted-Use Report Language

The auditor should add a separate paragraph at the end of the report that:

1. States that the report is intended solely for the information and use of the specified parties.
2. Identifies the specified parties.
3. States that the auditor's written communication is not intended to be, and should not be, used by nonspecified parties.

(The "AU-C 905 Illustrations" section at the end of the chapter contains an example of a restricted-use paragraph.)

The auditor should restrict by-product reports to those charged with governance, management, or others within the entity, regulatory agencies to whose jurisdiction the entity is subject, and parties to the contract or agreement. (AU-C 905.07)

Adding Other Specified Parties

After the engagement is completed or in the course of such an engagement, the client may ask the auditor to add other specified parties. An auditor should not agree to add other specified parties to a by-product report. (AU-C 905.08)

In addition, if the auditor adds other specified parties, he or she should obtain affirmative acknowledgment, ordinarily in writing, from the other parties about their understanding of the engagement, measurement or disclosure criteria, and the auditor's written communication. (AU-C 905.09)

If other parties are added after release of the auditor's written communication, the auditor may amend the auditor's written communication to add new parties. The auditor should also provide written acknowledgment to management of the addition and state that no subsequent or new procedures have been performed. (AU-C 905.10)

Limiting Report Distribution

The auditor should consider informing the entity that the auditor's written communication is not intended to be distributed to nonspecified parties. AU-C 905 makes clear that an auditor is not responsible for controlling, and cannot control, distribution of the auditor's written communication after its release. (AU-C 905.A7) The alert is designed to avoid misunderstandings related to the use of the written communication, particularly when taken out of the context in which it is intended to be used. An auditor may consider informing the entity or other specified parties that the written communication is not intended for distribution to parties other than those specified in the written communication.

Inclusion of a Separate Restricted-Use Communication and a Separate General-Use Communication in the Same Document

A separate restricted-use communication may be included in a document that contains a separate general-use communication. In such a case, the use of the general-use communication is not affected. (AU-C 905.A5)

COMBINED COMMUNICATION COVERING BOTH RESTRICTED-USE AND GENERAL-USE SUBJECT MATTER OR PRESENTATIONS

If the restricted-use and general-use communications are clearly differentiated within the combined communication, the alert that restricts the use may be limited to the communication in reports required to be restricted and the use of the general communication is not affected. (AU-C 905.A6) See Illustration 4 at the end of this chapter for an example.

AU-C 905 ILLUSTRATIONS

ILLUSTRATION 1. LIST OF SECTIONS RELATING TO THE RESTRICTED USE OF THE AUDITOR'S WRITTEN COMMUNICATION (SOURCE: AU-C 905 APPENDIX A)

Listed below are paragraphs in other sections that contain specific requirements to include an alert that restricts the use of the auditor's written communication or that otherwise address the inclusion of such alerts. The list is not a substitute for considering the requirements and related application and other explanatory material in the other sections.

- Paragraph .17 of Section 260, *The Auditor's Communication with Those Charged with Governance*
- Paragraphs .14d, .A32, and .A38–.A39 of Section 265, *Communicating Internal Control Related Matters Identified in an Audit*
- Paragraph .A16 of Section 725, *Supplementary Information in Relation to the Financial Statements as a Whole*
- Paragraphs .20, .A26–.A27, and .A33 of Section 800, *Special Considerations—Audits of Financial Statements Prepared in Accordance with Special Purpose Frameworks*
- Paragraphs .12–.13 and .A6–.A8 of Section 806, *Reporting on Compliance with Aspects of Contractual Agreements or Regulatory Requirements in Connection with Audited Financial Statements*
- Paragraphs .14f and .A6 of Section 915, *Reports on Application of Requirements of an Applicable Financial Reporting Framework*
- Paragraphs .33 and .A34 of Section 920, *Letters for Underwriters and Certain Other Requesting Parties*
- Paragraphs .30, .31i, and .A33 of Section 935, *Compliance Audits*

ILLUSTRATION 2. ILLUSTRATIVE AUDITOR'S WRITTEN COMMUNICATION

The following is an illustrative auditor's written communication encompassing the requirements in paragraph .14.

To Management and [*identify the body or individuals charged with governance, such as the entity's Board of Directors*] of ABC Company

In planning and performing our audit of the financial statements of ABC Company (the "Company") as of and for the year ended December 31, 20XX, in accordance with auditing standards generally accepted in the United States of America, we considered the Company's internal control over financial reporting (internal control) as a basis for designing audit procedures that are appropriate in the circumstances for the purpose of expressing our opinion on the financial statements, but not for the purpose of expressing an opinion on the effectiveness of the Company's internal control. Accordingly, we do not express an opinion on the effectiveness of the Company's internal control.

Our consideration of internal control was for the limited purpose described in the preceding paragraph and was not designed to identify all deficiencies in internal control that might be [*material weaknesses* or *material weaknesses or significant deficiencies*] and therefore [*material weaknesses* or *material weaknesses or significant deficiencies*] may exist that were not identified. However, as discussed below, we identified certain deficiencies in internal control that we consider to be [*material weaknesses* or *significant deficiencies* or *material weaknesses and significant deficiencies*].

A deficiency in internal control exists when the design or operation of a control does not allow management or employees, in the normal course of performing their assigned functions, to prevent, or detect and correct, misstatements on a timely basis. A material weakness is a deficiency, or a combination of deficiencies, in internal control, such that there is a reasonable possibility that a material misstatement of the entity's financial statements will not be prevented, or detected and corrected, on a timely basis. [*We consider the following deficiencies in the Company's internal control to be material weaknesses:*]

[*Describe the material weaknesses that were identified, and explain their potential effects.*]

[*A significant deficiency is a deficiency, or a combination of deficiencies, in internal control that is less severe than a material weakness, yet important enough to merit attention by those charged with governance. We consider the following deficiencies in the Company's internal control to be significant deficiencies:*]

[*Describe the significant deficiencies that were identified, and explain their potential effects.*]

[*If the auditor is communicating significant deficiencies and did not identify any material weaknesses, the auditor may state that none of the identified significant deficiencies are considered to be material weaknesses.*]

This communication is intended solely for the information and use of management, [*identify the body or individuals charged with governance*], others within the organization, and [*identify any governmental authorities to which the auditor is required to report*], and is not intended to be, and should not be, used by anyone other than these specified parties.

[*Auditor's signature*]

[*Auditor's city and state*]

[*Date of the auditor's report*]

Illustration 3. Illustrative No Material Weakness Communication

The following is an illustrative auditor's written communication indicating that no material weaknesses were identified during the audit of a not-for-profit organization.

To Management and [*identify the body or individuals charged with governance, such as the entity's Board of Directors*] of ABC Company [*NPO Organization*]

In planning and performing our audit of the financial statements of ABC Company (the "Company") [*NPO Organization (the Organization)*] as of and for the year ended December 31, 20XX, in accordance with auditing standards generally accepted in the United States of America, we considered the Company's [*Organization's*] internal control over financial reporting (internal control) as a basis for designing audit procedures that are appropriate in the circumstances for the purpose of expressing our opinion on the financial statements, but not for the purpose of expressing an opinion on the effectiveness of the Company's [*Organization's*] internal control. Accordingly, we do not express an opinion on the effectiveness of the Company's [*Organization's*] internal control.

A deficiency in internal control exists when the design or operation of a control does not allow management or employees, in the normal course of performing their assigned functions, to prevent, or detect and correct, misstatements on a timely basis. A material weakness is a deficiency, or a combination of deficiencies, in internal control, such that there is a reasonable possibility that a material misstatement of the entity's financial statements will not be prevented, or detected and corrected, on a timely basis.

Our consideration of internal control was for the limited purpose described in the first paragraph and was not designed to identify all deficiencies in internal control that might be material weaknesses. Given these limitations, during our audit we did not identify any deficiencies in internal control that we consider to be material weaknesses. However, material weaknesses may exist that have not been identified.

[*If one or more significant deficiencies have been identified, the auditor may add the following: Our audit was also not designed to identify deficiencies in internal control that might be significant deficiencies. A significant deficiency is a deficiency, or a combination of deficiencies, in internal control that is less severe than a material weakness, yet important enough to merit attention by those charged with governance. We communicated the significant deficiencies identified during our audit in a separate communication dated* [date]*.*]

This communication is intended solely for the information and use of management, [*identify the body or individuals charged with governance*], others within the organization, and [*identify any governmental authorities to which the auditor is required to report*], and is not intended to be, and should not be, used by anyone other than these specified parties.

[*Auditor's signature*]

[*Auditor's city and state*]

[*Date of the auditor's report*]

[*No amendments to paragraph .A40.*]

ILLUSTRATION 4. REPORT ON COMPLIANCE WITH ASPECTS OF CONTRACTUAL AGREEMENTS GIVEN IN A COMBINED REPORT, AND NO INSTANCES OF NONCOMPLIANCE WERE IDENTIFIED

Independent Auditor's Report

[*Appropriate addressee*]

Report on the Financial Statements

We have audited the accompanying financial statements of ABC Company, which comprise the balance sheet as of December 31, 20X1, and the related statements of income, changes in stockholders' equity, and cash flows for the year then ended, and the related notes to the financial statements.

Management's Responsibility for the Financial Statements

Management is responsible for the preparation and fair presentation of these financial statements in accordance with accounting principles generally accepted in the United States of America; this includes the design, implementation, and maintenance of internal control relevant to the preparation and fair presentation of financial statements that are free from material misstatement, whether due to fraud or to error.

Auditor's Responsibility

Our responsibility is to express an opinion on these financial statements based on our audit. We conducted our audit in accordance with auditing standards generally accepted in the United States of America. Those standards require that we plan and perform the audit to obtain reasonable assurance about whether the financial statements are free from material misstatement.

An audit involves performing procedures to obtain audit evidence about the amounts and disclosures in the financial statements. The procedures selected depend on the auditor's judgment, including the assessment of the risks of material misstatement of the financial statements, whether due to fraud or to error. In making those risk assessments, the auditor considers internal control relevant to the entity's preparation and fair presentation of the financial statements in order to design audit procedures that are appropriate in the circumstances, but not for the purpose of expressing an opinion on the effectiveness of the entity's internal control. Accordingly, we express no such opinion. An audit also includes evaluating the appropriateness of accounting policies used and the reasonableness of significant accounting estimates made by management, as well as evaluating the overall presentation of the financial statements.

We believe that the audit evidence we have obtained is sufficient and appropriate to provide a basis for our audit opinion.

Opinion

In our opinion, the financial statements referred to above present fairly, in all material respects, the financial position of ABC Company as of December 31, 20X1, and the results of its operations and its cash flows for the year then ended in accordance with accounting principles generally accepted in the United States of America.

Other Matter

In connection with our audit, nothing came to our attention that caused us to believe that ABC Company failed to comply with the terms, covenants, provisions, or conditions of sections XX to YY, inclusive, of the Indenture dated July 21, 20X0 with XYZ Bank, insofar as they relate to accounting matters. However, our audit was not directed primarily toward obtaining knowledge of such noncompliance. Accordingly, had we performed additional procedures, other matters may have come to our attention regarding the Company's noncompliance with the above-referenced terms, covenants, provisions, or conditions of the Indenture, insofar as they relate to accounting matters.

Restricted Use Relating to the Other Matter

The communication related to compliance with the aforementioned Indenture described in the Other Matter paragraph is intended solely for the information and use of the boards of directors and management of ABC Company and XYZ Bank and is not intended to be and should not be used by anyone other than these specified parties.

Report on Other Legal and Regulatory Requirements

[*Form and content of this section of the auditor's report will vary depending on the nature of the auditor's other reporting responsibilities.*]

[*Auditor's signature*]

[*Auditor's city and state*]

[*Date of the auditor's report*]

AU-C 910 Financial Statements Prepared in Accordance with a Financial Reporting Framework Generally Accepted in Another Country

AU-C ORIGINAL PRONOUNCEMENT

Source Statement on Auditing Standards (SAS) 124.

TECHNICAL ALERT

In October 2015, the Auditing Standards Board (ASB) issued SAS No. 130. SAS No. 130 contains amendments to this section. Any relevant changes are incorporated into the information that follows.

AU-C DEFINITIONS OF TERMS

AU-C 910 contains no definitions.

OBJECTIVES OF AU-C SECTION 910

AU-C Section 910.06 states that:

. . . the objective of the auditor, when engaged to report on financial statements prepared in accordance with a financial reporting framework generally accepted in another country, when such audited financial statements are intended for use outside the United States, is to address appropriately the special considerations that are relevant to

a. the acceptance of the engagement,
b. the planning and performance of the engagement, and
c. forming an opinion and reporting on the financial statements.

SCOPE

AU-C 910 applies to engagements for an auditor practicing in the United States to report on the financial statements that have been prepared in conformity with a financial reporting framework generally accepted in another country but not adopted by a body designated by the Council of the American Institute of Certified Public Accountants (AICPA). (AU-C 910.01)

REQUIREMENTS

TERMS OF ENGAGEMENT

Prior to accepting an engagement, the auditor must determine the acceptability of the financial reporting framework used and understand the purpose for which the financial statements are prepared and whether it is a fair presentation. The auditor must understand the individual users of the financial statements and management's steps to determine that the framework is acceptable. (AU-C 910.07)

The most difficult aspect of applying Section 910 in practice is the time and effort required to obtain an adequate understanding of the following:

1. Accounting principles generally accepted in the other country
2. Auditing standards of the other country
3. Audit reporting practices of the other country

In all these areas, AU-C 910 suggests that the auditor should consider consulting with persons with expertise in the area. (AU-C 910.A3) The need for consultation is a matter of professional judgment and depends, in part, on the formality and extensiveness of promulgated standards in the particular country.

In auditing financial statements prepared in conformity with accounting principles of another country, the auditor should:

1. Perform the procedures that are necessary to comply with the standards of US GAAS.
2. Modify such procedures as necessary for differences in financial statement assertions caused by the accounting principles of the other country.

NOTE: For example, procedures for testing deferred tax balances would not be needed if the other country's principles do not require or permit recognition of deferred taxes. (AU-C 910.A2)

(AU-C 910.09)

3. Obtain an understanding of the applied financial reporting framework by reading statutes or professional literature and, if necessary, by consulting with persons with appropriate expertise. (AU-C 910.10)

COMPLIANCE WITH FOREIGN AUDITING STANDARDS

If the auditor is asked to apply the auditing standards of another country in auditing financial statements prepared for use in the other country, the auditor should:

1. Obtain an understanding of the relevant statutes or professional literature that describes auditing standards generally accepted in that country.
2. Consider consulting persons having expertise in the auditing standards of the other country.
3. Comply with the standards of both the other country and US GAAS.

(AU-C 910.11)

Reporting

If financial statements are prepared for use only outside the United States or have only limited distribution within the United States, the auditor may report using either:

1. A US-style report modified to report on the financial reporting framework of another country, or
2. The report form of the other country.

(AU-C 910.12)

If the financial statements also are intended for use in the United States, the auditor should use the United States form of report that includes an emphasis-of-matter paragraph. The report should identify the financial reporting framework, refer to the note in the financial statements that describes the financial reporting framework, and indicate that the financial reporting framework differs from accounting principles readily accepted in the United States. (AU-C 910.13)

AU-C 910 ILLUSTRATIONS (SOURCE: AU-C 910.A11)

The following are illustrations of auditor's reports on financial statements prepared in accordance with a financial reporting framework generally accepted in another country.

1. US Form of Independent Auditor's Report to Report on Financial Statements Prepared in Accordance with a Financial Reporting Framework Generally Accepted in Another Country That Are Intended for Use Only Outside the United States
2. US Form of Independent Auditor's Report to Report on Financial Statements Prepared in Accordance with a Financial Reporting Framework Generally Accepted in Another Country That Also Are Intended for Use in the United States

Illustration 1. US Form of Independent Auditor's Report to Report on Financial Statements Prepared in Accordance with a Financial Reporting Framework Generally Accepted in Another Country That Are Intended for Use Only Outside the United States

Independent Auditor's Report

[*Appropriate addressee*]

We have audited the accompanying financial statements of ABC Company, which comprise the balance sheet as of December 31, 20X1, and the related statements of income, changes in stockholders' equity, and cash flows for the year then ended, and the related notes to the financial statements, which, as described in Note X to the financial statements, have been prepared on the basis of [*specify the financial reporting framework generally accepted*] in [*name of country*].

Management's Responsibility for the Financial Statements

Management is responsible for the preparation and fair presentation of these financial statements in accordance with [*specify the financial reporting framework generally accepted*] in [*name of country*]; this includes the design, implementation, and maintenance of internal control relevant to the preparation and fair presentation of financial statements that are free from material misstatement, whether due to fraud or to error.

Auditor's Responsibility

Our responsibility is to express an opinion on these financial statements based on our audit. We conducted our audit in accordance with auditing standards generally accepted in the United States of America (and in [*name of country*]). Those standards require that we plan and perform the audit to obtain reasonable assurance about whether the financial statements are free from material misstatement.

An audit involves performing procedures to obtain audit evidence about the amounts and disclosures in the financial statements. The procedures selected depend on the auditor's judgment, including the assessment of the risks of material misstatement of the financial statements, whether due to fraud or to error. In making those risk assessments, the auditor considers internal control relevant to the entity's preparation and fair presentation of the financial statements in order to design audit procedures that are appropriate in the circumstances, but not for the purpose of expressing an opinion on the effectiveness of the entity's internal control. Accordingly, we express no such opinion. An audit also includes evaluating the appropriateness of accounting policies used and the reasonableness of significant accounting estimates made by management, as well as evaluating the overall presentation of the financial statements.

We believe that the audit evidence we have obtained is sufficient and appropriate to provide a basis for our audit opinion.

Opinion

In our opinion, the financial statements referred to above present fairly, in all material respects, the financial position of ABC Company as of December 31, 20X1, and the results of its operations and its cash flows for the year then ended in accordance with [*specify the financial reporting framework generally accepted*] in [*name of country*].

[*Auditor's signature*]

[*Auditor's city and state*]

[*Date of the auditor's report*]

ILLUSTRATION 2. US FORM OF INDEPENDENT AUDITOR'S REPORT TO REPORT ON FINANCIAL STATEMENTS PREPARED IN ACCORDANCE WITH A FINANCIAL REPORTING FRAMEWORK GENERALLY ACCEPTED IN ANOTHER COUNTRY THAT ALSO ARE INTENDED FOR USE IN THE UNITED STATES

Independent Auditor's Report

[*Appropriate addressee*]

We have audited the accompanying financial statements of ABC Company, which comprise the balance sheet as of December 31, 20X1, and the related statements of income, changes in stockholders' equity, and cash flows for the year then ended, and the related notes to the financial statements, which, as described in Note X to the financial statements, have been prepared on the basis of [*specify the financial reporting framework generally accepted*] in [*name of country*].

Management's Responsibility for the Financial Statements

Management is responsible for the preparation and fair presentation of these financial statements in accordance with [*specify the financial reporting framework generally accepted*] in [*name of country*]; this includes the design, implementation, and maintenance of internal control relevant to the preparation and fair presentation of financial statements that are free from material misstatement, whether due to fraud or to error.

Auditor's Responsibility

Our responsibility is to express an opinion on these financial statements based on our audit. We conducted our audit in accordance with auditing standards generally accepted in the United States of America (and [*in name of country*]). Those standards require that we plan and perform the audit to obtain reasonable assurance about whether the financial statements are free from material misstatement.

An audit involves performing procedures to obtain audit evidence about the amounts and disclosures in the financial statements. The procedures selected depend on the auditor's judgment, including the assessment of the risks of material misstatement of the financial statements, whether due to fraud or to error. In making those risk assessments, the auditor considers internal control relevant to the entity's preparation and fair presentation of the financial statements in order to design audit procedures that are appropriate in the circumstances, but not for the purpose of expressing an opinion on the effectiveness of the entity's internal control. Accordingly, we express no such opinion. An audit also includes evaluating the appropriateness of accounting policies used and the reasonableness of significant accounting estimates made by management, as well as evaluating the overall presentation of the financial statements.

We believe that the audit evidence we have obtained is sufficient and appropriate to provide a basis for our audit opinion.

Opinion

In our opinion, the financial statements referred to above present fairly, in all material respects, the financial position of ABC Company as of December 31, 20X1, and the results of its operations and its cash flows for the year then ended in accordance with [*specify the financial reporting framework generally accepted*] in [*name of country*].

Emphasis of Matter

As discussed in Note X to the financial statements, the Company prepares its financial statements in accordance with [*specify the financial reporting framework generally accepted*] in [*name of country*], which differ(s) from accounting principles generally accepted in the United States of America. Our opinion is not modified with respect to this matter.

[*Auditor's signature*]

[*Auditor's city and state*]

[*Date of the auditor's report*]

AU-C 915 Reports on Application of Requirements of an Applicable Financial Reporting Framework

AU-C ORIGINAL PRONOUNCEMENTS

Sources Statements on Auditing Standards (SASs) 122, 123, and 125.

APPLICABILITY

Section 915 applies to providing *written* advice:

1. On the application of accounting principles to specified transactions (completed or proposed) involving facts and circumstances of a specific entity
2. On the type of report that may be rendered on a specific entity's financial statements

(AU-C 915.01)

The Section applies to these situations whether the advice is provided as part of a proposal to obtain a new client or as a separate engagement.

Section 915 applies to *oral* advice in the following circumstances:

1. The reporting accountant concludes the advice is intended to be used by a principal as an important factor in reaching a decision; and
2. The advice relates to the application of accounting principles to a specific transaction or the type of opinion that may be rendered on a specific entity's financial statements.

(AU-C 915.02)

Section 915 does not apply to:

1. A *continuing* accountant engaged to report on the financial statements of a specific entity
2. An engagement to assist in litigation involving accounting matters or provide expert testimony in litigation (i.e., litigation service engagements)
3. Advice provided to another accountant in public practice
4. Position papers on accounting principles or the type of opinion that may be rendered, including newsletters, articles, speeches, lectures, or other public presentations, and letters to standards-setting bodies

(AU-C 915.04-.05)

However, if position papers are intended to provide guidance on specific transactions or the type of opinion on a *specific* entity's financial statements, the Section applies.

When facing a hypothetical transaction, a reporting auditor cannot know whether a continuing accountant has reached a different conclusion on applying accounting principles to the same transaction or how the specific entity previously accounted for similar transactions. Therefore, written reports on hypothetical transactions are prohibited.

AU-C DEFINITIONS OF TERMS

Source: AU-C 915.08

For purposes of this Section, the terms have the meanings attributed as follows:

Continuing accountant. An accountant who has been engaged to report on the financial statements of a specific entity or entities of which the specific entity is a component.

Hypothetical transaction. A transaction or financial reporting issue that does not involve facts or circumstances of a specific entity.

Reporting accountant. An accountant, other than a continuing accountant, in the practice of public accounting, as described in ET Section 92, *Definitions*, who prepares a written report or provides oral advice on the application of the requirements of an applicable financial reporting framework to a specific transaction or on the type of report that may be issued on a specific entity's financial statements (a reporting accountant who is also engaged to provide accounting and reporting advice to a specific entity on a recurring basis is commonly referred to as an advisory accountant).

Specific transaction. A completed or proposed transaction or group of related transactions or a financial reporting issue involving facts and circumstances of a specific entity.

Written report. Any written communication that provides a conclusion on the appropriate application of the requirements of an applicable financial reporting framework to a specific transaction or on the type of report that may be issued on a specific entity's financial statements.

OBJECTIVE OF AU-C SECTION 915

AU-C Section 915.07 states that:

> *. . . the objective of the reporting accountant, when engaged to issue a written report or provide oral advice on the application of the requirements of an applicable financial reporting framework to a specific transaction or on the type of report that may be issued on a specific entity's financial statements, is to address appropriately*
>
> *a. the acceptance of the engagement.*
> *b. the planning and performance of the engagement.*
> *c. reporting on the specific transaction or type of report.*

In today's complex financial reporting environment, there is an increasing tendency for entities to consult with CPA firms other than their own auditors on accounting or financial reporting issues. This practice is sometimes called "opinion shopping"—a term that implies that the client will shop around until it finds an auditor who will agree with its position and then hire that auditor. A less pejorative term for the practice is obtaining a "second opinion." The implication of the term *second opinion* is that the motivation of the client arises from lack of clear-cut answers to accounting problems created by the fluid and constantly evolving environment of business today.

Section 915 addresses the concerns of financial statement users and regulators about opinion shopping. It would be inappropriate to prohibit second opinions because doing so would stifle the free exchange of ideas within the financial community and would restrict the ability of reporting entities and others to consider alternatives in determining appropriate financial reporting for new or emerging issues. Also, as a practical matter, the American Institute of Certified Public Accountants (AICPA) cannot afford to take action that might be viewed by the Federal Trade Commission as restricting competition.

Before providing advice to another CPA's client, a CPA should inform the entity of the need to consult with the other CPA and communicate with that CPA. The objective of this communication is primarily to determine whether the entity and its auditors have disagreed, and, if so, whether the disagreement is about facts or about how relevant accounting principles should be applied.

SAS 50 permitted reports on hypothetical transactions, which were reports on the application of accounting principles not involving facts and circumstances of a particular principal. The Securities and Exchange Commission (SEC) subsequently expressed concerns about the appropriate use of these reports and whether such reports were in the best interest of the public. In response to the SEC's concerns, the Auditing Standards Board issued SAS 97, *Amendment to Statement on Auditing Standards No. 50, Reports on the Application of Accounting Principles*, in June 2002. SAS 97 revised SAS 50 to prohibit written reports on hypothetical transactions.

REQUIREMENTS

ENGAGEMENT ACCEPTANCE

A CPA firm should adopt policies and procedures concerning the acceptance and approval of engagements to furnish a written report or oral advice on the application of accounting principles or the type of opinion to be rendered on financial statements.

It is important to understand the circumstances under which the written report or oral advice is requested and the intended use of the written report or oral advice. (AU-C 915.09) The reporting accountant should also understand the purpose of the request, the nature of the issue on which advice is requested, and whether there is a disagreement between the client and its continuing accountant. Before Section 915 was issued, many CPAs would not accept such an engagement if the client would not permit contact with the continuing accountant. However, some firms made a distinction between completed and proposed transactions and did not insist on contact before providing advice on proposed transactions. Section 915 now clearly requires contact with the other CPA in these circumstances because it applies to specific transactions, both completed and proposed.

APPLICABILITY TO PROPOSALS

For many practitioners, the most common situation in which Section 915 will apply is making a proposal for a new client. Not every proposal will be affected, but the requirements are applicable when a prospective client asks for the proposal to include the proposing firm's position on a specific accounting issue or the type of opinion that may be rendered on its financial statements in specific circumstances.

In all circumstances, before accepting an engagement, the successor auditor needs to communicate with the predecessor. However, when Section 915 applies, the communication should include more specific inquiries explicitly directed to disagreements about the subject on which a position is requested and should take place before the proposal is made rather than merely before acceptance of the audit engagement. In ordinary circumstances, communication does not take place until a predecessor has been terminated and does not take place during the proposal process. A request to include an opinion on accounting principles or type of audit opinion in a proposal changes the requirements.

Note that Section 915 focuses on accounting matters and the type of opinion that may be rendered. It does not broadly address auditing matters. This means that a proposal may discuss general matters of audit scope, such as overall approach, locations to be visited, and similar matters without creating a requirement to contact the continuing accountant before making the proposal.

Engagement, Acceptance, Planning, and Performance

1. The accountant should establish an understanding with the requesting party that management:
   a. Has responsibility for the accounting treatment.
   b. Acknowledges that the reporting accountant may need to consult with the continuing accountant and that management will authorize the continuing accountant to cooperate fully.
   c. Will notify those charged with governance and the continuing accountant about the nature of the engagement.

   (AU-C 915.11)
2. The reporting accountant should evaluate:
   a. The circumstances under which the written report or oral advice is requested.
   b. The request's purpose.
   c. The intended use of the written report or oral advice.

   (AU-C 915.09)
3. The reporting accountant should:
   a. Understand the form and substance of the transaction(s).
   b. Review applicable financial reporting framework.
   c. If appropriate, consult with other professionals or experts.
   d. If appropriate, perform research or other procedures to identify appropriate precedents or analogies.
   e. Request permission from the entity's management to consult with the continuing accountant and request the entity's management to authorize the continuing accountant to respond fully to the reporting accountant's request.
   f. Consult with the continuing accountant to determine the available facts needed for forming a conclusion.

   (AU-C 915.12)
4. When evaluating accounting principles for a specific transaction or determining the type of report that may be issued on a specific entity's financial statements, the reporting accountant should:
   a. Consult with the entity's continuing accountant to determine all the available facts relevant to forming a professional judgment.

b. Obtain available facts that the continuing accountant may be able to provide that include:

   1. The transaction's form and substance
   2. How management has applied accounting principles to similar transactions
   3. Whether management disputes the accounting method the continuing accountant recommends
   4. Whether the continuing accountant has arrived at a different conclusion than the reporting accountant

c. In communicating with the continuing accountant, follow the guidance on communications between predecessor and successor auditors.

(Section 315)

Reporting Standards

A written report should be addressed to the requesting party (for example, management or those charged with governance of the entity) and should ordinarily:

1. Briefly describe the engagement.
2. Identify the specific entity and describe the following:
   a. The transactions
   b. Relevant facts, circumstances, and assumptions
   c. Sources of information
3. Describe the appropriate accounting principles (including an identification of the country of origin) to be applied or type of opinion that may be rendered.
4. State that the responsibility for proper accounting treatment rests with preparers of financial statements who should consult their continuing accountants.
5. State that any differences in the facts, circumstances, or assumptions presented might change the report.
6. Include a separate paragraph at the end of the report that restricts the use of the report as required by AU-C 905 and that:
   a. States that the report is intended solely for the information and use of the specified parties.
   b. Identifies the parties.
   c. States that the report is not intended to be, and should not be, used by nonspecified parties.
7. If the reporting accountant is not independent of the entity, include a statement indicating the reporting accountant's lack of independence.

(AU-C 915.14)

Documentation

Section 915 does not impose any requirement to document the procedures used or information obtained to provide a basis for the professional judgment described in the report. However, the author recommends the following documentation:

1. A description of the problem, including all relevant facts and circumstances. (Preferably this should be prepared by the client.)
2. If applicable, a summary of the discussions with the continuing accountant.

3. A description of the procedures followed to determine the accounting practices that would be appropriate in the circumstances, including citations to relevant authoritative literature.

If the engagement is terminated before a report is issued, documentation of the engagement to that point is generally desirable but not essential.

AU-C 915 ILLUSTRATION (SOURCE: AU-C 915.A8)

Illustration 1. Illustrative Written Report to the Requesting Party

The following is an illustration of the reporting accountant's written report to the requesting party (for example, management or those charged with governance) on the application of the requirements of accounting principles generally accepted in the United States of America to a specific transaction.

Introduction

We have been engaged to report on the appropriate application of the requirements of accounting principles generally accepted in the United States of America to the specific transaction described below. This report is being issued to ABC Company for assistance in evaluating accounting policies for the described specific transaction. Our engagement has been conducted in accordance with Statement on Auditing Standards No. 122, Section 915, *Reports on Application of Requirements of an Applicable Financial Reporting Framework.*

Description of Transaction

The facts, circumstances, and assumptions relevant to the specific transaction as provided to us by the management of ABC Company are as follows:
[*Text discussing the facts, circumstances, and assumptions relevant to the specific transaction*]

Appropriate Accounting Principles

[*Text discussing accounting principles generally accepted in the United States of America and how they apply to the described transaction*]

Concluding Comments

The ultimate responsibility for the decision on the appropriate application of the requirements of accounting principles generally accepted in the United States of America for an actual transaction rests with the preparers of financial statements, who should consult with their continuing accountant. Our conclusion on the appropriate application of the requirements of accounting principles generally accepted in the United States of America for the described specific transaction is based solely on the facts provided to us as previously described; should these facts and circumstances differ, our conclusion may change.

Restricted Use

This report is intended solely for the information and use of those charged with governance and management of ABC Company and is not intended to be and should not be used by anyone other than these specified parties.

AU-C 920 Letters for Underwriters and Certain Other Requesting Parties

AU-C ORIGINAL PRONOUNCEMENTS

Sources Statements on Auditing Standards (SASs) 122, 125, and 129.

APPLICABILITY

Accountants, in comfort letters, describe procedures applied and findings obtained by applying those procedures. Negative assurances may be provided in certain circumstances. The procedures applied are described in the comfort letters. Examples of comfort letters are presented in the "AU-C 920 Illustrations" section of this chapter.

In addition to issuing a comfort letter to an underwriter, accountants may also issue a comfort letter to a broker-dealer or other financial intermediary acting as principal or agent in an offering or a placement of securities in connection with the following types of securities offerings:

1. Foreign offerings, including Regulation S, Eurodollar, and other offshore offerings
2. Transactions exempt from the registration requirements of Section 5 of the Securities Act of 1933 (the Act), including those pursuant to Regulation A, Regulation D, and Rule 144A
3. Securities offerings issued or backed by governmental, municipal, banking, tax-exempt, or other entities that are exempt from registration under the Act

In those offerings, the accountant may issue a comfort letter only if the party provides a representation letter that represents that the party's review process is substantially consistent with the review process under the 1933 Act.

An accountant is also permitted to issue a comfort letter in connection with acquisition transactions in which there is an exchange of stock and comfort letters that are requested by the buyer or seller, or both, as long as a representation letter is provided that represents that the party's review process is substantially consistent with the review process under the 1933 Act.

A comfort letter may also be addressed to parties with a statutory due diligence defense under Section 44.1 of the Act, other than a named underwriter, when a law firm or attorney for the requesting party issues a written opinion to the accountants that states that the party has a due diligence defense under Section 44.1 of the Act. If the requesting party cannot provide a law firm's or attorney's written opinion to the accountant, the requesting party should provide a representation letter.

When one of the parties identified in the preceding paragraphs (other than an underwriter or other party with due diligence responsibilities) requests a comfort letter but does not provide a representation letter, a special type of letter is permissible.

AU-C DEFINITIONS OF TERMS

Source: AU-C 920.07

For purposes of this section, the terms have the meanings attributed as follows:

Capsule financial information. Unaudited summarized interim financial information for periods subsequent to the periods covered by the audited financial statements or unaudited interim financial information included in the securities offering. Capsule financial information may be presented in narrative or tabular form and is often provided for the most recent interim period and for the corresponding period of the prior year.

Change period. The period ending on the cutoff date and ordinarily beginning, for balance sheet items, immediately after the date of the latest balance sheet in the securities offering and, for income statement items, immediately after the latest period for which such items are presented in the securities offering.

Closing date. The date on which the issuer of the securities or selling security holder delivers the securities to the underwriter in exchange for the proceeds of the offering.

Comfort letter. A letter issued by an auditor in accordance with this Section to requesting parties in connection with an entity's financial statements included in a securities offering.

Comparison date and comparison period. The date as of which, and period for which, data at the cutoff date and data for the change period are to be compared.

Cutoff date. The date through which certain procedures described in the comfort letter are to relate.

Effective date. The date on which the securities offering becomes effective.

Entity. The party whose financial statements are the subject of the engagement.

Negative assurance. A statement that, based on the procedures performed, nothing has come to the auditor's attention that has caused the auditor to believe that specified matters do not meet specified criteria (for example, that any material modifications should be made to the unaudited interim financial information for it to be in accordance with GAAP).

Requesting party. One of the following specified parties requesting a comfort letter, which has negotiated an agreement with the entity:

- An underwriter
- Other parties that are conducting a review process that is, or will be, substantially consistent with the due diligence process performed when the securities offering is, or if the securities offering was, being registered pursuant to the 1933 Act, as follows:

- A selling shareholder, sales agent, or other party with a statutory due diligence defense under Section 44.1 of the 1933 Act
- A broker-dealer or other financial intermediary acting as principal or agent in a securities offering in connection with the following types of securities offerings:
  - Foreign offerings, including Regulation S, Eurodollar, and other offshore offerings
  - Transactions that are exempt from the registration requirements of Section 5 of the 1933 Act, including those pursuant to Regulation A, Regulation D, and Rule 144A

- Offerings of securities issued or backed by governmental, municipal, banking, tax-exempt, or other entities that are exempt from registration under the 1933 Act
- The buyer or seller in connection with acquisition transactions in which there is an exchange of stock

Securities offerings. One of the following types of securities offerings:

- Registration of securities with the SEC under the 1933 Act
- Foreign offerings, including Regulation S, Eurodollar, and other offshore offerings
- Transactions that are exempt from the registration requirements of Section 5 of the 1933 Act, including those pursuant to Regulation A, Regulation D, and Rule 144A
- Offerings of securities issued or backed by governmental, municipal, banking, tax-exempt, or other entities that are exempt from registration under the 1933 Act
- Acquisition transactions in which there is an exchange of stock

Underwriter. As defined in the 1933 Act:

. . . any person who has purchased from an issuer with a view to, or offers or sells for an issuer in connection with, the distribution of any security, or participates or has a direct or indirect participation in any such undertaking, or participates or has a participation in the direct or indirect underwriting of any such undertaking; but such term shall not include a person whose interest is limited to a commission from an underwriter or dealer not in excess of the usual and customary distributors' or sellers' commission. As used in this paragraph, the term "issuer" shall include, in addition to an issuer, any person directly or indirectly controlling or controlled by the issuer, or any person under direct or indirect common control with the issuer.

Except when the context otherwise requires, the word *underwriter*, as used in this Section, refers to the managing, or lead, underwriter, who typically negotiates the underwriting agreement or purchase agreement (hereafter referred to as the *underwriting agreement*) for a group of underwriters whose exact composition is not determined until shortly before a securities offering becomes effective.

OBJECTIVES OF AU-C SECTION 920

AU-C Section 920.06 states that:

. . . the objectives of the auditor, when engaged to issue a letter to a requesting party in connection with an entity's financial statements included in a securities offering, are to

a. address appropriately the acceptance of the engagement and the scope of services; and
b. issue a letter with the appropriate form and content.

SCOPE

Engagements to issue comfort letters for underwriters and certain other requesting parties in connection with financial statements and financial statement schedules contained in registration statements filed with the Securities and Exchange Commission (SEC) under the Securities Act of 1933 (the Act) and certain other securities offerings. (See "Applicability" section for additional discussion.) (AU-C 920.01)

REQUIREMENTS: GENERAL

ENGAGEMENT ACCEPTANCE

The auditor is not required to accept an engagement to issue a comfort letter in connection with a financial statement included in a securities offering. A comfort letter should only be provided to underwriters and other parties meeting the definition of a requesting party (see "AU-C Definitions of Terms"). (AU-C 920.09)

REPRESENTATION LETTER

According to AU-C 920.11, if the party requesting the comfort letter is a party other than a named underwriter with a due diligence defense under Section 44.1 of the Act, but is one of the types of parties described in the "Applicability" section, the accountant should obtain either a written opinion from external legal counsel that the requesting party has a statutory due diligence defense under Section 44.1 of the 1933 Act or a representation letter that includes the following elements:

1. The letter should be addressed to the auditors.
2. The letter should contain the following:

   "This review process, applied to the information relating to the issuer is (will be) substantially consistent with the due diligence review process that we would perform if this placement of securities (or issuance of securities in an acquisition transaction) were being registered pursuant to the Securities Act of 1933 (the Act). We are knowledgeable with respect to that due diligence review process."

3. The letter should be signed by the requesting party.

When the accountants receive the representation letter, they should refer in the comfort letter to the requesting party's representations.

REPORTS TO OTHER PARTIES

When a party other than those described in the "Applicability" section requests a report, the accountant should not provide a comfort letter or the letter in Illustration 16 at the end of this chapter. Instead, the accountant should provide a report on agreed-upon procedures.

COMMUNICATIONS WITH UNDERWRITER

The accountant should suggest to the underwriter that they meet with the client to discuss the procedures to be followed related to the issuance of the comfort letter (procedures followed are described in the comfort letter). (AU-C 920.16) The underwriter should also provide the accountant with a draft of the underwriting agreement so that the accountant can indicate whether he or she will be able to furnish a letter in acceptable form.

DRAFT COMFORT LETTER

It is desirable for accountants to prepare a draft of the form of the comfort letter they expect to furnish as soon as they receive the draft of the underwriting agreement. The draft comfort letter should:

1. Deal, as completely as possible, with all matters to be covered in the final comfort letter.

2. Use exactly the same terms as those to be used in the final comfort letter, with the understanding that the comments in the final letter cannot be determined until the underlying procedures have been performed.
3. Be identified as a draft.
4. Not contain statements or implications that the accountant is carrying out such procedures as he or she considers necessary.

(AU-C 920.18-.19)

The following is a suggested form of the legend that may be placed on the draft comfort letter for identification and explanation of its purposes and limitations:

> This draft is furnished solely for the purpose of indicating the form of letter that we would expect to be able to furnish [*name of underwriter*] in response to their request, the matters to be covered in the letter, and the nature of the procedures that we would expect to carry out with respect to such matters. Based on our discussions with [*name of underwriter*], it is our understanding that the procedures outlined in this draft letter are those they wish us to follow. *Unless [*name of underwriter*] informs us otherwise, we shall assume that there are no additional procedures they wish us to follow. The text of the letter itself will depend, of course, on the results of the procedures, which we would not expect to complete until shortly before the letter is given and in no event before the cutoff date indicated therein.
>
> **If the accountant has not met with the underwriter, this sentence should be as follows*:
>
> In the absence of any discussions with [*name of underwriter*], we have set out in this draft letter those procedures referred to in the draft underwriting agreement (of which we have been furnished a copy) that we are willing to follow. (AU-C 920.20)

Auditor of the Group Financial Statements

If more than one auditor is involved in the audit of the financial statements and the reports of those accountants appear in the registration statement, the group auditor (the accountant reporting on the consolidated financial statements) should read the comfort letters of the component auditors who are reporting on components of the consolidated group. According to AU-C 920.21, the group auditor should state in his or her comfort letter that reading comfort letters of the component auditor was one of the procedures followed.

Shelf Registration

If the registrant has not chosen an underwriter by the effective date of a shelf registration statement, the accountant should not agree to furnish a comfort letter addressed to the client, legal counsel designated to represent the underwriting group, or a nonspecific addressee. The accountant may, however, agree to provide the client or legal counsel for the underwriting group with a draft comfort letter that describes the procedures performed by the accountant and the comments the accountant is willing to express based on those procedures. (AU-C 920.23) The following is a suggested form of the legend that should be placed on the draft comfort letter to describe the letter's purpose and limitations:

> This draft describes the procedures that we have performed and represents a letter we would be prepared to sign if the managing underwriter had been chosen and requested such a letter. The text of the final letter will depend, of course, on whether the managing underwriter who is selected requests that these and other procedures be performed to meet his or her needs and whether the managing underwriter requests that any of the procedures be updated to the date of issuance of the signed letter. (AU-C 920.A22)

Issuance of Letters or Reports under Other Standards

When issuing a comfort letter, the accountant may not issue any additional letters or reports under any other statements (SASs, Statements on Standards for Attestation Engagements [SSAEs], or Statements on Standards for Accounting and Review Services [SSARSs]) to the underwriter or other requesting parties in connection with the offering or placement of securities in which the accountant comments on items for which commenting is otherwise precluded by this Section.

REQUIREMENTS: FORMAT AND CONTENTS OF COMFORT LETTERS

Dating of Comfort Letter

The following apply to the date of the comfort letter:

1. Effective date. The letter normally is dated on or shortly before the effective date. (In rare instances, requests have been made to date letters on or shortly before the filing date.)
2. Cutoff date. The letter should state that the inquiries and other procedures described in the letter did not extend from the cutoff date (specified in the underwriting agreement) to the date of the letter. (AU-C 920.24)
3. Subsequent letters:
   a. A subsequent letter may be dated on or before the closing date.
   b. The specified procedures and inquiries noted in the comfort letter should be completed as of the cutoff date for each letter.
   c. Comments contained in an earlier letter may be incorporated by reference in a subsequent letter; but a subsequent letter should address only information in the most recently amended registration statement.

   (AU-C 920.A25-.A26)

Addressee

The following apply to determining the addressee of the comfort letter:

1. The letter should be addressed only to the requesting parties or both the requesting party and the entity. (An example of an appropriate form of address is "X Corporation and John Doe and Company, as Representative of Several Underwriters.") (AU-C 925.26)
2. The letter should not be addressed to or given to any parties other than the requesting party or both the requesting party and the entity.
3. A comfort letter for other accountants should be addressed in accordance with item 1 above, and copies should be given to the group auditor and his or her client.

Introductory Paragraph

The following apply to the introductory paragraph of the comfort letter:

1. It is good practice to refer to, but not repeat, the report on the financial statements, and to include an introductory paragraph that identifies the financial statements and the securities offering (AU-C 920.27-.28) similar to the following:

We have audited the [*identify the financial statements and financial statement schedules*] included (incorporated by reference) in the registration statement (No. 33-00000) on Form ___ filed by the company under the Securities Act of 1933 (the Act); our reports with respect thereto are also included (incorporated by reference) in that registration statement. The registration statement, as amended as of ____, is herein referred to as the registration statement.

2. If the audit report on the financial statements included in the registration statement is not the standard report—for instance, if an emphasis-of-matter paragraph has been added:
   a. Accountants should refer to that fact and discuss the content of the paragraph in the comfort letter.
   b. The accountants need not refer to or discuss explanatory paragraphs addressing the consistent application of accounting principles.
   c. If the SEC accepts a modified opinion on historical financial statements, the accountants should refer to the modification and discuss the subject matter in the comfort letter's opening paragraph.

   (AU-C 925.29)
3. The accountant should not repeat his or her opinion on the audited financial statements. (AU-C 920.30)
4. Negative assurance. The accountants should not give negative assurance concerning their audit report on the financial statements, nor should they give negative assurance concerning financial statements and financial statement schedules audited and reported on in the registration statement by other accountants.
5. Other reports issued by the accountants. The accountants may refer to their reports on:
   a. Condensed financial statements that are derived from audited financial statements
   b. Selected financial data
   c. Interim financial information
   d. Pro forma financial information
   e. A financial forecast
   f. Management's discussion and analysis (MD&A)
   g. If the above reports are not included (incorporated by reference) in the registration statement, they may be attached to the comfort letter. The accountant should not repeat the report in the comfort letter or otherwise imply that he or she is reporting as of the comfort letter date or that he or she is responsible for the sufficiency of the procedures for the underwriter's purposes. (AU-C 920.31)
6. The accountant should not mention, refer to, or attach to the comfort letter any restricted-use report in accordance with Section 905. (AU-C 920.33)

INDEPENDENCE

The following apply to statements on independence:

1. If, as is customary, the underwriting agreement in connection with an SEC filing requires a statement from the accountant concerning independence (AU 920.35), the following wording is appropriate:

   We are independent certified public accountants with respect to the XYZ Company, within the meaning of the Act and the applicable rules and regulations thereunder adopted by the SEC.

2. For a non-SEC filing, the following wording is appropriate:

   We are independent certified public accountants with respect to XYZ Company, under Rule 101 of the American Institute of Certified Public Accountants' (AICPA's) Code of Professional Conduct and its interpretations and rulings.

3. Accountants for previously nonaffiliated companies recently acquired by the registrant would make a statement similar to the following:

   As of [*date of the accountant's most recent report on the financial statements of his or her client*] and during the period covered by the financial statements on which we reported, we were independent certified public accountants with respect to [*name of client*] within the meaning of the Act and the applicable rules and regulations thereunder adopted by the SEC.

Compliance as to Form with SEC Requirements

The following apply to compliance with SEC requirements:

1. If the accountant is asked to express an opinion on whether the financial statements covered by his or her report comply as to form with pertinent accounting requirements adopted by the SEC, the following wording is appropriate:

   In our opinion [*include the phrase "except as disclosed in the registration statement," if applicable*], the [*identify the financial statements and financial statement schedules*] audited by us and included (incorporated by reference) in the registration statement comply as to form in all material respects with the applicable accounting requirements of the Act and the related rules and regulations adopted by the SEC. (AU-C 920.A41)

2. Material departures from pertinent rules and regulations adopted by the SEC should be disclosed in the comfort letter. (AU-C 920.38)
3. The accountant may provide positive assurance on compliance as to form with requirements under SEC rules and regulations only regarding those rules and regulations applicable to the form and content of financial statements and financial statement schedules that the accountant has audited. When the financial statements or financial statement schedules have not been audited, the accountant may only provide negative assurance on compliance as to form. (AU-C 920.39)
4. The auditor should not comment on compliance with the form of MD&A. (AU-C 920.40)

REQUIREMENTS: COMMENTING IN A COMFORT LETTER ON INFORMATION OTHER THAN AUDITED FINANCIAL STATEMENTS

General

The following apply to (1) unaudited interim financial information, (2) capsule financial information, (3) pro forma financial information, (4) financial forecasts, and (5) changes in capital stock, increases in long-term debt, and changes in other specified financial statement items.

1. Procedures performed by the accountant and criteria specified should be stated in the comfort letter. The auditor should also state that the interim period procedures may not disclose significant matters. (AU-C 920.41)
2. If, however, the accountants have been requested to provide negative assurance on interim financial information or capsule financial information, the procedures involved in a review need not be specified. (AU-C 920.A44)

3. If the underwriter requests that the accountant apply procedures in addition to those applicable to reviews of interim financial information, the accountant may perform those procedures and should describe them in the comfort letter. (AU-C 920.A46) The criteria specified by the underwriter should be included in the descriptions of procedures in the comfort letter.
4. The accountant should not make any statement indicating that he or she has applied any procedures deemed necessary for the requesting party's purpose. (AU-C 920.42a)
5. The accountant should not use terms such as *general review*, *limited review*, *reconcile*, *check*, or *test* to describe the work done unless the procedures required by those terms are described in the comfort letter. (AU-C 920.42b)
6. The accountant should not make a general statement that, as a result of carrying out procedures specified in the underwriting agreement and draft comfort letter, nothing else came to his or her attention that would be of interest to the underwriter. (AU-C 920.42c)

Knowledge of Internal Control

The accountant should obtain knowledge of a client's internal control over financial reporting as it relates to the preparation of both annual and interim financial information when commenting in the comfort letter on (1) unaudited interim financial information, including condensed information; (2) capsule financial information; (3) a financial forecast when historical financial statements provide a basis for one or more significant assumptions for the forecast; or (4) subsequent changes in capital stock, in long-term debt, and in other selected financial statement items. (AU-C 920.44)

Unaudited Interim Financial Information

The following apply to unaudited condensed interim financial information:

1. Accountants may comment in the form of negative assurance on this type of financial information only when they have conducted a review of the interim financial information. (AU-C 920.45) The negative assurance should be about whether any material modification should be made and whether the unaudited financial information "complies as to form in all material respects with the applicable accounting requirements of the 1933 Act and the related rules and regulations adopted by the SEC, if applicable." (AU-C 920.46b)
2. If the accountants have not conducted a review, they may not comment in the form of negative assurance. In those circumstances, the accountants are limited to reporting procedures performed and findings obtained. (AU-C 920.45)
3. The comfort letter should identify any unaudited interim financial information and should state that the information has not been audited in accordance with GAAS and no opinion is expressed concerning that information. (AU-C 920.48)
4. The comfort letter may state that the accountants have conducted review procedures. (AU-C 920.A53) If the letter states that the accountants issued a review report, the report should be attached unless the review report is included in the securities offering. (AU-C 920.47)

Capsule Financial Information

The following apply to capsule financial information:

1. Accountants may give negative assurance as to conformity with GAAP and may refer to whether the dollar amounts were determined on a basis substantially consistent with that of the corresponding amounts in the audited financial statements if (1) the capsule financial

information meets the minimum disclosure requirements of ASC 270, and (2) the accountants have reviewed the interim financial statements underlying the capsule financial information. (AU-C 920.49)

2. If a review was performed, the accountants may give negative assurance as to whether the dollar amounts were determined on a basis substantially consistent with that of the corresponding amounts in the audited financial statements. (AU-C 920.50)
3. If a review has not been performed, the accountants are limited to reporting procedures performed and findings obtained. (AU-C 920.50)

Pro Forma Financial Information

The following apply to pro forma financial information:

1. Accountants should not comment on this type of information unless they have appropriate knowledge of the accounting and reporting practices of the entity. (AU-C 920.52)
2. Accountants should not give negative assurance on the application of pro forma adjustments to historical amounts, the compilation of pro forma financial information, or whether the pro forma financial information complies as to form in all material respects with the applicable requirements of Rule 11-02 of Regulation S-X unless they have obtained the required knowledge described in item 1 above and have performed an audit of the annual financial statements or a review of interim financial statements of the entity to which the adjustments were applied. (AU-C 920.53)
3. For a business combination, the historical financial statements of each part of the combined entity on which the pro forma financial information is based should be audited or reviewed. (AU-C 920.53)
4. If the above requirements for giving negative assurance have not been met, the accountants are limited to reporting procedures performed and findings obtained. (AU-C 920.53)

Financial Forecasts

The following apply to financial forecasts:

1. To perform agreed-upon procedures on a financial forecast and comment on it, accountants should obtain the knowledge described in "Knowledge of Internal Control" earlier in this chapter and then perform the procedures prescribed in Section AT 301 for reporting on the compilation of a forecast. (AU-C 920.54)
2. The accountant's report on the forecast should be attached to the comfort letter. (AU-C 920.54)
3. Accountants may perform additional procedures on the forecast and report their findings in the comfort letter. (AU-C 920.54)
4. Accountants are not permitted to provide negative assurance on the results of procedures performed. They may also not provide negative assurance with respect to compliance of the forecast with Rule 11-03 of Regulation S-X unless they have performed an examination of the forecast in accordance with Section AT 301. (AU-C 920.56)
5. If the forecast is included in the registration statement, the forecast should be accompanied by an indication that the accountants have not examined the forecast and therefore do not express an opinion on it. If that statement is not included, the accountant should not issue a comfort letter. (AU-C 920.57)

SUBSEQUENT CHANGES

Comments on subsequent changes usually address:

1. Whether there have been any changes in capital stock, increases in long-term debt, or decreases in other specified financial statement items during the change period (see "AU-C Definitions of Terms").
2. Issues such as subsequent changes in the amounts of net current assets or stockholders' equity, net sales, total and per share amounts of income before extraordinary items, and net income.

Accountants generally will be asked to read minutes and make inquiries of company officials concerning the change period. The accountants should, therefore, base their comments solely on those limited procedures (AU-C 920.58), and clearly state this in the comfort letter.

The following apply to other aspects of subsequent changes:

1. Accountants may provide negative assurance on subsequent changes in specific financial statement items up to 135 days from the end of the most recent audit or review period. (AU-C 920.59)
2. For periods of 135 days or more, accountants may not provide negative assurance but may only report procedures performed and findings obtained. (AU-C 920.60)
3. Changes in an accounting principle during the change period should be stated in the comfort letter. (AU-C 920.A93-3)
4. Comments on subsequent changes are limited to those increases or decreases not disclosed in the registration statement. (AU-C 920.62)
5. The date and the period used to determine if subsequent changes occurred should be specified in both the draft and the final comfort letter. (AU-C 920.63)

TABLES, STATISTICS, AND OTHER FINANCIAL INFORMATION

The following apply to tables, statistics, and other financial information:

1. Accountants may comment only on the following:

   a. Information expressed in dollars, or percentages derived from those dollars, obtained from accounting records that are subject to the entity's internal control
   b. Information derived directly from the accounting records by analysis or computation (AU-C 920.65)
   c. Quantitative information obtained from an accounting record if the information is subject to the same controls as the dollar amounts (AU-C 920.66)

2. Accountants should not comment on matters such as the following:

   a. Any matter or information subject to legal interpretation
   b. Segment information or the appropriateness of allocations made to derive segment information included in financial statements
   c. Tables, statistics, and other financial information relating to an unaudited period, unless they have:

      1. Audited the client's financial statements for a period including or immediately prior to the unaudited period or have completed an audit for a later period.

2. Otherwise obtained knowledge of the client's internal control over financial reporting. (AU-C 920.67-68a)

3. Procedures followed by the accountants with respect to this information should be described in both the draft and the final comfort letter. The letter should also contain a statement that the accountants are not furnishing any assurances with respect to the sufficiency of the procedures for the underwriter's intended purpose. (AU-C 920.71c)
4. Regulation S-K requires the inclusion of certain financial information in registration statements. Accountants may comment and provide negative assurance about whether this information is in conformity with the disclosure requirements of Regulation S-K if the following conditions are met:

   a. The information has been derived from the accounting records subject to the entity's internal control over financial reporting or has been derived directly from the accounting records by analysis or computation.
   b. The information is capable of evaluation against reasonable criteria established by the SEC.

   (AU-C 920.72)

   Regulation S-K disclosure requirements that meet those conditions are:

   a. Item 301, *Selected Financial Data*
   b. Item 302, *Supplementary Financial Information*
   c. Item 402, *Executive Compensation*
   d. Item 503(d), *Ratio of Earnings to Fixed Charges*

   (AU-C 920.A81)

   Accountants should not comment in a comfort letter on compliance as to form of nonfinancial data presented in MD&A with SEC rules and regulations unless the accountant has examined or reviewed that data in accordance with AT 701. (AU-C 920.68b)
5. Specific information commented on should be identified by referring to specific captions, tables, page numbers, paragraphs, or sentences. Descriptions of the procedures followed and the findings obtained may be stated individually for each item of specific information commented on. (AU-C 920.69a)
6. Comments concerning tables, statistics, and other financial information included in the registration statement should include:

   a. A description of the procedures followed (AU-C 920.69b)
   b. The findings, ordinarily expressed in terms of agreement between items compared (AU-C 920.69c)
   c. Statements with respect to the acceptability of methods of allocation used in deriving the figures commented on:

      1. Whether comments on allocation may be made depends on the extent to which they are made in, or can be derived directly by analysis or computation from, the client's accounting records.
      2. Comments, if made, should make clear that the allocations are to a substantial extent arbitrary, that the allocation method used is not the only acceptable one, and that other acceptable methods of allocation might produce significantly different results.

   (AU-C 920.70)

REQUIREMENTS: OTHER MATTERS

Concluding Paragraph

It is desirable that the comfort letter conclude with a paragraph such as the following wording: (AU-C 920.74)

> This letter is solely for the information of the addressees and to assist the underwriters in conducting and documenting their investigation of the affairs of the company in connection with the offering of the securities covered by the offering memorandum, and it is not to be used, circulated, quoted, or otherwise referred to within or without the underwriting group for any other purpose, including, but not limited to, the registration, purchase, or sale of securities, nor is it to be filed with or referred to in whole or in part in the offering memorandum or any other document, except that reference may be made to it in the underwriting agreement or in any list of closing documents pertaining to the offering of the securities covered by the offering memorandum. (AU-C 920.A93-.A94)

Disclosure of Subsequently Discovered Matters

Accountants may discover matters that should be included in the final comfort letter but that were not mentioned in the draft comfort letter. If these matters are not to be disclosed in the registration statement, the accountant should let the client know that they will be mentioned in the final comfort letter. Also, the accountant should suggest that the underwriter be informed immediately. It is advisable for the accountant to be present when these matters are discussed between the client and the underwriter. (AU-C 920.75)

AU-C 920 ILLUSTRATIONS

The following illustrations of comfort letters are reprinted from AU-C 920.

1-A. Typical Comfort Letter for a 1933 Act Offering
1-B. Typical Comfort Letter for a Non-1933 Act Offering When the Required Representation Letter Has Been Obtained
2. Letter When a Short-Form Registration Statement Is Filed Incorporating Previously Filed Form 8-K by Reference
3. Letter Reaffirming Comments in Illustration 1-A as of a Later Date
4-A. Negative Assurance on Pro Forma Financial Information as to Compliance With the Applicable Accounting Requirements of Rule 11-02 of Regulation S-X
4-B. Negative Assurance on Pro Forma Financial Information as to Compliance With Pro Forma Bases as Described in the Pro Forma Financial Information
5. Comments on a Financial Forecast
6. Comments on Tables, Statistics, and Other Financial Information: Complete Description of Procedures and Findings
7. Comments on Tables, Statistics, and Other Financial Information: Summarized Description of Procedures and Findings Regarding Tables, Statistics, and Other Financial Information
8. Comments on Tables, Statistics, and Other Financial Information: Descriptions of Procedures and Findings Regarding Tables, Statistics, and Other Financial Information—Attached Securities Offering (or Selected Pages) Identifies Items to Which Procedures Were Applied through the Use of Designated Symbols

9. Alternate Wording When Auditor's Report on Audited Financial Statements Contains an Emphasis-of-Matter Paragraph
10. Alternate Wording When More Than One Auditor Is Involved
11. Alternate Wording When the SEC Has Agreed to a Departure from Its Accounting Requirements
12. Alternate Wording When Recent Earnings Data Are Presented in Capsule Form
13. Alternate Wording When Auditors Are Aware of a Decrease in a Specified Financial Statement Item
14. Alternate Wording of the Letter for Companies That Are Permitted to Present Interim Earnings Data for a 12-Month Period
15. Alternate Wording When the Procedures That the Requesting Party Has Requested the Auditor to Perform on Interim Financial Information Are Less Than a Review in Accordance with GAAS Applicable to Reviews of Interim Financial Information
16. Letter to a Requesting Party That Has Not Provided the Legal Opinion or the Representation Letter Required by Paragraph .11
17. Intentionally Omitted (see Illustration 1-B).
18. Alternate Wording When Reference to Examination of Annual Management's Discussion and Analysis and Review of Interim Management's Discussion and Analysis Is Made

Illustration 1-A. Typical Comfort Letter for a 1933 Act Offering

June 28, 20X6

[Addressee]

Dear Ladies and Gentlemen:

We have audited the consolidated financial statements of The Nonissuer Company, Inc. (the company) and subsidiaries, which comprise the consolidated balance sheets as of December 31, 20X5 and 20X4, and the related consolidated statements of income, changes in stockholders' equity, and cash flows for each of the years in the three-year period ended December 31, 20X5, and the related notes to the consolidated financial statements, all included in The Issuer Company's (the registrant) registration statement (no. 33-00000) on Form S-1 filed by the registrant under the Securities Act of 1933 (the Act); our report with respect thereto is also included in that registration statement. The registration statement, as amended on June 28, 20X6, is herein referred to as the registration statement.

In connection with the registration statement:

1. We are independent certified public accountants with respect to the company within the meaning of the 1933 Act and the applicable rules and regulations thereunder adopted by the SEC.
2. In our opinion [*include the phrase* "except as disclosed in the registration statement" *if applicable*], the consolidated financial statements audited by us and included in the registration statement comply as to form in all material respects with the applicable accounting requirements of the Act and the related rules and regulations adopted by the SEC.
3. We have not audited any financial statements of the company as of any date or for any period subsequent to December 31, 20X5; although we have conducted an audit for the year ended December 31, 20X5, the purpose (and, therefore, the scope) of the audit was to enable us to express our opinion on the consolidated financial statements as of December 31, 20X5, and for the year then ended, but not on the financial statements for any interim period within that year. Therefore, we are unable to and do not express any opinion on the unaudited condensed consolidated balance sheet as of March 31, 20X6, and the unaudited condensed consolidated statements of income, stockholders' equity, and cash flows for the three-month periods ended March 31, 20X6 and 20X5, included in the

registration statement, or on the financial position, results of operations, or cash flows as of any date or for any period subsequent to December 31, 20X5.

4. For purposes of this letter we have read the 20X6 minutes of meetings of the stockholders, the board of directors, and [*include other appropriate committees, if any*] of the company and its subsidiaries as set forth in the minute books at June 23, 20X6, officials of the company having advised us that the minutes of all such meetings through that date were set forth therein and having discussed with us the unapproved minutes of meetings held on [*dates*]; we have carried out other procedures to June 23, 20X6, as follows (our work did not extend to the period from June 24, 20X6 to June 28, 20X6, inclusive):

   a. With respect to the three-month periods ended March 31, 20X6 and 20X5, we have:

      1. Performed the procedures specified for a review in accordance with auditing standards generally accepted in the United States of America applicable to reviews of interim financial information on the unaudited condensed consolidated balance sheet as of March 31, 20X6, and the unaudited condensed consolidated statements of income, stockholders' equity, and cash flows for the three-month periods ended March 31, 20X6 and 20X5, included in the registration statement.
      2. Inquired of certain officials of the company who have responsibility for financial and accounting matters whether the unaudited condensed consolidated financial statements referred to in 4a(1) comply as to form in all material respects with the applicable accounting requirements of the Act and the related rules and regulations adopted by the SEC.

   b. With respect to the period from April 1, 20X6 to May 31, 20X6, we have:

      1. Read the unaudited consolidated financial statements of the company and subsidiaries for April and May of both 20X5 and 20X6 furnished us by the company, officials of the company having advised us that no such financial statements as of any date or for any period subsequent to May 31, 20X6, were available. [*If applicable:* The financial information for April and May of both 20X5 and 20X6 is incomplete in that it omits the statements of cash flows and other disclosures.]
      2. Inquired of certain officials of the company who have responsibility for financial and accounting matters whether the unaudited consolidated financial statements referred to in 4b(1) are stated on a basis substantially consistent with that of the audited consolidated financial statements included in the registration statement.

   The foregoing procedures do not constitute an audit conducted in accordance with generally accepted auditing standards. Also, they would not necessarily reveal matters of significance with respect to the comments in the following paragraph. Accordingly, we make no representations regarding the sufficiency of the foregoing procedures for your purposes.

5. Nothing came to our attention as a result of the foregoing procedures, however, that caused us to believe that:

   a. 1. Any material modifications should be made to the unaudited condensed consolidated financial statements described in 4a(1), included in the registration statement, for them to be in conformity with generally accepted accounting principles.
      2. The unaudited condensed consolidated financial statements described in 4a(1) do not comply as to form in all material respects with the applicable accounting requirements of the Act and the related rules and regulations adopted by the SEC.

   b. 1. At May 31, 20X6, there was any change in the capital stock, increase in long-term debt, or decrease in consolidated net current assets or stockholders' equity of the consolidated companies as compared with amounts shown in the March 31, 20X6 unaudited condensed consolidated balance sheet included in the registration statement, or

2. For the period from April 1, 20X6 to May 31, 20X6, there were any decreases, as compared to the corresponding period in the preceding year, in consolidated net sales or in income before extraordinary items or of net income, except in all instances for changes, increases, or decreases that the registration statement discloses have occurred or may occur.

6. As mentioned in 4b, company officials have advised us that no consolidated financial statements as of any date or for any period subsequent to May 31, 20X6 are available; accordingly, the procedures carried out by us with respect to changes in financial statement items after May 31, 20X6 have, of necessity, been even more limited than those with respect to the periods referred to in item 4. We have inquired of certain officials of the company who have responsibility for financial and accounting matters whether (a) at June 23, 20X6, there was any change in the capital stock, increase in long-term debt, or any decreases in consolidated net current assets or stockholders' equity of the consolidated companies as compared with amounts shown on the March 31, 20X6, unaudited condensed consolidated balance sheet included in the registration statement, or (b) for the period from April 1, 20X6 to June 23, 20X6, there were any decreases, as compared with the corresponding period in the preceding year, in consolidated net sales, or in income before extraordinary items or of net income. On the basis of these inquiries and our reading of the minutes as described in item 4, nothing came to our attention that caused us to believe that there was any such change, increase, or decrease, except in all instances for changes, increases, or decreases that the registration statement discloses have occurred or may occur.
7. This letter is solely for the information of the addressees and to assist the underwriters in conducting and documenting their investigation of the affairs of the company in connection with the offering of the securities covered by the registration statement, and it is not to be used, circulated, quoted, or otherwise referred to within or without the underwriting group for any other purpose, including but not limited to the registration, purchase, or sale of securities, nor is it to be filed with or referred to in whole or in part in the registration statement or any other document, except that reference may be made to it in the underwriting agreement or in any list of closing documents pertaining to the offering of the securities covered by the registration statement.

Illustration 1-B. Typical Comfort Letter for a Non-1933 Act Offering When the Required Representation Letter Has Been Obtained

This illustration is applicable when a comfort letter is issued in a non-1933 Act offering. It assumes the following:

- The offerer is not an SEC registrant.
- The requesting party has given the auditor a representation letter as required by paragraph .10 and described in paragraph .11.
- Interim financial information is included in the offering document, and the auditor has performed review procedures in accordance with GAAS applicable to reviews of interim financial information.
- The auditor did not perform an audit of the effectiveness of internal control over financial reporting in any period.
- There has not been a change in the application of a requirement of GAAP during the interim period. If there has been such a change, a reference to that change would be included in paragraph 4.

The cutoff date is June 23, 20X6, and the letter is dated June 28, 20X6. Each of the comments in the letter is in response to a request from the requesting party. For purposes of this illustration, the income statement items of the current interim period are to be compared with those of the corresponding period of the preceding year.

June 28, 20X6

[*Addressee*]

Dear Ladies and Gentlemen:

We have audited the consolidated financial statements of The Nonissuer Company, Inc. (the company) and subsidiaries, which comprise the consolidated balance sheets as of December 31, 20X5 and 20X4, and the related consolidated statements of income, changes in stockholders' equity, and cash flows for each of the years in the three-year period ended December 31, 20X5, and the related notes to the consolidated financial statements, all included [*or incorporated by reference*] in the offering memorandum for $30,000,000 of Senior Debt due May 30, 20X6. Our report with respect thereto is included in the offering memorandum. This offering memorandum, dated June 28, 20X6, is herein referred to as the Offering Memorandum.

This letter is being furnished in reliance upon your representation to us that:

a. You are knowledgeable with respect to the due diligence review process that would be performed if this placement of securities were being registered pursuant to the Securities Act of 1933 (the Act).
b. In connection with the offering of Senior Debt, the review process you have performed is substantially consistent with the due diligence review process that you would have performed if this placement of securities were being registered pursuant to the Act.

In connection with the Offering Memorandum:

1. We are independent certified public accountants with respect to the company under Rule 101 of the AICPA's Code of Professional Conduct and its interpretations and rulings.
2. We have not audited any financial statements of the company as of any date or for any period subsequent to December 31, 20X5; although we have conducted an audit for the year ended December 31, 20X5, the purpose (and, therefore, the scope) of the audit was to enable us to express our opinion on the consolidated financial statements as of December 31, 20X5, and for the year then ended, but not on the financial statements for any interim period within that year. Therefore, we are unable to and do not express any opinion on the unaudited condensed consolidated balance sheet as of March 31, 20X6, and the unaudited condensed consolidated statements of income, of cash flows, and of changes in stockholders' equity for the three-month periods ended March 31, 20X5 and 20X6, included in the Offering Memorandum, or on the financial position, results of operations, or cash flows as of any date or for any period subsequent to December 31, 20X5.
3. For purposes of this letter, we have read the 20X6 minutes of meetings of the stockholders, the board of directors, and [*include other appropriate committees, if any*] of the company and its subsidiaries as set forth in the minute books at June 23, 20X6, officials of the company having advised us that the minutes of all such meetings through that date were set forth therein and having discussed with us the unapproved minutes of meetings held on [*dates*]; we have carried out other procedures to June 23, 20X6, as follows (our work did not extend to the period from June 24, 20X6 to June 28, 20X6, inclusive):

   a. With respect to the three-month periods ended March 31, 20X6 and 20X5, we have:

      1. Performed the procedures specified for a review in accordance with auditing standards generally accepted in the United States of America applicable to reviews of interim financial information on the unaudited condensed consolidated balance sheet as of March 31, 20X6, and unaudited condensed consolidated statements of income, stockholders' equity, and cash flows for the three-month periods ended March 31, 20X6 and 20X5, included in the Offering Memorandum.

   b. With respect to the period from April 1, 20X6 to May 31, 20X6, we have:

      1. Read the unaudited consolidated financial statements of the company and subsidiaries for April and May of both 20X5 and 20X6 furnished to us by the company, officials of the company having advised us that no such financial statements as of any date or for any period subsequent to May 31, 20X6, were available. [*If applicable*: The financial information for

April and May of both 20X5 and 20X6 is incomplete in that it omits the statement of cash flows and other disclosures.]

2. Inquired of certain officials of the company who have responsibility for financial and accounting matters whether the unaudited consolidated financial statements referred to in 3b(1) are stated on a basis substantially consistent with that of the audited consolidated financial statements included in the Offering Memorandum.

The foregoing procedures do not constitute an audit conducted in accordance with GAAS. Also, they would not necessarily reveal matters of significance with respect to the comments in the following paragraph. Accordingly, we make no representations regarding the sufficiency of the foregoing procedures for your purposes.

4. Nothing came to our attention as a result of the foregoing procedures, however, that caused us to believe that:

   a. Any material modifications should be made to the unaudited condensed consolidated financial statements described in 3a(1), included in the Offering Memorandum, for them to be in conformity with generally accepted accounting principles.

      1. At May 31, 20X6, there was any change in the capital stock, increase in long-term debt, or decrease in consolidated net current assets or stockholders' equity of the consolidated companies as compared with amounts shown in the March 31, 20X6 unaudited condensed consolidated balance sheet included in the Offering Memorandum, or
      2. For the period from April 1, 20X6 to May 31, 20X6, there were any decreases, as compared to the corresponding period in the preceding year, in consolidated net sales, or in income before extraordinary items or of net income, except in all instances for changes, increases, or decreases that the Offering Memorandum discloses have occurred or may occur.

5. As mentioned in item 3b, company officials have advised us that no consolidated financial statements as of any date or for any period subsequent to May 31, 20X6 are available; accordingly, the procedures carried out by us with respect to changes in financial statement items after May 31, 20X6, have, of necessity, been even more limited than those with respect to the periods referred to in item 3. We have inquired of certain officials of the company who have responsibility for financial and accounting matters whether (a) at June 23, 20X6, there was any change in the capital stock, increase in long-term debt, or any decreases in consolidated net current assets or stockholders' equity of the consolidated companies as compared with amounts shown on the March 31, 20X6 unaudited condensed consolidated balance sheet included in the Offering Memorandum, or (b) for the period from April 1, 20X6 to June 23, 20X6, there were any decreases, as compared with the corresponding period in the preceding year, in consolidated net sales or in income before extraordinary items or of net income. On the basis of these inquiries and our reading of the minutes as described in item 3, nothing came to our attention that caused us to believe that there was any such change, increase, or decrease, except in all instances for changes, increases, or decreases that the Offering Memorandum discloses have occurred or may occur.
6. This letter is solely for the information of the addressees and to assist the requesting party in conducting and documenting their investigation of the affairs of the company in connection with the offering of the securities covered by the Offering Memorandum, and it is not to be used, circulated, quoted, or otherwise referred to for any purpose, including but not limited to the registration, purchase, or sale of securities, nor is it to be filed with or referred to in whole or in part in the Offering Memorandum or any other document, except that reference may be made to it in the Purchase Contract or in any list of closing documents pertaining to the offering of the securities covered by the Offering Memorandum.

Illustration 2. Letter When a Short-Form Registration Statement Is Filed Incorporating Previously Filed Form 8-K by Reference

This illustration is an example of modifications to the letter that the auditor of a nonissuer may provide when a registrant has acquired the nonissuer, and the registrant uses a short-form registration statement (for example, Form S-3) that incorporates a previously filed Form 8-K that includes the nonpublic company's financial statements. The auditor was independent of the nonissuer but is not independent with respect to the registrant.

June 28, 20X6

[*Addressee*]

Dear Ladies and Gentlemen:

We have audited the consolidated financial statements of The Nonissuer Company, Inc. (the company) and subsidiaries, which comprise the consolidated balance sheets as of December 31, 20X5 and 20X4, and the related consolidated statements of income, changes in stockholders' equity, and cash flows for each of the years in the three-year period ended December 31, 20X5, and the related notes to the consolidated financial statements, all included in The Issuer Company's (the registrant) current report on Form 8-K dated May 15, 20X6, and incorporated by reference in the registration statement (no. 33-00000) on Form S-3 filed by the registrant under the Securities Act of 1933 (the Act); our report with respect thereto is also incorporated by reference in that registration statement. The registration statement, as amended on June 28, 20X6, is herein referred to as the registration statement.

In connection with the registration statement:

1. As of [*insert date of the auditor's most recent report on the financial statements of the entity*] and during the period covered by the financial statements on which we reported, we were independent certified public accountants with respect to the company under Rule 101 of the AICPA's Code of Professional Conduct and its interpretations and rulings.
2. In our opinion, the consolidated financial statements audited by us and incorporated by reference in the registration statement comply as to form in all material respects with the applicable accounting requirements of the Act and the Securities Exchange Act of 1934 and the related rules and regulations adopted by the SEC.
3. We have not audited any financial statements of the company as of any date or for any period subsequent to December 31, 20X5; although we have conducted an audit for the year ended December 31, 20X5, the purpose (and, therefore, the scope) of the audit was to enable us to express our opinion on the consolidated financial statements as of December 31, 20X5, and for the year then ended, but not on the consolidated financial statements for any interim period within that year. Therefore, we are unable to and do not express any opinion on the unaudited condensed consolidated balance sheet as of March 31, 20X6, and the unaudited condensed consolidated statements of income, stockholders' equity, and cash flows for the three-month periods ended March 31, 20X6 and 20X5, included in the registrant's current report on Form 8-K dated May 15, 20X6, incorporated by reference in the registration statement, or on the financial position, results of operations, or cash flows as of any date or for any period subsequent to December 31, 20X5.
4. For purposes of this letter, we have read the 20X6 minutes of the meetings of the stockholders, the board of directors, and [*include other appropriate committees, if any*] of the company and its subsidiaries as set forth in the minute books at June 23, 20X6, officials of the company having advised us that the minutes of all such meetings through that date were set forth therein, and having discussed with us the unapproved minutes of meetings held on [*dates*]; we have carried out other procedures to June 23, 20X6, as follows (our work did not extend to the period from June 24, 20X6 to June 28, 20X6, inclusive):

With respect to the three-month periods ended March 31, 20X6 and 20X5, we have:

a. Performed a review in accordance with auditing standards generally accepted in the United States of America applicable to reviews of interim financial information on the unaudited condensed consolidated balance sheet as of March 31, 20X6, and the unaudited condensed consolidated statements of income, stockholders' equity, and cash flows for the three-month periods ended March 31, 20X6 and 20X5, included in the registrant's current report on Form 8-K dated May 15, 20X6, incorporated by reference in the registration statement.
b. Inquired of certain officials of the company who have responsibility for financial and accounting matters whether the unaudited condensed consolidated financial statements referred to in 4a comply as to form in all material respects with the applicable accounting requirements of the Securities Exchange Act of 1934 and the related rules and regulations adopted by the SEC.

The foregoing procedures do not constitute an audit conducted in accordance with GAAS. Also, they would not necessarily reveal matters of significance with respect to the comments in the following paragraph. Accordingly, we make no representations about the sufficiency of the foregoing procedures for your purposes.

5. Nothing came to our attention as a result of the foregoing procedures, however, that caused us to believe that:

   a. Any material modifications should be made to the unaudited condensed consolidated financial statements described in 4a, incorporated by reference in the registration statement, for them to be in conformity with GAAP.
   b. The unaudited condensed consolidated financial statements described in 4a do not comply as to form in all material respects with the applicable accounting requirements of the Securities Exchange Act of 1934 and the related rules and regulations adopted by the SEC.

6. This letter is solely for the information of the addressees and to assist the underwriters in conducting and documenting their investigation of the affairs of the company in connection with the offering of the securities covered by the registration statement, and for use of the auditors of the registrant in furnishing their letter to the underwriters, and it is not to be used, circulated, quoted, or otherwise referred to within the underwriting group for any other purpose, including but not limited to the registration, purchase, or sale of securities, nor is it to be filed with or referred to, in whole or in part, in the registration statement or any other document, except that reference may be made to it in the underwriting agreement or any list of closing documents pertaining to the offering of the securities covered by the registration statement.

ILLUSTRATION 3. LETTER REAFFIRMING COMMENTS IN ILLUSTRATION 1-A AS OF A LATER DATE

If more than one comfort letter is requested, the later letter may, in appropriate situations, refer to information appearing in the earlier letter without repeating such information. This illustration reaffirms and updates the information in Illustration 1-A.

July 25, 20X6

[*Addressee*]

Dear Ladies and Gentlemen:

We refer to our letter of June 28, 20X6, relating to the registration statement (no. 33-00000) of The Nonissuer Company, Inc. (the company). We reaffirm as of the date hereof (and as though made on the date hereof) all statements made in that letter except that, for the purposes of this letter:

a. The registration statement to which this letter relates is as amended on July 13, 20X6 [*effective date*].
b. The reading of minutes described in paragraph 4 of that letter has been carried out through July 20, 20X6 [*the new cutoff date*].

c. The procedures and inquiries covered in paragraph 4 of that letter were carried out to July 20, 20X6 [*the new cutoff date*] (our work did not extend to the period from July 21, 20X6 to July 25, 20X6 [*date of letter*], inclusive).
d. The period covered in paragraph 4*b* of that letter is changed to the period from April 1, 20X6 to June 30, 20X6, officials of the company having advised us that no such financial statements as of any date or for any period subsequent to June 30, 20X6, were available.
e. The references to May 31, 20X6 in paragraph 5*b* of that letter are changed to June 30, 20X6.
f. The references to May 31, 20X6 and June 23, 20X6 in paragraph 6 of that letter are changed to June 30, 20X6 and July 20, 20X6, respectively.

This letter is solely for the information of the addressees and to assist the underwriters in conducting and documenting their investigation of the affairs of the company in connection with the offering of the securities covered by the registration statement, and it is not to be used, circulated, quoted, or otherwise referred to within or without the underwriting group for any other purpose, including but not limited to the registration, purchase, or sale of securities, nor is it to be filed with or referred to, in whole or in part, in the registration statement or any other document, except that reference may be made to it in the underwriting agreement or any list of closing documents pertaining to the offering of the securities covered by the registration statement.

Illustration 4-A. Comments on Pro Forma Financial Information: Negative Assurance on Pro Forma Financial Information as to Compliance with the Applicable Accounting Requirements of Rule 11-02 of Regulation S-X

Illustration 4-A is applicable when the auditor is asked to provide negative assurance on (1) whether the pro forma financial information included in a registration statement complies as to form in all material respects with the applicable accounting requirements of Rule 11-02 of Regulation S-X, and (2) the application of pro forma adjustments to historical amounts in the compilation of the pro forma financial information (see paragraphs AU-C 920.52–.53). The material in this illustration is intended to be inserted between paragraphs 6 and 7 in Illustration 1-A or between paragraphs 5 and 6 in Illustration 1-B. The illustration assumes that the auditor has not previously reported on the pro forma financial information. If the auditor did previously report on the pro forma financial information, they may refer in the introductory paragraph of the comfort letter to the fact that they have issued a report, and the report may be attached to the comfort letter (see paragraph AU-C 920.A31–.A32). Therefore, in that circumstance, the procedures in 7b(1) and 7c ordinarily would not be performed, and the auditor would not separately comment on the application of pro forma adjustments to historical financial information because that assurance is encompassed in the auditor's report on pro forma financial information. The auditor may, however, agree to comment on compliance as to form with the applicable accounting requirements of Rule 11-02 of Regulation S-X.

7. At your request, we have:

   a. Read the unaudited pro forma condensed consolidated balance sheet as of March 31, 20X6, and the unaudited pro forma condensed consolidated statements of income for the year ended December 31, 20X5, and the three-month period ended March 31, 20X6, included in the registration statement.
   b. Inquired of certain officials of the company who have responsibility for financial and accounting matters about:

      (1) The basis for their determination of the pro forma adjustments and
      (2) Whether the unaudited pro forma condensed consolidated financial statements referred to in 6a comply as to form in all material respects with the applicable accounting requirements of Rule 11-02 of Regulation S-X.

c. Proved the arithmetic accuracy of the application of the pro forma adjustments to the historical amounts in the unaudited pro forma condensed consolidated financial statements.

The foregoing procedures are substantially less in scope than an examination, the objective of which is the expression of an opinion on management's assumptions, the pro forma adjustments, and the application of those adjustments to historical financial information. Accordingly, we do not express such an opinion. The foregoing procedures would not necessarily reveal matters of significance with respect to the comments in the following paragraph. Accordingly, we make no representation about the sufficiency of such procedures for your purposes.

8. Nothing came to our attention as a result of the procedures specified in item 7, however, that caused us to believe that the unaudited pro forma condensed consolidated financial statements referred to in 7a included in the registration statement do not comply as to form in all material respects with the applicable accounting requirements of Rule 11-02 of Regulation S-X and that the pro forma adjustments have not been properly applied to the historical amounts in the compilation of the unaudited pro forma condensed financial statements. Had we performed additional procedures or had we made an examination or review of the pro forma condensed consolidated financial statements, other matters might have come to our attention that would have been reported to you.

ILLUSTRATION 4-B. COMMENTS ON PRO FORMA FINANCIAL INFORMATION: NEGATIVE ASSURANCE ON PRO FORMA FINANCIAL INFORMATION AS TO COMPLIANCE WITH PRO FORMA BASES AS DESCRIBED IN THE PRO FORMA FINANCIAL INFORMATION

Illustration 4-B is applicable when the auditor is asked to provide negative assurance on (a) whether the pro forma financial information included in a securities offering complies as to form in all material respects with the pro forma bases described in the pro forma financial statements, and (b) the application of pro forma adjustments to historical amounts in the compilation of the pro forma financial information (see paragraphs .52–.53). The material in this example is intended to be inserted between paragraphs 5 and 6 in Illustration 1-B.

The example assumes that the auditor has not previously reported on the pro forma financial information. If the auditor did previously report on the pro forma financial information, the auditor may refer in the introductory paragraph of the comfort letter to the fact that the auditor has issued a report, and the report may be attached to the comfort letter (see paragraphs AU-C 920.A31–.A32). In that circumstance, the procedures in 6b(i) and 6c ordinarily would not be performed, and therefore the auditor would not separately comment on the application of pro forma adjustments to historical financial information because that assurance is encompassed in the auditor's report on pro forma financial information. The auditor may, however, agree to comment on compliance as to form with the pro forma bases described in the pro forma financial statements.

6. At your request, we have—

    a. Read the unaudited pro forma condensed consolidated balance sheet as of March 31, 20X6, and the unaudited pro forma condensed consolidated statements of income for the year ended December 31, 20X5, and the three-month period ended March 31, 20X6, included in the Offering Memorandum.
    b. Inquired of certain officials of the company who have responsibility for financial and accounting matters about

        i. the basis for their determination of the pro forma adjustments, and
        ii. whether the unaudited pro forma condensed consolidated financial statements referred to in 6a comply as to form in all material respects with the pro forma bases described in the pro forma condensed consolidated financial statements.

c. Proved the arithmetic accuracy of the application of the pro forma adjustments to the historical amounts in the unaudited pro forma condensed consolidated financial statements.

The foregoing procedures are substantially less in scope than an examination or review, the objective of which is the expression of an opinion or conclusion on management's assumptions, the pro forma adjustments, and the application of those adjustments to historical financial information. Accordingly, we do not express such an opinion or conclusion. The foregoing procedures would not necessarily reveal matters of significance with respect to the comments in the following paragraph. Accordingly, we make no representation about the sufficiency of such procedures for your purposes.

7. Nothing came to our attention as a result of the procedures specified in paragraph 6, however, that caused us to believe that the unaudited pro forma condensed consolidated financial statements referred to in 6a included in the Offering Memorandum do not comply in all material respects with the pro forma bases described in the pro forma condensed consolidated financial statements and that the pro forma adjustments have not been properly applied to the historical amounts in the compilation of the unaudited pro forma condensed consolidated financial statements. Had we performed additional procedures or had we made an examination or a review of the pro forma condensed consolidated financial statements, other matters might have come to our attention that would have been reported to you.

Illustration 5. Comments on a Financial Forecast

Illustration 5 is applicable when an auditor is asked to comment on a financial forecast (see paragraph .54). The material in this illustration is intended to be inserted between paragraphs 6 and 7 in Illustration 1-A and 5 and 6 in Illustration 1-B. The illustration assumes that the auditor has previously reported on the compilation of the financial forecast and that the report is attached to the letter (see paragraph .A33 and Illustration 15).

7. At your request, we performed the following procedure with respect to the forecasted consolidated balance sheet and consolidated statements of income and cash flows as of December 31, 20X6, and for the year then ending. With respect to forecasted rental income, we compared the occupancy statistics about expected demand for rental of the housing units to statistics for existing comparable properties and found them to be the same.
8. Because the procedure described above does not constitute an examination of prospective financial statements in accordance with standards promulgated by the AICPA, we do not express an opinion on whether the prospective financial statements are presented in conformity with AICPA presentation guidelines or on whether the underlying assumptions provide a reasonable basis for the presentation. Had we performed additional procedures or had we made an examination of the forecast in accordance with standards promulgated by the AICPA, matters might have come to our attention that would have been reported to you. Furthermore, there will usually be differences between the forecasted and actual results because events and circumstances frequently do not occur as expected, and those differences may be material.

Illustration 6. Comments on Tables, Statistics, and Other Financial Information: Complete Description of Procedures and Findings

Illustration 6 is applicable when the auditor is asked to comment on tables, statistics, or other compilations of information appearing in a registration statement (paragraphs .65–.71). Each of the comments is in response to a specific request. The paragraphs in this illustration are intended to follow paragraph 6 in Illustration 1-A or paragraph 5 in Illustration 1-B.

In some cases, the auditor may wish to combine in one paragraph the substance of paragraphs 6 and 8, shown as follows. This may be done by expanding the identification of items in paragraph 8 to provide the identification information included in paragraph 6. In such cases, the introductory sentences in paragraphs 6 and 8 and the text of paragraph 7 might be combined as follows: "For purposes of this letter, we have also read the following information and have performed the additional procedures stated below with respect to such information. Our audit of the consolidated financial statements . . ."

6. For purposes of this letter, we have also read the following, set forth in the securities offering on the indicated pages.

Item	*Page*	*Description*
a	4	"Capitalization." The amounts under the captions "Amount Outstanding as of May 31, 20X6" and "As Adjusted." The related notes, except the following in Note 2: "See Transactions with Interested Persons." From the proceeds of this offering the company intends to prepay $900,000 on these notes, pro rata. See "Use of Proceeds."
b	13	"History and Business—Sales and Marketing." The table following the first paragraph.
c	33	"Selected Financial Data."

7. Our audit of the consolidated financial statements for the periods referred to in the introductory paragraph of this letter comprised audit tests and procedures deemed necessary for the purpose of expressing an opinion on such financial statements as a whole. For none of the periods referred to therein, or any other period, did we perform audit tests for the purpose of expressing an opinion on individual balances of accounts or summaries of selected transactions such as those enumerated above, and, accordingly, we express no opinion thereon.
8. However, for purposes of this letter, we have performed the following additional procedures, which were applied as indicated with respect to the items enumerated above.

Item in 6	*Procedures and Findings*
a	We compared the amounts and numbers of shares listed under the caption, "Amount Outstanding as of May 31, 20X6," with the balances in the appropriate accounts in the company's general ledger and found them to be in agreement. We compared the amounts and numbers of shares listed under the caption, "Amount Outstanding as of May 31, 20X6," adjusted for the issuance of the debentures to be offered by means of the securities offering and for the proposed use of a portion of the proceeds thereof to prepay portions of certain notes, as described under "Use of Proceeds," with the amounts and numbers of shares shown under the caption, "As Adjusted," and found such amounts and numbers of shares to be in agreement. (However, we make no comments regarding the reasonableness of the "Use of Proceeds" or whether such use will actually take place.)
b	We compared the amounts of military sales, commercial sales, and total sales shown in the securities offering with the balances in the appropriate accounts in the company's accounting records for the respective fiscal years and for the unaudited interim periods and found them to be in agreement. We proved the arithmetic accuracy of the percentages of such amounts of military sales and commercial sales to total sales for the respective fiscal years and for the unaudited interim periods. We compared such computed percentages with the corresponding percentages appearing in the registration statement and found them to be in agreement.

c	We compared the amounts of net sales and income from continuing operations for the years ended December 31, 20X5, 20X4, and 20X3, with the respective amounts in the consolidated financial statements on pages 27 and 28 and the amounts for the years ended December 31, 20X2 and 20X1 with the respective amounts in the consolidated financial statements for 20X2 and 20X1 and found them to be in agreement. We compared the amounts of total assets, long-term obligations, and redeemable preferred stock at December 31, 20X5 and 20X4, with the respective amounts in the consolidated financial statements on pages 27 and 28 and the amounts at December 31, 20X3, 20X2, and 20X1, with the corresponding amounts in the consolidated financial statements for 20X3, 20X2, and 20X1 and found them to be in agreement. We compared the information included under the heading "Selected Financial Data" with the disclosure requirements of Item 301 of Regulation S-K. We also inquired of certain officials of the company who have responsibility for financial and accounting matters whether this information conforms in all material respects with the disclosure requirements of Item 301 of Regulation S-K. Nothing came to our attention as a result of the foregoing procedures that caused us to believe that this information does not conform in all material respects with the disclosure requirements of Item 301 of Regulation S-K.

9. It should be understood that we make no representations regarding questions of legal interpretation or regarding the sufficiency for your purposes of the procedures enumerated in the preceding paragraph; also, such procedures would not necessarily reveal any material misstatement of the amounts or percentages listed above. Further, we have addressed ourselves solely to the foregoing data as set forth in the registration statement and make no representations regarding the adequacy of disclosure or regarding whether any material facts have been omitted.

Illustration 7. Comments on Tables, Statistics, and Other Financial Information: Summarized Description of Procedures and Findings Regarding Tables, Statistics, and Other Financial Information

Illustration 7 illustrates, in paragraph 8a, a method of summarizing the descriptions of procedures and findings regarding tables, statistics, and other financial information in order to avoid repetition in the comfort letter. Each of the comments is in response to a specific request. The paragraphs in this illustration are intended to follow paragraph 6 in Illustration 1-A or paragraph 5 in Illustration 1-B.

Other methods of summarizing the descriptions may also be appropriately used. For example, the letter may present a matrix listing the financial information and common procedures employed and indicating the procedures applied to specific items.

6. For purposes of this letter, we have also read the following, set forth in the registration statement on the indicated pages.

Item	*Page*	*Description*
a	4	"Capitalization." The amounts under the captions "Amount Outstanding as of May 31, 20X6" and "As Adjusted." The related notes, except the following in Note 2: "See Transactions with Interested Persons." From the proceeds of this offering the company intends to prepay $900,000 on these notes, pro rata. See "Use of Proceeds."
b	13	"History and Business—Sales and Marketing." The table following the first paragraph.
c	33	"Selected Financial Data."

7. Our audit of the consolidated financial statements for the periods referred to in the introductory paragraph of this letter comprised audit tests and procedures deemed necessary for the purpose of expressing an opinion on such financial statements as a whole. For none of the periods referred to therein, or any other period, did we perform audit tests for the purpose of expressing an opinion on individual balances of accounts or summaries of selected transactions, such as those enumerated above, and, accordingly, we express no opinion thereon.
8. However, for purposes of this letter and with respect to the items enumerated in 6 above:
   a. Except for item 6a, we have (1) compared the dollar amounts either with the amounts in the audited consolidated financial statements described in the introductory paragraph of this letter or, for prior years, included in the company's accounting records, or with amounts in the unaudited consolidated financial statements described in paragraph 3 to the extent such amounts are included in or can be derived from such statements and found them to be in agreement; (2) compared the amounts of military sales, commercial sales, and total sales with amounts in the company's accounting records and found them to be in agreement; (3) compared other dollar amounts with amounts shown in analyses prepared by the company and found them to be in agreement; and (4) proved the arithmetic accuracy of the percentages based on the data in the previously mentioned financial statements, accounting records, and analyses.

      We compared the information in item 6c with the disclosure requirements of Item 301 of Regulation S-K. We also inquired of certain officials of the company who have responsibility for financial and accounting matters whether this information conforms in all material respects with the disclosure requirements of Item 301 of Regulation S-K. Nothing came to our attention as a result of the foregoing procedures that caused us to believe that this information does not conform in all material respects with the disclosure requirements of Item 301 of Regulation S-K.
   b. With respect to item 6a, we compared the amounts and numbers of shares listed under the caption "Amount Outstanding as of May 31, 20X6" with the balances in the appropriate accounts in the company's general ledger at May 31, 20X6, and found them to be in agreement. We compared the amounts and numbers of shares listed under the caption "Amount Outstanding as of May 31, 20X6," adjusted for the issuance of the debentures to be offered by means of the securities offering and for the proposed use of a portion of the proceeds thereof to prepay portions of certain notes, as described under "Use of Proceeds," with the amounts and numbers of shares shown under the caption, "As Adjusted" and found such amounts and numbers of shares to be in agreement. (However, we make no comments regarding the reasonableness of "Use of Proceeds" or whether such use will actually take place.)
9. It should be understood that we make no representations regarding questions of legal interpretation or regarding the sufficiency for your purposes of the procedures enumerated in the preceding paragraph; also, such procedures would not necessarily reveal any material misstatement of the amounts or percentages listed above. Further, we have addressed ourselves solely to the foregoing data as set forth in the registration statement and make no representations regarding the adequacy of disclosure or regarding whether any material facts have been omitted.

Illustration 8. Comments on Tables, Statistics, and Other Financial Information: Descriptions of Procedures and Findings Regarding Tables, Statistics, and Other Financial Information—Attached Securities Offering (or Selected Pages) Identifies Items to Which Procedures Were Applied through the Use of Designated Symbols

Illustration 8 illustrates an alternate format that could facilitate reporting when the auditor is requested to perform procedures on numerous statistics included in a securities offering. Each of the comments is in response to a specific request. The paragraph in Illustration 9 is intended to follow paragraph 6 in Illustration 1-A or paragraph 5 in Illustration 1-B.

7. For purposes of this letter, we have also read the items identified by you on the attached copy of the registration statement and have performed the following procedures, which were applied as indicated with respect to the symbols explained below:

   √ Compared the amount with ABC Company's financial statements for the period indicated included in the securities offering and found them to be in agreement.

8. Our audit of the consolidated financial statements for the periods referred to in the introductory paragraph of this letter comprised audit tests and procedures deemed necessary for the purpose of expressing an opinion on such financial statements as a whole. For none of the periods referred to therein, nor any other period, did we perform audit tests for the purpose of expressing an opinion on individual balances of accounts or summaries of selected transactions, such as those enumerated above, and, accordingly, we express no opinion thereon.

It should be understood that we make no representations regarding questions of legal interpretation or regarding the sufficiency for your purposes of the procedures enumerated in the preceding paragraph; also, such procedures would not necessarily reveal any material misstatement of the amounts or percentages listed above. Further, we have addressed ourselves solely to the foregoing data as set forth in the registration statement and make no representations regarding the adequacy of disclosure or regarding whether any material facts have been omitted.

[*The following is an extract from a securities offering that illustrates how an auditor can document procedures performed on numerous statistics included in the securities offering.*]

Summary Financial Information of ABC Company (in Thousands)

	ABC Company Year Ended December 31,		
Income statement data	*20X3*	*20X4*	*20X5*
Revenue from home sales	$104,110 √	$115,837 √	$131,032 √
Gross profit from sales	23,774 √	17,099 √	22,407 √
Income from home building net of tax	7,029 √	1,000 √	3,425 √

Illustration 9. Alternate Wording When Auditor's Report on Audit Financial Statements Contains an Emphasis-of-Matter Paragraph

Illustration 9 is applicable when the auditor's report on the audited financial statements included in the securities offering contains an emphasis-of-matter paragraph regarding a matter that would also affect the unaudited condensed consolidated interim financial statements included in the securities offering. The introductory paragraph would be revised as follows:

Our reports with respect thereto (which contain an emphasis-of-matter paragraph that describes a lawsuit to which the Company is a defendant, discussed in note 8 to the consolidated financial statements) are also included in the securities offering.

The matter described in the emphasis-of-matter paragraph would also be evaluated to determine whether it also requires mention in the comments on the unaudited condensed consolidated interim financial information (paragraph 5b of Illustration 1-A). If it is concluded that mention of such a matter in the comments on unaudited condensed consolidated financial statements is appropriate, a sentence would be added at the end of paragraph 5b in Illustration 1-A and paragraph 4b of Illustration 1-B:

Reference should be made to the introductory paragraph of this letter, which states that our audit report covering the consolidated financial statements as of and for the year ended December 31, 20X5, includes an emphasis-of-matter paragraph that describes a lawsuit to which the company is a defendant, discussed in note 8 to the consolidated financial statements.

Illustration 10. Alternate Wording When More Than One Auditor Is Involved

Illustration 10 applies when more than one auditor is involved in the audit of the financial statements of a business, and the group engagement team has obtained a copy of the comfort letter of the component auditors (see paragraph .21). Illustration 10 consists of an addition to paragraph 4, a substitution for the applicable part of paragraph 5, and an addition to paragraph 6 of Illustration 1-A paragraphs 3, 4, and 5 of Illustration 1-B, respectively.

[4]c. We have read the letter dated ___ of [*the other auditors*] with regard to [*the related company*].

5. Nothing came to our attention as a result of the foregoing procedures (which, so far as [*the related company*] is concerned, consisted solely of reading the letter referred to in 4c), however, that caused us to believe that . . .
6. . . . On the basis of these inquiries and our reading of the minutes and the letter dated ___ of [*the other auditors*] with regard to [*the related company*], as described in 4, nothing came to our attention that caused us to believe that there was any such change, increase, or decrease, except in all instances for changes, increases, or decreases that the registration statement discloses have occurred or may occur.

Illustration 11. Alternate Wording When the SEC Has Agreed to a Departure from Its Accounting Requirements

Illustration 11 is applicable when (1) there is a departure from the applicable accounting requirements of the 1933 Act and the related rules and regulations adopted by the SEC, and (2) representatives of the SEC have agreed to the departure. Paragraph 2 of Illustration 1-A would be revised to read as follows:

2. In our opinion [*include the phrase* except as disclosed in the registration statement *if applicable*], the consolidated financial statements and financial statement schedules audited by us and included (incorporated by reference) in the registration statement comply as to form in all material respects with the applicable accounting requirements of the Act and the related rules and regulations adopted by the SEC; however, as agreed to by representatives of the SEC, separate financial statements and financial statement schedules of ABC Company (an equity investee) as required by Rule 3-09 of Regulation S-X have been omitted.

Illustration 12. Alternate Wording When Recent Earnings Data Are Presented in Capsule Form

Illustration 12 is applicable when (1) the statement of income in the securities offering is supplemented by later information regarding sales and earnings (capsule financial information), (2) the auditor is asked to comment on that information (paragraphs .50–.51), and (3) the auditor has conducted a review in accordance with GAAS applicable to reviews of interim financial information of the financial statements from which the capsule financial information is derived. The same facts exist as in Illustration 1-A, except for the following:

- Sales and net income (no extraordinary items) share for the six-month periods ended June 30, 20X6 and 20X5 (both unaudited), are included in capsule form more limited than that specified by Financial Accounting Standards Board *Accounting Standards Codification 270, Interim Reporting*.
- No financial statements later than those for June 20X6 are available.
- The letter is dated July 25, 20X6, and the cutoff date is July 20, 20X6.

Paragraphs 4, 5, and 6 of Illustration 1-A would be revised to read as follows:

4. For purposes of this letter, we have read the 20X6 minutes of the meetings of the stockholders, the board of directors, and [*include other appropriate committees, if any*] of the company and its subsidiaries as set forth in the minute books at July 20, 20X6, officials of the company having advised us that the minutes of all such meetings through that date were set forth therein and discussed with us the unapproved minutes of meetings held on [*dates*]; we have carried out other procedures to July 20, 20X6, as follows (our work did not extend to the period from July 21, 20X6 to July 25, 20X6, inclusive):

   a. With respect to the three-month periods ended March 31, 20X6 and 20X5, we have:

      1. Performed the procedures specified for a review in accordance with auditing standards generally accepted in the United States of America applicable to reviews of interim financial information, on the unaudited condensed consolidated balance sheet as of March 31, 20X6, and the unaudited condensed consolidated statements of income, stockholders' equity, and cash flows for the three-month periods ended March 31, 20X6 and 20X5, included in the registration statement.
      2. Inquired of certain officials of the company who have responsibility for financial and accounting matters whether the unaudited condensed consolidated financial statements referred to in 4a(1) comply as to form in all material respects with the applicable accounting requirements of the Act and the related rules and regulations adopted by the SEC.

   b. With respect to the six-month periods ended June 30, 20X6 and 20X5, we have:

      1. Read the unaudited amounts for sales, net income, and earnings per share for the six-month periods ended June 30, 20X6 and 20X5, as set forth in paragraph [*identify location*].
      2. Performed the procedures specified for a review in accordance with auditing standards generally accepted in the United States of America, applicable to reviews of interim financial information, on the unaudited condensed consolidated balance sheet as of June 30, 20X6 and the unaudited condensed consolidated statements of income, stockholders' equity, and cash flows for the six-month periods ended June 30, 20X6 and 20X5, from which the unaudited amounts referred to in 4b(1) are derived.
      3. Inquired of certain officials of the company who have responsibility for financial and accounting matters whether the unaudited amounts referred to in 4b(1) are stated on a basis substantially consistent with that of the corresponding amounts in the audited consolidated statements of income.

   The foregoing procedures do not constitute an audit conducted in accordance with generally accepted auditing standards. Also, they would not necessarily reveal matters of significance with respect to the comments in the following paragraph. Accordingly, we make no representations regarding the sufficiency of the foregoing procedures for your purposes.

5. Nothing came to our attention as a result of the foregoing procedures, however, that caused us to believe that:

   a. (1) Any material modifications should be made to the unaudited condensed consolidated financial statements described in 4a(1), included in the registration statement, for them to be in conformity with generally accepted accounting principles.

(2) The unaudited condensed consolidated financial statements described in 4a(1) do not comply as to form in all material respects with the applicable accounting requirements of the Act and the related rules and regulations adopted by the SEC.

b. (1) The unaudited amounts for sales and net income for the six-month periods ended June 30, 20X6 and 20X5, referred to in 4b(1) do not agree with the amounts set forth in the unaudited condensed consolidated financial statements for those same periods.

(2) The unaudited amounts referred to in 4b(2) were not determined on a basis substantially consistent with that of the corresponding amounts in the audited consolidated statements of income.

c. At June 30, 20X6, there was any change in the capital stock, increase in long-term debt, or any decreases in consolidated net current assets or stockholders' equity of the consolidated companies as compared with amounts shown in the March 31, 20X6, unaudited condensed consolidated balance sheet included in the registration statement, except in all instances for changes, increases, or decreases that the registration statement discloses have occurred or may occur.

6. Company officials have advised us that no consolidated financial statements as of any date or for any period subsequent to June 30, 20X6 are available; accordingly, the procedures carried out by us with respect to changes in financial statement items after June 30, 20X6 have, of necessity, been even more limited than those with respect to the periods referred to in item 4. We have inquired of certain officials of the company who have responsibility for financial and accounting matters whether (1) at July 20, 20X6, there was any change in the capital stock, increase in long-term debt, or any decreases in consolidated net current assets or stockholders' equity of the consolidated companies as compared with amounts shown on the March 31, 20X6, unaudited condensed consolidated balance sheet included in the registration statement; or (2) for the period from July 1, 20X6 to July 20, 20X6, there were any decreases, as compared with the corresponding period in the preceding year, in consolidated net sales, or in income before extraordinary items or of net income. On the basis of these inquiries and our reading of the minutes as described in item 4, nothing came to our attention that caused us to believe that there was any such change, increase, or decrease, except in all instances for changes, increases, or decreases that the registration statement discloses have occurred or may occur.

ILLUSTRATION 13. ALTERNATE WORDING WHEN AUDITORS ARE AWARE OF A DECREASE IN A SPECIFIED FINANCIAL STATEMENT ITEM

Illustration 13 covers a situation in which auditors are aware of a decrease in a financial statement item on which they are requested to comment (see paragraphs .58–.64). The same facts exist as in Illustration 1-A, except for the decrease covered in the following change in paragraph 5b.

5. b. (1) At May 31, 20X6, there was any change in the capital stock, increase in long-term debt, or any decrease in consolidated stockholders' equity of the consolidated companies as compared with amounts shown in the March 31, 20X6 unaudited condensed consolidated balance sheet included in the registration statement, or

(2) For the period from April 1, 20X6 to May 31, 20X6, there were any decreases, as compared with the corresponding period in the preceding year, in consolidated net sales, or income before extraordinary items or of net income, except in all instances for changes, increases, or decreases that the registration statement discloses have occurred or may occur and except that the unaudited consolidated balance sheet as of May 31, 20X6, which we were furnished by the company, showed a decrease from March 31, 20X6 in consolidated net current assets as follows (in thousands of dollars):

	Current Assets	*Current Liabilities*	*Net Current Assets*
March 31, 20X6	$4,251	$1,356	$2,895
May 31, 20X6	3,986	1,732	2,254

6. As mentioned in 4b, company officials have advised us that no consolidated financial statements as of any date or for any period subsequent to May 31, 20X6, are available; accordingly, the procedures carried out by us with respect to changes in financial statement items after May 31, 20X6, have, of necessity, been even more limited than those with respect to the periods referred to in item 4. We have inquired of certain officials of the company who have responsibility for financial and accounting matters whether (a) at June 23, 20X6, there was any change in the capital stock, increase in long-term debt, or any decreases in consolidated net current assets or stockholders' equity of the consolidated companies as compared with amounts shown on the March 31, 20X6, unaudited condensed consolidated balance sheet included in the registration statement; or (b) for the period from April 1, 20X6 to June 23, 20X6, there were any decreases, as compared with the corresponding period in the preceding year, in consolidated net sales or in income before extraordinary items or of net income. On the basis of these inquiries and our reading of the minutes as described in item 4, nothing came to our attention that caused us to believe that there was any such change, increase, or decrease, except in all instances for changes, increases, or decreases that the registration statement discloses have occurred or may occur and except as described in the following sentence: We have been informed by officials of the company that there continues to be a decrease in net current assets that is estimated to be approximately the same amount as set forth in 5b [*or whatever other disclosure fits the circumstances*].

Illustration 14. Alternate Wording of the Letter for Companies That Are Permitted to Present Interim Earnings Data for a 12-Month Period

Certain types of companies are permitted to include earnings data for a 12-month period to the date of the latest balance sheet furnished in lieu of earnings data for both the interim period between the end of the latest fiscal year and the date of the latest balance sheet and the corresponding period of the preceding fiscal year. The following would be substituted for the applicable part of paragraph 3 of Illustration 1-A.

3. . . . was to enable us to express our opinion on the financial statements as of December 31, 20X5, and for the year then ended, but not on the financial statements for any period included in part within that year. Therefore, we are unable to and do not express any opinion on the unaudited condensed consolidated balance sheet as of March 31, 20X6, and the related unaudited condensed consolidated statements of income, stockholders' equity, and cash flows for the 12 months then ended included in the securities offering.

Illustration 15. Alternate Wording When the Procedures That the Requesting Party Has Requested the Auditor to Perform on Interim Financial Information Are Less Than a Review in Accordance with GAAS Applicable to Reviews of Interim Financial Information

Illustration 15 assumes that the requesting party has asked the auditor to perform specified procedures on the interim financial information and report thereon in the comfort letter. The letter is dated June 28, 20X6; procedures were performed through June 23, 20X6, the cutoff date. Because a review in accordance with GAAS applicable to reviews of interim financial information was not performed on the interim financial information as of March 31, 20X6, and for the quarter then ended, the auditor is limited to reporting procedures performed and findings obtained on the interim financial information. The following would be substituted for paragraph 4a of Illustration 1-A. Illustration 15 assumes there has not been a change in the application of a requirement of GAAP during the interim period. If there has been such a change, a reference to that change would be included in subparagraph 4a (2), which follows.

4. For purposes of this letter, we have read the 20X6 minutes of meetings of the stockholders, the board of directors, and [*include other appropriate committees, if any*] of the company and its subsidiaries as set forth in the minute books at June 23, 20X6, officials of the company having advised us that the minutes of all such meetings through that date were set forth therein and having discussed with us the unapproved minutes of meetings held on [*dates*]; we have carried out other procedures to June 23, 20X6, as follows (our work did not extend to the period from June 24, 20X6 to June 28, 20X6, inclusive):

   a. With respect to the three-month periods ended March 31, 20X6 and 20X5, we have:

      (1) Read the unaudited condensed consolidated balance sheet as of March 31, 20X6, and the unaudited condensed consolidated statements of income, stockholders' equity, and cash flows for the three-month periods ended March 31, 20X6 and 20X5, included in the registration statement [*or offering memorandum as applicable*], and agreed the amounts included therein with the company's accounting records as of March 31, 20X6 and 20X5, and for the three-month periods then ended.

      (2) Inquired of certain officials of the company who have responsibility for financial and accounting matters whether the unaudited condensed consolidated financial statements referred to in a(1): (a) are in conformity with generally accepted accounting principles applied on a basis substantially consistent with that of the audited consolidated financial statements included in the registration statement [*or offering memorandum as applicable*], and (b) comply as to form, in all material respects, with the applicable accounting requirements of the Act and the related rules and regulations adopted by the SEC. Those officials stated that the unaudited condensed consolidated financial statements (a) are in conformity with generally accepted accounting principles applied on a basis substantially consistent with that of the audited consolidated financial statements, and (b) comply as to form, in all material respects, with the applicable accounting requirements of the Act and the related rules and regulations adopted by the SEC.

   b. With respect to the period from April 1, 20X6 to May 31, 20X6, we have—

      i. Read the unaudited consolidated financial information of the company and subsidiaries for April and May of both 20X5 and 20X6 furnished us by the company, and agreed the amounts contained therein to the company's accounting records. Officials of the company have advised us that no financial statements as of any date or for any period subsequent to May 31, 20X6, were available. [*If applicable:* The financial information for April and May of both 20X5 and 20X6 is incomplete in that it omits the statements of cash flows and other disclosures.]

      ii. Inquired of certain officials of the company who have responsibility for financial and accounting matters whether (1) the unaudited consolidated financial information referred to in b(i) is stated on a basis substantially consistent with that of the audited consolidated financial statements included in the [*registration statement or* Offering Memorandum, *as applicable*]; (2) at May 31, 20X6, there was any change in the capital stock, increase in long-term debt, or any decrease in consolidated net current assets or stockholders' equity of the consolidated companies as compared with amounts shown in the March 31, 20X6 unaudited condensed consolidated balance sheet included in the [*registration statement or* Offering Memorandum, *as applicable*]; and (3) for the period from April 1, 20X6 to May 31, 20X6, there were any decreases, as compared with the corresponding period in the preceding year, in consolidated net sales or in income from continuing operations or of net income.

      Those officials stated that (1) the unaudited consolidated financial information referred to in 4b(i) is stated on a basis substantially consistent with that of the audited consolidated financial statements included in the [*registration statement or* Offering

Memorandum, *as applicable*]; (2) at May 31, 20X6, there was no change in the capital stock, no increase in long-term debt, and no decrease in net current assets or stockholders' equity of the consolidated companies as compared with amounts shown in the March 31, 20X6 unaudited condensed consolidated balance sheet included in the [*registration statement or* Offering Memorandum, *as applicable*]; and (3) there were no decreases for the period from April 1, 20X6 to May 31, 20X6, as compared with the corresponding period in the preceding year, in consolidated net sales or in income from continuing operations or of net income.

c. As mentioned in 4b(i), company officials have advised us that no financial statements as of any date or for any period subsequent to May 31, 20X6, are available; accordingly, the procedures carried out by us with respect to changes in financial statement items after May 31, 20X6, have, of necessity, been even more limited than those with respect to the periods referred to in 4a and 4b. We have inquired of certain officials of the company who have responsibility for financial and accounting matters whether (a) at June 23, 20X6, there was any change in the capital stock, increase in long-term debt, or any decreases in consolidated net current assets or stockholders' equity of the consolidated companies as compared with amounts shown in the March 31, 20X6 unaudited condensed consolidated balance sheet included in the [*registration statement or* Offering Memorandum, *as applicable*], or (b) for the period from April 1, 20X6 to June 23, 20X6, there were any decreases, as compared with the corresponding period in the preceding year, in consolidated net sales or in income from continuing operations or of net income. Those officials stated that (1) at June 23, 20X6, there was no change in the capital stock, no increase in long-term debt, and no decreases in consolidated net current assets or stockholders' equity of the consolidated companies as compared with amounts shown in the March 31, 20X6 unaudited condensed consolidated balance sheet, and (2) for the period from April 1, 20X6 to June 23, 20X6, there were no decreases, as compared with the corresponding period in the preceding year, in consolidated net sales or in income from continuing operations or of net income.

The foregoing procedures do not constitute an audit or a review conducted in accordance with generally accepted auditing standards. We make no representations regarding the sufficiency of the foregoing procedures for your purposes. Had we performed additional procedures or had we conducted an audit or a review of the company's March 31, April 30, or May 31, 20X6 and 20X5 condensed consolidated financial statements, other matters might have come to our attention that would have been reported to you.

5. At your request, we also—

a. Read the unaudited pro forma condensed consolidated balance sheet as of March 31, 20X6, and the unaudited pro forma condensed consolidated statements of income for the year ended December 31, 20X5, and the three-month period ended March 31, 20X6, included in the [*registration statement or* Offering Memorandum, *as applicable*].

b. Inquired of certain officials of the company and of XYZ Company (the company being acquired) who have responsibility for financial and accounting matters as to whether all significant assumptions regarding the business combination had been reflected in the pro forma adjustments and whether the unaudited pro forma condensed consolidated financial statements referred to in (a) comply as to form in all material respects with the [*applicable accounting requirements of Rule 11-02 of Regulation S-X or pro forma bases described in the pro forma condensed consolidated financial statements, as applicable*].

Those officials referred to above stated, in response to our inquiries, that all significant assumptions regarding the business combination had been reflected in the pro forma adjustments and that the unaudited pro forma condensed consolidated financial statements referred to in (a) comply as to form in all material respects with the [*applicable accounting requirements of Rule*

11-02 of Regulation S-X or pro forma bases described in the pro forma condensed consolidated financial statements, as applicable].

c. Compared the historical financial information for the company included on page 20 in the [*registration statement or* Offering Memorandum, *as applicable*] with historical financial information for the company on page 12 and found them to be in agreement.

   We also compared the financial information included on page 20 of the [*registration statement or* Offering Memorandum, *as applicable*] with the historical information for XYZ Company on page 13 and found them to be in agreement.

d. Proved the arithmetic accuracy of the application of the pro forma adjustments to the historical amounts in the unaudited pro forma condensed consolidated financial statements.

   The foregoing procedures are less in scope than an examination or review, the objective of which is the expression of an opinion or conclusion on management's assumptions, the pro forma adjustments, and the application of those adjustments to historical financial information. Accordingly, we do not express such an opinion or conclusion. We make no representation about the sufficiency of the foregoing procedures for your purposes. Had we performed additional procedures or had we made an examination or review of the pro forma financial information, other matters might have come to our attention that would have been reported to you.

ILLUSTRATION 16. LETTER TO A REQUESTING PARTY THAT HAS NOT PROVIDED THE LEGAL OPINION OR THE REPRESENTATION LETTER REQUIRED BY PARAGRAPH .11

Illustration 16 illustrates the letter to be provided in accordance with paragraph .11, in which the auditor does not provide negative assurance. This illustration assumes that these procedures are being performed at the request of the placement agent on information included in an offering circular in connection with a private placement of unsecured notes. The letter is dated June 30, 20X6; procedures were performed through June 25, 20X6, the cutoff date. The statements in paragraphs 4–8 of the example are illustrative of the statements required to be included by paragraph .12.

This illustration may also be used in connection with a filing under the 1933 Act when a party other than a named underwriter (for example, a selling shareholder) has not provided the auditor with the representation letter described in paragraph .11. In such a situation, this example may be modified to include the auditor's comments on independence and compliance as to form of the audited financial statements and financial statements schedules with the applicable accounting requirements of the 1933 Act and the related rules and regulations adopted by the SEC. Paragraph 1a(ii) may include an inquiry, and the response of company officials, on compliance as to form of the unaudited condensed interim financial statements.

June 30, 20X6

[*Addressee*]

Dear Ladies and Gentlemen:

We have audited the consolidated financial statements of The Nonissuer Company, Inc. (the company) and subsidiaries, which comprise the consolidated balance sheets as of December 31, 20X5 and 20X4, and the related consolidated statements of income, changes in stockholders' equity, and cash flows for each of the years in the three-year period ended December 31, 20X5, and the related notes to the consolidated financial statements, all included in the offering circular for $30,000,000 of notes due June 30, 20Z6. Our report with respect thereto is included in the offering circular. The offering circular dated June 30, 20X6, is herein referred to as the offering circular.

We are independent certified public accountants with respect to the company under Rule 101 of the AICPA's Code of Professional Conduct and its interpretations and rulings.

We have not audited any financial statements of the company as of any date or for any period subsequent to December 31, 20X5; although we have conducted an audit for the year ended December 31, 20X5, the purpose (and, therefore, the scope) of the audit was to enable us to express our opinion on the consolidated financial statements as of December 31, 20X5, and for the year then ended, but not on the financial statements for any interim period within that year. Therefore, we are unable to and do not express any opinion on the unaudited condensed consolidated balance sheet as of March 31, 20X6, and the unaudited condensed consolidated statements of income, stockholders' equity, and cash flows for the three-month periods ended March 31, 20X6 and 20X5, included in the offering circular, or on the financial position, results of operations, or cash flows as of any date or for any period subsequent to December 31, 20X5.

1. At your request, we have read the 20X6 minutes of meetings of the stockholders, the board of directors, and [*include other appropriate committees, if any*] of the company as set forth in the minute books at June 25, 20X6, officials of the company having advised us that the minutes of all such meetings through that date were set forth therein and having discussed with us the unapproved minutes of meetings held on [*dates*]; we have carried out other procedures to June 25, 20X6, as follows (our work did not extend to the period from June 26, 20X6 to June 30, 20X6, inclusive):

   a. With respect to the three-month periods ended March 31, 20X6 and 20X5, we have:

      1. Read the unaudited condensed consolidated balance sheet as of March 31, 20X6, and the unaudited condensed consolidated statements of income, stockholders' equity, and cash flows of the company for the three-month periods ended March 31, 20X6 and 20X5, included in the offering circular, and agreed the amounts included therein with the company's accounting records as of March 31, 20X6 and 20X5, and for the three-month periods then ended.
      2. Inquired of certain officials of the company who have responsibility for financial and accounting matters whether the unaudited condensed consolidated financial statements referred to in 1a(1) are in conformity with generally accepted accounting principles applied on a basis substantially consistent with that of the audited consolidated financial statements included in the offering circular. Those officials stated that the unaudited condensed consolidated financial statements are in conformity with generally accepted accounting principles applied on a basis substantially consistent with that of the audited consolidated financial statements.

   b. With respect to the period from April 1, 20X6 to May 31, 20X6, we have:

      1. Read the unaudited condensed consolidated financial statements of the company for April and May of both 20X5 and 20X6, furnished us by the company, and agreed the amounts included therein with the company's accounting records. Officials of the company have advised us that no financial statements as of any date or for any period subsequent to May 31, 20X6 were available. [*If applicable*: The financial information for April and May of both 20X5 and 20X6 is incomplete in that it omits the statements of cash flows and other disclosures.]
      2. Inquired of certain officials of the company who have responsibility for financial and accounting matters whether (a) the unaudited condensed consolidated financial statements referred to in 1b(1) are stated on a basis substantially consistent with that of the audited consolidated financial statements included in the offering circular, (b) at May 31, 20X6, there was any change in the capital stock, increase in long-term debt, or any decrease in consolidated net current assets or stockholders' equity of the consolidated companies as compared with amounts shown in the March 31, 20X6, unaudited condensed consolidated balance sheet included in the offering circular, and (c) for the period from April 1, 20X6 to May 31, 20X6, there were any decreases, as compared with the corresponding period in the preceding year, in consolidated net sales, or in income before extraordinary items or of net income.

      Those officials stated that (a) the unaudited condensed consolidated financial statements referred to in 1b(2) are stated on a basis substantially consistent with that of the audited consolidated financial statements included in the offering circular, (b) at May 31, 20X6, there was no change in the capital stock, no increase in long-term debt, and no decrease in consolidated net current assets or stockholders' equity of the consolidated companies as compared with amounts shown in the March 31, 20X6, unaudited condensed consolidated balance sheet included in the offering circular, and (c) there were no decreases for the period from April 1, 20X6 to May 31, 20X6, as compared with the corresponding period in the preceding year, in consolidated net sales, or in income before extraordinary items or of net income.

c. As mentioned in 1b, company officials have advised us that no financial statements as of any date or for any period subsequent to May 31, 20X6, are available; accordingly, the procedures carried out by us with respect to changes in financial statement items after May 31, 20X6, have, of necessity, been even more limited than those with respect to the periods referred to in 1a and 1b. We have inquired of certain officials of the company who have responsibility for financial and accounting matters whether (1) at June 25, 20X6, there was any change in the capital stock, increase in long-term debt, or any decreases in consolidated net current assets or stockholders' equity of the consolidated companies as compared with amounts shown on the March 31, 20X6, unaudited condensed consolidated balance sheet included in the offering circular, or (2) for the period from April 1, 20X6 to June 25, 20X6, there were any decreases, as compared with the corresponding period in the preceding year, in consolidated net sales or in income before extraordinary items or of net income.

Those officials referred to above stated that (1) at June 25, 20X6, there was no change in the capital stock, no increase in long-term debt, and no decreases in consolidated net current assets or stockholders' equity of the consolidated companies as compared with amounts shown on the March 31, 20X6, unaudited condensed consolidated balance sheet, and (2) there were no decreases for the period from April 1, 20X6 to June 25, 20X6, as compared with the corresponding period in the preceding year, in consolidated net sales or in income before extraordinary items or of net income.

2. For purposes of this letter, we have also read the items identified by you on the attached copy of the offering circular and have performed the following procedures, which were applied as indicated with respect to the symbols explained below:

 Compared the amount with the company's financial statements for the period indicated and found them to be in agreement.

 Compared the amount with the company's financial statements for the period indicated included in the offering circular and found them to be in agreement.

 Compared with a schedule or report prepared by the company and found them to be in agreement.

3. Our audit of the consolidated financial statements for the periods referred to in the introductory paragraph of this letter comprised audit tests and procedures deemed necessary for the purpose of expressing an opinion on such financial statements as a whole. For none of the periods referred to therein, nor for any other period, did we perform audit tests for the purpose of expressing an opinion on individual balances of accounts or summaries of selected transactions, such as those enumerated above, and, accordingly, we express no opinion thereon.
4. It should be understood that we have no responsibility for establishing (and did not establish) the scope and nature of the procedures enumerated in paragraphs 1–3 above; rather, the procedures enumerated therein are those the requesting party asked us to perform. Accordingly, we make no representations regarding questions of legal interpretation or regarding the sufficiency for your purposes of the procedures enumerated in the preceding paragraphs; also, such procedures would not necessarily reveal any material misstatement of the amounts or percentages listed above as set forth in the offering circular. Further, we have addressed ourselves solely to the foregoing data and make no representations regarding the adequacy of disclosures or whether any material facts have been

omitted. This letter relates only to the financial statement items specified above and does not extend to any financial statement of the company as a whole.

5. The foregoing procedures do not constitute an audit conducted in accordance with generally accepted auditing standards. Had we performed additional procedures or had we conducted an audit or a review of the company's March 31, April 30, or May 31, 20X6 and 20X5 condensed consolidated financial statements in accordance with generally accepted auditing standards, other matters might have come to our attention that would have been reported to you.
6. These procedures should not be taken to supplant any additional inquiries or procedures that you would undertake in your consideration of the proposed offering.
7. This letter is solely for your information and to assist you in your inquiries in connection with the offering of the securities covered by the offering circular, and it is not to be used, circulated, quoted, or otherwise referred to for any other purpose, including but not limited to the registration, purchase, or sale of securities, nor is it to be filed with or referred to, in whole or in part, in the offering circular or any other document, except that reference may be made to it in any list of closing documents pertaining to the offering of the securities covered by the offering document.
8. We have no responsibility to update this letter for events and circumstances occurring after June 25, 20X6.

ILLUSTRATION 17. INTENTIONALLY OMITTED

Illustration 17 from the AU Standards was redrafted in the Clarity (AU-C) Standards and appears in this volume as Illustration 1-B.

ILLUSTRATION 18. ALTERNATE WORDING WHEN REFERENCE TO EXAMINATION OF ANNUAL MANAGEMENT'S DISCUSSION AND ANALYSIS AND REVIEW OF INTERIM MANAGEMENT'S DISCUSSION AND ANALYSIS IS MADE

Illustration 18 is applicable when the auditor is making reference to an examination of annual MD&A and a review of interim MD&A. The same facts exist as in Illustration 1-A, except for the following:

- The auditor has examined the company's Management's Discussion and Analysis (MD&A) for the year ended December 31, 20X5, in accordance with AT Section 701, *Management's Discussion and Analysis*.
- The auditor has also performed reviews of the company's unaudited condensed consolidated financial statements in accordance with generally accepted auditing standards applicable to reviews of interim financial information and the company's MD&A for the three-month period ended March 31, 20X6, in accordance with AT Section 701.
- The accountant's reports on the examination and review of MD&A have been previously issued, but not distributed publicly; none of these reports is included in the securities offering. In this example, the auditor has elected to attach the previously issued reports to the comfort letter (see paragraph .A33).

Appropriate modifications would be made to the opening paragraph of the comfort letter if the auditor has performed a review of the company's annual MD&A.

The following would be substituted for the first paragraph of Illustration 1-A.

We have audited the consolidated financial statements of The Nonissuer Company, Inc. (the company) and subsidiaries, which comprise the consolidated balance sheets as of December 31, 20X5 and 20X4, and the related consolidated statements of income, changes in stockholders' equity, and cash flows for each of the years in the three-year period ended December 31, 20X5, the related notes to the consolidated financial statements, and the related financial statement schedules, all included in The Issuer Company's (the registrant) registration statement (no. 33-00000) on Form S-1 filed by the registrant under the Securities Act of 1933 (the Act); our reports with respect thereto are also included in that registration statement. The registration statement, as amended on June 28, 20X6, is herein referred to as the registration statement. Also, we have examined the company's Management's Discussion and Analysis (MD&A) for the year ended December 31, 20X5, included in the registration statement, as indicated in our report dated March 28, 20X6; our report with respect thereto is attached. We have also reviewed the unaudited condensed consolidated financial statements as of March 31, 20X6 and 20X5, and for the three-month periods then ended, included in the registration statement, as indicated in our report dated May 15, 20X6, and have also reviewed the company's MD&A for the three-month period ended March 31, 20X6, included in the registration statement, as indicated in our report dated May 15, 20X6; our reports with respect thereto are attached.

The following paragraph would be added after paragraph 3 of Illustration 1-A:

4. We have not examined any MD&A of the company as of or for any period subsequent to December 31, 20X5; although we have made an examination of the company's MD&A for the year ended December 31, 20X5, included in the registration statement, the purpose (and, therefore, the scope) of the examination was to enable us to express our opinion on such MD&A, but not on the MD&A for any interim period within that year. Therefore, we are unable to and do not express any opinion on the MD&A for the three-month period ended March 31, 20X6, included in the registration statement, or for any period subsequent to March 31, 20X6.

AU-C 925 Filings with the US Securities and Exchange Commission under the Securities Act of 1933

AU-C ORIGINAL PRONOUNCEMENT

Source Statement on Auditing Standards (SAS) 122.

AU-C DEFINITIONS OF TERMS

Source: AU-C 925.04

Auditor's consent. A statement signed and dated by the auditor that indicates that the auditor consents to the use of the auditor's report, and other references to the auditor, in a registration statement filed under the Securities Act of 1933.

Awareness letter. A letter signed and dated by the auditor to acknowledge the auditor's awareness that the auditor's review report on unaudited interim financial information is being used in a registration statement filed under the Securities Act of 1933. This letter is not considered to be part of the registration statement and is also commonly referred to as an *acknowledgment letter*.

Effective date of the registration statement. The date on which the registration statement filed under the Securities Act of 1933 becomes effective for purposes of evaluating the auditor's liability under Section 11 of the Securities Act of 1933.

OBJECTIVES OF AU-C SECTION 925

AU-C Section 925.03 states that:

> *. . . the objective of the auditor, in connection with audited financial statements of a nonissuer that are separately included or incorporated by reference in a registration statement filed under the Securities Act of 1933, is to perform specified procedures at or shortly before the effective date of the registration statement to sustain the burden of proof that the auditor has performed a reasonable investigation, as referred to in Section 11(b)(3)(B) of the Securities Act of 1933.*

REQUIREMENTS

ACCOUNTANT'S RESPONSIBILITY

In a filing under the Securities Act of 1933, the prospectus frequently contains a statement that certain information is included in reliance on the reports of certain named experts. The accountant should read the section containing that statement and all other sections of the prospectus to make certain that the issuer of the securities is not attributing to the accountant greater responsibility than he or she intended. (AU-C 925.08) There should be no implication that the financial statements have been prepared by the accountant or that they are not the direct representations of management.

Securities and Exchange Commission (SEC) work is complex and highly specialized. The accountant who performs this work should be familiar with the following accounting-related pronouncements of the SEC:

1. Regulation S-X
2. Regulation S-K
3. Financial Reporting Releases (FRRs)
4. Staff Accounting Bulletins (SABs)

ACCOUNTANT'S REPORT: REVIEW OF INTERIM FINANCIAL INFORMATION

In Accounting Series Release (ASR) 274, the SEC ruled that an accountant's report on a review of unaudited interim financial information is not considered part of the registration statement prepared or certified by an accountant or a report prepared or certified by an accountant within the meaning of Section 11 of the Securities Act of 1933. The SEC requires a statement to this effect whenever the accountant's review report is presented or incorporated by reference in a registration statement. The accountant should read the registration statement to ensure that such a statement has been made. (AU-C 925.A14.7)

SUBSEQUENT EVENTS PROCEDURES

Predecessor Auditor

An auditor who has not audited the financial statements for the most recent fiscal year, but whose reports on audits of prior years' financial statements are included in the registration statement, has a responsibility for material subsequent events from the date of the prior year financial statements through to the effective date. In accordance with procedures described in AU-C 560.19, the predecessor auditor should:

1. Read relevant parts of the prospectus and the registration statement, including the financial statements of the subsequent period.
2. Compare the financial statements for each period to be presented.
3. Obtain written representations from management.
4. Obtain a representation letter from the successor auditor regarding whether his or her audit revealed any matters that might materially affect the financial statements reported on by the predecessor or would require disclosure in the notes.
5. Not provide consent until any subsequently discovered facts until the auditor has satisfactorily completed his or her consideration of the facts.

NOTE: In addition to the three procedures above, the procedures in Section 508 under "Reissuance of Predecessor Auditor's Report" should be followed. Thus, the predecessor auditor should obtain a letter of representation from the management of the former client.

(AU-C 925.11-.12)

Current Auditor

The auditor should extend his or her procedures for subsequent events from the date of the audit report up to the effective date of the registration statement, or as close as possible to the effective date. Those procedures include the following:

1. Arrange with the client to be kept informed of the progress of the registration proceedings.
2. Read the entire prospectus and other relevant parts of the registration statement.
3. Inquire of and obtain written representations from officers and other executives responsible for financial and accounting matters about whether any events have occurred, other than those reflected or disclosed in the registration statement, that materially affect the audited financial statements in the registration statement or that should be disclosed to keep the financial statements from being misleading.

In addition to the preceding procedures, the auditor should have applied the subsequent events procedures described in Section 560, *Subsequent Events and Subsequently Discovered Facts*, up to the report date. They are as follows:

1. Compare latest interim financial statements to the statements being audited.
2. Understand management's procedures to identify subsequent events.
3. Ask officers and other executives responsible for financial and accounting matters whether:
    a. Any events have occurred that might affect the financial statements.
    b. Interim statements are prepared on same basis as annual statements.
    c. During the subsequent period there were any:
        (1) Unusual adjustments
        (2) Significant changes in:
            a. Capital stock
            b. Long-term debt
            c. Working capital
            d. Status of items accounted for on the basis of tentative or inconclusive data
            e. Existence of substantial contingent liabilities or commitments
            f. Ownership

(AU-C 925.A10)

4. Read minutes of meetings of those charged with governance. Inquire about matters dealt with at meetings for which minutes are not available.
5. Ask client's legal counsel about litigation, claims, and assessments (see Section 501, *Audit Evidence—Specific Considerations for Selected Items*). (AU-C 925.A10)
6. Obtain updated written representations from management (see Section 580, *Written Representations*) concerning subsequent events or information that has come to management's attention that would modify any previous representations.
7. Make additional inquiries or apply other procedures to the extent necessary to resolve issues raised in applying the foregoing procedures.

NOTE: Normally, an auditor obtains supplementary representation letters from the client and the client's lawyer that update the original letters from the report date to the effective date.

Response to Subsequent Events and Subsequently Discovered Facts: Audited Financial Statements

1. If, after the date of the report on audited financial statements, the auditor discovers subsequent events that require adjustment of or disclosure in the financial statements, he or she should follow the guidance in Section 560.
2. If, after the date of the report on audited financial statements, the auditor becomes aware that facts may have existed at the date of the report that might have affected the report had he or she then been aware of them, he or she should follow the guidance in Section 560.
3. In situations described in items 1 and 2, if the financial statements are adjusted or the required additional disclosure is made, the auditor should follow the guidance in Section 700 on dating the report.
4. In situations described in items 1 and 2, if the client refuses to adjust the financial statements or make the required additional disclosure, the auditor should apply the procedures described in Section 560. The auditor also should consider consulting with his or her lawyer about withholding consent to the use of the report on the audited financial statements in the registration statement. (AU-C 925.12)

Response to Subsequent Events and Subsequently Discovered Facts: Unaudited Financial Statements or Unaudited Interim Financial Information

If the accountant concludes that unaudited financial statements or unaudited interim financial information presented or incorporated by reference in a registration statement are not in conformity with the applicable financial reporting framework, he or she should insist that the statements or information be revised. (AU-C 925.13)

If the client refuses to make the revisions:

1. If the auditor has reported on a review of the interim financial information and the subsequently discovered facts would have affected the report had they been known to him or her at the date of the report, the accountant should refer to Section 560.
2. If the auditor has not reported on a review of the unaudited financial statements or interim financial information and the auditor's review is not included in the registration statements, the auditor should modify the report on the audited financial statements to describe the departure from the applicable financial reporting framework in the unaudited financial statements or interim financial information. (AU-C 925.15)
3. In situations described in items 1 or 2, the accountant should consider consulting with his or her lawyer about withholding consent to the use of the report on the audited financial statements in the registration statement. (AU-C 925.A11)

NOTE: This is sometimes called the reach-out theory of auditor responsibility. Even though the auditor is not explicitly reporting on the unaudited data, if he or she is aware of a GAAP departure in unaudited statements, the report should be modified to add a separate paragraph disclosing the departure. The opinion on the audited financial statements would remain unqualified. Naturally, the auditor's objective is to persuade the client to correct the departure. Should the client fail to do so, the auditor has no alternative but to add a paragraph to the audit report that describes the departure.

AU-C 925 ILLUSTRATION

ILLUSTRATION 1. ILLUSTRATIVE DISCLOSURES AND REPORTS (SOURCE: AU-C 925.15)

The following is an example of a typical "experts" section in a registration statement filed under the Securities Act of 1933:

Experts

The consolidated balance sheets of Company X as of December 31, 20X2 and 20X1, and the related consolidated statements of income and comprehensive income, changes in stockholders' equity, and cash flows for each of the three years in the period ended December 31, 20X2, included in this prospectus, have been so included in reliance on the report of ABC & Co., independent auditors, given on the authority of that firm as experts in auditing and accounting.

The following is an example of a disclosure for a registration statement filed under the Securities Act of 1933 that includes the auditor's review report on unaudited interim financial information when such disclosure is included in a separate section. This disclosure may also be included under a section titled "Experts":

Independent Auditors

With respect to the unaudited interim financial information of Company X for the three-month periods ended March 31, 20X3 and 20X2, included in this prospectus, ABC & Co. has reported that they have applied limited procedures in accordance with professional standards for a review of such information. However, their separate report dated May XX, 20X3, included herein, states that they did not audit and they do not express an opinion on that interim financial information. Accordingly, the degree of reliance on their report on such information should be restricted in light of the limited nature of the review procedures applied. ABC & Co. is not subject to the liability provisions of Section 11 of the Securities Act of 1933 for their report on the unaudited interim financial information because that report is not a "report" or a "part" of the registration statement prepared or certified by the accountants within the meaning of Sections 7 and 11 of the Act.

The following is an example of a typical description of the auditor's role when an issuer wishes to make reference to the auditor in an offering document prepared in connection with a securities offering that is not registered under the Securities Act of 1933:

Independent Auditors

The financial statements of Company X as of December 31, 20X2 and for the year then ended, included in this offering circular, have been audited by ABC & Co., independent auditors, as stated in their report appearing herein.

Although generally not necessary, the following is an example of language the auditor might use indicating that the auditor agrees to the inclusion of the auditor's report on the audited financial statements in offering materials prepared in connection with a securities offering that is not registered under the Securities Act of 1933:

We agree to the inclusion in the offering circular of our report, dated February 5, 20X3, on our audit of the financial statements of Company X.

AU-C 930 Interim Financial Information

AU-C ORIGINAL PRONOUNCEMENT

Source Statement on Auditing Standards (SAS) 122.

AU-C DEFINITION OF TERM

Source: AU-C 930.06

Interim financial information. Financial information prepared and presented in accordance with an applicable financial reporting framework that comprises either a complete or condensed set of financial statements covering a period or periods less than one full year or covering a 12-month period ending on a date other than the entity's fiscal year-end.

OBJECTIVE OF AU-C SECTION 930

AU-C Section 930.05 states that:

. . . the objective of the auditor when performing an engagement to review interim financial information is to obtain a basis for reporting whether the auditor is aware of any material modifications that should be made to the interim financial information for it to be in accordance with the applicable financial reporting framework through performing limited procedures.

SCOPE

AU-C 930 discusses the auditor's responsibilities when conducting a review of interim financial information. AU-C 930 applies when:

1. The entity's latest annual financial statements have been audited by the auditor or a predecessor;
2. The auditor has been engaged to audit the entity's current year financial statements, or the auditor audited the entity's latest annual financial statements and expects to audit the current year financial statements;
3. The client prepares its interim financial information in accordance with the same financial reporting framework as that used to prepare the annual financial statements, or the engagement of another auditor is not effective before the beginning of the period covered by the review; and
4. If the interim financial information is condensed information, then:

   a. The information conforms with an appropriate financial reporting framework;

b. It includes a note that the financial information does not represent complete financial statements and should be read in conjunction with the entity's latest annual audited financial statements; and
c. The information accompanies the entity's latest audited annual financial statements or those financial statements are made *readily available by the entity.*

(AU-C 930.02)

REQUIREMENTS: REVIEW PROCEDURES

UNDERSTANDING WITH CLIENT

A clear written understanding should be established with the client regarding the services to be performed in an engagement to review interim financial information. If an understanding has not been established with the client, the auditor should not accept or perform the engagement. (AU-C 930.09b)

The understanding is specifically required to include:

1. Objectives of the engagement
2. Responsibilities of management
3. Responsibilities of the auditor
4. Limitations of the engagement
5. Identification of the applicable financial reporting framework

(AU-C 930.10)

The understanding should state whether the auditor will provide a written or an oral report upon completion of the engagement.

Prior to accepting the engagement, the auditor should determine whether the financial reporting framework is appropriate. (AU-C 930.09A) The auditor also should obtain management's acknowledgment of its responsibility to establish and maintain controls that are sufficient to provide a reasonable basis for the preparation of reliable interim financial information in accordance with the applicable financial reporting framework. The auditor should obtain management's agreement to provide all information needed and access to individuals needed for inquiries. Management must also agree to include the auditor's review report on interim financial information that indicates that information has been reviewed by the auditor. The auditor should not accept the engagement if this is not the case. (AU-C 930.08)

NOTE: The best way to establish this understanding is to use an engagement letter (see "Techniques for Application").

TECHNIQUES FOR APPLICATION

The following aspects of conducting a review of interim financial information are discussed in this section:

1. Engagement letter
2. Analytical procedures
3. Extent of procedures
4. Subsequent discovery of facts existing at the date of report

5. Other information
6. Successor auditors
7. Additional guidance

ENGAGEMENT LETTER

It is prudent for the auditor to confirm the nature and scope of his or her engagement in a letter to the client. The engagement letter includes the following matters: (AU-C 930.A6)

1. The objective of the review is to provide the auditor with a basis for communicating whether he or she is aware of any material modifications that should be made to the interim financial information for it to conform to the applicable financial reporting framework.
2. The review includes obtaining sufficient knowledge of the entity's business and its internal control as it relates to the preparation of both annual and interim financial information to:
    a. Identify the types of potential material misstatements in the interim financial information and consider the likelihood of their occurrence.
    b. Select the inquiries and analytical procedures that will provide the auditor with a basis for communicating whether the auditor is aware of any material modifications that should be made to the interim financial information for it to conform to the applicable financial reporting framework.
3. The review engagement is limited in these areas:
    a. It does not provide a basis for expressing an opinion about whether the financial information is presented fairly, in all material respects, in conformity with the applicable financial reporting framework.
    b. It does not provide assurance that the auditor will become aware of all significant matters that would be identified in an audit.
    c. It does not provide assurance on internal control or to identify significant deficiencies and material weaknesses in internal control; however, the auditor is responsible for communicating to management and those charged with governance any significant deficiencies or material weaknesses in internal control that the auditor identified.
4. Management is responsible for:
    a. The interim financial information
    b. Establishing and maintaining effective internal control over financial reporting
    c. Compliance with laws and regulations
    d. Providing all financial records and related information to the auditor
    e. Providing a written representation letter to the auditor at the end of the engagement
    f. Adjusting the interim information to correct material misstatements
    g. Affirming in the management representation letter that any uncorrected misstatements are immaterial, both individually and in the aggregate to the interim financial statements as a whole
5. The auditor is responsible for conducting the review in accordance with standards established by the AICPA. A review of interim financial information consists principally of performing analytical procedures and making inquiries of persons responsible for financial and accounting matters. It is substantially less in scope than an audit conducted in accordance with auditing standards generally accepted in the United States of America, the objective of which is the

expression of an opinion regarding the financial information taken as a whole. Accordingly, the auditor will not express an opinion on the interim financial information.

6. The expected form of communication is a description of the expected form of the auditor's communication upon completion of the engagement, and a statement that, if the entity states in any form of communication containing the interim financial information that the information has been reviewed by the auditor or makes other reference to the auditor's association, the auditor's review report will be included in the document.

Knowledge of the Entity's Business and Internal Control

The auditor should have knowledge of the entity's business and internal control that is sufficient to:

- Identify types of potential material misstatements and the likelihood of such misstatements occurring.
- Determine the inquiries and analytical procedures to be performed. (The auditor should also use this knowledge to identify particular events, transactions, or assertions to determine where to direct inquiries or apply analytical procedures.)

(AU-C 930.11)

Planning the Review

When planning the review, the auditor should perform procedures to update his or her knowledge of the entity's business and its internal control. This knowledge should be sufficient to aid in determining the inquiries to be made and the analytical procedures to be performed, and identify relevant events, transactions, or assertions to subject to inquiries or analytical procedures. The auditor should read:

- Prior year's audit documentation (the auditor should also consider whether results of audit procedures performed impact the current year's financial statements)
- Documentation for prior interim period reviews of the current year
- Documentation of prior year's corresponding quarterly and year-to-date interim period reviews

NOTE: The auditor should specifically evaluate (1) corrected material misstatements; (2) issues identified in a summary of uncorrected misstatements (see Section 312); (3) identified risks of material misstatement due to fraud, including the risk of management override of controls; and (4) significant continuing financial accounting and reporting matters (e.g., significant deficiencies and material weaknesses).

- The most recent annual and comparable prior interim period financial information

The auditor should ask management about:

- Changes in business activities of the entity
- The identity of related parties and related-party transactions
- The nature and extent of significant changes in internal control, including changes in policies, procedures, or personnel, occurring after the prior annual audit or review of interim financial information

(AU-C 930.12)

The auditor should also consider the results of any audit procedures performed with respect to the current year's financial statements.

Initial Review of Interim Information

In an initial review of interim information, the auditor should perform procedures to enable him or her to obtain the understanding of the business and internal controls necessary to address the objectives of the review. In addition, the auditor should make inquiries of the predecessor auditor and, if permitted by the predecessor, review the predecessor's documentation for:

- The preceding annual audit, and
- Any prior interim periods in the current year reviewed by the predecessor

---

NOTE: The auditor may also want to review the predecessor's documentation for reviews of prior year's interim periods.

The auditor should specifically evaluate the nature of any (1) corrected material misstatements; (2) issues identified in any summary of uncorrected misstatements; (3) identified risks of material misstatement due to fraud, including the risk of management override of controls; and (4) significant continuing financial accounting and reporting matters (e.g., significant deficiencies or material weaknesses).

The inquiries and procedures performed in the initial review and the conclusions reached are solely the responsibility of the successor auditor. The successor auditor should not make reference in his or her report to the predecessor's work as the basis for the successor's report. If the predecessor does not respond to inquiries or make documentation available for review, the auditor should perform alternative procedures to obtain the required knowledge.

If the auditor has not audited the most recent annual financial statements, the auditor should obtain sufficient knowledge of the entity's internal control as it relates to preparing interim financial information. Such knowledge includes relevant aspects of the control environment, the entity's risk assessment process, control activities, information and communication, and monitoring. The auditor should be aware that internal control over the preparation of interim information may differ from that over annual financial information because different accounting principles may be permitted for interim financial information.

NOTE: The scope of the review may be restricted if the entity's internal control has deficiencies that are so significant that it is not practicable for the auditor to effectively perform necessary review procedures.

Required Review Procedures

The extent of procedures is influenced by significant changes in the client's accounting practices or in the nature or volume of its business activities. The following procedures should be tailored to the engagement based on the auditor's knowledge of the entity's business and internal control.

Analytical Procedures

The auditor should perform the following analytical procedures to identify and provide a basis for asking about the relationships and individual items that appear to be unusual and that may indicate a material misstatement in the interim financial information.

The auditor should compare:

- Quarterly interim financial information with comparable information for the immediately preceding interim period and the prior year's corresponding information. The auditor should factor in his or her knowledge of changes in the business or transactions.
- Recorded amounts or ratios developed from such amounts to the account's expectations.
- Disaggregated revenue data, such as comparing the current interim period's revenue reported by month and by operating segment with that of comparable prior periods.

The auditor should also consider plausible relationships among financial and relevant nonfinancial information.

(AU-C 930.13)

In applying analytical procedures, it is prudent for the auditor to develop a permanent file. The file contains the following:

1. Comparative financial information:
    a. Current quarter and preceding quarters
    b. Current quarter and year-to-date and the same periods of preceding years
    c. Current quarter and year-to-date and budgets for similar periods
2. Analysis of relationships: computation of relevant ratios (gross profit, net income, current, etc.) and comparison of these ratios with similar ratios of preceding years.
3. Sources of information for analytical procedures:
    a. Financial information for comparable prior periods giving consideration to known changes
    b. Anticipated results; for example, budgets or forecasts, including extrapolations from interim or annual data
    c. Relationships among elements of financial information within the period
    d. Information regarding the industry in which the client operates; for example, gross margin data
    e. Relationships of financial information with relevant nonfinancial information; for example, the relationship of sales to interest rates in the housing industry
4. Comparisons of disaggregated revenue data and other required procedures.

Inquiries and Other Procedures

The auditor should make the following inquiries of financial and accounting management: (AU-C 930.14)

- Has the interim financial information been prepared in conformity with the applicable financial reporting framework and, consistently applied?
- Are there any unusual or complex situations potentially affecting interim financial information?
- Have any significant transactions occurred or been recorded in the last several days of the interim period?
- Were uncorrected misstatements that were identified during the previous audit and interim review subsequently recorded? If so, when, and what were the final amounts of the adjustments?
- Were any issues identified while performing review procedures?

- Are there any subsequent events that could have a material effect on interim financial information?
- Does management know about any actual or suspected fraud involving management, employees who have significant roles in internal controls, or anyone else in a position to commit fraud that would materially affect the financial information?
- Does management know about any actual or suspected fraud alleged by anyone, including employees, former employees, analysts, regulators, or short sellers?
- Are there any significant journal entries and other adjustments?
- Are there any communications from regulatory agencies?
- Are there any significant deficiencies, including material weaknesses, in internal control relating to the preparation of both annual and interim financial information?
- Are there any changes in related parties?
- Are there any significant new related-party transactions?

The auditor should also read the following:

- Available minutes of meetings of stockholders, directors, and appropriate committees. The auditor should ask about issues discussed at meetings for which minutes are not available in order to identify issues that might affect interim financial information.
- The interim financial information to consider whether it conforms to the applicable financial reporting framework, based on the results of review procedures and other information that comes to the auditor's attention.
- Other information in documents containing the interim financial information, to consider whether the information or the manner of presentation is materially inconsistent with the interim financial information.

The auditor should also perform the following procedures:

- Obtain reports from component auditors engaged to perform a review of the interim financial information of significant components of the reporting entity, its subsidiaries, or its other investees. If reports have not been issued, the auditor should make inquiries of those auditors.
- Obtain evidence that the interim financial information agrees or reconciles with the accounting records. The auditor should consider asking management about the reliability of the records to which the interim information is compared or reconciled.

Inquiries Concerning Litigation, Claims, and Assessments

In a review, the auditor is ordinarily not required to send an inquiry letter to the entity's lawyer about litigation, claims, or assessments. However, it would be appropriate for the auditor to ask legal counsel about any specific matters that come to the auditor's attention that lead him or her to question whether there is a departure from the applicable financial reporting framework related to litigation, claims, or assessments. (AU-C 930.15)

Inquiries Concerning Going Concern Issues

The auditor should keep in mind that, although expectations from analytical procedures in a review are normally less precise than those of an audit, and the auditor is not required to corroborate management's responses with other evidence, the auditor should consider whether such responses are reasonable and consistent with other information from the review. (AU-C 930.17)

Although a review is not designed to identify conditions or events indicating substantial doubt about the entity's ability to continue as a going concern, such conditions may already exist, or the auditor may become aware of them while performing the review. In either case, the auditor should ask management about its plans for dealing with the adverse effects of conditions and events, and consider whether these matters are adequately disclosed in the interim financial information. (AU-C 930.16)

Extension of Interim Review Procedures

The auditor should keep in mind that, although expectations from analytical procedures in a review are normally less precise than those of an audit, and the auditor is not required to corroborate management's responses with other evidence, the auditor should consider whether such responses are reasonable and consistent with other information from the review. (AU-C 930.17)

During a review, an auditor may become aware of information that leads him or her to believe that the interim financial information may not be in conformity with the applicable financial reporting framework in all material respects. In this case, the auditor should make additional inquiries or perform other appropriate procedures to provide a basis for communicating whether he or she is aware of any material modifications that should be made to the interim information. (AU-C 930.18)

NOTE: For example, if an auditor questions whether a significant sales transaction is recorded in conformity with the applicable financial reporting framework, the auditor may perform procedures to resolve the question such as discussing the terms of the transaction with senior accounting and marketing personnel and/or reading the sales contract.

Timing of Review Procedures and Coordination with the Audit

Many review procedures can be performed before or at the same time that the entity is preparing interim financial information. Early performance of certain review procedures allows for early identification and consideration of significant accounting matters. Also, since the auditor performing the review is usually engaged to perform the year-end audit, the auditor may perform certain auditing procedures, such as reading the minutes of board of directors meetings, concurrently with the interim review.

Written Representations from Management

The auditor should obtain written representations from management for all interim financial information presented and for all periods covered by the review. According to AU 930.21, specific representations should cover the following:

Interim Financial Information

1. Management's acknowledgment of its responsibility for the fair presentation of the interim financial information in conformity with the applicable financial reporting framework
2. Management's belief that the interim financial information has been prepared and presented in conformity with the applicable financial reporting framework applicable to interim financial information

Internal Control

3. Management's acknowledgment of its responsibility to design, implement, and maintain controls that are sufficient to provide a reasonable basis for the preparation of reliable

interim financial information in accordance with the applicable financial reporting framework

4. Disclosure of all significant deficiencies, including material weaknesses, in the design or operation of internal controls as it relates to the preparation of both annual and interim financial information
5. Acknowledgment of management's responsibility for the design and implementation of programs and controls to prevent and detect fraud
6. Knowledge of fraud or suspected fraud affecting the entity involving (a) management, (b) employees who have significant roles in internal control, or (c) others where fraud could have a material effect on the interim financial information
7. Knowledge of any allegations of fraud or suspected fraud affecting the entity received in communications from employees, former employees, analysts, regulators, short sellers, or others
8. Disclosure to the auditor of the results of its assessment of the risk that the interim financial information may be materially misstated as a result of fraud
9. Disclosure to the auditor of all known instances of noncompliance or suspected noncompliance with laws and regulations whose effects should be considered when preparing interim financial information

Completeness of Information

10. Availability of all financial records, related data, and access
11. Completeness and availability of all minutes of meetings of stockholders, directors, and committees of directors or summaries of actions of recent meetings for which minutes have not yet been prepared
12. Communications with regulatory agencies concerning noncompliance with or deficiencies in financial reporting practices
13. Absence of unrecorded transactions

Recognition, Measurement, and Disclosure

14. Management's belief that the effects of any unrecorded financial statement misstatements aggregated by the auditor during the current review engagement and pertaining to the interim period(s) in the current year are immaterial, both individually and in the aggregate, to the interim financial information as a whole (a summary of such items should be included in or attached to the letter)
15. Plans or intentions that may materially affect the carrying value or classification of assets or liabilities
16. Information concerning related parties and related-party transactions and amounts receivable from or payable to related parties
17. Guarantees, whether written or oral, under which the entity is contingently liable
18. Significant estimates and material concentrations known to management that are required to be disclosed in accordance with the applicable financial reporting framework
19. Violations or possible violations of laws or regulations whose effects should be considered for disclosure in the interim financial information or as a basis for recording a loss contingency
20. Unasserted claims or assessments that are probable of assertion and must be disclosed in accordance with the applicable financial reporting framework

21. Other liabilities or gain or loss contingencies that are required to be accrued or disclosed by the applicable financial reporting framework
22. Satisfactory title to all owned assets, liens or encumbrances on such assets, and assets pledged as collateral
23. Compliance with aspects of contractual agreements that may affect the interim financial information

Subsequent Events

24. Information concerning subsequent events

The representation letter should be tailored to include additional representations specific to the entity's business or industry.

Evaluating the Results of Interim Review Procedures

During a review, the auditor may become aware of likely misstatements and should accumulate such misstatements for further evaluation. The account should evaluate misstatements individually and in the aggregate to determine whether a material modification to the interim financial statements is necessary for it to conform to the applicable financial reporting framework. (AU-C 930.19-.20) The auditor should use professional judgment in evaluating the materiality of uncorrected likely misstatements. When evaluating the materiality of uncorrected misstatements, the auditor should consider:

- The nature, cause, and amount of misstatements
- When the misstatement occurred (prior year or interim periods of the current year)
- Materiality judgments made in the prior or current year annual audit
- The potential effect of the misstatements on future interim or annual periods

When evaluating whether uncorrected likely misstatements, individually or in the aggregate, are material, the auditor should also consider:

- Whether it is appropriate to offset a misstatement of an estimated item with a misstatement of an item that can be precisely measured
- That accumulating immaterial misstatements in the balance sheet may contribute to material misstatements in the future

A review is incomplete and a review report cannot be issued if the auditor is not able to:

- Perform procedures necessary for a review engagement.
- Obtain required written representations from management.

In this case, the auditor should communicate that information, following the guidance below in "Requirements: Communication with Management and Those Charged with Governance."

Subsequent Discovery of Facts Existing at the Date of Report

If, subsequent to the date of the report, the auditor becomes aware of facts that existed at the date of the report that might have affected the report had he or she been aware of those facts, the auditor is well advised to refer to Section 560 for guidance.

Other Information

If interim financial information and the auditor's review report on such information appear in a document containing other information, the auditor might wish to refer to the guidance in Section 720, *Other Information in Documents Containing Audited Financial Statements.* For example, the SEC requires Form 10-Q to include a Management's Discussion and Analysis (MD&A) in addition to quarterly financial statements. The auditor might wish to read the MD&A and consider whether it is consistent with the auditor's knowledge obtained in reviewing the quarterly data.

Successor Auditors

Successor auditors must complete inquiries of the predecessor auditor before accepting an engagement to perform an initial review of interim information.

Additional Guidance

When performing reviews, the auditor may find that audit guidance for relevant sections is useful. Specifically, the auditor may wish to consider:

- Section 520, *Analytical Procedures*, when performing analytical procedures. The auditor should keep in mind that expectations developed during a review of interim information would ordinarily be less precise than those developed in an audit. In addition, the auditor is not required to corroborate management's answers with other evidence when performing a review, but should instead consider whether the response is reasonable and consistent with the results of other review procedures and the auditor's knowledge of the entity's business and its internal control.
- Section 260, *The Auditor's Communication with Those Charged with Governance*, when making communications to the audit committee.

Documentation

The auditor should prepare documentation for the review engagement. The form and content of such documentation should be designed to meet the particular engagement's circumstances. The auditor should use professional judgment when evaluating the quantity, type, and content of the documentation. However, such documentation should:

1. Discuss the nature, timing, and extent of procedures performed.
2. Explain the results of the procedures and the evidence obtained.
3. Include any significant findings or issues, such as indications that the interim financial information is materially misstated:

    a. Include any actions taken to address these findings.
    b. Include the basis for final conclusions reached.

4. Enable engagement team members with supervision and review responsibilities to understand the nature, timing, extent, and results of the review procedures performed.
5. Identify the engagement team members who performed and reviewed the work.
6. Identify the evidence obtained to support the conclusion that the interim financial information reviewed agreed or reconciled with accounting records.

(AU-C 930.42)

REQUIREMENTS: COMMUNICATION WITH MANAGEMENT AND THOSE CHARGED WITH GOVERNANCE

Required Communications

The auditor should determine whether any of the matters described in Section 260, *The Auditor's Communication with Those Charged with Governance*, as they relate to interim financial information, have been identified. (Examples of such matters include the process used by management for determining particularly sensitive accounting estimates or changes in significant accounting policies affecting the interim financial information. The presentation to those charged with governance should be similar to the presentation of uncorrected misstatements in the written representation letter.) If so, the auditor should communicate such matters to those charged with governance or be satisfied, through discussions with those charged with governance, that management has communicated these matters to those charged with governance.

Since the objective of a review is significantly different from that of an audit, any discussion about the quality of an entity's accounting principles for interim financial information would generally be limited to the impact of significant events, transactions, and changes in accounting estimates considered by the auditor when conducting the review. Interim review procedures do not provide assurance that the auditor will become aware of all matters affecting the auditor's judgment that would be identified as a result of an audit.

Reportable Conditions

If the auditor becomes aware of matters relating to internal control over financial reporting that might be of interest to those charged with governance, he or she should communicate those matters to the audit committee.

Communications to Management

The auditor should communicate with management as soon as practicable if he or she believes that material modification should be made to the interim financial information for it to conform with the applicable financial reporting framework, or that the entity issued the interim financial information before completion of the review, in those circumstances in which a review is required. (AU-C 930.24)

Lack of Appropriate Management Response

The auditor should inform those charged with governance of these matters as soon as practicable if management does not respond appropriately to the auditor's communication within a reasonable period of time. (AU-C 930.25)

Oral Communication

If the auditor identifies issues that need to be communicated to those charged with governance, this information should at least be sent to those charged with governance on a sufficiently timely basis to ensure that appropriate action can be taken. The auditor should document communications with those charged with governance if that communication is oral.

Lack of Appropriate Response from Those Charged with Governance

The auditor should decide whether to resign from the engagement related to interim financial information and whether to remain as the auditor of the entity's financial statements if those charged with governance do not respond appropriately to his or her communication within a reasonable period of time. The auditor may wish to consult with his or her attorney when making these decisions. (AU-C 930.26)

Fraud or Illegal Acts

If the auditor becomes aware of fraud, the auditor should communicate this to management. If the fraud involves senior management, or if it materially misstates the financial statements, then the auditor should communicate directly with those charged with governance. If the auditor becomes aware of a possible illegal act and the effect is not inconsequential, the auditor should make sure that those charged with governance are informed. (AU-C 930.27)

Significant Deficiencies or Material Weaknesses

If the auditor becomes aware of significant deficiencies, material weaknesses in internal control relating to the preparation of annual and interim financial information, or any other matters described in AU-C 260, then they should be communicated to management and those charged with governance. (AU-C 930.28)

REQUIREMENTS: AUDITOR'S REPORT

Description of Interim Financial Information

Each page of the interim financial information should be marked as "unaudited." (AU-C 930.31)

Date of Report and Addressee

The report should be addressed appropriately for the circumstances of the engagement and dated as of the date of completion of the review procedures. (AU-C 930.30)

Form of Auditor's Review Report

The auditor is not required to issue a report on a review of interim financial information; however, if the auditor does so, then according to AU 930.30 each page of the report should be clearly marked as unaudited, and the report should consist of the following:

1. A title that includes the word *independent.*
2. An introductory paragraph that
   - Identifies the entity whose interim financial information has been reviewed,
   - States that the interim financial information identified in the report was reviewed,
   - Identifies the interim financial information, and
   - Specifies the date or period covered by each financial statement composing the interim financial information.
3. A section with the heading "Management's Responsibility for the Financial Statements." This section should include an explanation that management is responsible for the preparation and fair presentation of the interim financial information in accordance with the applicable financial reporting framework and that this responsibility includes the design, implementation, and maintenance of internal control sufficient to provide a reasonable basis for the preparation and fair presentation of interim financial information in accordance with the applicable financial reporting framework.

4. A section with the heading "Auditor's Responsibility" that includes the following statements:
    - The auditor's responsibility is to conduct the review of interim financial information in accordance with auditing standards generally accepted in the United States of America applicable to reviews of interim financial information.
    - A review of interim financial information consists principally of applying analytical procedures and making inquiries of persons responsible for financial and accounting matters.
    - A review of interim financial information is substantially less in scope than an audit conducted in accordance with auditing standards generally accepted in the United States of America, the objective of which is an expression of an opinion regarding the financial information as a whole, and, accordingly, no such opinion is expressed.
5. A concluding section with an appropriate heading that includes a statement about whether the auditor is aware of any material modifications that should be made to the accompanying financial information so that it conforms to the applicable financial reporting framework. (This should include an identification of the country of origin of the accounting principles used.)
6. The manual or printed signature of the auditor's firm.
7. The city and state where the auditor practices.
8. The date of the review report.

Reference to Report of Another Auditor

When reporting on the review of interim financial information, the auditor may use and make reference to the review reports of other auditors.

Modification of the Review Report

A departure from the applicable financial reporting framework that has a material effect on the interim financial information requires the auditor to modify the review report; this includes both inadequate disclosure and changes in accounting principles that are not in conformity with the applicable financial reporting framework. The modified report should describe the nature of the departure and, if practicable, should state the effects of the departure on the interim financial information. (AU-C 930.35)

If there is substantial doubt about the entity's ability to continue as a going concern or a lack of consistency in the application of accounting principles affecting the interim financial information, the auditor does not have to add an additional paragraph in the report, provided that the interim financial information discloses the issue. (AU-C 930.A24) If there is inadequate disclosure within the interim financial information, then the auditor should modify the report and include the necessary information in the report.

If the auditor's report for the prior year-end indicated the existence of substantial doubt about the entity's ability to continue as a going concern, the supporting conditions continue to exist, and there is adequate disclosure of these conditions in the interim financial information, there is no need to modify the auditor's report. However, the auditor can emphasize the matter in the report.

If the auditor's report for the prior year did *not* indicate the existence of substantial doubt about the entity's ability to continue as a going concern, but conditions now indicate such an issue, and there is adequate disclosure of the situation in the interim financial information, then the auditor is not required to issue a modified report. However, the auditor can emphasize the matter in the report (see "AU-C 930 Illustrations").

Client Representation about Auditor's Review

If a client states in a written communication containing the reviewed interim financial information that the auditor has reviewed the interim financial information, the auditor should advise the entity that his or her report must also be included.

If the client does not agree to include the report, the auditor should:

- Request that neither the auditor's name nor reference to him or her be associated with the interim financial information.
- If the client does not comply, notify the client that the auditor does not permit either the use of his or her name or the reference.
- Communicate the client's noncompliance with the request to those charged with governance.
- Recommend that the client consult with legal counsel about applicable laws and regulations, if appropriate.
- Consider other appropriate actions.

(AU-C 930.38)

NOTE: In these circumstances, it is prudent for the auditor to consult with his or her lawyer.

If the auditor cannot complete the review and the client has represented that the auditor has reviewed interim financial information in a document filed with a regulatory agency or issued to stockholders or third parties, the auditor cannot issue the report and must notify the appropriate level of management as soon as practicable, and also consider following the steps noted immediately prior to this paragraph.

REQUIREMENTS: INTERIM FINANCIAL INFORMATION ACCOMPANYING AUDITED FINANCIAL STATEMENTS

Presentation of Interim Financial Information

Interim financial information ordinarily is presented as supplementary information outside the audited financial statements. Each page of the interim financial information should be clearly marked "unaudited." If this information is presented in a note to the audited financial statements, it should be clearly marked "unaudited."

The Auditor's Report

Because interim financial information is not audited and is not required to be fairly stated in conformity with the applicable financial reporting framework, the auditor need not modify the audit report for the review of interim financial information accompanying audited financial statements. However, the auditor should include an other-matter paragraph in the report in the following circumstances:

1. The interim financial information that has been reviewed is included in a document containing audited financial statements.

2. The interim financial information is not presented in conformity with the applicable financial reporting framework.
3. The auditor's separate review report is not presented with the information and addresses this issue.

(AU-C 930.40)

INTERPRETATIONS

There are no interpretations for this section. However, readers may want to reference the chapter on AU-C 570 for information on a relevant interpretation—see Interpretation No. 3 in the Interpretations section of that chapter.

AU-C 930 ILLUSTRATIONS

Illustrative Management Representation Letters for a Review of Interim Financial Information (AU-C 930.A56)

The following letters are presented for illustrative purposes only:

1. Short-Form Representation Letter for a Review of Interim Financial Information
2. Detailed Representation Letter for a Review of Interim Financial Information

These illustrations assume that the applicable financial reporting framework is accounting principles generally accepted in the United States of America, that no conditions or events exist that might be indicative of the entity's possible inability to continue as a going concern, and that no exceptions exist to the requested written representations. If circumstances differ from these assumptions, the representations would need to be modified to reflect the actual circumstances.

Illustration 1. Short-Form Representation Letter for a Review of Interim Financial Information

This representation letter is to be used in conjunction with the representation letter for the audit of the financial statements of the prior year. Management confirms the representations made in the representation letter for the audit of the financial statements of the prior year-end, as they apply to the interim financial information, and makes additional representations that may be needed for the interim financial information.

[*Date*]

To [*independent auditor*]:

This representation letter is provided in connection with your review of the [*consolidated*] balance sheet as of June 30, 20X1 and the related [*consolidated*] statements of income, changes in equity, and cash flows for the six-month period then ended of ABC Company for the purpose of reporting whether any material modifications should be made to the [*consolidated*] interim financial information for it to be in accordance with accounting principles generally accepted in the United States of America (US GAAP) [*including, if appropriate, an indication as to the appropriate form and content of interim financial information (for example, Article 10 of SEC Regulation S-X)*].

We confirm that[, to the best of our knowledge and belief, having made such inquiries as we considered necessary for the purpose of appropriately informing ourselves,] as of [*date of auditor's review report*]:

Interim Financial Information

1. We have fulfilled our responsibilities, as set out in the terms of the engagement letter dated [*insert date*] for the preparation and fair presentation of interim financial information in accordance with US GAAP; in particular the interim financial information is presented in accordance therewith.
2. We acknowledge our responsibility for the design, implementation, and maintenance of internal control relevant to the preparation and fair presentation of interim financial information that is free from material misstatement, whether due to fraud or to error.
3. The interim financial information has been adjusted or includes disclosures for all events subsequent to the date of the interim financial information for which US GAAP requires adjustment or disclosure.
4. The effects of uncorrected misstatements are immaterial, both individually and in the aggregate, to the interim financial information as a whole. A list of the uncorrected misstatements is attached to the representation letter.

   [*Any other matters that the auditor may consider appropriate*]

Information Provided

5. We have provided you with:
   - Access to all information of which we are aware that is relevant to the preparation and fair presentation of the interim financial information such as records, documentation, and other matters;
   - Minutes of the meetings of stockholders, directors, and committees of directors, or summaries of actions of recent meetings for which minutes have not yet been prepared;
   - Additional information that you have requested from us for the purpose of the review; and
   - Unrestricted access to persons within the entity of whom you determined it necessary to make inquiries.
6. We have disclosed to you all significant deficiencies or material weaknesses in the design or operation of internal control of which we are aware, as it relates to the preparation and fair presentation of both annual and interim financial information.
7. We have disclosed to you the results of our assessment of the risk that the interim financial information may be materially misstated as a result of fraud.
8. We have [*no knowledge of any*] [*disclosed to you all information of which we are aware in relation to*] fraud or suspected fraud that affects the entity and involves:
   - Management;
   - Employees who have significant roles in internal control; or
   - Others when the fraud could have a material effect on the interim financial information.
9. We have [*no knowledge of any*] [*disclosed to you all information in relation to*] allegations of fraud, or suspected fraud, affecting the entity's interim financial information communicated by employees, former employees, analysts, regulators, or others.
10. We have disclosed to you the identity of the entity's related parties and all the related-party relationships and transactions of which we are aware.
    [*Any other matters that the auditor may consider necessary*]
11. We have reviewed our representation letter to you dated [*date of representation letter relating to most recent audit*] with respect to the audited consolidated financial statements as of and for the year ended [*prior year-end date*]. We believe that representations [*references to applicable representations*] within that representation letter do not apply to the interim financial information referred to above. We now confirm those representations [*references to applicable representations*], as they

apply to the interim financial information referred to above, and incorporate them herein, with the following changes:

[*Indicate any changes.*]

12. [*Add any representations related to new accounting or auditing standards that are being implemented for the first time.*]

____

[*Name of chief executive officer and title*]

____

[*Name of chief financial officer and title*]

____

[*Name of chief accounting officer and title*]

Illustration 2. Detailed Representation Letter for a Review of Interim Financial Information

This representation letter is similar in detail to the management representation letter used for the audit of the financial statements of the prior year and, thus, need not refer to the written management representations received in the most recent audit.

[*Date*]

To [*independent auditor*]:

This representation letter is provided in connection with your review of the [*consolidated*] balance sheet as of June 30, 20X1 and the related [*consolidated*] statements of income, changes in equity, and cash flows for the six-month period then ended of ABC Company for the purpose of reporting whether any material modifications should be made to the [*consolidated*] interim financial information for it to be in accordance with accounting principles generally accepted in the United States of America (US GAAP) [*including, if appropriate, an indication as to the appropriate form and content of interim financial information (for example, Article 10 of SEC Regulation S-X)*].

We confirm that[, to the best of our knowledge and belief, having made such inquiries as we considered necessary for the purpose of appropriately informing ourselves,] as of [*date of auditor's review report*]:

Interim Financial Information

1. We have fulfilled our responsibilities, as set out in the terms of the engagement letter dated [*insert date*] for the preparation and fair presentation of the interim financial information in accordance with US GAAP; in particular the interim financial information is presented in accordance therewith.
2. We acknowledge our responsibility for the design, implementation, and maintenance of internal control relevant to the preparation and fair presentation of interim financial information that is free from material misstatement, whether due to fraud or to error.
3. Significant assumptions used by us in making accounting estimates, including those measured at fair value, are reasonable.
4. Related-party relationships and transactions have been appropriately accounted for and disclosed in accordance with the requirements of US GAAP.
5. The interim financial information has been adjusted or includes disclosures for all events subsequent to the date of the interim financial information for which US GAAP requires adjustment or disclosure.
6. The effects of uncorrected misstatements are immaterial, both individually and in the aggregate, to the interim financial information as a whole. A list of the uncorrected misstatements is attached to the representation letter.

[*Any other matters that the auditor may consider appropriate*]

Information Provided

7. We have provided you with:

   - Access to all information of which we are aware that is relevant to the preparation and fair presentation of the interim financial information such as records, documentation, and other matters;
   - Minutes of the meetings of stockholders, directors, and committees of directors, or summaries of actions of recent meetings for which minutes have not yet been prepared;
   - Additional information that you have requested from us for the purpose of the review; and
   - Unrestricted access to persons within the entity of whom you determined it necessary to make inquiries.

8. All transactions have been recorded in the accounting records and are reflected in the interim financial information.
9. We have disclosed to you all significant deficiencies or material weaknesses in the design or operation of internal control of which we are aware, as it relates to the preparation and fair presentation of both annual and interim financial information.
10. We have disclosed to you the results of our assessment of the risk that the interim financial information may be materially misstated as a result of fraud.
11. We have [*no knowledge of any*] [*disclosed to you all information of which we are aware in relation to*] fraud or suspected fraud that affects the entity and involves:

    - Management;
    - Employees who have significant roles in internal control; or
    - Others when the fraud could have a material effect on the interim financial information.

12. We have [*no knowledge of any*] [*disclosed to you all information in relation to*] allegations of fraud, or suspected fraud, affecting the entity's interim financial information communicated by employees, former employees, analysts, regulators, or others.
13. We have disclosed to you all known instances of noncompliance or suspected noncompliance with laws and regulations whose effects should be considered when preparing interim financial information.
14. There have been no communications from regulatory agencies concerning noncompliance with or deficiencies in financial reporting practices.
15. We have disclosed to you the identity of the entity's related parties and all the related-party relationships and transactions of which we are aware.

    [*Any other matters that the auditor may consider necessary*]

____

[*Name of chief executive officer and title*]

____

[*Name of chief financial officer and title*]

____

[*Name of chief accounting officer and title*]

Illustrations of Auditor's Review Reports on Interim Financial Information (Source: AU-C 930.A57)

1. A Review Report on Interim Financial Information
2. A Review Report on Condensed Comparative Interim Financial Information
3. A Review Report That Refers to a Component Auditor's Review Report on the Interim Financial Information of a Significant Component of a Reporting Entity
4. A Review Report on Comparative Interim Financial Information When the Prior Period Was Reviewed by Another Auditor

ILLUSTRATION 1. A REVIEW REPORT ON INTERIM FINANCIAL INFORMATION

Circumstances include the following:

- A review of interim financial information presented as a complete set of financial statements, including disclosures

Independent Auditor's Review Report

[*Appropriate addressee*]

Report on the Financial Statements

We have reviewed the accompanying [*describe the interim financial information or statements reviewed*] of ABC Company and subsidiaries as of September 30, 20X1, and for the three-month and nine-month periods then ended.

Management's Responsibility

The Company's management is responsible for the preparation and fair presentation of the interim financial information in accordance with [*identify the applicable financial reporting framework; for example, accounting principles generally accepted in the United States of America*]; this responsibility includes the design, implementation, and maintenance of internal control sufficient to provide a reasonable basis for the preparation and fair presentation of interim financial information in accordance with the applicable financial reporting framework.

Auditor's Responsibility

Our responsibility is to conduct our review in accordance with auditing standards generally accepted in the United States of America applicable to reviews of interim financial information. A review of interim financial information consists principally of applying analytical procedures and making inquiries of persons responsible for financial and accounting matters. It is substantially less in scope than an audit conducted in accordance with auditing standards generally accepted in the United States of America, the objective of which is the expression of an opinion regarding the financial information. Accordingly, we do not express such an opinion.

Conclusion

Based on our review, we are not aware of any material modifications that should be made to the accompanying interim financial information for it to be in accordance with [*identify the applicable financial reporting framework; for example, accounting principles generally accepted in the United States of America*].

[*Auditor's signature*]

[*Auditor's city and state*]

[*Date of the auditor's report*]

ILLUSTRATION 2. A REVIEW REPORT ON CONDENSED COMPARATIVE INTERIM FINANCIAL INFORMATION

The following is an example of a review report on a condensed balance sheet as of March 31, 20X1; the related condensed statements of income and cash flows for the three-month periods ended March 31, 20X1 and 20X0; and a condensed balance sheet derived from audited financial statements as of

December 31, 20X0. If the auditor's report on the preceding year-end financial statements was other than unmodified or included an emphasis-of-matter paragraph because of a going concern matter or an inconsistency in the application of accounting principles, the last paragraph of the illustrative report would be appropriately modified.

Independent Auditor's Review Report

[*Appropriate addressee*]

Report on the Financial Statements

We have reviewed the condensed consolidated financial statements of ABC Company and subsidiaries, which comprise the balance sheet as of March 31, 20X1, and the related condensed consolidated statements of income and cash flows for the three-month periods ended March 31, 20X1 and 20X0.

Management's Responsibility

The Company's management is responsible for the preparation and fair presentation of the condensed financial information in accordance with [*identify the applicable financial reporting framework; for example, accounting principles generally accepted in the United States of America*]; this responsibility includes the design, implementation, and maintenance of internal control sufficient to provide a reasonable basis for the preparation and fair presentation of interim financial information in accordance with the applicable financial reporting framework.

Auditor's Responsibility

Our responsibility is to conduct our reviews in accordance with auditing standards generally accepted in the United States of America applicable to reviews of interim financial information. A review of interim financial information consists principally of applying analytical procedures and making inquiries of persons responsible for financial and accounting matters. It is substantially less in scope than an audit conducted in accordance with auditing standards generally accepted in the United States of America, the objective of which is the expression of an opinion regarding the financial information. Accordingly, we do not express such an opinion.

Conclusion

Based on our reviews, we are not aware of any material modifications that should be made to the condensed financial information referred to above for it to be in accordance with [*identify the applicable financial reporting framework; for example, accounting principles generally accepted in the United States of America*].

***Report on Condensed Balance Sheet as of* [Date]**

We have previously audited, in accordance with auditing standards generally accepted in the United States of America, the consolidated balance sheet as of December 31, 20X0, and the related consolidated statements of income, changes in stockholders' equity, and cash flows for the year then ended (not presented herein); and we expressed an unmodified audit opinion on those audited consolidated financial statements in our report dated February 15, 20X1. In our opinion, the accompanying condensed consolidated balance sheet of ABC Company and subsidiaries as of December 31, 20X0, is consistent, in all material respects, with the audited consolidated financial statements from which it has been derived.

[*Auditor's signature*]

[*Auditor's city and state*]

[*Date of the auditor's report*]

ILLUSTRATION 3. A REVIEW REPORT THAT REFERS TO A COMPONENT AUDITOR'S REVIEW REPORT ON THE INTERIM FINANCIAL INFORMATION OF A SIGNIFICANT COMPONENT OF A REPORTING ENTITY

Circumstances include the following:

- A review of interim financial information presented as a complete set of financial statements, including disclosures.
- The auditor is making reference to another auditor's review report on the interim financial information of a significant component of a reporting entity.

Independent Auditor's Review Report

[*Appropriate addressee*]

Report on the Financial Statements

We have reviewed the accompanying [*describe the interim financial information or statements reviewed*] of ABC Company and subsidiaries as of September 30, 20X1, and for the three-month and nine-month periods then ended.

Management's Responsibility

The Company's management is responsible for the preparation and fair presentation of the interim financial information in accordance with [*identify the applicable financial reporting framework; for example, accounting principles generally accepted in the United States of America*]; this responsibility includes the design, implementation, and maintenance of internal control sufficient to provide a reasonable basis for the preparation and fair presentation of interim financial information in accordance with the applicable financial reporting framework.

Auditor's Responsibility

Our responsibility is to conduct our review in accordance with auditing standards generally accepted in the United States of America applicable to reviews of interim financial information. A review of interim financial information consists principally of applying analytical procedures and making inquiries of persons responsible for financial and accounting matters. It is substantially less in scope than an audit conducted in accordance with auditing standards generally accepted in the United States of America, the objective of which is the expression of an opinion regarding the financial information. Accordingly, we do not express such an opinion.

We were furnished with the report of other auditors on their review of the interim financial information of DEF subsidiary, whose total assets as of September 30, 20X1 and whose revenues for the three-month and nine-month periods then ended constituted 15%, 20%, and 22%, respectively, of the related consolidated totals.

Conclusion

Based on our review and the review report of other auditors, we are not aware of any material modifications that should be made to the accompanying interim financial information for it to be in accordance with [*identify the applicable financial reporting framework; for example, accounting principles generally accepted in the United States of America*].

[*Auditor's signature*]

[*Auditor's city and state*]

[*Date of the auditor's report*]

Illustration 4. A Review Report on Comparative Interim Financial Information When the Prior Period Was Reviewed by Another Auditor

Circumstances include the following:

- A review of interim financial information presented as a complete set of financial statements, including disclosures as of March 31, 20X1, and for the three-month period then ended.
- Comparative information is presented for the balance sheet as of December 31, 20X0, and for the statements of income and cash flows for the comparable interim period.
- The December 31, 20X0 financial statements were audited and the March 31, 20X0 interim financial information was reviewed by another auditor.

Independent Auditor's Review Report

[*Appropriate addressee*]

Report on the Financial Statements

We have reviewed the accompanying [*describe the interim financial information or statements reviewed*] of ABC Company and subsidiaries as of March 31, 20X1, and for the three-month period then ended. The consolidated statements of income and cash flows of ABC Company and subsidiaries for the three-month period ended March 31, 20X0 were reviewed by other auditors whose report dated June 1, 20X0 stated that based on their review, they were not aware of any material modifications that should be made to those statements in order for them to be in conformity with [*identify the applicable financial reporting framework; for example, accounting principles generally accepted in the United States of America*]. The consolidated balance sheet of the Company as of December 31, 20X0, and the related consolidated statements of income, changes in stockholders' equity, and cash flows for the year then ended (not presented herein), were audited by other auditors whose report dated March 15, 20X1 expressed an unmodified opinion on that statement.

Management's Responsibility

The Company's management is responsible for the preparation and fair presentation of the interim financial information in accordance with [*identify the applicable financial reporting framework; for example, accounting principles generally accepted in the United States of America*]; this responsibility includes the design, implementation, and maintenance of internal control sufficient to provide a reasonable basis for the preparation and fair presentation of interim financial information in accordance with the applicable financial reporting framework.

Auditor's Responsibility

Our responsibility is to conduct our review in accordance with auditing standards generally accepted in the United States of America applicable to reviews of interim financial information. A review of interim financial information consists principally of applying analytical procedures and making inquiries of persons responsible for financial and accounting matters. It is substantially less in scope than an audit conducted in accordance with auditing standards generally accepted in the United States of America, the objective of which is the expression of an opinion regarding the financial information. Accordingly, we do not express such an opinion.

Conclusion

Based on our review, we are not aware of any material modifications that should be made to the accompanying interim financial information as of and for the three months ended March 31, 20X1, for it to be in accordance with [*identify the applicable financial reporting framework; for example, accounting principles generally accepted in the United States of America*].

[*Auditor's signature*]

[*Auditor's city and state*]

[*Date of the auditor's report*]

Illustrations of Example Modifications to the Auditor's Review Report Due to Departures from the Applicable Financial Reporting Framework (AU-C 930.A58)

1. Modification Due to a Departure from the Applicable Financial Reporting Framework
2. Modification Due to Inadequate Disclosure
3. Emphasis-of-Matter Paragraph When a Going Concern Emphasis-of-Matter Paragraph Was Included in the Prior Year's Audit Report, and Conditions Giving Rise to the Emphasis-of-Matter Paragraph Continue to Exist
4. Emphasis-of-Matter Paragraph When a Going Concern Emphasis-of-Matter Paragraph Was Not Included in the Prior Year's Audit Report, and Conditions or Events Exist as of the Interim Reporting Date Covered by the Review That Might Be Indicative of the Entity's Possible Inability to Continue as a Going Concern

Illustration 1. Modification Due to a Departure from the Applicable Financial Reporting Framework

The following is an example of a modification of the auditor's review report due to a departure from the applicable financial reporting framework:

[*Basis for modification paragraph*]

Based on information furnished to us by management, we believe that the Company has excluded from property and debt in the accompanying balance sheet certain lease obligations that we believe should be capitalized to be in accordance with [*identify the applicable financial reporting framework; for example, accounting principles generally accepted in the United States of America*]. This information indicates that if these lease obligations were capitalized at September 30, 20X1, property would be increased by $_____, long-term debt would be increased by $_____, and net income would be increased (decreased) by $_____ and $_____, respectively, for the three-month and nine-month periods then ended.

[*Conclusion*]

Based on our review, with the exception of the matter(s) described in the preceding paragraph(s), we are not aware of any material modifications that should be made to the accompanying interim financial information for it to be in accordance with [*identify the applicable financial reporting framework; for example, accounting principles generally accepted in the United States of America*].

Illustration 2. Modification Due to Inadequate Disclosure

The following is an example of a modification of the auditor's review report due to inadequate disclosure:

[*Basis for modification paragraph*]

Management has informed us that the Company is presently defending a claim regarding [*describe the nature of the loss contingency*] and that the extent of the Company's liability, if any, and the effect on the accompanying interim financial information are not determinable at this time. The interim financial information fails to disclose these matters, which we believe are required to be disclosed in accordance with [*identify the applicable financial reporting framework; for example, accounting principles generally accepted in the United States of America*].

[*Conclusion*]

Based on our review, with the exception of the matter(s) described in the preceding paragraph(s), we are not aware of any material modifications that should be made to the accompanying interim financial information for it to be in accordance with [*identify the applicable financial reporting framework; for example, accounting principles generally accepted in the United States of America*].

Illustration 3. Emphasis-of-Matter Paragraph When a Going Concern Emphasis-of-Matter Paragraph Was Included in the Prior Year's Audit Report, and Conditions Giving Rise to the Emphasis-of-Matter Paragraph Continue to Exist

The following is an example of an emphasis-of-matter paragraph when a going concern emphasis-of-matter paragraph was included in the prior year's audit report, and conditions giving rise to the emphasis-of-matter paragraph continue to exist:

[*Emphasis-of-matter paragraph*]

Note 4 of the Company's audited financial statements as of December 31, 20X1, and for the year then ended, discloses that the Company was unable to renew its line of credit or obtain alternative financing at December 31, 20X1. Our auditor's report on those financial statements includes an emphasis-of-matter paragraph referring to the matters in note 4 of those financial statements and indicating that these matters raised substantial doubt about the Company's ability to continue as a going concern. As indicated in note 3 of the Company's unaudited interim financial information as of March 31, 20X2, and for the three months then ended, the Company was still unable to renew its line of credit or obtain alternative financing as of March 31, 20X2. The accompanying interim financial information does not include any adjustments that might result from the outcome of this uncertainty.

Illustration 4. Emphasis-of-Matter Paragraph When a Going Concern Emphasis-of-Matter Paragraph Was Not Included in the Prior Year's Audit Report, and Conditions or Events Exist as of the Interim Reporting Date Covered by the Review That Might Be Indicative of the Entity's Possible Inability to Continue as a Going Concern

The following is an example of an emphasis-of-matter paragraph when a going concern emphasis-of-matter paragraph was not included in the prior year's audit report, and conditions or events exist as of the interim reporting date covered by the review that might be indicative of the entity's possible inability to continue as a going concern:

[*Emphasis-of-matter paragraph*]

As indicated in note 3, certain conditions indicate that the Company may be unable to continue as a going concern. The accompanying interim financial information does not include any adjustments that might result from the outcome of this uncertainty.

AU-C 935 Compliance Audits

AU-C ORIGINAL PRONOUNCEMENTS

Sources Statements on Auditing Standards (SASs) 117, 122, 123, 125, and 130.

TECHNICAL ALERT

In October 2015, the Auditing Standards Board (ASB) issued SAS No. 130. SAS No. 130 contains amendments to this section. Any relevant changes are incorporated into the information that follows.

AU-C 935 DEFINITIONS OF TERMS

Source: AU-C 935.11

Applicable compliance requirements. Compliance requirements that are subject to the compliance audit.

Audit findings. The matters that are required to be reported by the auditor in accordance with the governmental audit requirement.

Audit risk of noncompliance. The risk that the auditor expresses an inappropriate audit opinion on the entity's compliance when material noncompliance exists. Audit risk of noncompliance is a function of the risks of material noncompliance and detection risk of noncompliance.

Compliance audit. A program-specific audit or an organization-wide audit of an entity's compliance with applicable compliance requirements.

Compliance requirements. Laws, regulations, rules, and provisions of contracts or grant agreements applicable to government programs with which the entity is required to comply.

Deficiency in internal control over compliance. A deficiency in internal control over compliance exists when the design or operation of a control over compliance does not allow management or employees, in the normal course of performing their assigned functions, to prevent, or detect and correct, noncompliance on a timely basis. A deficiency in *design* exists when (1) a control necessary to meet the control objective is missing, or (2) an existing control is not properly designed so that, even if the control operates as designed, the control objective would not be met. A deficiency in *operation* exists when a properly designed control does not operate as designed or the person performing the control does not possess the necessary authority or competence to perform the control effectively.

Detection risk of noncompliance. The risk that the procedures performed by the auditor to reduce audit risk of noncompliance to an acceptably low level will not detect noncompliance that exists and that could be material, either individually or when aggregated with other instances of noncompliance.

Government Auditing Standards. Standards and guidance issued by the Comptroller General of the United States, US Government Accountability Office for financial audits, attestation engagements, and performance audits. Government Auditing Standards also are known as generally accepted government auditing standards (GAGAS) or the "Yellow Book."

Government program. The means by which governmental entities achieve their objectives. For example, one of the objectives of the US Department of Agriculture is to provide nutrition to individuals in need. Examples of government programs designed to achieve that objective are the Supplemental Nutrition Assistance Program and the National School Lunch Program. Government programs that are relevant to this section are those in which a grantor or pass-through entity provides an award to another entity, usually in the form of a grant, contract, or other agreement. Not all government programs provide cash assistance; sometimes noncash assistance is provided (for example, a loan guarantee, commodities, or property).

Governmental audit requirement. A government requirement established by law, regulation, rule, or provision of contracts or grant agreements requiring that an entity undergo an audit of its compliance with applicable compliance requirements related to one or more government programs that the entity administers.

Grantor. A government agency from which funding for the government program originates.

Known questioned costs. Questioned costs specifically identified by the auditor. Known questioned costs are a subset of likely questioned costs.

Likely questioned costs. The auditor's best estimate of total questioned costs, not just the known questioned costs. Likely questioned costs are developed by extrapolating from audit evidence obtained, for example, by projecting known questioned costs identified in an audit sample to the entire population from which the sample was drawn.

Material noncompliance. In the absence of a definition of material noncompliance in the governmental audit requirement, a failure to follow compliance requirements or a violation of prohibitions included in the applicable compliance requirements that results in noncompliance that is quantitatively or qualitatively material, either individually or when aggregated with other noncompliance, to the affected government program.

Material weakness in internal control over compliance. A deficiency, or combination of deficiencies, in internal control over compliance, such that there is a reasonable possibility that material noncompliance with a compliance requirement will not be prevented, or detected and corrected, on a timely basis. In this section, a reasonable possibility exists when the likelihood of an event occurring is either reasonably possible or probable as defined as follows:

- **Reasonably possible.** The chance of the future event or events occurring is more than remote but less than likely.
- **Probable.** The future event or events are likely to occur.

Organization-wide audit. An audit of an entity's financial statements and an audit of its compliance with the applicable compliance requirements as they relate to one or more government programs that the entity administers.

Pass-through entity. An entity that receives an award from a grantor or other entity and distributes all or part of it to another entity to administer a government program.

Program-specific audit. An audit of an entity's compliance with applicable compliance requirements as they relate to one government program that the entity administers. The compliance audit portion of a program-specific audit is performed in conjunction with either an audit of the entity's or the program's financial statements.

Questioned costs. Costs that are questioned by the auditor because (1) there is a violation or possible violation of the applicable compliance requirements, (2) the costs are not supported by adequate documentation, or (3) the incurred costs appear unreasonable and do not reflect the actions that a prudent person would take in the circumstances.

Risk of material noncompliance. The risk that material noncompliance exists prior to the audit. This consists of two components:

- **Inherent risk of noncompliance.** The susceptibility of a compliance requirement to noncompliance that could be material, either individually or when aggregated with other instances of noncompliance, before consideration of any related controls over compliance.
- **Control risk of noncompliance.** The risk that noncompliance with a compliance requirement that could occur and that could be material, either individually or when aggregated with other instances of noncompliance, will not be prevented, or detected and corrected, on a timely basis by the entity's internal control over compliance.

Significant deficiency in internal control over compliance. A deficiency, or a combination of deficiencies, in internal control over compliance that is less severe than a material weakness in internal control over compliance, yet important enough to merit attention by those charged with governance.

OBJECTIVES OF AU-C SECTION 935

AU-C Section 935-10 states that:

. . . the auditor's objectives in a compliance audit are to

a. obtain sufficient appropriate audit evidence to form an opinion and report at the level specified in the governmental audit requirement on whether the entity complied in all material respects with the applicable compliance requirements; and

b. identify audit and reporting requirements specified in the governmental audit requirement that are supplementary to GAAS and Government Auditing Standards, if any, and perform procedures to address those requirements.

SCOPE

AU-C 935 applies to engagements to perform a compliance audit in accordance with generally accepted auditing standards (GAAS), the standards for financial audits under government auditing standards, or a governmental audit requirement that requires an auditor to express an opinion on compliance. It is not applicable when governmental audit requirements call for an examination under the Statements on Standards for Attestation Engagements (SSAEs) of an entity's internal controls over compliance. (AU-C 935.02-.03)

REQUIREMENTS

Application of AU-C Sections to a Compliance Audit

The auditor should adapt all AU-C Sections to the objectives of a compliance audit, with limited exceptions as listed in Illustration 1 at the end of this chapter. (AU-C 935.04)

Sources of Information Regarding Compliance Requirements

To gain an understanding of applicable compliance requirements, consult *The Compliance Supplement*, which is issued by the US Office of Management and Budget. It contains the compliance requirements applicable to many federal government programs. It also includes a number of sample audit procedures that are applicable to compliance requirements. The grantor agency may also have issued a program-specific audit guide that similarly contains compliance requirements and suggested audit procedures. (AU-C 935.A1)

Suggested Audit Procedures

If *The Compliance Supplement* or a program-specific audit guide is not available, the auditor may use the following procedures to obtain an understanding of the applicable compliance requirements:

1. Read the laws, regulations, rules, and contract provisions pertaining to the government program.
2. Make inquiries of management and other knowledgeable entity personnel.
3. Make inquiries of individuals outside the entity, such as government auditors, regulators, third-party specialists, and attorneys, regarding the laws and regulations applicable to entities within their jurisdictions.
4. Read the meeting minutes of the entity's governing body.
5. Read the audit documentation about applicable compliance requirements that were prepared during prior audits.
6. Discuss applicable compliance requirements with the auditors who performed prior audits.

(AU-C 935.A11)

Management's Responsibilities

Management is responsible for an entity's compliance with compliance requirements. This responsibility includes:

- *Compliance.* Comply with the compliance requirements of government programs.
- *Controls.* Maintain a control system that gives reasonable assurance that the entity administers government programs that are in compliance with compliance requirements.
- *Monitoring.* Evaluate and monitor compliance with the compliance requirements.
- *Corrective action.* Take corrective action in the event of noncompliance.

(AU-C 935.08)

The Compliance Audit Process Flow

The auditor should follow these steps when conducting a compliance audit:

1. *Materiality.* Establish material levels and apply them to the compliance audit based on the governmental audit requirements. (AU-C 935.13)

2. *Identification of programs.* Determine which government programs and compliance requirements to test. (AU-C 935.14)
3. *Performing procedures.* Perform risk assessment procedures to gain a sufficient understanding of the applicable compliance requirements and the entity's internal control over compliance. (AU-C 935.15) Also see if there are findings from previous audits, attestation engagements, or other monitoring that relate to the compliance audit. Additionally, gain an understanding of management's response to these findings that could have a material effect on the entity's compliance with applicable compliance requirements. Use this information to assess risk, as well as to determine the audit procedures for the compliance audit. (AU-C 935.16)
4. *Risk assessment.* Assess the risks of material noncompliance, whether due to fraud or to error, for each applicable compliance requirement. (AU-C 935.16)
5. *Material noncompliance risk.* Assess the risk of material noncompliance, whether due to fraud or to error, for each compliance requirement. (AU-C 935.17)
6. *Further audit procedures.* If there are risks of material noncompliance that are pervasive, then develop an overall response to these risks. (AU-C 935.18) The response should include further audit procedures, including tests of details, to obtain sufficient audit evidence. Tests of controls, analytical procedures, and risk assessment procedures are not sufficient. Test controls over compliance if there is an expectation of the operating effectiveness of controls over compliance, if substantive procedures alone do not provide sufficient evidence, or if these tests are mandated by a governmental audit requirement. (AU-C 935.19-.20)

NOTE: Sample tests of details can include the areas of grant disbursements or expenditures, eligibility files, cost allocation plans, and periodic reports filed with grantor agencies.

---

7. *Supplementary audit steps.* Determine if the governmental audit requirements include audit requirements that are in addition to GAAS and government auditing standards, and perform those procedures. If these requirements conflict with GAAS or government auditing standards, then use the GAAS or government auditing standards. (AU-C 935.21-.22)
8. *Written representations.* Request from management written representations that align with the governmental audit requirements. Include the following items in the request:

   a. Acknowledge management's responsibility for understanding and complying with the pertinent compliance requirements.
   b. Acknowledge management's responsibility for a system of controls that provides reasonable assurance of administering government programs as per their compliance requirements.
   c. State that management has identified and disclosed all of the programs related to the governmental audit requirements.
   d. State that management has made available all contracts and related correspondence relevant to the programs subject to the governmental audit requirements.
   e. State that management has disclosed all known noncompliance, or that there is no noncompliance.

f. State whether management believes the entity has complied with the compliance requirements.
g. State that management has made available all documentation related to compliance with the applicable compliance requirements.
h. State management's interpretation of compliance requirements that are subject to interpretation.
i. State that management has disclosed any grantor communications concerning possible noncompliance, through the date of the auditor's report.
j. State that management has disclosed the findings and related corrective actions taken for previous audits, attestation engagements, and monitoring related to the objectives of the compliance audit, through the date of the auditor's report.
k. State that management has disclosed all noncompliance with the compliance requirements subsequent to the period covered by the auditor's report, or state that there were no such cases.
l. State that management is responsible for taking corrective action on audit findings arising from the compliance audit.

(AU-C 935.23)

9. *Subsequent events.* Perform audit procedures through the date of the auditor's report to obtain evidence that subsequent events related to the entity's compliance have been identified. (AU-C 935.25)

NOTE: If the auditor becomes aware of noncompliance in the period subsequent to the report date that is of such significance that report users would be misled without this information (such as the discovery of noncompliance of such size that the grantor halted funding), then the auditor should discuss the matter with management and those charged with governance, and explain the noncompliance in an other-matters paragraph in the report. (AU-C 935.27)

---

10. *Evaluate evidence.* Evaluate the sufficiency and appropriateness of audit evidence. Then form an opinion on whether the entity materially complied with the compliance requirements. As part of this evaluation, review likely questioned costs, as well as known questioned costs. (AU-C 935.28)

NOTE: When evaluating evidence, the auditor can consider the frequency of noncompliance identified during the audit, the nature of the noncompliance, the adequacy of the entity's system for monitoring compliance, the effect of noncompliance on the entity, and whether any identified noncompliance with the applicable compliance requirements resulted in likely questioned costs that are material. (AU-C 935.29)

Material Noncompliance Risks

The auditor may consider the following factors when assessing the risks of material noncompliance:

1. Complexity of the applicable compliance requirements
2. Susceptibility of the applicable compliance requirements to noncompliance

3. The time period during which the entity has been subjected to the applicable compliance requirements
4. Observations about how the entity has complied with the requirements in prior years
5. The potential effect on the entity of noncompliance with the requirements
6. The degree of judgment involved in adhering to the compliance requirements
7. The assessment of the risks of material misstatement in the financial statement audit

(AU-C 935.A16)

Reporting Requirements

There are three types of compliance reports, which are (1) the report on compliance only, (2) the combined report on compliance and internal control over compliance, and (3) the separate report on internal control over compliance. The contents of these reports follow.

Report on compliance only. If the auditor is only reporting on compliance, then the report must:

- Have a title containing the word *independent.*
- Identify the government programs covered by the compliance audit.
- State the compliance requirements.
- State the period covered by the report.
- State that compliance with the compliance requirements is the responsibility of management.
- State that the auditor's responsibility is to express an opinion on the entity's compliance with the applicable compliance requirements, which is based on the compliance audit.
- State that the compliance audit was conducted in accordance with GAS, the standards applicable to financial audits in government accounting standards, and the governmental audit requirements.
- State that the compliance audit included an examination of evidence about the entity's compliance with such requirements, as well as other procedures considered necessary by the auditor.
- State that the auditor believes the compliance audit provides a reasonable basis for an opinion.
- State that the compliance audit does not provide a legal determination of the entity's compliance.
- State an opinion, at the level required by the governmental audit requirements, regarding whether the entity materially complied with the compliance requirements.
- If there is an opinion modification due to noncompliance, describe the noncompliance.
- If there is noncompliance that does not result in an opinion modification, describe it.
- Include the signature of the auditor's firm and the city and state where the auditor practices.
- Include the date of the report.

(AU-C 935.30)

Combined report on compliance and internal control over compliance. If the auditor combines the auditor's report on compliance with a report on internal control over compliance, then add the following items to the report just described for a report on compliance only:

- State that management is responsible for internal controls over compliance with the requirements of laws, regulations, rules, and contract provisions applicable to government programs.
- State that the auditor considered the entity's internal control over compliance with the applicable compliance requirements while planning and performing the audit, but only to determine procedures for expressing an opinion on compliance—not for expressing an opinion on the effectiveness of internal controls over compliance.
- State that the auditor is not expressing an opinion on internal control over compliance.
- State that the auditor's considerations were not designed to identify all deficiencies in internal control that might be significant deficiencies or material weaknesses in internal control over compliance.
- Define a "deficiency in internal control over compliance" and "material weakness in internal control over compliance."
- Describe identified material weaknesses in internal control over compliance.
- If there were significant deficiencies in internal controls over compliance, define "significant deficiency in internal control over compliance" and describe the deficiencies.
- If there were no material weaknesses in internal control over compliance, make a statement to that effect.
- If the report is developed solely for specific parties, state that the report is intended solely for the use of the specified parties, and that it is not intended for use by any other parties.

Separate report on internal control over compliance. If the auditor is required by the governmental audit requirements to report on internal control over compliance, and the auditor elects to issue a separate report on this matter, then add the following items to the report just described for a combined report on compliance and internal control over compliance:

- A title containing the word *independent*.
- A statement that the auditor audited the entity's compliance with the applicable compliance requirements for the named government program and specified time period, and refer to the auditor's report on compliance.
- A statement that the compliance audit was conducted in accordance with GAAS, those government auditing standards applicable to financial audits, and the governmental audit requirement.
- The signature of the auditor's firm.
- The date of the report.

(AU-C 935.32)

The auditor should also report noncompliance in the manner specified by the governmental audit requirements. Further, if the auditor communicates significant deficiencies or material weaknesses in internal control over compliance, government auditing standards require the auditor to obtain a response from the responsible officials regarding their views on the findings, conclusions, and recommendations in the auditor's report, and to include a copy of any written response in the auditor's report. (AU-C 935.33)

The auditor should modify his or her opinion on compliance in accordance with Section 705, *Modifications to the Opinion in the Independent Auditor's Reports*, if the audit identifies material noncompliance, or a restriction on the compliance audit's scope. (AU-C 935.34)

NOTE: If there is no governmental audit requirement to report on internal control over compliance, the auditor should still report significant deficiencies and material weaknesses in internal control over compliance to both management and those charged with governance.

In addition to the reporting noted above, the auditor should report to those charged with governance the auditor's responsibilities as noted in GAAS, government auditing standards, and the governmental audit requirements. This report should also include an overview of the planned scope and timing of the compliance audit, as well as significant findings arising from it.

NOTE: If a government agency has provided a report format that requires the auditor to make a statement for which there is no basis, reword the report or attach a properly worded separate report.

If the auditor reissues the report, include in it a note that the report replaces an earlier report, and explain why the report is replacing the prior report, as well as the changes from the prior report. Update the date of the reissued report if additional procedures were performed.

Documentation

The auditor should document all risk assessment procedures performed, as well as any responses to assessed risks of material noncompliance, any procedures performed to test compliance with the applicable compliance requirements, and the results of those procedures. Further, document materiality levels and the basis on which they were calculated. (AU-C 935.39-.42)

Reissuance of the Compliance Report

A reissued report should include an other-matter paragraph:

- Stating that the report is replacing a previously issued report,
- Describing the reasons why the report is being reissued, and
- Stating any changes from the previously issued report.

Dating a reissued report. The auditor's report date should be updated to reflect the date the auditor obtained sufficient appropriate audit evidence regarding the events that caused the auditor to perform the new procedures, if additional procedures are performed for all of the government programs being reported on.

If the additional procedures are performed to obtain sufficient appropriate audit evidence for only *some* of the government programs, the auditor should dual date the report. The updated report date should be the date the auditor obtained sufficient appropriate audit evidence regarding the government programs affected by the circumstances and referencing the government programs for which additional audit procedures have been performed. Reissuance of an auditor-prepared document required by the governmental audit requirement that is incorporated by reference into the auditor's report is considered to be a reissuance of the report. (AU-C 935.43)

AU-C ILLUSTRATIONS

ILLUSTRATION 1. AU-C SECTIONS THAT ARE NOT APPLICABLE TO COMPLIANCE AUDITS

AU-C Section	*Paragraphs Not Applicable to Compliance Audits*
210, *Terms of Engagement*	Paragraphs .06a and .08a
240, *Consideration of Fraud in a Financial Statement Audit*	Paragraphs .26 and .32b
250, *Consideration of Laws and Regulations in an Audit of Financial Statements*	All
315, *Understanding the Entity and Its Environment and Assessing the Risks of Material Misstatement*	Paragraphs .12c, .26–.27, and .33c
330, *Performing Audit Procedures in Response to Assessed Risks and Evaluating the Audit Evidence Obtained*	Paragraphs .13–.14, .19–.21, .26, and .31–.32
501, *Audit Evidence—Specific Considerations for Selected Items*	All
505, *External Confirmations*	All
510, *Opening Balances—Initial Audit Engagements, Including Reaudit Engagements*	Paragraphs .06, .08–.13, and .15–.17
540, *Auditing Accounting Estimates, Including Fair Value Accounting Estimates, and Related Disclosures*	All
550, *Related Parties*	All
560, *Subsequent Events and Subsequently Discovered Facts*	Paragraphs .09–.11 and .19–.20
570, *The Auditor's Consideration of an Entity's Ability to Continue as a Going Concern*	All
600, *Special Considerations—Audits of Group Financial Statements (Including the Work of Component Auditors)*	Paragraphs .25a, .38, .40c, .54, and .55c
700, *Forming an Opinion and Reporting on Financial Statements*	Paragraphs .14–.18, .21–.41, and .44–.58
705, *Modifications to the Opinion in the Independent Auditor's Report*	Paragraphs .18–.20
706, *Emphasis-of-Matter Paragraphs and Other-Matter Paragraphs in the Independent Auditor's Report*	Paragraphs .06–.07
708, *Consistency of Financial Statements*	All
720, *Other Information in Documents Containing Audited Financial Statements*	All
725, *Supplementary Information in Relation to the Financial Statements as a Whole*	All
730, *Required Supplementary Information*	All

800, *Special Considerations—Audits of Financial Statements Prepared in Accordance with Special Purpose Frameworks*	All
805, *Special Considerations—Audits of Single Financial Statements and Specific Elements, Accounts, or Items of a Financial Statement*	All
806, *Reporting on Compliance with Aspects of Contractual Agreements or Regulatory Requirements in Connection with Audited Financial Statements*	All
810, *Engagements to Report on Summary Financial Statements*	All
910, *Financial Statements Prepared in Accordance with a Financial Reporting Framework Generally Accepted in Another Country*	All
915, *Reports on Application of Requirements of an Applicable Financial Reporting Framework*	All
920, *Letters for Underwriters and Certain Other Requesting Parties*	All
925, *Filings with the US Securities and Exchange Commission under the Securities Act of 1933*	All
930, *Interim Financial Information*	All
940, *An Audit of Internal Control over Financial Reporting That Is Integrated with an Audit of Financial Statements*	All

ILLUSTRATION 2. ILLUSTRATIVE COMBINED REPORT ON COMPLIANCE WITH APPLICABLE REQUIREMENTS AND INTERNAL CONTROL OVER COMPLIANCE (UNMODIFIED OPINION ON COMPLIANCE; NO MATERIAL WEAKNESSES OR SIGNIFICANT DEFICIENCIES IN INTERNAL CONTROL OVER COMPLIANCE IDENTIFIED) (SOURCE: AU-C 935.A42)

The following is an illustrative combined report on compliance with applicable requirements and internal control over compliance that contains the elements in paragraphs .30–.31. This illustrative report contains an unmodified opinion on compliance with no material weaknesses or significant deficiencies in internal control over compliance identified. The AICPA Audit Guide Government Auditing Standards and Circular A-133 Audits contains illustrative language for other types of reports, including reports containing qualified or adverse opinions on compliance with either material weaknesses in internal control over compliance, significant deficiencies in internal control over compliance, or both identified.

Independent Auditor's Report

[*Addressee*]

Compliance

We have audited Example Entity's compliance with the [*identify the applicable compliance requirements or refer to the document that describes the applicable compliance requirements*] applicable to Example Entity's [*identify the government program(s) audited or refer to a separate schedule that identifies the program(s)*] for the year ended June 30, 20X1.

Management's Responsibility

Compliance with the requirements referred to above is the responsibility of Example Entity's management.

Auditor's Responsibility

Our responsibility is to express an opinion on Example Entity's compliance based on our audit.

We conducted our audit of compliance in accordance with auditing standards generally accepted in the United States of America, the standards applicable to financial audits contained in Government Auditing Standards issued by the Comptroller General of the United States, and [*insert the name of the governmental audit requirement or program-specific audit guide*]. Those standards and [*insert the name of the governmental audit requirement or program-specific audit guide*] require that we plan and perform the audit to obtain reasonable assurance about whether noncompliance with the compliance requirements referred to above that could have a material effect on [*identify the government program(s) audited or refer to a separate schedule that identifies the program(s)*] occurred. An audit includes examining, on a test basis, evidence about Example Entity's compliance with those requirements and performing such other procedures as we considered necessary in the circumstances. We believe that our audit provides a reasonable basis for our opinion. Our audit does not provide a legal determination of Example Entity's compliance with those requirements.

Opinion

In our opinion, Example Entity complied, in all material respects, with the compliance requirements referred to above that are applicable to [*identify the government program(s) audited*] for the year ended June 30, 20X1.

Internal Control over Compliance

Management of Example Entity is responsible for establishing and maintaining effective internal control over compliance with the compliance requirements referred to above. In planning and performing our audit, we considered Example Entity's internal control over compliance to determine the auditing procedures for the purpose of expressing our opinion on compliance, but not for the purpose of expressing an opinion on the effectiveness of internal control over compliance. Accordingly, we do not express an opinion on the effectiveness of Example Entity's internal control over compliance.

A deficiency in internal control over compliance exists when the design or operation of a control does not allow management or employees, in the normal course of performing their assigned functions, to prevent, or detect and correct, noncompliance on a timely basis. A material weakness in internal control over compliance is a deficiency, or combination of deficiencies in internal control over compliance, such that there is a reasonable possibility that material noncompliance with a compliance requirement will not be prevented, or detected and corrected, on a timely basis.

Our consideration of internal control over compliance was for the limited purpose described in the first paragraph of this section and was not designed to identify all deficiencies in internal control that might be deficiencies, significant deficiencies, or material weaknesses in internal control over compliance. We did not identify any deficiencies in internal control over compliance that we consider to be material weaknesses, as defined above.

The purpose of this report on internal control over compliance is solely to describe the scope of our testing of internal control over compliance and the results of that testing based on the [*insert the name of the governmental audit requirement or program-specific audit guide*]. Accordingly, this report is not suitable for any other purpose.

[*Signature*]

[*Auditor's city and state*]

[*Date*]

AU-C 940 An Audit of Internal Control over Financial Reporting That Is Integrated with an Audit of Financial Statements

AU-C ORIGINAL PRONOUNCEMENT

Source Statement on Auditing Standards (SAS) 130.

TECHNICAL ALERT

In October 2015, the Auditing Standards Board (ASB) released SAS No. 130, *An Audit of Internal Control over Financial Reporting That Is Integrated with an Audit of Financial Statements.* The SAS is effective for integrated audits for periods ending on or after December 15, 2016. SAS No. 130 is an outgrowth of the Attestation Standards Clarity Project and replaces AT 501 and its Interpretation 1. The ASB concluded that because AT 501 engagements must be integrated with an audit of financial statements, the content of AT 501 should be moved into generally accepted auditing standards (GAAS). AT 501 is withdrawn when SAS No. 130 becomes effective.

The new standard tracks closely with AT 501 and Public Company Accounting Oversight Board (PCAOB) AS No. 5 and requires the auditor to examine and report directly on the effectiveness of internal control over financial reporting (ICFR). It eliminates the option to examine and report on management's assessment about the effectiveness of ICFR; the auditor must examine and report directly on the effectiveness of ICFR.

AU-C 940 DEFINITIONS OF TERMS

Source: AU-C 940.05

Audit of ICFR. An audit of the design and operating effectiveness of an entity's internal control over financial reporting (ICFR).

Control objective. The aim or purpose of specified controls. Control objectives address the risks that the controls are intended to mitigate. In the context of ICFR, a control objective generally relates to a relevant assertion for a significant class of transactions, account balance, or disclosure and addresses the risk that the controls in a specific area will not provide reasonable assurance that a misstatement or omission in that relevant assertion is prevented, or detected and corrected, on a timely basis.

Criteria. The benchmarks used to measure or evaluate the subject matter. (Ref: par. .A5)

Detective control. A control that has the objective of detecting and correcting errors or fraud that have already occurred that could result in a misstatement of the financial statements.

Internal control over financial reporting (ICFR). A process effected by those charged with governance, management, and other personnel, designed to provide reasonable assurance regarding the preparation of reliable financial statements in accordance with the applicable financial reporting framework. ICFR includes those policies and procedures that:

i. Pertain to the maintenance of records that, in reasonable detail, accurately and fairly reflect the transactions and dispositions of the assets of the entity;
ii. Provide reasonable assurance that transactions are recorded as necessary to permit preparation of financial statements in accordance with the applicable financial reporting framework, and that receipts and expenditures of the entity are being made only in accordance with authorizations of management and those charged with governance; and
iii. Provide reasonable assurance regarding prevention, or timely detection and correction of unauthorized acquisition, use, or disposition of the entity's assets that could have a material effect on the financial statements.

ICFR has inherent limitations. It is a process that involves human diligence and compliance and is subject to lapses in judgment and breakdowns resulting from human failures. ICFR also can be circumvented by collusion or improper management override. Because of such limitations, there is a risk that material misstatements will not be prevented, or detected and corrected, on a timely basis by ICFR. (Ref: par. .A6–.A7)

Management's assessment about ICFR. Management's conclusion about the effectiveness of the entity's ICFR, based on suitable and available criteria. Management's assessment is included in management's report on ICFR. (Ref: par. .A8)

Preventive control. A control that has the objective of preventing errors or fraud that could result in a misstatement of the financial statements.

AU-C 940 OBJECTIVES

AU-C Section 940.04 states that the objectives of the auditor in an audit of ICFR are:

a. obtain reasonable assurance about whether material weaknesses exist as of the date specified in management's assessment about the effectiveness of ICFR (as of date) and

b. express an opinion on the effectiveness of ICFR in a written report, and communicate with management and those charged with governance as required by this section, based on the auditor's findings. (Ref: par. .A2–.A4)

SCOPE

AU-C 940 guidance applies only when:

- An auditor is engaged to perform an audit of ICFR, and
- That audit is integrated with the financial statements audit (integrated audit).

(AU-C 940.01)

REQUIREMENTS

The auditor's objective is to form an opinion on the effectiveness of an entity's ICFR. An entity's ICFR cannot be considered effective if a material weakness exists, so the auditor should plan to obtain sufficient evidence to obtain reasonable assurance about whether material weaknesses exist as of the date of management's assessment regarding ICFR. The auditor does not have to search for deficiencies that are less severe than a material weakness.

REQUIRED CONDITIONS FOR ENGAGEMENT ACCEPTANCE

The following conditions should be present for the auditor to accept the engagement to audit the effectiveness of an entity's internal control:

1. Management accepts responsibility for designing, implementing, and maintaining the effectiveness of the entity's ICFR.
2. Management evaluates the effectiveness of the entity's ICFR using suitable and available criteria.
3. Management supports its assessment about the effectiveness of ICFR with sufficient evidence and documentation.
4. Management provides a written assessment that accompanies the auditor's report containing its assessment of the entity's ICFR.
5. Management provides the auditor with:

    a. Access to all relevant information,
    b. Additional information the auditor may request, and
    c. Unrestricted access to internal staff from whom the auditor deems it necessary to obtain audit evidence.

6. The auditor determines that the as-of date is the same as the balance sheet date.

(AU-C 940.06)

When evaluating management's assessment, the auditor must use the same suitable and available criteria as was used by management. (AU-C 940.07)

If management refuses to provide a written assessment, the auditor should withdraw from the engagement. (AU-C 940.08) Withdrawal is *not* required if the engagement is required by law or regulation. In that case, the auditor should disclaim an opinion on ICFR. (AU-C 940.74)

EVIDENCE SUPPORTING MANAGEMENT'S ASSESSMENT

Management is responsible for documenting controls, which can be in the form of policy and procedure manuals, flowcharts, and decision tables. Management can also undertake ongoing monitoring activities to assess the effectiveness of ICFRs, report deficiencies, and take corrective actions. Both documentation and ongoing monitoring activities form the foundation for management's assessment regarding ICFR. (AU-C 940.A11-.A12)

INTEGRATING THE CONTROLS EXAMINATION WITH THE FINANCIAL STATEMENT AUDIT

The examination of ICFR should be integrated with the audit, such that the objectives of both engagements can be achieved at the same time. To do so, the auditor should design tests of controls that obtain sufficient evidence to support the auditor's opinion on ICFR, as well as the control risk assessments for the audit. (AU-C 940.09)

Risk Assessment

The auditor should devote the most attention to those areas where a material weakness could exist in an entity's ICFR. It is not necessary to test controls that would not present a reasonable possibility of material misstatement, even if those controls are deficient. (AU-C 940.15) The auditor must plan procedures based on the size and complexity of the organization, its business processes, and business units.

The auditor's planning should also include the results of the fraud risk assessment performed in the audit. The auditor should also evaluate whether the entity's controls adequately address the risk of misstatement due to fraud, and of management override of other controls. (AU-C 940.16) Examples of controls that can address these risks include:

- Controls over significant transactions, especially those resulting in late or unusual journal entries;
- Controls over journal entries made in the period-end closing process;
- Controls over related-party transactions;
- Controls related to significant estimates by management; and
- Controls that change management's willingness to inappropriately manage financial results.

(AU-C 940.A25)

Using the Work of Others

In the examination of ICFR, the auditor may use the work performed by internal auditors and other entity personnel, as well as third parties. The auditor's assessment of this work should include a review of the competence and objectivity of the individuals involved. *Competence* means the attainment and maintenance of a level of understanding, knowledge, and skill enabling a person to perform the tasks assigned to him or her, and *objectivity* means the ability to perform those tasks impartially and with intellectual honesty. (AU-C 940.A27)

The extent to which the auditor uses the work of others depends on the risk associated with the control being tested. As the risk increases, the auditor should rely more on his or her own work. (AU-C 940.A28)

Planning the Engagement

In planning the engagement, the auditor should consider factors such as the following:

1. Knowledge of the entity's ICFR obtained during other professional engagements
2. Matters affecting the industry in which the entity operates, such as financial reporting practices, economic conditions, laws and regulations, and technological changes
3. Matters relating to the entity's business, including its organization, operating characteristics, capital structure, and distribution methods
4. The extent of recent changes, if any, in the entity, its operations, or its ICFR
5. Preliminary judgments about materiality levels, inherent risk, and other factors relating to the determination of material weaknesses
6. Deficiencies previously communicated to those charged with governance
7. Legal or regulatory issues of which the entity is aware
8. The type and extent of evidential matter pertaining to the effectiveness of the entity's ICFR

9. Preliminary judgments about the effectiveness of ICFR
10. Public information about the entity impacting the evaluation of misstatements and the effectiveness of ICFR
11. Knowledge of the risks noted as part of the auditor's acceptance and retention evaluation
12. The level of complexity of the entity's operations

(AU-C 940.A21)

Use a Top-Down Approach

When selecting the controls to test, the auditor should use a top-down approach to the audit of ICFR. (AU-C 940.21) In sequence, this involves:

1. Starting at the financial statement level;
2. Utilizing the auditor's overall understanding of the risks to ICFR;
3. Focusing on entity-level controls;
4. Moving down to significant accounts and disclosures, and their related assertions;
5. Focusing on accounts, disclosures, and assertions that present a reasonable possibility of material misstatement of the financial statements and disclosures;
6. Verifying the auditor's understanding of the risks in the entity's processes; and
7. Selecting controls for testing that sufficiently address the assessed risk of material misstatement.

(AU-C 940.A33)

Entity-Level Controls

The auditor should test those entity-level controls that will assist in reaching a conclusion about the entity's level of ICFR. (AU-C 940.22) These controls include:

- Controls related to the control environment,
- Controls over management override,
- The entity's risk assessment process,
- Centralized processing and controls,
- Controls to monitor the results of operations,
- Controls to monitor other controls,
- Controls over the financial reporting process, and
- Programs and controls that address significant business control and risk management practices.

(AU-C 940.A35)

Control Environment

The auditor should evaluate the entity's control environment, since it has a significant impact on effective ICFR. This evaluation should include an assessment of whether management's operating style and ethical values promote effective ICFR, and whether those charged with governance understand and exercise oversight responsibility over financial reporting and ICFR. (AU-C 940.A41)

Financial Reporting Process

The auditor should evaluate the financial reporting process. This reporting process includes:

- Procedures to enter transaction totals in the general ledger
- Procedures that apply accounting policies

- Procedures related to journal entry creation
- Procedures for recording adjustments to the financial statements
- Procedures for preparing the financial statements

(AU-C 940.24)

Evaluating this reporting process should include an assessment of the processes used to create financial statements, the level of management participation, the locations participating in the process, the types of journal entries used, and the extent of oversight of the process.

Significant Accounts and Disclosures

The auditor should identify significant accounts and disclosures, and their relevant assertions, which requires the evaluation of the quantitative and qualitative risk factors related to each financial statement line item and disclosure. Risk factors to consider in this analysis for each account and related disclosure are:

- Size and composition of the account
- Susceptibility to misstatements caused by errors or fraud
- Nature of the account, class of transactions, or disclosure
- Volume of transaction activity, as well as the complexity and homogeneity of each of these transactions
- Exposure to losses
- Possibility of significant contingent liabilities
- Existence of related-party transactions
- Changes from the prior period

(AU-C 940.A50)

When an entity has multiple locations or business units, the auditor should conduct this analysis based on the consolidated financial statements.

Sources of Misstatement

The auditor should obtain an understanding of the likely sources of potential misstatements by understanding the flow of transactions, identifying the process points where misstatements could arise, and identifying the controls used to address those potential misstatements. The auditor directly performs this analysis or supervises the work of others who do so. (AU-C 940.29 and .30)

A good method for conducting this analysis is a walk-through of a transaction from its beginning until it appears in the financial statements. A walk-through can include such tasks as direct observation of processing steps, inspection of related documents, and recalculation. (AU-C 940.A56)

Selection of Controls to Be Tested

The auditor should test those controls that are important to the auditor's conclusion about whether the entity's controls sufficiently address the assessed risk of material misstatement. (AU-C 940.32) It may not be necessary to test all controls related to a relevant assertion if more than one control addresses the assessed risk. (AU-C 940.A59)

TESTING CONTROLS

The auditor should evaluate the design effectiveness of controls to determine if the controls, if prescribed as designed, can prevent, or detect and correct, misstatements in the financial statements. A test of operating effectiveness should include a determination of whether the control is operating as designed, and whether the person performing the control has the authority and competence to perform it effectively. This evaluation can include a walk-through that incorporates a mix of inquiry, operational observation, and documentation inspection. (AU-C 940.33 and .34)

For each test of control, the evidence needed depends upon the risk associated with the control; this is the risk that the control might not be effective, and, if not effective, that the risk of a material weakness exists. As a control's risk increases, so too should the level of evidence that the auditor obtains. (AU-C 940.35)

The auditor is not responsible for obtaining sufficient evidence to support an effectiveness opinion about each individual control, only about the entity's overall level of ICFR.

A number of factors affect the risk associated with each control, including:

- The nature and materiality of the misstatements that a control is intended to prevent, or detect and correct;
- The inherent risk associated with the related accounts and assertions;
- The presence of changes in the volume or nature of transactions adversely affecting control design or operating effectiveness;
- Whether the account has a history of errors;
- The effectiveness of controls that monitor other controls;
- The nature and frequency of the control;
- The degree to which the control relies on the effectiveness of other controls;
- The competence of the personnel who perform the control, and whether there have been changes in these personnel;
- Whether the control is automated, or requires manual monitoring; and
- The complexity of the control.

(AU-C 940.A66)

In the event of a control deviation, the auditor should determine the effect of the deviation on his or her assessment of the risk associated with the control being tested. An individual control does not necessarily have to operate without any deviation to be considered effective.

Importance of Types of Tests of Controls

Some types of tests produce greater evidence of the effectiveness of controls than others. The following tests are presented in order of effectiveness from most to least effective:

1. Reperformance of a control
2. Recalculation
3. Inspection of relevant documentation
4. Observation
5. Inquiry

(AU-C 940.A63)

A test of documentation may be dependent upon whether the control results in documentary evidence of its operation.

Timing and Extent of Tests of Controls

Testing a control over a longer period of time or testing close to the date of management's assessment provides additional evidence of control effectiveness. In general, the more extensively a control is tested, the greater the evidence obtained from that test. (AU-C 940.A78 and .A79)

Prior to the as-of date, management may upgrade the entity's controls. If the auditor determines that the new controls achieve stated control objectives and have been in existence long enough to assess their design and operating effectiveness, then there is no need to test the design and operating effectiveness of the superseded controls. However, if the operating effectiveness of the superseded controls is important to the auditor's control risk assessment in the financial statement audit, then testing of the superseded controls is appropriate. (AU-C 940.A80)

Interim Testing

Additional evidence needed to update the results of testing from an interim date to the entity's period end depends on the specific controls tested and the sufficiency of the evidence obtained prior to the as-of date, as well as the length of the remaining period and the possibility of significant ICFR changes subsequent to the interim testing. (AU-C 940.81)

Considerations for Subsequent Years' Testing

Information available in subsequent years' examinations might allow the auditor to assess risk as being lower than in the initial year of testing, which might lead to reduced testing in subsequent years.

The auditor should vary the nature, timing, and extent of controls testing in subsequent periods to introduce unpredictability into the testing. (AU-C 940.42) This may result in testing during different interim periods, changing the number and types of tests performed, or changing the combination of procedures used.

Evaluating Control Deficiencies

The auditor must evaluate identified control deficiencies and determine whether these deficiencies, individually or in combination, are material weaknesses. (AU-C 940.43)

The significance of a control deficiency depends on the magnitude of a potential misstatement and whether there is a reasonable possibility that existing controls will fail to prevent, or detect and correct, a misstatement. Thus, the severity of a deficiency depends on the *potential for a misstatement, not on whether a misstatement actually has occurred.* Accordingly, the absence of identified misstatement does not provide evidence that identified control deficiencies are not significant deficiencies or material weaknesses.

The key factors affecting the magnitude of a misstatement include the financial statement amounts exposed to the deficiency, as well as the volume of activity exposed to the deficiency.

The possibility of a deficiency resulting in a misstatement is impacted by a number of risk factors, which include:

- The nature of the financial statement accounts, transactions, and disclosures involved
- The cause and frequency of the exceptions
- The susceptibility of assets and liabilities to loss or fraud
- The subjectivity or complexity involved in determining the amounts involved
- The interaction of the control with other controls
- The interaction among deficiencies
- The possible future consequences of the deficiency
- The importance of controls to the financial reporting process

(AU-C 940.A91)

It is not necessary to quantify the probability of occurrence of a misstatement when evaluating deficiencies.

Multiple deficiencies affecting the same class of transaction, account balance, disclosure, or assertion increase the likelihood of material misstatement and may constitute a material weakness. (AU-C 940.47)

Compensating controls can reduce the effects of a deficiency, but they do not eliminate it. To have a mitigating effect, a compensation control should prevent, or detect and correct, a material misstatement.

Indicators of Material Weaknesses

There are certain key indicators of material weaknesses in ICFR. They include:

- Fraud by senior management, even if not material;
- Restatement of financial statements to correct for material misstatements that were caused by error or fraud;
- Identification of material misstatements that would not have been detected and corrected by ICFR; and
- Ineffective oversight of financial reporting and ICFR.

Forming an Opinion

The auditor should form an opinion on the effectiveness of ICFR. The source of this opinion should be the auditor's own tests and reports issued by internal audit. (AU-C 940.52)

The auditor should incorporate the results of substantive procedures performed in the audit of financial statements on the evaluation of ICFR. This evaluation should include:

- Risk assessments related to fraud
- Findings regarding illegal acts, noncompliance with regulations, and related-party transactions
- Indications of management bias related to accounting estimates and the selection of accounting principles
- Misstatements

However, the auditor cannot infer the effectiveness of a control from the above factors; that requires the direct testing of controls. (AU-C 940.54)

After forming an opinion, the auditor should examine management's report to ensure that it contains the following items:

- A statement regarding management's responsibility for ICFR
- A description of the subject matter of the audit
- An identification of the criteria against which ICFR is measured (such as the COSO *Internal Control—Integrated Framework*)
- Management's assessment about the effectiveness of ICFR
- A description of any material weaknesses
- The date as of which management makes its ICFR assessment

(AU-C 940.55)

If any of these items are missing or improperly presented, the auditor should request a revision. (AU-C 940.56) If this is not forthcoming, the auditor should modify the opinion and include an explanatory paragraph in his or her report. If management provides no report, then the auditor should withdraw from the engagement. (AU-C 940.74) Sample opinions are noted later in "Illustrations."

Management Representations and Responsibilities

The auditor should obtain written representations from management regarding the following items:

1. Acknowledgment of management's responsibility for the establishment and maintenance of ICFR
2. A statement that management has performed an evaluation of the effectiveness of the entity's ICFR, specifying the control criteria used
3. A statement that management did not use the auditor's procedures performed during the integrated audit as part of the basis for management's assertion
4. A statement of management's assessment about the effectiveness of the entity's ICFR based on the control criteria as of a specified date
5. A statement that management has disclosed to the auditor all deficiencies in the design or operation of ICFR, including separately disclosing all such deficiencies that it believes will be significant deficiencies or material weaknesses in ICFR
6. A description of any fraud resulting in a material misstatement to the entity's financial statements and any other fraud that does not result in a material misstatement to the entity's financial statements but does involve senior management or other employees who have a significant role in the entity's ICFR
7. A statement of whether the significant deficiencies and material weaknesses identified and communicated to management and those charged with governance during previous engagements have been resolved, and identifying any that have not
8. A statement whether there were, subsequent to the date being reported on, any changes in ICFR or other factors that might significantly affect ICFR, including any corrective actions taken by management with regard to significant deficiencies and material weaknesses

(AU-C 940.57)

A sample management representation letter is included in the "Illustrations" section of this chapter. Section 580, *Written Representations*, provides guidance on the date as of which management should sign such a representation letter and which members of management should sign it.

Communication of Deficiencies and Material Weaknesses

If the auditor identifies significant deficiencies or material weaknesses, he or she should communicate them in writing to management and those charged with governance (even if the items were remediated during the integrated audit). This communication should also include any such items that were previously communicated but not remediated. If the auditor concludes that the entity's oversight is ineffective, then the communication of these issues should also be extended to the board of directors. The communication should be made by the report release date. For a governmental entity, the communication should be made as soon as practicable, but no later than 60 days following the report release date. (AU-C 940.59-.61)

The auditor should also communicate to management in writing all nonmaterial and nonsignificant deficiencies no later than 60 days following the report release date, and inform those charged with governance when the communication was made. The communication to management does not need to include an itemization of those nonmaterial and nonsignificant deficiencies that were included in previous written communications. (AU-C 940.62)

The auditor should *not* issue a report indicating that no nonmaterial or material weaknesses were identified during the integrated audit. (AU-C 940.63)

REPORTING REQUIREMENTS

The auditor's examination report on the effectiveness of an entity's ICFR over financial reporting should include the following:

1. A title that includes the word *independent*
2. An addressee
3. An introductory paragraph that:
   a. Identifies the entity whose ICFR has been audited.
   b. States that the entity's ICFR has been audited.
   c. Identifies the as-of date.
   d. Identifies the criteria against which ICFR is measured.
4. A section headed "Management's Responsibility for Internal Control over Financial Reporting" that includes:
   a. A statement that management is responsible for designing, implementing, and maintaining effective ICFR and for its assessment about the effectiveness of ICFR
   b. A reference to management's report on ICFR
5. A section headed "Auditor's Responsibility" that includes:
   a. A statement that the auditor's responsibility is to express an opinion on the entity's ICFR based on the audit
   b. A statement that the examination was conducted in accordance with auditing standards generally accepted in the United States
   c. A statement that such standards require that the auditor plan and perform the examination to obtain reasonable assurance about whether effective ICFR was maintained in all material respects
   d. A description of the audit that includes stating that:
      i. An audit involves obtaining an understanding of ICFR, assessing the risk that a material weakness exists, testing and evaluating the design and operating effectiveness of ICFR based on the assessed risk, and performing such other procedures as the auditor considers necessary in the circumstances;
      ii. An audit of ICFR involves performing procedures to obtain audit evidence about whether a material weakness exists; and
      iii. The procedures selected depend on the auditor's judgment, including the assessment of the risks that a material weakness exists.
   e. A statement that the auditor believes the examination provides a reasonable basis for his or her opinion
6. A section headed "Definition and Inherent Limitations of Internal Control over Financial Reporting" that includes:
   a. A definition of ICFR (the auditor should use the same description of the entity's ICFR as management uses in its report)

   b. A statement that, because of inherent limitations, internal control may not prevent, or detect and correct, misstatements, and that projections of any assessment of effectiveness to future periods are subject to the risk that controls may become inadequate because of changes in conditions, or that the degree of compliance with the policies or procedures may deteriorate

7. A section headed "Opinion" that includes:

   a. The auditor's opinion on whether the entity maintained, in all material respects, effective ICFR as of the specified date, based on the criteria

8. The manual or printed signature of the auditor's firm
9. The city and state where the auditor practices
10. The date of the report

(AU-C 940.64)

The auditor can issue either a combined report or separate reports on an entity's financial statements and ICFR. If the auditor chooses to issue separate reports, then the following paragraph should be added to the financial statements reports:

> We also have audited, in accordance with auditing standards generally accepted in the United States of America, [*company name*]'s internal control over financial reporting as of December 31, 20X7, based on [*identify control criteria*], and our report dated [*date of report, which should be the same as the date of the report on the financial statements*] expressed [*include nature of the opinion*].

Again, if separate reports are issued, the auditor should add the following paragraph to the report on ICFR:

> We also have audited, in accordance with auditing standards generally accepted in the United States of America, the [*identify financial statement*] of [*company name*], and our report dated [*date of report, which should be the same as the date of the report on internal control*] expressed [*include nature of opinion*].

(AU-C 940.65)

The auditor should date the report no earlier than the date when he or she has collected sufficient evidence to support an opinion. The dates of the audit and ICFR reports should be the same. (AU-C 940.66)

Adverse Opinions

When ICFR is not effective because one or more material weaknesses exist, the auditor's report should also include the following information:

- The definition of a material weakness (see the earlier section, "AU-C 940 Definitions of Terms").
- A statement that one or more material weaknesses have been identified; the auditor need only refer to the material weaknesses described in management's report, as long as the referenced weaknesses are fairly presented.

(AU-C 940.66)

If material weaknesses have not been included in management's report, then the auditor's report should state that one or more material weaknesses have been identified but not included in management's report, and also note each weakness and the actual and potential effect on the presentation of the entity's financial statements. In this situation, the auditor should communicate the missing information to those charged with governance, noting that the information was not included in management's report. (AU-C 940.70)

Report Modifications

The auditor should issue a modified report if:

- One or more material weaknesses exist.
- Elements of management's report are either incomplete or improperly presented. If so, the auditor should include an other-matters paragraph in his or her report. (AU-C 940.72)
- There is a restriction on the engagement scope. If so, the auditor should either withdraw from the engagement or disclaim an opinion. If the latter, the auditor should state the reasons for the disclaimer; further, if the auditor concludes that a material weakness exists, the report should also include the definition of a material weakness, a description of those weaknesses identified, and their actual and potential impact on the entity's financial statements. The auditor should also communicate in writing that the audit of ICFR cannot be completed. (AU-C 940.73-.77)
- The auditor refers to the report of a component auditor as the basis for his or her own opinion. If so, the auditor should review Section 600, *Special Considerations—Audits of Group Financial Statements*, for guidance on this decision. (AU-C 940.78)
- There is other information in management's report or in a document containing management's report in addition to the elements subject to the auditor's evaluation. If so, the auditor should:

  - Disclaim an opinion on the additional information. Possible text for this purpose is:

    Other Matter

    We did not perform auditing procedures on [*describe additional information, such as management's cost-benefit statement*], and, accordingly, we do not express an opinion or provide any assurance on it.

    - If the additional information includes a material misstatement of fact, the auditor should communicate his or her views about the misstatement, in writing, to management and those charged with governance.

  - Read the additional information to identify material inconsistencies with management's report and material misstatements of fact when such information is included outside management's report in a document containing management's report and the related auditor's report. If, upon reading the additional information, the auditor becomes aware of an apparent material inconsistency or misstatement of fact, the auditor should apply the requirements in Section 720, *Other Information in Documents Containing Audited Financial Statements*, adapted as necessary to the audit of ICFR.

  (AU-C 940.80)

Examples of several of these reports are included in "Illustrations."

Other Topics

Subsequent Events

To determine the existence of changes to ICFR subsequent to the as-of date that might significantly affect ICFR, the auditor should review subsequent control reports by internal audit, independent auditors, regulatory agencies, and information from other sources. (AU-C 940.48)

If the auditor becomes aware, before the audit report date, of a material weakness that existed as of the management assessment date, the auditor should issue an adverse opinion. If the auditor cannot determine the impact of the item on the entity's ICFR as of the assessment date, the auditor should disclaim an opinion. (AU-C 940.49) If the material weakness arose between the as-of date and audit report date, then the auditor should include in his or her report an emphasis-of-matter paragraph describing the event and its effects. (AU-C 940.50)

Entities with Multiple Components

When the auditor is determining the entity locations where it should perform control tests, the group engagement team should assess the risk of material misstatement associated with the component. It is reasonable to eliminate from testing those components not presenting a reasonable possibility of material misstatement. (AU-C 940.81 and. 82)

The scope of the audit should include any entities acquired on or prior to the date of management's assessment, as well as operations accounted for as discontinued operations. (AU-C 940.85)

If the entity has equity method investments, the scope of the audit does not include the investee's controls, but does include controls over the reporting in the entity's financial statements, its portion of the investee's income or loss, the investment balance, adjustments to the income or loss and investment balance, and related disclosures. (AU-C 940.84)

Use of Service Organizations

If an entity outsources some or all of its information and communication systems, then the auditor should evaluate the activities of the service organization as part of the entity's ICFR. This requires obtaining an understanding of the service organization's controls that are relevant to the entity's ICFR, and of the entity's controls over the service organization. The auditor must obtain evidence that these controls are operating effectively. (AU-C 940.88 and .89) This can be done with one or more of the following procedures:

- Obtain a service auditor's report on controls placed in operation and tests of operating effectiveness, or a report on the application of procedures that describes tests of controls. In the former case, the auditor should assess the time period covered, the scope of the service auditor's work and applications addressed, the manner in which tested controls relate to the entity's controls, the service auditor's opinion on the effectiveness of the controls, and the service auditor's reputation, competence, and independence. In the latter case, the auditor should evaluate whether the report provides sufficient appropriate evidence.
- Test the entity's controls over the activities of the service organization.
- Test the service organization's controls.

(AU-C 940.90-.92)

If there is a significant period of time between the service auditor's test of controls and the management assessment date, the auditor should conduct additional procedures. This should include an inquiry of management to see if management has identified any changes in the service organization's controls during the intervening period, as well as the auditor's own investigations. If so, the auditor should evaluate the effect of the changes on the effectiveness of the entity's ICFR. (AU-C 940.93)

The auditor may elect to obtain additional evidence about the service organization's controls if there has been a significant amount of time between the date of the service auditor's report and the date of management's assessment, or if the activities of the service organization are significant to the entity. Other factors for the auditor to consider are the presence of errors in the service organization's transaction processing, and the significance of any changes made to the service organization's controls. (AU-C 940.94)

If the auditor decides to obtain additional evidence about the service organization's controls, possible options include:

- Evaluating the results of any procedures already performed by management
- Contacting the service organization directly for information, possibly including the performance of on-site procedures
- Requesting that a service auditor be engaged to supply the needed information

(AU-C 940.A146)

The auditor should not refer to the service auditor's report in his or her opinion on ICFR. (AU-C 940.96)

Automated Controls

Automated controls are less likely to break down than those performed manually. Also, given no programming changes or access to those programs, the auditor can avoid duplicating tests of automated controls that were performed in the prior year (though this requires testing of program change controls). (AU-C 940.97 and .98)

ILLUSTRATIONS

1. Unmodified Opinion on ICFR
2. Adverse Opinion on ICFR
3. Disclaimer of Opinion on ICFR
4. Unmodified Opinion on ICFR Making Reference to a Component Auditor
5. Combined Report Expressing an Unmodified Opinion on ICFR and an Unmodified Opinion on the Financial Statements
6. Written Communication of Significant Deficiencies and Material Weaknesses
7. Management Report

Illustrative Auditor's Reports (AU-C 940.A165)

The following illustrations assume that the audit of internal control over financial reporting (ICFR) and the audit of the financial statements were performed by the same auditor.

ILLUSTRATION 1. UNMODIFIED OPINION ON ICFR (AU-C 940.A165)

The following is an illustrative report expressing an unmodified opinion on ICFR.

Independent Auditor's Report

[Appropriate addressee]

Report on Internal Control over Financial Reporting[1]

We have audited ABC Company's internal control over financial reporting as of December 31, 20XX, based on [*identify criteria*].[2]

Management's Responsibility for Internal Control over Financial Reporting

Management is responsible for designing, implementing, and maintaining effective internal control over financial reporting, and for its assessment about the effectiveness of internal control over financial reporting, included in the accompanying [*title of management's report*].

Auditor's Responsibility

Our responsibility is to express an opinion on the entity's internal control over financial reporting based on our audit. We conducted our audit in accordance with auditing standards generally accepted in the United States of America. Those standards require that we plan and perform the audit to obtain reasonable assurance about whether effective internal control over financial reporting was maintained in all material respects.

An audit of internal control over financial reporting involves performing procedures to obtain audit evidence about whether a material weakness exists. The procedures selected depend on the auditor's judgment, including the assessment of the risks that a material weakness exists. An audit includes obtaining an understanding of internal control over financial reporting and testing and evaluating the design and operating effectiveness of internal control over financial reporting based on the assessed risk.

We believe that the audit evidence we have obtained is sufficient and appropriate to provide a basis for our audit opinion.

Definition and Inherent Limitations of Internal Control over Financial Reporting

An entity's internal control over financial reporting is a process effected by those charged with governance, management, and other personnel, designed to provide reasonable assurance regarding the preparation of reliable financial statements in accordance with [*applicable financial reporting framework, such as accounting principles generally accepted in the United States of America*]. An entity's internal control over financial reporting includes those policies and procedures that (1) pertain to the maintenance of records that, in reasonable detail, accurately and fairly reflect the transactions and dispositions of the assets of the entity; (2) provide reasonable assurance that transactions are recorded as necessary to permit preparation of financial statements in accordance with [*applicable financial reporting framework, such as accounting principles generally accepted in the United States of America*], and that receipts and expenditures of the entity are being made only in accordance with authorizations of management and those charged with governance; and (3) provide reasonable assurance regarding prevention, or timely detection and correction of unauthorized

---

1 https://publication.cpa2biz.com/content/link/ps/ad_940_definitions#ftn.ad_940_fn33

2 https://publication.cpa2biz.com/content/link/ps/ad_940_definitions#ftn.ad_940_fn34

acquisition, use, or disposition of the entity's assets that could have a material effect on the financial statements.

Because of its inherent limitations, internal control over financial reporting may not prevent, or detect and correct, misstatements. Also, projections of any assessment of effectiveness to future periods are subject to the risk that controls may become inadequate because of changes in conditions, or that the degree of compliance with the policies or procedures may deteriorate.

Opinion

In our opinion, ABC Company maintained, in all material respects, effective internal control over financial reporting as of December 31, 20XX, based on [*identify criteria*].

Report on Financial Statements

We also have audited, in accordance with auditing standards generally accepted in the United States of America, the [*identify financial statements*] of ABC Company, and our report dated [*date of report, which should be the same as the date of the report on the audit of ICFR*] expressed [*include nature of opinion*].

Report on Other Legal and Regulatory Requirements

[*Form and content of this section of the auditor's report will vary depending on the nature of the auditor's other reporting responsibilities.*]

[*Auditor's signature*]

[*Auditor's city and state*]

[*Date of the auditor's report*]

ILLUSTRATION 2. ADVERSE OPINION ON ICFR (AU-C 940.A165)

The following is an illustrative report expressing an adverse opinion on ICFR. In this example, the opinion on the financial statements is not affected by the adverse opinion on ICFR.

Independent Auditor's Report

[*Appropriate addressee*]

Report on Internal Control over Financial Reporting[3]

We have audited ABC Company's internal control over financial reporting as of December 31, 20XX, based on [*identify criteria*].[4]

Management's Responsibility for Internal Control over Financial Reporting

Management is responsible for designing, implementing, and maintaining effective internal control over financial reporting, and for its assessment about the effectiveness of internal control over financial reporting, included in the accompanying [*title of management's report*].

3 https://publication.cpa2biz.com/content/link/ps/ad_940_definitions#ftn.ad_940_fn35

4 https://publication.cpa2biz.com/content/link/ps/ad_940_definitions#ftn.ad_940_fn36

Auditor's Responsibility

Our responsibility is to express an opinion on the entity's internal control over financial reporting based on our audit. We conducted our audit in accordance with auditing standards generally accepted in the United States of America. Those standards require that we plan and perform the audit to obtain reasonable assurance about whether effective internal control over financial reporting was maintained in all material respects.

An audit of internal control over financial reporting involves performing procedures to obtain evidence about whether a material weakness exists. The procedures selected depend on the auditor's judgment, including the assessment of the risks that a material weakness exists. An audit includes obtaining an understanding of internal control over financial reporting and testing and evaluating the design and operating effectiveness of internal control over financial reporting based on the assessed risk.

We believe that the audit evidence we have obtained is sufficient and appropriate to provide a basis for our adverse audit opinion.

Definition and Inherent Limitations of Internal Control over Financial Reporting

An entity's internal control over financial reporting is a process effected by those charged with governance, management, and other personnel, designed to provide reasonable assurance regarding the preparation of reliable financial statements in accordance with [*applicable financial reporting framework, such as accounting principles generally accepted in the United States of America*]. An entity's internal control over financial reporting includes those policies and procedures that (1) pertain to the maintenance of records that, in reasonable detail, accurately and fairly reflect the transactions and dispositions of the assets of the entity; (2) provide reasonable assurance that transactions are recorded as necessary to permit preparation of financial statements in accordance with [*applicable financial reporting framework, such as accounting principles generally accepted in the United States of America*], and that receipts and expenditures of the entity are being made only in accordance with authorizations of management and those charged with governance; and (3) provide reasonable assurance regarding prevention, or timely detection and correction, of unauthorized acquisition, use, or disposition of the entity's assets that could have a material effect on the financial statements.

Because of its inherent limitations, internal control over financial reporting may not prevent, or detect and correct, misstatements. Also, projections of any assessment of effectiveness to future periods are subject to the risk that controls may become inadequate because of changes in conditions or that the degree of compliance with the policies or procedures may deteriorate.

Basis for Adverse Opinion

A material weakness is a deficiency, or a combination of deficiencies, in internal control over financial reporting, such that there is a reasonable possibility that a material misstatement of the entity's financial statements will not be prevented, or detected and corrected, on a timely basis. The following material weakness has been identified and included in the accompanying [*title of management's report*]. [*Identify the material weakness described in management's report.*][5]

Adverse Opinion

In our opinion, because of the effect of the material weakness described in the Basis for Adverse Opinion paragraph on the achievement of the objectives of [*identify criteria*], ABC Company has not maintained effective internal control over financial reporting as of December 31, 20XX, based on [*identify criteria*].

---

5 https://publication.cpa2biz.com/content/link/ps/ad_940_definitions#ftn.ad_940_fn37

Report on Financial Statements

We also have audited, in accordance with auditing standards generally accepted in the United States of America, the [*identify financial statements*] of ABC Company, and our report dated [*date of report, which should be the same as the date of the report on the audit of ICFR*] expressed [*include nature of opinion*]. We considered the material weakness identified above in determining the nature, timing, and extent of audit procedures applied in our audit of the 20XX financial statements, and this report does not affect such report on the financial statements.

Report on Other Legal and Regulatory Requirements

[*Form and content of this section of the auditor's report will vary depending on the nature of the auditor's other reporting responsibilities.*]

[*Auditor's signature*]

[*Auditor's city and state*]

[*Date of the auditor's report*]

Illustration 3. Disclaimer of Opinion on ICFR (AU-C 940.A165)

The following is an illustrative report expressing a disclaimer of opinion on ICFR. In this example, the auditor is applying paragraph .76 of this section because a material weakness was identified during the limited procedures performed by the auditor.

Independent Auditor's Report

[*Appropriate addressee*]

Report on Internal Control over Financial Reporting[6]

We were engaged to audit ABC Company's internal control over financial reporting as of December 31, 20XX, based on [*identify criteria*].[7]

Management's Responsibility for Internal Control over Financial Reporting

Management is responsible for designing, implementing, and maintaining effective internal control over financial reporting and for its assessment about the effectiveness of internal control over financial reporting included in the accompanying [*title of management's report*].

Auditor's Responsibility

Our responsibility is to express an opinion on ABC Company's internal control over financial reporting based on conducting the audit in accordance with auditing standards generally accepted in the United States of America. Because of the matter described in the Basis for Disclaimer of Opinion paragraph, however, we were not able to obtain sufficient appropriate audit evidence to provide a basis for an audit opinion.

Definition and Inherent Limitations of Internal Control over Financial Reporting

An entity's internal control over financial reporting is a process effected by those charged with governance, management, and other personnel, designed to provide reasonable assurance regarding the preparation of reliable financial statements in accordance with [*applicable financial reporting framework, such as accounting principles generally accepted in the United States of America*]. An entity's

6 https://publication.cpa2biz.com/content/link/ps/ad_940_definitions#ftn.ad_940_fn38

7 https://publication.cpa2biz.com/content/link/ps/ad_940_definitions#ftn.ad_940_fn39

internal control over financial reporting includes those policies and procedures that (1) pertain to the maintenance of records that, in reasonable detail, accurately and fairly reflect the transactions and dispositions of the assets of the entity; (2) provide reasonable assurance that transactions are recorded as necessary to permit preparation of financial statements in accordance with [*applicable financial reporting framework, such as accounting principles generally accepted in the United States of America*], and that receipts and expenditures of the entity are being made only in accordance with authorizations of management and those charged with governance; and (3) provide reasonable assurance regarding prevention, or timely detection and correction of unauthorized acquisition, use, or disposition of the entity's assets that could have a material effect on the financial statements.

Because of its inherent limitations, internal control over financial reporting may not prevent, or detect and correct, misstatements. Also, projections of any assessment of effectiveness to future periods are subject to the risk that controls may become inadequate because of changes in conditions, or that the degree of compliance with the policies or procedures may deteriorate.

Basis for Disclaimer of Opinion

[*Provide a description of the matter giving rise to the disclaimer of opinion.*]

Material Weakness

Because of the matter described above, we were not able to obtain sufficient appropriate audit evidence to provide a basis for an audit opinion. However, a material weakness has been identified. A material weakness is a deficiency, or a combination of deficiencies, in internal control over financial reporting, such that there is a reasonable possibility that a material misstatement of the entity's financial statements will not be prevented, or detected and corrected, on a timely basis. If one or more material weaknesses exist, an entity's internal control over financial reporting cannot be considered effective. The following material weakness has been included in the accompanying [*title of management's report*]. [*Identify the material weakness described in management's report and include a description of the material weakness, including its nature and its actual and potential effect on the presentation of the entity's financial statements issued during the existence of the material weakness.*]

Disclaimer of Opinion

Because of the significance of the matter described in the Basis for Disclaimer of Opinion paragraph, we have not been able to obtain sufficient appropriate audit evidence to provide a basis for an audit opinion. Accordingly, we do not express an opinion on the effectiveness of ABC Company's internal control over financial reporting.

Report on Financial Statements

We have audited, in accordance with auditing standards generally accepted in the United States of America, the [*identify financial statements*] of ABC Company, and our report dated [*date of report, which should be the same as the date of the report on the audit of ICFR*] expressed [*include nature of opinion*]. We considered the material weakness identified above in determining the nature, timing, and extent of audit procedures applied in our audit of the 20XX financial statements, and this report does not affect such report on the financial statements.

Report on Other Legal and Regulatory Requirements

[*Form and content of this section of the auditor's report will vary depending on the nature of the auditor's other reporting responsibilities.*]

[*Auditor's signature*]

[*Auditor's city and state*]

[*Date of the auditor's report*]

ILLUSTRATION 4. UNMODIFIED OPINION ON ICFR MAKING REFERENCE TO A COMPONENT AUDITOR (AU-C 940.A165)

The following is an illustrative report expressing an unmodified opinion on ICFR when the engagement partner decides to make reference to the report of a component auditor.

Independent Auditor's Report

[*Appropriate addressee*]

Report on Internal Control over Financial Reporting[8]

We have audited ABC Company's internal control over financial reporting as of December 31, 20XX, based on [*identify criteria*].[9]

Management's Responsibility for Internal Control over Financial Reporting

Management is responsible for designing, implementing, and maintaining effective internal control over financial reporting and for its assessment about the effectiveness of internal control over financial reporting included in the accompanying [*title of management's report*].

Auditor's Responsibility

Our responsibility is to express an opinion on the entity's internal control over financial reporting based on our audit. We did not audit the effectiveness of internal control over financial reporting of B Company, a wholly owned subsidiary, whose financial statements reflect total assets and revenues constituting 20% and 30%, respectively, of the related consolidated financial statement amounts as of and for the year ended December 31, 20XX. The effectiveness of B Company's internal control over financial reporting was audited by other auditors whose report has been furnished to us, and our opinion, insofar as it relates to the effectiveness of B Company's internal control over financial reporting, is based solely on the report of the other auditors. We conducted our audit in accordance with auditing standards generally accepted in the United States of America. Those standards require that we plan and perform the audit to obtain reasonable assurance about whether effective internal control over financial reporting was maintained in all material respects.

An audit of internal control over financial reporting involves performing procedures to obtain audit evidence about whether a material weakness exists. The procedures selected depend on the auditor's judgment, including the assessment of the risks that a material weakness exists. An audit includes obtaining an understanding of internal control over financial reporting and testing and evaluating the design and operating effectiveness of internal control over financial reporting based on the assessed risk.

We believe that the audit evidence we have obtained is sufficient and appropriate to provide a basis for our audit opinion.

Definition and Inherent Limitations of Internal Control over Financial Reporting

An entity's internal control over financial reporting is a process effected by those charged with governance, management, and other personnel, designed to provide reasonable assurance regarding the preparation of reliable financial statements in accordance with [*applicable financial reporting framework, such as accounting principles generally accepted in the United States of America*]. An entity's internal control over financial reporting includes those policies and procedures that (1) pertain to the maintenance of records that, in reasonable detail, accurately and fairly reflect the transactions and dispositions of the assets of the entity; (2) provide reasonable assurance that transactions are recorded as necessary to permit preparation of financial statements in accordance with [*applicable financial*

---

8 https://publication.cpa2biz.com/content/link/ps/ad_940_definitions#ftn.ad_940_fn40

9 https://publication.cpa2biz.com/content/link/ps/ad_940_definitions#ftn.ad_940_fn41

reporting framework, such as accounting principles generally accepted in the United States of America], and that receipts and expenditures of the entity are being made only in accordance with authorizations of management and those charged with governance; and (3) provide reasonable assurance regarding prevention, or timely detection and correction of unauthorized acquisition, use, or disposition of the entity's assets that could have a material effect on the financial statements.

Because of its inherent limitations, internal control over financial reporting may not prevent, or detect and correct, misstatements. Also, projections of any assessment of effectiveness to future periods are subject to the risk that controls may become inadequate because of changes in conditions, or that the degree of compliance with the policies or procedures may deteriorate.

Opinion

In our opinion, based on our audit and the report of the other auditors, ABC Company maintained, in all material respects, effective internal control over financial reporting as of December 31, 20XX, based on [*identify criteria*].

Report on Financial Statements

We also have audited, in accordance with auditing standards generally accepted in the United States of America, the [*identify financial statements*] of ABC Company, and our report dated [*date of report, which should be the same as the date of the report on the audit of ICFR*] expressed [*include nature of opinion*], based on our audit and the report of the other auditors.

Report on Other Legal and Regulatory Requirements

[*Form and content of this section of the auditor's report will vary depending on the nature of the auditor's other reporting responsibilities.*]

[*Auditor's signature*]

[*Auditor's city and state*]

[*Date of the auditor's report*]

ILLUSTRATION 5. COMBINED REPORT EXPRESSING AN UNMODIFIED OPINION ON ICFR AND AN UNMODIFIED OPINION ON THE FINANCIAL STATEMENTS (AU-C 940.A165)

The following is an illustrative combined report expressing an unmodified opinion on ICFR and an unmodified opinion on the financial statements. The circumstances include an audit of a complete set of general purpose financial statements (single year) prepared in accordance with accounting principles generally accepted in the United States of America.

Independent Auditor's Report

[*Appropriate addressee*]

Report on the Financial Statements and Internal Control[10]

We have audited the accompanying financial statements of ABC Company, which comprise the balance sheet as of December 31, 20XX, and the related statements of income, changes in stockholders' equity, and cash flows for the year then ended, and the related notes to the financial statements. We also

10 https://publication.cpa2biz.com/content/link/ps/ad_940_definitions#ftn.ad_940_fn42

have audited ABC Company's internal control over financial reporting as of December 31, 20XX, based on [*identify criteria*].[11]

Management's Responsibility for the Financial Statements and Internal Control over Financial Reporting

Management is responsible for the preparation and fair presentation of these financial statements in accordance with accounting principles generally accepted in the United States of America; this includes the design, implementation, and maintenance of effective internal control over financial reporting relevant to the preparation and fair presentation of financial statements that are free from material misstatement, whether due to fraud or to error. Management is also responsible for its assessment about the effectiveness of internal control over financial reporting, included in the accompanying [*title of management's report*].

Auditor's Responsibility

Our responsibility is to express an opinion on these financial statements and an opinion on the entity's internal control over financial reporting based on our audits. We conducted our audits in accordance with auditing standards generally accepted in the United States of America. Those standards require that we plan and perform the audits to obtain reasonable assurance about whether the financial statements are free from material misstatement and whether effective internal control over financial reporting was maintained in all material respects.

An audit of financial statements involves performing procedures to obtain audit evidence about the amounts and disclosures in the financial statements. The procedures selected depend on the auditor's judgment, including the assessment of the risks of material misstatement of the financial statements, whether due to fraud or to error. In making those risk assessments, the auditor considers internal control relevant to the entity's preparation and fair presentation of the financial statements in order to design audit procedures that are appropriate in the circumstances. An audit of financial statements also includes evaluating the appropriateness of accounting policies used and the reasonableness of significant accounting estimates made by management, as well as evaluating the overall presentation of the financial statements.

An audit of internal control over financial reporting involves performing procedures to obtain evidence about whether a material weakness exists. The procedures selected depend on the auditor's judgment, including the assessment of the risk that a material weakness exists. An audit of internal control over financial reporting also involves obtaining an understanding of internal control over financial reporting and testing and evaluating the design and operating effectiveness of internal control over financial reporting based on the assessed risk.

We believe that the audit evidence we have obtained is sufficient and appropriate to provide a basis for our audit opinions.

Definition and Inherent Limitations of Internal Control over Financial Reporting

An entity's internal control over financial reporting is a process effected by those charged with governance, management, and other personnel, designed to provide reasonable assurance regarding the preparation of reliable financial statements in accordance with accounting principles generally accepted in the United States of America. An entity's internal control over financial reporting includes those policies and procedures that (1) pertain to the maintenance of records that, in reasonable detail, accurately and fairly reflect the transactions and dispositions of the assets of the entity; (2) provide reasonable assurance that transactions are recorded as necessary to permit preparation of financial statements in accordance with accounting principles generally accepted in the United States of America, and that receipts and expenditures of the entity are being made only in accordance with authorizations of

---

11 https://publication.cpa2biz.com/content/link/ps/ad_940_definitions#ftn.ad_940_fn43

management and those charged with governance; and (3) provide reasonable assurance regarding prevention, or timely detection and correction of unauthorized acquisition, use, or disposition of the entity's assets that could have a material effect on the financial statements.

Because of its inherent limitations, internal control over financial reporting may not prevent, or detect and correct, misstatements. Also, projections of any assessment of effectiveness to future periods are subject to the risk that controls may become inadequate because of changes in conditions, or that the degree of compliance with the policies or procedures may deteriorate.

Opinions

In our opinion, the financial statements referred to above present fairly, in all material respects, the financial position of ABC Company as of December 31, 20XX, and the results of its operations and its cash flows for the year then ended in accordance with accounting principles generally accepted in the United States of America. Also, in our opinion, ABC Company maintained, in all material respects, effective internal control over financial reporting as of December 31, 20XX, based on [*identify criteria*].

Report on Other Legal and Regulatory Requirements

[*Form and content of this section of the auditor's report will vary depending on the nature of the auditor's other reporting responsibilities.*]

[*Auditor's signature*]

[*Auditor's city and state*]

[*Date of the auditor's report*]

Illustrative Written Communication of Significant Deficiencies and Material Weaknesses (AU-C 940.A156)

The following is an illustrative written communication of significant deficiencies and material weaknesses.

Illustration 6. Written Communication of Significant Deficiencies and Material Weaknesses (AU-C 940.A156)

To Management and [*identify the body or individuals charged with governance, such as the entity's board of directors*] of ABC Company:

In connection with our audit of ABC Company's (the Company) financial statements as of December 31, 20XX, and for the year then ended, and our audit of the Company's internal control over financial reporting as of December 31, 20XX (integrated audit), auditing standards generally accepted in the United States of America require that we advise you of the following matters relating to internal control over financial reporting (internal control) identified during our integrated audit.

Our responsibility is to plan and perform our integrated audit to obtain reasonable assurance about whether the financial statements are free from material misstatement, whether due to fraud or to error, and whether effective internal control was maintained in all material respects (that is, whether material weaknesses exist as of the date specified in management's assessment). The integrated audit is not designed to detect deficiencies that, individually or in combination, are less severe than a material weakness.

A deficiency in internal control exists when the design or operation of a control does not allow management or employees, in the normal course of performing their assigned functions, to prevent, or detect and correct, misstatements on a timely basis. A material weakness is a deficiency, or a combination of deficiencies, in internal control, such that there is a reasonable possibility that a material misstatement of the entity's financial statements will not be prevented, or detected and corrected, on a timely basis. [*We consider the following deficiencies in the Company's internal control to be material weaknesses:*]

[*Describe the material weaknesses that were identified during the integrated audit, and provide an explanation of their potential effects. The auditor may separately identify those material weaknesses that exist as of the date specified in management's assessment about ICFR by referring to the auditor's report.*]

[*A significant deficiency is a deficiency, or a combination of deficiencies, in internal control that is less severe than a material weakness, yet important enough to merit attention by those charged with governance. We consider the following deficiencies in the Company's internal control over financial reporting to be significant deficiencies:*]

[*Describe the significant deficiencies that were identified during the integrated audit, and provide an explanation of their potential effects.*]

This communication is intended solely for the information and use of management, [*identify the body or individuals charged with governance*], others within the organization, and [*identify any governmental authorities to which the auditor is required to report*], and is not intended to be and should not be used by anyone other than these specified parties.[12]

[*Auditor's signature*]

[*Auditor's city and state*]

[*Date*]

ILLUSTRATIVE MANAGEMENT REPORT (AU-C 940.A157)

The following is an illustrative management report containing the reporting elements described in paragraph .55 of this section with no material weaknesses reported.

ILLUSTRATION 7. MANAGEMENT REPORT (AU-C 940.A157)

Management's Report on Internal Control over Financial Reporting

ABC Company's internal control over financial reporting is a process effected by those charged with governance, management, and other personnel, designed to provide reasonable assurance regarding the preparation of reliable financial statements in accordance with [*applicable financial reporting framework, such as accounting principles generally accepted in the United States of America*]. An entity's internal control over financial reporting includes those policies and procedures that (1) pertain to the maintenance of records that, in reasonable detail, accurately and fairly reflect the transactions and dispositions of the assets of the entity; (2) provide reasonable assurance that transactions are recorded as necessary to permit preparation of financial statements in accordance with [*applicable financial reporting framework, such as accounting principles generally accepted in the United States of America*], and that receipts and expenditures of the entity are being made only in accordance with authorizations of management and those charged with governance; and (3) provide reasonable assurance regarding prevention, or timely detection and correction, of unauthorized acquisition, use, or disposition of the entity's assets that could have a material effect on the financial statements.

Management of ABC Company is responsible for designing, implementing, and maintaining effective internal control over financial reporting. Management assessed the effectiveness of ABC

12 https://publication.cpa2biz.com/content/link/ps/ad_940_definitions#ftn.ad_940_fn44

Company's internal control over financial reporting as of December 31, 20XX, based on [*identify criteria*].[13] Based on that assessment, management concluded that, as of December 31, 20XX, ABC Company's internal control over financial reporting is effective, based on [*identify criteria*].

Internal control over financial reporting has inherent limitations. Internal control over financial reporting is a process that involves human diligence and compliance and is subject to lapses in judgment and breakdowns resulting from human failures. Internal control over financial reporting also can be circumvented by collusion or improper management override. Because of its inherent limitations, internal control over financial reporting may not prevent, or detect and correct, misstatements. Also, projections of any assessment of effectiveness to future periods are subject to the risk that controls may become inadequate because of changes in conditions, or that the degree of compliance with the policies or procedures may deteriorate.

ABC Company

[*Report signers, if applicable*]

[*Date*]

13 https://publication.cpa2biz.com/content/link/ps/ad_940_definitions#ftn.ad_940_fn45

AT-C Preface

TECHNICAL ALERT

In April 2016, the Auditing Standards Board (ASB) issued Statement on Standards for Attestation Engagements (SSAE) No. 18, *Attestation Standards: Clarification and Recodification.* SSAE No. 18 is effective for practitioners' reports dated on or after May 1, 2017. SSAE No. 18 is the culmination of the attest clarity project, and it supersedes all of existing attestation standards except for:

- AT 501, whose content was moved to the auditing standards and codified as AU-C 940
- AT 701, which will not be clarified, but retained in its current form because it is a rarely performed engagement. The section number has been changed to AT-C Section 395.

AT-C ORGANIZATION

The AT-C sections are:

AT-C Preface	
Applicable to All Engagements	
AT-C Section 105	*Concepts Common to All Attestation Engagements*
Type of Service Performed	
AT-C Section 205	*Examination Engagements*
AT-C Section 210	*Review Engagements*
AT-C Section 215	*Agreed-Upon Procedures Engagements*
Subject-Matter-Specific Engagement	
AT-C Section 305	*Prospective Financial Information*
AT-C Section 310	*Reporting on Pro Forma Financial Information*
AT-C Section 315	*Compliance Attestation*
AT-C Section 320	*Reporting on an Examination of Controls at a Service Organization Relevant to User Entities' Internal Control over Financial Reporting*
AT-C Section 395	*Management's Discussion and Analysis*

ORGANIZATION OF EACH SECTION

Similar to the auditing standards and the accounting and review services clarifications, the ASB organized each AT-C section in a standard format:

- Objectives
- Definitions

- Requirements
- Application and other explanatory material

The application and explanatory paragraphs begin with an "A." prefix and follow the requirements section. The clarifications include the use of such formatting techniques as bulleted lists.

STRUCTURE OF THE CLARIFIED ATTESTATION STANDARDS

Similar to the clarified accounting and review standards, the clarified attestation standards begin with a section, 105, that contains content applicable to all attestation engagements. It continues with guidance specific to the type of service performed and with subject-matter-specific engagements. This means that, for each engagement, the practitioner must comply with at least two AT-C sections: AT-C 105 and either 205, 210, or 215. If a subject-matter engagement is involved, compliance with one of the four 300 sections is required.

Although the clarified attestation standards include four specific subject matters, practitioners may report on any subject matter assuming the following preconditions are met:

- The responsible party is other than the practitioner.
- The responsible party takes responsibility for the subject matter.
- The subject matter is appropriate.
- The evaluative subject matter is available and suitable.
- The practitioner expects to have unrestricted access to information and people who can provide the necessary evidence.
- The opinion, conclusion, or findings are contained in a written practitioners report.

SIGNIFICANT CHANGES

In addition to the restructuring and organizational changes outlined above, SSAE No. 18 makes some other significant changes, including:

- Review engagement guidance separated from examination engagements.
- Requirement for written representation letter. There is some flexibility in this requirement. See the discussion in the chapter on AT-C 105.
- Requirement to better identify risks of material misstatement in an examination engagement by obtaining a more in-depth understanding of the development of the subject matter.
- Detailed requirements similar to those in the SAS; for example, engagement letter or equivalent and written representations and examinations and reviews are now required.
- The requirement changed regarding scope limitations imposed by the engaging or responsible party. Practitioners are no longer required to withdraw. They may assess the effect and may either issue a qualified opinion, disclaim an opinion, or withdraw.

AT-C PREFACE

The AT-C Preface section gives an overview of the attestation standards, but does not contain requirements.

ATTESTATION ENGAGEMENT PURPOSE AND PREMISE

On the reliability of a subject matter or an assertion, an attestation engagement provides:

- An opinion (examination engagement),
- A conclusion (review engagement), or

- Findings (agreed-upon procedures engagement).

(AT-C Preface.07)

Responsibilities of the Responsible Party

The responsible party is the party responsible for the subject matter. There may be situations where no such party exists. In that case, a party with a reasonable basis for making a reasonable assertion may be deemed the responsible party. The responsible party has responsibility for:

- The subject matter and the presentation of the subject matter
- The assertion
- Measuring, evaluating, and presenting, free from material misstatement, the subject matter
- Providing the practitioner with:
  - Access to all relevant information
  - Any additional information requested by the practitioner
  - Unrestricted access to staff

(AT-C Preface.08)

Responsibilities of the Practitioner

The practitioner is responsible for conducting the attestation engagement in compliance with the requirements of the attestation standards. The practitioner is allowed to help the responsible party in developing or presenting the subject matter. (AT-C Preface.09)

Performance Requirements

As with other services, practitioners must:

- Have the appropriate competence and capabilities to perform the specific engagement,
- Comply with ethics requirements,
- Maintain professional skepticism, and
- Exercise professional judgment.

Reporting

Type of engagement	Conclusion	Procedures
Examination	Reasonable assurance—high but not absolute level of assurance	Extensive procedures
Review	Limited assurance	Extent of procedures less than in examination
Agreed-upon procedures	Description of the specified procedures and their results	Procedures determined by specified parties

Opinion in an Examination

At the end of an examination engagement, the practitioner expresses an opinion on whether the subject matter or an assertion about the subject matter is free from material misstatement. To obtain the reasonable assurance needed to express an opinion, the practitioner:

- Plans the work,
- Supervises other members of the engagement team,

- Identifies and assesses the risks of material misstatements, and
- Obtains sufficient appropriate evidence.

The procedures employed by the practitioner include:

- Inspection
- Observation
- Analysis
- Inquiry
- Reperformance
- Recalculation
- Confirmation with outside parties

(AT-C Preface.11)

Conclusions in a Review

The review report addresses whether any material modification should be made to the subject matter in order for it to be in accordance with the criteria or to an assertion about the subject matter in order for it to be fairly stated. A review conclusion provides limited assurance. To obtain this assurance, the practitioner:

- Plans the work,
- Supervises the team,
- Determines areas of increased risk of misstatements and focuses the procedures there,
- Obtains evidence through:
  - Inquiry
  - Analytical procedures
  - Other procedures

(AT-C Preface.12)

Agreed-Upon Procedures Report

As its title indicates, in an agreed-upon procedures report, the practitioner performs procedures determined by specified parties. The specified parties are the intended users of the report and are responsible for the adequacy of the procedures. The practitioner:

- Plans the work.
- Supervises the team.
- Applies the agree-upon procedures.

(AT-C Preface.13)

APPENDIX

Definitions of Terms

Appropriate party. Reference to this term should be read as the *responsible party* or the *engaging party*, as appropriate. See also **engaging party** and **responsible party**.

Appropriateness of evidence (in the context of Section 205, *Examination Engagements*). The measure of the quality of evidence, that is, its relevancy and reliability in providing support for the practitioner's opinion. See also **evidence**.

Appropriateness of review evidence (in the context of Section 210, *Review Engagements*). The measure of the quality of review evidence, that is, its relevancy and reliability in providing support for the practitioner's conclusion. See also **review evidence**.

Assertion. Any declaration or set of declarations about whether the subject matter is in accordance with (or based on) the criteria.

Attestation engagement. An examination, review, or agreed-upon procedures engagement performed under the attestation standards related to subject matter or an assertion that is the responsibility of another party. The following are the three types of attestation engagements:

1. *Examination engagement.* An attestation engagement in which the practitioner obtains reasonable assurance by obtaining sufficient appropriate evidence about the measurement or evaluation of subject matter against criteria in order to be able to draw reasonable conclusions on which to base the practitioner's opinion about whether the subject matter is in accordance with (or based on) the criteria or the assertion is fairly stated in all material respects.
2. *Review engagement.* An attestation engagement in which the practitioner obtains limited assurance by obtaining sufficient appropriate review evidence about the measurement or evaluation of subject matter against criteria in order to express a conclusion about whether any material modification should be made to the subject matter in order for it be in accordance with (or based on) the criteria or to the assertion in order for it to be fairly stated.
3. *Agreed-upon procedures engagement.* An attestation engagement in which a practitioner performs specific procedures on subject matter or an assertion and reports the findings without providing an opinion or a conclusion on it. The parties to the engagement (*specified parties*) agree upon and are responsible for the sufficiency of the procedures for their purposes.

See also **specified party** and **attestation standards**.

Attestation risk. In an examination or review engagement, the risk that the practitioner expresses an inappropriate opinion or conclusion, as applicable, when the subject matter or assertion is materially misstated.

Attestation standards. The Statements on Standards for Attestation Engagements (SSAEs), which are also known as the *attestation standards*, establish requirements and provide guidance for performing and reporting on examination, review, and agreed-upon procedures engagements (attestation engagements). Examples of subject matter for attestation engagements are a schedule of investment returns, the effectiveness of an entity's controls over the security of a system, or a statement of greenhouse gas emissions. The SSAEs apply only to attestation engagements performed under the SSAEs. They are issued under the "Compliance with Standards Rule" (ET sec. 1.310.001) of the AICPA Code of Professional Conduct, which requires an AICPA member who performs an attestation engagement to comply with standards promulgated by bodies designated by the AICPA Council. The AICPA Council has granted the Auditing Standards Board authority to promulgate the attestation standards, which are issued through a due process that includes deliberation in meetings open to the public, public exposure of proposed attestation standards, and a formal vote by an authorized standards-setting body. See also **attestation engagement**.

Carve-out method (in the context of Section 320, *Reporting on an Examination of Controls at a Service Organization Relevant to User Entities' Internal Control over Financial Reporting*). Method of addressing the services provided by a subservice organization, whereby management's description of the service organization's system identifies the nature of the services performed by the subservice organization and excludes from the description and from the scope of the service auditor's engagement the subservice organization's relevant control objectives and related controls.

Complementary subservice organization controls (in the context of Section 320). Controls that management of the service organization assumes, in the design of the service organization's system, will be implemented by the subservice organizations and are necessary to achieve the control objectives stated in management's description of the service organization's system.

Complementary user entity controls (in the context of Section 320). Controls that management of the service organization assumes, in the design of the service organization's system, will be implemented by user entities and are necessary to achieve the control objectives stated in management's description of the service organization's system.

Compliance with specified requirements (in the context of Section 315, *Compliance Attestation*). An entity's compliance with specified laws, regulations, rules, contracts, or grants.

Control objectives (in the context of Section 320). The aim or purpose of specified controls at the service organization. Control objectives address the risks that controls are intended to mitigate.

Controls at a service organization (in the context of Section 320). The policies and procedures at a service organization likely to be relevant to user entities' internal control over financial reporting. These policies and procedures are designed, implemented, and documented by the service organization to provide reasonable assurance about the achievement of the control objectives relevant to the services covered by the service auditor's report. In the context of Section 320, the policies and procedures include aspects of the information and communications component of user entities' internal control maintained by the service organization and control activities related to the information and communications component and may also include aspects of one or more of the other components of internal control at a service organization. For example, the definition of *controls at a service organization* may include aspects of the service organization's control environment, risk assessment, monitoring activities, and control activities when they relate to the services provided. Such definition does not, however, include controls at a service organization that are not related to the achievement of the control objectives stated in management's description of the service organization's system, for example, controls related to the preparation of the service organization's own financial statements.

Criteria. The benchmarks used to measure or evaluate the subject matter.

Criteria for the preparation of pro forma financial information (in the context of Section 310, *Reporting on Pro Forma Financial Information*). The basis disclosed in the pro forma financial information that management used to develop the pro forma financial information, including the assumptions underlying the pro forma financial information. Paragraph .11 of Section 310 contains the attributes of suitable criteria for an examination or review of pro forma financial information.

Documentation completion date. The date on which the practitioner has assembled for retention a complete and final set of documentation in the engagement file.

Engagement circumstances. The broad context defining the particular engagement, which includes the terms of the engagement; whether it is an examination, review, or agreed-upon procedures engagement; the characteristics of the subject matter; the criteria; the information needs of the intended users; relevant characteristics of the responsible party and, if different, the engaging party and their environment; and other matters—for example, events, transactions, conditions and practices, and relevant laws and regulations—that may have a significant effect on the engagement.

Engagement documentation. The record of procedures performed, relevant evidence obtained, and, in an examination or review engagement, conclusions reached by the practitioner, or in an agreed-upon procedures engagement, findings of the practitioner. (Terms such as *working papers* or *workpapers* are also sometimes used.)

Engagement partner. The partner or other person in the firm who is responsible for the attestation engagement and its performance and for the practitioner's report that is issued on behalf of the firm and who, when required, has the appropriate authority from a professional, legal, or regulatory body. *Engagement partner*, *partner*, and *firm* refer to their governmental equivalents when relevant. See also **firm** and **practitioner**.

Engagement team. All partners and staff performing the engagement and any individuals engaged by the firm or a network firm who perform attestation procedures on the engagement. This excludes a practitioner's external specialist and engagement quality control reviewer engaged by the firm or a network firm. The term *engagement team* also excludes individuals within the client's internal audit function who provide direct assistance.

Engaging party. The party(ies) that engage(s) the practitioner to perform the attestation engagement. See also **appropriate party** and **responsible party**.

Entity (in the context of Section 305, *Prospective Financial Information*). Any unit, existing or to be formed, for which financial statements could be prepared in accordance with generally accepted accounting principles or special purpose frameworks. For example, an entity can be an individual, partnership, corporation, trust, estate, association, or governmental unit.

Evidence. Information used by the practitioner in arriving at the opinion, conclusion, or findings on which the practitioner's report is based. See also **appropriateness of evidence** and **sufficiency of evidence**.

Financial forecast (in the context of Section 305). Prospective financial statements that present, to the best of the responsible party's knowledge and belief, an entity's expected financial position, results of operations, and cash flows. A financial forecast is based on the responsible party's assumptions reflecting conditions it expects to exist and the course of action it expects to take. A financial forecast may be expressed in specific monetary amounts as a single-point estimate of forecasted results or as a range, when the responsible party selects key assumptions to form a range within which it reasonably expects, to the best of its knowledge and belief, the item or items subject to the assumptions to actually fall. If a forecast contains a range, the range is not selected in a biased or misleading manner (for example, a range in which one end is significantly less expected than the other).

Financial projection (in the context of Section 305). Prospective financial statements that present, to the best of the responsible party's knowledge and belief, given one or more hypothetical assumptions, an entity's expected financial position, results of operations, and cash flows. A financial projection is sometimes prepared to present one or more hypothetical courses of action for evaluation, as in response to a question such as, "What would happen if . . . ?" A financial projection is based on the responsible party's assumptions reflecting conditions it expects would exist and the course of action it expects would be taken, given one or more hypothetical assumptions. A projection, like a forecast, may contain a range.

Firm. A form of organization permitted by law or regulation whose characteristics conform to resolutions of the Council of the AICPA and that is engaged in the practice of public accounting. See also **engagement partner** and **practitioner**.

Forecast (in the context of Section 305). Used alone, this term means forecasted information, which can be either a full presentation (a financial forecast) or a partial presentation. See also **financial forecast**.

Fraud. An intentional act involving the use of deception that results in a misstatement in the subject matter or the assertion.

General use. Use of a practitioner's report that is not restricted to specified parties.

General use of prospective financial statements (in the context of Section 305). Refers to the use of the statements by persons with whom the responsible party is not negotiating directly, for example, in an offering statement of an entity's debt or equity interests. See also **limited use of prospective financial statements** and **prospective financial statements**.

Guide (in the context of Section 305). The AICPA Guide *Prospective Financial Information*.

Hypothetical assumption (in the context of Section 305). An assumption used in a financial projection or in a partial presentation of projected information to present a condition or course of action that is not necessarily expected to occur but is consistent with the purpose of the projection.

Inclusive method (in the context of Section 320). Method of addressing the services provided by a subservice organization whereby management's description of the service organization's system includes a description of the nature of the services provided by the subservice organization as well as the subservice organization's relevant control objectives and related controls.

Internal audit function. A function of an entity that performs assurance and consulting activities designed to evaluate and improve the effectiveness of the entity's governance, risk management, and internal control processes.

Internal control over compliance (in the context of Section 315). An entity's internal control over compliance with specified requirements. The internal control addressed in Section 315 may include part of, but is not the same as, internal control over financial reporting.

Interpretive publications. Interpretive publications are not attestation standards. Interpretive publications are recommendations on the application of the attestation standards in specific circumstances, including engagements for entities in specialized industries. An interpretive publication is issued under the authority of the relevant senior technical committee after all members of the committee have been provided an opportunity to consider and comment on whether the proposed interpretive publication is consistent with the attestation standards. Examples of interpretive publications are interpretations of the attestation standards, exhibits to the attestation standards, attestation guidance included in AICPA guides, and attestation Statements of Position (SOPs). Interpretations of the attestation standards and exhibits are included within the sections of the attestation standards. AICPA Guides and attestation SOPs are listed in AT-C Appendix A, "AICPA Guides and Statements of Position," of the attestation standards. See also **other attestation publications**.

Key factors (in the context of Section 305). The significant matters on which an entity's future results are expected to depend. Such factors are basic to the entity's operations and, thus, encompass matters that affect, among other things, the entity's sales, production, service, and financing activities. Key factors serve as a foundation for prospective financial information and are the bases for the assumptions.

Limited use of prospective financial statements (in the context of Section 305). Refers to the use of prospective financial statements by the responsible party alone or by the responsible party and third parties with whom the responsible party is negotiating directly. Examples include use in negotiations for a bank loan, submission to a regulatory agency, and use solely within the entity. See also **general use of prospective financial statements** and **prospective financial statements**.

Management's description of a service organization's system and a service auditor's report on that description and on the suitability of the design of controls (referred to in the context of Section 320 as a *type 1 report*). A service auditor's report that comprises the following:

i. Management's description of the service organization's system
ii. A written assertion by management of the service organization about whether, based on the criteria:
   (1) Management's description of the service organization's system fairly presents the service organization's system that was designed and implemented as of a specified date.
   (2) The controls related to the control objectives stated in management's description of the service organization's system were suitably designed to achieve those control objectives as of the specified date.
iii. A service auditor's report that expresses an opinion on the matters in (ii)(1) and (ii)(2)

Management's description of a service organization's system and a service auditor's report on that description and on the suitability of the design and operating effectiveness of controls (referred to in the context of Section 320 as a *type 2 report*).

A service auditor's report that comprises the following:

i. Management's description of the service organization's system
ii. A written assertion by management of the service organization about whether, based on the criteria:
   (1) Management's description of the service organization's system fairly presents the service organization's system that was designed and implemented throughout the specified period.
   (2) The controls related to the control objectives stated in management's description of the service organization's system were suitably designed throughout the specified period to achieve those control objectives.

(3) The controls related to the control objectives stated in management's description of the service organization's system operated effectively throughout the specified period to achieve those control objectives.

iii. A service auditor's report that:

(1) Expresses an opinion on the matters in (ii)(1)–(ii)(3).
(2) Includes a description of the tests of controls and the results thereof.

Material noncompliance (in the context of Section 315). A failure to follow compliance requirements or a violation of prohibitions included in the specified requirements that results in noncompliance that is quantitatively or qualitatively material, either individually or when aggregated with other noncompliance.

Misstatement. A difference between the measurement or evaluation of the subject matter by the responsible party and the proper measurement or evaluation of the subject matter based on the criteria. Misstatements can be intentional or unintentional, qualitative or quantitative, and can include omissions. In certain engagements, a misstatement may be referred to as a *deviation*, *exception*, or *instance of noncompliance*. See also **risk of material misstatement**.

Modified opinion (in the context of Section 205). A qualified opinion, an adverse opinion, or a disclaimer of opinion.

Monitoring of controls (in the context of Section 320). A process to assess the effectiveness of internal control performance over time. It involves assessing the effectiveness of controls on a timely basis, identifying and reporting deficiencies to appropriate individuals within the service organization, and taking necessary corrective actions.

Network firm. A firm or other entity that belongs to a network, as defined in ET Section 0.400, *Definitions*.

Noncompliance with laws or regulations. Acts of omission or commission by the entity, either intentional or unintentional, that are contrary to the prevailing laws or regulations. Such acts include transactions entered into by, or in the name of, the entity or on its behalf by those charged with governance, management, or employees. *Noncompliance* does not include personal misconduct (unrelated to the subject matter) by those charged with governance, management, or employees of the entity.

Nonparticipant party (in the context of Section 215, *Agreed-Upon Procedures Engagements*). An additional specified party the practitioner is requested to add as a user of the report subsequent to the completion of the agreed-upon procedures engagement. See also **specified party**.

Other attestation publications. Publications other than interpretive publications. These include AICPA attestation publications not defined as interpretive publications; attestation articles in the *Journal of Accountancy* and other professional journals; continuing professional education programs and other instruction materials, textbooks, guidebooks, attestation programs, and checklists; and other attestation publications from state CPA societies, other organizations, and individuals. Other attestation publications have no authoritative status; however, they may help the practitioner understand and apply the attestation standards. The practitioner is not expected to be aware of the full body of other attestation publications. See also **interpretive publications**.

Other practitioner. An independent practitioner who is not a member of the engagement team who performs work on information that will be used as evidence by the practitioner performing the attestation engagement. This other practitioner may be part of the practitioner's firm, a network firm, or another firm.

Partial presentation (in the context of Section 305). A presentation of prospective financial information that excludes one or more of the applicable items required for prospective financial statements as described in Chapter 8, "Presentation Guidelines," of the AICPA Guide *Prospective Financial Information*.

Pervasive (in the context of Section 205). Describes the effects on the subject matter of misstatements or the possible effects on the subject matter of misstatements, if any, that are undetected due to an inability to obtain sufficient appropriate evidence. Pervasive effects on the subject matter are those that, in the practitioner's professional judgment,

a. Are not confined to specific aspects of the subject matter;
b. If so confined, represent or could represent a substantial proportion of the subject matter; or
c. In relation to disclosures, are fundamental to the intended users' understanding of the subject matter.

Practitioner. The person or persons conducting the attestation engagement, usually the engagement partner or other members of the engagement team, or, as applicable, the firm. When a section of the attestation standards expressly intends that a requirement or responsibility be fulfilled by the engagement partner, the term *engagement partner*, rather than *practitioner*, is used. *Engagement partner* and *firm* are to be read as referring to their governmental equivalents when relevant. See also **engagement partner** and **firm**.

Practitioner's specialist. An individual or organization possessing expertise in a field other than accounting or attestation, whose work in that field is used by the practitioner to assist the practitioner in obtaining evidence for the service being provided. A practitioner's specialist may be either a practitioner's internal specialist (who is a partner or staff, including temporary staff, of the practitioner's firm or a network firm) or a practitioner's external specialist. *Partner* and *firm* refer to their governmental equivalents when relevant.

Presentation guidelines (in the context of Section 305). The criteria for the presentation and disclosure of prospective financial information.

Presumptively mandatory requirements. The category of professional requirements with which the practitioner must comply in all cases in which such a requirement is relevant, except in rare circumstances discussed in paragraph .20 of Section 105, *Concepts Common to All Attestation Engagements*. The attestation standards use the word *should* to indicate a presumptively mandatory requirement. See also **attestation standards** and **unconditional requirements**.

Pro forma financial information (in the context of Section 310). A presentation that shows what the significant effects on historical financial information might have been had a consummated or proposed transaction (or event) occurred at an earlier date.

Professional judgment. The application of relevant training, knowledge, and experience within the context provided by attestation and ethical standards in making informed decisions about the courses of action that are appropriate in the circumstances of the attestation engagement.

Professional skepticism. An attitude that includes a questioning mind, being alert to conditions that may indicate possible misstatement due to fraud or error, and a critical assessment of evidence.

Projection (in the context of Section 305). This term can refer to either a financial projection or a partial presentation of projected information. See also **financial projection**.

Prospective financial information (in the context of Section 305). Any financial information about the future. The information may be presented as complete financial statements or limited to one or more elements, items, or accounts.

Prospective financial statements (in the context of Section 305). Either financial forecasts or financial projections, including the summaries of significant assumptions and accounting policies. Although prospective financial statements may cover a period that has partially expired, statements for periods that have completely expired are not considered to be prospective financial statements. Pro forma financial statements and partial presentations are not considered to be prospective financial statements. See also **general use of prospective financial statements** and **limited use of prospective financial statements**.

Reasonable assurance. A high but not absolute level of assurance.

Report release date. The date on which the practitioner grants the engaging party permission to use the practitioner's report.

Responsible party. The party(ies) responsible for the subject matter. If the nature of the subject matter is such that no such party exists, a party that has a reasonable basis for making a written assertion about the subject matter may be deemed to be the responsible party. See also **appropriate party** and **engaging party**.

Review evidence (in the context of Section 210). Information used by the practitioner in obtaining limited assurance on which the practitioner's review report is based. See also **appropriateness of review evidence** and **sufficiency of review evidence**.

Risk of material misstatement (in the context of Section 205). The risk that the subject matter is not in accordance with (or based on) the criteria in all material respects or that the assertion is not fairly stated in all material respects. See also **misstatement**.

Service auditor (in the context of Section 320). A practitioner who reports on controls at a service organization.

Service organization (in the context of Section 320). An organization or segment of an organization that provides services to user entities, which are likely to be relevant to those user entities' internal control over financial reporting.

Service organization's assertion (in the context of Section 320). A written assertion about the matters referred to in item ii of the definition of *management's description of a service organization's system and a service auditor's report on that description and on the suitability of* *the design and operating effectiveness of controls*, for a type 2 report, and, for a type 1 report, the matters referred to in part (b) of the definition of *management's description of a service organization's system and a service auditor's report on that description and on the suitability of the design of controls*.

Service organization's system (in the context of Section 320). The policies and procedures designed, implemented, and documented by management of the service organization to provide user entities with the services covered by the service auditor's report. Management's description of the service organization's system identifies the services covered, the period to which the description relates (or in the case of a type 1 report, the date to which the description relates), the control objectives specified by management or an outside party, the party specifying the control objectives (if not specified by management), and the related controls.

In the context of Section 320, the policies and procedures refer to the guidelines and activities for providing transaction processing and other services to user entities and include the infrastructure, software, people, and data that support the policies and procedures.

Specified party. The intended user(s) to whom use of the practitioner's written report is limited. See also **nonparticipant party**.

Statements on Standards for Attestation Engagements (SSAEs). See **attestation standards**.

Subject matter. The phenomenon that is measured or evaluated by applying criteria.

Subservice organization (in the context of Section 320). A service organization used by another service organization to perform some of the services provided to user entities that are likely to be relevant to those user entities' internal control over financial reporting.

Sufficiency of evidence (in the context of Section 205). The measure of the quantity of evidence. The quantity of the evidence needed is affected by the risks of material misstatement and also by the quality of such evidence. See also **evidence**.

Sufficiency of review evidence (in the context of Section 210). The measure of the quantity of review evidence. The quantity of the review evidence needed is affected by the risks of material misstatement and also by the quality of such evidence. See also **review evidence**.

Suitable criteria. The benchmarks used to measure or evaluate the subject matter that are established or developed by groups composed of experts that follow due process procedures, including exposure of the proposed criteria for public comment, are ordinarily considered suitable. Criteria promulgated by a body designated by the Council of the AICPA under the AICPA Code of Professional Conduct are, by definition, considered to be suitable. Suitable criteria exhibit all the following characteristics:

- *Relevance*. Criteria are relevant to the subject matter.
- *Objectivity*. Criteria are free from bias.
- *Measurability*. Criteria permit reasonably consistent measurements, qualitative or quantitative, of subject matter.
- *Completeness*. Criteria are complete when subject matter prepared in accordance with them does not omit relevant factors that could reasonably be expected to affect decisions of the intended users made on the basis of that subject matter.

Test of controls (in the context of Section 205). A procedure designed to evaluate the operating effectiveness of controls in preventing, or detecting and correcting, material misstatements in the subject matter.

Test of controls (in the context of Section 320). A procedure designed to evaluate the operating effectiveness of controls in achieving the control objectives stated in management's description of the service organization's system.

Type 1 report. See **management's description of a service organization's system and a service auditor's report on that description and on the suitability of the design of controls**.

Type 2 report. See **management's description of a service organization's system and a service auditor's report on that description and on the suitability of the design and operating effectiveness of controls**.

Unconditional requirements. The category of professional requirements with which the practitioner must comply in all cases in which such requirement is relevant. The attestation standards use the word *must* to indicate an unconditional requirement. See also **attestation standards** and **presumptively mandatory requirements**.

User auditor (in the context of Section 320). An auditor who audits and reports on the financial statements of a user entity.

User entity (in the context of Section 320). An entity that uses a service organization for which controls at the service organization are likely to be relevant to that entity's internal control over financial reporting.

Working papers or workpapers. See **engagement documentation**.

AT-C 105 Concepts Common to All Attestation Engagements

ORIGINAL PRONOUNCEMENT

Source Statement on Standards for Attestation Engagements (SSAE) 18.

APPLICABILITY AND WRITTEN ASSERTION

Section 105 applies to all engagements where a practitioner in public practice is engaged to issue an examination, review, or agreed-upon procedures report on another party's subject matter or assertion. (AT-C 105.01) The practitioner must request that the other party put the assertion in writing. The following table summarizes the practitioner's required course of action if a written assertion is not provided.

Written Assertion Not Provided (AT-C 105.02)		
Type of Engagement	**Engaging Party Is Responsible Party and Refuses to Provide Written Assertion**	**Engaging Party Is *Not* Responsible Party and Refuses to Provide Written Assertion**
Examination or review	Practitioner is required to withdraw from engagement.	Need not withdraw,* but must disclose refusal in report and restrict use of report to engaging party.
Agreed-upon procedures	Disclose refusal in the report.	Engagement letter should state that no written assertion will be provided. (AT-C 215.16)

* When possible to withdraw under laws or regulations.

OBJECTIVES

The overall objectives of a practitioner and attestation engagement are to:

a. *apply the requirements relevant to the attestation engagement;*
b. *report on the subject matter or assertion, and communicate as required by the applicable AT-C section, in accordance with the results of the practitioner's procedures; and*
c. *implement quality control procedures at the engagement level that provide the practitioner with reasonable assurance that the attestation engagement complies with professional standards and applicable legal and regulatory requirements.*

(AT-C 105.09)

DEFINITIONS OF TERMS

See the glossary in the Appendix to the chapter on the AT-C Preface for definitions of these terms relevant to this Section: *assertion, attestation engagement* (including *examination engagement, review engagement,* and *agreed-upon procedures engagement*), *attestation risk, criteria, documentation completion date, engagement circumstances, engagement documentation, engagement partner, engagement team, engaging party, evidence, firm, fraud, general use, internal audit function, misstatement, network firm, noncompliance with laws or regulations, other practitioner, practitioner, practitioner's specialist, professional judgment, professional skepticism, reasonable assurance, report release date, responsible party, specified party,* and *subject matter.*

REQUIREMENTS

Quality Control

As with other types of engagements, for attestation engagements the firm must have a quality control system in place that provides it with reasonable assurance of compliance with professional standards and legal and regulatory requirements and that the reports are appropriate. (AT-C 105.06) The type and extent of quality control systems depend on the size and nature of the firm and the nature of its engagements.

Compliance with Relevant AT-C Sections

As discussed in the chapter on the AT-C Preface, the practitioner must comply, depending on the type of engagement, with this Section and at least one other. (See the section on "Structure of the Clarified Attestation Standards" in the chapter on the AT-C Preface.) Practitioners should understand the relevant AT-C sections. (AT-C 105.12-.15)

Report Format Dictated by Law or Regulation

A practitioner may have an engagement where a report format is prescribed by law or by regulation. If the wording in the format is not acceptable, the practitioner should reword it or attach an appropriately worded practitioners report. (AT-C 105.18)

Professional Requirements in the Attestation Standards

The attestation standards, like other professional standards, assign two categories of responsibility to the requirements:

1. *Unconditional requirements.* The practitioner must comply with these requirements when relevant. To indicate this category, the Attestation Standards use the word *must.*
2. *Presumptively mandatory requirements.* The practitioner must comply with these standards when relevant except under rare circumstances. The standards use the word *should* for these requirements. In rare circumstances when the required procedure would be ineffective and the practitioners find it necessary to depart from these requirements, they should perform alternative procedures to satisfy the intent of the requirement. (AT-C 105.19 and .20)

Preconditions for an Attestation Engagement

Unless required by law or regulation to accept an engagement, the practitioner must be independent when performing an attestation engagement. (AT-C 105.24)

In order to meet the preconditions for an engagement, the practitioner must not be the responsible party, and the responsible party must take responsibility for the subject matter. In addition, the engagement must have the following characteristics:

1. The engagement must have an appropriate subject matter.
2. It must have criteria that are suitable and will be available to intended users.
3. The practitioner must expect to be able to obtain the evidence needed, including all relevant information the responsible party is aware of, information that the practitioner requests, and unrestricted access to staff within the appropriate party that the practitioner believes may have relevant information.
4. A written report will contain the practitioner's opinion, conclusion, or findings.

(AT-C 105.19)

In the absence of any of the above, the practitioner should work with the responsible party to try to resolve the issues. (AT-C 105.20)

In addition to meeting the preconditions, the engagement should be accepted only if the practitioner:

- Believes the relevant ethical requirements will be satisfied,
- Is satisfied that the engagement team has needed competence and capabilities, and
- Has an understanding with the engaging party.

(AT-C 105.27)

The practitioner may discover in the course of the engagement that one or more of the preconditions does not exist. In that case, the practitioner should attempt to resolve the issue and determine if it is appropriate to continue the engagement. If the issue is not resolved, but it is appropriate to continue with the engagement, the practitioner must determine what, if anything, must be communicated about the issue in the report. (AT-C 105.28)

Change in Terms of Engagement

A practitioner should agree to a change in engagement terms only if the engaging party presents a reasonable justification. Valid reasons for changes are:

- A change in circumstances, or
- A misunderstanding about the nature of the engagement.

For example, an engaging party may have misunderstood the nature of an attestation engagement, and finds that a consulting engagement would actually be more appropriate. That would be an acceptable reason for a change in engagement.

Invalid reasons include information that is:

- Incorrect,
- Incomplete, or
- Otherwise unsatisfactory.

The engagement should not be changed if the engaging party wants to avoid a modified opinion or disclaimer. (AT-C 105.A55)

Lacking agreement between the practitioner and the engaging party regarding a change in the terms of the engagement, the practitioner may withdraw from the engagement. If a practitioner changes the engagement to a lower level of service, he or she should:

- Comply with the standards relevant to the lower level of service,
- Issue a report appropriate to the lower level of service, and

- Not refer in the report to the change in service.

(AT-C 105.30)

Using the Work of an Other Practitioner

When using the work of an other practitioner, the practitioner should:

- Obtain an understanding that includes acknowledgment that the other practitioner will comply with relevant ethical requirements,
- Obtain an understanding of the other practitioner's competence,
- Evaluate the adequacy of the work,
- Communicate regarding the timing and scope of the engagement,
- Determine whether to reference the other practitioner in the report, and
- If assuming responsibility for the other practitioner's work, be involved in that work.

(AT-C 105.31)

The practitioner is responsible for the engagement, but if assuming responsibility for the work of an other practitioner or referring to that practitioner in the report, the practitioner should be certain to:

- Communicate clearly with the other practitioner, and
- Carefully evaluate the work of the other practitioner.

(AT-C 105.58)

Quality Control

Assignment of the Engagement Team and the Practitioner's Specialists

As with any engagement, the engagement partner is responsible for:

- Ensuring the competence and qualification of the engagement team and any outside specialists,
- Informing the engagement team members of their responsibilities, and
- Directing team members to bring areas of concern to the partner's attention.

(AT-C 105.32)

The engagement partner is also responsible for procedures, planning, performance, documentation, and consultation. (AT-C 105.33)

Documentation

Engagement documents should:

- Be prepared on a timely basis.
- Be assembled in an engagement documentation file no later than 60 days after the report release date.
- Not be altered or deleted before the end of the retention periods. If a practitioner must add or amend documentation, the practitioner should document the reason and who made the change.
- Include reasons for departures from presumptively mandatory requirements.

(AT-C 105.34-.41)

Engagement Quality Control Review

If the firm requires a quality control review, the engagement partner should discuss significant findings with the firm's quality control team. The engagement quality control review should:

- Consider discussing significant findings or issues with the engagement partner,
- Read the written subject matter or assertion,
- Read the report,
- Read documentation as appropriate,
- Evaluate conclusions reached, and
- Consider whether, based on the conclusions, the report is appropriate.

(AT-C 105.42)

Professional Skepticism and Professional Judgment

As with other types of engagements, the practitioner should execute the engagement with an attitude of skepticism and using professional judgment. (AT-C 105.43-.45)

INTERPRETATIONS

Responding to Requests for Reports on Matters Relating to Solvency (Issued May 1988; Amended February 1993; Revised January 2001; Revised November 2006; Revised December 2012; Revised April 2016, Effective for Practitioners' Reports Dated on or after May 1, 2017)

An accountant should not provide any form of assurance, through examination, review, or agreed-upon procedures, that an entity:

1. Is not insolvent at the time debt is incurred or would not be rendered insolvent thereby.
2. Does not have unreasonably small capital.
3. Has the ability to pay its debts as they mature.

An accountant may provide a client with various professional services that might be useful to the client in connection with a financing, but the scope of services and form of report have to conform to the requirements of the relevant professional standards.

If an accountant reports on the results of applying agreed-upon procedures, in addition to the normal requirements, the report should make clear that no representations are provided on questions of legal interpretation and no assurance is provided concerning the borrower's solvency, adequacy of capital, or ability to pay its debts.

Applicability of Attestation Standards to Litigation Services (July 1990; Revised January 2001; Revised April 2016, Effective for Practitioners' Reports Dated on or after May 1, 2017)

Attestation standards do not apply to litigation services unless the practitioner has been specifically engaged to express a written conclusion about the reliability of a written assertion that is the responsibility of another party and that conclusion and assertion are for the use of others who, under the rules of the proceedings, do not have an opportunity to analyze and challenge such work.

The attestation standards would apply if the practitioner is specifically requested by a litigant to issue an attestation services report.

A practitioner is not prohibited from providing expert testimony on matters relating to solvency. The prohibition on providing written reports related to solvency does not apply in a legal forum in which the legal definition and interpretation of matters relating to solvency can be analyzed and challenged by the opposing party.

PROVIDING ACCESS TO OR COPIES OF ENGAGEMENT DOCUMENTATION TO A REGULATOR (MAY 1996; REVISED JANUARY 2001; REVISED JANUARY 2002; REVISED DECEMBER 2012; REVISED APRIL 2016, EFFECTIVE FOR PRACTITIONERS' REPORTS DATED ON OR AFTER MAY 1, 2017)

A regulator's request for access to or photocopies of working papers in an attestation engagement should be treated in the same manner as a request related to audit working papers (see Section 230).

AT-C 205 Examination Engagements

OVERVIEW

Section 205 is the first of the level of service sections. These sections are:

- 205, Examination Engagements,
- 210, Review Engagements, and
- 215, Agreed-Upon Procedures Engagements

On every attestation engagement, the CPA must comply with Section 105, one of the level of service sections above, and any relevant subject matter section in the AT-C 300 section. Section 205 applies to all examination engagements and supplements the guidance in Section 105. See the chapter on the AT-C Preface for more information about the AT-C section structure.

OBJECTIVES

The practitioner's objectives in performing an examination engagement are to:

a. *obtain reasonable assurance about whether the subject matter as measured or evaluated against the criteria is free from material misstatement*

b. *express an opinion in a written report about whether*

  i. *the subject is in accordance with (or based on) the criteria, in all material respects, or*

  ii. *the responsible parties assertion is fairly stated in all material aspects, and*

c. *Communicate further as required by relevant AT-C sections.*

(AT-C 205.03)

DEFINITIONS OF TERMS

See the glossary in the Appendix to the chapter on the AT-C Preface for definitions of the following terms relevant to Section 205: *appropriateness of evidence*, *modified opinion*, *risk of material misstatement*, *sufficiency of evidence*, and *test of controls*.

REQUIREMENTS

INDEPENDENCE

Section 205 requires CPAs to be independent when performing attestation engagements unless required to perform the engagement by law or regulation. In that case, practitioners should disclaim an opinion, stating they are not independent. If practitioners provide the reasons for nonindependence, they must give all the reasons. (AT-C 205.06)

Terms of Engagement

The terms of engagement should be detailed in a written document and include:

- The objective
- The scope
- Practitioner's responsibilities
- A statement that the engagement will be conducted in accordance with the AICPA's attestation standards
- Responsibilities of the responsible party
- Responsibilities of the engaging party (if different from the responsible party)
- A statement about the inherent limitations of the engagement
- Identification of the measurement, evaluation, or disclosure criteria
- Acknowledgment that the engaging party agrees to provide the practitioner with a representation letter at the conclusion of the engagement

(AT-C 205.08)

The following is an example of an examination engagement letter.

Elements of the engagement letter	Sample engagement letter
	May 15, 20X1 Elizabeth Yu Chief Operating Officer Jade Imports 25 Smith Street San Francisco, CA Dear Ms. Yu: We are pleased to confirm our understanding of the services we are to provide for Jade Imports.
Scope	We will examine the physical inventory of Jade Imports as of May 31, 20X1.
A statement that the engagement will be conducted in accordance with the AICPA's attestation standards	Our examination will be conducted in accordance with attestation standards established by the American Institute of Certified Public Accountants.
Practitioner's responsibilities	Accordingly, it will include a physical count of inventory and other procedures we consider necessary to enable us to express an opinion as to whether your inventory and cash count is presented, in all material respects, in conformity with U.S. generally accepted accounting principles (GAAP), and whether it is fairly stated, in all material respects based on GAAP. If, for any reason, we are unable to complete the examination, we will not issue a report as a result of this engagement.
Limitations	[*Describe limitations on the use of the report, if any.*]

A statement about the inherent limitations of the engagement	Our engagement will not include a detailed inspection of every transaction and cannot be relied on to disclose all material errors, fraud, or other illegal acts that may exist. However, we will inform you of any material errors or fraud that comes to our attention. We will also inform you of any other illegal acts that come to our attention, unless clearly inconsequential.
Acknowledgment that the engaging party agrees to provide the practitioner with a representation letter at the conclusion of the engagement	At the end of the engagement, we will require a representation letter from management.
Responsibilities of the responsible party	We understand that you will provide us with the basic information required for our examination and that you are responsible for the accuracy and completeness of that information. We may advise you about appropriate criteria or assist in the development of the subject matter, but the responsibility for the subject matter remains with you. You are responsible for the presentation of the physical inventory in accordance with the GAAP, and for selecting the criteria and determining that such criteria are appropriate for your purposes. You are also responsible for making all management decisions and performing all management functions; for designating an individual who possesses suitable skill, knowledge, and experience to oversee the evaluation, adequacy, and results of those services; and for accepting responsibility for them.
Engagement partner	Bartholomew Sullivan is the engagement partner and is responsible for supervising the engagement and signing the report or authorizing another individual to sign it. We expect to begin our examination on approximately May 31, 20X1.
Fees	**Fees** We estimate that our fees for these services will range from $10,000 to $12,000. You will also be billed for travel and other out-of-pocket costs such as report production, word processing, postage, and so forth. Additional expenses are estimated to be $5,000. The fee estimate is based on anticipated cooperation from your personnel and the assumption that unexpected circumstances will not be encountered during the engagement. If significant additional time is necessary, we will discuss it with you and arrive at a new fee estimate before we incur the additional costs. Our invoices for these fees will be rendered each month as work progresses and are payable on presentation. In accordance with our firm policies, work may be suspended if your account becomes 30 days or more overdue and will not be resumed until your account is paid in full. If we elect to terminate our services for nonpayment, you will be obligated to compensate us for all time expended and to reimburse us for all out-of-pocket expenditures through the date of termination. **Subcontractors** We may from time to time, and depending on the circumstances, use third-party service providers in serving your account. We may share

	confidential information about you with these service providers, but remain committed to maintaining the confidentiality and security of your information. Accordingly, we maintain internal policies, procedures, and safeguards to protect the confidentiality of your personal information. In addition, we will secure confidentiality agreements with all service providers to maintain the confidentiality of your information, and we will take reasonable precautions to determine that they have appropriate procedures in place to prevent the unauthorized release of your confidential information to others. In the event that we are unable to secure an appropriate confidentiality agreement, you will be asked to provide your consent prior to the sharing of your confidential information with the third-party service provider. Furthermore, we will remain responsible for the work provided by any such third-party service providers. **Agreement** We appreciate the opportunity to be of service to you and believe this letter accurately summarizes the significant terms of our engagement. If you have any questions, please let us know. If you agree with the terms of our engagement as described in this letter, please sign the enclosed copy and return it to us. Sincerely, **Sullivan and Cregan, CPA** Bartholomew Sullivan, CPA Partner 800-555-1212 bsullivan@CPAFirm.com Enclosure **Response:** This letter correctly sets forth the understanding of Jade Imports. Authorized Signature: ________ Title: ________ Date: ________

Written Assertion

The practitioner should request a written assertion about the measurement or evaluation of the subject matter against the criteria. The following table summarizes the practitioner's course of action if a written assertion is not received. (AT-C 205.10)

Circumstance	Practitioner's Course of Action
Engaging party is responsible party and refuses to provide written assertion.	Withdraw if possible under law or regulation.
Engaging party is not the responsible party, and the responsible party refuses to provide a written assertion.	Need not withdraw. Disclose refusal in report and restrict the use of the report to the engaging party.

Planning the Engagement

AT-C 205.12 outlines the major steps in planning of an examination engagement.

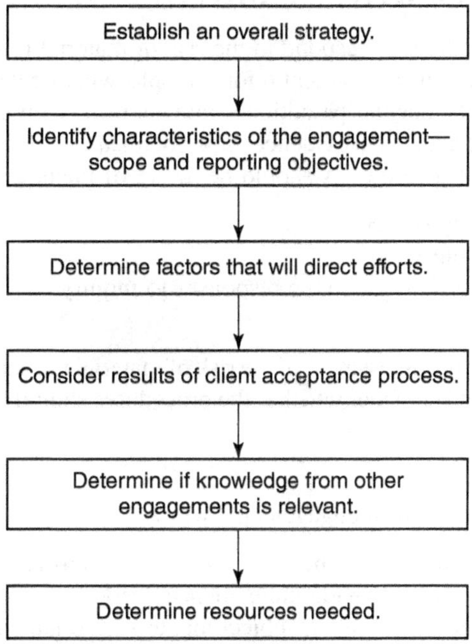

The plan developed by the practitioner should include the nature, timing, and extent of procedures, including risk assessment, further, and other procedures. (AT-C 205.13)

Risk Assessment Procedures

The practitioner must understand the subject matter sufficiently to:

- Identify and assess the risk of material misstatement, and
- Design and perform procedures to:
    - Respond to assessed risk.
    - Support the opinion.

        (AT-C 205.14)

This includes understanding internal control over the subject matter. For example, if the engagement involves an assertion regarding inventory, the practitioner should understand the relevant internal controls—their design and whether they have been implemented.

Materiality

Materiality should be considered when planning the strategy and if circumstances change during the course of the engagement.

Risks of Material Misstatement

Identifying and assessing the risk of material misstatement is critical in designing and performing further procedures that respond to risks of material misstatement. Evidence obtained should be sufficient to reduce risk to a level that gives practitioners the reasonable assurance needed to form an opinion. (AT-C 205.18 and .19)

Responding to Risk of Material Misstatement

When designing procedures to respond to the risk of material misstatement, the practitioner should look at the reasons for the assessment—for example, whether it is because of characteristics of the subject matter or whether the practitioner intends to rely on controls to determine other procedures. The amount of additional evidence to be obtained correlates with the level of assessed risk. (AT-C 205.22) Red flags the CPA should be aware of include:

- Inconsistency among sources
- Doubts about reliability
- Inconsistent, implausible, or vague responses to inquiry

(AT-C 205.23)

If practitioners change the assessment of the risk of material misstatement during the course of the engagement, they should consider whether the procedures should be changed. (AT-C 205.24)

Tests of Controls

Tests of controls are needed in engagements where:

- Practitioners intend to rely on the effectiveness of controls.
- Other procedures cannot provide the evidence needed.

  Of course, if the engagement subject matter is internal control, the CPA should test controls. (AT-C 205.24)

The practitioner should evaluate the results of tests of internal control to determine if the controls are reliable. When the practitioner intends to rely on controls and deviations in controls are found, other procedures are needed. The practitioner should also assess whether the results of the internal control tests affect the risk of material misstatements. (AT-C 205.25)

Other Procedures

Regardless of the results of internal control tests, practitioners should perform tests of details and/or analytical procedures. The exception to this is when the subject matter is internal control. (AT-C 205.26)

Analytical Procedures

Whenever using analytical procedures, practitioners should develop expectations and evaluate the reliability of the underlying data. Analytical procedures may produce results that are inconsistent with the findings of other tests. In that case the practitioner should resolve the differences through inquiry or performing other procedures. (AT-C 205.28)

Procedures Regarding Estimates

As discussed in the auditing section of this book, estimates are particularly risky because of their subjectivity. The practitioners should make sure that the responsible party has used appropriate criteria and methods to arrive at the estimate. (AT-C 205.29) If practitioners are responding to estimated assessed risk of material misstatement, they should make sure that events occurring through the date of the report have been considered. Practitioners should also:

- Test how the responsible party made the estimate.
- Test the data on which the estimate is based.
- Test the operating effectiveness of the related internal controls.
- Develop an expectation.

(AT-C 205.30)

SAMPLING

If sampling is used, the CPA should apply principles of good sampling technique:

- Determine that the sample size is sufficient.
- Select a representative sample.
- Treat an item as a deviation or misstatement if the practitioner is unable to apply the procedures.
- Investigate deviations.
- Evaluate results.

    At the end of the sampling process, the practitioner should evaluate whether the sample has provided a proper basis for conclusions about the population tested. (AT-C 205.31)

FRAUD, LAWS, AND REGULATIONS

The practitioner should assess whether any procedures indicate risk of material misstatement stemming from fraud or noncompliance with laws and regulations related to the subject matter. Practitioners should also ask the appropriate parties where they had knowledge of actual, suspected, or alleged fraud or noncompliance related to the subject matter. Practitioners should determine whether risk of material misstatement due to fraud or noncompliance is indicated by unusual or unexpected relationships within the subject matter or between the subject matter and related information. (AT-C 205.32)

RESPONDING TO FRAUD OR NONCOMPLIANCE

If practitioners identify fraud or suspect fraud, they should consider one or more of the following procedures:

- Discuss the finding with the appropriate parties.
- Ask that the appropriate party bring the matter to a third party, such as a legal counsel or a regulator.
- Assess how the finding affects other aspects of the engagement.
- Obtain legal advice.
- Communicate with a regulator.

    If practitioners are not satisfied with the results of these actions, they may consider withdrawing from the engagement or discussing noncompliance or suspected noncompliance in a separate paragraph in the report. (AT-C 205.A29 and .A30)

EVALUATING THE RELIABILITY OF THE ENTITY'S INFORMATION

In addition to assessing the information related to fraud, practitioners should evaluate the other information for accuracy, completeness, and whether it is sufficiently precise and detailed. (AT-C 205.35)

Using the Work of a Practitioner's Specialist

In the course of an examination engagement, it is not unusual for the practitioner to decide that a specialist—for example, a valuation expert—would add value to the process. Before using a specialist, the practitioner should assess whether the specialist has the relevant competence, capabilities, and objectivity. If the specialist is external, objectivity becomes even more important, and the practitioner should make additional inquiries.

To properly evaluate the specialist's work for the examination's purpose and the adequacy of the work, the practitioner should have enough understanding of the specialist's field. Practitioners should have a clear understanding with the specialist about:

- The work to be performed,
- Roles and responsibilities,
- The communication between the practitioner and the specialist, and
- The need for confidentiality.

  When the specialist completes his or her work, the practitioner should evaluate:

- The relevance of the findings, conclusions, and assumptions, and
- The reasonableness of the findings, conclusions, and assumptions.

  The practitioner should also evaluate the completeness and accuracy of source data used by the specialist—the old garbage in, garbage out saw is relevant. (AT-C 205.36) If the work is inadequate, practitioners should ask the specialist to do further work or practitioners should perform additional procedures themselves. (AT-C 205.37)

Using Internal Auditors

As in audits, practitioners may use internal auditors to:

- Obtain evidence, or
- Provide direct assistance.

Before using the internal auditors, the practitioner should assess:

- The level of competence,
- Objectivity of the internal audit function,
- If providing direct assistance, threats to internal auditors' objectivity, and
- Whether the internal audit function uses a systematic and disciplined approach.

(AT-C 205.39)

Practitioner should perform procedures to determine the adequacy of the work of the internal function. These procedures should include re-performance of some of the internal auditors' work. (AT-C 205.40)

Direct Assistance

Communicating with the Responsible Party

Before using internal auditors to provide direct assistance, the practitioner should obtain written affirmation from the responsible party that the internal auditor will follow the practitioner's direction without interference. (AT-C 205.41)

Responsibility of the Practitioner

Practitioners should direct, supervise, and review the work of the internal auditors providing direct assistance. (AT-C 205.42) Practitioners should perform more of the work where:

- More judgment is involved,
- Assessed risk of material misstatement is higher,
- The level of support for objectivity from the internal audit function's organizational status, policies, and procedures is lower, or
- The level of competence of the internal audit function is lower.

(AT-C 205.43)

Evaluate the Results of the Procedures

To evaluate the results of the procedures, practitioners should:

- Evaluate the internal audit function's work,
- Assess whether, if using internal auditors to provide direct assistance, practitioners have the proper level of involvement in the audit,
- Accumulate other than clearly trivial misstatements, and
- Evaluate whether the evidence gathered is sufficient and appropriate.

(AT-C 205.44-.46)

Considering Subsequent Events and Subsequently Discovered Facts

Practitioners should ask the responsible party or, if different, the engaging party if it is aware of any events subsequent to the examination and before the date of the practitioner's report that could significantly affect subject matter or an assertion. If practitioners become aware of such an event, they should make sure that adequate disclosure is made. (AT-C 205.48) After the date of the report, the practitioner has no responsibility to perform procedures, but should respond appropriately.

Written Representations

As with audits, it is important for practitioners to get representations in the form of a letter addressed to the practitioner. In the case of an examination, the representation should be made by the responsible party. The representation letter should be as of the date of the report and address the report's subject matter. (AT-C 205.54) The representation should include statements that:

- Include the assertion about the subject matter.
- All relevant matters are reflected in the measurement or evaluation of the subject matter or assertion.
- All known matters contradicting the subject matter or assertion and any communications from regulatory agencies or others affecting the subject matter or assertion have been disclosed to the practitioner.
- Acknowledge responsibility for:
    - The subject matter and the assertion,
    - Selecting the criteria when applicable, and
    - Determining that such criteria are appropriate for the responsible party's purposes.

- Any known events subsequent to the period (or point in time) of the subject matter being reported on that would have a material effect on the subject matter or assertion have been disclosed to the practitioner.
- The practitioner has been provided with all relevant information and access.
- If applicable, the responsible party believes the effects of uncorrected misstatements are immaterial, individually and in the aggregate, to the subject matter.
- If applicable, that significant assumptions used in making any material estimates are reasonable.
- The responsible party has disclosed to the practitioner:
    - All deficiencies in internal control relevant to the engagement of which the responsible party is aware;
    - Its knowledge of any actual, suspected, or alleged fraud or noncompliance with laws or regulations affecting the subject matter; and
    - Other matters the practitioner deems appropriate.

(AT-C 205.50)

If the engaging party is not the responsible party and the responsible party refuses to provide the required written representations, the practitioner should get oral responses from the responsible party. (AT-C 205.51)

Representations from the Responsible Party

If the engaging party is not the responsible party, the practitioner should get additional representations from the engaging party. These representations include statements that:

- Acknowledge that the responsible party is responsible for the subject matter and assertion.
- Acknowledge the engaging party's responsibility for selecting the criteria, when applicable.
- Acknowledge the engaging party's responsibility for determining that such criteria are appropriate for its purposes.
- The engaging party is not aware of any material misstatements in the subject matter or assertion.
- The engaging party has disclosed to the practitioner all known events subsequent to the period (or point in time) of the subject matter being reported on that would have a material effect on the subject matter or assertion.
- Address other matters as the practitioner deems appropriate.

(AT-C 205.52)

Assessment of the Written Representations

The practitioner should not just accept the representations. For material representations, the practitioner should make sure that they are reasonable and consistent with other information and that representing parties are sufficiently informed to make the statements. (AT-C 205.53)

Requested Representations Not Provided or Not Reliable

The written representations may not be provided or may raise doubt about competence, integrity, ethics, or diligence of the representing party. In that case, practitioners should take the steps listed in the following table.

Course of Action When Requested Representations Are Not Provided or Are Not Reliable	
Engaging Party Is the Responsible Party (AT-C 205.55A-.55C	**Engaging Party Is Not the Responsible Party (AT-C 205.56A and .56B)**
• Discuss the matter with the appropriate party; • Reevaluate the integrity of those from whom the representations were requested or received, and evaluate the effect that this may have on the reliability of representations and evidence in general; and • If any of the matters are not resolved to the practitioner's satisfaction, take appropriate action.	• If one or more of the requested representations are not provided in writing by the responsible party, but the practitioner receives satisfactory oral responses to the practitioner's inquiries sufficient to enable the practitioner to conclude that the practitioner has sufficient appropriate evidence to form an opinion about the subject matter, the practitioner's report should contain a separate paragraph that restricts the use of the report to the engaging party. • If one or more of the requested representations are provided neither in writing nor orally from the responsible party, a scope limitation exists, and the practitioner should determine the effect on the report, or the practitioner should withdraw from the engagement.

OTHER INFORMATION

There may be occasions where a party wants to include the practitioner's report in a document that contains the subject matter assertion and other information. A practitioner's report may appear in:

- Annual reports to holders of securities or beneficial interests
- Annual reports of organizations for charitable or philanthropic purposes
- Annual reports filed with regulatory authorities under the Securities Exchange Act of 1934
- Other documents to which the practitioner, at the client's request, devotes attention

If the practitioner is willing to include the report, the practitioner should read the other information for material inconsistency. If such an inconsistency exists or if there is a material misstatement of fact, then the practitioner should take appropriate action after discussing it with the responsible party. (AT-C 205.57)

FORMING AN OPINION

The practitioner issues an opinion on whether:

- The subject matter is in accordance with, or based on, the criteria in all material respects, or
- The assertion is fairly stated in all material aspects.

The practitioner should make sure that the evidence supports the conclusion that there are no uncorrected material misstatements, individually or in the aggregate. (AT-C 205.59)

The Report

The report should be written. If the report is an assertion, the assertion should be bound with the report. (AT-C 205.61-.62) The report should include the items listed in the left column in the following table.

Illustration: Practitioner's Examination Report on Subject Matter; Unmodified Opinion

Report Requirements	Sample Report
A title that includes the word independent	**Independent Accountant's Report** Other examples of acceptable titles include: Report of Independent Certified Public Accountant Independent Practitioner's Report
An appropriate addressee as required by the circumstances of the engagement	Jade Imports 25 Elizabeth Street San Francisco, CA
An identification or description of the subject matter or assertion being reported on, including the point in time or period of time to which the measurement or evaluation of the subject matter or assertion relates	We have examined [*identify the subject matter, for example, the accompanying schedule of investment returns of XYZ Company for the year ended December 31, 20XX*].
An identification of the criteria against which the subject matter was measured or evaluated	The inventory will be measured based on U.S. generally accepted accounting principles.
The responsible party and its responsibility for the subject matter in accordance with (or based on) the criteria or for its assertion	XYZ Company's management is responsible for presenting the schedule of inventory in accordance with (or based on) U.S. generally accepted accounting principles.
The practitioner's responsibility to express an opinion on the subject matter or assertion, based on the practitioner's examination	Our responsibility is to express an opinion on [*identify the subject matter, for example, the schedule of investment returns*] based on our examination.
The practitioner's examination was conducted in accordance with attestation standards established by the AICPA.	Our examination was conducted in accordance with attestation standards established by the American Institute of Certified Public Accountants.
AICPA attestation standards require that the practitioner plan and perform the examination to obtain reasonable assurance about whether: *(1) The subject matter is in accordance with (or based on) the criteria, in all material respects (or equivalent language regarding the subject matter and criteria, such as the language used in the examples in paragraph .A82) or* *(2) The responsible party's assertion is fairly stated, in all material respects.*	Those standards require that we plan and perform the examination to obtain reasonable assurance about whether the inventory is in accordance with (or based on) the criteria, in all material respects.

Description of the nature of the engagement	An examination involves performing procedures to obtain evidence about inventory. The nature, timing, and extent of the procedures selected depend on our judgment, including an assessment of the risks of material misstatement of inventory, whether due to fraud or to error. We believe that the evidence we obtained is sufficient and appropriate to provide a reasonable basis for our opinion. [*Include a description of significant inherent limitations, if any, associated with the measurement or evaluation of the subject matter against the criteria.*]
Emphasis of matter	[*Additional paragraph(s) may be added to emphasize certain matters relating to the attestation engagement or the subject matter.*]
The practitioner's opinion about whether the subject matter is in accordance with (or based on) the criteria, in all material respects, or the responsible party's assertion is fairly stated, in all material respects.	In our opinion, [*identify the subject matter, for example, the schedule of investment returns of XYZ Company for the year ended December 31, 20XX or the schedule of investment returns referred to above*], is presented in accordance with (or based on) [*identify the criteria, for example, the ABC criteria set forth in Note 1*], in all material respects.
The manual or printed signature of the practitioner's firm	Bartholomew Sullivan, CPA
The city and state where the practitioner practices	San Francisco, CA
The date of the report. (The report should be dated no earlier than the date on which the practitioner has obtained sufficient appropriate evidence on which to base the practitioner's opinion, including evidence that the attestation documentation has been reviewed. If applicable, the written presentation of the subject matter has been prepared, and the responsible party has provided a written assertion or, in the circumstances described previously, an oral assertion.)	June 25, 20X1

Restricted Use Paragraph

If a restricted use paragraph is called for, the alert should be presented in a separate paragraph that restricts the use of the report. The alert should:

- State that the report is intended solely for the information and use of specified parties, identify those parties, and state that no other party should use the report. (AT-C 205.65)

Circumstances that call for restricted use include when:

- The criteria are appropriate only for those who participated in their establishment or are presumed to have an adequate understanding of the criteria.
- The criteria are available only to specified parties.
- The engaging party is not the responsible party and the responsible party provides only oral representations. Those circumstances should disclosed in the report, and the report should be restricted to the engaging party. (AT-C 205.84)

(AT-C 205.64)

Modified Opinions

A modified opinion includes a separate paragraph in the report that describes the reason for the modification. (AT-C 205.69)

Type of Opinion	Circumstances	Opinion	Practitioner's Responsibility in Report
Modified	Is unable to obtain sufficient appropriate evidence to reach a conclusion. Concludes that the subject matter does not meet or is not based on the criteria in all material aspects.	Separate paragraph that describes the matter(s) giving rise to the modification.	Separate paragraph
Qualified	Has obtained sufficient appropriate evidence, but concludes that misstatements, individually or in the aggregate, are material, but not pervasive to the subject matter. Is unable to obtain sufficient appropriate evidence on which to base the opinion, but concludes that the possible effects on the subject matter of undetected misstatements, if any, could be material, but not pervasive.		Statement that the practitioner believes that the evidence that petitioner has obtained is sufficient and appropriate to provide a basis for the practitioner's modified opinion.
Adverse	Has obtained sufficient appropriate evidence, but concludes that misstatements, individually or in the aggregate, are both material and pervasive to the subject matter.	State that because of the significance of the matter giving rise to the modification, the subject matter is not presented in accordance, or based on, the criteria in all material aspects.	Same statement as for qualified opinion.

Disclaimer	Is unable to obtain sufficient appropriate evidence on which to base the opinion, and concludes that the possible effects on the subject matter of any undetected misstatements could be both material and pervasive. Engaging party is the responsible party and refuses to provide written assertion, and the practitioner cannot withdraw because of law or regulation.	Statement that because of the significance of the matter giving rise to the modification, the practitioner has not been able to obtain sufficient appropriate evidence to provide a basis for an examination opinion, and, accordingly, the practitioner does not express an opinion on the subject matter.	See Illustration 6 at the end of this chapter for appropriate language.
(AU-C 205.68-.83)			

When the practitioner modifies the opinion but also has a scope limitation, the report should include both a description of:

- The scope limitation and
- The matter that caused the subject matter to be materially misstated.

(AT-C 205.78)

If there are one or more material misstatements based on the criteria, practitioners should express a qualified for adverse opinion directly on the subject matter. (AT-C 207.80)

A reference to an external specialist may be included in a modified report if it is relevant to an understanding of the modification. (AT-C 205.81)

Communicating with the Responsible and Engaging Partners

Practitioners should communicate the following to the responsible party:

- Known or suspected fraud
- Known noncompliance with laws or regulations
- Uncorrected misstatements
- Internal control deficiencies relevant to the subject matter. (If internal control deficiencies are not relevant to the subject matter, the practitioner should use judgment about whether or not to communicate.)

  This information should be given to the engaging party if the responsible party is not the engaging party. (AT-C 205.85)

Documentation

The form and content of documentation depends on the particular engagement's circumstances. Practitioners should use professional judgment when determining the quantity, type, and content of the documentation. Documentation is the principal record of the procedures applied, information obtained, and conclusion reached. The documentation provides the primary support for the report and assists in the conduct and supervision of the engagement. It should be sufficient to:

- Understand the nature, timing, extent, and results of procedures performed.
- Identify which engagement team members performed the work and the date it was completed.

It should also include documentation of:

- The discussions with the responsible party or others about significant findings or issues, including when the discussions were held and with whom.
- Who reviewed the engagement work performed, the date of the review, and the extent of the review.
- Documentation regarding the responsible party's refusal to provide one or more written representations or doubt about the reliability of the responsible party's representations.
- Documentation regarding the responsible party's responses to requests for written representation under AT-C 205.51. (See the "Written Representations" section in this chapter.)

INTERPRETATIONS

Reporting on Attestation Engagements Performed in Accordance with Government Auditing Standards (December 2004; Revised January 2008)

When an auditor performs an attestation engagement in accordance with generally accepted government auditing standards, the scope paragraph of the report should be modified to indicate that the work was "conducted in accordance with attestation standards established by the American Institute of Certified Public Accountants and the standards applicable to attestation engagements contained in *Government Auditing Standards* issued by the Comptroller General of the United States."

Reporting on the Design of Internal Control (Issued December 2008; Revised December 2012; Revised April 2016, Effective for Practitioners' Reports Dated on or after May 1, 2017)

The auditor cannot report on the suitability of the design of an entity's internal control, based on the risk assessment procedures performed to gain an understanding of the entity and its environment, since these procedures do not provide a sufficient basis of information to make such a report.

If the auditor is asked to sign a prescribed form developed by the party to whom the reports are to be submitted regarding the design of an entity's internal controls, the auditor should either revise the form or attach a separate report that conforms to the auditor's professional standards.

The auditor should not submit a report about an entity's ability to establish suitable internal controls.

ILLUSTRATIONS (AT-C 205.A121)

ILLUSTRATION 1. PRACTITIONER'S EXAMINATION REPORT ON SUBJECT MATTER; UNMODIFIED OPINION

Independent Accountant's Report

[*Appropriate addressee*]

We have examined [identify the subject matter, for example, the accompanying schedule of investment returns of XYZ Company for the year ended December 31, 20XX]. XYZ Company's management is responsible for [*identify the subject matter, for example, presenting the schedule of investment returns*] in accordance with (or based on) [*identify the criteria, for example, the ABC criteria set forth in Note 1*]. Our responsibility is to express an opinion on [*identify the subject matter, for example, the schedule of investment returns*] based on our examination.

Our examination was conducted in accordance with attestation standards established by the American Institute of Certified Public Accountants. Those standards require that we plan and perform the examination to obtain reasonable assurance about whether [*identify the subject matter, for example, the schedule of investment returns*] is in accordance with (or based on) the criteria, in all material respects. An examination involves performing procedures to obtain evidence about [*identify the subject matter, for example, the schedule of investment returns*]. The nature, timing, and extent of the procedures selected depend on our judgment, including an assessment of the risks of material misstatement of [*identify the subject matter, for example, the schedule of investment returns*], whether due to fraud or to error. We believe that the evidence we obtained is sufficient and appropriate to provide a reasonable basis for our opinion.

[*Include a description of significant inherent limitations, if any, associated with the measurement or evaluation of the subject matter against the criteria.*]

[*Additional paragraph(s) may be added to emphasize certain matters relating to the attestation engagement or the subject matter.*]

In our opinion, [*identify the subject matter, for example, the schedule of investment returns of XYZ Company for the year ended December 31, 20XX or the schedule of investment returns referred to above*], is presented in accordance with (or based on) [*identify the criteria, for example, the ABC criteria set forth in Note 1*], in all material respects.

[*Practitioner's signature*]

[*Practitioner's city and state*]

[*Date of practitioner's report*]

ILLUSTRATION 2. PRACTITIONER'S EXAMINATION REPORT ON AN ASSERTION; UNMODIFIED OPINION

Independent Accountant's Report

[*Appropriate addressee*]

We have examined management of XYZ Company's assertion that [*identify the assertion, including the subject matter and the criteria, for example, the accompanying schedule of investment returns of XYZ Company for the year ended December 31, 20XX, is presented in accordance with (or based on) the ABC criteria set forth in Note 1*]. XYZ Company's management is responsible for its assertion. Our responsibility is to express an opinion on management's assertion based on our examination.

Our examination was conducted in accordance with attestation standards established by the American Institute of Certified Public Accountants. Those standards require that we plan and perform the examination to obtain reasonable assurance about whether management's assertion is fairly stated, in all material respects. An examination involves performing procedures to obtain evidence about management's assertion. The nature, timing, and extent of the procedures selected depend on our judgment, including an assessment of the risks of material misstatement of management's assertion, whether due to fraud or to error. We believe that the evidence we obtained is sufficient and appropriate to provide a reasonable basis for our opinion.

[*Include a description of significant inherent limitations, if any, associated with the measurement or evaluation of the subject matter against the criteria.*]

[*Additional paragraph(s) may be added to emphasize certain matters relating to the attestation engagement or the subject matter.*]

In our opinion, management's assertion that [*identify the assertion, including the subject matter and the criteria, for example, the accompanying schedule of investment returns of XYZ Company for the year ended December 31, 20XX, is presented in accordance with (or based on) the ABC criteria set forth in Note 1*] is fairly stated, in all material respects.

[*Practitioner's signature*]

[*Practitioner's city and state*]

[*Date of practitioner's report*]

ILLUSTRATION 3. PRACTITIONER'S EXAMINATION REPORT IN WHICH THE PRACTITIONER EXAMINES MANAGEMENT'S ASSERTION AND REPORTS DIRECTLY ON THE SUBJECT MATTER; UNMODIFIED OPINION

Independent Accountant's Report

[*Appropriate addressee*]

We have examined management of XYZ Company's assertion that [*identify the assertion, including the subject matter and the criteria, for example, the accompanying schedule of investment returns of XYZ Company for the year ended December 31, 20XX, is presented in accordance with (or based on) the ABC criteria set forth in Note 1*]. XYZ Company's management is responsible for its assertion. Our responsibility is to express an opinion on [*identify the subject matter, for example, the accompanying schedule of investment returns of XYZ Company for the year ended December 31, 20XX*], based on our examination.

Our examination was conducted in accordance with attestation standards established by the American Institute of Certified Public Accountants. Those standards require that we plan and perform the examination to obtain reasonable assurance about whether [*identify the subject matter, for example, the schedule of investment returns*] is presented in accordance with (or based on) the criteria, in all material respects. An examination involves performing procedures to obtain evidence about [*identify the subject matter, for example, the schedule of investment returns*]. The nature, timing, and extent of the procedures selected depend on our judgment, including an assessment of the risks of material misstatement of [*identify the subject matter, for example, the schedule of investment returns*], whether due to fraud or to error. We believe that the evidence we obtained is sufficient and appropriate to provide a reasonable basis for our opinion.

[*Include a description of significant inherent limitations, if any, associated with the measurement or evaluation of the subject matter against the criteria.*]

[*Additional paragraph(s) may be added to emphasize certain matters relating to the attestation engagement or the subject matter.*]

In our opinion, [*identify the subject matter, for example, the accompanying schedule of investment returns of XYZ Company for the year ended December 31, 20XX or the schedule of investment returns referred to above*] is presented in accordance with (or based on) [*identify the criteria, for example, the ABC criteria set forth in Note 1*], in all material respects.

[*Practitioner's signature*]

[*Practitioner's city and state*]

[*Date of practitioner's report*]

ILLUSTRATION 4. PRACTITIONER'S EXAMINATION REPORT ON SUBJECT MATTER; UNMODIFIED OPINION; USE OF THE PRACTITIONER'S REPORT IS RESTRICTED TO SPECIFIED PARTIES

Independent Accountant's Report

[*Appropriate addressee*]

We have examined [*identify the subject matter, for example, the number of widgets sold by XYZ Company to ABC Company (or tons of coal mined by XYZ Company ... or gallons of gas sold in the United States by XYZ Company to ABC Company) during the year ended December 31, 20XX,*] to determine whether it has been calculated in accordance with (or based on) [*identify the criteria, for example, the agreement dated (date) between ABC Company and XYZ Company, as further described in Note 1*]. XYZ Company's management is responsible for [*identify the subject matter, for example, calculating the number of widgets sold*]. Our responsibility is to express an opinion on [*identify the subject matter, for example, the number of widgets sold by XYZ Company to ABC Company (or tons of coal mined by XYZ Company ... or gallons of gas sold in the United States by XYZ Company to ABC Company) during the year ended December 31, 20XX,*] based on our examination.

Our examination was conducted in accordance with attestation standards established by the American Institute of Certified Public Accountants. Those standards require that we plan and perform the examination to obtain reasonable assurance about whether [*identify the subject matter, for example, the number of widgets sold, tons of coal mined, or gallons of gas sold*] is in accordance with (or based on) the criteria, in all material respects. An examination involves performing procedures to obtain evidence about [*identify the subject matter, for example, the number of widgets sold, tons of coal mined, or gallons of gas sold*]. The nature, timing, and extent of the procedures selected depend on our judgment, including an assessment of the risks of material misstatement of [*identify the subject matter, for example, the number of widgets sold by XYZ Company to ABC Company (or tons of coal mined by XYZ Company, or gallons of gas sold in the United States by XYZ Company to ABC Company*], whether due to fraud or to error. We believe that the evidence we obtained is sufficient and appropriate to provide a reasonable basis for our opinion.

[*Include a description of significant inherent limitations, if any, associated with the measurement or evaluation of the subject matter against the criteria.*]

[*Additional paragraph(s) may be added to emphasize certain matters relating to the attestation engagement or the subject matter.*]

In our opinion, [*identify the subject matter, for example, the number of widgets sold by XYZ Company to ABC Company (or tons of coal mined by XYZ Company, or gallons of gas sold in the United States by XYZ Company to ABC Company) during the year ended December 31, 20XX,*] has been calculated in accordance with (or based on) [*identify the criteria, for example, the agreement dated (date) between ABC Company and XYZ Company, as further described in Note 1*], in all material respects.

This report is intended solely for the information and use of [*identify the specified parties, for example, ABC Company and XYZ Company*], and is not intended to be and should not be used by anyone other than the specified parties.

[*Practitioner's signature*]

[*Practitioner's city and state*]

[*Date of practitioner's report*]

Illustration 5. Practitioner's Examination Report on Subject Matter; Qualified Opinion

The following is an illustrative practitioner's report for an examination engagement in which the practitioner expresses a qualified opinion because conditions exist that, individually or in combination, result in one or more material, but not pervasive, misstatements of the subject matter based on (or in certain engagements, deviations from, exceptions to, or instances of noncompliance with) the criteria.

Independent Accountant's Report

[*Appropriate addressee*]

We have examined [*identify the subject matter, for example, the accompanying schedule of investment returns of XYZ Company for the year ended December 31, 20XX*]. XYZ Company's management is responsible for [*identify the subject matter, for example, presenting the schedule of investment returns*] in accordance with (or based on) [*identify the criteria, for example, the ABC criteria set forth in Note 1*]. Our responsibility is to express an opinion on [*identify the subject matter, for example, the schedule of investment returns*] based on our examination.

Our examination was conducted in accordance with attestation standards established by the American Institute of Certified Public Accountants. Those standards require that we plan and perform the examination to obtain reasonable assurance about whether [*identify the subject matter, for example, the schedule of investment returns*] is presented in accordance with (or based on) the criteria, in all material respects. An examination involves performing procedures to obtain evidence about [*identify the subject matter, for example, the schedule of investment returns*]. The nature, timing, and extent of the procedures selected depend on our judgment, including an assessment of the risks of material misstatement of [*identify the subject matter, for example, the schedule of investment returns*], whether due to fraud or to error. We believe that the evidence we obtained is sufficient and appropriate to provide a reasonable basis for our opinion.

[*Include a description of significant inherent limitations, if any, associated with the measurement or evaluation of the subject matter against the criteria.*]

[*Additional paragraph(s) may be added to emphasize certain matters relating to the attestation engagement or the subject matter.*]

Our examination disclosed [*describe condition(s) that, individually or in the aggregate, resulted in a material misstatement or deviation from the criteria*].

In our opinion, except for the material misstatement [*or deviation from the criteria*] described in the preceding paragraph, [*identify the subject matter, for example, the accompanying schedule of investment returns of XYZ Company for the year ended December 31, 20XX, or the schedule of investment returns referred to above*], is presented in accordance with (or based on) [*identify the criteria, for example, the ABC criteria set forth in Note 1*], in all material respects.

[*Practitioner's signature*]

[*Practitioner's city and state*]

[*Date of practitioner's report*]

ILLUSTRATION 6. PRACTITIONER'S EXAMINATION REPORT; PRACTITIONER ENGAGED TO REPORT ON SUBJECT MATTER; DISCLAIMER OF OPINION BECAUSE OF SCOPE LIMITATION

Independent Accountant's Report

[*Appropriate addressee*]

We were engaged to examine [*identify the subject matter, for example, the accompanying schedule of investment returns of XYZ Company for the year ended December 31, 20XX*], in accordance with (or based on) [*identify the criteria, for example, the ABC criteria set forth in Note 1*]. XYZ Company's management is responsible for [*identify the subject matter, for example, presenting the schedule of investment returns*]. Our responsibility is to express an opinion on [*identify the subject matter, for example, the schedule of investment returns*] based on conducting the examination in accordance with attestation standards established by the American Institute of Certified Public Accountants.

[*The first sentence of the practitioner's report has been revised to state, "We were engaged to examine" rather than "We have examined." The standards under which the practitioner conducts an examination have been identified at the end of the second sentence of the report, rather than in a separate sentence in the second paragraph of the report.*]

[*The report should omit statements*

indicating what those standards require of the practitioner.

indicating that the practitioner believes the evidence obtained is sufficient and appropriate to provide a reasonable basis for the practitioner's opinion.

describing the nature of an examination engagement.]

[*Include a paragraph to describe scope limitations.*]

Because of the limitation on the scope of our examination discussed in the preceding paragraph, the scope of our work was not sufficient to enable us to express, and we do not express, an opinion on whether [*identify the subject matter, for example, the accompanying schedule of investment returns of XYZ Company for the year ended December 31, 20XX, or the schedule of investment returns referred to above*] is in accordance with (or based on) [*identify the criteria, for example, the ABC criteria set forth in Note 1*], in all material respects.

[*Practitioner's signature*]

[*Practitioner's city and state*]

[*Date of practitioner's report*]

AT-C 210 Review Engagements

ORIGINAL PRONOUNCEMENT

Source Statement on Standards for Attestation Engagements (SSAE) 18.

APPLICABILITY

AT-C 210's guidance applies to all review engagements and supplements the guidance in Section 105. On every attestation engagement, the CPA must comply with Section 105, one of service sections numbered in the 200s, and any relevant subject matter section in the AT-C 300 section. (AT-C 210.01) See the chapter on AT-C Preface for more information about the AT-C section structure.

NOTE: Practitioners should not perform reviews of:

a. Prospective financial information,
b. Internal control, or
c. Compliance with requirements of specified laws, regulations, rules, contracts, or grants. (AT-C 210.07)

Guidance on those engagements can be found in other AT-C Sections.

DEFINITIONS OF TERMS

See the glossary in the Appendix to the chapter on the AT-C Preface for definitions of the following terms relevant to this Section: *appropriateness of review evidence*, *review evidence*, and *sufficiency of review evidence*.

OBJECTIVES OF SECTION 215

In conducting a review engagement, the practitioner's objectives are to:

a. obtain limited assurance about whether any material modifications should be made to the subject matter in order for it to be in accordance with (or based on) the criteria;
b. express a conclusion in a written report about whether the practitioner is aware of any material modifications that should be made to

    i. the subject matter in order for it to be in accordance with (or based on) the criteria or
    ii. the responsible party's assertion in order for it to be fairly stated; and

c. communicate further as required by relevant AT-C sections.

(AT-C 210.03)

REQUIREMENTS

Terms of Engagement

The terms of engagement should be detailed in a written document and include:

- Identification of the measurement, evaluation, or disclosure criteria
- A statement that the engagement will be conducted in accordance with the AICPA's attestation standards
- Practitioner's responsibilities
- Responsibilities of the responsible party

Responsibilities of the engaging partner (if different from the responsible party)

- A statement that a review is substantially less in scope than an examination and, therefore, does not provide reasonable assurance
- Acknowledgment that the engaging party agrees to provide the practitioner with a representation letter at the conclusion of the engagement

(AT-C 210.09)

Elements of the engagement letter	Sample engagement letter
Date *Name, title, and address of individual signing on behalf of client*	May 15, 20X1 Elizabeth Yu, CFO Jade Imports 25 Smith Street San Francisco, CA Dear Ms. Yu:
Scope	We are pleased to confirm our understanding of the services we are to provide for Jade Imports. We will review the schedule of inventory of Jade Imports as of May 31, 20X1.
Engagement will be conducted in accordance with the AICPA's attestation standards	Our review will be conducted in accordance with attestation standards established by the American Institute of Certified Public Accountants.
Practitioner's responsibilities	Accordingly, it will include a physical count of inventory and other procedures we consider necessary to enable us to express an opinion as to whether your inventory is presented, in all material respects, in conformity with U.S. generally accepted accounting principles (GAAP), and whether it is fairly stated, in all material respects based on GAAP. If, for any reason, we are unable to complete the review, we will not issue a report as a result of this engagement.
Responsibilities of the responsible party	We understand that you will provide us with the basic information required for our review and that you are responsible for the accuracy and completeness of that information. We may advise you about appropriate criteria or assist in the development of the subject matter, but the responsibility for the subject matter remains with you.

	You are responsible for the presentation of the physical inventory in accordance with GAAP and for selecting the criteria and determining that such criteria are appropriate for your purposes. You are also responsible for making all management decisions and performing all management functions; for designating an individual who possesses suitable skill, knowledge, or experience to oversee the evaluating the adequacy and results of those services and accepting responsibility for them.
A review is substantially less in scope than an examination, and, therefore, does not provide reasonable assurance	A review differs significantly from, and is substantially less in scope than, an examination, the objective of which is the expression of an opinion on [*subject matter or assertion*]. Accordingly, we will not express such an opinion. We will not evaluate the [*subject matter or assertion*] to determine if they are appropriate for the Company's purposes. Consequently, we make no representation regarding the sufficiency of the [*subject matter or assertion*] either for the purpose of this engagement or for any other purpose.
A statement about the inherent limitations of the engagement	Our engagement cannot be relied upon to disclose errors, fraud, or noncompliance with laws and regulations that may exist. However, we will inform the Company of any material errors, fraud, or noncompliance with laws and regulations that come to our attention, unless they are clearly inconsequential.
Acknowledgment that the engaging party agrees to provide the practitioner with a representation letter at the conclusion of the engagement	At the conclusion of our engagement, we will require a representation letter from the management that, among other things, will confirm management's responsibility for the presentation of the inventory in accordance with GAAP.
Engagement partner	Bartholomew Sullivan is the engagement partner and is responsible for supervising the engagement and signing the report or authorizing another individual to sign it. We expect to begin our review on approximately May 31, 20X1.
Fees—Optional	**Fees** We estimate that our fees for these services will range from $10,000 to $12,000. You will also be billed for travel and other out-of-pocket costs such as report production, word processing, postage, etc. Additional expenses are estimated to be $5,000. The fee estimate is based on anticipated cooperation from your personnel and the assumption that unexpected circumstances will not be encountered during the engagement. If significant additional time is necessary, we will discuss it with you and arrive at a new fee estimate before we incur the additional costs. Our invoices for these fees will be rendered each month as work progresses and are payable on presentation. In accordance with our firm policies, work may be suspended if your account becomes 30 days or more overdue and will not be resumed until your account is paid in full. If we elect to terminate our services for nonpayment, you will be obligated to compensate us for all time expended and to reimburse us for all out-of-pocket expenditures through the date of termination.

Third-party service providers—Optional	**Subcontractors** We may from time to time, and depending on the circumstances, use third-party service providers in serving your account. We may share confidential information about you with these service providers, but remain committed to maintaining the confidentiality and security of your information. Accordingly, we maintain internal policies, procedures, and safeguards to protect the confidentiality of your personal information. In addition, we will secure confidentiality agreements with all service providers to maintain the confidentiality of your information and we will take reasonable precautions to determine that they have appropriate procedures in place to prevent the unauthorized release of your confidential information to others. In the event that we are unable to secure an appropriate confidentiality agreement, you will be asked to provide your consent prior to the sharing of your confidential information with the third-party service provider. Furthermore, we will remain responsible for the work provided by any such third-party service providers.
Request for agreement signature	**Agreement** We appreciate the opportunity to be of service to you and believe this letter accurately summarizes the significant terms of our engagement. If you have any questions, please let us know. If you agree with the terms of our engagement as described in this letter, please sign the enclosed copy and return it to us.
Signature and contract information of the practitioner	Sincerely, **Sullivan and Cregan, CPA** Bartholomew Sullivan, CPA Partner 800-555-1212 bsullivan@CPAFirm.com Enclosure
Acknowledgement of the responsible party	**Response:** This letter correctly sets forth the understanding of Jade Imports. Authorized Signature: ________________________ Title: ________________________ Date: ________________________

Written Assertion

The practitioner should request a written assertion about the measurement or evaluation of the subject matter against the criteria. The table below summarizes the practitioner's course of action if a written assertion is not received. (AT-C 210.11)

Circumstance	Practitioner's Course of Action
Engaging party is the responsible party and refuses to provide written assertion.	Withdraw if possible under law or regulation.
Engaging party is not the responsible party, and the responsible party refuses to provide a written assertion.	Need not withdraw. Disclose refusal in report and restrict the use of the report to the engaging party.

PLANNING THE ENGAGEMENT

AT-C 210.13 and .14 outline the major steps in planning a review engagement.

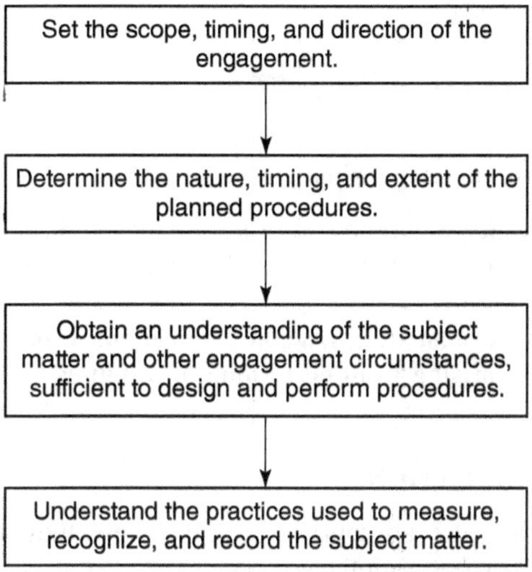

MATERIALITY

Materiality should be assessed when planning and performing the review engagement and when evaluating whether any material modifications are needed. (AT-C 210.14)

PROCEDURES

In review engagements, practitioners express limited assurance that the subject matter is in accordance with, or based on, the criteria or the assertion is fairly stated. Practitioners must acquire sufficient evidence to support the conclusion. (AT-C 210.15) When deciding on procedures to use, practitioners should consider:

- The subject matter
- The practices used by the responsible party to measure, recognize, and record the subject matter
- Engagement circumstances
- The risk that the practitioner may fail to modify the report when the subject matter is materially misstated.

(AT-C 210.16)

ANALYTICAL PROCEDURES

Analytical procedures are often seen as the foundation of a review engagement. Practitioners should:

- Determine the suitability of specific procedures.
- Assess the reliability of the underlying data.
- Develop expectations.

(AT-C 210.19)

When inconsistencies or deviations from expectations surface, practitioners should:

- Ask the responsible party about them.
- Assess the responsible party's response.
- Consider other procedures.

(AT-C 210.20)

Inquiries

Practitioners should ask the responsible party:

- How the subject matter was prepared in accordance with, or based on, the criteria
- Which practices are used by the responsible party to measure, recognize, and record the subject matter
- Whether there have been any relevant communications form regulatory agencies or others
- Any other questions arising from performing procedures

(AT-C 210.21)

Fraud, Laws, and Regulations

Practitioners should ask the appropriate parties where they had knowledge of actual, suspected, or alleged fraud or noncompliance related to the subject matter. Practitioners should respond appropriately to such matters. (AT-C 210.23 and .24)

Responding to Fraud or Noncompliance

If practitioners identify fraud or suspect fraud, they should consider one or more of the following procedures:

- Discuss the finding with the appropriate parties.
- Ask that the appropriate party bring the matter to a third party, such as legal counsel or regulator.
- Assess how the finding affects other aspects of the engagement.
- Obtain legal advice.
- Communicate with a regulator.

If practitioners are not satisfied with the results of these actions, practitioners may consider withdrawing from the engagement or discussing noncompliance or suspected noncompliance in a separate paragraph in the report. (AT-C 210.A31 and .A32)

Evaluating the Reliability of the Entity's Information

In addition to assessing the information related to fraud, practitioners should evaluate the other information attained for accuracy, completeness, or other problems. If the practitioners find problematic items, they should ask the responsible party to assess the effect of those items on the subject matter. When practitioners believe there may be a material misstatement, they should perform additional procedures. (AT-C 210.25-.26)

Using the Work of a Practitioner's Specialist or Internal Auditor

Practitioners using practitioner's specialists or internal auditors should apply the guidance in the chapter on AT-C 205.

EVALUATING THE RESULTS OF PROCEDURES

During the engagement, practitioners should compile a schedule of identified misstatements, other than those that are clearly trivial. The objective of this schedule is to determine if those misstatements are material to the subject matter, either individually or in the aggregate.

In addition to looking at misstatements for materiality, practitioners should make sure they have accumulated sufficient and appropriate evidence to support the conclusion. (AT-C 210.28-.29)

CONSIDERING SUBSEQUENT EVENTS AND SUBSEQUENTLY DISCOVERED FACTS

Practitioners should ask the responsible party or, if different, the engaging party, if they are aware of any events subsequent to the review and before the date of the practitioner's report that could significantly affect subject matter or an assertion. If practitioners become aware of such an event, they should make sure that adequate disclosure is made. After the date of the report, practitioners have no responsibility to perform procedures, but should respond appropriately. (AT-C 210.31 and .32)

WRITTEN REPRESENTATIONS

As with audits, it is important for practitioners to get representations in the form of a written letter addressed to the practitioner. In the case of a review, the representation should be made by the responsible party. The representation letter should be as of the date of the report and address the report's subject matter. (AT-C 210.37) The representation should include statements that:

- Include the assertion about the subject matter.
- All relevant matters are reflected in the measurement or evaluation of the subject matter or assertion.
- All known matters contradicting the subject matter or assertion and any communication from regulatory agencies or others affecting the subject matter or assertion have been disclosed to the practitioner.
- Acknowledge responsibility for:
  - The subject matter and the assertion,
  - Selecting the criteria when applicable, and
  - Determining that such criteria are appropriate for the responsible party's purposes.
- Any known events subsequent to the period (or point in time) of the subject matter being reported on that would have a material effect on the subject matter or assertion have been disclosed to the practitioner.
- It has provided the practitioner with all relevant information and access.
- If applicable, that the responsible party believes the effects of uncorrected misstatements are immaterial, individually and in the aggregate, to the subject matter.
- If applicable, that significant assumptions used in making any material estimates are reasonable.
- The responsible party has disclosed to the practitioner:
  - All deficiencies in internal control relevant to the engagement of which the responsible party is aware;
  - Its knowledge of any actual, suspected, or alleged fraud or noncompliance with laws or regulations affecting the subject matter; and
  - Other matters the practitioner deems appropriate.

(AU-C 210.33)

If the engaging party is not the responsible party and the responsible party refuses to provide the required written representations, the practitioner should get oral responses from the responsible party. (AT-C 210.34)

Representations from the Responsible Party

If the engaging party is not the responsible party, the practitioner should get additional representations from the engaging party. These representations include statements that:

- Acknowledge that the responsible party is responsible for the subject matter and assertion.
- Acknowledge the engaging party's responsibility for selecting the criteria, when applicable.
- Acknowledge the engaging party's responsibility for determining that such criteria are appropriate for its purposes.
- Acknowledge that the engaging party is not aware of any material misstatements in the subject matter or assertion.
- Acknowledge that the engaging party has disclosed to the practitioner all known events subsequent to the period (or point in time) of the subject matter being reported on that would have a material effect on the subject matter or assertion.
- Address other matters as the practitioner deems appropriate.

(AT-C 205.52)

Assessment of the Written Representations

The practitioners should not just accept the representations. For material representations, practitioners should make sure that they are reasonable and consistent with other information, and that representing parties are sufficiently informed to make the statements. (AT-C 205.53)

Requested Representations Not Provided or Not Reliable

The written representations may not be provided or may raise doubt about competence, integrity, ethics, or diligence of the representing party. In that case, practitioners should take the steps listed in the following table.

Course of Action When Requested Representations Are Not Provided or Are Not Reliable	
Engaging Party Is the Responsible Party (AT-C 210.38)	**Engaging Party Is Not the Responsible Party (AT-C 210.39)**
• Discuss the matter with the appropriate party; • Reevaluate the integrity of those from whom the representations were requested or received and evaluate the effect that this may have on the reliability of representations and evidence in general; and • If any of the matters are not resolved to the practitioner's satisfaction, take appropriate action.	• If one or more of the requested representations are not provided in writing by the responsible party, but the practitioner receives satisfactory oral responses to the practitioner's inquiries sufficient to enable the practitioner to conclude that the practitioner has sufficient appropriate evidence to form a conclusion about the subject matter, the practitioner's report should contain a separate paragraph that restricts the use of the report to the engaging party.

	• If one or more of the requested representations are provided neither in writing nor orally from the responsible party, a scope limitation exists, and the practitioner should determine the effect on the report, or the practitioner should withdraw from the engagement.

OTHER INFORMATION

There may be occasions where a party wants to include the practitioner's report in a document that contains the subject matter assertion and other information. A practitioner's report may appear in:

- Annual reports to holders of securities or beneficial interests
- Annual reports of organizations for charitable or philanthropic purposes
- Annual reports filed with regulatory authorities under the Securities Exchange Act of 1934
- Other documents to which the practitioner, at the client's request, devotes attention

If the practitioner is willing to include the report, the practitioner should read the other information for material inconsistency. If such an inconsistency exists or if there is a material misstatement of fact, then the practitioner should take appropriate action after discussing it with the responsible party. (AT-C 210.40)

FORMING A CONCLUSION

Practitioners form a conclusion on whether there are any material modifications that should be made in order for:

- The subject matter to be in accordance with, or based on, the criteria, or
- The assertion for it to be fairly stated.

The practitioner should make sure that the evidence supports the conclusion that there are no uncorrected material misstatements, individually or in the aggregate. Practitioners should also evaluate whether the presentation of the subject matter or assertion is misleading. (AT-C 210.42 and .43)

THE REPORT

The report should be written. In a review, the practitioner's conclusion should be expressed in the form of negative assurance (see illustrations of review reports). The practitioner should state whether any information came to his or her attention that indicated:

1. The subject matter is not based on (or in conformity with) the criteria or
2. The assertion is not presented in all material respects based on established or stated criteria.

If the report is an assertion, the assertion should be bound with the report or clearly stated in the report. (AT-C 210.44 and .45) The report should include the items listed in the left column in the following table.

Illustration: Practitioner's Review Report on Subject Matter; Unmodified Opinion

Report Requirements	Sample Report
A title that includes the word independent	**Independent Accountant's Report** Other examples of acceptable titles include: Report of Independent Certified Public Accountant Independent Practitioner's Report
An appropriate addressee as required by the circumstances of the engagement	Elizabeth Yu Jade Imports 25 Elizabeth Street San Francisco, CA
An identification or description of the subject matter or assertion being reported on, including the point in time or period of time to which the measurement or evaluation of the subject matter or assertion relates	We have reviewed the schedule of physical inventory as of May 31, 20X1.
The responsible party and its responsibility for the subject matter in accordance with (or based on) the criteria or for its assertion	Jade Imports' management is responsible for presenting the schedule of physical inventory in accordance with U.S. generally accepted accounting principles.
An identification of the criteria against which the subject matter was measured or evaluated	The inventory is measured based on U.S. generally accepted accounting principles.
The practitioner's responsibility to express a conclusion on the subject matter or assertion, based on the practitioner's review	Our responsibility is to express an opinion on the schedule of physical inventory based on our review.
The practitioner's review was conducted in accordance with attestation standards established by the AICPA.	Our review was conducted in accordance with attestation standards established by the American Institute of Certified Public Accountants.
AICPA attestation standards require that the practitioner plan and perform the review to obtain limited assurance about whether: (1) *The subject matter is in accordance with (or based on) the criteria, in all material respects (or equivalent language regarding the subject matter and criteria, such as the language used in the examples in paragraph .A65), or* (2) *The responsible party's assertion in order for it to be fairly stated.*	Those standards require that we plan and perform the review to obtain limited assurance about whether any material modifications should be made to the schedule of physical inventory in order for it to be in accordance with the criteria.
Limitations of a review	A review is substantially less in scope than an examination, the objective of which is to obtain reasonable assurance about whether the schedule of physical inventory is in accordance with, or based on, the criteria, in all material respects, or the responsible party's assertion is fairly stated, in all material respects in order to

	express an opinion. Accordingly, the practitioner does not express such an opinion. The review provides a reasonable basis for the practitioner's conclusion.
Significant inherent limitations, if any, associated with the measurement or evaluation of the subject matter against the criteria	[*Include a description of significant inherent limitations, if any.*]
Other matters	[*Additional paragraph(s) may be added to emphasize certain matters relating to the attestation engagement or the subject matter.*]
The practitioner's conclusion	Based on our review, we are not aware of any material modification that should be made to the accompanying schedule of physical inventory of Jade Imports as of May 31, 2016 in order for it to be in accordance with U.S. GAAP.
The manual or printed signature of the practitioner's firm	Bartholomew Sullivan, CPA
The city and state where the practitioner practices	San Francisco, CA
The date of the report	June 25, 20X1*

* The report should be dated no earlier than the date on which:

- The practitioner has obtained sufficient appropriate review evidence on which to base the practitioner's conclusion, including evidence that the attestation documentation has been reviewed;
- If applicable, the written presentation of the subject matter has been prepared; and
- The responsible party has provided a written assertion or, in circumstances described previously, an oral assertion.

Restricted Use Paragraph

If a restricted use paragraph is called for, the alert should be presented in a separate paragraph that restricts the use of the report. The alert should:

- State that the report is intended solely for the information and use of specified parties,
- Identify those parties, and
- State that other party should not use the report. (ADT-C 210.48)

Circumstances that call for restricted use include when:

- The criteria are appropriate only for those who participated in their establishment or are presumed to have an adequate understanding of the criteria.
- The criteria are available only to specified parties.
- The engaging party is not the responsible party and the responsible party provides only oral representations. Those circumstances should disclosed in the report, and the report should be restricted to the engaging party. (AU-C 205.84)

(AT-C 210.47)

MODIFIED OPINIONS

A modified conclusion includes a separate paragraph in the report that describes the reason for the modification. (AT-C 205.69)

Type of Opinion	Circumstances	Opinion	Practitioner's Responsibility in Report
Modified	Concludes that the subject matter is misstated and incorrect.	Separate paragraph that describes the matter(s) giving rise to the modification.	Separate paragraph
Qualified	Has obtained sufficient appropriate evidence, but concludes that misstatements, individually or in the aggregate, are material, but not pervasive to the subject matter.		Statement that the practitioner believes that the evidence petitioner has obtained is sufficient and appropriate to provide a basis for the practitioners modified opinion.
None—Withdraw if possible	Misstatements, individually or in the aggregate, are both material and pervasive to the subject matter. Is unable to obtain sufficient appropriate evidence to reach a conclusion.		
(AU-C 210.51-.58)			

Communicating with the Responsible and Engaging Partners

Practitioners should communicate the following to the responsible party:

- Known or suspected fraud
- Known noncompliance with laws or regulations
- Uncorrected misstatements

This information should be given to the engaging party if the responsible party is not the engaging party. (AT-C 210.61)

DOCUMENTATION

The form and content of documentation depends on the particular engagement's circumstances. Practitioners should use professional judgment when determining the quantity, type, and content of the documentation. Documentation is the principal record of the procedures applied, information obtained, and conclusion reached. The documentation provides the primary support for the report and assists in the conduct and supervision of the engagement. It should be sufficient to:

- Understand the nature, timing, extent, and results of procedures performed.
- Identify which engagement team members performed the work and the date it was completed.

It should also include documentation of:

- The discussions with the responsible party or others about significant findings or issues, including when the discussions were held and with whom.
- Who reviewed the engagement work performed, the date of the review, and the extent of the review.
- Documentation regarding the responsible party's refusal to provide one or more written representations or doubt about the reliability of the responsible party's representations.
- Documentation regarding the responsible party's responses to requests for written representation under AT-C 205.51. (See the "Written Representations" section in this chapter.)

ILLUSTRATIONS—ILLUSTRATIVE PRACTITIONER'S REVIEW REPORTS

ILLUSTRATION 1. PRACTITIONER'S REVIEW REPORT ON SUBJECT MATTER; UNMODIFIED CONCLUSION

The following is an illustrative practitioner's review report in which the practitioner has reviewed the subject matter and is reporting on the subject matter.

Independent Accountant's Review Report

Board of Directors
Jade Imports

We have reviewed [*identify the subject matter, for example, the accompanying schedule of investment returns of Jade Imports for the year ended December 31, 20XX*]. Jade Imports' management is responsible for [*identify the subject matter, for example, presenting the schedule of investment returns*] in accordance with (or based on) [*identify the criteria, for example, the ABC criteria set forth in Note 1*]. Our responsibility is to express a conclusion on [*identify the subject matter, for example, the schedule of investment returns*] based on our review.

Our review was conducted in accordance with attestation standards established by the American Institute of Certified Public Accountants. Those standards require that we plan and perform the review to obtain limited assurance about whether any material modifications should be made to [*identify the subject matter, for example, the schedule of investment returns*] in order for it to be in accordance with (or based on) the criteria. A review is substantially less in scope than an examination, the objective of which is to obtain reasonable assurance about whether [*identify the subject matter, for example, the schedule of investment returns*] is in accordance with (or based on) the criteria, in all material respects, in order to express an opinion. Accordingly, we do not express such an opinion. We believe that our review provides a reasonable basis for our conclusion.

[*Include a description of significant inherent limitations, if any, associated with the measurement or evaluation of the subject matter against the criteria.*]

[*Additional paragraph(s) may be added to emphasize certain matters relating to the attestation engagement or the subject matter.*]

Based on our review, we are not aware of any material modifications that should be made to [*identify the subject matter, for example, the accompanying schedule of investment returns of Jade Imports for the year ended December 31, 20X1*], in order for it be in accordance with (or based on) [*identify the criteria, for example, the ABC criteria set forth in Note 1*].

Sullivan and Cregan, CPAs
San Francisco, CA
June 25, 20X2

ILLUSTRATION 2. PRACTITIONER'S REVIEW REPORT ON AN ASSERTION; UNMODIFIED CONCLUSION; USE OF THE REPORT IS RESTRICTED TO SPECIFIED PARTIES

Independent Accountant's Review Report

Board of Directors
Jade Imports

We have reviewed management of Jade Imports' assertion that [*identify the assertion, including the subject matter and the criteria, for example, the accompanying schedule of investment returns of Jade Imports for the year ended December 31, 20XX, is presented in accordance with (or based on) the ABC criteria set forth in Note 1*]. Jade Imports' management is responsible for its assertion. Our responsibility is to express a conclusion on management's assertion based on our review.

Our review was conducted in accordance with attestation standards established by the American Institute of Certified Public Accountants. Those standards require that we plan and perform the review to obtain limited assurance about whether any material modifications should be made to management's assertion in order for it to be fairly stated. A review is substantially less in scope than an examination, the objective of which is to obtain reasonable assurance about whether management's assertion is fairly stated, in all material respects, in order to express an opinion. Accordingly, we do not express such an opinion. We believe that our review provides a reasonable basis for our conclusion.

[*Include a description of significant inherent limitations, if any, associated with the measurement or evaluation of the subject matter against the criteria.*]

[*Additional paragraph(s) may be added to emphasize certain matters relating to the attestation engagement or the subject matter.*]

Based on our review, we are not aware of any material modifications that should be made to management of Jade Imports' assertion in order for it to be fairly stated.

This report is intended solely for the information and use of [*identify the specified parties, for example, Pearl River Emporium and Jade Imports*], and is not intended to be, and should not be, used by anyone other than the specified parties.

Sullivan and Cregan, CPAs
San Francisco, CA
June 25, 20X2

ILLUSTRATION 3. PRACTITIONER'S REVIEW REPORT ON SUBJECT MATTER; QUALIFIED CONCLUSION

Independent Accountant's Review Report

Board of Directors
Jade Imports

We have reviewed [*identify the subject matter, for example, the accompanying schedule of investment returns of Jade Imports for the year ended December 31, 20XX*]. Jade Imports' management is responsible for [*identify the subject matter, for example, presenting the schedule of investment returns*] based on [*identify the criteria, for example, the ABC criteria set forth in Note 1*]. Our responsibility is to express a conclusion on [*identify the subject matter, for example, the schedule of investment returns*] based on our review.

Our review was conducted in accordance with attestation standards established by the American Institute of Certified Public Accountants. Those standards require that we plan and perform the review to obtain limited assurance about whether any material modifications should be made to [*identify the subject matter, for example, the schedule of investment returns*] in order for it to be in accordance with (or based on) the criteria. A review is substantially less in scope than an examination, the objective of which is to obtain reasonable assurance about whether [*identify the subject matter, for example, the schedule of investment returns*] is in accordance with (or based on) the criteria, in all material respects, in order to express an opinion. Accordingly, we do not express such an opinion. We believe that our review provides a reasonable basis for our conclusion.

[*Include a description of significant inherent limitations, if any, associated with the measurement or evaluation of the subject matter against the criteria.*]

[*Additional paragraph(s) may be added to emphasize certain matters relating to the attestation engagement or the subject matter.*]

Our review identified [*describe condition(s) that, individually or in the aggregate, resulted in a material misstatement, or deviation from, the criteria*].

Based on our review, except for the matter(s) described in the preceding paragraph, we are not aware of any material modifications that should be made to [*identify the subject matter, for example, the accompanying schedule of investment returns of Jade Imports for the year ended December 31, 20XX*], in order for it to be in accordance with (or based on) [*identify the criteria, for example, the ABC criteria set forth in Note 1*].

Sullivan and Cregan, CPAs
San Francisco, CA
June 25, 20X2

AT-C 215 Agreed-Upon Procedures Engagements

ORIGINAL PRONOUNCEMENT

Source Statement on Standards for Attestation Engagements (SSAE) 18.

APPLICABILITY

AT-C 215 applies when performing all agreed-upon procedures engagements, except engagements to issue comfort letters to underwriters. Guidance for those engagements can be found in AU-C 920. On every attestation engagement, the practitioners must comply with Section 105, one of service sections numbered in the 200s, and any relevant subject matter section in the section. (AT-C 210.01) See the chapter on the AT-C Preface for more information about the AT-C section structure.

If practitioners engage to perform agreed-upon procedures as part of or in addition to another type of service, AT-C 215 applies only to the agreed-upon procedures service. The report on agreed-upon procedures may be combined with a report on other services as long as the service can be clearly distinguished. (AT-C 215.03)

DEFINITIONS OF TERMS

See the "Definitions of Terms" section in the Appendix to the chapter on the AT-C Preface for a definition of the term *nonparticipant party*, relevant to this Section.

OBJECTIVES OF AT-C SECTION 215

In conducting an agreed-upon services engagement, the practitioner's objectives are to:

a. apply to the subject matter procedures that are established by specified parties who are responsible for the sufficiency of the procedures for their purposes;
b. issue a written practitioner's report that describes the procedures applied and the practitioner's findings; and
c. communicate further as required by relevant AT-C sections.

REQUIREMENTS

INDEPENDENCE

Section 215 requires practitioners to be independent when performing attestation engagements unless required to perform the engagement by law or regulation. In that case, practitioners should disclaim an opinion, stating they are not independent. If the practitioners provide the reasons for nonindependence, they must give all the reasons. (AT-C 215.09)

PRECONDITIONS

In addition to the preconditions specified in AT-C 105, the following preconditions must be met:

- The specified parties agree on the procedures and take responsibility for the sufficiency of the agree-upon procedures.
- The practitioner determines that the procedure can be:
  - Performed,
  - Reported on according to the guidance in Section 215, and
  - Expected to result in reasonably consistent findings.
- The practitioner agrees to apply the specified parties' materiality limit, if any, for reporting purposes.
- Use of the report is restricted to specified parties.

(AT-C 215.10)

TERMS OF ENGAGEMENT

The terms of engagement should be detailed in an engagement letter or other written agreement, including:

a. The nature of the engagement
b. Identification of:
   i. The subject matter or assertion,
   ii. The responsible party,
   iii. The criteria to be used, and
   iv. Specified parties
c. Acknowledgment by the specified parties of their responsibility for the sufficiency of the procedures
d. The practitioner's responsibilities
e. That the engagement will be conducted in accordance with attestation standards established by the AICPA
f. Enumeration of (or referring to) the procedures
g. Disclaimers expected to be included in the practitioner's report
h. Use restrictions
i. Assistance to be provided to the practitioner
j. Any involvement of a practitioner's external specialist
k. The specified parties' agreed-upon materiality limits, if applicable

(AT-C 215.14)

Sample Engagement Letter

May 31, 20X1
Elizabeth Yu
Chief Operating Officer
Jade Imports
25 Smith Street
San Francisco, CA
Dear Ms. Yu,

This engagement letter confirms our understanding of the terms and objectives of our engagement and limitations of the services that Sullivan, CPAs will provide to Jade Imports. This engagement is solely to assist you and the Board of Directors in determining if the accounts receivable trial balance accurately reflects amounts due from customers as of May 31, 20X1. The Company and members of the Board of Directors shall be referred to collectively as the "Parties."

Scope of Services

We will apply the agreed-upon procedures described in the attached schedule (schedule A) to accounts receivable of Jade Imports as of May 31, 20X1, prepared in accordance with US Generally Accepted Accounting Principles (GAAP). You may specify changes to the scope or nature of the agreed-upon procedures. If this occurs, we will amend schedule A to address the change in agreed-upon procedures.

Our engagement to apply the agreed-upon procedures will be performed in accordance with Statements on Standards for Attestation Engagements issued by the AICPA.

When we complete our procedures, we will issue a report describing the agreed-upon procedures and our findings. Bartholomew Sullivan is responsible for supervising the engagement and authorizing the signing of our report.

Limitations of the Agreed-Upon Procedures

The performance of agreed-upon procedures does not constitute an examination, and we will not express an opinion on the accounts receivable balance as of May 31, 20X1. Moreover, we have no obligation to perform any procedures beyond those listed in schedule A. Our report will contain a paragraph indicating that had we performed additional procedures, other matters might have come to our attention that would have been reported to you. Also, our report is intended solely for the use of the Parties and should not be used by anyone other than the Parties.

We will not evaluate the agreed-upon procedures to determine if they are appropriate for the Parties' purposes. Consequently, we make no representation regarding the sufficiency of the agreed-upon procedures either for the purpose of this engagement or for any other purpose.

Our engagement cannot be relied upon to disclose errors, fraud, or noncompliance with laws and regulations that may exist. However, we will inform the Parties of any material errors, fraud, or noncompliance with laws and regulations that come to our attention, unless they are clearly inconsequential.

Responsibility for Agreed-Upon Procedures

The Parties acknowledge that they specified the agreed-upon procedures, and they are solely responsible for the sufficiency of the procedures.

You are responsible for the following:

- Making all management decisions and performing all management functions in connection with the services and information provided resulting from this engagement
- Designating an individual with suitable skill, knowledge, and/or experience to oversee our services
- Evaluating the adequacy and results of the services performed
- Accepting responsibility for the results of the services performed
- Designing, implementing, and maintaining internal control relevant to the preparation and fair presentation of the information provided to us
- Preventing and detecting fraud
- Identifying and ensuring that the Company complies with applicable laws and regulations
- Making all financial records and related information available to us and for the accuracy and completeness of that information

At the conclusion of our engagement, we will require a representation letter from the Company's management that, among other things, will confirm management's responsibility for the presentation of the schedule of accounts receivable in accordance with GAAP.

If the above terms are acceptable to the Parties and the services outlined are in accordance with your understanding (including the description of agreed-upon procedures in schedule A), please sign the enclosed copy of this letter in the space provided and return it to us.

Sincerely yours,
Bartholomew Sullivan
ACCEPTED AND AGREED:

This engagement letter sets forth the entire understanding of the Parties with respect to the services to be provided by Sullivan, CPAs:

By Jade Imports:
Signature: ____________________
Print Name: ____________________
Title: ____________________
Date: ____________________
By [*Name of specified party(ies)*]:
Signature: ____________________
Print Name: ____________________
Title: ____________________
Date: ____________________

____

Schedule A

The scope of this engagement is limited to the following agreed-upon procedures:

- Confirmation of accounts receivable from customers
- Comparison of the accounts receivable aged trial balance of accounts receivable with results of the confirmations received from customers

REQUESTING A WRITTEN ASSERTION

Practitioners should get written assertions from the responsible party. Those assertions should describe the measurement or evaluation of the subject matter against the criteria; for example:

> The accounts receivable trial balance accurately reflects amounts due from customers as of December 31, 20X1.

If the engaging party is not the responsible party and practitioners know that the responsible party will not provide a written assertion, the engagement letter should specify that no written assertion will be provided. (AT-C 215.15 and .16)

PROCEDURES

The procedures agreed upon by the practitioner and the specified parties may be as limited or as extensive as the specified parties wish. Mere reading of an assertion or specified information, however, is not sufficient to permit a practitioner to report on the results of applying agreed-upon procedures.

The procedures to be performed are specified in the engagement letter. However, during the course of the engagement, the procedures may be changed. If so, those changes should be agreed to in writing with the specified party. Procedures should be clearly stated and not open to interpretation. (AT-C 215.17-.19) Section 215 provides some examples of appropriate and inappropriate procedures, listed in the following table.

Appropriate Procedures	Inappropriate Procedures
Execution of a sampling application after agreeing on relevant parameters	Mere reading of the work performed by others solely to describe their findings
Inspection of specified documents evidencing certain types of transactions or detailed attributes thereof	Evaluating the competency or objectivity of another party
Confirmation of specific information with third parties	Obtaining an understanding about a particular subject
Comparison of documents, schedules, or analyses with certain specified attributes	Interpreting documents outside the scope of the practitioner's professional expertise
Performance of specific procedures on work performed by others	
Performance of mathematical computations	
(AT-C 215.A17)	(AT-C 215.A18)

The procedures should be sufficient to provide a reasonable basis or the findings in the report. (AT-C 215.20)

Involvement of a Practitioner's External Specialist

The practitioners and the specified parties should explicitly agree to involving a specialist in assisting practitioners in performing an agreed-upon procedures engagement. Practitioners should not agree to merely read the specialist's report solely to describe or repeat the specialist's findings in his or her report. The latter does not constitute assistance to the practitioner. (AT-C 215.21)

A description of the nature of the assistance provided should be included in the report. (AT-C 215.22)

Involvement of Internal Auditors or Other Practitioners

Practitioners must perform the agreed-upon procedures included in their report. Internal auditors or others may prepare schedules and accumulate data or provide other information for the practitioner, but cannot perform agreed-upon procedures reported on by the practitioner. (AT-C 215.23)

The Practitioner's Report

The practitioner's report should be dated as of the date of completion of the agreed-upon procedures. (AT-C 215.34) The practitioner's agreed-upon procedures report should be written in the form of procedures and findings. Section 215 does not mandate a specific format but does list elements that are required. The report should include:

a. A title that includes the word *independent*.
b. An appropriate addressee as required by the circumstances of the engagement.
c. An identification of the subject matter or assertion and the nature of an agreed-upon procedures engagement.
d. An identification of the specified parties.
e. A statement that the procedures performed were those agreed to by the specified parties identified in the report.
f. A statement that identifies the responsible party and its responsibility for the subject matter or its assertion.
g. A statement that:
    i. The sufficiency of the procedures is solely the responsibility of the parties specified in the report.
    ii. The practitioner makes no representation regarding the sufficiency of the procedures either for the purpose for which the report has been requested or for any other purpose.
h. A list of the procedures performed (or reference thereto) and related findings.
i. When applicable, a description of any agreed-upon materiality limits.
j. A statement that:
    i. The agreed-upon procedures engagement was conducted in accordance with attestation standards established by the American Institute of Certified Public Accountants.
    ii. The practitioner was not engaged to and did not conduct an examination or review, the objective of which would be the expression of an opinion or conclusion, respectively, on the subject matter.
    iii. The practitioner does not express such an opinion or conclusion.
    iv. Had the practitioner performed additional procedures, other matters might have come to the practitioner's attention that would have been reported.
k. When applicable, a description of the nature of the assistance provided by a practitioner's external specialist, as discussed in paragraphs .21 and .22.

l. When applicable, reservations or restrictions concerning procedures or findings.

m. An alert, in a separate paragraph, that restricts the use of the report. The alert should:
   i. State that the practitioner's report is intended solely for the information and use of the specified parties,
   ii. Identify the specified parties for whom use is intended, and
   iii. State that the report is not intended to be, and should not be, used by anyone other than the specified parties.

n. When the engagement is also performed in accordance with Government Auditing Standards, the alert that restricts the use of the report should include the following information, rather than the information required by paragraph .35m:
   i. A description of the purpose of the report, and
   ii. A statement that the report is not suitable for any other purpose.

o. The manual or printed signature of the practitioner's firm.
p. The city and state where the practitioner practices.
q. The date of the report. The report should be dated no earlier than the date on which the practitioner completed the procedures and determined the findings, including that:
   i. The attestation documentation has been reviewed,
   ii. If applicable, the written presentation of the subject matter has been prepared, and
   iii. The responsible party has provided a written assertion, unless the responsible party refuses to provide an assertion.

(AT-C 215.35)

Other requirements are as follows:

1. If applicable, and if the practitioner does not withdraw from the engagement or change the engagement to another form of engagement, disclose in the report that the responsibility party refuses to provide a written assertion (see the section "Requesting a Written Assertion"). (AT-C 215.36)
2. If, in connection with the application of agreed-upon procedures, matters come to the practitioner's attention by other means that significantly contradict the subject matter (or written assertions), include this matter in the report. (AT-C 215.41)

RESTRICTIONS ON THE PERFORMANCE OF PROCEDURES

Practitioners should attempt to have specified parties agree to any modification of the agreed-upon procedures when circumstances impose restrictions on the performance of those procedures. If an agreement cannot be obtained (for example, when the agreed-upon procedures are published by a regulatory agency that will not modify those procedures), the practitioner should either describe any restrictions in his or her report or withdraw from the engagement. (AT-C 215.37)

ADDING SPECIFIED PARTIES

Practitioners may be asked to consider adding another party as a specified party (a nonparticipant party—see the "Definitions of Terms" section in the Appendix to the AT-C Preface chapter) after the completion of the agreed-upon procedures engagement. If practitioners agree to add the nonparticipant party as a specified party, they should obtain affirmative acknowledgment from that party, normally in writing, agreeing to the procedures performed and agreeing to take responsibility for the sufficiency of those procedures.

If a nonparticipant party is added after the practitioner has issued the report, the practitioner may reissue the report or provide written acknowledgment that a party has been added. If the report is reissued, the report date should not be changed. If written acknowledgment is provided, the acknowledgment ordinarily should state that no procedures have been performed subsequent to the date of the report. (AT-C 215.38-.40)

Knowledge of Outside Matters

If matters come to the practitioner's attention by other means outside the agreed-upon procedures that significantly contradict the assertion referred to in the report, the practitioner should include the matter in the report. (AT-C 215.41)

INTERPRETATION

Third-Party Due Diligence Services Related to Asset-Backed Securitizations: SEC Release No. 34-72936

The Securities and Exchange Commission (SEC) issued Release No. 34-72936, *Nationally Recognized Statistical Rating Organizations.* The release acknowledges that certain procedures often performed by practitioners as agreed-upon procedures engagements related to asset-backed securitizations (ABS) are considered third-party *due diligence services.* These include due diligence services that relate to checking the accuracy of the information or data about the assets provided by the securitizer or originator of the assets.

The release requires:

- The issuer or underwriter of any ABS to make publicly available the findings and conclusions of any third-party due diligence report obtained by the issuer or underwriter.
- Any third-party due diligence service provider to complete Form ABS Due Diligence-15E.

The release goes on to state:

> The Commission understands there may be particular considerations that would need to be taken into account under applicable professional standards that govern certain services provided by the accounting profession. The requirements and limitations resulting from relevant professional standards generally are described within the reports issued and, to the extent such requirements or limitations are based upon professional standards, the Commission would not object to the inclusion of the same description in the written certifications.

The procedures or findings of due diligence services conducted as agreed-upon procedures engagements are made public through the EDGAR system and/or through the process by which the nationally recognized statistical rating organization (NRSRO) publishes its credit ratings.

In response to the SEC release, the American Institute of Certified Public Accountants (AICPA) issued an interpretation in February 2015. The interpretation guides practitioners in how to respond to certain aspects of the release and potential conflicts with professional standards.

On the SEC form for due diligence services performed as an agreed-upon procedures engagement, the practitioner should include all of the elements in paragraph .31 of AT Section 201 and clarifying wording.

The use of an agreed-upon-procedures report may need to be restricted. If that is the case, the practitioner may want to inform the client that restricted-use reports are not intended for distribution to nonspecified parties, regardless of whether the report is included in a document containing a separate general-use report. A restricted-use report should alert readers to the restriction on the use of the report by indicating that the report is not intended to be and should not be used by anyone other than the specified parties.

ILLUSTRATIONS

EXHIBIT—ILLUSTRATIVE PRACTITIONER'S AGREED-UPON PROCEDURES REPORTS (AT-C 215.A48)

ILLUSTRATION 1. PRACTITIONER'S AGREED-UPON PROCEDURES REPORT RELATED TO A STATEMENT OF INVESTMENT PERFORMANCE STATISTICS

Independent Accountant's Report on Applying Agreed-Upon Procedures

[*Appropriate addressee*]

We have performed the procedures enumerated below, which were agreed to by [*identify the specified party(ies), for example, the audit committees and managements of ABC Inc. and XYZ Fund*], on [*identify the subject matter, for example, the accompanying Statement of Investment Performance Statistics of XYZ Fund for the year ended December 31, 20X1*]. XYZ Fund's management is responsible for [*identify the subject matter, for example, the Statement of Investment Performance Statistics for the year ended December 31, 20X1*]. The sufficiency of these procedures is solely the responsibility of the parties specified in this report. Consequently, we make no representation regarding the sufficiency of the procedures enumerated below either for the purpose for which this report has been requested or for any other purpose.

[*Include paragraphs to enumerate procedures and findings.*]

This agreed-upon procedures engagement was conducted in accordance with attestation standards established by the American Institute of Certified Public Accountants. We were not engaged to and did not conduct an examination or review, the objective of which would be the expression of an opinion or conclusion, respectively, on [*identify the subject matter, for example, the accompanying Statement of Investment Performance Statistics of XYZ Fund for the year ended December 31, 20X1*]. Accordingly, we do not express such an opinion or conclusion. Had we performed additional procedures, other matters might have come to our attention that would have been reported to you.
[*Additional paragraph(s) may be added to describe other matters.*]

This report is intended solely for the information and use of [*identify the specified party(ies), for example, the audit committees and managements of ABC Inc. and XYZ Fund*], and is not intended to be, and should not be, used by anyone other than the specified parties.
[*Practitioner's signature*]

[*Practitioner's city and state*]

[*Date of practitioner's report*]

ILLUSTRATION 2. PRACTITIONER'S AGREED-UPON PROCEDURES REPORT RELATED TO CASH AND ACCOUNTS RECEIVABLE

Independent Accountant's Report on Applying Agreed-Upon Procedures

[*Appropriate addressee*]

We have performed the procedures enumerated below, which were agreed to by [*identify the specified party(ies), for example, the boards of directors and managements of ABC Company and XYZ Company*], on [*identify the subject matter, for example, the cash and accounts receivable information of

XYZ Company as of December 31, 20XX, included in the accompanying information provided to us by management of ABC Company]. XYZ Company is responsible for [*identify the subject matter, for example, the cash and accounts receivable information of XYZ Company as of December 31, 20XX, included in the accompanying information provided to us by management of ABC Company*]. The sufficiency of these procedures is solely the responsibility of the parties specified in this report. Consequently, we make no representation regarding the sufficiency of the procedures enumerated below either for the purpose for which this report has been requested or for any other purpose.

The procedures and the associated findings are as follows:

Cash

1. For the four bank accounts listed below, we obtained:
   a. The December 31, 20XX, bank reconciliations from XYZ Company management and
   b. The December 31, 20XX, general ledger from XYZ Company management.
2. We performed the following procedures:
   a. Obtained a bank confirmation directly from each bank of the cash on deposit as of December 31, 20XX.
   b. Compared the balance confirmed by the bank to the amount shown on the respective bank reconciliations.
   c. Mathematically checked the bank reconciliations.
   d. Compared the cash balances per book listed in the reconciliations below to the respective general ledger account balances.

Cash December 31, 20XX	
Bank	Cash Balance per Book
DEF National Bank, general ledger account 123	$5,000
LMN State Bank, general ledger account 124	3,776
RST Trust Company regular account, general ledger account 125	86,912
RST Trust Company payroll account, general ledger account 126	5,000
	$110,688

We found no exceptions as a result of the procedures.

Accounts Receivable

3. We obtained the accounts receivable aged trial balance as of December 31, 20XX, from XYZ Company (attached as exhibit A). We mathematically checked that the individual customer account balance subtotals in the aged trial balance of accounts receivable agreed to the total accounts receivable per the aged trial balance. We compared the total accounts receivable per the accounts receivable aged trial balance to the total accounts receivable per general ledger account 250.
   We found no exceptions as a result of the procedures.
4. We obtained the accounts receivable subsidiary ledger as of December 31, 20XX, from XYZ Company. We compared the individual customer account balance subtotals shown in the accounts receivable aged trial balance (exhibit A) as of December 31, 20XX, to the balances shown in the accounts receivable subsidiary ledger.
   We found no exceptions as a result of the procedures.
5. We selected 50 customer account balances from exhibit A by starting at the eighth item and selecting every fifteenth item thereafter until 50 were selected. The sample size selected represents 9.8% of the aggregate amount of the customer account balances. We obtained the corresponding invoices from

XYZ Company and traced the aging (according to invoice dates) for the 50 customer account balances shown in exhibit A to the details of outstanding invoices in the accounts receivable subsidiary ledger.

We found no exceptions as a result of the procedures.

6. We mailed confirmations directly to the customers representing the 150 largest customer account balance subtotals selected from the accounts receivable aged trial balance, and we received responses as indicated below. As agreed, any individual differences in a customer account balance of less than $300 were to be considered minor, and no further procedures were performed.

   Of the 150 customer balances confirmed, we received responses from 140 customers; 10 customers did not reply.

   No exceptions were identified in 120 of the confirmations received. The differences in the remaining 20 confirmation replies were less than $300.

   For the 10 customers that did not reply, we traced the items constituting the outstanding customer account balance to invoices and supporting shipping documents.

   A summary of the confirmation results according to the respective aging categories is as follows.

Accounts Receivable December 31, 20X1			
Aging Categories	**Customer Account Balances**	**Confirmations Requested**	**Confirmations Received**
Current	$156,000	$76,000	$ 65,000
Past Due:			
Less than one month	60,000	30,000	19,000
One to three months	36,000	18,000	10,000
More than three months	48,000	48.000	8,000
	$300,000	$172,000	$102,000

This agreed-upon procedures engagement was conducted in accordance with attestation standards established by the American Institute of Certified Public Accountants. We were not engaged to and did not conduct an examination or a review, the objective of which would be the expression of an opinion or conclusion, respectively, on [*identify the subject matter, for example, the cash and accounts receivable information of XYZ Company as of December 31, 20XX, included in the accompanying information provided to us by management of ABC Company*]. Accordingly, we do not express such an opinion or conclusion. Had we performed additional procedures, other matters might have come to our attention that would have been reported to you.

[*Additional paragraph(s) may be added to describe other matters.*]

This report is intended solely for the information and use of [*identify the specified party(ies), for example, the boards of directors and managements of ABC Company and XYZ Company*], and is not intended to be and should not be used by anyone other than the specified parties.

[*Practitioner's signature*]

[*Practitioner's city and state*]

[*Date of practitioner's report*]

ILLUSTRATION 3. PRACTITIONER'S AGREED-UPON PROCEDURES REPORT IN CONNECTION WITH CLAIMS OF CREDITORS

Independent Accountant's Report on Applying Agreed-Upon Procedures

[*Appropriate addressee*]

We have performed the procedures enumerated below, which were agreed to by [*identify the specified party(ies), for example, the Trustee of XYZ Company*], on [*identify the subject matter, for example, the claims of creditors of XYZ Company as of May 31, 20XX, as set forth in the accompanying Schedule A*]. XYZ Company is responsible for maintaining records of [*identify the subject matter, for example, the claims of creditors of XYZ Company as of May 31, 20XX, as set forth in the accompanying Schedule A*]. The sufficiency of these procedures is solely the responsibility of the party specified in this report. Consequently, we make no representation regarding the sufficiency of the procedures enumerated below either for the purpose for which this report has been requested or for any other purpose.

The procedures and associated findings are as follows:

1. Obtained the general ledger and the accounts payable trial balance as of May 31, 20XX, from XYZ Company. Compared the total of the accounts payable trial balance to the total accounts payable balance in general ledger account 450.
   The total of the accounts payable trial balance agreed with the total accounts payable balance in the general ledger account number 450.
2. Obtained the claim form submitted by creditors in support of the amounts claimed from XYZ Company. Compared the creditor name and amounts from the claim form to the respective name and amounts shown in the accounts payable trial balance obtained in procedure 1. For any differences identified, requested XYZ Company to provide supporting detail. Compared such identified differences to the supporting detail provided.
   All differences noted are presented in column 3 of Schedule A. Except for those amounts shown in column 4 of Schedule A, all such differences were agreed to [*describe supporting detail*].
3. Using the claim form obtained in procedure 2, compared the name and amount to invoices, and, if applicable, receiving reports, provided by XYZ Company.
   No exceptions were found as a result of this procedure.

This agreed-upon procedures engagement was conducted in accordance with attestation standards established by the American Institute of Certified Public Accountants. We were not engaged to and did not conduct an examination or review, the objective of which would be the expression of an opinion or conclusion, respectively, on [*identify the subject matter, for example, the claims of creditors of XYZ Company as of May 31, 20XX, as set forth in the accompanying Schedule A*]. Accordingly, we do not express such an opinion or conclusion. Had we performed additional procedures, other matters might have come to our attention that would have been reported to you.

[*Additional paragraph(s) may be added to describe other matters.*]

This report is intended solely for the information and use of [*identify the specified party(ies), for example, the Trustee of XYZ Company*], and is not intended to be, and should not be, used by anyone other than the specified party.

[*Practitioner's signature*]

[*Practitioner's city and state*]

[*Date of practitioner's report*]

AT-C 305 Prospective Financial Information

ORIGINAL PRONOUNCEMENT

Source Statement on Standards for Attestation Engagements (SSAE) 18.

APPLICABILITY

AT-C 305's guidance applies to all examination and agreed-upon procedures engagements on prospective financial information, and supplements the guidance in Section 105. On *every* attestation engagement, CPAs must comply with Section 105 and one of the service sections. For Section 305, CPAs must also comply with Section 205 on examination engagements or Section 215 on agreed-upon procedure engagements. (AT-C 305.01) See the chapter on the AT-C Preface for more information about the AT-C section structure.

Prospective financial information included in this section may be prospective financial statements or partial presentations.

Except for the introduction and definitions paragraphs, the guidance in this section is divided between examination engagements and agreed-upon procedures engagements.

DEFINITIONS OF TERMS

See the "Definitions of Terms" section in the Appendix to the chapter on the AT-C Preface for definitions of the following terms relevant to this Section: *entity*, *financial forecast*, *financial projection*, *Guide*,[1] *hypothetical assumption*, *key factors*, *partial presentation*, *presentation guidelines*, *prospective financial information*, and *prospective financial statements*.

To apply the guidance in Section 305, it is important to understand the differences between a forecast and a projection.

Financial Forecast	Financial Projection
Based on the responsible party's reasonable expectations	Based on the responsible party's knowledge and one or more hypothetical assumptions.
Acceptable for *general use*, that is, use by those with whom the responsible party is not negotiating directly. Also, acceptable for limited use.	Not acceptable for general use. Acceptable for only *limited use*, that is, by the responsible party alone or with third parties with whom the responsible party is negotiating directly.

1 The Guide referred to in this section is the AICPA Guide *Prospective Financial Information*.

OBJECTIVES—EXAMINATION ENGAGEMENTS

The objectives of AT-C 305 for examination engagements are to:

a. obtain reasonable assurance about whether, in all material respects,

i. the prospective financial information is presented in accordance with the guidelines for the presentation of prospective financial information established by the AICPA (AICPA presentation guidelines) and

ii. the assumptions underlying the forecast are suitably supported and provide a reasonable basis for the responsible party's forecast, or the assumptions underlying the projection are suitably supported and provide a reasonable basis for the responsible party's projection, given the hypothetical assumptions. (Ref: par. .A2)

b. express an opinion in a written report on the matters in "a."

(AT-C 305.08)

Practitioners do not address whether the prospective results can be achieved.

OBJECTIVIES—AGREED-UPON PROCEDURES ENGAGEMENTS

The objectives of AT-C 305 for examination engagements are:

a. Apply to the prospective financial information procedures that are established by specified parties who are responsible for the sufficiency of the procedures for their purposes, and

b. Issue a written report that describes the procedures applied and the practitioner's findings.

(AT-C 305.07)

REQUIREMENTS: EXAMINATION OF PROSPECTIVE FINANCIAL STATEMENTS

PRECONDITIONS FOR AN EXAMINATION ENGAGEMENT

Practitioners should not agree to the use of their names in conjunction with a financial projection that the practitioner believes will be distributed to those not negotiating directly with the responsible party. (AT-C 305.10)

Acceptable Examination Engagements

Practitioners may accept an engagement to examine:

- A forecast or projection if the responsible party has agreed to disclose the significant assumption
- A financial projection if the responsible party has agreed to identify in the presentation the hypothetical assumptions and the limitation on the usefulness of the projection
- A partial presentation if it describes the limitation on its usefulness

Change in Circumstances after Acceptance of the Engagement

At times, practitioners may encounter changes after accepting an engagement. The following table summarizes those possible changes and the practitioners' responses.

Examination Engagements	
Circumstances after Accepting the Engagement	***Course of Action***
Forecast or projection discloses *none* of the significant assumptions.	Withdraw from the engagement. If required to perform the engagement by law or regulation, express an adverse opinion.
Forecast or projection fails to disclose *one or more* significant assumptions.	Describe the assumptions in the report and express an adverse opinion.
Projection fails to describe or identify which of the assumptions is/are hypothetical or to describe the limitations on the usefulness of the projection.	Withdraw from the engagement. If required to perform the engagement by law or regulation, express an adverse opinion.
(AT-C 305.12-.14)	

TRAINING AND PROFICIENCY

Practitioners should:

- Understand the preparation and presentation guidelines in the Guide.
- Possess a sufficient level of knowledge of the industry.
- Obtain knowledge of the key factors on which the financial information is based.

(AT-C 305.15-.17)

REQUESTING A WRITTEN ASSERTION

Practitioners should withdraw, if possible under law or regulation, if the responsible party refuses to provide written assertions. (AT-C 305.18)

PROCEDURES

The following diagrams list the procedures for forecasts and projections.

Procedures for Forecasts

Evaluate whether the responsible party has a reasonably objective basis for the forecast.

↓

Determine whether sufficiently objective assumptions can be developed for each key factor.

↓

Perform procedures necessary to report on whether assumptions:
- *Are suitable supported.*
- *Provide a reasonable basis for the forecast.*

↓

Evaluate whether the preponderance of information supports each significant assumption.

↓

Evaluate whether the hypothetical assumptions are consistent with the purpose of the presentation.

↓

Evaluate in the aggregate whether the assumptions provide a reasonable basis for the forecast.

↓

Evaluate the assumptions related to an expired portion of the prospective period.

↓

Perform procedures to obtain reasonable assurance about whether:
- The presentation reflects the identified assumptions.
- Computations are mathematically accurate.
- Assumptions are internally consistent.
- Accounting principles are appropriate.
- Information is presented in accordance with AICPA guidance.
- Assumptions are adequately disclosed.

↓

Conclude whether prospective financial information should be revised because of:
- Mathematical errors
- Unreasonable or internally inconsistent assumptions
- Inappropriate or incomplete presentation
- Inadequate disclosure

Procedures for Projections

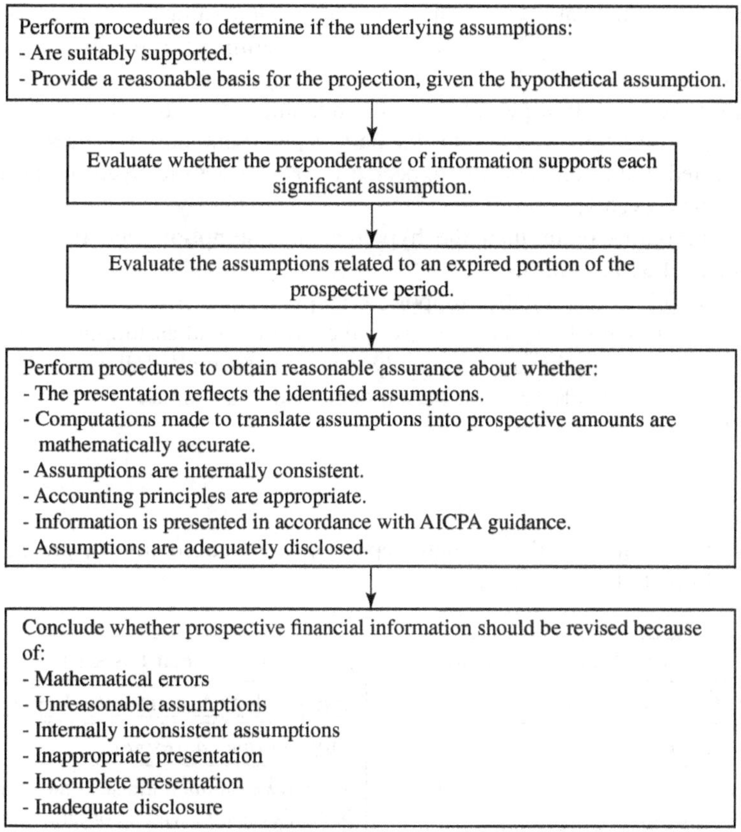

WRITTEN REPRESENTATIONS

In addition to the representations required by AT-C 205, practitioners should request the following representations.

Written Representations for Forecasts

a. The forecast presents the expected financial position, results of operations, and cash flows for the forecast period;
b. The forecast reflects the responsible party's judgment, based on present circumstances, of the expected conditions and the expected course of action;
c. The assumptions are reasonable and suitably supported;
d. If the forecast contains a range, the item or items subject to the assumptions are reasonably expected to fall within the range; and
e. The range was not selected in a biased or misleading manner.

Written Representations for Projections

a. The projection presents the hypothetical assumptions;
b. The projection indicates which of the hypothetical assumptions, if any, are improbable;
c. The projection presents the limitations of the usefulness of the presentation;
d. The projection presents the expected financial position, results of operations, and cash flows for the projection period given the hypothetical assumptions;
e. The projection reflects the responsible party's judgment, based on present circumstances, of expected conditions and the expected course of action given the occurrence of the hypothetical events;
f. The assumptions other than the hypothetical assumptions are reasonable, given the hypothetical assumptions;
g. The assumptions are suitably supported; and
h. If the projection contains a range, given the hypothetical assumptions, the item or items subject to the assumption are reasonably expected to actually fall within the range, and that the range was not selected in a biased or misleading manner.

(AT-C 305.28-.29)

REPORT

According to AT 301.33, the standard report on the examination of prospective financial statements should include the following:

Practitioner's Examination Report on a Financial Forecast	
Title that includes the word *independent*	**Independent Accountant's Report**
Appropriate addressee	[*Appropriate addressee*]
An identification of the prospective financial information being reported on	We have examined the accompanying forecast of XYZ Company, which comprises the forecasted balance sheet as of December 31, 20X1, and the related forecasted statements of income, stockholders' equity, and cash flows for the year then ending, . . .
An indication that the criteria against which the prospective financial information was measured or evaluated are the AICPA guidelines for the presentation of a forecast or projection	. . . based on the guidelines for the presentation of a forecast established by the American Institute of Certified Public Accountants.
A statement that identifies: i. The responsible party and its responsibility for preparing and presenting the prospective financial information in accordance with the AICPA guidelines ii. The practitioner's responsibility, which is to express an opinion on the prospective financial information, based on the practitioner's examination	XYZ Company's management is responsible for preparing and presenting the forecast in accordance with the guidelines for the presentation of a forecast established by the American Institute of Certified Public Accountants. Our responsibility is to express an opinion on the forecast based on our examination.

Practitioner's Examination Report on a Financial Forecast	
A statement that: i. The practitioner's examination was conducted in accordance with attestation standards established by the AICPA. ii. Those standards require that the practitioner plan and perform the examination to obtain reasonable assurance about whether the forecast (or projection) is presented in accordance with the AICPA guidelines in all material respects. iii. The practitioner believes the evidence obtained is sufficient and appropriate to provide a reasonable basis for the opinion.	Our examination was conducted in accordance with attestation standards established by the American Institute of Certified Public Accountants. Those standards require that we plan and perform the examination to obtain reasonable assurance about whether the forecast is presented in accordance with the guidelines for the presentation of a forecast established by the American Institute of Certified Public Accountants, in all material respects.
A description of the nature of an examination engagement	An examination involves performing procedures to obtain evidence about the forecast. The nature, timing, and extent of the procedures selected depend on our judgment, including an assessment of the risks of material misstatement of the forecast, whether due to fraud or to error. We believe that the evidence we obtained is sufficient and appropriate to provide a reasonable basis for our opinion.
The practitioner's opinion about: i. Whether the forecast (or projection) is presented, in all material respects, in accordance with the AICPA guidelines for the presentation of a forecast or projection, and ii. Whether the underlying assumptions are suitably supported and provide a reasonable basis for the forecast or a reasonable basis for the projection given the hypothetical assumptions.	In our opinion, the accompanying forecast is presented, in all material respects, in accordance with the guidelines for the presentation of a forecast established by the American Institute of Certified Public Accountants, and the underlying assumptions are suitably supported and provide a reasonable basis for management's forecast.
A statement indicating that the prospective results may not be achieved and describing other significant inherent limitations, if any.	There will usually be differences between the forecasted and actual results because events and circumstances frequently do not occur as expected, and those differences may be material.
A statement that the practitioner has no responsibility to update the report for events and circumstances occurring after the date of the report.	We have no responsibility to update this report for events and circumstances occurring after the date of this report.
The manual or printed signature of the practitioner's firm	Sullivan and Cregan, CPAs
The city and state where the practitioner practices	San Francisco, CA
The date of the report*	February 15, 20X2
(AT-C 305.33)	

* The report should be dated no earlier than the date on which the practitioner has obtained sufficient appropriate evidence on which to base the practitioner's opinion.

Report on an Examination of a Projection

An illustration of a report on an examination of a projection is presented at the end of this chapter. For a projection, the practitioner should express an opinion on whether the hypothetical assumptions provide a reasonable basis for the projection. In addition to the required elements listed above for a practitioner's report on an examination of a forecast, a report on an examination of a projection should include:

a. Identification of the hypothetical assumptions,
b. A description of the special purpose for which the projection was prepared, and
c. An alert, in a separate paragraph, that restricts the use of the report. The alert should:
    i. State that the report is intended solely for the information and use of the specified parties,
    ii. Identify the specified parties for whom use is intended, and
    iii. State that the report is not intended to be, and should not be, used by anyone other than the specified parties.
d. When the engagement is also performed in accordance with Government Auditing Standards, the alert that restricts the use of the report should include the following information, rather than the information required by paragraph .33c:
    i. A description of the purpose of the report, and
    ii. A statement that the report is not suitable for any other purpose.

(AT-C 305.33)

Modified Opinions

Modified Opinions—Examination Engagements	
Circumstance	***Opinion***
Prospective financial statements:	
Depart from AICPA presentation guidelines.	Issue a qualified opinion or an adverse opinion.
Fail to disclose significant assumptions.	Issue an adverse opinion.
Misapply accounting principles.	Issue an adverse opinion.
Are such that the practitioner is unable to obtain sufficient appropriate evidence.	Disclaim an opinion and describe the limitation.
One or more of the significant assumptions are not suitably supported or do not provide a reasonable basis for the *forecast*.	Issue an adverse opinion.
One or more of the significant assumptions do not provide a reasonable basis for the *projection*, given the hypothetical assumptions.	Issue an adverse opinion.
(AT-C 305.35)	

Qualified Opinion

A practitioner's report with a qualified opinion should include a separate explanatory paragraph that states all substantive reasons for the qualification and describes the departure from AICPA presentation guidelines. The opinion should include the words *except* or *exception* and should refer to the separate explanatory paragraph. (AT-C 305.A36)

Adverse Opinion

A practitioner's report with an adverse opinion should include a separate explanatory paragraph that states all substantive reasons for the adverse opinion. The opinion should state that the presentation is not in conformity with AICPA presentation guidelines and should refer to the separate explanatory paragraph.

If the assumptions do not provide a reasonable basis for the financial statements, the opinion paragraph should make that statement. If a significant assumption is not disclosed, the practitioner should describe the assumption in the report.

(AT-C 305.A36)

Disclaimer of Opinion

A practitioner's report with a disclaimer of opinion should include a separate explanatory paragraph that states how the examination did not comply with appropriate standards. The disclaimer of opinion paragraph should state that the scope of the examination was not sufficient to enable the practitioner to express an opinion on the presentation of or the assumptions underlying the forecast or projection. The disclaimer of opinion should include a direct reference to the separate explanatory paragraph. (AT-C 305.A38)

If there is a scope limitation and also material departures from presentation guidelines, the practitioner should describe the departures in the report.

Modification of Standard Examination Report

There are circumstances under which the practitioner should modify the report without modifying the opinion included in the report. The circumstances and the modifications are explained next.

Emphasis of a Matter

The practitioner may present explanatory information or other informative material regarding the prospective financial statements in a separate paragraph of the report.

Prospective Financial Information Contains a Range

If prospective financial information contains a range, the report should state in a separate paragraph that the responsible party has chosen to present that information in a range. AT Section 305's guidance suggests the following:

> As described in the summary of significant assumptions, management of XYZ Company has elected to portray forecasted [*describe the financial statement element or elements for which the expected results of one or more assumptions fall within a range, and identify assumptions expected to fall within a range, for example, revenue in the amounts of $X,XXX and $Y,YYY, which is predicated upon occupancy rates of XX percent and YY percent of available apartments*] rather than as a single

point estimate. Accordingly, the accompanying forecast presents forecasted financial position, results of operations, and cash flows [*describe one or more assumptions expected to fall within a range, for example, "at such occupancy rates"*]. However, there is no assurance that the actual results will fall within the range of [*describe one or more assumptions expected to fall within a range, for example, occupancy rates*] presented.
(AT-C 305.A33)

Examination Is Part of Larger Engagement

If the practitioner's examination of prospective financial statements is part of a larger engagement (for example, a financial feasibility study or business acquisition study), the practitioner may expand the report on the examination of the prospective financial statements to describe the entire engagement. (AT-C 305.A20)

REQUIREMENTS: APPLYING AGREED-UPON PROCEDURES TO PROSPECTIVE FINANCIAL STATEMENTS

PRECONDITIONS FOR AN AGREED-UPON PROCEDURES ENGAGEMENT

A practitioner may accept an engagement to apply agreed-upon procedures to prospective financial statements when the preconditions specified in Section 105 and Section 215 are met and the prospective financial information includes a summary of significant assumptions. (AT-C 305.38)

Practitioner's Report on Agreed-Upon Procedures

Practitioners do not offer an opinion or a conclusion in an agreed-upon procedures engagement. The practitioner's report on the results of applying agreed-upon procedures should include the elements listed in the following.

Practitioner's Report on Agreed-Upon Procedures	
Title that includes the word *independent*	**Independent Accountant's Agreed-Upon Procedures Report**
Appropriate addressee	[*Appropriate addressee*]
A statement that the procedures performed were those agreed to by the specified parties identified in the report	We have performed the procedures enumerated below, which were agreed to by the boards of directors of Jade Imports and Pearl River Emporium, on . . .
Identification of the prospective financial information and the nature of an agreed-upon procedures engagement	. . . the forecasted balance sheet as of December 31, 20X1 and the related forecasted statements of income, stockholders' equity, and cash flows for the year then ending.
A statement that identifies the responsible party and its responsibility for preparing and presenting the forecast (or projection) in accordance with the guidelines for the presentation of a forecast (or projection) established by the AICPA	Jade Imports' management is responsible for preparing and presenting the forecast in accordance with the guidelines for the presentation of a forecast established by the American Institute of Certified Public Accountants.

Practitioner's Report on Agreed-Upon Procedures	
The sufficiency of the procedures is solely the responsibility of the parties specified in the report.	The sufficiency of these procedures is solely the responsibility of those parties specified in this report.
The practitioner makes no representation regarding the sufficiency of the procedures.	Consequently, we make no representation regarding the sufficiency of the procedures enumerated below either for the purpose for which this report has been requested or for any other purpose.
A list of the procedures performed (or reference thereto) and related findings	
The agreed-upon procedures engagement was conducted in accordance with attestation standards established by the AICPA.	This agreed-upon procedures engagement was conducted in accordance with attestation standards established by the American Institute of Certified Public Accountants.
The practitioner was not engaged to and did not conduct an examination or a review, the objective of which would be the expression of an opinion or a conclusion, respectively, on whether the presentation of the forecast is in accordance with guidelines for the presentation of a forecast established by the AICPA, whether the underlying assumptions are suitably supported, and whether the underlying assumptions provide a reasonable basis for the forecast or a reasonable basis for the projection given the hypothetical assumptions.	We were not engaged to and did not conduct an examination or a review, the objective of which would be the expression of an opinion or a conclusion, respectively, about whether the forecast is presented in accordance with the guidelines for the presentation of a forecast established by the American Institute of Certified Public Accountants or whether the underlying assumptions are suitably supported or provide a reasonable basis for management's forecast. Accordingly, we do not express such an opinion or conclusion. Had we performed additional procedures, other matters might have come to our attention that would have been reported to you.
A statement indicating that the prospective results may not be achieved and describing other significant inherent limitations, if any	There will usually be differences between the forecasted and actual results because events and circumstances frequently do not occur as expected, and those differences may be material.
A statement that the practitioner has no responsibility to update the report for events and circumstances occurring after the date of the report	We have no responsibility to update this report for events and circumstances occurring after the date of this report.
An alert, in a separate paragraph, that restricts the use of the report. The alert should state that the report is intended solely for the information and use of the specified parties, identify those parties, and state that the report is not intended to be, and should not be, used by anyone other than the specified parties.	This report is intended solely for the information and use of the boards of directors of Jade Imports and Pearl River Emporium, and is not intended to be, and should not be, used by anyone other than these specified parties.
The manual or printed signature of the practitioner's firm	Sullivan and Cregan, CPAs

Practitioner's Report on Agreed-Upon Procedures	
The city and state where the practitioner practices	San Francisco, CA
The date of the report*	February 15, 20X2
AT-C 305.39	

* The report should be dated no earlier than the date on which the practitioner completed the procedures and determined the findings.

When applicable, the report should include:

- A description of any agreed-upon materiality limits, and
- A description of the nature of the assistance provided by a practitioner's external specialist.

ILLUSTRATION

ILLUSTRATION 1. PRACTITIONER'S EXAMINATION REPORT ON A FINANCIAL PROJECTION

The following is an illustrative practitioner's report for an examination of a financial projection that does not contain a range.

Independent Accountant's Report

Board of Directors
Jade Imports

We have examined the accompanying projection of Jade Imports, which comprises [*identify the statements—for example, the projected balance sheet as of December 31, 20X1 and the related projected statements of income, stockholders' equity, and cash flows for the year then ending*] based on the guidelines for the presentation of a projection established by the American Institute of Certified Public Accountants. Jade Imports' management is responsible for preparing and presenting the projection based on the granting of the requested loan as described in the summary of significant assumptions in accordance with the guidelines for the presentation of a projection established by the American Institute of Certified Public Accountants. The projection was prepared for the purpose of negotiating a loan to expand Jade Imports' flagship store. Our responsibility is to express an opinion on the projection based on our examination.

Our examination was conducted in accordance with attestation standards established by the American Institute of Certified Public Accountants. Those standards require that we plan and perform the examination to obtain reasonable assurance about whether the projection is presented in accordance with the guidelines for the presentation of a projection established by the American Institute of Certified Public Accountants, in all material respects. An examination involves performing procedures to obtain evidence about the projection. The nature, timing, and extent of the procedures selected depend on our judgment, including an assessment of the risks of material misstatement of the projection, whether due to fraud or to error. We believe that the evidence we obtained is sufficient and appropriate to provide a reasonable basis for our opinion.

In our opinion, assuming the granting of the requested loan for the purpose of expanding Jade Imports' flagship store, the projection referred to above is presented, in all material respects, in accordance with the guidelines for the presentation of a projection established by the American Institute of Certified Public Accountants, and the underlying assumptions are suitably supported and provide a reasonable basis for management's projection given the hypothetical assumption(s).

Even if the loan is granted and the store is expanded, there will usually be differences between the projected and actual results because events and circumstances frequently do not occur as expected, and those differences may be material. We have no responsibility to update this report for events and circumstances occurring after the date of this report.

The accompanying projection and this report are intended solely for the information and use of [*identify specified parties, for example, Jade Imports and California State Bank*], and are not intended to be and should not be used by anyone other than these specified parties.

Sullivan and Cregan, CPAs
San Francisco, CA
June 25, 20X2

AT-C 310 Reporting on Pro Forma Financial Information

ORIGINAL PRONOUNCEMENT

Source Statement on Standards for Attestation Engagements (SSAE) 18.

APPLICABILITY

AT-C 310 applies to reports on an examination or a review of pro forma financial information, except for those listed below and supplements the guidance in Section 105. For Section 310, CPAs must also comply with Section 205 on examination engagements or Section 210 on review engagements. See the chapter on the AT-C Preface for more information on the AT-C section structure. (AT-C 310.04)

This section does not apply to the third type of service engagement in the 200s section: agreed-upon procedure engagements related to pro forma financial information. For those engagements, practitioners should comply with Sections 105 and 215. This section also does not apply to:

- Comfort letters or performing procedures on pro forma financial information in connection with an offering. For those engagements, practitioners should look to the guidance in AU-C Section 920.
- Pro forma financial information presented outside the basic financial statements but within the same document where the practitioner is not engaged to report on the pro forma financial information. In those situations, practitioners should look to the guidance in AU-C Sections 720 and 925.
- Transactions consummated after the balance sheet date reflected in the historical financial statements.
- The applicable financial reporting framework that requires the presentation of pro forma financial information in the financial statements or the accompanying notes.

(AT-C 310.02)

Common uses of pro forma information might be to show the effects of a:

- Business combination,
- Change in capitalization,
- Disposition of a significant portion of a business,
- Change in form or status of a business (for example, from a division to a separate entity), or
- Proposed sale of securities and application of the proceeds.

DEFINITION OF TERMS

See the "Definitions of Terms" section in the Appendix to the chapter on the AT-C Preface for definitions of the following terms relevant to this Section: *criteria for the preparation of pro forma financial information* and *pro forma financial information.*

OBJECTIVES OF AN EXAMINATION ENGAGEMENT

A practitioner's objectives in an examination of pro forma financial information are to:

a. obtain reasonable assurance about whether, in accordance with (or based on) the criteria

i. management's assumptions provide a reasonable basis for presenting the significant effects directly attributable to the underlying transaction (or event), (Ref: par. .A1)
ii. and, in all material respects

(1) the related pro forma adjustments give appropriate effect to those assumptions, and
(2) the pro forma amounts reflect the proper application of those adjustments to the historical financial statement amounts.

b. express an opinion in a written report on the matters in paragraph .05a above
(AT-C 310.05)

As with all examinations, the objectives of an examination of pro forma financial information are to obtain reasonable assurance and express an opinion.

OBJECTIVES OF A REVIEW ENGAGEMENT

A practitioner's objectives in a review of pro forma financial information are:

a. obtain limited assurance about whether, in accordance with (or based on) the criteria, any material modifications should be made to

i. management's assumptions in order for them to provide a reasonable basis for presenting the significant effects directly attributable to the underlying transaction (or event),
ii. the related pro forma adjustments in order for them to give appropriate effect to those assumptions, or
iii. the pro forma amounts in order for them to reflect the proper application of those adjustments to the historical financial statement amounts.

b. express a conclusion in a written report on the matters in paragraph .06a above
(AT-C 310.06)

As with all reviews, the objectives of a review of pro forma information are to obtain limited assurance and express a conclusion.

REQUIREMENTS

PRECONDITIONS FOR EXAMINATION AND REVIEW ENGAGEMENTS

A practitioner may *examine* or *review* pro forma financial information if all three of the following conditions are achieved:

1. The document including the pro formas also includes, or the documents are readily available, complete historical financial statements (or incorporates them by reference) of the entity for the most recent year available. If pro formas are for an interim period,

historical interim information for that period is also presented (or incorporated by reference). If the circumstances are a business combination, the document includes historical data for significant constituent parts of the combined entity.

2. The historical financial statements on which the pro forma information is based have been audited in the case of an examination of pro forma information or reviewed in the case of a review of pro forma information by a practitioner. The audit (or review report, if issued) should be included in the document containing pro forma information or be readily available.

NOTE: The level of assurance on the pro formas should be no greater than the level on the related historical statements.

---

3. The practitioner reporting on the pro forma information should have an appropriate level of knowledge of the entity's accounting and financial reporting practices.

(AT-C 310.08 and .09)

PROCEDURES FOR EXAMINATIONS AND REVIEW ENGAGEMENTS

The procedures for an examination or review include:

1. Obtaining an understanding of the underlying transaction or event.
2. Obtaining a level of knowledge of each significant constituent part of the combined entity in a business combination.
3. Discussing with management their assumptions about the effects of the transaction or event.
4. Evaluating whether pro forma adjustments are included for all significant effects of the transaction or event.
5. Obtaining sufficient evidence in support of such adjustments.

NOTE: In considering the level of attestation risk the practitioner is willing to accept in a pro forma information engagement, the level of assurance on the underlying historical financial statements is a key factor. Accordingly, the procedures the practitioner should apply to the assumptions and pro forma adjustments are substantially the same for either an examination or a review engagement. The evidence needed is a matter of judgment and may vary with the level of service involved.

---

6. Evaluating whether the presentation of management's assumptions is sufficiently clear and comprehensive, and
7. Evaluating whether management's assumptions are consistent with each other and with the data used to develop them.
8. Determining whether computations of pro forma adjustments are mathematically correct and that the pro forma column reflects proper application of the adjustments.
9. Reading the pro forma financial information and evaluating the appropriateness of the descriptions of:

    a. The underlying transaction or event,
    b. The pro forma adjustments, and
    c. The significant assumptions and significant uncertainties about those assumptions

10. Evaluating whether the source of the historical information base is appropriately identified.

(AT-C 310.13)

Request for a Written Assertion

If management does not provide the written assertion requested by management, the practitioner should withdraw from the engagement, if possible under law or regulation. (AT-C 310.10)

Request for a Written Representation

In addition to the representations required by Sections 205 or 210, practitioners should obtain management's written representations on:

a. Their responsibility for the assumptions.
b. Assertion that the assumptions provide a reasonable basis for presenting all of the significant effects directly attributable to the transaction or event.
c. Assertion that the related pro forma adjustments give appropriate effect to the assumptions.
d. Assertion that the pro forma column reflects the proper application of adjustments.
e. The pro forma assertions are consistent with the entity's financial reporting framework and its accounting policies.
f. Pro forma financial information is appropriately presented and significant effects of the transaction or event are appropriately disclosed.

(AT-C 310.14)

If management refuses to provide a written representation, the practitioner's scope is limited. In that case:

- For an examination engagement, the limitation precludes an unmodified opinion and may be sufficient for withdrawal from the engagement, if possible under laws or regulation.
- For a review engagement, the limitation is sufficient for withdrawal from the engagement.

(AT-C 310.15)

Form of Report on Pro Forma Financial Information

The report on the pro forma information and the report on historical financial information may be combined. If they are combined and the date of completion of the examination or review procedures of financial information is after the date of the completion of the audit or review of historical financial information, the practitioner should dual date the report as follows:

> February 15, 20X1, except for the paragraphs regarding pro forma financial information for which the date is March 29, 20X1.

(AT-C 310.16)

The following are a series of examples of examination and agreed-upon procedure reports on pro forma financial information, based on AT-C 310.A24.

Practitioner's Examination Report on Pro Forma Financial Information: Unmodified Opinion

The practitioner's report on pro forma financial information should include the items listed in the left column of the table below. If the practitioner is disclaiming an opinion, the statement that the examination was conducted under AICPA standards and what they require and the description of the objectives and limitations of pro forma information should be omitted.

Practitioner's Examination Report on Pro Forma Financial Information: Unmodified Opinion	
A title that includes the word *independent*	**Independent Accountant's Report**
An appropriate addressee as required by the circumstances of the engagement	Board of Directors Jade Imports
A reference to the pro forma adjustments included in the pro forma financial information	We have examined the pro forma adjustments giving effect to . . .
A reference to management's description of the transaction (or event) to which the pro forma adjustments give effect. (The description is included in the pro forma financial information.)	. . . the underlying transaction (or event) described in Note 1 and the application of those adjustments to the historical amounts in the accompanying pro forma condensed balance sheet of Jade Imports as of December 31, 20X1, and . . .
An identification or description of the pro forma financial information being reported on, including the point in time or period of time to which the measurement or evaluation of the pro forma financial information relates	. . . the related pro forma condensed statement of income for the year then ended (pro forma financial information),
An identification of the criteria against which the pro forma financial information was measured or evaluated	. . . based on the criteria in Note 1.
A reference to the financial statements from which the historical financial information is derived, a statement that such financial statements were audited, and, if applicable, whether the financial statements were audited by another auditor. (The report on pro forma financial information should refer to any modification in the auditor's report on the historical financial statements. In the case of a business combination, this paragraph applies to each significant constituent part of the combined entity.)	The historical condensed financial statements are derived from the historical financial statements of Jade Imports, which were audited by us, and of Pearl River Emporium, which were audited by other accountants, appearing elsewhere herein [*or "and are readily available"*].
The pro forma adjustments are based on management's assumptions.	The pro forma adjustments are based on management's assumptions described in Note 1.
Identification of management and its responsibility	Jade Imports' management is responsible for the pro forma financial information.
The practitioner's responsibility	Our responsibility is to express an opinion on the pro forma financial information based on our examination.
The practitioner's examination was conducted in accordance with attestation standards established by the AICPA	Our examination was conducted in accordance with attestation standards established by the American Institute of Certified Public Accountants.
AICPA standards requirements	Those standards require that we plan and perform the examination to obtain reasonable assurance about whether, based on the criteria in Note 1, . . .

Management's assumptions provide a reasonable basis for presenting the significant effects directly attributable to the underlying transaction (or event), and, in all material respects, the related pro forma adjustments give appropriate effect to those assumptions, and the pro forma amounts reflect the proper application of those adjustments to the historical financial statement amounts.	. . . management's assumptions provide a reasonable basis for presenting the significant effects directly attributable to the underlying transaction (or event), and, in all material respects, the related pro forma adjustments give appropriate effect to those assumptions, and the pro forma amounts reflect the proper application of those adjustments to the historical financial statement amounts.
Description of the examination's procedures	An examination involves performing procedures to obtain evidence about management's assumptions, the related pro forma adjustments, and the pro forma amounts in the pro forma condensed balance sheet of Jade Imports as of December 31, 20X1, and the related pro forma condensed statement of income for the year then ended. The nature, timing, and extent of the procedures selected depend on our judgment, including an assessment of the risks of material misstatement of the pro forma financial information, whether due to fraud or to error.
Practitioner's belief that the evidence is sufficient and appropriate to provide a reasonable basis for the practitioner's opinion	We believe that the evidence we obtained is sufficient and appropriate to provide a reasonable basis for our opinion.
A description of the objectives and limitations of pro forma financial information	The objective of this pro forma financial information is to show what the significant effects on the historical financial information might have been had the underlying transaction (or event) occurred at an earlier date. However, the pro forma condensed financial statements are not necessarily indicative of the results of operations or related effects on financial position that would have been attained had the above-mentioned transaction (or event) actually occurred at such earlier date.
The practitioner's opinion	In our opinion, based on the criteria in Note 1, management's assumptions provide a reasonable basis for presenting the significant effects directly attributable to the above-mentioned transaction (or event) described in Note 1, and, in all material respects, the related pro forma adjustments give appropriate effect to those assumptions, and the pro forma amounts reflect the proper application of those adjustments to the historical financial statement amounts in the pro forma condensed balance sheet of Jade Imports as of December 31, 20X1, and the related pro forma condensed statement of income for the year then ended.

The manual or printed signature of the practitioner's firm	Sullivan and Cregan, CPAs
The city and state where the practitioner practices	San Francisco, CA
The date of the report*	March 25, 20X2

* The report should be dated no earlier than the date on which the practitioner has obtained sufficient appropriate evidence on which to base the practitioner's opinion, including evidence that:

- The attestation documentation has been reviewed,
- The pro forma financial information has been prepared, and
- Management has provided a written assertion.

When the circumstances identified in Section 205 regarding a restricted-use alert are applicable, the alert should be in a separate paragraph, restricting the use of the report or describing the purpose of the report.

PRACTITIONER'S REVIEW REPORT: UNMODIFIED CONCLUSION

Practitioner's Review Report on Pro Forma Financial Information: Unmodified Conclusion	
A title that includes the word *independent*	**Independent Accountant's Report**
An appropriate addressee	Board of Directors Jade Imports
A reference to the pro forma adjustments included in the pro forma financial information	We have reviewed the pro forma adjustments giving effect to the transaction (or event) . . .
A reference to management's description of the transaction (or event) to which the pro forma adjustments give effect. (The description is included in the pro forma financial information.)	. . . described in Note 1 and the application of those adjustments to the historical amounts in the accompanying pro forma condensed balance sheet of X Company as of March 31, 20X2, and the related pro forma condensed statement of income for the three months then ended (pro forma financial information), . . .
An identification or description of the pro forma financial information being reported on, including the point in time or period of time to which the measurement or evaluation of the pro forma financial information relates	. . . and the related pro forma condensed statement of income for the three months then ended (pro forma financial information), . . .
An identification of the criteria against which the pro forma financial information was measured or evaluated	. . . based on the criteria in Note 1.
A reference to the financial statements from which the historical financial information is derived and a statement that such financial statements were audited or reviewed, as applicable.*	These historical condensed financial statements are derived from the historical unaudited financial statements of X Company, which were reviewed by us, and of Y Company, which were reviewed by other accountants, appearing elsewhere herein [*or "and are readily available"*].

The pro forma adjustments are based on management's assumptions.	The pro forma adjustments are based on management's assumptions as described in Note 1.
Identification of management and its responsibility for the pro forma financial information	X Company's management is responsible for the pro forma financial information.
The practitioner's responsibility to express a conclusion on the pro forma financial information based on the practitioner's review	Our responsibility is to express a conclusion based on our review.
The practitioner's review was conducted in accordance with attestation standards established by the AICPA.	Our review was conducted in accordance with attestation standards established by the American Institute of Certified Public Accountants.
Requirements of AICPA standards	Those standards require that we plan and perform our review to obtain limited assurance about whether, based on the criteria in Note 1, any material modifications should be made to management's assumptions in order for them to provide a reasonable basis for presenting the significant effects directly attributable to the underlying transaction (or event); the related pro forma adjustments, in order for them to give appropriate effect to those assumptions; or the pro forma amounts, in order for them to reflect the proper application of those adjustments to the historical financial statement amounts.
Degree of assurance	A review is substantially less in scope than an examination, the objective of which is to obtain reasonable assurance about whether, based on the criteria, management's assumptions provide a reasonable basis for presenting the significant effects directly attributable to the underlying transaction (or event), and, in all material respects, the related pro forma adjustments give appropriate effect to those assumptions, and the pro forma amounts reflect the proper application of those adjustments to the historical financial statement amounts, in order to express an opinion.
Accordingly, the practitioner does not express such an opinion.	Accordingly, we do not express such an opinion.
The practitioner believes that the review provides a reasonable basis for the practitioner's conclusion.	We believe that our review provides a reasonable basis for our conclusion.

A description of the objectives and limitations of pro forma financial information	The objective of this pro forma financial information is to show what the significant effects on the historical financial information might have been had the underlying transaction (or event) occurred at an earlier date. However, the pro forma condensed financial statements are not necessarily indicative of the results of operations or related effects on financial position that would have been attained had the above-mentioned transaction (or event) actually occurred at such earlier date.
The practitioner's conclusion	Based on our review, we are not aware of any material modifications that should be made to management's assumptions in order for them to provide a reasonable basis for presenting the significant effects directly attributable to the above-mentioned transaction (or event) described in Note 1, the related pro forma adjustments in order for them to give appropriate effect to those assumptions, or the pro forma amounts, in order for them to reflect the proper application of those adjustments to the historical financial statement amounts in the pro forma condensed balance sheet of X Company as of March 31, 20X2, and the related pro forma condensed statement of income for the three months then ended, based on the criteria in Note 1.
The manual or printed signature of the practitioner's firm	Sullivan and Cregan, CPAs
The city and state where the practitioner practices	San Francisco, CA
The date of the report**	June 15, 20X2

* If the practitioner issued a review report on the historical financial statements, the report should include a statement that a review report was issued, and, if applicable, whether the financial statements were reviewed by another accountant. (The report on pro forma financial information should refer to any modification in the accountant's report on the historical financial information. In the case of a business combination, this paragraph applies to each significant constituent part of the combined entity.)

** The report should be dated no earlier than the date on which the practitioner has obtained sufficient appropriate review evidence on which to base the practitioner's conclusion, including evidence that:

- The attestation documentation has been reviewed,
- The pro forma financial information has been prepared, and
- Management has provided a written assertion.

ILLUSTRATIONS

ILLUSTRATION 1. PRACTITIONER'S EXAMINATION REPORT ON PRO FORMA FINANCIAL INFORMATION AT YEAR-END WITH A REVIEW OF PRO FORMA FINANCIAL INFORMATION FOR A SUBSEQUENT INTERIM DATE: UNMODIFIED OPINION AND UNMODIFIED CONCLUSION

Independent Accountant's Report

[*Appropriate addressee*]

We have examined the pro forma adjustments giving effect to the transaction (or event) described in Note 1 and the application of those adjustments to the historical amounts in the accompanying pro forma condensed balance sheet of X Company as of December 31, 20X1, and the related pro forma condensed statement of income for the year then ended (pro forma financial information) based on the criteria in Note 1. The historical condensed financial statements are derived from the historical financial statements of X Company, which were audited by us, and of Y Company, which were audited by other accountants, appearing elsewhere herein [*or "and are readily available"*]. The pro forma adjustments are based on management's assumptions described in Note 1. X Company's management is responsible for the pro forma financial information. Our responsibility is to express an opinion on the pro forma financial information based on our examination.

Our examination was conducted in accordance with attestation standards established by the American Institute of Certified Public Accountants. Those standards require that we plan and perform the examination to obtain reasonable assurance about whether, based on the criteria in Note 1, management's assumptions provide a reasonable basis for presenting the significant effects directly attributable to the underlying transaction (or event), and, in all material respects, the related pro forma adjustments give appropriate effect to those assumptions, and the pro forma amounts reflect the proper application of those adjustments to the historical financial statement amounts. An examination involves performing procedures to obtain evidence about management's assumptions, the related pro forma adjustments, and the pro forma amounts in the pro forma condensed balance sheet of X Company as of December 31, 20X1, and the related pro forma condensed statement of income for the year then ended. The nature, timing, and extent of the procedures selected depend on our judgment, including an assessment of the risks of material misstatement of the pro forma financial information, whether due to fraud or to error. We believe that the evidence we have obtained is sufficient and appropriate to provide a reasonable basis for our opinion.

In addition, we have reviewed the pro forma adjustments and the application of those adjustments to the historical amounts in the accompanying pro forma condensed balance sheet of X Company as of March 31, 20X2, and the related pro forma condensed statement of income for the three months then ended (pro forma financial information), based on the criteria in Note 1. The historical condensed financial statements are derived from the historical financial statements of X Company, which were reviewed by us, and of Y Company, which were reviewed by other accountants,[1] appearing elsewhere herein [*or "and are readily available"*]. The pro forma adjustments are based on management's assumptions as described in Note 1. X Company's management is responsible for the pro forma financial information. Our responsibility is to express a conclusion based on our review.

Our review was conducted in accordance with attestation standards established by the American Institute of Certified Public Accountants. Those standards require that we plan and perform our review to obtain limited assurance about whether, based on the criteria in Note 1, any material modifications should

1 https://publication.cpa2biz.com/content/link/ps/atc_section_300#ftn.atc_310_fn20

be made to management's assumptions in order for them to provide a reasonable basis for presenting the significant effects directly attributable to the underlying transaction (or event); the related pro forma adjustments, in order for them to give appropriate effect to those assumptions; or the pro forma amounts, in order for them to reflect the proper application of those adjustments to the historical financial statement amounts. A review is substantially less in scope than an examination, the objective of which is to obtain reasonable assurance about whether, based on the criteria, management's assumptions provide a reasonable basis for presenting the significant effects directly attributable to the underlying transaction (or event), and, in all material respects, the related pro forma adjustments give appropriate effect to those assumptions, and the pro forma amounts reflect the proper application of those adjustments to the historical financial statement amounts, in order to express an opinion. Accordingly, we do not express such an opinion on the pro forma adjustments or on the application of such adjustments to the pro forma condensed balance sheet as of March 31, 20X2, and the pro forma condensed statement of income for the three months then ended. We believe that our review provides a reasonable basis for our conclusion.

The objective of this pro forma financial information is to show what the significant effects on the historical financial information might have been had the underlying transactions (or event) occurred at an earlier date. However, the pro forma condensed financial statements are not necessarily indicative of the results of operations or related effects on financial position that would have been attained had the above-mentioned transaction (or event) actually occurred at such earlier date.

In our opinion, based on the criteria in Note 1, management's assumptions provide a reasonable basis for presenting the significant effects directly attributable to the above-mentioned transaction (or event) described in Note 1, and, in all material respects, the related pro forma adjustments give appropriate effect to those assumptions, and the pro forma amounts reflect the proper application of those adjustments to the historical financial statement amounts in the pro forma condensed balance sheet of X Company as of December 31, 20X1, and the related pro forma condensed statement of income for the year then ended.

Based on our review, we are not aware of any material modifications that should be made to management's assumptions in order for them to provide a reasonable basis for presenting the significant effects directly attributable to the above-mentioned transaction (or event) described in Note 1, the related pro forma adjustments in order for them to give appropriate effect to those assumptions, or the pro forma amounts in order for them to reflect the proper application of those adjustments to the historical financial statement amounts in the pro forma condensed balance sheet of X Company as of March 31, 20X2, and the related pro forma condensed statement of income for the three months then ended based on the criteria in Note 1.

[*Practitioner's signature*]

[*Practitioner's city and state*]

[*Date of practitioner's report*]

Illustration 2. Practitioner's Examination Report: Qualified Opinion Because of a Scope Limitation

Independent Accountant's Report

[*Appropriate addressee*]

We have examined the pro forma adjustments giving effect to the transaction (or event) described in Note 1 and the application of those adjustments to the historical amounts in the accompanying pro forma condensed balance sheet of X Company as of December 31, 20X1, and the related pro forma condensed statement of income for the year then ended (pro forma financial information), based on the criteria in Note 1. The historical condensed financial statements are derived from the historical financial statements of X Company, which were audited by us, and of Y Company, which were audited by other accountants, appearing elsewhere herein [*or "and are readily available"*]. The pro forma adjustments are based upon management's assumptions described in Note 1. X Company's management is responsible for the pro forma financial information. Our responsibility is to express an opinion on the pro forma financial information based on our examination.

Except as discussed below, our examination was conducted in accordance with attestation standards established by the American Institute of Certified Public Accountants. Those standards require that we plan and perform the examination to obtain reasonable assurance about whether, based on the criteria in Note 1, management's assumptions provide a reasonable basis for presenting the significant effects directly attributable to the underlying transaction (or event), and, in all material respects, the related pro forma adjustments give appropriate effect to those assumptions, and the pro forma amounts reflect the proper application of those adjustments to the historical financial statement amounts. An examination involves performing procedures to obtain evidence about management's assumptions, the related pro forma adjustments, and the pro forma amounts in the pro forma condensed balance sheet of X Company as of December 31, 20X1, and the related pro forma condensed statement of income for the year then ended. The nature, timing, and extent of the procedures selected depend on our judgment, including an assessment of the risks of material misstatement of the pro forma financial information, whether due to fraud or to error. We believe that the evidence we obtained is sufficient and appropriate to provide a reasonable basis for our opinion.

We were unable to perform the examination procedures we considered necessary with respect to the assumptions relating to the proposed loan described in Adjustment E in Note 1.

The objective of this pro forma financial information is to show what the significant effects on the historical financial information might have been had the underlying transaction (or event) occurred at an earlier date. However, the pro forma condensed financial statements are not necessarily indicative of the results of operations or related effects on financial position that would have been attained had the above-mentioned transaction (or event) actually occurred at such earlier date.

In our opinion, based on the criteria in Note 1, except for the effects of such changes, if any, as might have been determined to be necessary had we been able to satisfy ourselves as to the assumptions relating to the proposed loan, management's assumptions provide a reasonable basis for presenting the significant effects directly attributable to the above-mentioned transaction (or event) described in Note 1, and, in all material respects, the related pro forma adjustments give appropriate effect to those assumptions, and the pro forma amounts reflect the proper application of those adjustments to the historical financial statement amounts in the pro forma condensed balance sheet of X Company as of December 31, 20X1, and the related pro forma condensed statement of income for the year then ended.

[*Practitioner's signature*]

[*Practitioner's city and state*]

[*Date of practitioner's report*]

Illustration 3. Practitioner's Examination Report: Qualified Opinion Because of Reservations about the Propriety of the Assumptions

Independent Accountant's Report

[*Appropriate addressee*]

[*Same first three paragraphs as examination report in Illustration 1*]

As discussed in Note 1 to the pro forma financial statements, the pro forma adjustments reflect management's assumption that X Division of the acquired company will be sold. The net assets of this division are reflected at their historical carrying amount; generally accepted accounting principles require these net assets to be recorded at fair value less cost to sell.

In our opinion, based on the criteria in Note 1, except for inappropriate valuation of the net assets of X Division, management's assumptions described in Note 1 provide a reasonable basis for presenting the significant effects directly attributable to the above-mentioned transaction (or event) described in Note 1, and, in all material respects, the related pro forma adjustments give appropriate effect to those assumptions, and the pro forma amounts reflect the proper application of those adjustments to the historical financial statement amounts in the pro forma condensed balance sheet of X Company as of December 31, 20X1, and the related pro forma condensed statement of income for the year then ended.

[*Practitioner's signature*]

[*Practitioner's city and state*]

[*Date of the practitioner's report*]

Illustration 4. Practitioner's Examination Report: Disclaimer of Opinion Because of a Scope Limitation

Independent Accountant's Report

[*Appropriate addressee*]

We were engaged to examine the pro forma adjustments giving effect to the transaction (or event) described in Note 1 and the application of those adjustments to the historical amounts in the accompanying pro forma financial condensed balance sheet of X Company as of December 31, 20X1, and the related pro forma condensed statement of income for the year then ended (pro forma financial information), based on the criteria in Note 1. The historical condensed financial statements are derived from the historical financial statements of X Company, which were audited by us, and of Y Company, which were audited by other accountants, appearing elsewhere herein [*or "and are readily available"*]. The pro forma adjustments are based on management's assumptions described in Note 1. X Company's management is responsible for the pro forma financial information.

As discussed in Note 1 to the pro forma financial statements, the pro forma adjustments reflect management's assumptions that the elimination of duplicate facilities would have resulted in a 30% reduction in operating costs. Management could not supply us with sufficient evidence to support this assertion.

[*The third paragraph in the practitioner's examination report in example 1 is intentionally omitted from the report with a disclaimer of opinion.*]

Because we were unable to evaluate management's assumptions regarding the reduction in operating costs and other assumptions related thereto, the scope of our work was not sufficient to enable us to express, and we do not express, an opinion on whether, based on the criteria in Note 1, management's assumptions provide a reasonable basis for presenting the significant effects directly attributable to the above-mentioned transaction (or event) described in Note 1, or on whether, in all material respects, the related pro forma adjustments give appropriate effect to those assumptions, and the pro forma amounts reflect the proper application of those adjustments to the historical financial statement amounts in the pro forma condensed balance sheet of X Company as of December 31, 20X1, and the related pro forma condensed statement of income for the year then ended.

[*Practitioner's signature*]

[*Practitioner's city and state*]

[*Date of practitioner's report*]

AT-C 315 Compliance Attestation

ORIGINAL PRONOUNCEMENT

Source Statement on Standards for Attestation Engagements (SSAE) 18, *Attestation Standards: Revision and Recodification.*

APPLICABILITY

This Section provides guidance for engagements related to either:

- Compliance with requirements of specified laws, regulations, rules, contracts, or grants (specified requirements), or
- The effectiveness of internal control over compliance with specified requirements.

(AT-C 315.01)

A practitioner may be engaged to perform agreed-upon procedures to assist users in evaluating management's written assertion about an entity's compliance with specified requirements, the effectiveness of internal control over compliance, or both. A practitioner also may be engaged to examine compliance with specified requirements or a written assertion thereon. For example, some electronic funds transfer associations or networks require their members who process transactions to complete a compliance exam.

On *every* attestation engagement, CPAs must comply with Section 105 and one of the service sections. For Section 315, CPAs must comply with Section 205 on examination engagements or Section 215 on agreed-upon procedure engagements. (AT-C 315.04) See the chapter on the AT-C Preface for more information about the AT-C section structure.

The Statement does *not* apply to:

1. Reviews.
2. Examination engagements to report on an entity's internal control over compliance with specified requirements.
3. Situations in which an auditor reports on specified requirements based solely on an audit of financial statements. See AU-C 806.
4. Engagements where a governmental audit requirement requires an auditor to express an opinion on compliance in accordance with AU-C Section 935, *Compliance Audits.*

(AT-C 315.02)

DEFINITIONS OF TERMS

See the glossary in the Appendix to the chapter on the AT-C Preface for definitions of the following terms relevant to this Section: *compliance with specified requirements*, *internal control over compliance*, and *material noncompliance*.

OBJECTIVES OF AN EXAMINATION ENGAGEMENT

The practitioner's objectives in performing examination engagements under Section 315 are to:

a. *obtain reasonable assurance about whether the entity complied with the specified requirements, in all material respects,*
b. *express an opinion in a written report about whether*
   i. *the entity complied with the specified requirements, in all material respects, or*
   ii. *management's assertion about its compliance with the specified requirements is fairly stated, in all material respects.*

   (AT-C 315.06)

OBJECTIVES OF AN AGREED-UPON PROCEDURES ENGAGEMENT

The practitioner's objectives in performing agreed-upon procedures engagements under Section 315 are:

a. *apply to an entity's compliance with specified requirements or an entity's internal control over compliance with specified requirements procedures that are established by specified parties who are responsible for the sufficiency of the procedures for their purposes and*
b. *issue a written report that describes the procedures applied and the practitioner's findings.*

(AT-C 315.07)

REQUIREMENTS—EXAMINATION ENGAGEMENTS

PRECONDITIONS FOR EXAMINATION ENGAGEMENTS

To accept an engagement to examine compliance with specified requirements, in addition to the requirements in Sections 105 and 205, practitioners should make sure that management accepts responsibility for the entity compliance with:

- Specified requirements and
- The entity's internal control over compliance

Practitioners must also make sure that management evaluates the entity's compliance with specified requirements. (AT-C 315.10)

WRITTEN ASSERTION—EXAMINATION ENGAGEMENTS

The responsible party's refusal to provide a written assertion as part of an examination engagement constitutes a limitation on the scope of the engagement. Such a limitation should cause the practitioner to withdraw from the engagement. An exception exists if an examination of an entity's compliance with specified requirements is required by law or regulation. In this case, the practitioner should disclaim an opinion on compliance unless he or she obtains evidential matter that warrants expressing an adverse opinion. (AT-C 315.10)

Note that assertions should not be subjective, using qualifying language such as "substantially complied."

REASONABLE ASSURANCE—EXAMINATION ENGAGEMENT

If practitioners are examining compliance with specified requirements, they should seek reasonable assurance of the entity's compliance in all material respects. The examination should include procedures designed to detect intentional and unintentional material noncompliance. (AT-C 315.11)

PROCEDURES—EXAMINATION ENGAGEMENTS

AT-C 315.12-.16 outline procedures to perform.

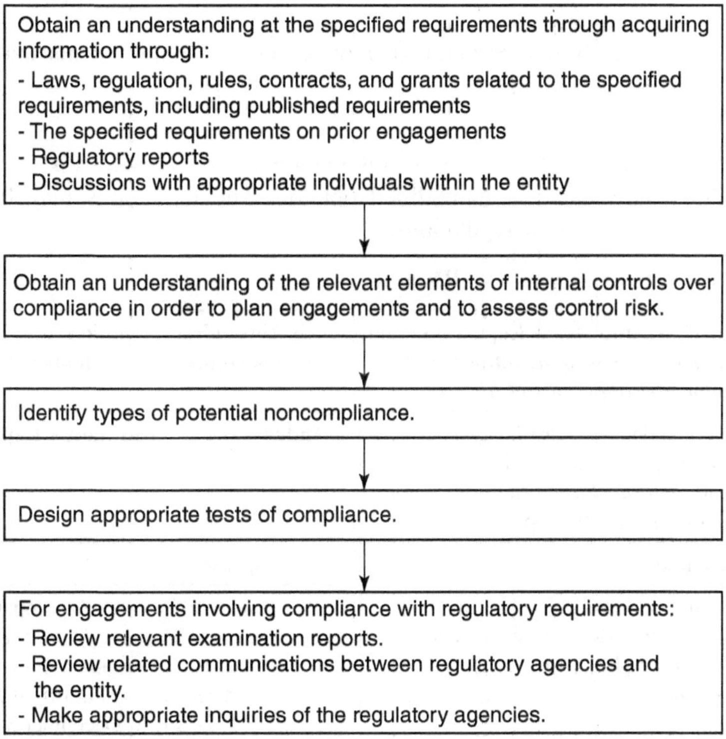

The practitioner should gain an understanding of the parts of the internal control related to compliance with the specified requirements, mentioned above, by:

a. Inquiries
b. Inspection of documents
c. Observation of activities

For an entity with multiple components, determine if it is necessary to examine all components for compliance. In making this determination, consider:

a. To what degree do the specified compliance requirements apply at the component level?
b. What are your judgments about materiality?
c. How centralized are the records?
d. How effective is the control environment, particularly management's direct control over the exercise of authority delegated to others and its ability to supervise activities at various locations effectively?
e. What are the nature and the extent of operations conducted at the various components?
f. How similar are controls over compliance for different components?

Written Representations—Examination Engagements

Practitioners should request the written representations in Section 205 and representations that:

- Acknowledge management's responsibility for establishing and maintaining effective internal control over compliance.
- State that management has performed an evaluation of the entity's compliance with specified requirements.
- State management's interpretation of any compliance requirements that have varying interpretations.

(AT-C 315.17)

The responsible party's refusal to furnish the required representations is a scope limitation. Practitioners should not issue an unmodified opinion. The limitations may be sufficient to withdraw, if permitted by law or regulations.

Practitioner's Examination Report

Practitioner's Examination Report on Compliance; Unmodified Opinion **Practitioner is reporting on subject matter (an entity's compliance with specified requirements during a period of time).**	
A title that includes the word *independent* An identification of the specified requirements against which compliance was measured or evaluated. (Ref: par. .A21)	**Independent Accountant's Report**
An appropriate addressee	[*Appropriate addressee*]
Identification of the compliance matters that are being reported on or the assertion about such matters, including the point in time or period of time to which the measurement or evaluation of compliance relates	We have examined XYZ Company's compliance with [*identify the specified requirements, for example, the requirements listed in Attachment 1*] during the period January 1, 20X1, to December 31, 20X1.
Identification of management and its responsibility	Management of XYZ Company is responsible for XYZ Company's compliance with the specified requirements.
The practitioner's responsibility	Our responsibility is to express an opinion on XYZ Company's compliance with the specified requirements based on our examination.
A statement that the examination was conducted in accordance with attestation standards established by the AICPA	Our examination was conducted in accordance with attestation standards established by the American Institute of Certified Public Accountants.
AICPA standards' requirements	Those standards require that we plan and perform the examination to obtain reasonable assurance about whether XYZ Company complied, in all material respects, with the specified requirements referenced above.
The practitioner believes the evidence obtained is sufficient and appropriate to provide a reasonable basis for the practitioner's opinion.	We believe that the evidence we obtained is sufficient and appropriate to provide a reasonable basis for our opinion.

A description of the nature of an examination engagement	An examination involves performing procedures to obtain evidence about whether XYZ Company complied with the specified requirements. The nature, timing, and extent of the procedures selected depend on our judgment, including an assessment of the risks of material noncompliance, whether due to fraud or error.
A statement that the examination does not provide a legal determination on the entity's compliance with specified requirements	Our examination does not provide a legal determination on XYZ Company's compliance with specified requirements.
The practitioner's opinion about whether, in all material respects the entity complied with the specified requirements or management's assertion about the entity's compliance with specified requirements is fairly stated	In our opinion, XYZ Company complied, in all material respects, with [*identify the specified requirements, for example, the requirements listed in Attachment 1*] during the period January 1, 20X1 to December 31, 20X1.
The manual or printed signature of the practitioner's firm	[*Practitioner's signature*]
The city and state where the practitioner practices	[*Practitioner's city and state*]
The date of the report*	[*Date of practitioner's report*]

* The report should be dated no earlier than the date on which the practitioner has obtained sufficient appropriate evidence on which to base the practitioner's opinion, including evidence that:

- The attestation documentation has been reviewed, and
- Management has provided a written assertion.

When the circumstances identified in Section 205 regarding a restricted-use alert are applicable, the alert should be in a separate paragraph, restricting the use of the report or describing the purpose of the report.

The practitioner should add a statement that describes significant inherent limitations, if any, associated with the measurement or evaluation of the entity's compliance with specified requirements or its assertion thereon.

ILLUSTRATION

ILLUSTRATION 1. PRACTITIONER'S EXAMINATION REPORT ON AN ASSERTION ABOUT COMPLIANCE; UNMODIFIED OPINION

The following is an illustrative practitioner's examination report for an engagement in which the practitioner is reporting on the management's assertion about compliance with specified requirements and management's assertion accompanies the report.

Independent Accountant's Report

[*Appropriate addressee*]

We have examined management of XYZ Company's assertion that XYZ Company complied with [*identify the specified requirements, for example, the requirements listed in Attachment 1*] during the period January 1, 20X1 to December 31, 20X1.[1] XYZ Company's management is responsible for its assertion. Our responsibility is to express an opinion on management's assertion about XYZ Company's compliance with the specified requirements based on our examination.

Our examination was conducted in accordance with attestation standards established by the American Institute of Certified Public Accountants. Those standards require that we plan and perform the examination to obtain reasonable assurance about whether management's assertion about compliance with the specified requirements is fairly stated, in all material respects. An examination involves performing procedures to obtain evidence about whether management's assertion is fairly stated, in all material respects. The nature, timing, and extent of the procedures selected depend on our judgment, including an assessment of the risks of material misstatement of management's assertion, whether due to fraud or to error. We believe that the evidence we obtained is sufficient and appropriate to provide a reasonable basis for our opinion.

Our examination does not provide a legal determination on XYZ Company's compliance with the specified requirements.

In our opinion, management's assertion that XYZ Company complied with [*identify the specified requirements, for example, the requirements listed in Attachment 1*], is fairly stated, in all material respects.

[*Practitioner's signature*]

[*Practitioner's city and state*]

[*Date of practitioner's report*]

Frequently, criteria will be contained in the compliance requirements, in which case it is not necessary to repeat the criteria in the practitioner's report; however, if the criteria are not included in the compliance requirement, the report should identify the criteria. (Ref: par. .A21–.A23)

Modified Opinions

A practitioner may find material noncompliance. In that case, the practitioner should modify the option in accordance with the guidance in Section 205 and describe the material noncompliance.

REQUIREMENTS: AGREED-UPON PROCEDURES ENGAGEMENT

Preconditions for an Agreed-Upon Engagement

To accept an engagement to apply agreed-upon procedures related to compliance with specified requirements or internal control over compliance with specified requirements, the practitioner must comply with the requirements in Sections 105 and 215 and determine that management:

1. Accepts responsibility for the entity's compliance with specified requirements and the entity's internal control over compliance.
2. Evaluates the entity's compliance with specified requirements or the effectiveness of the entity's internal control over compliance.

1 https://publication.cpa2biz.com/content/link/ps/atc_section_300#ftn.atc_315_fn20

Understanding with Specified Parties

A written management representation letter is required in agreed-upon procedures engagements relating to compliance matters. In that letter management should:

- Acknowledge its responsibility for establishing and maintain effective internal control over compliance.
- State that it has performed an evaluation of:
  - The entity's compliance with specified requirements, or
  - The entity's controls for establishing and maintaining internal control over compliance and detecting noncompliance with requirements, as applicable.
- State that its interpretation of any compliance requirements complies with varying interpretations.
- State that it has disclosed any known noncompliance occurring subsequent to the period covered by the practitioner's report.

(AT-C 315.25)

The Agreed-Upon Procedures Report

The practitioner's report on agreed-upon procedures on an entity's compliance with specified requirements or about the effectiveness of an entity's internal control over compliance should be in the form of procedures and findings. The report should be dated as of the date of completion of the agreed-upon procedures. According to AT-C 315.26, the practitioner's report should contain the following elements:

a. A title that includes the word *independent.*
b. An appropriate addressee as required by the circumstances of the engagement.
c. An identification of the compliance matters that are being reported on or the assertion about such matters, including the point in time or period of time to which the measurement or evaluation of compliance relates.
d. An identification of the specified requirements against which compliance was measured or evaluated. (Ref: par. .A21)
e. A statement that identifies:
   i. Management and its responsibility for compliance with the specified requirements (when reporting on the subject matter) or for its assertion (when reporting on the assertion).
   ii. The practitioner's responsibility to express an opinion on the entity's compliance with the specified requirements or on management's assertion about the entity's compliance with the specified requirements, based on the practitioner's examination.
f. A statement that:
   i. The examination was conducted in accordance with attestation standards established by the American Institute of Certified Public Accountants.
   ii. Those standards require that the practitioner plan and perform the examination to obtain reasonable assurance about whether:

(1) The entity complied with the specified requirements, in all material respects, or
(2) Management's assertion about compliance with the specified requirements is fairly stated, in all material respects.

iii. The practitioner believes the evidence obtained is sufficient and appropriate to provide a reasonable basis for the practitioner's opinion.

g. A description of the nature of an examination engagement.
h. A statement that describes significant inherent limitations, if any, associated with the measurement or evaluation of the entity's compliance with specified requirements or its assertion thereon.
i. A statement that the examination does not provide a legal determination on the entity's compliance with specified requirements.
j. The practitioner's opinion about whether, in all material respects:

   i. The entity complied with the specified requirements, or
   ii. Management's assertion about the entity's compliance with specified requirements is fairly stated.

k. When the circumstances identified in Section 205 are applicable, an alert in a separate paragraph that restricts the use of the report or describes the purpose of the report, as applicable.[2]
l. The manual or printed signature of the practitioner's firm.

m. The city and state where the practitioner practices.
n. The date of the report. The report should be dated no earlier than the date on which the practitioner has obtained sufficient appropriate evidence on which to base the practitioner's opinion, including evidence that:

   i. The attestation documentation has been reviewed, and
   ii. Management has provided a written assertion.

The following are illustrations of two agreed-upon procedures reports.

ILLUSTRATIONS

ILLUSTRATION 2. PRACTITIONER'S AGREED-UPON PROCEDURES REPORT RELATED TO COMPLIANCE

The following is an illustrative practitioner's agreed-upon procedures report related to an entity's compliance with specified requirements in which the procedures and findings are enumerated, rather than referenced.

Independent Accountant's Report on Applying Agreed-Upon Procedures

[*Appropriate addressee*]

We have performed the procedures enumerated below, which were agreed to by [*identify the specified parties, for example, the management and board of directors of XYZ Company*], related to XYZ

2 https://publication.cpa2biz.com/content/link/ps/atc_section_300#ftn.atc_315_fn8

Company's compliance with [*identify the specified requirements, for example, the requirements listed in Attachment 1*] during the period January 1, 20X1 to December 31, 20X1.[3] XYZ Company's management is responsible for its compliance with those requirements. The sufficiency of these procedures is solely the responsibility of those parties specified in this report. Consequently, we make no representations regarding the sufficiency of the procedures enumerated below either for the purpose for which this report has been requested or for any other purpose.

[*Include paragraphs to enumerate procedures and findings.*]

This agreed-upon procedures engagement was conducted in accordance with attestation standards established by the American Institute of Certified Public Accountants. We were not engaged to and did not conduct an examination or review, the objective of which would be the expression of an opinion or conclusion, respectively, on compliance with specified requirements. Accordingly, we do not express such an opinion or conclusion. Had we performed additional procedures, other matters might have come to our attention that would have been reported to you.

This report is intended solely for the information and use of [*identify the specified parties, for example, the management and board of directors of XYZ Company*] and is not intended to be, and should not be, used by anyone other than the specified parties.

[*Practitioner's signature*]

[*Practitioner's city and state*]

[*Date of practitioner's report*]

ILLUSTRATION 3. PRACTITIONER'S AGREED-UPON PROCEDURES REPORT RELATED TO INTERNAL CONTROL OVER COMPLIANCE

The following is an illustrative practitioner's agreed-upon procedures report related to an entity's internal control over compliance in which the procedures and findings are enumerated rather than referenced.

Independent Accountant's Report on Applying Agreed-Upon Procedures

[*Appropriate addressee*]

We have performed the procedures enumerated below, which were agreed to by [*identify the specified parties, for example, the management and board of directors of XYZ Company*], related to XYZ Company's internal control over compliance with [*identify the specified requirements for example, the requirements listed in Attachment 1*], as of December 31, 20X1.[4] XYZ Company's management is responsible for its internal control over compliance with those requirements. The sufficiency of these procedures is solely the responsibility of the parties specified in this report. Consequently, we make no representations regarding the sufficiency of the procedures enumerated below either for the purpose for which this report has been requested or for any other purpose.
[*Include paragraphs to enumerate procedures and findings.*]

This agreed-upon procedures engagement was conducted in accordance with attestation standards established by the American Institute of Certified Public Accountants. We were not engaged to and did not conduct an examination or review, the objective of which would be the expression of an opinion or conclusion, respectively, on internal control over compliance with specified requirements. Accordingly,

3 https://publication.cpa2biz.com/content/link/ps/atc_section_300#ftn.atc_315_fn21

4 https://publication.cpa2biz.com/content/link/ps/atc_section_300#ftn.atc_315_fn22

we do not express such an opinion or conclusion. Had we performed additional procedures, other matters might have come to our attention that would have been reported to you.

This report is intended solely for the information and use of [*identify the specified parties, for example, the management and board of directors of XYZ Company*] and is not intended to be, and should not be, used by anyone other than the specified parties.

[*Practitioner's signature*]

[*Practitioner's city and state*]

[*Date of practitioner's report*]

AT-C 320 Reporting on an Examination of Controls at a Service Organization Relevant to User Entities' Internal Control over Financial Reporting

ORIGINAL PRONOUNCEMENT

Source Statement on Standards for Attestation Engagements (SSAE) 18.

APPLICABILITY

AT-C 320 applies to examination engagements to report on controls at organizations that provide services to user entities when those controls are likely to be relevant to user entities' internal control over financial reporting. (AT-C 320.01)

For Section 320, CPAs must comply with Section 105 and Section 205 on examination engagements. (AT-C 320.02) See the chapter on the AT-C Preface for more information about the AT-C section structure.

Section 320 does not address engagements to examine or apply agreed-upon procedures to a user entity's transactions or balances maintained by a service organization or agree-upon procedures engagements related to controls of a service organization.

DEFINITIONS OF TERMS

See the glossary in the Appendix to the chapter on the AT-C Preface for definitions of the following terms relevant to this Section: *carve-out method, complementary user entity controls, control objectives, controls at a service organization, inclusive method, internal audit function, management's description of a service organization's system and a service auditor's report on that description and on the suitability of the design of controls (referred to in this section as a* type 1 report*), management's description of a service organization's system and a service auditor's report on that description and on the suitability of the design and operating effectiveness of controls (referred to in this section as a* type 2 report*), service auditor, service organization, service organization's assertion, service organization's system, subservice organization, test of controls, user auditor*, and *user entity*.

OBJECTIVES OF AT-C SECTION 320

The objectives of the service auditor are to:

a. *obtain reasonable assurance about whether, in all material respects, based on suitable criteria:*

- *Management's description of the service organization's system fairly presents the service organization's system that was designed and implemented throughout the specified period (or in the case of a type 1 report, as of a specified date)*
- *The controls related to the control objectives stated in management's description of the service organization's system were suitably designed to provide reasonable assurance that the control objectives would be achieved if the controls operated effectively throughout the specified period (or in the case of a type 1 report, as of a specified date)*
- *When included in the scope of the engagement, the controls operated effectively to provide reasonable assurance that the control objectives stated in management's description of the service organization's system were achieved throughout the specified period.*

b. *Express an opinion in a written report about the matters in paragraph "a" above.*

(AT-C 320.07)

REQUIREMENTS

MANAGEMENT AND THOSE CHARGED WITH GOVERNANCE

The service auditor should determine the appropriate person within the management of the service organization or governance structure with whom to interact on representations, communications, and other matters. When making that determination, the service auditor should consider the responsibilities and the knowledge of the individuals. (AT-C 320.09)

PRECONDITIONS

The service auditor should accept or continue an engagement to report on the controls of a service organization if:

1. The auditor's initial knowledge of the engagement indicates that the scope of the engagement and management's description of the system used will not be so limited that it will be unlikely to be useful.
2. Management acknowledges and accepts its responsibility for:
   a. A description of the service organization's system and related assertion,
   b. Having a reasonable basis for its assertion,
   c. Selecting and stating the criteria to be used,
   d. Specifying the control objectives,
   e. Identifying risks that threaten achievement of the control objectives, and
   f. Providing a written assertion that will be included in management's description of the service organization's system, both of which will be provided to user entities.

(AT-C 320.10)

If management's description of the system includes the services provided by a subservice organization and its related control and objectives, management's acknowledgement and acceptance of the items in 2b above should include the subservice organization. (AT-C 320.11)

Request to Change the Scope of the Engagement

As with Section 105, if management requests a scope change before the engagement is complete, the service auditor should be satisfied that there is a justifiable reason for the change before agreeing to it. (AT-C 320.12)

Requesting a Written Assertion

If management refuses to provide a written assertion, the service auditor should withdraw from the engagement, when withdrawal is possible under law or regulations. (AT-C 320.13)

Assessing the Suitability of the Criteria

The service auditor should ascertain whether management has used suitable criteria:

1. To prepare the description of the organization's system
2. To evaluate whether controls were designed to achieve control objectives
3. For a type 2 report, to evaluate whether controls operated effectively throughout the specified period to achieve control objectives

(AT-C 320.14)

The service auditor should determine the following when assessing the suitability of criteria to evaluate whether management's description of a system is fairly presented:

1. Whether the description of the system reflects how it was designed and implemented, including the following items (if applicable):
   a. The types of services provided
   b. The procedures by which services are provided
   c. Information used in the performance of the procedures
   d. How the system captures and addresses significant events and conditions other than transactions
   e. The process by which reports and other information are prepared for user entities
   f. Services performed by a subservice organization
   g. The control objectives and controls designed to achieve the objectives of the system
   h. Other aspects of the controls, risk assessment, and other systems that are relevant to the services provided
2. For a type 2 report, whether the system description includes relevant details of changes to the system during the period addressed by the description
3. Whether the description of the system does not omit or distort relevant information

(AT-C 320.15)

When assessing the suitability of criteria, the service auditor should determine if the criteria address whether:

- Any risks threatening the control objectives have been identified, and
- The identified controls would provide reasonable assurance that these risks would not keep the control objectives from being achieved.

When making this assessment, the service auditor should verify whether the criteria include whether the controls were consistently applied throughout the period, including whether these controls were applied by those with appropriate competence and authority. (AT-C 320.16 and .17)

Materiality

The service auditor should evaluate materiality for:

- Management's description of the organization's system,
- The suitability of the controls, and
- (For a type 2 report) the operating effectiveness of the controls needed to achieve the objectives stated in the description.

(AT-C 320.19)

Obtaining an Understanding of the Service Organization's System and Assessing the Risk of Material Misstatement

The service auditor should acquire an understanding of the organization's system, including those controls included in the engagement scope.

The understanding should include processes used to:

- Prepare the description of the service organization's system.
- Identify controls.
- Assess the suitability of the controls' design.
- For a type 2 report, assess the operating effectiveness of controls.

(AT-C 320.20)

Using the Work of the Internal Audit Function

If there is an internal audit function within the service organization, the service auditor should understand its responsibilities in order to determine whether it can be relevant to the engagement. This includes an evaluation of:

1. The internal audit function's responsibilities
2. How the internal audit function fits in the service organization's structure
3. The activities performed by the internal audit function as it relates to the service organization

(AT-C 320.21)

To gain an understanding of the procedures performed and findings, the service auditor should read the reports of the internal audit function and regulatory examinations. (AT-C 320.23)

Obtaining Evidence Regarding Management's Description of the Service Organization's System

The service auditor should read management's description of the organization's system and evaluate whether those elements of the description that are within the engagement scope are presented fairly. This assessment should address whether:

1. The control objectives stated in the description are reasonable.
2. The controls stated in the description were implemented.
3. Any complementary user entity controls are adequately described.
4. Any services performed by a subservice organization are adequately described, as well as whether the inclusive or carve-out methods were used.

(AT-C 320.25)

The service auditor should use inquiries and other procedures to determine whether the system has been implemented. (AT-C 320.26)

Obtaining Evidence Regarding the Design of Controls

The service auditor should determine which controls are needed to achieve the control objectives for the system, and assess whether these controls were suitably designed by identifying and evaluating those risks threatening control objectives and evaluating the linkage of the controls with those risks. (AT-C 320.27)

Obtaining Evidence Regarding the Operating Effectiveness of Controls

For a type 2 engagement, the service auditor tests those controls that management has identified in its description are needed to achieve the control objectives of the system, as well as assess their effectiveness throughout the period. (AT-C 320.28) The service auditor should inquire about control changes implemented during the period covered by the service auditor's report. If the changes are significant, he or she should ascertain whether they are included in management's description of the system. If not, the service auditor should describe the changes in the report. If any superseded controls were relevant for meeting control objectives, the service auditor should test the controls prior to the change. If it is not possible to do so, the service auditor should determine the impact on the report. (AT-C 320.29)

Evaluating the Reliability of Information Produced by the Service Organization

When designing and testing controls, the service auditor should do the following:

1. Perform other procedures to procure evidence about how a control was applied, the consistency of application, and by whom or by what means it was applied.
2. Determine whether the controls depend on other controls, and whether the service auditor should obtain evidence about the effectiveness of those other controls.
3. Determine a method for selecting items to be tested to meet procedure objectives.

To determine the extent of tests of controls and whether sampling can be used, the service auditor should consider the characteristics of the population of controls to be tested. (AT-C 320.31)

Nature and Causes of Deviations

The service auditor should investigate any deviations identified, and ascertain whether:

1. Deviations are within the expected rate of deviation.
2. Additional testing is needed to conclude whether the controls related to the objectives operated effectively in the specified period.
3. The testing provides a basis for concluding that a control did not operate effectively in the specified period.

(AT-C 320.32)

If the service auditor learns that any identified deviations were the result of fraud, he or she should assess the risk that management's description of the system is not fairly presented, that the controls are not suitably designed, and (in a type 2 engagement) that the controls are not operating effectively. (AT-C 320.33)

The service auditor may learn of nontrivial:

- Noncompliance with laws or regulations,
- Fraud, or
- Uncorrected misstatements

attributable to service organization personnel that may affect user entities.

If so, the service auditor should assess the effects on:

- Management's assertion,
- Management's description of the service organization's system,
- The achievement of the control objectives, and
- The service auditor's report.

(AT-C 320.34)

SUBSEQUENT EVENTS

The service auditor should inquire of management whether there have been any events during the period between management's description of the organization's system and the date of the auditor's report that could have a significant effect on management's assertion. The service auditor should disclose such items in the report. (AT-C 320.35)

WRITTEN REPRESENTATIONS

The service auditor should obtain from management written representations that management has disclosed any situations where:

a. There are instances of legal or regulatory noncompliance or uncorrected errors.
b. There is knowledge of actual or suspected management or employee acts that may adversely affect the fairness of the description of the organization's system or the achievement of its control objectives.

(AT-C 320.36)

If there is a subservice organization providing services to a service organization, and management uses the inclusive method, then the service auditor should obtain written representations from the management of the subservice organization. (AT-C 320.37)

Written representations should be organized as a representation letter that is addressed to the service auditor, and the letter should be dated as of the same date as the service auditor's report.

If management will not provide written representations, the service auditor should discuss the matter with management, evaluate the effect of the refusal on his or her assessment of the integrity of management, and take such actions as disclaiming an opinion or withdrawing from the engagement. (AT-C 320.38)

THE SERVICE AUDITOR'S TYPE 2 REPORT

The service auditor's type 2 report should contain the information in the left column of the following table.

A title that includes the word *independent*	**Independent Service Auditor's Report on XYZ Service Organization's Description of Its [*type or name of*] System and the Suitability of the Design and Operating Effectiveness of Controls**
An appropriate addressee	XYZ Service Organization

Management's description of the service organization's system, the function performed by the system, and the period to which the description relates	*Scope* We have examined XYZ Service Organization's description of its [*type or name of*] system entitled "XYZ Service Organization's Description of Its [*type or name of*] System" for processing user entities' transactions [*or identification of the function performed by the system*] throughout the period [*date*] to [*date*] (description) and the suitability of the design and operating effectiveness of the controls included in the description to achieve the related control objectives stated in the description . . .
The criteria identified in management's assertion against which the fairness of the presentation of the description and the suitability of the design and operating effectiveness of the controls to achieve the related control objectives stated in the description were evaluated	. . . based on the criteria identified in "XYZ Service Organization's Assertion" (assertion). The controls and control objectives included in the description are those that management of XYZ Service Organization believes are likely to be relevant to user entities' internal control over financial reporting, and the description does not include those aspects of the [*type or name of*] system that are not likely to be relevant to user entities' internal control over financial reporting.
A statement that the controls and control objectives included in the description are those that management believes are likely to be relevant to user entities' internal control over financial reporting, and the description does not include those aspects of the system that are not likely to be relevant to user entities' internal control over financial reporting. If management's description of the service organization's system refers to the need for complementary user entity controls, a statement that the service auditor has not evaluated the suitability of the design or operating effectiveness of complementary user entity controls, and that the control objectives stated in the description can be achieved only if complementary user entity controls are suitably designed and operating effectively, along with the controls at the service organization. A reference to management's assertion and a statement regarding management's responsibility.	*Service Organization's Responsibilities* In [*section number where the assertion is presented*], XYZ Service Organization has provided an assertion about the fairness of the presentation of the description and suitability of the design and operating effectiveness of the controls to achieve the related control objectives stated in the description. XYZ Service Organization is responsible for preparing the description and assertion, including the completeness, accuracy, and method of presentation of the description and assertion, providing the services covered by the description, specifying the control objectives and stating them in the description, identifying the risks that threaten the achievement of the control objectives, selecting the criteria stated in the assertion, and designing, implementing, and documenting controls that are suitably designed and operating effectively to achieve the related control objectives stated in the description.
Service auditor's responsibilities	*Service Auditor's Responsibilities* Our responsibility is to express an opinion on the fairness of the presentation of the description and on the suitability of the design and operating effectiveness of the controls to achieve the related control objectives stated in the description, based on our examination.

Examination was conducted in accordance with attestation standards established by the AICPA.	Our examination was conducted in accordance with attestation standards established by the American Institute of Certified Public Accountants.
Requirements of the AICPA standards	Those standards require that we plan and perform the examination to obtain reasonable assurance about whether, in all material respects, based on the criteria in management's assertion, the description is fairly presented and the controls were suitably designed and operating effectively to achieve the related control objectives stated in the description throughout the period [*date*] to [*date*].
The evidence is sufficient and appropriate to provide a reasonable basis for the opinion.	We believe that the evidence we obtained is sufficient and appropriate to provide a reasonable basis for our opinion.
Procedures involved in examination of management's description of a service organization's system and the suitability of the design and operating effectiveness of the service organization's controls to achieve the related control objectives stated in the description	An examination of a description of a service organization's system and the suitability of the design and operating effectiveness of controls involves: • Performing procedures to obtain evidence about the fairness of the presentation of the description and the suitability of the design and operating effectiveness of the controls to achieve the related control objectives stated in the description, based on the criteria in management's assertion. • Assessing the risks that the description is not fairly presented and that the controls were not suitably designed or operating effectively to achieve the related control objectives stated in the description. • Testing the operating effectiveness of those controls that management considers necessary to provide reasonable assurance that the related control objectives stated in the description were achieved. • Evaluating the overall presentation of the description, suitability of the control objectives stated in the description, and suitability of the criteria specified by the service organization in its assertion.
A description of the inherent limitations of controls	*Inherent Limitations* The description is prepared to meet the common needs of a broad range of user entities and their auditors who audit and report on user entities' financial statements and may not, therefore, include every aspect of the system that each individual user entity may consider important in its own particular environment. Because of their

	nature, controls at a service organization may not prevent, or detect and correct, all misstatements in processing or reporting transactions [*or identification of the function performed by the system*]. Also, the projection to the future of any evaluation of the fairness of the presentation of the description, or conclusions about the suitability of the design or operating effectiveness of the controls to achieve the related control objectives, is subject to the risk that controls at a service organization may become ineffective.
A reference to a description of the service auditor's tests of controls and the results thereof that includes: • Identification of controls tested • Whether items tested represent all or a selection of items in the population • Nature of the tests in sufficient detail to enable user auditors to determine the effect of such tests on their risk assessments • Any identified deviations in the operation of controls included in the description, extent of testing performed by the service auditor that led to the identification of the deviations (including the number of items tested), and the number and nature of the deviations noted (even if, on the basis of tests performed, the service auditor concludes that the related control objective was achieved) • If the work of the internal audit function has been used in tests of controls to obtain evidence, a description of internal auditor's work and service auditor's procedures with respect to that work.	*Description of Tests of Controls* The specific controls tested and the nature, timing, and results of those tests are listed in [*section number where the description of tests of controls is presented*].
The service auditor's opinion (The information in bold relates to engagements where subservice organizations are involved.)	*Opinion* In our opinion, in all material respects, based on the criteria described in XYZ Service Organization's assertion: a. The description fairly presents the [*type or name of*] system that was designed and implemented throughout the period [*date*] to [*date*]. b. The controls related to the control objectives stated in the description were suitably designed to provide reasonable assurance that the control objectives would be achieved if the controls operated effectively throughout the period [*date*] to [*date*] ***and subservice organizations and user entities applied the complementary controls assumed in the design of XYZ Service***

	***Organization's controls throughout the period* [date] *to* [date].** c. The controls operated effectively to provide reasonable assurance that the control objectives stated in the description were achieved throughout the period [*date*] to [*date*] ***if complementary subservice organization and user entity controls assumed in the design of XYZ Service Organization's controls operated effectively throughout the period* [date] *to* [date]**.
An alert, in a separate paragraph, that restricts the use of the report	*Restricted Use* This report, including the description of tests of controls and results thereof in [*section number where the description of tests of controls is presented*], is intended solely for the information and use of management of XYZ Service Organization, user entities of XYZ Service Organization's [*type or name of*] system during some or all of the period [*date*] to [*date*], and their auditors who audit and report on such user entities' financial statements or internal control over financial reporting and have a sufficient understanding to consider it, along with other information, including information about controls implemented by user entities themselves, when assessing the risks of material misstatement of user entities' financial statements. This report is not intended to be, and should not be, used by anyone other than the specified parties.
The manual or printed signature of the service auditor's firm.	[*Service auditor's signature*]
The city and state where the service auditor practices.	[*Service auditor's city and state*]
The date of the report.*	[*Date of the service auditor's report*]

* The report should be dated no earlier than the date on which the service auditor has obtained sufficient appropriate evidence on which to base the service auditor's opinion, including evidence that:

- Management's description of the service organization system has been prepared,
- Management has provided a written assertion, and
- The attestation documentation has been reviewed.

OTHER MATTERS IN THE REPORT

A statement is added to the service auditor's report when information that is not covered by the report is included in the description of the service organization's system. This paragraph would follow the Scope paragraph in the preceding table.	The information included in [*section number where the other information is presented*], "Other Information Provided by XYZ Service Organization," is presented by management of XYZ Service Organization to provide additional information and is not a part of XYZ Service

	Organization's description of its [*name or type of*] system made available to user entities during the period [*date*] to [*date*]. Information about XYZ Service Organization's [*describe the nature of the information, for example, business continuity planning, privacy practices, and so on*] has not been subjected to the procedures applied in the examination of the description of the [*name or type of*] system and of the suitability of the design and operating effectiveness of controls to achieve the related control objectives stated in the description of the [*name or type of*] system.
A statement is added to the service auditor's report when the service organization uses a subservice organization, the carve-out method is used to present the subservice organization, and complementary subservice organization controls are required to meet the control objectives. This paragraph would follow the Scope paragraph in the preceding table.	XYZ Service Organization uses a subservice organization to [*identify the function or service provided by the subservice organization*]. The description includes only the control objectives and related controls of XYZ Service Organization and excludes the control objectives and related controls of the subservice organization. The description also indicates that certain control objectives specified by XYZ Service Organization can be achieved only if complementary subservice organization controls assumed in the design of XYZ Service Organization's controls are suitably designed and operating effectively, along with the related controls at XYZ Service Organization. Our examination did not extend to controls of the subservice organization, and we have not evaluated the suitability of the design or operating effectiveness of such complementary subservice organization controls.
A statement is added to the assertion when complementary user entity controls are required to meet the control objectives. This paragraph would follow the Scope paragraph in the preceding table.	The description indicates that certain control objectives specified in the description can be achieved only if complementary user entity controls assumed in the design of XYZ Service Organization's controls are suitably designed and operating effectively, along with related controls at the service organization. Our examination did not extend to such complementary user entity controls, and we have not evaluated the suitability of the design or operating effectiveness of such complementary user entity controls.

Modified Opinions

The service auditor should modify the opinion, as well as modify the service auditor's report, to clearly describe all of the reasons for a modification under the following circumstances:

1. Management's description of the system is not fairly presented.
2. The controls are not suitably designed to provide reasonable assurance that the control objectives would be achieved.
3. For a type 2 report, the controls did not operate effectively throughout the specified period to achieve the stated control objectives.
4. The service auditor is unable to obtain sufficient evidence.

(AT-C 320.42)

If the service auditor plans to disclaim an opinion because of lack of evidence, and has concluded that some aspects of the description are not fairly presented, or some controls were not suitably designed to provide reasonable assurance regarding control objectives, or (for a type 2 report) some controls did not operate effectively throughout the specified period, then the service auditor should identify these findings in the report. (AT-C 320.43)

If the service auditor plans to disclaim an opinion, then the service auditor should not identify the procedures performed, nor describe characteristics of the engagement in the report. (AT-C 320.44)

Other Communication Responsibilities

If the service auditor is aware of incidents of legal or regulatory noncompliance, fraud, or uncorrected errors attributable to management or other personnel that are not trivial and that may affect user entities, then the service auditor should determine the effect of these incidents on the description of the organization's system, control objectives, and the service auditor's report. Further, the service auditor should take appropriate action if this information has not been communicated to affected user entities and management refuses to do. (AT-C 320.45)

ILLUSTRATION

Illustration 1. Type 1 Service Auditor's Report

Independent Service Auditor's Report[1] on XYZ Service Organization's Description of Its [*type or name of*] System and the Suitability of the Design of Controls

To: XYZ Service Organization

We have examined XYZ Service Organization's description of its [*type or name of*] system entitled, "XYZ Service Organization's Description of Its [*type or name of*] System," for processing user entities' transactions [*or identification of the function performed by the system*] as of [*date*] (description) and the suitability of the design of the controls included in the description to achieve the related control objectives stated in the description, based on the criteria identified in "XYZ Service Organization's Assertion" (assertion). The controls and control objectives included in the description are those that management of XYZ Service Organization believes are likely to be relevant to user entities' internal control over financial reporting, and the description does not include those aspects of the [*type or name of*] system that are not likely to be relevant to user entities' internal control over financial reporting.

---

1 https://publication.cpa2biz.com/content/link/ps/atc_section_300#ftn.atc_320_fn33

[*A statement such as the following is added to the service auditor's report when information that is not covered by the report is included in the description of the service organization's system.*]

***The information included in* [section number where the other information is presented]*, "Other Information Provided by XYZ Service Organization," is presented by management of XYZ Service Organization to provide additional information and is not a part of XYZ Service Organization's description of its* [name or type of] *system made available to user entities as of* [date]*. Information about XYZ Service Organization's* [describe the nature of the information, for example, business continuity planning, privacy practices, and so on] *has not been subjected to the procedures applied in the examination of the description of the* [name or type of] *system and of the suitability of the design of controls to achieve the related control objectives stated in the description of the* [name or type of] *system*.**

[*A statement such as the following is added to the report when the service organization uses a subservice organization, the carve-out method is used to present the subservice organization, and complementary subservice organization controls are required to meet the control objectives.*]

XYZ Service Organization uses a subservice organization to* [identify the function or service provided by the subservice organization]*. The description includes only the control objectives and related controls of XYZ Service Organization and excludes the control objectives and related controls of the subservice organization. The description also indicates that certain control objectives specified by XYZ Service Organization can be achieved only if complementary subservice organization controls assumed in the design of XYZ Service Organization's controls are suitably designed and operating effectively, along with the related controls at XYZ Service Organization. Our examination did not extend to controls of the subservice organization, and we have not evaluated the design or operating effectiveness of such complementary subservice organization controls.

[*A statement such as the following is added to the assertion when complementary user entity controls are required to meet the control objectives.*]

The description indicates that certain control objectives specified in the description can be achieved only if complementary user entity controls assumed in the design of XYZ Service Organization's controls are suitably designed and operating effectively, along with related controls at the service organization. Our examination did not extend to such complementary user entity controls, and we have not evaluated the suitability of the design or operating effectiveness of such complementary user entity controls.

Service Organization's Responsibilities

In [*section number where assertion is presented*], XYZ Service Organization has provided an assertion about the fairness of the presentation of the description and suitability of the design of the controls to achieve the related control objectives stated in the description. XYZ Service Organization is responsible for preparing the description and its assertion, including the completeness, accuracy, and method of presentation of the description and assertion, providing the services covered by the description, specifying the control objectives and stating them in the description, identifying the risks that threaten the achievement of the control objectives, selecting the criteria stated in the assertion, and designing, implementing, and documenting controls that are suitably designed and operating effectively to achieve the related control objectives stated in the description.

Service Auditor's Responsibilities

Our responsibility is to express an opinion on the fairness of the presentation of the description and on the suitability of the design of the controls to achieve the related control objectives stated in the description, based on our examination.

Our examination was conducted in accordance with attestation standards established by the American Institute of Certified Public Accountants. Those standards require that we plan and perform the examination to obtain reasonable assurance about whether, in all material respects, based on the criteria in management's assertion, the description is fairly presented and the controls were suitably designed to achieve the related control objectives stated in the description as of [*date*]. We believe that the evidence we obtained is sufficient and appropriate to provide a reasonable basis for our opinion.

An examination of a description of a service organization's system and the suitability of the design of controls involves:

- Performing procedures to obtain evidence about the fairness of the presentation of the description and the suitability of the design of the controls to achieve the related control objectives stated in the description, based on the criteria in management's assertion.
- Assessing the risks that the description is not fairly presented and that the controls were not suitably designed to achieve the related control objectives stated in the description.
- Evaluating the overall presentation of the description, suitability of the control objectives stated in the description, and suitability of the criteria specified by the service organization in its assertion.

Inherent Limitations

The description is prepared to meet the common needs of a broad range of user entities and their auditors who audit and report on user entities' financial statements and may not, therefore, include every aspect of the system that each individual user entity may consider important in its own particular environment. Because of their nature, controls at a service organization may not prevent, or detect and correct, all misstatements in processing or reporting transactions [*or identification of the function performed by the system*]. Also, the projection to the future of any evaluation of the fairness of the presentation of the description, or conclusions about the suitability of the design of the controls to achieve the related control objectives, is subject to the risk that controls at a service organization may become ineffective.

Other Matter

We did not perform any procedures regarding the operating effectiveness of controls stated in the description and, accordingly, do not express an opinion thereon.

Opinion

In our opinion, in all material respects, based on the criteria described in XYZ Service Organization's assertion:

a. The description fairly presents the [*type or name of*] system that was designed and implemented as of [*date*].
b. The controls related to the control objectives stated in the description were suitably designed to provide reasonable assurance that the control objectives would be achieved if the controls operated effectively as of [*date*] ***and subservice organizations and user entities applied the complementary controls assumed in the design of XYZ Service Organization's controls as of* [date].**

Restricted Use

This report is intended solely for the information and use of management of XYZ Service Organization, user entities of XYZ Service Organization's [*type or name of*] system as of [*date*], and their auditors who audit and report on such user entities' financial statements or internal control over financial reporting and have a sufficient understanding to consider it, along with other information, including information about controls implemented by user entities themselves, when assessing the risks of material misstatements of user entities' financial statements. This report is not intended to be, and should not be, used by anyone other than the specified parties.

[*Service auditor's signature*]

[*Service auditor's city and state*]

[*Date of the service auditor's report*]

AT-C Section 395 (Designated for AT Section 701) *Management's Discussion and Analysis (MD&A)—A Summary*[1,2]

ORIGINAL PRONOUNCEMENT

Source Statement on Standards for Attestation Engagements (SSAE) 18.

TECHNICAL ALERT

Because practitioners rarely perform attest engagements to report on a company's management's discussion and analysis for Securities and Exchange Commission (SEC) reporting, the Auditing Standards Board (ASB) did not clarify this section. It merely changed the section number.

APPLICABILITY

AT-C 395 applies when a practitioner is engaged by a public entity that prepares Management's Discussion and Analysis (MD&A) in accordance with the rules and regulations adopted by the Securities and Exchange Commission (SEC) (or a nonpublic entity following the same requirements) to perform either an examination or a review of MD&A. A practitioner engaged to perform agreed-upon procedures on MD&A should follow the guidance in Section 21r.

---

1 *The SSAE on examination or review of MD&A is essentially a detailed manual on how to perform examinations and reviews, and only the highlights are summarized here. A practitioner seeking to provide these services should refer to SSAE 18 and the SEC's rules and regulations on MD&A. Only the considerations for a public entity are covered here. The considerations for a nonpublic entity are very similar because only the SEC has, at this point, issued rules and regulations that provide guidance on the presentation of MD&A.*

2 *Practitioners should be aware that, on April 15, 2002, the SEC issued "Commission Statement about Management's Discussion and Analysis of Financial Condition and Results of Operations." The release sets forth certain views of the SEC regarding disclosures that should be considered by registrants. Disclosure matters covered in the release are liquidity and capital resources, including off-balance-sheet arrangements; certain trading activities that include non-exchange-traded contracts accounted for at fair value; and the effects of transactions with related and certain other parties. The release can be found on the SEC's website at* www.sec.gov.

DEFINITION OF TERM

MD&A. Management's Discussion and Analysis of Financial Condition and Results of Operations adopted by the SEC and found in Item 303 of Regulation S-K, as interpreted by Financial Reporting Release (FRR) 36.

OBJECTIVES OF AT SECTION 395

The SEC adopted requirements for MD&A in 1974 to have management provide a narrative explanation of the financial statements. The idea was to allow the user to see the company's financial position and operating results through management's eyes.

Two levels of service are possible—an examination or a review. A review report is restricted as to use and is not intended to be filed with the SEC. An examination report is intended for general use, but at this stage, whether there will be a significant demand for this service is unknown. The SEC does not require a practitioner's report on MD&A—the narrative presentation is management's responsibility and not a part of the audited financial statements.

According to AT 395.05, the practitioner's objective in an examination of MD&A is to express an opinion on the presentation taken as a whole by reporting whether:

1. The presentation includes, in all material respects, the required elements of the rules and regulations adopted by the SEC.
2. The historical financial amounts included in the presentation have been accurately derived, in all material respects, from the entity's financial statements.
3. The underlying information, determinations, estimates, and assumptions of the entity provide a reasonable basis for the disclosures contained in the presentation.

The objective of a review of MD&A is to provide negative assurance on these three items.

NOTE: "Negative assurance" indicates that no information came to the accountant's attention that would cause him or her not to believe the three statements.

An examination of MD&A would generally be expected to relate to the MD&A for annual periods, but a review might relate to the MD&A for annual or interim periods or some combination.

In an examination, the practitioner seeks to obtain reasonable assurance by accumulating sufficient evidence to support the disclosures and assumptions, thus limiting attestation risk to an appropriately low level. A review consists principally of applying analytical procedures and making inquiries, and does not provide assurance that a practitioner would become aware of all significant matters that would be disclosed in an examination.

SSAE 10 made only minor changes to this section, including modifying the reports in this section to conform to changes made by Statement on Auditing Standards (SAS) 93, *Omnibus Statement on Auditing Standards—2000.*

REQUIREMENTS: EXAMINATION

ACCEPTANCE

To accept an engagement to examine MD&A, the practitioner should audit the financial statements for at least the latest period to which the MD&A presentation relates, and the financial statements for the other periods covered by the MD&A presentation should have been audited by the practitioner or a predecessor auditor.

Performance

According to AT 395.41, the practitioner should do the following:

1. Obtain an understanding of the rules and regulations adopted by the SEC for MD&A and management's method of preparing MD&A.
2. Plan the engagement by developing an overall strategy considering factors such as matters affecting the entity's industry and similar knowledge obtained during the audit of financial statements.
3. Consider relevant portions of internal control applicable to the preparation of MD&A.
4. Obtain sufficient evidence, including testing completeness, by comparing the content of the MD&A to the information obtained in the audit of financial statements and considering whether the explanations in the MD&A are consistent with this information.
5. Consider the effect of events subsequent to the balance sheet date by extending subsequent events review procedures in the audit to the MD&A information.
6. Obtain written representations from management concerning its responsibility for MD&A, completeness of minutes, events subsequent to the balance sheet date, and other matters the practitioner considers relevant to the MD&A presentation.
7. Form an opinion about whether the MD&A presentation meets the objectives for an opinion on such a presentation.

Reporting

The financial statements for the periods covered by the MD&A presentation and the related auditors' report should accompany the presentation or be incorporated by reference to information filed with a regulatory agency.

The report should include the elements as found in the example in Illustration 1.

REQUIREMENTS: REVIEW

Acceptance

A practitioner may accept an engagement to review an MD&A presentation for an annual period under the same circumstances as an examination.

To accept an engagement to review the MD&A presentation for an interim period, both of the following points should occur:

1. The practitioner should either:

    a. Review and report on the historical financial statements for the related comparative interim periods or
    b. Audit the interim financial statements

2. The practitioner or a predecessor auditor either has already examined or will examine the MD&A presentation for the most recent fiscal year.

Performance

According to AT 395.76, the practitioner should do the following:

1. Obtain an understanding of the rules and regulations adopted by the SEC for MD&A and management's method of preparing MD&A.
2. Plan the engagement, considering factors such as matters affecting the industry, the types of information management reports to external analysts, and matters identified during the audit or review of historical financial statements.
3. Consider relevant portions of the entity's internal control applicable to the MD&A.
4. Apply analytical procedures and make inquiries of management and others.
5. Consider the effects of events subsequent to the balance sheet date.
6. Obtain written representations from management.
7. Form a conclusion as to whether any information came to the practitioner's attention that would cause him or her to believe the objectives related to the MD&A presentation were not achieved.

Reporting

The financial statements for the periods covered by the MD&A presentation and the related auditors' or accountants' reports should accompany the presentation or be incorporated by reference to information filed with a regulatory agency.

The report should include the elements as found in the examples in Illustrations 2 and 3.

ILLUSTRATIONS

The following reports are adapted from SSAE 10:[3]

1. An illustration of the wording of a standard examination report
2. A standard review report on an annual MD&A presentation
3. A standard review report on an MD&A presentation for an interim period

Illustration 1. Standard Examination Report

Report of Independent Registered Public Accounting Firm

To the Audit Committee, Board of Directors, and Shareholders
Widget Company
Main City, USA

We have examined Widget Company's Management's Discussion and Analysis taken as a whole, included [*incorporated by reference*] in the Company's [*insert description of registration statement or document*]. Management is responsible for the preparation of the Company's Management's Discussion

3 *If the entity is a nonissuer and complies with GAAS rather than the standards of the PCAOB, the references in the report to the PCAOB's standards should be changed to refer to "auditing standards generally accepted in the United States of America" and "attestation standards established by the American Institute of Certified Public Accountants."*

and Analysis pursuant to the rules and regulations adopted by the Securities and Exchange Commission. Our responsibility is to express an opinion on the presentation based on our examination. We have audited, in accordance with the standards of the Public Company Accounting Oversight Board (United States), the financial statements of Widget Company as of December 31, 20X2 and 20X1, and for each of the years in the three-year period ended December 31, 20X2; in our report dated February 15, 20X3, we expressed an unqualified opinion on those financial statements.[4]

Our examination of Management's Discussion and Analysis was conducted in accordance with attestation standards established by the Public Company Accounting Oversight Board and, accordingly, included examining, on a test basis, evidence supporting the historical amounts and disclosures in the presentation. An examination also includes assessing the significant determinations made by management as to the relevancy of information to be included and the estimates and assumptions that affect reported information. We believe that our examination provides a reasonable basis for our opinion.

The preparation of Management's Discussion and Analysis requires management to interpret the criteria, make determinations as to the relevancy of information to be included, and make estimates and assumptions that affect reported information. Management's Discussion and Analysis includes information regarding the estimated future impact of transactions and events that have occurred or are expected to occur, expected sources of liquidity and capital resources, operating trends, commitments, and uncertainties. Actual results in the future may differ materially from management's present assessment of this information because events and circumstances frequently do not occur as expected.[5]

In our opinion, the Company's presentation of Management's Discussion and Analysis includes, in all material respects, the required elements of the rules and regulations adopted by the Securities and Exchange Commission; the historical financial amounts included therein have been accurately derived, in all material respects, from the Company's financial statements; and the underlying information, determinations, estimates, and assumptions of the Company provide a reasonable basis for the disclosures contained therein.

Smith and Jones
March 1, 20X3

---

4 *If prior financial statements were audited by other auditors, this sentence would be replaced by the following*:

We have audited, in accordance with the standards of the Public Company Accounting Oversight Board (United States), the financial statements of Widget Company as of and for the year ended December 31, 20X2, and in our report dated Month XX, 20X3, we expressed an unqualified opinion on those financial statements. The financial statements of Widget Company as of December 31, 20X1, and for each of the years in the two-year period then ended were audited by other auditors, whose report dated Month XX, 20X2, expressed an unqualified opinion on those financial statements.

If the practitioner's opinion on the financial statements is based on the report of other auditors, this sentence would be replaced by the following:

We have audited, in accordance with the standards of the Public Company Accounting Oversight Board (United States), the financial statements of Widget Company as of December 31, 20X2 and 20X1, and for each of the years in the three-year period ended December 31, 20X2, and in our report dated Month XX, 20X3, we expressed an unqualified opinion on those financial statements based on our audits and the report of other auditors.

5 *The following sentence should be added to the beginning of the explanatory paragraph if the entity is a nonpublic entity*:

Although Widget Company is not subject to the rules and regulations of the Securities and Exchange Commission, the accompanying Management's Discussion and Analysis is intended to be a presentation in accordance with the rules and regulations adopted by the Securities and Exchange Commission.

Illustration 2. Standard Review Report on an Annual MD&A Presentation

Report of Independent Registered Public Accounting Firm

To the Board of Directors
Widget Company
Main City, USA

We have reviewed Widget Company's Management's Discussion and Analysis taken as a whole, included [*incorporated by reference*] in the Company's [*insert description of registration statement or document*]. Management is responsible for the preparation of the Company's Management's Discussion and Analysis pursuant to the rules and regulations adopted by the Securities and Exchange Commission. We have audited, in accordance with the standards of the Public Company Accounting Oversight Board (United States), the financial statements of Widget Company as of December 31, 20X2 and 20X1, and for each of the years in the three-year period ended December 31, 20X2, and in our report dated February 15, 20X3, we expressed an unqualified opinion on those financial statements.

We conducted our review of Management's Discussion and Analysis in accordance with attestation standards established by the Public Company Accounting Oversight Board. A review of Management's Discussion and Analysis consists principally of applying analytical procedures and making inquiries of persons responsible for financial, accounting, and operational matters. It is substantially less in scope than an examination, the objective of which is the expression of an opinion on the presentation. Accordingly, we do not express such an opinion.

The preparation of Management's Discussion and Analysis requires management to interpret the criteria, make determinations as to the relevancy of information to be included, and make estimates and assumptions that affect reported information. Management's Discussion and Analysis includes information regarding the estimated future impact of transactions and events that have occurred or are expected to occur, expected sources of liquidity and capital resources, operating trends, commitments, and uncertainties. Actual results in the future may differ materially from management's present assessment of this information because events and circumstances frequently do not occur as expected.[6]

Based on our review, nothing came to our attention that caused us to believe that the Company's presentation of Management's Discussion and Analysis does not include, in all material respects, the required elements of the rules and regulations adopted by the Securities and Exchange Commission; that the historical financial amounts included therein have not been accurately derived, in all material respects, from the Company's financial statements; or that the underlying information, determinations, estimates, and assumptions of the Company do not provide a reasonable basis for the disclosures contained therein.

This report is intended solely for the information and use of [*list or refer to the specified parties*] and is not intended to be, and should not be, used by anyone other than the specified parties.

Smith and Jones
March 1, 20X3

---

6 *The following sentence should be added to the beginning of the explanatory paragraph if the entity is a nonpublic entity:*

Although Widget Company is not subject to the rules and regulations of the Securities and Exchange Commission, the accompanying Management's Discussion and Analysis is intended to be a presentation in accordance with the rules and regulations adopted by the Securities and Exchange Commission.

ILLUSTRATION 3. STANDARD REVIEW REPORT ON AN INTERIM MD&A PRESENTATION

Report of Independent Registered Public Accounting Firm

To the Audit Committee, Board of Directors, and Shareholders
Widget Company
Main City, USA

We have reviewed Widget Company's Management's Discussion and Analysis taken as a whole, included in the Company's [*insert description of registration statement or document*]. Management is responsible for the preparation of the Company's Management's Discussion and Analysis pursuant to the rules and regulations adopted by the Securities and Exchange Commission. We have reviewed, in accordance with the standards of the Public Company Accounting Oversight Board, the interim financial information of Widget Company as of June 30, 20X3 and 20X2, and for the three-month and six-month periods then ended and have issued our report thereon dated July 15, 20X3.

We conducted our review of Management's Discussion and Analysis in accordance with attestation standards established by the Public Company Accounting Oversight Board. A review of Management's Discussion and Analysis consists principally of applying analytical procedures and making inquiries of persons responsible for financial, accounting, and operational matters. It is substantially less in scope than an examination, the objective of which is the expression of an opinion on the presentation. Accordingly, we do not express such an opinion.

The preparation of Management's Discussion and Analysis requires management to interpret the criteria, make determinations as to the relevancy of information to be included, and make estimates and assumptions that affect reported information. Management's Discussion and Analysis includes information regarding the estimated future impact of transactions and events that have occurred or are expected to occur, expected sources of liquidity and capital resources, operating trends, commitments, and uncertainties. Actual results in the future may differ materially from management's present assessment of this information because events and circumstances frequently do not occur as expected.[7]

Based on our review, nothing came to our attention that caused us to believe that the Company's presentation of Management's Discussion and Analysis does not include, in all material respects, the required elements of the rules and regulations adopted by the Securities and Exchange Commission; that the historical financial amounts included therein have not been accurately derived, in all material respects, from the Company's financial statements; or that the underlying information, determinations, estimates, and assumptions of the Company do not provide a reasonable basis for the disclosures contained therein.

This report is intended solely for the information and use of [*list or refer to the specified parties*] and is not intended to be, and should not be, used by anyone other than the specified parties.

Smith and Jones
March 1, 20X3

---

[7] *The following sentence should be added to the beginning of the explanatory paragraph if the entity is a nonpublic entity:*

Although Widget Company is not subject to the rules and regulations of the Securities and Exchange Commission, the accompanying Management's Discussion and Analysis is intended to be a presentation in accordance with the rules and regulations adopted by the Securities and Exchange Commission.

AT 20 Defining Professional Requirements in Statements on Standards for Attest Engagements

ORIGINAL PRONOUNCEMENT

Source Statement on Standards for Attestation Engagements (SSAE) 13, *Defining Professional Requirements in Statements on Standards for Attest Engagements.*

TECHNICAL ALERT

In April 2016, the Auditing Standards Board (ASB) issued SSAE No. 18, *Attestation Standards: Clarification and Recodification.* SSAE No. 18 is effective for practitioners' reports dated on or after May 1, 2017. SSAE No. 18 is the culmination of the attestation clarity project, and it supersedes all of existing attestation standards except for:

- AT 501, whose content was moved to the auditing standards and codified as AU-C 940.
- AT 701, which will not be clarified, but retained in its current form because it is a rarely performed engagement. The section number has been changed to AT-C Section 395.

The clarified standards use the prefix "AT-C" and can be found in the AT-C chapters of this book.

DEFINING PROFESSIONAL REQUIREMENTS IN STATEMENTS ON STANDARDS FOR ATTESTATION ENGAGEMENTS

AT Section 20 clarifies that the SSAEs use two categories of professional requirements to describe the degree of responsibility the standards impose on auditors.

- *Unconditional requirements.* The practitioner is required to comply with an unconditional requirement in all cases in which the circumstances exist to which the unconditional requirement applies. SSAEs use the words *must* or *is required* to indicate an unconditional requirement.
- *Presumptively mandatory requirements.* The practitioner also is required to comply with a presumptively mandatory requirement in all cases in which the circumstances exist to which the presumptively mandatory requirement applies; however, in rare circumstances, the practitioner may depart from a presumptively mandatory requirement provided the practitioner documents his or her justification for the departure and how the alternative

procedures performed in the circumstances were sufficient to achieve the objectives of the presumptively mandatory requirement. SSAEs use the word *should* to indicate a presumptively mandatory requirement.

The term "should consider" means that the consideration of the procedure or action is presumptively required, whereas carrying out of the procedure or action is not.

AT Section 20 also clarifies that explanatory material, which is defined within SSAEs, is intended to explain the objective of the professional requirements, rather than imposing a professional requirement for the practitioner to perform.

AT 50 SSAE Hierarchy

ORIGINAL PRONOUNCEMENT

Source Statement on Standards for Attestation Engagements (SSAE) 14, *SSAE Hierarchy*.

TECHNICAL ALERT

In April 2016, the Auditing Standards Board (ASB) issued SSAE No. 18, *Attestation Standards: Clarification and Recodification.* SSAE No. 18 is effective for practitioners' reports dated on or after May 1, 2017. SSAE No. 18 is the culmination of the attestation clarity project, and it supersedes all of existing attestation standards except for:

- AT 501, whose content was moved to the auditing standards and codified as AU-C 940.
- AT 701, which will not be clarified, but retained in its current form because it is a rarely performed engagement. The section number has been changed to AT-C Section 395.

The clarified standards use the prefix "AT-C" and can be found in the AT-C chapters of this book.

ATTESTATION STANDARDS

The eleven attestation standards do not supersede existing standards in SASs and SSARSs. The practitioner who is engaged to perform an engagement subject to these existing standards should follow such standards and not look to the eleven attestation standards or the discussion of them in AT Section 101 for guidance.

The eleven standards are classified as follows:

General: 1 through 5.
Fieldwork: 6 and 7.
Reporting: 8 through 11.

1. *First general standard.* The engagement shall be performed by a practitioner who must have adequate technical training and proficiency to perform the attestation engagement. (AT 101.19)
2. *Second general standard.* The engagement shall be performed by a practitioner who must have adequate knowledge of the subject matter. (AT 101.21)
3. *Third general standard.* The practitioner must have reason to believe that the subject matter is capable of evaluation against reasonable criteria that are suitable and available to users. (AT 101.23)
4. *Fourth general standard.* The practitioner must maintain an independence in mental attitude in all matters relating to the engagement. (AT 101.35)

5. *Fifth general standard.* The practitioner must exercise due professional care in the planning and performance of the engagement and the preparation of the report. (AT 101.39)
6. *First standard of fieldwork.* The practitioner must adequately plan the work and must properly supervise any assistants. (AT 101.42)
7. *Second standard of fieldwork.* The practitioner must obtain sufficient evidence to provide a reasonable basis for the conclusion that is expressed in the report. (AT 101.51)
8. *First standard of reporting.* The practitioner must identify the subject matter or the assertion being reported on and state the character of the engagement in the report. (AT 101.63)
9. *Second standard of reporting.* The practitioner must state the practitioner's conclusion about the subject matter or the assertion in relation to the criteria against which the subject matter was evaluated in the report. However, if conditions exist that, individually or in combination, result in one or more material deviations from the criteria, the practitioner should modify the report and should ordinarily express his or her conclusion directly on the subject matter, not on the assertion. (AT 101.66)
10. *Third standard of reporting.* The practitioner must state all of the practitioner's significant reservations about the engagement, the subject matter, and, if applicable, the assertion related thereto in the report. (AT 101.71)
11. *Fourth standard of reporting.* The practitioner must state in the report that the report is intended solely for the information and use of the specified parties under the following circumstances:
    - When the criteria used to evaluate the subject matter are determined by the practitioner to be appropriate only for a limited number of parties who either participated in their establishment or can be presumed to have an adequate understanding of the criteria
    - When the criteria used to evaluate the subject matter are available only to specified parties
    - When reporting on subject matter and a written assertion has not been provided by the responsible party
    - When the report is on an attestation engagement to apply agreed-upon procedures to the subject matter

    (AT 101.78)

ATTESTATION INTERPRETATIONS

Attestation interpretations consist of:

- Interpretations of the SSAEs
- Appendixes to the SSAEs
- Attestation guidance in the AICPA audit and accounting guides
- AICPA attestation Statements of Position

Practitioners should consider the attestation interpretations and be prepared to explain how they complied with the provisions addressed by the guidance.

OTHER ATTESTATION PUBLICATIONS

Other attest publications have no authoritative status, but they may help the practitioner apply the standards. They include:

- AICPA attestation publications not included in the list above
- Attestation articles in the AICPA's *Journal of Accountancy*
- Attestation articles in the CPA Letter
- Continuing professional education courses and other instruction materials
- Textbooks, guidebooks, attest programs, and checklists
- Attestation publications from state CPA societies, other organizations, and individuals

AT 101 Attest Engagements

ORIGINAL PRONOUNCEMENTS

Sources Statement on Standards for Attestation Engagements (SSAE) 10, *Attestation Standards: Revision and Recodification*, as amended by SSAE 11, January 2002, and SSAE 12.

TECHNICAL ALERT

In April 2016, the Auditing Standards Board (ASB) issued SSAE No. 18, *Attestation Standards: Clarification and Recodification.* SSAE No. 18 is effective for practitioners' reports dated on or after May 1, 2017. SSAE No. 18 is the culmination of the attestation clarity project, and it supersedes all of existing attestation standards except for:

- AT 501, whose content was moved to the auditing standards and codified as AU-C 940.
- AT 701, which will not be clarified, but retained in its current form because it is a rarely performed engagement. The section number has been changed to AT-C Section 395.

The clarified standards use the prefix "AT-C" and can be found in the AT-C chapters of this book.

APPLICABILITY

AT 101 applies to attest engagements, as defined below, are performed by a certified public accountant in the practice of public accounting (practitioner). See AT Section 301, *Financial Forecasts and Projections*, for additional guidance on applicability when engaged to provide an attest service on a financial forecast or projection.

NOTE: Practitioners performing agreed-upon procedures must follow the general, fieldwork, and reporting standards for attest engagements described in the section, but should refer to AT Section 201 for specific guidance on performing such engagements. When a practitioner accepts an attest engagement for a government body or agency and agrees to follow specified government standards, guides, procedures, statutes, rules, and regulations, the practitioner must follow those governmental requirements as well as the applicable attestation standards.

DEFINITIONS OF TERMS

Assertion. A declaration or set of related declarations about whether the subject matter is based on, or in conformity with, the selected criteria.

NOTE: A conclusion on the reliability of a written assertion may refer to that assertion or to the subject matter to which the assertion relates. However, if there are one or more material deviations from the criteria, the practitioner should modify the report and should ordinarily express his or her conclusion directly on the subject matter, not on management's assertion.

Attest engagement. An engagement in which a practitioner is engaged to issue or does issue an examination, a review, or an agreed-upon procedures report on subject matter, or an assertion about the subject matter, that is the responsibility of another party.

NOTE: Professional services that are not covered by this section include the following:

1. *Services performed under Statements on Auditing Standards (SASs).*
2. *Services performed under Statements on Standards for Accounting and Review Services (SSARSs).*
3. *Services performed under the Statement on Standards for Consulting Services (SSCSs), including litigation services.*
4. *Engagements to advocate a client's position, such as representing the client when dealing with the Internal Revenue Service (IRS).*
5. *Engagements to prepare tax returns or provide tax advice.*

Attestation risk. The risk that the practitioner may unknowingly fail to appropriately modify his or her attest report on an assertion that is materially misstated. It consists of the risk (inherent and control risk) that the assertion contains errors that could be material and the risk (detection risk) that the practitioner will not detect such errors.

Criteria. The standards or benchmarks used to measure and present the subject matter and against which the practitioner evaluates the subject matter.

Responsible party. The person or persons (either as individuals or representatives of the entity) responsible for the subject matter. If no such party exists due to the nature of the subject matter, then a party who has a reasonable basis for making a written assertion about the subject matter may provide such an assertion.

Subject matter. Examples of the subject matter of an attest engagement include:

- Historical or prospective performance or condition, such as prospective financial information, performance measurements, and backlog data
- Physical characteristics, such as a narrative description or square footage of facilities
- Historical events, such as the price of a market basket or goods on a certain date
- Analyses, such as breakeven analyses
- Systems and processes, such as internal control
- Behavior, such as corporate governance or compliance with laws and regulations

OBJECTIVES OF SECTION 101

At one time, attest services provided by CPAs were limited to expressing a positive opinion on historical financial statements on the basis of an audit made in accordance with generally accepted auditing standards (GAAS). However, CPAs are increasingly requested to provide assurance on representations other than historical financial statements and in forms other than the positive opinion. The main objective of adopting the attestation standards was to provide guidance and establish a broad framework for the variety of attest services demanded of CPAs.

There are eleven attestation standards and two levels of attest assurance that can be reported for general distribution, as follows:

1. Positive assurance in reports that express conclusions on the basis of an *examination*.
2. Moderate assurance in reports that express conclusions on the basis of a *review*.

The guidance on attest services also provides for reports based on agreed-upon procedures or agreed-upon criteria, as long as the use of the report is limited to the parties who agreed upon the procedures or criteria.

In 1999, the Auditing Standards Board issued SSAE 9, *Amendments to SSAE Nos. 1, 2, and 3*. SSAE 9:

- Provided the option of reporting directly on the subject matter of the assertion, while still permitting practitioners to report on management's assertion. (The practitioner would continue to be required to obtain management's assertion as a condition of engagement performance.)
- Eliminated the requirement for a separate presentation of management's assertion in certain cases where the assertion is included in the introductory paragraph of the practitioner's report. (This limited approach to direct reporting was modified by SSAE 10.)
- Conformed the reporting guidance to include reporting elements similar to those required in auditor reports on historical financial statements as contained in Section 508, *Reports on Audited Financial Statements*.
- Provided guidance on the relationship between SSAEs and the Statements on Quality Control Standards.

In 2001, the Auditing Standards Board issued SSAE 10, *Attestation Standards: Revision and Recodification*. SSAE 10 superseded SSAEs 1 through 9 and renumbered the AT sections in the American Institute of Certified Public Accountants' (AICPA's) *Codification*. The primary driver behind the issuance of SSAE 10 was not the need for substantive changes, but the need to make the guidance among attest services more consistent. The revisions to this section included:

- Changing the title of this section to Attest Engagements.
- Changing the definition of an attest engagement.
- Clarifying that the attestation standards may be applied to a broad range of subject matter.
- Clarifying the relationship between the responsible party, the client (if different from the responsible party), and the practitioner.
- Clarifying that the essential elements of criteria referred to in the third general standard are that the criteria must be suitable and available to users, and the subject matter must be capable of reasonably consistent measurement.
- Providing guidance on restricting the use of the report when a practitioner performs and reports on engagements when a written assertion cannot be obtained.
- Permitting true direct reporting on the subject matter. (There is no requirement to make reference to an assertion in the practitioner's report. The practitioner would also be permitted to report on the written assertion.)
- Expanding guidance on the circumstances in which the use of attest reports should be restricted to specified parties.

Additional changes made by SSAE 10 are described in AT Sections 201 to 701. In 2002, the Auditing Standards Board issued SSAE 11, *Attest Documentation*. SSAE 11 incorporates in the attestation standards the concepts and terminology in AU-C Section 230, *Audit Documentation*.

In 2002, SSAE 12, *Amendment to Statement on Standards for Attestation Engagements No. 10, Attestation Standards: Revision and Recodification*, was issued. SSAE 12 clarifies that although an effective quality control system will assist in complying with attestation standards, a deficiency in or noncompliance with the quality control system does not, by itself, indicate that an engagement was not performed according to the appropriate standards.

REQUIREMENTS

A practitioner who is engaged to issue or does issue an examination, a review, or an agreed-upon procedures report on subject matter, or an assertion about the subject matter that is the responsibility of another party, should do so in accordance with the eleven attestation standards described later in this section.

Any professional engagement which results in an expression of assurance must be performed under the applicable AICPA standards. Reports issued in connection with other professional standards should be clearly distinguished from attest reports.

An identified responsible party is a prerequisite for an attest engagement. A practitioner may accept an examination, a review, or an agreed-upon procedures engagement on subject matter or a related assertion if one of the following is met:

- The client is responsible for the subject matter. If, due to the nature of the subject matter, a responsible party does not otherwise exist, then the client must have a reasonable basis for providing a written assertion about the subject matter.
- If the client is not responsible for the subject matter, then he or she must be able to provide the practitioner, or have a responsible third party provide the practitioner, with evidence of the third party's responsibility for the subject matter.

NOTE: The practitioner should not take on the role of the responsible party in an attest engagement.

The practitioner should obtain written acknowledgment or other evidence (e.g., reference to legislation, a regulation, or a contract) of the responsible party's responsibility for the subject matter.

The eleven attestation standards are a natural extension of, *but do not supersede*, the ten standards in GAAS. Further, they do not supersede existing standards in SASs and SSARSs. The practitioner who is engaged to perform an engagement subject to these existing standards should follow such standards and not look to the eleven attestation standards or the discussion of them in AT Section 101 for guidance.

ATTESTATION STANDARDS

The eleven standards are classified as follows:
General: 1 through 5.
Fieldwork: 6 and 7.
Reporting: 8 through 11.

1. *First general standard.* The engagement shall be performed by a practitioner who must have adequate technical training and proficiency to perform the attestation engagement. (AT 101.19)

2. *Second general standard.* The engagement shall be performed by a practitioner who must have adequate knowledge of the subject matter. (AT 101.21)
3. *Third general standard.* The practitioner must have reason to believe that the subject matter is capable of evaluation against reasonable criteria that are suitable and available to users. (AT 101.23)

   a. *Suitable* criteria must be:

      1. *Objective*—Free from bias.
      2. *Measurable*—Permit reasonably consistent measurements (qualitative or quantitative) of subject matter. The practitioner should consider whether the criteria are sufficiently precise to permit people having competence in and using the same measurement criterion to be able to obtain materially similar measurements.
      3. *Complete*—Relevant factors that would alter a conclusion about the subject matter are not omitted.
      4. *Relevant*—Be relevant to the subject matter.

      Criteria issued by a body designated by the Council under the AICPA's Code of Professional Conduct, or issued by regulatory agencies and other bodies composed of experts that follow due-process procedures, are considered suitable. Other criteria that lack authoritative support should be evaluated according to the characteristics described above. Regardless of who establishes the criteria, the responsible party or client is responsible for selecting the criteria. The client is responsible for determining whether the criteria are appropriate for its purpose.

   b. The criteria must be *available* to users in one or more of the following ways:

      1. Publicly
      2. Through inclusion in a clear manner in the presentation of the subject matter or the assertion, or in the practitioner's report
      3. By being well understood by most users, although not formally available

      If the criteria are available only to specified parties, such as the terms of a contract or criteria issued by an industry association and available only to those in the industry, the practitioner's report should be restricted to parties that have access to the criteria.

4. *Fourth general standard.* The practitioner must maintain an independence in mental attitude in all matters relating to the engagement. (AT 101.35)
5. *Fifth general standard.* The practitioner must exercise due professional care in the planning and performance of the engagement and the preparation of the report. (AT 101.39)
6. *First standard of fieldwork.* The practitioner must adequately plan the work and must properly supervise any assistants. (AT 101.42) Factors to be considered in planning an attest engagement include the following: (AT 101.45)

   a. The criteria to be used
   b. Preliminary judgments about attestation risk and materiality
   c. Nature of the subject matter or the items within the assertion that are likely to require revision or adjustment
   d. Conditions that may require extension or modification of attest procedures
   e. Nature of report (see reporting standards) to be issued

7. *Second standard of fieldwork.* The practitioner must obtain sufficient evidence to provide a reasonable basis for the conclusion that is expressed in the report. (AT 101.51)

NOTE: The scope paragraph should be omitted, and paragraphs describing the scope restrictions should be included.

In establishing an appropriate combination of procedures to accumulate evidence and appropriately restrict attestation risk, the practitioner should consider the following:

a. Evidence obtained from sources outside an entity, such as through confirmation, provides greater assurance of an assertion's reliability than evidence secured solely from within the entity.
b. Information obtained from the attester's direct personal knowledge, such as through physical examination, observation, computation, operating tests, or inspection, is more persuasive than information obtained indirectly.
c. The more effective the controls over the subject matter are, the more assurance they provide about the subject matter or the assertion.

   In an attest engagement designed to provide a high level of assurance (an examination), the practitioner should select from *all* available procedures any combination that can limit attestation risk to an appropriately low level.

   In an attest engagement designed to provide a moderate level of assurance (a review), the practitioner's procedures are ordinarily limited to inquiries and analytical procedures and do not include search and verification procedures, such as confirmation and physical examination.

NOTE: In an attest engagement designed solely to meet the needs of specified parties who have participated in establishing the nature and scope of the engagement, the practitioner is required to perform only those procedures that have been designed or agreed to by the parties.

If the practitioner cannot obtain a written assertion from the responsible party, the practitioner should consider the effects on his or her ability to obtain sufficient evidence to form a conclusion about the subject matter. If the practitioner's client is the responsible party, the practitioner should ordinarily conclude that a scope limitation exists. If the practitioner's client is not the responsible party, the practitioner may be able to conclude that he or she has sufficient evidence to form a conclusion about the subject matter.

8. *First standard of reporting.* The practitioner must identify the subject matter or the assertion being reported on and state the character of the engagement in the report. (AT 101.63) The statement of the character of the attest engagement includes:

   a. A description of the nature and scope of the work performed, and
   b. A reference to the professional standards governing the engagement (see the "Illustrations" section).

NOTE: When the assertion does not accompany the practitioner's report, the first paragraph of the report should also contain a statement of the assertion. This requirement would be met by using a hot link *within the practitioner's report to management's assertion.*

---

9. *Second standard of reporting.* The practitioner must state the practitioner's conclusion about the subject matter or the assertion in relation to the criteria against which the subject matter was evaluated in the report. However, if conditions exist that, individually or in combination, result in one or more material deviations from the criteria, the practitioner should modify the report and should ordinarily express his or her conclusion directly on the subject matter, not on the assertion. (AT 101.66)

10. *Third standard of reporting.* The practitioner must state all of the practitioner's significant reservations about the engagement, the subject matter, and, if applicable, the assertion related thereto in the report. (AT 101.71)

Reservations about the engagement include unresolved problems that the practitioner had in complying with the attestation, other interpretative standards, or specified agreed-upon procedures.

Reservations about the engagement also include scope limitations. Scope restrictions may require the practitioner:

a. To qualify the assurance provided,
b. To disclaim any assurance, or
c. To withdraw from the examination or review engagement.

Ordinarily, if the scope limit is pervasive or imposed by the client, a disclaimer of opinion or withdrawal is appropriate.

In a review engagement, the review is incomplete and the practitioner should withdraw from the engagement when:

- The practitioner is unable to perform the necessary inquiry and analytical procedures.
- The client is the responsible party and does not provide a written assertion.

Reservations about the subject matter or assertion refer to questions about whether the subject matter or assertion is fairly stated, in all material respects, based on established or stated criteria, including adequacy of disclosure. They can result in either qualified or adverse opinions.

Reservations also include questions about measurement, form, arrangement, content, or underlying judgments and assumptions applicable to the subject matter or the assertion. Reservations may require modification of the practitioner's report.

11. *Fourth standard of reporting.* The practitioner must state in the report that the report is intended solely for the information and use of the specified parties under the following circumstances: (AT 101.78)

- When the criteria used to evaluate the subject matter are determined by the practitioner to be appropriate only for a limited number of parties who either participated in their establishment or can be presumed to have an adequate understanding of the criteria
- When the criteria used to evaluate the subject matter are available only to specified parties
- When reporting on subject matter and a written assertion has not been provided by the responsible party
- When the report is on an attestation engagement to apply agreed-upon procedures to the subject matter

A number of circumstances may affect the need to restrict a report, including:

- The purpose of the report
- The criteria used in preparation of the subject matter
- The extent to which the procedures performed are known or understood
- The potential for the report to be misunderstood when taken out of context

Although a practitioner should consider informing the client that restricted-use reports are not intended for distribution to nonspecified parties, regardless of whether they are included in a document containing a separate general-use report, a practitioner is not responsible for controlling a client's distribution of restricted-use reports.

Restricted-use reports should contain:

a. A statement indicating that the report is intended solely for the information and use of the specified parties
b. An identification of the specified parties to whom use is restricted
c. A statement that the report is not intended to be and should not be used by anyone other than these specified parties

---

NOTE: A practitioner may restrict the use of any report.

If a practitioner issues a single combined report covering both subject matter or presentations that require restrictions and those that do not require restrictions, the use of a single combined report should be restricted to the specified parties.

If a separate restricted-use report is included in a document that contains a general-use report, this does not affect the intended use of either report (i.e., the restricted-use report remains restricted and the general-use report continues to be for general use).

Examination Reports

In an attest engagement designed to achieve a high level of assurance (an examination), the practitioner's conclusion should be expressed in the form of an opinion (see "Illustrations: Examination Reports").

The practitioner should clearly state, in his or her opinion, whether (1) the subject matter is based on (or in conformity with) the criteria, in all material respects, or (2) the assertion is presented (or fairly stated), in all material respects, based on the criteria. Reports may be qualified or modified because of the subject matter, the assertion, or the engagement. Reports also may emphasize certain matters relating to the engagement.

The form of the practitioner's report depends on whether the practitioner's opinion is on the subject matter or assertion. According to AT 101.85, the practitioner's examination report on subject matter should include the following:

- A title that includes the word *independent*
- An identification of the subject matter and the responsible party
- Statements that:
  - The subject matter is the responsibility of the responsible party.
  - The practitioner's responsibility is to express an opinion on the subject matter based on his or her examination.

    - The examination was conducted in accordance with attestation standards established by the AICPA, and, accordingly, included procedures that the practitioner considered necessary in the circumstances.
    - The practitioner believes the examination provides a reasonable basis for his or her opinion.

- The practitioner's opinion on whether the subject matter is based on (or in conformity with) the criteria in all material respects
- A statement restricting the use of the report to specified parties when the criteria used to evaluate the subject matter are determined to be appropriate only for a limited number of parties who understand the criteria, or when such criteria are available only to the specified parties; the report should also be restricted when a written assertion has not been provided by the responsible party, and a statement to that effect should be included in the introductory paragraph.
- The manual or printed signature of the practitioner's firm
- The date of the examination report

Under AT 101.86, the practitioner's examination report on an assertion should include the following:

- A title that includes the word *independent*
- An identification of the assertion and the responsible party (when the assertion does not accompany the practitioner's report, the first paragraph of the report should also contain a statement of the assertion)
- Statements that:
    - The assertion is the responsibility of the responsible party.
    - The practitioner's responsibility is to express an opinion on the assertion based on his or her examination.
    - The examination was conducted in accordance with attestation standards established by the AICPA, and, accordingly, included procedures that the practitioner considered necessary in the circumstances.
    - The practitioner believes the examination provides a reasonable basis for his or her opinion.
- The practitioner's opinion on whether the assertion is presented (or fairly stated), in all material respects, based on the criteria
- A statement restricting the use of the report to specified parties when the criteria used to evaluate the subject matter are appropriate only for a limited number of parties who understand the criteria, or when such criteria are available only to the specified parties
- The manual or printed signature of the practitioner's firm
- The date of the examination report

The practitioner is not precluded from examining an assertion but opining directly on the subject matter.

Review Reports

In an attest engagement designed to achieve only a moderate level of assurance (a review), the practitioner's conclusion should be expressed in the form of negative assurance (see "Illustrations: Review Reports"). The practitioner should state whether any information came to his or her attention that indicated (1) the subject matter is not based on (or in conformity with) the criteria or (2) the assertion is not presented in all material respects based on established or stated criteria.

According to AT 101.89, the practitioner's review report on subject matter should include:

- A title that includes the word *independent*
- An identification of the subject matter and the responsible party
- Statements that:
  - The subject matter is the responsibility of the responsible party.
  - The review was conducted in accordance with attestation standards established by AICPA.
  - A review is substantially less in scope than an examination, the objective of which is an expression of opinion on the subject matter, and, accordingly, no such opinion is expressed.
- A statement about whether the practitioner is aware of any material modifications that should be made to the subject matter in order for it to be based on (or in conformity with), in all material respects, the criteria, other than those modifications, if any, indicated in his or her report
- A statement restricting the use of the report to specified parties when the criteria used to evaluate the subject matter are appropriate only for a limited number of parties who understand the criteria, or when such criteria are available only to the specified parties. The report should also be restricted when a written assertion has not been provided by the responsible party, and a statement to that effect should be included in the introductory paragraph.
- The manual or printed signature of the practitioner's firm
- The date of the examination report

Under AT 101.90, the practitioner's review report on an assertion should include the following:

- A title that includes the word *independent*
- An identification of the assertion and the responsible party (when the assertion does not accompany the practitioner's report, the first paragraph of the report should also contain a statement of the assertion)
- Statements that:
  - The assertion is the responsibility of the responsible party.
  - The review was conducted in accordance with attestation standards established by AICPA.
  - A review is substantially less in scope than an examination, the objective of which is an expression of opinion on the assertion, and accordingly, no such opinion is expressed.
- A statement about whether the practitioner is aware of any material modifications that should be made to the assertion in order for it to be presented (or fairly stated), in all material respects, based on (or in conformity with) the criteria, other than those modifications, if any, indicated in his or her report
- A statement restricting the use of the report to specified parties when the criteria used to evaluate the subject matter are appropriate only for a limited number of parties who understand the criteria, or when such criteria are available only to the specified parties
- The manual or printed signature of the practitioner's firm
- The date of the review report

RELATIONSHIP TO QUALITY CONTROL STANDARDS

Attestation and quality control standards are related, since attestation standards relate to the conduct of individual attest engagements and quality control standards relate to the firm's whole attest practice. The quality control policies and procedures that a firm adopts may affect both the conduct of individual attest engagements and the conduct of a firm's attest practice as a whole. Therefore, SSAE 10 requires firms to adopt a system of quality control in the conduct of their attest practice. However, deficiencies in or noncompliance with the quality control system do not, by themselves, indicate that an engagement was not performed according to the appropriate standards.

ATTEST DOCUMENTATION

The practitioner should prepare and maintain documentation of the attest engagement. The form and content of the attest documentation will depend on the particular engagement's circumstances. The practitioner should use professional judgment in determining the quantity, type, and content of attest documentation.

Attest documentation is the principal record of the procedures applied, information obtained, and conclusions or findings reached by the practitioner. It serves to provide the primary support for the practitioner's report and assist in the conduct and supervision of the engagement. It should be sufficient to:

- Allow members of the engagement team with supervisory and review responsibilities to understand the nature, timing, extent, and results of attest procedures performed, and the information obtained, and
- Indicate which engagement team members performed and reviewed the work.

Attest documentation, which may be in paper or electronic form, includes work programs, analyses, memoranda, letters of confirmation and representation, abstracts or copies of the entity's documents, and schedules or commentaries prepared or obtained by the practitioner.

The practitioner owns the attest documentation, and some states recognize this right of ownership in their statutes. However, the practitioner has an ethical, and sometimes legal, obligation to maintain the confidentiality of the client or responsible party. The practitioner should adopt reasonable procedures to maintain the confidentiality of information contained in the attest documentation and to prevent unauthorized access to that documentation. The practitioner should also retain the attest documentation for a period sufficient to meet the needs of his or her practice, and to satisfy any pertinent legal or regulatory requirements for records retention. (The practitioner should be able to access electronic documentation throughout the retention period.)

Sometimes attest documentation may serve as a source of reference for the client, but such documentation should not be considered as part of, or a substitute for, the client's accounting records.

When performing an examination of prospective financial statements, attest documentation ordinarily should indicate that the practitioner considered the process by which the entity develops its prospective financial statements in determining the scope of the engagement.

NOTE: Although the requirement to maintain attest documentation is stated in SSAE 10, changes have been made by SSAE 11, which reflect the concepts and terms used in SAS 96.

Establishing an Understanding with the Client

According to AT 101.46, the practitioner should establish an understanding with the client on the services to be performed for each engagement that includes:

1. The objectives of the engagement
2. Management's responsibilities
3. Practitioner's responsibilities
4. Limitations of the engagement

The understanding should be documented, preferably through a written communication with the client. If the practitioner believes that an understanding has not been established, he or she should not accept the engagement.

Representation Letter

In an examination or review engagement, a practitioner should consider obtaining a representation letter from the responsible party. According to AT 101.60, examples of representations that may be included are:

- A statement acknowledging responsibility for the subject matter and the assertion (if applicable)
- A statement acknowledging responsibility for selecting the criteria (if applicable)
- A statement acknowledging responsibility for determining that such criteria are appropriate for its purposes, where the responsible party is the client
- The assertion about the subject matter based on the selected criteria
- A statement that all known matters contradicting the assertion and any communication from regulatory agencies affecting the subject matter or the assertion have been disclosed to the practitioner
- Availability of all records relevant to the subject matter
- A statement that any known events subsequent to the period (or point in time) of the subject matter being reported on that would have a material effect on the subject matter (or assertion, if applicable) have been disclosed to the practitioner

If the client is not the responsible party, the practitioner should consider obtaining a representation letter from the client. According to AT 101.61, examples of representations included in the letter are:

- A statement that any known material subsequent events have been disclosed
- A statement acknowledging the client's responsibility for selecting the criteria, if applicable
- A statement acknowledging the client's responsibility for determining that such criteria are appropriate

If the responsible party or client refuses to furnish necessary written representations in an examination engagement, the practitioner should consider the impact on the ability to issue a conclusion about the subject matter. If the representation is necessary to obtain sufficient evidence to issue a report, the responsible party or client's refusal may cause the practitioner to disclaim an opinion or withdraw. However, in other circumstances, a qualified opinion may be appropriate. The practitioner should also consider whether the refusal affects his or her ability to rely on other representations.

If the engagement is a review and a scope limitation exists, the practitioner should withdraw from the engagement.

NOTE: Written representations are part of the evidential matter that the practitioner obtains.

Other Information in a Client-Prepared Document Containing the Practitioner's Attest Report

A practitioner's report may appear in:

- Annual reports to holders of securities or beneficial interests
- Annual reports of organizations for charitable or philanthropic purposes
- Annual reports filed with regulatory authorities under the Securities Exchange Act of 1934
- Other documents to which the practitioner, at the client's request, devotes attention

In this case, the auditor should do the following:

1. Read the other information.

NOTE: This is the knowledgeable study of information by an auditor who has an understanding of the client's business, organization, and operating characteristics, as well as its financial characteristics.

2. Consider whether the other information is materially inconsistent with information in the audited financial statements. This consideration includes the manner of presentation of both the other information and comparable information in the financial statements.
3. If there is a material inconsistency:

   a. Determine whether the financial statements, the report, or both require revision.

   NOTE: This means the auditor should decide if the difference is caused by a misstatement in the financial statements.

   b. Request that the client revise the other information if it, rather than the financial statements, is misstated.
   c. If the other information is not revised, consider other actions such as:

      1. Revising the report to include an explanatory paragraph describing the material inconsistency
      2. Withholding the use of the report in the document
      3. Withdrawing from the engagement

4. If the auditor's reading makes him or her aware of a material misstatement of fact, the auditor should:

   a. Discuss the matter with the client.
   b. Consider that:

      1. He or she may not have the expertise to assess the validity of the statement.
      2. There may be no standards by which to assess its presentation.
      3. There may be valid differences of judgment or opinion.

NOTE: This means that concluding there is a material misstatement is much more subjective than concluding there is a material inconsistency.

c. Request that the client seek the advice of legal counsel on the matter.
d. If the auditor concludes after discussion with the client that there is, in fact, a material misstatement of fact, he or she should consider steps such as:
    1. Notifying the client in writing of his or her views.
    2. Consulting his or her own legal counsel on what other action is appropriate.

SUBSEQUENT EVENTS

Subsequent events are events or transactions that occur after the point in time or period of time of the subject matter being tested but not before the date of the practitioner's report that have a material effect on the subject matter and therefore require adjustment or disclosure in the financial statements.

The two types of events that a practitioner must consider are:

1. Events that provide additional evidence about conditions that existed at the point in time or during the period of time of the subject matter being tested. The practitioner should use this information in considering whether the subject matter is presented in conformity with the criteria and may affect the presentation of the subject matter, the assertion, or the practitioner's report.
2. Events that provide evidence about conditions that arose after the point in time or period of time of the subject matter being tested that need to be disclosed to keep the subject matter from being misleading. This type of subsequent event will not normally affect the practitioner's report if the information is disclosed.

The practitioner is not responsible for detecting subsequent events. However, the practitioner should ask the responsible party if that party is aware of any subsequent events through the date of the practitioner's report that would have a material effect on the subject matter or assertion. If a representation letter is obtained, the letter should include a representation concerning subsequent events.

If the practitioner subsequently becomes aware of conditions that existed at the date of the practitioner's report that might have affected the report had the practitioner been aware of them, the practitioner should consider the guidance in AU-C Section 560, *Subsequent Events and Subsequently Discovered Facts*.

INTERPRETATIONS

DEFENSE INDUSTRY QUESTIONNAIRE ON BUSINESS ETHICS AND CONDUCT (ISSUED AUGUST 1987; AMENDED FEBRUARY 1989; MODIFIED MAY 1989; REVISED JANUARY 2001; REVISED NOVEMBER 2006)

This interpretation provides detailed guidance to a practitioner engaged to examine or review a defense contractor's responses to a questionnaire related to principles of business ethics and conduct adopted by certain companies in the defense industry.

Responding to Requests for Reports on Matters Relating to Solvency (Issued May 1988; Amended February 1993; Revised January 2001; Revised November 2006)

An accountant should not provide any form of assurance, through examination, review, or agreed-upon procedures, that an entity:

1. Is not insolvent at the time debt is incurred or would not be rendered insolvent thereby.
2. Does not have unreasonably small capital.
3. Has the ability to pay its debts as they mature.

An accountant may provide a client with various professional services that might be useful to a client in connection with a financing, but the scope of services and form of report have to conform to the requirements of the relevant professional standards.

If an accountant reports on the results of applying agreed-upon procedures, in addition to the normal requirements, the report should make clear that no representations are provided on questions of legal interpretation and no assurance is provided concerning the borrower's solvency, adequacy of capital, or ability to pay its debts.

Applicability of Attestation Standards to Litigation Services (July 1990; Revised January 2001)

Attestation standards do not apply to litigation services unless the practitioner has been specifically engaged to express a written conclusion about the reliability of a written assertion that is the responsibility of another party, and that conclusion and assertion are for the use of others who, under the rules of the proceedings, do not have an opportunity to analyze and challenge such work. The attestation standards would apply if the practitioner is specifically requested by a litigant to issue an attestation services report.

A practitioner is not prohibited from providing expert testimony on matters relating to solvency. The prohibition on providing written reports related to solvency does not apply in a legal forum in which the legal definition and interpretation of matters relating to solvency can be analyzed and challenged by the opposing party.

Providing Access to, or Photocopies of, Working Papers to a Regulator (May 1996; Revised January 2001; Revised January 2002)

A regulator's request for access to or photocopies of working papers in an attestation engagement should be treated in the same manner as a request related to audit working papers (see Section 230).

Attest Engagements on Financial Information Included in XBRL Instance Documents (September 2003)

NOTE: This interpretation was issued after the date that the PCAOB issued Release No. 2003-006, which recognized AICPA standards as interim transitional standards. Therefore, this guidance is not considered authoritative for practitioners with public company clients.

This interpretation provides guidance on the practitioner's considerations when he or she is engaged to examine and report on whether an Instance Document accurately reflects underlying financial information. (XBRL is the business reporting part of Extensible Markup Language [XML], a freely licensable open technology standard, which makes it possible to store and transfer data. An entity's financial information is made available in XBRL in a machine-readable format called an "Instance Document," which can then be distributed electronically through e-mail, on a website, etc.)

The practitioner should first make sure that the subject matter is capable of evaluation against suitable and available criteria. Two criteria, XBRL taxonomies and XBRL International Technical Specifications, meet these criteria. Some entities may create their own taxonomies, which the practitioner must evaluate to determine if they are "suitable and available."

The interpretation offers examples of procedures that the practitioner should consider performing to obtain sufficient evidential matter to form an opinion, such as:

- Comparing the rendered (i.e., converted from machine language) Instance Document to the financial information
- Tracing and agreeing the Instance Document's tagged information to the financial information
- Testing that the financial information is tagged and included in the Instance Document
- Testing that tagging is consistent
- Testing that extension or custom taxonomy meets the XBRL International Technical Specification

When reporting on such an engagement, the practitioner should note whether the underlying financial information has been audited or reviewed. If so, reference to the audit or review should be made. If not, the practitioner should disclaim an opinion on the underlying financial information. If there is information in the Instance Document not covered by the practitioner's report, it should be clearly identified.

Examples of reports for these types of engagements are shown in Examination Reports Illustrations 8 and 9.

Reporting on Attestation Engagements Performed in Accordance with Government Auditing Standards (December 2004; Revised January 2008)

When an auditor performs an attestation engagement in accordance with generally accepted government auditing standards, the scope paragraph of the report should be modified to indicate that the work was "conducted in accordance with attestation standards established by the American Institute of Certified Public Accountants and the standards applicable to attestation engagements contained in *Government Auditing Standards* issued by the Comptroller General of the United States."

Reporting on the Design of Internal Control (December 2008)

The auditor cannot report on the suitability of the design of an entity's internal control, based on the risk assessment procedures performed to gain an understanding of the entity and its environment, since these procedures do not provide a sufficient basis of information to make such a report.

If the auditor is asked to sign a prescribed form developed by the party to whom the reports are to be submitted regarding the design of an entity's internal controls, the auditor should either revise the form or attach a separate report that conforms to the auditor's professional standards.

The auditor should not submit a report about an entity's ability to establish suitable internal controls.

Including a Description of Tests of Controls or Other Procedures, and the Results Thereof, in an Examination Report (July 2010)

The circumstances of a specific engagement are relevant to a practitioner's consideration of whether to include a description of tests of controls or other procedures performed, as well as the results of those tests, in the examination report. The practitioner should consider the following when determining whether to include this description:

- Whether there has been a request for this information
- Whether there is a business need for requesting it
- Whether report recipients have sufficient knowledge of the engagement to understand the description
- Whether including the description in the report will cause a misunderstanding of the opinion
- Whether tests of controls or other procedures by the practitioner directly relate to the engagement

Adding this description to the report may increase the need to restrict the use of the report to specific parties.

ILLUSTRATIONS: EXAMINATION REPORTS

These illustrations are adapted from SSAE 10.

Illustration 1. Standard Examination Report on Subject Matter for General Use

This report pertains to subject matter for which suitable criteria exist and are available to all users through inclusion in a clear manner in the presentation of the subject matter. A written assertion has been obtained from the responsible party.

Independent Accountant's Report

To the Board of Directors
Widget Company
Main City, USA

We have examined the accompanying schedule of investment returns of Widget Company for the year ended December 31, 20X1. Widget Company's management is responsible for the schedule of investment returns. Our responsibility is to express an opinion on this statement based on our examination.

Our examination was conducted in accordance with attestation standards established by the American Institute of Certified Public Accountants and, accordingly, included examining, on a test basis, evidence supporting Widget Company's schedule of investment returns and performing such other procedures as we considered necessary in the circumstances. We believe that our examination provides a reasonable basis for our opinion.

[*Additional paragraph(s) may be added to emphasize certain matters relating to the attest engagement or the subject matter.*]

In our opinion, the schedule referred to above presents, in all material respects, the investment returns of Widget Company for the year ended December 31, 20X1, based on the [XXX] criteria set forth in Note 1.

Smith and Jones
February 15, 20X2

ILLUSTRATION 2. STANDARD EXAMINATION REPORT ON AN ASSERTION FOR GENERAL USE

This report pertains to subject matter for which suitable criteria exist and are available to all users through inclusion in a clear manner in the presentation of the subject matter. A written assertion has been obtained from the responsible party.

Independent Accountant's Report

To the Board of Directors
Widget Company
Main City, USA

We have examined management's assertion that the accompanying schedule of investment returns of Widget Company for the year ended December 31, 20X1, is presented in accordance with [XXX] criteria set forth in Note 1. Widget Company's management is responsible for the assertion. Our responsibility is to express an opinion on the assertion based on our examination.

Our examination was conducted in accordance with attestation standards established by the American Institute of Certified Public Accountants and, accordingly, included examining, on a test basis, evidence supporting management's assertions and performing such other procedures as we considered necessary in the circumstances. We believe that our examination provides a reasonable basis for our opinion.

[*Additional paragraph(s) may be added to emphasize certain matters relating to the attest engagement or the assertion.*]

In our opinion, management's assertion referred to above is fairly stated, in all material respects, based on the [XXX] criteria set forth in Note 1.

Smith and Jones
February 15, 20X2

ILLUSTRATION 3. EXAMINATION REPORT FOR GENERAL USE

The introductory paragraph states the practitioner has examined management's assertion, but the practitioner opines directly on the subject matter. The report pertains to subject matter for which suitable criteria exist and are available to all users through inclusion in a clear manner in the presentation of the subject matter. A written assertion has been obtained from the responsible party.

Independent Accountant's Report

To the Board of Directors
Widget Company
Main City, USA

We have examined management's assertion that the accompanying schedule of investment returns of Widget Company for the year ended December 31, 20X1, is presented in accordance with the [XXX] criteria set forth in Note 1. Widget Company's management is responsible for the assertion. Our responsibility is to express an opinion on this statement based on our examination.

Our examination was conducted in accordance with attestation standards established by the American Institute of Certified Public Accountants and, accordingly, included examining, on a test basis, evidence supporting Widget Company's schedule of investment returns and performing such other procedures as we considered necessary in the circumstances. We believe that our examination provides a reasonable basis for our opinion.

[*Additional paragraph(s) may be added to emphasize certain matters relating to the attest engagement or the assertion.*]

In our opinion, the schedule referred to above presents, in all material respects, the investment returns of Widget Company for the year ended December 31, 20X1, based on the [XXX] criteria set forth in Note 1.

Smith and Jones
February 15, 20X2

ILLUSTRATION 4. EXAMINATION REPORT ON SUBJECT MATTER; USE OF REPORT RESTRICTED

In this example, use of the report is restricted because although suitable criteria exist, the criteria are available only to specified parties. A written assertion has been obtained from the responsible party.

Independent Accountant's Report

To the Board of Directors
Widget Company
Main City, USA

We have examined the accompanying schedule of investment returns of Widget Company for the year ended December 31, 20X1. Widget Company's management is responsible for the schedule of investment returns. Our responsibility is to express an opinion on this statement based on our examination.

Our examination was conducted in accordance with attestation standards established by the American Institute of Certified Public Accountants and, accordingly, included examining, on a test basis, evidence supporting Widget Company's schedule of investment returns and performing such other procedures as we considered necessary in the circumstances. We believe that our examination provides a reasonable basis for our opinion.

[*Additional paragraph(s) may be added to emphasize certain matters relating to the attest engagement or the assertion.*]

In our opinion, the schedule referred to above presents, in all material respects, the investment returns of Widget Company for the year ended December 31, 20X1, based on the criteria referred to in the investment management agreement between Widget Company and Basic Investment Managers, Ltd., dated November 15, 20X1.

This report is intended solely for the information and use of Widget Company and Basic Investment Managers, Ltd. and is not intended to be and should not be used by anyone other than these specified parties.

Smith and Jones
February 15, 20X2

ILLUSTRATION 5. EXAMINATION REPORT: QUALIFIED OPINION

In this example, the opinion is qualified because conditions exist that, individually or in combination, result in one or more material misstatements or deviations from the criteria. The report is for general use and pertains to subject matter for which suitable criteria exist and are available to all users through inclusion in a clear manner in the presentation of the subject matter. A written assertion has been obtained from the responsible party.

Independent Accountant's Report

To the Board of Directors
Widget Company
Main City, USA

We have examined the accompanying schedule of investment returns of Widget Company for the year ended December 31, 20X1. Widget Company's management is responsible for the schedule of investment returns. Our responsibility is to express an opinion based on our examination.

Our examination was conducted in accordance with attestation standards established by the American Institute of Certified Public Accountants and, accordingly, included examining, on a test basis, evidence supporting Widget Company's schedule of investment returns and performing such other procedures as we considered necessary in the circumstances. We believe that our examination provides a reasonable basis for our opinion.

Our examination disclosed the following [*describe condition(s) that, individually or in the aggregate, resulted in a material misstatement or deviation from the criteria*].

In our opinion, except for the material misstatement (or deviation from the criteria) described in the preceding paragraph, the schedule referred to above presents, in all material respects, the investment returns of Widget Company for the year ended December 31, 20X1, based on the [XXX] criteria set forth in Note 1.

Smith and Jones
February 15, 20X2

ILLUSTRATION 6. EXAMINATION REPORT: DISCLAIMER OF OPINION

This example illustrates a disclaimer of opinion because of a scope restriction. The report pertains to subject matter for which suitable criteria exist and are available to all users through inclusion in a clear manner in the presentation of the subject matter.

Independent Accountant's Report

To the Board of Directors
Widget Company
Main City, USA

We were engaged to examine the accompanying schedule of investment returns of Widget Company for the year ended December 31, 20X1. Widget Company's management is responsible for the schedule of investment returns.

Because of the restriction on the scope of our examination discussed in the preceding paragraph, the scope of our work was not sufficient to enable us to express, and we do not express, an opinion on whether the schedule referred to above presents, in all material respects, the investment returns of Widget Company for the year ended December 31, 20X1, based on the [XXX] criteria set forth in Note 1.

Smith and Jones
February 15, 20X2

ILLUSTRATION 7. EXAMINATION REPORT: SUBJECT MATTER IS THE RESPONSIBILITY OF A PARTY OTHER THAN THE CLIENT

In this example, the report is restricted as to use, since a written assertion has not been provided by the responsible party. The subject matter pertains to criteria that are suitable and are available to the client.

Independent Accountant's Report

To the Board of Directors
Widget Company
Main City, USA

We have examined the accompanying schedule of investment returns of Widget Company for the year ended December 31, 20X1. Widget Company's management is responsible for the schedule of investment returns. Widget management did not provide us a written assertion about their schedule of investment returns for the year ended December 31, 20X1. Our responsibility is to express an opinion based on our examination.

Our examination was conducted in accordance with attestation standards established by the American Institute of Certified Public Accountants and, accordingly, included examining, on a test basis, evidence supporting Widget Company's schedule of investment returns and performing such other procedures as we considered necessary in the circumstances. We believe that our examination provides a reasonable basis for our opinion.

[*Additional paragraph(s) may be added to emphasize certain matters relating to the attest engagement or the subject matter.*]

In our opinion, the schedule referred to above presents, in all material respects, the investment returns of Widget Company for the year ended December 31, 20X1, based on the [XXX] criteria set forth in Note 1.

This report is intended solely for the information and use of the management and the board of directors of Widget Company and is not intended to be and should not be used by anyone other than these specified parties.

Smith and Jones
February 15, 20X2

ILLUSTRATION 8. EXAMINATION REPORT ON SUBJECT MATTER FOR AN ENGAGEMENT ON FINANCIAL INFORMATION INCLUDED IN AN XBRL INSTANCE DOCUMENT

The following illustration, adapted from an interpretation of AT 101, assumes that the underlying financial information was audited by the practitioner.

Independent Accountant's Report

To the Board of Directors
Widget Company
Main City, USA

We have examined the accompanying XBRL Instance Document of Widget Company that reflects the data presented in the financial statements of Widget Company as of December 31, 20X1, and for the year then ended. Widget Company's management is responsible for the XBRL Instance Document. Our responsibility is to express an opinion based on our examination.

Our examination was conducted in accordance with attestation standards established by the American Institute of Certified Public Accountants and, accordingly, included examining, on a test basis, evidence supporting the XBRL Instance Document and performing such other procedures as we considered necessary in the circumstances. We believe that our examination provides a reasonable basis for our opinion.

In our opinion, the XBRL Instance Document of Widget Company referred to above accurately reflects, in all material respects, the data presented in the financial statements in conformity with the [*identify criteria*].

We have also audited, in accordance with auditing standards generally accepted in the United States of America, the financial statements of Widget Company as of December 31, 20X1, and for the year then ended, and in our report dated February 15, 20X2, we expressed an unqualified opinion on those financial statements. [*If the report is other than unqualified, disclose this and the reasons behind the modified opinion.*]

Smith and Jones
February 15, 20X2

Illustration 9. Examination Report on Management's Assertions for an Engagement on Financial Information Included in an XBRL Instance Document

The following illustration, adapted from an interpretation of AT 101, assumes that the underlying financial information was audited by the practitioner.

Independent Accountant's Report

To the Board of Directors
Widget Company
Main City, USA

We have examined management's assertion that the accompanying XBRL Instance Document accurately reflects the data presented in the financial statements of Widget Company as of December 31, 20X1 and for the year then ended in conformity with XBRL US Consumer and Industrial Taxonomy and the XBRL International Technical Specifications 2.0. Widget Company's management is responsible for the assertion. Our responsibility is to express an opinion on the assertion based on our examination.

We have also audited, in accordance with auditing standards generally accepted in the United States of America, the financial statements of Widget Company as of December 31, 20X1, and for the year then ended; in our report dated February 15, 20X2, we expressed an unmodified opinion on those financial statements.

Our examination was conducted in accordance with attestation standards established by the American Institute of Certified Public Accountants and, accordingly, included examining, on a test basis, evidence supporting the XBRL Instance Document and performing such other procedures as we considered necessary in the circumstances. We believe that our examination provides a reasonable basis for our opinion.

In our opinion, management's assertion referred to above is fairly stated, in all material respects, in conformity with XBRL US Consumer and Industrial Taxonomy and the XBRL International Technical Specifications 2.0.

Smith and Jones
February 15, 20X2

ILLUSTRATIONS: REVIEW REPORTS

These illustrations are adapted from SSAE 10.

ILLUSTRATION 1. STANDARD REVIEW REPORT ON SUBJECT MATTER FOR GENERAL USE

This report pertains to subject matter for which suitable criteria exist and are available to all users through inclusion in a clear manner in the presentation of the subject matter. A written assertion has been obtained from the responsible party.

Independent Accountant's Report

To the Board of Directors
Widget Company
Main City, USA

We have reviewed the accompanying schedule of investment returns of Widget Company for the year ended December 31, 20X1. Widget Company's management is responsible for the schedule of investment returns.

Our review was conducted in accordance with attestation standards established by the American Institute of Certified Public Accountants. A review is substantially less in scope than an examination, the objective of which is the expression of an opinion on Widget Company's schedule of investment returns. Accordingly, we do not express such an opinion.

[*Additional paragraph(s) may be added to emphasize certain matters relating to the attest engagement or the subject matter.*]

Based on our review, nothing came to our attention that caused us to believe that the schedule of investment returns of Widget Company for the year ended December 31, 20X1, is not presented, in all material respects, in conformity with the [XXX] criteria set forth in Note 1.

Smith and Jones
February 15, 20X2

ILLUSTRATION 2. REVIEW REPORT: SUBJECT MATTER IS THE RESPONSIBILITY OF A PARTY OTHER THAN THE CLIENT

This review report is restricted as to use since a written assertion has not been provided by the responsible party. The subject matter pertains to criteria that are suitable and are available to the client.

Independent Accountant's Report

To the Board of Directors
Widget Company
Main City, USA

We have reviewed the accompanying schedule of investment returns of Widget Company for the year ended December 31, 20X1. Widget Company's management is responsible for the schedule of investment returns. Widget Company's management did not provide us a written assertion about their schedule of investment returns for the year ended December 31, 20X1.

Our review was conducted in accordance with attestation standards established by the American Institute of Certified Public Accountants. A review is substantially less in scope than an examination, the objective of which is the expression of an opinion on Widget Company's schedule of investment returns. Accordingly, we do not express such an opinion.

[*Additional paragraph(s) may be added to emphasize certain matters relating to the attest engagement or the subject matter.*]

Based on our review, nothing came to our attention that caused us to believe that the schedule of investment returns of Widget Company for the year ended December 31, 20X1, is not presented, in all material respects, in conformity with the [XXX] criteria set forth in Note 1.

This report is intended solely for the information and use of the management and the board of directors of Widget Company and is not intended to be and should not be used by anyone other than these specified parties.

Smith and Jones
February 15, 20X2

ILLUSTRATION 3. REVIEW REPORT ON AN ASSERTION

Although suitable criteria exist for the subject matter, the report is restricted since the criteria are available only to specified parties. A written assertion has been obtained from the responsible party.

Independent Accountant's Report

To the Board of Directors
Widget Company
Main City, USA

We have reviewed management's assertion that the accompanying schedule of investment returns of Widget Company for the year ended December 31, 20X1, is presented in accordance with the [XXX] criteria referred to in Note 1. Widget Company's management is responsible for the assertion.

Our review was conducted in accordance with attestation standards established by the American Institute of Certified Public Accountants. A review is substantially less in scope than an examination, the objective of which is the expression of an opinion on management's opinion. Accordingly, we do not express such an opinion.

[*Additional paragraph(s) may be added to emphasize certain matters relating to the attest engagement or the assertion.*]

Based on our review, nothing came to our attention that caused us to believe that management's assertion referred to above is not fairly stated, in all material respects, based on the [XXX] criteria referred to in the investment management agreement between Widget Company and Basic Investment Managers, Ltd., dated November 15, 20X1.

This report is intended solely for the information and use of Widget Company and Basic Investment Managers, Ltd. and is not intended to be and should not be used by anyone other than these specified parties.

Smith and Jones
February 15, 20X2

AT 201 Agreed-Upon Procedures Engagements[1,2]

ORIGINAL PRONOUNCEMENT

Source Statement on Standards for Attestation Engagements (SSAE) 10, *Attestation Standards: Revision and Recodification*, as amended by SSAE 11.

TECHNICAL ALERT

In April 2016, the Auditing Standards Board (ASB) issued SSAE No. 18, *Attestation Standards: Clarification and Recodification.* SSAE No. 18 is effective for practitioners' reports dated on or after May 1, 2017. SSAE No. 18 is the culmination of the attestation clarity project, and it supersedes all of existing attestation standards except for:

- AT 501, whose content was moved to the auditing standards and codified as AU-C 940.
- AT 701, which will not be clarified, but retained in its current form because it is a rarely performed engagement. The section number has been changed to AT-C Section 395.

The clarified standards use the prefix "AT-C" and can be found in the AT-C chapters of this book.

APPLICABILITY

AT 201 applies when performing all agreed-upon procedures engagements, except the following:

1. Situations in which an accountant reports on specified compliance requirements based solely on an audit (see AU-C Section 806, *Reporting on Compliance with Aspects of*

---

1 *Statement of Position (SOP) 01-3*, Performing Agreed-Upon Procedures Engagements That Address Internal Control over Derivative Transactions as Required by the New York State Insurance Law, *provides guidance to practitioners on performing an agreed-upon procedures engagement that enables insurance companies to meet the requirements of the New York Derivative Law (the Law) that amends Article 14 of the New York Insurance Law. The Law requires insurers who enter into derivative transactions to file with the State of New York Insurance Department (Department) a statement describing an independent CPA's assessment of the insurance company's internal control over derivative transactions. This assessment is considered part of the evaluation of internal control prescribed by Section 307(b) of the New York State Insurance Law. An assessment is required regardless of whether the derivative transactions are material to the insurer's financial statements.*

2 *See the chapter on the AT-C Preface for an important update on the clarified attestation standards and their effective dates.*

Contractual Agreements or Regulatory Requirements in Connection with Audited Financial Statements)

2. Engagements for which the objective is to report in accordance with AU-C Section 935, *Compliance Audits*, unless the terms of the engagement specify that the engagement be performed pursuant to SSAEs
3. Engagements covered by AU-C Section 920, Letters for Underwriters and Certain Other Requesting Parties
4. Certain professional services that would not be considered as falling under this section as described in AT 101.04

When performing agreed-upon procedures on prospective information or compliance matters, the practitioner should refer to AT Section 301, *Forecasts and Projections*, and AT Section 601, *Compliance Attestation*.

DEFINITIONS OF TERMS

Agreed-upon procedures engagement. An agreed-upon procedures engagement is one in which a practitioner is engaged by a client to issue a report of findings based on specific procedures performed on subject matter. The client engages the practitioner to assist specified parties in evaluating subject matter or an assertion. The specified parties assume responsibility for the sufficiency of the agreed-upon procedures. In this type of engagement, the practitioner does not perform an examination or review and does not provide an opinion or negative assurance about the assertion. The practitioner's report is in the form of procedures and findings.

Assertion. An assertion is any declaration or set of declarations about whether the subject matter is based on, or in conformity with, the criteria selected.

OBJECTIVES OF AT SECTION 201

This section presents attestation standards and provides guidance to a practitioner concerning performance and reporting in all agreed-upon engagements, except those noted above in "Effective Date" and "Applicability." It was issued because of the diversity in practice in performing and reporting on agreed-upon procedures engagements.

SSAE 10 revised this section to include:

- Eliminating the requirement for the practitioner to obtain a written assertion in an agreed-upon procedures engagement.
- Providing guidance on engagements to apply agreed-upon procedures to specified elements, accounts, or items of a financial statement previously covered by Statement on Auditing Standards (SAS) 75, *Engagements to Apply Agreed-Upon Procedures to Specified Elements, Accounts, or Items of a Financial Statement*. (SAS 75 was withdrawn as part of SAS 93, *Omnibus Statement on Auditing Standards—2000*.)

SSAE 11 amended this section to delete the guidance on working papers. Documentation requirements for attest engagements are now covered in AT Section 101, *Attest Engagements*.

REQUIREMENTS

STANDARDS

The practitioner should follow the general, fieldwork, and reporting standards for attestation engagements (see AT Section 101) in performing and reporting on agreed-upon procedures engagements as interpreted in this section.

SUBJECT MATTER

In an agreed-upon procedures engagement, the agreed-upon procedures are applied to the specific subject matter using the selected criteria. The subject matter may take many different forms and be at a point in time or covering a period of time. However, the subject matter and the criteria must meet the conditions in the third general standard (see AT Section 101). The criteria may be stated with the enumerated procedures or referred to in the practitioner's report.

ASSERTION

In general, a written assertion is not required in an agreed-upon procedures engagement, except when another attest standard specifically requires it (see AT Section 601). If, however, the practitioner asks that the responsible party provide an assertion, the assertion may be presented in writing in a representation letter or another written communication from the responsible party (such as a statement, narrative description, or schedule, appropriately identifying what is being presented and the point in time or period of time covered). The responsible party's refusal to furnish a written assertion is a scope limitation that requires the practitioner to withdraw from the engagement.

ACCEPTANCE OF ENGAGEMENT

The practitioner may perform an agreed-upon procedures attestation engagement if:

1. The practitioner establishes an understanding with the client about the services to be performed.
2. He or she has adequate knowledge of the subject matter to which the agreed-upon procedures are to be applied.
3. He or she is independent (ordinarily engagement team independence, not firm-wide independence).
4. One of the following conditions is met:
   a. The client is responsible for the subject matter, or has a reasonable basis for providing a written assertion about the subject matter when a responsible party does not exist due to the nature of the subject matter.
   b. The client is not responsible for the subject matter but is able to provide the practitioner, or have a third party who is responsible for the subject matter provide the practitioner, with evidence of the third party's responsibility for the subject matter.
5. The practitioner and the specified parties agree upon the nature, timing, and extent of procedures performed or to be performed. Furthermore, the procedures agreed to should not be overly subjective and possibly open to varying interpretations. The practitioner should not report on the engagement if the specified users do not agree to the procedures.
6. The specified parties take responsibility for the sufficiency of the agreed-upon procedures for their purposes.

7. The specific subject matter to which the procedures are to be applied is subject to reasonably consistent measurement.
8. Criteria to be used in the determination of findings are agreed upon between the practitioner and the specified parties.
9. The procedures to be applied to the specific subject matter are expected to result in reasonably consistent findings using the criteria.
10. Evidence related to the specific subject matter to which the procedures are applied is expected to exist to provide a reasonable basis for expressing the findings in the practitioner's report.
11. If applicable, the practitioner and the specified parties agree to any materiality limits for reporting purposes.
12. The report is restricted to the specified parties.
13. For agreed-upon procedures engagements on prospective financial information, a summary of significant assumptions is included in the prospective financial statements (see AT Section 301).

Involvement of a Specialist

The practitioner and the specified parties should explicitly agree to involving a specialist, if any, in assisting the practitioner in performing an agreed-upon procedures engagement. The practitioner should not agree to merely read the specialist's report solely to describe or repeat the specialist's findings in his or her own report. The latter does not constitute assistance to the practitioner.

Involvement of Internal Auditors or Others

Except as referred to in the prior section, the practitioner must perform the agreed-upon procedures included in his or her report. Internal auditors or others may prepare schedules and accumulate data or provide other information for the practitioner, but cannot perform agreed-upon procedures reported on by the practitioner.

Elements of Practitioner's Report

According to AT 201.38, the practitioner's report on agreed-upon procedures should be in the form of procedures and findings. The report should contain the following elements:

1. A title that includes the word *independent*
2. Identification of the specified parties
3. Identification of the subject matter (or the written assertion related thereto) and the character of the engagement
4. Identification of the responsible party
5. A statement that the subject matter is the responsibility of the responsible party
6. A statement that the procedures performed were those agreed to by the specified parties identified in the report
7. A statement that the agreed-upon procedures engagement was conducted in accordance with attestation standards established by the AICPA
8. A statement that the sufficiency of the procedures is solely the responsibility of the specified parties, and a disclaimer of responsibility for the sufficiency of those procedures

9. A list of procedures performed (or reference thereto) and all related findings; negative assurance should not be given, and vague or ambiguous language in reporting findings should be avoided
10. If applicable, a description of any agreed-upon materiality limits
11. A statement that the practitioner was not engaged to, and did not, conduct an examination of the subject matter, the objective of which would be the expression of an opinion, a disclaimer of opinion on the assertion, and a statement that if the practitioner had performed additional procedures, other matters might have come to his or her attention that would have been reported
12. A statement of restrictions on the use of the report because it is intended to be used solely by the specified parties
13. For an agreed-upon procedures engagement on prospective financial information, all items included in AT Section 301
14. If applicable, a description of the nature of the assistance provided by a specialist
15. If applicable, and if the practitioner does not withdraw from the engagement, a description of any restrictions (not agreed to) or reservations on the performance of the procedures
16. The manual or printed signature of the practitioner's firm
17. The date of the report

Other requirements are as follows:

1. If desired, include explanatory language about matters such as disclosure of stipulated facts, assumptions, or interpretations; description of the conditions of records, controls, or data; explanation that the practitioner has no responsibilities to update the report; and explanation of sampling risk.
2. If applicable, and if the practitioner does not withdraw from the engagement or change the engagement to another form of engagement, disclose in the report the inability to obtain representations from the responsible party (see the section "Representation Letter").
3. If, in connection with the application of agreed-upon procedures, matters come to the practitioner's attention by other means that significantly contradict the subject matter (or written assertions), include this matter in the report.

Dating of Report

The practitioner's report should be dated as of the date of completion of the agreed-upon procedures.

Adding Specified Parties

The practitioner may be asked to consider adding another party as a specified party (a nonparticipant party) after the completion of the agreed-upon procedures engagement. If the practitioner agrees to add the nonparticipant party as a specified party, he or she should obtain affirmative acknowledgment from that party, normally in writing, agreeing to the procedures performed and agreeing to take responsibility for the sufficiency of those procedures.

If a nonparticipant party is added after the practitioner has issued his or her report, the practitioner may reissue the report or provide written acknowledgment that a party has been added. If the report is reissued, the report date should not be changed. If written acknowledgment is provided, the acknowledgment ordinarily should state that no procedures have been performed subsequent to the date of the report.

Restrictions on the Performance of Procedures

The practitioner should attempt to have specified parties agree to any modification of the agreed-upon procedures when circumstances impose restrictions on the performance of those procedures. If an agreement cannot be obtained (for example, when the agreed-upon procedures are published by a regulatory agency that will not modify those procedures), the practitioner should either describe any restrictions in his or her report or withdraw from the engagement.

Representation Letter

Practitioners may find that a representation letter is useful in obtaining representations from the responsible party. Generally, a representation letter is not required for this type of engagement. However, a representation letter is required in an agreed-upon procedures engagement related to compliance with specified requirements (see AT Section 601). If the practitioner decides to request a representation letter from the responsible party and that party refuses to furnish one, the practitioner should do one of the following:

1. Disclose in the accountant's report the inability to obtain representations from the responsible party.
2. Withdraw from the engagement (required for an agreed-upon procedures engagement related to compliance with specified requirements).
3. Change to another form of engagement.

Knowledge of Outside Matters

If matters come to the practitioner's attention by other means outside the agreed-upon procedures that significantly contradict the assertion referred to in the report, the practitioner should include the matter in the report.

Change from Another Engagement (Attest or Nonattest) to an Agreed-Upon Procedures Engagement

Before agreeing to change another type of engagement to an agreed-upon procedures engagement, the practitioner should consider the following:

1. Are there certain procedures performed as part of the other engagement that are not appropriate to include in an agreed-upon procedures engagement?
2. What are the reasons given for the request, especially any scope restrictions or restrictions on matters to be reported related to the other engagement?
3. What additional effort is required to complete the other engagement?
4. What is the reason for changing from a general-use to a restricted-use report?
5. Is it appropriate to accept a change in engagement if agreed-upon procedures are substantially complete (or effort to complete the procedures is relatively insignificant)?

INTERPRETATION

Third-Party Due Diligence Services Related to Asset-Backed Securitizations: SEC Release No. 34-72936

The Securities and Exchange Commission (SEC) issued Release No. 34-72936, *Nationally Recognized Statistical Rating Organizations*. The release acknowledges that certain procedures often performed by practitioners as agreed-upon procedures engagements related to asset-backed securitizations (ABS) are considered third-party *due diligence services*. These include due diligence services that relate to checking the accuracy of the information or data about the assets provided by the securitizer or originator of the assets.

The release requires:

- The issuer or underwriter of any ABS to make publicly available the findings and conclusions of any third-party due diligence report obtained by the issuer or underwriter.
- Any third-party due diligence service provider to complete Form ABS Due Diligence-15E.

The release goes on to state:

> The Commission understands there may be particular considerations that would need to be taken into account under applicable professional standards that govern certain services provided by the accounting profession. The requirements and limitations resulting from relevant professional standards generally are described within the reports issued and, to the extent such requirements or limitations are based upon professional standards, the Commission would not object to the inclusion of the same description in the written certifications.

The procedures or findings of due diligence services conducted as agreed-upon procedures engagements are made public through the EDGAR system and/or through the process by which the nationally recognized statistical rating organization (NRSRO) publishes its credit ratings.

In response to the SEC release, the AICPA issued an interpretation in February 2015. The interpretation guides practitioners in how to respond to certain aspects of the release and potential conflicts with professional standards.

On the SEC form for due diligence services performed as an agreed-upon procedures engagement, the practitioner should include all of the elements in paragraph .31 of AT Section 201 and clarifying wording.

The use of an agreed-upon-procedures report may need to be restricted. If that is the case, the practitioner may want to inform his or her client that restricted-use reports are not intended for distribution to nonspecified parties, regardless of whether they are included in a document containing a separate general-use report. A restricted-use report should alert readers to the restriction on the use of the report by indicating that the report is not intended to be and should not be used by anyone other than the specified parties.

TECHNIQUES FOR APPLICATION

MEANING OF INDEPENDENCE

Independence requirements for an agreed-upon procedures engagement are less stringent than the independence requirements for other attest and audit engagements; refer to the Code of Professional Conduct, Interpretation 101.11, *Modified Application of Rule 101 for Engagements Performed in Accordance with Statements on Standards for Attestation Engagements* (revised February 2012, effective April 30, 2012).

ENGAGEMENT LETTER

The practitioner should establish a clear understanding regarding the terms of engagement, preferably in an engagement letter. Engagement letters should be addressed to the client, and, in some circumstances, to all specified parties. According to AT 201.10, the practitioner should consider including the following matters in the engagement letter:

1. Nature of the engagement
2. Identification of the subject matter (or the assertion related thereto), the responsible party, and the criteria to be used
3. Identification of specified parties
4. Specified parties' acknowledgment of their responsibility for the sufficiency of the procedures
5. Responsibilities of the practitioner
6. Reference to attestation standards established by AICPA
7. Agreement on procedures by enumerating, or referring to, the procedures
8. Disclaimers expected to be included in the practitioner's report
9. Use restrictions
10. Assistance to be provided to the practitioner
11. Involvement of a specialist, if applicable
12. Agreed-upon materiality limits, if applicable

COMMUNICATION WITH SPECIFIED PARTIES

Ordinarily, the practitioner should communicate directly with, and obtain affirmative acknowledgment from, each of the specified parties. This may be accomplished by:

1. Meeting with the specified parties
2. Distributing a draft of the anticipated report to the specified parties and obtaining their agreement
3. Distributing a copy of the engagement letter to the specified parties and obtaining their agreement

If the practitioner is unable to communicate directly with all of the specified parties, he or she should consider doing one or more of the following:

1. Comparing the procedures to be applied to written requirements of the specified parties
2. Discussing the procedures to be applied with appropriate representatives of the specified parties
3. Reviewing relevant contracts with, or correspondence from, the specified parties

PROCEDURES TO BE PERFORMED

The procedures agreed upon by the practitioner and the specified parties may be as limited or as extensive as the specified parties wish. Mere reading of an assertion or specified information, however, is not sufficient to permit a practitioner to report on the results of applying agreed-upon procedures.

Appropriate procedures might include:

1. Executing a sampling application after agreeing on relevant parameters
2. Inspecting specified documents
3. Confirming information with third parties
4. Comparing documents, schedules, or analyses with specified attributes
5. Performing specific procedures on work performed by others, including the work of internal auditors
6. Making mathematical computations

Examples of inappropriate procedures include evaluating the competency or objectivity of another party or interpreting documents outside the scope of the practitioner's professional expertise.

Representation Letter

Although, as a general rule, a representation letter is not required, it is advisable to obtain one. According to AT 201.38, examples of matters that might appear in a representation letter include:

1. A statement acknowledging responsibility for the subject matter or the assertion
2. A statement acknowledging responsibility for selecting the criteria and for determining that the criteria are appropriate
3. The assertion about the subject matter based on the criteria selected
4. A statement that all known matters contradicting the subject matter or the assertion and any communication from regulatory agencies affecting the subject matter or the assertion have been disclosed to the practitioner
5. Availability of all records relevant to the subject matter and the agreed-upon procedures
6. Other matters the practitioner deems appropriate

Report on Agreed-Upon Procedures in a Document Containing Financial Statements

When the practitioner consents to the inclusion of his or her report on agreed-upon procedures in a document containing the entity's financial statements, the practitioner is associated with those financial statements. For a public entity, the practitioner should include his or her audit report (see AU-C Section 700, *Forming an Opinion and Reporting on Financial Statements*), review report (see AU-C Section 930, *Interim Financial Information*), or unaudited disclaimer in such document. For a private entity, the practitioner should include his or her audit report (see AU-C Section 700), review report (see AR Section 60-90), or compilation report (see AR Section 60-90) in such document. If the practitioner has not audited, reviewed, or compiled the private entity financial statements, the document should state that the practitioner has not audited, reviewed, or compiled the financial statements and assumes no responsibility for them. All combined reports (agreed-upon procedure and other reports) should be restricted to specified parties (see AT Section 101).

ILLUSTRATIONS

Illustration 1. Accountant's Standard Report on an Agreed-Upon Procedures Engagement (from SSAE 10)

Independent Accountant's Report on Applying Agreed-Upon Procedures

To the Managements of Widget Inc. and Basic Fund:

We have performed the procedures enumerated below, which were agreed to by the audit committees and managements of Widget Inc., and Basic Fund, solely to assist you in evaluating the accompanying Statement of Investment Performance Statistics of Basic Fund (prepared in accordance with the criteria specified therein) for the year ended December 31, 20X1. Basic Fund's management is responsible for the statement of investment performance statistics. This agreed-upon procedures engagement was conducted in accordance with attestation standards established by the American Institute of Certified Public Accountants. The sufficiency of these procedures is solely the responsibility of the parties specified in the report. Consequently, we make no representation regarding the sufficiency of the procedures described below either for the purpose for which this report has been requested or for any other purpose.

The procedures and associated findings are as follows:

[*Include paragraphs to enumerate procedures and findings.*]

We were not engaged to and did not conduct an examination, the objective of which would be the expression of an opinion on the accompanying Statement of Investment Performance Statistics of Basic Fund. Accordingly, we do not express such an opinion. Had we performed additional procedures, other matters might have come to our attention that would have been reported to you.

This report is intended solely for the information and use of the audit committees and managements of Widget Inc. and Basic Fund, and is not intended to be and should not be used by anyone other than these specified parties.

Smith and Jones
February 15, 20X2

NOTE: The following are additional illustrations of reporting on applying agreed-upon procedures to elements, accounts, or items of a financial statement.

ILLUSTRATION 2. REPORT IN CONNECTION WITH A PROPOSED ACQUISITION

Independent Accountant's Report on Applying Agreed-Upon Procedures

To the Board of Directors and Management of Widget Company:

We have performed the procedures enumerated below, which were agreed to by the Board of Directors and management of Widget Company, solely to assist you in connection with the proposed acquisition of Generic Company as of December 31, 20X1. Generic Company is responsible for its cash and accounts receivable records. This agreed-upon procedures engagement was conducted in accordance with attestation standards established by the American Institute of Certified Public Accountants. The sufficiency of these procedures is solely the responsibility of the parties specified in this report. Consequently, we make no representation regarding the sufficiency of the procedures described below either for the purpose for which this report has been requested or for any other purpose.

The procedures and the associated findings are as follows:

Cash

1. We obtained confirmation of the cash on deposit from the following banks, and we agreed the confirmed balance to the amount shown on the bank reconciliations maintained by Generic Company. We mathematically checked the bank reconciliations and compared the resultant cash balance per book to the respective general ledger account balances.

Bank	*General ledger account balances as of December 31, 20X1*
XY Bank	$ 2,500
AB Bank	4,200
Town Trust Company regular account	67,341
Town Trust Company payroll account	11,240
	$ 85,281

We found no exceptions as a result of the procedures.

Accounts Receivable

2. We added the individual customer account balances shown in an aged trial balance of accounts receivable (identified as Exhibit A) and compared the resultant total with the balance in the general ledger account.

   We found no difference.
3. We compared the individual customer account balances shown in the aged trial balance of accounts receivable (Exhibit A) as of December 31, 20X1 to the balances shown in the accounts receivable subsidiary ledger.

   We found no exceptions as a result of the comparisons.
4. We traced the aging (according to invoice dates) for 50 customer account balances shown in Exhibit A to the details of outstanding invoices in the accounts receivable subsidiary ledger. The balances selected for tracing were determined by starting at the eighth item and selecting every fifteenth item thereafter.

   We found no exceptions in the aging of the amounts of the 50 customer account balances selected. The sample size traced was 9.8% of the aggregate amount of the customer account balances.
5. We mailed confirmations directly to the customers representing the 150 largest customer account balances selected from the accounts receivable trial balance, and we received responses as indicated in the following paragraph and table. We also traced the items constituting the outstanding customer account balance to invoices and supporting shipping documents for customers from which there was no reply. As agreed, any individual differences in a customer account balance of less than $300 were to be considered minor, and no further procedures were performed.

   Of the 150 customer balances confirmed, we received responses from 140 customers; 10 customers did not reply. No exceptions were identified in 120 of the confirmations received. The differences disclosed in the remaining 20 confirmation replies either were minor in amount (as defined above) or were reconciled to the customer account balance without proposed adjustment thereto. A summary of the confirmation results according to the respective aging categories is as follows:

	Accounts receivable December 31, 20X1		
Aging categories	*Customer account balances*	*Confirmations requested*	*Confirmations received*
Current	$225,000	$115,000	$ 90,000
Past due:			
Less than one month	52,000	27,000	20,000
One to three months	36,000	20,000	9,000
More than three months	24,000	24,000	7,000
	$337,000	$186,000	$126,000

We were not engaged to and did not conduct an audit, the objective of which would be the expression of an opinion on cash and accounts receivable. Accordingly, we do not express such an opinion. Had we performed additional procedures, other matters might have come to our attention that would have been reported to you.

This report is intended solely for the information and use of the board of directors and management of Widget Company and is not intended to be and should not be used by anyone other than these specified parties.

Smith and Jones
February 15, 20X2

Illustration 3. Report in Connection with Claims of Creditors

Independent Accountant's Report on Applying Agreed-Upon Procedures

To the Trustees of Widget Company:

We have performed the procedures described below, which were agreed to by the Trustees of Widget Company with respect to the claims of creditors, solely to assist you in determining the validity of claims of Widget Company as of May 31, 20X1 as set forth in the accompanying Schedule A. Widget Company is responsible for maintaining records of claims submitted by creditors of Widget Company. This agreed-upon procedures engagement was conducted in accordance with attestation standards established by the American Institute of Certified Public Accountants. The sufficiency of these procedures is solely the responsibility of the party specified in this report. Consequently, we make no representation regarding the sufficiency of the procedures described below either for the purpose for which this report has been requested or for any other purpose.

The procedures and associated findings are as follows:

1. Compare the total of the trial balance of accounts payable at May 31, 20X1, prepared by Widget Company, to the balance in the related general ledger account.

   The total of the accounts payable trial balance agreed with the balance in the related general ledger account.
2. Compare the amounts for claims received from creditors (as shown in claim documents provided by Widget Company) to the respective amounts shown in the trial balance of accounts payable. Using the data included in the claims documents and in Widget Company's accounts payable detail records, reconcile any differences found to the accounts payable trial balance.

   All differences noted are presented in column 3 of Schedule A. Except for those amounts shown in column 4 of Schedule A, all such differences were reconciled.
3. Obtain the documentation submitted by creditors in support of the amounts claimed and compare it to the following documentation in Widget Company's files: invoices, receiving reports, and other evidence of receipt of goods or services.

   No exceptions were found as a result of these comparisons.

We were not engaged to and did not conduct an audit, the objective of which would be the expression of an opinion on the claims of creditors set forth in the accompanying Schedule A. Accordingly, we do not express such an opinion. Had we performed additional procedures, other matters might have come to our attention that would have been reported to you.

This report is intended solely for the information and use of the Trustees of Widget Company and is not intended to be and should not be used by anyone other than this specified party.

Smith and Jones
February 15, 20X2

AT 301 Financial Forecasts and Projections

ORIGINAL PRONOUNCEMENT

Source Statement on Standards for Attestation Engagements (SSAE) 10, *Attestation Standards: Revision and Recodification*, as amended by SSAEs 11 and 17.

TECHNICAL ALERT

In April 2016, the Auditing Standards Board (ASB) issued SSAE No. 18, *Attestation Standards: Clarification and Recodification.* SSAE No. 18 is effective for practitioners' reports dated on or after May 1, 2017. SSAE No. 18 is the culmination of the attestation clarity project, and it supersedes all of existing attestation standards except for:

- AT 501, whose content was moved to the auditing standards and codified as AU-C 940.
- AT 701, which will not be clarified, but retained in its current form because it is a rarely performed engagement. The section number has been changed to AT-C Section 395.

The clarified standards use the prefix "AT-C" and can be found in the AT-C chapters of this book.

APPLICABILITY

AT 301 requires the practitioner to report when the practitioner *submits* to the client or others prospective financial statements that the practitioner has assembled or assisted in assembling, and also believes the prospective financial statements might be used by a third party. This section also provides standards for a practitioner engaged to examine, compile, or apply agreed-upon procedures to partial presentations. (See the section "Definitions of Terms.")

There are several circumstances in which the pronouncement does not apply, as explained in the following paragraphs.

The Statement does not apply to a financial analysis of a potential project where the practitioner obtains the information, makes the assumptions, and assembles the presentation. This type of analysis is not for general use; *however*, if the responsible party (see below) reviews and adopts the assumptions and presentation, or bases its assumption and presentation on the analysis, the Statement does apply.

The Statement does not apply to engagements involving prospective financial statements used solely in connection with litigation services if the practitioner's work is subject to analysis and challenge by all parties. This exception does not apply if:

1. The practitioner is specifically engaged to issue or does issue an examination, a compilation, or an agreed-upon procedures report on prospective financial statements.

2. The prospective financial statements are for use by third parties who, under the rules of the proceedings, do not have the opportunity for analysis and challenge by each party.

The Statement also does not apply to services involving the following:

1. Prospective financial statements restricted to internal use
2. Current year budgets presented with interim period historical financial statements

DEFINITIONS OF TERMS

For purposes of this section, the following definitions apply.

Assembly. Manual or computer processing of mathematical or other clerical functions related to the presentation of prospective financial statements.

Compilation of prospective financial statements. A professional service that involves:

1. Assembling prospective financial statements
2. Performing required procedures (see later sections), including reading the prospective financial statements and the accompanying summary of significant assumptions and accounting policies, and considering whether they appear to be presented in conformity with American Institute of Certified Public Accountants (AICPA) presentation guidelines (see AICPA *Guide for Prospective Financial Information*) and are not obviously inappropriate
3. Issuing a compilation report

A compilation does not provide assurance that the practitioner will become aware of significant matters that might be disclosed by more extensive procedures, such as those performed in an examination of prospective financial statements.

Entity. Any unit, *existing or to be formed*, for which financial statements could be prepared in accordance with generally accepted accounting principles or a special purpose framework. It may be an individual, partnership, corporation, trust, estate, association, or governmental unit.

Examination of prospective financial statements. A professional service that involves:

1. Evaluating the preparation of the prospective financial statements
2. Evaluating the support underlying the assumptions
3. Evaluating the presentation of the financial statements for conformity with AICPA presentation guidelines (see AICPA *Guide for Prospective Financial Information*)
4. Issuing an examination report

An examination provides the practitioner with a basis for reporting on whether, in his or her opinion, the prospective financial statements are presented in conformity with AICPA guidelines and the assumptions provide a reasonable basis for the responsible party's forecast or projection given the hypothetical assumptions.

Financial forecast. Prospective financial statements that present, to the best of the responsible party's (see below) knowledge and belief, an entity's expected financial position (see following entry), results of operations, and cash flows. It is based on the responsible party's assumptions about the conditions it expects to exist and the course of action it expects to take. A financial forecast may be expressed in specific monetary amounts as a single point estimate of forecasted results or as a range.

Financial projection. Prospective financial statements that present, to the best of the responsible party's knowledge and belief, *given one or more hypothetical assumptions* (see entry later in this section), an entity's expected financial position, results of operations, and cash flows. Ordinarily, it is prepared to answer the question, "What would happen if . . . ?" A financial projection may contain a range.

General use of prospective financial statements. Use of prospective financial statements by persons with whom the responsible party is not negotiating directly (e.g., prospective financial statements in an offering statement for an entity's debt or equity securities). Recipients of general-use prospective financial statements are unable to ask the responsible party directly about the presentation. *Only a financial forecast is appropriate for general use.*

Hypothetical assumption. An assumption used in a financial projection to present a condition or a course of action that may not occur but is consistent with the purpose of the projection.

Key factors. Significant matters on which an entity's future results are expected to depend. Key factors encompass matters that affect items such as sales, production, service, and financing activities. They are the foundation for prospective financial statements and are the bases for assumptions.

Limited use of prospective financial statements. Use of prospective financial statements by the responsible party alone or by the responsible party and *third parties with whom the responsible party is negotiating directly* (e.g., prospective financial statements used in loan negotiations, submission to a regulatory agency, or solely within the entity). *Financial forecasts and financial projections are appropriate for limited use.*

Partial presentation. A presentation of prospective financial information that excludes one or more of the items required for prospective financial statements (see "Requirements: General"). Partial presentations are not ordinarily appropriate for general use and should be restricted for use by specified parties who will be negotiating directly with the responsible party.

Prospective financial statement. Financial forecasts or financial projections (see earlier entry), *including* summaries of significant assumptions and accounting policies. Prospective financial statements may cover a period that has *partially* expired. The following are *not* prospective financial statements:

1. Statements for periods that have completely expired
2. Pro forma financial statements (see AT Section 401)
3. Partial presentations

Responsible party. Person or persons responsible for the assumptions underlying prospective financial statements. Ordinarily, the responsible party is management; however, it can be outsiders, such as a party considering acquiring the entity.

OBJECTIVES OF AT SECTION 301

For many years, practitioners have been requested to provide and have provided services relating to forecasts and projections. There was, however, little in the authoritative literature to guide the practitioner in these types of engagements for some time. In 1980, the AICPA issued a guide on reviews of financial forecasts, but many areas of practice were not covered by that guide. There was a need for more comprehensive guidance. Section 301 provides that guidance.

The section does the following:

1. Defines a financial forecast and a financial projection, and related terms.
2. Establishes procedures and reporting standards for prospective financial statements that require the following services:

a. Compilation
b. Examination
c. Application of agreed-upon procedures

The service that was previously called a *review* was renamed an *examination*, because that is the highest level of service available. Now there is no review service.

SSAE 10 revised this section to include:

- Changing elements of the standard reports to conform to those elsewhere in the attestation standards
- Making the section applicable to partial presentations of prospective financial information
- Changing references to statements of changes in financial position to statements of cash flows

Additional guidance for practitioners' services relating to prospective financial statements is found in the AICPA *Guide for Prospective Financial Information.*

SSAE 11 amended this section to delete the guidance on working papers. Documentation requirements for attest engagements are now covered in Section 101, *Attest Engagements.*

REQUIREMENTS: GENERAL

A practitioner should perform one of the services described in this Statement—compilation, examination, or application of agreed-upon procedures—whenever he or she does the following:

1. Submits to the client or others prospective financial statements that he or she has assembled, or assisted in assembling, that are, or reasonably might be, expected to be used by others.
2. Reports on prospective financial statements that are, or reasonably might be, expected to be used by others.

A practitioner may *not* compile, examine, or apply agreed-upon procedures to prospective financial statements that omit the summary of significant assumptions.

A practitioner should *not* compile, examine, or apply agreed-upon procedures to a financial projection that excludes either an identification of hypothetical assumptions or a description of the limitations on the usefulness of the presentation.

A practitioner may *not* consent to the use of his or her name in conjunction with a financial projection if the projection is to be used by persons not negotiating directly (general use) with the responsible party *unless* the projection is used to supplement a forecast.

Prospective financial statements preferably should be in the format of the historical financial statements. According to AT 301, Appendix A, paragraph 1, at a minimum, however, the following must be presented:

1. Sales or gross revenues
2. Gross profit or cost of sales
3. Unusual or infrequently occurring items
4. Provision for income taxes
5. Discontinued operations or extraordinary items
6. Income from continuing operations
7. Net income
8. Basic and diluted earnings per share, if applicable
9. Significant changes in financial position (for example, see AICPA *Guide for Prospective Financial Information*)

10. Summary of significant assumptions
11. Summary of significant accounting policies
12. A description of what the responsible party intends the prospective financial statements to present
13. A statement that the assumptions are based on the responsible party's judgment at the time the prospective information was prepared
14. A caveat that the prospective results may not be achieved

A presentation that omits any of items 1 through 9 is a partial presentation, which would not ordinarily be appropriate for general use. If an omitted applicable minimum item is derivable from the information presented, the presentation would not be deemed to be a partial presentation. A presentation that contains items 1 through 9 but omits 10 through 14 is *not* a partial presentation and is subject to the provisions of this section applicable to complete presentations.[1]

PARTIAL PRESENTATIONS

A practitioner who is engaged to or does compile, examine, or apply agreed-upon procedures to a partial presentation should follow the guidance in this section for complete presentations and make modifications necessary to reflect the nature of the presentation.

Procedures on a partial presentation may be affected by the nature of the information presented. When engaged to compile or examine a partial presentation, the practitioner should consider whether key factors affecting elements, accounts, or items that are interrelated with those in the partial presentation he or she has been engaged to examine or compile have been evaluated, including key factors that may not necessarily be obvious to the partial presentation. (An example of this might be productive capacity relative to a sales forecast.) The practitioner should also consider whether all significant assumptions have been disclosed. The scope of the examination or compilation of some partial presentations may need to be similar to that for the examination or compilation of a presentation of prospective financial statements.

Because partial presentations are generally for limited use, reports on partial presentations of both forecasted and projected information should describe any limitations on the presentation's usefulness.

NOTE: Chapter 23 of the AICPA Guide for Prospective Financial Information *explains how to apply the guidance for complete prospective financial statements to partial presentations.*

REQUIREMENTS: COMPILATION OF PROSPECTIVE FINANCIAL STATEMENTS

STANDARDS

The following standards apply to the compilation of prospective financial statements and the practitioner's report on these statements:

1. The person or persons performing the compilation should have adequate technical training and proficiency to compile prospective financial statements.

---

[1] *Complete presentation guidelines for entities that choose to issue prospective financial statements are included in the AICPA Audit and Accounting Guide,* Guide for Prospective Financial Information. *The* Guide *also presents presentation guidelines for partial presentations.*

2. The practitioner should exercise due professional care in performing the compilation and preparing the report.
3. The work should be adequately planned, and assistants should be properly supervised.
4. The practitioner should perform the applicable compilation procedures.
5. The practitioner's report should conform to the guidance described in the following section.

NOTE: Applicable compilation procedures should be performed (see Appendix B of this chapter).

Practitioner's Report

According to AT 301.18, the standard report on the compilation of prospective financial statements should include the following:

1. An identification of the prospective financial statements
2. A statement that the practitioner has compiled the prospective financial statements in accordance with attestation standards established by the AICPA
3. A statement that a compilation is limited in scope and does not enable the practitioner to express an opinion or any other form of assurance on the prospective financial statements or the assumptions
4. A warning that the prospective results may not be achieved
5. A statement that the practitioner assumes no responsibility to update the report for events and circumstances occurring after the date of the report
6. The manual or printed signature of the practitioner's firm
7. The date of the compilation report

Other requirements are as follows:

1. The date of the practitioner's report is the date of completion of the practitioner's compilation procedures.
2. If prospective financial statements contain a range, the practitioner's report should include a separate paragraph related to the circumstances.
3. For the compilation of a projection, the practitioner's report should include a statement describing the special purpose for which the projection was prepared, as well as a separate paragraph that restricts the use of the report to the specified parties.
4. A practitioner who is not independent may issue a compilation report. A separate paragraph of the report is as follows and may also include the reasons for independence impairment:

    We are not independent with respect to XYZ Company.

5. If prospective financial statements contain presentation deficiencies or omit disclosures other than those relating to significant assumptions, the practitioner's report should disclose the deficiency or omission.
6. If prospective financial statements are presented on a special purpose framework other than generally accepted accounting principles (GAAP) and this is not disclosed, the practitioner's report should disclose the basis of presentation.

Examples of compilation reports on prospective financial statements are presented in Illustrations 1–3.

REQUIREMENTS: EXAMINATION OF PROSPECTIVE FINANCIAL STATEMENTS

STANDARDS

The practitioner should follow the general, fieldwork, and reporting standards for attestation engagements described in AT Section 101.

NOTE: Standards concerning technical training and proficiency and planning the examination engagement, as well as applicable examination procedures, are described in Appendix C of this chapter.

ACCOUNTANT'S REPORT

According to AT 301.33, the standard report on the examination of prospective financial statements should include the following:

1. A title that includes the word *independent*.
2. An introductory paragraph with statements that:
   a. Identify the prospective financial statements.
   b. Identify the responsible party.
   c. The prospective financial statements are the responsibility of the responsible party.
   d. The practitioner's responsibility is to express an opinion on the prospective financial statements based on his or her examination.
3. A scope paragraph with statements that:
   a. The examination was made in accordance with attestation standards established by the AICPA, and accordingly, included such procedures as the practitioner considered necessary in the circumstances.
   b. The practitioner believes that the examination provides a reasonable basis for his or her opinion.
4. An opinion paragraph that presents:
   a. The practitioner's opinion that the prospective financial statements are presented in conformity with AICPA presentation guidelines (see AICPA *Guide for Prospective Financial Statements*) and that the underlying assumptions provide a reasonable basis for the forecast. If a projection is presented, the practitioner's opinion should be that the underlying assumptions provide a reasonable basis for the projection given the hypothetical assumptions.
   b. A warning that the prospective results may not be achieved.
   c. A statement that the practitioner assumes no responsibility to update the report for events and circumstances occurring after the date of the report.
5. The manual or printed signature of the practitioner's firm.
6. The date of the examination or report.

Other requirements are as follows:

1. The date of the practitioner's report is the date of completion of the practitioner's examination procedures.

2. If prospective financial statements contain a range, the practitioner's report should include a separate paragraph that describes the responsible party's election to present a range and the assumptions involved.
3. For the examination of a projection, the practitioner's report should include a statement describing the special purpose for which the projection was prepared and a separate paragraph that restricts the report to the specified parties.

MODIFICATIONS OF PRACTITIONER'S OPINION

The practitioner should modify his or her opinion in the following circumstances.

1. If prospective financial statements depart from AICPA presentation guidelines, issue a qualified opinion or an adverse opinion.
2. If prospective financial statements fail to disclose significant assumptions, issue an adverse opinion.
3. If one or more of the significant assumptions do not provide a reasonable basis for the forecast, issue an adverse opinion.
4. If one or more of the significant assumptions do not provide a reasonable basis for the projection, given the hypothetical assumptions, issue an adverse opinion.
5. If there is a scope limitation, disclaim an opinion and describe the limitation.
6. If there is a departure from GAAP (e.g., failure to capitalize a capital lease), issue an adverse opinion.

Examples of modified reports on prospective financial statements are presented in "Illustrations."

Qualified Opinion

A practitioner's report with a qualified opinion should include a separate explanatory paragraph that states all substantive reasons for the qualification and describes the departure from AICPA presentation guidelines. The opinion should include the words *except* or *exception* and should refer to the separate explanatory paragraph.

NOTE: A qualified opinion cannot be issued for a measurement (GAAP) departure, unreasonable or omitted assumption, or scope limitation.

Adverse Opinion

A practitioner's report with an adverse opinion should include a separate explanatory paragraph that states all substantive reasons for the adverse opinion. The opinion should state that the presentation is not in conformity with AICPA presentation guidelines and should refer to the separate explanatory paragraph.

If the assumptions do not provide a reasonable basis for the financial statements, the opinion paragraph should make that statement.

If a significant assumption is not disclosed, the practitioner should describe the assumption in the report.

Disclaimer of Opinion

A practitioner's report with a disclaimer of opinion should include a separate explanatory paragraph that states how the examination did not comply with appropriate standards. The disclaimer of opinion paragraph should state that the scope of the examination was not sufficient to enable the practitioner to express an opinion on the prospective financial statements. The disclaimer of opinion should include a direct reference to the separate explanatory paragraph.

If there is a scope limitation and also material departures from presentation guidelines, the practitioner should describe the departures in the report.

Modification of Standard Examination Report

There are circumstances under which the practitioner should modify the report without modifying the opinion included in the report. The circumstances and the modifications are explained in this section.

Emphasis of a Matter

The practitioner may present explanatory information or other informative material regarding the prospective financial statements in a separate paragraph of the report.

Part of Examination Made by Another Accountant

If more than one practitioner is involved in the examination, the guidance provided in Section 543, *Part of Audit Performed by Other Independent Auditors*, is generally applicable.

Comparative Historical Financial Information

Prospective financial statements may be included in a document that also contains audited, reviewed, or compiled historical financial statements and the practitioner's report on those financial statements. In addition, the historical financial statements in the document may also be summarized and presented comparatively with the prospective financial statements. In these circumstances, the concluding sentence of the last paragraph of the practitioner's report on the examination of the prospective financial statements is as follows:

> *The historical financial statements for the year ended December 31, 20X1 (from which the historical data are derived) and our report thereon are set forth on pages xx–xx of this document.*

Examination is Part of Larger Engagement

If the practitioner's examination of prospective financial statements is part of a larger engagement (for example, a financial feasibility study or business acquisition study), the practitioner may expand the report on the examination of the prospective financial statements to describe the entire engagement.

Examples of reports on the examination of prospective financial statements are presented in "Illustrations."

REQUIREMENTS: APPLYING AGREED-UPON PROCEDURES TO PROSPECTIVE FINANCIAL STATEMENTS (SEE ALSO AT SECTION 201)

General

A practitioner may accept an engagement to apply agreed-upon procedures to prospective financial statements only when the following conditions are met:

1. Is the practitioner independent?
2. Do the specified parties and the practitioner agree upon the procedures to be performed by the practitioner, and do the specified parties take responsibility for the sufficiency of the procedures to be performed?

3. Is the use of the report restricted to the specified parties involved?
4. Do the prospective financial statements include a summary of significant assumptions?
5. Are the prospective financial statements to which the procedures are to be applied subject to reasonably consistent evaluation against criteria that are suitable and available to the specified parties?
6. Are the criteria to be used in the determination of findings agreed upon between the practitioner and the specified parties?
7. Are the procedures to be applied to the prospective financial statements expected to result in reasonably consistent findings using the criteria?
8. Is evidential matter expected to exist to provide a reasonable basis for expressing the findings in the practitioner's report?
9. Where applicable, do the practitioner and the specified parties agree on any materiality limits for reporting purposes?

The practitioner ordinarily should meet with the specified parties to discuss procedures to be followed. If the practitioner is not able to discuss the procedures directly with all specified parties who will receive the report, he or she should apply one of the following or similar procedures:

1. Discuss the procedures to be applied with appropriate representatives of the specified parties.
2. Review relevant correspondence from the specified parties.
3. Compare the procedures to written requirements of the specified parties.
4. Distribute a draft of the report or a copy of the client's engagement letter to the specified parties and obtain their agreement.

While the agreed-upon procedures generally may be as extensive or limited as the parties specify, mere reading of the prospective financial statements is not a procedure sufficient to permit a practitioner to report on the results of applying agreed-upon procedures to those statements.

Practitioner's Report

The practitioner's report on the results of applying agreed-upon procedures should include the elements as indicated in the example report presented in Illustration 11.

REQUIREMENTS: OTHER

PRACTITIONER-SUBMITTED DOCUMENT

If a practitioner-submitted document contains the practitioner's compilation, review, or audit report on historical financial statements and prospective financial statements, the practitioner should compile, examine, or apply agreed-upon procedures to the prospective financial statements and report accordingly. However, the practitioner does not have to compile, examine, or apply agreed-upon procedures to the prospective financial statements if (1) they are labeled "budget," (2) the budget is only for the current fiscal year, and (3) the budget is presented with current year interim financial statements. In these circumstances, the practitioner should report on the budget and indicate that he or she did not compile or examine it and disclaim an opinion or any other form of assurance.

The budgeted information may omit the summaries of significant assumptions and accounting polices required by the AICPA presentation guidelines as long as the omission is not undertaken with the intention of misleading a user of the budgeted information and is disclosed in the practitioner's report (see Illustration 12).

CLIENT-PREPARED DOCUMENT

If a client-prepared document contains the practitioner's compilation, review, or audit report on historical financial statements and prospective financial statements, the practitioner should not consent to the use of his or her name in the document unless one of the following conditions exist:

1. The practitioner (or another practitioner) has compiled, examined, or applied agreed-upon procedures to the prospective financial statements and the report of the practitioner accompanies them or is included in the document.
2. The prospective financial statements are accompanied by an indication by the responsible party or the practitioner that the practitioner has not compiled, examined, or applied agreed-upon procedures to the prospective financial statements and that the practitioner assumes no responsibility for them.

If the practitioner audited historical financial statements that accompany prospective financial statements that he or she did not compile, examine, or apply agreed-upon procedures to, he or she should refer to Section 550, *Other Information in Documents Containing Audited Financial Statements*, and determine if that pronouncement applies.

If a client-prepared document contains the practitioner's report on prospective financial statements and historical financial statements, the practitioner should not consent to the use of his or her name in the document unless one of the following conditions exists:

1. The practitioner (or another practitioner) has compiled, reviewed, or audited the historical financial statements and the report of the practitioner accompanies them or is included in the document.
2. The historical financial statements are accompanied by an indication by the responsible party or the practitioner that the practitioner has not compiled, reviewed, or audited the historical financial statements and that the practitioner assumes no responsibility for them.

Inconsistent Information

An entity may publish documents that contain information other than historical financial statements in addition to the compiled or examined prospective financial statements and the practitioner's report thereon. In these circumstances, the practitioner should read the other information and consider whether there are inconsistencies with the information appearing in the prospective financial statements.

If the practitioner examined prospective financial statements included in a document containing inconsistent information, the practitioner should consider whether the prospective financial statements, the practitioner's report, or both require revision. Depending on the conclusion reached, the practitioner should consider other actions, such as issuing an adverse opinion, disclaiming an opinion because of a scope limitation, withholding use of the practitioner's report in the document, or withdrawing from the engagement.

If the practitioner compiled the prospective financial statements included in the document containing inconsistent information, the practitioner should try to obtain additional or revised information. If the additional or revised information is not received, the practitioner should withhold use of the compilation report or withdraw from the compilation engagement.

Material Misstatement of Fact

If, in the document containing the compiled or examined prospective financial statements, the practitioner becomes aware of information he or she believes is a material misstatement of fact, he or she should discuss the matter with the responsible party. If the practitioner concludes that there is a valid basis for concern, he or she should suggest that the responsible party consult with a party whose advice might be useful, such as the entity's attorney.

If, after discussing the possible material misstatement of fact, the practitioner concludes that a material misstatement of fact exists, he or she should consider notifying the responsible party in writing and consulting his or her attorney.

INTERPRETATIONS

There are no interpretations for this section. The AICPA has issued the *Prospective Financial Information Guide*, which provides comprehensive guidance for engagements related to prospective financial statements.

ILLUSTRATIONS

The illustrations on the following pages are adapted from SSAE 10 (AT 300.19–.56).

NOTE: These report forms are appropriate whether the presentation is based on GAAP or a special purpose framework. If the responsible party is other than management, the references to management in these reports should be changed to refer to the party who assumes responsibility for the assumptions.

ILLUSTRATION 1. STANDARD REPORT: COMPILATION OF FORECAST (DOES NOT CONTAIN A RANGE)

To the Board of Directors of Widget Company
Main City, USA

Independent Accountant's Report

We have compiled the accompanying forecasted balance sheet, statements of income, retained earnings, and cash flows of Widget Company as of December 31, 20X1, and for the year then ending, in accordance with attestation standards established by the American Institute of Certified Public Accountants.[2]

A compilation is limited to presenting in the form of a forecast information that is the representation of management and does not include evaluation of the support for the assumptions underlying the forecast. We have not examined the forecast, and, accordingly, do not express an opinion or any other form of assurance on the accompanying statements or assumptions. Furthermore, there will usually be differences between the forecasted and actual results, because events and circumstances frequently do not occur as expected, and those differences may be material. We have no responsibility to update this report for events and circumstances occurring after the date of this report.

Smith and Jones
February 15, 20X2

2 *When the presentation is summarized as discussed in "Requirements: General," this sentence might read, "We have compiled the accompanying summarized forecast of Widget Company as of December 31, 20X1, and for the year then ended in accordance with attestation standards established by the American Institute of Certified Public Accountants."*

ILLUSTRATION 2. STANDARD REPORT: COMPILATION OF PROJECTION (DOES NOT CONTAIN A RANGE)

To the Board of Directors of Widget Company
Main City, USA

Independent Accountant's Report

We have compiled the accompanying projected balance sheet, statements of income, retained earnings, and cash flows for Widget Company as of December 31, 20X1, and for the year then ending, in accordance with attestation standards established by the American Institute of Certified Public Accountants.[3] The accompanying projection and this report were prepared for the Anytown National Bank for the purpose of negotiating a loan to expand Widget Company's plant.

A compilation is limited to presenting in the form of a projection information that is the representation of management and does not include evaluation of the support for the assumptions underlying the projection. We have not examined the projection and, accordingly, do not express an opinion or any other form of assurance on the accompanying statements or assumptions. Furthermore, even if the loan is granted and the plant is expanded, there will usually be differences between the projected and actual results, because events and circumstances frequently do not occur as expected, and those differences may be material. We have no responsibility to update this report for events and circumstances occurring after the date of this report.

The accompanying projection and this report are intended solely for the information and use of Widget Company and Anytown National Bank and are not intended to be and should not be used by anyone other than these specified parties.

Smith and Jones
February 15, 20X2

ILLUSTRATION 3. STANDARD COMPILATION REPORT: SEPARATE PARAGRAPH—PROSPECTIVE FINANCIAL STATEMENTS CONTAIN A RANGE

As described in the summary of significant assumptions, management of Widget Company has elected to portray forecasted revenue at the amounts of $X, XXX and $Y, YYY, which is predicated upon occupancy rates of XX% and YY% of available apartments, rather than as a single point estimate. Accordingly, the accompanying forecast presents forecasted financial position, results of operations, and cash flows at such occupancy rates. However, there is no assurance that the actual results will fall within the range of occupancy rates presented.

Smith and Jones
February 15, 20X2

---

3 *When the presentation is summarized as discussed in "Requirements: General," this sentence might read, "We have compiled the accompanying summarized projection of Widget Company as of December 31, 20X1, and for the year then ended in accordance with attestation standards established by the American Institute of Certified Public Accountants."*

ILLUSTRATION 4. STANDARD REPORT: EXAMINATION OF FORECAST

To the Board of Directors of Widget Company
Main City, USA

Independent Accountant's Report

We have examined the accompanying forecasted balance sheet, statements of income, retained earnings, and cash flows of Widget Company as of December 31, 20X1, and for the year then ending.[4] Widget's management is responsible for the forecast. Our responsibility is to express an opinion on the forecast based on our examination.

Our examination was conducted in accordance with attestation standards established by the American Institute of Certified Public Accountants and, accordingly, included such procedures as we considered necessary to evaluate both the assumptions used by management and the preparation and presentation of the forecast. We believe that our examination provides a reasonable basis for our opinion.

In our opinion, the accompanying forecast is presented in conformity with guidelines for presentation of a forecast established by the American Institute of Certified Public Accountants, and the underlying assumptions provide a reasonable basis for management's forecast. However, there will usually be differences between the forecasted and actual results, because events and circumstances frequently do not occur as expected, and those differences may be material. We have no responsibility to update this report for events and circumstances occurring after the date of this report.

Smith and Jones
February 15, 20X2

ILLUSTRATION 5. STANDARD REPORT: EXAMINATION OF PROJECTION

To the Board of Directors of Widget Company
Main City, USA

Independent Accountant's Report

We have examined the accompanying projected balance sheet, statements of income, retained earnings, and cash flows of Widget Company as of December 31, 20X1, and for the year then ending.[5] Widget's management is responsible for the projection, which was prepared for the purpose of obtaining a loan. Our responsibility is to express an opinion on the projection based on our examination.

Our examination was conducted in accordance with attestation standards for an examination of a projection established by the American Institute of Certified Public Accountants and, accordingly, included such procedures as we considered necessary to evaluate both the assumptions used by management and the preparation and presentation of the projection. We believe that our examination provides a reasonable basis for our opinion.

In our opinion, the accompanying projection is presented in conformity with guidelines for presentation of a projection established by the American Institute of Certified Public Accountants, and the underlying assumptions provide a reasonable basis for management's projection assuming the granting of the requested loan for the purpose of expanding Widget Company's plant as described in the

---

4 *When the presentation is summarized as discussed in "Requirements: General," this sentence might read, "We have examined the accompanying summarized forecast of Widget Company as of December 31, 20X1, and for the year then ending."*

5 *When the presentation is summarized as discussed in "Requirements: General," this sentence might read, "We have examined the accompanying summarized projection of Widget Company as of December 31, 20X1, and for the year then ending."*

summary of significant assumptions. However, even if the loan is granted and the plant is expanded, there will usually be differences between the projected and actual results, because events and circumstances frequently do not occur as expected, and those differences may be material. We have no responsibility to update this report for events and circumstances occurring after the date of this report.

The accompanying projection and this report are intended solely for the information and use of the board of directors and are not intended to be and should not be used by anyone other than these specified parties.

Smith and Jones
February 15, 20X2

Illustration 6. Standard Examination Report: Separate Paragraph—Prospective Financial Statements (Forecast) Contain a Range

As described in the summary of significant assumptions, management of Widget Company has elected to portray forecasted revenue at the amounts of $X, XXX and $Y, YYY, which is predicated upon occupancy rates of XX% and YY% of available apartments rather than as a single point estimate. Accordingly, the accompanying forecast presents forecasted financial position, results of operations, and cash flows at such occupancy rates. However, there is no assurance that the actual results will fall within the range of occupancy rates presented.

Smith and Jones
February 15, 20X2

Illustration 7. Examination Report: Qualified Opinion on Forecast

To the Board of Directors of Widget Company
Main City, USA

Independent Accountant's Report

We have examined the accompanying forecasted balance sheet, statements of income, retained earnings, and cash flows of Widget Company as of December 31, 20X1, and for the year then ending. Widget Company's management is responsible for the forecast. Our responsibility is to express an opinion on the forecast based on our examination.

Our examination was conducted in accordance with attestation standards established by the American Institute of Certified Public Accountants and, accordingly, included such procedures as we considered necessary to evaluate both the assumptions used by management and the preparation and presentation of the forecast. We believe that our examination provides a reasonable basis for our opinion.

The forecast does not disclose reasons for the significant variation in the relationship between income tax expense and pretax accounting income as required by generally accepted accounting principles.

In our opinion, except for the omission of the disclosure of the reasons for the significant variation in the relationship between income tax expense and pretax accounting income as discussed in the preceding paragraph, the accompanying forecast is presented in conformity with guidelines for presentation of a forecast established by the American Institute of Certified Public Accountants and the underlying assumptions provide a reasonable basis for management's forecast. However, there will usually be differences between the forecasted and actual results, because events and circumstances frequently do not occur as expected, and those differences may be material. We have no responsibility to update this report for events and circumstances occurring after the date of this report.

Smith and Jones
February 15, 20X2

ILLUSTRATION 8. EXAMINATION REPORT: ADVERSE OPINION ON FORECAST

To the Board of Directors of Widget Company
Main City, USA

Independent Accountant's Report

We have examined the accompanying forecasted balance sheet, statements of income, retained earnings, and cash flows of Widget Company as of December 31, 20X1, and for the year then ending. Widget Company's management is responsible for the forecast. Our responsibility is to express an opinion on the forecast based on our examination.

Our examination was conducted in accordance with attestation standards for an examination of a financial forecast established by the American Institute of Certified Public Accountants and, accordingly, included such procedures as we considered necessary to evaluate both the assumptions used by management and the preparation and presentation of the forecast. We believe that our examination provides a reasonable basis for our opinion.

As discussed under the caption "Sales" in the summary of significant forecast assumptions, the forecasted sales include, among other things, revenue from the Company's federal defense contracts continuing at the current level. The Company's present federal defense contracts will expire in March 20X2. No new contracts have been signed and no negotiations are under way for new federal defense contracts. Furthermore, the federal government has entered into contracts with another company to supply the items being manufactured under the Company's present contracts.

In our opinion, the accompanying forecast is not presented in conformity with guidelines for presentation of a financial forecast established by the American Institute of Certified Public Accountants because management's assumptions, as discussed in the preceding paragraph, do not provide a reasonable basis for management's forecast. We have no responsibility to update this report for events or circumstances occurring after the date of this report.

Smith and Jones
February 15, 20X2

ILLUSTRATION 9. EXAMINATION REPORT: DISCLAIMER OF OPINION ON FORECAST

To the Board of Directors of Widget Company
Main City, USA

Independent Accountant's Report

We were engaged to examine the accompanying forecasted balance sheet, statements of income, retained earnings, and cash flows of Widget Company as of December 31, 20X1, and for the year then ending. Widget Company's management is responsible for the forecast.

As discussed under the caption "Income From Investee" in the summary of significant forecast assumptions, the forecast includes income from an equity investee constituting 23% of forecasted net income, which is management's estimate of the Company's share of the investee's income to be accrued for 20X1. The investee has not prepared a forecast for the year ending December 31, 20X1, and we were therefore unable to obtain suitable support for this assumption.

Because, as described in the preceding paragraph, we are unable to evaluate management's assumption regarding income from an equity investee and other assumptions that depend thereon, the scope of our work was not sufficient to express, and we do not express, an opinion with respect to the presentation of or the assumptions underlying the accompanying forecast. We have no responsibility to update this report for events and circumstances occurring after the date of this report.

Smith and Jones
February 15, 20X2

Illustration 10. Expansion of Practitioner's Report on or for a Financial Feasibility Study[6]

Independent Accountant's Report

The Board of Directors
Example Hospital
Maintown, Texas

We have prepared a financial feasibility study of Example Hospital's plans to expand and renovate its facilities. The study was undertaken to evaluate the ability of Example Hospital (the Hospital) to meet the Hospital's operating expenses, working capital needs, and other financial requirements, including the debt service requirements associated with the proposed $25,000,000 [*legal title of bonds*] issue, at an assumed average annual interest rate of 10.0% during the five years ending December 31, 20X5.

The proposed capital improvements program (the Program) consists of a new two-level addition, which is to provide 50 additional medical-surgical beds, increasing the complement to 275 beds. In addition, various administrative support service areas in the present facilities are to be remodeled. The Hospital administration anticipates that construction is to begin June 30, 20X1, and to be completed by December 31, 20X2.

The estimated total cost of the Program is approximately $30,000,000. It is assumed that the $25,000,000 of revenue bonds that the Example Hospital Finance Authority proposes to issue would be the primary source of funds for the Program. The responsibility for payment of debt service on the bonds is solely that of the Hospital. Other necessary funds to finance the Program are assumed to be provided from the Hospital's funds, from a local fund drive, and from interest earned on funds held by the bond trustee during the construction period.

Our procedures included analysis of:

- Program history, objectives, timing, and financing
- The future demand for the Hospital's services, including consideration of:
  - Economic and demographic characteristics of the Hospital's defined service area
  - Locations, capacities, and competitive information pertaining to other existing and planned area hospitals
  - Physician support for the Hospital and its programs
  - Historical utilization levels
- Planning agency applications and approvals
- Construction and equipment costs, debt service requirements, and estimated financing costs
- Staffing patterns and other operating considerations
- Third-party reimbursement policy and history
- Revenue/expense/volume relationships

We also participated in gathering other information, assisted management in identifying and formulating its assumptions, and assembled the accompanying financial forecast based on those assumptions.

6 *This form of report is also applicable to other entities such as hotels or stadiums. Although the illustrated report format and language should not be departed from in any significant way, the language used should be tailored to fit the circumstances that are unique to a particular engagement (e.g., the description of the proposed capital improvement program, the proposed financing of the program, the specific procedures applied by the practitioner, and any explanatory comments included in emphasis-of-matter paragraphs).*

The accompanying financial forecast for the annual periods ending December 31, 20X1 through 20X5, is based on assumptions that were provided by or reviewed with and approved by management. The financial forecast includes:

- Balance sheets
- Statements of operations
- Statements of cash flows
- Statements of changes in net assets

We have examined the financial forecast. Example Hospital's management is responsible for the forecast. Our responsibility is to express an opinion on the forecast based on our examination.

Our examination was conducted in accordance with attestation standards established by the American Institute of Certified Public Accountants (AICPA) and, accordingly, included such procedures as we considered necessary to evaluate both the assumptions used by management and the preparation and presentation of the forecast. We believe that our examination provides a reasonable basis for our opinion.

Legislation and regulations at all levels of government have affected and may continue to affect revenues and expenses of hospitals. The financial forecast is based on legislation and regulations currently in effect. If future legislation or regulations related to hospital operations are enacted, such legislation or regulation could have a material effect on future operations.

The interest rate, principal payments, Program costs, and other financing assumptions are described in the section entitled "Summary of Significant Forecast Assumptions and Rationale." If actual interest rates, principal payments, and funding requirements are different from those assumed, the amount of the bond issue and debt service requirements would need to be adjusted accordingly from those indicated in the forecast. If such interest rates, principal payments, and funding requirements are lower than those assumed, such adjustments would not adversely affect the forecast.

Our conclusions are presented below:

- In our opinion, the accompanying financial forecast is presented in conformity with guidelines for presentation of a financial forecast established by the AICPA.
- In our opinion, the underlying assumptions provide a reasonable basis for management's forecast. However, there will usually be differences between the forecasted and actual results, because events and circumstances frequently do not occur as expected, and those differences may be material.
- The accompanying financial forecast indicates that sufficient funds could be generated to meet the Hospital's operating expenses, working capital needs, and other financial requirements, including the debt service requirements associated with the proposed $25,000,000 bond issue, during the forecast periods. However, the achievement of any financial forecast is dependent on future events, the occurrence of which cannot be assured.

We have no responsibility to update this report for events and circumstances occurring after the date of this report.

Smith and Jones
February 15, 20X2

ILLUSTRATION 11. PRACTITIONER'S REPORT: APPLYING AGREED-UPON PROCEDURES TO A FORECAST

Independent Practitioner's Report on Applying Agreed-Upon Procedures

Board of Directors—Widget Corporation
Board of Directors—Basic Company

At your request, we have performed certain agreed-upon procedures, as enumerated below, with respect to the forecasted balance sheet and the related forecasted statements of income, retained earnings, and cash flows of Generic Company, a subsidiary of Basic Company, as of December 31, 20X1, and for the year then ending. These procedures, which were agreed to by the Boards of Directors of Widget Corporation and Basic Company, were performed solely to assist you in evaluating the forecast in connection with the proposed sale of Generic Company to Widget Corporation. [*Client*]'s management is responsible for the forecast.

This agreed-upon procedures engagement was conducted in accordance with attestation standards established by the American Institute of Certified Public Accountants (AICPA). The sufficiency of these procedures is solely the responsibility of the specified parties. Consequently, we make no representation regarding the sufficiency of the procedures described below either for the purpose for which this report has been requested or for any other purpose.

[*Include paragraphs to enumerate procedures and findings.*]

We were not engaged to, and did not, conduct an examination, the objective of which would be the expression of an opinion on the accompanying prospective financial statements. Accordingly, we do not express an opinion on whether the prospective financial statements are presented in conformity with AICPA presentation guidelines or on whether the underlying assumptions provide a reasonable basis for the presentation. Had we performed additional procedures, other matters might have come to our attention that would have been reported to you. Furthermore, there will usually be differences between the forecasted and actual results, because events and circumstances frequently do not occur as expected, and those differences may be material. We have no responsibility to update this report for events and circumstances occurring after the date of this report.

This report is intended solely for the information and use of the Boards of Directors of Basic Company and Widget Corporation and is not intended to be and should not be used by anyone other than these specified parties.

Smith and Jones
February 15, 20X2

ILLUSTRATION 12. STANDARD PARAGRAPHS ADDED TO PRACTITIONER'S REPORT IN A PRACTITIONER-SUBMITTED DOCUMENT: BUDGETED FINANCIAL STATEMENTS—SUMMARIES OF SIGNIFICANT ASSUMPTIONS AND ACCOUNTING POLICIES OMITTED

The accompanying budgeted balance sheet, statements of income, retained earnings, and cash flows of Widget Company as of December 31, 20X1, and for the six months then ending, have not been compiled or examined by us, and, accordingly, we do not express an opinion or any other form of assurance on them.

Management has elected to omit the summaries of significant assumptions and accounting policies required under established guidelines for presentation of prospective financial statements. If the omitted summaries were included in the budgeted information, they might influence the user's conclusion about the company's budgeted information. Accordingly, this budgeted information is not designed for those who are not informed about such matters.

APPENDICES

The following appendices are reproduced with permission from SSAE 10. Appendix B is concerned with compilation of prospective financial statements, and Appendix C is concerned with examination of prospective financial statements. The appendices deal with the following:

1. Training and proficiency of the practitioners
2. Planning the engagement
3. Procedures to be applied

Appendix A from the Statement is included in "Requirements: General" (list of fourteen minimum presentation requirements).

APPENDIX B: TRAINING AND PROFICIENCY, PLANNING AND PROCEDURES APPLICABLE TO COMPILATIONS

Training and Proficiency

1. The practitioner should be familiar with the guidelines for the preparation and presentation of prospective financial statements. The guidelines are contained in the AICPA *Guide for Prospective Financial Information*.
2. The practitioner should possess or obtain a level of knowledge of the industry and the accounting principles and practices of the industry in which the entity operates or will operate, that will enable him to compile prospective financial statements that are in appropriate form for an entity operating in that industry.

Planning the Compilation Engagement

3. To compile the prospective financial statements of an existing entity, the practitioner should obtain a general knowledge of the nature of the entity's business transactions and the key factors upon which its future financial results appear to depend. He or she should also obtain an understanding of the accounting principles and practices of the entity to determine if they are comparable to those used within the industry in which the entity operates.
4. To compile the prospective financial statements of a proposed entity, the practitioner should obtain knowledge of the proposed operations and the key factors upon which its future results appear to depend and that have affected the performance of entities in the same industry.

Compilation Procedures

5. In performing a compilation of prospective financial statements the practitioner should, where applicable:

   a. Establish an understanding with the client, preferably in writing, regarding the services to be performed. The understanding should include the objectives of the engagement, the client's responsibilities, the practitioner's responsibilities, and the limitations of the engagement. The practitioner should document the understanding, preferably through a written communication with the client. If the practitioner believes an understanding with the client has not been established, he or she should decline to accept or perform the engagement.
   b. Inquire about the accounting principles used in the preparation of the prospective financial statements.

      1. For existing entities, compare the accounting principles used to those used in preparation of previous historical financial statements and inquire whether such principles are the same as those expected to be used in the historical financial statements covering the prospective period.

2. For entities to be formed or entities formed that have not commenced operations, compare specialized industry accounting principles used, if any, to those typically used in the industry. Inquire about whether the accounting principles used for the prospective financial statements are those that are expected to be used when, or if, the entity commences operations.

c. Ask how the responsible party identifies the key factors and develops its assumptions.
d. List, or obtain a list of, the responsible party's significant assumptions providing the basis for the prospective financial statements and consider whether there are any obvious omissions in light of the key factors upon which the prospective results of the entity appear to depend.
e. Consider whether there appear to be any obvious internal inconsistencies in the assumptions.
f. Perform, or test the mathematical accuracy of, the computations that translate the assumptions into prospective financial statements.
g. Read the prospective financial statements, including the summary of significant assumptions, and consider whether:

1. The statements, including the disclosures of assumptions and accounting policies, appear to be not presented in conformity with the AICPA presentations guidelines for prospective financial statements.[7]
2. The statements, including the summary of significant assumptions, appear to be not obviously inappropriate in relation to the practitioner's knowledge of the entity and its industry and, for a:

a. *Financial forecast*, the expected conditions and course of action in the prospective period.
b. *Financial projection*, the purpose of the presentation.

h. If a significant part of the prospective period has expired, inquire about the results of operations or significant portions of the operations (such as sales volume), and significant changes in financial position, and consider their effect in relation to the prospective financial statements. If historical financial statements have been prepared for the expired portion of the period, the practitioner should read such statements and consider those results in relation to the prospective financial statements.
i. Confirm his or her understanding of the statements (including assumptions) by obtaining written representations from the responsible party. Because the amounts reflected in the statements are not supported by historical books and records but rather by assumptions, the practitioner should obtain representations in which the responsible party indicates its responsibility for the assumptions. The representations should be signed by the responsible party at the highest level of authority who the practitioner believes is responsible for and knowledgeable, directly or through others, about matters covered by the representations.

---

7 *Presentation guidelines for entities that issue prospective financial statements are set forth and illustrated in the AICPA* Guide for Prospective Financial Information.

1. For a *financial forecast*, the representations should include the responsible party's assertion that the financial forecast presents, to the best of the responsible party's knowledge and belief, the expected financial position, results of operations, and cash flows for the forecast period and that the forecast reflects the responsible party's judgment, based on present circumstances, of the expected conditions and its expected course of action. The representations should also include a statement that the forecast is presented in conformity with guidelines for presentation of a forecast established by the American Institute of Certified Public Accountants. The representations should also include a statement that the assumptions on which the forecast is based are reasonable. If the forecast contains a range, the representation should also include a statement that, to the best of the responsible party's knowledge and belief, the item or items subject to the assumption are expected to actually fall within the range and that the range was not selected in a biased or misleading manner.
2. For a *financial projection*, the representations should include the responsible party's assertion that the financial projection presents, to the best of the responsible party's knowledge and belief, the expected financial position, results of operations, and cash flows for the projection period given the hypothetical assumptions, and that the projection reflects its judgment based on present circumstances, of expected conditions, and its expected course of action given the occurrence of the hypothetical events. The representations should also:

   a. Identify the hypothetical assumptions and describe the limitations on the usefulness of the presentation.
   b. State that the assumptions are appropriate.
   c. Indicate if the hypothetical assumptions are improbable.
   d. If the projection contains a range, include a statement that, to the best of the responsible party's knowledge and belief, given the hypothetical assumptions, the item or items subject to the assumption are expected to actually fall within the range and that the range was not selected in a biased or misleading manner.

   The representations should also include a statement that the projection is presented in conformity with guidelines for presentation of a projection established by the AICPA.

j. Consider, after applying the above procedures, whether he has received representations or other information that appears to be obviously inappropriate, incomplete, or otherwise misleading and, if so, attempt to obtain additional or revised information. If he does not receive such information, the practitioner should ordinarily withdraw from the compilation engagement.[8] (Note that the omission of disclosures, other than those relating to significant assumptions, would not require the practitioner to withdraw; see "Requirements.")

---

[8] *The accountant need not withdraw from the engagement if the effect of such information on the prospective financial statements does not appear to be material.*

APPENDIX C: TRAINING AND PROFICIENCY, PLANNING, AND PROCEDURES APPLICABLE TO EXAMINATIONS

Training and Proficiency

1. The practitioner should be familiar with the guidelines for the preparation and presentation of prospective financial statements. The guidelines are contained in the AICPA *Guide for Prospective Financial Information.*
2. The practitioner should possess or obtain a level of knowledge of the industry and the accounting principles and practices of the industry in which the entity operates or will operate that will enable him to examine prospective financial statements that are in appropriate form for an entity operating in that industry.

Planning an Examination Engagement

3. Planning the examination engagement involves developing an overall strategy for the expected scope and conduct of the engagement. To develop such a strategy, the practitioner needs to have sufficient knowledge to enable him to adequately understand the events, transactions, and practices that, in his judgment, may have a significant effect on the prospective financial statements.
4. Factors to be considered by the practitioners in planning the examination include:

   a. The accounting principles to be used and the type of presentation.
   b. The anticipated level of attestation risk[9] related to the prospective financial statements.
   c. Preliminary judgments about materiality levels.
   d. Items within the prospective financial statements that are likely to require revision or adjustment.
   e. Conditions that may require extension or modification of the practitioner's examination procedures.
   f. Knowledge of the entity's business and its industry.
   g. The responsible party's experience in preparing prospective financial statements.
   h. The length of the period covered by the prospective financial statements.
   i. The process by which the responsible party develops its prospective financial statements.

5. The practitioner should obtain knowledge of the entity's business, accounting principles, and the key factors upon which its future financial results appear to depend. The practitioner should focus on such areas as:

   a. The availability and cost of resources needed to operate. Principal items usually include raw materials, labor, short-term and long-term financing, and plant and equipment.
   b. The nature and condition of markets in which the entity sells its goods or services, including final consumer markets if the entity sells to intermediate markets.

---

[9] *Attestation risk is the risk that the practitioner may unknowingly fail to appropriately modify his or her examination report on prospective financial statements that are materially misstated, that is, that are not presented in conformity with AICPA presentation guidelines or have assumptions that do not provide a reasonable basis for management's forecast, or management's projection given the hypothetical assumptions. It consists of (1) the risk (consisting of inherent risk and control risk) that the prospective financial statements contain errors that could be material and (2) the risk (detection risk) that the accountant will not detect such errors.*

c. Factors specific to the industry, including competitive conditions, sensitivity to economic conditions, accounting policies, specific regulatory requirements, and technology.
d. Patterns of past performance for the entity or comparable entities, including trends in revenue and costs, turnover of assets, uses and capacities of physical facilities, and management policies.

Examination Procedures

6. The practitioner should establish an understanding with the responsible party regarding the services to be performed. The understanding should include the objectives of the engagement, the responsible party's responsibilities, the practitioner's responsibilities, and the limitations of the engagement. The practitioner should document the understanding, preferably through a written communication with the responsible party. If the practitioner believes an understanding with the responsible party has not been established, he or she should decline to accept or perform the engagement. If the responsible party is different than the client, the practitioner should establish the understanding with both the client and the responsible party, and the understanding also should include the client's responsibilities.
7. The practitioner's objective in an examination of prospective financial statements is to accumulate sufficient evidence to limit attestation risk to a level that is, in his or her professional judgment, appropriate for the level of assurance that may be imparted by his or her examination report. In a report on an examination of prospective financial statements, he or she provides assurance only about whether the prospective financial statements are presented in conformity with AICPA presentation guidelines and whether the assumptions provide a reasonable basis for management's forecast, or a reasonable basis for management's projection given the hypothetical assumptions. He or she does not provide assurance about the achievability of the prospective results because events and circumstances frequently do not occur as expected and achievement of the prospective results is dependent on the actions, plans, and assumptions of the responsible party.
8. In the examination of prospective financial statements, the practitioner should select from all available procedures—that is, procedures that assess inherent and control risk and restrict detection risk—any combination that can limit attestation risk to such an appropriate level. The extent to which examination procedures will be performed should be based on the practitioner's consideration of:

   a. The nature and materiality of the information to the prospective financial statements taken as a whole.
   b. The likelihood of misstatements.
   c. Knowledge obtained during current and previous engagements.
   d. The responsible party's competence with respect to prospective financial statements.
   e. The extent to which the prospective financial statements are affected by the responsible party's judgment (i.e., its judgment in selecting the assumptions used to prepare the prospective financial statements).
   f. The adequacy of the responsible party's underlying data.

9. The practitioner should perform those procedures he considers necessary in the circumstances to report on whether the assumptions provide a reasonable basis for the:

a. **Financial forecast.** The practitioner can form an opinion that the assumptions provide a reasonable basis for the forecast if the responsible party represents that the presentation reflects, to the best of its knowledge and belief, its estimate of expected financial position, results of operations, and cash flows for the prospective period[10] and the practitioner concludes, based on his examination:

   1. That the responsible party has explicitly identified all factors expected to materially affect the operations of the entity during the prospective period and has developed appropriate assumptions with respect to such factors.[11]
   2. That the assumptions are suitably supported.

b. **Financial projection given the hypothetical assumptions.** The practitioner can form an opinion that the assumptions provide a reasonable basis for the financial projection, given the hypothetical assumptions, if the responsible party represents that the presentation reflects, to the best of its knowledge and belief, expected financial position, results of operations, and cash flows for the prospective period, given the hypothetical assumptions,[12] and the practitioner concludes, based on his examination:

   1. That the responsible party has explicitly identified all factors that would materially affect the operations of the entity during the prospective period if the hypothetical assumptions were to materialize and has developed appropriate assumptions with respect to such factors.
   2. That the other assumptions are suitably supported given the hypothetical assumptions. However, as the number and significance of the hypothetical assumptions increase, the practitioner may not be able to satisfy himself about the presentation as a whole by obtaining support for the remaining assumptions.

10. The practitioner should evaluate the support for the assumptions.

   a. **Financial forecast.** The practitioner can conclude that assumptions are suitably supported if the preponderance of information supports each significant assumption.
   b. **Financial projection.** In evaluating support for assumptions other than hypothetical assumptions, the practitioner can conclude that they are suitably supported if the preponderance of information supports each significant assumption, given the hypothetical assumptions. The practitioner need not obtain support for the hypothetical assumptions, although he should consider whether they are consistent with the purpose of the presentation.

---

10 *If the forecast contains a range, the representation should also include a statement that, to the best of the responsible party's knowledge and belief, the item or items subject to the assumption are expected to actually fall within the range and that the range was not selected in a biased or misleading manner.*

11 *An attempt to list all assumptions is inherently not feasible. Frequently, basic assumptions that have enormous potential impact are considered to be implicit, such as conditions of peace and absence of natural disasters.*

12 *If the projection contains a range, the representation should also include a statement that, to the best of the responsible party's knowledge and belief, given the hypothetical assumptions, the item or items subject to the assumption are expected to actually fall within the range and that range was not selected in a biased or misleading manner.*

11. In evaluating the support for assumptions, the practitioner should consider:

    a. Whether sufficient pertinent sources of information about the assumptions have been considered. Examples of external sources the practitioner might consider are government publications, industry publications, economic forecasts, existing or proposed legislation, and reports of changing technology. Examples of internal sources are budgets, labor agreements, patents, royalty agreements and records, sales backlog records, debt agreements, and actions of the board of directors involving entity plans.
    b. Whether the assumptions are consistent with the sources from which they are derived.
    c. Whether the assumptions are consistent with each other.
    d. Whether the historical financial information and other data used in developing the assumptions are sufficiently reliable for that purpose. Reliability can be assessed by inquiry and analytical or other procedures, some of which may have been completed in past examinations or reviews of the historical financial statements. If historical financial statements have been prepared for an expired part of the prospective period, the practitioner should consider the historical data in relation to the prospective results for the same period, where applicable. If the prospective financial statements incorporate such historical financial results and that period is significant to the presentation, the practitioner should make a review of the historical information in conformity with the applicable standards for review.[13]
    e. Whether the historical financial information and other data used in developing the assumptions are comparable over the periods specified or whether the effects of any lack of comparability were considered in developing the assumptions.
    f. Whether the logical arguments, or theory, considered with the data supporting the assumptions are reasonable.

12. In evaluating the preparation and presentation of the prospective financial statements, the practitioner should perform procedures that will provide reasonable assurance that the:

    a. Presentation reflects the identified assumptions.
    b. Computations made to translate the assumptions into prospective amounts are mathematically accurate.
    c. Assumptions are internally consistent.
    d. Accounting principles used in the:

        1. *Financial forecast* are consistent with the accounting principles expected to be used in the historical financial statements covering the prospective period and those used in the most recent historical financial statements, if any.
        2. *Financial projection* are consistent with the accounting principles expected to be used in the prospective period and those used in the most recent historical financial

---

[13] *If the entity is a public company, the accountant should perform the procedures in AU-C Section 930,* Interim Financial Information. *If the entity is nonpublic, the accountant should perform the procedures in SSARS 1,* Compilation and Review of Financial Statements (AR Section 60–90).

[14] *The accounting principles used in a financial projection need not be those expected to be used in the historical financial statements for the prospective period if use of different principles is consistent with the purpose of the presentation.*

[15] *Presentation guidelines for entities that issue prospective financial statements are set forth and illustrated in the* AICPA Guide for Prospective Financial Information.

statements, if any, or that they are consistent with the purpose of the presentation.[14]

e. Presentation of the prospective financial statements follows the AICPA guidelines applicable for such statements.[15]
f. Assumptions have been adequately disclosed based on AICPA presentation guidelines for prospective financial statements.

13. The practitioner should consider whether the prospective financial statements, including related disclosures, should be revised because of:

    a. Mathematical errors.
    b. Unreasonable or internally inconsistent assumptions.
    c. Inappropriate or incomplete presentation.
    d. Inadequate disclosure.

14. The practitioner should obtain written representations from the responsible party acknowledging its responsibility for both the presentation and the underlying assumptions. The representations should be signed by the responsible party at the highest level of authority whom the practitioner believes is responsible for and knowledgeable, directly or through others in the organization, about the matters covered by the representations. Appendix B, paragraph 5i, describes the specific representations to be obtained for a financial forecast and a financial projection. See "Disclaimer of Opinion" under "Requirements: Examination of Prospective Financial Statements" for guidance on the form of report to be rendered if the practitioner is not able to obtain the required representations.

AT 401 Reporting on Pro Forma Financial Information

ORIGINAL PRONOUNCEMENT

Source Statement on Standards for Attestation Engagements (SSAE) 10, *Attestation Standards: Revision and Recodification.*

TECHNICAL ALERT

In April 2016, the Auditing Standards Board (ASB) issued SSAE No. 18, *Attestation Standards: Clarification and Recodification.* SSAE No. 18 is effective for practitioners' reports dated on or after May 1, 2017. SSAE No. 18 is the culmination of the attestation clarity project, and it supersedes all of existing attestation standards except for:

- AT 501, whose content was moved to the auditing standards and codified as AU-C 940.
- AT 701, which will not be clarified, but retained in its current form because it is a rarely performed engagement. The section number has been changed to AT-C Section 395.

The clarified standards use the prefix "AT-C" and can be found in the AT-C chapters of this book.

APPLICABILITY

AT 401 applies to reports on an examination or a review of pro forma financial information. When pro forma information is provided outside the financial statements and the accountant is not engaged to report on it, the guidance in Section 550, *Other Information in Documents Containing Audited Financial Statements*, applies.

DEFINITION OF TERM

Pro forma financial information. Shows "what the significant effects on historical financial information *might have been* had a *consummated or proposed* transaction (or event) occurred at an earlier date." (Emphasis added.)

OBJECTIVES OF AT SECTION 401

A high rate of mergers and acquisitions in the late 1980s increased the need for guidance on pro forma financial information. The Auditing Standards Board issued an SSAE, *Reporting on Pro*

Forma Financial Information (the Statement), in 1988. The attestation statement applies to the accountant's involvement with all presentations of pro forma financial information, including information required by Article 11 of Securities and Exchange Commission (SEC) Regulation S-X.

The statement explains the application of the general guidance for attestation engagements to engagements to report on pro forma information. The permitted levels of service that the accountant can provide related to pro forma information are a *review* or an *examination*.

The statement does not apply to the generally accepted accounting principles (GAAP) requirements in historical financial statements related to disclosure of a transaction consummated after the balance sheet date to achieve a more meaningful presentation, such as presentation of earnings per share revised for a subsequent stock split.

Use of Pro Forma Information

Pro forma information might be used to show the effects of a business combination, change in capitalization, disposition of a significant portion of a business, a change in form or status of a business (for example, from a division to a separate entity), or a proposed sale of securities and application of the proceeds.

REQUIREMENTS

Conditions for Reporting and the Accountant's Objectives

A practitioner may *examine* or *review* pro forma financial information if all three of the following conditions are achieved:

1. The document including the pro formas also includes complete historical financial statements (or incorporates them by reference) of the entity for the most recent year. If pro formas are for an interim period, historical interim information for that period is also presented (or incorporated by reference). If the circumstances are a business combination, the document includes historical data for significant constituent parts of the combined entity.
2. The historical financial statements on which the pro forma information is based have been audited or reviewed by a practitioner.

NOTE: The level of assurance on the pro formas should be no greater than the level on the related historical statements. For a nonpublic entity, the review may be performed under AR Sections 60–90.

3. The practitioner reporting on the pro forma information should have an appropriate level of knowledge of the entity's accounting and financial reporting practices.

NOTE: Generally this knowledge will be the result of having audited or reviewed the historical statements. If the practitioner was not the auditor or reviewer of the historical statements, the practitioner "should consider whether, under the particular circumstances, he or she can acquire sufficient knowledge."

ENGAGEMENT OBJECTIVES

Examination

The objective of a practitioner's *examination* of pro forma information is to provide reasonable assurance that:

1. Management's assumptions provide a reasonable basis for presenting the significant effects of the underlying transaction or event.
2. Pro forma adjustments give appropriate effect to the assumptions.
3. The pro forma column (historical information modified by adjustments) reflects the proper application of the adjustments.

Review

The objective of a practitioner's *review* of pro forma information is to provide negative assurance on the three aspects of the pro forma information listed in the preceding paragraph.

NOTE: "Negative assurance" indicates that no information came to the practitioner's attention that would cause him or her not to believe the three statements.
The objectives of an examination or review do not focus on the final pro forma column alone. The assurance is not that the pro forma column conforms with established criteria. The practitioner's objectives relate to the three separate aspects of a pro forma presentation:

- *Assumptions (reasonable)*
- *Adjustments (give effect to assumptions)*
- *Final column (application of adjustments is proper)*

PROCEDURES

The procedures for an examination or review include:

1. Obtaining an understanding of the underlying transaction or event.
2. Obtaining a level of knowledge of each significant constituent part of the combined entity in a business combination.
3. Discussing with management their assumptions about the effects of the transaction or event.
4. Evaluating whether pro forma adjustments are included for all significant effects of the transaction or event.
5. Obtaining sufficient evidence in support of such adjustments.

NOTE: In considering the level of attestation risk the practitioner is willing to accept in a pro forma information engagement, the level of assurance on the underlying historical financial statements is a key factor. Accordingly, the procedures the practitioner should apply to the assumptions and pro forma adjustments are substantially the same for either an examination or a review engagement. The evidence needed is a matter of judgment and may vary with the level of service involved.

---

6. Evaluating whether the presentation of management's assumptions is sufficiently clear and comprehensive, and whether management's assumptions are consistent with each other and with the data used to develop them.

7. Determining whether computations of pro forma adjustments are mathematically correct and that the pro forma column reflects proper application of the adjustments.
8. Obtaining management's written representations on:
   a. Their responsibility for the assumptions
   b. Assertion that the assumptions provide a reasonable basis for presenting all of the significant effects directly attributable to the transaction or event
   c. Assertion that the related pro forma adjustments give appropriate effect to the assumptions
   d. Assertion that the pro forma column reflects the proper application of adjustments
   e. Their belief that significant effects of the transaction or event are appropriately disclosed
9. Reading the pro forma financial information and evaluating the appropriateness of the descriptions of:
   a. The underlying transaction or event,
   b. The pro forma adjustments, and
   c. The significant assumptions and significant uncertainties about those assumptions.

   Also, evaluating whether the source of the historical information base is appropriately identified.

FORM OF REPORT ON PRO FORMA FINANCIAL INFORMATION

According to AT 401.12, a practitioner's examination report on pro forma financial information should include:

1. A title that includes the word *independent.*
2. An identification of the pro forma financial information.
3. A reference to the financial statements from which the historical financial information is derived and a statement as to whether such financial statements were audited. (The report on pro forma financial information should refer to any modification in the practitioner's report on the historical financial information.)
4. An identification of the responsible party and a statement that the responsible party is responsible for the pro forma financial information.
5. Statements that:
   a. The practitioner's responsibility is to express an opinion on the pro forma financial information based on his or her examination.
   b. The examination of the pro forma financial information was conducted in accordance with attestation standards established by the AICPA and, accordingly, included such procedures as the practitioner considered necessary in the circumstances.
   c. The practitioner believes that the examination provides a reasonable basis for his or her opinion.
6. A separate paragraph explaining the objective of pro forma financial information and its limitations.
7. The practitioner's opinion as to whether management's assumptions provide a reasonable basis for presenting the significant effects directly attributable to the transaction (or event), whether the related pro forma adjustments give appropriate effect to those assumptions, and whether the pro forma column reflects the proper application of those adjustments to the historical financial statements.

8. The manual or printed signature of the practitioner's firm.
9. The date of the examination report.

According to AT 401.13, a practitioner's review report on pro forma financial information should include the following:

1. A title that includes the word *independent.*
2. An identification of the pro forma financial information.
3. A reference to the financial statements from which the historical financial information is derived and a statement as to whether such financial statements were audited or reviewed. (The report on pro forma financial information should refer to any modification in the practitioner's report on the historical financial information.)
4. An identification of the responsible party and a statement that the responsible party is responsible for the pro forma financial information.
5. A statement that the review of the pro forma financial information was conducted in accordance with attestation standards established by the AICPA.
6. A statement that a review is substantially less in scope than an examination, the objective of which is the expression of an opinion on the pro forma financial information and, accordingly, the practitioner does not express such an opinion.
7. A separate paragraph explaining the objective of pro forma financial information and its limitations.
8. The practitioner's conclusion as to whether any information came to the practitioner's attention to cause him or her to believe that management's assumptions do not provide a reasonable basis for presenting the significant effects directly attributable to the transaction (or event), or that the related pro forma adjustments do not give appropriate effect to those assumptions, or that the pro forma column does not reflect the proper application of those adjustments to the historical financial statements.
9. The manual or printed signature of the firm.
10. The date of the review report.

The practitioner's report on the pro forma financial information:

- Should be dated as of the completion of the appropriate procedures
- May be added to the practitioner's report on historical financial information or may appear separately

If the reports are combined and the date of completion of procedures on the pro forma financial information is after the completion of fieldwork for the audit or review of the historical financial information, the combined report should be dual dated, as shown in the following:

February 15, 20X2, except for the paragraphs regarding pro forma financial information as to which the date is March 20, 20X2.

See "Illustrations" for example reports on examinations (Illustration 1) and reviews (Illustration 2) of pro forma information.

NOTE: A practitioner's report may combine a review of some pro forma information and an examination of other pro forma information (for example, an examination of annual pro formas with a review of quarterly pro forma information). An example of such a report is presented in Illustration 3.

Report Modifications

A practitioner should modify the report (qualify, adverse, or disclaim) or withdraw from the engagement for (1) restrictions on the scope of the engagement, or (2) reservations about the propriety of the assumptions or the conformity of the presentation with those assumptions, including inadequate disclosure of significant matters. Examples of modified reports appear as Illustrations 4 through 7.

NOTE: Uncertainty about whether the transaction/event will be consummated does not require a report modification.

INTERPRETATIONS

There are no interpretations for this section.

TECHNIQUES FOR APPLICATION

Presentation of Pro Forma Financial Information

Pro forma financial information:

1. Should be labeled to distinguish it from historical financial information
2. Should describe the transaction or event that is presented as pro forma, the source of the historical information on which it is based, significant assumptions underlying the information, and any significant uncertainties
3. Should indicate that it should be read in conjunction with the related historical information
4. Should indicate that it is not necessarily indicative of results that would have been obtained if the transaction had taken place earlier

---

NOTE: For presentation of pro forma information for a public company, the practitioner should also refer to Article 11 of Regulation S-X.

Nonaudit and Nonreview Clients

Can a practitioner who has not audited or reviewed the historical base financial statements have a sufficient level of knowledge of the entity's accounting and financial reporting practices to accept a pro forma review or examination engagement? The knowledge would have to be obtained to permit the practitioner to report on the pro forma information. A practitioner may be able to obtain this knowledge in some cases. For example, if the 20X1 pro forma information were based on historical financial statements audited by someone else, but the practitioner has audited the historical financial statements for 20X2, and as part of that audit, reviewed the workpapers of the predecessor auditors, the practitioner should have obtained an appropriate level of knowledge.

Most Recent Year Historical Financial Statements

There is a requirement that the historical financial statements for the most recent year be included in the document containing the pro forma financial information. If the historical financial statements for the most recent year are not yet available, can the practitioner accept the engagement to report on the pro formas? Yes. The Statement indicates that the historical financial statements for the preceding year should be included if financial statements for the most recent year are not available.

COMPILED HISTORICAL FINANCIAL STATEMENTS

An entity with audited financial statements acquires a small closely held business for which the practitioner has compiled the financial statements. Is it permissible for the practitioner to accept an engagement to report on pro forma financial information? No, not if the operating results of the closely held business are material to the combined entity. The historical base should be audited or reviewed. Compilation is not enough, but the practitioner can accept the engagement if he or she is able to perform a retroactive review or audit.

QUALIFIED REPORT ON HISTORICAL FINANCIAL STATEMENTS

The practitioner's report on pro forma financial information refers to the financial statements from which the historical financial information was derived, and states whether the financial statements were audited or reviewed. If the report on the historical financial statements was a qualified opinion or was otherwise modified, a reference to the modification should be included in the report on pro forma information.

ILLUSTRATIONS

The following are examples of reports on pro forma financial information (adapted from SSAE 10, AT 400 Appendices A–E).

ILLUSTRATION 1. REPORT ON EXAMINATION OF PRO FORMA FINANCIAL INFORMATION

To the Board of Directors of Widget Company
Main City, USA

Independent Accountant's Report

We have examined the pro forma adjustments reflecting the transaction [*or event*] described in Note 1 and the application of those adjustments to the historical amounts in [*the assembly of*] the accompanying pro forma condensed balance sheet of Widget Company as of December 31, 20X1, and the pro forma condensed statement of income for the year then ended. The historical condensed financial statements are derived from the historical financial statements of Widget Company, which were audited by us, and of Basic Company, which were audited by other accountants, appearing elsewhere herein [*or incorporated by reference*]. Such pro forma adjustments are based upon management's assumptions described in Note 2. Widget Company's management is responsible for the pro forma financial information. Our responsibility is to express an opinion on the pro forma financial information based on our examination.

Our examination was conducted in accordance with attestation standards established by the American Institute of Certified Public Accountants and, accordingly, included such procedures as we considered necessary in the circumstances. We believe that our examination provides a reasonable basis for our opinion.

The objective of this pro forma financial information is to show what the significant effects on the historical financial information might have been had the transaction [*or event*] occurred at an earlier date. However, the pro forma condensed financial statements are not necessarily indicative of the results of operations or related effects on financial position that would have been attained had the above-mentioned transaction [*or event*] actually occurred earlier.

In our opinion, management's assumptions provide a reasonable basis for presenting the significant effects directly attributable to the above-mentioned transaction [*or event*] described in Note 1, the related pro forma adjustments give appropriate effect to those assumptions, and the pro forma column reflects the proper application of those adjustments to the historical financial statement amounts in the pro forma condensed balance sheet as of December 31, 20X1, and the pro forma condensed statement of income for the year then ended.

Smith and Jones
February 15, 20X2

NOTE: Additional paragraph(s) may be added before the opinion paragraph to emphasize certain matters relating to the attest engagement or the subject matter.

Illustration 2. Report on Review of Pro Forma Financial Information

To the Board of Directors of Widget Company
Main City, USA

Independent Accountant's Report

We have reviewed the pro forma adjustments reflecting the transaction [*or event*] described in Note 1 and the application of those adjustments to the historical amounts in [*the assembly of*] the accompanying pro forma condensed balance sheet of Widget Company as of March 31, 20X2, and the pro forma condensed statement of income for the three months then ended. These historical condensed financial statements are derived from the historical unaudited financial statements of Widget Company, which were reviewed by us, and of Basic Company, which were reviewed by other accountants, appearing elsewhere herein [*or incorporated by reference*]. Such pro forma adjustments are based on management's assumptions as described in Note 2. Widget Company's management is responsible for the pro forma financial information.

Our review was conducted in accordance with attestation standards established by the American Institute of Certified Public Accountants. A review is substantially less in scope than an examination, the objective of which is the expression of an opinion on management's assumptions, the pro forma adjustments, and the application of those adjustments to historical financial information. Accordingly, we do not express such an opinion.

The objective of this pro forma financial information is to show what the significant effects on the historical financial information might have been had the transaction [*or event*] occurred at an earlier date. However, the pro forma condensed financial statements are not necessarily indicative of the results of operations or related effects on financial position that would have been attained had the above-mentioned transaction [*or event*] actually occurred earlier.

Based on our review, nothing came to our attention that caused us to believe that management's assumptions do not provide a reasonable basis for presenting the significant effects directly attributable to the above-mentioned transaction [*or event*] described in Note 1, that the related pro forma adjustments do not give appropriate effect to those assumptions, or that the pro forma column does not reflect the proper application of those adjustments to the historical financial statement amounts in the pro forma condensed balance sheet as of March 31, 20X2, and the pro forma condensed statement of income for the three months then ended.

Smith and Jones
February 15, 20X2

Illustration 3. Report on Examination of Pro Forma Financial Information at Year-End with a Review of Pro Forma Financial Information for a Subsequent Interim Date

To the Board of Directors of Widget Company
Main City, USA

Independent Accountant's Report

We have examined the pro forma adjustments reflecting the transaction [*or event*] described in Note 1 and the application of those adjustments to the historical amounts in [*the assembly of*] the accompanying pro forma condensed balance sheet of Widget Company as of December 31, 20X1, and the pro forma condensed statement of income for the year then ended. The historical condensed financial statements are derived from the historical financial statements of Widget Company, which were audited by us, and of Basic Company, which were audited by other accountants, appearing elsewhere herein [*or incorporated by reference*]. Such pro forma adjustments are based upon management's assumptions described in Note 2. Widget Company's management is responsible for the pro forma financial information. Our responsibility is to express an opinion on the pro forma financial information based on our examination.

Our examination was conducted in accordance with attestation standards established by the American Institute of Certified Public Accountants and, accordingly, included such procedures as we considered necessary in the circumstances. We believe that our examination provides a reasonable basis for our opinion.

In addition, we have reviewed the related pro forma adjustments and the application of those adjustments to the historical amounts in [*the assembly of*] the accompanying pro forma condensed balance sheet of Widget Company as of March 31, 20X2, and the pro forma condensed statement of income for the three months then ended. The historical condensed financial statements are derived from the historical financial statements of Widget Company, which were reviewed by us, and Basic Company, which were reviewed by other accountants, appearing elsewhere herein [*or incorporated by reference*]. Such pro forma adjustments are based upon management's assumptions as described in Note 2. Our review was conducted in accordance with attestation standards established by the American Institute of Certified Public Accountants. A review is substantially less in scope than an examination, the objective of which is the expression of an opinion on management's assumptions, the pro forma adjustments, and the application of those adjustments to historical financial information. Accordingly, we do not express such an opinion on the pro forma adjustments or the application of such adjustments to the pro forma condensed balance sheet as of March 31, 20X2, and the pro forma condensed statement of income for the three months then ended.

The objective of this pro forma financial information is to show what the significant effects on the historical information might have been had the transaction [*or event*] occurred at an earlier date. However, the pro forma condensed financial statements are not necessarily indicative of the results of operations or related effects on financial position that would have been attained had the above-mentioned transaction [*or event*] actually occurred earlier.

In our opinion, management's assumptions provide a reasonable basis for presenting the significant effects directly attributable to the above-mentioned transaction [*or event*] described in Note 1, the related pro forma adjustments give appropriate effect to those assumptions, and the pro forma column reflects the proper application of those adjustments to the historical financial statement amounts in the pro forma condensed balance sheet as of December 31, 20X1, and the pro forma condensed statement of income for the year then ended.

Based on our review, nothing came to our attention that caused us to believe that management's assumptions do not provide a reasonable basis for representing the significant effects directly attributable to the above-mentioned transaction [*or event*] described in Note 1, that the related pro forma adjustments do not give appropriate effect to those assumptions, or that the pro forma column does not reflect the proper application of those adjustments to the historical financial statement amounts in the pro forma condensed balance sheet as of March 31, 20X2, and the pro forma condensed statement of income for the three months then ended.

Smith and Jones
February 15, 20X2

ILLUSTRATION 4. REPORT ON EXAMINATION OF PRO FORMA FINANCIAL INFORMATION GIVING EFFECT TO A BUSINESS COMBINATION TO BE ACCOUNTED FOR AS A POOLING OF INTERESTS

Independent Accountant's Report

We have examined the pro forma adjustments reflecting the proposed business combination to be accounted for as a pooling of interests described in Note 1 and the application of those adjustments to the historical amounts in the accompanying pro forma condensed balance sheet of X Company as of December 31, 20X1, and the pro forma condensed statements of income for each of three years in the period then ended. These historical condensed financial statements are derived from the historical financial statements of X Company, which were audited by us, and of Y Company, which were audited by other accountants, appearing elsewhere herein [*or incorporated by reference*]. Such pro forma adjustments are based upon management's assumptions described in Note 2. X Company's management is responsible for the pro forma financial information. Our responsibility is to express an opinion on the pro forma financial information based on our examination.

Our examination was conducted in accordance with attestation standards established by the American Institute of Certified Public Accountants and, accordingly, included such procedures as we considered necessary in the circumstances. We believe that our examination provides a reasonable basis for our opinion.

The objective of this pro forma financial information is to show what the significant effects on the historical financial information might have been had the transactions [*or event*] occurred at an earlier date.

[*Additional paragraph(s) may be added to emphasize certain matters relating to the attest engagement or the subject matter.*]

In our opinion, the accompanying condensed pro forma financial statements of X Company as of December 31, 20X1, and for each of the three years in the period then ended give appropriate effect to the pro forma adjustments necessary to reflect the proposed business combination on a pooling of interests basis as described in Note 1 and the pro forma column reflects the proper application of those adjustments to the historical financial statements.

[*Signature*]

[*Date*]

ILLUSTRATION 5. REPORT ON EXAMINATION OF PRO FORMA FINANCIAL INFORMATION—SCOPE LIMITATION QUALIFICATION

To the Board of Directors of Widget Company
Main City, USA

Independent Accountant's Report

We have examined the pro forma adjustments reflecting the transaction [*or event*] described in Note 1 and the application of those adjustments to the historical amounts in [*the assembly of*] the accompanying pro forma condensed balance sheet of Widget Company as of December 31, 20X1, and the pro forma condensed statement of income for the year then ended. The historical condensed financial statements are derived from the historical financial statements of Widget Company, which were audited by us, and of Basic Company, which were audited by other accountants, appearing elsewhere herein [*or incorporated by reference*]. Such pro forma adjustments are based upon management's assumptions described in Note 2. Widget Company's management is responsible for the pro forma financial information. Our responsibility is to express an opinion on the pro forma financial information based on our examination.

Except as described below, our examination was conducted in accordance with attestation standards established by the American Institute of Certified Public Accountants and, accordingly, included such procedures as we considered necessary in the circumstances. We believe that our examination provides a reasonable basis for our opinion.

We are unable to perform the examination procedures we considered necessary with respect to assumptions relating to the proposed loan described as Adjustment E in Note 2.

The objective of this pro forma financial information is to show what the significant effects on the historical financial information might have been had the transaction [*or event*] occurred at an earlier date. However, the pro forma condensed financial statements are not necessarily indicative of the results of operations or related effects on financial position that would have been attained had the above-mentioned transaction [*or event*] actually occurred earlier.

In our opinion, except for the effects of such changes, if any, as might have been determined to be necessary had we been able to satisfy ourselves as to the assumptions relating to the proposed loan, management's assumptions provide a reasonable basis for presenting the significant effects directly attributable to the above-mentioned transaction [*or event*] described in Note 1, the related pro forma adjustments give appropriate effect to those assumptions, and the pro forma column reflects the proper application of those adjustments to the historical financial statement amounts in the pro forma condensed balance sheet as of December 31, 20X1, and the pro forma condensed statement of income for the year then ended.

Smith and Jones
February 15, 20X2

ILLUSTRATION 6. REPORT ON EXAMINATION OF PRO FORMA FINANCIAL INFORMATION—QUALIFICATION—PROPRIETY OF ASSUMPTIONS

To the Board of Directors of Widget Company
Main City, USA

Independent Accountant's Report

We have examined the pro forma adjustments reflecting the transaction [*or event*] described in Note 1 and the application of those adjustments to the historical amounts in [*the assembly of*] the accompanying pro forma condensed balance sheet of Widget Company as of December 31, 20X1, and the pro forma condensed statement of income for the year then ended. The historical condensed financial statements are derived from the historical financial statements of Widget Company, which were audited by us, and of Basic Company, which were audited by other accountants, appearing elsewhere herein [*or incorporated by reference*]. Such pro forma adjustments are based upon management's assumptions described in Note 2. Widget Company's management is responsible for the pro forma financial information. Our responsibility is to express an opinion on the pro forma financial information based on our examination.

Our examination was conducted in accordance with attestation standards established by the American Institute of Certified Public Accountants and, accordingly, included such procedures as we considered necessary in the circumstances. We believe that our examination provides a reasonable basis for our opinion.

The objective of this pro forma financial information is to show what the significant effects on the historical financial information might have been had the transaction [*or event*] occurred at an earlier date. However, the pro forma condensed financial statements are not necessarily indicative of the results of operations or related effects on financial position that would have been attained had the above-mentioned transaction [*or event*] actually occurred earlier.

As discussed in Note 2 to the pro forma financial statements, the pro forma adjustments reflect management's assumption that X Division of the acquired company will be sold. The net assets of this division are reflected at their historical carrying amount; generally accepted accounting principles require these net assets to be recorded at estimated net realizable value.

In our opinion, except for inappropriate valuation of net assets of X Division, management's assumptions described in Note 2 provide a reasonable basis for presenting the significant effects directly attributable to the above-mentioned transaction [*or event*] described in Note 1, the related pro forma adjustments give appropriate effect to those assumptions, and the pro forma column reflects the proper application of those adjustments to the historical financial statement amounts in the pro forma condensed balance sheet as of December 31, 20X1, and the pro forma condensed statement of income for the year then ended.

Smith and Jones
February 15, 20X2

Illustration 7. Disclaimer of Opinion on Pro Forma Financial Information—Scope Limitation

To the Board of Directors of Widget Company
Main City, USA

Independent Accountant's Report

We were engaged to examine the pro forma adjustments reflecting the transaction [*or event*] described in Note 1 and the application of those adjustments to the historical amounts in [*the assembly of*] the accompanying pro forma condensed balance sheet of Widget Company as of December 31, 20X1, and the pro forma condensed statement of income for the year then ended. The historical condensed financial statements are derived from the historical financial statements of Widget Company, which were audited by us, and of Basic Company, which were audited by other accountants, appearing elsewhere herein [*or incorporated by reference*]. Such pro forma adjustments are based upon management's assumptions described in Note 2. Widget Company's management is responsible for the pro forma financial information.

As discussed in Note 2 to the pro forma financial statements, the pro forma adjustments reflect management's assumptions that the elimination of duplicate facilities would have resulted in a 30% reduction in operating costs. Management could not supply us with sufficient evidence to support this assertion.

The objective of this pro forma financial information is to show what the significant effects on the historical financial information might have been had the transaction [*or event*] occurred at an earlier date. However, the pro forma condensed financial statements are not necessarily indicative of the results of operations or related effects on financial position that would have been attained had the above-mentioned transaction [*or event*] actually occurred earlier.

Since we were unable to evaluate management's assumptions regarding the reduction in operating costs and other assumptions related thereto, the scope of our work was not sufficient to express, and therefore, we do not express, an opinion on the pro forma adjustments, management's underlying assumptions regarding those adjustments, and the application of those adjustments to the historical financial statement amounts in the pro forma condensed financial statement amounts in the pro forma condensed balance sheet as of December 31, 20X1, and the pro forma condensed statement of income for the year then ended.

Smith and Jones
February 15, 20X2

AT 501 An Examination of an Entity's Internal Control over Financial Reporting That Is Integrated with an Audit of Its Financial Statements

> *IMPORTANT NOTE: The guidance in this section applies to engagements for nonissuers. Auditors of issuers and public entities subject to Securities and Exchange Commission (SEC) rules should refer to the guidance in Public Company Accounting Oversight Board (PCAOB) 5,* An Audit of Internal Control over Financial Reporting That Is Integrated with an Audit of Financial Statements, *and should NOT follow the guidance in this section for the purpose of complying with Section 404 of the Sarbanes-Oxley Act.*

ORIGINAL PRONOUNCEMENT

Source Statement on Standards for Attestation Engagements (SSAE) 15, *An Examination of an Entity's Internal Control over Financial Reporting That Is Integrated with an Audit of Its Financial Statements*

TECHNICAL ALERT

In April 2016, the Auditing Standards Board (ASB) issued SSAE No. 18, *Attestation Standards: Clarification and Recodification.* SSAE No. 18 is effective for practitioners' reports dated on or after May 1, 2017. SSAE No. 18 is the culmination of the attestation clarity project, and it supersedes all of existing attestation standards except for:

- AT 501, whose content was moved to the auditing standards and codified as AU-C 940.
- AT 701, which will not be clarified, but retained in its current form because it is a rarely performed engagement. The section number has been changed to AT-C Section 395.

The clarified standards use the prefix "AT-C" and can be found in the AT-C chapters of this book.

APPLICABILITY

AT 501 is applicable when an independent accountant is engaged to issue or does issue an examination report on the design and operating effectiveness of an entity's internal control over financial reporting that is integrated with an audit of financial statements.

NOTE: A practitioner may also be engaged to examine the effectiveness of an entity's internal control over financial reporting as of a date other than the end of an entity's fiscal year. If so, the examination should still be integrated with the financial statement audit.

Review engagements are prohibited, but agreed-upon procedures engagements are not.

This statement does not affect the auditor's responsibility for considering or communicating internal control related matters in an audit. See Section 265, *Communicating Internal Control Related Matters Identified in an Audit.*

For reports on the processing of transactions at service organizations, AU-C Section 402, *Audit Considerations Relating to an Entity Using a Service Organization*, continues to apply. For reports on the suitability of the design of internal controls or on controls over the effectiveness and efficiency of operations, AT Section 101, *Attest Engagements*, applies. For reports on controls over compliance with laws and regulations, AT Section 601, *Compliance Attestation*, applies.

DEFINITIONS OF TERMS

Control objective. The aim or purpose of specified controls. It normally addresses the risks that a control is designed to mitigate. For internal control, it addresses the risk that controls will not provide reasonable assurance that a misstatement or omission is either prevented, or detected and corrected on a timely basis.

Deficiency. A *deficiency* exists when the design or operation of a control does not allow management or employees to either prevent, or detect and correct, misstatements on a timely basis. A *design deficiency* exists when either (1) a control needed to meet a control objective is missing; or (2) an existing control is incorrectly designed so that, even if the control operates as designed, the control objective would not be met.[1] An *operation deficiency* exists when a properly designed control does not operate as designed, or when the person performing the control does not have the authority or competence to perform the control correctly.

Detective control. A control whose objective is to detect and correct errors or fraud that have already occurred, which could result in a misstatement of the financial statements.

Internal control over financial reporting. A process designed to provide reasonable assurance regarding the preparation of reliable financial statements in accordance with the applicable financial reporting framework. The controls should address the proper maintenance of records, transaction recordation, and prevention of unauthorized assets usage, resulting in the prevention of misstatements in the financial statements.

Management's assertion. Management's statement about the effectiveness of the entity's internal control, and which is included in management's report on internal control.

Material weakness. A deficiency in internal control resulting in a reasonable possibility that a material misstatement of the entity's financial statements will not be prevented, or detected and corrected.

Preventive control. A control having the objective of preventing errors or fraud that could result in a misstatement of the financial statements.

Relevant assertion. An assertion in the financial statements that has a reasonable possibility of containing a misstatement that would cause the financial statements to be materially misstated.

Significant account or disclosure. An account balance or disclosure that has a reasonable possibility that it could contain a misstatement, either individually or in aggregate with others, that has a material effect on the financial statements.

Significant deficiency. A deficiency or combination of deficiencies in internal control that is less severe than a material weakness, but is important enough to merit the attention of those charged with governance.

OBJECTIVES OF AT SECTION 501

The history of public reporting on internal control has been long and controversial. In the mid-1940s there was a debate about whether an auditor had a duty to modify the audit report to disclose serious deficiencies in accounting control. In the late 1960s, several large banks included accountants' reports on internal control in their annual reports. These reports were brief and stated, in effect, that the accountants had reviewed controls and believed that the control systems were effective.

There was disagreement about the desirability of this type of reporting. Some accountants believed that reports on internal control served no useful purpose unless the recipients were in a position to do something about internal control effectiveness.

In late 1971, Statement on Accounting Procedure (SAP) 49 was issued to put an effective halt to the small but growing practice of public reporting on internal control. It required two caveat paragraphs on the limitations of accounting control, and the only form of assurance permitted was negative assurance on the absence of material weaknesses. Critics of the accounting profession, most notably officials of the Securities and Exchange Commission (SEC), publicly derided the report as a triumph of technical precision over meaningful reporting and common sense.

There were no significant developments in the area until the illegal payments scandal broke in the mid-1970s. One outcome of the scandal was passage of the Foreign Corrupt Practices Act of 1977. The Act adopted the accounting profession's definition of internal accounting control and required that all public companies have a system of internal accounting control sufficient to meet the objectives stated in the definition.

The SEC began what appeared to be a concerted drive to require independent accountants to report publicly on the internal accounting systems of public companies. Despite the momentum of the illegal payments scandal, the drive faltered because of unanticipated strong opposition from public companies and lack of support from large CPA firms. Ultimately, the SEC backtracked and withdrew its proposals. In response to the Foreign Corrupt Practices Act and related SEC proposals, however, the accounting profession had started several initiatives, and many of them had been virtually completed before the SEC's withdrawal.

In 1977, even before passage of the Act was achieved, Statement on Auditing Standards (SAS) 20 had been issued. It imposed a responsibility on the auditor to communicate material weaknesses in accounting control to management.

In the mid-1980s, SAS 30 was issued. It provided a vehicle for an accountant to issue a positive opinion on accounting control. The unmodified opinion stated:

> *In our opinion, the system of internal accounting control of XYZ Company and subsidiaries in effect at* [date], *taken as a whole, was sufficient to meet the objectives stated above insofar as those objectives pertain to the prevention or detection of errors or irregularities in amounts that would be material in relation to the consolidated financial statements.*

However, this report was largely of academic interest only. Without the pressure of an SEC requirement, there was little incentive even for public companies to engage an independent accountant to express an opinion on an internal accounting control system. Small and privately owned companies never had any great interest in such reports. The report was a service that was all dressed up but had no place to go.

In the wake of the savings and loan crisis in the late 1980s, there was considerable regulatory and legislative activity to help reduce fraudulent financial reporting. A National Commission on Fraudulent Financial Reporting, known as the Treadway Commission, was created. The Commission's report, issued in 1987, included as one of its recommendations the requirement for a management report on internal control. Legislators and regulators agreed. The Federal Deposit Insurance Corporation (FDIC) Improvement Act of 1991 affecting financial institutions was passed, and the SEC issued another rule proposal, Report of Management's Responsibilities, proposing a requirement for public companies to provide such a management report publicly. However, a common definition of "internal control" was needed to make such management reporting consistent. A group called the Committee of Sponsoring Organizations of the Treadway Commission (COSO) developed a common definition to provide a standard for reporting. Their report, *Internal Control—Integrated Framework*, was issued in 1992.

SSAE 2 was issued by the American Institute of Certified Public Accountants (AICPA) in 1993. This Statement substantially changed the approach to reporting on control by requiring that management issue its report and the accountant provide an opinion on management's assertion. This parallels the audit process in which management issues the financial statements and the auditor provides an opinion on the statements. The report continued to include caveat paragraphs about the inherent limitation of internal control similar to those required by SAP 49 and SAS 30.

SSAE 6 was issued in 1995 to make the guidance compatible with the COSO definitions and criteria for internal control. Theoretically, management may use any reasonable criteria for effective internal control established by a recognized body. However, COSO is the only recognized body specifically identified in the SSAEs.

SSAE 9 was issued by the AICPA in 1999. This SSAE enabled the practitioner to report directly on a specified subject matter, such as internal control, rather than management's assertion. The practitioner continued to be required to obtain management's assertion in order to perform the engagement. SSAE 9 also eliminated the requirement for a separate presentation of management's assertion in certain cases where the assertion is included in the introductory paragraph of the practitioner's report.

SSAE 10, revisions to this section include clarifying that:

- The responsible party's refusal to provide a written assertion as part of an examination engagement should cause the practitioner to withdraw from the engagement. (An exception exists if an examination of internal control is required by law or regulation. In this case, the practitioner should disclaim an opinion unless he or she obtains evidential matter that warrants expressing an adverse opinion.)
- The responsible party's refusal to furnish the required representations constitutes a limitation on the scope of the engagement.
- If, in a multiple-party arrangement, the practitioner's client is not the responsible party, the practitioner has no responsibility to communicate reportable conditions to the responsible party. (However, the practitioner is not precluded from making that communication.)

SSAE 15, *An Examination of an Entity's Internal Control over Financial Reporting That Is Integrated with an Audit of Its Financial Statements*, was issued in 2008, and provides a broad array of detailed changes to and supersedes SSAE 10.

REQUIREMENTS

The auditor's objective is to form an opinion on the effectiveness of an entity's internal control. An entity's internal control cannot be considered effective if a material weakness exists, so the auditor should plan an examination designed to obtain sufficient evidence to obtain reasonable assurance about whether material weaknesses exist as of the date of management's assertion regarding internal control. The auditor does not have to search for deficiencies that are less severe than a material weakness.

An engagement conducted in accordance with this section should comply with the general, fieldwork, and reporting standards in AT Section 101.

The Section (1) establishes conditions that should be met for an auditor to examine the effectiveness of an entity's internal control over financial reporting and (2) establishes the engagement performance and reporting requirements for the engagement.

REQUIRED CONDITIONS FOR ENGAGEMENT ACCEPTANCE

The following conditions should be present for the auditor to accept the engagement to examine the effectiveness of an entity's internal control. These are:

1. Management accepts responsibility for the effectiveness of the entity's internal control.
2. Management evaluates the effectiveness of the entity's internal control using suitable criteria.
3. Management supports its assertion about internal control effectiveness with sufficient evidence.
4. Management provides a report containing its assertion about the effectiveness of the entity's internal control.

If management refuses to provide a written assertion, the auditor should withdraw from the engagement. Withdrawal is *not* required if the engagement is required by law or regulation. In that case, the auditor should disclaim an opinion on internal control.

Evidence Supporting Management's Assertion

Management is responsible for documenting controls, which can be in the form of policy and procedure manuals, flowcharts, and decision tables. Management can also undertake ongoing monitoring activities to assess the effectiveness of internal controls, report deficiencies, and take corrective actions. Both documentation and ongoing monitoring activities form the foundation for management's assertion regarding internal control.

Integrating the Controls Examination with the Financial Statement Audit

The examination of internal control should be integrated with the audit, such that the objectives of both engagements can be achieved at the same time. To do so, the auditor should design tests of controls that obtain sufficient evidence to support the auditor's opinion on internal control, as well as the control risk assessment for the audit. The date of management's assertion should match the balance sheet date of the period covered by the financial statements.

Risk Assessment

The auditor should devote the most attention to those areas where a material weakness could exist in an entity's internal control. It is not necessary to test controls that would not present a reasonable possibility of material misstatement, even if those controls are deficient. The auditor must plan procedures based on the size and complexity of the organization, its business processes, and business units.

The auditor's planning should also include the results of the fraud risk assessment performed in the audit. The auditor should also evaluate whether the entity's controls adequately address the risk of misstatement due to fraud, and of management override of other controls. Examples of controls that can address these risks include:

- Controls over significant transactions, especially those resulting in late or unusual journal entries;
- Controls over journal entries made in the period-end closing process;
- Controls over related-party transactions;
- Controls related to significant estimates by management; and
- Controls that change management's willingness to inappropriately manage financial results.

Using the Work of Others

In the examination of internal controls, the auditor may use the work performed by internal auditors and other entity personnel, as well as third parties. The auditor's assessment of this work should include a review of the competence and objectivity of the individuals involved. *Competence* means the attainment and maintenance of a level of understanding, knowledge, and skills enabling a person to perform the tasks assigned to him or her, and *objectivity* means the ability to perform those tasks impartially and with intellectual honesty.

The extent to which the auditor uses the work of others depends on the risk associated with the control being tested. As the risk increases, the auditor should rely more on his or her own work.

Planning the Engagement

In planning the engagement, the auditor should consider factors such as the following:

1. Knowledge of the entity's internal control obtained during other professional engagements
2. Matters affecting the industry in which the entity operates, such as financial reporting practices, economic conditions, laws and regulations, and technological changes
3. Matters relating to the entity's business, including its organization, operating characteristics, capital structure, and distribution methods
4. The extent of recent changes, if any, in the entity, its operations, or its internal control
5. Preliminary judgments about materiality levels, inherent risk, and other factors relating to the determination of material weaknesses
6. Deficiencies previously communicated to management
7. Legal or regulatory issues of which the entity is aware
8. The type and extent of evidential matter pertaining to the effectiveness of the entity's internal control
9. Preliminary judgments about the effectiveness of internal control
10. Public information about the entity impacting the evaluation of misstatements and the effectiveness of internal control
11. Knowledge of the risks noted as part of the auditor's acceptance and retention evaluation
12. The level of complexity of the entity's operations

The auditor should use a top-down approach to selecting the controls to be tested. In sequence, this involves:

1. Starting at the financial statement level;
2. Utilizing the auditor's overall understanding of the risks to internal control;
3. Focusing on entity-level controls;
4. Moving down to significant accounts and disclosures, and their related assertions;
5. Focusing on accounts, disclosures, and assertions that present a reasonable possibility of material misstatement of the financial statements and disclosures;
6. Verifying the auditor's understanding of the risks in the entity's processes; and
7. Selecting controls for testing that sufficiently address the assessed risk of material misstatement.

Entity-Level Controls

The auditor should test those entity-level controls that will assist in reaching a conclusion about the entity's level of internal control. These controls include:

- Controls related to the control environment,
- Controls over management override,
- The entity's risk assessment process,
- Centralized processing and controls,
- Controls to monitor the results of operations,
- Controls to monitor other controls,
- Controls over the financial reporting process, and
- Programs and controls that address significant business control and risk management practices.

Control Environment

The auditor should evaluate the entity's control environment, since it has a significant impact on effective internal control. This evaluation should include an assessment of whether management's operating style and ethical values promote effective internal control, and whether those charged with governance understand and exercise oversight responsibility over financial reporting and internal control.

Financial Reporting Process

The auditor should evaluate the financial reporting process. This reporting process includes:

- Procedures to enter transaction totals in the general ledger
- Procedures that apply accounting policies
- Procedures related to journal entry creation
- Procedures for recording adjustments to the financial statements
- Procedures for preparing the financial statements

Evaluating this reporting process should include an assessment of the processes used to create financial statements, the level of management participation, the locations participating in the process, the types of journal entries used, and the extent of oversight of the process.

Significant Accounts and Disclosures

The auditor should identify significant accounts and disclosures, and their relevant assertions, which requires the evaluation of the quantitative and qualitative risk factors related to each financial statement line item and disclosure. Risk factors to consider in this analysis for each account and related disclosure are:

- Size and composition of the account
- Susceptibility to misstatements caused by errors or fraud
- Volume of transaction activity, as well as the complexity and homogeneity of each of these transactions
- Exposure to losses
- Possibility of significant contingent liabilities
- Existence of related-party transactions
- Changes from the prior period

When an entity has multiple locations or business units, the auditor should conduct this analysis based on the consolidated financial statements.

Sources of Misstatement

The auditor should obtain an understanding of the likely sources of potential misstatements by understanding the flow of transactions, identifying the process points where misstatements could arise, and identifying the controls used to address those potential misstatements. The auditor directly performs this analysis or supervises the work of others who do so. A good method for conducting this analysis is a walk-through of a transaction from its beginning until it appears in the financial statements. A walk-through can include such tasks as direct observation of processing steps, inspection of related documents, and recalculation.

Selection of Controls to Be Tested

The auditor should test those controls that are important to the auditor's conclusion about whether the entity's controls sufficiently address the assessed risk of material misstatement. It may not be necessary to test all controls related to a relevant assertion if more than one control addresses the assessed risk.

TESTING CONTROLS

The auditor should evaluate the design effectiveness of controls to determine if the controls, if prescribed as designed, can prevent, or detect and correct, misstatements in the financial statements. A test of operating effectiveness should include a determination of whether the control is operating as designed, and whether the person performing the control has the authority and competence to perform it effectively. This evaluation can include a walk-through that incorporates a mix of inquiry, operational observation, and documentation inspection.

For each test of control, the evidence needed depends upon the risk associated with the control; this is the risk that the control might not be effective, and if not effective, that the risk of a material weakness exists. As a control's risk increases, so too should the level of evidence that the auditor obtains.

The auditor is not responsible for obtaining sufficient evidence to support an effectiveness opinion about each individual control, only about the entity's overall level of internal control.

A number of factors affect the risk associated with each control, including:

- The nature and materiality of the misstatements that a control is intended to prevent, or detect and correct;
- The inherent risk associated with the related accounts and assertions;
- The presence of changes in the volume or nature of transactions adversely affecting control design or operating effectiveness;
- Whether the account has a history of errors;
- The effectiveness of controls that monitor other controls;
- The nature and frequency of the control;
- The degree to which the control relies on the effectiveness of other controls;
- The competence of the personnel who perform the control, and whether there have been changes in these personnel;
- Whether the control is automated, or requires manual monitoring; and
- The complexity of the control.

In the event of a control deviation, the auditor should determine the effect of the deviation on his or her assessment of the risk associated with the control being tested. An individual control does not necessarily have to operate without any deviation to be considered effective.

Importance of Types of Tests of Controls

Some types of tests produce greater evidence of the effectiveness of controls than others. The following tests are presented in order of effectiveness from most to least effective:

1. Reperformance of a control
2. Recalculation
3. Inspection of relevant documentation
4. Observation
5. Inquiry

A test of documentation may be dependent upon whether the control results in documentary evidence of its operation.

Timing and Extent of Tests of Controls

Testing a control over a longer period of time, or testing close to the date of management's assertion provides additional evidence of control effectiveness. In general, the more extensively a control is tested, the greater the evidence obtained from that test.

Prior to the date of management's assertion, management may upgrade the entity's controls. If the auditor determines that the new controls achieve stated control objectives and have been in existence long enough to assess their design and operating effectiveness, then there is no need to test the design and operating effectiveness of the superseded controls. However, if the operating effectiveness of the superseded controls is important to the auditor's control risk assessment in the financial statement audit, then testing of the superseded controls is appropriate.

Interim Testing

Additional evidence needed to update the results of testing from an interim date to the entity's period-end depends on the specific controls tested and the sufficiency of the evidence obtained prior to the as-of date, as well as the length of the remaining period and the possibility of significant internal control changes subsequent to the interim testing.

Considerations for Subsequent Years' Testing

Information available in subsequent years' examinations might allow the auditor to assess risk as being lower than in the initial year of testing, which might lead to reduced testing in subsequent years.

The auditor should vary the nature, timing, and extent of controls testing in subsequent periods to introduce unpredictability into the testing. This may result in testing during different interim periods, changing the number and types of tests performed, or changing the combination of procedures used.

FORMING AN OPINION

The auditor should form an opinion on the effectiveness of internal control. The source of this opinion should be the auditor's own tests and reports issued by internal audit. After forming an opinion, the auditor should examine management's report to ensure that it contains the following items:

- A statement regarding management's responsibility for internal control
- A description of the subject matter of the examination
- An identification of the criteria against which internal control is measured (such as the COSO *Internal Control—Integrated Framework*)
- Management's assertion about the effectiveness of internal control
- A description of any material weaknesses
- The date as of which management makes its internal control assertion

If any of these items are missing or improperly presented, the auditor should request a revision. If this is not forthcoming, the auditor should include an explanatory paragraph in his or her report. If management provides no report, then the auditor should withdraw from the engagement. Sample opinions are noted later in "Illustrations."

Management Representations and Responsibilities

The auditor should obtain written representations from management regarding the following items:

1. Acknowledgment of management's responsibility for the establishment and maintenance of internal control
2. A statement that management has performed an evaluation of the effectiveness of the entity's internal control, specifying the control criteria used
3. A statement that management did not use the auditor's procedures performed during the integrated audit as part of the basis for management's assertion
4. A statement of management's assertion about the effectiveness of the entity's internal control based on the control criteria as of a specified date
5. A statement that management has disclosed to the auditor all deficiencies in the design or operation of internal control, including separately disclosing all such deficiencies that it believes will be significant deficiencies or material weaknesses in internal control
6. A description of any fraud resulting in a material misstatement to the entity's financial statements and any other fraud that does not result in a material misstatement to the entity's financial statements, but which involves senior management, or other employees who have a significant role in the entity's internal control

7. A statement of whether the significant deficiencies and material weaknesses identified and communicated to management and those charged with governance during previous engagements have been resolved, and identifying any that have not
8. A statement whether there were, subsequent to the date being reported on, any changes in internal control or other factors that might significantly affect internal control, including any corrective actions taken by management with regard to significant deficiencies and material weaknesses

A sample management representation letter is included in Illustration 11. Section 333, *Management Representations*, provides guidance on the date as of which management should sign such a representation letter and which members of management should sign it.

Communication of Deficiencies and Material Weaknesses

If the auditor identifies significant deficiencies or material weaknesses, he or she should communicate them in writing to management and those charged with governance (even if the items were remediated during the audit). This communication should also include any such items that were previously communicated but not remediated. If the auditor concludes that the entity's oversight is ineffective, then the communication of these issues should also be extended to the board of directors. The communication should be made by the report release date. For a governmental entity, the communication should be made as soon as practicable, but no later than 60 days following the report release date.

The auditor should also communicate in writing all nonmaterial and nonsignificant deficiencies to management no later than 60 days following the report release date, and inform those charged with governance when the communication was made. The communication to management does not need to include an itemization of those nonmaterial and nonsignificant deficiencies that were included in previous written communications.

The auditor should *not* issue a report indicating that no nonmaterial or material weaknesses were identified during the integrated audit.

EVALUATING CONTROL DEFICIENCIES

The auditor must evaluate identified control deficiencies and determine whether these deficiencies, individually or in combination, are material weaknesses.

The significance of a control deficiency depends on the magnitude of a potential misstatement and whether there is a reasonable possibility that existing controls will fail to prevent, or detect and correct, a misstatement. Thus, the severity of a deficiency depends on the *potential for a misstatement, not on whether a misstatement actually has occurred*. Accordingly, the absence of identified misstatement does not provide evidence that identified control deficiencies are not significant deficiencies or material weaknesses.

The key factors affecting the magnitude of a misstatement include the financial statement amounts exposed to the deficiency, as well as the volume of activity exposed to the deficiency.

The possibility of a deficiency resulting in a misstatement is impacted by a number of risk factors, which include:

- The nature of the financial statement accounts, transactions, and disclosures involved
- The susceptibility of assets and liabilities to loss or fraud
- The subjectivity or complexity involved in determining the amounts involved
- The interaction of the control with other controls

- The interaction among deficiencies
- The possible future consequences of the deficiency

It is not necessary to quantify the probability of occurrence of a misstatement when evaluating deficiencies.

Multiple deficiencies affecting the same account, disclosure, or assertion increase the likelihood of material misstatement and may constitute a material weakness.

Compensating controls can reduce the effects of a deficiency, but they do not eliminate it. To have a mitigating effect, a compensation control should prevent, or detect and correct, a material misstatement.

Indicator of Material Weaknesses

There are certain key indicators of material weaknesses in internal control. They include:

- Fraud by senior management, even if not material,
- Restatement of financial statements due to correct for material misstatements that were caused by error or fraud,
- Identification of material misstatements that would not have been detected and corrected by internal control, and
- Ineffective oversight of financial reporting and internal control.

REPORTING REQUIREMENTS

The auditor's examination report on the effectiveness of an entity's internal control over financial reporting should include the following:

1. A title that includes the word *independent*
2. A statement that management is responsible for maintaining effective internal control and for evaluating the effectiveness of internal control
3. An identification of management's assertion on internal control that accompanies the auditor's report, including a reference to management's report
4. A statement that the auditor's responsibility is to express an opinion on the entity's internal control (or on management's assertion) based on his or her examination
5. A statement that the examination was conducted in accordance with attestation standards established by AICPA
6. A statement that such standards require that the auditor plan and perform the examination to obtain reasonable assurance about whether effective internal control was maintained in all material respects
7. A statement that an examination includes obtaining an understanding of internal control, assessing the risk that a material weakness exists, testing and evaluating the design and operating effectiveness of internal control based on the assessed risk, and performing such other procedures as the auditor considers necessary in the circumstances
8. A statement that the auditor believes the examination provides a reasonable basis for his or her opinion
9. A definition of internal control (the auditor should use the same description of the entity's internal control as management uses in its report)

10. A statement that, because of inherent limitations, internal control may not prevent, or detect and correct, misstatements, and that projections of any evaluation of effectiveness to future periods are subject to the risk that controls may become inadequate because of changes in conditions, or that the degree of compliance with the policies or procedures may deteriorate
11. The auditor's opinion on whether the entity maintained, in all material respects, effective internal control as of the specified date, based on the control criteria; or the auditor's opinion on whether management's assertion about the effectiveness of the entity's internal control as of the specified date is fairly stated, in all material respects, based on the control criteria
12. The manual or printed signature of the auditor's firm
13. The date of the report

The auditor can issue either a combined report or separate reports on an entity's financial statements and internal control. If he or she chooses to issue separate reports, then the following paragraph should be added to the financial statements reports:

> *We also examined* [or audited] *in accordance with attestation standards established by the American Institute of Certified Public Accountants,* [company name]*'s internal control over financial reporting as of December 31, 20X7, based on* [identify control criteria] *and our report dated* [date of report, which should be the same as the date of the report on the financial statements] *expressed* [include nature of the opinion].

Again, if separate reports are issued, the auditor should add the following paragraph to the report on internal control:

> *We also have audited, in accordance with auditing standards generally accepted in the United States of America, the* [identify financial statement] *of* [company name] *and our report dated* [date of report, which should be the same as the date of the report on internal control] *expressed* [include nature of opinion].

When internal control is not effective, the auditor cannot express an opinion on management's assertion, and so should report directly on the effectiveness of internal control. The auditor's report should also include the following information:

- The definition of a material weakness (see the earlier section, "Definitions of Terms").
- A statement that one or more material weaknesses have been identified; the auditor need only refer to the material weaknesses described in management's report, as long as the referenced weaknesses are fairly presented.

If material weaknesses have not been included in management's report, then the auditor's report should state that one or more material weaknesses have been identified but not included in management's report, and also note each weakness and the actual and potential effect on the presentation of the entity's financial statements. In this situation, the auditor should communicate the missing information to those charged with governance, noting that the information was not included in management's report.

The auditor should date the report no earlier than the date when he or she has collected sufficient evidence to support an opinion. The dates of the audit and internal control reports should be the same.

Report modifications. The auditor should issue a modified report if:

- Management's report is either incomplete or improperly presented. If so, the auditor should include an explanatory paragraph in his or her report.
- There is a restriction on the engagement scope. If so, the auditor should either withdraw from the engagement or disclaim an opinion. If the latter, the auditor should state the reasons for the disclaimer; further, if the auditor concludes that a material weakness exists, the report should also include the definition of a material weakness, a description of those weaknesses identified, and their actual and potential impact on the entity's financial statements. The auditor should also communicate in writing that the examination of internal control cannot be completed.
- The auditor includes the report of another audit within his or her own report. If so, the auditor should review Section 543, *Part of Audit Performed by Other Independent Auditors*, for guidance on this decision.
- There is other information in management's report that is subject to the auditor's evaluation. If so, the auditor should disclaim an opinion on the additional information. Possible text for this purpose is "We do not express an opinion or any other form of assurance on [*describe additional information*]." If the additional information includes a material misstatement of fact, the auditor should communicate his or her views about the misstatement, in writing, to management and those charged with governance.

Examples of several of these reports are included in "Illustrations."

OTHER TOPICS

Subsequent Events

To determine the existence of changes to internal control in subsequent periods, the auditor should review subsequent control reports by internal audit, independent auditors, regulatory agencies, and information from other sources.

If the auditor becomes aware, before the audit report date, of a material weakness that existed as of the management assertion date, the auditor should issue an adverse opinion. If the auditor cannot determine the impact of the item on the entity's internal control as of the assertion date, the auditor should disclaim an opinion. If the material weakness arose between the assertion date and audit report date, then the auditor should include in his or her report a paragraph describing the event and its effects.

Multiple Location Entities

When the auditor is determining the entity locations where it should perform control tests, it is necessary to assess the risk of material misstatement associated with the entity location. It is reasonable to eliminate from testing those locations not presenting a reasonable possibility of material misstatement.

The scope of the controls examination should include any entities acquired on or prior to the date of management's assertion, as well as operations accounted for as discontinued operations.

If the entity has equity method investments, the examination scope does not include the investee's controls, but does include controls over the reporting of the entity's financial statements, its portion of the investee's income or loss, the investment balance, adjustments to the income or loss and investment balance, and related disclosures.

Use of Outsourced Services

If an entity outsources some or all of its information and communication systems, then the auditor should evaluate the controls of the service organization as part of the controls of the entity. This requires obtaining an understanding of the service organization's controls that are relevant to the entity's internal control, and of the entity's controls over the service organization.

The auditor must obtain evidence that these controls are operating effectively. This can be done with one or more of the following procedures:

- Obtain a service auditor's report on controls placed in operation and tests of operating effectiveness, or a report on the application of procedures that describes tests of controls. In the former case, the auditor should assess the time period covered, the scope of the examination and applications addressed, the manner in which tested controls relate to the entity's controls, the service auditor's opinion on the effectiveness of the controls, and the service auditor's reputation, competence, and independence. In the latter case, the auditor should evaluate whether the report provides sufficient appropriate evidence.
- Test the entity's controls over the activities of the service organization.
- Test the service organization's controls.

If there is a significant period of time between the service auditor's test of controls and the management assertion date, the auditor should conduct additional procedures. This should include an inquiry of management to see if management has identified any changes in the service organization's controls during the intervening period, as well as the auditor's own investigations. If so, the auditor should evaluate the effect of the changes on the effectiveness of the entity's internal control.

The auditor may elect to obtain additional evidence about the service organization's controls if there has been a significant amount of time between the dates of the service auditor's report and management's assertion, or if the activities of the service organization are significant to the entity. Other factors for the auditor to consider are the presence of errors in the service organization's transaction processing, and the significance of any changes made to the service organization's controls.

If the auditor decides to obtain additional evidence about the service organization's controls, possible options include:

- Evaluating the results of any procedures already performed by management
- Contacting the service organization directly for information, possibly including the performance of on-site procedures
- Requesting that a service auditor be engaged to supply the needed information

The auditor should not refer to the service auditor's report in his or her opinion on internal control.

Automated Controls

Automated controls are less likely to break down than those performed manually. Also, given no programming changes or access to those programs, the auditor can avoid duplicating tests of automated controls that were performed in the prior year (though this requires testing of program change controls).

Effect of Substantive Procedures on Controls Conclusion

The auditor should incorporate the results of substantive procedures performed in the audit of financial statements on the evaluation of internal control. This evaluation should include:

- Risk assessments related to fraud
- Findings regarding illegal acts and related-party transactions
- Indications of management bias related to accounting estimates and the selection of accounting principles
- Misstatements

However, the auditor cannot infer the effectiveness of a control from the above factors; that requires the direct testing of controls.

INTERPRETATIONS

Reporting under Section 112 of the Federal Deposit Insurance Corporation Improvement Act (Issued September 2010)

To comply with the integrated audit requirement in AT Section 501, when an insured depository institution (IDI) uses the consolidated holding company's financial statements to satisfy the audited financial statements requirement, the auditor would be required to perform procedures necessary to obtain sufficient appropriate audit evidence to express an opinion on the financial statements and their internal control over financial reporting. When these financial statements are not prepared for external distribution, financial statements may consist of the financial information of the IDI in a reporting package or equivalent schedules and analyses that include the information needed for the preparation of the holding company's consolidated financial statements, including disclosures. Materiality is based on the financial information of the IDI, rather than the financial statements of the holding company. If the auditor cannot obtain sufficient audit evidence with respect to the financial information of the IDI, he or she is required to withdraw from the engagement or disclaim an opinion on the effectiveness of the IDI's internal control over financial reporting.

When an IDI does not prepare financial statements for external distribution, the auditor is still required to evaluate its period-end financial reporting process, which includes the IDI's procedures for preparing financial information for purposes of the consolidated holding company's financial statements.

The illustrative reports of Section 501 may be used to report on the effectiveness of the IDI's internal control over financial reporting. The requirement to add a paragraph to the internal control report that references the financial statement audit does not apply when the auditor does not issue a separate auditor's report on the IDI's financial statements.

ILLUSTRATIONS

The following are illustrations of opinions on internal control, communications of significant deficiencies and material weaknesses, and a management report. They are adapted from the SSAE 15 appendices (AT Section 501, Appendices A, B, and D).

ILLUSTRATION 1. UNQUALIFIED OPINION ON INTERNAL CONTROL

Independent Auditor's Report

We have examined XYZ Company's internal control over financial reporting as of December 31, 20XX, based on [*identify criteria*]. XYZ Company's management is responsible for maintaining effective internal control over financial reporting, and for its assertion of the effectiveness of internal control over financial reporting, included in the accompanying [*title of management's report*]. Our responsibility is to express an opinion on XYZ Company's internal control over financial reporting based on our examination.

We conducted our examination in accordance with attestation standards established by the American Institute of Certified Public Accountants. Those standards require that we plan and perform the examination to obtain reasonable assurance about whether effective internal control over financial reporting was maintained in all material respects. Our examination included obtaining an understanding of internal control over financial reporting, assessing the risk that a material weakness exists, and testing and evaluating the design and operating effectiveness of internal control based on the assessed risk. Our examination also included performing such other procedures as we considered necessary in the circumstances. We believe that our examination provides a reasonable basis for our opinion.

An entity's internal control over financial reporting is a process effected by those charged with governance, management, and other personnel, designed to provide reasonable assurance regarding the preparation of reliable financial statements in accordance with [*applicable financial reporting framework, such as accounting principles generally accepted in the United States of America*]. An entity's internal control over financial reporting includes those policies and procedures that (1) pertain to the maintenance of records that, in reasonable detail, accurately and fairly reflect the transactions and dispositions of the assets of the entity; (2) provide reasonable assurance that transactions are recorded as necessary to permit preparation of financial statements in accordance with [*applicable financial reporting framework, such as accounting principles generally accepted in the United States of America*], and that receipts and expenditures of the entity are being made only in accordance with authorizations of management and those charged with governance; and (3) provide reasonable assurance regarding prevention or timely detection of and correction of unauthorized acquisition, use, or disposition of the entity's assets that could have a material effect on the financial statements.

Because of its inherent limitations, internal control over financial reporting may not prevent, or detect and correct, misstatements. Also, projections of any evaluation of effectiveness to future periods are subject to the risk that controls may become inadequate because of changes in conditions, or that the degree of compliance with the policies or procedures may deteriorate.

In our opinion, XYZ Company maintained, in all material respects, effective internal control over financial reporting as of December 31, 20XX, based on [*identify criteria*].

We also have audited, in accordance with auditing standards generally accepted in the United States of America, the [*identify financial statements*] of XYZ Company and our report dated [*date of report, which should be the same as the date of the report on the examination of internal control*] expressed [*include nature of opinion*].

[*Signature*]

[*Date*]

ILLUSTRATION 2. UNQUALIFIED OPINION ON MANAGEMENT'S ASSERTION

Independent Auditor's Report

We have examined management's assertion, included in the accompanying [*title of management report*], that XYZ Company maintained effective internal control over financial reporting as of December 31, 20XX, based on [*identify criteria*]. XYZ Company's management is responsible for maintaining effective internal control over financial reporting, and for its assertion of the effectiveness of internal control over financial reporting, included in the accompanying [*title of management's report*]. Our responsibility is to express an opinion on management's assertion based on our examination.

We conducted our examination in accordance with attestation standards established by the American Institute of Certified Public Accountants. Those standards require that we plan and perform the examination to obtain reasonable assurance about whether effective internal control over financial reporting was maintained in all material respects. Our examination included obtaining an understanding of internal control over financial reporting, assessing the risk that a material weakness exists, and testing and evaluating the design and operating effectiveness of internal control based on the assessed risk. Our examination also included performing such other procedures as we considered necessary in the circumstances. We believe that our examination provides a reasonable basis for our opinion.

An entity's internal control over financial reporting is a process effected by those charged with governance, management, and other personnel, designed to provide reasonable assurance regarding the preparation of reliable financial statements in accordance with [*applicable financial reporting framework, such as accounting principles generally accepted in the United States of America*]. An entity's internal control over financial reporting includes those policies and procedures that (1) pertain to the maintenance of records that, in reasonable detail, accurately and fairly reflect the transactions and dispositions of the assets of the entity; (2) provide reasonable assurance that transactions are recorded as necessary to permit preparation of financial statements in accordance with [*applicable financial reporting framework, such as accounting principles generally accepted in the United States of America*], and that receipts and expenditures of the entity are being made only in accordance with authorizations of management and those charged with governance; and (3) provide reasonable assurance regarding prevention or timely detection and correction of unauthorized acquisition, use, or disposition of the entity's assets that could have a material effect on the financial statements.

Because of its inherent limitations, internal control over financial reporting may not prevent, or detect and correct, misstatements. Also, projections of any evaluation of effectiveness to future periods are subject to the risk that controls may become inadequate because of changes in conditions, or that the degree of compliance with the policies or procedures may deteriorate.

In our opinion, management's assertion that XYZ Company maintained effective internal control over financial reporting as of December 31, 20XX, is fairly stated, in all material respects, based on [*identify criteria*].

We also have audited, in accordance with auditing standards generally accepted in the United States of America, the [*identify financial statements*] of XYZ Company and our report dated [*date of report, which should be the same as the date of the report on the examination of internal control*] expressed [*include nature of opinion*].

[*Signature*]

[*Date*]

Illustration 3. Adverse Opinion on Internal Control

Independent Auditor's Report

We have examined XYZ Company's internal control over financial reporting as of December 31, 20XX, based on [*identify criteria*]. XYZ Company's management is responsible for maintaining effective internal control over financial reporting, and for its assertion of the effectiveness of internal control over financial reporting, included in the accompanying [*title of management's report*]. Our responsibility is to express an opinion on XYZ Company's internal control over financial reporting based on our examination.

We conducted our examination in accordance with attestation standards established by the American Institute of Certified Public Accountants. Those standards require that we plan and perform the examination to obtain reasonable assurance about whether effective internal control over financial reporting was maintained in all material respects. Our examination included obtaining an understanding of internal control over financial reporting, assessing the risk that a material weakness exists, and testing and evaluating the design and operating effectiveness of internal control based on the assessed risk. Our examination also included performing such other procedures as we considered necessary in the circumstances. We believe that our examination provides a reasonable basis for our opinion.

An entity's internal control over financial reporting is a process effected by those charged with governance, management, and other personnel, and designed to provide reasonable assurance regarding the preparation of reliable financial statements in accordance with [*applicable financial reporting framework, such as accounting principles generally accepted in the United States of America*]. An entity's internal control over financial reporting includes those policies and procedures that (1) pertain to the maintenance of records that, in reasonable detail, accurately and fairly reflect the transactions and dispositions of the assets of the entity; (2) provide reasonable assurance that transactions are recorded as necessary to permit preparation of financial statements in accordance with [*applicable financial reporting framework, such as accounting principles generally accepted in the United States of America*], and that receipts and expenditures of the entity are being made only in accordance with authorizations of management and those charged with governance; and (3) provide reasonable assurance regarding prevention, or timely detection and correction of unauthorized acquisition, use, or disposition of the entity's assets that could have a material effect on the financial statements.

Because of its inherent limitations, internal control over financial reporting may not prevent, or detect and correct, misstatements. Also, projections of any evaluation of effectiveness to future periods are subject to the risk that controls may become inadequate because of changes in conditions, or that the degree of compliance with the policies or procedures may deteriorate.

A material weakness is a deficiency, or a combination of deficiencies, in internal control over financial reporting, such that there is a reasonable possibility that a material misstatement of the entity's financial statements will not be prevented, or detected and corrected on a timely basis. The following material weakness has been identified and included in the accompanying [*title of management's report*].

[*Identify the material weakness described in management's report.*]

In our opinion, because of the effect of the material weakness described above on the achievement of the objectives of the control criteria, XYZ Company has not maintained effective internal control over financial reporting as of December 31, 20XX, based on [*identify criteria*].

We also have audited, in accordance with auditing standards generally accepted in the United States of America, the [*identify financial statements*] of XYZ Company. We considered the material weakness identified above in determining the nature, timing, and extent of audit tests applied in our audit of the 20XX financial statements, and this report does not affect our report dated [*date of report, which should be the same as the date of the report on the examination of internal control*], which expressed [*include nature of opinion*].

[*Signature*]

[*Date*]

ILLUSTRATION 4. DISCLAIMER OF OPINION ON INTERNAL CONTROL

Independent Auditor's Report

We were engaged to examine XYZ Company's internal control over financial reporting as of December 31, 20XX, based on [*identify criteria*]. XYZ Company's management is responsible for maintaining effective internal control over financial reporting, and for its assertion of the effectiveness of internal control over financial reporting, included in the accompanying [*title of management's report*].

[*Paragraph that describes the substantive reasons for the scope limitation*] Accordingly, we were unable to perform auditing procedures necessary to form an opinion on XYZ Company's internal control over financial reporting as of December 31, 20XX.

An entity's internal control over financial reporting is a process effected by those charged with governance, management, and other personnel, designed to provide reasonable assurance regarding the preparation of reliable financial statements in accordance with [*applicable financial reporting framework, such as accounting principles generally accepted in the United States of America*]. An entity's internal control over financial reporting includes those policies and procedures that (1) pertain to the maintenance of records that, in reasonable detail, accurately, and fairly reflect the transactions and dispositions of the assets of the entity; (2) provide reasonable assurance that transactions are recorded as necessary to permit preparation of financial statements in accordance with [*applicable financial reporting framework, such as accounting principles generally accepted in the United States of America*], and that receipts and expenditures of the entity are being made only in accordance with authorizations of management and those charged with governance; and (3) provide reasonable assurance regarding prevention, or timely detection and correction of unauthorized acquisition, use, or disposition of the entity's assets that could have a material effect on the financial statements.

Because of its inherent limitations, internal control over financial reporting may not prevent, or detect and correct, misstatements. Also, projections of any evaluation of effectiveness to future periods are subject to the risk that controls may become inadequate because of changes in conditions, or that the degree of compliance with the policies or procedures may deteriorate.

A material weakness is a deficiency, or a combination of deficiencies, in internal control over financial reporting, such that there is a reasonable possibility that a material misstatement of the entity's financial statements will not be prevented, or detected and corrected, on a timely basis. If one or more material weaknesses exist, an entity's internal control over financial reporting cannot be considered effective. The following material weakness has been identified and included in the accompanying [*title of management's report*].

[*Identify the material weakness described in management's report and include a description of the material weakness, including its nature and its actual and potential effect on the presentation of the entity's financial statements issued during the existence of the material weakness.*]

Because of the limitation on the scope of our audit described in the second paragraph, the scope of our work was not sufficient to enable us to express, and we do not express, an opinion on the effectiveness of XYZ Company's internal control over financial reporting.

We have audited, in accordance with auditing standards generally accepted in the United States of America, the [*identify financial statements*] of XYZ Company and our report dated [*date of report*] expressed [*include nature of opinion*]. We considered the material weakness identified above in determining the nature, timing, and extent of audit tests applied in our audit of the 20XX financial statements, and this report does not affect such report on the financial statements.

[*Signature*]

[*Date*]

Illustration 5. Unqualified Opinion on Internal Control Based, in Part, on the Report of Another Auditor

Independent Auditor's Report

We have examined XYZ Company's internal control over financial reporting as of December 31, 20XX, based on [*identify criteria*]. XYZ Company's management is responsible for maintaining effective internal control over financial reporting, and for its assertion of the effectiveness of internal control over financial reporting, included in the accompanying [*title of management's report*]. Our responsibility is to express an opinion on XYZ Company's internal control over financial reporting based on our examination. We did not examine the effectiveness of internal control over financial reporting of ABC Company, a wholly owned subsidiary, whose financial statements reflect total assets and revenues constituting 20% and 30%, respectively, of the related consolidated financial statement amounts as of and for the year ended December 31, 20XX. The effectiveness of ABC Company's internal control over financial reporting was examined by other auditors whose report has been furnished to us, and our opinion, insofar as it relates to the effectiveness of ABC Company's internal control over financial reporting, is based solely on the report of the other auditors.

We conducted our examination in accordance with attestation standards established by the American Institute of Certified Public Accountants. Those standards require that we plan and perform the examination to obtain reasonable assurance about whether effective internal control over financial reporting was maintained in all material respects. Our examination included obtaining an understanding of internal control over financial reporting, assessing the risk that a material weakness exists, and testing and evaluating the design and operating effectiveness of internal control based on the assessed risk. Our examination also included performing such other procedures as we considered necessary in the circumstances. We believe that our examination and the report of the other auditors provide a reasonable basis for our opinion.

An entity's internal control over financial reporting is a process effected by those charged with governance, management, and other personnel, designed to provide reasonable assurance regarding the preparation of reliable financial statements in accordance with [*applicable financial reporting framework, such as accounting principles generally accepted in the United States of America*]. An entity's internal control over financial reporting includes those policies and procedures that (1) pertain to the maintenance of records that, in reasonable detail, accurately and fairly reflect the transactions and dispositions of the assets of the entity; (2) provide reasonable assurance that transactions are recorded as necessary to permit preparation of financial statements in accordance with [*applicable financial reporting framework, such as accounting principles generally accepted in the United States of America*], and that receipts and expenditures of the entity are being made only in accordance with authorizations of management and those charged with governance; and (3) provide reasonable assurance regarding prevention, or timely detection and correction of unauthorized acquisition, use, or disposition of the entity's assets that could have a material effect on the financial statements.

Because of its inherent limitations, internal control over financial reporting may not prevent, or detect and correct, misstatements. Also, projections of any evaluation of effectiveness to future periods are subject to the risk that controls may become inadequate because of changes in conditions, or that the degree of compliance with the policies or procedures may deteriorate.

In our opinion, based on our examination and the report of the other auditors, XYZ Company maintained, in all material respects, effective internal control over financial reporting as of December 31, 20XX, based on [*identify criteria*].

We also have audited, in accordance with auditing standards generally accepted in the United States of America, the [*identify financial statements*] of XYZ Company and our report dated [*date of report, which should be the same as the date of the report on the examination of internal control*] expressed [*include nature of opinion*].

[*Signature*]

[*Date*]

ILLUSTRATION 6. COMBINED REPORT EXPRESSING AN UNQUALIFIED OPINION ON INTERNAL CONTROL AND ON THE FINANCIAL STATEMENTS

Independent Auditor's Report

We have audited the accompanying balance sheet of XYZ Company as of December 31, 20XX, and the related statements of income, retained earnings, and cash flows for the year then ended. We also have audited XYZ Company's internal control over financial reporting as of December 31, 20XX, based on [*identify criteria*]. XYZ Company's management is responsible for these financial statements, for maintaining effective internal control over financial reporting, and for its assertion of the effectiveness of internal control over financial reporting, included in the accompanying [*title of management's report*]. Our responsibility is to express an opinion on these financial statements and an opinion on XYZ Company's internal control over financial reporting based on our audits.

We conducted our audit of the financial statements in accordance with auditing standards generally accepted in the United States of America and our audit of internal control over financial reporting in accordance with attestation standards established by the American Institute of Certified Public Accountants. Those standards require that we plan and perform the audits to obtain reasonable assurance about whether the financial statements are free of material misstatement and whether effective internal control over financial reporting was maintained in all material respects. Our audit of the financial statements included examining, on a test basis, evidence supporting the amounts and disclosures in the financial statements, assessing the accounting principles used and significant estimates made by management, as well as evaluating the overall financial statement presentation. Our audit of internal control over financial reporting included obtaining an understanding of internal control over financial reporting, assessing the risk that a material weakness exists, and testing and evaluating the design and operating effectiveness of internal control based on the assessed risk. Our audits also included performing such other procedures as we considered necessary in the circumstances. We believe that our audits provide a reasonable basis for our opinions.

An entity's internal control over financial reporting is a process effected by those charged with governance, management, and other personnel, designed to provide reasonable assurance regarding the preparation of reliable financial statements in accordance with [*applicable financial reporting framework, such as accounting principles generally accepted in the United States of America*]. An entity's internal control over financial reporting includes those policies and procedures that (1) pertain to the maintenance of records that, in reasonable detail, accurately and fairly reflect the transactions and dispositions of the assets of the entity; (2) provide reasonable assurance that transactions are recorded as necessary to permit preparation of financial statements in accordance with [*applicable financial reporting framework, such as accounting principles generally accepted in the United States of America*], and that receipts and expenditures of the entity are being made only in accordance with authorizations of management and those charged with governance; and (3) provide reasonable assurance regarding prevention, or timely detection and correction, of unauthorized acquisition, use, or disposition of the entity's assets that could have a material effect on the financial statements.

Because of its inherent limitations, internal control over financial reporting may not prevent, or detect and correct, misstatements. Also, projections of any evaluation of effectiveness to future periods are subject to the risk that controls may become inadequate because of changes in conditions, or that the degree of compliance with the policies or procedures may deteriorate.

In our opinion, the financial statements referred to above present fairly, in all material respects, the financial position of XYZ Company as of December 31, 20XX, and the results of its operations and its cash flows for the year then ended in conformity with accounting principles generally accepted in the United States of America. Also in our opinion, XYZ Company maintained, in all material respects, effective internal control over financial reporting as of December 31, 20XX, based on [*identify criteria*].

[*Signature*]

[*Date*]

Illustration 7. Communication of Significant Deficiencies and Material Weaknesses

In connection with our audit of XYZ Company's (the "Company") financial statements as of December 31, 20XX, and for the year then ended, and our audit of the Company's internal control over financial reporting as of December 31, 20XX ("integrated audit"), the standards established by the American Institute of Certified Public Accountants require that we advise you of the following internal control matters identified during our integrated audit.

Our responsibility is to plan and perform our integrated audit to obtain reasonable assurance about whether the financial statements are free of material misstatement, whether caused by error or by fraud, and whether effective internal control over financial reporting was maintained in all material respects (that is, whether material weaknesses exist as of the date specified in management's assertion). The integrated audit is not designed to detect deficiencies that, individually or in combination, are less severe than a material weakness. However, we are responsible for communicating to management and those charged with governance significant deficiencies and material weaknesses identified during the integrated audit. We are also responsible for communicating to management deficiencies that are of a lesser magnitude than a significant deficiency, unless previously communicated, and inform those charged with governance when such a communication was made.

A deficiency in internal control over financial reporting exists when the design or operation of a control does not allow management or employees, in the normal course of performing their assigned functions, to prevent, or detect and correct, misstatements on a timely basis. [*A material weakness is a deficiency, or a combination of deficiencies, in internal control over financial reporting, such that there is a reasonable possibility that a material misstatement of the Company's financial statements will not be prevented, or detected and corrected on a timely basis. We believe the following deficiencies constitute material weaknesses:*]

[*Describe the material weaknesses that were identified during the integrated audit. The auditor may separately identify those material weaknesses that exist as of the date of management's assertion by referring to the auditor's report.*]

[*A significant deficiency is a deficiency, or a combination of deficiencies, in internal control over financial reporting that is less severe than a material weakness, yet important enough to merit attention by those charged with governance. We consider the following deficiencies to be significant deficiencies:*]

[*Describe the significant deficiencies that were identified during the integrated audit.*]

This communication is intended solely for the information and use of management, [*identify the body or individuals charged with governance*], others within the organization, and [*identify any specified governmental authorities*] and is not intended to be and should not be used by anyone other than these specified parties.

Illustration 8. Management Report

Management's Report on Internal Control over Financial Reporting

XYZ Company's internal control over financial reporting is a process effected by those charged with governance, management, and other personnel, and designed to provide reasonable assurance regarding the preparation of reliable financial statements in accordance with [*applicable financial reporting framework, such as accounting principles generally accepted in the United States of America*]. An entity's internal control over financial reporting includes those policies and procedures that (1) pertain to the maintenance of records that, in reasonable detail, accurately and fairly reflect the transactions and dispositions of the assets of the entity; (2) provide reasonable assurance that transactions are recorded as necessary to permit preparation of financial statements in accordance with [*applicable financial reporting framework, such as accounting principles generally accepted in the United States of America*], and that receipts and expenditures of the entity are being made only in accordance with authorizations of management and those charged with governance; and (3) provide reasonable assurance regarding prevention, or timely detection and correction of unauthorized acquisition, use, or disposition of the entity's assets that could have a material effect on the financial statements.

Management is responsible for establishing and maintaining effective internal control over financial reporting. Management assessed the effectiveness of XYZ Company's internal control over financial reporting as of December 31, 20XX, based on the framework set forth by the Committee of Sponsoring Organizations of the Treadway Commission in *Internal Control—Integrated Framework.* Based on that assessment, management concluded that, as of December 31, 20XX, XYZ Company's internal control over financial reporting is effective based on the criteria established in *Internal Control—Integrated Framework.*

XYZ Company
[*Report signers, if applicable*]

[*Date*]

AT 601 Compliance Attestation

ORIGINAL PRONOUNCEMENT

Source	Statement on Standards for Attestation Engagements (SSAE) 10, *Attestation Standards: Revision and Recodification.*
Effective Date	This statement is currently effective.

TECHNICAL ALERT

In April 2016, the Auditing Standards Board (ASB) issued SSAE No. 18, *Attestation Standards: Clarification and Recodification.* SSAE No. 18 is effective for practitioners' reports dated on or after May 1, 2017. SSAE No. 18 is the culmination of the attestation clarity project, and it supersedes all of existing attestation standards except for:

- AT 501, whose content was moved to the auditing standards and codified as AU-C 940.
- AT 701, which will not be clarified, but retained in its current form because it is a rarely performed engagement. The section number has been changed to AT-C Section 395.

The clarified standards use the prefix "AT-C" and can be found in the AT-C chapters of this book.

APPLICABILITY

AT 601 is applicable to agreed-upon procedures related to either or both of the following:

1. Compliance with requirements of specified laws, regulations, rules, contracts, or grants (specified requirements)
2. The effectiveness of internal control over compliance with specified requirements

AT 601 also is applicable to engagements to examine the entity's compliance with specified requirements or a written assertion thereon.

The Statement does *not* apply to the following:

1. Audits performed in accordance with generally accepted auditing standards (GAAS)
2. Engagements to report in accordance with specific compliance requirements based solely on audit of financial statements, as addressed in AU-C Section 806, *Reporting on Compliance with Aspects of Contractual Agreements or Regulatory Requirements in Connection with Audited Financial Statements*
3. Engagements to report in accordance with AU-C Section 935, *Compliance Audits*
4. Engagements covered by AU-C Section 920, *Letters for Underwriters and Certain Other Requesting Parties* (comfort letters)

5. The report that encompasses the internal control over compliance for a broker or dealer in securities as required by Rule 17a-5 of the Securities Exchange Act of 1934

NOTE: An accountant is discouraged from accepting an engagement to examine the effectiveness of internal control over compliance or an assertion thereon because reasonable criteria for evaluation are typically not available. If such an engagement is accepted, the appropriate guidance is in AT 101 in American Institute of Certified Public Accountants (AICPA) publications (AT Section 101 herein). Additionally, AT 601 (AT Section 601 herein) may be helpful, but it is intended for reporting on internal control over financial reporting, not over compliance.

DEFINITIONS OF TERMS

Attestation risk.[1] The risk that the practitioner may unknowingly fail to modify appropriately his or her opinion. It is composed of inherent risk, control risk, and detection risk.

Control risk.[1] The risk that material noncompliance that could occur will not be prevented or detected on a timely basis by the entity's internal control.

Detection risk.[1] The risk that the practitioner's procedures will lead him or her to conclude that material noncompliance does not exist when, in fact, such noncompliance does exist.

Inherent risk.[1] The risk that material noncompliance with specified requirements could occur, assuming there are no related controls.

Internal control over compliance. The process by which management obtains reasonable assurance of compliance with specified requirements.

Specified requirements. A term that is used to refer to an entity's compliance with requirements of specified laws, regulations, rules, contracts, or grants.

OBJECTIVES OF AT SECTION 601

This SSAE provides guidance for engagements related to either (1) compliance with requirements of specified laws, regulations, rules, contracts, or grants (specified requirements) or (2) the effectiveness of internal control over compliance with specified requirements.

A practitioner may be engaged to perform agreed-upon procedures to assist users in evaluating management's written assertion about an entity's compliance with specified requirements, the effectiveness of internal control over compliance, or both. A practitioner also may be engaged to examine compliance with specified requirements or a written assertion thereon. For example, some electronic funds transfer associations or networks require their members who process transactions to complete a compliance exam.

This section clarifies that:

- The responsible party's refusal to furnish the required representations constitutes a limitation on the scope of the engagement.
- The responsible party's refusal to provide a written assertion as part of an examination engagement should cause the practitioner to withdraw from the engagement. (An exception exists if an examination of an entity's compliance with specified requirements is required by law or regulation. In this case, the practitioner should disclaim an opinion on

---

1 *Terms that are related to risk in an examination engagement.*

compliance unless he or she obtains evidential matter that warrants expressing an adverse opinion.)

- If the engagement is to perform agreed-upon procedures and:
  - The client is the responsible party, that party's refusal to provide an assertion requires that the practitioner withdraw from the engagement.
  - The client is not the responsible party, the practitioner is not required to withdraw, but should consider the effects of the refusal on the engagement and report.

REQUIREMENTS: GENERAL (APPLICABLE TO BOTH AGREED-UPON PROCEDURES AND EXAMINATION ENGAGEMENTS)

GENERAL

An engagement conducted in accordance with this section should comply with the general, fieldwork, and reporting standards in AT Section 101.

CRITERIA

The practitioner cannot accept an agreed-upon procedures or an examination engagement unless reasonable criteria have been established by a recognized body or are stated in or attached to the practitioner's report.

PROHIBITED ENGAGEMENTS

A practitioner should not accept an engagement to perform a review (see AT Section 101) about compliance with specified requirements or about the effectiveness of internal control over compliance or assertions thereon.

USING THE WORK OF A SPECIALIST

The practitioner should follow the guidance of AU-C Section 620, *Using the Work of an Auditor's Specialist*, if he or she decides that a specialist is necessary for an engagement covered by this section.

MANAGEMENT'S REPRESENTATIONS

According to AT 601.68, for both an agreed-upon procedures engagement and an examination engagement, the practitioner should obtain the responsible party's written representations that:

1. Acknowledge the responsible party's responsibility for complying with the specified requirements.
2. Acknowledge the responsible party's responsibility for establishing and maintaining effective internal control over compliance.
3. State that the responsible party has performed an evaluation of (1) the entity's compliance with specified requirements, or (2) the entity's internal controls for ensuring compliance and detecting noncompliance with requirements, as applicable.
4. State the responsible party's assertion about the entity's compliance with the specified requirements or about the effectiveness of the internal control over compliance, as applicable, based on the stated or established criteria.
5. State that the responsible party has disclosed to the practitioner all known noncompliance.

6. State that the responsible party has made available all documentation related to compliance with specified requirements.
7. State the responsible party's interpretation of any compliance requirements that have varying interpretations.
8. State that the responsible party has disclosed any communications from regulatory agencies, internal auditors, and other practitioners concerning possible noncompliance with the specified requirements, including communications received between the end of the period addressed in the written assertion and the date of the practitioner's report.
9. State that the responsible party has disclosed any known noncompliance occurring subsequent to the period for which, or date as of which, the responsible party selects to make its assertion.

AU-C Section 580, *Written Representations*, provides guidance on the dating and signatories of the representation letter.

The responsible party's refusal to furnish the required representations is a scope limitation. In an examination engagement, the practitioner ordinarily should disclaim an opinion or withdraw. However, based on the nature of the representations or circumstances, a qualified opinion may be appropriate.

In an agreed-upon procedures engagement in which the practitioner's client is the responsible party, the responsible party's refusal to provide written assertions is a scope limitation sufficient to cause the practitioner to withdraw. When the practitioner's client is not the responsible party, the practitioner:

- Is not required to withdraw, but should consider the effects of the responsible party's refusal on his or her report, as well as the ability to rely on other representations of the responsible party.
- May also want to obtain written representations from the client (e.g., knowledge of any noncompliance).

Other Information in a Client-Prepared Document

The practitioner's report on either compliance with specified requirements or the effectiveness of internal control over compliance or written assertions thereon may be included in a client-prepared document that includes other information. In those circumstances, the practitioner should read the other information and follow the procedures discussed in Section 101.

REQUIREMENTS: AGREED-UPON PROCEDURES ENGAGEMENT

Conditions for Acceptance

A practitioner may accept an agreed-upon procedures engagement related to an entity's compliance with specified requirements or the effectiveness of internal control over compliance, if the responsible party:

1. Accepts responsibility for the entity's compliance with specified requirements and the effectiveness of the entity's internal control over compliance.
2. Evaluates the entity's compliance with specified requirements or the effectiveness of the entity's internal control over compliance.

In addition, the conditions that apply to acceptance of all agreed-upon procedures engagements have to be met (see AT Section 201).

NOTE: A written management representation letter is required in agreed-upon procedures engagements relating to compliance matters.

The practitioner should obtain a written assertion about compliance with specified requirements or internal control over compliance from the responsible party. The written assertion may be provided in the representation letter or in a separate report accompanying the practitioner's report. If the client is the responsible party, that party's refusal to provide an assertion requires that the practitioner withdraw from the engagement. If the engagement is required by law or regulation withdrawal is *not* required. If the client is not the responsible party, the practitioner does not have to withdraw but should consider the effects of the refusal on the engagement and report.

Understanding with Specified Parties

The specified parties should participate in establishing the procedures to be performed and take responsibility for the adequacy of those procedures. The practitioner should determine whether the specified parties understand the procedures to be performed by discussing the nature of management's assertion and the procedures with the specified parties (see "Techniques for Application").

Understanding the Specified Compliance Requirements

The practitioner should obtain an understanding of the specified compliance requirements stated in management's assertion. To obtain this understanding, the practitioner should consider the following:

1. Laws, regulations, rules, contracts, and grants relevant to the specified compliance requirements
2. Knowledge about the specified compliance requirements obtained from the following:
    a. Prior engagements and regulatory reports
    b. Discussions with appropriate individuals within the entity
    c. Discussions with appropriate individuals outside the entity, such as regulators or specialists

Scope Restrictions

The practitioner should attempt to obtain agreement from the specified parties for modification of the agreed-upon procedures if circumstances impose restrictions on the scope of those procedures. If an agreement for modification cannot be obtained, the practitioner should describe the restrictions in the attestation report or withdraw from the engagement.

Subsequent Events

If the practitioner becomes aware of noncompliance related to management's assertion that occurs after the period addressed by that assertion but before the date of the report, he or she should consider including that information in the report. According to AT 601.24, the practitioner has no obligation to perform procedures to detect noncompliance in the subsequent period.

PRACTITIONER'S REPORT

The practitioner's report on agreed-upon procedures on an entity's compliance with specified requirements or about the effectiveness of an entity's internal control over compliance should be in the form of procedures and findings. The report should be dated as of the date of completion of the agreed-upon procedures. According to AT 601.24, the practitioner's report should contain the following elements:

1. A title that includes the word *independent*
2. Identification of the specified parties
3. Identification of the subject matter of the engagement (or management's assertion thereon), including the period or point in time addressed,[2] and a reference to the character of the engagement
4. An identification of the responsible party
5. A statement that the subject matter is the responsibility of responsible party
6. A statement that the procedures, which were agreed to by the specified parties identified in the report, were performed to assist the specified parties in evaluating the entity's compliance with the specified requirements or the effectiveness of its internal control over compliance
7. A statement that the agreed-upon procedures engagement was conducted in accordance with attestation standards established by the AICPA
8. A statement that the sufficiency of the procedures is solely the responsibility of the specified parties and a disclaimer of responsibility for the sufficiency of those procedures
9. A list of the procedures performed (or reference thereto) and related findings. The practitioner should not provide negative assurance
10. Where applicable, a description of any agreed-upon materiality limits
11. A statement that the practitioner was not engaged to and did not conduct an examination of the entity's compliance with specified requirements or about the effectiveness of an entity's internal control over compliance, a disclaimer of opinion thereon, and a statement that if the practitioner had performed additional procedures, other matters might have come to his or her attention that would have been reported
12. A statement restricting the use of the report to the specified parties (however, if the report is a matter of public record, the practitioner should include the following sentence: "However, this report is a matter of public record and its distribution is not limited.")
13. Where applicable, reservations or restrictions concerning procedures or findings
14. Where applicable, a description of the nature of the assistance provided by the specialist
15. The manual or printed signature of the practitioner's firm
16. The date of the report

REQUIREMENTS: EXAMINATION ENGAGEMENT

CONDITIONS FOR ENGAGEMENT PERFORMANCE

According to AT 601.10, a practitioner may accept an examination engagement related to an entity's compliance with specified requirements if the following conditions are met:

---

[2] *Generally, management's assertion about compliance with specified requirements will address a period of time, whereas an assertion about internal control over compliance will address a point in time.*

1. The responsible party accepts responsibility for the entity's compliance with specified requirements and the effectiveness of the entity's internal control over compliance.
2. The responsible party evaluates the entity's compliance with specified requirements.
3. Sufficient evidential matter exists or could be developed to support the responsible party's evaluation.

A practitioner may examine the effectiveness of the entity's internal control over compliance or an assertion thereon only if he or she has reason to believe that the subject matter is capable of reasonably consistent evaluation against criteria that are suitable and available to users. If such criteria exist for internal control over compliance, the practitioner should perform the engagement in accordance with AT Section 101. AT Section 501 may also be helpful on such an engagement.

The practitioner should obtain a written assertion about compliance with specified requirements or internal control over compliance from the responsible party. The written assertion may be provided in a representation letter to the practitioner or in a separate report accompanying the practitioner's report. The responsible party's written assertion may take various forms but should be specific enough that users having competence in and using the same or similar measurement and disclosure criteria ordinarily would be able to arrive at materially similar conclusions.

The responsible party's refusal to provide a written assertion as part of an examination engagement should cause the practitioner to withdraw from the engagement, regardless of whether the client is the responsible party. An exception exists if an examination of an entity's compliance with specified requirements is required by law or regulation. In this case, the practitioner should disclaim an opinion on compliance unless he or she obtains evidential matter that warrants expressing an adverse opinion. If the practitioner expresses an adverse opinion and the responsible party does not provide an assertion, the practitioner's report should be restricted.

Extent of Evidence

To express an opinion on an entity's compliance (or assertion related thereto), the practitioner should accumulate sufficient evidence about the entity's compliance with specified requirements and limit attestation risk to an appropriately low level.

Assessment of Inherent Risk

The practitioner should consider factors affecting inherent risk similar to the factors an auditor would consider when planning an audit of financial statements (see AU-C Section 240, *Consideration of Fraud in a Financial Statement Audit*). According to AT 601.33, in addition, the practitioner should consider the following factors:

1. The complexity of the specified compliance requirements
2. The length of time the entity has been subject to the specified compliance requirements
3. Prior experience with the entity's compliance
4. Potential impact of noncompliance

Assessment of Control Risk

The practitioner should assess control risk. To assess control risk for compliance with specified requirements and to plan the engagement, the practitioner should obtain an understanding of those parts of the internal control related to compliance.

Engagement Procedures

According to AT 601.39, in an examination of the entity's compliance with specified requirements, the practitioner should do the following:

1. Obtain an understanding of the specified compliance requirements.
2. Plan the engagement.
3. Consider relevant portions of the entity's internal control over compliance.
4. Obtain sufficient evidence including testing compliance with specified requirements.
5. Consider subsequent events.
6. Form an opinion about whether the entity complied, in all material respects, with specified requirements (or whether the responsible party's assertion about such compliance is fairly stated in all material respects) based on the specified criteria.

Subsequent Events

The practitioner should consider information about subsequent events that comes to his or her attention between the end of the period addressed by the practitioner's report and prior to the issuance of the report.

The practitioner has no responsibility to detect noncompliance after the period being reported on but before the date of the report. However, if the practitioner becomes aware of this type of noncompliance, and its nature and significance may make management's assertion misleading, the practitioner should include in the report an explanatory paragraph describing the nature of the noncompliance.

Practitioner's Report

According to AT 601.55, the practitioner's report on an examination, which is ordinarily addressed to the entity, should include the following:

1. A title that includes the word *independent*
2. An identification of the specified compliance requirements, including the period covered, and of the responsible party[3]
3. A statement that compliance with the specified requirements is the responsibility of the entity's management
4. A statement that the practitioner's responsibility is to express an opinion on the entity's compliance with those requirements based on his or her examination
5. A statement that the examination was conducted in accordance with attestation standards established by the AICPA and, accordingly, included examining, on a test basis, evidence about the entity's compliance with those requirements and performing such other procedures as the practitioner considered necessary in the circumstances
6. A statement that the practitioner believes the examination provides a reasonable basis for his or her opinion
7. A statement that the examination does not provide a legal determination on the entity's compliance
8. The practitioner's opinion on whether the entity complied, in all material respects, with specified requirements based on the specified criteria

---

[3] *A practitioner also may be engaged to report an entity's compliance with specified requirements as of a point in time. In this case, the reports in "Illustrations" should be adapted as appropriate.*

9. A statement restricting the use of the report to the specified parties when the criteria used to evaluate compliance:
   a. Are determined by the practitioner to be appropriate only for a limited number of parties who either participated in establishing the criteria or who can be assumed to have an adequate understanding of the criteria
   b. Are available only to specified parties
10. The manual or printed signature of the practitioner's firm
11. The date of the examination report

The practitioner's report should be dated as of the date of completion of the examination procedures.

REPORT MODIFICATIONS

The practitioner should modify the standard report whenever any one of the following conditions exist:

1. There is material noncompliance with specified requirements (qualified or adverse opinion).
2. The scope of the engagement is restricted (qualified or disclaimer of opinion).
3. The practitioner refers to the report of another practitioner as the basis, in part, for the report (see Illustration 5 in AT Section 501).

INTERPRETATIONS

There are no interpretations for this section.

TECHNIQUES FOR APPLICATION

PLANNING THE ENGAGEMENT—GENERAL

For either an agreed-upon procedures engagement or an examination, the practitioner should properly plan the engagement. In planning the engagement, the practitioner should consider doing the following:

1. Discuss the purpose of the engagement with management.
2. Read or obtain an understanding of relevant laws and documents.
3. Obtain an engagement letter.
4. Design a program of procedures to be applied.

AGREED-UPON PROCEDURES ENGAGEMENT

In this type of engagement, the practitioner should try to meet with the specified parties or a representative of the specified parties to establish the procedures. If a meeting is not possible, the practitioner should do one of the following:

1. Compare the procedures to be applied to written requirements of the specified parties.
2. Review relevant contracts with or correspondence from the specified parties.
3. Distribute a draft of the anticipated report or a copy of a proposed engagement letter to the specified parties with a request for their comments.

4. Discuss the procedures to be applied with appropriate representatives of the specified parties involved.

The manner in which the procedures are established should be documented in the practitioner's workpapers.

At the conclusion of this type of engagement, the practitioner should obtain a management representation letter. If the management refuses, the practitioner should withdraw from the engagement.

Planning the Examination Engagement

The practitioner should consider the following when planning the engagement:

1. For an entity with multiple components, determine if it is necessary to examine all components for compliance. In making this determination, consider:
    a. To what degree do the specified compliance requirements apply at the component level?
    b. What are our judgments about materiality?
    c. How centralized are the records?
    d. How effective is the control environment, particularly management's direct control over the exercise of authority delegated to others and its ability to supervise activities at various locations effectively?
    e. What are the nature and extent of operations conducted at the various components?
    f. How similar are controls over compliance for different components?
2. Determine the need to use the work of a specialist (see AU-C Section 620, *Using the Work of an Auditor's Specialist*).
3. Identify the existence of an internal audit function and the extent to which internal auditors are involved in monitoring compliance with specified requirements (see AU-C Section 610, *The Auditor's Consideration of the Internal Audit Function in an Audit of Financial Statements*).
4. Obtain an understanding of the parts of the internal control related to compliance with the specified requirements. This understanding may be obtained by:
    a. Inquiries
    b. Inspection of documents
    c. Observation of activities
5. Identify types of potential noncompliance.
6. Assess control risk. If the practitioner wishes to assess control risk below the maximum, he or she should perform tests of controls.

Examination Procedures

The nature of procedures and the sufficiency of evidence are matters of practitioner judgment. Procedures to be considered include the following:

1. For engagements involving regulatory requirements:
    a. Review communication between regulatory agencies and the entity.
    b. Review examination reports of the regulatory agencies.
    c. If appropriate, make inquiries of regulatory agencies including inquiries about examinations in progress.
    d. Make inquiries of entity's outside and inside counsel responsible for such matters.

2. Identify subsequent events for the period from the reporting period to the date of the report that would provide evidence about compliance during the period under examination. Information concerning subsequent events would be obtained from the following sources:
   a. Relevant internal auditors' reports issued during the subsequent period
   b. Other practitioners' reports identifying noncompliance, issued during the subsequent period
   c. Regulatory agencies' reports on the entity's noncompliance, issued during the subsequent period
   d. Information about the entity's noncompliance, obtained through other professional engagements for that entity
3. If the specified requirements relate to financial statement matters, compare the relevant parts of these statements with the specified requirements.
4. Obtain a management representation letter. If management refuses, the practitioner should consider issuing a qualified opinion or a disclaimer of opinion.

MATERIALITY

Materiality in an examination of compliance differs from materiality in an audit. In an examination, the practitioner should consider the:

1. Nature of the compliance requirements, which may or may not be quantifiable in monetary terms.
2. Nature and frequency of noncompliance, including sampling risks.
3. Qualitative considerations, including user needs and expectations.

ILLUSTRATIONS

The following illustrations are adapted from SSAE 10 (AT Section 601).

ILLUSTRATION 1. AGREED-UPON PROCEDURES REPORT IN WHICH THE PROCEDURES AND FINDINGS CONCERNING COMPLIANCE WITH SPECIFIED REQUIREMENTS ARE ENUMERATED[4]

To the Board of Directors of Widget Company
Main City, USA

Independent Accountant's Report on Applying Agreed-Upon Procedures

We have performed the procedures enumerated below, which were agreed to by [*list specified parties*], solely to assist the specified parties in evaluating Widget Company's compliance with [*list specified requirements*] during the year ended December 31, 20X1. Management is responsible for Widget Company's compliance with those requirements. This agreed-upon procedures engagement was

4 *In some agreed-upon procedures engagements, the practitioner may issue one report on a combined management assertion about compliance with specified requirements and the effectiveness of internal control over compliance. The practitioner's combined report should address both specified requirements and internal control over compliance.*

performed in accordance with attestation standards established by the American Institute of Certified Public Accountants. The sufficiency of these procedures is solely the responsibility of the parties specified in this report. Consequently, we make no representation regarding the sufficiency of the procedures described below either for the purpose for which this report has been requested or for any other purpose.

[*Include paragraphs to enumerate procedures and findings.*]

We were not engaged to, and did not, perform an examination, the objective of which would be the expression of an opinion on compliance. Accordingly, we do not express such an opinion. Had we performed additional procedures, other matters might have come to our attention that would have been reported to you.

This report is intended solely for the information and use of [*list or refer to specified parties*] and is not intended to be and should not be used by anyone other than these specified parties.

Smith and Jones
February 15, 20X2

ILLUSTRATION 2. AGREED-UPON PROCEDURES REPORT IN WHICH THE PROCEDURES AND FINDINGS CONCERNING THE EFFECTIVENESS OF INTERNAL CONTROL OVER COMPLIANCE ARE ENUMERATED[5]

To the Board of Directors of Widget Company
Main City, USA

Independent Accountant's Report on Applying Agreed-Upon Procedures

We have performed the procedures enumerated below, which were agreed to by [*list specified parties of report*], solely to assist the specified parties in evaluating the effectiveness of Widget Company's internal control over compliance with [*list specified requirements*] as of December 31, 20X1. Management is responsible for Widget Company's internal control over compliance with those requirements. This agreed-upon procedures engagement was performed in accordance with attestation standards established by the American Institute of Certified Public Accountants. The sufficiency of these procedures is solely the responsibility of the parties specified in the report. Consequently, we make no representation regarding the sufficiency of the procedures described below either for the purpose for which this report has been requested or for any other purpose.

[*Include paragraphs to enumerate procedures and findings.*]

We were not engaged to, and did not, perform an examination, the objective of which would be the expression of an opinion on the effectiveness of internal control over compliance. Accordingly, we do not express such an opinion. Had we performed additional procedures, other matters might have come to our attention that would have been reported to you.

This report is intended solely for the information and use of [*list or refer to specified parties*] and is not intended to be and should not be used by anyone other than these specified parties.

Smith and Jones
February 15, 20X2

---

[5] *In some agreed-upon procedures engagements, the practitioner may issue one report on a combined management assertion about compliance with specified requirements and the effectiveness of internal control over compliance. The practitioner's combined report should address both specified requirements and internal control over compliance.*

Illustration 3. Examination Report Expressing an Opinion on Compliance with Specified Requirements

To the Board of Directors of Widget Company
Main City, USA

Independent Accountant's Report

We have examined Widget Company's compliance with [*list specified compliance requirements*] during the year ended December 31, 20X1. Management is responsible for Widget Company's compliance with those requirements. Our responsibility is to express an opinion on Widget Company's compliance based on our examination.

Our examination was conducted in accordance with attestation standards established by the American Institute of Certified Public Accountants and, accordingly, included examining, on a test basis, evidence about Widget Company's compliance with those requirements and performing such other procedures as we considered necessary in the circumstances. We believe that our examination provides a reasonable basis for our opinion. Our examination does not provide a legal determination on Widget Company's compliance with specified requirements.

In our opinion, Widget Company complied in all material respects with the aforementioned requirements for the year ended December 31, 20X1.

Smith and Jones
February 15, 20X2

Illustration 4. Examination Report When Expressing an Opinion on Management's Assertion about Compliance with Specified Requirements

To the Board of Directors of Widget Company
Main City, USA

Independent Accountant's Report

We have examined management's assertion, included in the accompanying [*title of management report*], that Widget Company complied with [*list specified compliance requirements*] during the year ended December 31, 20X1. Management is responsible for Widget Company's compliance with those requirements. Our responsibility is to express an opinion on management's assertion about Widget Company's compliance based on our examination.

Our examination was conducted in accordance with attestation standards established by the American Institute of Certified Public Accountants and, accordingly, included examining, on a test basis, evidence about Widget Company's compliance with those requirements and performing such other procedures as we considered necessary in the circumstances. We believe that our examination provides a reasonable basis for our opinion. Our examination does not provide a legal determination on Widget Company's compliance with specified requirements.

In our opinion, management's assertion that Widget Company complied with the aforementioned requirements during the year ended December 31, 20X1 is fairly stated, in all material respects.

Smith and Jones
February 15, 20X2

Illustration 5. Modified Report When Practitioner Has Identified Material Noncompliance and Management Has Appropriately Modified Its Assertion

To the Board of Directors of Widget Company
Main City, USA

Independent Accountant's Report

We have examined Widget Company's compliance with [*list specified compliance requirements*] for the year ended December 31, 20X1. Management is responsible for compliance with those requirements. Our responsibility is to express an opinion on Widget Company's compliance based on our examination.

Our examination was conducted in accordance with attestation standards established by the American Institute of Certified Public Accountants and, accordingly, included examining, on a test basis, evidence about Widget Company's compliance with those requirements and performing such other procedures as we considered necessary in the circumstances. We believe that our examination provides a reasonable basis for our opinion. Our examination does not provide a legal determination on Widget Company's compliance with specified requirements.

Our examination disclosed the following material noncompliance with [*type of compliance requirement*] applicable to Widget Company during the year ended December 31, 20X1. [*Describe noncompliance.*]

In our opinion, except for the material noncompliance described in the third paragraph, Widget Company complied, in all material respects, with the aforementioned requirements for the year ended December 31, 20X1.

Smith and Jones
February 15, 20X2

Illustration 6. Adverse Report When Practitioner Has Identified Material Noncompliance and Management Has Appropriately Modified Its Assertion

To the Board of Directors of Widget Company
Main City, USA

Independent Accountant's Report

We have examined Widget Company's compliance with [*list of specified compliance requirements*] for the [*period*] ended [*date*]. Management is responsible for compliance with these requirements. Our responsibility is to express an opinion on Widget Company's compliance based on our examination.

Our examination was conducted in accordance with attestation standards established by the American Institute of Certified Public Accountants and, accordingly, included examining, on a test basis, evidence about Widget Company's compliance with those requirements and performing such other procedures as we considered necessary in the circumstances. We believe that our examination provides a reasonable basis for our opinion. Our examination does not provide a legal determination on Widget Company's compliance with specified requirements.

Our examination disclosed the following material noncompliance with [*type of compliance requirement*] applicable to Widget Company during the [*period*] ended [*date*]. [*Describe noncompliance.*]

In our opinion, because of the effect of the noncompliance described in the third paragraph, Widget Company has not complied with the aforementioned requirements for the [*period*] ended [*date*].

Smith and Jones
February 15, 20X2

AT 701 Management's Discussion and Analysis (MD&A)—A Summary[1]

ORIGINAL PRONOUNCEMENT

Source Statement on Standards for Attestation Engagements (SSAE) 10, *Attestation Standards: Revision and Recodification.*

TECHNICAL ALERT

In April 2016, the Auditing Standards Board (ASB) issued SSAE No. 18, *Attestation Standards: Clarification and Recodification.* SSAE No. 18 is effective for practitioners' reports dated on or after May 1, 2017. SSAE No. 18 is the culmination of the attestation clarity project, and it supersedes all of existing attestation standards except for:

- AT 501, whose content was moved to the auditing standards and codified as AU-C 940.
- AT 701, which will not be clarified, but retained in its current form because it is a rarely performed engagement. The section number has been changed to AT-C Section 395.

The clarified standards use the prefix "AT-C" and can be found in the AT-C chapters of this book.

APPLICABILITY

AT 701 applies when a practitioner is engaged by a public entity that prepares Management's Discussion and Analysis (MD&A) in accordance with the rules and regulations adopted by the Securities and Exchange Commission (SEC) (or a nonpublic entity following the same requirements) to either perform an examination or review of MD&A. A practitioner engaged to perform agreed-upon procedures on MD&A should follow the guidance in Section 201.

[1] *The SSAE on examination or review of MD&A is essentially a detailed manual on how to perform examinations and reviews, and only the highlights are summarized here. A practitioner seeking to provide these services should refer to SSAE 10 and the SEC's rules and regulations on MD&A. Only the considerations for a public entity are covered here. The considerations for a nonpublic entity are very similar because only the SEC has, at this point, issued rules and regulations that provide guidance on the presentation of MD&A.*

DEFINITION OF TERM

MD&A. Management's Discussion and Analysis of Financial Condition and Results of Operations adopted by the SEC and found in Item 303 of Regulation S-K, as interpreted by Financial Reporting Release (FRR) 36.

OBJECTIVES OF AT SECTION 701

The SEC adopted requirements for MD&A in 1974 to have management provide a narrative explanation of the financial statements. The idea was to allow the user to see the company's financial position and operating results through management's eyes.

Two levels of service are possible—an examination or a review. A review report is restricted as to use and is not intended to be filed with the SEC. An examination report is intended for general use, but at this stage, whether there will be a significant demand for this service is unknown. The SEC does not require a practitioner's report on MD&A—the narrative presentation is management's responsibility and not a part of the audited financial statements.

According to AT 701.05, the practitioner's objective in an examination of MD&A is to express an opinion on the presentation taken as a whole by reporting whether:

1. The presentation includes, in all material respects, the required elements of the rules and regulations adopted by the SEC.
2. The historical financial amounts included in the presentation have been accurately derived, in all material respects, from the entity's financial statements.
3. The underlying information, determinations, estimates, and assumptions of the entity provide a reasonable basis for the disclosures contained in the presentation.

The objective of a review of MD&A is to provide negative assurance on these three items.

NOTE: "Negative assurance" indicates that no information came to the accountant's attention that would cause him or her not to believe the three statements.

An examination of MD&A would generally be expected to relate to the MD&A for annual periods, but a review might relate to the MD&A for annual or interim periods or some combination.

In an examination, the practitioner seeks to obtain reasonable assurance by accumulating sufficient evidence to support the disclosures and assumptions, thus limiting attestation risk to an appropriately low level. A review consists principally of applying analytical procedures and making inquiries and does not provide assurance that a practitioner would become aware of all significant matters that would be disclosed in an examination.

SSAE 10 made only minor changes to this section, including modifying the reports in this section to conform to changes made by Statement on Auditing Standards (SAS) 93, *Omnibus Statement on Auditing Standards—2000.*

REQUIREMENTS: EXAMINATION

ACCEPTANCE

To accept an engagement to examine MD&A, the practitioner should audit the financial statements for at least the latest period to which the MD&A presentation relates and the financial statements for the other periods covered by the MD&A presentation should have been audited by the practitioner or a predecessor auditor.

PERFORMANCE

According to AT 701.41, the practitioner should do the following:

1. Obtain an understanding of the rules and regulations adopted by the SEC for MD&A and management's method of preparing MD&A.
2. Plan the engagement by developing an overall strategy considering factors such as matters affecting the entity's industry and similar knowledge obtained during the audit of financial statements.
3. Consider relevant portions of internal control applicable to the preparation of MD&A.
4. Obtain sufficient evidence, including testing completeness, by comparing the content of the MD&A to the information obtained in the audit of financial statements and considering whether the explanations in the MD&A are consistent with this information.
5. Consider the effect of events subsequent to the balance sheet date by extending subsequent events review procedures in the audit to the MD&A information.
6. Obtain written representations from management concerning its responsibility for MD&A, completeness of minutes, events subsequent to the balance sheet date, and other matters the practitioner considers relevant to the MD&A presentation.
7. Form an opinion about whether the MD&A presentation meets the objectives for an opinion on such a presentation.

REPORTING

The financial statements for the periods covered by the MD&A presentation and the related auditors' report should accompany the presentation or be incorporated by reference to information filed with a regulatory agency.

The report should include the elements as found in the example in Illustration 1.

REQUIREMENTS: REVIEW

ACCEPTANCE

A practitioner may accept an engagement to review an MD&A presentation for an annual period under the same circumstances as an examination.

To accept an engagement to review the MD&A presentation for an interim period, both of the following points should occur:

1. The practitioner should either:

   a. Review and report on the historical financial statements for the related comparative interim periods or
   b. Audit the interim financial statements.

2. The practitioner or a predecessor auditor either has already examined or will examine the MD&A presentation for the most recent fiscal year.

PERFORMANCE

According to AT 701.76, the practitioner should do the following:

1. Obtain an understanding of the rules and regulations adopted by the SEC for MD&A and management's method of preparing MD&A.
2. Plan the engagement, considering factors such as matters affecting the industry, the types of information management reports to external analysts, and matters identified during the audit or review of historical financial statements.
3. Consider relevant portions of the entity's internal control applicable to the MD&A.
4. Apply analytical procedures and make inquiries of management and others.
5. Consider the effects of events subsequent to the balance sheet date.
6. Obtain written representations from management.
7. Form a conclusion as to whether any information came to the practitioner's attention that would cause him or her to believe the objectives related to the MD&A presentation were not achieved.

REPORTING

The financial statements for the periods covered by the MD&A presentation and the related auditors' or accountants' reports should accompany the presentation or be incorporated by reference to information filed with a regulatory agency.

The report should include the elements as found in the examples in Illustrations 2 and 3.

INTERPRETATIONS

There are no interpretations for this section.

ILLUSTRATIONS

The following reports are adapted from SSAE 10:[2]

1. An illustration of the wording of a standard examination report
2. A standard review report on an annual MD&A presentation
3. A standard review report on an MD&A presentation for an interim period

ILLUSTRATION 1. STANDARD EXAMINATION REPORT

Report of Independent Registered Public Accounting Firm

To the Audit Committee, Board of Directors, and Shareholders
Widget Company
Main City, USA

We have examined Widget Company's Management's Discussion and Analysis taken as a whole, included [*incorporated by reference*] in the Company's [*insert description of registration*

[2] *If the entity is a nonissuer and complies with GAAS rather than the standards of the PCAOB, the references in the report to the PCAOB's standards should be changed to refer to "auditing standards generally accepted in the United States of America" and "attestation standards established by the American Institute of Certified Public Accountants."*

statement or document]. Management is responsible for the preparation of the Company's Management's Discussion and Analysis pursuant to the rules and regulations adopted by the Securities and Exchange Commission. Our responsibility is to express an opinion on the presentation based on our examination. We have audited, in accordance with the standards of the Public Company Accounting Oversight Board (United States), the financial statements of Widget Company as of December 31, 20X2 and 20X1, and for each of the years in the three-year period ended December 31, 20X2; in our report dated February 15, 20X3, we expressed an unqualified opinion on those financial statements.[3]

Our examination of Management's Discussion and Analysis was conducted in accordance with attestation standards established by the Public Company Accounting Oversight Board and, accordingly, included examining, on a test basis, evidence supporting the historical amounts and disclosures in the presentation. An examination also includes assessing the significant determinations made by management as to the relevancy of information to be included and the estimates and assumptions that affect reported information. We believe that our examination provides a reasonable basis for our opinion.

The preparation of Management's Discussion and Analysis requires management to interpret the criteria, make determinations as to the relevancy of information to be included, and make estimates and assumptions that affect reported information. Management's Discussion and Analysis includes information regarding the estimated future impact of transactions and events that have occurred or are expected to occur, expected sources of liquidity and capital resources, operating trends, commitments, and uncertainties. Actual results in the future may differ materially from management's present assessment of this information because events and circumstances frequently do not occur as expected.[4]

In our opinion, the Company's presentation of Management's Discussion and Analysis includes, in all material respects, the required elements of the rules and regulations adopted by the Securities and Exchange Commission; the historical financial amounts included therein have been accurately derived,

---

3 *If prior financial statements were audited by other auditors, this sentence would be replaced by the following*:

We have audited, in accordance with the standards of the Public Company Accounting Oversight Board (United States), the financial statements of Widget Company as of and for the year ended December 31, 20X2, and in our report dated Month XX, 20X3, we expressed an unqualified opinion on those financial statements. The financial statements of Widget Company as of December 31, 20X1, and for each of the years in the two-year period then ended were audited by other auditors, whose report dated Month XX, 20X2, expressed an unqualified opinion on those financial statements.

If the practitioner's opinion on the financial statements is based on the report of other auditors, this sentence would be replaced by the following:

We have audited, in accordance with the standards of the Public Company Accounting Oversight Board (United States), the financial statements of Widget Company as of December 31, 20X2 and 20X1, and for each of the years in the three-year period ended December 31, 20X2, and in our report dated Month XX, 20X3, we expressed an unqualified opinion on those financial statements based on our audits and the report of other auditors.

4 *The following sentence should be added to the beginning of the explanatory paragraph if the entity is a nonpublic entity*:

Although Widget Company is not subject to the rules and regulations of the Securities and Exchange Commission, the accompanying Management's Discussion and Analysis is intended to be a presentation in accordance with the rules and regulations adopted by the Securities and Exchange Commission.

in all material respects, from the Company's financial statements; and the underlying information, determinations, estimates, and assumptions of the Company provide a reasonable basis for the disclosures contained therein.

Smith and Jones
March 1, 20X3

ILLUSTRATION 2. STANDARD REVIEW REPORT ON AN ANNUAL MD&A PRESENTATION

Report of Independent Registered Public Accounting Firm

To the Board of Directors
Widget Company
Main City, USA

We have reviewed Widget Company's Management's Discussion and Analysis taken as a whole, included [*incorporated by reference*] in the Company's [*insert description of registration statement or document*]. Management is responsible for the preparation of the Company's Management's Discussion and Analysis pursuant to the rules and regulations adopted by the Securities and Exchange Commission. We have audited, in accordance with the standards of the Public Company Accounting Oversight Board (United States), the financial statements of Widget Company as of December 31, 20X2 and 20X1, and for each of the years in the three-year period ended December 31, 20X2, and in our report dated February 15, 20X3, we expressed an unqualified opinion on those financial statements.

We conducted our review of Management's Discussion and Analysis in accordance with attestation standards established by the Public Company Accounting Oversight Board. A review of Management's Discussion and Analysis consists principally of applying analytical procedures and making inquiries of persons responsible for financial, accounting, and operational matters. It is substantially less in scope than an examination, the objective of which is the expression of an opinion on the presentation. Accordingly, we do not express such an opinion.

The preparation of Management's Discussion and Analysis requires management to interpret the criteria, make determinations as to the relevancy of information to be included, and make estimates and assumptions that affect reported information. Management's Discussion and Analysis includes information regarding the estimated future impact of transactions and events that have occurred or are expected to occur, expected sources of liquidity and capital resources, operating trends, commitments, and uncertainties. Actual results in the future may differ materially from management's present assessment of this information because events and circumstances frequently do not occur as expected.[5]

Based on our review, nothing came to our attention that caused us to believe that the Company's presentation of Management's Discussion and Analysis does not include, in all material respects, the required elements of the rules and regulations adopted by the Securities and Exchange Commission; that

---

5 *The following sentence should be added to the beginning of the explanatory paragraph if the entity is a nonpublic entity*:

Although Widget Company is not subject to the rules and regulations of the Securities and Exchange Commission, the accompanying Management's Discussion and Analysis is intended to be a presentation in accordance with the rules and regulations adopted by the Securities and Exchange Commission.

the historical financial amounts included therein have not been accurately derived, in all material respects, from the Company's financial statements; or that the underlying information, determinations, estimates, and assumptions of the Company do not provide a reasonable basis for the disclosures contained therein.

This report is intended solely for the information and use of [*list or refer to the specified parties*] and is not intended to be, and should not be, used by anyone other than the specified parties.

Smith and Jones
March 1, 20X3

ILLUSTRATION 3. STANDARD REVIEW REPORT ON AN INTERIM MD&A PRESENTATION

Report of Independent Registered Public Accounting Firm

To the Audit Committee, Board of Directors, and Shareholders
Widget Company
Main City, USA

We have reviewed Widget Company's Management's Discussion and Analysis taken as a whole, included in the Company's [*insert description of registration statement or document*]. Management is responsible for the preparation of the Company's Management's Discussion and Analysis pursuant to the rules and regulations adopted by the Securities and Exchange Commission. We have reviewed, in accordance with the standards of the Public Company Accounting Oversight Board, the interim financial information of Widget Company as of June 30, 20X3 and 20X2, and for the three-month and six-month periods then ended and have issued our report thereon dated July 15, 20X3.

We conducted our review of Management's Discussion and Analysis in accordance with attestation standards established by the Public Company Accounting Oversight Board. A review of Management's Discussion and Analysis consists principally of applying analytical procedures and making inquiries of persons responsible for financial, accounting, and operational matters. It is substantially less in scope than an examination, the objective of which is the expression of an opinion on the presentation. Accordingly, we do not express such an opinion.

The preparation of Management's Discussion and Analysis requires management to interpret the criteria, make determinations as to the relevancy of information to be included, and make estimates and assumptions that affect reported information. Management's Discussion and Analysis includes information regarding the estimated future impact of transactions and events that have occurred or are expected to occur, expected sources of liquidity and capital resources, operating trends, commitments, and uncertainties. Actual results in the future may differ materially from management's present assessment of this information because events and circumstances frequently do not occur as expected.[6]

Based on our review, nothing came to our attention that caused us to believe that the Company's presentation of Management's Discussion and Analysis does not include, in all material respects, the

---

6 *The following sentence should be added to the beginning of the explanatory paragraph if the entity is a nonpublic entity:*

Although Widget Company is not subject to the rules and regulations of the Securities and Exchange Commission, the accompanying Management's Discussion and Analysis is intended to be a presentation in accordance with the rules and regulations adopted by the Securities and Exchange Commission.

required elements of the rules and regulations adopted by the Securities and Exchange Commission; that the historical financial amounts included therein have not been accurately derived, in all material respects, from the Company's financial statements; or that the underlying information, determinations, estimates, and assumptions of the Company do not provide a reasonable basis for the disclosures contained therein.

This report is intended solely for the information and use of [*list or refer to the specified parties*] and is not intended to be, and should not be, used by anyone other than the specified parties.

Smith and Jones
March 1, 20X3

AT 801 Reporting on Controls at a Service Organization

ORIGINAL PRONOUNCEMENT

Source Statement on Standards for Attestation Engagements (SSAE) 16, *Reporting on Controls at a Service Organization.*

TECHNICAL ALERT

In April 2016, the Auditing Standards Board (ASB) issued SSAE No. 18, *Attestation Standards: Clarification and Recodification.* SSAE No. 18 is effective for practitioners' reports dated on or after May 1, 2017. SSAE No. 18 is the culmination of the attestation clarity project, and it supersedes all of existing attestation standards except for:

- AT 501, whose content was moved to the auditing standards and codified as AU-C 940.
- AT 701, which will not be clarified, but retained in its current form because it is a rarely performed engagement. The section number has been changed to AT-C Section 395.

The clarified standards use the prefix "AT-C" and can be found in the AT-C chapters of this book.

APPLICABILITY

AT 801 applies to examination engagements to report on controls at organizations that provide services to user entities when those controls are likely to be relevant to user entities' internal control over financial reporting.

DEFINITIONS OF TERMS

Carve-out method. A method for reviewing the services provided by a subservice organization, where management's definition identifies the nature of the services performed and excludes its control objectives and controls from the scope of the service auditor's engagement.

Complementary user entity controls. Controls that the management of a subservice entity assumes will be implemented by entities using the services of the subservice entity.

Control objectives. The purpose of specific controls.

Controls at a service organization. The policies and procedures used by a service organization that are likely to be relevant to the internal control over the financial reporting of user entities.

Controls at a subservice organization. The policies and procedures used by a subservice organization that are likely to be relevant to the internal control over the financial reporting of user entities.

Criteria. The standard against which the service auditor evaluates subject matter.

Inclusive method. A method of reviewing the services provided by a subservice organization, where management's definition of the organization's system includes a description of the services provided by the subservice organization and its control objectives and related controls.

Internal audit function. A service organization's internal auditors and others who perform activities similar to those performed by internal auditors.

Report on management's description of a service organization's system and the suitability of the design of controls. A report that includes management's description of a service organization's system, a written assertion about whether management's description fairly presents the system, and whether controls were suitably designed to achieve control objectives, as well as a service auditor's report expressing an opinion on the preceding items.

Report on management's description of a service organization's system and the suitability of the design and operating effectiveness of controls. A report that includes management's description of a service organization's system, a written assertion about whether management's description fairly presents the system, and whether controls were suitably designed to achieve control objectives, as well as a service auditor's report expressing an opinion on the preceding items and a description of the tests of controls and related results.

Service auditor. A practitioner who reports on the controls of a service organization.

Service organization. Either an organization or a segment of an organization that provides services to user entities; the services are likely to be relevant to the internal control over financial reporting of user entities.

Service organization's system. The policies and procedures used by the management of a service organization to provide user entities with the services addressed by a service auditor's report.

Subservice organization. A service organization that is used by another service organization to perform some services that it provides to user entities; these services are likely to be relevant to the internal controls over financial reporting of user entities.

Test of controls. A procedure to evaluate the operating effectiveness of controls in achieving the control objectives described in management's description of the system of a service organization.

User auditor. An auditor who audits and reports on the financial statements of an entity.

User entity. An entity that makes use of a service organization.

OBJECTIVES OF AT SECTION 801

According to AT 801.06, the objectives of the service auditor are to obtain reasonable assurance about whether, in all material respects, based on suitable criteria:

- Management's description of the service organization's system fairly presents the system that was designed and implemented throughout the specified period.
- The controls related to the control objectives stated in management's description of the service organization's system were suitably designed throughout the specified period.
- When included in the scope of the engagement, the controls operated effectively to provide reasonable assurance that the control objectives stated in management's description of the service organization's system were achieved throughout the specified period.

The service auditor also has the objective of reporting in accordance with his or her findings.

REQUIREMENTS

MANAGEMENT AND THOSE CHARGED WITH GOVERNANCE

The service auditor should determine the appropriate person within the management of the service organization or governance structure with whom to interact.

ACCEPTANCE AND CONTINUANCE

The service auditor should accept or continue an engagement to report on the controls of a service organization if:

1. The auditor has the competency and capability to perform the engagement.
2. The auditor's initial knowledge of the engagement indicates that the criteria used will be suitable, he or she will have access to appropriate evidence, and the scope of the engagement will not be so limited that it will be unlikely to be useful.
3. Management agrees to the terms of the engagement by its acceptance of responsibility for a description of the service organization's system and related assertion, having a reasonable basis for its assertion, selecting and stating the criteria to be used, specifying the control objectives, identifying risks that threaten achievement of the control objectives, providing the auditor with access to all information and people requested by the auditor, making written representations, and providing a written assertion that will be included in management's description of the service organization's system.

If management refuses to provide a written assertion, the service auditor should withdraw from the engagement. If there is a legal or regulatory restriction on withdrawing, then the service auditor should disclaim an opinion.

If management requests a scope change before the engagement is complete, the service auditor should be satisfied regarding the reason for the change before agreeing to it.

ASSESSING THE SUITABILITY OF THE CRITERIA

The service auditor should ascertain whether management has used suitable criteria:

1. To prepare the description of the organization's system
2. To evaluate whether controls were designed to achieve control objectives
3. For a type 2 report, to evaluate whether controls operated effectively throughout the specified period to achieve control objectives

The service auditor should determine the following when assessing the suitability of criteria to evaluate whether management's description of a system is fairly presented:

1. Whether the description of the system presents how it was designed and implemented, including the following items (if applicable):

   a. The types of services provided
   b. The procedures by which services are provided
   c. The related accounting records
   d. How the system captures and addresses significant events and conditions
   e. The process by which reports and other information are prepared for user entities
   f. The control objectives and controls designed to achieve the objectives of the system

g. Other aspects of the controls, risk assessment, and other systems that are relevant to the services provided

2. For a type 2 report, whether the system description includes relevant details of changes to the system during the period addressed by the description
3. Whether the description of the system does not omit or distort relevant information

When assessing the suitability of criteria, the service auditor should determine if the criteria address whether any risks threatening the control objectives have been identified, and if the identified controls would provide reasonable assurance that these risks would not keep the control objectives from being achieved. When making this assessment, the service auditor should verify whether the criteria include whether the controls were consistently applied throughout the period, including whether these controls were applied by those with appropriate competence and authority.

The service auditor should evaluate materiality for management's description of the organization's system, the suitability of the controls, and (for a type 2 report) the operating effectiveness of the controls needed to achieve the objectives stated in the description.

Obtaining an Understanding of the Service Organization's System

The service auditor should acquire an understanding of the organization's system, including those controls included in the engagement scope.

Obtaining Evidence Regarding Management's Description of the Service Organization's System

The service auditor should read management's description of the organization's system and evaluate whether those elements of the description that are within the engagement scope are presented fairly. This assessment should address whether:

1. The control objectives stated in the description are reasonable
2. The controls stated in the description were implemented
3. Any complementary user entity controls are adequately described
4. Any services performed by a subservice organization are adequately described, as well as whether the inclusive or carve-out methods were used

The service auditor should use inquiries and other procedures to determine whether the system has been implemented.

Obtaining Evidence Regarding the Design of Controls

The service auditor should determine which controls are needed to achieve the control objectives for the system, and assess whether these controls were suitably designed by identifying those risks threatening control objectives and evaluating the linkage of the controls with those risks.

Obtaining Evidence Regarding the Operating Effectiveness of Controls

For a type 2 engagement, the service auditor tests those controls that he or she has determined are needed to achieve the control objectives of the system, as well as assess their effectiveness throughout the period. The service auditor should inquire about control changes implemented during the period covered by the service auditor's report. If the changes are significant, he or she should ascertain whether they are included in management's description of the system. If not, the service auditor should describe the changes in his or her report. If any superseded controls were relevant for meeting control objectives, the service auditor should test the controls prior to the change. If it is not possible to do so, the service auditor should determine the impact on his or her report.

When designing and testing controls, the service auditor should do the following:

1. Perform other procedures to procure evidence about how a control was applied, the consistency of application, and by whom or by what means it was applied.
2. Determine whether the controls depend on other controls, and whether he or she should obtain evidence about the effectiveness of those other controls.
3. Determine a method for selecting items to be tested to meet procedure objectives.

To determine the extent of tests of controls and whether sampling can be used, the service auditor should consider the characteristics of the population of controls to be tested.

The service auditor should investigate any deviations identified, and ascertain the following:

1. Whether deviations are within the expected rate of deviation
2. Whether additional testing is needed to conclude whether the controls related to the objectives operated effectively in the specified period
3. Whether the testing provides a basis for concluding that a control did not operate effectively in the specified period

If the service auditor learns that any identified deviations were the result of intentional acts, he or she should assess the risk that management's description of the system is not fairly presented, that the controls are not suitably designed, and (in a type 2 engagement) that the controls are not operating effectively.

Using the Work of the Internal Audit Function

If there is an internal audit function within the service organization, the service auditor should understand its responsibilities in order to determine whether it can be relevant to the engagement. This includes an evaluation of:

1. The technical competence and objectivity of the internal auditors
2. Whether they perform their work with due professional care
3. Whether there will be effective communication between the service auditor and the internal auditors

If the work of the internal auditor is likely to be adequate for the purposes of the engagement, the service auditor should evaluate the impact of internal audit work in terms of the work performed by the internal auditors, the significance of that work to the service auditor's conclusions, and the amount of subjectivity used by the internal auditors in their work.

To ascertain the adequacy of specific work done by the internal auditors for use by the service auditor, the service auditor should evaluate whether:

1. The work was done by auditors with adequate training and proficiency.
2. The work was properly supervised and documented.
3. There is sufficient evidence from which to draw conclusions.

4. Conclusions reached and reports written are appropriate in the circumstances.
5. Exceptions were properly resolved.

When the service auditor uses the work of the internal audit function, he or she should not reference that work in the opinion, since the service auditor has sole responsibility for the opinion. For a type 2 report, the service auditor should describe his or her use of the internal auditors in the report section that describes tests of controls and the results thereof.

Written Representations

The service auditor should obtain from management the following written representations:

1. Reaffirmation of the assertion in management's description of the service organization's system
2. That management has provided the service auditor with all relevant information and access
3. That management has disclosed any situations where there:
   a. Are instances of legal or regulatory noncompliance or uncorrected errors
   b. Is knowledge of actual or suspected management or employee acts that may adversely affect the fairness of the description of the organization's system or the achievement of its control objectives
   c. Are any control design deficiencies
   d. Are instances where controls have not operated as described
   e. Are subsequent events that could have a significant effect on management's assertion

If there is a subservice organization providing services to a service organization, and management uses the inclusive method, then the service auditor should obtain written representations from the management of the subservice organization.

Written representations should be organized as a representation letter that is addressed to the service auditor, and the letter should be dated as of the same date as the service auditor's report.

If management does not provide written representations, the service auditor should discuss the matter with management, evaluate the effect of the refusal on his or her assessment of the integrity of management, and take such actions as disclaiming an opinion or withdrawing from the engagement.

Other Information

The service auditor should use other information to identify inconsistencies with or misstatements in management's description of the service organization's system. If there are inconsistencies or misstatements, the service auditor should discuss the matter with management. This may call for further appropriate action.

Subsequent Events

The service auditor should inquire of management whether there have been any events during the period between management's description of the organization's system and the date of the auditor's report that could have a significant effect on management's assertion. The service auditor should disclose such items in his or her report.

The service auditor is not responsible for events subsequent to the date of his or her report.

Documentation

The service auditor should prepare documentation that is sufficient to enable an experienced service auditor with no previous connection to the engagement to understand:

1. The nature, timing, and extent of any procedures used
2. The results of procedures performed and evidence obtained
3. Significant findings or issues, conclusions reached, and the judgments made in reaching those conclusions

The service auditor should record the following when documenting procedures performed:

1. The characteristics of items or matters being tested
2. Who performed the work and when he or she did so
3. Who reviewed the work and when he or she did so

If the service auditor used the internal audit staff, he or she should document the conclusions reached regarding the adequacy of the internal audit function and the procedures completed to do so.

The service auditor should document the discussion of significant findings or issues with management, as well as the names of the persons involved and the date of each discussion.

The service auditor should document how he or she addressed any inconsistency in the information examined and the final conclusion.

The service auditor should assemble all engagement documentation into an engagement file and complete the related administration no later than 60 days after the release date of the service auditor's report. The service auditor should not delete or discard documentation after assembling the final engagement file. If the service auditor must modify or add to the existing documentation after the file has been completed, he or she should document the reasons for the change, and when and by whom they were made and reviewed.

Preparing the Service Auditor's Report

The service auditor's type 2 report should contain the following information:

1. A title that includes the word *independent*
2. An addressee
3. Identification of the following items:
   a. Management's description of the service organization's system and the function performed by that system
   b. Any parts of management's description of the system that are not addressed by the service auditor's report
   c. Any information included in a document containing the service auditor's report that is not addressed by the report
   d. The criteria
   e. Any services performed by a subservice organization, and whether the carve-out or inclusive methods were used: If the carve-out method was employed, a statement that management's description of the organization's system does not include the control objectives and related controls located at subservice organizations, and that the service auditor's procedures do not address the subservice organization. If the inclusive method was employed, a statement that management's description of the organization's system

includes the subservice organization's control objectives and related controls, and that the service auditor's procedures addressed the subservice organization.

4. If management's description of the organization's system notes the need for complementary user entity controls, a statement that the service auditor has not evaluated the suitability of the design or effectiveness of complementary user entity controls, and that the stated control objectives can only be achieved if complementary user entity controls are suitably designed and operate effectively (as well as the controls of the service organization)
5. A reference to the assertion by management, as well as a statement that management is responsible for:
   a. Preparing the description of the service organization's system and the assertion
   b. Providing the services covered by the description of the service organization's system
   c. Specifying the control objectives and stating them in the description of the system
   d. Identifying the risks that threaten the accomplishment of the control objectives
   e. Selecting the criteria
   f. Designing, implementing, and documenting controls that are designed and operate effectively enough to achieve the objectives stated in the description of the organization's system
6. A statement that the service auditor's responsibility is to express an opinion on the fairness of the presentation of management's description of the system of the service organization, and on the suitability of the design and operating effectiveness stated in the description, based on the examination by the service auditor
7. A statement that the examination was conducted in accordance with the attestation standards established by the AICPA, and that those standards require the service auditor to plan and perform this examination in order to obtain reasonable assurance as to whether management's description of the organization's system is fairly presented and controls suitably designed and operated during the specified period in order to achieve related control objectives
8. A statement that an examination of management's description of the organization's system and the suitability of the design and effectiveness of the controls in achieving control objectives involves the performance of procedures to obtain evidence about the fairness of the presentation of the description and suitability of the design and effectiveness of the controls to achieve the related control objectives stated in the description
9. A statement that the examination included assessing the risks that management's description is not fairly presented and that the controls were not suitably designed or operated effectively to achieve the related control objectives
10. A statement that the examination included testing the effectiveness of the controls that the service auditor considered necessary to provide reasonable assurance that the related control objectives were achieved
11. A statement that an examination engagement of this type also includes the evaluation of the overall presentation of management's description of the service organization's system, as well as the suitability of the control objectives stated in the description
12. A statement that the service auditor believes that the examination provides a reasonable basis for his or her opinion
13. A statement about the inherent limitations of controls

14. The service auditor's opinion on whether, in all material respects, based on the criteria described in management's assertion:
    a. Management's description of the system fairly presents the system that was designed and implemented throughout the period
    b. The controls related to the control objectives statement in management's description were suitably designed to provide reasonable assurance that the control objectives would be achieved if they operated effectively throughout the specified period
    c. The controls the service auditor tested operated effectively throughout the specified period
    d. The application of complementary user entity controls is necessary to achieve the control objectives stated in management's description, then make reference to this condition
15. A reference to a description of the service auditor's tests of controls and the results, including:
    a. The identification of tested controls and the nature of the tests in enough detail to enable user auditors to determine the effects of such tests on their risk assessments
    b. The identification of any deviations in the operation of controls included in the description, the extent of the testing that identified the deviations, and the number and nature of deviations noted
16. A statement restricting the use of the service auditor's report to the management of the service organization, user entities of the service organization during the period covered by the report, and the independent auditors of those user entities
17. The date of the report
18. The name of the service auditor and the city and state where the auditor maintains the office that is responsible for the engagement

The service auditor's type 1 report should contain the following information:

1. A title that includes the word *independent*
2. An addressee
3. Identification of the following items:
    a. Management's description of the service organization's system and the function performed by that system
    b. Any parts of management's description of the system that are not addressed by the service auditor's report
    c. Any information included in a document containing the service auditor's report that is not addressed by the report
    d. The criteria
    e. Any services performed by a subservice organization, and whether the carve-out or inclusive methods were used: If the carve-out method was employed, a statement that management's description of the organization's system does not include the control objectives and related controls located at subservice organizations, and that the service auditor's procedures do not address the subservice organization. If the inclusive method was employed, a statement that management's description of the organization's system include the subservice organization's control objectives and related controls and that the service auditor's procedures addressed the subservice organization.

4. If management's description of the organization's system notes the need for complementary user entity controls, a statement that the service auditor has not evaluated the suitability of the design or effectiveness of complementary user entity controls, and that the stated control objectives can only be achieved if complementary user entity controls are suitably designed and operate effectively (as well as the controls of the service organization)
5. A reference to the assertion by management, as well as a statement that management is responsible for:
   a. Preparing the description of the service organization's system and the assertion
   b. Providing the services covered by the description of the service organization's system
   c. Specifying the control objectives and stating them in the description of the system
   d. Identifying the risks that threaten the accomplishment of the control objectives
   e. Selecting the criteria
   f. Designing, implementing, and documenting controls that are designed and operate effectively enough to achieve the objectives stated in the description of the organization's system
6. A statement that the service auditor's responsibility is to express an opinion on the fairness of the presentation of management's description of the system of the service organization, and on the suitability of the design and operating effectiveness stated in the description, based on the examination by the service auditor
7. A statement that the examination was conducted in accordance with the attestation standards established by the AICPA, and that those standards require the service auditor to plan and perform this examination in order to obtain reasonable assurance as to whether management's description of the organization's system is fairly presented and controls suitably designed and operated during the specified period in order to achieve related control objectives
8. A statement that the service auditor has not performed any procedures regarding the operating effectiveness of controls and, therefore, expresses no opinion about them
9. A statement that an examination of management's description of the organization's system and the suitability of the design and effectiveness of the controls in achieving control objectives involves the performance of procedures to obtain evidence about the fairness of the presentation of the description and suitability of the design and effectiveness of the controls to achieve the related control objectives stated in the description
10. A statement that the examination included assessing the risks that management's description is not fairly presented and that the controls were not suitably designed or operated effectively to achieve the related control objectives
11. A statement that an examination engagement of this type also includes the evaluation of the overall presentation of management's description of the service organization's system, as well as the suitability of the control objectives stated in the description
12. A statement that the service auditor believes that the examination provides a reasonable basis for his or her opinion
13. A statement about the inherent limitations of controls
14. The service auditor's opinion on whether, in all material respects, based on the criteria described in management's assertion:
    a. Management's description of the system fairly presents the system that was designed and implemented as of the specified date

b. The controls related to the control objectives statement in management's description were suitably designed to provide reasonable assurance that the control objectives would be achieved if they operated effectively as of the specified date
c. The application of complementary user entity controls is necessary to achieve the control objectives stated in management's description, then make reference to this condition

15. A statement restricting the use of the service auditor's report to the management of the service organization, user entities of the service organization as of the end of the period covered by the report, and the independent auditors of those user entities
16. The date of the report
17. The name of the service auditor and the city and state where the auditor maintains the office that is responsible for the engagement

The service auditor should date the report no earlier than the date on which he or she obtained sufficient appropriate evidence to support the opinion.

The service auditor should modify his or her opinion, as well as modify the service auditor's report, to clearly describe all of the reasons for a modification under the following circumstances:

1. Management's description of the system is not fairly presented.
2. The controls are not suitably designed to provide reasonable assurance that the control objectives would be achieved.
3. For a type 2 report, the controls do not operate effectively throughout the specified period to achieve the stated control objectives.
4. The service auditor is unable to obtain sufficient evidence.

If the service auditor plans to disclaim an opinion due to lack of evidence, and has concluded that some aspects of the description are not fairly presented, or some controls were not suitably designed to provide reasonable assurance regarding control objectives, or (for a type 2 report) some controls did not operate effectively throughout the specified period, then he or she should identify these findings in his or her report.

If the service auditor plans to disclaim an opinion, then he or she should not identify the procedures performed, nor describe characteristics of the engagement in the report.

OTHER COMMUNICATION RESPONSIBILITIES

If the service auditor is aware of incidents of legal or regulatory noncompliance, fraud, or uncorrected errors attributable to management or other personnel that are not trivial and that may affect user entities, then he or she should determine the effect of these incidents on the description of the organization's system, control objectives, and the service auditor's report. Further, the service auditor should take appropriate action if this information has not been communicated to affected user entities..

ILLUSTRATIONS

The following reports are adapted from SSAE 16.

1. An illustration of the wording of a type 2 service auditor's report.
2. An illustration of the wording of a type 1 service auditor's report.

ILLUSTRATION 1. TYPE 2 SERVICE AUDITOR'S REPORT

Independent Service Auditor's Report on a Description of a Service Organization's System and the Suitability of the Design and Operating Effectiveness of Controls

To: XYZ Service Organization

Scope

We have examined XYZ Service Organization's description of its [*type or name of*] system for processing user entities' transactions [*or identification of the function performed by the system*] through the period [*date*] to [*date*] [*description*] and the suitability of the design and operating effectiveness of controls to achieve the related control objectives stated in the descriptions.

Service Organization's Responsibilities

On page XX of the description, XYZ Service Organization has provided an assertion about the fairness of the presentation of the description and suitability of the design and operating effectiveness of the controls to achieve the related control objectives stated in the description. XYZ Service Organization is responsible for preparing the description and the assertion, including the completeness, accuracy, and method of presentation of the description and the assertion, providing the services covered by the description, specifying the control objectives and stating them in the description, identifying the risks that threaten the achievement of the control objectives, selecting the criteria, and designing, implementing, and documenting controls to achieve the related control objectives stated in the description.

Service Auditor's Responsibilities

Our responsibility is to express an opinion on the fairness of the presentation of the description and on the suitability of the design and operating effectiveness of the controls to achieve the related control objectives stated in the description, based on our examination. We conducted our examination in accordance with attestation standards established by the American Institute of Certified Public Accountants. Those standards require that we plan and perform our examination to obtain reasonable assurance about whether, in all material respects, the description is fairly presented and the controls were suitably designed and operating effectively to achieve the related control objectives stated in the description throughout the period [*date*] to [*date*].

An examination of a description of a service organization's system and the suitability of the design and operating effectiveness of the service organization's controls to achieve the related control objectives stated in the description involves performing procedures to obtain evidence about the fairness of the presentation of the description and the suitability of the design and operating effectiveness of those controls to achieve the related control objectives stated in the description. Our procedures included assessing the risks that the description is not fairly presented and that the controls were not suitably designed or operating effectively to achieve the related control objectives stated in the description. Our procedures also included testing the operating effectiveness of those controls that we consider necessary to provide reasonable assurance that the related control objectives stated in the description were achieved. An examination engagement of this type also includes evaluating the overall presentation of the description and the suitability of the control objectives stated therein, and the suitability of the criteria specified by the service organization and described at page [*aa*]. We believe that the evidence we obtained is sufficient and appropriate to provide a reasonable basis for our opinion.

Inherent Limitations

Because of their nature, controls at a service organization may not prevent, or detect and correct, all errors or omissions in processing or reporting transactions [*or identification of the function performed by the system*]. Also, the projection to the future of any evaluation of the fairness of the presentation of the description, or conclusions about the suitability of the design or operating effectiveness of the controls to achieve the related control objectives is subject to the risk that controls at a service organization may become inadequate or fail.

Opinion

In our opinion, in all material respects, based on the criteria described in XYZ Service Organization's assertion on page [*aa*],

1. The description fairly presents the [*type or name of*] system that was designed and implemented throughout the period [*date*] to [*date*].
2. The controls related to the control objectives stated in the description were suitably designed to provide reasonable assurance that the control objectives would be achieved if the controls operated effectively throughout the period [*date*] to [*date*].
3. The controls tested, which were those necessary to provide reasonable assurance that the control objectives stated in the description were achieved, operated effectively throughout the period [*date*] to [*date*].

Descriptions of Tests of Controls

The specific controls tested and the nature, timing, and results of those tests are listed on pages [*yy–zz*].

Restricted Use

This report, including the description of tests of controls and results thereof on pages [*yy–zz*], is intended solely for the information and use of XYZ Service Organization, user entities of XYZ Service Organization's [*type or name of*] system during some or all of the period [*date*] to [*date*], and the independent auditors of such user entities, who have a sufficient understanding to consider it, along with other information including information about controls implemented by user entities themselves, when assessing the risks of material misstatements of user entities' financial statements. This report is not intended to be and should not be used by anyone other than these specified parties.

Smith and Jones
March 1, 20X3

Following is a modification of the scope paragraph in a type 2 service auditor's report if the description refers to the need for complementary user entity controls (new language is shown in boldface italics):

> We have examined XYZ Service Organization's description of its [*type or name of*] system for processing user entities' transactions [*or identification of the function performed by the system*] throughout the period [*date*] to [*date*] (description) and the suitability of the design and operating effectiveness of controls to achieve the related control objectives stated in the description. ***The description indicates that certain control objectives specified in the description can be achieved only if complementary user entity controls contemplated in the design of XYZ Service Organization's controls are suitably designed and operating effectively, along with related controls at the service organization. We have not evaluated the suitability of the design or operating effectiveness of such complementary user entity controls.***

Following is a modification of the applicable subparagraphs of the opinion paragraph of a type 2 service auditor's report if the application of complementary user entity controls is necessary to achieve the related control objectives stated in the description of the service organization's system (new language is shown in boldface italics):

2. The controls related to the control objectives stated in the description were suitably designed to provide reasonable assurance that those control objectives would be achieved if the controls operated

effectively throughout the period [*date*] to [*date*] ***and user entities applied the complementary user entity controls contemplated in the design of XYZ Service Organization's controls throughout the period* [date] *to* [date].**

3. The controls tested, which, ***together with the complementary user entity controls referred to in the scope paragraph of this report, if operating effectively***, were those necessary to provide reasonable assurance that the control objectives stated in the description were achieved, operated effectively throughout the period [*date*] to [*date*].

Following is a modification of the paragraph that describes the responsibilities of management of the service organization for use in a type 2 service auditor's report when the control objectives have been specified by an outside party (new language is shown in boldface italics):

> On page XX of the description, XYZ Service Organization has provided an assertion about the fairness of the presentation of the description and suitability of the design and operating effectiveness of the controls to achieve the related control objectives stated in the description. XYZ Service Organization is responsible for preparing the description and for its assertion, including the completeness, accuracy, and method of presentation of the description and assertion, as well as for providing the services covered by the description, selecting the criteria, and designing, implementing, and documenting controls to achieve the related control objectives stated in the description. ***The control objectives have been specified by* [name of party specifying the control objectives] *and are stated on page* [aa] *of the description*.**

ILLUSTRATION 2. TYPE 1 SERVICE AUDITOR'S REPORT

Independent Service Auditor's Report on a Description of a Service Organization's System and the Suitability of the Design of Controls

To: XYZ Service Organization

Scope

We have examined XYZ Service Organization's description of its [*type or name of*] system for processing user entities' transactions [*or identification of the function performed by the system*] as of [*date*], and the suitability of the design of controls to achieve the related control objectives stated in the descriptions.

Service Organization's Responsibilities

On page XX of the description, XYZ Service Organization has provided an assertion about the fairness of the presentation of the description and suitability of the design of the controls to achieve the related control objectives stated in the description. XYZ Service Organization is responsible for preparing the description and for its assertion, including the completeness, accuracy, and method of presentation of the description and the assertion, providing the services covered by the description, specifying the control objectives and stating them in the description, identifying the risks that threaten the achievement of the control objectives, selecting the criteria, and designing, implementing, and documenting controls to achieve the related control objectives stated in the description.

Service Auditor's Responsibilities

Our responsibility is to express an opinion on the fairness of the presentation of the description and on the suitability of the design of the controls to achieve the related control objectives stated in the description, based on our examination. We conducted our examination in accordance with attestation standards established by the American Institute of Certified Public Accountants. Those standards require that we plan and perform our examination to obtain reasonable assurance about whether, in all material respects, the description is fairly presented and the controls were suitably designed to achieve the related control objectives stated in the description as of [*date*].

An examination of a description of a service organization's system and the suitability of the design of the service organization's controls to achieve the related control objectives stated in the description involves performing procedures to obtain evidence about the fairness of the presentation of the description of the system and the suitability of the design of the controls to achieve the related control objectives stated in the description. Our procedures included assessing the risks that the description is not fairly presented and that the controls were not suitably designed to achieve the related control objectives stated in the description. Our procedures also included assessing the risks that the description is not fairly presented and that the controls were not suitably designed to achieve the related control objectives stated in the description. An examination engagement of this type also includes evaluating the overall presentation of the description and the suitability of the control objectives stated therein, and the suitability of the criteria specified by the service organization and described at page [*aa*].

We did not perform any procedures regarding the operating effectiveness of the controls stated in the description and, accordingly, do not express an opinion thereon.

We believe that the evidence we obtained is sufficient and appropriate to provide a reasonable basis for our opinion.

Inherent Limitations

Because of their nature, controls at a service organization may not prevent, or detect and correct, all errors or omissions in processing or reporting transactions [or identification of the function performed by the system]. The projection to the future of any evaluation of the fairness of the presentation of the description, or conclusions about the suitability of the design of the controls to achieve the related control objectives is subject to the risk that controls at a service organization may become inadequate or fail.

Opinion

In our opinion, in all material respects, based on the criteria described in XYZ Service Organization's assertion:

1. The description fairly presents the [*type or name of*] system that was designed and implemented as of [*date*], and
2. The controls related to the control objectives stated in the description were suitably designed to provide reasonable assurance that the control objectives would be achieved if the controls operated effectively as of [*date*].

Restricted Use

This report is intended solely for the information and use of XYZ Service Organization, user entities of XYZ Service Organization's [*type or name of*] system as of [*date*], and the independent auditors of such user entities, who have a sufficient understanding to consider it, along with other information including information about controls implemented by user entities themselves, when obtaining an understanding of user entities' information and communication systems relevant to financial reporting. This report is not intended to be and should not be used by anyone other than these specified parties.

Smith and Jones
March 1, 20X3

Following is a modification of the scope paragraph in a type 1 report if the description of the service organization's system refers to the need for complementary user entity controls (new language is shown in boldface italics):

We have examined XYZ Service Organization's description of its [*type or name of*] system (description) made available to user entities of the system for processing their transactions [*or identification of the function performed by the system*] as of [*date*], and the suitability of the design of controls to achieve the related control objectives stated in the description. ***The description indicates that certain complementary user entity controls must be suitably designed and implemented at user entities for related controls at the service organization to be considered suitably designed to achieve the related control objectives. We have not evaluated the suitability of the design or operating effectiveness of such complementary user entity controls.***

Following is a modification of the applicable subparagraph in the opinion paragraph of a type 1 report if the application of complementary user entity controls is necessary to achieve the related control objectives stated in management's description of the service organization's system (new language is shown in boldface italics):

2. The controls related to the control objectives stated in the description were suitably designed to provide reasonable assurance that those control objectives would be achieved if the controls operated effectively as of [*date*] ***and user entities applied the complementary user entity controls contemplated in the design of XYZ Service Organization's controls as of*** **[date].**

Following is a modification of the paragraph that describes management of XYZ Service Organization's responsibilities to be used in a type 1 report when the control objectives have been specified by an outside party (new language is shown in boldface italics):

On page XX of the description, XYZ Service Organization has provided an assertion about the fairness of the presentation of the description and suitability of the design of the controls to achieve the related control objectives stated in the description. XYZ Service Organization is responsible for preparing the description and assertion, including the completeness, accuracy, and method of presentation of the description and assertion, providing the services covered by the description, selecting the criteria, and designing, implementing, and documenting controls to achieve the related control objectives stated in the description. ***The control objectives have been specified by*** **[name of party specifying the control objectives]** ***and are stated on page*** **[aa]** ***of the description.***

Illustration 3. Modified Service Auditor's Reports

The following examples of modified service auditor's reports are for guidance only and are not intended to be exhaustive or applicable to all situations. They are based on the illustrative reports above.

Example 1: Qualified Opinion for a Type 2 Report—The Description of the Service Organization's System Is Not Fairly Presented in All Material Respects

The following is an illustrative paragraph describing the basis for the qualified opinion. The paragraph would be inserted before the modified opinion paragraph. All other report paragraphs are unchanged.

Basis for Qualified Opinion

The accompanying description states on page [*mn*] that XYZ Service Organization uses operator identification numbers and passwords to prevent unauthorized access to the system. Based on inquiries of staff personnel and observation of activities, we have determined that operator identification numbers and passwords are employed in applications A and B but are not required to access the system in applications C and D.

Opinion

In our opinion, except for the matter described in the preceding paragraph, and based on the criteria described in XYZ Service Organization's assertion on page [*aa*], in all material respects . . .

Example 2: Qualified Opinion—The Controls Are Not Suitably Designed to Provide Reasonable Assurance That the Control Objectives Stated in the Description of the Service Organization's System Would Be Achieved If the Controls Operated Effectively

The following is an illustrative paragraph describing the basis for the qualified opinion. The paragraph would be inserted before the modified opinion paragraph. All other report paragraphs are unchanged.

Basis for Qualified Opinion

As discussed on page [*mn*] of the accompanying description, from time to time, XYZ Service Organization makes changes in application programs to correct deficiencies or to enhance capabilities. The procedures followed in determining whether to make changes, in designing the changes, and in implementing them do not include review and approval by authorized individuals who are independent from those involved in making the changes. There also are no specified requirements to test such changes or provide test results to an authorized reviewer prior to implementing the changes. As a result the controls are not suitably designed to achieve the control objective, "Controls provide reasonable assurance that changes to existing applications are authorized, tested, approved, properly implemented, and documented."

Opinion

In our opinion, except for the matter described in the preceding paragraph, and based on the criteria described in XYZ Service Organization's assertion on page [*aa*], in all material respects . . .

Example 3: Qualified Opinion for a Type 2 Report—The Controls Did Not Operate Effectively throughout the Specified Period to Achieve the Control Objectives Stated in the Description of the Service Organization's System

The following is an illustrative paragraph describing the basis for the qualified opinion. The paragraph would be inserted before the modified opinion paragraph. All other report paragraphs are unchanged.

Basis for Qualified Opinion

XYZ Service Organization states in its description that it has automated controls in place to reconcile loan payments received with the various output reports. However, as noted on page [*mn*] of the description of tests of controls and results thereof, this control was not operating effectively throughout the period [*date*] to [*date*] due to a programming error. This resulted in the nonachievement of the control objective, "Controls provide reasonable assurance that loan payments received are properly recorded" throughout the period January 1, 20X1, to April 30, 20X1. XYZ Service Organization implemented a change to the program performing the calculation as of May 1, 20X1, and our tests indicate that it was operating effectively throughout the period May 1, 20X1, to December 31, 20X1.

Opinion

In our opinion, except for the matter described in the preceding paragraph, and based on the criteria described in XYZ Service Organization's assertion on page [*aa*], in all material respects . . .

Example 4: Qualified Opinion—The Service Auditor Is Unable to Obtain Sufficient Appropriate Evidence

The following is an illustrative paragraph describing the basis for the qualified opinion. The paragraph would be inserted before the modified opinion paragraph. All other report paragraphs are unchanged.

Basis for Qualified Opinion

XYZ Service Organization states in its description that it has automated controls in place to reconcile loan payments received with the output generated. However, electronic records of the performance of this reconciliation for the period from [*date*] to [*date*] were deleted as a result of a computer processing error and, therefore, we were unable to test the operation of this control for that period. Consequently, we were unable to determine whether the control objective, "Controls provide reasonable assurance that loan payments received are properly recorded" was achieved throughout the period [*date*] to [*date*].

Opinion

In our opinion, except for the matter described in the preceding paragraph, and based on the criteria described in XYZ Service Organization's assertion on page [*aa*], in all material respects . . .

ILLUSTRATION 4. REPORT PARAGRAPHS FOR SERVICE ORGANIZATIONS THAT USE A SUBSERVICE ORGANIZATION

Following are modifications of the illustrative type 2 report in Example 1 of Appendix A for use in engagements in which the service organization uses a subservice organization (new language is shown in boldface italics):

Example 1: Carve-Out Method

Scope

We have examined XYZ Service Organization's description of its system for processing user entities' transactions [*or identification of the function performed by the system*] throughout the period [*date*] to [*date*] (description) and the suitability of the design and operating effectiveness of controls to achieve the related control objectives stated in the description.

XYZ Service Organization uses a computer processing service organization for all of its computerized application processing. The description on pages* [bb–cc] *includes only the controls and related control objectives of XYZ Service Organization and excludes the control objectives and related controls of the computer processing service organization. Our examination did not extend to controls of the computer processing service organization.

All other report paragraphs are unchanged.

Example 2: Inclusive Method

Scope

We have examined XYZ Service Organization's ***and ABC Subservice Organization's*** description of its **[*their*]** [*type or name of*] system for processing user entities' transactions [*or identification of the function performed by the system*] throughout the period [*date*] to [*date*] (description) and the suitability of the design and operating effectiveness of ***XYZ Service Organization's and ABC Subservice Organization's*** controls to achieve the related control objectives stated in the description. *ABC Subservice Organization is an independent service organization that provides computer processing services to XYZ Service Organization. XYZ Service Organization's description includes a description of ABC Subservice Organization's* [type or name of] *system used by XYZ Service Organization to process transactions for its user entities, as well as relevant control objectives and controls of ABC Subservice Organization.*

XYZ Service Organization's Responsibilities

On page XX of the description, XYZ Service Organization [***and ABC Subservice Organization***] has [***have***] provided an assertion [***their assertions***] about the fairness of the presentation of the description and suitability of the design and operating effectiveness of the controls to achieve the related control objectives stated in the description. XYZ Service Organization ***and ABC Subservice Organization are*** responsible for preparing the description and assertion***s***, including the completeness, accuracy, and method of presentation of the description and assertion***s***, providing the services covered by the description, specifying the control objectives and stating them in the description, identifying the risks that threaten the achievement of the control objectives, selecting the criteria, and designing, implementing, and documenting controls to achieve the related control objectives stated in the description.

Inherent Limitations

Because of their nature, controls at a service organization ***or subservice organization*** may not prevent, or detect and correct, all errors or omissions in processing or reporting transactions. Also, the projection to the future of any evaluation of the fairness of the presentation of the description or any conclusions about the suitability of the design or operating effectiveness of the controls to achieve the related control objectives is subject to the risk that controls at a service organization ***or subservice organization*** may become ineffective or fail.

Opinion

In our opinion, in all material respects, based on the criteria specified in XYZ Service Organization***'s and ABC Subservice Organization's*** assertions on page [*aa*]:

1. The description fairly presents ***XYZ Service Organization's*** [*type or name of*] system ***and ABC Subservice Organization's [type or name of] system used by XYZ Service Organization to process transactions for its user entities [or identification of the function performed by the service organization's system]*** that [***were***] was designed and implemented throughout the period [*date*] to [*date*].
2. The controls related to the control objectives ***of XYZ Service Organization and ABC Subservice Organization*** stated in the description were suitably designed to provide reasonable assurance that the control objectives would be achieved if the controls operated effectively throughout the period [*date*] to [*date*].
3. The controls ***of XYZ Service Organization and ABC Subservice Organization that*** we tested, which were those necessary to provide reasonable assurance that the control objectives stated in the description were achieved, operated effectively throughout the period [*date*] to [*date*].

All other report paragraphs are unchanged.

ILLUSTRATION 5. ASSERTIONS BY MANAGEMENT OF A SERVICE ORGANIZATION

The assertion by management of the service organization may be included in management's description of the service organization's system or may be attached to the description. The following illustrative assertions are intended for assertions that are included in the description.

The following illustrative management assertions are for guidance only and are not intended to be exhaustive or applicable to all situations.

Example 1: Assertion by Management of a Service Organization for a Type 2 Report

XYZ Service Organization's Assertion

We have prepared the description of XYZ Service Organization's [*type or name of*] system (description) for user entities of the system during some or all of the period [*date*] to [*date*], and their user auditors who have a sufficient understanding to consider it, along with other information, including information about controls implemented by user entities of the system themselves, when assessing the risks of material misstatements of user entities' financial statements. We confirm, to the best of our knowledge and belief, that:

1. The description fairly presents the [*type or name of*] system made available to user entities of the system during some or all of the period [*date*] to [*date*] for processing their transactions [*or identification of the function performed by the system*]. The criteria we used in making this assertion were that the description:

   a. Presents how the system made available to user entities of the system was designed and implemented to process relevant transactions, including:

      1. The classes of transactions processed
      2. The procedures, within both automated and manual systems, by which those transactions are initiated, authorized, recorded, processed, corrected as necessary, and transferred to the reports presented to user entities of the system
      3. The related accounting records, supporting information, and specific accounts that are used to initiate, authorize, record, process, and report transactions; this includes the correction of incorrect information and how information is transferred to the reports presented to user entities of the system
      4. How the system captures and addresses significant events and conditions, other than transactions
      5. The process used to prepare reports or other information provided to user entities of the system
      6. Specified control objectives and controls designed to achieve those objectives
      7. Other aspects of our control environment, risk assessment process, information and communication systems (including the related business processes), control activities, and monitoring controls that are relevant to processing and reporting transactions of user entities of the system

   b. Does not omit or distort information relevant to the scope of the [*type or name of*] system, while acknowledging that the description is prepared to meet the common needs of a broad range of user entities of the system and the independent auditors of those user entities, and may not, therefore, include every aspect of the [*type or name of*] system that each individual user entity of the system and its auditor may consider important in its own particular environment.

2. The description includes relevant details of changes to the service organization's system during the period covered by the description when the description covers a period of time.
3. The controls related to the control objectives stated in the description were suitably designed and operated effectively throughout the period [*date*] to [*date*] to achieve those control objectives. The criteria we used in making this assertion were that

   a. The risks that threaten the achievement of the control objectives stated in the description have been identified by the service organization;
   b. The controls identified in the description would, if operating as described, provide reasonable assurance that those risks would not prevent the control objectives stated in the description from being achieved; and
   c. The controls were consistently applied as designed, including whether manual controls were applied by individuals who have the appropriate competence and authority.

Example 2: Assertion by Management of a Service Organization for a Type 1 Report

XYZ Service Organization's Assertion

We have prepared the description of XYZ Service Organization's [*type or name of*] system (description) for user entities of the system as of [*date*], and their user auditors who have a sufficient understanding to consider it, along with other information including information about controls implemented by user entities themselves, when obtaining an understanding of user entities' information and communication systems relevant to financial reporting. We confirm, to the best of our knowledge and belief, that:

1. The description fairly presents the [*type or name of*] system made available to user entities of the system as of [*date*] for processing their transactions [*or identification of the function performed by the system*]. The criteria we used in making this assertion were that the description:
   a. Presents how the system made available to user entities of the system was designed and implemented to process relevant transactions, including:
      1. The classes of transactions processed
      2. The procedures, within both automated and manual systems, by which those transactions are initiated, authorized, recorded, processed, corrected as necessary, and transferred to the reports presented to user entities of the system
      3. The related accounting records, supporting information, and specific accounts that are used to initiate, authorize, record, process, and report transactions; this includes the correction of incorrect information and how information is transferred to the reports provided to user entities of the system
      4. How the system captures and addresses significant events and conditions, other than transactions
      5. The process used to prepare reports or other information provided to user entities of the system
      6. Specified control objectives and controls designed to achieve those objectives
      7. Other aspects of our control environment, risk assessment process, information and communication systems (including the related business processes), control activities, and monitoring controls that are relevant to processing and reporting transactions of user entities of the system
   b. Does not omit or distort information relevant to the scope of the [*type or name of*] system, while acknowledging that the description is prepared to meet the common needs of a broad range of user entities of the system and the independent auditors of those user entities, and may not, therefore, include every aspect of the [*type or name of*] system that each individual user entity of the system and its auditor may consider important in its own particular environment
2. The controls related to the control objectives stated in the description were suitably designed as of [*date*] to achieve those control objectives. The criteria we used in making this assertion were that:
   a. The risks that threaten the achievement of the control objectives stated in the description have been identified by the service organization.
   b. The controls identified in the description would, if operating as described, provide reasonable assurance that those risks would not prevent the control objectives stated in the description from being achieved.

AR-C 60 General Principles for Engagements Performed in Accordance with Statements on Standards for Accounting and Review Services

ORIGINAL PRONOUNCEMENT

Source Statement on Standards for Accounting and Review Services (SSARS) 21, effective for SSARS engagements for financial statements for periods ending on or after December 15, 2015, with early application permitted.

TECHNICAL ALERT

General information and background on SSARS No. 21 can be found in the Preface. This technical alert focuses on SSARS No. 21 changes to AR-C Section 60. Old AR Section 60 did not contain guidance on engagement acceptance and continuance. With SSARS No. 21, clarified Section 60:

- Contains specific guidance on engagement acceptance and continuance that applies to *all* SSARS engagements.
- Covers ethical requirements, professional judgment, conduct of the engagement, and engagement level quality control.
- Requires a signed engagement letter for all SSARS engagements.

Note that an engagement letter is required, but the period that the engagement letter covers is left to the accountant's judgment. However, evergreen letters are strongly discouraged because they may result in misunderstandings with the client. Annual letters are strongly encouraged.

OBJECTIVES AND LIMITATIONS OF SSARS ENGAGEMENTS

AR-C section 60 establishes a framework and provides guidance for the performance of all SSARS engagements. Specific requirements for performing and reporting on SSARS engagements are in other AR-C sections. SSARS engagements include an accountant's preparation, compilation, and review of management's financial statements. Note that certain reviews of interim financial information are out of scope of the SSARS. (See the chapter on AR-C Section 90.) The accountant may be engaged to prepare, compile, or review either a complete set of financial statements or an individual financial statement, and for varying time periods. (AR-C 60.A10)

Sources of Guidance. In addition to the SSARS themselves, accountants should look to interpretive publications which are issued by the ARSC after careful review. These interpretations and exhibits are included in the relevant AR-C sections. Accountants may also look to other publications for guidance. Although these publications are not authoritative, they are developed by experts and may be helpful. The accountant should, of course, exercise professional judgment in the selection and use of these publications. Appendix C, at the end of this book, includes a list of AICPA Alerts, Technical Practice Aids, checklists, and other publications available through www.cpa2biz.com. (AR-C 60.17-.18 and .A33-.A36)

FUNDAMENTAL REQUIREMENTS

CONDUCT OF THE ENGAGEMENT IN ACCORDANCE WITH SSARS

SSARS defines two types of requirements:

1. *Unconditional.* These must be complied with.
2. *Presumptively mandatory requirements.* As the adjectives implies, these requirements are presumed to be mandatory except in rare circumstances where the accountant judges it necessary to depart because the required procedure would be ineffective.

(AR-C 60.15-.16)

QUALITY CONTROL IN A SSARS ENGAGEMENT

Similar to quality control requirements for audit engagements, in SSARS engagements the engagement partner must take responsibility for:

- Overall quality
- Direction, supervision, planning, and performance
- The appropriateness of the report
- Performance in compliance with the firm's quality control procedures

The last includes appropriate procedures related to:

- Acceptance and continuance of client relationships and engagements,
- Appropriate conclusions,
- Competence of the engagement team, and
- Maintenance of documentation.

(AR-C 60.20-.22)

The accountant should possess a level of industry-specific accounting knowledge to compile or review financial statements that are appropriate for an entity operating in that industry. An accountant should not accept an engagement if his or her preliminary knowledge of the engagement indicates that ethical requirements for professional competence will not be met. However, the accountant can sometimes use the work of experts to satisfy the competency requirement. If so, the accountant should be satisfied that persons carrying out selected aspects of the engagement possess the required skills and knowledge, and that the accountant has adequate involvement in the engagement. (AR-C 60.21)

Practice Pointer. The engagement partner should keep an eye out throughout the engagement for ethical noncompliance on the part of engagement staff. If any ethical issues come to the partner's attention through observation or inquiry, the partner should take appropriate action. So too, if something comes to the partner's attention which would have caused the firm to decline the engagement, that fact should be brought to the attention of the firm for prompt and appropriate action.

Acceptance and Continuance of Client Relationships and Engagements

An accountant cannot accept a SSARS engagement if:

- The accountant believes ethical requirements will not be satisfied,
- Necessary information is likely to be unavailable or unreliable, or
- The accountant doubts management's integrity and it is likely to affect the engagement.

(AR-C 60.24)

Before accepting a SSARS engagement, the accountant should review these preconditions and:

- Determine that the engagement team has the necessary professional competence. This includes industry-specific accounting knowledge.
- Determine whether the reporting framework is acceptable

(AR-C 60.25a and .25b)

When assigning staff to an engagement, the partner should consider the team's understanding of and experience with similar engagements, professional standards, legal and regulatory requirements, the client's industry, and the firm's quality control policies and procedures. This evaluation may be done in the light of the teams experience and/or training.

Except for certain reviews of interim financial statements discussed in the chapter on Section 90, the accountant is responsible for conducting the engagement in accordance with SSARS. (AR-C 60.25c) Throughout an engagement, the accountant needs to exercise professional judgment and to document it in accordance with the specific requirements of AU-C Sections 70, 80, and 90. (AU-C 60.A19) The accountant also needs to be alert for ethical compliance on the part of engagement team members. (AR-C 60.22)

Practice Pointer. It is possible that some of the above requirements are already incorporated through the firm's quality control manual. Firms should review the requirements and make appropriate updates to their quality control procedures.

The accountant is also responsible for obtaining management's agreement that it understands its responsibilities as a condition of accepting the engagement. Management's responsibilities include:

- *Preparation and presentation.* Management is responsible for the preparation and presentation of the financial statements in accordance with the applicable financial reporting framework.
- *Internal controls.* Management is responsible for internal controls relevant to the preparation and presentation of the financial statements.
- *Fraud.* Management is responsible for preventing and detecting fraud.
- *Legal compliance.* Management is responsible for complying with applicable laws and regulations.
- *Accuracy.* Management is responsible for the accuracy and completeness of information provided.

- *Records availability.* Management is responsible for making financial and related records available to the accountant.
- *Access.* Management is responsible for providing unrestricted access to anyone to whom the accountant needs to make inquiries.

(AR-C 60.25c)

APPENDIX—DEFINITIONS OF TERMS FOR AR-C SECTIONS 60 THROUGH 90 (SOURCE: AR-C 60–90)

Analytical procedures. Evaluations of financial information through analysis of plausible relationships among both financial and nonfinancial data. Analytical procedures also encompass such investigation, as is necessary, of identified fluctuations or relationships that are inconsistent with other relevant information or that differ from expected values by a significant amount.

Applicable financial reporting framework. The financial reporting framework adopted by management and, when appropriate, those charged with governance, in the preparation and fair presentation of the financial statements that is acceptable in view of the nature of the entity and the objective of the financial statements or that is required by law or regulation.

Basic financial statements. Financial statements excluding supplementary information and required supplementary information.

Comparative financial statements. A complete set of financial statements for one or more prior periods included for comparison with the financial statements of the current period.

Designated accounting standards-setter. A body designated by the Council of the AICPA to promulgate accounting principles generally accepted in the United States of America pursuant to the "Compliance with Standards Rule" (et sec. 1.310.001) and the "Accounting Principles Rule" (et sec. 1.320.001) of the AICPA Code of Professional Conduct.

Emphasis-of-matter paragraph. A paragraph included in the accountant's review report that is required by SSARSs, or is included at the accountant's discretion, and that refers to a matter appropriately presented or disclosed in the financial statements that, in the accountant's professional judgment, is of such importance that it is fundamental to the users' understanding of the financial statements.

Engagement partner. The partner or other person in the firm who is responsible for the engagement and its performance and for the report that is issued on behalf of the firm and who, when required, has the appropriate authority from a professional, legal, or regulatory body.

Engagement team. All accountants and staff performing the engagement and any individuals engaged by the firm who perform procedures on the engagement.

Errors. Mistakes in the financial statements, including arithmetical or clerical mistakes, and mistakes in the application of accounting principles, including inadequate disclosures.

Experienced accountant. An individual (whether internal or external to the firm) who has practical review experience and a reasonable understanding of:

a. Review processes,
b. SSARSs and applicable legal and regulatory requirements,
c. The business environment in which the entity operates, and
d. Review and financial reporting issues relevant to the entity's industry.

Financial reporting framework. A set of criteria used to determine measurement, recognition, presentation, and disclosure of all material items appearing in the financial statements (for example, accounting principles generally accepted in the United States of America [US GAAP], International Financial Reporting Standards promulgated by the International Accounting Standards Board, or a special purpose framework).

Financial statements. A structured representation of historical financial information, including related notes, intended to communicate an entity's economic resources and obligations at a point in time or the changes therein for a period of time in accordance with a financial reporting framework. The related notes ordinarily comprise a summary of significant accounting policies and other explanatory information. The term *financial statements* ordinarily refers to a complete set of financial statements as determined by the requirements of the applicable financial reporting framework but can also refer to a single financial statement.

Firm. A form of organization permitted by law or regulation whose characteristics conform to resolutions of the Council of the AICPA and that is engaged in the practice of public accounting.

Fraud. An intentional act that results in a misstatement in financial statements.

Generally accepted accounting principles (GAAP). Reference to *generally accepted accounting principles* in SSARSs means generally accepted accounting principles promulgated by bodies designated by the Council of the AICPA pursuant to the "Compliance with Standards Rule" (et sec. 1.310.001) and the "Accounting Principles Rule" (et sec. 1.320.001) of the AICPA Code of Professional Conduct.

Historical financial information. Information expressed in financial terms regarding a particular entity, derived primarily from that entity's accounting system, about economic events occurring in past time periods or about economic conditions or circumstances at points in time in the past.

Interpretive publications. Interpretations of SSARSs; the AICPA *Guide Compilation and Review Engagements*, guidance on reviews, compilations, and engagements to prepare financial statements included in AICPA Audit and Accounting Guides; and AICPA Statements of Position, to the extent that those statements are applicable to such engagements.

Management. The person(s) with executive responsibility for the conduct of the entity's operations. For some entities, management includes some or all of those charged with governance (for example, executive members of a governance board or an owner-manager).

Misstatement. A difference between the amount, classification, presentation, or disclosure of a reported financial item and the amount, classification, presentation, or disclosure that is required for the item to be presented fairly in accordance with the applicable financial reporting framework. Misstatements can arise from fraud or from error.

Misstatements also include those adjustments of amounts, classifications, presentations, or disclosures that, in the accountant's professional judgment, are necessary for the financial statements to be presented fairly, in all material respects.

Noncompliance. Acts of omission or commission by the entity, either intentional or unintentional, which are contrary to the prevailing laws or regulations. Such acts include transactions entered into, by, or in the name of, the entity or on its behalf by those charged with governance, management, or employees. *Noncompliance* does not include personal misconduct (unrelated to the business activities of the entity) by those charged with governance, management, or employees of the entity.

Other-matter paragraph. A paragraph included in the accountant's review report that is required by SSARSs, or is included at the accountant's discretion, and that refers to a matter other than those presented or disclosed in the financial statements that, in the accountant's professional judgment, is relevant to users' understanding of the review, the accountant's responsibilities, or the accountant's review report.

Other preparation, compilation, and review publications. Publications other than interpretive publications. These include AICPA accounting and review publications not defined as interpretive publications; the AICPA's annual Alert *Developments in Review, Compilation, and Financial Statement Preparation Engagements*; articles addressing reviews, compilations, and engagements to prepare financial statements in the *Journal of Accountancy* and other professional journals; continuing professional education programs and other instruction materials, textbooks, guidebooks, programs for reviews, compilations, and engagements to prepare financial statements, and checklists; and other publications addressing reviews, compilations, and engagements to prepare financial statements from state CPA societies, other organizations, and individuals.

Professional judgment. The application of relevant training, knowledge, and experience, within the context provided by SSARSs and ethical standards, in making informed decisions about the courses of action that are appropriate in the circumstances of the review, compilation, or engagement to prepare financial statements.

Report release date. The date the accountant grants the entity permission to use the accountant's review report in connection with the financial statements.

Required supplementary information. Information that a designated accounting standards-setter requires to accompany an entity's basic financial statements. Required supplementary information is not part of the basic financial statements; however, a designated accounting standards-setter considers the information to be an essential part of financial reporting for placing the basic financial statements in an appropriate operational, economic, or historical context. In addition, authoritative guidelines for the methods of measurement and presentation of the information have been established.

Review documentation. The record of review procedures performed, relevant review evidence obtained, and conclusions the accountant reached (terms such as *working papers* or *workpapers* are also sometimes used).

Review evidence. Information used by the accountant to provide a reasonable basis for obtaining limited assurance.

Special purpose framework. A financial reporting framework other than GAAP that is one of the following bases of accounting:

a. **Cash basis.** A basis of accounting that the entity uses to record cash receipts and disbursements and modifications of the cash basis having substantial support (for example, recording depreciation on fixed assets).
b. **Tax basis.** A basis of accounting that the entity uses to file its tax return for the period covered by the financial statements.
c. **Regulatory basis.** A basis of accounting that the entity uses to comply with the requirements or financial reporting provisions of a regulatory agency to whose jurisdiction the entity is subject (for example, a basis of accounting that insurance companies use pursuant to the accounting practices prescribed or permitted by a state insurance commission). (Ref: par. .A4)
d. **Contractual basis.** A basis of accounting that the entity uses to comply with an agreement between the entity and one or more third parties other than the accountant.
e. **Other basis.** A basis of accounting that uses a definite set of logical, reasonable criteria that is applied to all material items appearing in financial statements.

The cash basis, tax basis, regulatory basis, and other basis of accounting are commonly referred to as *other comprehensive bases of accounting* (OCBOA).

Specified parties. The intended users of the accountant's review report.

Subsequent events. Events occurring between the date of the financial statements and the date of the accountant's review report.

Subsequently discovered facts. Facts that become known to the accountant after the date of the accountant's review report that, had they been known to the accountant at that date, may have caused the accountant to revise the accountant's review report.

Supplementary information. Information presented outside the basic financial statements, excluding required supplementary information, that is not considered necessary for the financial statements to be fairly presented in accordance with the applicable financial reporting framework.

Those charged with governance. The person(s) or organization(s) (for example, a corporate trustee) with responsibility for overseeing the strategic direction of an entity and the obligations related to the accountability of the entity. This includes overseeing the financial reporting process. Those charged with governance may include management personnel (for example, executive members of a governance board or an owner-manager).

Updated report. A report issued by a continuing accountant that takes into consideration information that the accountant becomes aware of during the accountant's current engagement and that re-expresses the accountant's previous conclusions or, depending on the circumstances, expresses different conclusions on the financial statements of a prior period reviewed by the accountant as of the date of the accountant's current report.

Written representation. A written statement by management provided to the accountant to confirm certain matters or to support other review evidence. Written representations in this context do not include financial statements, the assertions therein, or supporting books and records.

AR-C 70 Preparation of Financial Statements

ORIGINAL PRONOUNCEMENT

Source Statement on Standards for Accounting and Review Services (SSARS) 21, effective for SSARS engagements for periods ending on or after December 15, 2015, with early application permitted.

OBJECTIVES AND LIMITATIONS OF PREPARATION ENGAGEMENTS

It is important to note that the requirements in AR-C 60 apply to all SSARS engagements, including preparation engagements. In addition to the guidance in this chapter, readers should apply the requirements in the chapter on Section 60 to preparation engagements.

TECHNICAL ALERT

General information and background on SSARS No. 21 can be found in the Preface. This technical alert focuses on the SSARS No. 21 creation of AR-C Section 70, *Preparation of Financial Statements*. This is a new section that establishes a fourth SSARS engagement and:

- Applies when an accountant in public practice is engaged to prepare financial statements.
- Does not apply when an accountant prepares financial statements:
  - And is also engaged to perform an audit, review, or compilation of those financial statements.
  - Solely for submission to taxing authorities.
  - For inclusion in written personal financial plans prepared by the accountants.
  - In conjunction with business valuation services. (AR-C 70.01)
- Does not require a report—even when the financial statements are expected to be used by or provided to a third party.
- Requires:
  - A legend on each page of the financial statements stating that no assurance is provided or
  - The issuance of a disclaimer on the financial statements.
- Does not require the accountant to be independent. (AR-C 70.03)
- Can be applied to financial statements with or without disclosures.

Note that Section 70 does not apply when the accountant is not in public practice.

DEFINITIONS OF TERMS

See the chapter on AR-C 60 for the definitions for terms related to Sections 60–90.

DETERMINING THE TYPE OF ENGAGEMENT

It is important to determine whether the entity has engaged the accountant to assist in preparing the financial statements (a bookkeeping service) or to actually prepare the financial statements. To aid practitioners in making that distinction and others, AR-C 70.A19 includes the following chart. Accountants are also cautioned to exercise professional judgment when determining the type of engagement.

Illustration

Examples of Accountant Services for Which AR-C Section 70 Applies	Examples of Accountant Services for Which AR-C Section 70 Does Not Apply
Preparation of financial statements prior to audit or review by another accountant	Preparation of financial statements when the accountant is engaged to perform an audit, review, or compilation of such financial statements
Preparation of financial statements for an entity to be presented alongside the entity's tax return	Preparation of financial statements with a tax return solely for submission to taxing authorities
Preparation of personal financial statements for presentation alongside a financial plan	Personal financial statements that are prepared for inclusion in written personal financial plans prepared by the accountant
	Financial statements prepared in conjunction with litigation services that involve pending or potential legal or regulatory proceedings
	Financial statements prepared in conjunction with business valuation services
	Maintaining depreciation schedules
	Preparing or proposing certain adjustments, such as those applicable to deferred income taxes, depreciation, or leases
Preparation of a single financial statement, such as a balance sheet or income statement, or preparing financial statements with substantially all disclosures omitted	Drafting financial statement notes
Using the information in a general ledger to prepare financial statements outside of an accounting software system	Entering general ledger transactions or processing payments (general bookkeeping) in an accounting software system

Section 70 may also be applied to specified elements, accounts, or items of a financial statement; supplementary and required supplementary information; and pro forma and prospective financial information. (AR-C 70.A1)

REQUIREMENTS

In addition to complying with AR-C 70, the accountant engaged to prepare financial statements must also comply with the requirements in AR-C 60.08. The following table outlines the steps in an engagement to prepare financial statements. The steps are discussed in more detail in the sections following the illustration.

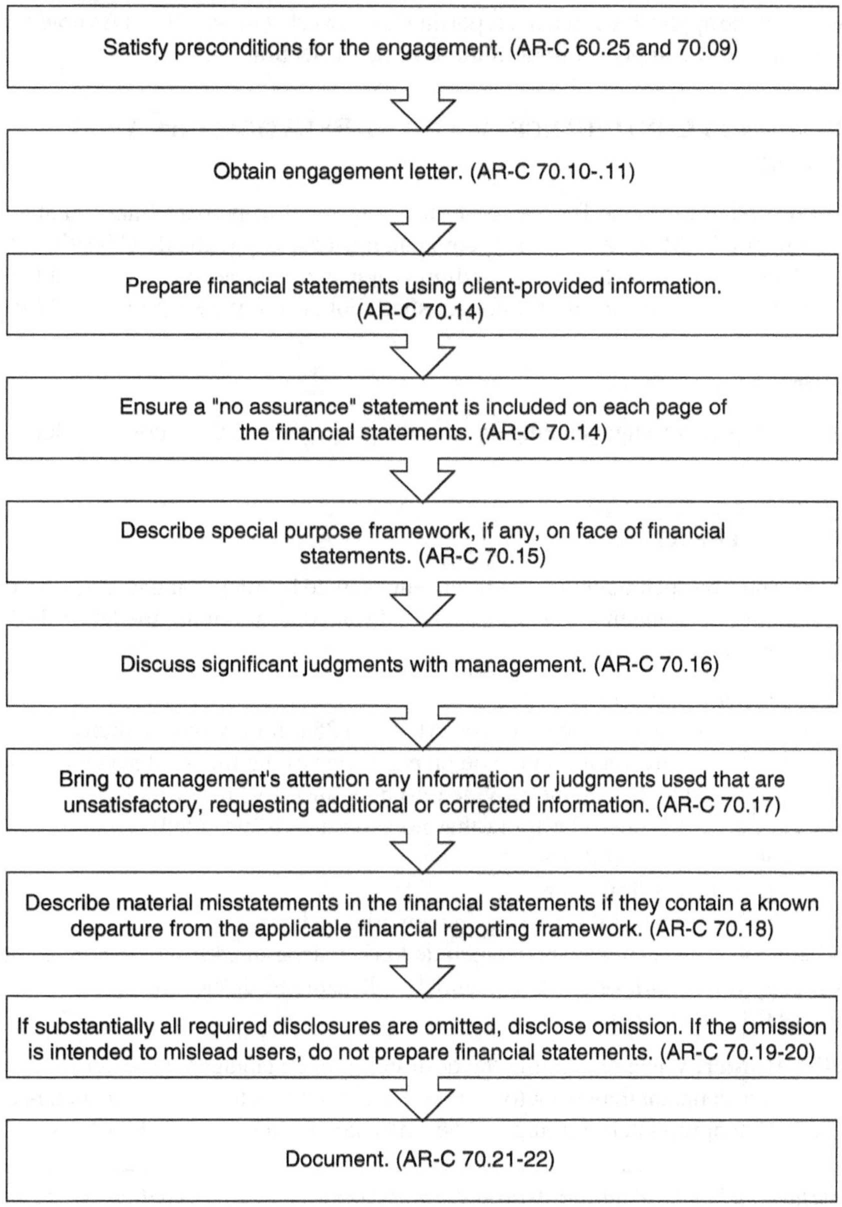

Illustration—Steps in an Engagement to Prepare Financial Statements

Note that a preparation engagement does not require the accountant to verify the accuracy or completeness of management's information. The accountant is also not required to gather information to express an opinion or conclusion on the financial statements. (AR-C 70.04)

Quality Control in a Preparation Engagement

As with other engagements, the accountant should either have or obtain an adequate understanding of the applicable financial reporting framework. (AR-C 70.12) As noted previously, accountants must also comply with the requirements in Section 60.

Acceptance and Continuance of Client Relationships and Preparation Engagements

Note: Preconditions for performance of an engagement to prepare financial statements are included in paragraphs AR-C 60.25. The accountant must comply with AR-C Section 60.25. If the accountant does not believe those preconditions are met, the accountant should discuss the situation with management and, if still not satisfied, not accept the engagement. (AR-C 70.09)

Independence

Because a preparation engagement is not an attest engagement, the accountant does not need to be independent.

Engagement Terms

The terms must be documented in a written letter signed by management or those charged with governance and the accountant or the accountant's firm. At a minimum, the letter should include the following elements:

- The engagement objective
- Responsibilities of management (see AR-C 60.25a in previous chapter)
- Management's agreement to include on each page of the financial statements a statement that indicates the accountant provided no assurance (or, if not included, the accountant must issue a disclaimer clarifying that no assurance is provided)
- Accountant's responsibilities
- The engagement's limitations
- The applicable financial reporting framework used
- Whether the financial statements include known departures from the applicable financial reporting framework or omit substantially all required disclosures

  (AR-C 70.10-.11)

Practice Pointer. When explaining the desirability of an engagement letter for a preparation engagement, the accountant may want to point out that it reduces the risk of misunderstanding and of management inappropriately relying on the financial statements. (AR-C 70.A5)

NOTE: If the prepared financial statements are not to be used by a third party, include in the engagement letter an acknowledgment by management that the statements are not to be used by a third party. (AR-C 70.A6)

Preparing Financial Statements

A report is not required in a preparation engagement, but the accountant must include on each page of the financial statements a statement that "no assurance is provided." The following are suggested legends that may appear on the bottom of each page:

- No assurance is provided by XYZ CPA on these financial statements.
- XYZ CPA did not perform an audit or review or compilation engagement on these financial statements, and no assurance is provided on them.

If the accountant cannot include a "no assurance" statement, the accountant must either issue a disclaimer or perform a compilation engagement.

(AR-C 70.14)

Documentation Requirements

A preparation engagement has few required documentation requirements. However, the documentation must include:

- The engagement letter or other written documentation of the terms agreed to with management
- A copy of the accountant-prepared financial statements
- The accountant should also document departures from presumptively mandatory requirements (mentioned above), noting the justification for the departure and how alternative procedures were sufficient. These departures should be rare.

  (AR-C 70.21-.22)

Here are other items to consider including:

- While preparing the financial statements, the accountant may assist management in making significant judgments regarding amounts or disclosures included in the financial statements. The accountant should discuss those with management to ensure that management understands and take responsibility for them. The accountant may want to document those cases. (AR-C 70.A18)
- Support for journal entries and disclosures.
- Any other items required by firm policy.

ILLUSTRATION (AR-C 70.A20)

Illustration 1. An Engagement Letter for an Engagement to Prepare Financial Statements in Accordance with Accounting Principles Generally Accepted in the United States of America

To the appropriate representative of ABC Company:

You have requested that we prepare the financial statements of ABC Company (the Company), which comprise the balance sheet as of December 31, 20X2, and the related statements of income, changes in stockholders' equity, and cash flows for the year then ended and the related notes to the financial statements. We are pleased to confirm our acceptance and our understanding of this engagement by means of this letter.

Our Responsibilities

The objective of our engagement is to prepare financial statements in accordance with accounting principles generally accepted in the United States of America based on information provided by you. We will conduct our engagement in accordance with Statements on Standards for Accounting and Review Services (SSARSs) promulgated by the Accounting and Review Services Committee of the AICPA and comply with the AICPA's Code of Professional Conduct, including the ethical principles of integrity, objectivity, professional competence, and due care.

We are not required to, and will not, verify the accuracy or completeness of the information you will provide to us for the engagement or otherwise gather evidence for the purpose of expressing an opinion or a conclusion. Accordingly, we will not express an opinion or a conclusion or provide any assurance on the financial statements.

Our engagement cannot be relied upon to identify or disclose any financial statement misstatements, including those caused by fraud or error, or to identify or disclose any wrongdoing within the Company or noncompliance with laws and regulations.

Management Responsibilities

The engagement to be performed is conducted on the basis that management acknowledges and understands that our role is to prepare financial statements in accordance with accounting principles generally accepted in the United States of America. Management has the following overall responsibilities that are fundamental to our undertaking the engagement to prepare your financial statements in accordance with SSARSs:

a. The selection of accounting principles generally accepted in the United States of America as the financial reporting framework to be applied in the preparation of financial statements
b. The prevention and detection of fraud
c. To ensure that the Company complies with the laws and regulations applicable to its activities
d. The accuracy and completeness of the records, documents, explanations, and other information, including significant judgments, you provide to us for the engagement to prepare financial statements
e. To provide us with:
    i. Access to all information of which you are aware that is relevant to the preparation and presentation of the financial statements, such as records, documentation, and other matters,
    ii. Additional information that may be requested for the purpose of the preparation of the financial statements, and
    iii. Unrestricted access to persons within the Company with whom we determine it is necessary to communicate.

The financial statements will not be accompanied by a report. However, you agree that the financial statements will clearly indicate that no assurance is provided on them.

[*If the accountant expects to issue a disclaimer, instead of the preceding paragraph, the following may be added:*

As part of our engagement, we will issue a disclaimer that will state that the financial statements were not subjected to an audit, review, or compilation engagement by us and, accordingly, we do not express an opinion or a conclusion, nor do we provide any assurance on them.]

Other Relevant Information

Our fees for these services . . .

[*The accountant may include language, such as the following, regarding limitation of, or other arrangements regarding, the liability of the accountant or the entity, such as indemnification to the accountant for liability arising from knowing misrepresentations to the accountant by management (regulators may restrict or prohibit such liability limitation arrangements):*

You agree to hold us harmless and to release, indemnify, and defend us from any liability or costs, including attorney's fees, resulting from management's knowing misrepresentations to us.]

Please sign and return the attached copy of this letter to indicate your acknowledgment of, and agreement with, the arrangements for our engagement to prepare the financial statements described herein, and our respective responsibilities.

Sincerely yours,

____

[*Signature of accountant or accountant's firm*]

Acknowledged and agreed on behalf of ABC Company by:

______

[*Signed*]

[*Name and Title*]

____

[*Date*]

AR-C 80 Compilation Engagements

ORIGINAL PRONOUNCEMENTS

Source Statement on Standards for Accounting and Review Services (SSARS) 21, effective for SSARS engagements for periods ending on or after December 15, 2015, with early application permitted.

OBJECTIVES AND LIMITATIONS OF PREPARATION ENGAGEMENTS

It is important to note that the requirements in AR-C 60 apply to all SSARS engagements, including compilation engagements. Readers should apply the requirements in the chapter on Section 60 to compilation engagements in addition to the guidance in this chapter.

Section 80 applies when an accountant has been *engaged* to compile financial statements. Section 80 may also apply to other historical or prospective financial information. When performing a compilation engagement, the accountant does not provide any assurance as to the accuracy or completeness of management's information or gather evidence to express an opinion or a conclusion on the financial statements. (AR-C 80.01-.02) Rather, the accountant's objective in a compilation engagement is "to apply accounting and financial reporting expertise to assist management in the presentation of financial statements and report without undertaking to obtain or provide any assurance that there are no material modifications that should be made to the financial statements in order for them to be in accordance with the applicable financial reporting framework." (AR-C 80.04)

TECHNICAL ALERT

General information and background on SSARS No. 21 can be found in the Preface. This technical alert focuses on SSARS No. 21 changes to AR-C 80, *Compilation Engagements*. Section 80:

- Applies when the accountant is *engaged* to perform a compilation engagement.
- Eliminates the need for the accountant to determine whether he or she has prepared financial statements by eliminating the submission criterion.
- Always requires a report, but the standard report is shortened to one paragraph and does not include headers, thus differentiating it from audit and review reports.
- Requires additional paragraphs when:
  - The financial statements are prepared in accordance with a special purpose framework,
  - Management elects to omit substantially all disclosures required by the applicable financial reporting framework,
  - The accountant's independence is impaired,
  - There is a known departure from the applicable financial reporting framework, and

- Supplementary information accompanies the financial statements and the accountant's compilation report.

DEFINITIONS OF TERMS

See the chapter on AR-C 60 for the definitions for terms related to Sections 60–90.

REQUIREMENTS

A compilation is a service where accountants apply their accounting and financial reporting expertise to assist management in presenting financial statements without obtaining or providing any assurance that there are no material modifications to be made to the financial statements for them to be in conformity with the applicable financial reporting framework. A compilation differs significantly from a review or an audit of financial statements. A compilation does not contemplate performing inquiry, analytical procedures, or other procedures performed in a review. Additionally, a compilation does *not* contemplate:

- Obtaining an understanding of the entity's internal control;
- Assessing fraud risk;
- Testing accounting records by obtaining sufficient appropriate audit evidence through inspection, observation, confirmation, or the examination of source documents (for example, canceled checks or bank images); or
- Other procedures ordinarily performed in an audit.

Therefore, a compilation does not provide a basis for obtaining or providing any assurance regarding the financial statements.

INDEPENDENCE

For a compilation engagement, accountants must determine whether they are independent of the entity. (AR-C 80.07)

Reporting When the Accountant Is Not Independent

When issuing a compilation report where the accountant is not independent of the entity for which the report is being compiled, the accountant should modify the last paragraph of the accountant's report to indicate a lack of independence, such as "I am not independent with respect to ABC Company." It is acceptable to elaborate on this statement and describe why the accountant is not independent, such as pointing out that the accountant has a direct financial interest in the entity, or a family member is employed by the entity. If the accountant chooses to describe the reasons for the lack of independence, he or she must include *all* the reasons. (AR-C 80.22-.23)

ACCEPTANCE AND CONTINUANCE OF CLIENT RELATIONSHIPS

Accountants must comply with the requirements in the chapter on AR-C 60 related to acceptance and continuance of a client. They must also obtain the acknowledgment of management that it understands its responsibility:

- For the financial statements' fair presentation in accordance with the applicable financial reporting framework and the applicable disclosures.

- Unless a different understanding is reached, to include the compilation report in any document containing financial statements that indicates the accountant has performed a compilation.
(AR-C 80.08)

If the accountant is not satisfied with any of the above conditions or those in AR-C 60 and cannot resolve the issues, he or she should not accept the engagement. (AR-C 80.09)

Establishing an Understanding

The accountant must both establish and document *in writing* an understanding with management regarding compilation engagement services. The written agreement should be signed by the accountant or the accountant's firm and management or those charged with governance. Such written communications reduce the risk that management may inappropriately rely on the accountant to protect the entity against some types of risks, or expect the accountant to perform some tasks that are actually management's responsibility. The documentation should include the following:

- *Objective.* The objective is to assist management in presenting financial information in the form of financial statements.
- *Limitations of the compilation engagement.* The accountant does not obtain any assurance that there are no material modifications that should be made.
- *Accountant's responsibilities.* (Also see the chapter on AR-C 60.)
- *Management's responsibilities.* Management is responsible for the items listed above in the section on "Acceptance and Continuance of Client Relationships" and in AR-C 60.25c found in the related section in the chapter on AR-C 60.
- *Identification of the applicable financial reporting framework.*
- *Form and content of the report.* The accountant should make clear that there are circumstances where the report may differ from the standard report.
- *Other.* If applicable, also note fees and billings, any limitations on the liability of the accountant or the client, conditions under which others may access compilation-related documents, and other services to be provided that relate to regulatory requirements. It may also be necessary to include the existence of any material departures from the applicable financial reporting framework, the omission of disclosures, and references to any supplementary information.
(AR-C 80.09)

NOTE: If the compiled financial statements are not to be used by a third party, include in the engagement letter an acknowledgment by management that the statements are not to be used by a third party. (AR-C 80.A8)

Examples of engagement letters for compilation services are in the "Illustrations" section at the end of this chapter.

Compilation Performance Requirements

In order to assist the client, the accountant should understand the applicable financial reporting framework and the accounting policies used by the entity. In a compilation engagement, the accountant has no responsibility to obtain evidence about the accuracy or completeness of the financial statements. The accountant is required to read the financial statements and consider whether they appear to be correct in form and free of obvious material errors. (AR-C 80.13)

If an accountant performs a compilation, he or she must provide a written report or communication or else withdraw from the engagement.

The accountant should have knowledge of the following topics in order to perform a compilation engagement:

- *Industry knowledge.* Have an understanding of the industry in which the client operates that is sufficient to compile financial statements that are appropriate for an entity in that industry. This does not prevent an accountant from accepting an engagement in an industry where the accountant has no previous experience, but does mean that the accountant should obtain the required level of knowledge. The knowledge can be obtained through experience, publications, continuing professional education, or knowledgeable individuals. (AR-C 80.12 and .A12)
- *Client knowledge.* Have an understanding of the client's business and the accounting principles and practices used by it (including any differences in the client's business model from normal industry practices). This requires a general understanding of the client's operating characteristics and the nature of its assets, liabilities, revenues, and expenses.

Inadequate Information

Although the accountant is not required to corroborate information, if he or she believes the information provided is unsatisfactory, the accountant should request additional information. (AR-C 80.14) If management does not provide information requested and the accountant cannot complete the engagement, the accountant should withdraw. (AR-C 80.16a)

Revisions

During the course of the engagement, the accountant may become aware that:

- The financial statements do not adequately refer to or describe the applicable financial reporting framework,
- Revisions are needed for financial statements to be in accordance with accounting requirements, or
- The financial statements are otherwise misleading.
(AR-C 80.15)

In those cases, the accountant should propose revisions and ask management to revise the financials. However, if:

- Management does not make the revisions and chooses not to disclose the departures, and
- The accountant chooses not to disclose the departures in the compilation report,

the accountant should withdraw and give the reasons to management. (AR-C 80.16)

Documentation in a Compilation Engagement

The accountant should prepare documentation for each compilation engagement in enough detail to provide a clear understanding of the work completed. The type of documentation depends on the circumstances of the engagement, but should at least include the engagement letter, a copy of the financial statements, and a copy of the accountant's report. (AR-C 80.38) The accountant may also consider including significant findings and issues and communications to management regarding fraud or illegal acts that came to the accountant's attention.

Reporting on the Financial Statements

Basic Report

If an accountant reports on compiled financial statements, they should be accompanied by a written report. This report should contain the following items:

- *Title.* The title indicates that it is the accountant's compilation report.
- *Addressee.* The report is addressed based on the circumstances of the engagement.
- *Introductory paragraph.* This section identifies the entity whose financial statements have been compiled, notes that the statements have been compiled, identifies the financial statements that have been compiled, specifies the dates or period covered by them, and includes a statement that the accountant has not audited or reviewed the financial statements, was not required to perform procedures to verify the accuracy or completeness of the information, and therefore does not express an opinion, conclusion, or provide any assurance about whether the financial statements are in accordance with the applicable financial reporting framework.

NOTE: If financial statements are prepared in accordance with a special purpose framework, they are not appropriate in form unless the financial statements include a description of the special purpose framework, including a summary of significant differences from generally accepted accounting principles (GAAP).

- *Management's responsibility.* This section states that management is responsible for the preparation and fair presentation of the financial statements in accordance with the applicable financial reporting framework, as well as for internal controls relevant to the preparation and presentation of the financial statements.
- *Accountant's responsibility.* This section states that the accountant performed the compilation in accordance with SSARS.

NOTE: Each page of the financial statements that were compiled by the accountant should be labeled "See accountant's compilation report" or "See independent accountant's compilation report."

- *Accountant's signature.* The written document should include the signature of the accounting firm or the accountant.
- *City and state.* Where the accountant practices.
- *Report date.* The date the accountant completed the required procedures.

(AR-C 80.17)

(Examples of compilation reports are shown at the end of the chapter in the "Illustrations" section.)

Substantially All Required Disclosures Omitted

If an entity requests that the accountant compile financial statements that omit substantially all disclosures, the accountant may still compile the financial statements provided that the omissions are not, to the accountant's knowledge, intended to be misleading to statement users. When issuing such financial statements, the accountant should include in the compilation report a separate paragraph stating that:

- Management has elected to omit substantially all disclosures,
- The omitted disclosures might influence user conclusions about the company's financial results, and
- The financial statements are not designed for those who are not informed about such matters.
  (AR-C 80.24-.25)

NOTE: If management elects to include only a few disclosures, they should be labeled "Selected Information—Substantially All Disclosures Required by [identify the applicable financial reporting framework] *Are Not Included." (AR-C 80.A32)*

Compilation Report—Special Purpose Framework

When an accountant is compiling financial statements that have been prepared using a special purpose framework, then the presentation should be in accordance with AR-C 80. The financial statements should include:

- A description of the basis of presentation,
- A summary of significant accounting policies, and
- A description of the differences between the special purpose framework and GAAP.

If the financial statements contain items similar to GAAP, then management should include disclosures similar to GAAP. If the items above are not included and unless the entity elects to omit substantially all disclosures, the accountant should modify the report. (AR-C 80.18)

For financial statements prepared on a contractual basis of accounting, the accountant should modify the report if the financial statements do not adequately explain significant interpretations of the contract. (AR-C 80.19) When the financial statements are prepared on a regulatory or contractual basis of accounting, the financial statements should reference management's responsibility for determining the framework is acceptable and describe the purpose for which the financial statements are prepared or reference a note with that information. (AR-C 80.20)

The report should include a separate paragraph that indicates that the financial statements are prepared in accordance with the special purpose framework and refer to the financial statement note describing the framework and state that the special purpose framework is a basis of accounting other than GAAP. (AR-C 80.24)

Departures from the Applicable Financial Reporting Framework

If an accountant becomes aware of a departure from the applicable financial reporting framework that is material to the financial statements, the accountant should consider whether modification of the accompanying report is an adequate disclosure of the issue. If so, the issue can be disclosed in a separate paragraph of the report. The accountant does not have to determine the effects of this departure if management has not done so, as long as the accountant states in the report that he or she has not made such a determination. If the effects are known, they should be disclosed. If the accountant believes that modification of the standard report is not an adequate method for indicating the deficiency, the accountant should withdraw from the review engagement and provide no further services regarding those financial statements. (AR-C 80.27-30)

Reporting When Compiled Financial Statements Are Not to Be Used by a Third Party

If there is no expectation that compiled financial statements are to be used by a third party, the accountant does not have to issue a compilation report. However, the accountant should include a reference on each page of the financial statements that restricts their use, such as "Restricted for Management's Use Only."

If the accountant learns that the financial statements have been distributed to third parties, then the accountant should discuss the matter with management to determine the best course of action, which may include the return of the financial statements. If the accountant requests the return of the financial statements and the client does not comply, then the accountant should notify the third parties that the financial statements were not intended for use by third parties.

Emphasizing a Matter

Section 80 does not preclude an emphasis-of-matter paragraph. The accountant may elect to emphasize a matter disclosed in the financial statements. If so, the accountant should include explanatory information in a separate paragraph of the accountant's report. Examples of items that might be emphasized are uncertainties, significant transactions with other parties, important subsequent events, and the comparability of the financial statements with those of a prior period.

NOTE: An emphasis paragraph is never mandatory in a compilation report.

Restricting the Compilation Report

Although not required, an accountant's report may include an alert that restricts the use of the report. If a report is restricted, the accountant should include a paragraph in the report stating that the report is intended solely for the information and use of the specified parties.

If the accountant issues a combined report that addresses subjects requiring a use restriction and subject matter not requiring such a restriction, then the accountant should apply the use restriction to the entire report.

If a restricted-use report is included in a general-use report, then the restricted-use report is still restricted, and the general-use report is still available for general use.

If the accountant is asked to include additional parties in the distribution of a restricted-use report, and the engagement has already been completed, the accountant may agree to do so, based on such criteria as their identity, knowledge of disclosure criteria, and the intended use of the report. If the accountant includes additional parties, the accountant should obtain acknowledgment from the other parties of their understanding of the nature of the engagement, disclosure criteria, and the related report. This may require reissuance of the report (though not with a new report date). If the accountant instead issues written acknowledgment that the new parties have been added as specified parties, then he or she should state that no procedures have been performed subsequent to the report date.

NOTE: The accountant is not responsible for controlling a client's distribution of restricted-use reports.

An Entity's Ability to Continue as a Going Concern

If the accountant learns that an uncertainty may exist about an entity's ability to continue as a going concern for a period not to exceed one year beyond the date of the compiled financial statements, then the accountant should request that management consider the possible effects of this uncertainty on the financial statements, including the need for a related disclosure. (AR-C 80. A15) The accountant should then consider the reasonableness of management's response; if the response is unreasonable, the accountant should withdraw from the engagement and provide no further services relating to those financial statements. It is acceptable to emphasize an uncertainty about an entity's ability to continue as a going concern.

Subsequent Events

In a compilation engagement, the accountant does not have responsibility regarding subsequent events. However, the accountant may become aware of a material subsequent event either during the performance of compilation procedures or subsequent to the date of the compilation report but prior to its release. If so, the accountant should request that management consider the effects of the event on the financial statements and related disclosures. If the subsequent event is not adequately accounted for in the financial statements or related disclosures, and management's response is not reasonable, then the accountant should withdraw from the engagement and provide no further services relating to those financial statements.

If the subsequent event has a material impact on the financial statements, the accountant should include an explanatory paragraph in the compilation report.

Subsequent Discovery of Facts Existing at the Report Date

The accountant may become aware of facts subsequent to the report date that may have existed at that date, and which might have caused him or her to believe that information supplied by the entity was incomplete or incorrect. If so, the accountant should:

- Determine whether the information is reliable,
- Determine whether the facts existed as of the report date,
- Discuss the matter with management,
- Request cooperation with the investigation, and
- Obtain additional or revised information if the effect of the matter is such that the accountant's report or the financial statements would have been affected and the accountant believes that persons using the financial statements would attach importance to the information.

If the accountant decides that further action should be taken to prevent further use of the financial statements or the accountant's report, then advise the client to disclose these facts and their impact to those persons using or likely to use the financial statements. This may call for the issuance of revised financial statements, or inclusion of the disclosure in the financial statements of the subsequent period (if their issuance is imminent), or notification that the existing financial statements should not be used and that revised statements will be issued shortly.

If the client refuses to make these disclosures, then notify appropriate personnel at the highest levels within the entity of the refusal and that the accountant will take immediate steps to prevent further use of the financial statements and accountant's report. Barring alternative recommendations by the accountant's attorney, the accountant should take these steps:

1. Notify the client that the accountant's report can no longer be associated with the financial statements.
2. Notify those regulatory agencies having jurisdiction over the client that they can no longer rely on the accountant's report.
3. Notify each known user of the financial statements that the financial statements and the accountant's report can no longer be used.

These notifications should include a description of the subsequently acquired information and its effect on the financial statements. The descriptions should be as factual as possible, and avoid any comments about the conduct or motives of any persons involved. Alternatively, if the client has not cooperated, it is acceptable not to describe the subsequently acquired information, but rather to indicate that the client has not cooperated in substantiating the information, and that, assuming the information is true, the accountant believes the compilation report can no longer be used or associated with the financial statements. It is not necessary to make this disclosure unless the accountant believes the financial statements are likely to be misleading.

Supplementary Information

If the compiled financial statements are accompanied by supplementary information, the accountant should indicate the degree of responsibility that he or she is taking for this information in an other-matter paragraph or in a separate report on the supplementary information. If the accountant has compiled the supplementary information, then the accountant should refer to the supplementary information in the accountant's report or issue a separate report for this information. If a separate report is issued for this purpose, the accountant should state in it that the other information accompanying the financial statements is only presented for the purposes of additional analysis and that the information has been compiled from information that is the representation of management, without audit or review, and that the accountant does not express an opinion or provide any assurance on the information. (AR-C 80.32-33)

If the accountant has compiled the financial statements, but not the supplementary information, an other-matter paragraph is required. That paragraph should indicate that the supplementary information:

- Is presented for additional analysis, but is not a required part of the basic financial statements;
- Is management's representation; and
- Was not subject to the compilation engagement and the accountant does not express an opinion or provide any assurance on the supplementary information.
(AR-C 80.34)

Required Supplementary Information

The accountant is not required to apply procedures to required supplementary information that accompanies compiled financial statements. When required supplementary information is omitted from financial statements that omit substantially all disclosures required by US GAAP, the accountant may not combine the paragraph discussing the omission of substantially all disclosures with the paragraph referring to the omission of the required supplementary information. Following are illustrative report paragraphs for required supplementary information.

The Required Supplementary Information Is Included and the Accountant Did Not Compile the Required Supplementary Information

[*Identify the applicable financial reporting framework (for example, accounting principles generally accepted in the United States of America)*] require that [*identify the required supplementary information*] on page XX be presented to supplement the basic financial statements. Such information, although not a part of the basic financial statements, is required by [*identify the designated accounting standard setter*], who considers it to be an essential part of financial reporting and for placing the basic financial statements in an appropriate operational, economic, or historical context. Such information was not audited, reviewed, or compiled by me (us) and, accordingly, I (we) do not express an opinion or provide any assurance on it. (AR-C 80.36a-c)

The Required Supplementary Information Is Included, the Accountant Compiled the Required Supplemental Information, and No Material Departures from the Prescribed Guidelines Regarding the Required Supplementary Information Have Been Identified

[*Identify the applicable financial reporting framework (for example, accounting principles generally accepted in the United States of America)*] require that [*identify the required supplementary information*] on page XX be presented to supplement the basic financial statements. Such information, although not a part of the basic financial statements, is required by [*identify the designated accounting standard setter*], who considers it to be an essential part of financial reporting and for placing the basic financial statements in an appropriate operational, economic, or historical context. Such information has been compiled by me (us) without audit or review and, accordingly, I (we) do not express an opinion or provide any assurance on it.

All Required Supplementary Information Is Omitted

Include, in a separate paragraph, a statement that:

Management has omitted [*describe the missing required supplementary information*] that [*identify the applicable financial reporting framework (for example, accounting principles generally accepted in the United States of America)*] require to be presented to supplement the basic financial statements. Such missing information, although not a part of the basic financial statements, is required by [*identify the designated accounting standard setter*], who considers it to be an essential part of financial reporting and for placing the basic financial statements in an appropriate operational, economic, or historical context. (AR-C 80.36a-c)

Some Required Supplementary Information Is Omitted and Some Is Presented in Accordance with the Prescribed Guidelines Regarding the Required Supplementary Information

[*Identify the applicable financial reporting framework (for example, accounting principles generally accepted in the United States of America)*] require that [*identify the included supplementary information*] be presented to supplement the basic financial statements. Such information, although not a part of the basic financial statements, is required by [*identify designated accounting standard setter*], who considers it to be an essential part of financial reporting for placing the basic financial statements in an appropriate operational, economic, or historical context. Such information was not audited, reviewed, or compiled by me (us) and, accordingly, I (we) do not express an opinion or provide any assurance on it.

Management has omitted [*describe the missing required supplementary information*] that [*identify the applicable financial reporting framework*] require to be presented to supplement the basic financial statements. Such missing information, although not a part of the basic financial statements, is required by [*identify designated accounting standard setter*], who considers it to be an essential part of financial reporting for placing the basic financial statements in an appropriate operational, economic, or historical context. (AR-C 80.36d)

Material Departures from the Prescribed Guidelines Regarding the Required Supplementary Information Were Identified While Compiling the Required Supplementary Information

[*Identify the applicable financial reporting framework (for example, accounting principles generally accepted in the United States of America)*] require that the [*identify the supplementary information*] on page XX be presented to supplement the basic financial statements. Such information, although not a part of the basic financial statements, is required by [*identify designated accounting standards setter*], who considers it to be an essential part of financial reporting for placing the basic financial statements in an appropriate operational, economic, or historical context. Such information was compiled by me (us) without audit or review and, accordingly, I (we) do not express an opinion or provide any assurance on it.

> However, during my (our) compilation, I (we) did become aware of the following material departures from the prescribed guidelines regarding the required supplementary information [*identify the required supplementary information and describe the material departures from the prescribed guidelines regarding the required supplementary information*]. (AR-C 80.36e)

Communicating to Management and Others

When the accountant is made aware that fraud or illegal acts may have occurred, he or she should bring the issue to the attention of management, though it is not necessary to report illegal acts that are clearly inconsequential. If fraud or an illegal act involves senior management, then notification goes to a higher level within the entity. If fraud or an illegal act involves an owner of the entity, the accountant should consider resigning from the engagement. Further, whenever there is evidence of fraud or an illegal act, the accountant should consider consulting with legal counsel.

Communication of these matters can be oral or in writing. If oral, the accountant should document the conversation.

NOTE: There may be a duty to disclose fraud or illegal acts to outside parties to comply with legal and regulatory requirements, or in response to a subpoena, or to a successor accountant when the successor decides to communicate with the predecessor accountant.

Change in Engagement from Audit or Review to Compilation

An accountant may originally be engaged to audit or review an entity's financial statements, and then be requested, before the completion of the engagement, to change the engagement to a compilation. Before agreeing to this change, consider the following:

- The reason for the request, especially the implications of the scope restriction.
- The remaining incremental effort and cost required to complete the audit or review.

If the audit or review procedures are substantially complete or the completion cost is insignificant, the accountant should consider the propriety of accepting a change to a compilation engagement.

A change in circumstances impacting the entity's need for an audit or review, or a misunderstanding about the nature of the engagement, is a reasonable basis for requesting an engagement change to compilation services. If the accountant accepts the engagement change and issues a report, the report should not refer to the original engagement and audit or review procedures performed, or to the scope limitations resulting from the change.

NOTE: The accountant is normally precluded from issuing a compilation report if the client did not provide a signed representation letter as part of an audit or review, or if the accountant has been prohibited from corresponding with the entity's legal counsel as part of an audit.

ILLUSTRATIONS

CHECKLIST FOR A COMPILATION ENGAGEMENT

Note: Ensure that requirements in AR-C 60 are met.

Step No.	*Action/Decision*
1.	Determine whether the firm is independent. If the firm is not, see step 10. If the firm is, see step 11.
2.	Obtain an understanding in writing with the client about the engagement. (For a new client, determine if communication with the predecessor accountant is desirable.) (AR-C 80.09)
3.	Acquire the necessary knowledge of the client industry's accounting principles and practices. (AR-C 80.A12)
4.	Acquire a general understanding of the nature of the client's business transactions, the form of the accounting records, the stated qualifications of the accounting personnel, the accounting basis used, and the form and content of the financial statements. (It is not necessary to make inquiries or perform other procedures; however, if the accountant becomes aware that information supplied by the entity is incorrect, incomplete, or unsatisfactory, the accountant should obtain additional or revised information.) (AR-C 80.14)
5.	Read the financial statements and determine if they appear to be appropriate in form and free from obvious material error. (AR-C 80.13)
6.	Consider whether all disclosures required by GAAP are provided. If they are not, go to step 7. If they are, go to step 8.
7.	If the client has engaged the accountant to prepare financial statements that omit all or substantially all of the disclosures required by GAAP, indicate this in a separate paragraph in the report. Indicate that if the disclosure had been included, they might affect the user's conclusions and that, therefore, the financial statements are not designed for those not informed about such matters. (AU-C 80.25) If most, but not all, disclosures are omitted, the omission should be treated in the report like a departure from GAAP. (AR-C 80.26) Notes to the financial statements should be labeled "Selected Information—Substantially All Disclosures Required by Generally Accepted Accounting Principles Are Not Included." (AR-C 80.31)
8.	Consider whether the financial statements contain material departures from GAAP. If they do, go to step 9. If they do not, go to step 10.
9.	Request the client to revise the financial statements. Failing that, modify the report by adding a separate paragraph that describes the departure. If the effect of the departure has been determined by management or is known by the accountant, disclose the dollar effects in the report. If the effect of the departure has not been determined, state that in the report. (AR-C 80.27-.30) (The report need not be modified for uncertainties, going concern matters, or inconsistencies if they are properly disclosed—see step 6.) Withdraw from the engagement if the departures are designed to mislead financial statement users.
10.	If the firm is not independent, add a separate, final paragraph to the report stating "We are not independent with respect to XYZ Company." (AR-C 80.22) If the accountant decides to explain why he or she is not independent, *all* the reasons for the lack of independence should be disclosed. (AR-C 80.23)
11.	Sign and date (manual, stamped, electronic, or typed signature) the report using the date the compilation was completed. (AR-C 80.17g and .17i) Include the city and state where the accountant practices.
12.	Issue the financial statements and related compilation report.

NOTE: This checklist is designed for a GAAP basis compilation. If the accounting basis is a special purpose framework, questions should be added to address (1) disclosure of the basis of accounting and (2) appropriate titles for the financial statements.

Exhibit A—Illustrative Engagement Letters (Ref: par. .A1) .A42	
Illustration 1	An Engagement Letter for a Compilation Engagement with Respect to Financial Statements Prepared in Accordance with Accounting Principles Generally Accepted in the United States of America
Illustration 2	An Engagement Letter for a Compilation Engagement with Respect to Financial Statements Prepared in Accordance with Accounting Principles Generally Accepted in the United States of America, Except the Financial Statements Omit the Statement of Cash Flows and Substantially All Disclosures Required by US GAAP and in Which the Accountant's Independence Is Impaired
Illustration 3	An Engagement Letter for a Compilation Engagement with Respect to Financial Statements Prepared in Accordance with the Tax Basis of Accounting
The illustrative engagement letters in this exhibit are intended as illustrations that may be used in conjunction with the considerations outlined in Statements on Standards for Accounting and Review Services. The engagement letter will vary according to individual requirements and circumstances, and the illustrations are drafted to refer to a compilation engagement for a single reporting period. The accountant may seek legal advice about whether a proposed letter is suitable.	

Illustration 1. An Engagement Letter for a Compilation Engagement with Respect to Financial Statements Prepared in Accordance with Accounting Principles Generally Accepted in the United States of America

To the appropriate representative of management of ABC Company:

You have requested that we prepare the financial statements of ABC Company, which comprise the balance sheet as of December 31, 20XX, and the related statements of income, changes in stockholders' equity, and cash flows for the year then ended, and the related notes to the financial statements, and perform a compilation engagement with respect to those financial statements. We are pleased to confirm our acceptance and our understanding of this engagement by means of this letter.

Our Responsibilities

The objective of our engagement is to:

a. Prepare financial statements in accordance with accounting principles generally accepted in the United States of America based on information provided by you, and
b. Apply accounting and financial reporting expertise to assist you in the presentation of financial statements without undertaking to obtain or provide any assurance that there are no material modifications that should be made to the financial statements in order for them to be in accordance with accounting principles generally accepted in the United States of America.

We will conduct our compilation engagement in accordance with Statements on Standards for Accounting and Review Services (SSARSs) promulgated by the Accounting and Review Services Committee of the AICPA and comply with the AICPA's Code of Professional Conduct, including the ethical principles of integrity, objectivity, professional competence, and due care.

We are not required to, and will not, verify the accuracy or completeness of the information you will provide to us for the engagement or otherwise gather evidence for the purpose of expressing an opinion or a conclusion. Accordingly, we will not express an opinion or a conclusion, nor will we provide any assurance on the financial statements.

Our engagement cannot be relied upon to identify or disclose any financial statement misstatements, including those caused by fraud or error, or to identify or disclose any wrongdoing within the entity or noncompliance with laws and regulations.

Your Responsibilities

The engagement to be performed is conducted on the basis that you acknowledge and understand that our role is to prepare financial statements in accordance with accounting principles generally accepted in the United States of America and assist you in the presentation of the financial statements in accordance with accounting principles generally accepted in the United States of America. You have the following overall responsibilities that are fundamental to our undertaking the engagement in accordance with SSARSs:

a. The selection of accounting principles generally accepted in the United States of America as the financial reporting framework to be applied in the preparation of the financial statements
b. The preparation and fair presentation of financial statements in accordance with accounting principles generally accepted in the United States of America and the inclusion of all informative disclosures that are appropriate for accounting principles generally accepted in the United States of America
c. The design, implementation, and maintenance of internal control relevant to the preparation and fair presentation of the financial statements
d. The prevention and detection of fraud
e. To ensure that the entity complies with the laws and regulations applicable to its activities
f. The accuracy and completeness of the records, documents, explanations, and other information, including significant judgments, you provide to us for the engagement
g. To provide us with:
    i. Access to all information of which you are aware is relevant to the preparation and fair presentation of the financial statements, such as records, documentation, and other matters
    ii. Additional information that we may request from you for the purpose of the compilation engagement
    iii. Unrestricted access to persons within the entity of whom we determine it necessary to make inquiries

You are also responsible for all management decisions and responsibilities and for designating an individual with suitable skills, knowledge, and experience to oversee our preparation of your financial statements. You are responsible for evaluating the adequacy and results of the services performed and accepting responsibility for such services.

Our Report

As part of our engagement, we will issue a report that will state that we did not audit or review the financial statements and that, accordingly, we do not express an opinion or a conclusion, nor do we provide any assurance on them.

You agree to include our accountant's compilation report in any document containing financial statements that indicates that we have performed a compilation engagement on such financial statements and, prior to inclusion of the report, to ask our permission to do so.

Other Relevant Information

Our fees for these services . . .

[*The accountant may include language, such as the following, regarding limitation of or other arrangements regarding the liability of the accountant or the entity, such as indemnification to the accountant for liability arising from knowing misrepresentations to the accountant by management (regulators may restrict or prohibit such liability limitation arrangements):*

You agree to hold us harmless and to release, indemnify, and defend us from any liability or costs, including attorney's fees, resulting from management's knowing misrepresentations to us.]

Please sign and return the attached copy of this letter to indicate your acknowledgment of, and agreement with, the arrangements for our engagement to prepare the financial statements described herein and to perform a compilation engagement with respect to those same financial statements, and our respective responsibilities.

Sincerely yours,

____

[*Signature of accountant or accountant's firm*]

Acknowledged and agreed on behalf of ABC Company by:

____

[*Signed*]

[*Name and title*]

____

[*Date*]

Illustration 2. An Engagement Letter for a Compilation Engagement with Respect to Financial Statements Prepared in Accordance with Accounting Principles Generally Accepted in the United States of America, Except the Financial Statements Omit the Statement of Cash Flows and Substantially All Disclosures Required by US GAAP and in Which the Accountant's Independence Is Impaired

To the appropriate representative of management of ABC Company:

You have requested that we prepare the financial statements of ABC Company, which comprise the balance sheet as of December 31, 20XX, and the related statements of income and changes in stockholders' equity for the year then ended, and perform a compilation engagement with respect to those financial statements. These financial statements will not include a statement of cash flows and related notes to the financial statements. We are pleased to confirm our acceptance and our understanding of this engagement by means of this letter.

Our Responsibilities

The objective of our engagement is to:

a. Prepare financial statements in accordance with accounting principles generally accepted in the United States of America based on information provided by you, and
b. Apply accounting and financial reporting expertise to assist you in the presentation of financial statements without undertaking to obtain or provide any assurance that there are no material modifications that should be made to the financial statements in order for them to be in accordance with accounting principles generally accepted in the United States of America.

We will conduct our compilation engagement in accordance with Statements on Standards for Accounting and Review Services (SSARSs) promulgated by the Accounting and Review Services Committee of the AICPA and comply with the AICPA's Code of Professional Conduct, including the ethical principles of integrity, objectivity, professional competence, and due care.

We are not required to, and will not, verify the accuracy or completeness of the information you will provide to us for the engagement or otherwise gather evidence for the purpose of expressing an opinion or a conclusion. Accordingly, we will not express an opinion or a conclusion, nor will we provide any assurance on the financial statements.

Our engagement cannot be relied upon to identify or disclose any financial statement misstatements, including those caused by fraud or error, or to identify or disclose any wrongdoing within the entity or noncompliance with laws and regulations.

Your Responsibilities

The compilation engagement to be performed is conducted on the basis that you acknowledge and understand that our role is to prepare financial statements in accordance with accounting principles generally accepted in the United States of America and assist you in the presentation of the financial statements in accordance with accounting principles generally accepted in the United States of America. You have the following overall responsibilities that are fundamental to our undertaking the engagement in accordance with SSARSs:

a. The selection of accounting principles generally accepted in the United States of America as the financial reporting framework to be applied in the preparation of the financial statements
b. The preparation and fair presentation of financial statements in accordance with accounting principles generally accepted in the United States of America
c. The design, implementation, and maintenance of internal control relevant to the preparation and fair presentation of the financial statements
d. The prevention and detection of fraud
e. To ensure that the entity complies with the laws and regulations applicable to its activities
f. The accuracy and completeness of the records, documents, explanations, and other information, including significant judgments, you provide to us for the engagement
g. To provide us with:
    i. Access to all information of which you are aware is relevant to the preparation and fair presentation of the financial statements, such as records, documentation, and other matters
    ii. Additional information that we may request from you for the purpose of the compilation engagement
    iii. Unrestricted access to persons within the entity of whom we determine it necessary to make inquiries

Our Report

As part of our engagement, we will issue a report that will state that we did not audit or review the financial statements and that, accordingly, we do not express an opinion or a conclusion, nor do we provide any assurance on them. We will disclose that we are not independent in our report.

You agree to include our accountant's compilation report in any document containing financial statements that indicates that we have performed a compilation engagement on such financial statements and, prior to inclusion of the report, to ask our permission to do so.

Other Relevant Information

Our fees for these services . . .

[*The accountant may include language, such as the following, regarding limitation of, or other arrangements regarding, the liability of the accountant or the entity, such as indemnification to the accountant for liability arising from knowing misrepresentations to the accountant by management (regulators may restrict or prohibit such liability limitation arrangements):*

You agree to hold us harmless and to release, indemnify, and defend us from any liability or costs, including attorneys' fees, resulting from management's knowing misrepresentations to us.]

Please sign and return the attached copy of this letter to indicate your acknowledgment of, and agreement with, the arrangements for our engagement to prepare the financial statements described herein and to perform a compilation engagement with respect to those same financial statements, and our respective responsibilities.

Sincerely yours,

____

[*Signature of accountant or accountant's firm*]

Acknowledged and agreed on behalf of ABC Company by:

____

[*Signed*]

[*Name and title*]

____

[*Date*]

Illustration 3. An Engagement Letter for a Compilation Engagement with Respect to Financial Statements Prepared in Accordance with the Tax Basis of Accounting

To the appropriate representative of management of ABC Company:

You have requested that we prepare the financial statements of ABC Company, which comprise the statement of assets, liabilities, and equity—tax basis as of December 31, 20XX, and the related statements of operations and related earnings—tax basis, and cash flows—tax basis for the year then ended, and the related notes to the financial statements and perform a compilation engagement with respect to those financial statements. We are pleased to confirm our acceptance and our understanding of this compilation engagement by means of this letter.

Our Responsibilities

The objective of our engagement is to:

a. Prepare financial statements in accordance with the tax basis of accounting based on information provided by you, and
b. Apply accounting and financial reporting expertise to assist you in the presentation of financial statements without undertaking to obtain or provide any assurance that there are no material modifications that should be made to the financial statements in order for them to be in accordance with the tax basis of accounting.

We will conduct our compilation engagement in accordance with Statements on Standards for Accounting and Review Services (SSARSs) promulgated by the Accounting and Review Services Committee of the AICPA and comply with the AICPA's Code of Professional Conduct, including the ethical principles of integrity, objectivity, professional competence, and due care.

We are not required to, and will not, verify the accuracy or completeness of the information you will provide to us for the engagement or otherwise gather evidence for the purpose of expressing an opinion or a conclusion. Accordingly, we will not express an opinion or a conclusion, nor will we provide any assurance on the financial statements.

Our engagement cannot be relied upon to identify or disclose any financial statement misstatements, including those caused by fraud or error, or to identify or disclose any wrongdoing within the entity or noncompliance with laws and regulations.

Your Responsibilities

The engagement to be performed is conducted on the basis that you acknowledge and understand that our role is to prepare financial statements in accordance with the tax basis of accounting and assist you in the presentation of the financial statements in accordance with the tax basis of accounting. You have the following overall responsibilities that are fundamental to our undertaking the engagement in accordance with SSARSs:

a. The selection of the tax basis of accounting as the financial reporting framework to be applied in the preparation of the financial statements
b. The preparation and fair presentation of financial statements in accordance with the tax basis of accounting
c. The inclusion of all informative disclosures that is appropriate for the tax basis of accounting. This includes:
    i. A description of the tax basis of accounting, including a summary of significant accounting policies, and how the tax basis of accounting differs from accounting principles generally accepted in the United States of America, the effects of which need not be quantified and
    ii. Informative disclosures similar to those required by accounting principles generally accepted in the United States of America.
d. The design, implementation, and maintenance of internal control relevant to the preparation and fair presentation of the financial statements
e. The prevention and detection of fraud
f. To ensure that the entity complies with the laws and regulations applicable to its activities
g. The accuracy and completeness of the records, documents, explanations, and other information, including significant judgments, you provide to us for the compilation engagement
h. To provide us with:
    i. Access to all information of which you are aware is relevant to the preparation and fair presentation of the financial statements, such as records, documentation, and other matters
    ii. Additional information that we may request from you for the purpose of the compilation engagement
    iii. Unrestricted access to persons within the entity of whom we determine it necessary to make inquiries

You are also responsible for all management decisions and responsibilities and for designating an individual with suitable skills, knowledge, and experience to oversee our preparation of your financial statements. You are responsible for evaluating the adequacy and results of the services performed and accepting responsibility for such services.

Our Report

As part of our engagement, we will issue a report that will state that we did not audit or review the financial statements and that, accordingly, we do not express an opinion or a conclusion, nor do we provide any assurance on them.

You agree to include our accountant's compilation report in any document containing financial statements that indicates that we have performed a compilation engagement on such financial statements and, prior to inclusion of the report, to ask our permission to do so.

Other Relevant Information

Our fees for these services . . .

[*The accountant may include language, such as the following, regarding limitation of, or other arrangements regarding, the liability of the accountant or the entity, such as indemnification to the accountant for liability arising from knowing misrepresentations to the accountant by management (regulators may restrict or prohibit such liability limitation arrangements):*

You agree to hold us harmless and to release, indemnify, and defend us from any liability or costs, including attorneys' fees, resulting from management's knowing misrepresentations to us.]

Please sign and return the attached copy of this letter to indicate your acknowledgment of, and agreement with, the arrangements for our engagement to prepare the financial statements described herein and perform a compilation engagement with respect to those same financial statements and our respective responsibilities.

Sincerely yours,

____

[*Signature of accountant or accountant's firm*]

Acknowledged and agreed on behalf of ABC Company by:

____

[*Signed*]

[*Name and title*]

____

[*Date*]

[*Revised, February 2015, to include additional required engagement letter elements.*]

Exhibit B—Illustrative Examples of the Accountant's Compilation Report on Financial Statements (Ref: par. .A22, .A30, .A32, and .A34) .A43	
Illustration 1	An Accountant's Compilation Report on Comparative Financial Statements Prepared in Accordance with Accounting Principles Generally Accepted in the United States of America
Illustration 2	An Accountant's Compilation Report on Comparative Financial Statements Prepared in Accordance with the AICPA's Financial Reporting Framework for Small- and Medium-Sized Entities
Illustration 3	An Accountant's Compilation Report on Comparative Financial Statements Prepared in Accordance with the Tax Basis of Accounting, and Management Has Elected to Omit Substantially All Disclosures Ordinarily Included in Financial Statements Prepared in Accordance with the Tax Basis of Accounting
Illustration 4	An Accountant's Compilation Report on Comparative Financial Statements Prepared in Accordance with Accounting Principles Generally Accepted in the United States of America When the Accountant's Independence Is Impaired, and the Accountant Determines to Not Disclose the Reasons for the Independence Impairment
Illustration 5	An Accountant's Compilation Report on Comparative Financial Statements Prepared in Accordance with the AICPA's Financial Reporting Framework for Small- and Medium-Sized Entities When the Accountant's Independence Has Been Impaired Due to the Accountant Having a Financial Interest in the Entity,

	and the Accountant Decides to Disclose the Reason for the Independence Impairment
Illustration 6	An Accountant's Compilation Report on Comparative Financial Statements, and the Accountant Is Aware of Departures from Accounting Principles Generally Accepted in the United States of America

Illustration 1. An Accountant's Compilation Report on Comparative Financial Statements Prepared in Accordance with Accounting Principles Generally Accepted in the United States of America

Management is responsible for the accompanying financial statements of XYZ Company, which comprise the balance sheets as of December 31, 20X2 and 20X1 and the related statements of income, changes in stockholders' equity, and cash flows for the years then ended, and the related notes to the financial statements in accordance with accounting principles generally accepted in the United States of America. I (We) have performed compilation engagements in accordance with Statements on Standards for Accounting and Review Services promulgated by the Accounting and Review Services Committee of the AICPA. I (We) did not audit or review the financial statements, nor was (were) I (we) required to perform any procedures to verify the accuracy or completeness of the information provided by management. Accordingly, I (we) do not express an opinion or a conclusion, nor provide any form of assurance on these financial statements.

[*Signature of accounting firm or accountant, as appropriate*]

[*Accountant's city and state*]

[*Date of the accountant's report*]

Illustration 2. An Accountant's Compilation Report on Comparative Financial Statements Prepared in Accordance with the AICPA's Financial Reporting Framework for Small- and Medium-Sized Entities

Management is responsible for the accompanying financial statements of XYZ Company, which comprise the statements of financial position as of December 31, 20X2 and 20X1 and the related statements of operations and cash flows for the years then ended, and the related notes to the financial statements in accordance with the AICPA's Financial Reporting Framework for Small- and Medium-Sized Entities, and for determining that the AICPA's Financial Reporting Framework for Small- and Medium-Sized Entities is an acceptable financial reporting framework. I (We) have performed compilation engagements in accordance with Statements on Standards for Accounting and Review Services promulgated by the Accounting and Review Services Committee of the AICPA. I (We) did not audit or review the financial statements, nor was (were) I (we) required to perform any procedures to verify the accuracy or completeness of the information provided by management. Accordingly, I (we) do not express an opinion or a conclusion, nor provide any form of assurance on these financial statements.

I (We) draw attention to Note X of the financial statements, which describes the basis of accounting. The financial statements are prepared in accordance with the AICPA's Financial Reporting Framework for Small- and Medium-Sized Entities, which is a basis of accounting other than accounting principles generally accepted in the United States of America.

[*Signature of accounting firm or accountant, as appropriate*]

[*Accountant's city and state*]

[*Date of the accountant's report*]

Illustration 3. An Accountant's Compilation Report on Comparative Financial Statements Prepared in Accordance with the Tax Basis of Accounting, and Management Has Elected to Omit Substantially All Disclosures Ordinarily Included in Financial Statements Prepared in Accordance with the Tax Basis of Accounting

Management is responsible for the accompanying financial statements of XYZ Partnership, which comprise the statements of assets, liabilities, and partners' capital—tax basis as of December 31, 20X2 and 20X1 and the related statements of revenue and expenses—tax basis, and changes in partners' capital—tax basis for the years then ended in accordance with the tax basis of accounting, and for determining that the tax basis of accounting is an acceptable financial reporting framework. I (We) have performed compilation engagements in accordance with Statements on Standards for Accounting and Review Services promulgated by the Accounting and Review Services Committee of the AICPA. I (We) did not audit or review the financial statements, nor was (were) I (we) required to perform any procedures to verify the accuracy or completeness of the information provided by management. Accordingly, I (we) do not express an opinion or a conclusion, nor provide any form of assurance on these financial statements.

The financial statements are prepared in accordance with the tax basis of accounting, which is a basis of accounting other than accounting principles generally accepted in the United States of America. Management has elected to omit substantially all the disclosures ordinarily included in financial statements prepared in accordance with the tax basis of accounting. If the omitted disclosures were included in the financial statements, they might influence the user's conclusions about the company's assets, liabilities, equity, revenue, and expenses. Accordingly, the financial statements are not designed for those who are not informed about such matters.

[*Signature of accounting firm or accountant, as appropriate*]

[*Accountant's city and state*]

[*Date of the accountant's report*]

Illustration 4. An Accountant's Compilation Report on Comparative Financial Statements Prepared in Accordance with Accounting Principles Generally Accepted in the United States of America When the Accountant's Independence Is Impaired, and the Accountant Determines to Not Disclose the Reasons for the Independence Impairment

Management is responsible for the accompanying financial statements of XYZ Company, which comprise the balance sheets as of December 31, 20X2 and 20X1 and the related statements of income, changes in stockholders' equity, and cash flows for the years then ended, and the related notes to the financial statements in accordance with accounting principles generally accepted in the United States of America. I (We) have performed compilation engagements in accordance with Statements on Standards for Accounting and Review Services promulgated by the Accounting and Review Services Committee of the AICPA. I (We) did not audit or review the financial statements, nor was (were) I (we) required to perform any procedures to verify the accuracy or completeness of the information provided by management. Accordingly, I (we) do not express an opinion or a conclusion, nor provide any form of assurance on these financial statements.

I am (we are) not independent with respect to XYZ Company.

[*Signature of accounting firm or accountant, as appropriate*]

[*Accountant's city and state*]

[*Date of the accountant's report*]

ILLUSTRATION 5. AN ACCOUNTANT'S COMPILATION REPORT ON COMPARATIVE FINANCIAL STATEMENTS PREPARED IN ACCORDANCE WITH THE AICPA'S FINANCIAL REPORTING FRAMEWORK FOR SMALL- AND MEDIUM-SIZED ENTITIES WHEN THE ACCOUNTANT'S INDEPENDENCE HAS BEEN IMPAIRED DUE TO THE ACCOUNTANT HAVING A FINANCIAL INTEREST IN THE ENTITY, AND THE ACCOUNTANT DECIDES TO DISCLOSE THE REASON FOR THE INDEPENDENCE IMPAIRMENT

Management is responsible for the accompanying financial statements of XYZ Company, which comprise the statements of financial position as of December 31, 20X2 and 20X1, and the related statements of operations and cash flows for the years then ended, and the related notes to the financial statements in accordance with the AICPA's Financial Reporting Framework for Small- and Medium-Sized Entities, and for determining that the AICPA's Financial Reporting Framework for Small- and Medium-Sized Entities is an acceptable financial reporting framework. I (We) have performed compilation engagements in accordance with Statements on Standards for Accounting and Review Services promulgated by the Accounting and Review Services Committee of the AICPA. I (We) did not audit or review the financial statements, nor was (were) I (we) required to perform any procedures to verify the accuracy or completeness of the information provided by management. Accordingly, I (we) do not express an opinion or a conclusion, nor provide any form of assurance on these financial statements.

I (We) draw attention to Note X of the financial statements, which describes the basis of accounting. The financial statements are prepared in accordance with the AICPA's Financial Reporting Framework for Small- and Medium-Sized Entities, which is a basis of accounting other than accounting principles generally accepted in the United States of America.

I am (we are) not independent with respect to XYZ Company, as during the year ended December 31, 20X2, I (a member of the engagement team) had a direct financial interest in XYZ Company.

[*Signature of accounting firm or accountant, as appropriate*]

[*Accountant's city and state*]

[*Date of the accountant's report*]

ILLUSTRATION 6. AN ACCOUNTANT'S COMPILATION REPORT ON COMPARATIVE FINANCIAL STATEMENTS, AND THE ACCOUNTANT IS AWARE OF DEPARTURES FROM ACCOUNTING PRINCIPLES GENERALLY ACCEPTED IN THE UNITED STATES OF AMERICA

Management is responsible for the accompanying financial statements of XYZ Company, which comprise the balance sheets as of December 31, 20X2 and 20X1 and the related statements of income, changes in stockholders' equity, and cash flows for the years then ended, and the related notes to the financial statements in accordance with accounting principles generally accepted in the United States of America. I (We) have performed compilation engagements in accordance with Statements on Standards for Accounting and Review Services promulgated by the Accounting and Review Services Committee of the AICPA. I (We) did not audit or review the financial statements, nor was (were) I (we) required to perform any procedures to verify the accuracy or completeness of the information provided by management. Accordingly, I (we) do not express an opinion or a conclusion, nor provide any form of assurance on these financial statements.

Accounting principles generally accepted in the United States of America require that land be stated at cost. Management has informed me (us) that XYZ Company has stated its land at appraised value and that if accounting principles generally accepted in the United States of America had been followed, the land account and stockholders' equity would have been decreased by $500,000.

[*Signature of accounting firm or accountant, as appropriate*]

[*Accountant's city and state*]

[*Date of the accountant's report*]

AR-C 90 Review of Financial Statements

ORIGINAL PRONOUNCEMENT

Statement on Standards for Accounting and Review Services (SSARS) 21, effective for SSARS engagements for periods ending on or after December 15, 2015.

OBJECTIVES AND LIMITATIONS OF REVIEW ENGAGEMENTS

It is important to note that the requirements in AR-C 60 apply to all SSARS engagements, including review engagements. In addition to the guidance in this chapter, readers should apply the requirements in the chapter on Section 60 to review engagements.

The accountant's objective when performing a review of financial statements is to *obtain limited assurance as a basis for reporting whether the accountant is aware of any material modifications that should be made to the financial statements for them to be in accordance with the applicable financial reporting framework, primarily through the performance of inquiry and analytical procedures.*

(AR-C 90.04)

Certain reviews of interim financial information are out of the scope of the SSARS. This Section does not apply to the review of interim financial statements in the following situations:

1. The entity's latest annual financial statements were audited by the accountant or a predecessor.
2. The accountant either has been engaged to audit the entity's current year financial statements or audited the entity's latest annual financial statements and, when it is expected that the current year financial statements will be audited, the appointment of another accountant to audit the current year financial statements is not effective prior to the beginning of the period covered by the review.
3. The entity prepares its interim financial information in accordance with the same financial reporting framework as that used to prepare the annual financial statements.

In these situations, the accountant should perform reviews in accordance with AU-C 930, *Interim Financial Information.* (AR-C 90.02)

AR-C Section 90 may be applied to reviews of other historical financial information, such as:

- Specific elements, accounts, or items of a financial statement,
- Supplementary information,
- Required supplementary information,
- Financial information contained in a tax return, and
- Single financial statements as long as the accountant's scope is not limited.

(AR-C 90.01, 90.A1, and 90.A2)

TECHNICAL ALERT

SSARS No. 21

General information and background on SSARS No. 21 can be found in the Preface. This technical alert focuses on SSARS No. 21 changes to AR-C Section 90. Those changes include:

- Changes to the review report:
  - Use of headings
  - Name the city and state of the issuing office
  - Emphasis-of-matter paragraph required for:
    - Financial statements prepared with a special purpose framework,
    - Change in reference to a departure from the applicable financial reporting framework,
    - Comparative statements where the prior period is audited,
    - A known material departure from the framework,
    - Financial statement revised for a subsequently discovered fact that becomes known after the release date and the report changes from the original,
    - Supplementary information,
    - Required supplementary information, and
    - A matter appropriately reflected in the financial statements, but that is fundamental to the user's understanding
  - Other-matter paragraph to communicate a matter not reflected in the financial statements that is relevant to the user's understanding of the review, the accountant's responsibilities, or the review report
  - If other-matter or emphasis-of-matter paragraph is expected to be included, communicate with management the expected content of those paragraphs
  - For special purpose framework financial statements, modify the report when the financial statements do not include a description of a special purpose framework, a summary of significant accounting policies, and an adequate description of how the framework differs from GAAP
  - The report required to reference management's responsibility for determining the acceptability of the framework
  - Other-matter paragraph that restricts the use of the review report if the financial statements are prepared using a contractual or regulatory basis of accounting or measurement or disclosure criteria determined by the accountant to be suitable for a limited number of users or available only to specified parties
- Additional guidance on supplementary information, including reporting requirements
- Elimination of guidance relating to fraud and illegal acts
- Provision that, in addition to financial statements, reviews may also be applied to other historical information

Interpretation—Section 9090

In February 2016, the Accounting and Review Services Committee (ARSC) issued AR-C Interpretation No. 1 of AR-C Section 90, Consideration Related to Reviews Performed in

Accordance with International Standard Review Engagements (ISRE) 2400 (Revised), *Engagements to Review Historical Financial Statements.*

The Interpretation addresses the question of whether an accountant may refer to the ISREs in a review report. The ARSC decided that a practitioner may review financial statements in accordance with both SSARSs and another set of standards, such as ISRE 2400 (Revised), and should refer to those standards in the review report paragraph "Accountant's Responsibility."

DEFINITIONS OF TERMS

See the chapter on AR-C 60 for the definitions of terms related to Sections 60–90.

REQUIREMENTS

Following is an overview of the review engagement process. See content that follows the checklist for detailed information.

Illustration Checklist for a Review Engagement

Step No.	*Action/Decision*
1.	Obtain an understanding with the client in writing regarding the engagement. (For a new client, determine if communication with the predecessor accountant is desirable.)
2.	Determine whether the firm is independent. If the firm is, go to step 3. If the firm is not, do not issue a review report.
3.	Acquire the necessary knowledge of the client industry's accounting principles and practices.
4.	Acquire an understanding of the client's business, including (a) a general understanding of the entity's organization, (b) its operating characteristics, and (c) the nature of its assets, liabilities, revenues, and expenses.
5.	Develop expectations for the planned analytical procedures, apply appropriate inquiry and analytical procedures to obtain a reasonable basis for expressing limited assurance that no material modifications should be made to the financial statements, and compare expectations to recorded amounts or ratios developed from recorded amounts.
6.	Read the financial statements to determine whether, based on the information presented, they appear to conform to the applicable financial reporting framework. Obtain reports of other accountants for subsidiaries, investees, and so on, if any. Indicate division of responsibility if reference is made to other accountants.
7.	Perform additional procedures if information appears to be incorrect, incomplete, or otherwise unsatisfactory.
8.	Describe in the working papers matters covered in steps 5 and 7. Also, describe unusual matters that were considered and how they were resolved.
9.	Determine whether the inquiry and analytical procedures considered necessary to achieve limited assurance are incomplete or restricted in any way.
10.	Document the review engagement as required by SSARS.
11.	Consider whether the financial statements contain departures from the applicable financial reporting framework, including disclosure departures. If they do, go to step 12. If they do not, go to step 13.

12. Request that the client revise the financial statements. Failing that, consider modifying the review report by adding a separate paragraph or paragraphs. If the effect of the departure has been determined by management or is known by the accountant, disclose the dollar effects in the report. (However, the report need not be modified for uncertainties, going concern matters, or inconsistencies if they are properly disclosed.) Withdraw from the engagement if the departures are designed to mislead financial statement users.
13. Obtain a representation letter from the client.
14. Mark each page of the financial statements, including notes to the financial statements, "See Accountant's Review Report."
15. Sign and date (manual, stamped, electronic, or typed signature) the report using the date the inquiry and analytical procedures were completed.
16. Issue the financial statements and the related review report.

The accountant is required to comply with the Section 90 provisions when he or she has been engaged to review financial statements. A review is a service in which the accountant obtains limited assurance that there are no material modifications to be made to the financial statements for them to be in conformity with the applicable financial reporting framework. In a review engagement, the accountant should accumulate review evidence to obtain a limited level of assurance.

A review differs significantly from an audit of financial statements in which the auditor obtains a high level of assurance (expressed in the auditor's report as obtaining reasonable assurance) that the financial statements are free of material misstatement. A review does not contemplate obtaining an understanding of the entity's internal control; assessing fraud risk; testing accounting records by obtaining sufficient appropriate audit evidence through inspection, observation, confirmation, or the examination of source documents (for example, canceled checks or bank images); or other procedures ordinarily performed in an audit. Accordingly, in a review, the accountant does not obtain assurance that he or she will become aware of all significant matters that would be disclosed in an audit. In a review engagement, the accountant performs sufficient procedures to provide a limited assurance that there are no material modifications required for the financial statements to be in conformity with the applicable financial reporting framework. Professional judgment is needed to determine the specific nature, timing, and extent of review procedures.

NOTE: The nature, timing, and extent of procedures for gathering review evidence are limited relative to an audit.

MATERIALITY

Generally, misstatements and omissions are considered material if (individually or in aggregate) they could reasonably be expected to influence the economic decisions of users. The accountant's judgments about materiality are made in light of surrounding circumstances, in the context of the applicable financial reporting framework, and are affected by the size or nature of a misstatement. Further, the accountant's judgments about materiality are based on a consideration of the information needs of users as a group (not individually). When making these judgments, it is reasonable for the accountant to assume that users have a reasonable knowledge of business and economic activities, understand that financial statements are prepared at certain levels of materiality, recognize the uncertainties in some forms of measurement, and make reasonable economic decisions on the basis of the information contained within financial statements. These considerations may be dealt with in more detail in individual financial reporting frameworks. (AR-C 90.A4)

INDEPENDENCE

An accountant whose independence is impaired cannot perform a review. If the accountant becomes aware during the engagement that independence is impaired, the accountant should withdraw. (AR-C 90.07) The AICPA Code of Conduct provides guidance on independence and can be accessed at http://pub.aicpa.org/codeofconduct/Ethics.aspx. (AR-C 90.A10)

ACCEPTANCE AND CONTINUANCE OF CLIENT RELATIONSHIPS

When assessing whether to accept or continue a client, accountants must comply not only with the Section 90 requirements but also with the AR-C 60.25 requirements detailed in the chapter on AR-C 60. Accountants cannot accept a review engagement if management imposes a scope imitation that will prevent the accountant from obtaining enough evidence to support a review report. (ARC-C 90.08) They must also obtain the acknowledgment of management that it understands its responsibilities:

- For the financial statements' fair presentation in accordance with the applicable financial reporting framework and the applicable disclosures.
- If the financial statements use a special purpose framework, the disclosures must include:
  - A description of the framework, including significant policies and how it differs from GAAP, and disclosures similar to GAAP for those items similar to GAAP;
  - If prepared on a contractual basis, a description of any significant contract interpretations; and
  - Any additional disclosures necessary to achieve fair presentation.
- To provide a letter of representation.
- Unless a different understanding is reached, to include the review report in any document containing financial statements that indicates the financial statements have been reviewed by the accountant.

(AR-C 90.09)

If the accountants are not satisfied with any of the above conditions or those in AU-C 60.25 and cannot resolve the issues, they should not accept the engagement. (AR-C 90.10)

ESTABLISHING AN UNDERSTANDING WITH THE CLIENT

An accountant must establish a written understanding with management for a review engagement. This document should include the following items:

- *Objective.* To obtain limited assurance that there are no material modifications to be made to the financial statements.

- *Management responsibilities.* See the previous section "Acceptance and Continuance of Client Relationships" and the information on AR-C 60.25 in the Section 60 chapter.
- *Accountant responsibilities.* The accountant is responsible for conducting the engagement in accordance with SSARSs issued by the AICPA and comply with the AICPA's Code of Professional Conduct.
- *Limitations of a review engagement.* A review primarily involves applying analytical procedures to management's financial data and making inquiries of management. It is less in scope than an audit, which involves the expression of an opinion regarding the financial statements as a whole. A review does not involve gaining an understanding of an entity's internal control, nor of assessing fraud risk, testing accounting records, or the examination of source documents or other procedures performed in an audit. Thus, an accountant engaged in a review will not express an opinion regarding the financial statements as a whole. A review engagement cannot be relied upon to disclose errors, fraud, or illegal acts.
- *Material errors.* The accountant will inform management of any material errors or evidence of fraud or illegal acts, but need not report illegal acts that are clearly inconsequential.
- *Identification of the applicable financial reporting framework; review report.* The expected form and content and a statement that the report may differ from the expected form and contact.

(AR-C 90.12)

The engagement letter should be signed by the accountant or the accountant's firm and management or those charged with governance. (AR-C 90.12)

A review engagement letter may include other matters, such as fees and billings, limitations on the liabilities of the parties, references to supplementary information, and additional services related to regulatory requirements. The engagement letter should reference supplementary information.

Sample review engagement letters are shown later in the "Illustrations" section at the end of this chapter.

Change in Engagement from Audit to Review

An accountant may be engaged to audit a client's financial statements, and then, before the completion of the audit, is requested to change the engagement to a review. Before agreeing to this change, the accountant should consider the reason for the client's request and the additional audit effort and cost needed to complete the audit. A change in the entity's circumstances that affects its need for an audit or a misunderstanding about the nature of an audit are normally considered reasonable grounds for requesting a change in engagement. (AR-C 90.A135-.A136)

If the audit procedures are substantially complete or additional costs are minimal, then consider the propriety of accepting a change in the engagement. Also, evaluate the possibility that information affected by the scope restriction may be incorrect, incomplete, or unsatisfactory.

NOTE: When an accountant has been engaged to audit an entity's financial statements and has been prohibited from contacting the entity's legal counsel, the accountant, except in rare circumstances, is precluded from issuing a review report on the financial statements. (AR-C 90)

If the accountant accepts the change to a review engagement and subsequently issues a review report, he or she should not refer to the original engagement, or any audit procedures performed, or scope limitations resulting from the changed engagement. (AR-C 90.88-.89)

ILLUSTRATION—CHECKLIST FOR CHANGE IN ENGAGEMENT FROM AUDIT/REVIEW TO REVIEW/COMPILATION

Step No.	*Action/Decision*
1.	Consider (a) the reason given for the client's request, (b) the additional effort required to complete the engagement, and (c) the estimated additional cost to complete the engagement.
2.	Determine whether the request for the change is caused by (a) a change in circumstances affecting the need for an audit or review, (b) a misunderstanding as to the nature of alternative services, or (c) restrictions caused by the client or by circumstances on the scope of the engagement. If (a) or (b)—which provide a reasonable basis for requesting a change—go to step 3. If (c), go to step 4.
3.	Consider issuing an appropriate compilation or review report. Make no mention in the report of the original engagement, the procedures performed, or the scope limitations. Go to step 5.
4.	Evaluate the possibility that the information affected by the scope restriction may be incorrect, incomplete, or otherwise unsatisfactory. If the client prohibited you from corresponding with the company's legal counsel or refused to sign a client representation letter, except in rare circumstances, do not issue a review or compilation report.
5.	If the audit or review is substantially complete or the cost to complete is insignificant, consider the propriety of accepting a changed engagement.
6.	Revise the engagement letter regarding the nature of the services to be rendered.

COMMUNICATION WITH MANAGEMENT AND THOSE CHARGED WITH GOVERNANCE

If the accountant becomes aware during review procedures that fraud or illegal acts may have occurred, the accountant should bring the matter to the attention of management. If these acts involve senior management, then they should be reported to those at a higher level within the entity, or those charged with governance. If these acts involve the owner of the business, then consider resigning from the engagement, and also consider consulting with legal counsel. The communication may be oral or written; if oral, then document it.

The accountant should communicate, on a timely basis, any significant matters. (AR-C 90.13) It may be necessary to disclose certain matters to outside parties in order to comply with legal and regulatory requirements. (AR-C 90.A25)

NOTE: Unless required to by law or regulation, the accountant may need management's consent to provide a third party with a copy of the accountant's written communication with management. (AR-C 90.26)

Review Performance Requirements

The review procedures require an understanding of the entity and the environment in which it operates and are tailored to the industry in which the client operates.

Understanding the Industry

The accountant should have an understanding of the industry in which the client operates. He or she may accept a review engagement in an industry where the accountant has no previous experience, but then has a responsibility to obtain the required level of knowledge. (AR-C 90.14) For example, if a client operates in the construction industry, the accountant needs to understand the specialized accounting guidance used in that industry. To that end, the accountant may want to read the AICPA guide and other publications and/or take a continuing professional education course.

Knowledge of the Entity

The accountant should also obtain sufficient knowledge about the client's business and accounting principles and practices to identify areas with a greater likelihood of material misstatements and determine appropriate review procedures. (AR-C 90.15) This understanding should encompass the client's organization, operating characteristics, assets, liabilities, revenue, and expenses. The accountant should take note of unusual client accounting policies and procedures. (AR-C 90.16) The accountant should understand the entity's form of business, who is involved in the organization and their functions, principals, management, and related parties. The accountant should also acquire knowledge about the entity's operating locations, production methods, distribution systems, compensation methods, and so forth.

Designing and Performing Review Procedures[1]

The accountant designs and performs analytical procedures, makes inquiries, and performs other procedures to accumulate review evidence for obtaining limited assurance that no material modifications are needed. These procedures should be focused in those areas with increased risks of misstatements. The accountant can identify those areas through knowledge of the entity, understanding of the client's industry, and awareness of risks in the general business environment. (AR-C 90.17-.18) Although Section 90 emphasizes inquiries and analytical procedures, circumstances may dictate that the accountant perform procedures used in an audit. If that is the case, the engagement remains a review.

Analytical Procedures. Analytical procedures involve comparisons of the accountant's expectations with recorded amounts or derived ratios. The accountant develops expectations for this comparison by identifying and using plausible relationships that are reasonably expected to exist based on the accountant's knowledge of the client's industry and of the client. Sources of information for developing expectations include financial information for comparable prior periods, forecasted results, disaggregated revenue data, relationships among types of financial information, industry information, and relationships between financial and nonfinancial information (such as sales per employee). (AR-C 90.19)

---

1 *Useful checklists for inquiries and analytical procedures can be found in the "Illustrations" section at the end of the chapter.*

The accountant should:

- Determine the suitability of procedures for the intended purpose
- Evaluate the reliability of the data
- Develop an expectation
- Determine if the expectation is precise enough to provide assurance
- Determine the deviation from the expectation that is acceptable
  (AR-C 90.20)

Practice Pointer. Before using industry data, the accountant may want to investigate whether the standards are relevant to the way the company does business. For example, the data may include information on companies that manufacture in another country, whereas the client uses local resources. (AR-C 90.21)

Investigating Results. If the accountant's analytical procedures identify fluctuations or relationships that are inconsistent with other information or which differ significantly from expected amounts, the accountant should investigate these issues through management inquiries and other procedures. The accountant does not have to corroborate management's responses with other evidence, but that need may arise if the responses are not satisfactory or are inconsistent with other data.

Inquiries of Management. When conducting review procedures, the accountant should make inquiries of knowledgeable management regarding:

a. Whether the financial statements were prepared in conformity with the applicable financial reporting framework
b. Unusual or complex situations that affect the financial statements
c. Significant transactions occurring during the period, especially those occurring near the end of the reporting period
d. The status of uncorrected misstatements that were identified during the previous engagement
e. Questions that arose during other review procedures
f. Material events subsequent to the date of the financial statements
g. Fraud affecting the entity which could have a material effect on the financial statements
h. Significant journal entries
i. Communications from regulatory agencies
j. Allegations of fraud or suspected fraud
k. Instances of noncompliance with laws and regulations affecting the financial statements
l. Related parties and significant related party transactions
m. Litigation, claims, and assessments
n. Reasonableness of significant assumptions
o. Action taken at meetings of stockholders, boards, or committees affecting the financial statements
p. Any other matters
   (AR-C 90.22)

NOTE: The accountant is not required to corroborate management's responses with other information, but should consider the reasonableness and consistency of management's responses in view of the results of other procedures, as well as the accountant's knowledge of the client's business and industry. (AR-C 90.23)

Other Procedures

The accountant should also:

- Read the financial statements and consider whether they appear to conform with the applicable financial reporting framework,
- Obtain reports from those accountants who have been engaged to audit or review the financial statements of significant components, and
- Reconcile the financial statements to underlying accounting records.

(AR-C 90.24-.26)

If the accountant becomes aware that some information is incorrect, incomplete, or unsatisfactory in some other way, he or she should request that management consider the effect of these matters on the financial statements. If the accountant believes the financial statements may be materially misstated, he or she must then perform additional procedures to obtain limited assurance that there are no material modifications required. (AR-C 90.29-.31) If the accountant instead concludes that the financial statements are materially misstated and management does not revise them, then consider whether modification of the standard report is sufficient for disclosing the issue, or whether he or she should withdraw from the review engagement and provide no further services regarding those financial statements. (See also the section later in this chapter on reports on known departures from the applicable financial reporting framework.)

Written Representations

Management must provide written representations for all financial statements and periods covered by the accountant's review report as of the date of the accountant's review report. The letter should be addressed to the accountant and signed by those members of management who are responsible for and knowledgeable about the topics in the representation letter. Typically, the CEO and CFO sign the representation letter. The accountant should receive the signed letter from management before releasing the report.

The representation letter should include at least these items:

- Management has fulfilled its responsibility for the preparation and presentation of the financial statements in accordance with the applicable financial reporting framework.
- Management believes that the financial statements are fairly presented in accordance with the applicable financial reporting framework.
- Management acknowledges that it is responsible for the internal controls relevant to the preparation and presentation of the financial statements.
- Management acknowledges that it is responsible for preventing and detecting fraud.
- All transactions have been recorded and are reflected in the financial statements.
- Management has disclosed (or does not have) knowledge of any fraud, suspected fraud, or any allegations of fraud affecting the entity that involves management or others where fraud could have a material effect on the financial statements.
- Management responds fully and truthfully to all inquiries.
- The information provided is complete and management has provided all access requested.
- Management has disclosed any instance of suspected or actual noncompliance with laws and regulations that might affect the financial statements.
- Management has attached to the representation letter a summary of material uncorrected misstatements.

- Management's belief as to whether the uncorrected misstatements are material.
- Management has disclosed all known or possible litigation that might affect the financial statements.
- Management's belief as to the reasonableness of as significant assumptions used in estimates.
- Management has disclosed related parties, relationships, and transactions and has accounted for and disclosed those relationships and transactions.
- Information is provided concerning subsequent events.

(AR-C 90.34)

The representation letter is usually modified to include additional representations that are specific to the client's business or industry or as the accountant deems necessary. (AR-C 90.35 and .A59)

If the accountant does not issue the review report for a significant period of time after completing all review-related inquiries and procedures, he or she should consider obtaining an updated representation letter from the client. Further, if the client requests that the accountant reissue the review report on the financial statements of a prior period and those statements will be comparatively presented with the reviewed financial statements of a later period, this calls for an updated representation letter. (AR-C 90.A57)

If management does not provide a written representation letter or the accountant has reason to doubt management's integrity, the accountant should withdraw from the engagement. (AR-C 90.37)

A sample representation letter is included in the "Illustrations" section at the end of this chapter.

NOTE: If the current management team was not present during all periods being reported on, the accountant should still obtain written representations from them for all periods addressed by the review report.

Documentation in a Review Engagement

The accountant should provide sufficient documentation of a review engagement to clearly show the work performed, the review evidence obtained and its source, and the accountant's conclusions. It should include the following:

- *Engagement letter.* The signed engagement letter.
- *Procedures.* The nature, timing, and extent of procedures. The analytical procedures performed, including the accountant's expectations,[2] comparison results, and management's responses to the accountant's inquiries about inconsistent relationships or fluctuations from expected amounts. Also note any additional review procedures due to unexpected differences in initial results.
- *Significant matters.* The significant matters covered in the accountant's inquiry procedures and management's responses.
- *Significant findings.* Any findings or issues that the accountant considers to be significant and conclusions and professional judgments.

---

2 *Failure to document expectations is a common peer review comment. See AICPA* Compilation and Review Developments—2013/14, *Copyright AICPA 2014.*

- *Fraud or noncompliance.* Any written or oral communications with management regarding fraud or noncompliance that came to the accountant's attention.
- *Review report.* Communications with management regarding expectations to include an emphasis-of-matter paragraph or other-matter paragraph.
- *Other accountants.* Communication with other accountants who audited or reviewed the financial statements of significant components.
- *Representation letter.*[3]
- *A copy of the reviewed financial statements and the accountant's report.*

(AR-C 90.91-.92 and .A138-.A142)

NOTE: An oral explanation is not sufficient support for an accountant's work, but it can be used to clarify information contained in the documentation.

Reporting on the Financial Statements

The accountant should accompany reviewed financial statements with a written report that includes the following information:

- *Title.* The report title indicates that it is the accountant's review report and includes the word *independent*, such as "Independent Accountant's Review Report."
- *Addressee.* The report is addressed as required under the terms of the engagement.
- *Introductory paragraph.* The introductory paragraph identifies the entity whose financial statements were reviewed, states that the financial statements were reviewed, identifies which statements were reviewed, specifies the date or period covered by the financial statements, states that a review primarily involves applying analytical procedures to management's financial data and making inquiries of management, and states that a review is substantially less in scope than an audit; the objective of an audit is to express an opinion regarding the financial statements as a whole, and that the accountant does not express such an opinion.
- *Management's responsibilities for the financial statements.* The report uses that heading and states that management is responsible for the preparation and fair presentation of the financial statements in accordance with the applicable financial reporting framework, as well as for the internal controls relevant to the preparation and fair presentation of the financial statements.
- *Accountant's responsibility.* The report uses that heading and states that the accountant is responsible for conducting the review in accordance with SSARSs issued by AICPA. Also, it states that those standards require the accountant to perform the procedures to obtain limited assurance that there are no material modifications that should be made to the financial statements. Further, it states that the accountant believes that the results of his or her procedures provide a reasonable basis for the report.
- *Engagement results.* This is a section with an appropriate heading and states that, based on his or her review, the accountant is not aware of any material modifications that should be made to the financial statements so that they will be in conformity with the applicable financial reporting framework, other than those modifications listed in the report.

---

3 *Failure to obtain written representations from management is another common peer review comment. Ibid.*

- *Accountant's signature.* The manual or printed signature of the accountant or accounting firm, along with the city and state where the accountant practices.
- *Report date.* The date of the review report, which should be no earlier than the date the accountant completed sufficient procedures to obtain limited assurance.

(AR-C 90.39)

NOTE: GAAP financial statements must comply with the subsequent events guidance in the FASB's ASC 855. ASC 855 requires disclosure of the date through which subsequent events have been evaluated. Therefore, the report date can never be earlier than management's subsequent event date.

Several sample review reports are included at the end of this chapter in the "Illustrations" section.

Emphasizing a Matter

It is acceptable for an accountant to emphasize a matter in the review report, though it should be presented in a separate paragraph. (AR-C 90.52) Examples of such items are uncertainties, significant transactions with related parties, and important subsequent events. An emphasis paragraph is never required; it is added solely at the accountant's discretion. (AR-C 90.53)

Emphasis-of-matter paragraphs should appear immediately after the accountant's conclusion under a heading such as "Emphasis of a Matter" or other appropriate heading. The paragraph should emphasize a clear reference to the matter and where it can be found and that the report is not modified because of the matter emphasized. An other-matter paragraph should appear after the conclusion paragraph and any emphasis-of-matter paragraph.

Special Purpose Framework

A special purpose framework includes the cash, tax, regulatory, and other bases of accounting formerly known as other comprehensive basis of accounting (OCBOA) and contractual basis of accounting. If a client prepares financial statements in accordance with a special purpose framework, they are not appropriate in form unless the statements include:

- A description of the framework,
- A description of significant accounting policies,
- A summary of the primary differences from GAAP, and
- Informative disclosures similar to those required by GAAP.

If those items are not included, the accountant should modify the report. (AR-C 90.40) If financial statements are prepared on a contractual basis and they do not adequately describe significant interpretations of the contract, the accountant must modify the report. (AR-C 90.41) The review report should reference management's responsibility for determining the acceptability of the framework and describe the purpose for which the financial statements are prepared or refer to a note that does so. (AR-C 90.42) The review report should also include an emphasis-of-matter paragraph, with an appropriate heading, that states the financial statements are prepared using a special reporting framework, refers to the note describing the framework, and that the basis is other than GAAP. (AR-C 90.43)

Restricting the Use of the Review Report

If an accountant's report is not restricted to specific parties, then it is for *general use*. The report is for *restricted use* if it is intended only for specific third parties. The accountant should designate the review report as being for restricted use when the report or presentation is based on disclosure criteria contained in a contractual agreement or regulatory provisions that are not in conformity with an applicable financial reporting framework. (AR-C 90.44) The alert should be included when the subject matter of the report is based on measurement or disclosure criteria that the accountant decides are suitable for a limited number of people who can be expected to understand the criteria or measurement or disclosure criteria available to specified parties. (AR-C 90.61)

A restricted report should contain a separate paragraph, an alert, that includes a statement indicating that the report is intended solely for the information and use of the specified parties, which identifies the parties to whom the report is restricted, and which states that the report is not intended to be and should not be used by anyone other than the specified parties. (AR-C 90.62)

If the accountant is asked to consider adding other parties to the recipient list for a restricted report, the accountant may agree to do so, based on the consideration of such factors as identity of the other parties, and the intended use of the report. (AR-C 90.A111)

If the other parties are added after the release of the review report, the accountant may:

- Amend the report to add the other parties and not change the report date, or
- Provide other written acknowledgment that the other parties have been added (and state that no procedures have been performed subsequent to the date of the report).

(AR-C 90.64)

NOTE: The accountant is not responsible for controlling a client's distribution of restricted-use reports. (AR-C 90.A109)

Going Concern Considerations

During a review, it may come to the accountant's attention that there is uncertainty regarding an entity's ability to continue as a going concern for a reasonable period of time. The time period is dictated by the financial reporting framework or, if not specified in the framework, a reasonable period of time not to exceed one year past the date of the financial statements. (AR-C 90.65)

If there is a going concern uncertainty, the accountant should request that management consider the effects on the financial statements.

The accountant should consider the reasonableness of management's resulting response, including the adequacy of any related disclosures. If the accountant concludes that management's conclusions are unreasonable or the related disclosure of the situation is not adequate, he or she should consider whether modification of the review report is adequate to disclose the going concern issue. If the accountant concludes that the entity's disclosures are inadequate, a departure from the applicable financial reporting framework exists and the accountant should follow that guidance. (AR-C 90.66-.68)

NOTE: It is also acceptable to emphasize an uncertainty about a going concern issue, provided that the uncertainty is disclosed in the financial statements. An emphasis paragraph is not required and added solely at the accountant's discretion. (AR-C 90.A114)

Known Departures from the Applicable Financial Reporting Framework

The accountant may become aware of a departure from the applicable financial reporting framework, including inadequate disclosure of going concern issues and other matters. If so, the accountant should consider whether modification of the report is adequate. If it is, the departure should be disclosed in a separate paragraph of the report. The separate paragraph should disclose the effects of the departure if they have been determined by management or known by the accountant. If the effects are not known, the accountant should state that. The accountant should withdraw from the engagement if he or she believes the disclosures are inadequate. (AR-C 90.56-.59)

Subsequent Events

Before the review report date, the accountant may become aware of subsequent events that have a material effect on the reviewed financial statements. If so, the accountant should request that management consider the effects on the financial statements. If the accountant concludes that the subsequent event is not properly reflected in the financial statements, he or she should follow the guidance for known departures from the applicable financial reporting framework. (AR-C 90.69-.70)

Subsequent Discovery of Facts Existing at the Report Date

Subsequent to the review report date, the accountant may become aware of facts that existed on the report date, which may have caused him or her to believe the information originally supplied by the entity was unsatisfactory.

Discovered before the Report Release Date. After the date of the accountant's review report, the accountant has no obligation to perform other review procedures, unless new information comes to his or her attention. However, if such new information becomes known before the release date, the accountant should determine whether it is reliable and whether it existed at the report date. The accountant should request cooperation from management to investigate the new information. If the information would have affected the review report or the financial statements, and the accountant believes the persons using the financial statements would consider the information to be important and management revises the financial statements, then the accountant should perform procedures. The accountant should also either date the review report as of a later date or dual date the report. If management does not revise the financial statements as needed, the accountant should modify the review report appropriately. (AR-C 90.71-.73)

Discovered after the Report Release Date. The accountant should discuss the issue with management, determine if the financial statements need revision, and, if so, find out how management intends to address the matter. If management revises the financial statements, the accountant should date the review report as of a later date or dual date the report. (AR-C 90.75a)

If the financial statements were made available before revision and have been made available to third parties, the accountant should assess the timeliness and appropriateness of management's action to ensure that those who received the financial statements have been notified not to use the financial statements. If management has not taken appropriate action, the accountant should inform management that he or she will try to prevent further use of the review report. (AR-C 90.74-.77)

Supplementary Information

If the financial statements are accompanied by supplementary information, the accountant should indicate the degree of responsibility that he or she is taking for it. The accountant includes an explanation of the supplementary information in either an other-matter paragraph in the review report or a separate report, which states the information is the representation of management and that either:

- The supplementary data are presented only for purposes of additional analysis and have been subjected to the inquiry and analytical procedures applied in the review of the financial statements, the information is the representation of management, the accountant is not aware of any material modifications that should be made to it, the information has not been audited and the auditor does not express an opinion on it, or
- The supplementary data are presented only for purposes of additional analysis and have not been subjected to the inquiry and analytical procedures applied in the review of the financial statements, but were instead compiled from information that is the representation of management, without audit or review, and the accountant does not express an opinion, a conclusion, or provide any assurance on the data.
(AR-C 90.80-.82)

Required Supplementary Information That Accompanies Reviewed Financial Statements

SSARS do not require the accountant to apply procedures to any information presented for supplementary analysis purposes, including required supplementary information. However, the accountant should modify the accountant's review report by including an other-matter paragraph that, as applicable:

- Refers to the required supplementary information and states the accountant performed a compilation or review of the information or the accountant did not perform a compilation, review, or audit on the information;
- States the required supplementary information is omitted or some is missing; and
- Indicates the accountant has identified departures from the guidelines or has unresolved doubts about whether the information is presented in accordance with the prescribed guidelines.
(AR-C 90.83)

The accountant should present that other matter paragraph after the paragraph that reports the results of the engagement. It may read as follows:

THE REQUIRED SUPPLEMENTARY INFORMATION IS INCLUDED

[*Identify the applicable financial reporting framework (for example, accounting principles generally accepted in the United States of America)*] require that [*identify the required supplementary information*] on page XX be presented to supplement the basic financial statements. Such information, although not a part of the basic financial statements, is required by [*identify the designated accounting standards setter*], who considers it to be an essential part of financial reporting and for placing the basic financial statements in an appropriate operational, economic, or historical context. Such information was not audited, reviewed, or compiled by me (*us*) and, accordingly, I (*we*) do not express an opinion or provide any assurance on it. (AR-C 90.84a-c)

SOME REQUIRED SUPPLEMENTARY INFORMATION IS OMITTED AND SOME IS PRESENTED IN ACCORDANCE WITH THE PRESCRIBED GUIDELINES REGARDING THE REQUIRED SUPPLEMENTARY INFORMATION

[*Identify the applicable financial reporting framework (for example, accounting principles generally accepted in the United States of America)*] require that [*identify the included supplementary information*] be presented to supplement the basic financial statements. Such information, although not a part of the basic financial statements, is required by [*identify designated accounting standards setter*], who considers it to be an essential part of financial reporting for placing the basic financial statements in an appropriate operational, economic, or historical context. Such information was not audited, reviewed, or compiled by me (us) and, accordingly, I (we) do not express an opinion or provide any assurance on it.

Management has omitted [*describe the missing required supplementary information*] that [*identify the applicable financial reporting framework*] require to be presented to supplement the basic financial statements. Such missing information, although not a part of the basic financial statements, is required by [*identify designated accounting standard setter*], who considers it to be an essential part of financial reporting for placing the basic financial statements in an appropriate operational, economic, or historical context. The results of our review of the basic financial statements are not affected by this missing information.

MEASUREMENT OR PRESENTATION OF THE REQUIRED SUPPLEMENTARY INFORMATION DEPARTS MATERIALLY FROM THE PRESCRIBED GUIDELINES

Add a statement that material departures from described guidelines exist. (AR-C 90.84e)

ACCOUNTANT HAS UNRESOLVED DOUBTS ABOUT COMPLIANCE WITH GUIDELINES

If the accountant has unresolved doubts about whether the required supplementary information is measured or presented in accordance with the prescribed guidelines, the accountant should add a statement that he or she has doubts about whether material modifications should be made to the required supplementary information for it to be presented in accordance with guidelines established by [*identify designated accounting standards setter*]. (AR-C 90.84f)

ALL REQUIRED SUPPLEMENTARY INFORMATION OMITTED

Management has omitted [*describe the missing required supplementary information*] that [*identify the applicable financial reporting framework (for example, accounting principles generally accepted in the United States of America)*] require to be presented to supplement the basic financial statements. Such missing information, although not a part of the basic financial statements, is required by [*identify the designated accounting standard setter*], who considers it to be an essential part of financial reporting and for placing the basic financial statements in an appropriate operational, economic, or historical context. The results of our review of the basic financial statements are not affected by this missing information. (AR-C 90.85)

ILLUSTRATIONS: REVIEW ENGAGEMENT

Illustration 1	Inquiries for a Review
Illustration 2	Suggested Analytical Procedures
Engagement Letters (AR-C 90.A145)	
Illustration 3	An Engagement Letter for a Review Engagement with Respect to Financial Statements Prepared in Accordance with Accounting Principles Generally Accepted in the United States of America
Illustration 4	An Engagement Letter for a Review Engagement with Respect to Financial Statements Prepared in Accordance with the Tax Basis of Accounting

Representation Letter (AR-C 90.A146)	
Illustration 5	Representation Letter
Review Reports (AR-C 90.A147)	
Illustration 6	An Accountant's Review Report on Comparative Financial Statements Prepared in Accordance with Accounting Principles Generally Accepted in the United States of America When a Review Has Been Performed for Both Periods
Illustration 7	An Accountant's Review Report on Single-Year Financial Statements Prepared in Accordance with Accounting Principles Generally Accepted in the United States of America
Illustration 8	An Accountant's Review Report on Single-Year Financial Statements Prepared in Accordance with the Tax Basis of Accounting
Illustration 9	An Accountant's Review Report on Interim Financial Statements Prepared in Accordance with Accounting Principles Generally Accepted in the United States of America
Illustration 10	An Accountant's Review Report on Comparative Financial Statements Disclosing a Departure from Accounting Principles Generally Accepted in the United States of America
Illustration 11	An Accountant's Review Report on Comparative Consolidated Financial Statements in Which the Accountant Makes Reference to the Work of Other Accountants Who Were Engaged to Review the Financial Statements of a Significant Component

Illustration 1. Inquiries for a Review

1. General:

   a. Have there been any changes in the entity's business activities?
   b. Are there any unusual or complex situations that may have an effect on the financial statements (for example, business combinations, restructuring plans, or litigation)?
   c. What procedures are in place related to recording, classifying, and summarizing transactions and accumulating information related to financial statements disclosures?
   d. Have the financial statements been prepared in conformity with the applicable financial reporting framework? Have there been any changes in accounting principles and methods of applying those principles?
   e. Have there been any instances of fraud or illegal acts within the entity?
   f. Have there been any allegations or suspicions that fraud or illegal acts might have occurred or might be occurring within the entity? If so, where and how?
   g. Are any entities other than the reporting entity commonly controlled by the owners? If so, has an evaluation been performed to determine whether those other entities should be consolidated into the financial statements of the reporting entity?
   h. Are there any entities other than the reporting entity in which the owners have significant investments (for example, variable interest entities)? If so, has an evaluation been performed to determine whether the reporting entity is the primary beneficiary related to the activities of these other entities?
   i. Have any significant transactions occurred or been recognized near the end of the reporting period?

2. Cash and cash equivalents:

    a. Is the entity's policy regarding the composition of cash and cash equivalents in accordance with Financial Accounting Standards Board Statement ASC 305? Has the policy been applied on a consistent basis?
    b. Are all cash and cash equivalents accounts reconciled on a timely basis?
    c. Have old or unusual reconciling items between bank balances and book balances been reviewed and adjustments made where necessary?
    d. Has there been a proper cutoff of cash receipts and disbursements?
    e. Has a reconciliation of intercompany transfers been prepared?
    f. Have checks written but not mailed as of the financial statement date been properly reclassified into the liability section of the balance sheet?
    g. Have material bank overdrafts been properly reclassified into the liability section of the balance sheet?
    h. Are there compensating balances or other restrictions on the availability of cash and cash equivalents balances? If so, has consideration been given to reclassifying these amounts as noncurrent assets?
    i. Have cash funds been counted and reconciled with control accounts?

3. Receivables:

    a. Has an adequate allowance for doubtful accounts been properly reflected in the financial statements?
    b. Have uncollectible receivables been written off through a charge against the allowance account or earnings?
    c. Has interest earned on receivables been properly reflected in the financial statements?
    d. Has there been a proper cutoff of sales transactions?
    e. Are there receivables from employees or other related parties? Have receivables from owners been evaluated to determine if they should be reflected in the equity section (rather than the asset section) of the balance sheet?
    f. Are any receivables pledged, discounted, or factored? Are recourse provisions properly reflected in the financial statements?
    g. Have receivables been properly classified between current and noncurrent?
    h. Have there been significant numbers of sales returns or credit memoranda issued subsequent to the balance sheet date?
    i. Is the accounts receivable subsidiary ledger reconciled to the general ledger account balance on a regular basis?

4. Inventory:

    a. Are physical inventory counts performed on a regular basis, including at the end of the reporting period? Are the count procedures adequate to ensure an appropriate count? If not, how have amounts related to inventories been determined for purposes of financial statement presentation? If so, what procedures were used to take the latest physical inventory and what date was that inventory taken?
    b. Have general ledger control accounts been adjusted to agree with the physical inventory count? If so, were the adjustments significant?
    c. If the physical inventory counts were taken at a date other than the balance sheet date, what procedures were used to determine changes in inventory between the date of physical inventory counts and the balance sheet date?
    d. Were consignments in or out considered in taking physical inventories?
    e. What is the basis of valuing inventory for purposes of financial statement presentation?
    f. Does inventory cost include material, labor, and overhead where applicable?

g. Has inventory been reviewed for obsolescence or cost in excess of net realizable value? If so, how are these costs reflected in the financial statements?
h. Have proper cutoffs of purchases, goods in transit, and returned goods been made?
i. Are there any inventory encumbrances?
j. Is scrap inventoried and controlled?

5. Prepaid expenses:

a. What is the nature of the amounts included in prepaid expenses?
b. How are these amounts being amortized?

6. Investments:

a. What is the basis of accounting for investments reported in the financial statements (for example, securities, joint ventures, or closely held businesses)?
b. Are derivative instruments properly measured and disclosed in the financial statements? If those derivatives are utilized in hedge transactions, have the documentation or assessment requirements related to hedge accounting been met?
c. Are investments in marketable debt and equity securities properly classified as trading, available-for-sale, and held-to-maturity?
d. How were fair values of the reported investments determined? Have unrealized gains and losses been properly reported in the financial statements?
e. If the fair values of marketable debt and equity securities are less than cost, have the declines in value been evaluated to determine whether the declines are other-than-temporary?
f. For any debt securities classified as held-to-maturity, does management have the positive ability and intent to hold the securities until they mature? If so, have those debt securities been properly measured?
g. Have gains and losses related to disposal of investments been properly reflected in the financial statements?
h. How was investment income determined? Is investment income properly reflected in the financial statements?
i. Has appropriate consideration been given to the classification of investments between current and noncurrent?
j. For investments made by the reporting entity, have consolidation, equity, or cost method accounting requirements been considered?
k. Are any investments encumbered?

7. Property and equipment:

a. Are property and equipment items properly stated at depreciated cost or other proper value?
b. When was the last time a physical inventory of property and equipment was taken?
c. Are all items reflected in property and equipment held for use? If not, have items that are held for sale been properly reclassified from property and equipment?
d. Have gains or losses on disposal of property and equipment been properly reflected in the financial statements?
e. What are the criteria for capitalization of property and equipment? Have the criteria been consistently and appropriately applied?
f. Are repairs and maintenance costs properly reflected as an expense in the income statement?
g. What depreciation methods and rates are utilized in the financial statements? Are these methods and rates appropriate and applied on a consistent basis?
h. Are there any unrecorded additions, retirements, abandonments, sales, or trade-ins?
i. Does the entity have any material lease agreements? If so, have those agreements been properly evaluated for financial statement presentation purposes?

j. Are there any asset retirement obligations associated with tangible long-lived assets? If so, has the recorded amount of the related asset been increased because of the obligation, and is the liability properly reflected in the liability section of the balance sheet?
k. Has the entity constructed any of its property and equipment items? If so, have all components of cost been reflected in measuring these items for purposes of financial statement presentation, including but not limited to capitalized interest?
l. Has there been any significant impairment in value of property and equipment items? If so, has any impairment loss been properly reflected in the financial statements?
m. Are any property and equipment items mortgaged or otherwise encumbered? If so, are these mortgages and encumbrances properly reflected in the financial statements?

8. Intangibles and other assets:

a. What is the nature of the amounts included in other assets?
b. Do these assets represent costs that will benefit future periods? What is the amortization policy related to these assets? Is this policy appropriate?
c. Have other assets been properly classified between current and noncurrent?
d. Are intangible assets with finite lives being appropriately amortized?
e. Are the costs associated with computer software properly reflected as intangible assets (rather than property and equipment) in the financial statements?
f. Are the costs associated with goodwill (and other intangible assets with indefinite lives) properly reflected as intangible assets in the financial statements? Has amortization ceased related to these assets?
g. Has there been any significant impairment in value of these assets? If so, has any impairment loss been properly reflected in the financial statements?
h. Are any of these assets mortgaged or otherwise encumbered?

9. Accounts and short-term notes payable and accrued liabilities:

a. Have significant payables been reflected in the financial statements?
b. Are loans from financial institutions and other short-term liabilities properly classified in the financial statements?
c. Have significant accruals (for example, payroll, interest, provisions for pension and profit-sharing plans, or other post-retirement benefit obligations) been properly reflected in the financial statements?
d. Has a liability for employees' compensation for future absences been properly accrued and disclosed in the financial statements?
e. Are any liabilities collateralized or subordinated? If so, are those liabilities disclosed in the financial statements?
f. Are there any payables to employees and related parties?

10. Long-term liabilities:

a. Are the terms and other provisions of long-term liability agreements properly disclosed in the financial statements?
b. Have liabilities been properly classified between current and noncurrent?
c. Has interest expense been properly accrued and reflected in the financial statements?
d. Is the company in compliance with loan covenants and agreements? If not, is the noncompliance properly disclosed in the financial statements?
e. Are any long-term liabilities collateralized or subordinated? If so, are these facts disclosed in the financial statements?
f. Are there any obligations that, by their terms, are due on demand within one year from the balance sheet date? If so, have these obligations been properly reclassified into the current liability section of the balance sheet?

11. Income and other taxes:

    a. Do the financial statements reflect an appropriate provision for current and prior-year income taxes payable?
    b. Have any assessments or reassessments been received? Are there tax authority examinations in process?
    c. Are there any temporary differences between book and tax amounts? If so, have deferred taxes on these differences been properly reflected in the financial statements?
    d. Do the financial statements reflect an appropriate provision for taxes other than income taxes (for example, franchise, sales)?
    e. Have all required tax payments been made on a timely basis?

12. Other liabilities, contingencies, and commitments:

    a. What is the nature of the amounts included in other liabilities?
    b. Have other liabilities been properly classified between current and noncurrent?
    c. Are there any guarantees, whether written or verbal, whereby the entity must stand ready to perform or is contingently liable related to the guarantee? If so, are these guarantees properly reflected in the financial statements?
    d. Are there any contingent liabilities (for example, discounted notes, drafts, endorsements, warranties, litigation, and unsettled asserted claims)? Are there any potential unasserted claims? Are these contingent liabilities, claims, and assessments properly measured and disclosed in the financial statements?
    e. Are there any material contractual obligations for construction or purchase of property and equipment or any commitments or options to purchase or sell company securities? If so, are these facts clearly disclosed in the financial statements?
    f. Is the entity responsible for any environmental remediation liability? If so, is this liability properly measured and disclosed in the financial statements?
    g. Does the entity have any agreement to repurchase items that previously were sold? If so, have the repurchase agreements been taken into account in determining the appropriate measurements and disclosures in the financial statements?
    h. Does the entity have any sales commitments at prices expected to result in a loss at the consummation of the sale? If so, are these commitments properly reflected in the financial statements?
    i. Are there any violations, or possible violations, of laws or regulations the effects of which should be considered for financial statement accrual or disclosure?

13. Equity:

    a. What is the nature of any changes in equity accounts during each reporting period?
    b. What classes of stock (other ownership interests) have been authorized?
    c. What is the par or stated value of the various classes of stock (other ownership interests)?
    d. Do amounts of outstanding shares of stock (other ownership interests) agree with subsidiary records?
    e. Have pertinent rights and privileges of ownership interests been properly disclosed in the financial statements?
    f. Does the entity have any mandatorily redeemable ownership interests? If so, have these ownership interests been evaluated so that a proper determination has been made related to whether these ownership interests should be measured and reclassified to the liability section of the balance sheet? Are redemption features associated with ownership interests clearly disclosed in the financial statements?
    g. Have dividend (distribution) and liquidation preferences related to ownership interests been properly disclosed in the financial statements?

h. Do disclosures related to ownership interests include any applicable call provisions (prices and dates), conversion provisions (prices and rates), unusual voting rights, significant terms of contracts to issue additional ownership interests, or any other unusual features associated with the ownership interests?
i. Are syndication fees properly reflected in the financial statements as a reduction of equity (rather than an asset)?
j. Have any stock options or other stock compensation awards been granted to employees or others? If so, are these options or awards properly measured and disclosed in the financial statements?
k. Has the entity made any acquisitions of its own stock? If so, are the amounts associated with these reacquired shares properly reflected in the financial statements as a reduction in equity? Is the presentation in accordance with applicable state laws?
l. Are there any restrictions or appropriations on retained earnings or other capital accounts? If so, are these restrictions or appropriations properly reflected in the financial statements?

14. Revenue and expenses:

a. What is the entity's revenue recognition policy? Is the policy appropriate? Has the policy been consistently applied and appropriately disclosed?
b. Are revenues from sales of products and rendering of services recognized in the appropriate reporting period (that is, when the products have been delivered and when the services have been performed)?
c. Were any sales recorded under a "bill and hold" arrangement? If yes, have the criteria been met to record the transaction as a sale?
d. Are purchases and expenses recognized in the appropriate reporting period (that is, matched against revenue) and properly classified in the financial statements?
e. Do the financial statements include discontinued operations? If so, are amounts associated with discontinued operations properly displayed in the income statement?
f. Does the entity have any gains or losses that would necessitate the display of comprehensive income (for example, gains/losses on available-for-sale securities or cash flow hedge derivatives)? If so, have these items been properly displayed within comprehensive income (rather than included in the determination of net income)?

15. Other:

a. Have events occurred subsequent to the balance sheet date that would require adjustment to, or disclosure in, the financial statements?
b. Have actions taken at stockholders, committees of directors, or comparable meetings that affect the financial statements been reflected in the financial statements?
c. Are significant estimates and material concentrations (for example, customers or suppliers) properly disclosed in the financial statements?
d. Are there plans or intentions that may materially affect the carrying amounts or classification of assets and liabilities reflected in the financial statements?
e. Have there been material transactions between or among related parties (for example, sales, purchases, loans, or leasing arrangements)? If so, are these transactions properly disclosed in the financial statements?
f. Are there uncertainties that could have a material impact on the financial statements? Is there any change in the status of previously disclosed material uncertainties? Are all uncertainties, including going concern matters that could have a material impact on the financial statements, properly disclosed in the financial statements?
g. Are barter or other nonmonetary transactions properly recorded and disclosed?

Illustration 2. Suggested Analytical Procedures (AR-C 90.A143)

- Comparing financial statements with statements for comparable prior period(s).
- Comparing current financial information with anticipated results, such as budgets or forecasts (for example, comparing tax balances and the relationship between the provision for income taxes and pretax income in the current financial information with corresponding information in (1) budgets, using expected rates, and (2) financial information for prior periods).
- Comparing current financial information with relevant nonfinancial information.
- Comparing ratios and indicators for the current period with expectations based on prior periods; for example, performing gross profit analysis by product line and operating segment using elements of the current financial information and comparing the results with corresponding information for prior periods. Examples of key ratios and indicators are the current ratio, receivables turnover or days' sales outstanding, inventory turnover, depreciation to average fixed assets, debt to equity, gross profit percentage, net income percentage, and plant operating rates.
- Comparing ratios and indicators for the current period with those of entities in the same industry.
- Comparing relationships among elements in the current financial information with corresponding relationships in the financial information of prior periods; for example, expense by type as a percentage of sales, assets by type as a percentage of total assets, and percentage of change in sales to percentage of change in receivables.
- Analytical procedures may include such statistical techniques as trend analysis or regression analysis and may be performed manually or with the use of computer-assisted techniques.

Illustration 3. An Engagement Letter for a Review Engagement with Respect to Financial Statements Prepared in Accordance with Accounting Principles Generally Accepted in the United States of America

To the appropriate representative of management of ABC Company:

You have requested that we prepare the financial statements of ABC Company, which comprise the balance sheet as of December 31, 20XX, and the related statements of income, changes in stockholders' equity, and cash flows for the year then ended, and the related notes to the financial statements and perform a review engagement with respect to those financial statements. We are pleased to confirm our acceptance and understanding of this engagement by means of this letter.

Our Responsibilities

The objective of our engagement is to:

a. Prepare financial statements in accordance with accounting principles generally accepted in the United States of America based on information provided by you, and
b. Obtain limited assurance as a basis for reporting whether we are aware of any material modifications that should be made to the financial statements in order for the statements to be in accordance with accounting principles generally accepted in the United States of America.

We will conduct our engagement in accordance with Statements on Standards for Accounting and Review Services (SSARSs) promulgated by the Accounting and Review Services Committee of the AICPA and comply with the AICPA's Code of Professional Conduct, including ethical principles of integrity, objectivity, professional competence, and due care.

A review engagement includes primarily applying analytical procedures to your financial data and making inquiries of company management. A review engagement is substantially less in scope than an audit engagement, the objective of which is the expression of an opinion regarding the financial statements as a whole. A review engagement does not contemplate obtaining an understanding of the entity's internal control; assessing fraud risk; testing accounting records by obtaining sufficient appropriate audit evidence through inspection, observation, confirmation, or the examination of source documents; or other procedures ordinarily performed in an audit engagement. Accordingly, we will not express an opinion regarding the financial statements.

Our engagement cannot be relied upon to identify or disclose any financial statement misstatements, including those caused by error or fraud, or to identify or disclose any wrongdoing within the entity or noncompliance with laws and regulations. However, we will inform the appropriate level of management of any material errors and any evidence or information that comes to our attention during the performance of our review procedures that indicates fraud may have occurred. In addition, we will report to you any evidence or information that comes to our attention during the performance of our review procedures regarding noncompliance with laws and regulations that may have occurred, unless they are clearly inconsequential.

Your Responsibilities

The engagement to be performed is conducted on the basis that you acknowledge and understand that our role is to prepare financial statements in accordance with accounting principles generally accepted in the United States of America and to obtain limited assurance as a basis for reporting whether we are aware of any material modifications that should be made to the financial statements in order for the statements to be in accordance with accounting principles generally accepted in the United States of America. You have the following overall responsibilities that are fundamental to our undertaking the engagement in accordance with SSARSs:

a. The selection of accounting principles generally accepted in the United States of America as the financial reporting framework to be applied in the preparation of the financial statements
b. The preparation and fair presentation of the financial statements in accordance with accounting principles generally accepted in the United States of America and the inclusion of all informative disclosures that are appropriate for accounting principles generally accepted in the United States of America
c. The design, implementation, and maintenance of internal control relevant to the preparation and fair presentation of the financial statements
d. The prevention and detection of fraud
e. To ensure that the entity complies with the laws and regulations applicable to its activities
f. The accuracy and completeness of the records, documents, explanations, and other information, including significant judgments, you provide to us for the engagement
g. To provide us with:
    i. Access to all information of which you are aware is relevant to the preparation and fair presentation of the financial statements, such as records, documentation, and other matters
    ii. Additional information that we may request from you for the purpose of the review engagement
    iii. Unrestricted access to persons within the entity of whom we determine it necessary to make inquiries
h. To provide us, at the conclusion of the engagement, with a letter that confirms certain representations made during the review

You are also responsible for all management decisions and responsibilities, and for designating an individual with suitable skills, knowledge, and experience to oversee our preparation of your financial statements. You are responsible for evaluating the adequacy and results of services performed and accepting responsibility for such services.

Our Report

[*Insert appropriate reference to the expected form and content of the accountant's review report. Example follows.*]

We will issue a written report upon completion of our review of ABC Company's financial statements. Our report will be addressed to the board of directors of ABC Company. We cannot provide assurance that an unmodified accountant's review report will be issued. Circumstances may arise in which it is necessary for us to report known departures from accounting principles generally accepted in the United States of America, add an emphasis-of-matter or other-matter paragraph(s), or withdraw from the engagement. If, for any reason, we are unable to complete the review of your financial statements, we will not issue a report on such statements as a result of this engagement.

You agree to include our accountant's review report in any document containing financial statements that indicates that such financial statements have been reviewed by us and, prior to inclusion of the report, to ask our permission to do so.

Other Relevant Information

Our fees for these services . . .

[*The accountant may include language, such as the following, regarding limitation of or other arrangements regarding the liability of the accountant or the entity, such as indemnification to the accountant for liability arising from knowing misrepresentations to the accountant by management (regulators may restrict or prohibit such liability limitation arrangements):*

You agree to hold us harmless and to release, indemnify, and defend us from any liability or costs, including attorney's fees, resulting from management's knowing misrepresentations to us.]

Please sign and return the attached copy of this letter to indicate your acknowledgement of, and agreement with, the arrangements for our engagement to prepare the financial statements described herein and to perform a review of those same financial statements and our respective responsibilities.

Sincerely yours,

____

[*Signature of accountant or accountant's firm*]

Acknowledged and agreed on behalf of ABC Company by:

____

[*Signed*]

[*Name and title*]

____

[*Date*]

ILLUSTRATION 4. AN ENGAGEMENT LETTER FOR A REVIEW ENGAGEMENT WITH RESPECT TO FINANCIAL STATEMENTS PREPARED IN ACCORDANCE WITH THE TAX BASIS OF ACCOUNTING

To the appropriate representative of management of ABC Company:

You have requested that we prepare the financial statements of ABC Company, which comprise the statement of assets, liabilities, and equity—tax basis as of December 31, 20XX, and the related statements of operations and retained earnings—tax basis, and cash flows—tax basis for the year then ended, and the related notes to the financial statements and to perform a review engagement with respect to those financial statements. We are pleased to confirm our acceptance and our understanding of this engagement by means of this letter.

Our Responsibilities

The objective of our engagement is to:

a. Prepare financial statements in accordance with the tax basis of accounting based on information provided by you, and
b. Obtain limited assurance as a basis for reporting whether we are aware of any material modifications that should be made to the financial statements in order for the statements to be in accordance with the tax basis of accounting.

We will conduct our review engagement in accordance with Statements on Standards for Accounting and Review Services (SSARSs) promulgated by the Accounting and Review Services Committee of the AICPA and comply with the AICPA's Code of Professional Conduct, including ethical principles of integrity, objectivity, professional competence, and due care.

A review engagement includes primarily applying analytical procedures to your financial data and making inquiries of company management. A review engagement is substantially less in scope than an audit engagement, the objective of which is the expression of an opinion regarding the financial statements as a whole. A review engagement does not contemplate obtaining an understanding of the entity's internal control; assessing fraud risk; testing accounting records by obtaining sufficient appropriate audit evidence through inspection, observation, confirmation, or the examination of source documents; or other procedures ordinarily performed in an audit engagement. Accordingly, we will not express an opinion regarding the financial statements.

Our engagement cannot be relied upon to identify or disclose any financial statement misstatements, including those caused by error or fraud, or to identify or disclose any wrongdoing within the entity or noncompliance with laws and regulations. However, we will inform the appropriate level of management of any material errors and any evidence or information that comes to our attention during the performance of our review procedures that indicates fraud may have occurred. In addition, we will report to you any evidence or information that comes to our attention during the performance of our review procedures regarding noncompliance with laws and regulations that may have occurred, unless they are clearly inconsequential.

Your Responsibilities

The engagement to be performed is conducted on the basis that you acknowledge and understand that our role is to prepare financial statements in accordance with the tax basis of accounting and to obtain limited assurance as a basis for reporting whether we are aware of any material modifications that should be made to the financial statements in order for the statements to be in accordance with the tax basis of accounting. You have the following overall responsibilities that are fundamental to our undertaking the engagement in accordance with SSARSs:

a. The selection of the tax basis of accounting as the financial reporting framework to be applied in the preparation of the financial statements
b. The preparation and fair presentation of the financial statements in accordance with the tax basis of accounting and the inclusion of all informative disclosures that are appropriate for the tax basis of accounting. This includes:
    i. A description of the tax basis of accounting, including a summary of significant accounting policies, and how the tax basis of accounting differs from accounting principles generally accepted in the United States of America, the effects of which need not be qualified

   ii. Informative disclosures similar to those required by accounting principles generally accepted in the United States of America

c. The design, implementation, and maintenance of internal control relevant to the preparation and fair presentation of the financial statements
d. The prevention and detection of fraud
e. To ensure that the entity complies with the laws and regulations applicable to its activities
f. The accuracy and completeness of the records, documents, explanations, and other information, including significant judgments, you provide to us for the engagement
g. To provide us with:

   i. Access to all information of which you are aware is relevant to the preparation and fair presentation of the financial statements, such as records, documentation, and other matters
   ii. Additional information that we may request from you for the purpose of the review engagement
   iii. Unrestricted access to persons within the entity of whom we determine it necessary to make inquiries

h. To provide us, at the conclusion of the engagement, with a letter that confirms certain representations made during the review

You are also responsible for all management decisions and responsibilities and for designating an individual with suitable skills, knowledge, and experience to oversee our preparation of your financial statements. You are responsible for evaluating the adequacy and results of the services performed and accepting responsibility for such services.

Our Report

[*Insert appropriate reference to the expected form and content of the accountant's review report. Example follows.*]

We will issue a written report upon completion of our review of ABC Company's financial statements. Our report will be addressed to the board of directors of ABC Company. We cannot provide assurance that an unmodified accountant's review report will be issued.

Circumstances may arise in which it is necessary of us to report known departures from the tax basis of accounting, add an emphasis-of-matter or other-matter paragraph(s), or withdraw from the engagement. If, for any reason, we are unable to complete the review of your financial statements, we will not issue a report on such statements as a result of this engagement.

You agree to include our accountant's review report in any document containing financial statements that indicates that such financial statements have been reviewed by us and, prior to inclusion of the report, to ask our permission to do so.

Other Relevant Information

Our fees for these services . . .

[*The accountant may include language, such as the following, regarding limitation of or other arrangements regarding the liability of the accountant or the entity, such as indemnification to the accountant for liability arising from knowing misrepresentations to the accountant by management (regulators may restrict or prohibit such liability limitation arrangements):*

You agree to hold us harmless and to release, indemnify, and defend us from any liability or costs, including attorney's fees, resulting from management's knowing misrepresentations to us.]

Please sign and return the attached copy of this letter to indicate your acknowledgment of, and agreement with, the arrangements for our engagement to prepare the financial statements described herein and to perform a review with respect to those same financial statements and our respective responsibilities.

Sincerely yours,

____

[*Signature of accountant or accountant's firm*]

Acknowledged and agreed on behalf of ABC Company by:

____

[*Signed*]

[*Name and title*]

____

[*Date*]

Illustration 5. Representation Letter (AU-C 90.A61)

[*Entity letterhead*]
[*To accountant*]
[*Date*]

This representation letter is provided in connection with your review of the financial statements of ABC Company, which comprise the balance sheets as of December 31, 20X2 and 20X1, and the related statements of income, changes in stockholders' equity and cash flows for the years then ended, and the related notes to the financial statements, for the purpose of obtaining limited assurance as a basis for reporting whether you are aware of any material modifications that should be made to the financial statements in order for the statements to be in accordance with accounting principles generally accepted in the United States of America.

Certain representations in this letter are described as being limited to matters that are material. Items are considered material, regardless of size, if they involve an omission or misstatement of accounting information that, in the light of surrounding circumstances, makes it probable that the judgment of a reasonable person relying on the information would be changed or influenced by the omission or misstatement.

We represent that to the best of our knowledge and belief, having made such inquiries as we considered necessary for the purpose of appropriately informing ourselves, as of [*date of accountant's review report*]:

Financial Statements

- We acknowledge our responsibility and have fulfilled our responsibilities for the preparation and fair presentation of the financial statements in accordance with accounting principles generally accepted in the United States of America.
- We acknowledge our responsibility and have fulfilled our responsibilities for the design, implementation, and maintenance of internal control relevant to the preparation and fair presentation of financial statements that are free from material misstatement, whether due to fraud or error.
- We acknowledge our responsibility for the design, implementation, and maintenance of internal control to prevent and detect fraud.
- Significant assumptions used by us in making accounting estimates, including those measured at fair value, are reasonable.
- Related party relationships and transactions have been appropriately accounted for and disclosed in accordance with the requirements of accounting principles generally accepted in the United States of America.

- Guarantees, whether written or oral, under which the company is contingently liable have been properly accounted for and disclosed in accordance with the requirements of accounting principles generally accepted in the United States of America.
- Significant estimates and material concentrations known to management that are required to be disclosed in accordance with FASB *Accounting Standards Codification* (ASC) 275, *Risks and Uncertainties*, have been properly accounted for and disclosed in accordance with the requirements of accounting principles generally accepted in the United States of America. [*Significant estimates are estimates at the balance sheet date that could change materially within the next year.* Concentrations *refer to volumes of business, revenues, available sources of supply, or markets or geographic areas for which events could occur that would significantly disrupt normal finances within the next year.*]
- All events subsequent to the date of the financial statements and for which accounting principles generally accepted in the United States of America requires adjustment or disclosure have been adjusted or disclosed.
- The effects of uncorrected misstatements are immaterial, both individually and in the aggregate, to the financial statements as a whole.
- The effects of all known actual or possible litigation and claims have been accounted for and disclosed in accordance with accounting principles generally accepted in the United States of America.

[*Any other matters that the accountant may consider appropriate.*]

Information Provided

- We have responded fully and truthfully to all inquiries made to us by you during your review.
- We have provided you with:
    - Access to all information, of which we are aware, that is relevant to the preparation and fair presentation of the financial statements, such as records, documentation, and other matters;
    - Minutes of meetings of stockholders, directors, and committees of directors or summaries of actions of recent meetings for which minutes have not yet been prepared;
    - Additional information that you have requested from us for the purpose of the review; and
    - Unrestricted access to persons within the entity from whom you determined it necessary to obtain review evidence.
- All transactions have been recorded in the accounting records and are reflected in the financial statements.
- We have [*no knowledge of any*] [*disclosed to you all information that we are aware of regarding*] fraud or suspected fraud that affects the entity and involves:
    - Management,
    - Employees who have significant roles in internal control, or
    - Others when the fraud could have a material effect on the financial statements.
- We have [*no knowledge of any*] [*disclosed to you all information that we are aware of regarding*] allegations of fraud, or suspected fraud, affecting the entity's financial statements as a whole communicated by employees, former employees, analysts, regulators, or others.
- We have no plans or intentions that may materially affect the carrying amounts or classification of assets and liabilities.
- We have disclosed to you all known instances of noncompliance or suspected noncompliance with laws or regulations whose effects should be considered when preparing financial statements.
- We [*have disclosed to you all known actual or possible*] [*are not aware of any pending or threatened*] litigation and claims whose effects should be considered when preparing the financial statements [*and we have not consulted legal counsel concerning litigation or claims*].

- We have disclosed to you any other material liabilities or gain or loss contingencies that are required to be accrued or disclosed by FASB ASC 450, *Contingencies*.
- We have disclosed to you the identity of the entity's related parties and all the related party relationships and transactions of which we are aware.
- No material losses exist (such as from obsolete inventory or purchase or sale commitments) that have not been properly accrued or disclosed in the financial statements.
- The company has satisfactory title to all owned assets, and no liens or encumbrances on such assets exist, nor has any asset been pledged as collateral, except as disclosed to you and reported in the financial statements.
- We have complied with all aspects of contractual agreements that would have a material effect on the financial statements in the event of noncompliance.
- We are in agreement with the adjusting journal entries that you have recommended, and they have been posted to the company's accounts (if applicable).

[*Any other matters that the accountant may consider necessary*]

____

[*Name of chief executive officer and title*]

____

[*Name of chief financial officer and title*]

Representation letters ordinarily are tailored to include additional appropriate representations from management relating to matters specific to the entity's business or industry.

ILLUSTRATION 6. AN ACCOUNTANT'S REVIEW REPORT ON COMPARATIVE FINANCIAL STATEMENTS PREPARED IN ACCORDANCE WITH ACCOUNTING PRINCIPLES GENERALLY ACCEPTED IN THE UNITED STATES OF AMERICA WHEN A REVIEW HAS BEEN PERFORMED FOR BOTH PERIODS

Independent Accountant's Review Report

____

[*Appropriate addressee*]

I (We) have reviewed the accompanying financial statements of XYZ Company, which comprise the balance sheets as of December 31, 20X2 and 20X1, and the related statements of income, changes in stockholders' equity, and cash flows for the years then ended, and the related notes to the financial statements. A review includes primarily applying analytical procedures to management's (owners') financial data and making inquiries of company management (owners). A review is substantially less in scope than an audit, the objective of which is the expression of an opinion regarding the financial statements as a whole. Accordingly, I (we) do not express such an opinion.

Management's Responsibility for the Financial Statements

Management (Owners) is (are) responsible for the preparation and fair presentation of these financial statements in accordance with accounting principles generally accepted in the United States of America; this includes the design, implementation, and maintenance of internal control relevant to the preparation and fair presentation of financial statements that are free from material misstatement whether due to fraud or error.

Accountant's Responsibility

My (Our) responsibility is to conduct the review engagements in accordance with Statements on Standards for Accounting and Review Services promulgated by the Accounting and Review Services Committee of the AICPA. Those standards require me (us) to perform procedures to obtain limited assurance as a basis for reporting whether I am (we are) aware of any material modifications that should be made to the financial statements for them to be in accordance with accounting principles generally accepted in the United States of America. I (We) believe that the results of my (our) procedures provide a reasonable basis for my (our) conclusion.

Accountant's Conclusion

Based on my (our) reviews, I am (we are) not aware of any material modifications that should be made to the accompanying financial statements in order for them to be in accordance with accounting principles generally accepted in the United States of America.

[*Signature of accounting firm or accountant, as appropriate*]

[*Accountant's city and state*]

[*Date of the accountant's review report*]

ILLUSTRATION 7. AN ACCOUNTANT'S REVIEW REPORT ON SINGLE-YEAR FINANCIAL STATEMENTS PREPARED IN ACCORDANCE WITH ACCOUNTING PRINCIPLES GENERALLY ACCEPTED IN THE UNITED STATES OF AMERICA

Independent Accountant's Review Report

____

[*Appropriate addressee*]

I (We) have reviewed the accompanying financial statements of XYZ Company, which comprise the balance sheet as of December 31, 20XX, and the related statements of income, changes in stockholders' equity, and cash flows for the year then ended, and the related notes to the financial statements. A review includes primarily applying analytical procedures to management's (owners') financial data and making inquiries of company management (owners). A review is substantially less in scope than an audit, the objective of which is the expression of an opinion regarding the financial statements as a whole. Accordingly, I (we) do not express such an opinion.

Management's Responsibility for the Financial Statements

Management (Owners) is (are) responsible for the preparation and fair presentation of these financial statements in accordance with accounting principles generally accepted in the United States of America; this includes the design, implementation, and maintenance of internal control relevant to the preparation and fair presentation of financial statements that are free from material misstatement whether due to fraud or error.

Accountant's Responsibility

My (Our) responsibility is to conduct the review engagement in accordance with Statements on Standards for Accounting and Review Services promulgated by the Accounting and Review Services Committee of the AICPA. Those standards require me (us) to perform procedures to obtain limited assurance as a basis for reporting whether I am (we are) aware of any material modifications that should be made to the financial statements for them to be in accordance with accounting principles generally accepted in the United States of America. I (We) believe that the results of my (our) procedures provide a reasonable basis for my (our) conclusion.

Accountant's Conclusion

Based on my (our) review, I am (we are) not aware of any material modifications that should be made to the accompanying financial statements in order for them to be in accordance with accounting principles generally accepted in the United States of America.

[*Signature of accounting firm or accountant, as appropriate*]

[*Accountant's city and state*]

[*Date of the accountant's review report*]

Illustration 8. An Accountant's Review Report on Single-Year Financial Statements Prepared in Accordance with the Tax Basis of Accounting

Independent Accountant's Review Report

____

[*Appropriate addressee*]

I (We) have reviewed the accompanying financial statements of XYZ Partnership, which comprise the statement of assets, liabilities, and partners' capital—tax basis as of December 31, 20XX, and the related statements of revenue and expenses—tax basis, and partners' capital—tax basis for the year then ended, and the related notes to the financial statements. A review includes primarily applying analytical procedures to management's (partners') financial data and making inquiries of partnership management (owners). A review is substantially less in scope than an audit, the objective of which is the expression of an opinion regarding the financial statement as a whole. Accordingly, I (we) do not express such an opinion.

Management's Responsibility for the Financial Statements

Management (Partners) is (are) responsible for the preparation and fair presentation of these financial statements in accordance with the basis of accounting the partnership uses for income tax purposes; this includes determining that the basis of accounting the partnership uses for income tax purposes is an acceptable basis for the preparation of financial statements in the circumstances. Management (Partners) is (are) also responsible for the design, implementation, and maintenance of internal control relevant to the preparation and fair presentation of financial statements that are free from material misstatement, whether due to fraud or error.

Accountant's Responsibility

My (Our) responsibility is to conduct the review engagement in accordance with Statements on Standards for Accounting and Review Services promulgated by the Accounting and Review Services Committee of the AICPA. Those standards require me (us) to perform procedures to obtain limited assurance as a basis for reporting whether I am (we are) aware of any material modifications that should be made to the financial statements for them to be in accordance with the basis of accounting the partnership uses for income tax purposes. I (We) believe that the results of my (our) procedures provide a reasonable basis for my (our) conclusion.

Accountant's Conclusion

Based on my (our) review, I am (we are) not aware of any material modifications that should be made to the accompanying financial statements in order for them to be in accordance with the basis of accounting the partnership uses for income tax purposes.

Basis of Accounting

I (We) draw attention to Note X of the financial statements, which describes the basis of accounting. The financial statements are prepared in accordance with the basis of accounting the partnership uses for income tax purposes, which is a basis of accounting other than accounting principles generally accepted in the United States of America. Our conclusion is not modified with respect to this matter.

[*Signature of accounting firm or accountant, as appropriate*]

[*Accountant's city and state*]

[Date of the accountant's review report]

ILLUSTRATION 9. AN ACCOUNTANT'S REVIEW REPORT ON INTERIM FINANCIAL STATEMENTS PREPARED IN ACCORDANCE WITH ACCOUNTING PRINCIPLES GENERALLY ACCEPTED IN THE UNITED STATES OF AMERICA

Independent Accountant's Review Report

____

[*Appropriate addressee*]

I (We) have reviewed the accompanying financial statements of XYZ Company, which comprise the balance sheet as of September 30, 20XX, and the related statements of income, changes in stockholders' equity, and cash flows for the three and nine months then ended, and the related notes to the financial statements. A review includes primarily applying analytical procedures to management's (owners') financial data and making inquiries of company management (owners). A review is substantially less in scope than an audit, the objective of which is the expression of an opinion regarding the financial statements as a whole. Accordingly, I (we) do not express such an opinion.

Management's Responsibility for the Financial Statements

Management (Owners) is (are) responsible for the preparation and fair presentation of these financial statements in accordance with accounting principles generally accepted in the United States of America; this includes the design, implementation, and maintenance of internal control relevant to the preparation and fair presentation of financial statements that are free from material misstatement whether due to fraud or error.

Accountant's Responsibility

My (Our) responsibility is to conduct the review engagements in accordance with Statements on Standards for Accounting and Review Services promulgated by the Accounting and Review Services Committee of the AICPA. Those standards require me (us) to perform procedures to obtain limited assurance as a basis for reporting whether I am (we are) aware of any material modifications that should be made to the financial statements for them to be in accordance with accounting standards generally accepted in the United States of America. I (We) believe that the results of my (our) procedures provide a reasonable basis for my (our) conclusion.

Accountant's Conclusion

Based on my (our) review, I am (we are) not aware of any material modifications that should be made to the accompanying financial statements in order for them to be in accordance with accounting principles generally accepted in the United States of America.

[*Signature of accounting firm or accountant, as appropriate*]

[*Accountant's city and state*]

[*Date of the accountant's review report*]

ILLUSTRATION 10—AN ACCOUNTANT'S REVIEW REPORT ON COMPARATIVE FINANCIAL STATEMENTS DISCLOSING A DEPARTURE FROM ACCOUNTING PRINCIPLES GENERALLY ACCEPTED IN THE UNITED STATES OF AMERICA

Independent Accountant's Review Report

____

[*Appropriate addressee*]

I (We) have reviewed the accompanying financial statements of XYZ Company, which comprise the balance sheets as of December 31, 20X2 and 20X1, and the related statements of income, changes in stockholders' equity, and cash flows for the years then ended, and the related notes to the financial statements. A review includes primarily applying analytical procedures to management's (owners') financial data and making inquiries of company management (owners). A review is substantially less in scope than an audit, the objective of which is the expression of an opinion regarding the financial statements as a whole. Accordingly, I (we) do not express such an opinion.

Management's Responsibility for the Financial Statements

Management (Owners) is (are) responsible for the preparation and fair presentation of these financial statements in accordance with accounting principles generally accepted in the United States of America; this includes the design, implementation, and maintenance of internal control relevant to the preparation and fair presentation of financial statements that are free from material misstatement whether due to fraud or error.

Accountant's Responsibility

My (Our) responsibility is to conduct the review engagements in accordance with Statements on Standards for Accounting and Review Services promulgated by the Accounting and Review Services Committee of the AICPA. Those standards require me (us) to perform procedures to obtain limited assurance as a basis for reporting whether I am (we are) aware of any material modifications that should be made to the financial statements for them to be in accordance with accounting principles generally accepted in the United States of America. I (We) believe that the results of my (our) procedures provide a reasonable basis for my (our) conclusion.

Accountant's Conclusion

Based on my (our) reviews, except for the issue noted in the Known Departure From Accounting Principles Generally Accepted in the United States of America paragraph, I am (we are) not aware of any material modifications that should be made to the accompanying financial statements in order for them to be in accordance with accounting principles generally accepted in the United States of America.

Known Departure from Accounting Principles Generally Accepted in the United States of America

As disclosed in Note X to these financial statements, accounting principles generally accepted in the United States of America require that inventory cost consist of material, labor, and overhead. Management has informed me (us) that the inventory of finished goods and work in process is stated in the accompanying financial statements at material and labor cost only, and that the effects of this departure from accounting principles generally accepted in the United States of America on financial position, results of operations, and cash flows have not been determined.

Or:

As disclosed in Note X to these financial statements, the company has adopted [*description of newly adopted method*], whereas it previously used [*description of previous method*]. Although the [*description of newly adopted method*] is in accordance with accounting principles generally accepted in the United States of America, the company does not appear to have reasonable justification for making a change as required by FASB Accounting Standards Codification 250, *Accounting Changes and Error Corrections.*

[*Signature of accounting firm or accountant, as appropriate*]

[*Accountant's city and state*]

[*Date of the accountant's review report*]

ILLUSTRATION 11. AN ACCOUNTANT'S REVIEW REPORT ON COMPARATIVE CONSOLIDATED FINANCIAL STATEMENTS IN WHICH THE ACCOUNTANT MAKES REFERENCE TO THE WORK OF OTHER ACCOUNTANTS WHO WERE ENGAGED TO REVIEW THE FINANCIAL STATEMENTS OF A SIGNIFICANT COMPONENT

Independent Accountant's Review Report

____

[*Appropriate addressee*]

I (We) have reviewed the accompanying consolidated financial statements of XYZ Company and its subsidiaries, which comprise the consolidated balance sheets as of December 31, 20X2 and 20X1, and the related consolidated statements of income, changes in stockholders' equity, and cash flows for the years then ended, and the related notes to the financial statements. A review includes primarily applying analytical procedures to management's (owners') financial data and making inquiries of company management (owners). A review is substantially less in scope than an audit, the objective of which is the expression of an opinion regarding the financial statements as a whole. Accordingly, I (we) do not express such an opinion.

Management's Responsibility for the Financial Statements

Management (Owners) is (are) responsible for the preparation and fair presentation of these consolidated financial statements in accordance with accounting principles generally accepted in the United States of America; this includes the design, implementation, and maintenance of internal control relevant to the preparation and fair presentation of consolidated financial statements that are free from material misstatement whether due to fraud or error.

Accountant's Responsibility

My (Our) responsibility is to conduct the review engagements in accordance with Statements on Standards for Accounting and Review Services (SSARSs) promulgated by the Accounting and Review

Services Committee of the AICPA. We have not reviewed the financial statements of B Company, a wholly owned subsidiary, whose financial statements reflect total assets constituting 20 percent and 22 percent, respectively, of consolidated total assets at December 31, 20X2 and 20X1, and total revenues constituting 18 percent and 20 percent, respectively, of consolidated total revenues for the years then ended. These statements were reviewed by other accountants, whose report has been furnished to me (us), and our conclusion, insofar as it relates to the amounts included for B Company, is based solely on the report of the other accountants.

SSARSs require me (us) to perform procedures to obtain limited assurance as a basis for reporting whether I am (we are) aware of any material modifications that should be made to the consolidated financial statements for them to be in accordance with accounting principles generally accepted in the United States of America. I (We) believe that the results of my (our) procedures provide a reasonable basis for my (our) conclusion.

Accountant's Conclusion

Based on my (our) reviews, and the report of other accountants, I am (we are) not aware of any material modifications that should be made to the accompanying consolidated financial statements in order for them to be in accordance with accounting principles generally accepted in the United States of America.

[*Signature of accounting firm or accountant, as appropriate*]

[*Accountant's city and state*]

[*Date of the accountant's review report*]

AR-C 120 Compilation of Pro Forma Financial Information

ORIGINAL PRONOUNCEMENTS

Sources Statement on Standards for Accounting and Review Services (SSARSs) 22.

APPLICABILITY

AR-C 120 is applicable when an accountant is engaged to compile or issue a compilation report on pro forma financial information.

TECHNICAL ALERT

As part of the SSARS clarity project, SSARS No. 21 superseded all AR sections except for AR 120. In September 2016, the ARSC issued SSARS No. 22, which put the guidance in clarified format. The standard is effect for reports dated on or after May 1, 2017.

OBJECTIVES OF AR-C SECTION 120

It is important to note that the requirements in AR-C 60 apply to all SSARS engagements, including compilation engagements. Readers should apply the requirements in the chapter on Section 60 to compilation engagements in addition to the guidance in this chapter.

The objective of the accountant in a compilation of pro forma financial information is to apply accounting and financial reporting expertise to assist management in the presentation of pro forma financial information and report in accordance with this section without undertaking to obtain or provide any assurance on the pro forma financial information. (AR-C 120.03)

Entities issue pro forma information to show what the significant effects on historical financial information might have been had a consummated or proposed transaction or event occurred at an earlier date—for example, a business combination or the disposal of a portion of the business.

REQUIREMENTS

GENERAL GUIDANCE

Independence

For a pro forma engagement, accountants must determine whether they are independent of the entity. (AR-C 120.06)

ACCEPTANCE AND CONTINUANCE OF CLIENT RELATIONSHIPS

Accountants must comply with the requirements in the chapter on AR-C 60 related to acceptance and continuance of a client. They must also obtain the acknowledgment of management that it understands its responsibility:

a. The preparation and fair presentation of pro forma financial information in accordance with the applicable financial reporting framework
b. To include the following in any document that contains the pro forma financial information:
    i. The complete financial statements of the entity for the most recent year (or for the preceding year if financial statements for the most recent year are not yet available) or such financial statements are readily available
    ii. If pro forma financial information is presented for an interim period, either historical interim financial information for that period (which may be in condensed form) or that such interim information is readily available
    iii. In the case of a business combination, the relevant historical financial information for the significant constituent parts of the combined entity
c. To ensure that the financial statements of the entity (or, in the case of a business combination, of each significant constituent part of the combined entity) on which the pro forma financial information is based have been subjected to a compilation, review, or an audit engagement
d. To include the accountant's compilation or review report or the auditor's report on the financial statements (or to have readily available) in any document containing the pro forma financial information
e. To present a summary of significant assumptions with the pro forma financial information
f. To obtain the accountant's permission prior to including the accountant's compilation report in any document containing the pro forma financial information that indicates that the entity's accountant has performed a compilation engagement on such pro forma financial information (AR-C 120.07)

Reporting Obligation

An accountant may prepare or assist in the preparation of pro forma financial information and submitting such a preparation to management *without* the issuance of a compilation report, unless the accountant has been engaged to perform a compilation. However, in deciding whether to issue a compilation report, the accountant should consider how such a presentation of pro forma financial information will be used. If the accountant believes that he or she will be associated with the information, he or she should consider issuing a compilation report so a user will not infer a level of assurance that does not exist.

Additionally, the historical financial statements of the entity on which the compiled pro forma information is based must have been compiled, reviewed, or audited and the related report should be included in the document containing the pro forma financial information.

Understanding with the Entity

The accountant should both establish and document an understanding with management. Such written communications reduce the risk that management may inappropriately rely on the accountant to protect the entity against some types of risks, or expect the accountant to perform some tasks that are actually management's responsibility. The documentation should include the following:

a. The objectives of the engagement
b. The responsibilities of management set forth in paragraph .25c of AR-C section 60 and paragraph 7 of this section
c. The responsibilities of the accountant
d. The limitations of the compilation engagement
e. Identification of the applicable financial reporting framework for the preparation of the pro forma financial information
f. The expected form and content of the accountant's compilation report and a statement that there may be circumstances in which the report may differ from its expected form and content (AR-C 120.09)

Performance Requirements

Before completing a compilation of pro forma financial information, he or she must adhere to the compilation requirements contained in AR-C 80.17-.31, which require the accountant to possess a level of knowledge of the accounting principles and practices of the client's industry that will enable him or her to perform the compilation. The accountant should also understand:

1. The nature of the entity's business transactions
2. The form of its accounting records
3. The stated qualifications of its accounting personnel
4. The accounting basis of its financial statements
5. The form and content of the financial statements

The accountant should read the presentation of the pro forma financial information, including the summary of significant assumptions, and consider whether the information appears to be in appropriate form and free of obvious material mistakes.

Reporting Requirements

The basic elements of a report on compiled pro forma financial information are as follows:

- *Title.* The title indicates that it is the accountant's compilation report.
- *Addressee.* The report is addressed based on the circumstances of the engagement.
- *Introductory paragraph.* Identifies the entity whose pro forma financial information has been compiled, notes that the information has been compiled, identifies the information that has been compiled, specifies the dates or period covered, references the financial statements from which the historical financial information is derived, and includes a statement on whether such financial statements were compiled, that pro forma information was not audited or reviewed, and, therefore, the accountant does not express an opinion or provide any assurance about whether the pro forma information is in accordance with the applicable financial reporting framework. (If the report on historical information contains a modification, the report on pro forma information should refer to that modification.)
- *Management's responsibility.* States that management is responsible for the preparation and fair presentation of the pro forma information in accordance with the applicable financial reporting framework, as well as for internal controls relevant to the preparation and presentation of the financial statements.

- *Accountant's responsibility.* States that the accountant's responsibility is to conduct the compilation in accordance with SSARS, as well as a statement that the objective of a compilation is to assist management in presenting pro forma information without obtaining or providing assurance that there are no material modifications that should be made to the financial statements.
- *Objective paragraph.* A separate paragraph explaining the objective and limitations of pro forma information.
- *Accountant's signature.* The signature of the accounting firm or the accountant.
- *Report date.* The date of the compilation report.

If the accountant is not independent, the report should be modified. In deciding whether or not he or she is independent, the accountant should refer to the AICPA Code of Professional Conduct.

ILLUSTRATIONS

ILLUSTRATION 1. ENGAGEMENT LETTER FOR A COMPILATION ON PRO FORMA FINANCIAL INFORMATION

The following is an example compilation report on pro forma financial information.

[*Appropriate salutation*]

You have requested that we prepare the pro forma financial information of ABC Company (the Company) and perform a compilation engagement with respect to that pro forma financial information. We are pleased to confirm our acceptance and our understanding of this engagement by means of this letter.

Pro forma financial information is a presentation that shows what the significant effects on historical financial information might have been had a consummated or proposed transaction (or event) occurred at an earlier date.

Our Responsibilities

The objective of our engagement is to

a. prepare the pro forma financial information in accordance with accounting principles generally accepted in the United States of America, and
b. perform a compilation engagement on the pro forma financial information we prepared in which we will apply accounting and financial reporting expertise to assist you in the presentation of the pro forma financial information and report without undertaking to obtain or provide any assurance that there are no material modifications that should be made to the pro forma financial information in order for it to be in accordance with accounting principles generally accepted in the United States of America.

We will conduct our engagement in accordance with Statements on Standards for Accounting and Review Services (SSARSs) promulgated by the Accounting and Review Services Committee of the American Institute of Certified Public Accountants (AICPA) and comply with the AICPA's Code of Professional Conduct, including the ethical principles of integrity, objectivity, professional competence, and due care.

We are not required to, and will not, verify the accuracy or completeness of the information you will provide to us for the engagement or otherwise gather evidence for the purpose of expressing an opinion or a conclusion. Accordingly, we will not express an opinion or provide any assurance on the pro forma financial information.

Our engagement cannot be relied upon to identify or disclose any pro forma financial information misstatements, including those caused by fraud or error, or to identify or disclose any wrongdoing within the Company or noncompliance with laws and regulations.

Management Responsibilities

The engagement to be performed is conducted on the basis that management acknowledges and understands that our role is to prepare the pro forma financial information in accordance with accounting principles generally accepted in the United States of America and perform a compilation engagement on the pro forma financial information we prepared. Management has the following overall responsibilities that are fundamental to our undertaking the engagement in accordance with SSARSs:

a. For the preparation and fair presentation of the pro forma financial information in accordance with accounting principles generally accepted in the United States of America and for the selection of accounting principles generally accepted in the United States of America as the applicable financial reporting framework
b. To include the following in any document that contains the pro forma financial information:
   i. The complete financial statements of the entity for the most recent year (or for the preceding year if financial statements for the most recent year are not yet available) or such financial statements are readily available
   ii. If pro forma financial information is presented for an interim period, either historical interim financial information for that period (which may be in condensed form) or that such interim information is readily available
   iii. In the case of a business combination, the relevant historical financial information for the significant constituent parts of the combined entity
c. To ensure that the financial statements of the entity (or, in the case of a business combination, of each significant constituent part of the combined entity) on which the pro forma financial information is based have been subjected to a compilation, review, or an audit engagement
d. To include the accountant's compilation or review report or the auditor's report on the financial statements (or make readily available) in any document containing the pro forma financial information
e. To present a summary of significant assumptions with the pro forma financial information
f. To obtain the accountant's permission prior to including the accountant's compilation report in any document containing the pro forma financial information that indicates that the entity's a

ILLUSTRATION 2. COMPILATION REPORT ON PRO FORMA FINANCIAL INFORMATION

Compilation report on pro forma financial information reflecting a business combination prepared in accordance with accounting principles generally accepted in the United States of America:

Accountant's Compilation Report

[*Appropriate salutation*]

Management is responsible for the accompanying pro forma condensed balance sheet of XYZ Company as of December 31, 20X1, and the related pro forma condensed statement of income for the year then ended (pro forma financial information), based on the criteria in Note 1. The historical condensed financial statements are derived from the financial statements of XYZ Company, on which I (we) performed a compilation engagement, and of ABC Company, on which other accountants performed a compilation engagement. The pro forma adjustments are based on management's assumptions described in Note 1. (We) have performed a compilation engagement in accordance with Statements on Standards for Accounting and Review Services promulgated by the Accounting and

Review Services Committee of the AICPA. I (we) did not examine or review the pro forma financial information nor was (were) I (we) required to perform any procedures to verify the accuracy or completeness of the information provided by management. Accordingly, I (we) do not express an opinion, a conclusion, nor provide any form of assurance on the pro forma financial information.

The objective of this pro forma financial information is to show what the significant effects on the historical financial information might have been had the underlying transaction (or event) occurred at an earlier date. However, the pro forma condensed financial statements are not necessarily indicative of the results of operations or related effects on financial position that would have been attained had the above mentioned transaction (or event) actually occurred at such earlier date.

[Additional paragraph(s) may be added to emphasize certain matters relating to the compilation engagement or the subject matter.]

[*Signature of accounting firm or accountant, as appropriate*]

[*Accountant's city and state*]

[*Date of the accountant's report*]

APPENDIX A: CROSS-REFERENCES TO SASs, SSAEs, AND SSARSs

Statements on Auditing Standards (SASs)

No.	*Date issued*	*Title*	*Section*
117	Dec. 2009	Compliance Audits[1]	720
118	Feb. 2010	*Other Information in Documents Containing Audited Financial Statements*	725
119	Feb. 2010	*Supplementary Information in Relation to the Financial Statements as a Whole*	730
120	Feb. 2010	*Required Supplementary Information*	935
122	Oct. 2011	*Codification of Auditing Standards and Procedures*	Throughout
123	Oct. 2011	*Omnibus Statement on Auditing Standards—2011*	200, 260, 705, 720, 915, 935
124	Oct. 2011	*Financial Statements Prepared in Accordance with a Financial Reporting Framework Generally Accepted in Another Country*	910
125	Dec. 2011	*Alert That Restricts the Use of the Auditor's Written Communication*	260, 265, 725, 800, 806, 905, 915, 920, 935
126	July 2012	*The Auditor's Consideration of an Entity's Ability to Continue as a Going Concern*	570
127	Jan. 2013	*Omnibus Statement of Auditing Standards—2013*	600, 800
128	Feb. 2014	*Using the Work of Internal Auditors*	610
129	July 2014	*Amendments to SAS No. 122 Section 920, Letters for Underwriters and Certain Other Requesting Parties, as Amended*	920
130	Oct. 2015	*An Audit of Internal Control over Financial Reporting That Is Integrated with an Audit of Financial Statements*	940
131	Jan. 2016	*Amendment to Auditing Standards No. 122 Section 700, Forming an Opinion and Reporting on Financial Statements*	700

1 *To address practice issues, clarified SAS Nos. 117, 118, 119, and 120 were issued before the clarified Omnibus SAS in 2011. SAS No. 122 changed the numbers of AU sections 801, 550, 551, and 558, but did not supersede the guidance in SAS Nos. 117, 118, 119, and 120.*

Statements on Standards for Attestation Engagements (SSAEs)

No.	*Date issued*	*Title*	*AT Sections*
1–9	Various	Superseded by SSAE 10	
10	Jan. 2001	*Attestation Standards: Revision and Recodification*	101, 201, 301, 401, 601, 701
11	Jan. 2002	*Attest Documentation*	101.100-.108, 201.27-.30, 301.17, 301.32
12	Sept. 2002	*Amendment to SSAE 10, Attestation Standards: Revision and Recodification*	101.17-.19, 201, 301
13	Dec. 2005	*Defining Professional Requirements in Statements on Standards for Attestation Engagements*	20
14	Nov. 2006	*SSAE Hierarchy*	50
15	Sept. 2008	*An Examination of an Entity's Internal Control over Financial Reporting That Is Integrated with an Audit of Its Financial Statements*	501
16	Apr. 2010	*Reporting on Controls at a Service Organization*	801
17	Dec. 2010	*Reporting on Compiled Prospective Financial Statements When the Practitioner's Independence Is Impaired*	301.23
18	Apr. 2016	*Attestation Standards: Clarification and Recodification*[2]	AT-C Sections: Preface, 105, 205, 210, 215, 305, 310, 315, 320, 395

Statements on Standards for Accounting and Review Services (SSARSs)

No.	*Date issued*	*Title*	*Guide Section*
1	Dec. 1978	Superseded by SSARS No. 19	
2–4	Various	Superseded by SSARS No. 21	
5	July 1982	(Deleted by SSARS 7)	
6–13	Various	Superseded by SSARS No. 21	
14	July 2005	*Compilations of Pro Forma Financial Information*	AR 120[3]
15–20	Various	Superseded by SSARS No. 21	
21	Oct. 2014	*Statements on Standards for Accounting and Review Services*	AR-C 60, 70, 80, 90
22	Sept. 2016	*Compilation of Pro Forma Financial Information*	AR-C 120

2 *SSAE No. 18 does not supersede chapter 7, "Managements Discussion and Analysis" of SSAE No. 10, codified as section 701, and retained as AT-C section 395.*

3 *Upon implementation of SSARS No. 21, all other SSARS are superseded with the exception of AR 120. AR 120 will be superseded by a clarity SSARS in the future.*

APPENDIX B: LIST OF AICPA AUDIT AND ACCOUNTING GUIDES AND AICPA STATEMENTS OF POSITION—AUDITING AND ATTESTATION[1]

Along with auditing Interpretations of Statements on Auditing Standards (SASs), which are integrated in the appropriate sections, the auditing guidance in the following American Institute of Certified Public Accountants (AICPA) Audit and Accounting Guides and auditing Statements of Positions are recommendations on how to apply the SASs in specific circumstances and for entities in specialized industries that are issued under the authority of the Auditing Standards Board (ASB). Auditors who do not follow the guidance in an applicable interpretive publication should be prepared to explain how they complied with the relevant SAS requirements addressed by such guidance.

AICPA Audit and Accounting Guides summarize the practices applicable to specific industries and describe relevant matters, conditions, and procedures unique to these industries. In addition, general audit and accounting guides listed below may be of interest to CPAs performing audit and attest engagements. Guides are available from the AICPA:

Airlines
Analytical Procedures
Assessing and Responding to Audit Risk in a Financial Statement Audit
Assets Required to Be Used in Research and Development Activities
Audit Sampling
Auditing Revenue in Certain Industries
Brokers and Dealers in Securities
Construction Contractors
Depository and Lending Institutions: Banks and Savings Institutions, Credit Unions, Finance Companies, and Mortgage Companies
Employee Benefit Plans
Entities with Oil and Gas Producing Activities
Gaming
Government Auditing Standards and Single Audits
Health Care Entities
Investment Companies
Life and Health Insurance Entities
Not-for-Profit Entities
Property and Liability Insurance Entities
Special Considerations in Auditing Financial Instruments
State and Local Governments
Testing Goodwill for Impairment
Valuation of Privately Held Company Equity Securities Issues as Compensation

[1] *Accounting Statements of Position are not included in this listing.*

STATEMENTS OF POSITION—AUDITING AND ATTESTATION

Auditing and Attestation Statements of Position are issued to achieve one or more of several objectives: to revise, clarify, or supplement guidance in previously issued Audit and Accounting Guides; to describe and provide implementation guidance for specific types of audit and attestation engagements; or to provide guidance on specialized areas in audit and attestation engagements. The auditing and attestation guidance in a Statement of Position has the same authority as auditing and attestation guidance in an Audit and Accounting Guide.

SOP No.	Topic	Title
00-1	Health Care	*Auditing Health Care Third-Party Revenues and Related Receivables*
92-8	Insurance	*Auditing Property/Casualty Insurance Entities' Statutory Financial Statements Applying Certain Requirements of the NAIC Annual Statement Instructions*
04-1	Insurance	*Auditing the Statement of Social Insurance*

To order the AICPA publications, call 888-777-7077 or go to www.aicpa.org.

APPENDIX C: OTHER AUDITING PUBLICATIONS[1]

List of Current AICPA Risk Alerts, AICPA Technical Practice Aids, and Other Publications

Current AICPA Risk Alerts reviewed by AICPA Audit and Attestation Standards staff

- Employee Benefit Plans Industry Developments
- General Accounting and Auditing Developments
- Government Auditing Standards and Single Audit Developments
- Not-for-Profit Entities Industry Developments
- Understanding the Responsibilities of Auditors for Audits of Group Financial Statements

AICPA Technical Practice Aids, Accounting and Auditing Publications Technical Questions and Answers

- TIS Section 8000, *Audit Field Work*
- TIS Section 9000, *Auditor's Reports*

Other Publications

- *2011 Yellow Book Independence—Nonaudit Services Documentation*
- *Applying OCBOA in State and Local Governmental Financial Statements*
- *Audits of Futures Commission Merchants, Introducing Brokers, and Commodity Pools*
- *Documenting and Testing Compliance and Internal Control over Compliance in a Single Audit*
- *Establishing and Maintaining a System of Quality Control for a CPA Firm's Accounting and Auditing Practice*
- *Internal Control for Today's Smart Business*
- *Preparing and Reporting on Cash- and Tax-Basis Financial Statements*
- *Using (SOC 1® Report) in Audits of Employee Benefit Plans*

[1] *See the chapter on AU-C 200 for more information on the "GAAS hierarchy."*

INDEX